قُرْاٰنُ مَجِيدٌ

THE HOLY QURAN

WITH

ENGLISH TRANSLATION

AND

COMMENTARY

VOLUME 2

SURAH AL-IMRAN – SURAH AL-TAUBA

Published under the auspices of
Hazrat Mirza Tahir Ahmad
Fourth successor of the Promised Messiah
and Supreme Head of the Worldwide
Ahmadiyyah Movement in Islam

Published by
ISLAM INTERNATIONAL PUBLICATIONS LIMITED

The first volume comprising the first nine chapters alongwith an introduction appeared in 1947. The book was found to be too voluminous to be easily handled and, therefore, for the convenience of the readers it was split up into two parts. Vol: I part I was reprinted in 1964 in Pakistan (the present book) containing the introduction & the first two chapters, and Vol: I part II dealing with the next seven chapters (now vol: 2) was reprinted in 1965.

First Published in U. K. in 1988 by
ISLAM INTERNATIONAL PUBLICATIONS LTD.
Islamabad
Sheephatch Lane
Tilford, Surrey GU10 2AQ
and Printed in Great Britain by
Unwin Brothers
Woking, Surrey.

British Library Cataloguing in Publication Data
[Koran. English & Arabic, 1988]
The Holy Quran with English Translation
and Commentary.
I. Alhaj, Mirza Bashir-ud-Din Mahmud Ahmad
1889 - 1965
297'. 1227

ISBN 1-85372-045-3

PUBLISHER'S NOTE

This five volume commentary of the Holy Quran is an English translation of the commentary on the Holy Quran by the Second Head of the Ahmadiyya Community, Hazrat Mirza Bashiruddin Mahmood Ahmad, Khalifatul Masih II.

His published work on the Holy Quran comprises a ten volume commentary in Urdu *(Tafseer-e-Kabir)* covering the following Surahs; *Al-Fatihah & Al-Baqarah, Yunus* to *Al-Ankabut* and from *Al-Naba* to *Al-Nas*. The present English commentary is based on that commentary. As far as the remaining Surahs are concerned, that is chapters; *Al-i-Imran* to *Al-Taubah* and from *Al-Ahqaf* to *Al-Mursalat*, the compiling Editors have made use of the extensive notes prepared by the late Hazrat Khalifatul Masih II in preparing a detailed and comprehensive commentary which he was unfortunately unable to complete in his life time. The commentary of such chapters is nonetheless based on his own deliberations.

This commentary is a unique master piece. It is an excellent exegesis on the true meaning of the Holy Quran. Although no commentary can ever claim to encompass the final interpretation of the Holy Quran, the manner in which this rich treasure has been prised open by an author who had deep insight into the meaning of the Holy Quran, has certainly set the standard by which all future commentaries ought to be judged.

An index and the following listings have been added in the present edition at the end of the fifth volume:

Table of contents of the Index

Alphabetical listing of Chapters of the Holy Quran.

Important Arabic words and expressions explained in the commentary

The Index of subjects.

The Publishers acknowledge and sincerely thank the following members of U. S. A. Jamaat in particular and their helpers in general for the very careful and hard work in preparing these listings and the index so exhaustively:

Aisha Sharif, Nyceemah Yaqub, Aisha Hakim, Shakura Nooriah, Salma Ghani, Kadija el Hadi, Rafia Ramah, Khulat Alladin, Dhiya Tahira, Uzma Saeed, Farzana Qader and Fatima Haneef.

The publishers also wish to acknowledge the work of M. Zafar Mahmood and Munir-ud-Din Shams Add. Vakil-ul-Ishaat in revising the index and listings and then checking the proofs with the cooperation of Lajna and Ansar of U. K. May Allah bless them all.

The cost of publishing this five-volume commentary has been met jointely by members of the Ahmadiyya Community in the United States of America and the United Kingdom on the happy occasion of thanks giving Centenary Jubilee Celebrations of the world-wide Ahmadiyya Community in Islam.

The funds generated from its sale will be recicled in the further publication of the Holy Quran. May Allah grant abundant reward to all those who have contributed towards this publication.

CONTENTS

PREFACE

This book forms Volume II of the Commentary of the Qur'an. It comprise seven Chapters — From *Sura* Al 'Imran to *Sura* Al-Tauba.

The annotations of the Text have been generally divided into two parts. The first deals with Important Words in the verse under comment. These words, along with other words derived from the same root, particularly those occurring in other parts of the Qur'ān, have been explained and examples given to illustrate their different uses. These explanations are based on the standard lexicons of the Arabic language, such as the Lisān al-'Arab, the Tāj al-'Arūs, the Mufradāt of Imām Rāghib, the Arabic-English Lexicon by E. W. Lane and the Aqrab al-Mawārid. As regards the Translation, the procedure has been to base the meaning of every word first on the corroborative testimony of other parts of the Qur'ān and secondly on the context. The words printed in italics have been introduced to explain the meaning of the Text, there being no words corresponding to them in the original.

The second part consists of explanatory Notes or Commentary. Every Note first derives its authority from the tenor and spirit of the Qur'ān as expressed in various other places. Next to the Qur'ān precedence is given to the Ḥadīth and then come the standard dictionaries of the Arabic language. Last of all, recourse has been had to the evidence of history which was necessary for the explanation of such verses as refer to well-known historical events.

In the course of the preparation of these Notes light has been thrown from time to time on the order which runs through the verses of each Chapter, the one following the other in natural sequence; and a careful perusal of these Notes will convince the reader that the Qur'ān forms a thoroughly coherent and consistent reading.

A system of cross-references has been introduced. These cross-references have been placed below the Text and the Translation. They give at a glance the various places where the subject of a particular verse has been dealt with in the Qur'ān.

An Introduction is prefixed to each Chapter, in addition to the General Introduction which serves as an introduction to the whole Book. The Introduction to each Chapter dicusses the place and date of its revelation and gives a summary of its contents and the relation it has with the Chapters preceding or following it. It also provides sufficient material for the reader to understand and realize that not only the verses of the various Chapters but also the specific position of each Chapter itself is governed by an intelligent order.

The Editor thanks M. Muḥammad Aḥmad Jalīl, Professor, Jāmi'ah Aḥmadiyya, Rabwah, West Pakistan, for his taking great pains in correcting the proofs. Thanks are also due to Dr. A. J. Arberry, the well-known Orientalist, and Sir Ronald Storrs, K.C.M.G., C.B.E., ex-High Commissioner of Palestine for the valuable suggestions they made in regard to the Translation of the Text, and to Mr. F. W. Bustin, Editor, The Civil & Military Gazette, Lahore, who kindly revised the manuscript.

MALIK GHULAM FARID
(*The Editor*)

SYSTEM OF TRANSLITERATION

In transliterating Arabic words we have followed the system adopted by the Royal Asiatic Society.

ا at the beginning of a word, pronounced as *a, i, u* preceded by a very slight aspiration, like *h* in the English word 'honour'.

ث *th*, pronounced like *th* in the English word 'thing'.

ح *ḥ*, a guttural aspirate, stronger than h.

خ *kh*, pronounced like the Scotch *ch* in 'loch'.

ذ *dh*, pronounced like the English *th* in 'that', 'with'.

ص *ṣ*, strongly articulated s.

ض *ḍ*, similar to the English *th* in 'this'.

ط *ṭ*, strongly articulated palatal t.

ظ *ẓ*, strongly articulated z.

ع ʻ, a strong guttural, the pronunciation of which must be learnt by the ear.

غ *gh*, a sound approached very nearly in the *rʻgrasseyeʻ* in French, and in the German *r*. It requires the muscles of the throat to be in the 'gargling' position whilst pronouncing it.

ق *q*, a deep guttural *k* sound.

ء ʼ, a sort of catch in the voice.

Short vowels are represented by *a* for ◌َ (like *u* in 'bud') ; *i* for ◌ِ (like *i* in 'bid') ; u for ◌ُ (like *oo* in 'wood') ; the long vowels by *ā* for ◌ or ا (like *a* in 'father') ; *ī* for ي (like *ee* in 'deep') ; *ai* for ◌ي (like *i* in 'site') ; *ū* for و (like *oo* in 'root'); au for و ◌ (resembling *ou* in 'sound').

The consonants not included in the above list have the same phonetic value as in the principal languages of Europe.

CHAPTER 3

ĀL ʻIMRĀN

(*Revealed after Hijra*)

Connection with the Preceding Chapter

This chapter has a twofold connection with the preceding chapter, Al-Baqara, *i.e.* (1) there is a link between the whole chapter, Āl ʻImrān and the whole chapter, Al-Baqara, and (2) there is a link between the concluding portion of Al-Baqara and the opening verses of Āl ʻImrān. In fact the order in the Quran is of two kinds : either the topic with which one chapter is concluded is continued in the following chapter, or the subject-matter of the whole preceding chapter is dealt with in the next. This twofold connection exists between *Sūras*, Al-Baqara and Āl ʻImrān.

The connection of the whole subject-matter of Āl ʻImrān with that of Al-Baqara mainly consists in a description of the causes that led to the transfer of prophethood from the Mosaic to the Islamic dispensation. This was the main theme of Al-Baqara, and in explanation the degenerate condition of the Jews was dealt with at some length in that *Sūra*. But in Al-Baqara little light was shed on Christianity, which constitutes the culmination of the Mosaic dispensation. This omission could have given rise to doubts in the minds of some people that though Judaism which constituted the beginning of the Mosaic dispensation had become corrupt, its culmination, the Christian faith, was still pure ; and hence, there was no necessity to introduce and establish a new religion—Islam. To remove this seemingly legitimate doubt, the hollowness of the current Christian doctrines has been fully exposed in Āl ʻImrān. But as the Christian faith seeks to base its superiority as much on the nobility of its detailed practical teaching as on the excellence of its tenets and doctrines, so after Āl ʻImrān this subject has been dealt with in chapter Al-Nisā to which reference will be made at its proper place. Anyhow, the falsity of the Christian doctrines having been established in Āl ʻImrān, the chapter proceeds to show that, as the Christian faith which had reformed and regenerated Judaism had itself become corrupt and degenerate, it could not prove a bar in the way of the introduction of a new and better dispensation. On the contrary, it constituted a strong testimony to the need for the introduction of a new Law. Consequently, the divine attributes of "Living" and "Self-Subsisting and All-Sustaining" in the very beginning of Āl ʻImrān are intended to repudiate Christian doctrines.

The second kind of connection *viz.* that of the concluding portion of Al-Baqara with the opening portion of Āl ʻImrān is apparent from the fact that the former *Sūra* had concluded with some prayers in which prayer for national reformation and for the triumph of Islam over its enemies formed the main subject ; and by placing the divine attributes of "Living" and "Self-Subsisting and All-Sustaining" in the beginning of Āl ʻImrān, Muslims have been assured that God will certainly come to their aid and that by His help alone can success be achieved, because He being "Living" and "Self-Subsisting and All-Sustaining," His power knows no weakening. Similarly, verse 5 of the present chapter, which purports to say that a grievous punishment is in store for those who have rejected the Signs of God and that God possesses the power to take revenge, points to the acceptance of the prayer embodied in the concluding words of the last chapter *i.e. So help us against the disbelieving people.*

Title and Date of Revelation

This *Sūra* is known by several names in the Ḥadīth. Like Al-Baqara, it is also known by the name Al-Zahrā (the Bright One) which is indicative of the strong similarity existing between the themes of the two *Sūras* and their subject-matter. The chapter is also known by the names *Al-Amān* (Peace), *Al-Kanz* (the Treasure), *Al-Muʿīna* (the Helper), *Almujādala* (the Pleading), *Al-Istighfār* (the Seeking of Forgiveness), and *Ṭayyiba* (the Pure). The *Sūra* was revealed at Medina.

Subject-Matter

This chapter, like its predecessor, opens with the abbreviated letters *Alif Lām Mīm* (I am Allah, the All-Knowing) which is intended to draw our attention to the divine attribute of knowledge ; and mention of the attributes " Living " and " Self-Subsisting and All-Sustaining " is meant to point out that in this *Sūra* the divine attribute of knowledge has been substantiated by God's attributes of "Living" and "Self-Subsisting and All-Sustaining" *i.e.* the fact that God is "Living" and "Self-Subsisting and All-Sustaining" constitutes proof of His being " All-Knowing ", because death and decay are born of lack of knowledge. He Who is " Living " and " Self-Subsisting and All-Sustaining " will necessarily be " All-Knowing " because if there had been another " all-knowing " being like Him, he too would have possessed the power to provide means for his everlasting subsistence (2 : 3). Then the chapter goes on to say (a) that whereas the Torah and the Gospels have proceeded from a true source, the followers of these Books, Jews and Christians, have strayed away from the right path as regards their doctrines and deeds ; (b) that consequently divine punishment would overtake them, and (c) that the belief that connection with these Books will save them from God's punishment is a vain hope, because these Books having become abrogated, are unable to satisfy the needs and requirements of the time (4—7). Further the *Sūra* says that there is going to be a sort of spiritual duel between the Quran and these Books and that in this duel the Quran will prove to be far superior to them and will prevail over them when set against them because it embodies teachings which the latter lack (8—12). The *Sūra* proceeds to tell Muslims that they should banish the doubt from their minds that, in view of the numerical superiority of Jews and Christians and the preponderance of the means at their disposal, Muslims would not prevail against them, because God had already granted them predominance over enemies who were also more powerful and larger in number. The same phenomenon will be repeated now. Further, God says that national victories do not result from material means but from the superiority of national morals. Hence final victory will come to Muslims because, though they lack the former they are in ample possession of the latter (13—18). Again, the Quran says that belief in the Oneness of God forms one of the important and major means of victory, and with this Muslims have been blessed. So as Muslims possess true religion, no power on earth can defeat them (19-20). The chapter proceeds to dwell upon the theme that nobody can prevail against God and His Messenger because opposition to them means opposition to justice and justice cannot suffer defeat (21—23).

Furthermore, the chapter says that the enemies of Islam labour under the delusion that their national usages and customs are superior to those of Muslims. They seem to ignore the fact that in this world there is no escape from the law of cause and effect, and they cannot hope to succeed by flouting this law (24—28). It further says that there exists a great difference between the good morals of Muslims and the bad morals of disbelievers ; the former, therefore, should always be on their guard against being influenced by the depravity of the latter lest they incur God's wrath (29—31). The *Sūra* continues the subject and develops it further when it says that the way to progress and prosperity for Muslims does not lie in imitating other peoples but in strictly following Islam and the Holy Prophet (32-33). The above statement is not an empty assertion, because history bears testimony to the fact that victory has always come by following God's Messengers (34-35). After this a clear and detailed exposition of the real subject is taken in hand with a brief reference to the beginning of Christianity, the refutation of which is the main theme here (36—64). Then the attention of the People of the Book has been drawn to the fact that when Muslims also believe in the truth of the origin and source of their faith, there is no reason for them to fight each other. On the contrary, they should both preach to disbelievers the doctrine of the Oneness of God, on which they agree, and keep within bounds their respective doctrines where they disagree (65). Then some light is thrown on the evil consequences of differences and enmity which possess no reasonable basis, and it is made clear that such enmity leads to foolish beliefs and dulls the brain and impairs righteousness (66—81). The Quran further says that every Messenger has always had a pledge taken from his followers that when God bestows on them " Book and Wisdom," they should also accept the truth that follows in its wake, failing which God's punishment would descend on them (82—90) ; and the chapter warns Christians that they cannot hope to remain the " chosen ones " of God and retain His love if they refuse to accept the New Truth. Muslims, however, adhere to this teaching and believe in all the Messengers and, in fact, no other course is acceptable to God. It asks how a person who has subscribed to the view that truth has always continued to be revealed by God can now, with justification, defy this principle ; and declares that, if one does so, one will certainly incur God's displeasure and His punishment (91-92). Then the *Sūra* goes on to say that real good consists in sacrificing that thing in the way of God which is most dear to one and thus real sacrifice is the sacrifice of one's feelings, customs and beliefs (93). It further says that matters regarding which the People of the Book dispute and quarrel with Muslims carry no weight because originally some of them were regarded as permissible by their own forefathers. If the latter succeeded in obtaining salvation in spite of them, why cannot Muslims ? (94—96). The subject is further developed where God says that Muslims and Jews have a meeting-point in Abraham, and since it was Abraham who laid the foundations of the Ka'ba, why should the Israelites quarrel with Muslims on the basis of unreal and unsubstantial differences and why should they prefer deception and tyranny to cool and dispassionate consideration of truth (97—100). Then a note of warning is sounded to Muslims that the People of the Book have gone so far in opposition to them that, if they had their way, they would certainly lead them astray. But Muslims cannot go astray because they are the recipients of God's new revelation. They are, therefore, admonished to put up patiently with all opposition and oppression, strengthen their connection with God and establish their mutual relations on a firmer basis because they will stand in sore need of a united front when confronted with a severe attack from Christians (101—110). Muslims are further told that before that time comes, they should strengthen their ranks by conveying the message of Islam to as many people as possible and this should be done in two ways : (*a*) there should be a special party of preachers among Muslims who should dedicate their lives to the propagation of Islam ; (*b*) Muslims should preach their faith as best they can. Herein lies the success of Islam (111). Muslims are further warned against harbouring the delusion that, in the event of their fight with Christians, the Jews would help them. On the contrary, the latter would spare no pains to harass and oppress them. They would, however, fail to do Muslims any real harm and would themselves meet with disgrace and humiliation (112-113). The Quran does not fail to recognize good wherever it is found and says that all the People of the Book are not bad. Some among them are good and these will get their reward from God (114—116). But those who are evilly disposed will come to grief and will be disgraced. Muslims are admonished to have nothing to do with such people lest they become influenced by their bad morals. They should, however, have no fear of them, because they would not be able to do Muslims any substantial harm (117—121).

Then a brief reference is made to the Battle of Badr, and Muslims are told that, just as in the face of extremely adverse circumstances God protected and helped them against the idolaters of Mecca at Badr and vouchsafed them a clear victory over them, the same will happen with regard to the People of the Book. God's mercy and forgiveness will accompany Muslims and His punishment will fall on their enemies (122—130). Muslims are further told that Jews and Christians depend for their power and might on interest. But the taking and giving of interest runs counter to good morals. They should, therefore, derive their power from helping the poor (131—133). Secondly, Christians depend on Atonement, a doctrine born of the view that repentance will not be accepted. By taking interest the People of the Book oppress God's servants and by subscribing to the dogma of the non-acceptance of repentance they declare God to be cruel like themselves. Muslims are enjoined to avoid this doctrine and to ask forgiveness of God if they happen to commit a sinful act (134—137). They are further comforted by the knowledge that God has always destroyed the enemies of His Messengers. They should do their duty, make suitable sacrifices and employ the material means at their disposal and leave the rest to God. He would see that victory comes to them ; they are only required to make as much effort as should demonstrate the depth and sincerity of their faith (138—144). Further, God says that in the vast chain of truth, the Holy Prophet is but a link and if he should happen to die or be killed in battle (though in conformity with God's promise he could not be killed), Muslims should not lose heart because believers have, throughout the ages, been fighting the enemies of truth in adverse circumstances and as a result have always achieved both worldly and spiritual prosperity (145—152). Then the incident of Uhud is mentioned and the lesson is driven home to Muslims that sometimes a slight exhibition of weakness results in dire consequences (153—156), and they are admonished that on such occasions of crisis they should completely avoid mutual recrimination as it is calculated to undermine national spirit ; and he who does so is not a friend of his community(157—159). Another rule of conduct to be observed is that in time of warfare leaders should behave more leniently than usual towards their followers and should have proper regard for their susceptibilities, so that the enemy may get no opportunity to create discord among them and all things should be done after mutual consultation (160). Then the former subject is repeated, *viz.*, that no success is possible without God's help, therefore the demands of religion and morality should not be disregarded from considerations of petty worldly gains (161—164). God then reminds Muslims of the great good He has done to them inasmuch as He has raised for them a perfect Messenger. They should follow him and eschew the path of disturbers of peace that they may achieve success (165—169). Then the Quran lays down a great principle, *viz.*, that those who lose their lives while fighting for the cause of truth are entitled to special respect. It is these people who get eternal life and it is they who exhibit such morals as give life to their community (170—173). After that we are told that in every community there are some weak people, so we should not be afraid of the existence of some weak members in our ranks (174—180). Again, a reference is made to the People of the Book and we are told that their religious condition has become so corrupt that, while on the one hand they claim to be God's own chosen people, on the other, they hesitate to spend their money in His way. Muslims are enjoined to take a lesson from this (181-183). The moral depravity of these people is further contrasted with their claim that they are commanded to give their allegiance only to that Messenger who should demand the greatest sacrifice of them. God says that such Messengers did appear among them, but they refused to accept them (184—185). The theme of sacrifice is further developed where God says that it is foolish to be afraid of making sacrifices for national causes. The greatest of sacrifices is to suffer death, but death is sure to come upon every one, with the difference that the good continue to make progress even after death. Why then should one be afraid of it ? (186). Muslims are then warned that they will have to be tried ; and they should not think that they would achieve success without passing through the ordeal of trials and tribulations (187). God further says that He had commanded the People of the Book to preach and propagate these teachings but, when they themselves consigned them to oblivion, how could they preach them to others ? These people seek to be praised for deeds which they have not done. But instead of praise they will meet with disgrace and destruction because he who does not live up to his professions is never honoured (188—190). In the next few verses the special qualities and characteristics of true believers are described and Muslims are taught certain prayers, the offering of which is essential for progress and prosperity (191—195). They are told that if they pray with sincerity, their prayers will be accepted and, with God's help, they will defeat and bring low their enemy, however strong (196—199). But all the People of the Book are not bad. Though a majority of them are bad, some of them are good. These latter will get their reward from God (200). The *Sūra* concludes with rules of conduct by observing which Muslims can achieve success and predominance (201).

سُوْرَةُ اٰلِ عِمْرَانَ مَدَنِيَّةٌ

1. In the name of Allah, the Gracious, the Merciful.[293]

بِسْمِ اللّٰهِ الرَّحْمٰنِ الرَّحِيْمِ ۝

2. *Alif Lām Mīm.[293A]

الٓمّٓ ۝

3. *Allah is He beside Whom there is no God, the Living, the Self-Subsisting and All-Sustaining.[294]

اللّٰهُ لَاۤ اِلٰهَ اِلَّا هُوَ الْحَيُّ الْقَيُّوْمُ ۝

*See 2 : 2   *See 2 : 256.

---

293. Commentary :
     See note under **1 : 1**

293A. Commentary :
     See note under **2 : 2**

294. Important Words :
For the meaning of الحي and القيوم see **2 : 256.**

Commentary :

The verse contains a strong refutation of the divinity of Jesus. This doctrine being one of the main topics dealt with in this chapter, the *Sūra* fittingly opens with such attributes of God as cut at the very root of this doctrine. These attributes *i.e.* (1) the Living or the Ever-Living, and (2) the Self-Subsisting and All-Sustaining, prove on the one hand that God, the possessor of these attributes, should need no partner or helper ; and on the other that Jesus, who was subject to the law of birth and death, being thus neither ever-living nor self-subsisting and all-sustaining, could not be divine.

These attributes also prove the hollowness of the doctrine of Atonement which is a corollary of the above doctrine. Jesus, it is said, suffered death to atone for the sins of mankind. If that is so, he could not be God, for God is Ever-Living and cannot suffer death, permanent

or temporary. It is futile to say that the death of Jesus meant only the separation of the god-Jesus from his physical habitat. The connection between the god-Jesus and his physical body was, according to Christian belief, in its very nature, a temporary one and was bound to break one day, even if Jesus had not died on the Cross. So the mere breaking up of this connection could serve no useful purpose. It must be some other death which brought redemption to his sinful followers. That death, according to the Christians themselves, came upon Jesus when after his crucifixion he descended into Hades or Hell (Acts 2 : 31 and the Book of Common Prayer, Article on Religion, III). Thus, far from being immune from death, which is God's exclusive prerogative, Jesus suffered death both in its literal and figurative sense. He not only died but descended into Hades. Again he not only suffered from grief and pain but also disgrace and humiliation.

Similarly, the attribute of القيوم (the Self-Subsisting and All-Sustaining) proves the falsity of the Christian doctrine. God, being Self-Subsisting and All-Sustaining, should not only live by Himself without the support of any other being but all others should receive support from Him. But Jesus can never be

4. *He has sent down to thee the Book containing the truth *and* fulfilling that which precedes it; and He sent down the Torah and the Gospel before *this*, as a guidance to the people; and He has sent down *the Discrimination.[295]

نَزَّلَ عَلَيْكَ الْكِتٰبَ بِالْحَقِّ مُصَدِّقًا لِّمَا بَيْنَ يَدَيْهِ وَاَنْزَلَ التَّوْرٰىةَ وَالْاِنْجِيْلَ ۙ مِنْ قَبْلُ هُدًى لِّلنَّاسِ وَاَنْزَلَ الْفُرْقَانَ ۚ

*4 : 106; 5 : 49; 29 : 52; 39 : 3.   *2 : 54, 186; 8 : 42; 21 : 49; 25 : 2.

proved to possess these attributes. Like other mortals, he was born of a woman, lived on food and drink, suffered pain and humiliation, asked others to pray for the alleviation of his sufferings, and finally, as the Christians say, died on the Cross. The New Testament bears ample testimony to all these facts. But God being Ever-Living, Self-Subsisting and All-Sustaining is above all this.

295. Important Words :

بِالْحَق (containing the truth). الْحَق is derived from حَق *i.e.* it was or became just, proper, right, true, authentic, genuine, substantial or real; or it was or became an established or confirmed truth or fact; or it was or became binding, incumbent or due. So حَق means, a truth; an established fact; a right; equity and justice; a thing that is decreed or destined; a thing suitable to the requirements of wisdom, justice, truth and right. الْحَق is one of the names of God, meaning the Really Existing God; or the Creator according to the requirements of wisdom, justice and right. The word is also applied to the Quran and the religion of Islam (Lane). See also 2 : 181.

تَوْرٰاة (Torah) is believed to be a Hebrew word. In Arabic it is said to be derived from ورى. They say ورى النار *i.e.* the fire burnt. ورى الزند means, he made the fire-producing wood or steel produce fire. ورى الخبر means, he concealed the news. ورى عن كذا means, he meant one thing but by using equivocal expressions made the listener think of another (Aqrab). In view of these significations of the

word, تَوْرٰاة (Torah) is so called probably because in its pristine purity reading it and acting upon its teaching kindled in the heart of man the fire of divine love. Possibly, the word also contains a hint that bright prophecies about the advent of the final Law-giving Prophet lie hidden in the Book. In Hebrew the root meaning of the word is "to teach," the word Torah meaning, "instruction or precept or law" (Gesenius). Torah is the name applied to the five books of Moses: Genesis, Exodus, Leviticus, Numbers and Deuteronomy. The name may have its origin in the popular Jewish belief that "the original Pentateuch, like everything celestial, consisted of fire, being written in block letters of flame upon a white ground of fire" (Jew. Enc. xii. 197.). The name Torah is also sometimes applied to the Ten Commandments.

اِنْجِيل (Gospel) is probably of Greek origin from which the English form "Evangel" (good news) is derived. The word Evangel was formerly freely used in place of Gospel. but is now archaic. In Arabic نجله ابوه (*najalahū*) means, his father begot him. نجل الشيئ means, he laid bare or disclosed the thing. نجل الارض means, he tore open or ploughed the land for the purpose of sowing seed. نجل الرجل (*najila*) means, the man's eyes were large and beautiful. The word اِنْجِيل which, according to Aqrab, is a Greek word underived from any Arabic root, means بشارة *i.e.* good news.

مُصَدِّقا (fulfilling). See 2 : 42.

5. Surely, those who deny the Signs of Allah shall have a severe punishment. And [a]Allah is Mighty, Possessor of the power to requite.[296]

اِنَّ الَّذِیۡنَ کَفَرُوۡا بِاٰیٰتِ اللہِ لَہُمۡ عَذَابٌ شَدِیۡدٌ ۟ وَاللہُ عَزِیۡزٌ ذُو انۡتِقَامٍ ۞

---

[a]5 : 96 ; 14 : 48 ; 39 : 38.

الفرقان (Discrimination). See 2 : 54.

Commentary :

The expression بالحق rendered as " containing the truth " (lit. " with truth ") means : (1) that the Quran comprises true teachings which are based on eternal truth and are incapable of being successfully assailed ; (2) that the Quran has been sent rightly, meaning that the first recipients of it were the fittest people to receive it ; (3) that it has come in the fulness of time and fulfils a true need ; (4) that it has come to stay and no effort on the part of its opponents can succeed in destroying or tampering with it. See Important Words above.

انجیل means " good news," and the Gospels are so called because they contained not only " good news " for those who accepted Jesus, but also because they contained prophecies about the advent of the Greatest of the Prophets whose coming Jesus described as the coming of the Lord Himself (Matt. 21 : 40) or as the advent of the kingdom of God (Mark, 1 : 15). They also contain prophecies about the advent in the Latter Days of Jesus' own counterpart, the Promised Messiah.

The word انجیل occurring in the verse does not refer to the present four Gospels which were written by the followers of Jesus long after his so-called crucifixion and which give merely an account of his life and teachings. The word refers to the actual revelation received by Jesus from God. The present Gospels do indeed contain a part of that revelation, but divine words have become so mixed up with the sayings of Jesus himself that in many cases it is difficult to distinguish between the two. The Gospels contain a good deal of matter which is admittedly not of divine origin.

The saying of the Holy Prophet صدورهم انا جیلهم i.e. " the breasts of my Companions are like Gospels " (Lisān), sheds some light on the significance and position of Injīl. This saying of the Prophet means that the breasts of his Companions were repositories of his life-history and teachings which are indeed a great gospel. It may be inferred from this that the position of the present Gospels is analogous to that of the collections of Ḥadīth, such as Bukhārī, Muslim, etc.

The clause, *He sent down the Torah and the Gospel before this as a guidance*, means that before the Quran was revealed, the Torah and the Gospels provided spiritual guidance for men but that their place was now taken by the Quran which has come as a guidance for all time and all mankind.

The words, *and He has sent down the Discrimination*, placed at the end of the verse refer to the Quran, the coming down of which has already been mentioned in the beginning of the verse. The idea has been repeated here to point out that the Quran has come to take the place of the previous scriptures, the word " Discrimination " also pointing to the same fact. The word may also refer to the heavenly Signs vouchsafed to Islam to establish its truth.

For an explanation of the term مصدق (fulfilling) see 2 : 42.

296. Important Words :

ذوانتقام (Possessor of the power to requite). انتقام is the noun-infinitive from نقم i.e. he took vengeance. They say نقم منه or

363

6. Surely, *nothing in the earth or in the heavens is hidden from Allah.²⁹⁷

إِنَّ اللّٰهَ لَا يَخْفٰى عَلَيْهِ شَيْءٌ فِى الْاَرْضِ وَلَا فِى السَّمَآءِ ۞

7. *He it is Who fashions you in the wombs as He wills; there is no God but He, the Mighty, the Wise,²⁹⁸

هُوَ الَّذِيْ يُصَوِّرُكُمْ فِى الْاَرْحَامِ كَيْفَ يَشَآءُ لَآ اِلٰهَ اِلَّا هُوَ الْعَزِيْزُ الْحَكِيْمُ ۞

---

*14 : 39; 40 : 17; 64 : 5; 86 : 8.   *22 : 6; 23 : 12—15; 39 : 7; 40 : 65; 64 : 4.

انتقم منه meaning, he wreaked vengeance on him; he punished him; he inflicted penal retribution on him for what he had done. نقمة and انتقام both mean, vengeance or penal retribution or punishment (Aqrab & Lane).

Commentary :

After the coming down of the Quran as a "Discrimination" and as "fulfilling" what is in the previous scriptures, referred to in the preceding verse, the persistent rejection of the Holy Prophet becomes indeed deserving of great punishment, and the verse points out that the God of Islam being "Mighty" and "Possessor of the power to requite," those who have rejected the truth must be prepared for divine requital.

297. Commentary :

God is not only Mighty and the Possessor of the power to requite but He is also All-Knowing, which is a necessary attribute for the successful exercise of power and the infliction of punishment. The verse thus constitutes yet another argument against the alleged divinity of Jesus. Nothing is hidden from God, His knowledge encompassing everything; but Jesus, according to his own admission, did not know many things (Mark 11 : 12,13). He even did not know when the Judgement Day was to be (Matt. 24 : 36). Such lack of knowledge is

evidently incompatible with the dignity of God.

298. Important Words :

يصور (fashions) is derived from صار. They say صار الشيء meaning : (1) he made the thing inclined ; (2) he divided or cut the thing into parts or pieces. صوره means, he formed or fashioned it ; he gave it a shape. صوّره تصويرا means, he fashioned it and gave it a definite shape. الصورة means, the image or form or shape of a thing by which it is distinguished from other things (Aqrab & Lane).

Commentary :

تصوير (fashioning) and خلق (creating) are two different things as is clear from 7 : 12 and 82 : 89. خلق which takes place before تصوير means creating a thing and giving it a general physical form, whereas تصوير signifies detailed formation and the endowing of a child with moral and spiritual faculties. Thus خلق and تصوير are inter-related like body and soul. Medical research has shown that there exists some subtle relationship between the physical features of a man and his morals. The clause, *He it is Who fashions you in the wombs*, would, therefore, mean that after God brings into existence a body in the womb, He endows it with faculties and capacities necessary to fulfil its destiny. So it is in

8. He it is Who has sent down to thee the Book; *a*in it there are verses that are decisive in meaning—they are the basis of the Book—and there are *b*others that are susceptible of different interpretations. But those in whose hearts is perversity pursue such thereof as are susceptible of different interpretations, seeking discord and seeking *wrong* interpretation of it. And none knows *c*its *right* interpretation except Allah *d*and those who are firmly grounded in knowledge; they say, 'We believe in it; the whole is from our Lord.'—And none heed except those gifted with understanding.—299

هُوَ الَّذِىٓ اَنْزَلَ عَلَيْكَ الْكِتٰبَ مِنْهُ اٰيٰتٌ مُّحْكَمٰتٌ هُنَّ اُمُّ الْكِتٰبِ وَ اُخَرُ مُتَشٰبِهٰتٌ فَاَمَّا الَّذِيْنَ فِىْ قُلُوْبِهِمْ زَيْغٌ فَيَتَّبِعُوْنَ مَا تَشَابَهَ مِنْهُ ابْتِغَآءَ الْفِتْنَةِ وَ ابْتِغَآءَ تَاْوِيْلِهٖ وَمَا يَعْلَمُ تَاْوِيْلَهٗٓ اِلَّا اللّٰهُ وَالرّٰسِخُوْنَ فِى الْعِلْمِ يَقُوْلُوْنَ اٰمَنَّا بِهٖ كُلٌّ مِّنْ عِنْدِ رَبِّنَا وَمَا يَذَّكَّرُ اِلَّآ اُولُوا الْاَلْبَابِ ۝

---

*a*11 : 2.   *b*39 : 24.   *c*7 : 54 ; 18 : 79.   *d*4 : 163.

---

the womb of his mother that the foundations of a man's future are laid, and it is to this fact that the Holy Prophet referred when he said that when the formation of the child in the womb begins, the angels ask God whether they should write it down as lucky or ill-fated (Bukhārī).

As the formation of the child takes place in the womb of the mother, naturally it is affected by its environment, *i.e.*, the physical and moral condition of the mother. So Jesus, whose body, like that of other human beings, was formed in the womb of a woman, could not escape being affected by the limitations and failings inherent in woman. Now as the Bible holds woman to be morally inferior to man, for it was through Eve that Satan deceived Adam (Gen. 3 : 12, 13), Jesus could not but have partaken of the failings and weaknesses of his mother. Thus the fatherless birth of Jesus proved, if anything, that Jesus was by nature more inclined to sin than other men. This is why, in his discussion with the Christians of Najrān, the Holy Prophet pointedly referred to the birth of Jesus as an argument

disproving his divinity. He is reported to have said to them : "Do you not know that it was a woman who conceived Jesus, just as a woman conceives a child, and then she was delivered of him just as a woman is delivered of a child " (Jarīr, iii. 101).

The clause, *there is no God but He*, has been placed as a natural consequence of the preceding clause. When it is God Who fashions children in the wombs of their mothers, no child born of a woman could claim to be divine.

299. Important Words :

مُحْكَمٰت (decisive in meaning) is derived from اَحْكَمَ which again is derived from حَكَمَ which means, he decided or he judged; he prevented or restrained or withheld. اَحْكَمَهُ means, he rendered it firm, stable and secure; he restrained it. Hence مُحْكَم means : (1) that which has been made secure from change or alteration ; (2) that in which there is no ambiguity or possibility of doubt; (3) that which is clear in meaning and decisive in exposition (Aqrab, Mufradāt & Lane).

ام (basis) is the noun-infinitive from ام (*amma*) *i.e.* he aimed at or sought or took himself to. ام possesses a variety of meanings some of which are: (1) mother; (2) source or origin or basis of a thing; (3) anything which is a means of sustenance and support or of reformation and correction for another; (4) anything to which other things surrounding it are linked (Aqrab & Mufradāt).

متشابهات (susceptible of different inter-pretations) is the plural of متشابهة which is derived from شبه. They say شبهه به *i.e.* he made it to be like that; he likened it to that. شبه عليه الامر means, he rendered the affair confused or obscure or ambiguous to him. تشابه الرجلان means, the two men were so like each other that it was difficult to distinguish one from the other. متشابهة means, mutually resembling. Thus the expression متشابهة is used about (1) that phrase, sentence or verse which is susceptible of different, though concordant, interpre-tations; or (2) that whose parts resemble or are concordant with one another; or (3) that whose true significance bears a similarity to a sense which is not meant; or (4) that of which the true meaning is known only by referring it to what is termed محكم (decisive); or (5) that which cannot be rightly understood without repeated consideration (Aqrab, Lane & Mufradāt).

زيغ (perversity) is the noun-infinitive from زاغ which means, he declined or deviated, or turned aside from the right course. So زيغ means, deviation from the truth or the right course; crookedness; doubt. ازاغه means, he made him deviate from the right course (Aqrab & Mufradāt).

تأويله (its interpretation). تأويل is the noun-infinitive from اول which is derived from آل *i.e.* he or it turned or returned. اوله means, he caused it or him to turn or return. اول الكلام means, he interpreted or explained the speech or writing. اول الرويا

means, he interpreted the dream. تأويل means; (1) interpretation or explanation; (2) conjecture about the meaning of a speech or writing; (3) turning away a speech or writing from its right interpretation; (4) inter-pretation of a dream; (5) end, result or sequel of a thing (Lane & Aqrab). In the present verse the word تأويل occurs twice, the first-mentioned تأويل giving the second or the third meaning, while the second-mentioned gives the first or the fifth meaning.

الراسخون (firmly grounded) is the plural of الراسخ which is derived from رسخ *i.e.* he or it was or became firm, stable or estab-lished. رسخ الشيئ means, the thing became firmly established. رسخ العلم فى قلبه means, knowledge became firmly established, or sank deep, in his heart. الراسخ فى العلم is one whose knowledge is extensive and deep-rooted, being firmly established and based on sure ground (Aqrab & Mufradāt).

Commentary :

The verse, which was revealed when a party of Christians from Najrān visited the Holy Prophet in Medina (Jarīr), serves a fourfold purpose: (1) it gives the genesis of the later Christian doctrines and explains how the true original doctrines became perverted; (2) it tells how the critics of Islam, particularly the Christians, distort true Islamic teachings in order to find an excuse for attacking Islam; (3) it warns Muslims to take a lesson from the history of Christians; and (4) it supplies a sure and trustworthy principle of interpreting revealed Books, or, for that matter, any writing or speech, in a right manner.

What proved the perversion of the Christian faith was that expressions like "son of God" etc. used metaphorically were taken literally and the simple and straightforward faith of Jesus was transformed out of all recognition, the متشابهة being given the place of محكم.

Again, it is on record that when the party of

Christians, referred to above, visited the Holy Prophet and had a discussion with him on the godhead of Jesus, they, like clever casuists, who when it suits their purpose tear a passage from its context and then base their arguments on it, asked the Holy Prophet if the words كلمة الله (word of God) and روح (spirit) were used about Jesus in the Quran, and, receiving an answer in the affirmative, joyfully exclaimed that the divinity of Jesus was thereby proved. They did not care to ponder over the explanation of these words in their context, which did not at all bear out the sense which they thought they possessed. It is to such objectionable practices that allusion is made in this verse, which lays down the golden rule that, in order to prove a controversial point, the decisive and clearly worded parts of a scripture should be taken into consideration, and that if they are found to contradict the construction put upon a certain ambiguous passage quoted in support of an argument, that interpretation should be rejected and the passage should be so interpreted as to make it harmonize with the decisive and clearly worded parts of the text.

This golden rule should always be observed whenever it is required to interpret or explain a passage which is susceptible of several interpretations and is not easily comprehensible. Its observance is all the more necessary when a seemingly difficult and knotty verse of the Quran is sought to be explained. Any interpretation which clashes with other verses of the Quran and runs counter to the clearly worded parts thereof should be rejected and only that interpretation which is in harmony with its basic principles should be accepted.

According to the verse, the Quran has two sets of verses. Some are محكم (decisive in meaning) and others متشابهة (capable of different interpretations). The right way to interpret a متشابهة verse is that only such interpretation of it should be accepted as agrees with the verses that are محكم and all other interpretations should be dismissed as incorrect. It is on record that one day the Holy Prophet, on hearing people disputing about the interpretation of certain verses of the Quran, angrily said : " Thus were ruined those who have gone before you. They interpreted certain parts of their scriptures in such a manner as to make them contradict other parts. But the Quran has been so revealed that different parts of it should corroborate one another. So do not reject any truth by making one part contradict the other. Act on what you understand thereof and refer that which you do not understand to those who know and understand it " (Musnad).

The above ḥadīth also refutes the theory of abrogation, for it speaks of the Quran as a Book of which all parts corroborate one another and condemns those who think that some of its verses contradict others. To Ahmad, the Holy Founder of the Ahmadiyya Movement, goes the credit of exploding the so-called abrogation theory. He and his disciples have given convincing explanations of those verses which were previously regarded as abrogated.

It may be noted here that in 39 : 24 the whole Quran is called متشابهة and in 11 : 2 all the Quranic verses have been described as محكم. This should not be taken as contradicting the verse under comment, according to which some verses of the Quran are محكم and others متشابهة. The apparent inconsistency is easily explained. So far as the real significance of the Quranic verses is concerned the whole of the Quran is محكم (decisive), inasmuch as all its verses contain decisive and eternal truths. In another sense, however, the whole of the Quran is متشابهة inasmuch as the Quranic verses have been so worded as to give, at one and the same time, several meanings equally true and good. The Quran is also متشابهة (i.e. mutually resembling) in the sense that there is no contradiction or inconsistency in it, its different verses

9. 'Our Lord, let not our hearts become perverse after Thou hast guided us ; and bestow on us mercy from Thyself ; surely, Thou alone art the Bestower.[300]

رَبَّنَا لَا تُزِغْ قُلُوۡبَنَا بَعۡدَ اِذۡ هَدَيۡتَنَا وَهَبۡ لَنَا مِنۡ لَّدُنۡكَ رَحۡمَةً ۚ اِنَّكَ اَنۡتَ الۡوَهَّابُ ۝

affording support to one another. But parts of it are certainly محكم or متشابهة for different readers according to their mental and spiritual capacities, as the present verse points out.

As regards prophecies, those that are couched in plain and direct language, susceptible of only one meaning, would be regarded as محكم and those that are described in figurative or metaphorical language, capable of more than one interpretation, would be regarded as متشابهة. The prophecies described in metaphorical language should, therefore, be interpreted in the light of the prophecies that have been clearly and literally fulfilled and also in the light of the basic and fundamental principles of Islam. For an example of محكم prophecies, the reader is referred to 58 : 22 ; whereas 28 : 86 contains a متشابهة prophecy.

The term محكم may also be applied to such verses as embody full and complete commandments while متشابهة verses are those which give only part of a certain commandment, and require to be read in conjunction with other verses to make a complete injunction.

Moreover, محكمات (decisive verses) generally deal with the Law and the doctrines of Faith, while متشابهات generally deal with topics of secondary importance or describe incidents in the lives of Prophets or the history of peoples and, while so doing, sometimes make use of idioms and phrases capable of different meanings. Such verses should not be so interpreted as to contradict the clear-worded tenets of the Faith.

The Arabic clause which has been translated as, *and none knows its right interpretation except Allah and those who are firmly grounded in knowledge; they say, 'We believe in it ; the whole is from our Lord'*, may be rendered in two ways, according as the pause is made after the word الله (Allah) or after the word العلم (knowledge). If the pause is made after the العلم (knowledge), the clause would be translated as above and the term متشابهات would in this case apply to verses pertaining to events of the past or verses containing general exhortation. If, however, the pause is made after الله (Allah), the term متشابهات would refer to prophecies of which the real interpretation is known to God only. In this case the clause would be translated as, "and none knows its interpretation except Allah ; and those who are firmly grounded in knowledge say, 'We believe in it, the whole is from our Lord." Grammatically both constructions are correct.

Finally, it may be noted that the use of metaphors, the main basis of متشابهة verses, in religious scriptures is necessary ; (1) to assure vastness of meaning in the fewest of words ; (2) to add beauty and grace to the style ; and (3) to provide for the people a trial (ابتلا) without which spiritual development and perfection is not possible.

300. Important Words :

الوهاب (Bestower) is derived from وهب i.e. he gave or he bestowed. وهب له مالا means, he gave or bestowed property on him. هبة which is the noun-infinitive from وهب means : (1) the act of giving a person something without receiving anything in return ; (2) the thing so given. الوهاب which is the intensive form of واهب (giver) means, one who gives greatly and extensively,

10. ' Our Lord, *a*Thou wilt certainly assemble mankind together on the Day about which there is no doubt ; surely Allah breaks not His promise.'[301]

رَبَّنَآ اِنَّكَ جَامِعُ النَّاسِ لِيَوۡمٍ لَّا رَيۡبَ فِيۡهِ ۚ اِنَّ اللّٰهَ لَا يُخۡلِفُ الۡمِيۡعَادَ ۟

---

*a*3 : 26 ; 4 : 88 ; 45 : 27.

(Aqrab). The word is used about God because He gives to each and every one of His creatures according to his deserts and none is overlooked (Mufradāt).

Commentary :

The verse, which comprises a very important prayer, comes as a fitting sequel to the preceding verse. It points out the great truth that not unoften a people receive a favour or blessing from God, which sometimes later proves a means of stumbling for them. They abuse the favour of God or misinterpret divine guidance and thus bring about their ruin. This is what happened to the Christians ; and Muslims are warned to be watchful against this source of error and ever to pray to God to protect them against it. See also 1 : 7.

The verse also hints that dissension and straying away from the truth would be the lot of Muslims if they subordinated decisive verses to those ambiguous, and fundamentals to matters of secondary importance. This is why the Holy Prophet used to recite this prayer constantly, which fact implied an instruction to his followers to do the same. Indeed, there could be no greater tragedy than, having once found the right path, to go astray, and, having once received divine favour, to become the object of His anger.

The verse also draws attention to the fact that the error of interpreting متشابهات in a manner which is at variance with محكمات (see preceding verse) can only be avoided through the purification of the heart and through

prayer. The right knowledge of the Quran is vouchsafed only to those who are pure of heart. In this connection see also 56 : 80.

301. Important Words :

جَامِع (wilt assemble) is derived from جمع *i.e.* he collected or he assembled. جمع الشيئ means, he assembled and arranged the thing. God is called جامع because He will bring together all men on the Day of Judgement and will give them their reward or punishment as they deserve. The central mosque of a town is also called جامع because people gather there for Prayers, particularly for Friday Prayer from the entire neighbourhood. جمعة (Friday) is also so called because on that day people assemble for the weekly worship (Tāj & Aqrab).

مِيعاد (promise) is derived from وعد *i.e.* he promised. Generally وعد means, he promised a good thing ; and اوعد means, he threatened with something evil. ميعاد means, time or place of promise or appointment (Aqrab). It also means, promise (Lane).

Commentary :

The prayer contained in the preceding verse becomes all the more essential because man has to give an account of his actions before God on the Day of Reckoning when He will bring together men of all ages and all lands. An examination is a very hard thing but it becomes harder still if held in the presence of a gathering comprising the whole of mankind.

R. 2   11. Those who disbelieve— ^a*their possessions and their children shall not avail them at all against Allah ; and it is they that are the fuel of the Fire.*[302]

اِنَّ الَّذِيْنَ كَفَرُوْا لَنْ تُغْنِيَ عَنْهُمْ اَمْوَالُهُمْ وَلَآ اَوْلَادُهُمْ مِّنَ اللّٰهِ شَيْئًا ۚ وَاُولٰٓئِكَ هُمْ وَقُوْدُ النَّارِ ۙ ۞

12. ^b*Their case* is like the case of the people of Pharaoh and those before them ; they rejected Our Signs ; so Allah punished them for their sins, and Allah is severe in punishing.[303]

كَدَاْبِ اٰلِ فِرْعَوْنَ ۙ وَالَّذِيْنَ مِنْ قَبْلِهِمْ ۚ كَذَّبُوْا بِاٰيٰتِنَا ۚ فَاَخَذَهُمُ اللّٰهُ بِذُنُوْبِهِمْ ۗ وَاللّٰهُ شَدِيْدُ الْعِقَابِ ۞

---

^a3 : 117 ; 58 : 18 ; 92 : 12 ; 111 : 3.   ^b8 : 53, 55.

---

302. Important Words :

تُغْنِيَ (shall avail) is derived from غِنٰى *i.e.* he became free from want ; or he was in a state of competence or sufficiency ; or he became rich. اِغْنَاه means, he made him free from want ; or put him in a state of sufficiency or competence ; or he made him rich. مَا يُغْنِيْ عَنْكَ هٰذَا means, this shall not suffice or satisfy thee ; or shall not stand thee in good stead ; or shall not avail or profit thee (Tāj).

Commentary :

As these verses have particular reference to Christians, the word "disbelievers" occurring in this verse may apply to them. Thus the verse contains a great prophecy ; for though at the time of its revelation Christians were not strong or numerous, yet the time was to come when they were destined to be so. Indeed they became the wealthiest people in the whole world and their progeny has spread over entire continents. But that cannot protect them from God's punishment. Their very wealth and number have become the cause of their destruction and, as predicted in the verse, they are now being punished with fire in the form of shots, shells and incendiary bombs. The verse may also refer to the Day of Judgement, spoken of in the preceding verse, when

nothing shall avail the Christian nations against the punishment of God.

The verse may also apply to the infidels of Mecca, all of whose efforts against the Holy Prophet came to naught, whose wealth fell into Muslim hands and whose children joined the fold of Islam in large numbers. In this case "fire" would mean either the fire of Hell or the fire of war which they themselves had kindled against Islam but which finally proved their own ruin.

303. Important Words :

دَاْب (case) is the noun-infinitive from دَأَب. They say دَأَب فِى الْعَمَل *i.e.* (1) he laboured and strove hard and exerted and wearied himself in the work ; (2) he remained constant in it. دَأْب means, working hard and constantly ; habit, custom or manner ; case, affair or condition (Aqrab).

Commentary :

In the previous verse disbelievers were warned that their wealth and their numbers would prove of no avail against God's punishment. The present verse points to the fact that this warning was no idle threat. Disbelievers in the past had met with a similar fate. Just as the efforts of Pharaoh and his people against Moses proved futile and their wealth, numbers

13. Say to those who disbelieve, *a*' You shall be overcome and gathered unto Hell; and an evil place of rest it is'.[304]

قُلْ لِّلَّذِيْنَ كَفَرُوْا سَتُغْلَبُوْنَ وَ تُحْشَرُوْنَ اِلٰى جَهَنَّمَ ۚ وَ بِئْسَ الْمِهَادُ ۝

14. Certainly there was for you a Sign in *b*the two armies that encountered each other, one army fighting in the cause of Allah and the other disbelieving, whom they saw to be twice as many as themselves, actually with *their* eyes. *Thus* *c*Allah strengthens with His aid whomsoever He pleases. In that surely is a lesson for those who have eyes.[305]

قَدْ كَانَ لَكُمْ اٰيَةٌ فِيْ فِئَتَيْنِ الْتَقَتَا ۚ فِئَةٌ تُقَاتِلُ فِيْ سَبِيْلِ اللّٰهِ وَ اُخْرٰى كَافِرَةٌ يَّرَوْنَهُمْ مِّثْلَيْهِمْ رَأْيَ الْعَيْنِ ۚ وَ اللّٰهُ يُؤَيِّدُ بِنَصْرِهٖ مَنْ يَّشَاءُ ۚ اِنَّ فِيْ ذٰلِكَ لَعِبْرَةً لِّاُولِي الْاَبْصَارِ ۝

---

*a*8 : 37 ; 54 : 46.   *b*8 : 42, 43.   *c*8 : 27.

---

and power could not save them from destruction, so would the endeavours of those who rejected the Holy Prophet not only fail to retard the progress of Islam but would pave the way for their own ruin.

304. Important Words :

تُحْشَرُوْن (gathered) is derived from حشر i.e., he gathered. حشر الناس means, he gathered together the people; he forced them to emigrate i.e. he banished them. حشر الجمع means, he drove the gathering from one place to another. حشرت الوحوش means, the animals were gathered and made to depart; they died or perished. يوم الحشر means, the Day of Congregation i.e. of Resurrection (Aqrab).

مهاد (place of rest) is derived from مهد. They say مهد الفراش i.e. he spread and made even (i.e. prepared) the bedding. مهاد means, bed; bedding; a low-lying piece of land (Aqrab).

Commentary :

The verse speaks of the end of the disbelievers. Islam will triumph over them in this world; and in the next Hell will be their abode.

305. Important Words :

عبرة (lesson) is the noun-infinitive from عبر. They say عبر i.e. he crossed it, or he passed over it from one side to the other. اعتبر means, he took warning; he took what he saw as an indication of what was concealed. عبرة therefore means, (1) an admonition or exhortation; (2) an admonition or exhortation by which one takes warning; (3) a thing by the state or condition of which one is admonished, reminded, directed or guided (Aqrab & Lane).

Commentary :

This verse refers to the Battle of Badr in which 313 ill-equipped and ill-armed Muslims inflicted a crushing defeat on a well-equipped and well-armed Meccan force, 1,000 strong. This fulfilled two prophecies—one contained in an earlier revelation of the Quran and the other in the Bible. The Quranic revelation said : *Do they say, ' We are a victorious host ? '. Nay, the hosts will be routed and will show their backs . . . . The day when they will be dragged into the Fire on their faces, (and it will be said to them) 'taste ye the touch of burning'* (54 : 45—49). And the Biblical prophecy

said : " In the forest of Arabia shall ye lodge,
O ye travelling companies of Dedanim. The
inhabitants of the land of Tema brought water
to him that was thirsty, they prevented with
their bread him that fled. For they fled from
the swords, from the drawn sword, and from
the bent bow, and from the grievousness of
war. For thus hath the Lord said unto me,
Within a year, according to the years of a
hireling, and all the glory of Kedar shall fail ;
and the residue of the number of archers, the
mighty men of the children of Kedar, shall
be diminished : for the Lord God of Israel
hath spoken it " (Isa. 21 : 13--17).

In accordance with this prophecy, about a
year after the flight of the Holy Prophet from
Mecca, the power of Kedar (the progenitor of
the Meccan tribes) was broken at Badr and
their glory departed. The Quranic prophecy
was also literally fulfilled ; for, after the Meccan
host was routed at Badr the ring-leaders
of the Quraish who fell in the battle, had to be
actually dragged along the ground and cast into
a well for burial, It was on this occasion that,
addressing their dead bodies the Holy Prophet
said, " God has made true the promise He had
made to us. Have you also found to be true
that which was promised to you ? " (Bukhārī).

The Quran describes the Day of Badr as the
day of " Discrimination " (8 : 42), because on
that day a great prophecy, accompanied by
great results, was fulfilled in extremely
unfavourable circumstances. The defeat of
the infidels was as unexpected and complete
as was the victory of the Muslims. Truly has
the Battle of Badr been reckoned among the
greatest battles in history. It virtually decided
the fate of the Meccans and of the whole of
Arabia. The power of the Quraish was broken
for ever and the New Faith rose high and
powerful in the land ; and all this came about
exactly as it had been prophesied.

The clause, *whom they saw to be twice as many
as themselves,* points out that the Meccan army
appeared to the Muslims to be less than their
actual strength *i.e.* only twice instead of thrice
the number of the Muslims, as was actually the
case. This was quite in harmony with divine will
which designed that the encounter should take
place and the few weak and ill-equipped
Muslims, seeing the full strength of the enemy,
should not become discouraged (8 : 45). What
happened was that one-third of the Meccan
army was behind a rising piece of land and
the Muslims could see only two-thirds of them
i.e. 600 or twice as many as their own number.
The Muslims were thus naturally heartened by
seeing the Meccan army only twice their own
number because they knew that in fulfilment
of His promise (8 : 67-68) God would surely
vouchsafe to them victory over an enemy
double their number.

The words, *actually with their eyes,* have
been added to point out that it was not in a
vision or a dream that the Muslims saw the
disbelievers to be less than their actual number
but in a state of actual wakefulness, which
naturally proved more heartening than would
have been the case if they had seen them so
only in a dream or vision, which very often
has an interpretation other than what actually
appears.

15. [a]Beautified for men is the love of desired things—women and children, and stored-up heaps of gold and silver, and pastured horses and cattle and crops. [b]That is the provision of the present life; but it is Allah with Whom is an excellent home.[306]

زُيِّنَ لِلنَّاسِ حُبُّ الشَّهَوَاتِ مِنَ النِّسَآءِ وَالْبَنِيْنَ وَالْقَنَاطِيْرِ الْمُقَنْطَرَةِ مِنَ الذَّهَبِ وَالْفِضَّةِ وَالْخَيْلِ الْمُسَوَّمَةِ وَالْأَنْعَامِ وَالْحَرْثِ ذٰلِكَ مَتَاعُ الْحَيٰوةِ الدُّنْيَا وَاللّٰهُ عِنْدَهُ حُسْنُ الْمَاٰبِ ۝

---

[a]18:47; 57:21.   [b]3:186; 9:38; 10:71.

---

306. Important Words:

الشهوات (desired things) is the plural of شهوة being derived from شها. They say شها i.e. he desired it; he desired it eagerly and intensely; he longed for it. شهوة means: (1) desire, or intense desire, or longing for a thing; (2) the thing desired or the object of desire. Sometimes the word is used in a bad sense indicating a low desire or gratification of venereal lust (Aqrab & Lane).

قناطير (heaps) and مقنطرة (stored-up) are both derived from قنطر. They say قنطر الرجل i.e. the man possessed, or came into possession of, great wealth. قنطر الشئ means, he tied up the thing, or he vaulted it. قناطير is the plural of قنطار meaning, heaped-up wealth. It also signifies a measure varying in weight and value at different times and in different countries. مقنطرة when added to قناطير intensifies the meaning, pointing to the greatness of heaped-up wealth. It also means, collected together or stored-up, giving also the sense of completeness and perfection (Aqrab & Lane).

Commentary:

The verse enumerates some of the things of this world which engross man's attention and often turn him away from God. These are particularly the things to the acquisition of which men, more specially in Christian countries, have applied their time and energy. As already pointed out, it is the Christians that are chiefly addressed in this *Sūra*. Islam does not prohibit the use, or even the seeking, of the good things of this world; but it certainly condemns the action of those who become engrossed in them and make them the very object of their life. Elsewhere the Quran refers to the Christian people as "those whose efforts are all lost in the life of this world" (18:105).

As to the question, who is the "beautifier" referred to in the clause, *beautified for men*, it may be noted that though the natural beauty in all things comes from God, yet here the "beautifier" is Satan, for in the present verse the question is not of "simple beauty" but of "engrossing beauty," not simply of the desired things of the world but of the abnormal love for them; and it is certainly Satan who endows the things of this world with engrossing beauty and creates in the hearts of men special love for them. God is only the beautifier of good deeds and good things, and the creator, in the heart of man, of dislike for evil ones (49:8, also 16:64).

16. Say, 'Shall I inform you of [a]something better than that?' For those who fear God, there are gardens with their Lord, beneath which rivers flow; therein shall they abide; and [b]pure spouses and [c]Allah's pleasure. And Allah is Mindful of His servants,[307]

قُلْ اَؤُنَبِّئُكُمْ بِخَيْرٍ مِّنْ ذٰلِكُمْ لِلَّذِيْنَ اتَّقَوْا عِنْدَ رَبِّهِمْ جَنّٰتٌ تَجْرِيْ مِنْ تَحْتِهَا الْاَنْهٰرُ خٰلِدِيْنَ فِيْهَا وَاَزْوَاجٌ مُّطَهَّرَةٌ وَّرِضْوَانٌ مِّنَ اللّٰهِ ۚ وَاللّٰهُ بَصِيْرٌ بِالْعِبَادِ ۝

17. Those who say, 'Our Lord, we do believe; [d]forgive us, therefore, our sins and save us from the punishment of the Fire;'[308]

اَلَّذِيْنَ يَقُوْلُوْنَ رَبَّنَآ اِنَّنَآ اٰمَنَّا فَاغْفِرْ لَنَا ذُنُوْبَنَا وَقِنَا عَذَابَ النَّارِ ۝

---

[a]18 : 47 ; 19 : 77. [b]See 2 : 26. [c]3 : 163, 175 ; 5 : 3 ; 9 : 72 ; 48 : 30 ; 59 : 9.
[d]3 : 194 ; 7 : 156 ; 23 : 110 ; 60 : 6.

---

307. Important Words :

رِضْوَان (pleasure) is derived from رَضِىَ i.e. he was pleased; he was well pleased; he was satisfied or contented; he regarded (him) with good-will or favour. رِضْوَان which is the noun-infinitive from رَضِىَ means, the state of being well pleased; satisfaction; good-will (Lane). As رِضْوَان signifies abundant pleasure or satisfaction, the word has come to be used in the Quran in connection with God only (Mufradāt). رِضْوَان is also the name of the keeper or guardian-angel of Paradise (Lane).

Commentary :

Though Islam does not object to the acquisition of the good things of this world, yet the good things of the life to come are far greater and nobler for man. And greater still is the pleasure or good-will of God which the Quran mentions as the greatest blessing (9 : 72). For one who succeeds in attaining it, even worldly things become a source of peace of mind. The Companions of the Holy Prophet attained it (9 : 100) and so they have been rightly called "the best people" (3 : 111).

308. Important Words :

ذُنُوْب (faults) which is the plural of ذَنْب (fault) is derived from the root ذَنَب (dhanaba). They say ذَنَبَهُ (dhanaba-hū) i.e. he followed his tail, not quitting its track; he followed him in any case, never quitting his track, the word ذَنَب (dhanab) meaning a tail, or, in man, the part of the body corresponding to the tail. ذَنْب (dhanb) means a fault, a misdeed, an offence, a thing for which one is blamable, if one does it intentionally. It differs from اِثْم (sin) in that whereas ذَنْب may be either intentional or committed through inadvertence, اِثْم is peculiarly intentional (Lane). According to Al-Rāghib, ذَنْب means, such errors and mistakes as bring about a harmful result or make one liable to be called to account (Mufradāt). Really ذَنْب (dhanb) signifies such failings or shortcomings as adhere to human nature, just as ذَنَب dhanab (tail, or in man, the corresponding part of the body) adheres to the body i.e. natural failings and shortcomings in man.

18. ^aThe steadfast, and the truthful, and the humble, and those who spend in the way of God, and those ^bwho seek forgiveness in the latter part of the night.[309]

اَلصّٰبِرِيْنَ وَالصّٰدِقِيْنَ وَالْقٰنِتِيْنَ وَالْمُنْفِقِيْنَ وَالْمُسْتَغْفِرِيْنَ بِالْاَسْحَارِ ۝

19. Allah bears witness that there is no God but He—and *also do* the angels and those possessed of knowledge—^cMaintainer of justice; there is no God but He, the Mighty, the Wise.[310]

شَهِدَ اللّٰهُ اَنَّهٗ لَآ اِلٰهَ اِلَّا هُوَ وَالْمَلٰٓئِكَةُ وَاُولُوا الْعِلْمِ قَآئِمًۢا بِالْقِسْطِ لَآ اِلٰهَ اِلَّا هُوَ الْعَزِيْزُ الْحَكِيْمُ ۝

---

^a33 : 36. ^b51 : 18, 19. ^c5 : 9 ; 7 : 30.

---

309. Important Words :

الْاَسْحَار (latter part of the night) is the plural of السحر *i.e.* the time before dawn. الاسحار is in the plural number but has been translated as singular for the sake of convenience. السحر also means, the side or end of a thing (Aqrab).

Commentary :

The qualities or attributes of a true believer mentioned in this verse represent four stages of spiritual progress : (1) When a man embraces true faith, he is very often subjected to persecution ; therefore, the first stage through which he has to pass is that of " patience and steadfastness." (2) When persecution comes to an end and a believer is free to act as he pleases, he carries into practice the teachings which he was unable fully to act upon before. Thus the second stage relates to " living truthfully " *i.e.* living up to one's conviction. (3) When, as a result of faithfully carrying out the commandments of their Faith, true believers attain to power, even then humility does not take leave of them. They remain as " humble " in spirit as ever. (4) Nay, their sense of service still increases. They " spend " whatever Allah has given them for the welfare of humanity. But, as the concluding words of the verse point out, all this time they

continue praying to God in the stillness of the night to forgive any falling short, on their part, of the high ideal of the service of humanity.

A true Muslim is expected to display all these qualities. He must show an unflinching patience and steadfastness under the severest trials and must live up to his conviction and carry into actual practice the noble ideals of his religion. Again, he must spend what God has given him of wealth, knowledge, influence, etc., in the service of humanity and must at the same time never be remiss in the discharge of the duties he owes to God. He should not only pray during the fixed hours of the day but should also pass parts of his nights in prayer and worship of the Lord. Special stress is laid in the Quran on the Prayer in the latter part of the night (17 : 80 ; 73 : 3—7). The word الاسحار (lit. latter parts of nights) has been used in the plural number to hint that a true believer should not be satisfied with praying in the latter part of the night only once or twice but should make it a habit to rise regularly for the *Tahajjud* Prayers.

310. Commentary :

The one central and indisputable fact in nature and the basic principle of every true religion is the Unity of God. The whole creation and the

375

20. Surely, ^athe *true* religion with Allah is complete submission. And those who were given the Book did not disagree but after knowledge had come to them, out of mutual envy. And whoso denies the Signs of Allah, then surely Allah is quick at reckoning.³¹¹

إِنَّ الدِّيْنَ عِنْدَ اللّٰهِ الْإِسْلَامُ ثَقَّ وَمَا اخْتَلَفَ الَّذِيْنَ اُوْتُوا الْكِتٰبَ اِلَّا مِنْ بَعْدِ مَا جَآءَهُمُ الْعِلْمُ بَغْيًا بَيْنَهُمْ وَمَنْ يَّكْفُرْ بِاٰيٰتِ اللّٰهِ فَاِنَّ اللّٰهَ سَرِيْعُ الْحِسَابِ ۞

---

^a3 : 86.

consummate order pervading it bear an undeniable testimony to this fundamental truth. The angels who are the bearers of the message of truth to the Prophets, the Messengers of God who propagate it in the world, and those good people who receive and imbibe true knowledge from God's Messengers, all add their testimony to the testimony of God. Similarly, all are united in testifying to the falsehood of the idea of setting up gods with God, be it in the form of plurality, trinity, or duality of gods. All true testimony must point and does point to the Oneness of the Creator.

311. Important Words :

اِسْلَام (complete submission) which is derived from اَسْلَمَ which again is derived from سَلِمَ signifies : (1) complete submission to God ; (2) the religion of Islam, the latter meaning being also based on the first-mentioned meaning (Tāj). See also 2 : 113.

Commentary :

The verse throws light on the fact that though other religious systems also claim to inculcate belief in the Oneness of God and submission to His will, yet it is only in Islam, the religion brought by the Holy Prophet, that the idea of submission to God's will has found its consummation ; for complete submission requires complete manifestation of God's attributes and it is in Islam alone that such manifestation has taken place. So Islam alone of all religious systems deserves to be called the religion of God in the real sense of the term. All true religions were indeed more or less *Islam* in their original form and their adherents *Muslims* in the literal sense of the term, but not till the time when religion became complete in all its different aspects was any faith given the name of Islam, which was reserved for the final dispensation perfected in the Quran.

The clause, *And those who were given the Book did not disagree but after knowledge had come to them, out of mutual envy*, signifies that if Jews and Christians had been truly submissive to the will of God, as they claim to be, they would not have refused to accept Islam, which is submission to divine will in its completest and most perfect form. By their rejection of Islam they have brought ruin upon themselves and have been deprived of God's grace and bounties of which they had had an ample share before.

376

21. But if they dispute with thee, say, ^a'I have submitted myself to Allah, and *also* those who follow me.' And say to those who have been given the Book and to the unlearned, 'Have you submitted?' If they submit, then they will surely be guided; but if they turn back, then ^bthy duty is only to convey the message. And Allah is Watchful of His servants.[312]

22. Surely, those who deny the Signs of Allah and ^cseek to kill the Prophets unjustly, and seek to kill such men as enjoin equity—announce to them a painful punishment.[313]

---

*a*4 : 126.   *b*5 : 93, 100 ; 13 : 41 ; 16 : 83.   *c*See 2 : 62.

---

312. Important Words :

امين (the unlearned), see 2 : 79.

الذين اوتوا الكتاب (those who have been given the Book) *i.e.* the People of the Book. The two expressions *i.e.* الذين اوتوا الكتاب and امين comprise the whole of mankind. الذين اوتوا الكتاب are those people who possess and profess to follow a revealed scripture; and امیون are those who accept and follow no such Book.

Commentary :

If the People of the Book and those who follow no revealed scripture were to submit to God, they would surely accept the Holy Prophet and be rightly guided, the former because clear prophecies are found in their scriptures regarding him and the latter because of the combined testimony of nature, human conscience and common sense. Submission to God is the source of all true guidance. One stumbles and loses the right path only when one deviates from the course of submission, bowing to authorities other than God.

313. Important Words :

یقتلون (seek to kill). See 2 : 62.

بشرهم (announce to them). See 2 : 26

Commentary :

Disbelievers are here warned that if they do not accept the Signs of God and persist in rejecting and fighting His Messengers and are not prepared to accept the arbitrament of divine revelation and of reason, they cannot escape divine punishment. No Prophet of God, whatever circumstances faced him, ever failed in his mission. No amount of persecution or attempts to murder the Prophets ever succeeded in arresting or retarding the progress of their faith. The history of religion provides a standing testimony to this fact; and the Holy Prophet of Islam—the Greatest of all Prophets—was not going to be an exception. The expression فبشرهم بعذاب الیم translated as "announce to them a painful punishment" literally means, "give them the glad tidings of a painful punishment." The word بشر (give

377

23. Those are they *a*whose deeds shall come to naught in this world and in the next, and they shall have no helpers.[314]

اُولٰٓئِكَ الَّذِيْنَ حَبِطَتْ اَعْمَالُهُمْ فِى الدُّنْيَا وَالْاٰخِرَةِ وَمَا لَهُمْ مِّنْ نّٰصِرِيْنَ ۝

24. Dost thou not know of those who have been given *their* portion of the Book? *b*They are called to the Book of Allah that it may judge between them, but a party of them turn away in aversion.[315]

اَلَمْ تَرَ اِلَى الَّذِيْنَ اُوْتُوْا نَصِيْبًا مِّنَ الْكِتٰبِ يُدْعَوْنَ اِلٰى كِتٰبِ اللهِ لِيَحْكُمَ بَيْنَهُمْ ثُمَّ يَتَوَلّٰى فَرِيْقٌ مِّنْهُمْ وَ هُمْ مُّعْرِضُوْنَ ۝

*a*2 : 218; 7 : 148; 18 : 106.   *b*24 : 49.

---

glad tidings) has been used with a twofold purpose : (1) to signify that the promised punishment is extraordinarily great, the word بشارة literally meaning a news that changes the colour of the skin of the listener ; (2) to point to the fact that the disbelievers have been deprived of a great blessing. They were invited to God's favour which was truly glad tidings but, having rejected it, they incurred His wrath and brought punishment on their heads.

314. Commentary :

Disbelievers have no faith in the retribution of the life to come ; so as a proof of the fact that their deeds will not avail them at all on the Day of Resurrection, they are told that in the present life also their efforts to destroy Islam will prove futile and this will be evidence of the fact that in the life to come their works will be of no use to them. Two facts have been foretold, one relating to this life and the other to the life to come. When the former turns out to be true, the latter will also have to be regarded as true. It must not, however, be thought that all the works of disbelievers will come to naught ; for, elsewhere the Quran says, *Whosoever does a tittle of good will have its reward* (99 : 8). This shows that the present verse refers to such works only as are performed to destroy or weaken Islam or such works as are opposed to the teachings of Islam.

315. Commentary :

The expression, *portion of the Book*, may refer to (1) the prophecies contained in the Bible concerning the Holy Prophet which formed a portion of the Book ; or (2) the genuine portion of the Bible, because only a part of it had remained safe from interpolation and this alone could be called a part of the true Book ; or (3) the expression may also mean that as compared with the Quran, which is the Book *par excellence*, being the eternal and perfect divine Book, the Bible is but a portion and a part. In view of these different explanations, the verse would give different meanings : (a) that when the attention of Jews and Christians is drawn to the prophecies embodied in their scriptures they refuse to be guided by them. Or (b) that if the People of the Book had adhered to the genuine portion of their own scriptures the criteria laid down therein for testing the truth of a claimant to prophethood would have surely led them to accept the Holy Prophet. Or (c) that if they had faithfully acted on the teachings of their own scriptures, which was in fact a part of the perfect and eternal teachings contained in the Quran, they would have certainly recognized the truth of the New Faith.

25. That is because they say, ^a' The Fire shall not touch us, except for a limited number of days.' And what they used to forge has deceived them regarding their religion.[316]

ذٰلِكَ بِاَنَّهُمْ قَالُوْا لَنْ تَمَسَّنَا النَّارُ اِلَّا اَيَّامًا مَّعْدُوْدٰتٍ ۫ وَّغَرَّهُمْ فِيْ دِيْنِهِمْ مَّا كَانُوْا يَفْتَرُوْنَ ۞

26. How *will they fare* ^bwhen We will gather them together on the Day about which there is no doubt; and when every soul shall be paid in full what it has earned, and they shall not be wronged?[317]

فَكَيْفَ اِذَا جَمَعْنٰهُمْ لِيَوْمٍ لَّا رَيْبَ فِيْهِ ۫ وَوُفِّيَتْ كُلُّ نَفْسٍ مَّا كَسَبَتْ وَهُمْ لَا يُظْلَمُوْنَ ۞

27. Say, ' O Allah, ^cLord of sovereignty, Thou givest sovereignty to whomsoever Thou pleasest; and Thou takest away sovereignty from whomsoever Thou pleasest. Thou exaltest whomsoever Thou pleasest and Thou abasest whomsoever Thou pleasest. In Thy hand is all good. Thou surely hast power to do all things.[317A]

قُلِ اللّٰهُمَّ مٰلِكَ الْمُلْكِ تُؤْتِي الْمُلْكَ مَنْ تَشَآءُ وَتَنْزِعُ الْمُلْكَ مِمَّنْ تَشَآءُ ۫ وَتُعِزُّ مَنْ تَشَآءُ وَتُذِلُّ مَنْ تَشَآءُ ۫ بِيَدِكَ الْخَيْرُ ۫ اِنَّكَ عَلٰى كُلِّ شَيْءٍ قَدِيْرٌ ۞

---

^a2:81; 5:19. ^b3:10; 4:88; 45:27. ^c2:285; 5:19,41; 35:14; 40:17; 48:15.

---

316. Commentary:

Both Jews and Christians persuaded themselves to believe that they would be safe against the punishment of the Hereafter, the Jews thinking themselves immune owing to their being the favoured ones of God on account of their being the descendants of His Prophets, and the Christians deluding themsleves with the idea that Jesus, " the son of God," had washed away their sins with his supposed death on the Cross. The false notion of each proved their ruin.

317. Commentary:

The People of the Book are here called upon to imagine how they will fare when they will have to render an account of their deeds before God on the Day of Judgement and will find to their mortification that the fact of their being descendants of God's Prophets or their belief in the crucifixion of Jesus will not save them from the punishment of Hell.

The clause, *When every soul shall be paid in full what it has earned*, shows that the reference to forgers of lies mentioned in the previous verse is particularly to Christians. This verse is an emphatic contradiction of the doctrine that the blood of any one, and not one's own good works, can be a means of salvation.

317A Commentary:

See under next verse.

28. *a*'Thou makest the night pass into the day and makest the day pass into the night. And *b*Thou bringest forth the living from the dead and bringest forth the dead from the living. And Thou givest to whomsoever Thou pleasest without measure.'³¹⁸

تُوۡلِجُ الَّیۡلَ فِی النَّهَارِ وَتُوۡلِجُ النَّهَارَ فِی الَّیۡلِ وَتُخۡرِجُ الۡحَیَّ مِنَ الۡمَیِّتِ وَتُخۡرِجُ الۡمَیِّتَ مِنَ الۡحَیِّ وَتَرۡزُقُ مَنۡ تَشَآءُ بِغَیۡرِ حِسَابٍ ۞

*a*7 : 55 ; 13 : 4 ; 22 : 62 ; 35 : 14 ; 39 : 6 ; 57 : 7.   *b*6 : 96 ; 10 : 32 ; 30 : 20.

318. Commentary :

This and the preceding verse point to the immutable divine law that nations rise and fall as they conform to, or defy, the will of God, Who is the source of all power and glory. They also refer to the fulfilment of a great prophecy. A nation which had enjoyed temporal and spiritual sovereignty for a long time was going to be abased, because it had persistently violated the divine law and had become spiritually dead ; and in place of it another nation, till now very low in the scale of humanity, was going to be raised to the highest pinnacle of temporal and spiritual power. The sovereignty or kingdom mentioned in the preceding verse refers to both the temporal and spiritual kingdom which was promised to the progeny of Abraham and which the Israelites had enjoyed for a long time. That kingdom was now going to be transferred to the House of Ishmael to find its completest manifestation in Islam. A living nation had suffered death and another, as good as dead, had arisen into life.

The word النهار (day) represents prosperity and power, and الليل (night) signifies the loss of power combined with decline and decadence. By using this simile, the Quran draws attention to the fact that a people who wish that the night of woes and miseries should never overtake them and that they should never continue to enjoy the day of prosperity and glory, should so place themselves in front of the Divine Sun as to continue to be illuminated by its ever-effulgent light. In this connection it may also be noted that the Quranic expression, *Thou makest the night pass into the day and makest the day pass into the night,* does not merely signify alternate ending and beginning of day and night but also the conversion of part of the day into night and *viceversa,* thus hinting at the lengthening of the one at the cost of the other.

The clause, *And Thou givest to whomsoever thou pleasest without measure,* holds out a promise to Muslims that the glory of Islam will be unparalleled and will last for ever. Islam will never be displaced as a religion and Muslims will always continue to be one of the most exalted peoples of the earth till the end of time. The appearance of Ahmad, the Promised Messiah, at a time when the temporal power of Islam was at its lowest ebb and Muslims had also become morally and spiritually degenerate, was in fulfilment of this very promise. Through him Islam has found a new life. It will now bloom and blossom till whole nations shall come under its spiritual sway, and Muslims shall regain their pristine glory and shall become the most dominant people on the face of the earth.

29. ^aLet not the believers take disbelievers for friends in preference to believers,—and whoever does that has no connection with Allah—except that you cautiously guard against them. And Allah cautions you against His punishment; and to Allah is the returning.[319]

لَا يَتَّخِذِ الْمُؤْمِنُوْنَ الْكٰفِرِيْنَ اَوْلِيَآءَ مِنْ دُوْنِ الْمُؤْمِنِيْنَ ۚ وَمَنْ يَّفْعَلْ ذٰلِكَ فَلَيْسَ مِنَ اللّٰهِ فِيْ شَيْءٍ اِلَّاۤ اَنْ تَتَّقُوْا مِنْهُمْ تُقٰىةً ۗ وَيُحَذِّرُكُمُ اللّٰهُ نَفْسَهٗ ۗ وَاِلَى اللّٰهِ الْمَصِيْرُ ۝

30. Say, ^b'Whether you conceal what is in your breasts or reveal it, Allah knows it; and He knows whatever is in the heavens and whatever is in the earth. And Allah has power to do all things.'[320]

قُلْ اِنْ تُخْفُوْا مَا فِيْ صُدُوْرِكُمْ اَوْ تُبْدُوْهُ يَعْلَمْهُ اللّٰهُ ۗ وَيَعْلَمُ مَا فِي السَّمٰوٰتِ وَمَا فِي الْاَرْضِ ۗ وَاللّٰهُ عَلٰى كُلِّ شَيْءٍ قَدِيْرٌ ۝

^a3 : 119 ; 4 : 140, 145.   ^b27 : 75 ; 28 : 70.

---

319. Important Words :

نَفْسَهٗ (His punishment). نَفْس is the noun-infinitive from نَفُسَ (nafusa) which literally means, it was or became loved and highly esteemed. نَفِسَ بِه (nafisa) means, he was tenacious or niggardly of it. نَفْس means, the soul; the spirit; the mind; the body; a person or being; a person's or being's self; brother or relative, or one belonging to one's own religion; purpose, will or desire; punishment, etc. (Aqrab & Lane).

Commentary :

With the advent of political power to Islam, as promised in the preceding verses, the contracting of political alliances became necessary for the Muslim State. The verse under comment embodies the guiding principle that no Muslim State should enter into any treaty or alliance with a non-Muslim State which should in any way injure, or conflict with, the interests of other Muslim States. The interests of Islam should transcend all other interests.

The phrase, *in preference to believers*, means: (1) that Muslims should not form friendly relations with disbelievers in preference to believers, shunning the latter and seeking the former; (2) that they should not form any connection with disbelievers in a way that may harm the interests of Muslims. They are, however, free to contract friendly relations with such non-Muslims as are friendly to them, according to the exigencies of time and circumstances (60 : 9, 10).

The verse also instructs Muslims to be on their guard against the plots and machinations of disbelievers. The expression, *except that you cautiously guard against them*, refers not to the power of the enemy but to his cunning against which Muslims should always be on their guard.

The clause وَيُحَذِّرُكُمُ اللّٰهُ نَفْسَهٗ rendered as, *And Allah cautions you against His punishment*, may also be translated as "and Allah cautions or warns you concerning Himself", meaning that if you do not faithfully accept the guidance of God, and make friends with disbelievers in preference to believers, you will lose God, Who will in that case have no connection with you.

320. Commentary :

This and the succeeding verse are addressed to the enemies of Islam. They are warned

31. *Beware of* the Day ᵃwhen every soul shall find itself confronted with *all* the good it has done and *all* the evil it has done. It will wish there were a great distance between it and that *evil*. And Allah cautions you against His punishment. And Allah is Most Compassionate to His servants.³²¹

يَوْمَ تَجِدُ كُلُّ نَفْسٍ مَّا عَمِلَتْ مِنْ خَيْرٍ مُّحْضَرًا ۖ وَّمَا عَمِلَتْ مِنْ سُوْٓءٍ ۛ تَوَدُّ لَوْ اَنَّ بَيْنَهَا وَبَيْنَهٗٓ اَمَدًۢا بَعِيْدًا ۗ وَيُحَذِّرُكُمُ اللّٰهُ نَفْسَهٗ ۗ وَاللّٰهُ رَءُوْفٌۢ بِالْعِبَادِ ۩

R. 4   32. Say, ᵇ'If you love Allah, follow me : *then* will Allah love you and forgive you your faults. And Allah is Most Forgiving, Merciful.'³²²

قُلْ اِنْ كُنْتُمْ تُحِبُّوْنَ اللّٰهَ فَاتَّبِعُوْنِيْ يُحْبِبْكُمُ اللّٰهُ وَيَغْفِرْ لَكُمْ ذُنُوْبَكُمْ ۗ وَاللّٰهُ غَفُوْرٌ رَّحِيْمٌ ۞

33. Say, ᶜ'Obey Allah and His Messenger :' but if they turn away, then *remember that* Allah loves not the disbelievers.³²³

قُلْ اَطِيْعُوا اللّٰهَ وَالرَّسُوْلَ ۚ فَاِنْ تَوَلَّوْا فَاِنَّ اللّٰهَ لَا يُحِبُّ الْكٰفِرِيْنَ ۞

ᵃ18 : 50.   ᵇ4 : 70.   ᶜ4 : 60; 5 : 93; 8 : 47; 24 : 55; 58 : 14.

that all their open or secret machinations against Islam shall come to naught, for the obvious reason that the Almighty and the All-Knowing God had promised to protect it.

321. Important Words :

رَءُوف (Most Compassionate) is one of the attributes of God. It is derived from رَأَف meaning, he pitied him or had compassion on him; he pitied or compassionated him tenderly or in the utmost degree (Lane & Aqrab).

Commentary :

For the meaing of the clause, *And Allah cautions you against His punishment*, see 3 : 29 above.

322. Commentary :

The verse is most important inasmuch as it pertains to the attainment of the love of God which is considered by Islam to be the highest goal of human life. It constitutes an open and unqualified challenge to mankind, particularly to Christians, who claim to be under the direct leadership of the "son of God," while they and the Jews both call themselves "the children of Allah and His beloved ones" (5 : 19). The verse emphatically declares that the goal pertaining to the attainment of divine love is now impossible of achievement except by accepting Islam and following the Holy Prophet Muhammad (peace and blessings of God be on him!). Those who seek to love God and attain to His nearness must follow the guidance of the Prophet of Islam, which will make them the beloved ones of God. This is the only door now left open for the attainment of divine love; and as God loves only pure souls, such men as sincerely follow Islam and act upon its teachings will be purified by Him and have their faults forgiven them.

323. Commentary :

In contrast to the previous verse, the present verse tells us of the end of those who do not

34. Allah did choose Adam and Noah and the family of Abraham and the family of ' Imrān above all peoples,—[324]

إِنَّ اللهَ اصْطَفٰى اٰدَمَ وَنُوْحًا وَّاٰلَ اِبْرٰهِيْمَ وَاٰلَ عِمْرٰنَ عَلَى الْعٰلَمِيْنَ ۞

love God and refuse to obey Him and His Messenger. They are disbelievers and are deprived of God's love.

324. Important Words :

عمران ('Imrān) may possibly refer to two persons : (1) Amram of the Bible, who was a son of Kohath and a grandson of Levi. He was the father of Moses, Aaron and Miriam, Moses being the youngest of the three (Jew. Enc. under Amram; also Exod. 6 : 18-20); (2) 'Imrān, the father of Mary, mother of Jesus. This ' Imrān was the son of Yoshhim or Yoshim (Jarīr & Kathīr).

Commentary :

From this verse onward the Quranic narration narrows down specifically to the Christian people, the present verse beautifully beginning with the mention of Adam and ending with that of " the family of 'Imrān." 'Imrān, as stated above, was (1) the name of the father of Moses and (2) of the father of Mary. The Quran has chosen this name with a twofold purpose : (1) to include, besides Moses, a reference to Aaron, the elder brother of Moses, and (2) to use it as a sort of preamble for introducing the story of Mary, the mother of Jesus, and, through it, that of Jesus himself. The repetition of the name "'Imrān " in the verse following the succeeding one also points to the same conclusion.

It is significant that whereas the verse mentions the names of Adam and Noah singly and individually, it refers to Abraham and 'Imrān as heads of families. This has

been done in order to point out that the latter names include references to certain individuals from among their progeny. Thus the expression "family of Abraham " not only refers to Abraham personally but also to his sons and grandsons, Ishmael, Isaac, Jacob and Joseph. It may also include a reference to the Holy Prophet of Islam who was likewise descended from Abraham. Similarly, the words " family of 'Imrān " refer to Aaron, Moses and Jesus. 'Imrān himself is not included, as he was not a Prophet. See also 3 : 36.

The verse also helps to clarify the meaning of such Quranic expressions as "Allah chose or exalted this or that person or this or that people above all peoples," for, here Adam and Noah and the family of Abraham and the family of 'Imrān have all been spoken of as being chosen above all peoples. As all these cannot possibly be above all others, for that would be a contradiction in terms, the only inference is that each one of the above-mentioned individuals and families was exalted above the men or the peoples of his or their age only and not above the peoples of all ages.

The verse also serves to point out that just as Adam and Noah and Abraham and the children of 'Imrān were successful in spite of the opposition of the people, so will God make the Prophet of Islam successful in spite of the hostility of the enemies of Islam and will prove that he and his Companions were His chosen people.

35. A *a*race, co-related with one another. And Allah is All-Hearing, All-Knowing.[325]

ذُرِّيَّةً بَعْضُهَا مِنْ بَعْضٍ ۗ وَاللّٰهُ سَمِيعٌ عَلِيمٌ ۞

36. *Remember* when *the* woman of 'Imrān said, ' My Lord, I have vowed to Thee what is in my womb to be dedicated to Thy service. So do accept *it* of me ; verily, Thou alone art All-Hearing, All-Knowing'.[326]

إِذْ قَالَتِ امْرَأَتُ عِمْرَانَ رَبِّ إِنِّي نَذَرْتُ لَكَ مَا فِي بَطْنِي مُحَرَّرًا فَتَقَبَّلْ مِنِّي ۚ إِنَّكَ أَنْتَ السَّمِيعُ الْعَلِيمُ ۞

*a*6 : 88 ; 19 : 59.

---

325. Commentary :

The word ذرية (a race) has been put in the verse not as مبتدا but as حال. The verse must, therefore, be considered a part of the preceding one and would literally mean, " while these were or are a race co-related with one another," the inference being that the individuals and families mentioned in the preceding verse were chosen by God because they all belonged to the same stock, the stock of good and righteous people.

326. Important Words :

محررا (dedicated to special service) is derived from حر *i.e.* it became hot ; or he became free. حرر means, he wrote ; or he wrote well and elegantly and accurately. حرر رقبة means, he freed a slave. حرر ابنه means, he dedicated his son for the worship of God and the service of the church or the temple ; or he devoted him to that service as long as he should live. محرر means, freed from slavery ; emancipated ; a child devoted by the parent to the service of the church or the temple ; or one divorced from all affairs of the world and dedicated to the service of the temple (Lane, Mufradāt & Jarīr). It was a custom among the Israelites that those who were dedicated to the service of the temple remained unmarried (Gospel of Mary, 5 : 6 ; and Bayān under 3 : 36).

امرأة (woman) is derived from مرأ *i.e.* it (the food) was wholesome. مرء or امرأ means, a man. مرأة or امرأة means, a woman ; a perfect woman ; a wife (Lane).

عمران ('Imrān). In the present verse the word is either the abbreviated form of آل عمران (the family of 'Imrān, father of Moses) just as they use the word "Israel" for " the children of Israel " (see 2 : 41), or it refers to 'Imrān, the father of Mary. See also 3 : 34

Commentary :

In this verse the mother of Mary whose name was Hanna (Enc. Bib.) has been spoken of as امرأة عمران (woman of 'Imrān) while in 19 : 29, Mary herself has been addressed as اخت هارون (sister of Aaron). 'Imrān (Amram) and Aaron were respectively the father and brother of Moses, while he had also a sister named Miriam. Being ignorant of Arabic idiom and Quranic style, Christian writers, who ascribe the authorship of the Quran to the Holy Prophet, think that in his ignorance he confused Mary, mother of Jesus, with Mary or Miriam, the sister of Moses. Thus they pretend to have discovered a serious anachronism in the Quran—an absurd charge, inasmuch as quite a number of passages can be cited to show that the Quran considers Moses and Jesus as two Prophets separated from each other by a long line of Prophets (*e.g.* 2 : 88 ; 5 : 44—46).

These Christian writers are not the first to make this "discovery." The "credit" for it goes to the Christians of Najrān who, as long as 1,350 years ago, raised the same objection and received a prompt reply. It is on record that when the Holy Prophet sent Mughīra to Najrān, the Christians of that place asked him: "Do you not read in the Quran Mary (mother of Jesus) being mentioned as the sister of Aaron, while you know that Jesus was born a long, long time after Moses?" "I did not know the answer," says Mughīra, "and on my return to Medina I enquired about it of the Holy Prophet who readily answered, 'Why did you not tell them that the Israelites used to name their children after their deceased Prophets and saints?'" (Tirmidhī). In fact, there is actually a tradition to the effect that the husband of Hanna and the father of Mary was named 'Imrān whose father (i.e. Mary's grandfather) had the name Yoshhim or Yoshim (Jarīr & Kathīr). Thus this 'Imrān is different from the 'Imrān who was the father of Moses and whose own father was Kohath (Exod. 6 : 18-20).

The fact that Hanna's husband, or for that matter Mary's father, has been named Joachim in the Christian scriptures (Gospel of the Birth of Mary and the Enc. Brit. under Mary) should not perplex us as Joachim is the same as Yoshim mentioned by Ibn Jarīr as the father of 'Imrān. The Christian scriptures give the name of the grandfather instead of the father, which is not an uncommon practice. Besides, there are instances in the Bible of one person being known by two names. Gideon, for instance, was also called Jerubbaal (Judg. 7:1). So there should be no surprise if the second name of Joachim happened to be 'Imrān.

Moreover, like individuals, families, too, are sometimes known after the names of their distinguished ancestors. In the Bible the name Israel sometimes stands for the Israelites (Deut. 6 : 3, 4) and Kedar for the Ishmaelites (Isa. 21 : 16 ; 42 : 11). Similarly, Jesus has been called the son of David (Matt. 1 : 1). So the words امرأة عمران may also mean امرأة آل عمران i.e. a woman from the family of 'Imrān, or a perfect woman from the family of 'Imrān. This explanation finds further strength from the fact that the words آل عمران (family of 'Imrān) have been used by the Quran only two verses before the present one. So the word آل (family) was dropped here owing to the nearness of reference. And it is admitted that Hanna, the mother of Mary, who was the cousin of Elisabeth (John's mother) belonged to the House of Aaron and through him to that of 'Imrān (Luke 1 :5, 36.)

The vow of Mary's mother seems to have been taken under the influence of the Essenes who were generally held in high esteem by the people of that time, and who practised celibacy and excluded women from their membership, and dedicated their lives to the service of religion and their fellow-beings (Enc. Bib. and Jew. Enc.). It is remarkable that the teachings of the Gospels have much in common with those of the Essenes. It is also clear from the meaning of the word محرر as given under Important Words above, that Mary's mother had vowed the dedication of her child's life to the service of the temple, and as such she intended the child never to marry, which shows that Mary was meant to belong to the priestly class. This is why, elsewhere in the Quran, she is called the sister of Aaron and not of Moses (19 : 29) though both were real brothers, for whereas Moses was the founder of the Jewish Law, Aaron was the head of the Jewish priestly class (Enc. Bib. and Enc. Brit. under Aaron). Thus Mary, mother of Jesus, was the sister of Aaron not in the sense that she was his real sister but in the sense that, like Aaron, she also belonged to the priestly order.

37. But when she was delivered of it, she said, ' My Lord, I am delivered of a female,'—and Allah knew best what she had brought forth and the male *she was thinking of* was not like the female *she had brought forth*— 'and I have named her Mary, and I commit her and her offspring to Thy protection from Satan, the rejected. '327

فَلَمَّا وَضَعَتْهَا قَالَتْ رَبِّ اِنِّیْ وَضَعْتُهَاۤ اُنْثٰیؕ وَاللّٰهُ اَعْلَمُ بِمَا وَضَعَتْ وَ لَیْسَ الذَّكَرُ كَالْاُنْثٰیۚ وَاِنِّیْ سَمَّیْتُهَا مَرْیَمَ وَاِنِّیْۤ اُعِیْذُهَا بِكَ وَ ذُرِّیَّتَهَا مِنَ الشَّیْطٰنِ الرَّجِیْمِ ۝

---

327. Important Words :

مَرْیَم (Mary) was the mother of Jesus. She was probably named after the sister of Moses and Aaron, known as Mariam (later pronunciation Miriam). The word, which is probably a compound one consisting of مر and م possesses, in Hebrew, a variety of interpretations, some of them being "bitter sea"; "drop of the sea"; "star of the sea"; "bitterness"; "mistress" or "lady". From two alternative roots Mariam might also mean, "the rebellious", or "the corpulent" (Enc. Bib. under Mary). It also means "exalted" (Cruden's Concordance). Muslim traditionists ascribe to the word the meaning of "pious worshipper" (Kashshāf).

الرَّجِیْم (the rejected) is passive participle from رجم. They say رجمه *i.e.* he pelted him with stones; he smote and killed him; he drove him away; he cursed him; he boycotted or forsook him; he reviled or abused him. رجم الرجل means, the man said a thing on conjecture. رجم القبر means, he put up a stone at the tomb to serve as a sign. الرَّجِیْم means : (1) one whom God has driven away from His presence and mercy *i.e.* the one rejected ; (2) one whom God has cursed ; (3) one who has been forsaken and abandoned ; and (4) one who has been pelted with stones (Aqrab & Lane). It also means, one driven away or deprived of all goodness and virtue (Mufradāt).

Commentary :

Mary's mother had made the vow in the hope that she would be blessed with a son whom she would dedicate to the service of God. Instead a daughter was born to her. So she was naturally perplexed.

The words, *Allah knew best what she had brought forth*, form a parenthetical clause spoken by God whereas the following words, *the male was not like the female*, may be taken to have been either spoken by God or by Mary's mother. Most probably they are God's words and mean as rendered in the text, that the female child she had brought forth was superior to the male child she desired to have. If taken to have been spoken by Mary's mother, they would mean that the female child she had given birth to could not be like the male child she desired, inasmuch as a boy only was fitted to do the special service to which she desired to dedicate him.

The clause, *I have named her Mary*, contains an implied prayer to God to make the girl as exalted and as good and virtuous as the name Mary, meaning exalted or a pious worshipper, signified.

The words, *I commit her and her offspring to Thy protection from Satan, the rejected*, offer some difficulty. If Mary's mother intended her child to be dedicated to the service of God, she must have known that the child would remain unmarried for life. What is, then, the sense in offering prayer for the child's offspring? The most probable explanation is that God had told her in a vision that her daughter would grow up to womanhood and would have a child, whereupon she prayed that Mary and her child might both be granted God's protection from Satan, the rejected. In spite of this, however, she appears to have left the future of Mary in God's hand and dedicated her, as she had originally intended, to the service of God (3: 38 ; 3: 45 ; also Gospel of the Birth of Mary). This must have been an exceptional case, for ordinarily only males were eligible for such dedication. The assumption that Mary's mother had a vision that her daughter would have a son is not unfounded. It finds mention in the Gospel of Mary (3: 5) though perhaps in a somewhat different form.

There was nothing unusual about the prayer of Hanna, Mary's mother, that Mary and her offspring might be protected from satanic influences. All pious parents are actuated by such a desire for their children and pray that they should grow up to lead good and virtuous lives. But unfortunately this simple and natural prayer of Mary's mother, coupled with a saying of the Holy Prophet to the effect that Mary and her son Jesus were free from the touch of Satan, has given rise to widespread misunderstanding and has been made the basis of an entirely erroneous and misleading belief among a section of Muslims, besides affording to Christians a welcome excuse for attack on Islam. A section among the latter-day Muslims has come to believe that of all men and women, Jesus and his mother, Mary, alone were immune from the evil influences of Satan.

As hinted above, this doctrine is based on a tradition of the Holy Prophet which says: "No child is born but Satan touches it at the time of its birth and makes it cry, except Jesus and his mother Mary" (Bukhārī). Unfortunately, this saying of the Holy Prophet has been shorn of its true setting and utterly misunderstood. These words of the Prophet, besides being not strictly relevant as they refer

only to the touch of Satan at the time of the birth of a child and not absolutely, were necessitated by the fact that the Jews, out of their enmity towards Jesus, charged him and his mother with the infamous accusation that, God forbid, Mary led an immoral life, and conceived out of rightful wedlock, and that consequently Jesus, her son, had an illegal birth. It was to refute this filthy charge that the Holy Prophet uttered the above-quoted words. So this saying of the Prophet is not intended to be general but has only a particular significance with a specific setting. In fact this ḥadīth mentions the names of Jesus and his mother Mary only by way of citing an instance and what is meant is that all mortals born of a woman are likely to come under the influence of Satan except such as possess moral and spiritual qualities like unto those possessed by Mary and her son. Arabic language is not wanting in instances where a person is named not in his individual capacity but as representing a class of people (Kashshāf & Manāwī). The names of Jesus and Mary have been specifically chosen because of the aspersion cast at them by the wicked Jews. Another equally good interpretation is that the words "no child is born" occurring in this ḥadīth are, as hinted above, not general but have been used in a restricted sense, signifying not all children absolutely but only such children as were born out of wedlock in the days of Jesus, and the name of Mary has been added because it was her abnormal conception that occasioned such birth of Jesus. Another saying of the Holy Prophet supports this interpretation. Says he, "every child is born in the likeness of Islam; it is only his parents that make him a Christian, a Jew or a Fire-Worshipper" (Bukhārī). So the "touch" of Satan referred to in the foregoing ḥadīth cannot be general; it must be taken in a restricted sense.

38. So her Lord accepted her with a gracious acceptance and caused her to grow an excellent growth and made Zachariah her guardian. Whenever Zachariah visited her in the chamber, he found with her provisions. He said, 'O Mary, whence hast thou this?' She replied, 'It is from Allah'. Surely, Allah gives to whomsoever He pleases without measure.[328]

فَتَقَبَّلَهَا رَبُّهَا بِقَبُوْلٍ حَسَنٍ وَّ اَنْبَتَهَا نَبَاتًا حَسَنًا وَّ كَفَّلَهَا زَكَرِيَّا ۙ كُلَّمَا دَخَلَ عَلَيْهَا زَكَرِيَّا الْمِحْرَابَ وَجَدَ عِنْدَهَا رِزْقًا ۚ قَالَ يٰمَرْيَمُ اَنّٰى لَكِ هٰذَا ۚ قَالَتْ هُوَ مِنْ عِنْدِ اللّٰهِ ۚ اِنَّ اللّٰهَ يَرْزُقُ مَنْ يَّشَآءُ بِغَيْرِ حِسَابٍ ۞

That Jesus and his mother are not alone in being free from the touch of Satan is clear from a number of Quranic verses and several sayings of the Holy Prophet. To quote only one instance from each, the Quran says: (O Satan,) surely thou shalt have no power over My servants, except such of the erring ones as choose to follow thee (15 : 43). And the Holy Prophet says : "If a person goes in unto his wife praying, 'O my Lord, keep me away from Satan and so too, keep away the child you grant me,' and the wife conceives on such an occasion, the child born will be free from the touch of Satan " (Bukhārī).

As for himself personally the Holy Prophet says, " Every one of you has a satan attached to him (who tries to lead him astray) but God has helped me against my satan who has turned a Muslim i.e. obedient and submissive " (Musnad). This means that so far as the Holy Prophet was concerned Satan had become virtually non-existent. This is certainly a much more exalted position than mere protection against the attack of Satan. Truly has the Prophet remarked, "If Moses and Jesus had been alive, they would have found themselves forced to follow me " (Kathīr).

Finally, it may be noted that though Islam declares all Prophets of God to be virtually safe from the influence of Satan, the Bible does not ascribe this protection to Jesus; for the New Testament clearly states at a number of places that he was tempted by the Devil for no less than forty days (e.g. Mark 1 : 12, 13).

328. **Important Words :**

كفّلها (made him her guardian) is derived from كفل. They say كفله i.e. he was or became responsible for him; he became his guardian. كفل خالدا زيدا means, he made Zaid the guardian of Khālid; he gave Khālid in the guardianship of Zaid (Aqrab).

زكريا (Zachariah or Zacharias) was the name of an Israelite holy person whom the Quran presents as a Prophet (6 : 86-90) but of whom the Bible speaks only as a priest (Luke 1 : 5). The person presented as a Prophet by the Bible is Zechariah (the Book Zech. 1 : 1; mark the difference in spelling) of whom the Quran, however, makes no mention. زكريا of the Quran was the father of Yaḥyā (John) who was a cousin of Jesus.

المحراب (chamber) is derived from حرب for which see 2 : 280. محراب means, a room in the uppermost story of a house; a chamber to which one ascends by stairs; the chief sitting place in a room or a house; the place or niche where the Imām stands while leading the Prayers in a mosque; a mosque or a place of worship (Aqrab & Lane). محراب (chamber of Prayer or the place of the Imām in a mosque) is probably so called because it is

39. There *and then* did Zachariah pray to His Lord, saying, *a*' My Lord, grant me from Thyself pure offspring; surely, Thou art the Hearer of prayer.'[329]

هُنَالِكَ دَعَا زَكَرِيَّا رَبَّهٗ ۚ قَالَ رَبِّ هَبْ لِیْ مِنْ لَّدُنْكَ ذُرِّيَّةً طَيِّبَةً ۚ اِنَّكَ سَمِيْعُ الدُّعَآءِ ۝

40. And the angels called to him as *b*he stood praying in the chamber: *c*' Allah gives thee glad tidings of Yaḥyā, *d*who shall testify to the truth of a word from Allah,—noble and chaste and a Prophet, from among the righteous.'[330]

فَنَادَتْهُ الْمَلٰٓئِكَةُ وَهُوَ قَآئِمٌ يُّصَلِّیْ فِی الْمِحْرَابِ ۙ اَنَّ اللهَ يُبَشِّرُكَ بِيَحْيٰى مُصَدِّقًۢا بِكَلِمَةٍ مِّنَ اللهِ وَسَيِّدًا وَّحَصُوْرًا وَّنَبِيًّا مِّنَ الصّٰلِحِيْنَ ۝

---

*a*19 : 6, 7 ; 21 : 90, 91.   *b*19 : 13.   *c*19 : 8 ; 21 : 91.   *d*3 : 46 ; 4 : 172.

---

a place where one fights the forces of evil or where one gets divorced from the affairs and concerns of the world, the word حرب meaning fighting as well as being despoiled or deprived of all possessions (Mufradāt).

Commentary :

Many fantastic stories have been woven round Mary's reply to Zachariah's question as to whence she got the gifts he found lying about her. The gifts were evidently brought by worshippers visiting the place and there was also nothing extraordinary in her reply that the gifts were from Allah, for every good thing that comes to man is really from God, He being the final agency. In fact, from a girl of Mary's religious upbringing any other reply would rather have been surprising. The accounts of Mary having been provided with heavenly fruits by angels are, therefore, nothing but the figment of the Commentators' own minds and find no support whatsoever from the Quran or the sayings of the Holy Prophet. The pious reply of the child, however, made a deep impression on the mind of Zachariah and awakened in the depths of his soul the latent and natural desire of possessing a similarly virtuous child of his own.

The words, *Surely Allah gives to whomsoever He pleases without measure*, are most probably

the words of God and not those of Mary. But if they are Mary's words, they make her reply all the more impressive and Zachariah's earnest prayer, referred to in the following verse, all the more justified.

329. Commentary :

Deeply touched by the little girl's reply, Zachariah was moved there and then to pray to God to be blessed with a pious child like Mary. The prayer was probably repeated over a length of period as it is mentioned in varying words in different parts of the Quran (3 : 39 ; 19 : 5—7 ; 21 : 90). This finds further support in the fact that whereas the first prayer was offered when Mary was yet a child, the birth of a son to Zachariah actually took place when Mary had grown up to woman-hood, Jesus and John (Yaḥyā) being nearly of the same age. Or what is equally probable, the prayer of Zachariah was accepted at the very beginning and God gave him the promise of a child at the very first prayer offered ; but, after the manner of pious men, he still continued to pray for the bestowal of the promised gift.

330. Important Words :

يحيى (Yaḥyā or John) is the name of the Prophet who appeared before Jesus to serve

41. He said, [a]'My Lord, how shall I have a son, when age has overtaken me, and my wife is barren?' He answered, 'Such is *the way of* Allah: He does what He pleases.'[331]

قَالَ رَبِّ اَنّٰى يَكُوْنُ لِىْ غُلٰمٌ وَّقَدْ بَلَغَنِىَ الْكِبَرُ وَامْرَاَتِىْ عَاقِرٌ ۚ قَالَ كَذٰلِكَ اللّٰهُ يَفْعَلُ مَا يَشَآءُ ۞

---

[a]19 : 9, 10.

as his harbinger in fulfilment of the Biblical prophecy (Mal. 3 : 1 and 4 : 5). The Hebrew form is يوحنا which in that language means, God has been gracious (Enc. Brit.). The name Yaḥyā was given by God Himself and was meant to point to a distinctive characteristic of his (19 : 8). In Arabic the word is derived from the root حياة (life) and means, he lives or he shall live. The implication in the name was that he would not die in childhood but would live to the age of manhood or that he would lead a righteous life. The fact that Yaḥyā did not die a natural death but was killed (Matt. 14 : 10) shows yet another implication in the name *i.e.* that he would die the death of a martyr and would thus live for ever in the sight of God. Says the Quran, *Think not of those who have been slain in the cause of Allah as dead. Nay, they are living in the presence of their Lord and are granted gifts from Him* (3 : 170). Yaḥyā is probably the only known Israelite Prophet who was actually killed, as hinted in the Quranic verse, *We have not made anyone before him of that name* (19 : 8 ; cf. Luke 1 : 61).

حصور (chaste) is derived from حصر *i.e.* he was or became unable to express his mind by reason of shame, etc. حصر عنه means, he became impeded and was unable to do it. حصر عن المرأة means, he abstained or kept away from sexual intercourse with the woman, whether intentionally or through impotence. حصر بالسر means, he concealed the secret and refrained from divulging it. حصره means, he prevented or restrained him. حصور therefore, means, one who has no sexual inter-

course with women, though able to have it, abstaining from them from a motive of chastity and for the sake of shunning worldly pleasures ; or one who is prevented from having it by impotence ; or one who does not desire them ; one very careful and cautious, who abstains or refrains from a thing through fear, etc.; concealer of a secret or secrets ; one who abstains from evil passions and frivolous games and sport (Lane & Aqrab).

Commentary :

The description of Yaḥyā (John) given in the verse *i.e.* سيدا (noble or great), and حصورا (chaste or refrainer from evil passions), and نبيا (Prophet) and من الصلحين (righteous), agrees with that given in Luke (1 : 13—17, 76). In Luke we have, " he (John or Yaḥyā) shall be great in the sight of God . . . he shall drink neither wine nor strong drink . . . he shall be filled with the Holy Ghost . . . and he shall be called the prophet of the Most High." The Quran also describes Yaḥyā as one *who shall testify to the truth of a word from Allah* (3 : 40). And John came in exact fulfilment of Malachi's prophecy : " Behold I will send you Elijah the prophet before the great and terrible day of the Lord come " (Mal. 4 : 5). The Quranic expression حصور in the sense of " concealer of a secret " also points to the above description, for Yaḥyā (John) was the bearer of the hidden news of the coming of Jesus.

331. Important Words :

غلام (son) is derived from غلم *i.e.* he became excited by lust or carnal desire. اغتلم الشراب

42. ^aHe said, ' My Lord, appoint a token for me.' He replied, 'Thy token shall be that thou shalt not speak to men for three days ^bexcept by signs. And remember thy Lord much and glorify Him in the evening and in the early morning.'³³²

قَالَ رَبِّ اجْعَلْ لِّيْ اٰيَةً ۚ قَالَ اٰيَتُكَ اَلَّا تُكَلِّمَ النَّاسَ ثَلٰثَةَ اَيَّامٍ اِلَّا رَمْزًا ۚ وَاذْكُرْ رَّبَّكَ كَثِيْرًا وَّ سَبِّحْ بِالْعَشِيِّ وَالْاِبْكَارِ ۞

^a19 : 11.   ^b19 : 12.

means, the beverage became strong in its influence upon the head. غلام means : (1) a young man, one whose moustache is growing forth ; (2) a son, a male child ; (3) a man of middle age ; (4) a male slave or servant (Lane).

Commentary :

Zachariah's question contained in the words, *how shall I have a son ?* implies no disbelief on his part in God's promise, as alleged by the Bible (Luke 1 : 20). It is simply a spontaneous expression of innocent surprise at the divine promise. It also contains a veiled prayer that he might live long enough to see the child born and grow up into a young man. Zachariah has referred to his old age and the barrenness of his wife to make God's mercy take a practical shape all the more speedily.

The expression كذالك الله يفعل ما يشاء may be rendered in three ways : (1) thus Allah does what He pleases ; (2) this is really so, but Allah does what He pleases ; (3) such is the way of Allah, He does what He pleases.

332. Commentary :

It appears from the Bible that tokens or signs for the fulfilment of certain prophecies used to be fixed in former times. Sometimes certain phenomena of nature were fixed as such tokens. For instance, Gen. 9 : 17 fixes the rainbow as a token for the fulfilment of God's promise that there shall be no more flood to destroy the earth. God also appointed the observance of circumcision as a token for the bestowal of the blessings which He promised Abraham and his seed (Gen. 17 : 11). Again, the observance of the Sabbath was fixed as a sign for the divine covenant made with the Israelites (Exod. 31 : 13—17). Similarly, at Zachariah's request God appointed a token for the fulfilment of His promise. Zachariah was to abstain from speaking for three days, and then was the promise to be fulfilled. He was not deprived of his power of speech, as the Gospels seem to allege, as a punishment for his not believing the words of God (Luke 1 : 20—22).

As to the question why the token of keeping silent and refraining from the use of the tongue was fixed for Zachariah, it may be briefly noted that, *firstly*, it was intended to afford Zachariah a suitable opportunity for passing his time in meditation and prayer—a condition particularly helpful in attracting divine mercy and grace. *Secondly*, refraining from speech has also been found helpful, in some cases, in making one regain lost vitality and health. The practice seems to have been in vogue among the Jews of those times (19 : 27) and is even now resorted to by certain people among Hindus and others. Islam does not recognize such practices as tend to suspend the useful activities of man, but it certainly discourages talkativeness (Tirmidhī, ch. on *Birr wa'l-Ṣila*).

R 5.   **43.** And *remember* when the angels said, ' O Mary, Allah has chosen thee and purified thee and *^a*chosen thee above the women of all peoples.³³³

وَاِذۡ قَالَتِ الۡمَلٰٓئِكَةُ يٰمَرۡیَمُ اِنَّ اللّٰهَ اصۡطَفٰكِ وَ طَهَّرَكِ وَاصۡطَفٰكِ عَلٰی نِسَآءِ الۡعٰلَمِیۡنَ ۝

44. ' O Mary, be obedient to thy Lord and prostrate thyself and worship *God alone* with those who worship.'^{333A}

یٰمَرۡیَمُ اقۡنُتِیۡ لِرَبِّكِ وَاسۡجُدِیۡ وَارۡكَعِیۡ مَعَ الرّٰكِعِیۡنَ ۝

45. *^b*This is of the tidings of things unseen which We reveal to thee. And thou wast not with them when they cast their arrows, *^c*as to which of them should be the guardian of Mary, nor wast thou with them when they disputed with one another.³³⁴

ذٰلِكَ مِنۡ اَنۡۢبَآءِ الۡغَیۡبِ نُوۡحِیۡهِ اِلَیۡكَ ؕ وَ مَا كُنۡتَ لَدَیۡهِمۡ اِذۡ یُلۡقُوۡنَ اَقۡلَامَهُمۡ اَیُّهُمۡ یَكۡفُلُ مَرۡیَمَ ۪ وَ مَا كُنۡتَ لَدَیۡهِمۡ اِذۡ یَخۡتَصِمُوۡنَ ۝

---

*^a*3 : 34.   *^b*11 : 50 ; 12 : 103.   *^c*3 : 38.

333. Commentary :

As Yaḥyā (John) was the forerunner of Jesus (Mal. 3 : 1 ; 4 : 5), the Quran has first mentioned the prophecy relating to him and then has proceeded to give a detailed account of the birth and prophethood of Jesus along with a brief mention of his mother, Mary, which is meant as a preliminary to the real subject. In the present verse the word " chosen " has been used twice. This is not without purpose. In the first instance the word has been used in regard to Mary without reference to any other person, signifying her exalted position absolutely ; while in the second case it has been used to express her high position in relation to the other women of her time. It need not be mentioned that, according to the usage of the Quran, the word ' ālamīn (peoples) does not here refer to all times and all ages, but only to the specific time in which Mary lived. See also 2 : 48.

The use of the word الملائكة (angels) in the plural number is also not purposeless. If the mere conveying of a message was intended, only one angel could act as a message-bearer.

Why then did God order a number of them to speak to Mary ? In the Quranic idiom the use of the plural number signifies that, as God intended to bring about, through her son, a great change in the world affecting various spheres of life, He ordered all the different angels connected with the relevant spheres to take part in conveying the message, thus calling upon all of them to help in bringing about the desired change. See note on angels in 2 : 31.

333A. Important Words :

ارکعی (worship God alone). See 2 : 44.

334. Important Words :

اقلامهم (their arrows). اقلام is the plural of قلم (an arrow). They say قلم الشیء *i.e.* he cut the thing. قلم الظفر means, he clipped the superfluous part of the nail (Aqrab). القلم means : (1) a reed used for writing after being pared or shaped into a pen *i.e.* a reed-pen ; (2) a headless arrow used for drawing lots ; (3) an arrow or a dart (Aqrab). It was customary among Arabs to use arrows for drawing lots as well as in gambling, etc.

46. When the angels said, 'O Mary, ^aAllah gives thee glad tidings of ^ba word from Him ; his name shall be the Messiah, Jesus, son of Mary, honoured in this world and in the next, and of those who are granted nearness *to God* ; [335]

اِذْ قَالَتِ الْمَلَٰٓئِكَةُ يَٰمَرْيَمُ اِنَّ اللّٰهَ يُبَشِّرُكِ بِكَلِمَةٍ مِّنْهُ ۖ اسْمُهُ الْمَسِيحُ عِيسَى ابْنُ مَرْيَمَ وَجِيهًا فِى الدُّنْيَا وَالْاٰخِرَةِ وَمِنَ الْمُقَرَّبِينَ ۝

^a19 : 20.   ^b3 : 40 ; 4 : 172.

Commentary :

Many of the facts which the Quran has brought to light regarding Mary are not found in the previous scriptures. Hence, they are here spoken of as "things unseen." As narrated in the verses that follow, Mary had become pregnant, while leading a life of dedication in the temple. The priests grew most anxious when they came to know of the startling fact. They feared scandal and disputed among themselves and cast lots to decide as to who should take charge of her and arrange her disposal in marriage with some suitable person. One Joseph, a carpenter, as mentioned in the Gospels, was hit upon as a suitable person to be her husband and was persuaded to accept the awkward situation. All this was naturally done in secret and so it was a غیب (a thing unseen) which the Quran has brought to light.

335. Important Words :

كلمة (word) means, a word ; an expression ; a proposition ; a sentence ; a saying ; an argument ; an assertion ; an expression of opinion (Lane) ; also, a decree ; a commandment (Mufradāt). See also 2 : 38.

المسیح (Messiah) is derived from مسح. They say مسح الشیئ *i.e.* he wiped off the dirt from the thing with his hand ; or he passed his hand over it. مسح الشیئ بالماء means, he passed his hand, wetted with water, over the thing. مسحه means, he anointed him or it with oil. مسح فى الارض means, he set forth journeying through the land. مسح البیت means, he

compassed or went round the House of God. مسحه بالسیف means, he struck him with the sword and killed him. مسحه الله means, God created him blessed and goodly ; and contrarily, God created him accursed and foul. مسیح therefore, means : (1) one anointed *i.e.* wiped over with some such thing as oil ; (2) a king ; (3) one beautiful in the face ; (4) one who journeys or travels much ; (5) one very truthful ; (6) one erring greatly ; (7) one created blessed and goodly ; (8) one created accursed and foul (Lane). المسیح الدجال means, Antichrist ; one erring greatly and created accursed and foul ; one travelling much spreading false ideas. المسیح is the Arabic form of Messiah which represents the Hebrew Māshīah *i.e.* anointed one (Enc. Bib. & Enc. Rel. and Eth.)

عیسى (Jesus) is probably a Hebrew name in which it has the form الیسوع or یسوع from which the inverted Arabic form is عیسى. In Arabic the word may be considered to have been derived from the root عیس or عوس. The word العیس means, white camels, the whiteness of whose hair is mixed with a dark shade, and these are looked upon as particularly good animals. عاس الرجل ماله means, the man managed his property well. عاس معیشته means, he improved and bettered his life (Aqrab & Lisān). Jesus is the Greek form of Joshua and Jeshua (Enc. Bib.)

ابن مریم (son of Mary) is a surname of Jesus known in Arabic as *Kunyat*. Jesus has been called *Ibn Maryam* probably because, being born without the agency of a male parent, he could not but be known after his mother. For the word Mary see 3 : 43.

Commentary :

The word كلمة (word) as used in this verse requires some explanation, particularly because it has been quoted by Christian missionaries in support of the ridiculous allegation that by using it the Quran has recognized the sonship of Jesus. The occasion on which the verse was revealed would throw some light on the significance of the word.

The first 83 verses of this *Sūra* were revealed when the Christian deputation from Najrān visited Medina and had a discussion with the Holy Prophet about the status and personality of Jesus. Being silenced on other points, they asked the Holy Prophet whether the word *Kalima* had been used in the Quran concerning Jesus, and, receiving a reply in the affirmative, they triumphantly shouted that they had won and rose to depart without waiting for the explanation of this much-misunderstood word. The occasion and circumstances of the revelation of the relevant verses clearly show that they were revealed not in support, but in refutation and repudiation, of the Christian doctrine of the divinity of Jesus. The words كلمة (word) and روح (mercy) occurring together in 4 : 172 make it clear beyond the shadow of a doubt that they have been used to destroy and repudiate the doctrine of the divinity and sonship of Jesus rather than establish it. The full verse referred to above runs as follows : *O People of the Book, exceed not the limits in your religion, and say not of Allah anything but the truth. Verily the Messiah, Jesus, son of Mary, was only a Messenger of God and a fulfilment of His word (كلمة) which He sent down to Mary and a mercy (روح) from Him. So believe in Allah and His Messengers and say not, 'They are three.' Desist, it will be better for you ; verily Allah is* the only one God. *Far is it from His holiness that He should have a son. To Him belongs whatever is in the heavens and whatever is in the earth, and sufficient is Allah as a guardian.* The words speak for themselves.

Curiously enough, some Christian writers have asserted that the Holy Prophet did not understand the real significance of the word *Kalima*. The word is Arabic ; and to say that an Arab of the Holy Prophet's knowledge and intelligence did not know the meaning or significance of this word is simply absurd. It is a fact that neither the Holy Prophet nor any of his followers ever attached to this word any extraordinary significance which might exalt Jesus over the rest of humanity. Large numbers of Christians have accepted Islam in the past. While studying the Quran, they must have come across this word several times but none of them ever took it in the sense in which our Christian critics pretend to take it, and none of them ever believed in the godhood of Jesus on account of this expression having been used in the Quran.

The great lexicographist, the author of *Tāj al-'Arūs*, says that Jesus has been called *Kalimat Allah* because his words were helpful to the cause of religion. Just as a person who helps the cause of religion by his valour is called *Saif Allah* (the sword of God) or *Asad Allah* (the lion of God), so is the expression *Kalimat Allah*. According to the same authority, Jesus was called *Kalimat Allah* also because his birth did not take place through the agency of a male parent but by the direct "command" of God (19 :21, 22).

Besides the literal meanings given above the Quran has used this word in the following senses : (1) "a sign" as in 66 : 13 and 8 : 8 ; (2) "punishment" as in 10 : 97 ; (3) "plan" or "design" as in 9 : 40 ; (4) "glad tidings" as in 7 : 138 ; (5) "creation of God" as in 31 : 28 and 18 : 110 ; (6) "a mere word of mouth" or "a mere assertion" as in 23 : 101.

47. 'And [a]he shall speak to the people in the cradle and when of middle age, and he shall be of the righteous.'[336]

وَيُكَلِّمُ النَّاسَ فِي الْمَهْدِ وَكَهْلًا وَّمِنَ الصّٰلِحِيْنَ

[a]5 : 111.

Taken in any of the above senses, the word كلمة (*Kalima*) in no way gives to Jesus a status higher than that of other Prophets.

Again, if Jesus has been called *Kalima* (word) in the Quran, the Holy Prophet has been called *dhikr i.e.* a book or a good speech (65 : 11, 12), which evidently consists of many *Kalimas* (words). In fact, if *Kalimat Allah* is taken in the sense of "word of God", the utmost we can say is that God expressed Himself through Jesus just as He expressed Himself through other Prophets. Words are nothing but a vehicle for the expression of thoughts. They do not form part of our being nor do they become incarnated.

The personal pronoun in the expression اسمه (his name) occurring in the verse, being in the masculine gender, evidently cannot refer to *Kalima*, which is in the feminine gender. It can only refer to the person about whom the glad tidings was given. The relevant clause of the verse may, therefore, also be rendered as " O Mary, Allah gives thee glad tidings with a word (*i.e.* by means of a revelation) from Him ; his (*i.e.* the promised one's) name shall be the Messiah, Jesus, son of Mary."

Jesus has been called *Masîḥ* (Messiah) in this verse and the word *Masîḥ*, as given under Important Words above, means one who travels much. Thus Jesus was given this name because he was to travel much. But if in pursuance of the Gospel narrative, Jesus' ministry be admitted to have been confined to only three years and his travels to only a few Palestinian or Syrian towns, the title of *Masîḥ* in no way fits him. Recent historical research, has, however, established the fact that after having recovered from the shock and the wounds of crucifixion, Jesus travelled far and wide in the East and finally reached Kashmir to give his message to the lost tribes of Israel who lived in these parts. In this connection see also 23 : 51, where Jesus is spoken of as having been afforded shelter in a hilly tract of land. مسيح (*Masîḥ*) also means "one anointed." As the birth of Jesus was out of the ordinary and was liable to be looked upon as illegitimate, therefore, to remove this possible accusation, he was spoken of as "being anointed" with God's own anointment, even as all true Prophets of God are anointed. Jesus has been so spoken of also because, like a thing anointed with oil, the water of sin could not penetrate him. It could only just touch his skin but could not sink into it nor remain there (Matt. 4 : 1—11). In contrast to it, the high spiritual rank of the Holy Prophet of Islam may be judged from a well-known saying of his wherein he says that his Satan had turned Muslim and urged him to do nothing but good (Musnad & Muslim), meaning that not only could no satanic touch harm him but that Satan had become virtually non-existent for him. Nay, it means even more ; for, the words signify that the Holy Prophet had been provided with such a powerful spiritual transformer that even satanic suggestions were converted into veritable forces of virtue in him.

The expression, *of those who are granted nearness to God*, also gives to Jesus no higher position than that of a righteous servant of God. All people advanced in righteousness have been spoken of in the Quran as being granted nearness to God (56 : 11, 12).

336. **Important Words :**

المهد (cradle) is the noun-infinitive from the

verb مهد . They say مهد المكان i.e. he made the place plain, even or smooth for himself. مهد فراشا means, he spread a bed for himself and made it even and smooth. مهد لنفسه خيرا means, he prepared good things for himself. مهد له منزلة سنية means, he prepared or established for him a high station or position. مهد لنفسه also means, he gained or earned or sought to earn sustenance, etc. for himself. المهد means, a place prepared for a child and made plain, even or smooth that he may sleep in it; a child's cradle; a bed; a thing spread to lie, recline or sit upon; a piece of plain ground or a smooth expanse (Lane & Aqrab). In its verbal senses the infinitive مهد would also mean, making a thing even and smooth; preparing a thing; preparation; gaining or earning a sustenance, etc.

كهلا (of middle age) is the noun-infinitive from كهل i.e. he was or became of middle age. اكتهل الرجل means, the man attained middle age. اكتهل النبات means, the plant became tall and full grown and blossomed. كهل means, one who is of middle age, or one who is of the age when a person's hair becomes intermixed with hoariness; or one who is between thirty or thirty-four and 51 years of age (Lane & Aqrab); or one who is between 40 and 51 years of age (Tha'labī).

Commentary :

It is evident that by the words, *he shall speak*, the Quran does not mean simple utterance of words; for such speaking is done by all children and all grown up men except the few congenitally dumb. The expression is, therefore, meant to refer to a particular kind of speaking *i.e.* speaking wisely or speaking words of wisdom. Similarly the clause, *in the cradle and when of middle age*, refers to the two periods of childhood and manhood when Jesus would speak words of wisdom, thus indirectly hinting that he would not die young but would live to a good ripe age. According to Ibn

Qayyim, a scholar of great eminence, some scholars have denied the crucifixion and (the so-called) ascension of Jesus at the age of 30 or 33 on the ground that Jesus was, according to the Quran, to speak to men when he was a *Kahl i.e.* of middle age. This shows that these scholars look upon Tha'labī's definition as the correct one. See Important Words above.

That Jesus spoke words of wisdom in his childhood has nothing miraculous or supernatural about it. Many intelligent and well brought up children speak like that. Luke supplies an instance of how Jesus spoke in childhood: "And when they had fulfilled the days, the child Jesus tarried behind in Jerusalem. And it came to pass that after three days they found him in the temple, sitting in the midst of the doctors, both hearing them and asking them questions. And all that heard him were astonished at his understanding and answers" (Luke, 2:43—47).

The Quranic reference to the two distinct periods of Jesus' life may also be taken to hint that his speaking in the latter period was to be of a different nature from that in the former. In the latter period he was to speak to men as a Prophet of God. Thus the glad tidings given to Mary consisted in the fact that Jesus was not only destined to be an intelligent child but was also to live to a ripe age as a righteous servant of God.

It should, however, be noted that the expression "in the cradle" does not necessarily mean childhood. The word مهد (cradle) has not been used in the verse literally but only broadly to signify the period of unripe age *i.e.* that preceding كهل or full-grown manhood. In fact, as shown under Important Words, مهد does not originally mean a cradle. That meaning is rather secondary, the primary meaning being the state or period of preparation when one is, as it were, being prepared and

48. She said, ' My Lord, ^ahow shall I have a son, when no man has touched me ? ' He said, " Such is *the way of Allah*, He creates what He pleases. ^bWhen He decrees a thing, He says to it, ' Be ' and it is.[337]

قَالَتۡ رَبِّ اَنّٰی یَکُوۡنُ لِیۡ وَلَدٌ وَّلَمۡ یَمۡسَسۡنِیۡ بَشَرٌ ؕ قَالَ کَذٰلِکِ اللّٰهُ یَخۡلُقُ مَا یَشَآءُ ؕ اِذَا قَضٰۤی اَمۡرًا فَاِنَّمَا یَقُوۡلُ لَهٗ کُنۡ فَیَکُوۡنُ ۝

---

^a19 : 21.   ^bSee 2 : 118.

---

made even and smooth for the duties of ripe age. The fact that the Quran has mentioned the two periods (*i.e.* "in the cradle " and " middle age ") side by side also shows that there is no intervening period between them. The entire period before کهلا (middle age) is that of مهد *i.e.* a period of preparation ; otherwise the verse would become a dispraise rather than praise ; for in that case the insinuation would be that Jesus did not speak wisely in the period lying between childhood and middle age.

Finally, it may be noted that, according to the Quran and authentic Ḥadīth, Jesus did not die on the Cross at the age of 33 but lived up to a very old age, but of this we would speak later at its proper place.

337. Commentary :

The news of a son, however happy in ordinary circumstances, greatly perplexed Mary who was not only as yet unmarried but was also meant to remain so for life. The verse reflects her justified perplexity. It also shows that Jesus had no father, as hinted in Mary's words, *no man has touched me*. Having been dedicated to the service of the temple, Mary could not, consistently with her vow of celibacy, marry. If she was to marry and have children in due course, there was no occasion for her to be surprised when the birth of a child was announced to her by the angel in a vision. No normal girl would be surprised, if she were told in a vision that a son would be born to her ; for she would naturally infer that the promised child would be born to her after marriage. In the Gospel of Mary, the vow of celibacy is clearly referred to. In chapter 5 of the said Gospel we read that when the high priest made a public order that all the virgins living in the temple who had reached their fourteenth year should return home, all the other virgins yielded obedience to this command, but " Mary the virgin of the Lord " alone answered that she could not comply with it ; and for this refusal of hers she assigned the reason that both she and her parents had devoted her to the service of the Lord, and that she had vowed virginity to the Lord, which vow she was resolved never to break (Gospel of Mary, 5 : 4, 5, 6).

Mary's subsequent marriage with Joseph was thus contrary to the vow and against her own wish. She was, however, compelled by circumstances to marry when found with child. The priests had to arrange her marriage with Joseph in order to avoid scandal. It does not, however, appear from the Gospels how Joseph was prevailed upon to consent, for he was obviously in the dark about her being pregnant at the time of marriage (Matt. 1 : 18, 19). Presumably some plausible excuse was found to justify the breaking of the vow.

Christians and Jews are both agreed that the birth of Jesus was something out of the ordinary—the Christians holding it as supernatural and the Jews as illegitimate (Jew. Enc.). Even in the family birth register, Jesus' birth was

49. "And [a]He will teach him the Book and the Wisdom and the Torah and the Gospel ;[338]

وَيُعَلِّمُهُ الْكِتٰبَ وَالْحِكْمَةَ وَالتَّوْرٰبةَ وَالْاِنْجِيْلَ ۞

[a]5 : 111.

recorded as such (Talmud). This fact alone should constitute a sufficient proof of Jesus' birth being out of the ordinary. But it was neither supernatural nor illegitimate. To quote only one medical authority : " Medical men have not ruled out altogether the possibility of natural parthenogenesis or the production of a child by a female, without any relation to a male. Such a statement off-hand appears ridiculous, yet its possibility, from a purely biological standpoint, under certain conditions, cannot be disregarded. Dr. Timme calls attention to this possibility as the result of a certain type of tumors, known as *arrhenoblastoma* (from the Greek words for " male " and " germ ") which are occasionally found in the female pelvis or lower body. These tumors are capable of generating male sperm-cells. Naturally, if these male sperm-cells were alive and active and came in contact with the female's own egg-cell or ovum, conception might occur. There is nothing illogical in this process of reasoning . . . Dr. Timme states that there are twenty authentic cases reported in Europe in which an *arrhenoblastoma* had been found to develop male sperm-cells. . . . The *arrhenoblastoma* is a tumor that contains blastodermic cells. . . These cells are creative structures and are capable of development at any time and the fact, therefore, that *arrhenoblastoma* containing these " embryonic cells " might create testicular tissue, capable of producing male sperm-cells

seems scientifically not impossible. . . . . If living male sperm-cells are produced in a female body by *arrhenoblastoma*, the possibility of self-fertilization of a woman, even though a virgin, cannot be denied. That is to say, her own body would produce the same result as though sperm-cells from a man's body had been transferred to hers in the more usual way, or by a physician's aid " (American Medical Journal).

There are cases on record of children having been born without fathers : " A young girl of great moral purity became pregnant without the slightest knowledge of the source. . . . There is a case of pregnancy in an unmarried woman, who successfully resisted an attempt at criminal connection and yet became impregnated and gave birth to a perfectly formed female child" (Anomalies and Curiosities of Medicine by George M. Gould, A.M., M.D., and Walter L. Payle, A.M., M.D., published by W. B. Saunders & Co., London).

338. **Commentary :**

The word كتاب (Book) signifies both " the Book " and the " art of writing." If the word be here taken to mean " the Book," then it would apply to the "Torah," the Law of Moses, and in this case the concluding words, " the Torah and the Gospel " would be taken as explanatory, the word " Torah " standing for the " Book " and the word " Gospel " for " Wisdom."

50. [a]"And *will make him* a Messenger to the children of Israel, (to say): [b]'I come to you with a Sign from your Lord, which is, that I will fashion out for you *a creation* out of clay after the manner of a bird, then I will breathe into it *a new spirit* and it will become a soaring being by the command of Allah; and I will heal the night-blind and the leprous, and I will quicken the dead, by the command of Allah; and I will announce to you what you will eat and what you will store up in your houses. Surely therein is a Sign for you, if you be believers.[339]

وَرَسُوۡلًا اِلٰى بَنِىۡۤ اِسۡرَآءِیۡلَ ۙ اَنِّىۡ قَدۡ جِئۡتُكُمۡ بِاٰیَةٍ مِّنۡ رَّبِّكُمۡ ۙ اَنِّىۡۤ اَخۡلُقُ لَكُمۡ مِّنَ الطِّیۡنِ كَهَیۡئَةِ الطَّیۡرِ فَاَنۡفُخُ فِیۡهِ فَیَكُوۡنُ طَیۡرًۢا بِاِذۡنِ اللّٰهِ ۚ وَاُبۡرِئُ الۡاَكۡمَهَ وَالۡاَبۡرَصَ وَاُحۡىِ الۡمَوۡتٰى بِاِذۡنِ اللّٰهِ ۚ وَاُنَبِّئُكُمۡ بِمَا تَاۡكُلُوۡنَ وَمَا تَدَّخِرُوۡنَ ۙ فِىۡ بُیُوۡتِكُمۡ ؕ اِنَّ فِىۡ ذٰلِكَ لَاٰیَةً لَّكُمۡ اِنۡ كُنۡتُمۡ مُّؤۡمِنِیۡنَ ۝

---

[a]43 : 60 ; 61 : 7.   [b]5 : 111.

---

339. Important Words :

اَخۡلُقُ (I fashion out) is derived from خلق. They say خلقه meaning: (1) he measured it, or he determined its measure or proportion (*e.g.* they say خلق الادیم meaning, he determined the leather with a view to cutting it); (2) he designed or fashioned or planned it; (3) he made it according to a certain measure or design; (4) He (God) produced or created or brought into existence a thing or being without there being any previously existing pattern or model or similitude *i.e.* He originated it; (5) he forged or fabricated a story or a lie, etc.; (6) he made a thing smooth, even and equable (Lane & Lisān).

الطین (clay) is derived from طان *i.e.* he made his work or deed good; he performed or executed his work or deed well. طانه الله على الخیر means, God created him with a disposition or adaptation to that which is good *i.e.* created him with a good natural disposition. طانه means, he coated or plastered it with clay or mud. طین means, clay, earth, mould, soil or mud. طینة means, any material substance of which anything having form consists; the natural constitution or disposition

of a thing. The term ابن الطین is sometimes used to signify Adam (Lane). Figuratively الطین may signify such persons as possess docile natures suitable for being moulded into any good shape like pliable clay.

الطیر (bird) which is the plural of طائر (a bird) and is also sometimes used as singular is derived from طار *i.e.* (1) he or it flew or moved in the air by means of wings; (2) he or it ran or moved quickly or fled. طار عقله means, his reason fled. طارت الابل means, the she-camel conceived. طار لكل منهم سهمه means, the share of each came to him. طیر or الطیر is both the plural of طائر (bird) and the noun-infinitive from the verb طار. So طیر means: (1) flying birds, insects, etc.; (2) a flying bird, insect, etc., for طیر is sometimes also used as singular; (3) as an infinitive-noun طیر would also give the different meanings conveyed by its verbal forms (Lane).

هیئة (manner) is the noun-infinitive from هاء. They say هاء الرجل meaning, the man was or became of good form and appearance or other properties denoted by هیئة, the noun-infinitive. هاء الیه means, he desired or longed to see or find him or it. هیّأ means, he gave him or he made him have a garb or guise, etc.; he prepared or arranged it and put it in a good state. تهيأ لام means, he became prepared for the thing or the matter. هيئة means, form, fashion, appearance or figure; guise or garb; state, condition or case; manner, mode or quality (Aqrab & Lane).

ابرى (I heal) is derived from برى i.e. he was or became clear or free from a thing. برى من المرض means, he became free from disease i.e. he recovered from it. برى من الدين means, he became clear of debt. ابرأه means, he cured or healed him of the disease; he declared him innocent or free from the defect attributed to him; he acquitted him (Aqrab & Lane).

اكمه (blind) is derived from كمه i.e. he became blind; or his eyes did not see at night. كمه فلان also means, he was or became deprived of reason or understanding. كمه النهار means, the day became dark i.e. the sun became overcast with clouds. اكمه means, one who cannot see at night; one who is born blind; one who becomes blind afterwards; one who is deprived of reason and understanding (Aqrab & Mufradāt).

ابرص (leprous) is derived from برص i.e. he was or became affected with برص (leprosy) viz. a sort of whiteness that appears upon parts of the body by reason of a corrupt state of health or constitution. The moon is sometimes called الابرص because of its white hue. ارض برصاء means, a land of which the herbage has become depastured at several places so that it has become bare thereof (Aqrab & Lane). A variety of leprosy of the Hebrews (probably identical with modern leprosy) was characterized by the presence of smooth, shining, depressed white patches or scales, the hair on which participated in the whiteness, while the skin and adjacent flesh became insensible (Webster).

تأكلون (you will eat) is derived from اكل

i.e. he ate; he ate up; he devoured; he consumed; he wore away, etc. The Holy Prophet is reported to have said, امرت بقرية تأكل القرى i.e. I have been commanded to emigrate to a town (Medina) which shall devour (i.e. subdue and conquer) other towns (Lane).

Commentary :

With this verse begins an account of Jesus' ministry as a Prophet of God. By using the words, *a Messenger to the children of Israel*, the verse makes it clear that Jesus' mission was confined to the House of Israel. He was not a World-Messenger. In fact, as the Gospel itself states, he expressly ordered his disciples not to preach his message to any but the Israelites : "These twelve Jesus sent forth, and commanded them, saying, 'Go not into the way of the Gentiles, and into any city of the Samaritans enter ye not : but go rather to the lost sheep of the house of Israel'" (Matt. 10:5-6). It cannot be argued that this prohibition was confined to the lifetime of Jesus and that after his death his disciples were at liberty to preach to all the nations of the world, for this supposition is belied by the Gospel itself : "But when they persecute you in this city, flee ye into another : for verily I say unto you, Ye shall not have gone over the cities of Israel, till the Son of man be come" (Matt. 10 : 23). According to this verse, the followers of Jesus were enjoined to confine their preaching to the children of Israel till the time of his second coming. The same injunction is contained in Matt. 15:24; 18:11, 12; 19:28; Acts 3:25, 26; 13:46; Luke 19:10; 15:4; 22:28—30.

Only in Matt. 28:19 there appears some ambiguity about the mission of Jesus but on deeper reflection it becomes clear that here too it is the tribes of Israel that are meant, and not all peoples and all nations. The early disciples understood these words of Jesus in this very sense : "Now they which were scattered abroad upon the persecution that arose about Stephen travelled as far as Phenice, and Cyprus, and Antioch, preaching the word to none but unto the Jews only" (Acts 11 : 19).

For a clear understanding of the other parts of the present verse *i.e.* making birds of clay, etc., it is necessary to remember that it was Jesus' habit to talk in parables—a way of talking which was predicted in the previous scriptures to be a characteristic of his speech. Says the Gospel : "All these things spake Jesus unto the multitudes in parables; and without a parable spake he not unto them : that it might be fulfilled which was spoken by the prophet, saying, I will open my mouth in parables" (Matt. 13 : 34, 35). Later historians also have referred to this peculiar characteristic of Jesus : "In his popular addresses Jesus would make free use of parables. He spoke in parables to all classes but especially to the people. Without parables he was not wont to speak to them" (Enc. Bib. under Jesus). With this torch-light of history in our hands, it does not remain difficult for us to understand or explain the "signs" of Jesus as mentioned in the present verse.

There is no mention in the Bible of the miracle of creating birds popularly believed to have been performed by Jesus. If Jesus had really created birds, there is no reason why the Bible should have omitted to mention it, particularly when the creation of birds was a miracle the like of which had never been shown before by any Messenger of God. The mention of such a miracle would certainly have established his superiority over other Prophets and would have lent some support to the claim to divinity which has been foisted upon him by his later followers. Of the different meanings of خلق (*khalq*)—measuring, determining, designing or fashioning; making and creating, etc., —given under Important Words above, it is in the former sense that this word has been

used in this verse. In the sense of "creating" the act of *khalq* has not been attributed in the Quran to any other being or thing except God. In fact, the Quran has laid the greatest emphasis on this exclusive attribute of God Who has been again and again declared to be the sole "Creator" of all things. All others to whom creation has been attributed are declared by the Quran to have been themselves created by God and to be devoid of all power to create anything (e.g. see 13 : 17 ; 16 : 21 ; 22 : 74 ; 25 : 4 ; 31 : 11, 12 ; 35 : 41 and 46 : 5). Even the silly notion that the power of creating, though the unshared prerogative of God, might have been temporarily delegated by Him to another is rejected by the Quran with the contempt it deserves (39 : 30 & 16 : 72).

In the light of the above explanation, and keeping in view the figurative sense of "clay," for which see Important Words above, the clause, *I will fashion out for you a creation out of clay after the manner of a bird, then I will breathe into it (a new spirit) and it will become a soaring being*, would mean that if ordinary men of humble origin but possessing the inherent power of growth and development came into contact with Jesus and accepted his message, they would undergo a complete transformation in their lives. From men grovelling in the dust and not seeing beyond their material cares and mundane concerns, they would become converted into birds soaring high into the lofty regions of the spiritual firmament. And this is exactly what happened. The humble and despised fishermen of Galilee, under the impact of the ennobling teaching of their Master, began soaring like birds, preaching to the world of Israel the word of God and bravely facing all sorts of hardships and privations and making sacrifices that should adorn the history of any nation. Says Jesus : "I say unto you, Take no thought for your life, what ye shall eat, and what ye shall drink ;

nor yet for your body, what ye shall put on. Is not the life more than meat, and the body than raiment ? Behold the fowls of the air : for they sow not, neither do they reap, nor gather into barns ; yet your heavenly Father feedeth them. Are ye not much better than they ? " (Matt. 6 : 25 , 26).

The miracle relating to the making of birds from clay may be interpreted in another way as well. In the time of Jesus people had a special liking for the practice of occult sciences —hypnotism, mesmerism, etc. So it is possible that God granted him special power of this kind in order to impress the people and make them believe in him. In this case the sign of making birds would mean that Jesus made small clay models of birds and then through a sort of mesmerism made them appear to fly in the air. But this did not convert them into really living birds ; for as soon as the influence was removed, they fell down to the ground like so many lumps of earth. This miracle of Jesus was more or less like the miracle of the rod of Moses which was temporarily made to look like a real serpent but was actually not so. But whatever the significance of the sign, it was performed, as the verse clearly puts it, *by the command of Allah*, and Jesus possessed no power of creation. (For fuller description see Izāla by Ahmad, the Promised Messiah).

As for healing the blind and the leprous, it appears from the Bible that persons suffering from certain diseases (leprosy, etc.) were considered unclean and were therefore not allowed to come in contact with other men. If, therefore, the word ابرئ be taken to mean " I declare to be free ", the clause would signify that the legal or social disabilities and disadvantages under which persons suffering from such maladies laboured were removed by Jesus. If, however, the word be interpreted as "I heal," then the clause would mean that Jesus used to heal persons suffering from these dis-

eases. But as indicated above, Jesus used to speak in metaphors. So just as the " creation " spoken of is spiritual creation, the diseases mentioned are spiritual diseases. The Prophets of God are spiritual physicians ; they give eyes to those that have lost spiritual sight, and they give hearing to those who are spiritually deaf, and they restore life to those who are spiritually dead (see also Matt. 13 : 15). In this case the word اكمه (blind or one who is blind at night) would stand for such person as possesses the light of faith but being weak, cannot stand trials. He sees in the day time *i.e.* so long as there are no trials and the sun of faith shines forth unclouded ; but when the night comes on *i.e.* when there are trials, and sacrifices have to be made, he loses his spiritual vision and stands still (*cf.* 2 : 21). Similarly, the word ابرص (leprous) would, in the spiritual sense, stand for one who is imperfect in faith, having patches of diseased skin among healthy ones. But even if these words be taken in their physical sense, Jesus is proved to possess no peculiar power. All Prophets heal diseases and ailments by the power of prayer. In this case, however, the word اكمه (blind) would be taken in the sense of one who cannot see at night or one whose sight is weak.

The clause, *I will quicken the dead*, does not mean that Jesus actually brought the dead to life. Those actually dead are never restored to life in this world. Such a belief is diametrically opposed to the whole Quranic teaching (23 : 100, 101 ; 21 : 96 ; 39 : 59, 60 ; 2 : 29 ; 40 : 12 ; 45 : 27). The sayings of the Holy Prophet are also clear on this point. For instance, it is related that when Jābir's father, who was a Companion of the Holy Prophet, was killed in the Battle of Uhud and the lad was much grieved, the Holy Prophet consolingly told him that God had lovingly spoken to his father in the other world and had asked him to beg of Him anything he liked, for that would be given him. Thereupon Jābir's father said, "Grant me, my Lord, another lease of life on earth that I may again be killed in Thy way." God replied, "I would certainly have done so, but the word has gone forth from Me that the dead shall not be sent back to the earth" (Tirmidhī & Mājah).

That the so-called dead who are reported to have been raised by Jesus were not actually dead is clear from the Gospels as well. The incident described in Matt. 9 : 23-25 sheds some light on it. As a matter of fact, Prophets are only sent to give life to those who are spiritually dead. Jesus, Moses, Abraham and, above all, the Holy Prophet of Islam brought about a complete change in the lives of their followers. This, in religious language, is termed raising the dead to life. Literally, too, the word مُوتَى (the dead) does not necessarily mean those physically dead. It is also used about those who are dead spiritually, morally or intellectually. The Quran freely speaks of the quickening of the dead in the sense of granting life to the spiritually dead (e.g. 3 : 28 ; 6 : 123 ; 8 : 43 ; 25 : 50 ; 36 : 71). In 8 : 25 the Holy Prophet himself has been spoken of as giving life to the dead. Says the Quran : *O ye who believe, respond to Allah and the Messenger when he calls you that he may give you life.* Here it is spiritual and intellectual life that is meant, for Muslims do not believe that the Holy Prophet ever brought an actually dead person to life.

The miracles of Jesus, as mentioned in this verse, have been stated in a natural order. First of all is mentioned the change in the outlook and way of life of those that came in contact with him. From men of the world, they became men of God. They rose from the dust and began soaring in the air. Then are mentioned some of the more common spiritual diseases of which Jesus cured the people ; the blind were given spiritual sight and those having diseased skins were healed. Finally, the spiritually dead are declared to have received through Jesus a new life. Thus not only a natural order but a sort of progressive order is found in the verse, the climax, so for as individual reformation is concerned, being reached with the miracle relating to the quickening of the dead. But if the verse be interpreted literally, no arrangement seems to exist in the order in which the miracles are described here, i.e., (1) the creation of birds out of clay ; (2) the healing of the blind ; (3) the healing of those suffering from leprosy i.e. those who had patches of disease on their skin ; and (4) the raising of the dead to life.

The true climax, however, reaches in the miracle or sign mentioned in the clause, *I will announce to you what you will eat and what you will store up in your houses.* According to *Abū'l Baqā* the words نَبَأ (news) and اَنْبَأ (he gave the news) are used in the Quran for announcing matters of great importance (Kulliyāt). This shows that what Jesus is here represented as announcing to the people are matters of supreme importance to his followers. The language of the verse being parabolic, the word تَأكُلُون (you will eat) will be taken figuratively, meaning, "you will subdue or conquer" (see under Important Words above). Thus the clause, *I will announce to you what you will eat,* would mean, "I will let you know what you will subdue or conquer" i.e. "I will announce to you the conquests you are destined to make in future." The other expression, i.e., I will also let you know *what you will store up in your houses,* would mean, "I will let you know the deeds which you should or would leave behind for posterity."

The entire clause may have yet another meaning. It may mean that Jesus told his disciples : (1) what they should eat i.e. what they should spend to meet their physical needs, and (2) what they should store up i.e. what they should lay up as a spiritual treasure in Heaven. In other words, Jesus told them that their earnings

51. 'And *I come* ^afulfilling that which is before me, namely, the Torah ; and to allow you some of that which was forbidden to you ; and I come to you with a sign from your Lord ; so fear Allah and obey me.'³⁴⁰

وَمُصَدِّقًا لِّمَا بَيْنَ يَدَىَّ مِنَ التَّوْرٰىةِ وَلِاُحِلَّ لَكُمْ بَعْضَ الَّذِىْ حُرِّمَ عَلَيْكُمْ وَجِئْتُكُمْ بِاٰيَةٍ مِّنْ رَّبِّكُمْ ۖ فَاتَّقُوا اللّٰهَ وَاَطِيْعُوْنِ ۞

^a5 : 47 ; 61 : 7.

should be honestly and lawfully acquired and that they should spend their savings in the way of God, having no thought for the morrow which should be left to God (see Matt. 6 : 25, 26 as quoted above).

340. Commentary :

Jesus came in fulfilment of the prophecies of the previous Prophets contained in the Torah. But he brought no new Law, being a follower of Moses in this respect. He himself was conscious of this limitation of his authority. Says he : " Think not that I am come to destroy the law or the prophets : I am not come to destroy, but to fulfil. For verily I say unto you, till heaven and earth pass away, one jot or one tittle shall in no wise pass away from the law, till all be fulfilled " (Matt. 5 : 17, 18). The expression, *to allow you some of that which was forbidden to you*, does not, therefore, refer to any change or modification in the Mosaic Law. The reference is only to those things which the Jews had themselves rendered unlawful for themselves. Elsewhere the Quran says, *So because of the transgression of the Jews, We forbade them pure things which had been allowed to them* (4 :161). Again, *Truly I am come to you with wisdom and to make clear to you some of that about which you differ* (43 : 64). These verses show that there were differences among the various sects of the Jews regarding the

lawfulness or otherwise of certain things and that by their iniquities and transgressions they had deprived themselves of certain divine blessings. Jesus thus came as a judge to decide in what matters the Jews had deviated from the right path and to tell them that the blessings of which they had been deprived would be restored to them, if they followed him.

Among Islamic sources the following well-known Commentaries support our interpretation of the verse : " Jesus did not abrogate any portion of the Torah ; he simply made lawful to the Jews those things about which they used to disagree among themselves through error " (Kathīr, under present verse). Again, " The words, *that which was forbidden to you*, refer to those things which the learned men after Moses had declared to be unlawful, giving the innovation the force of Law ; Jesus restored the true commandments of the Torah, as they had been revealed by God " (Muḥīṭ). Yet again, " Jesus followed the Law of Moses. He used to observe the Sabbath, and turn his face to the Temple and he used to say to the Jews, I do not teach you even a single word which is not in accord with the Law of Moses ; I only remove from you the burden laid on you as a result of the innovations you made after Moses " (Fatḥ).

52. 'Surely, [a]Allah is my Lord and your Lord ; so worship Him : this is the right path.' " 341

اِنَّ اللّٰهَ رَبِّیْ وَرَبُّکُمْ فَاعْبُدُوْهُ ط هٰذَا صِرَاطٌ مُّسْتَقِیْمٌ ۟

53. And when Jesus perceived their disbelief, he said, [b]'Who will be my helpers in the cause of Allah ?' The disciples answered, 'We are the helpers of Allah. We have believed in Allah. And bear thou witness that we are obedient.342

فَلَمَّاۤ اَحَسَّ عِیْسٰی مِنْهُمُ الْکُفْرَ قَالَ مَنْ اَنْصَارِیْۤ اِلَی اللّٰهِ ط قَالَ الْحَوَارِیُّوْنَ نَحْنُ اَنْصَارُ اللّٰهِ ۚ اٰمَنَّا بِاللّٰهِ ۚ وَاشْهَدْ بِاَنَّا مُسْلِمُوْنَ ۟

---

[a]5 : 73, 118 ; 19 : 37 ; 43 : 65.   [b]5 : 112 ; 61 : 15.

---

341. Commentary :

This verse clearly refutes the later Christian doctrine of the Trinity and the Sonship of Jesus ascribed to him. Jesus looks upon himself to be as human and as subservient to God as any other mortal.

342. Important Words :

الْحَوَارِیُّوْن (disciples) is the plural of حَوَارِیْ (a disciple) which is derived from حَارَ which means, he or it returned ; or he became perplexed. حَارَالثَّوْب means, he washed the cloth and rendered it white. حَوَارِیْ means: (1) one who whitens clothes by washing them i.e. a washerman ; (2) one who has been tried and found to be free from vice or fault ; (3) a person of pure and unsullied character ; (4) one who advises or counsels or acts honestly and faithfully ; (5) a true and sincere friend or helper ; (6) a select friend and helper of a Prophet ; (7) a relation. The disciples of Jesus were called حَوَارِیُّوْن because they helped him in his work, or because they were white or pure of heart, or because they made the hearts of other people white and pure by

their noble teachings and good example, or (as some have thought) because some of them were washermen by profession (Lane, Aqrab & Mufradāt). The Quran has used the word in the sense of helpers, as the words that follow indicate.

Commentary :

In this verse the Quran has cleared the disciples of Jesus of the serious lapses asribed to them in the Gospels. They were sincere helpers in the cause of God, believing in the mission of Jesus and making no secret of their faith.

The word حَوَارِیْ as explained under Important Words above, signifies a reliable helper and disciple of a Prophet. From an authentic saying of the Holy Prophet the word appears to have also been once applied by him to one of his trustworthy and distinguished Companions, Zubair b. ' Awwām, who, on an occasion of great danger, went alone boldly in the enemy camp on an extremely cold and dark night and brought back necessary information (Bukhārī).

54. 'Our Lord, we believe in that which Thou hast sent down and we follow this Messenger. So write us down among those who bear witness.'[343]

رَبَّنَاۤ اٰمَنَّا بِمَاۤ اَنۡزَلۡتَ وَاتَّبَعۡنَا الرَّسُوۡلَ فَاكۡتُبۡنَا مَعَ الشّٰهِدِیۡنَ ۝

55. And [a]they planned and Allah also planned; and Allah is the best of planners.[344]

وَمَكَرُوۡا وَمَكَرَ اللّٰهُ ؕ وَاللّٰهُ خَیۡرُ الۡمٰکِرِیۡنَ ۝

---

[a]8 : 31; 27 : 51.

---

343. Commentary :

Not only did the disciples of Jesus heartily respond to his call for aid, but also bore witness to his truth both by words of mouth and by their good example and faithful conduct. The verse also makes it clear that the disciples looked upon Jesus as only a Messenger of God with no claim to divinity.

344. Important Words :

مَكَرُوۡا (they planned) and مَكَرَ (he planned) are from the same root. مَكَرَ means, he plotted or planned secretly with a view to circumventing the other; he practised an evasion or a device or a machination; he exercised art or cunning or skill in the management or ordering of affairs with excellent consideration and deliberation; he tried to do harm or mischief secretly. مَكَرَ اللّٰه (God planned) may also mean, God requited the machination of a person or a people (Lane) See also 2 : 16. مَكَر is of two kinds: (1) مَكَر مَحۡمُوۡد i.e. a good plan by which a good object is sought, and (2) مَكَر مَذۡمُوۡم i.e. an evil plan by which an evil object is sought (Mufradāt). In view of the above, the word مَكَر when used with regard to the enemies of Jesus would signify their wicked designs and evil machinations to destroy his mission and bring him to ruin; and when used with regard to God, it would signify the plan of God to frustrate the evil designs of the Jews and bring punishment on their heads.

Commentary :

The Jews had planned that Jesus should die an accursed death on the Cross (Deut. 21 : 23), but God's plan was that he should be saved from that death. The plan of the Jews was frustrated and God's plan was successful, because Jesus did not die on the Cross but came down alive, dying a natural death, full of years, in Kashmir, far away from the scene of his crucifixion.

56. 'When Allah said, 'O Jesus, *a*I will cause thee to die *a natural death* and *b*will exalt thee to Myself, and will clear thee from *the charges of* those who disbelieve, and will place those who follow thee above those who disbelieve, until the Day of Resurrection ; *c*then to Me shall be your return, and I will judge between you concerning that wherein you differ.[345]

اِذۡ قَالَ اللّٰهُ یٰعِیۡسٰۤی اِنِّیۡ مُتَوَفِّیۡکَ وَ رَافِعُکَ اِلَیَّ وَ مُطَهِّرُکَ مِنَ الَّذِیۡنَ کَفَرُوۡا وَ جَاعِلُ الَّذِیۡنَ اتَّبَعُوۡکَ فَوۡقَ الَّذِیۡنَ کَفَرُوۤا اِلٰی یَوۡمِ الۡقِیٰمَۃِ ثُمَّ اِلَیَّ مَرۡجِعُکُمۡ فَاَحۡکُمُ بَیۡنَکُمۡ فِیۡمَا کُنۡتُمۡ فِیۡهِ تَخۡتَلِفُوۡنَ ۝

*a*3:194; 4:16; 7:127; 8:51; 10:47, 105; 12:102; 13:41; 16:29, 33; 22:6; 39:43; 40:68, 78; 47:28.   *b*4:159; 7:177; 19:57.   *c*5:49; 6:165; 11:24; 31:16; 39:8.

345. Important Words :

مُتَوَفِّیۡکَ (cause thee to die) is derived from وَفیٰ *i.e.* he fulfilled or performed ; or he was faithful, etc. توفّی اللّٰہ زیدا means, قبض روحه *i.e.* God took away the soul of Zaid, namely, He caused him to die. When God is the subject and a human being the object, توفّی has no other meaning than that of taking away the soul, whether in sleep or death. See note on 2 : 235. So مُتَوَفِّیۡکَ means, I will cause thee to die. Ibn 'Abbās, a cousin of the Holy Prophet and a scholar of great eminence, has translated مُتَوَفِّیۡکَ as مُمِیۡتُکَ *i.e.* I will cause thee to die (Bukhārī). Similarly, Zamakhsharī, an Arab linguist of great repute, says : "The expression مُتَوَفِّیۡکَ means, I will protect thee from being killed by the people and will grant thee full lease of life ordained for thee, and will cause thee to die a natural death, not by being killed" (Kashshāf). In fact, all Arabic lexicographers are agreed on the point that the word توفّی as used in the aforesaid manner, can bear no other interpretation. Not a single instance from the whole of Arabic literature can be shown of this expression having been used in any other sense. Outstanding scholars and Commentators like (1) Ibn 'Abbās, (2) Imām Mālik (3) Imām Bukhārī, (4) Imām ibn Ḥazm, (5) Imām ibn Qayyim, (6) Qatāda,

(7) Wahab, and others are of the same view (see 1. Bukhārī, ch. on *Tafsīr*; 2. Bukhārī, ch. on *Bad' al-Khalq*; 3. Biḥār ; 4. Al-Muḥallā, Cairo, i. 23; 5. Ma'ād, p. 19 ; 6. Manthūr ii. 7. Kathīr). According to Fatḥ al-Bayān, those Commentators who have tried to put other meanings into the word توفّی, as used in the aforesaid manner, have done so on account of their belief that Jesus has been taken up to heaven alive ; otherwise, the word possesses no other meaning but that of taking away the soul or causing to die. The expression has been used at no less than 25 different places in the Quran and in no less than 23 of them the meaning is to take away the soul at the time of death. Only at two places the meaning is to take the soul away at the time of sleep ; but here the qualifying word "sleep" or "night" has been added (6 : 61 ; 39 : 43).

رَافِعُکَ (will exalt thee). رَافِع is the active participle from رفع. They say رفعه *i.e.* he raised him or it; he elevated him or it; he lifted it ; he uplifted it ; he exalted or honoured him ; he took it up, etc. Thus رفع is the antonym of وضع *i.e.* he put it down ; he debased it. The Holy Prophet says :

اِنَّ اللّٰہَ یَرۡفَعُ بِہٰذَا الۡقُرۡآنِ اَقۡوَامًا وَ یَضَعُ اَقۡوَامًا

i.e. Allah will, by means of this Quran, exalt some peoples and humble others (Mājah).

Again he says :

من تواضع لله رفعه الله الى السماء السابعة

i.e. he who truly humbles himself for the sake of God, God would lift him to the seventh heaven *i.e.* would exalt him to the highest spiritual station ('Ummāl, ii. 25). The Quran has described the Day of Resurrection as خافضة رافعة meaning, it shall debase some and exalt others (56 : 4). In the Quran we also have فى بيوت اذن الله ان ترفع *i.e. in houses with regard to which Allah has commanded that they be exalted* (24 : 37). Again العمل الصالح يرفعه *i.e.* the righteous work of a man exalts him (35 : 11). Even in our daily Prayers we pray اللهم ارفعنى *i.e.* O God, exalt me. In fact, when the رفع of a man is spoken of as being to or towards God, the meaning is invariably his spiritual elevation, because God being not material or confined to a place, no physical elevation to Him is possible. Jesus himself has denied the possibility of his rising physically to heaven. Says he : "And no man hath ascended up to heaven but he that came down from heaven, even the son of man which is in heaven " (John 3 : 13).

Commentary :

This verse has been linked up with the preceding one with the word اذ (when), thus indicating that it provides what is known as ظرف for the concluding clause of that verse *i.e. Allah is the best of planners.* The present verse thus relates to the occasion when Jesus was being made a victim of the evil machinations of his enemies who were plotting to have him crucified and thereby prove him to have come to an accursed end (Deut. 21 : 22, 23). " Nay ", says God to Jesus as stated in the verse under comment, " thine enemy shall not be permitted to kill thee on the Cross and thereby prove thee to be low and debased spiritually. On the contrary, I will cause thee to die a natural death and will exalt thee in My presence. . . ."

This is the only possible meaning of the verse in conformity with the context. Unfortunately, however, the verse is one of those which have heavily suffered from misinterpretation. Meanings have been sought to be put upon its words which they are simply incapable of bearing. It is now an admitted fact that, through the free intermixture of Muslims and Christians and the conversion *en masse* of hundreds of thousands of Christians to Islam, the belief that Jesus had risen up to heaven alive found widespread credence among Muslims, the misunderstanding of the prophecy about the second advent of Jesus lending support to it.

There is no gainsaying the fact that Jesus is dead, and not alive in heaven. The Holy Porphet is reported to have said, " Had Moses and Jesus been now living, they would have found themselves forced to follow me " (Kathīr). He even fixed the age of Jesus as 120 ('Ummāl). The Quran, in as many as 30 verses, has completely demolished the absurd belief of the physical ascension of Jesus and his supposed life in heaven. The arrangement of words in the verse under comment also leaves no doubt about the death of Jesus. Four distinct promises have been made to him in the verse : (1) his being saved from death on the Cross and dying thereafter a natural death ; (2) his exaltation in God's presence ; (3) his exoneration from the false charges of his enemies, and (4) the domination of his followers over his rejectors. The last three promises have already been fulfilled ; but what of the first ? It is idle to speak of تقديم and تاخير (*i.e.* the first-mentioned promise to be read after the others) without any justifying reason. It is idle also to claim that متوفيك here means " I will cause thee to sleep." The Quranic idiom spurns the idea. Indeed such a meaning makes the verse almost ridiculous.

The verse beautifully describes in four brief words the frustration of the plans of the Jews

57. 'Then as for those who disbelieve, I will punish them with a
severe punishment in this world and
in the next, and they shall have no
helpers'.346

58. 'And as for those who believe and
do good works, ^aHe will pay them their
full rewards. And Allah loves not the
wrongdoers.'

59. That is what We recite unto
thee of the Signs and the wise
Reminder. 347

فَاَمَّا الَّذِيْنَ كَفَرُوْا فَاُعَذِّبُهُمْ عَذَابًا شَدِيْدًا فِى الدُّنْيَا وَالْاٰخِرَةِ ۖ وَمَا لَهُمْ مِّنْ نّٰصِرِيْنَ ۞

وَاَمَّا الَّذِيْنَ اٰمَنُوْا وَعَمِلُوا الصّٰلِحٰتِ فَيُوَفِّيْهِمْ اُجُوْرَهُمْ ۖ وَاللهُ لَا يُحِبُّ الظّٰلِمِيْنَ ۞

ذٰلِكَ نَتْلُوْهُ عَلَيْكَ مِنَ الْاٰيٰتِ وَالذِّكْرِ الْحَكِيْمِ ۞

---

^a4 : 174 ; 35 : 31 ; 39 : 11, 70.

---

referred to in the preceding verse. They had
planned (1) to bring about the death of Jesus
by crucifixion; and (2) to be thus able to say
that because he was a false prophet, he died an
accursed death on the Cross (Deut. 21 : 22,
23). They also sought (3) to bring false charges
against him, especially the heinous charge of an
illegitimate birth; and (4) to be thus able to
compass the destruction of his entire movement.
They were completely foiled in all these designs.
Jesus died, not on the Cross, but a natural
death, respected and revered by devoted followers. He was cleared of the false charges
imputed to him and has ever been regarded as
one of the sacred band of God's great Prophets.
Last of all, his followers have for centuries
held his rejectors, the Jews, under their heels.

The words, *those who follow thee*, originally
referred to the Christians and the words, *those
who disbelieve*, to the Jews. Later, however,
when Islam made its appearance, the words
those who follow thee, naturally came to include
Muslims, who believe in the divine mission
of Jesus; and history tells us that Muslims
and Christians have both dominated the Jews
whenever and wherever they have come in
contact with them.

The prophecy about giving dominance to the

believers in Jesus over his rejectors was, however, to be fulfilled in its completest form at the
time of his second advent which has now taken
place in the person of Ahmad, the Promised
Messiah, whose message is for all the nations of
the world. The clause, *those who disbelieve*,
would, therefore, now apply to all those from
among Jews, Christians, Muslims, Hindus,
Buddhists and others who reject the Second
Messiah who has come in fulfilment of the
prophecies of both Jesus and the Holy Prophet
of Islam. No wonder then that the words:
"O Jesus, I will cause thee to die (a natural
death).........and will place those who follow
thee above those who disbelieve" also formed
part of the revelation vouchsafed to Ahmad
(Izāla, p. 192).

346. **Commentary:**

The words, *those who disbelieve*, here refer to
Jews, who have suffered great hardships
throughout the ages. The tale of their woes and
afflictions at the hands of Titus about 70
years after the crucifixion of Jesus pales into
insignificance before the sufferings to which
they have been subjected in some parts of
Europe in our own time.

347. **Commentary:**

The story of Jesus, as narrated in the Quran

60. Surely, the case of Jesus with Allah is like the case of Adam. He created him out of dust, then He said to him, ' Be ', and he was.[348]

اِنَّ مَثَلَ عِيْسَى عِنْدَ اللّٰهِ كَمَثَلِ اٰدَمَ خَلَقَهٗ مِنْ تُرَابٍ ثُمَّ قَالَ لَهٗ كُنْ فَيَكُوْنُ ۝

61. [a]This is the truth from thy Lord, so be thou not of those who doubt.[349]

اَلْحَقُّ مِنْ رَّبِّكَ فَلَا تَكُنْ مِّنَ الْمُمْتَرِيْنَ ۝

---

[a]2:148; 6:115; 10:95.

---

is not a mere thing of the past. It is meant to shed new light on events that form the basis of the doctrines of a large section of humanity as well as to provide a lesson for the future.

348. Commentary :

The word مثل (case) is used to express resemblance, which may be of different kinds and different degrees. Sometimes, the thing likened is equal to that to which it is likened, sometimes the former is superior to the latter, and sometimes the latter is superior to the former. So it is not necessary that the thing likened to another should be equal, or even similar, to the latter in all respects. The likeness between Adam and Jesus referred to in this verse, may, therefore, not be stretched too far.

In the verse the word 'Adam' primarily stands for man i.e. the sons of Adam generally. Jesus is thus declared to be like other mortals who have all been created from dust (40 : 68), and so there can be no divinity about him. If, however, the word 'Adam' be taken to refer to the progenitor of the human race, then the verse would be taken to point to the resemblance between Jesus and Adam in being born without the agency of a male parent. In this case, the fact that Jesus had a mother would not affect the likeness which, as stated above, need not be complete in all respects.

The words, then He said to him, " Be " and he

was, show that the command refers, not to the birth of Jesus (for the fact of his creation has already been mentioned in the words خلقه i.e. He created him, occurring in the preceding part of the verse) but to his death. The use of the word كن (Be) in relation to death should not sound odd, for, according to the teaching of Islam, death is not the end of life but simply a change, the beginning of a new life. The meaning in this case would be that after having created Jesus and having allowed him the prescribed lease of life in this world, God caused him to die and took his soul away to the next world. The expression, "Be" and he was, may also refer to the creation or birth of Jesus in the sense that, after giving him the human form in the womb of his mother, God said to him " Be " i.e. become quickened with life, whereupon he became alive. Again, the reference may also be to the spiritual life i.e. after creating Jesus in the form of a man God called upon him to become a Prophet, which was the ultimate end of his creation, and consequently he became a Prophet. Whatever the interpretation, the verse constitutes a clear refutation of the Christian belief in the divinity of Jesus on the plea of his unusual birth.

As for the creation of man from تراب (dust), we shall give a suitable note when we come to the verses directly dealing with the subject.

349. Important Words :

ممترين (those who doubt) means : (1) those who doubt ; (2) those who contest and raise

62. Now whoso disputes with thee concerning him, after what has come to thee of knowledge, say to him, ' Come, let us call our sons and your sons, and our women and your women, and our people and your people ; then let us pray fervently and *invoke the curse of Allah on those who lie.'350

فَمَنْ حَآجَّكَ فِيهِ مِنْ بَعْدِ مَا جَآءَكَ مِنَ الْعِلْمِ فَقُلْ تَعَالَوْا نَدْعُ اَبْنَآءَنَا وَاَبْنَآءَكُمْ وَنِسَآءَنَا وَنِسَآءَكُمْ وَاَنْفُسَنَا وَاَنْفُسَكُمْ ۫ ثُمَّ نَبْتَهِلْ فَنَجْعَلْ لَّعْنَتَ اللّٰهِ عَلَى الْكٰذِبِيْنَ ۝

---

62 : 7, 8.

---

objections (see also 2 : 148). Both meanings are applicable here.

Commentary :

As حق (truth) also signifies an established fact or an established truth (2 : 148 & 3 : 4), the verse hints that as now the fact has been established beyond doubt or controversy that there was nothing in Jesus above an ordinary mortal, so there is truly no possibility of doubt or difference of opinion in the matter.

350. Important Words :

نبتهل (let us pray fervently) is derived from بهل . They say بهله i.e. he left him to his own will ; or he left him to himself ; he cursed him. ابتهل means, he prayed or supplicated humbly and earnestly and fervently, with energy and effort. باهله means, he cursed him, being also cursed by the latter. مباهلة means, the act of invoking God's curse on each other i.e. on whichever party is the wrongdoer (Aqrab & Lane).

انفسنا و انفسكم (our people and your people). The words are the plural of نفس and mean : (1) our souls and your souls ; (2) ourselves and yourselves ; (3) our people and your people ; (4) our co-religionists and your co-religionists (Lane). See also 2 : 55 and 3 : 29. Here, as the context shows, the words give the last-mentioned meaning.

Commentary :

The present discussion on Christian doctrines

with which this *Sūra* began has been brought to a close in this verse. The reference, as mentioned above, is to the Christian deputation from Najrân which consisted of sixty persons and was headed by their chief, 'Abdul Masîḥ known as Al-'Âqib. They met the Holy Prophet in his Mosque and the discussion on the doctrine of the divinity of Jesus continued at some length. When the question had been fully discussed and the members of the deputation were found to be still insisting on their false doctrine, the Holy Prophet, in obedience to the divine command contained in the present verse, invited them as a last resort to join him in a sort of prayer-contest technically known as مباهلة i.e. invoking the curse of God on the holders of false beliefs. As, however, the Christians did not appear to be sure of their ground, they declined to accept the challenge, thus indirectly admitting the falsity of their doctrine (Zurqānī, Khamîs & Bayān under 3:3). On this occasion, the Holy Prophet brought out 'Alī, Fāṭima, Ḥasan and Ḥusain (Khamîs & Zurqānī) as well as Abū Bakr, 'Umar, 'Uthmān and others ('Asākir) in the field and is reported to have said : " If the Christians had accepted the challenge of مباهلة and agreed to pray to God to send His punishment on the lying party, God would have surely destroyed the liars before a year had passed" (Bukhārī, Muslim & Tirmidhī).

It may be noted that the prayer-contest

63. This certainly is the true account. There is none worthy of worship save Allah; and surely it is Allah Who is the Mighty, the Wise.[351]

اِنَّ هٰذَا لَهُوَ الْقَصَصُ الْحَقُّ ۚ وَمَا مِنْ اِلٰهٍ اِلَّا اللّٰهُ ۚ وَاِنَّ اللّٰهَ لَهُوَ الْعَزِيْزُ الْحَكِيْمُ ۝

known as مباهلة is in the nature of seeking God's arbitration in fundamental religious differences. When other methods of settlement fail, the parties approach Almighty God to decide between them according to His eternal scheme of helping the righteous and destroying the wicked. The act of cursing is thus not in the form of abusing but an earnest supplication to God to uphold the truth and destroy falsehood—to amputate the diseased limb in order to save the healthy one. Thus مباهلة is a very serious affair and should be resorted to in very rare cases, subject to the following conditions, which are deducible from the present verse as well as from the relevant sayings of the Holy Prophet: (1) the point in dispute should be a matter of supreme and fundamental religious importance and should be based on clear scriptural authority; (2) the matter should first be fully argued and discussed between the parties; (3) the مباهلة should take place only if and when after the aforesaid discussion each party still continues to adhere to its views, definitely holding the other party to be in the wrong; (4) for the actual contest the parties should assemble in a suitable place together with the members of their families and a suitable number of others holding similar views, and there solemnly invoke the curse of God on the party sticking to falsehood.

As to the form or time of punishment which, as a result of مباهلة, must overtake the offending party, the verse sheds no light. The matter rests entirely with God. From the above-quoted tradition, however, it may be deduced that if any period at all is to be fixed, it should be not less than a year. But the form of punishment must still rest on divine

will. The Heavenly Judge reserves the right of deciding each individual case as He thinks fit. The result is left to speak for itself.

It may be noted here incidentally that during the discussions with the Christian deputation from Najrān the Holy Prophet allowed them to pray in his Mosque in their own way, which they did facing the East—an act of religious toleration unparalleled in the history of all religion (Zurqānī).

351. Important Words :

القصص (account) is the noun-infinitive from قص . They say قص الشعر i.e. he cut or clipped the hair. قص عليه الخبر means, he related or narrated the news to him. قص أثره means, he followed after his track, or he followed him step by step. قصص (qaṣaṣ) means, the act of narrating; narration or account; track or footsteps. قصص (qiṣaṣ) with different vowel point, is the plural of قصة meaning, a story, a narrative, etc. (Aqrab & Lane).

Commentary :

This verse partially repeats the sense of verse 3 : 61 above in order to impress upon the reader that the discomfiture of the Christian deputation in the challenge of مباهلة mentioned in 3 : 62 sets the seal upon the conclusion that Islam has truly triumphed over Christianity, and that there is no god but Allah Who, being "Mighty and Wise," needs no son or helper.

As stated in the verse, the facts narrated in the above verses constitute "the true account" about Jesus and not impossible things which his followers out of excessive love, or his enemies out of inveterate hatred, have attributed to him.

64. But if they turn away, then *remember that* Allah knows the mischief-makers well.[352]

فَإِنْ تَوَلَّوْا فَإِنَّ اللّٰهَ عَلِيْمٌۢ بِالْمُفْسِدِيْنَ ۩

65. Say, 'O People of the Book! come to a word equal between us and you— that we worship none but Allah, and that we associate no partner with Him, and that *a*some of us take not others for Lords beside Allah.' But if they turn away, then say, ' Bear witness that we have submitted *to God*.'[353]

قُلْ يٰۤاَهْلَ الْكِتٰبِ تَعَالَوْا اِلٰى كَلِمَةٍ سَوَآءٍۢ بَيْنَنَا وَبَيْنَكُمْ اَلَّا نَعْبُدَ اِلَّا اللّٰهَ وَلَا نُشْرِكَ بِهٖ شَيْئًا وَّلَا يَتَّخِذَ بَعْضُنَا بَعْضًا اَرْبَابًا مِّنْ دُوْنِ اللّٰهِ فَإِنْ تَوَلَّوْا فَقُوْلُوا اشْهَدُوْا بِاَنَّا مُسْلِمُوْنَ ۩

---

*a*9:31.

352. Commentary :

The clause, *then remember that Allah knows the mischief-makers well*, embodies a solemn warning. God being All-Knowing, each and every act of the wrongdoers is known to Him and He will judge them accordingly.

353. Important Words :

ارباب (Lords) is the plural of رب (Lord) for which see 1 : 2. رب means, lord, master or owner ; a chief or ruler to whom obedience is rendered ; one who fosters, brings up, or nourishes (Lane & Aqrab).

Commentary :

This verse is wrongly considered by some to provide a basis for a compromise between Islam on the one hand and Christianity and Judaism on the other. It is argued that if these faiths become united in the doctrine of the Oneness of God, the verse permits the sacrifice of other Islamic teachings as being of comparatively little importance. Nothing can be farther from the truth. The Quran, the Ḥadīth, and the facts of history are all united in belying this ridiculous assumption. It is simply unthinkable that compromise in matters of faith could be allowed by any religion worth the name, particularly with a people who, in the immediately preceding verses, have been severely condemned for their beliefs and who are so forcefully challenged to a prayer-contest to invoke the curse of God upon those who lie in their beliefs. The Holy Prophet, while writing his missionary epistle to Heraclius, used this very verse, yet he forcefully invited the latter to accept Islam and threatened him with divine punishment if he refused to do so (Bukhārī). This shows beyond doubt that the mere fact of his believing in the Oneness of God, could not, according to the Holy Prophet, save Heraclius from God's punishment. Elsewhere the Quran emphatically declares that *surely the (true) religion with Allah is Islam (i.e. complete submission) ; and whoso seeks a religion other than Islam, it shall not be accepted from him, and in the life to come he shall be among the losers* (3 : 20 & 86). Can anything be clearer ?

The truth is that this verse is intended to suggest an easy and simple method by which Jews and Christians can arrive at a right decision regarding the truth of Islam. Christians, in spite of claiming belief in the unity of Godhead, felt satisfied in believing in the divinity of Jesus ; and Jews, notwithstanding their claim to be monotheists, gave blind allegiance to their priests and divines, practically placing them in the position of God Himself.

66. O People of the Book! ^awhy do you dispute concerning Abraham, when the Torah and the Gospel were not revealed till after him ? Will you not then understand ?[354]

يَـٰٓأَهْلَ ٱلْكِتَـٰبِ لِمَ تُحَآجُّونَ فِىٓ إِبْرَٰهِيمَ وَمَآ أُنزِلَتِ ٱلتَّوْرَىٰةُ وَٱلْإِنجِيلُ إِلَّا مِنۢ بَعْدِهِۦٓ أَفَلَا تَعْقِلُونَ ٦٦

^a2 : 141.

The verse exhorts both these communities to come back to their original belief in the Oneness of God and give up the worship of false deities who stand in the way of their accepting Islam. Thus, instead of seeking a compromise with these faiths, the verse virtually invites Christians and Jews to the faith of Islam, by drawing their attention to the doctrine of the Oneness of God which being, at least in its outer form, the common fundamental doctrine of all, could serve as a meeting ground for further approach.

It was exactly on these lines that Ahmad, the Promised Messiah, in his "Message of Peace," made an offer to the Hindus of India to enter into an agreement with the Muslims of his way of thinking to the effect that they (Hindus) would respect and honour the Holy Prophet of Islam and would look upon him as a true Messenger of God, even as he and his followers believed in Rama and Krishna as God's Elect.

Special emphasis has been laid in the verse under comment on the Oneness of God—a doctrine on which in theory all revealed religions seem to agree, but regarding the details of which no two faiths are found to concur. Most religions claim to be monotheistic ; but under the outer veneer of monotheism, polytheism very often lies hidden in most hideous forms. It is the simple faith of Islam alone which is really and truly monotheistic in all its aspects and which strongly condemns the association with God of anything or any being in His person, attributes, worship or works. It is most unfortunate, however, that in spite of Islam being such a strictly monotheistic faith, a section of present-day Muslims has drifted away into the quagmire of what cannot but be termed idol-worship in the wider sense of the word.

Incidentally, it may be noted that the letter mentioned by Bukhārī and other Muslim traditionists as having been addressed by the Holy Prophet to Heraclius in the words of this verse inviting him to accept Islam has recently been discovered and found to contain the exact words quoted by Bukhārī (R. Rel. vol. v. no. 8). This furnishes a strong proof of the essential authenticity of Bukhārī and, for that matter, of other accepted works of Hadīth.

354. **Commentary :**

As the context shows, the words, *concerning Abraham*, mean concerning the religion of Abraham. He was neither a follower of the Torah nor a follower of the Gospel ; for both these Books were revealed long after him. Still the People of the Book disputed among themselves as to the religion of Abraham, each party claiming that he believed as they did.

67. Behold! you are those who disputed about that whereof you had knowledge. Why then do you *now* dispute about that whereof you have no knowledge *at all*? Allah knows, and you know not.[355]

هَاَنْتُمْ هٰٓؤُلَاۤءِ حَاجَجْتُمْ فِيْمَا لَكُمْ بِهٖ عِلْمٌ فَلِمَ تُحَاۤجُّوْنَ فِيْمَا لَيْسَ لَكُمْ بِهٖ عِلْمٌ ۚ وَاللّٰهُ يَعْلَمُ وَاَنْتُمْ لَا تَعْلَمُوْنَ ۝

68. Abraham was neither a Jew *a*nor a Christian, but *b*he was ever inclined *to God* and obedient *to Him*, and he was not of those who associate gods with God.[356]

مَا كَانَ اِبْرٰهِيْمُ يَهُوْدِيًّا وَّلَا نَصْرَانِيًّا وَّلٰكِنْ كَانَ حَنِيْفًا مُّسْلِمًا ۗ وَمَا كَانَ مِنَ الْمُشْرِكِيْنَ ۝

69. Surely, the nearest of men to Abraham are those who followed him, and *c*this Prophet and those who believe; and Allah is the friend of believers.[357]

اِنَّ اَوْلَى النَّاسِ بِاِبْرٰهِيْمَ لَلَّذِيْنَ اتَّبَعُوْهُ وَهٰذَا النَّبِيُّ وَالَّذِيْنَ اٰمَنُوْا ۗ وَاللّٰهُ وَلِيُّ الْمُؤْمِنِيْنَ ۝

*a*2:141.   *b*3:96; 4:126; 6:162; 16:121, 124.   *c*16:124.

355. Commentary:

The verse administers a rebuke to the Jews with whom disputation about religious questions had become a habit and a pastime. The rebuke purports to say: Is not your appetite for bickering and quarrelling about Biblical principles and tenets, with which you are at least conversant to some extent, satisfied that you have begun to meddle with matters about which you know nothing? The reference is either to the Quranic teaching or to their claim about Abraham referred to in the preceding verse.

356. Important Words:

حنيفا (ever inclined to God). See 2:136.

Commentary:

If Abraham can be said to belong to any of the present faiths, it is Islam; for, (1) Islam is a name with a meaning bearing on the inner spirit of the faith—submission or obedience to the will of God; (2) Abraham himself used the word مسلم for himself and also for his son Ishmael, from whom the Holy Prophet of Islam is descended (2:129); and (3) he prayed that from among his progeny a مسلم (Muslim) people may come forth (2:129). But he was obviously not a Muslim in the sense that he followed in detail the religion brought by the Holy Prophet.

The clause, *he was not of those who associate gods with God*, is a sort of rebuke to Jews and Christians who, in spite of calling themselves monotheists, virtually practised polytheism and still did not hesitate to claim Abraham as one of themselves.

357. Important Words:

اولى (nearest). See 4:136.

Commentary:

Though in a technical sense Abraham was neither a Jew nor a Christian nor yet a Muslim for he lived long before these faiths came into existence, yet taking in view the inner spirit of the faith he was certainly most nearly related to Islam and its Holy Founder. Jews

70. ^aA section of the People of the Book would fain lead you astray ; but they lead astray none except themselves, only they perceive not.³⁵⁸

وَدَّتْ طَّآئِفَةٌ مِّنْ اَهْلِ الْكِتٰبِ لَوْ يُضِلُّوْنَكُمْ وَمَا يُضِلُّوْنَ اِلَّا اَنْفُسَهُمْ وَمَا يَشْعُرُوْنَ ۝

71. ^bO People of the Book ! why do you deny the Signs of Allah, while you are witnesses thereof ?³⁵⁹

يٰاَهْلَ الْكِتٰبِ لِمَ تَكْفُرُوْنَ بِاٰيٰتِ اللّٰهِ وَاَنْتُمْ تَشْهَدُوْنَ ۝

72. O People of the Book ! ^cwhy do you confound truth with falsehood and ^dhide the truth knowingly ?³⁶⁰

يٰاَهْلَ الْكِتٰبِ لِمَ تَلْبِسُوْنَ الْحَقَّ بِالْبَاطِلِ وَتَكْتُمُوْنَ الْحَقَّ وَاَنْتُمْ تَعْلَمُوْنَ ۝

---

^a4 : 90.   ^b3 : 99.   ^c2 : 43.   ^dSee 2 : 43.

---

and Christians had no right to claim him as their spiritual progenitor when all their beliefs and practices were at such variance with his teaching.

358. Commentary :

The simplicity, straightforwardness and perfection of the faith of Islam very often create such strong feelings of appreciation in the hearts of the People of the Book that they feel irresistibly drawn towards it but, being inimical and jealous, their appreciation often takes the queer though not unpsychological course that they begin to wish that Muslims may become like themselves.

Taking the word ضلالة in the sense of ruin (see 2 : 27), the expression يضلونكم (lead you astray) may also be rendered as "lead you to ruin" and the next clause, *but they lead astray none except themselves*, may in that case mean that by seeking to ruin the Muslims, they only ruin themselves, because the rise of one's enemy signifies one's own fall.

359. Commentary :

Rejection of God's Signs is a heinous crime for anyone, but it becomes still more heinous for him who is a direct witness thereof.

360. Commentary :

By means of the signs mentioned in their scriptures about the Holy Prophet, the People of the Book could easily know that Muhammad (peace and blessings of God be on him!) was indeed the Promised Prophet, yet because of enmity and jealousy they would not recognize him and insisted on mixing up truth with falsehood rather than accept the truth in its unalloyed purity.

73. And a section of the People of the Book say, 'Believe in that which has been revealed unto the believers in the early part of the day and disbelieve in the latter part thereof; perchance they may return;[361]

وَقَالَت طَّآئِفَةٌ مِّنۡ اَهۡلِ الۡكِتٰبِ اٰمِنُوۡا بِالَّذِىۤ اُنۡزِلَ عَلَى الَّذِيۡنَ اٰمَنُوۡا وَجۡهَ النَّهَارِ وَاكۡفُرُوۡۤا اٰخِرَهٗ لَعَلَّهُمۡ يَرۡجِعُوۡنَ ۚ ۝

74. 'And [a]obey none but him who follows your religion';—Say, 'Surely, the *true* guidance, the guidance of Allah, is that one be given the like of that which has been given to you'— 'or [b]they would dispute with you before your Lord.' Say, 'All bounty is in the hand of [c]Allah. He gives it to whomsoever He pleases. And Allah is Bountiful, All-Knowing.[362]

وَلَا تُؤۡمِنُوۡۤا اِلَّا لِمَنۡ تَبِعَ دِيۡنَكُمۡ قُلۡ اِنَّ الۡهُدٰى هُدَى اللّٰهِ اَنۡ يُّؤۡتٰۤى اَحَدٌ مِّثۡلَ مَاۤ اُوۡتِيۡتُمۡ اَوۡ يُحَآجُّوۡكُمۡ عِنۡدَ رَبِّكُمۡ قُلۡ اِنَّ الۡفَضۡلَ بِيَدِ اللّٰهِ يُؤۡتِيۡهِ مَنۡ يَّشَآءُ وَاللّٰهُ وَاسِعٌ عَلِيۡمٌ ۝

[a]2:121.   [b]2:77.   [c]57:30.

---

361. Commentary:

This verse refers to one of the attempts of the Jews to lead Muslims astray. This attempt pertained to a clever ruse on their part to strike a blow at the growing power of Islam. The Jews were held in esteem by the pagan Arabs for their religious learning. They took undue advantage of this and thought of a device to turn Muslims away from their faith by outwardly embracing Islam in the early part of a day and recanting it in its latter part, seeking in this way to make the unlettered Arabs believe that something must have been seriously wrong with Islam, otherwise these learned men would not have so hurriedly given it up. Devices like these have been employed by the enemies of truth in all ages, but they have never succeeded.

362. Commentary:

The construction of this verse, though seemingly rather complicated, is designed to make it capable of different interpretations.

We will give here those most apparent :—

(1) The clause, *And obey none but him who follows your religion,* is a continuation of the concluding clause of the preceding verse. Thereafter comes a parenthetical clause beginning with the words, *Say, surely the true guidance,* and ending with the words, *the like of that which has been given to you.* Then comes again the speech of the Jews in the words, *Or they would dispute with you before your Lord,* the verse finally ending with the divine commandment, *Say, All bounty, etc.* The style is peculiar to the Quran and is intended to produce a good psychological effect.

The words, *that one be given the like of that which has been given to you,* which Muslims are bidden to say are in fitting contrast to the words of the Jews quoted in the beginning of the verse *i.e. obey none but him who follows your religion.* Jews make God a national deity, debarring all others from His favours, whereas Muslims believe in Him as the Lord of all, basing His right to greatness on the

75. ^a'He chooses for His mercy whomsoever He pleases. And Allah is Lord of exceeding bounty.'[363]

يَخْتَصُّ بِرَحْمَتِهِ مَنْ يَّشَآءُ ۗ وَ اللّٰهُ ذُوالْفَضْلِ الْعَظِيْمِ ۝

^a2 : 106.

---

bestowal of His favours in whatever form and to whatever people they may come. Moreover, they believe that the fold of Islam, which is Allah's universal guidance, is open to all peoples. The words of the Jews, *Or they would dispute with you before your Lord,* mean that if the Jews follow any dispensation other than their own, they would thereby prove their own guilt in the sight of God, for in that case they would be tacitly admitting that the door of God's favours is open to others as well, and thus they would make themselves liable to punishment for rejecting Islam. The words, *All bounty is in the hand of Allah,* mean that the bestowing of the gift of prophethood upon a people is in the hand of God alone and He confers it on those who are deserving of it.

(2) According to another interpretation, only the words قل ان الهدى هدى الله which in this case would be translated as "Say, the true guidance is the guidance of Allah," would be considered as being parenthetical and the following words *i.e. that one be given the like of that which has been given to you,* etc., would be taken to form part of the speech of the Jews. In this case the clause would signify that the Jews say to one another that the guidance that has come to the House of Israel, or the favours that have been bestowed on them, can never be vouchsafed to any other people. They are the exclusive privilege of Israel.

(3) Yet another interpretation is obtained, if the speech of the Jews is taken to end with the words, *obey none but him who follows your religion,* the succeeding clauses being considered to be all divine speech put in the mouth of believers. In this case the words فتقبلوه would be considered to be understood before the clause او يحاجوكم عند ربكم and the entire expression would mean, "so they should accept it, or they should dispute with you before your Lord", signifying that, as true guidance is the guidance contained in the Quran, so either the Jews should accept it or they and Muslims should place their case before God for decision *i.e.* they should have a مباهلة (*Mubahala*) *i.e.* a prayer-contest with them and pray to God to help the righteous and destroy the wicked as already explained in 3 : 62.

363. Commentary :

The word "bounty" here refers to the gift of revelation. The People of the Book are told that if God is pleased to grant prophethood to a people other than themselves, they can have no cause to grumble nor any ground for complaint. The word "exceeding" (lit. great) hints that since God is "Lord of exceeding bounty," it is in the fitness of things that His gifts and favours should descend on all peoples, at one time on this people and at another on that. The word also hints that God being "Lord of exceeding bounty" the time had now come for one universal dispensation for all mankind.

76. Among the People of the Book there is he who, if thou trust him with a treasure, will return it to thee; and among them there is he who, if thou trust him with a dīnār, will not return it to thee, unless thou keep standing over him. That is because they say, 'We are not liable to blame in the matter of the unlearned;' and they utter a lie against Allah knowingly.[364]

وَمِنْ اَهْلِ الْكِتٰبِ مَنْ اِنْ تَأْمَنْهُ بِقِنْطَارٍ يُّؤَدِّهٖ اِلَيْكَ وَمِنْهُمْ مَّنْ اِنْ تَأْمَنْهُ بِدِيْنَارٍ لَّا يُؤَدِّهٖ اِلَيْكَ اِلَّا مَا دُمْتَ عَلَيْهِ قَآئِمًا ذٰلِكَ بِاَنَّهُمْ قَالُوْا لَيْسَ عَلَيْنَا فِي الْاُمِّيّٖنَ سَبِيْلٌ وَيَقُوْلُوْنَ عَلَى اللّٰهِ الْكَذِبَ وَهُمْ يَعْلَمُوْنَ ۞

77. Nay, but *a*whoso fulfils his pledge and fears *God*—verily, Allah loves the God-fearing.[365]

بَلٰى مَنْ اَوْفٰى بِعَهْدِهٖ وَاتَّقٰى فَاِنَّ اللّٰهَ يُحِبُّ الْمُتَّقِيْنَ ۞

---

*a*5:2; 6:153; 13:21; 16:92; 17:35.

---

364. **Commentary:**

The words, *We are not liable to blame in the matter of the unlearned*, refer to a notion prevalent among Jews in the time of the Holy Prophet that it was no sin to rob the gentile Arabs of their possessions, because the latter followed a false religion. The Jews believed that they were at liberty to do as they liked concerning Muslims and would not be called to account for it. Possibly they deduced this queer doctrine from the Jewish law of usury, which makes an invidious distinction between a Jew and a non-Jew regarding the giving and taking of interest (Exod. 22:25; Lev. 25:36, 37; Deut. 23:20, 21).

Another meaning of this verse is obtained if we take the words "trust," "treasure," "dīnār" etc. in a figurative sense. The Bible contains not only prophecies about the Holy Prophet of Islam but also clear injunctions to the People of the Book to accept him when he made his appearance. This was in the nature of a "trust" with them. But when the Promised Prophet appeared, they refused to surrender that trust, except a few of them who accepted Islam. These it is that are spoken of as returning the treasure they are trusted with, whereas those who not only rejected the Holy Prophet but even refused to admit that their scriptures contained any prophecies about him are likened to such as would not even return a "dīnār" entrusted to them unless you *keep standing over them i.e.* unless you force them in argument to admit the truth.

365. **Commentary:**

In this verse believers are exhorted not to follow the bad example of Jews but to deal equitably with all peoples alike. All treaties and covenants and all obligations should be loyally fulfilled and all pledges properly redeemed.

The verse also refutes the Jewish notion that they are superior to other nations and lays down the golden rule that all human beings as such are equal and it is only personal qualities that make a difference. In fact, all rivalry between different nations and the consequent tension and war are the result of the pernicious notion that some nations are superior to others by virtue of their descent.

78. *As for* those who take *ª*a paltry price in exchange of their covenant with Allah and their oaths, they shall have no portion in the life to come, and *ᵇ*Allah will neither speak to them nor look upon them on the Day of Resurrection, nor will He purify them; and for them shall be a grievous punishment.366

إِنَّ الَّذِيْنَ يَشْتَرُوْنَ بِعَهْدِ اللّٰهِ وَاَيْمَانِهِمْ ثَمَنًا قَلِيْلًا اُولٰٓئِكَ لَا خَلَاقَ لَهُمْ فِي الْاٰخِرَةِ وَلَا يُكَلِّمُهُمُ اللّٰهُ وَلَا يَنْظُرُ اِلَيْهِمْ يَوْمَ الْقِيٰمَةِ وَلَا يُزَكِّيْهِمْ ۪ وَلَهُمْ عَذَابٌ اَلِيْمٌ ۝

79. And, surely, among them is a section *ᶜ*who twist their tongues while reciting the Book : that you may think it to be part of the Book, while it is not part of the Book. And they say ' It is from Allah ; ' while it is not from Allah ; and they utter a lie against Allah knowingly.367

وَاِنَّ مِنْهُمْ لَفَرِيْقًا يَّلْوٗنَ اَلْسِنَتَهُمْ بِالْكِتٰبِ لِتَحْسَبُوْهُ مِنَ الْكِتٰبِ وَمَا هُوَ مِنَ الْكِتٰبِ ۚ وَيَقُوْلُوْنَ هُوَ مِنْ عِنْدِ اللّٰهِ وَمَا هُوَ مِنْ عِنْدِ اللّٰهِ ۚ وَيَقُوْلُوْنَ عَلَى اللّٰهِ الْكَذِبَ وَهُمْ يَعْلَمُوْنَ ۝

---

*ª*See 2 : 42.   *ᵇ*2 : 175 ; 23 : 109.   *ᶜ*2 : 76 ; 4 : 47 ; 5 : 42.

Figuratively, the verse also hints that the People of the Book can no longer enjoy God's pleasure unless they faithfully tender the evidence that is with them regarding the Holy Prophet and accept the New Faith. See also the preceding verse.

366. Commentary :

Those who break God's covenant and withhold true evidence really do so only to earn worldly benefits, which are indeed a paltry price.

The word خلاق literally meaning an abundant portion of what is good (see 2 : 201), has been used here to show that disbelievers will not have a portion of good works large enough to secure salvation for them; otherwise the Quran makes it clear that no work of man, whether good or bad, is truly lost (*e.g.* 99 : 8, 9).

The words, *Allah will neither speak to them nor look upon them on the Day of Resurrection,* mean that God will not speak to them words

of kindness and will not look upon them with mercy and compassion. In fact, the looking of God upon a person cannot but mean the bestowing of His grace and favour upon him. The breakers of God's covenants and the withholders of true evidence will not receive such a look from Him. The words, *nor will He purify them,* mean that He will not adjudge them as pure.

367. Commentary :

The clause, *who twist their tongues while reciting the Book,* alludes to an evil practice of some Jews in the time of the Holy Prophet. They would recite a passage in Hebrew in such a manner as would deceive the hearers into believing that it was the Torah that was being recited. The word "Book" used thrice in this verse means "a passage in Hebrew" in the first place and "the Torah" in the last two. The passage is spoken of as "the Book" because the Jews tried to make it appear as such.

80. It is not *possible* for a man that Allah should give him the Book and dominion and prophethood, *and* then [a]he should say to men, 'Be servants to me and not to Allah;' but he *would say,* 'Be solely devoted to the Lord because you teach the Book and because you study *it.*'368

مَا كَانَ لِبَشَرٍ اَنْ يُّؤْتِيَهُ اللّٰهُ الْكِتَابَ وَالْحُكْمَ وَ النُّبُوَّةَ ثُمَّ يَقُوْلَ لِلنَّاسِ كُوْنُوْا عِبَادًا لِّيْ مِنْ دُوْنِ اللّٰهِ وَلٰكِنْ كُوْنُوْا رَبَّانِيِّنَ بِمَا كُنْتُمْ تُعَلِّمُوْنَ الْكِتَابَ وَ بِمَا كُنْتُمْ تَدْرُسُوْنَ ۟

---

[a]5 : 117, 118.

---

368. Important Words :

ربانين (solely devoted to the Lord) is the plural of ربانى which is a relative noun derived from رب (Lord) just as لحيانى (long-bearded) and شعرانى (having long hair) are derived from لحية (beard) and شعر (hair) respectively. Keeping in view the different meanings of رب (see 1 : 2 and 3 : 65) the word ربانى would mean, one who devotes himself to religious service, or applies himself to acts of devotion ; one who possesses a knowledge of God ; one who is learned in religious matters ; a good or righteous man ; a worshipper of the Lord ; a teacher of others who begins to nourish people with the small matters of knowledge or science before taking the great ones ; a learned man who not only practises what he knows but also instructs others ; one of high rank in knowledge ; a lord or master ; a leader ; a reformer (Lane, Sībwaih & Mubarrad).

The expression ما كان له (it is not possible for him) is, according to Arabic idiom, used in three senses : (1) it does not become him ; as in the hadīth ما كان لابن ابى قحافة ان يصلى بين يدى رسول الله صلم *i.e.* it does not become the son of Abū Quḥāfa (*i.e.* Abū Bakr) to lead the Faithful in Prayers in the presence of the

Prophet of God (Bukhārī) ; (2) it is rationally impossible for him to do so ; or, it does not stand to reason that he should have done so ; (3) he cannot possibly do so, *i.e.*, it is physically impossible for him to do so. It is in the second sense that the expression has been used in this verse. See also 2 : 35.

Commentary :

It is quite inconceivable that a man whom God has raised as a Prophet and to whom He has given a revealed Book for the guidance of men should teach them to take him as God beside Allah. Such a supposition would imply a serious reflection on God Himself Who chose for His Messenger a man who undid the very work which he had been commissioned to do, and who, instead of calling upon men to worship God, set himself up as God and called upon them to adore him. Such a thing can never occur. A Prophet would always exhort men to become the devotees of God only.

The words, *because you teach the Book and because you study it,* show that it is the duty of all those who succeed in acquiring spiritual knowledge to impart it to others and not to let men grope in the darkness of ignorance.

81. Nor *is it possible for* him that he should bid you take the angels and the Prophets for Lords. Would he enjoin you to disbelieve after you have submitted *to God* ?[369]

R. 9   82. And *remember the time* ᵃwhen Allah took a covenant from *the people through* the Prophets, *saying,* 'Whatever I give you of the Book and Wisdom *and* then there comes to you a Messenger, fulfilling what is with you, you shall believe in him and help him.' *And* He said, 'Do you agree, and do you accept the responsibility which I lay upon you in this *matter* ?' They said, 'We agree'; He said, 'Then bear witness and I am with you among the witnesses.'[370]

*a*5 : 13.

369. Commentary :

It is an act of great infidelity to regard angels and Prophets as Lords, and to put them in the place of Almighty God. A true Prophet can never be guilty of such an offence. It is the height of unreason to believe that a person whose very mission is to turn infidels into believers and who does not hesitate to defy the whole world for the achievement of this noble end should first make men the devotees of God and then seek to turn them into his own adorers.

370. Important Words :

ميثاق النبين (covenant from the people through the Prophets) literally means, covenant of the Prophets. According to Arabic usage, the expression اخذ الله ميثاق النبين (lit. Allah took the covenant of the Prophets) may refer either to a covenant which the Prophets of God entered into with Him, or to a covenant which God took from the people through their Prophets. In this verse the words are used in the latter sense, which is supported by another

reading of ميثاق النبين as reported by Ubayy bin Ka'b and 'Abdullah bin Mas'ūd, *i.e.,* ميثاق الذين اوتوا الكتاب meaning, the covenant of those who were given the Book (Muḥīṭ). This rendering is supported by the words that follow *i.e. and then there comes to you a Messenger fulfilling what is with you,* because it was to the people and not to their Prophets that the Messenger of God came. The meaning given above gains further support from the fact that as other Prophets were dead at the time of the Holy Prophet, they could naturally render him no help and there was thus no sense in taking any covenant from them to this effect.

Commentary :

This verse is considered to apply to other Prophets in general and to the Holy Prophet in particular. Both applications are correct. The verse lays down a general rule. The advent of every Prophet takes place in fulfilment of certain prophecies made by a previous Prophet in which he enjoins his followers to

83. Now *whoso turns away after this, then, surely, those are the transgressors.[371]

قَمَنْ تَوَلّٰى بَعْدَ ذٰلِكَ فَأُولٰٓئِكَ هُمُ الْفٰسِقُوْنَ ۞

84. Do they seek a religion other than Allah's, while to Him submits whosoever is in the heavens and the earth, willingly or unwillingly, and to Him shall they be returned?[372]

اَفَغَيْرَ دِيْنِ اللّٰهِ يَبْغُوْنَ وَلَهٗٓ اَسْلَمَ مَنْ فِي السَّمٰوٰتِ وَالْاَرْضِ طَوْعًا وَّكَرْهًا وَّاِلَيْهِ يُرْجَعُوْنَ ۞

*5 : 48; 24 : 56.

accept the next Prophet when he makes his appearance. If the Prophet comes in fulfilment of the prophecies contained in the scriptures of one people only, as was the case with Jesus and other Israelite Prophets, then only that people are bound to accept and help him; but if the scriptures of all religions predict the coming of a Prophet, as in the case of the Holy Prophet, then all nations are bound to accept him.

The Holy Prophet appeared in fulfilment of the prophecies not only of the Israelite Prophets (Isa. 21 : 13—15. Deut. 18 : 18; 33 : 2. John 14 : 25, 26; 16 : 7—13) but also of the Aryan Seers and Buddhist and Zoroastrian Sages. We have the following prophecy in *Dasātīr*, the sacred scripture of the Parsis: "When the people of Iran will begin to do such (*i.e.* evil) deeds, there shall appear from among the Arabs a man whose followers shall abolish the crown, the throne, the kingdom, and the religion of Iran. The headstrong shall become humble and a house without idols shall take the place of idol-houses and fire-temples, and to it shall they turn their faces in worship" (Safrang Dasātīr, p. 188, Sirājī Press, Delhi). The words are too clear to need comment. A similar prophecy is found in Jāmāspi, a work of Jāmāsp, the first successor of Zoroaster (Jāmāspi, published by Nizām al-Mashā'ikh, Delhi, 1330 A.H.).

The word مصدّقا (fulfilling; for the meaning

of which see 2 : 42) has been used here to denote the criterion by which a true claimant to prophethood is distinguished from a false one. But if the word is taken in the sense of "verifying or confirming or declaring to be true" as is sometimes done, this verification or confirmation can be no test of knowing a true Prophet from an impostor, for even an impostor can declare the previous scriptures to be true. The word has, therefore, been rightly translated here as "fulfilling" for it is only by "fulfilling" in his person the prophecies contained in the previous scriptures that a claimant can prove his truth, it being beyond the power of an impostor to fulfil the previous prophecies in his person.

371. Commentary:

The word فاسقون (transgressors) used in this verse may also be rendered as disobedient or breakers of promise. Both these meanings are applicable here.

372. Commentary:

As in the physical world man must submit to the laws of nature, whether he wills it or not, and he knows by experience that such submission is useful for him, it is only reasonable that in spiritual matters also, wherein he has been granted a certain amount of freedom, he should obey the laws and commands of Allah and thus win His pleasure to his own eventual benefit.

85. Say, *a*'We believe in Allah and in that which has been revealed to us, and that which was revealed to Abraham and Ishmael and Isaac and Jacob and the Tribes, and that which was given to Moses and Jesus and other Prophets from their Lord. We make no distinction between any of them and to Him we submit.'373

قُلْ اٰمَنَّا بِاللّٰهِ وَمَاۤ اُنْزِلَ عَلَيْنَا وَمَاۤ اُنْزِلَ عَلٰۤى اِبْرٰهِيْمَ وَاِسْمٰعِيْلَ وَاِسْحٰقَ وَيَعْقُوْبَ وَالْاَسْبَاطِ وَمَاۤ اُوْتِىَ مُوْسٰى وَعِيْسٰى وَالنَّبِيُّوْنَ مِنْ رَّبِّهِمْ ۖ لَا نُفَرِّقُ بَيْنَ اَحَدٍ مِّنْهُمْ ۖ وَنَحْنُ لَهٗ مُسْلِمُوْنَ ۝

86. And *b*whoso seeks a religion other than Islam, it shall not be accepted from him, and in the life to come he shall be among the losers.374

وَمَنْ يَّبْتَغِ غَيْرَ الْاِسْلَامِ دِيْنًا فَلَنْ يُّقْبَلَ مِنْهُ ۖ وَهُوَ فِى الْاٰخِرَةِ مِنَ الْخٰسِرِيْنَ ۝

---

*a*2 : 137 ; 2 : 286.   *b*3 : 20 ; 5 : 4.

373. Commentary :

The Jews refused to believe in non-Israelite Prophets as the words, *obey none but him who follows your religion* (3 : 74) show. In the present verse the charge has been pressed home to Jews that whereas they rejected all but the Israelite Prophets, Islam requires its followers to believe in all the Prophets of God, irrespective of the country or the race or the community to which they belonged or of the time in which they lived. Again, Islam requires them not only to believe in the Prophets that have passed away but also in any that may appear in future. A great contrast indeed, between the catholicity of Islam and the narrow-mindedness of Judaism !

The words, *We make no distinction between any of them*, should not be understood to mean that Islam considers all Prophets to be of equal spiritual rank. This view is contrary to 2 : 254 in which some Prophets have been declared

to possess a higher spiritual rank than others. So the words refer only to discrimination as regards believing in them and not as regards their rank.

374. Commentary :

The Jews and Christians used to say that they were not bound to accept Islam because it was the Quran that verified the Torah and the Gospel and not the Torah and the Gospel that verified the Quran. Apart from the fact that the Quran does not "verify" the previous scriptures, in the sense in which they understood it, their sense of false security has been shattered in this verse and it has been declared unequivocally that Islam is now the only religion acceptable to God. Even if the word اسلام (Islam) is here taken to signify not "the religion of Islam" but "submission and resignation to the will of God," the present verse makes it binding on the People of the Book to accept Islam, as it alone now represents the will of the Supreme Being.

87. How shall Allah guide a people who have disbelieved after believing and who had borne witness that the Messenger was true and to whom clear proofs had come? And Allah guides not the wrong-doing people.[375]

كَيْفَ يَهْدِى اللهُ قَوْمًا كَفَرُوْا بَعْدَ اِيْمَانِهِمْ وَ شَهِدُوْۤا اَنَّ الرَّسُوْلَ حَقٌّ وَّجَآءَهُمُ الْبَيِّنٰتُ ؕ وَاللهُ لَا يَهْدِى الْقَوْمَ الظّٰلِمِيْنَ ۝

88. Of such the reward is that on them shall be the ᵃcurse of Allah and of angels and of men, all together.[375A]

اُولٰٓئِكَ جَزَآؤُهُمْ اَنَّ عَلَيْهِمْ لَعْنَةَ اللهِ وَالْمَلٰٓئِكَةِ وَالنَّاسِ اَجْمَعِيْنَ ۙ۝

89. ᵇThey shall abide thereunder. Their punishment shall not be lightened nor shall they be reprieved;[375B]

خٰلِدِيْنَ فِيْهَا ۚ لَا يُخَفَّفُ عَنْهُمُ الْعَذَابُ وَ لَا هُمْ يُنْظَرُوْنَ ۙ۝

90. ᶜExcept those who repent thereafter and amend. And surely Allah is Most Forgiving, Merciful.[376]

اِلَّا الَّذِيْنَ تَابُوْا مِنْۢ بَعْدِ ذٰلِكَ وَ اَصْلَحُوْا ۛ فَاِنَّ اللهَ غَفُوْرٌ رَّحِيْمٌ ۝

ᵃ2:162; 4:53; 5:79.   ᵇ2:163.   ᶜ2:161; 4:147; 5:40; 24:6.

375. Commentary:

Certainly a people who at first believe in the truth of a Prophet and proclaim their belief openly and become witnesses of heavenly Signs but afterwards reject that Prophet through fear of men or other worldly considerations lose all title to be again guided to the right path. The verse lays down a general principle that God lets a person go astray only when the latter knowingly allows disbelief and wickedness to get hold of him and does not try to improve his ways.

375A. Commentary:

For an explanation of the expression, *the curse of Allah and of angels and of men*, see under 2:162.

375B. Commentary:

See 2:163.

376. Commentary:

The curse and punishment spoken of in the preceding verses are conditional and will last as long as the condition that has brought them about lasts.

The words, *and amend*, show that mere repentance and sorrow at what is past is not sufficient to secure divine forgiveness. Sinners must not only express genuine regret for past faults but also promise to abandon evil ways in future. Nay, they should do more. They should try to reform others as well, for the word اصلحوا rendered as "amend" not only signifies amending one's own ways but also reforming others (see 2:161). If a person is really sincere in his repentance and realizes the true value of virtue, he cannot stop at being good himself but would also try to make others good, if only to protect his own environment.

91. ^aSurely, those who disbelieve after they have believed and then increase in disbelief, their repentance shall not be accepted, and these are they who have gone astray.[377]

92. *As for* ^bthose who have disbelieved, and die while they are disbelievers, there shall not be accepted from any one of them *even* an earth-full of gold though he offer it in ransom. It is these for whom shall be a grievous punishment, and they shall have no helpers.[378]

R. 10   93. ^cNever shall you attain to righteousness unless you spend out of that which you love; and whatever you spend, Allah surely knows it well.[379]

---

^a4 : 138 ; 63 : 4.   ^b2 : 162 ; 4 : 19 ; 47 : 35.   ^c9 : 34, 111 ; 63 : 11.

---

377. Commentary:

The verse does not mean that the repentance of apostates shall in no case be accepted because this inference runs counter to 3 : 90 according to which repentance is acceptable at every stage. So the reference in the words, *their repentance shall not be accepted,* is to those persons only who make a profession of repentance but are not sincere in it, and, instead of reinforcing their profession by bringing about a real and practical change in their lives, actually increase in disbelief. The words, *these are they who have gone astray,* placed at the end of the verse corroborate this inference, for they show that in spite of a lip-profession of repentance they still continue to follow a course of error. Such repentance cannot be genuine and hence cannot be accepted.

378. Commentary:

This verse further explains the true significance of repentance. So long as death does not overtake one and the door of performing good works is open, the door of repentance is also open. But in no case will mere lip-repentance of disbelievers or their alms be accepted. If there is no faith in the heart, mere giving of alms or mere apparently good works cannot win the pleasure of God, even if one spends large quantities of gold.

379. Important Words:

البر (righteousness) means, goodness of a high order (Mufradāt). The Holy Prophet has explained the word بر as *i.e.* حسن الخلق the excellence of moral qualities (Muslim & Musnad). See also 2 : 45, 178. As true belief is the basis of all goodness, so the word البر may also be taken to mean true belief.

Commentary:

Since the word البر means, goodness or righteousness of a high order or excellence of morals, the verse purports to say that though God is cognizant of, and suitably rewards, each and every thing that one spends in the cause of Allah, yet the goodness of a high order,

94. All food was lawful to the children of Israel, except what Israel forbade himself before the Torah was sent down. Say, 'Bring, then, the Torah and read it, if you are truthful.'[380]

كُلُّ الطَّعَامِ كَانَ حِلًّا لِّبَنِيْ اِسْرَآءِيْلَ اِلَّا مَا حَرَّمَ اِسْرَآءِيْلُ عَلٰى نَفْسِهٖ مِنْ قَبْلِ اَنْ تُنَزَّلَ التَّوْرٰىةُ ۚ قُلْ فَاْتُوْا بِالتَّوْرٰىةِ فَاتْلُوْهَاۤ اِنْ كُنْتُمْ صٰدِقِيْنَ ۝

most acceptable in His sight, can be achieved only by spending out of things, be they material or otherwise, which one loves most, for the obvious reason that such spending involves the greatest sacrifice.

In the preceding verse it is said, *there shall not be accepted from any one of them even an earthfull of gold, though he offer it in ransom.* From this some people might conclude that spending in the cause of God was of no use. To remove this possible misunderstanding it is pointed out here that spending in the cause of God is a highly meritorious act and spending what is best naturally brings the highest good. The preceding verse refers only to such disbelievers as die in their disbelief.

The verse may be interpreted in three ways : (1) if البر is taken to mean true faith, the verse would mean that as disbelievers think more of their worldly interests than of God, they are unable to recognize the truth of Islam. Thus the verse signifies that in order to attain true faith, which is the essence of all righteousness and the highest form of good, one must be prepared to sacrifice everything that one holds dear. (2) If البر is taken in the sense of goodness of a high order, the verse would mean that though whatever is spent in the cause of God is an act of righteousness, yet the highest stage of righteousness can be attained only by spending in the way of God that which one loves best. (3) If, however, the word البر is taken to mean high morals, the verse would signify that high morals cannot be attained without inculcating a true spirit of sacrifice.

It is on record in the Ḥadīth that when this verse was revealed, Abū Ṭalḥa, a Companion of the Holy Prophet, stood up and addressing him said, " O Messenger of God, my garden known as Bi'r Rauḥā (this garden was situated opposite to the Mosque at Medina) is to me the dearest of my property and I hereby give it in charity " (Bukhārī, ch. on *Tafsīr*). This illustrates how the early converts to Islam strove to practise the highest good, as the Quran enjoined upon them.

380. Important Words :

كل (all) is a very common Arabic word used to express two senses : (1) all members of a group ; (2) all parts of an individual thing. The word may generally be rendered as, all ; whole ; each ; every one, etc. It is also sometimes used in the sense of not " all " but " the majority of ", and rarely even in the sense of " some " or " part of " (Aqrab & Tāj).

Commentary :

The preceding verses emphasize the importance of complete submission to the will of God. The highest good cannot be attained without the sacrifice of most beloved things, including personal and national sentiments. The present verse cites an apt illustration. Whereas God had allowed " all food " to the Jews, the Israelites forbade themselves parts thereof on the ground that Jacob, for personal and medical considerations, abstained from partaking of them. But as the word Israel, primarily the name of Jacob, is also used about his children and descendants and has been so used in the Bible, it may also be taken in this

95. Now whoso forges a lie against Allah after this, then it is these that are the wrongdoers.[381]

فَمَنِ افْتَرٰى عَلَى اللّٰهِ الْكَذِبَ مِنْ بَعْدِ ذٰلِكَ فَأُولٰٓئِكَ هُمُ الظّٰلِمُوْنَ ۹۵

96. Say, 'Allah has spoken the truth: follow, therefore, the religion of Abraham, *who was* ever inclined *to God*; and he was not of those who associate gods with God.'[382]

قُلْ صَدَقَ اللّٰهُ فَاتَّبِعُوْا مِلَّةَ اِبْرٰهِيْمَ حَنِيْفًا وَمَا كَانَ مِنَ الْمُشْرِكِيْنَ ۹۶

---

*a*See 3 : 68.

---

sense in the second clause of the present verse.

By saying, *All food was lawful to the children of Israel*, the Quran also refutes an objection of the People of the Book, which served as an obstacle in the way of their accepting Islam. There were certain kinds of food which the Jews abstained from eating but which were allowed by Islam. One such thing was the sciatic nerve, to which reference is made in Gen. 32 : 32. Jacob suffered from sciatica, and, therefore, for medical reasons he forbade himself the use of the sciatic nerve as food. This was a personal matter but the children of Israel followed his example blindly and made it a rule of conduct to abstain from the eating of the sinew. It was not forbidden by Law, the abstention being purely voluntary.

Moreover, the incident which led to the abandonment of the sciatic nerve as food by Israel and later by the Israelites took place long before the Torah was revealed. The Torah itself does not forbid it but merely mentions it as a practice of the Jews who had, therefore, no right to object to its use by the Muslims. The objection, if valid, also held good against Abraham and many other Prophets. Besides, there are some foods which were used by Abraham and his descendants but were later forbidden by the Torah. The camel is an instance of this kind. Hence, the verse purports to say that if certain foods used by the patriarchs are allowed to other peoples, the Jews have no right to object.

It may be pointed out here that there is a difference of meaning between كل طعام (*kullu-ṭaʿāmin*) and الطعام كل (*kull al-ṭaʿāmi*) as used in the present verse. The former means, every kind of food, while the latter means, all food *i.e.* the whole food. It appears that the Jews objected that the Muslims ate the whole meat, not excepting even the nerve.

381. Commentary:

The word ذٰلك (this) refers to the statement made in the preceding verse. To say that such and such parts of food were disallowed by God whereas He had not forbidden them, or even without directly attributing any commandant to God persistently to abstain from partaking of a lawful food without just reason virtually amounted to forging a lie against God which only wrongdoers could resort to.

382. Commentary:

By saying that Abraham was ever obedient to God, the verse hints that he did not prohibit the eating of any particular meat of his own accord, as the Israelites have done. So by differing from the Israelites in this matter, Islam does not go against the way and the practice of the Prophets of God, particularly that of Abraham.

By saying that Abraham did not associate gods with God, the Jews are reminded that it

97. Surely, ^athe first House founded for mankind is that at Becca, abounding in blessings and a guidance for all peoples.³⁸³

98. In it are manifest signs ; ^bit is the place of Abraham ; and ^cwhoso enters it, enters peace. And ^dpilgrimage to the House is a duty which men—those who can find a way thither—owe to Allah. And whoever disbelieves, *let him remember* that Allah is surely independent of all creatures.³⁸⁴

اِنَّ اَوَّلَ بَیۡتٍ وُّضِعَ لِلنَّاسِ لَلَّذِیۡ بِبَکَّةَ مُبٰرَکًا وَّهُدًی لِّلۡعٰلَمِیۡنَ ۞

فِیۡهِ اٰیٰتٌۢ بَیِّنٰتٌ مَّقَامُ اِبۡرٰهِیۡمَ ۚ وَمَنۡ دَخَلَهٗ کَانَ اٰمِنًا ؕ وَلِلّٰهِ عَلَی النَّاسِ حِجُّ الۡبَیۡتِ مَنِ اسۡتَطَاعَ اِلَیۡهِ سَبِیۡلًا ؕ وَمَنۡ کَفَرَ فَاِنَّ اللّٰهَ غَنِیٌّ عَنِ الۡعٰلَمِیۡنَ ۞

---

^a5 : 98 ; 27 : 92 ; 28 : 58 ; 29 : 68 ; 106 : 4, 5.   ^b2 : 126.   ^c14 : 36 ; 28 : 58 ; 29 : 68.   ^d22 : 28.

---

is they themselves who set up gods with God and go against the religion of Abraham, to whom the will of his Master was all in all.

383. Important Words :

بَکَّة (Becca) is the name given to the valley of Mecca. The word is probably derived from بَكَّ . They say بَكَّهُ *i.e.* he pushed him into a narrow and crowded place. بَكَّ عُنُقَهُ means, he dealt blows on his neck and broke it. بَاكَ الْقَوْمُ عَلَی الشَّیٔ means, the people crowded round the thing. The valley of مَكَّة (Mecca) is called بَکَّة (Becca) probably on account of the crowding of the people there, or because it used to break the necks of the tyrants (Aqrab). The word بَکَّة (Becca) is also considered by some to be the same as Mecca, its میم having been changed into ب . These two letters are interchangeable as in لَازِم and لَازِب .

Commentary :

See note on 2 : 128 with regard to the antiquity of the Ka'ba.

In this verse, the Quran draws the attention of the People of the Book to the antiquity of the Ka'ba in order to point out that the real and original centre of God's religion is the Ka'ba, those adopted by Jews and Christians being of later origin. Just as certain foods which Jews abstained from were not originally forbidden but came subsequently to be held unlawful, similarly their *Qibla* was not the original *Qibla* but was adopted as such at a subsequent time.

384. Commentary :

After alluding to the historical evidence in favour of the Ka'ba, the Quran proceeds to state that reason also demands that the Ka'ba should be adopted as the *Qibla*. The verse gives three reasons to show that the Ka'ba is entitled to be adopted as the *Qibla* or the centre of God's religion.

The first reason, as hinted in the words, *the place of Abraham*, is that Abraham came and prayed here. Jews and Christians, to both of whom Abraham is worthy of great reverence, have to admit that Abraham visited the place. Therefore it cannot be denied that it is a blessed place.

The second reason, referred to in the words *whoso enters it enters peace*, is that the Ka'ba not only promises but also affords peace and security to those who enter it. This promise has been literally fulfilled. Temporally, God has ever protected it against wars and invasions both in ancient and modern times. The way in which Abraha, ruler of Yemen, and his hosts were destroyed when they tried to invade the Ka'ba and the way in which this territory, which then formed a part of the dominion of Turkey, was kept outside the conflict during the last World War (1914–18) afford remarkable instances of how miraculously God protects the Ka'ba. Unlike the sacred places of other nations, it has never fallen into the hands of a people who would not revere it. Even in the Days of Ignorance when the different tribes of pagan Arabia were constantly at war with one another, the territory of the Ka'ba was held to be sacred and no fighting was allowed therein. Spiritually, also, it is a place of security for those who enter it in the spiritual sense, *i.e.* embrace the religion of Islam. They become recipients of divine favours and enjoy security from the punishment of God.

The third reason which entitles the Ka'ba to be adopted as the *Qibla* is hinted at in the words, *pilgrimage to the House is a duty which men . . . . . . owe to God.* The verse contains an implied promise on the part of God that the Ka'ba shall ever continue to be the centre to which men of different countries and diverse nations will resort for Pilgrimage. The fulfilment of this promise is proof of the fact that the Ka'ba has indeed been designed by God to be the *Qibla* of all nations.

Every Muslim who can find a way to Mecca is bound to perform Pilgrimage to the Ka'ba once in his lifetime. If he performs it more than once, it is regarded as a supererogatory act of devotion.

The words, *who can find a way thither,* embody three conditions: (1) one should have the necessary conveyance for performing the journey; (2) one should have the necessary money to bear the expenses; and (3) there should be peace and security on the way (Dāwūd). If a person is sick, he is supposed to have no "way" and Pilgrimage does not become obligatory on him.

The words, *and whoever disbelieves (let him remember) that Allah is surely independent of all creatures,* signify that whoever refuses to accept the Ka'ba as the *Qibla,* in spite of the arguments given in its favour, should remember that these commandments have been given for the good of man himself; so if he does not act upon them, he only harms himself and does no harm to God, Who is "independent of all creatures."

The object of Pilgrimage is to accustom men to leave their home and country and suffer separation from relatives and friends for the sake of God. The Pilgrimage to Mecca is also a symbol of the respect shown to places where the will of God was specially manifested and a reminder of the incidents connected with that manifestation. It reminds believers of the long and hazardous journey of Abraham and Ishmael to the desert valley of Mecca and of Ishmael's being left in that desert by Abraham; it tells them in speechless eloquence how those who make sacrifices in the way of God are protected and honoured by Him; and it fosters their faith in the power and might of God. Again, the pilgrim, on finding himself near the place which has, from the beginning of the world, been dedicated to the worship of God, is sure to experience a peculiar spiritual association with those who have, through centuries, been bound together by the love and remembrance of God.

Beside this, the Pilgrimage to Mecca has great social and political significance; for Muslims from all parts of the world who meet here once a year can exchange views and establish and renew relations of love and brotherhood. They have opportunities of acquainting themselves with the problems that confront Muslims in different countries, of copying one another's good points, profiting by one another's experience and of co-operating with one another. It is, however, a matter of great regret that

99. Say, a'O People of the Book! why deny ye the Signs of Allah, while Allah is Watchful of what you do? '385

قُلْ يٰٓاَهْلَ الْكِتٰبِ لِمَ تَكْفُرُوْنَ بِاٰيٰتِ اللّٰهِ ۖ وَاللّٰهُ شَهِيْدٌ عَلٰى مَا تَعْمَلُوْنَ ۟

100. Say, 'O People of the Book! bwhy hinder ye the believers from the path of Allah, seeking to make it crooked, while you are witnesses thereof? And Allah is not unmindful of what you do. '386

قُلْ يٰٓاَهْلَ الْكِتٰبِ لِمَ تَصُدُّوْنَ عَنْ سَبِيْلِ اللّٰهِ مَنْ اٰمَنَ تَبْغُوْنَهَا عِوَجًا وَّاَنْتُمْ شُهَدَآءُ ۗ وَمَا اللّٰهُ بِغَافِلٍ عَمَّا تَعْمَلُوْنَ ۟

101. cO ye who believe! if you obey any party of those who have been given the Book, they will turn you again into disbelievers after you have believed.387

يٰٓاَيُّهَا الَّذِيْنَ اٰمَنُوْۤا اِنْ تُطِيْعُوْا فَرِيْقًا مِّنَ الَّذِيْنَ اُوْتُوا الْكِتٰبَ يَرُدُّوْكُمْ بَعْدَ اِيْمَانِكُمْ كٰفِرِيْنَ ۟

---

a3 : 71.   b7 : 46, 87 ; 8 : 48 ; 9 : 34 ; 14 : 4 ; 22 : 26.   c2 : 110 ; 3 : 150.

---

at present little advantage is being taken of this aspect of the Pilgrimage.

385. Important Words:

شهيد (Watchful), for which see also 2 : 24, is here used for the first time in connection with God. The word is derived from شهد which means, he gave information or decisive information of what he had witnessed or seen ; he declared what he knew ; he gave testimony or evidence ; he saw or watched or witnessed or beheld a thing ; he was present at a place. شهيد means, one who gives information of, or declares, what he knows or has seen or witnessed ; one who gives decisive information ; one who sees or beholds a thing ; witness or an eye-witness ; one possessing much knowledge ; a martyr slain in the cause of God. When used about God the word signifies, the Faithful ; the Trusty in testimony ; He from Whose knowledge nothing is hidden (Lane). Other similar words used by the Quran about God are (1) وكيل meaning Guardian (e.g. 3 : 174) ; and (2) رقيب meaning Watcher (e.g. 4 : 2) ; and (3) حفيظ also meaning

Guardian or Keeper (e.g. 11 : 58 and 4 : 81). See also 2 : 24 ; 4 : 2 ; 3 : 174 and 4 : 81.

Commentary :

The words لم تكفرون rendered as, why deny ye, may also be rendered as, why are you ungrateful respecting . . . .

The institution of Pilgrimage and other forms of worship prescribed by Islam are all for the good of man, but in his ignorance he refuses to recognize, or be thankful for, this good.

386. Commentary :

The words تبغونها عوجا (seeking to make it crooked) may also be translated as, you seek in it crookedness, i.e., you desire that there should appear crookedness in Islam ; or you desire to turn the truths of this religion from their real import and to pervert its tenets.

387. Commentary :

The words, any party of those who have been given the Book, refer to that party of the People of the Book who were most hostile to Islam, there being a section of them who

102. How would you disbelieve, while to you are rehearsed the Signs of Allah, and His Messenger is present among you ? *a*And he who holds fast to Allah is indeed guided to the right path.[388]

وَكَيْفَ تَكْفُرُونَ وَأَنْتُمْ تُتْلٰى عَلَيْكُمْ اٰيٰتُ اللّٰهِ وَ فِيْكُمْ رَسُوْلُهٗ ؕ وَمَنْ يَّعْتَصِمْ بِاللّٰهِ فَقَدْ هُدِيَ اِلٰى صِرَاطٍ مُّسْتَقِيْمٍ ۝

R. 11 103. O ye who believe! fear Allah as He should be feared ; and *b*let not death overtake you except when you are in a state of submission.[389]

يٰۤاَيُّهَا الَّذِيْنَ اٰمَنُوا اتَّقُوا اللّٰهَ حَقَّ تُقٰتِهٖ وَلَا تَمُوْتُنَّ اِلَّا وَاَنْتُمْ مُّسْلِمُوْنَ ۝

*a*4 : 147, 176. *b*2 : 133.

---

had turned believers and others who were indifferent. Muslims have already been warned of this danger in 2 : 110.

388. Commentary :

The words, *who holds fast to Allah*, have two meanings : (1) whoever preserves himself from sin by acting on God's commandments ; (2) whoever connects himself with Allah and cleaves firmly to Him, thereby securing for himself an everlasting source of rise and progress.

389. Commentary :

As the spiritual degradation of the Jews was due to lack of تقوی or God-fearingness, Muslims are warned to be ever-watchful in this respect. The words rendered as, *Fear Allah as He should be feared*, embody a strong appeal in favour of تقوی (righteousness) and signify that on the one hand we should have a firm conviction that if we are remiss God will visit our sins with His punishment; and on the other we should also have a firm faith in His mercy and forgiveness. There is a tradition related by 'Abdullah bin 'Abbās which explains

the above words as meaning: "God should be obeyed, and should not be disobeyed. We should be grateful to Him, and should not show ingratitude to Him. We should remember Him and not forget Him " (Kathīr). The words also mean that one should not fear any reproach with respect to God, and should observe equity for God's sake even if by doing so one may have to injure one's own self or one's parents or children or other near relatives.

The words, *let not death overtake you except when you are in a state of submission*, mean that we should be ever resigned to the will of God, so that when death overtakes us, it should find us obedient and resigned to His will. As the hour of death is not known, one can be sure of dying in a state of resignation to God only if one is continually in that condition, hence the expression means that one should always remain obedient to God. It may also mean that our love of obedience to God should be such that He, out of regard for our feelings, may not let death come upon us at a time when we are not perfectly resigned to Him.

104. And ^ahold fast, all together, by the rope of Allah and be not divided; and ^bremember the favour of Allah which He bestowed upon you when you were enemies and ^cHe united your hearts in love so that by His grace you became *as* brothers; and you were on the brink of a pit of fire and He saved you from it. Thus does Allah explain to you His commandments that you may be guided.³⁹⁰

وَاعْتَصِمُوۡا بِحَبۡلِ اللّٰهِ جَمِيۡعًا وَّلَا تَفَرَّقُوۡا ۪ وَاذۡكُرُوۡا نِعۡمَتَ اللّٰهِ عَلَيۡكُمۡ اِذۡ كُنۡتُمۡ اَعۡدَآءً فَاَلَّفَ بَيۡنَ قُلُوۡبِكُمۡ فَاَصۡبَحۡتُمۡ بِنِعۡمَتِهٖۤ اِخۡوَانًا ۚ وَكُنۡتُمۡ عَلٰى شَفَا حُفۡرَةٍ مِّنَ النَّارِ فَاَنۡقَذَكُمۡ مِّنۡهَا ؕ كَذٰلِكَ يُبَيِّنُ اللّٰهُ لَكُمۡ اٰيٰتِهٖ لَعَلَّكُمۡ تَهۡتَدُوۡنَ ۟

---

^a3 : 106 ; 6 : 160 ; 8 : 47.   ^b2 : 232.   ^c8 : 64.

---

390. Important Words:

حَبْل (rope). They say حَبَلَهُ *i.e.* he bound or tied him with a rope or cord. حَبَلَ الصَّيْدَ means, he caught the game with a snare or net. حَبِلَتِ الْمَرْاَةُ means, the woman became pregnant. حَبْل means, a rope or cord or anything with which a thing is tied or made fast; a bond or cause of union or link of connection, such as a bond of love or friendship; mutual connection by such a bond; a covenant or compact; an obligation by which one becomes responsible for the safety of a person or thing; a promise or assurance of security or safety; an artery, vein or nerve (Lane). It also means alliance and protection (Aqrab).

Commentary:

Another cause of the spiritual degradation of the Israelites was that they did not remain united but split up into sections, finding fault with one another. The verse warns Muslims against that danger. The Holy Prophet is reported to have said : "The Book of God is the rope of Allah which has been extended from the heavens to the earth" (Jarīr, iv. 30). Broadly speaking, there are three things which may be taken to have been here meant by the rope of God, by holding fast to which Muslims may remain united and be safe

against disunion and disruption : (1) the Quran ; (2) the Messenger of God ; (3) the Successors to the Messenger of God.

The similitude may have reference to sea-life. Ropes are thrown to save the life of a drowning man. When a man falls into the sea or when a boat is wrecked by a storm, people in the boat or those standing on the shore throw out ropes to those who are struggling for their lives in the sea. The similitude is thus incidentally a refutation of the objection that the Quran restricts its similitudes to such objects only as were known to the desert-dwellers of Arabia.

It may be noted here that whenever the Quran speaks of the open or secret hostility of the enemies of Islam, it exhorts Muslims to be strong of faith; for it is at such times that one is likely to waver and show weakness in resolution. Thus after referring to the hostility of the People of the Book (3 : 100, 101) the Quran exhorts Muslims : (1) to fear God as He should be feared (3 : 103) ; (2) to be constant in obedience to God (3 : 103) ; and (3) to hold fast to the rope of God and preserve themselves from disunion (3 : 104).

The words, *remember the favour of Allah*, signify that as one can appreciate a boon of

105. And let there be among you a body of men *who should invite to goodness, and enjoin equity and forbid evil. And it is they who shall prosper.[391]

وَلْتَكُنْ مِنْكُمْ اُمَّةٌ يَّدْعُوْنَ اِلَى الْخَيْرِ وَيَأْمُرُوْنَ بِالْمَعْرُوْفِ وَيَنْهَوْنَ عَنِ الْمُنْكَرِ وَاُولٰٓئِكَ هُمُ الْمُفْلِحُوْنَ ۞

*3 : 111, 115; 7 : 158; 9 : 71; 31 : 18.

God properly only when one experiences the disadvantages that result from its absence, so the Quran reminds Muslims of the discord and enmity that existed between them before they became united in Islam.

The words, *He united your hearts in love*, show that according to Islam it is no great virtue to bear no malice or hatred to others. Nor does Islam inculcate a life of seclusion and detachment. What it requires is positive love for, and active sympathy with, fellow beings. One who is devoid of this is really devoid of true faith.

391. Commentary :

The word خیر (goodness) here signifies Islam, because goodness in general is included in the word معروف (equity) used immediately after it. In fact, the true Faith (Islam) is the only goodness in the true sense of the word. The verse purports to say that as by making you enter the fold of Islam God has delivered you from a pit of fire, you should also try to deliver others from the fire of disbelief.

The words, *And let there be among you a body of men who should invite to goodness*, do not mean that the duty of preaching is confined to a few only. What is meant is that, whereas all should try to preach and propagate the truth of Islam, there should be a party of men among Muslims who should be wholly and solely devoted to this work.

As for the method of preaching, the Quran says elsewhere, *Call unto the way of thy Lord with wisdom and goodly exhortation and argue with them (the disbelievers) in a way that is best* (16 : 126). And the Holy Prophet is reported to have said, "If any one of you sees anything evil, let him remove it with his hand. If he cannot do it with his hand, then let him forbid it with his tongue. If he cannot do even that, then let him at least detest it in his mind, and that is the weakest kind of faith " (Muslim).

The verse also suggests a way by following which Muslims can maintain their unity. So long as a Muslim people have their attention concentrated on the preaching of Islam and doing good, they will live in peace among themselves, for disunion is mostly born of idleness and a false sense of security.

Each and every individual Muslim is not enjoined here to devote himself wholly to the preaching of Islam ; for if it were so, Muslims could not earn their livelihood nor take part in other healthy pursuits of life. So, though all must contribute their quota, only a section of the community is required to devote itself exclusively to the work of preaching.

106. And be not like those *who became divided and who disagreed *among themselves* after clear proofs had come to them. And it is they for whom there shall be a great punishment.³⁹²

وَلَا تَكُوْنُوْا كَالَّذِيْنَ تَفَرَّقُوْا وَاخْتَلَفُوْا مِنْۢ بَعْدِ مَا جَآءَهُمُ الْبَيِّنَٰتُ ۚ وَاُولٰٓئِكَ لَهُمْ عَذَابٌ عَظِيْمٌ ۞

107. On the day *when some faces shall be white, and some faces shall be black. As for those whose faces will be black, *it will be said to them* : ' Did you disbelieve after believing ? Taste, then, the punishment because of your disbelief. '³⁹³

يَّوْمَ تَبْيَضُّ وُجُوْهٌ وَّتَسْوَدُّ وُجُوْهٌ ۚ فَاَمَّا الَّذِيْنَ اسْوَدَّتْ وُجُوْهُهُمْ ۚ اَكَفَرْتُمْ بَعْدَ اِيْمَانِكُمْ فَذُوْقُوا الْعَذَابَ بِمَا كُنْتُمْ تَكْفُرُوْنَ ۞

---

*a*3 : 104 ; 6 : 160 ; 8 : 47.   *b*10 : 27, 28 ; 39 : 61 ; 80 : 39—43.

---

392. Commentary :

The Quran does not merely give general philosophic teachings but actually refers to historical facts to bring home to the Faithful the gravity of the dangers that proved the ruin of peoples gone by. The verse, therefore, aptly refers to the dissensions of the People of the Book, and Muslims are enjoined to avoid them. The Holy Prophet says: "Whoso separates himself from the body of the Muslims even by the space of a span, throws off from his neck the rope of Muslim brotherhood (Dāwūd). Again, "whoso severs his connection (with the community of the Muslims) will be cast into the Fire " (Tirmidhī, ch. on *Fitan*).

393. Important Words :

تبيض (shall be white) is derived from باض. They say باض فلانا *i.e.* he exceeded him in whiteness. ابيض means, he or it turned white. بياض signifies whiteness, and ابيض means white (Aqrab). The expression ابيض وجهه means, his face became white, meaning, his face became expressive of joy *i.e.* he became joyful (Lane).

تسود (will turn black) is derived from ساد.

They say ساد فلانا *i.e.* he exceeded him in blackness. اسود means, he or it turned black. سواد means, blackness, and اسود means, black (Aqrab). اسود وجهه means, his face became black, meaning, his face became expressive of grief or sorrow (Lane). Whiteness is sometimes used to denote a good and happy condition ; while blackness is a token of a bad condition and failure (Aqrab under بياض)

Commentary :

The Quran itself explains "whiteness" and "blackness" as emblematic of "happiness" and "sorrow" respectively (see 3 : 108 and 16 : 59 and also compare 75 : 23 and 80 : 39, 40). Similarly, when a person does a deed for which he is praised, the Arabs say of him ابيض وجه فلان *i.e.* the face of such a one has become white or قد بيض الله وجه فلان *i.e.* God has made the face of such a one white. On the contrary, if a person does a deed for which he is reproached, it is said of him اسود وجهه *i.e.* his face has become black, or سود الله وجهه *i.e.* Allah has blackened his face. Thus the words يوم تبيض وجوه و تسود وجوه (lit. when some faces shall turn white and some faces shall

435

108. And ^aas for those whose faces will be white, they will be in the mercy of Allah ; therein will they abide.

وَاَمَّا الَّذِيْنَ ابْيَضَّتْ وُجُوْهُهُمْ فَفِيْ رَحْمَةِ اللّٰهِ هُمْ فِيْهَا خٰلِدُوْنَ ۝

109. These are the Signs of Allah, We rehearse them to thee while they comprise the truth ; and Allah wills not any wrong to *His* creatures.³⁹⁴

تِلْكَ اٰيٰتُ اللّٰهِ نَتْلُوْهَا عَلَيْكَ بِالْحَقِّ وَمَا اللّٰهُ يُرِيْدُ ظُلْمًا لِّلْعٰلَمِيْنَ ۝

110. And ^bto Allah belongs whatever is in the heavens and whatever is in the earth, and to Allah shall *all* affairs be returned *for decision.*³⁹⁵

وَلِلّٰهِ مَا فِى السَّمٰوٰتِ وَمَا فِى الْاَرْضِ وَاِلَى اللّٰهِ تُرْجَعُ الْاُمُوْرُ ۝

---

^a10 : 27.　^b3 : 130, 190 ; 4 : 132 ; 57 : 11.

---

turn black) mean, when some will be praised for their deeds, and some will be reproached ; or they mean, when some will rejoice and some will grieve.

The present verse speaks of discord and disagreement mentioned in the preceding verse as disbelief ; for the ultimate end of such disagreement and dissension is nothing but disbelief.

394. Important Words :

The words بالحق (lit. ' with truth ' and translated as, while they comprise the truth) signify, *firstly*, that these Signs or words of God are full of truths ; *secondly*, that they have come as a matter of right i.e. you had a right to receive them ; *thirdly* that, this was the proper time for their recital. See also 3 : 4

The words, *Allah wills not any wrong*, mean that by calling upon mankind to accept the Holy Prophet, God does not intend to cause them harm ; in fact, He desires to have mercy on them. The interests of mankind required that a Prophet should have been sent to them.

395. Commentary :

As whatever is in the heavens and in the earth belongs to God, so it was in the fitness of things that finally a Prophet with a universal mission should have been raised. The previous system of raising separate Prophets for separate peoples and separate periods was meant only by way of preparation. Now was the time of one God and one Prophet.

111. *a*You are the best people raised for the good of mankind ; *b*you enjoin what is good and forbid evil and believe in Allah. And if the People of the Book had believed, it would have, surely, been better for them. Some of them are believers, but most of them are disobedient.³⁹⁶

كُنْتُمْ خَيْرَ اُمَّةٍ اُخْرِجَتْ لِلنَّاسِ تَأْمُرُوْنَ بِالْمَعْرُوْفِ وَتَنْهَوْنَ عَنِ الْمُنْكَرِ وَتُؤْمِنُوْنَ بِاللّٰهِ وَلَوْ اٰمَنَ اَهْلُ الْكِتٰبِ لَكَانَ خَيْرًا لَّهُمْ مِنْهُمُ الْمُؤْمِنُوْنَ وَاَكْثَرُهُمُ الْفٰسِقُوْنَ ۝

112. They cannot harm you save a slight hurt; and *c*if they fight you, they shall show you their backs. Then they shall not be helped.³⁹⁷

لَنْ يَّضُرُّوْكُمْ اِلَّاۤ اَذًى وَاِنْ يُّقَاتِلُوْكُمْ يُوَلُّوْكُمُ الْاَدْبَارَ ثُمَّ لَا يُنْصَرُوْنَ ۝

*a*2 : 144.   *b*3 : 105, 115 ; 7 : 158 ; 9 : 71 ; 31 : 18.   *c*59 : 13.

396. Commentary :

The verse not only claims that the Muslims are the best people—a great claim indeed— but also gives reasons for it. These reasons are : (1) Muslims have been raised for the good of others ; (2) they have been raised not for the good of any one people or any one country but for the good of all mankind ; (3) it has been made their duty to enjoin what is good and forbid evil and believe in one God. The history of Islam bears ample testimony to the fact that Muslims fulfilled all the hopes expressed in this verse. They were not only the torch-bearers of Islam to the four corners of the world but they also contributed to the betterment of other peoples in a most remarkable manner. The renaissance of the West was mostly, if not entirely, due to their influence (*e.g.* The Making of Humanity by Robert Briffault).

The greatness of a people is proportionate to the magnitude of their work. As Muslims were to bring about the good of all mankind, they have been declared the greatest of all peoples. In fact, the real purpose of a Muslim's life is to do good to humanity. As Islam is the greatest good, so Muslims have been enjoined to convey its message to the whole world. They are also required to enjoin what is good and forbid what is evil. There are other people also who claim to enjoin good and forbid evil, but their aim in doing so is to contribute to the strength or betterment of their own respective communities. The Quran warns Muslims against having such restricted motives by adding the words, *and you believe in Allah,* i.e. your preaching should be for God's sake only Who is the Lord of the worlds.

The assignment of this great task to Muslims also implies the appearance of divine Messengers among them from time to time, for it is heavenly Messengers alone who can best perform this duty; and it is through them that we can properly realize the true significance of this task.

It may also be pointed out here that, according to this verse, the excellence of the Muslim people is governed by, and is subject to, the above conditions i.e. preaching Islam to mankind and enjoining what is good and forbidding what is evil ; mere lip-profession of Islam cannot entitle anyone to claim excellence.

397. Commentary :

The words, *they cannot harm you save a slight*

113. ^aSmitten shall they be with abasement wherever they are found, unless they have protection from Allah, or protection from men. They have incurred the wrath of Allah, and smitten are they with wretchedness. ^bThat is because they would reject the Signs of Allah and kill the Prophets unjustly. That is because they rebelled and used to transgress.[398]

ضُرِبَتْ عَلَيْهِمُ الذِّلَّةُ اَيْنَ مَا ثُقِفُوٓا اِلَّا بِحَبْلٍ مِّنَ اللّٰهِ وَحَبْلٍ مِّنَ النَّاسِ وَبَآءُوْ بِغَضَبٍ مِّنَ اللّٰهِ وَضُرِبَتْ عَلَيْهِمُ الْمَسْكَنَةُ ذٰلِكَ بِاَنَّهُمْ كَانُوْا يَكْفُرُوْنَ بِاٰيٰتِ اللّٰهِ وَيَقْتُلُوْنَ الْاَنْۢبِيَآءَ بِغَيْرِ حَقٍّ ذٰلِكَ بِمَا عَصَوْا وَّكَانُوْا يَعْتَدُوْنَ ۝

---

^a2 : 62, 91 ; 5 : 61 ; 7 : 168.   ^b2 : 62, 92 ; 3 : 22.

---

hurt, signify that Jews, in spite of their great enmity to Islam, will not be able to do Muslims more than a slight injury, and this is what actually happened.

The words, *they shall show you their backs*, contain a prophecy which met with its fulfilment three times by the defeat at Medina of the hostile Jewish tribes who made common cause with the Arab tribes. They were guilty of treachery and met with the punishment they deserved.

The words are equally applicable to the enemies of Islam in general. Preaching of the divine message can bring upon Muslims only temporary trouble. If they persevere in preaching with sincerity and patience, they are sure to come out successful in their endeavour. On the other hand, if the enemies of Islam take up arms against Muslims for their preaching of Islam, God will help the latter against their enemies and grant them victory.

398. Important Words :

حبل (protection). See 3 : 104.

مسكنة (wretchedness) is derived from سكن *i.e.* he or it was or became still or silent or motionless. مسكنة means, the state of a مسكين ; lowliness or submissiveness; lowness, abasement or humiliation; paucity of property; evil state or condition; weakness ; poverty of mind, etc. (Lane). It also means disgrace

and wretchedness (Aqrab); also loss of the power of movement (Mufradāt).

Commentary :

This verse contains an important and far-reaching prophecy regarding Jews. They are for ever doomed to disgrace and humiliation. They have ever to live in subjection to other Powers. The history of the Jewish people from the time of the Holy Prophet up to the present day bears woeful testimony to the truth of this awful prophecy. In all countries and in all ages, the present age of enlightenment and toleration not being excepted, they have been the victims of bitter persecution and have been subjected to diverse kinds of disgrace and humiliation. Their practice of usury has also made them the hated of all nations.

The word حبل rendered here as " protection" is full of significance and is applicable in almost all its different meanings for which see 3 : 104. Generally speaking, the divine rope, or in other words, " protection from Allah," refers to Islam; and "protection from men " refers to the protection of non-Muslim Powers. The latter may be illustrated by the Treaty of Versailles, which afforded the Jews a temporary protection, while the former was made possible through a section of them accepting the Holy Prophet. In the present age, the Promised Messiah (Holy Founder of the Ahmadiyya Movement in Islam), whom

114. *a*They are not *all* alike. Among the People of the Book there is a party who stand *by their covenant ;* they recite the word of Allah in the hours of night and prostrate themselves *before Him.*399

115. They believe in Allah and the Last Day, and *b*enjoin what is good and forbid evil, and *c*chasten, vying with one another, to good works. And these are among the righteous.

لَيْسُوْا سَوَآءً مِنْ اَهْلِ الْكِتٰبِ اُمَّةٌ قَآئِمَةٌ يَّتْلُوْنَ اٰيٰتِ اللّٰهِ اٰنَآءَ الَّيْلِ وَ هُمْ يَسْجُدُوْنَ ۝

يُؤْمِنُوْنَ بِاللّٰهِ وَالْيَوْمِ الْاٰخِرِ وَيَأْمُرُوْنَ بِالْمَعْرُوْفِ وَيَنْهَوْنَ عَنِ الْمُنْكَرِ وَيُسَارِعُوْنَ فِي الْخَيْرٰتِ ؕ وَاُولٰٓئِكَ مِنَ الصّٰلِحِيْنَ ۝

---

*a*4 : 163.   *b*3 : 105, 111 ; 9 : 71.   *c*21 : 91 ; 23 : 62 ; 35 : 33.

God has raised as the saviour of mankind, is the emblem of protection for the Jews. They can save themselves by accepting him.

The word مسكنة rendered as "wretchedness" also signifies, humiliation, disgrace, and loss of the power of movement. All these have been the fate of the Jews. They have often been expelled from countries, and even today in Russia there are certain districts which they are not permitted to enter. The recent persecution of the Jews in Germany and other countires of Europe is only too well-known to need a reference.

The clause, *kill the Prophets unjustly*, refers not only to the attempt of the Jews to crucify Jesus, but also to their plots to kill the Holy Prophet of Islam.

The verse also serves as a warning to Muslims that if they rejected the Promised Messiah, who has come in the spirit and power of Jesus as well as of the Holy Prophet and whose duty it is to preach and rejuvenate Islam, they would also be smitten with the same disgrace which

has been the lot of the Jews for their rejection of Jesus and the Holy Prophet.

399. Important Words :

امة قائمة (a party who stand by the covenant) may give a number of meanings besides the one given in the text *e.g.* : (1) a party or people who perform well the duties entrusted to them ; (2) a people who stand up for Prayer in the latter part of the night, an act of worship highly commended both in the Quran and the sayings of the Holy Prophet.

Commentary :

The words, *a party who stand by their covenant,* refer to those among the Jews who embraced Islam (see the next verse and also 4 : 163). The view finds further support from the words, *and prostrate themselves before Him*, for سجدة (prostration) was not included in the worship performed by Jews. The exhortation to Mary conveyed in the words, *and prostrate thyself* (3 : 44), was only an exceptional commandment specifically meant for her.

116. And *whatever good they do, they shall not be denied its due reward; and Allah well knows the God-fearing. 400

وَمَا يَفْعَلُوْا مِنْ خَيْرٍ فَلَنْ يُّكْفَرُوْهُ ۗ وَاللّٰهُ عَلِيْمٌ ۢ بِالْمُتَّقِيْنَ ۞

117 *As for those who disbelieve, their possessions and their children shall not avail them aught against Allah; and these are the inmates of the Fire; therein shall they abide. 401

اِنَّ الَّذِيْنَ كَفَرُوْا لَنْ تُغْنِيَ عَنْهُمْ اَمْوَالُهُمْ وَلَا اَوْلَادُهُمْ مِّنَ اللّٰهِ شَيْئًا ۗ وَاُولٰٓئِكَ اَصْحٰبُ النَّارِ ۚ هُمْ فِيْهَا خٰلِدُوْنَ ۞

118. *The likeness of what they spend for the present life is as the likeness of a wind wherein there is intense cold, which smites the harvest of a people who have wronged themselves and destroys it. And Allah has not wronged them, but they wrong themselves. 402

مَثَلُ مَا يُنْفِقُوْنَ فِيْ هٰذِهِ الْحَيٰوةِ الدُّنْيَا كَمَثَلِ رِيْحٍ فِيْهَا صِرٌّ اَصَابَتْ حَرْثَ قَوْمٍ ظَلَمُوْا اَنْفُسَهُمْ فَاَهْلَكَتْهُ ۗ وَمَا ظَلَمَهُمُ اللّٰهُ وَلٰكِنْ اَنْفُسَهُمْ يَظْلِمُوْنَ ۞

---

*28 : 85 ; 99 : 8.   *3 : 11 ; 58 : 18.   *10 : 25 ; 68 : 18—21.

400. Commentary :

The verse shows that Islam is not a national or tribal religion, but that whoever joins it, no matter from what nation or creed he comes, will receive the same reward as any other follower of the Faith, provided, of course, he acts righteously. In Islam no preferential or prejudicial treatment is meted out to the members of any particular nationality. A Jew, and for that matter any other man, after embracing Islam, is on a par with an Arab Muslim.

401. Commentary :

If disbelievers employ their wealth and their children in opposition to God, these shall not serve as protection against divine punishment which must overtake them. But if they employ their wealth and their children in order to win the pleasure of God, this is sure ultimately to lead to their guidance. A Companion of the Holy Prophet is reported to have once said to him that in the Days of Ignorance *i.e.*, before he accepted Islam, he had given a hundred camels in charity and asked him whether that charity would bring him any reward. The Holy Prophet promptly replied, " Your acceptance of Islam is a result of the very charity you practised " (Bukhārī, ch. on *Zakāt*).

402. Important Words :

صِرّ (intense cold). They say صَرَّ الْبَابُ *i.e.* the door made a sound or a creaking sound. صَرَّ الطَّائِرُ means, the bird (hawk or falcon) uttered its cry. صِرّ means, it (plant) became smitten with intense cold; or he (a person) had an iron collar put round his neck. So صِرّ means: (1) intense cold; (2) cold that smites the herbage and

119. O ye who believe! ^atake not others than your own people as intimate friends : ^bthey will not fail to corrupt you. They love to see you in trouble. Hatred has already shown itself through *the utterances of* their mouths and what their breasts conceal is greater still. We have made clear to you Our commandments, if you will understand :⁴⁰³

يَا أَيُّهَا الَّذِيْنَ اٰمَنُوْا لَا تَتَّخِذُوْا بِطَانَةً مِّنْ دُوْنِكُمْ لَا يَأْلُوْنَكُمْ خَبَالًا ۚ وَدُّوْا مَا عَنِتُّمْ ۚ قَدْ بَدَتِ الْبَغْضَاءُ مِنْ أَفْوَاهِهِمْ ۖ وَمَا تُخْفِيْ صُدُوْرُهُمْ أَكْبَرُ ۚ قَدْ بَيَّنَّا لَكُمُ الْاٰيٰتِ إِنْ كُنْتُمْ تَعْقِلُوْنَ ۝

---

^a3 : 29 ; 4 : 140, 145. ^b9 : 47.

---

destroys it ; (3) sound or noise ; (4) a wind with an excessively loud sound ; (5) fire (Lane & Lisān).

Commentary :

The idea underlying this verse is that the efforts of the disbelievers against Islam will react only against themselves. Whatever they do and whatever they spend with a view to injuring or destroying Islam will only injure the disbelievers themselves. God sent Islam for the good of the people, but by rejecting it they are bringing about their own ruin.

403. Important Words :

بِطَانَة (intimate friends) is derived from بطن i.e. it was or became hidden. بطانة means, a lining ; an inner vest ; a close and intimate friend or friends ; a friend or friends to whom one reveals one's secrets (Aqrab).

خبال (corruption) is derived from خبل. They say خبله i.e. he made him or it corrupt or evil. خبله الحزن means, the grief affected and vitiated his reason. خبل الرجل عن كذا means, he confined the man and prevented him from it. خبال means, corruption or bad condition whether of body or reason or actions ; loss or deterioration ; ruin or destruction ; fatal poison (Aqrab).

عنت (in trouble) is derived from عنت. They say عنت الشيئ i.e. the thing became bad

or corrupt. عنت فلان means, misfortune befell him and he got into trouble. عنت زيد means Zaid met with a calamity and was ruined, عنت العظم means, the bone became weak and broke after it was in a good condition. عنت الرجل means, the man committed a sin (Aqrab). See also 2 : 221.

Commentary :

The words لا يألونكم خبالا rendered as, *they will not fail to corrupt you*, may also mean : (1) they have no scruple in ruining you ; (2) they leave no stone unturned to spoil your work ; (3) they will do what they can to corrupt your religion ; (4) they are always busy in injuring you.

The words ودوا ما عنتم (they love to see you in trouble) may, in the light of the meanings given under Important Words above, mean : (1) they love to see you fall into calamity and misfortune ; (2) they love to see you perish ; (3) they love to see you become weak and broken ; (4) they love to see you become sinful.

Obviously, this verse refers to avoiding such non-Muslims only as are at war with Muslims or such as seek to injure Islam in any other way. It does not require Muslims to have absolutely no relations with any non-Muslim. Elsewhere, the Quran says : *Allah forbids you*

120. Behold, you are those who love them, but they love you not. ᵃAnd you believe in all the Book. When they meet you, they say, ' We believe;' but when they are alone, they bite their finger-tips at you for rage. Say, ' Perish in your rage'. Surely, Allah knows well what is hidden in *your* breasts.⁴⁰⁴

121. ᵇIf anything good befall you, it grieves them; and if an evil befall you, they rejoice thereat. But if you be steadfast and righteous, their designs will not harm you at all : surely, Allah encompasses *all* that they do.⁴⁰⁵

هَاأَنتُمْ أُوْلَاءِ تُحِبُّونَهُمْ وَلَا يُحِبُّونَكُمْ وَتُؤْمِنُونَ بِالْكِتَابِ كُلِّهِ ۖ وَإِذَا لَقُوكُمْ قَالُوا آمَنَّا ۖ وَإِذَا خَلَوْا عَضُّوا عَلَيْكُمُ الْأَنَامِلَ مِنَ الْغَيْظِ ۚ قُلْ مُوتُوا بِغَيْظِكُمْ ۗ إِنَّ اللَّهَ عَلِيمٌ بِذَاتِ الصُّدُورِ ۝

إِن تَمْسَسْكُمْ حَسَنَةٌ تَسُؤْهُمْ وَإِن تُصِبْكُمْ سَيِّئَةٌ يَفْرَحُوا بِهَا ۖ وَإِن تَصْبِرُوا وَتَتَّقُوا لَا يَضُرُّكُمْ كَيْدُهُمْ شَيْئًا ۗ إِنَّ اللَّهَ بِمَا يَعْمَلُونَ مُحِيطٌ ۝

ᵃ2 : 15, 77 ; 5 : 62.   ᵇ9 : 50.

---

not respecting those who have not fought against you on account of your religion and who have not driven you out from your homes, that you be kind to them and deal equitably with them. Surely Allah loves those who are equitable (60 : 9).

404. Commentary :

As borne out by the context, words like " and they do not believe in all the Book " must be taken to be understood after the words, *you believe in all the Book.*

The words, *perish in your rage*, have been addressed to such Jews as are the enemies of Islam and seek to destroy it. The words are meant as a rebuke. When every effort has been made to reform them, and they would not

listen, then they should suffer the consequences of their blind hostility.

405. Commentary :

The enemies of Islam, both open and secret, are grieved to see the success of believers and try to minimize it. But when Muslims meet with some failure, they rejoice and try to exaggerate it. Their object is to dishearten and discourage believers.

The words, *Allah encompasses their deeds,* signify that God will bring to nought all their doings and destroy them. Muslims should not therefore fear them. All machinations of the enemies of Islam are known to God, Who will frustrate them.

3 122. And *remember the time* when thou didst go forth early in the morning from thy household, assigning to the believers their positions for battle. And Allah is All-Hearing, All-Knowing ;[406]

وَاِذْ غَدَوْتَ مِنْ اَهْلِكَ تُبَوِّئُ الْمُؤْمِنِيْنَ مَقَاعِدَ لِلْقِتَالِ ۗ وَاللّٰهُ سَمِيْعٌ عَلِيْمٌ ۞

406. Commentary :

In the preceding verses Muslims have been taught the lesson of patience, perseverance and righteousness. If they act upon it, they will succeed and no enemy can injure them. Now the same lesson is brought home to them by an illustration from their current history.

The verse refers to the important Battle of Uḥud, which was fought in the third year of Hijra. After sustaining a crushing defeat at Badr, the Quraish of Mecca began to make preparations in earnest for another attack on the Holy Prophet and his followers at Medina. Accordingly, next year a well-equipped army of 3,000 warriors marched against Medina under the leadership of Abū Sufyān. When the Holy Prophet heard of it, he consulted his Companions as to the best way of meeting the enemy. The majority of the older Companions were of the opinion that they should remain in the city and defend themselves. 'Abdullah bin Ubayy bin Salūl, leader of the hypocrites, was also of the same opinion. The Holy Prophet also held the same view. He had seen in a dream that the Muslim army had suffered a loss, although it had also inflicted loss on the enemy. So he desired to remain in the city and there wait for the enemy. But the majority of his followers, mostly young men and such of the older people as had not taken part in the Battle of Badr, were eager to march out of Medina and meet the enemy in pitched battle. The Holy Prophet respected the wishes of the majority and decided to march out. Later, however, the majority thought better of the

matter and veered round to the opinion of the Holy Prophet. But now the Holy Prophet refused to change his mind, saying that it did not behove a Prophet of God to put down his armour after he had once put it on till God decided between him and the enemy. So he marched out of Medina with a force of 1,000 men. A large party of Jews, who were apparently in alliance with the Muslims, wished to join him. But the Holy Prophet did not accept their help. They were a treacherous people and God had just warned him against them, saying, *They will not fail to corrupt you ; they love to see you in trouble* (3 : 119).

When the Holy Prophet had proceeded some distance, 'Abdullah bin Ubayy, leader of the hypocrites, deserted and returned to Medina on the pretext that his advice to stay in Medina had been ignored and that the help of the Jews, whom he had brought as reinforcement, had also been rejected. This reduced the Muslim army to only 700 men. At this sudden defection on the part of 'Abdullah, a tribe from the Khazraj called *Banū Ḥāritha*, and a tribe from the Aus called *Banū Salma*, in spite of being sincere Muslims, showed signs of wavering and thought of deserting, but God saved them from such defection (3 : 123).

On entering the valley of Uḥud, the Holy Prophet arrayed his men in battle order with their backs towards the hill and their faces towards Medina. As a further precaution, he stationed 50 archers at a certain point on the hill in the rear of the Muslim army under the leadership of 'Abdullah bin Jubair, with express orders not to quit the place until so ordered by the Prophet himself, even if they saw the

123. When two of your groups meditated cowardice, although Allah was their friend. And upon Allah should the believers rely.[407]

اِذْ هَمَّتْ طَّآئِفَتٰنِ مِنْكُمْ اَنْ تَفْشَلَا وَاللهُ وَلِيُّهُمَا وَعَلَى اللهِ فَلْيَتَوَكَّلِ الْمُؤْمِنُوْنَ ۞

Meccans fleeing before the Muslims or even if they saw the Muslims being defeated and their bodies being eaten by birds.

As was the custom in Arabia, the battle commenced with single combats, resulting in the death of several disbelievers and some Muslims. Then the enemy made a general assault, which was repeated thrice, and each time they were completely repulsed. The battle waged hot, but at last the enemy force broke and they were forced to flee, pursued by the Muslims, so much so that some of the latter began to collect the booty.

When the party stationed on the hill in the rear of the army saw this, they thought of leaving their position, thinking that as the battle was over the object of the Holy Prophet's commandment was fulfilled and their presence on the hill was no longer needed. Their leader remonstrated with them and asked them to stick to the place in obedience to the Holy Prophet's command. But they paid no heed to his words and left the place. A few, however, remained behind with him on the hill. Khālid bin Walīd, who was among the disbelievers, having not yet embraced Islam, at once saw his opportunity and with a party of disbelievers attacked and killed the few men with their leader who had remained behind, and fell on the Muslims from the rear. Seeing this, the fleeing Meccans also took heart and returned to the attack, and in the confusion that followed some one mischievously shouted that the Prophet had been killed. This disheartened the believers, some of whom fled to Medina, and others left the battlefield, overwhelmed with grief at the supposed death of their Holy Master. Many, however, not desiring to live when the Prophet was dead, rushed into the ranks of the enemy and died fighting bravely.

The confusion was so complete that the Holy Prophet was at one time left with only twelve Companions; at another time, he had only two Companions with him and was thus practically left all alone. All this time, he was the centre of the enemy's attacks, but the few Companions that stood by him shielded him with their bodies and, standing like statues of stone, received all the arrows and all the blows on their bodies which became pierced like sieves. But they did not swerve even by the fraction of an inch from their place lest by so doing they should expose the body of the Holy Prophet. Whenever any one of them fell, his place was promptly taken by another. The Holy Prophet was also wounded. One of his teeth was broken by a stone and a ring of his helmet was smashed into his face by a ruthless blow. When the Companions who still remained in or near the battlefield learned that their Master was alive, a section of them gathered round him and, repelling the attacks of the enemy, slowly took him to a safe place on the hillside. Then the enemy withdrew. More than seventy of the Companions fell in the battle, including Ḥamza, the valiant uncle of the Holy Prophet; and many were wounded. But as later events showed, this calamity, however great in itself, did not prove a check to the forward march of Islam. The rest of the battle is described in the succeeding verses.

407. **Important Words:**

يَتَوَكَّلْ (should rely) is derived from وَكَلَ (wakala). They say وَكَلَ اِلَيْهِ الْاَمْرَ i.e. he left the matter

124. ^aAnd Allah had already helped you at Badr ^bwhen you were weak. So take Allah for your protector that you may be grateful.[408]

وَلَقَدْ نَصَرَكُمُ اللّٰهُ بِبَدْرٍ وَّاَنْتُمْ اَذِلَّةٌ ۚ فَاتَّقُوا اللّٰهَ لَعَلَّكُمْ تَشْكُرُوْنَ ۞

---

^a8 : 8, 11; 9 : 25.　　^b2 : 250

to him for disposal as he might think fit. وكله بكذا (wakkalahū) means, he appointed him his وكيل or agent for the disposal or management of such and such a matter. توكل بالامر means, he became responsible, or accepted responsibility, for the management of the affair. توكل على الله means, he relied on God; he put his trust in Him; he submitted himself to Him. The infinitive noun توكل signifies relying on, and trusting in, God alone, to the exclusion of worldly means (Aqrab & Lane).

Commentary :

The two groups mentioned here were, as stated above, the two tribes of *Banū Salma* and *Banū Hāritha*, belonging respectively to Aus and Khazraj. Their idea of returning (referred to in the note under the preceding verse) was not due to any doubt on their part with regard to the truth of Islam, but was merely due to weakness born of attending circumstances. But as they were sincere believers, God saved them from yielding to this weakness. See also note on 3 : 122.

The clause, *upon Allah should the believers rely*, does not mean that a Muslim should neglect material means and confine himself to praying to God and waiting for His help. This is a misguided conception of توكل (trusting in God) which finds no support in Islamic teachings. What Islam teaches is this, that a true believer should use all the available means of attaining an object but should, at the same time, not rely upon them. He should trust in

God alone looking upon worldly means as only being effective under the will of God. " Tie the knees of your camel and then trust in God ", says the Holy Prophet—an extremely difficult position but nevertheless the only right way of demonstrating true faith in God !

408. Important Words :

بدر (Badr) literally means the full moon. The verb form بدر from which the noun form is derived gives the sense of making haste. They say بدر الى الشىء *i.e.* he hastened towards it. *Badr*, in the sense of full moon, is so called because it hastens to rise before the sun sets and to set before the sun rises. Badr is also the name of a place on the route between Mecca and Medina. It takes its name from a spring which belonged to a man named Badr. The Battle of Badr referred to here took place near this place.

Commentary :

These words are addressed to Muslims through the Holy Prophet, who actually used them after the Battle of Uḥud. They remind the Faithful that God had granted them victory at Badr while they were much weaker than at the time of the Battle of Uḥud, because they behaved obediently, patiently and God-fearingly on that occasion. So the setback at Uḥud was due to their own weakness and the disobedience, though not quite intentional, which some of them showed to their Master. But the words also imply a promise of help in future if the Muslims repent of their mistake and behave like true believers.

125. When thou didst say to the believers, ^a'Will it not suffice you that your Lord should help you with three thousand angels sent down *from on high*?'⁴⁰⁹

اِذْ تَقُوْلُ لِلْمُؤْمِنِيْنَ اَلَنْ يَّكْفِيَكُمْ اَنْ يُّمِدَّكُمْ رَبُّكُمْ بِثَلٰثَةِ اٰلٰفٍ مِّنَ الْمَلٰٓئِكَةِ مُنْزَلِيْنَ ۞

126. Yea, if you be steadfast and righteous and they come upon you immediately in hot haste, your Lord will help you with five thousand angels, attacking vehemently.⁴¹⁰

بَلٰٓى اِنْ تَصْبِرُوْا وَتَتَّقُوْا وَيَأْتُوْكُمْ مِّنْ فَوْرِهِمْ هٰذَا يُمْدِدْكُمْ رَبُّكُمْ بِخَمْسَةِ اٰلٰفٍ مِّنَ الْمَلٰٓئِكَةِ مُسَوِّمِيْنَ ۞

---

^a8 : 10.

409. Commentary :

The verse means that if the Meccans made another attack upon Muslims sometime after Uhud, God would help the la.ter by sending down a force of three thousand angels. It is a mistake to think that these words refer to the Battle of Badr which has been mentioned in the preceding verse only incidentally in order to cite an illustration of how God helped steadfast Muslims in times of danger. Moreover, the number of angels sent at the Battle of Badr was, according to 8 : 10, one thousand and not three thousand, as here stated. The fulfilment of the present promise is referred to in 3 : 152 below.

410. Important Words :

فور (immediately) is derived from فار. They say فارالماء *i.e.* the water gushed forth from the earth. فارت القدر means, the conter ts of the cooking pot vehemently boiled and rose high in it. فورة means, the intensity of heat or anger or the like. فورة النهار means, the first part of the day. فور signifies the state or condition that comes without delay. The Arabs say رجع من فوره *i.e.* he returned or turned back immediately without tarrying (Aqrab).

مسومين (attacking vehemently) is derived from سوم. They say سوم الفرس *i.e.* he branded the horse with a brand. سوم الخيل means, he let loose the horses for grazing, سوم عليهم means, he suddenly and vehemently attacked them and wrought havoc among them (Aqrab). In the verse under comment the word is used in the last-mentioned sense.

Commentary :

The verse signifies that if the disbelievers returned to the attack at once, without giving the Muslims any opportunity to recoup themselves, God would help the latter with five thousand angels. The difference in the number of angels,—in the preceding verse the number mentioned being 3,000—was due to the difference in the condition of the Muslims. They were at that time exhausted and wounded and, therefore, needed greater help than they would have needed, if the enemy attack had been delayed.

The enemy did indeed think of returning, but God prevented them from doing so. Briefly stated, the facts are that when the Quraish were retracing their steps towards Mecca, members of the Arab tribes living in the vicinity of Medina asked them about the result of the battle, and when they declared that they were victorious, these men put them to shame by saying, "If you have been really

127. And ^aAllah has made it only as glad tidings for you and to put your hearts at rest thereby; and help comes from Allah alone, the Mighty, the Wise.⁴¹¹

وَمَا جَعَلَهُ اللّٰهُ اِلَّا بُشْرٰى لَكُمْ وَلِتَطْمَئِنَّ قُلُوبُكُمْ بِهٖ ۚ وَمَا النَّصْرُ اِلَّا مِنْ عِنْدِ اللّٰهِ الْعَزِيْزِ الْحَكِيْمِ ۟

128. *God will do so* that He might cut off a part of the disbelievers or abase them so that they might go back frustrated.⁴¹²

لِيَقْطَعَ طَرَفًا مِّنَ الَّذِيْنَ كَفَرُوْٓا اَوْ يَكْبِتَهُمْ فَيَنْقَلِبُوْا خَآئِبِيْنَ ۟

---

^a8 : 11.

---

victorious, where are the spoils ? What have you brought from the battlefield ? " Touched to tne quick by this taunt, the Quraish decided to retrieve their shame by attacking the Muslims once more. When the Holy Prophet came to know of this, on the day following the battle, he gave immediate orders to march and directed that only those of his followers who had taken part in the Battle of Uḥud should join him. The Muslims went as far as Ḥamrā' al-Asad, a place about eight miles from Medina. The Meccans were, however, so overawed by this unexpectedly bold and prompt appearance of the Holy Prophet and his followers that they decided to retreat hastily to Mecca. This was due to the fear which the angels had inspired in their hearts. Otherwise there was no reason for them to flee from an enemy upon whom they had inflicted so heavy a loss only a day before and who, besides being very much reduced in number, were utterly exhausted and were suffering from grievous wounds as a result of the previous day's fighting.

A recent Commentator, having translated the words, هذا من فورهم as "in a headlong manner," has applied them to the Battle of Aḥzāb. This is not right. The fact is that verses 125 and 126, as already explained, are both connected with the Battle of Uḥud and relate to the time immediately following it. The word بلى (yea) occurring in the beginning of the verse also denotes a connection between the verses and supplies the answer to the question in 3 : 125, viz : *will it not suffice you?* Thus the word بلى would here mean "yes, it will suffice, and so will suffice a force of 5,000 angels if the enemy were to return to the attack at this very moment."

411. Commentary :

The verse is intended to warn Muslims against treating angels as gods or even as an independent source of help. Help comes from Allah alone ; angels are entirely subservient to Him and do nothing by their own will. They come only by the command of God and do only what God commands them. The way in which angels help men is that they strengthen their hearts and fill their enemies with awe and fear. If God had so willed, a single angel would have been enough to help the Muslims, but He promised to send as many as five thousand angels in order to cheer and strengthen their hearts and to hint that a very large number of the hidden forces of nature were working in their favour. For the work and duties of angels see 2 : 31.

It may incidentally be noted here that some believers, and even some disbelievers, are reported to have actually seen the angels at the Battle of Badr. (Jarīr, iv. 47). See also 8 : 11.

412. Important Words :

يكبت (abase) is derived from كبت . They

447

129. Thou hast no concern in the matter: He may turn to them in mercy or punish them, for they are wrongdoers.[413]

لَيْسَ لَكَ مِنَ الْاَمْرِ شَىْءٌ اَوْ يَتُوْبَ عَلَيْهِمْ اَوْ يُعَذِّبَهُمْ فَاِنَّهُمْ ظٰلِمُوْنَ ۝

say كبّ i.e. (1) he overthrew or prostrated him; (2) he humbled or abased him; (3) he turned him away; (4) he turned him back with his fury; (5) he destroyed him or caused him to perish (Aqrab).

Commentary:

The words, *or abase them*, mean that if the disbelievers attacked the Muslims, they would be punished and a part of them killed, and if they did not attack the Muslims, they would retreat in abasement and disgrace. Actually, it was the lesser of the two alternatives that came to pass; for when the Holy Prophet, learning that the Meccans were contemplating an immediate attack on Medina marched out with his followers, the Meccans fled in disgrace and abasement (see note on 3 : 126).

The verse also shows that God sometimes makes conditional prophecies *i.e.* He predicts two alternative events of which only one is to occur, according as circumstances demand. In the present case, God knew that only the latter alternative would come to pass, yet He did not foretell it definitely. The coming of the angels, it may be noted further, was meant as a guarantee of the punishment or disgrace of the enemy, as the case might be.

413. Commentary:

This verse is erroneously supposed to contain a sort of admonition or warning to the Holy Prophet for his having prayed to God for the destruction of the Meccans. There is no mention of any such prayer here, nor was there any occasion for such a prayer. In fact, a Prophet never prays for the destruction of any people without the permission of God.

The words are meant only as an answer to those who attributed the reverse of the Muslims at Uḥud to the alleged error of their leaving the city against the advice of experienced men. The Quran says that the result was brought about by the supreme wisdom of God and that the Holy Prophet had nothing to do with the matter. One good result of this reverse was that many were guided to acceptance of Islam, seeing how God helped the Holy Prophet and how He afforded him protection although he was left alone in the battle.

The verse also contains a reply to the hypocrites, ʿAbdullah bin Ubayy and his followers, who had deserted the Holy Prophet at Uḥud, saying that he had not followed their advice. It tells them that it was God Who was helping the Prophet, and Who, even after the reverse at Uḥud, had fulfilled His promise regarding the ignominious retreat of the Meccans referred to in the preceding verse.

The words, *that He might cut off a part of the disbelievers*, and, *or abase them*, occurring in the preceding verse correspond to the words *He may turn to them in mercy*, and, *or punish them*, occurring in the present verse in the reverse order, the suggestion being that the part that will be cut off will be those who are to be punished by God, while those whom God will temporarily abase and who will return unsuccessful will be those to whom God is finally to turn in mercy; *i.e.* by returning safe, though unsuccessful, they will be afforded an opportunity to repent. Accordingly, we find that many of those who escaped alive were afterwards converted to Islam, and among them were men like Khālid, son of Walīd; ʿIkrima, son of Abū Jahl; ʿAbd al-Raḥmān, son of Abū Bakr, and many others who later made a name in the history of Islam. Abū Sufyān, Commander

130. [a]And to Allah belongs whatever is in the heavens and whatever is in the earth. He forgives whomsoever He pleases and punishes whomsoever He pleases, and Allah is most Forgiving, Merciful.[414]

وَلِلّٰهِ مَا فِى السَّمٰوٰتِ وَمَا فِى الْاَرْضِ یَغْفِرُ لِمَنْ یَّشَآءُ وَیُعَذِّبُ مَنْ یَّشَآءُ ۚ وَاللّٰهُ غَفُوْرٌ رَّحِیْمٌ ۝

4. 131. O ye who believe ! [b]devour not interest involving diverse additions ; and fear Allah that you may prosper.[415]

یٰۤاَیُّهَا الَّذِیْنَ اٰمَنُوْا لَا تَاْکُلُوا الرِّبٰۤوا اَضْعَافًا مُّضٰعَفَةً ۪ وَّاتَّقُوا اللّٰهَ لَعَلَّکُمْ تُفْلِحُوْنَ ۝

---

[a]3 : 110, 190 ; 4 : 132 ; 57 : 11.   [b]2 : 276 ; 30 : 40.

---

of the Meccan army, was also among them.

The verse also throws light on the general nature of prophecies made by the Prophets of God. There is often an element of contingency or uncertainty in them; sometimes it is hidden and sometimes expressed as in the present verse. A clear alternative is put forward here in the form of mercy and punishment to be shown according to the will of God. The reason for this is that prophecies do not proceed from a mechanical or rigid source which is arbitrary and inflexible, but from God, Who possesses both the quality of mercy and the power to punish, which He exercises, according as circumstances demand. In keeping with this principle, the Prophets of God hold out the hope of salvation on condition of genuine repentance, even when they utter unqualified predictions about the doom of their enemies.

414. Commentary :

As Master and Owner, Allah is more inclined to forgiveness and mercy than to punishment, although He has sometimes to resort to the latter for the ultimate good of mankind.

415. Important Words.

الرِّبٰوا (interest). See 2 : 276.

اَضْعَافًا مُّضٰعَفَةً (involving diverse additions). اَضْعَاف is the plural of ضِعْف which originally means, the like of a thing. In its wider significance, the word means the like of a thing or more than that indefinitely. So اَضْعَاف means, manifold or simply a great addition, the addition being unlimited. مُضٰعَفَة is the infinitive of ضَاعَف . They say ضَاعَفَهُ i.e. he doubled it, or trebled it, or redoubled it, or simply increased it indefinitely (Aqrab & Tāj). The expression اَضْعَافًا مُضٰعَفَة would mean, increased manifold ; or increased indefinitely. It should be noted that the words اَضْعَافًا مُضٰعَفَة are not used here as a qualifying phrase to restrict the meaning of رِبٰوا (interest) so as to confine it to a particular kind of interest. They are used as a descriptive clause to point to the inherent nature of رِبٰوا (interest) which involves a continual increase that never ends.

Commentary :

The charging of interest, although now legalized by Christian nations, was prohibited by Moses (see Exod. 22. 25 ; Lev. 25 : 36, 37 ; Deut ; 23 : 19).

The verse does not mean that usury is permissible at a moderate rate, only a high rate being disallowed. All interest is prohibited, whether moderate or excessive; and the words اَضْعَافًا مُضٰعَفَة rendered as, involving diverse additions, have been added only to point to the practice that was actually in vogue in

132. And *a*fear the Fire prepared for the disbelievers.[416]

وَاتَّقُوا النَّارَ الَّتِي أُعِدَّتْ لِلْكَافِرِينَ ۝

133. And *b*obey Allah and the Messenger that you be shown mercy.

وَأَطِيعُوا اللَّهَ وَالرَّسُولَ لَعَلَّكُمْ تُرْحَمُونَ ۝

134. *c*And vie with one another in asking for forgiveness from your Lord, and for a Paradise whose price is the heavens and the earth, prepared for the God-fearing—[417]

وَسَارِعُوا إِلَى مَغْفِرَةٍ مِّن رَّبِّكُمْ وَجَنَّةٍ عَرْضُهَا السَّمَاوَاتُ وَالْأَرْضُ أُعِدَّتْ لِلْمُتَّقِينَ ۝

---

*a*2:25; 66:7.   *b*See 3:33.   *c*57:22.   See also 2:26.

the time of the Prophet. Thus the extreme limit has been mentioned merely to bring out its heinousness whereas, in fact, all interest is prohibited, as clearly stated in 2:276—281.

The mention of the prohibition of interest while dealing with the subject of war is significant. We find that in 2:276—281 also the prohibition of interest has been mentioned in connection with the question of war. This shows that war and interest are closely related to one another—a fact amply borne out by the history of modern times. As a matter of fact, interest is one of the causes of war, and it also helps to prolong it. If there were no lending and borrowing at interest, wars could not be prolonged. If it is asked how the expenses of war are to be met in Islam, if money is not to be borrowed on interest, the answer is that when an aggressive war is forced upon Muslims, they are required to make free contributions for the sake of their religion and country. Suitable taxes also provide a fair means to meet the expenses of war, and taxes automatically prove a check on the undue prolongation of hostilities. See also 2:276, 277; 2:279, 280.

The mention of the prohibition of interest in connection with wars also shows that the verses of the Quran have not been thrown together

at random but that there runs a wise and natural order through them.

416. Commentary:

In 2:276 also the prohibition of interest has been followed by a warning against fire. Evidently it is the fire of war that is primarily meant here. The word "disbelievers" besides being general may also here mean those who disobey the divine commandment relating to interest.

417. Important Words:

عرض (price). The verb عرض gives a number of meanings. They say عرض الشيء عليه *i.e.* he showed him the thing. عرض له عارض means, some difficulty confronted him, or came across his way, or some accident happened to him. عرض means : (1) price of a thing in a form other than money ; (2) breadth or width ; (3) vastness ; (4) goods ; (5) a valley ; (6) side of a mountain (Aqrab).

Commentary:

This verse is an answer to those who, obsessed by their present environments, think that commerce and other affairs of the world cannot be carried on without interest. God says that by following the teachings of Islam Muslims can and will enjoy all sorts of benefits.

The verse is an invitation to follow the commandments of Islam, which has been

135. Those who spend in prosperity and adversity, and those who suppress anger and pardon men ; and Allah loves those who do good ;[418]

الَّذِينَ يُنْفِقُونَ فِي السَّرَّآءِ وَالضَّرَّآءِ وَالْكَاظِمِينَ الْغَيْظَ وَالْعَافِينَ عَنِ النَّاسِ وَاللهُ يُحِبُّ الْمُحْسِنِينَ ۝

spoken of as leading to "forgiveness" and "Paradise". The former implies freedom from pain and afflictions; the latter stands for bliss.

The word عرض rendered as "price" gives, as shown above, a number of meanings. The idea is that the blessings of Paradise will not be limited. While in Paradise, a man will feel happy wherever he may be. On the contrary in this world, we find that a man often possesses the necessary means of enjoyment while at home, but when he is on journey, he is often put to inconvenience. Such will not be the case in Paradise.

The clause also means that believers will be granted a Paradise which will comprise both heaven and earth, i.e., the believers will be in Paradise both on this earth and in the life to come.

There is a tradition to the effect that once certain Companions asked the Holy Prophet, "If Paradise encompasses the heavens and the earth, where is Hell ?" To this the Prophet replied : "Where is the night when the day comes ?" (Kathīr). This reply throws very interesting light on the nature of Heaven and Hell. The Holy Prophet has also said that the smallest reward of the inmates of Paradise will be as immense as the space between heaven and earth.

418. Important Words.

العافين (those who pardon) is derived from عفو which means, to obliterate or remove traces of a thing (Aqrab). See also 2 : 188.

A man is said to exercise the quality of عفو when he obliterates from his mind, or totally forgets, the sins or mistakes committed against him by others. When used with reference to God, the word signifies not only obliteration of sins but also obliteration of all traces thereof.

Commentary :

The verse describes three stages of dealing with other people. In the first stage, a spiritual wayfarer, when offended against, restrains or suppresses his anger. In the second stage, he goes a step further and grants forgiveness and free pardon to the offender. In the third stage, he not only grants the offender complete pardon, but also does a suitable act of kindness to him and bestows some favour upon him. These three stages are well illustrated by an incident in the life of Ḥasan, son of 'Alī and grandson of the Holy Prophet. A slave of his once committed an offence, and Ḥasan became very angry and decided to punish him. Thereupon, the slave recited the first part of the verse i.e. those who suppress anger. Hearing these words, Ḥasan withheld his hand and stood still where he was. Then the slave recited the second part i.e. and pardon men. Hearing this, Ḥasan promptly complied with the divine behest by saying, "Go, I pardon thee." Then the slave recited the last part of the verse i.e. and Allah loves those who do good. In obedience to this command of God, Ḥasan at once set the slave free, saying, "You are a free man and may go where you like" (Bayān, i. 366).

451

136. And those who, *when they commit a foul deed or wrong themselves, remember Allah and implore forgiveness for their sins,—and *who can forgive sins except Allah?—and do not persist knowingly in what they have done,[419]

137. *It is these whose reward is forgiveness from their Lord, and gardens beneath which rivers flow, wherein they shall abide; and how good is the reward of those who work![420]

وَالَّذِيْنَ اِذَا فَعَلُوْا فَاحِشَةً اَوْ ظَلَمُوْٓا اَنْفُسَهُمْ ذَكَرُوا اللّٰهَ فَاسْتَغْفَرُوْا لِذُنُوْبِهِمْ ۗ وَمَنْ يَّغْفِرُ الذُّنُوْبَ اِلَّا اللّٰهُ ۚ وَلَمْ يُصِرُّوْا عَلٰى مَا فَعَلُوْا وَهُمْ يَعْلَمُوْنَ ۝

اُولٰٓئِكَ جَزَآؤُهُمْ مَّغْفِرَةٌ مِّنْ رَّبِّهِمْ وَجَنّٰتٌ تَجْرِيْ مِنْ تَحْتِهَا الْاَنْهٰرُ خٰلِدِيْنَ فِيْهَا ۚ وَنِعْمَ اَجْرُ الْعٰمِلِيْنَ ۝

*7 : 202. *14 : 11; 39 : 54; 61 : 13. *39 : 75.

419. Commentary :

This verse embodies a refutation of the Christian doctrine of Atonement. The words, *remember Allah*, mean that righteous persons are at once reminded of Allah whenever they happen to commit a sin. As a matter of fact, though even good men may occasionally fall into sin, their hearts are not dead and they are always ready to repent. So if they happen to commit a sin, it is due only to a temporary lapse, and not because they love to indulge in sin. Thus so long as a man "remembers God" immediately after he commits a sin and feels sincere remorse and compunction at his evil deed, there is always time for his repentance to be accepted. But when he goes on sinning until he loses all sense of sin and ceases to feel compunction and remorse at his evil deeds, he loses the power to repent and is doomed, unless God should work some special change in him.

The words, *and who can forgive sins except Allah?* have been introduced as a parenthetical clause to exhort sinners to repent They are not made to repent through fear, but by

being reminded of divine forgiveness. When God is Gracious and Forgiving, why should not man repent ?

The words, *do not persist knowingly*, imply that whenever good men happen to commit an error, they do not try to justify their conduct, but frankly admit their mistake and then reform themselves. The verse does not, however, mean that a man should confess his sins to others. What is meant is that one should confess one's guilt to oneself *i.e.* one should feel that one has been in the wrong and should not proceed to defend one's conduct when some one else, or, for that matter, when one's own conscience reproaches one for one's misdeeds. Those truly righteous never try to deceive themselves.

420. Commentary :

When a man truly turns to God, after committing a sin, and sincerely repents of his misdeeds, he is forgiven by God. The verse makes it further clear that forgiveness is only the first stage. God leads those who repent to higher stages of spiritual progress and promises them Heaven.

138. Surely, ^athere have been *many* dispensations before you ; ^bso travel through the earth and see how evil was the end of those who treated *the Prophets* as liars.[421]

قَدْ خَلَتْ مِنْ قَبْلِكُمْ سُنَنٌ فَسِيْرُوْا فِى الْاَرْضِ فَانْظُرُوْا كَيْفَ كَانَ عَاقِبَةُ الْمُكَذِّبِيْنَ ۝

139. This, *the Quran*, is ^ca clear demonstration to men, and ^da guidance and ^ean admonition to the God-fearing.[422]

هٰذَا بَيَانٌ لِّلنَّاسِ وَهُدًى وَّمَوْعِظَةٌ لِّلْمُتَّقِيْنَ ۝

140. ^fSlacken not, nor grieve ; and you shall certainly have the upper hand, if you are believers.[423]

وَلَا تَهِنُوْا وَلَا تَحْزَنُوْا وَاَنْتُمُ الْاَعْلَوْنَ اِنْ كُنْتُمْ مُّؤْمِنِيْنَ ۝

---

^a7 : 39 ; 13 : 31 ; 41 : 26 ; 46 : 19.   ^b6 : 12 ; 12 : 110 ; 27 : 70.   ^c5 : 16 ; 36 : 70.
^d2 : 3, 186 ; 31 : 4.   ^e24 : 35.   ^f4 : 105 ; 47 : 36.

---

421. Important Words :

سُنَن (dispensations) is the plural of سُنَّة which is derived from سَنَّ. They say سَنَّ i.e. he whetted or sharpened it (knife, appetite, etc.). سَنَّ الْعُقْدَة means, he undid the knot. سَنَّ الْاَمْر means, he made known or manifested the matter or the affair or the case. سَنَّ الشَّيْئَ means, he shaped or formed or fashioned the thing. سَنَّ الطَّرِيْقَة means, he followed or pursued that way or course. سَنَّ عَلَيْهِمْ سُنَّة means, he established or instituted or prescribed for them a law or custom or mode of conduct. سُنَّة means, (1) face or form ; (2) way or course or rule of conduct ; (3) way of acting instituted or pursued by a people and followed by others after them ; (4) character or conduct or nature or disposition ; (5) law or religious law or dispensation (Aqrab & Tāj).

Commentary :

The clause, *there have been many dispensations before you*, means that there have gone before you men who followed different ways and possessed diverse characters ; or there have passed before you many dispensations and many nations following different systems or laws. So you should journey in the earth and see what class of men were saved and who perished and what was the end of those who persisted in evil.

422. Commentary :

The pronoun هٰذَا (this) may be taken to refer to (1) the Quran, or (2) the verse immediately preceding, or (3) the subject of repentance discussed in the foregoing verses.

The word مُتَّقِيْن (God-fearing or righteous) does not here necessarily apply to Muslims only. It extends to all persons who earnestly desire to guard against things that are fraught with danger to their souls and who take heed of their spiritual good. It is only such persons as are likely to benefit by admonition.

423. Important Words :

اِن (if) is a common Arabic word giving a number of meanings : (1) if, (2) not, (3) verily, (4) because, (5) when, etc. (Lane).

Commentary :

The expression, *Slacken not, nor grieve*, embodies a very important principle of national or, for that matter, personal strength, the words

141. *a*If you have received an injury, surely the *disbelieving* people have already received a similar injury. And such days We cause to alternate among men *that they may be admonished,* and that Allah may distinguish those who believe and may take witnesses from among you ; and Allah loves not the unjust ;[424]

اِنْ يَّمْسَسْكُمْ قَرْحٌ فَقَدْ مَسَّ الْقَوْمَ قَرْحٌ مِّثْلُهُ ۖ وَتِلْكَ الْاَيَّامُ نُدَاوِلُهَا بَيْنَ النَّاسِ وَلِيَعْلَمَ اللّٰهُ الَّذِيْنَ اٰمَنُوْا وَيَتَّخِذَ مِنْكُمْ شُهَدَآءَ ۖ وَاللّٰهُ لَا يُحِبُّ الظّٰلِمِيْنَ ۞

---

*a*4 : 105.

"slacken not " pertaining to future dangers and the words "grieve not " to past errors and misfortunes. Nations fall only when, either through lack of true realization of their responsibilities they begin to slacken, or through brooding over the past, they give way to despair. The words warn against both these dangers.

The clause, *you shall certainly have the upper hand,* means that if Muslims follow the above advice, they will certainly be victorious in the end. Intervening failures are indeed no failures if the final triumph is assured. Muslims had apparently met with a reverse at Uḥud, so God exhorts the Faithful to let no sort of weakness get hold of them on account of that reverse, either in body or in actions or in faith.

The Arabic clause rendered as, *if you are believers,* may also be rendered as " because you are believers ". In this case the verse would embody a more positive promise of victory.

424. Important Words :

يعلم (distinguish) is derived from علم which ordinarily means, he knew, but is also used in the sense of distinguishing. Ibn Jarīr says under this verse that the expression لا علم *i.e.* لا عرف هذا من هذا means, that I may distinguish 'Abdullah from 'Umar. The word is used in this sense in 2 : 144 and 2 : 221 also. In fact, God, being Omniscient, does not stand in need of knowing a thing,

for everything is ever known to Him. It is only distinguishing between two things that is meant. Even, however, if علم is taken here in the sense of knowing, the expression may be explained by the fact that knowledge is of two kinds. One kind of knowledge consists of knowing a thing before it comes into existence ; and the other kind consists of knowing it when, and as, it actually comes into existence. Here it is the latter kind of knowledge that is meant.

Commentary :

Elsewhere (in 3 : 166 below) it is said that Muslims inflicted upon disbelievers an injury double of what they themselves suffered. This refers to the Battle of Badr, when seventy Meccans were killed and seventy were taken prisoner, thus making a total of 140. In the Battle of Uḥud, on the other hand, seventy Muslims were killed, but none of them were taken prisoner. Thus Muslims had inflicted on the disbelievers a double injury in the Battle of Badr compared with what they themselves suffered in the Battle of Uḥud. Counting, however, only those killed in the two battles, the loss to Muslims and disbelievers has been spoken of in the present verse as similar. Or the verse might be taken to refer to the nature or quality of the misfortune, which was alike in both cases. In that case verse 166 below might be taken to refer to quantity and the present verse to quality.

142. And that Allah may purify those who believe, and destroy the disbelievers.[425]

وَلِيُمَحِّصَ اللّٰهُ الَّذِيۡنَ اٰمَنُوۡا وَيَمۡحَقَ الۡكٰفِرِيۡنَ ۞

143. [a]Do you suppose that you will enter Heaven while Allah has not yet distinguished those of you that strive *in the way of Allah* and has not yet distinguished the steadfast?[426]

اَمۡ حَسِبۡتُمۡ اَنۡ تَدۡخُلُوا الۡجَنَّةَ وَلَمَّا يَعۡلَمِ اللّٰهُ الَّذِيۡنَ جٰهَدُوۡا مِنۡكُمۡ وَيَعۡلَمَ الصّٰبِرِيۡنَ ۞

---

[a]2 : 215 ; 9 : 16.

The word " days " is used both for the " days of success " and the " days of misfortune ". Here either of these may be taken, but preferably the latter.

The words, *And such days We cause to alternate*, mean that even believers sometimes suffer reverses. If it were not so, then there would be little credit in being a believer. No effort is required to find or see the sun, and so one deserves no reward for it. In matters of faith, therefore, there is always present an element of secrecy, and only those who are seriously and earnestly desirous of knowing the truth can discern and accept it. Hence, they become deserving of reward in the sight of God. The words also implied a prophecy that the reverse at Uḥud was to be followed by victory for the Muslims ; and so it actually came to pass.

The words, *Allah may distinguish those who believe*, signify that misfortunes are also intended to make the faith of true believers evident to all. When believers endure trials with patience and steadfastness and do not swerve from the path of faith, their sincerity becomes evident. Trials also serve to distinguish true believers from hypocrites. If there had been no trials, the hypocrisy of men like 'Abdullah bin Ubayy and his associates would have remained undetected and unknown.

The word شهداء (witnesses) does not

here mean martyrs, for a true Muslim is always a martyr if killed in the cause of God. Moreover, there is no sense in saying that the reverse at Uḥud was meant to take martyrs from among Muslims. Here, therefore, the word means witnesses. The Faithful bear witness to the truth of Islam by their steadfastness and by the noble example they set in times of misfortune. They are eloquent witnesses to the truth of Islam.

The word *unjust* at the end of the verse signifies that in view of the facts stated above it is unjust to find fault with Islam on the basis of such reverses.

425. Commentary :

The reverse suffered at Uḥud cleansed Muslims of their sins. It served as a sort of atonement for their sins. Moreover, the Battle of Uḥud made some disbelievers realize that Islam was God's religion. The very Meccans who took a leading part against the Muslims in that battle became ultimate y converted to Islam. Their hearts were conquered and disbelief was thereby destroyed.

426. Commentary :

It is trials and afflictions which prove the worth of man ; and there can be no advancement or spiritual purification without them.

144. And you used to wish for this death before you met it; now you have seen it while you were *actually* looking for *it*.[427]

وَلَقَدْ كُنْتُمْ تَمَنَّوْنَ الْمَوْتَ مِنْ قَبْلِ اَنْ تَلْقَوْهُ فَقَدْ رَاَيْتُمُوْهُ وَاَنْتُمْ تَنْظُرُوْنَ ۞

R. 15 145. *a*And Muhammad is only a Messenger. Verily, *all* Messengers have passed away before him. If then he die or be slain, will you turn back on your heels? *b*And he who turns back on his heels shall not harm Allah at all. And Allah will certainly reward the grateful.[428]

وَمَا مُحَمَّدٌ اِلَّا رَسُوْلٌ قَدْ خَلَتْ مِنْ قَبْلِهِ الرُّسُلُ اَفَاۡئِنْ مَّاتَ اَوْ قُتِلَ انْقَلَبْتُمْ عَلٰۤى اَعْقَابِكُمْ وَمَنْ يَّنْقَلِبْ عَلٰى عَقِبَيْهِ فَلَنْ يَّضُرَّ اللّٰهَ شَيْئًا ۣ وَسَيَجْزِى اللّٰهُ الشّٰكِرِيْنَ ۞

---

*a*5 : 76. *b*2 : 144, 218 ; 5 : 55 ; 47 : 39.

---

427. Important Words :

تَنْظُرُوْنَ (looking for) is derived from نظر which ordinarily means, he saw or he looked. نَظَرَ اليه or نَظَرَهُ means, he looked at, or he looked towards, him in order to see him; or he extended or stretched his sight towards him whether he saw him or not. نَظَرَهُ also means, he waited for him or it. دارى تَنْظُرُ دارَه means, my house faces his house (Aqrab & Lane).

Commentary :

The word مَوْت (death) here stands for war, for the result of war is death. War was death particularly for the Muslims, who were extremely weak, both in equipment and numbers compared with their powerful enemy. In Zurqānī we read that when before the Battle of Uḥud the Holy Prophet proposed to fight the enemy from inside Medina, some of his Companions, particularly those who had not taken part in the Battle of Badr, said, "We had longed for this day. So go out with us to our enemies, so that they may not think that we have played the coward" (Zurqānī, i. 22). It is to this longing of the Muslims that reference is made in the words, *you used to wish for this death.* This longing meant that the Muslims wished to achieve something

in the way of God, but God here reprimands them by saying that now they have seen that they could do nothing by themselves. This is why Islam teaches that one should never desire encounter with the enemy; but that if and when the occasion actually comes, one should be brave and steadfast. The Holy Prophet says: "Do not desire encounter with the enemy; rather ask for peace and security from Allah. But when you meet the enemy, then be steadfast and patient and know that Paradise lies under the shadow of the swords *i.e.* if you die fighting in the cause of God, He will surely grant you bliss and happiness in the life to come (Muslim, ch. on *Jihād*).

The pronoun in the words, *seen it,* refers to fighting. It signifies that you have now seen fighting and have, as a result of that, realized that without the help of God you possess no power to fight the enemy and can achieve nothing. The closing words, *while you were actually looking for it,* are intended to cheer up the spirits of believers. The reverse only brought them the thing they were actually looking for.

428. Commentary :

As already mentioned (3 : 122), the false report

was spread at Uḥud that the Holy Prophet was killed. The verse refers to this incident and purports to say that although the report about the death of the Prophet was untrue, yet even if it had been true, that should not have made the Faithful waver in their faith. Muhammad was only a Prophet ; and as other Prophets before him had died, so would he. But the God of Islam ever lives.

It is also on record that when, seven years later, the Holy Prophet died, 'Umar stood up in the Mosque at Medina with a drawn sword in his hand, and said, "Whoever will say that the Prophet of God is dead, I will cut off his head. He is not dead, but has gone to his Lord (i.e. he has ascended to heaven) even as Moses had gone to his Lord, and he would come back and punish the hypocrites." At this stage, Abū Bakr, who happened to be away at the time of the Prophet's death, hurriedly came back, went straight into the Prophet's chamber and, seeing that he was really dead, kissed his forehead, saying, "Sweet art thou in death as thou wert in life, and surely God will not bring on thee two deaths." Then he came out, strong and firm, asked 'Umar to sit down and, addressing the Companions, who were gathered in the Mosque, recited to them this very verse i.e. *Muhammad is only a Messenger ; verily all Messengers have passed away before him ; if then he die or be slain, will you turn back on your heels ?* meaning, that in the circumstances it was no wonder that the Holy Prophet also had passed away. Hearing this timely recital, 'Umar, and all others, were convinced of the death of the Holy Prophet and were overpowered with grief. Thus the verse incidentally proves that the Prophets that lived before the Holy Prophet had all died ; for if any of them had been alive, the verse could not have been quoted as proof of the Holy Prophet's death.

The verse also negatives the idea that any Prophet has risen to heaven; for it was used to falsify 'Umar's contention to the effect that the Holy Prophet was not dead but had risen to heaven. The verse thus proves, without a shadow of doubt, that Jesus too, who was one of the Prophets that had appeared before the Holy Prophet, is not physically alive in the heavens, as some present-day Muslims, following the Christian belief, erroneously think. He is certainly dead, as proved by this verse and the consensus of the Companions' opinion on the occasion of the death of the Holy Prophet.

In fact, religion does not depend on any personality. It belongs to God alone. That is why the Quran says that if the Holy Prophet dies or is killed, it will be no ground for Muslims to turn away from Islam ; for the Prophet is only a Measenger and the religion is God's. Elsewhere, however, the Quran clearly says: *And Allah will protect thee from men* (5 : 68). These two verses are not at variance with each other. What the Quran intends to emphasize in the present verse is the fundamental truth of Islamic teachings. Muslims had seen how pure and true these teachings were. Their truth was evident and they could not have become false even if the Holy Prophet had been slain. For instance, the fundamental teaching of Islam is the Unity of God. Now, this truth could not become an untruth if the Prophet were killed. But apart from this announcement in principle, the Prophet could not be killed, for God had definitely promised to protect him.

It should also be remembered that immunity from being murdered is not given in the Quran as a criterion of a Prophet's truth. People are required to accept a Prophet in his lifetime, and therefore they must have proofs of his truth in his lifetime, so that, by witnessing them, they may believe in him. They cannot wait till the time of his death in order to know whether he is a true or a false claimant.

146. And no soul can die except by Allah's leave,—a decree with a fixed term. *a*And whoever desires the reward of the present world, We will give him thereof; and whoever desires the reward of the life to come, We will give him thereof; and We will surely reward the grateful.[429]

وَمَا كَانَ لِنَفْسٍ اَنْ تَمُوْتَ اِلَّا بِاِذْنِ اللّٰهِ كِتٰبًا مُّؤَجَّلًا ؕ وَمَنْ يُّرِدْ ثَوَابَ الدُّنْيَا نُؤْتِهٖ مِنْهَا ۚ وَمَنْ يُّرِدْ ثَوَابَ الْاٰخِرَةِ نُؤْتِهٖ مِنْهَا ؕ وَسَنَجْزِى الشّٰكِرِيْنَ ﴿۱۴۶﴾

147. And many a Prophet there has been beside whom fought numerous companies *of their followers*. *b*They slackened not for aught that befell them in the way of Allah, nor did they weaken, nor did they humiliate themselves *before the enemy*. And Allah loves the steadfast.[430]

وَكَاَيِّنْ مِّنْ نَّبِيٍّ قٰتَلَ مَعَهٗ رِبِّيُّوْنَ كَثِيْرٌ ۚ فَمَا وَهَنُوْا لِمَا اَصَابَهُمْ فِيْ سَبِيْلِ اللّٰهِ وَمَا ضَعُفُوْا وَمَا اسْتَكَانُوْا ؕ وَاللّٰهُ يُحِبُّ الصّٰبِرِيْنَ ﴿۱۴۷﴾

---

*a*3 : 149 ; 4 : 135 ; 42 : 21.   *b*4 : 105.

Once a Prophet has furnished clear proofs of his truth in his lifetime, his claim is established and nothing can undo those proofs. Only if a Prophet were murdered before he had been able to give any proof of his truth could we conclude that he had proved a failure and was not a true claimant. But such a thing has never happened.

The enemy rejoiced when the report went round that the Prophet had been slain, but that supposed death of the Prophet turned out to be the veritable "life" of Islam. It fulfilled a great purpose. It prepared Muslims for the actual passing of the Holy Prophet. If this event had not occurred, the death of the Holy Prophet would have proved an unbearable trial for Muslims. In fact this painful experience brought in disguise many blessings for Islam. At the Battle of Uḥud, it brought to light the unshakable faith of the believers; at the time of his death it served to save Islam from going to pieces; and now that Islam is to all appearances dead, it is serving as a means of

breathing new life into it, by proving that Jesus, whom Christians have deified, is dead, like all other Prophets that lived before Islam.

429. Commentary :

The preceding verse spoke of the possible death of the Holy Prophet. But that was mentioned only as a matter of principle. Otherwise, how could the Holy Prophet, whom God had promised to protect, die except by His leave? Whenever death comes, it comes with the permission of God; but that permission could not be yet given in the case of the Holy Prophet. There is a fixed time for it and the enmity or the secret machinations of disbelievers could not hasten that time.

430. Important Words :

ربيون (companies of followers) is the plural of ربّى (ribbī) which is derived from رب for which see 1 : 2. ربّى means, one related to ربة *i.e.* a company or a large company or a numerous company. Thus ربيون means, those forming a large company or a large body of persons

148. And they uttered not a word except that they said : *a*'Our Lord, forgive us our errors and our excesses in our conduct, and make firm our steps and help us against the disbelieving people.'[431]

وَمَا كَانَ قَوْلَهُمْ اِلَّا اَنْ قَالُوْا رَبَّنَا اغْفِرْ لَنَا ذُنُوْبَنَا وَاِسْرَافَنَا فِيْ اَمْرِنَا وَثَبِّتْ اَقْدَامَنَا وَانْصُرْنَا عَلَى الْقَوْمِ الْكٰفِرِيْنَ ۝

149. *b*So Allah gave them the reward of this world, as also an excellent reward of the next ; and Allah loves those who do good.[432]

فَاٰتٰهُمُ اللّٰهُ ثَوَابَ الدُّنْيَا وَحُسْنَ ثَوَابِ الْاٰخِرَةِ ؕ وَاللّٰهُ يُحِبُّ الْمُحْسِنِيْنَ ۝

150. *c*O ye who believe ! if you obey those who have disbelieved, they will cause you to turn back on your heels, and you will become losers.[433]

يٰۤاَيُّهَا الَّذِيْنَ اٰمَنُوْۤا اِنْ تُطِيْعُوا الَّذِيْنَ كَفَرُوْا يَرُدُّوْكُمْ عَلٰۤى اَعْقَابِكُمْ فَتَنْقَلِبُوْا خٰسِرِيْنَ ۝

---

*a*2 : 251, 287.   *b*3 : 146.   *c*2 : 110 ; 3 : 101.

---

i.e. followers (Aqrab). It also signifies learned, pious and patient men (Lane).

اِسْتَكَانُوْا (did humiliate themselves) is derived from سكن which means, he or it became still or stationary ; or the word is derived from كان which means, he or it came into existence ; or he or it was in a certain condition. اِسْتَكَانَ means, he was or became lowly, humble, humiliated, or in a state of abasement (Aqrab).

Commentary :

The verse exhorts believers to profit by the good example set by their righteous predecessors. The latter were not found lacking in preparations for fighting in the cause of Allah nor were they slack in actual fighting or wanting in steadfastness.

431. Commentary :

Each part of the prayer contained in this verse corresponds to the points mentioned in the previous one. In fact, success comes only by the help and grace of God. Human effort alone is not enough.

It should, however, be noted that, corresponding to the last part of the prayer in this verse, there is mentioned no corresponding effort on the part of believers in the preceding verse, thus indicating that final victory and success come solely through the grace of God and are not the result of our actions.

432. Commentary :

The rewards of the next life are of various degrees, and such believers as have been described above will get the best of them. The word حسن rendered as "excellent" does not necessarily indicate superlative degree but is also used to express an intensified sense absolutely.

433. Commentary :

It should be noted that Muslims are not enjoined here to have no dealings with non-Muslims ; they are only warned against following such disbelievers as are enemies of Islam. They should remain on the alert against these, though they need not fear them, because God is on their side, as pointed out in the next verse.

151. Nay, ^aAllah is your Protector, and He is the best of helpers.

بَلِ اللهُ مَوْلٰىكُمْ ۚ وَهُوَ خَيْرُ النّٰصِرِيْنَ ۝

152. ^bWe shall strike terror into the hearts of those that have disbelieved because they associate partners with Allah, for which He has sent down no authority. Their abode is the Fire; and evil is the habitation of the wrongdoers.⁴³⁴

سَنُلْقِيْ فِيْ قُلُوْبِ الَّذِيْنَ كَفَرُوا الرُّعْبَ بِمَاۤ اَشْرَكُوْا بِاللهِ مَا لَمْ يُنَزِّلْ بِهٖ سُلْطٰنًا ۚ وَمَأْوٰىهُمُ النَّارُ ۚ وَبِئْسَ مَثْوَى الظّٰلِمِيْنَ ۝

153. And Allah had surely made good to you His promise when you were slaying and destroying them by His leave, until, when you became lax and disagreed among yourselves concerning the order and you disobeyed after He had shown you that which you loved, *He withdrew His help.* Among you were those who desired the present world, and among you were those who desired the next. Then He turned you away from them, that He might try you—and He has surely pardoned you, and Allah is Gracious to the believers—⁴³⁵

وَلَقَدْ صَدَقَكُمُ اللهُ وَعْدَهٗۤ اِذْ تَحُسُّوْنَهُمْ بِاِذْنِهٖ ۚ حَتّٰۤى اِذَا فَشِلْتُمْ وَتَنَازَعْتُمْ فِى الْاَمْرِ وَعَصَيْتُمْ مِّنْ بَعْدِ مَاۤ اَرٰىكُمْ مَّا تُحِبُّوْنَ ۚ مِنْكُمْ مَّنْ يُّرِيْدُ الدُّنْيَا وَمِنْكُمْ مَّنْ يُّرِيْدُ الْاٰخِرَةَ ۚ ثُمَّ صَرَفَكُمْ عَنْهُمْ لِيَبْتَلِيَكُمْ ۚ وَلَقَدْ عَفَا عَنْكُمْ ۚ وَاللهُ ذُوْ فَضْلٍ عَلَى الْمُؤْمِنِيْنَ ۝

^a8:41; 9:51; 22:79. ^b8:13; 59:3.

---

434. Commentary:

The words, *because they associate partners with Allah*, signify that he who associates gods with God can never be truly brave, for he lacks complete devotion to any one. It is only complete devotion that can inspire a person to make sacrifices. As a believer is completely devoted to the One God, therefore, he is ever ready to make every kind of sacrifice in His cause.

Moreover, it is through lack of perseverance that idolaters go from one god to another, and perseverance is an essential concomitant of bravery. Where there is no perseverance, there is no bravery. Again, idolaters are rebels in setting up gods with God, and a rebel's

heart is never at rest; and a heart that is not at ease cannot be brave. Yet again, polytheism springs from superstitious fear and one possessed of that sort of fear can never be truly brave.

It should, however, be remembered that it is only relative bravery that is meant here; otherwise even among idolaters and polytheists, there are men who possess bravery and courage, but their courage and bravery is inferior to that of true believers who put faith in One God and believe in His great powers and in the life after death.

435. Commentary:

The word "promise" occurring in the verse refers to the general promise of victory

154. When you were running away and looked not back at anyone while the Messenger was calling out to you from your rear, then He gave you a sorrow in recompense for a sorrow, *that you might not grieve for what escaped you, nor for what befell you. And Allah is well aware of what you do.[436]

اِذْ تُصْعِدُوْنَ وَلَا تَلْوٗنَ عَلٰۤى اَحَدٍ وَّالرَّسُوْلُ يَدْعُوْكُمْ فِيْۤ اُخْرٰىكُمْ فَاَثَابَكُمْ غَمًّۢا بِغَمٍّ لِّكَيْلَا تَحْزَنُوْا عَلٰى مَا فَاتَكُمْ وَلَا مَاۤ اَصَابَكُمْ ۖ وَاللّٰهُ خَبِيْرٌۢ بِمَا تَعْمَلُوْنَ ۟۵۲

*57 : 24.

---

and success repeatedly given to Muslims.

The clause, *when you became lax*, refers to the party of archers posted at the rear of the Muslim army at Uḥud, and signifies that they could not resist the temptation of taking part in the actual fighting and in collecting the booty, and their failure to control that desire was an act of cowardice on their part. It is indeed the heart which is the seat of true bravery and courage. Says the Holy Prophet: "Strong is not he who overthrows his rival in a wrestling match, but strong is he who controls himself in times of anger" (Bukhārī ch. on *Adab*). The word, *order*, in the clause, *you disagreed among yourselves concerning the order*, may refer either to the order of the Holy Prophet given to the party of archers not to leave their station without his permission or to the import of the order *i.e.* whether the Holy Prophet really meant them to stay there even after the battle had been won, some saying that he did mean that and others alleging that he did not.

The words, *you disobeyed*, signify that they paid no heed to their leader, 'Abdullah bin Jubair, who, in compliance with the order of the Prophet, directed them not to quit the place, in spite of the fact that victory was within sight. They could not control themselves and so brought misfortune on the Muslims.

The words, *those who desired the present world*

etc., refer to the party that quitted the place at which they had been stationed. The Arabic clause may also be rendered as meaning that some members of the party desired the nearer thing *i.e.* taking part in fighting and collecting the booty, while others (*viz.* 'Abdullah bin Jubair and those of his comrades who did not quit their post) desired what was farther off *i.e.* they thought of the ultimate consequence of disobeying the command of the Holy Prophet. Some were short-sighted, while others were far-sighted.

The words, *He turned you away from them*, signify that God imposed the reverse in order to make this incident a lesson for the future.

436. Important Words:

تُصْعِدُوْنَ (you were running away) is derived from اَصْعَدَ which again is derived from صَعِدَ which primarily means, he ascended or climbed a height, etc. اَصْعَدَ فِى الارض means, he went from a low piece of land to one that is high, both physically and figuratively; or adversely, he descended or went down into the land. اَصْعَدَ فِى العدو means, he exerted himself in running. اَصْعَدَ also means, he went forth or went away in any direction (Lane).

اَثَابَ (gave in recompense) is from the same root as ثَوَاب and مَثُوبَة and مَثَابَة and means, he gave in reward or recompense or return; or he gave as a substitute (Aqrab). See also 2 : 104 and 2 : 126.

Commentary :

The words, *When you were running away and looked not back at anyone,* refer to the incident which happened when in the Battle of Uḥud the Muslims were attacked from both the rear and the front and their ranks were broken and many of them were fleeing in different directions. At first, when the Muslims heard that the enemy was coming from behind, they turned back to attack the enemy, but it so happened that a large body of Muslims was also coming from the rear at that time. In the confusion of the hour, these were mistaken for the enemy and attacked. Such was the confusion and the panic that even the voice of the Holy Prophet was not heeded.

The words, *gave you a sorrow in recompense for a sorrow,* refer to the report of the Holy Prophet's death in the Battle of Uḥud. Thus the first-mentioned "sorrow", which was later in occurring, refers to the false report of the Holy Prophet's death and the second-mentioned "sorrow", which was first in occurring, refers to the sorrow that the Companions of the Holy Prophet—the archers stationed at the back—caused him by having failed faithfully to follow his order. One sorrow came in recompense of the other. The report of the Holy Prophet's death referred to above spread when a Muslim, named Muṣ'ab bin 'Umair, the Companion who carried the flag, was killed, being mistaken for the Holy Prophet. The second-mentioned "sorrow" does not obviously refer to the wounds received by the Holy Prophet, for the wounds were received not before but after the archers left their station and after the above-mentioned erroneous report about the death of the Holy Prophet.

The sorrow which certain Muslims caused the Holy Prophet by paying no heed to his voice when at the ensuing disorder he called out to them from the rear, was

also recompensed. When the Muslims did not pay heed to the call of the Prophet, God caused them to think for a while that he was dead, which was to them a punishment similar to their offence. If they did not pay heed to the voice of the divine Messenger, of what use to them was his existence in this world ? Thus when they heard of the reported death of the Holy Prophet, their thoughts naturally and immediately turned to the great benefits which they had received and were receiving through him and they were at once made to realize not only the greatness of his rank but also the magnitude of their own mistake.

The Arabic words غَمًّا بِغَمٍّ rendered as, *a sorrow in recompense for a sorrow,* may also be rendered as " a sorrow in addition to another sorrow " *i.e.* one sorrow coming after another. In that case, the words would mean that God so designed that the sorrow pertaining to the unfounded report of the Holy Prophet's death should come immediately after the sorrow of a reverse so that the latter sorrow, which later proved to be unfounded, should obliterate the effect of the former sorrow, thus effacing the harmful effects of the defeat.

The clause, *what escaped you,* refers to victory which the Muslims lost after they had almost gained it. So great was the joy of the Muslims at the safety of the Holy Prophet that they actually forgot their sorrow at the loss of victory. Similarly, the clause, *what befell you,* refers to the loss of their men in the battle-field. The Muslims lost 70 killed, while the Meccans lost only about 20. The words may also refer to the wounds received by the Muslims on that occasion.

The words, *that you might not grieve,* may also signify that, having received some punishment then and there for the offence committed, the Muslims might feel secure from punishment in the Hereafter.

155. Then after the sorrow, [a]He sent down peace on you—a slumber that overcame a party of you, while the other party was anxious concerning their own selves, thinking wrongly of Allah *like unto* the thought of ignorance. They said, ' Is there for us any part in the government *of affairs?* ' Say, ' All government belongs to Allah.' They hide in their minds what they disclose not to thee. They say, [b]'If we had any part in the government *of affairs,* we should not have been killed here.' Say, ' If you had remained in your homes, surely those on whom fighting had been enjoined would have gone forth to their death-beds,' *that Allah might bring about His decree* and that Allah might test what was in your breasts and that He might purge what was in your hearts. And Allah knows well what is in the minds;[437]

ثُمَّ اَنْزَلَ عَلَيْكُمْ مِّنْ بَعْدِ الْغَمِّ اَمَنَةً نُّعَاسًا يَّغْشٰى طَآئِفَةً مِّنْكُمْ وَطَآئِفَةٌ قَدْ اَهَمَّتْهُمْ اَنْفُسُهُمْ يَظُنُّوْنَ بِاللّٰهِ غَيْرَ الْحَقِّ ظَنَّ الْجَاهِلِيَّةِ يَقُوْلُوْنَ هَلْ لَّنَا مِنَ الْاَمْرِ مِنْ شَيْءٍ قُلْ اِنَّ الْاَمْرَ كُلَّهٗ لِلّٰهِ يُخْفُوْنَ فِيْ اَنْفُسِهِمْ مَّا لَا يُبْدُوْنَ لَكَ يَقُوْلُوْنَ لَوْ كَانَ لَنَا مِنَ الْاَمْرِ شَيْءٌ مَّا قُتِلْنَا هٰهُنَا قُلْ لَّوْ كُنْتُمْ فِيْ بُيُوْتِكُمْ لَبَرَزَ الَّذِيْنَ كُتِبَ عَلَيْهِمُ الْقَتْلُ اِلٰى مَضَاجِعِهِمْ وَلِيَبْتَلِىَ اللّٰهُ مَا فِيْ صُدُوْرِكُمْ وَلِيُمَحِّصَ مَا فِيْ قُلُوْبِكُمْ وَاللّٰهُ عَلِيْمٌ بِذَاتِ الصُّدُوْرِ ۝

---

[a]8 : 12.   [b]3 : 169.

---

437. Important Words :

امر (government) means: (1) order or command; (2) matter or affair; (3) state or condition; (4) authority, government or management. اولوا الامر means, those who hold command or exercise authority (Aqrab). قتل (fighting) being noun-infinitive means both to kill and to be killed. Another reading of the word قتل here is قاتل (Muḥīṭ, iii. 90 & Kashshāf) which shows that the word قتل (qatl) has been used here in the sense of fighting and not killing. The word قتل has been used elsewhere also in the Quran in the sense of fighting (see 2 : 192). See also Jarīr under 3 : 155.

Commentary :

The words, *a slumber that overcame a party of you,* refer to an incident connected with the Battle of Uḥud. Abū Ṭalḥa says, " I lifted my head on the day of Uḥud and began to look about, and there was none among us on that day but was bending down his head with slumber." This incident has been narrated by Tirmidhī, Nasaī and others (see Kathīr, ii. 303). As sleep or slumber is a symbol of peaceful condition, being a sign of hearts that are calm and at rest, the Quran refers to this incident as a sort of favour. The incident evidently occurred when the battle was practically over and the Muslims had returned to the neighbouring height.

The reference in the words, *the other party,* is to the hypocrites who were at Medina and who had not taken part in the battle. When they heard of the reverse which overtook the Muslims and of the reported death of the

Holy Prophet, they, in spite of rejoicing at the misfortune that had befallen the Muslims, became anxious about their own lives and feared what would happen to them in case the Meccans should attack Medina. The words cannot apply to the party of Muslims that took part in the battle, of whom the Quran says, *He has surely pardoned you and Allah is Gracious to the believers* (3 : 153 above).

The words, *Is there for us any part in the government of affairs?*, uttered by the hypocrites mean, "nobody listens to our opinion in matters of administration; we had advised the Muslims not to go out of Medina to fight, but our advice was ignored, with the result that they were defeated". The sentence might also mean, "now (*i.e.* after this reverse) real government and power have gone into the hands of the idolaters and nothing has been left for us."

The words, *All government belongs to Allah*, signify that the decision in all matters rests with God; or that whatever might happen in the intervening period God has ordained that eventually power and government shall be vouchsafed to Muslims, who will have dominion in the land.

The words, *we should not have been killed here*, mean, "If we had any voice in the management of affairs and if our advice had been accepted, our brethren would not have been killed in battle," it being insinuated that while they were wise, the Muslims were simply foolish. The words may also be understood to mean, "if we were to have any government (as the Prophet had promised), we should not have been defeated in the battle." By saying so the hypocrites hinted that the prophecies of the Holy Prophet regarding the triumph of Islam had turned out to be false.

It may be noted here that by saying, *we should not have been killed here*, the hypocrites did not evidently mean that they themselves would not have been killed. What they meant was that their brethren or comrades who were killed would not have been killed. This shows that by the slaying of one's self is sometimes meant the slaying of one's brethren or companions. This explains the words اقتلوا انفسكم in 2 : 55, and تقتلون انفسكم in 2 : 86. See also note on 2 : 55.

The divine words, *If you had remained in your homes*, refer to the hypocrites; and by the words, *those on whom fighting had been enjoined*, are meant the true believers. The injunction referred to is contained in 2 : 191.

In the clause, *would have gone forth to their death-beds*, the word مضاجع (death-beds) has been used in order to point to the abject cowardice of the hypocrites on the one hand, and the steadfast devotion of the true believers on the other. It reminds the hypocrites that whereas they returned to Medina, thinking that fighting in the existing circumstances was sure death, such was the faith of the true believers that even if the hypocrites had kept back from the very beginning they would have cheerfully gone forth to the battle-field, or the place of death, as it was commonly thought to be. All this happened that God might purify and ennoble the Faithful.

156. Those of you who turned their backs on the day when the two hosts met, surely it was Satan who sought to make them slip because of certain doings of theirs. But certainly Allah has already pardoned them. Verily Allah is Most Forgiving, Forbearing.[438]

اِنَّ الَّذِیۡنَ تَوَلَّوۡا مِنۡکُمۡ یَوۡمَ الۡتَقَی الۡجَمۡعٰنِ ۙ اِنَّمَا اسۡتَزَلَّهُمُ الشَّیۡطٰنُ بِبَعۡضِ مَا کَسَبُوۡا ۚ وَلَقَدۡ عَفَا اللّٰهُ عَنۡهُمۡ ؕ اِنَّ اللّٰهَ غَفُوۡرٌ حَلِیۡمٌ ﴿۱۵۵﴾

7 157. O ye who believe! be not like those who have disbelieved, and who say of their brethren when they travel in the land or go forth to war: ' Had they been with us, they would not have died or been slain :' *This is so*, that Allah may make it a cause of regret in their hearts. And Allah gives life and causes death and Allah is Mindful of what you do.[439]

یٰۤاَیُّهَا الَّذِیۡنَ اٰمَنُوۡا لَا تَکُوۡنُوۡا کَالَّذِیۡنَ کَفَرُوۡا وَقَالُوۡا لِاِخۡوَانِهِمۡ اِذَا ضَرَبُوۡا فِی الۡاَرۡضِ اَوۡ کَانُوۡا غُزًّی ۚ لَّوۡ کَانُوۡا عِنۡدَنَا مَا مَاتُوۡا وَمَا قُتِلُوۡا ۚ لِیَجۡعَلَ اللّٰهُ ذٰلِکَ حَسۡرَةً فِیۡ قُلُوۡبِهِمۡ ؕ وَاللّٰهُ یُحۡیٖ وَیُمِیۡتُ ؕ وَاللّٰهُ بِمَا تَعۡمَلُوۡنَ بَصِیۡرٌ ﴿۱۵۶﴾

438. Commentary :

The "slipping" spoken of in the verse refers to the disobeying of the order given to the party stationed on the hill at the back of the main body of the Faithful. It may also refer to the running away of some Muslims from the battle-field. But God, out of His great mercy, and considering all the attending circumstances, pardoned them all.

The words, *because of certain doings of theirs*, contain an implied praise. These men were truly righteous people. It was only " some" of their misdeeds that brought them this temporary disgrace. All their doings were not bad ; only some were bad. The words also embody a warning that a true believer should not rest satisfied even if most of his deeds are righteous. He is never quite out of danger unless all of his deeds are good. He can, however, hope for forgiveness, if he manages to make the majority of his deeds good.

439. Commentary :

The expression, *when they travel in the land,* means, when they travel in the land in the cause of God. This meaning is supported by the context.

The idea contained in the words, *so that Allah may make it a cause of regret in their hearts,* is that when Muslims refused to act upon the advice of disbelievers not to fight, and instead, came forth in large numbers to fight in the way of God, the disbelievers were naturally grieved at their failure to win them over to their way of thinking.

The interpretation of the clause, *and Allah gives life and causes death*, would vary according to the different meanings of the words موت (death) and حیاة (life) occurring in it. If the death referred to in the verse is taken in the sense of destruction, the clause would mean that with the death of a few Muslims, Islam would not go to ruin. God has decreed to vouchsafe victory to Muslims and the death in fighting of a number of the victorious army cannot possibly result in their destruction. If, however, death

158. And if you are slain in the cause of Allah or you die, ^asurely forgiveness from Allah and mercy shall be better than what they hoard.⁴⁴⁰

159. And if you die or be slain, ^bsurely unto Allah shall you be gathered together.⁴⁴¹

160. And it is by the great mercy of Allah that thou art kind towards them, and if thou hadst been rough *and* hard-hearted, they would surely have dispersed from around thee. So pardon them and ask forgiveness for them, and ^cconsult them in matters of administration; and when thou art determined, then put thy trust in Allah. Surely, Allah loves those who put their trust in Him.⁴⁴²

وَلَئِنْ قُتِلْتُمْ فِيْ سَبِيْلِ اللّٰهِ اَوْ مُتُّمْ لَمَغْفِرَةٌ مِّنَ اللّٰهِ وَرَحْمَةٌ خَيْرٌ مِّمَّا يَجْمَعُوْنَ ۞

وَلَئِنْ مُّتُّمْ اَوْ قُتِلْتُمْ لَاِلَى اللّٰهِ تُحْشَرُوْنَ ۞

فَبِمَا رَحْمَةٍ مِّنَ اللّٰهِ لِنْتَ لَهُمْ وَلَوْ كُنْتَ فَظًّا غَلِيْظَ الْقَلْبِ لَانْفَضُّوْا مِنْ حَوْلِكَ فَاعْفُ عَنْهُمْ وَاسْتَغْفِرْ لَهُمْ وَشَاوِرْهُمْ فِى الْاَمْرِ فَاِذَا عَزَمْتَ فَتَوَكَّلْ عَلَى اللّٰهِ اِنَّ اللّٰهَ يُحِبُّ الْمُتَوَكِّلِيْنَ ۞

---

^a10 : 59 ; 43 : 33.　　^b5 : 97 ; 6 : 73 ; 8 : 25 ; 23 : 80.　　^c42 : 39.

is here taken to mean "disgrace" then the clause would mean that God's votaries and true servants never meet with disgrace, because all honour is in His hands and He gives it to whomsoever He pleases. Truly speaking, he who fights and lays down his life in the cause of truth can in no sense be regarded as dead, because such a one gives his life for the sake of Him Who is the controller of all life and death. Such a person can never die ; for though physically he may die, spiritually he lives for ever. In this connection see also 2 : 155.

440. Commentary :

The words, *forgiveness from Allah and mercy shall be better than what they hoard,* mean that hypocrites are afraid of death because of the wealth and property which they have to leave behind ; whereas, if believers are killed in the cause of Allah, they will get what is incomparably greater than what hypocrites are greedily

hoarding up, or what Muslims themselves may have collected in the form of wealth and other worldly things. There is thus no reason for true believers to be afraid of death.

441. Commentary :

The pronoun "you" includes both hypocrites and believers ; for all will be gathered unto God for reward or punishment, as the case may be.

442. Important Words :

شَاوِرْ (consult) is derived from شور which means, he gathered or extracted honey from the comb, and separated it from the wax شار الدابة means, he rode the beast in order to ascertain its true worth. اشار اليه means he pointed towards him or it. شار عليه means, he gave him advice ; he offered him counsel. شاوره means, he consulted him he sought his opinion or advice ; he discussed with him in order to find out his opinion. مشورة means, good counsel o consultation. شورى means, mutual consultation (Aqrab).

فتوكّل (then put thy trust). For the meaning of توكّل see 3 : 123.

Commentary :

The verse gives an insight into the beautiful character of the Holy Prophet, of which the most effable and prominent trait was his all-comprehensive mercy. He was full of the milk of human kindness and was not only kind towards his Companions and followers but was also full of mercy for his enemies who were always on the look-out to stab him in the back. It is on record that he took no action even against those treacherous hypocrites who had deserted him in the Battle of Uḥud. He even consulted them in affairs of State.

The verse also constitutes an effective answer to the charge of the hypocrites that the Holy Prophet attached no importance to their advice and did what he liked. The Quran refutes this charge by saying that if the Holy Prophet had not been kind and gentle towards them, they would have left him long ago. Thus their continuing to remain with him falsified their accusation and proved that the Prophet's treatment of them was very kind and that in conformity with the divine command (see also 42 : 39) he used to consult them regarding affairs of State, with the result that many of them afterwards repented of their deeds and became sincere Muslims. The injunction about consultation contained in the present verse, although general in application, refers to the hypocrites of Medina in particular.

It may be noted that Islam stands alone in including the institution of مشورة (consultation) among its fundamental principles. It lays down as a rule that both the Prophet and his Successors should, whenever necessary, consult their followers in important affairs of State. A religion claiming to be universal is bound to contain such a teaching; for persons of different classes and different communities continue to enter its fold, and if these are consulted in matters of moment, it is calculated not only to add to their experience and practical wisdom, but also to increase and keep alive their interest in affairs of State. This is why the Holy Prophet used to consult his followers in all important matters, as he did before the Battles of Badr, Uḥud, and Aḥzāb, and also when a false accusation was brought against his wife, 'Ā'isha. Baihaqī reports : " Certainly Allah and His Messenger did not stand in need of the advice of anybody, but God has made it (the seeking of advice) a source of mercy for men. Those who hold consultation will not stray away from the path of rectitude, while those who do not are liable to do so." Abū Huraira says : " The Holy Prophet was most solicitous in consulting others in all matters of importance " (Manthūr, ii. 90).

'Umar, the Second Successor of the Holy Prophet, is reported to have said : لا خلافة الا بالمشورة i.e. " There is no Khilāfat without consultation " (Izālat al-Khifā 'an Khilāfat al-Khulafā). Thus the holding of consultation in matters of consequence is an important injunction of Islam and is binding on both spiritual and temporal Chiefs, though they are not bound to accept that consultation, as the words, when thou art determined, then put thy trust in Allah, show. The Khalīfa must seek the advice of leading Muslims, but the final decision always rests with him. He is not bound to accept in full or in part the advice tendered to him by a majority of them. This view has ever been held by the main body of Muslims throughout the centuries and finds ample support in the sayings of the Holy Prophet as well as in his practice and in that of his Rightly-guided Successors.

The objection, that if the Khalīfa is not

bound to act upon the advice of the majority, what is the use of his seeking advice, or of others offering it, is unwise and beside the point. The verse gives to the *Khalīfa* the right to reject advice if he is convinced that it is in the interest of religion or the community to do so. Normally, he respects the views of the majority, but the Islamic شورى or مشاورة (*Shūra* or *Mushāwarat*) is not a parliament in the sense in which the word is generally understood in the West. Islam enjoins only consultation and not decision by votes, which are two different things. Consultation is meant to help the *Khalīfa* to know the views of his followers and to enable him to respect them as far as possible. It is not at all intended to tie his hands. It is on record that the Holy Prophet rejected the advice of the majority of his followers on certain occasions, and on others he even refused to accept their unanimous opinion. For instance, regarding the treatment of the prisoners of Badr he accepted the advice of Abū Bakr and rejected that of 'Umar, 'Abdullah bin Rawāha and Sa'd bin Mu'ādh (Musnad, i. 283). At Ḥudaibiya, he signed the treaty in clear opposition to the advice of his Companions (Bukhārī, ch. on *Shurūṭ.*) Similarly, Abū Bakr discarded the almost unanimous advice of the Muslims by sending the expedition to Syria under Usāma, immediately after the death of the Holy Prophet (Athīr, ii. 139). In contrast to this, it is also on record that the Holy Prophet sometimes sacrificed his own view to that of his followers as he did in marching out of Medina for the Battle of Uḥud.

The context of the verse, however, shows that here the injunction was primarily meant with regard to the hypocrites, and nobody could say that the Holy Prophet was bound to do what the hypocrites advised him.

The advantages of consultation are : (1) The *Khalīfa* or the *Amīr* comes to know the views of his followers. (2) He is helped in arriving at a correct decision. (3) Representative Muslims get an opportunity to think about, and take personal interest in, important State affairs, thus receiving most useful training in matters of administration. (4) The *Khalīfa* is enabled to judge the mental and administrative capabilities of different individuals, which help him to assign the right work to the right man. (5) It enables him to know the aptitudes, aspirations and tendencies as well as the moral and spiritual condition of the different members of his community, and thus he becomes able to effect an improvement, wherever necessary, in his people.

The meaning of expressions like, *put thy trust in Allah*, is generally misunderstood. In the language of the Quran توكل (trusting in God) does not consist in disregarding the material means of doing a thing. On the contrary, توكل as taught by Islam means that a person should first make use of all the resources at his command and then place his trust in God to bless his efforts with success, believing all the time that the means can be successful only if and when God wills it and that the true cause and the real source of all success is God alone.

The words, *put thy trust in Allah*, as used in the present context, also hint that if the Prophet or the *Khalīfa* were to be bound to accept the counsel of his followers, it would be against the spirit of توكل (trusting in God). In fact, one who is bound to act in accordance with the advice of another cannot be said to be trusting in God so far as acting on that advice is concerned.

161. If Allah help you, none shall overcome you ; but if He forsake you, then who is there that can help you beside Him ? In Allah, then, let the believers put their trust.[443]

اِنْ یَّنْصُرْکُمُ اللّٰہُ فَلَا غَالِبَ لَکُمْ ۚ وَاِنْ یَّخْذُلْکُمْ فَمَنْ ذَا الَّذِیْ یَنْصُرُکُمْ مِّنْ بَعْدِہٖ ؕ وَعَلَی اللّٰہِ فَلْیَتَوَکَّلِ الْمُؤْمِنُوْنَ ۝

162. And it is not possible for a Prophet to act dishonestly, and whoever acts dishonestly shall bring with him that about which he has been dishonest on the Day of Resurrection. [a]Then shall every soul be fully paid what it has earned ; and they shall not be wronged.[444]

وَمَا کَانَ لِنَبِیٍّ اَنْ یَّغُلَّ ؕ وَمَنْ یَّغْلُلْ یَاْتِ بِمَا غَلَّ یَوْمَ الْقِیٰمَۃِ ۚ ثُمَّ تُوَفّٰی کُلُّ نَفْسٍ مَّا کَسَبَتْ وَہُمْ لَا یُظْلَمُوْنَ ۝

---

[a]3 : 26 ; 14 : 52 ; 40 : 18.

---

443. Commentary :

The words من بعده translated as, *beside Him*, literally mean " after Him " and may also be rendered as " in opposition to Him ". The verse throws further light on the philosophy of توکل (trusting in God). In spite of making use of the necessary means, a true believer should, and in fact does, put his trust in God alone.

444. Commentary :

The verse can be interpreted in two ways. The archers stationed by the Holy Prophet at the mount of Uḥud to protect the rear of the Muslim army left their post when they saw the Meccan army in full flight. They thought that by leaving the mount at that stage they would not be contravening the spirit of the Prophet's orders, which were to the effect that they were not to leave their post in any circumstances. They further thought that as, according to Arab custom, a soldier was entitled to the possession of the booty he laid his hand on during the fight, they might be deprived of

their share of the spoils of war if they stuck to their post. This precipitate action of the archers implied an apprehension on their part that the Prophet might ignore their right to the booty and might thus prove faithless to them. It is this apprehension that the verse condemns in the words, *And it is not possible for a Prophet to act dishonestly*. But no imputation of actual faithlessness to the Holy Prophet is implied. The verse simply purports to say that it was far from the Prophet to ignore the rights to the booty of those whom he himself had stationed at a certain place.

The verse may also be taken as a rebuke to the hypocrites who deserted the Holy Prophet in the Battle of Uḥud. In this case, the implication would be that while the hypocrites had proved faithless to the Prophet by leaving him in the lurch, the Prophet would not prove faithless to God by refusing to fight in His cause even when weak and deserted. This meaning is also supported by the context.

163. ^aIs he who follows the pleasure of Allah like him who draws on himself the wrath of Allah and whose abode is Hell ? And an evil retreat it is !⁴⁴⁵

164. They have *different* grades *of grace* with Allah ; and Allah sees what they do.⁴⁴⁶

165. Verily, Allah has conferred a favour on the believers by ^braising among them a Messenger from among themselves who recites to them His Signs, and purifies them and teaches them the Book and Wisdom ; and, before that, they were surely in manifest error.⁴⁴⁷

---

^a2 : 208, 266 ; 3 : 16 ; 5 : 3, 17 ; 9 : 72.   ^b2 : 130, 152 ; 9 : 128 ; 62 : 3 ; 65 : 12.

---

445. Commentary :

The words, *who follows the pleasure of Allah*, apply to the Holy Prophet and his true followers who, undaunted by the defection of the hypocrites at Uḥud, which considerably weakened their ranks, proceeded to fight the enemies of Islam. The hypocrites, on the other hand, by their act of desertion, drew upon themselves the wrath of God. They turned away from the fire of war, but a much worse fire awaited them in Hell. They retreated from the battle-field in order to seek security, but their retreat proved to be the gate of Gehenna for them.

The expression كمن باء بسخط من الله rendered as, *like him who draws on himself the wrath of Allah*, may also be translated as "like him who turns (or returns) with the wrath of Allah." The latter rendering would help further to clarify the explanation given above.

446. Commentary :

The words هم درجات literally mean, they are

different grades. Actually, however, they mean, they are the possessors of different grades of grace, the word اولوا (possessors) being understood before the word درجات. The word اولوا has been dropped to intensify the meaning, as if the holders of these grades of grace were the very grades personified.

447. Commentary :

The expression, *by raising among them a Messenger from among themselves*, is intended to awaken in the hearts of Muslims a desire to follow the example of the Holy Prophet, who was like them and one of them. The Prophet was not only a man like them but was actually one of them. If he could rise to such spiritual heights, why could not they ?

All Messengers of God are raised from among human beings and they possess the same faculties and are actuated by the same desires and aspirations as other human beings, and therefore they can serve as true models for their fellow-beings. But a so-called "son of

166. What! ^awhen a misfortune befalls you—and you had inflicted the double of that—you say, whence is this? Say, It is from your own selves. Surely, Allah has power over all things.[448]

اَوَلَمَّاۤ اَصَابَتۡكُمۡ مُّصِيۡبَةٌ قَدۡ اَصَبۡتُمۡ مِّثۡلَيۡهَا ۙ قُلۡتُمۡ اَنّٰى هٰذَا ؕ قُلۡ هُوَ مِنۡ عِنۡدِ اَنۡفُسِكُمۡ ؕ اِنَّ اللّٰهَ عَلٰى كُلِّ شَىۡءٍ قَدِيۡرٌ ۝

---

^a4 : 80.

God" does not possess the same desires and the same faculties as we have, and cannot therefore be a model for us. Our model should be from our own kind. He who is not of our kind, being a divine being, free from human passions and human weaknesses, cannot be held out to us as a model for imitation.

The verse also points to the fulfilment of the prayer of Abraham contained in 2 : 130 in which the different functions of the Promised Prophet have been mentioned just as they are mentioned here.

448. Commentary :

The words, and you had inflicted the double of that, refer to the Battle of Badr, wher 70 Meccans were killed and 70 taken captive. At Uḥud, 70 Muslims were killed, none being taken prisoner. Thus the Muslims had inflicted a double loss on the Meccans.

The fact that no Muslim was taken prisoner at Uḥud demonstrates their high sense of honour. They preferred death to dishonour. They would die fighting rather than lay down their arms. Some of them were found killed on the battle-field with as many as eighty wounds on their bodies. How could such men allow themselves to be taken prisoner by the enemy? It is most significant that in all the different battles that were fought by Muslims till the time of 'Uthmān—and they were many, and hundreds of thousands of men took part in them—the number of Muslim prisoners did not exceed a few hundred.

The expression, It is from your own selves, seems to contradict the succeeding verse where it is said, And that which befell you on the day when two parties met was by Allah's command, and also 4 : 79, 80 where it is said: And if some good befalls them, they say, ' this, is from Allah' and if evil befall them, they say, ' this is from thee'. Say, All is from Allah. What has happened to these people that they come not near understanding anything? Whatever of good comes to thee is from Allah, and whatever of evil befalls thee is from thyself. On a deeper reflection, however, no conflict or contradiction is found to exist ; for the different statements, apparently contradictory, have been made from different view-points. As for the real cause of man's actions, both the good and evil actions are said to emanate from him, because he is their doer; but as it is God Who, as the final Judge, brings about the results of man's actions, whether good or bad, they can equally be said to proceed from Him. In this sense, both the good and evil results of man's actions would be attributed to God. Again, as God has created all things for our good and it is through their misuse that we suffer, therefore the evil that befalls us can legitimately be said to proceed from our ownselves. But when that evil is removed by the right use of the things provided by God and good results ensue, then that good must be attributed to God, for it is He Who has endowed things with the properties by the right use of which we benefit. In this sense good results will be attributed to God and

167. And that which befell you, on the day when the two parties met, was by Allah's command; and *this was so* that He might distinguish the believers;[449]

وَمَاۤ اَصَابَكُمۡ يَوۡمَ الۡتَقَى الۡجَمۡعٰنِ فَبِاِذۡنِ اللّٰهِ وَلِيَعۡلَمَ الۡمُؤۡمِنِيۡنَ ۝

168. And that He might distinguish the hypocrites. And it was said to them, 'Come ye, fight in the cause of Allah and repel *the attack of the enemy*;' they said, 'If we knew how to fight, we would surely follow you.' They were, that day, nearer to disbelief than to belief. [a]They say with their mouths what is not in their hearts. And Allah knows well what they conceal.[450]

وَلِيَعۡلَمَ الَّذِيۡنَ نَافَقُوۡا ۚ وَقِيۡلَ لَهُمۡ تَعَالَوۡا قَاتِلُوۡا فِىۡ سَبِيۡلِ اللّٰهِ اَوِ ادۡفَعُوۡا ۚ قَالُوۡا لَوۡ نَعۡلَمُ قِتَالًا لَّاتَّبَعۡنٰكُمۡ ۚ هُمۡ لِلۡكُفۡرِ يَوۡمَئِذٍ اَقۡرَبُ مِنۡهُمۡ لِلۡاِيۡمَانِ ۚ يَقُوۡلُوۡنَ بِاَفۡوَاهِهِمۡ مَّا لَيۡسَ فِىۡ قُلُوۡبِهِمۡ ۗ وَاللّٰهُ اَعۡلَمُ بِمَا يَكۡتُمُوۡنَ ۝

---

[a]48 : 12.

evil ones to man. Thus all the three assertions, though apparently contradicting one another, prove to be true.

449. Commentary :

The "meeting of the parties" refers to the Battle of Uḥud which is under review here.

The clause ليعلم المؤمنين rendered as, *that He might distinguish the believers*, does not mean, "that He might know the believers", as generally translated. According to Quranic idiom, the expression simply means that Allah might mark out, or make known, or distinguish believers from disbelievers. See also note on 3 : 141.

450. Commentary :

Trials come to bring about a distinction between true believers and those weak of faith or insincere. In this way, the sufferings of the Muslims at Uḥud proved a blessing in disguise. They served to distinguish the true believers from the hypocrites who had so far remained intermixed with the true believers. While professing to be true Muslims, they were, at heart, enemies of Islam; and their passing for Muslims was injurious to the Muslim community. The believers, taking them for true Muslims, remained unaware of the secret machinations by which they sought to injure the cause of Islam. So it was in the interests of Islam that their hypocrisy became unmasked and the Muslims became on their guard against them. On the other hand, just as the exposure of the hypocrites proved beneficial to the believers, similarly the coming to light of their own sincerity and devotion served a most useful purpose. It served not only to disappoint the enemies of Islam who came to realize that with such devoted followers they could make no headway against Islam, but it also opened their eyes to its truth; for it became clear to them that a religion which could inspire its votaries with such selfless zeal and steadfast devotion could not but be true.

The particle او rendered as "and" in the clause, *fight in the cause of Allah and repel the attack of the enemy*, literally means "or" and is equivalent to "in other words", or "what is the same thing" etc. It is used here: (1) to explain the meaning of the

169. *It is these* who said of their brethren, while they *themselves* remained behind, ' If they had obeyed us, *they would not have been slain.' Say, *b*' Then avert death from yourselves, if you are truthful.'⁴⁵¹

اَلَّذِیْنَ قَالُوْا لِاِخْوَانِهِمْ وَقَعَدُوْا لَوْ اَطَاعُوْنَا مَا قُتِلُوْا قُلْ فَادْرَءُوْا عَنْ اَنْفُسِکُمُ الْمَوْتَ اِنْ کُنْتُمْ صَادِقِیْنَ ۱۶۹

---

*a*3 : 155.   *b*4 : 79.

---

preceding clause *i.e. fight in the cause of Allah.* So the whole sentence would read something like this : "It was said to them (the hypocrites), Come ye, fight in the cause of Allah, which was the same thing as repelling the attack of the enemy". This rendering would go to prove that the Companions of the Holy Prophet waged no aggressive war and all their fighting was undertaken in self-defence. (2) Or the word او (and) is used here in the sense of " at least." According to this rendering, the sentence would mean : " Fight in the cause of Allah ; and if you cannot fight in the cause of Allah, at least fight in defence of your own homes and hearths," *i.e.,* your own interests require that you should defend Medina against the attack of the enemy. (3) Or as rendered in the text the word is used in the sense of " and ". With this meaning of او, the whole sentence would mean, " fight in the cause of Allah and repel the attack of the enemy."

The expression لو نعلم قتالا translated in the text as, *If we knew how to fight,* may have three meanings : (1) If we knew that there would be fighting *i.e.* we thought there would be no fighting. By using this expression the hypocrites meant that seeing the strength of the enemy, the Muslims would at once run away and there will be no fighting. (2) If we knew it to be a fight *i.e.* it was no fight in which the Muslims were going to be engaged, but certain destruction in view of the appalling difference between the numbers and equipment of the opposing forces. (3) Or, as rendered in the text, the expression may mean, if we knew how to fight. In this case, it must be taken to have been used ironically, signifying : " We are unaware of the art of war ; if we had been acquainted with it, we would have fought along with you."

The allusion in the verse is obviously to the defection at Uḥud of a party of 300 hypocrites under their leader 'Abdullah bin Ubayy, who, at a crucial moment, deserted the Muslims and went back to Medina, saying, " He (the Prophet) has disregarded my advice and has followed the advice of mere lads." Seeing this, 'Abdullah bin 'Amr, father of Jābir, approached him and asked him not to desert the Prophet in that manner, upon which 'Abdullah replied in the very words quoted by the Quran *i.e.* لو نعلم قتالا لاتبعناکم meaning, " If we knew there would be fighting, we would have surely followed you." At this 'Abdullah b. 'Amr exclaimed, saying : " God's curse be upon you. Surely, He Himself will help His Messenger " (Jarīr, iii. 104.).

451. Commentary :

The word اخوان (brethren) may refer to both the Muslims and the hypocrites. If taken to refer to the Muslims, the expression قالوا لاخوانهم (said of their brethren) would either mean, "said concerning their brethren, the Muslims", or it would mean " said to their brethren, the Muslims ". If, however, it is taken to refer to the hypocrites, the expression would mean,

170. ^aThink not of those, who have been slain in the cause of Allah, as dead. Nay, they are living, in the presence of their Lord, *and* are granted gifts *from Him,*[452]

وَلَا تَحْسَبَنَّ الَّذِيْنَ قُتِلُوْا فِيْ سَبِيْلِ اللّٰهِ اَمْوَاتًا ۚ بَلْ اَحْيَاءٌ عِنْدَ رَبِّهِمْ يُرْزَقُوْنَ ۝

171. Jubilant because of that which Allah has given them of His bounty ; and rejoicing for those who have not yet joined them from behind them, because on ^bthem shall come no fear, nor shall they grieve.[453]

فَرِحِيْنَ بِمَآ اٰتٰىهُمُ اللّٰهُ مِنْ فَضْلِهٖ ۙ وَيَسْتَبْشِرُوْنَ بِالَّذِيْنَ لَمْ يَلْحَقُوْا بِهِمْ مِّنْ خَلْفِهِمْ ۙ اَلَّا خَوْفٌ عَلَيْهِمْ وَلَا هُمْ يَحْزَنُوْنَ ۝

---

^a2 : 155.   ^b2 : 63 ; 6 : 49 ; 7 : 50 ; 46 : 14.

"said to their own brethren" *i.e.* talked among themselves.

The expression, *Then avert death from yourselves,* embodies a prophecy about the destruction of the hypocrites. The clause would thus signify, "You stayed in your homes in order to save yourselves. Now, the time of your destruction has arrived. So protect yourselves if you can."

452. Important Words :

اموات (dead) is the plural of ميت which besides meaning a dead person, also means : (1) one whose blood has not been avenged ; (2) one who leaves behind no successors ; (3) one stricken with sorrow and grief. See also 2 : 29.

Commentary :

According to the above three significations of the word اموانا (dead) the verse would mean : (1) that the blood of Muslim martyrs shall certainly be avenged ; (2) that their place shall be taken by others equally zealous ; (3) that these martyrs, though apparently dead, are leading happy lives in the presence of their Lord.

As martyrs lay down their lives for the sake of God, therefore they are granted in the next world a special kind of life which is different

from, and superior to, that of ordinary believers.

453. Important Words :

فرحين (jubilant) is the plural of فرح which is the verbal adjective from the verb فرح (*Fariḥa*) meaning, he rejoiced ; he was glad and jubilant ; he exulted and behaved proudly. فرحين therefore, means, (1) exultant and proud ; (2) glad and jubilant, being well-pleased and satisfied (Lane & Aqrab). The word is used here in the latter sense.

يستبشرون (they rejoice) is derived from بشر. The word استبشر means, (1) he rejoiced or became rejoiced by receiving good and happy news ; (2) he gave or conveyed good news so as to make the hearer rejoice at it (Aqrab & Lane). See also 2 : 26.

Commentary :

Taking the word يستبشرون (they rejoice) in the first-mentioned sense, (see Important Words above) the verse would mean, they (the martyrs) are glad that their brethren, who are left behind in the world and will follow them later, will soon be victorious and will triumph over their enemies *i.e.* after death the veils have been removed and the martyrs have become definitely aware of the victories

172. They rejoice at the favour of Allah and *His* bounty, and *at the fact* that [a]Allah suffers not the reward of the believers to be lost.[454]

يَسْتَبْشِرُوْنَ بِنِعْمَةٍ مِّنَ اللّٰهِ وَفَضْلٍ وَّاَنَّ اللّٰهَ لَا يُضِيْعُ اَجْرَ الْمُؤْمِنِيْنَ ۞

173. *As to* those who [b]answered the call of Allah and the Messenger after they had received an injury—such of them as do good and act righteously shall have a great reward ;[455]

اَلَّذِيْنَ اسْتَجَابُوْا لِلّٰهِ وَالرَّسُوْلِ مِنْۢ بَعْدِ مَاۤ اَصَابَهُمُ الْقَرْحُ ۛ لِلَّذِيْنَ اَحْسَنُوْا مِنْهُمْ وَاتَّقَوْا اَجْرٌ عَظِيْمٌ ۞

---

[a]7 : 171; 9 : 120; 11 : 116.   [b]8 : 25.

---

in store for Muslims. According to the second signification of the word, the verse would mean, they give good tidings to their brethren by appearing to them in dreams. The verse may also mean, they receive good tidings concerning their brethren. *i.e.* the angels of God keep them informed of the later successes and victories of Islam.

454. Commentary :

The expression, *Allah suffers not the reward of the believers to be lost,* means that the works of the believers will not go in vain. They will certainly bring their due reward.

455. Commentary :

The reference in this and the next verse is to the two expeditions led by the Holy Prophet against the Meccans as a result of the Battle of Uḥud. The first was undertaken on the day immediately following that battle. When the Meccans withdrew from Uḥud, and took their way back to Mecca, they were, as narrated above, taunted by the Arab tribes for having brought no booty and no prisoners of war from a battle in which they claimed to have won a victory. The Meccans, thereupon, thought of returning to Medina with a view to re-attacking the Muslims and completing their victory. The Holy Prophet, who had also anticipated the return of the Meccans, at once called upon his Companions to join him in the pursuit of the enemy and most

wisely restricted the call to only such able-bodied Muslims as had taken part in the Battle of Uḥud. So on the following day, he left Medina with 250 men. When the Meccans heard of the Muslims advancing towards them, they lost heart and fled. The Holy Prophet went as far as Ḥamrā' al-Asad, a distance of about eight miles from Medina on the route to Mecca, and seeing that the enemy had fled, returned to Medina.

The second expedition came a year later. Before leaving the battle-field of Uḥud, Abū Sufyān, commander of the Meccan army, had promised the Muslims another engagement next year at Badr. But the ensuing year being a year of famine, he could not keep his appointment. So he sent Nu'aim b. Mas'ūd to Medina to terrify the Muslims by spreading false rumours of great preparations having been made by the Meccans. This clumsy ruse completely failed to frighten the Muslims, who came to Badr at the appointed time only to find that the Meccans had not appeared. The Muslims profited by this opportunity by taking part in trafficking at the great annual fair that used to be held there every year and returned prosperous as well as triumphant to Medina. This expedition is known in history as the expedition of *Badr al-Ṣughrā,* (*i.e.* the smaller Badr), to distinguish it from the great Battle of Badr which had taken place about two years earlier.

174. Those to whom men said, ' People have mustered against you, therefore fear them,' but this *only* increased their faith and they said, ' Sufficient for us is Allah, and an excellent guardian is He.'[456]

175. So they returned with a mighty favour from Allah and a great bounty, while no evil had touched them ; and they followed [a]the pleasure of Allah ; and Allah is the Lord of great bounty.[457]

176. It is Satan who only frightens [b]his friends ; so fear them not but fear Me, if you are believers.[458]

---

[a]2 : 208,266 ; 3 : 16, 163 ; 5 : 3,17 ; 9 : 72 ; 57 : 21,28.   [b]7 : 28 ; 16 : 101 ; 35 : 7.

---

456. Important Words :

وكيل (guardian). is derived from وكل . They say وكل اليه الامر *i.e.* he left the matter to him and did not interfere in it. كلنى الى كذا means, leave thou me to manage this thing as I may deem proper. وكيل means, one to whom the management of an affair is left or consigned ; guardian ; agent or deputy. الوكيل is one of of the names of God meaning, Guardian ; One Who watches or looks after the affairs of the Faithful ; One sufficing for His servants (Aqrab & Lane).

Commentary :

The reference here is to the false rumours spread by Nu'aim bin Mas'ūd that the Meccans had made great preparations against the Muslims and were about to attack them. See also the preceding verse.

457. Commentary :

As stated above, the Muslims returned from *Badr al-Ṣughrā* after having made great profit by trading at the annual fair held there. This is hinted in the word " bounty ". The words, *no evil had touched them*, mean that there was no fighting, the Meccans having failed to appear.

458. Commentary :

The expression يخوف اولياءه rendered in the text as, *Satan only frightens his friends*, may mean : (1) Satan tries to make believers fear disbelievers, who are his friends ; (2) he frightens disbelievers themselves *i.e.* he becomes the cause of their fear, for the friends of Satan can never be brave. In the latter case the pronoun " them " in, *so fear them not*, would refer to the noun الناس (people) in 3 : 174 above.

177. ªAnd let not those who hastily fall into disbelief grieve thee ; surely, they cannot harm Allah in any way. Allah desires not to assign any portion for them in the life to come ; and they shall have a severe punishment.⁴⁵⁹

وَلَا يَحْزُنْكَ الَّذِيْنَ يُسَارِعُوْنَ فِي الْكُفْرِ اِنَّهُمْ لَنْ يَّضُرُّوا اللّٰهَ شَيْئًا يُرِيْدُ اللّٰهُ اَلَّا يَجْعَلَ لَهُمْ حَظًّا فِي الْاٰخِرَةِ وَلَهُمْ عَذَابٌ عَظِيْمٌ ۞

178. Surely, ᵇthose who have purchased disbelief at the price of faith cannot harm Allah at all ; and they shall have a grievous punishment.⁴⁶⁰

اِنَّ الَّذِيْنَ اشْتَرَوُا الْكُفْرَ بِالْاِيْمَانِ لَنْ يَّضُرُّوا اللّٰهَ شَيْئًا وَلَهُمْ عَذَابٌ اَلِيْمٌ ۞

179. And let not the disbelievers think that ᶜOur granting them respite is good for them ; the result of Our granting them respite will only be that they will increase in sin ; and they shall have an humiliating punishment.⁴⁶¹

وَلَا يَحْسَبَنَّ الَّذِيْنَ كَفَرُوْا اَنَّمَا نُمْلِيْ لَهُمْ خَيْرٌ لِّاَنْفُسِهِمْ اِنَّمَا نُمْلِيْ لَهُمْ لِيَزْدَادُوْا اِثْمًا وَلَهُمْ عَذَابٌ مُّهِيْنٌ ۞

ª5 : 42.   ᵇ2 : 17, 87 ; 14 : 29.   ᶜ22 : 45.

---

459. Commentary :

The clause, *who hastily fall into disbelief*, refers to the hypocrites and the weak in faith whom the slightest trial throws into disbelief. The word "portion" means "portion of grace and God's mercy."

460. Commentary :

As in the preceding verse, the word Allah in the clause, *cannot harm Allah*, stands either for the cause of Allah or for the Holy Prophet and the believers, because God is evidently above being harmed. The expression has been used to show that those who try to do harm to Islam or to the Holy Prophet and his followers, really try to do harm to God Himself, for the obvious reason that the cause of the Holy Prophet or that of Islam is the cause of God Himself.

461. Important Words :

The paticle ل (*lām*) in the expression ليزدادوا

here denotes not purpose but result or consequence : as in the well-known Arabic couplet :

لدوا للموت وابنوا للخراب فكلكم يسير الى تباب

i.e. Bear children that they should die and build houses that they should fall into ruins, for all of you are marching towards destruction. Thus the verse would mean : We grant them respite that they should mend their ways, but the result is that they increase in sin. Such ل (*lām*) is known as لام عاقبت in Arabic.

The particle ل may, in one sense, also denote cause, as an Arab would say خرجت من البلد لمخافة شر *i.e.* I left the town because of the fear of evil. In this sense, the clause would mean, We grant them respite because they have increased in evil, *i.e.*, their increasing in evil has been the cause of Our granting them respite so that they may have an opportunity to mend their ways and reform themselves.

180. ^aAllah would not leave the believers as you are, until He separated the wicked from the good. Nor would Allah ^breveal to you the unseen. But Allah chooses of His Messengers whom He pleases. Believe, therefore, in Allah and His Messengers. If you believe and be righteous, you shall have a great reward.[462]

مَا كَانَ اللّٰهُ لِيَذَرَ الْمُؤْمِنِيْنَ عَلٰى مَآ اَنْتُمْ عَلَيْهِ حَتّٰى يَمِيْزَ الْخَبِيْثَ مِنَ الطَّيِّبِ ۗ وَمَا كَانَ اللّٰهُ لِيُطْلِعَكُمْ عَلَى الْغَيْبِ وَلٰكِنَّ اللّٰهَ يَجْتَبِيْ مِنْ رُّسُلِهٖ مَنْ يَّشَآءُ ۖ فَاٰمِنُوْا بِاللّٰهِ وَرُسُلِهٖ ۚ وَاِنْ تُؤْمِنُوْا وَتَتَّقُوْا فَلَكُمْ اَجْرٌ عَظِيْمٌ ۝

^a8 : 38 ; 29 : 3-4. ^b72 : 27-28.

---

462. Important Words :

لِيُطْلِعَكُمْ (would reveal to you). يَطْلَعُ is derived from طَلَعَ which means, he appeared ; he rose ; he ascended. اَطْلَعَهُ عَلَيْهِ means, he revealed it to him or he made him acquainted with it ; or lifted him high up so that he might have a clear view of it. The expression لِيُطْلِعَكُمْ عَلَى الْغَيْبِ therefore, would mean, that He should cause you to ascend the unseen ; or lift you high up to have a clear view of the unseen i.e. cause you to obtain mastery of the unseen ; or in other words, reveal to you the secrets of the unseen in abundance.. Elsewhere the Quran says لَا يُظْهِرُ عَلٰى غَيْبِهٖ اَحَدًا i.e. God discloses not the unseen to any one in abundance (72 : 27). Here too the word used i.e. يُظْهِرُ points to mastery of a thing or having a thing in abundance.

Commentary :

The sentence, *Allah would not leave the believers as you are*, signifies that the trials and tribulations through which Muslims have so far passed would not soon end. There are yet many more in store for them, and they will continue to come till true believers are discriminated from hypocrites and those weak in faith.

The expression, *Allah chooses of His Messengers whom He pleases*, does not mean that some of the Messengers are chosen and others not, but that of the persons whom He has ordained to be sent as His Messengers, He chooses the one suited for the particular age in which he is sent. Or the particle مِنْ (of) may be taken to give the sense of intensification or emphasis without restricting the sense to a specified section of the class. In that case the sentence will read as, Allah does choose as His Messengers whom He pleases. It must be remembered that all Messengers are raised under a special divine decree.

When it was stated that God intended to separate the wicked from the good by revealing His will to His Messengers, the question was asked by disbelievers, why did not God reveal Himself to them ? To this question God has given the answer that He reveals His will only to His Messengers and the Elect. All are not pure or ennobled enough to receive His revelation.

478

181. And let not those, *a*who are niggardly with respect to what Allah has given them of His bounty, think that it is good for them ; nay, it is evil for them. That with respect to which they were niggardly shall be put as a collar round their necks on the Day of Resurrection. And to Allah belongs the heritage of the heavens and the earth, and Allah is well aware of what you do.[463]

182. And surely Allah has heard the utterance of those who said, *b*'Allah is poor and we are rich'—We shall record what they have said, and *c*their attempts to kill the Prophets unjustly; and We shall say, 'Taste ye the punishment of burning.'[464]

وَلَا يَحْسَبَنَّ الَّذِيْنَ يَبْخَلُوْنَ بِمَا اٰتٰىهُمُ اللّٰهُ مِنْ فَضْلِهٖ هُوَ خَيْرًا لَّهُمْ ۚ بَلْ هُوَ شَرٌّ لَّهُمْ ۚ سَيُطَوَّقُوْنَ مَا بَخِلُوْا بِهٖ يَوْمَ الْقِيٰمَةِ ۗ وَلِلّٰهِ مِيْرَاثُ السَّمٰوٰتِ وَالْاَرْضِ ۗ وَاللّٰهُ بِمَا تَعْمَلُوْنَ خَبِيْرٌ ۝

لَقَدْ سَمِعَ اللّٰهُ قَوْلَ الَّذِيْنَ قَالُوْٓا اِنَّ اللّٰهَ فَقِيْرٌ وَّنَحْنُ اَغْنِيَآءُ ۘ سَنَكْتُبُ مَا قَالُوْا وَقَتْلَهُمُ الْاَنْبِيَآءَ بِغَيْرِ حَقٍّ ۙ وَّنَقُوْلُ ذُوْقُوْا عَذَابَ الْحَرِيْقِ ۝

---

*a*4 : 38 ; 17 : 30 ; 25 : 68.   *b*5 : 65.   *c*4 : 156.

---

463. Important Words :

میراث (heritage) is derived from ورث *i.e.* he inherited. ورث مال ابیه or ورث اباه means, he inherited the property of his father. They say ورثت مجده *i.e.* I inherited his glory. ورث عن ابیه or ورث من ابیه means, he inherited from his father, or he inherited part of the property of his father. اورثه الشیئ means, he made him inherit the thing. اورثه المرض ضعفا means, the disease occasioned him, as its result, weakness. ورث and ارث and تراث and میراث all mean, what is inherited; an inheritance; a heritage whether property, rank, quality, nobility, etc. وارث means, an heir. الوارث as an epithet applied to God means, He Who remains after the creatures have perished (Lane). Primarily الوراثة signifies the transfer of property, etc. from one to another without sale or gift. The Arabs say ورثت علما من فلان *i.e.* I gained or acquired knowldege from such a one (Mufradāt).

Commentary :

The chief obstacle in the way of the hypocrites to accept Islam was that constant calls were made on Muslims to spend money in the cause of God and make sacrifices for it. They are told in this verse that their unwillingness to spend would eventually do them no good nor would it save their possessions from destruction.

The sentence, *And to Allah belongs the heritage of the heavens and the earth*, obviously does not mean that Allah will receive heavens and earth in inheritance from some one else. The word میراث rendered as heritage here signifies ownership. The word also means portion allotted to one, as in the verse الذین *i.e.* those who shall inherit Paradise (23 : 12). Now Paradise is not inherited by any one ; it is only received as an allotted portion from God.

464. Commentary :

The words, *Allah has heard the utterance of those*, have been used by way of rebuke and warning, meaning that God is not unaware of these impudent utterances and that the

183. That is because of that which your hands have sent on before yourselves, and *the truth is* that *a*Allah is not at all unjust to *His* Servants—465

ذٰلِكَ بِمَا قَدَّمَتْ اَیْدِیْکُمْ وَاَنَّ اللّٰهَ لَیْسَ بِظَلَّامٍ لِّلْعَبِیْدِ ۟

184. Those who say, 'Allah has charged us not to believe in any Messenger until he bring us an offering which fire devours.' Say,' There have already come to you Messengers before me with *b*clear Signs and with that which you speak of. Why, then, did you seek to kill them, if you are truthful ? '466

اَلَّذِیْنَ قَالُوْۤا اِنَّ اللّٰهَ عَهِدَ اِلَیْنَاۤ اَلَّا نُؤْمِنَ لِرَسُوْلٍ حَتّٰی یَاْتِیَنَا بِقُرْبَانٍ تَاْکُلُهُ النَّارُ قُلْ قَدْ جَآءَکُمْ رُسُلٌ مِّنْ قَبْلِیْ بِالْبَیِّنٰتِ وَ بِالَّذِیْ قُلْتُمْ فَلِمَ قَتَلْتُمُوْهُمْ اِنْ کُنْتُمْ صٰدِقِیْنَ ۟

---

*a*8 : 52 ; 41 : 47 ; 50 : 30.   *b*5 : 33 ; 14 : 10 ; 40 : 84.

---

utterers will certainly have to answer for them.

The words, *Allah is poor and we are rich*, were uttered by the Jews on behalf of the hypocrites and as an expression of their thoughts when the latter were called upon to spend their wealth in the cause of Allah (3 : 181). These words also express the thoughts of those niggardly persons and the weak of faith who join a new religion but find it hard to comply with its ever-growing monetary demands and sometimes cry out in impatience: "Has Allah become poor that we are asked to spend our hard-earned money in His cause"? In fact, one of the principal causes of the opposition to a new religious movement is reluctance on the part of the people to undergo the sacrifices of money and comfort that the new faith demands.

The words, *We shall record what they have said*, signify that God will not let such mischievous utterances go unpunished, implying that what is forgiven is, as it were, not recorded.

465. Commentary :

The expression, *Allah is not at all unjust to His servants*, falsifies the inference to which

the statement of the disbelievers mentioned in the previous verse gives rise. They seem to say that if Islam had been true, God Himself would have helped it and would not have asked others to help it with their money. To this objection the answer is given that if the Prophet is an impostor and yet God is helping him to thrive and prosper, it means that God is doing a great wrong to the people by granting respite to an impostor and by allowing the people to be led astray by helping a wrong cause. But as God cannot be unjust, so the cause of Islam must be, and is, a right cause.

466. Commentary :

The enemies of truth never admit their defeat. They continue to seek new pretexts for refusing to believe in it. When the Jews were told that they had opposed the Prophets of God through covetousness (3 : 181-182), they retorted by saying that they did not oppose Muslims through covetousness but because, unlike them, the Muslims devoured even the animals which they offered as sacrifices, instead of burning them at the altar according to the Jewish Law (Lev. 1 : 11-17). Thus it was not they but the Muslims who were greedy and

185. ^aAnd if they accuse thee of lying, even so were accused of lying Messengers before thee who came with clear Signs and books of wisdom and the shining Book.[467]

فَاِنْ كَذَّبُوْكَ فَقَدْ كُذِّبَ رُسُلٌ مِّنْ قَبْلِكَ جَآءُوْ بِالْبَيِّنٰتِ وَ الزُّبُرِ وَ الْكِتٰبِ الْمُنِيْرِ ۝

---

^a35 : 5,26.

---

covetous and they could not, therefore, consistently with the Law of Moses, accept the Prophet who did not observe that Law.

The Quran answers this objection by saying that the observance of the law about burnt offerings was no criterion to test the truth of a Prophet, because that could easily be done by an impostor. It was بينات (clear Signs) only that demonstrated and established the truth of a claimant. But even if observance of burnt offerings was the criterion of a true Prophet, the Jews had no right to raise an objection ; for in that case the question arose, why did they reject those Prophets who strictly conformed to that law? The fact that the Jewish demand referred to in the words, *that which you speak of*, has been mentioned in the verse separately from *clear Signs*, shows that what the Jews spoke of was not a miracle, but that they were only referring to the law about burnt offerings, and not to the miracle of fire descending from heaven to consume a sacrifice, as is generally but wrongly believed.

467. Important Words :

زبر (books of wisdom) is the plural of زبور which is derived from زبر. They say زبر البئر *i.e.* he cased or lined the well with stones or bricks, etc. زبر البناء means, he raised the wall by placing layers of stones or bricks on one another. زبر الكتاب means, he wrote the writing or the book.

زبر السائل means, he chid or scolded the beggar. زبور (*zabūr*) means, a writing or a book : a book of wisdom and intellectual science, not containing legal statutes, ordinances or commandments. Based on its verbal senses, the word would also mean a book that protects and beautifies a source of knowledge just as a casing protects and beautifies a well ; or a book that contains warnings. The word is particularly used about the Book of David containing the Psalms. زبور (*zubūr*) is the plural of زبر (*zibr*) which means, a writing or a book ; also wisdom and reason (Aqrab & Lane).

Commentary :

It is worthy of note that unlike its predecessor the present verse makes no reference to a burnt offering after the word بينات (clear Signs) which shows that a burnt offering formed no proof of the truth of a claimant to prophethood.

It will be noted that whereas the words زبر (books of wisdom) and بينات (clear Signs) are both in the plural number, the word الكتاب المنير (the shining Book) has been put in the singular number, the reason being that all the Israelite Prophets followed one Book of Law only, viz., the Torah given to Moses, while each of them came with separate clear Signs as well as with separate Books or revelations containing things of wisdom and warnings.

186. ^aEvery soul shall taste of death. And you shall be paid in full your rewards only on the Day of Resurrection. So whosoever is removed away from the Fire and is made to enter Heaven has indeed attained his goal. ^bAnd the life of this world is nothing but an illusory enjoyment.⁴⁶⁸

187. ^cYou shall surely be tried in your possessions and in your persons and ^dyou shall surely hear many hurtful things from those who were given the Book before you and from those who set up equals to God. But if you show fortitude and act righteously, that indeed is a matter of strong determination.⁴⁶⁹

188. And *remember* when Allah took a covenant from those who were given the Book, *saying,* 'You shall make this *Book* known to the people and not conceal it.' But ^ethey threw it away behind their backs, and bartered it for a paltry price. Evil is that which they have purchased. ⁴⁷⁰

---

^a21 : 36 ; 29 : 58.   ^b4 : 174 ; 35 : 31 ; 39 : 36.   ^c2 : 156 ; 8 : 29 ; 64 : 16.   ^d5 : 83.   ^e2 : 102.

---

468. Commentary :

Death is perhaps the most certain pheno- menon in nature and yet man's attitude towards it is of disregard and indifference. The worldly life has been here called a vain and illusory thing, because on the face of it it appears to be a very attractive and sweet thing, but when one becomes engrossed in seeking its pleasures and profits, one finds it bitter and deceptive.

469. Commentary :

Tests and trials are necessary and serve a four-fold purpose : (1) They distinguish the waverers and the weak of faith from those sincere and steadfast votaries whose faith is strong and firm. (2) They become a means of spiritual advancement for those sincere in faith. (3) Those who are tried come to know of the strength or otherwsie of their own faith and are thus enabled to shape their conduct accordingly. (4) Trials also establish the title to reward of those deserving it.

Indeed there never was a Prophet who, along with his followers, was not called upon to put up with abuse and hardships.

470. Commentary :

The reference here is to no particular covenant but to a general covenant taken from the followers of every Prophet that they would

189. Think not that those ᵃwho exult in what they have done, and love to be praised for what they have not done—think not that they are secure from punishment. They shall suffer a grievous chastisement.⁴⁷¹

لَا تَحۡسَبَنَّ الَّذِيۡنَ يَفۡرَحُوۡنَ بِمَاۤ اَتَوۡا وَّيُحِبُّوۡنَ اَنۡ يُّحۡمَدُوۡا بِمَا لَمۡ يَفۡعَلُوۡا فَلَا تَحۡسَبَنَّهُمۡ بِمَفَازَةٍ مِّنَ الۡعَذَابِ ۚ وَلَهُمۡ عَذَابٌ اَلِيۡمٌ ﴿۱۸۹﴾

190. ᵇAnd to Allah belongs the kingdom of the heavens and the earth; and Allah has power over all things.⁴⁷²

وَلِلّٰهِ مُلۡكُ السَّمٰوٰتِ وَالۡاَرۡضِ ۗ وَاللّٰهُ عَلٰى كُلِّ شَيۡءٍ قَدِيۡرٌ ﴿۱۹۰﴾

191. ᶜIn the creation of the heavens and the earth and in the alternation of the night and the day there are indeed signs for men of understanding;⁴⁷³

اِنَّ فِيۡ خَلۡقِ السَّمٰوٰتِ وَالۡاَرۡضِ وَاخۡتِلَافِ الَّيۡلِ وَالنَّهَارِ لَاٰيٰتٍ لِّاُولِى الۡاَلۡبَابِ ﴿۱۹۱﴾

ᵃ61 : 3-4.   ᵇ5 : 18-19, 121 ; 24 : 43 ; 42 : 50.   ᶜ2 : 165 ; 3 : 28 ; 45 : 6.

---

preach and promulgate the message they had accepted and would live up to it. The pronoun "it" in the clause, *and not conceal it*, may refer either to the Book or the covenant.

471. Important Words :

مَفَازَة (secure) is derived from فَازَ which means, he was successful and gained what he desired. فَازَ مِنۡهُ means, he escaped it (danger, etc.), or he became secure from it. So مَفَازَة means, a place or state of security or escape ; a means of success and prosperity (Aqrab).

Commentary :

The expression "think not" mentioned twice in the verse not only makes the sentence more clear but also adds to it beauty and force. Such people as exult in evil deeds and have no anxiety and no desire for their spiritual welfare, being satisfied with false praise only, must not consider themselves secure from divine punishmentne.

472. Commentary :

After having dealt, at some length, with the incidents connected with the Battle of Uḥud and the hardships that the Muslims had to suffer as a result thereof, God comforts them with the declaration that their intervening sufferings are only a passing phase and the final victory will surely be theirs, because to God belongs the kingdom of the heavens and the earth and He has graciously decreed to bestow both spiritual and temporal blessings on Muslims.

473. Commentary :

The lesson implied in the creation of the heavens and the earth and in the alternation of night and day is that man has been created both for spiritual and temporal progress, and that if he acts righteously, his period of darkness and affliction must needs be followed by one of sunshine and happiness. For further explanation of this verse see next verse.

192. [a]Those who remember Allah standing, sitting, and *lying* on their sides, and ponder over the creation of the heavens and the earth. [b]"Our Lord, Thou hast not created this in vain; *Nay*, Holy art Thou; save us, then, from the punishment of the Fire.[474]

الَّذِيْنَ يَذْكُرُوْنَ اللهَ قِيَامًا وَّقُعُوْدًا وَّعَلٰى جُنُوْبِهِمْ وَيَتَفَكَّرُوْنَ فِيْ خَلْقِ السَّمٰوٰتِ وَالْاَرْضِ رَبَّنَا مَا خَلَقْتَ هٰذَا بَاطِلًا سُبْحٰنَكَ فَقِنَا عَذَابَ النَّارِ ۝

---

[a]4 : 104; 10 : 13; 39 : 10; 62 : 11.   [b]38 : 28.

---

474. Important Words :

باطلا (in vain) is derived from بطل meaning, it was or became false or vain, or void or futile or devoid of virtue or of no account. They say ذهب دمه باطلا meaning, his blood went for nothing *i.e.* went unretaliated. بطل فى حديثه means, he jested or was not serious in his discourse. باطل therefore, means: false, spurious, vain, useless, void and of no account (Lane).

Commentary :

Such a grand system to which an allusion has been made in the previous verse could certainly not have been brought into being without a definite purpose. The phenomenon of day and night referred to in the preceding verse affords an illustration of how this purpose is served. With the rising of the sun the whole world is illuminated, and men begin to work. Then night falls and the light of the sun is hidden from our view and men go to sleep, but even then some heavenly bodies are busy doing their allotted work. Thus both during day and night heavenly bodies perform their appointed functions and loyally serve man. The whole universe having been created to serve man, the creation of man also must have a great purpose. Of men some are bright in themselves like the sun, and there are others who possess no intrinsic light of their own but borrow it from others. Such men as place themselves in right relation to the Sun of the spiritual realm get lighted, while those that keep away from it are left in the dark.

When man ponders over the spiritual implication of the physical phenomenon of the creation of heavens and earth, the alternation of day and night and the consummate order that pervades the universe, he is deeply impressed by the great wisdom of the Creator, and from the inmost depths of his being rises the cry: *Our Lord, Thou hast not created this in vain.* Then apprehension takes hold of him lest he should become deprived of the light of the spiritual Sun and he cries out: *Save us from the punishment of Fire,* which is nothing but being overtaken by spiritual darkness and moral degradation.

193. "Our Lord, whomsoever Thou causest to enter the Fire, him Thou hast surely disgraced. And the wrong-doers shall have no helpers.[475]

رَبَّنَآ اِنَّكَ مَنْ تُدْخِلِ النَّارَ فَقَدْ اَخْزَيْتَهٗ ۙ وَمَا لِلظّٰلِمِيْنَ مِنْ اَنْصَارٍ ۝

194. "Our Lord, we have heard a Crier calling unto faith, 'Believe ye in your Lord', and we have believed. Our Lord, forgive us, therefore, our errors and remove from us our evils and in death number us with the righteous.[476]

رَبَّنَآ اِنَّنَا سَمِعْنَا مُنَادِيًا يُّنَادِيْ لِلْاِيْمَانِ اَنْ اٰمِنُوْا بِرَبِّكُمْ فَاٰمَنَّا ۖ رَبَّنَا فَاغْفِرْ لَنَا ذُنُوْبَنَا وَكَفِّرْ عَنَّا سَيِّاٰتِنَا وَتَوَفَّنَا مَعَ الْاَبْرَارِ ۝

195. "Our Lord, give us ᵃwhat Thou hast promised to us through Thy Messengers; and disgrace us not on the Day of Resurrection. Surely, Thou breakest not Thy promise."

رَبَّنَا وَاٰتِنَا مَا وَعَدْتَّنَا عَلٰى رُسُلِكَ وَلَا تُخْزِنَا يَوْمَ الْقِيٰمَةِ ۗ اِنَّكَ لَا تُخْلِفُ الْمِيْعَادَ ۝

ᵃ14:48; 40:52.

475. Commentary :

A true believer dreads nothing so much as the displeasure of God which is like fire that burns up all traces of goodness, and this fire is the heritage of the wrongdoers only, whom nothing can save from punishment.

476. Important Words :

ذنوب (errors), which is of lighter significance and which generally refers to natural weaknesses and ordinary mistakes and omissions, may represent those dark recesses in us where the light of the sun does not properly reach; while سيئات (evils) which is a comparatively stronger word, may mean the clouds of dust which hide the light of the sun from our view. See also 2:81 & 3:17.

Commentary :

In 3:191 above the word *"day"* in the expression, *the alternation of the night and the day*, is placed after the word "*night*," which points to the fact that the spiritual wayfarer, after having passed through the night of trials and sins, finally basks in the light of the spiritual Sun by accepting and following the divine Crier. But, as the present verse points out, he is afraid lest his weaknesses should retard his progress or lest the dust of his sins and the clouds of his misdeeds should intervene and hide from him the light and warmth of the spiritual Sun, so he humbly prays God to disperse the dust of his sins and drive away the clouds of his misdeeds.

The expression توفنا مع الابرار rendered as, *in death number us with the righteous*, literally means, cause us to die with the righteous, meaning, cause us to die when we are righteous, or let not death come upon us except when we are righteous.

485

196. So their Lord answered their *prayers, saying,* ^a' I will allow not the work of any worker from among you, whether male or female, to be lost. You are from one another. ^bThose, therefore, who have emigrated, and have been driven out from their homes, and have been persecuted in My cause, and have fought and been killed, I will surely remove from them their evils and ^cwill cause them to enter gardens through which streams flow—a reward from Allah, and with Allah is the best of rewards.'[477]

197. ^dLet not the moving about of the disbelievers in the land deceive thee.[478]

198. It is a small *and brief* advantage, then Hell shall be their abode. What an evil place of rest ![479]

فَاسْتَجَابَ لَهُمْ رَبُّهُمْ اَنِّيْ لَاۤ اُضِيْعُ عَمَلَ عَامِلٍ مِّنْكُمْ مِّنْ ذَكَرٍ اَوْ اُنْثٰي بَعْضُكُمْ مِّنْ بَعْضٍ ۚ فَالَّذِيْنَ هَاجَرُوْا وَ اُخْرِجُوْا مِنْ دِيَارِهِمْ وَ اُوْذُوْا فِيْ سَبِيْلِيْ وَ قٰتَلُوْا وَ قُتِلُوْا لَاُكَفِّرَنَّ عَنْهُمْ سَيِّاٰتِهِمْ وَلَاُدْخِلَنَّهُمْ جَنّٰتٍ تَجْرِيْ مِنْ تَحْتِهَا الْاَنْهٰرُ ۚ ثَوَابًا مِّنْ عِنْدِ اللّٰهِ ؕ وَ اللّٰهُ عِنْدَهٗ حُسْنُ الثَّوَابِ ۞

لَا يَغُرَّنَّكَ تَقَلُّبُ الَّذِيْنَ كَفَرُوْا فِي الْبِلَادِ ۞

مَتَاعٌ قَلِيْلٌ ۟ ثُمَّ مَأْوٰىهُمْ جَهَنَّمُ ؕ وَبِئْسَ الْمِهَادُ ۞

---

^a4 : 125 ; 16 : 98 ; 20 : 113.   ^b16 : 42.   22 : 59, 60.   ^cSee 2 : 26.   ^d40 : 5.

477. Commentary :

As this *Sūra* mainly deals with Christian doctrines and ideals and their way of life, and as Christianity, in spite of its claims to the contrary, gives woman a status definitely inferior to that of man, the insistence on the equality of the status of woman with man in the spiritual sphere forms a fitting sequel to it. At several places in the Quran, believing men and believing women are addressed in the same language and are made equally subject to the same commandments and entitled to the same rights and privileges. Briefly, Islam recognizes the equality of the social and religious rights of man and woman. The words, *you are from one another*, are intended to emphasize the equality of status mentioned in the preceding part of the verse.

The verse also constitutes an effective refutation of the charges of the Shias against the Holy Prophet's Companions whose failings and shortcomings, if any, were all forgiven by God in view of the good works they performed.

478. Commentary :

The verse, besides relating to the time of the Holy Prophet, has also a most appropriate application to the present dazzling material progress of Christian nations in all departments of life, and warns Muslims not to be deceived or overawed by the glamour of this transitory and fleeting progress.

479. Commentary :

The prosperity of Christian nations is only temporary, and the verse hints at the dreadful punishment which is in store for them and which has now actually begun to overtake them.

199. But ^athose who fear their Lord shall have gardens through which streams flow; therein shall they abide—an entertainment from Allah. And that which is with Allah is still better for the righteous.⁴⁸⁰

لٰكِنِ الَّذِيْنَ اتَّقَوْا رَبَّهُمْ لَهُمْ جَنّٰتٌ تَجْرِيْ مِنْ تَحْتِهَا الْاَنْهٰرُ خٰلِدِيْنَ فِيْهَا نُزُلًا مِّنْ عِنْدِ اللّٰهِ وَمَا عِنْدَ اللّٰهِ خَيْرٌ لِّلْاَبْرَارِ ۝

200. ^bAnd surely among the People of the Book there are some who believe in Allah and in what has been sent down to you and in what was sent down to them, humbling themselves before Allah. They barter not the Signs of Allah for a paltry price. ^cIt is these who shall have their reward with their Lord. Surely, Allah is swift in account.⁴⁸¹

وَاِنَّ مِنْ اَهْلِ الْكِتٰبِ لَمَنْ يُّؤْمِنُ بِاللّٰهِ وَمَا اُنْزِلَ اِلَيْكُمْ وَمَا اُنْزِلَ اِلَيْهِمْ خٰشِعِيْنَ لِلّٰهِ لَا يَشْتَرُوْنَ بِاٰيٰتِ اللّٰهِ ثَمَنًا قَلِيْلًا اُولٰٓئِكَ لَهُمْ اَجْرُهُمْ عِنْدَ رَبِّهِمْ اِنَّ اللّٰهَ سَرِيْعُ الْحِسَابِ ۝

---

^aSee 2:26.   ^b3:111.   ^c57:29.

---

480. Important Words:

نُزُل Nuzul (entertainment) is the noun-infinitive from نَزَلَ (nazala) meaning, he alighted, descended or came down; he lodged or settled in a place. نُزُل means, guests; place where guests are made to lodge; food prepared for guests; a blessed food (Lane & Aqrab).

اَبْرَار (the righteous) is the plural of بَرّ (a righteous person). Though for the sake of brevity the word has been translated here as "the righteous", it really signifies "highly righteous persons". See also 2:45, 178.

Commentary:

Righteous people will be, as it were, the guests of God, being housed and fed by Him with blessed food. This, as the verse puts it, will be an entertainment from Allah; but what is actually with Allah for the particularly righteous people is still better.

It must be noted that the verse mentions two classes of good people: (1) الَّذِيْنَ اتَّقَوْا i.e. those who fear God, viz., ordinarily righteous persons; and (2) الْاَبْرَار i.e. those who are highly righteous. For the former the words used are مِنْ عِنْدِ اللّٰهِ i.e. they will have entertainment from God, whereas for the latter the words used are عِنْدَ اللّٰهِ i.e. the highly righteous will, as it were, live with God Himself and enjoy His company.

481. Commentary:

The verse embodies a prophecy to the effect that many Christians and Jews will finally accept Islam.

The Arabic words rendered here as, Allah is swift in account, when used in regard to disbelievers, would mean that God is swift at taking account and dealing out punishment; but when used about believers they would mean that God is quick in settling accounts and giving out rewards.

201. O ye who believe! be steadfast and strive to excel in steadfastness and [a]be on *your* guard and fear Allah that you may prosper.[482]

يٰۤاَيُّهَا الَّذِيۡنَ اٰمَنُوا اصۡبِرُوۡا وَصَابِرُوۡا وَرَابِطُوۡا ۟ وَاتَّقُوا اللّٰهَ لَعَلَّكُمۡ تُفۡلِحُوۡنَ ۟

[a]8 : 61.

482. Important Words :

صَابِرُوۡا (strive to excel in steadfastness) is derived from صبر which means, he was patient or steadfast; or he exercised restraint over himself; or he bore hardships with patience. صَابَرَهُ means, he excelled him in patience and steadfastness; he excelled him in patiently bearing hardships; he vide with him in patience or steadfastness (Lane & Aqrab).

رَابِطُوۡا (be on your guard) is derived from ربط meaning, he tied or bound or made fast a thing; he tied or bound a beast with a rope in order that it might not run away and be kept handy. ربط جأشه means, he strengthened or fortified his heart. ربط الله على قلبه means, God strengthened his heart with patience and steadfastness. رابط الامر means, he kept or applied himself constantly or assiduously to the thing or affair. رابط الفريقان means, the two parties tied their horses at their respective frontiers, each in preparation for the other. رابطوا would therefore mean, persevere in fighting against your enemy; or tie your horses in readiness at the frontier; or keep post or remain at the frontier of the enemy in preparation; or apply yourselves constantly and assiduously to the obligations of your religion; or be mindful of the times of Prayer (Lane & Aqrab).

Commentary :

The verse, which is the last of the present *Sūra*, is important and mentions the essential means for the attainment of national goal. Taken in the physical sense, it signifies that in order to attain their goal, Muslims should not only be patient and steadfast and make greater sacrifices than their opponents but should always be on their guard and should particularly be watchful about strengthening their frontiers. Taken in the spiritual sense, the injunctions contained in the verse would mean that Muslims should not only hold fast to their religion and faithfully act upon its teachings but should also zealously carry the message of Islam to non-Muslims and establish missions in their countries, at the same time vigorously defending themselves against all their attacks. The reference particularly is to the Christian people who have proved to be the most bitter enemies of Islam.

The five requisites of success mentioned in the verse are: (1) exercise of patience and steadfastness absolutely; (2) showing greater patience and greater steadfastness than the enemy; (3) applying constantly and assiduously to the service of religion and community; (4) keeping vigilant watch at the frontiers, both for the purposes of defence and attack; and (5) leading lives of righteousness and fearing God. Ah, what a panacea for the ills of Islam but how woefully neglected !

CHAPTER 4

AL-NISĀ

(*Revealed after Hijra*)

Date and Place of Revelation.

This *Sūra* consists of 177 verses including *Bismillah*. 'Ā'isha is reported by Bukhārī to have said that this chapter was revealed when, after her marriage with the Holy Prophet, she had come into his house; and as 'Ā'isha came into the Holy Prophet's house some time after the *Hijra*, the chapter proves to be wholly of Medinite origin. Qurṭubī says that the verse, *Verily Allah commands you to give over the trusts to those entitled to them* (4 : 58), belongs to Meccan revelations and was revealed at the time of the fall of Mecca. This is a case of faulty nomenclature, for everything revealed after *Hijra* is Medinite, even though it may have been revealed at Mecca. The Rev. E. M. Wherry, Noeldeke and some other European scholars are agreed on its being of the Medinite period and regard it as having been revealed between the fourth and fifth years of the *Hijra*. Noeldeke, however, is inclined to place some of its verses among the Meccan revelations because in them " Jews are referred to in a friendly spirit." Wherry thinks that the words " O people " occurring in verse 134 of this *Sūra* show that it was revealed at Mecca because this form of address has been exclusively used in the Meccan *Sūras*.

The fact, however, remains that this is a Medinite *Sūra* and some of its parts were revealed very late in the Holy Prophet's ministry. European scholars are wrong in inferring from the form of address, *viz.* " O people," used in this *Sūra* that some of its verses belong to the Meccan period. Similarly, their inference that, because in some of its verses Jews are referred to in a friendly spirit, therefore those verses must belong to the Meccan period, carries no weight. The inference that the above-mentioned form of address was used only at Mecca has no basis inasmuch as this form of address has also been used in *Sūras* which by the consensus of the opinion of scholars belong to the Medinite period, *viz.*, chapters *Al-Baqara* and *Al-Ḥajj*, (*e.g.* 2 : 22; 22:2), though because this form of address has been used in these *Sūras*, these European scholars regard some of their verses also as having been revealed at Mecca. But to say that because a certain verse uses the expression " O people " it must, in spite of all contrary evidence, belong to the Meccan period is anything but reasonable.

The truth, however, is that as long as the Holy Prophet was at Mecca, very few of the commandments of the *Sharī'at* had been revealed and the people of Mecca were the principal addressees. Therefore in the Meccan *Sūras* the words " O people " were frequently employed as a form of address. But with the Holy Prophet's coming to Medina, Muslims became welded into an organised community, therefore at Medina the form of address " O people " generally became changed into " O ye who believe." This change was quite natural. But with the Prophet's advent to Medina, disbelievers were not altogether ignored. At Medina also they used to enquire of the Holy Prophet about many things and their questions were answered and those answers are recorded in the Quran. So whenever in Medina an answer to a certain question was revealed in which, along with Muslims, disbelievers were also addressed, the form of

489

address consisted of the words "O people." But when the revealed answer or commandment concerned only Muslims, the words "O ye who believe" were used. So there was no reason for the words "O people" to be definitely given up at Medina; and to fix Mecca as the place of revelation of a specific *Sūra* because of these words having been used in it is simply arbitrary.

Similarly, the inference of Noeldeke that because Jews have been referred to in some of the verses of this *Sūra* in a friendly spirit, therefore those verses must belong to the Meccan period, is ill-based. In the verses which deal with Jews, the Quran maintains an attitude of uniform fairness to them whether those verses belong to the Meccan or the Medinite period. For instance, it is in a Medinite *Sūra* i.e. *Al-Baqara*, that occurs the verse, *And the Jews say, 'the Christians stand on nothing,' and the Christians say, 'the Jews stand on nothing' while they both read the same Book* (2:114). In this verse the Quran has been scrupulously fair towards both Jews and Christians. So the argument that because in a certain verse Jews have been referred to in a friendly spirit, therefore that verse must necessarily belong to the Meccan period, carries no weight.

Subject-Matter.

As in *Āl 'Imrān*, the Christian Faith constitutes the main theme of this *Sūra*. But in this *Sūra* greater space has been assigned to a comparison of the detailed teachings of the two religions, Islam and Christianity, with special reference to the progress and domination of Christianity in the Latter Days. As in the Latter Days, Christianity was loudly to profess and proclaim its superiority over Islam on the basis of its teachings regarding women, this chapter largely deals with them, and even a cursory glance over these teachings establishes the fact that even in this respect Islamic teachings are infinitely superior to those of Christianity. And as the subject of orphans is intimately connected with that of women, it has also received special mention here. The *Sūra* is the first among divine revelations to safeguard the rights of women. They are not only given the right of inheritance along with men but have also been declared to be the masters and arbiters of their property.

The second main topic dealt with in this chapter is that of hypocrisy. As in the Latter Days Christianity was to gain world-wide predominance and a large number of Muslims were to live under Christian governments and, as a result of their subservience to Christian rulers and their fear of Christian criticism of Islam, they were to adopt an hyprocritical attitude towards their own faith, the subject of hypocrisy has been particularly treated in this chapter along with that of women, and light is thrown on the depths to which an hypocrite sinks spiritually and temporally. Pointed reference has also been made to the ultimate success of Islam, when shame and abasement will seize these weak-hearted and hypocritical Muslims who feared men more than their Creator.

Towards the end of the *Sūra* a somewhat detailed mention is made of the crucifixion of Jesus, and it is declared that the religious predominance of Christianity is due to the belief that Jesus is not dead but living. This belief is shown to be utterly unfounded because as Jesus is proved not to have died on the Cross, but to have died a natural death, the question of his resurrection simply does not arise. In the concluding verses of this *Sūra* it is declared that this false doctrine will in the end be obliterated and the doctrine of the Oneness of God will reign supreme in the world.

سُوْرَةُ النِّسَآءِ مَدَنِيَّةٌ

1. In the name of Allah, the Gracious, the Merciful.[483]

بِسْمِ اللّٰهِ الرَّحْمٰنِ الرَّحِيْمِ ۝

2. O ye people! ^afear your Lord, ^bWho created you from a single soul and created therefrom its mate, and from them twain spread many men and women ; and fear Allah, in whose name you appeal to one another, and *fear Him particularly* respecting ties of relationship. Verily, Allah watches over you.[484]

يَآيُّهَا النَّاسُ اتَّقُوْا رَبَّكُمُ الَّذِيْ خَلَقَكُمْ مِّنْ نَّفْسٍ وَّاحِدَةٍ وَّخَلَقَ مِنْهَا زَوْجَهَا وَبَثَّ مِنْهُمَا رِجَالًا كَثِيْرًا وَّنِسَآءً ۚ وَاتَّقُوا اللّٰهَ الَّذِيْ تَسَآءَلُوْنَ بِهٖ وَالْاَرْحَامَ ۚ اِنَّ اللّٰهَ كَانَ عَلَيْكُمْ رَقِيْبًا ۝

---

^a33 : 71 ; 59 : 19.　　^b7 : 190 ; 16 : 73 ; 30 : 22 ; 39 : 7.

483. Important Words :

　　　See under 1 : 1.

484. Important Words :

رقيبا (Watcher) is derived from رقب . They say رقبه *i.e.* he watched him ; or guarded him ; or waited for him ; or he kept or preserved it. رقيب is one of God's attributes meaning, Watcher, Guardian, Keeper ; One from Whom nothing is hidden. رقيب also means, an observer ; a spy (Lane & Aqrab).

Commentary :

The words نفس واحدة (single soul) may signify : (1) Adam ; or (2) man and woman taken together, because when two things jointly perform one function, they may be spoken of as one. For instance, 2 : 62 speaks of one food, while it consisted of *Manna* and quails ; or (3) man and woman taken individually, because mankind may be said to have been created from one "single soul" in the sense that each and every individual is created from the seed of man who is "one soul" and is also born of woman who is likewise "one soul."

The expression, *and created therefrom its mate,*

does not mean that woman was created out of the body of man but that she belonged to the same kind and species as man, having the same nature and the same propensities. The meaning of this expression becomes clear when elsewhere we read in the Quran : *And Allah has made for you mates from among yourselves* (16 : 73) ; and *He has made for you pairs of your own selves, and of the cattle also pairs* (42 : 12). This means that, like other human beings, a wife was provided for Adam from his own species. And just as other men's wives are not created from their ribs, so was the wife of Adam not created out of his ribs ; and just as our wives have been made from ourselves in the sense that they are of the same kind as ourselves, so was the wife of Adam created from his rib in the sense that she belonged to the same race as Adam did. The preposition من (from) which has given rise to this misconception has been used in the Quran not only about Adam but about other men as well (*e.g.* 4 : 60 ; 9 : 128 ; 10 : 3 ; 62 : 3, 4.), and in both cases it should mean the same thing *i.e.* belonging to the same kind or species. The Quran

491

3. And ^agive to the orphans their property and exchange not the bad for the good, and devour not their property with your own. Surely, it is a great sin.[485]

وَ اٰتُوا الْيَتٰمٰۤى اَمْوَالَهُمْ وَ لَا تَتَبَدَّلُوا الْخَبِيثَ بِالطَّيِّبِ وَ لَا تَاْكُلُوۤا اَمْوَالَهُمْ اِلٰۤى اَمْوَالِكُمْ اِنَّهٗ كَانَ حُوْبًا كَبِيْرًا ۝

^a4 : 11, 128 ; 6 : 153 ; 17 : 35.

lends no support whatever to the view that Eve was actually created from the rib of Adam, as is clear from the following verses: *We have created you in pairs* (78 : 9); *And of everything have We created pairs* (51 : 50), which means that, just as God created a mate for every living thing, so did He make one for Adam. He did not need to depart from this law in respect of Adam and to create a female for him out of his own body.

The idea of Eve having been created out of the rib of Adam seems to have arisen from a saying of the Holy Prophet to the effect "Women have been created from a rib, and surely, the most crooked part of a rib is the highest part thereof. If you set yourself to straighten it, you will break it" (Bukhārī, ch. on *Nikāḥ*). This ḥadīth is, however, an argument against the above view rather than in favour of it, for it makes no mention of Eve, and speaks of all women, and it is clear that every woman has not been created from a rib.

The expression "created from a rib" is evidently figurative and must not be taken literally. What it means is only that, like unto a rib, there is a sort of crookedness in the nature of woman and that this very crookedness lends charm to her. An analogous Quranic expression, *viz.*: خلق الانسان من عجل *i.e.* "man is made of (lit. from) haste" (21 : 38) helps to illustrate the point. These words clearly do not mean that man has been created out of a substance called عجل or haste. They mean only that man is hasty by nature. The above view has been supported by Majma' al

Biḥār, Baḥr al-Muḥīṭ and Sirāj al-Wahhāj, which all agree that in the above ḥadīth the Arabic word ضلع means a certain crookedness of manners, the word itself meaning crookedness.

In fact, this ḥadīth refers to a certain peculiarity of woman, *viz.*, her affectation of displeasure and coquetry. This "crookedness" has been spoken of in the ḥadīth as the highest or the best trait in her character, and those who take affectation of anger on her part as an expression of her real anger and begin to deal harshly with her for that reason, in fact destroy woman's most attractive and winning feature.

The verse places "the fear of God," side by side with "respect for the ties of relationship", thus emphasizing the importance of good treatment of relatives, on which the Quran lays so much stress. The Holy Prophet used to recite this verse when delivering a marriage sermon in order to remind the parties of their duties to one another.

485. Important Words:

حُوبًا (sin) is derived from حاب meaning, he sinned; he did what was unlawful. حوب means: (1) a great sin or simply sin or crime; (2) wrong or injustice; (3) perdition, destruction or death; (4) disease; (5) a trial, trouble or affliction (Lane & Aqrab).

Commentary :

After mentioning two favours of God in the previous verse, *viz.*, the multiplying of many men and women from a "single soul," and preserving them from destruction by instituting

4. And if you fear that you will not be fair in dealing with the orphans, then marry of women as may be agreeable to you, two, or three, or four; and *a*if you fear you will not deal justly, then *marry only* one or what your right hands possess. That is the nearest *way* for you to avoid injustice.[486]

وَإِنْ خِفْتُمْ اَلَّا تُقْسِطُوْا فِي الْيَتٰمٰى فَانْكِحُوْا مَا طَابَ لَكُمْ مِّنَ النِّسَآءِ مَثْنٰى وَثُلٰثَ وَرُبٰعَ فَاِنْ خِفْتُمْ اَلَّا تَعْدِلُوْا فَوَاحِدَةً اَوْ مَا مَلَكَتْ اَيْمَانُكُمْ ۭ ذٰلِكَ اَدْنٰى اَلَّا تَعُوْلُوْا ۞

---

*a*4 : 130.

ties of relationship, the Quran proceeds to emphasize the need of protecting posterity by safeguarding the rights and interests of orphans.

The expression, *and exchange not the bad for the good*, means that if you do not give the orphans their property, the result will be that your own pure possessions will become impure and you yourselves will suffer in the long run.

The words, *devour not their property with your own*, contain a warning to guardians not to mix up the property of orphans with their own with the intention of misappropriating it. The clause also hints that if the guardian of an orphan possesses sufficient means of subsistence, he should not take anything out of the property of his ward as a compensation for his guardianship.

486. Important Words :

طَابَ (as may be agreeable). طَابَ الشَّيْئُ means, the thing was or became pleasing, delightful, agreeable or delicious. طَابَتْ بِهِ نَفْسِى means, my mind or my soul became pleased and satisfied with it. طَابَ الْعَيْشُ لِفُلَانٍ means, life became pleasant and free from cares for such a one طَابَ عَنِ الشَّيْئِ نَفْسًا means, he willingly parted with the thing (Aqrab & Lane).

مَثْنٰى (two) is derived from ثَنٰى . They say ثَنَاهُ *i.e.* he doubled it or folded it ; or he turned one part of it upon another. ثَنٰى signifies the repetition of a thing, doing it one

time after another, or a thing or affair done twice. مَثْنٰى means اِثْنَانِ اِثْنَانِ *i.e.* two and two ; two and two together ; or two at a time and two at a time. Similarly, ثُلَاثَ means, three and three ; three and three together ; or three at a time and three at a time ; and so is the meaning of رُبَاعَ (Lane & Aqrab). The expression مَثْنٰى وَثُلَاثَ وَرُبَاعَ would thus mean, two at a time or three at time or four at a time.

تَعُوْلُوْا (do injustice) is derived from عَالَ which means : (1) he had a family or a large family ; (2) he sustained and supported the family ; (3) he was or became poor ; (4) he acted unjustly and wrongfully, or he deviated from the right course.

Commentary :

The verse is important inasmuch as it permits polygamy under special circumstances. Islam allows (though it certainly does not enjoin) a man to have more than one wife up to four at a time. As the permission concerning polygamy has been given in connection with the subject of orphans, it should be taken to be primarily based on the question of the care of that much-neglected class of society. There are cases when the interests of orphans can best be protected by marrying one or more wives from among the female wards or from other women as the exigencies of circumstances may require. This can generally happen in one of the following cases :

(1) A man has a number of orphans, including girls, to look after. He is unmarried and there is danger of his falling into temptation. In this case he should marry one or more girls, as the case may be, from among his wards and thus protect himself from falling into sin or from betraying his trust and acting wrongfully towards his wards.

(2) He is married, but his wife fails to treat the orphans properly. He may in such a case also marry one of his female wards so that they may have a good and separate home of their own.

(3) Some of his younger relations, *e.g.*, brothers or sisters, become orphans and he finds that he or his existing wife cannot properly look after them. In such an eventuality, he may marry a suitable woman of mature age who may treat them like a mother. It is on record that in similar circumstances Jābir, a young man and one of the Holy Prophet's distinguished Companions, married a widow of mature age and when the Prophet asked him why he had not married a young girl, Jābir replied that he had done so that his wife might look after his brothers and sisters who were left orphans by the death of his father. The Holy Prophet was much pleased at this act of Jābir and prayed for him (Bukhārī, ch. on *Buyū'*).

4. If a person is afraid that the orphans under his care being strangers to him, he may not treat them as kindly as he should do, he may establish direct relationship with them by marrying one of the female wards.

(5) If a person has a large number of orphans under his care and he finds that he cannot do full justice to them without marrying more wives than one, he is permitted to do so to the limit of four.

The words, *two or three or four*, signify that the last number marks the utmost limit. It is related that after this verse was revealed, the Holy Prophet asked those of his Companions who had more than four wives to keep any four of them they liked and divorce the rest, so that the number might not exceed four (Tirmidhī, ch. on *Nikāḥ*).

A general note on polygamy is appropriate here. Though the verse mentions polygamy in connection with the subject of orphans, yet other situations may also arise in which polygamy may become a necessary remedy for many social or moral evils.

If only the objects of marriage itself be considered, the permission of the Quran to its followers to wed more wives than one, appears to be not only justifiable but in some cases desirable and even necessary; nay, in such cases it may become positively injurious to the best interests of individuals and of the community not to take advantage of this permission. According to the Quran, the objects of marriage are four, *i.e.*, (1) protection against physical, moral and spiritual maladies; (2) peace of mind and the availability of a loving companion ; (3) procreation of children ; and (4) widening of the circle of relationship.

With respect to the first-mentioned object, the Quran says : " *And allowed to you are those beyond that* (*i.e.* the cases mentioned in the earlier verses) *that you seek them by means of your property—marryiny them properly* (and guarding yourselves against animal passions) *and not committing fornication* (and not indulging in unrestricted gratification) (4 : 25). The word حصنين occurring in the verse quoted above is derived from أحصان which means, to seek protection from the attacks of an enemy by entering into a fort. Thus Islam regards marriage as a sort of fort, or a means of protection against moral and spiritual diseases. With respect to this object the Quran further says : *They* (your wives) *are a garment for you and you are a garment for them* (2 : 188). Now the dress of a person serves a three-fold purpose: (1) It protects him against the inclemency of weather; (2) it serves as an embellishment and adornment; and (3) it covers one's private parts and any defects that may be in one's physical formation. With respect to the second object the Quran says : *And of His Signs is this, that He has created wives for you from among yourselves that you may find peace of mind in them and He has engendered love and tenderness between you* (30 : 22). About the third object it says : *Your wives are a tilth for you; so approach your tilth when and how you like* (2 : 224).

Now every one can easily conceive that one or all of the above-mentioned four objects of marriage, *i.e.*, (1) protection against physical, moral and spiritual diseases; (2) procreation and propagation of the human race ; (3) company of a life-long and loving companion and (4) widening of the circle of relationship are, sometimes, not realized in the case of one wife only. It is a hard fact which cannot be denied that there are persons whose sexual instinct is too strong to be satisfied with one wife. This is a physical necessity inherent in man and it is playing with fire to make light of this, the most powerful of all physical instincts. The only sane and proper course open to a man whose sexual powers are abnormally strong is to marry another, if one wife does not satisfy him. Such cases may be rare but you cannot ignore their existence altogether. And a perfect religious system, as Islam claims to be, has to provide for the physical and spiritual requirements of all sorts of people. Again, if the wife of a person becomes a permanent invalid or suffers from a contagious disease, the object of marriage is certainly defeated if such a person does not marry another wife. Indeed, no course is left to him but either to contract another lawful marriage or, failing successfully to combat the attacks of his passions, to lead a dissolute life. And an ailing wife cannot make a good companion either, because however worthy of regard and com-

passion she may be, her company cannot give peace of mind to her husband in all respects. In the third instance, if the wife of a person happens to be barren, the natural and perfectly legitimate desire of the husband to have an issue to succeed him and perpetuate his name remains unfulfilled in the absence of a polygamous marriage. It is to meet the requirements of all such persons that Islam has allowed the contraction of plural matrimonial relations. If, however, in any of these cases a husband divorces his first wife, it would be a shame and disgrace for him. For instance, in the case of an invalid wife it would mean that he lived with her as long as she was whole and deserted her at a time when she most needed his protection. The only honourable course in such a case would be to look after the diseased wife tenderly and marry another woman who may fulfil the functions of a wife.

It will thus be seen that the objects of a polygamous marriage are, to a certain extent, the same as those of a monogamous marriage. When one or all of those objects are not realized by a monogamous marriage, a polygamous marriage becomes a necessity and is allowed. There are, however, other reasons also which may render it necessary for a person to have one or more wives in addition to the one whom he dearly loves and who also fulfils the objects of marriage. Those reasons are : (*a*) to protect orphans ; (*b*) to provide husbands for marriageable widows and (*c*) to supplement the decreasing manhood of a family or community.

It is manifestly clear from the verse under comment in which permission is given to marry more wives than one that polygamy is resorted to particularly with a view to taking under one's protection orphans left unprotected. The verse clearly states : *If you fear that you will not be fair in dealing with orphans* (under your protection), *then marry of women. as may be agreeable to you, two or three or four;*

5. And ^agive the women their dowries willingly. But if they, of their own pleasure, remit to you a part thereof, then enjoy it as something pleasant and wholesome.[487]

وَاٰتُوا النِّسَآءَ صَدُقٰتِهِنَّ نِحْلَةً ۚ فَاِنۡ طِبْنَ لَكُمۡ عَنۡ شَیۡءٍ مِّنۡهُ نَفۡسًا فَكُلُوۡهُ هَنِیۡٓئًا مَّرِیۡٓئًا ۝

---

*a*4 : 25-26 ; 60 : 11.

---

and if you fear you will not deal justly (between your wives) *then marry only one.* The words hint that the mother of such orphans as are left in the guardianship of a person should preferably be married by him so that he should become directly related to, and more intimately connected with, them and thus become more interested in their welfare than he otherwise could be.

Again, the Quran says : *And marry widows from among you* (24 : 33). To provide husbands for widows is thus another object which the institution of polygamy fulfils. Muslims were perpetually engaged in fighting in the time of the Holy Prophet. Many fell in wars and left behind widows and orphans without near relations to look after them. The preponderance of women over men and an exceptionally large number of orphans with no one to look after them, which is the inevitable result of war, necessitated that, to save the Muslim society from moral degeneration, polygamous marriages should be encouraged. The last World War also vindicated this useful institution of Islam. It left an abnormally large number of young women without husbands. Indeed, the great preponderance of females over males in the West, due to the appalling loss of manhood caused by the War, is responsible for the present awful laxity of morals which is eating into the vitals of Western society. Young girls fail to get suitable husbands. But natural passions must be satisfied. The result is dissolution and depravity. In view of the moral depravity prevailing in many countries, who has the hardihood to deny the wisdom of the Islamic

institution of polygamy ? Many indescribable moral and physical evils have arisen in the West as the result of this preponderance of women over men, the only proper remedy for which is polygamy.

The institution of polygamy is also intended to meet the serious situation that follows in the wake of a war, when, besides other aspects of decline, the manhood of a nation becomes so depleted as to threaten national destruction. The fall of birth-rate, which is a potent cause of the decay of a people and from which some Western countries are badly suffering, can be effectively remedied only by resorting to polygamy. The West will never recover from the terrible moral and social diseases from which it is suffering as well as from the appalling numerical decline facing certain countries and communities, unless, setting aside all false notions and false sentiments, it submits to the Islamic injunctions about polygamy. It is a sacrifice demanded of men and women alike—a sacrifice in which personal and passing sentiments are required to be partly ignored for the wider and permanent interests of whole communities and countries.

487. Important Words :

صَدُقٰت (dowries) which is the plural of صَدُقَة (*ṣaduqa*) and not صَدَقَة (*ṣadaqa*), as might be wrongly supposed, is derived from صدق. They say صدق فى الحديث *i.e.* he was true in his speech, or he spoke the truth, or he spoke truthfully. صدق فى القتال means, he fought well ; he gave a good account of himself in the fight ; he was true to his duty in the fight. صدق فى الوعد

means, he was truthful in his promise. The expression صدقه النصيحة والاخاء means, he was sincere to him in his advice and brotherly affection. See also 2 : 32. صدقة (ṣadaqa) of which the plural is صدقات (ṣadaqāt) means, anything given to win the pleasure of God and a good reward from Him; alms and charity; Zakāt, i.e., the prescribed tax of Islam for helping the poor, etc. صدقة (ṣaduqa) of which the plural is صدقات (ṣaduqāt) as in the present verse, means, dowry or nuptial gift i.e. a gift that is given to or for a bride (Lane & Aqrab). Another word for it is صداق (or مهر) which Islam prescribes for every marriage tie, making it binding on the husband to pay to his wife. It is so called because it is a symbol of truthfulness and sincerity on the part of the husband.

نحلة (willingly) is derived from نحل. The expression نحل المراة means, he gave his wife her مهر or dowry. They say نحل فلانا i.e. he gave such a one willingly and cheerfully without expecting a return. نحلة means, giving a thing willingly and cheerfully without expecting a return ; payment of the dowry to a wife ; a free gift. نحلة is distinguishable from هبة (a free gift) in that every هبة is نحلة but every نحلة is not هبة (Aqrab & Mufradāt).

Commentary :

The verse may be taken to be addressed to both the husband and the relations of the wife. In the latter case, it would mean that the relations of a woman should not spend her dowry received from the husband to meet their own needs, but should faithfully hand it over to her. Some persons receive the dowry of their female wards from their husbands and then, instead of giving it to them, keep it for themselves. Primarily, however, the verse is addressed to the husband whom it requires to pay the agreed dowry to his wife willingly, cheerfully and without demur. Some people fix dowries for their wives and then hesitate or even refuse to pay them, expecting them and even urging them to forego the right. The verse condemns this evil practice.

The word نحلة (paying the dowry willingly and cheerfully) also points to the amount of the dowry being reasonable i.e. it should be well within the means of the husband so that its payment may not be a painful burden to him. He should be in a position to pay it willingly and cheerfully.

The clause, *if they, of their own pleasure, remit to you a part thereof*, applies to those wives who voluntarily and willingly give up or pay back anything out of the agreed dowry. It does not apply to a case in which the wife is asked or made to relinquish the whole or part of the dowry before it has been actually paid to her. According to 'Umar, a woman might claim back her dowry even after she has given it up, if she has done so under any vestige of pressure.

The words, *then enjoy it as something pleasant and wholesome*, imply a compliment to such husbands as evoke a willing and voluntary response from their wives owing to their kind and loving treatment of them. In such cases the wives are so pleased with their husbands that they offer to them a part of their dowry out of their own free will, as a token of the true love that exists between them.

6. And give not to the foolish your property which Allah has made for you a means of support; but feed them therewith and clothe them and speak to them words of kind advice.[488]

وَلَا تُؤۡتُوا السُّفَهَآءَ اَمۡوَالَكُمُ الَّتِیۡ جَعَلَ اللّٰهُ لَكُمۡ قِیٰمًا وَّارۡزُقُوۡهُمۡ فِیۡهَا وَاكۡسُوۡهُمۡ وَقُوۡلُوۡا لَهُمۡ قَوۡلًا مَّعۡرُوۡفًا ۝

488. Important Words :

فِیٰمًا (means of support) is derived from قَام i.e. he stood up. قَام بالامر means, he undertook or managed the affair. قَام علیه means, he took care of him or it. قَام بالیتیم means, he supported or maintained the orphan (Lane). So قِیٰام would mean, the act or state of standing; a means of support or sustenance.

Commentary :

The verse speaks of the property of the orphans as "your property," hinting thereby that the guardians of orphans should be very careful about spending the orphans' property and should in this respect treat it as their own. The expression "your property" may also signify "the property of the orphans which is in your custody." It is also possible that the expression has been used here to include all property whether belonging to the orphans or to their guardians.

As special emphasis was laid in the preceding verses on the care and good treatment of orphans, there was a likelihood that some Muslims might too readily give orphans their money on demand from them. This verse cautions guardians against such a hasty step, because, being young and inexperienced, orphans might waste their money and might also thereby spoil their character. Muslims are, therefore, bidden to meet the legitimate needs of orphans but not to squander away their money, which is a means of their support and maintenance. The same injunction applies to the children or persons of weak understanding in general, the reason being the same in both cases.

The word سفهاء translated as "foolish" but properly meaning, "those who cannot take proper care of their possessions", has been substituted for the word "orphans" in the present verse to supply the needed reason for the injunction, as well as to make it of general application, including in its scope all such persons as are unable to take care of their possessions.

In the case of grown-up imbeciles, the verse would be taken to be addressed to the State which should take effective steps to set up institutions like Courts of Wards to look after the property of such persons as cannot manage it themselves.

7.   And prove the orphans until they attain *the age of* marriage ; then, if you find in them sound judgement, deliver to them their property ; and devour it not in extravagance and haste against their growing up. And whoso is rich, let him abstain ; and whoso is poor, let him eat *thereof* with equity.   And when you deliver to them their property, then take witnesses in their presence.   And Allah is sufficient as a Reckoner.[489]

وَابْتَلُوا الْيَتٰمٰى حَتّٰى اِذَا بَلَغُوا النِّكَاحَ ۚ فَاِنْ اٰنَسْتُمْ مِنْهُمْ رُشْدًا فَادْفَعُوٓا اِلَيْهِمْ اَمْوَالَهُمْ ۚ وَلَا تَاْكُلُوْهَآ اِسْرَافًا وَّبِدَارًا اَنْ يَّكْبَرُوا ۚ وَمَنْ كَانَ غَنِيًّا فَلْيَسْتَعْفِفْ ۚ وَمَنْ كَانَ فَقِيْرًا فَلْيَاْكُلْ بِالْمَعْرُوْفِ ۚ فَاِذَا دَفَعْتُمْ اِلَيْهِمْ اَمْوَالَهُمْ فَاَشْهِدُوا عَلَيْهِمْ ۚ وَكَفٰى بِاللّٰهِ حَسِيْبًا ۝

---

489. Commentary :

Guardians of orphans are enjoined to continue to test them so that if, after having reached the age of puberty, which according to some authorities is 18 years and according to others 21, they are found to be capable of taking charge of their property, it should be handed over to them.   But in no circumstances is it to be made over to them before puberty is attained and before they are so mature of intellect as to take care of and manage their property.   If even at the mature age of 18 or 21, they are found to be incapable of managing their property, it may be withheld from them for a further period, with the sanction of the State.

The verse also warns guardians not to squander away in haste the money of their wards before they are old enough to take charge of it.   The guardian is, however, allowed a reasonable wage, if he is poor, which should be in proportion to the amount of work he does and to the value of the ward's property.

But if the guardian is a person of ample means, he should take nothing out of the orphan's property. In that case, his should be a labour of love, done in hope of reward from God. This verse is not a repetition but an explanation of 4 : 3 which contains a prohibitory injunction for such guardians as possess sufficient income, with the addition that it allows a certain remuneration for guardians of meagre means.

The words, *when you deliver to them their property, then take witnesses in their presence,* have been added as a safeguard against all possible frauds as well as misunderstandings. The property should be handed over to the wards in the presence of reliable witnesses when both the wards and the witnesses are present as the word " presence " hints.

The verse ends with a stern warning in the words, *Allah is sufficient as a Reckoner.* So all concerned should fear the All-Seeing and All-Knowing God.   Indeed, the fear of being called to account before God is the only true basis of all righteousness and the real and most effective preventive against sin and iniquity. One should fear not only the punishment of God but also losing His love and mercy.

8. *For men is a share of that which parents and near relations leave ; and for women is a share of that which parents and near relations leave, whether it be little or much—a determined share.⁴⁹⁰

لِلرِّجَالِ نَصِیۡبٌ مِّمَّا تَرَکَ الۡوَالِدٰنِ وَالۡاَقۡرَبُوۡنَ ۙ وَلِلنِّسَآءِ نَصِیۡبٌ مِّمَّا تَرَکَ الۡوَالِدٰنِ وَالۡاَقۡرَبُوۡنَ مِمَّا قَلَّ مِنۡہُ اَوۡ کَثُرَ ؕ نَصِیۡبًا مَّفۡرُوۡضًا ۝

9. And when *other* relations and orphans and the poor are present at the division *of heritage*, give them *something* therefrom and speak to them words of kindness.⁴⁹¹

وَاِذَا حَضَرَ الۡقِسۡمَۃَ اُولُوا الۡقُرۡبٰی وَالۡیَتٰمٰی وَالۡمَسٰکِیۡنُ فَارۡزُقُوۡہُمۡ مِّنۡہُ وَقُوۡلُوۡا لَہُمۡ قَوۡلًا مَّعۡرُوۡفًا ۝

10. And let those fear *God* who, if they should leave behind them their own weak offspring, would be anxious for them. Let them, therefore, fear Allah and let them say the right word.⁴⁹²

وَلۡیَخۡشَ الَّذِیۡنَ لَوۡ تَرَکُوۡا مِنۡ خَلۡفِہِمۡ ذُرِّیَّۃً ضِعٰفًا خَافُوۡا عَلَیۡہِمۡ ۪ فَلۡیَتَّقُوا اللّٰہَ وَلۡیَقُوۡلُوۡا قَوۡلًا سَدِیۡدًا ۝

*4 : 34.

---

490. Commentary :

This verse, without giving the details, forms the basis of the Islamic law of inheritance. Detailed rules are given in the succeeding verses. The verse lays down the general principle of the social equality of man and woman. Both are entitled to a suitable share in the property.

491. Commentary :

The *Sūra* began by enjoining men and women to treat one another with kindness. Next, it exhorted believers to take care of orphans, for these matters have an important bearing upon social order. The present verse treats of yet another social subject of importance.

By the words, *relations and orphans and the poor*, are here meant those distant relatives, and those orphans and poor persons who, being not among the testator's lawful heirs, are not entitled to receive any part of his property as of right. The verse, though not giving a legal right of inheritance to them, exhorts all true Muslims, while making a will about the division of their property, to set apart a portion of it for orphans and the poor and

such distant relatives as are entitled to no legal share. A testator, however, can leave by will not more than one-third of his property to other than his lawful heirs (Bukhārī, ch. on *Waṣāya*).

According to Ibn 'Abbās, Ibn Musayyib, Ibn Sa'īd and Abū Ja'far, the time referred to in the verse is when a person is about to make his will regarding the division of his property (Muḥīṭ). If nothing can be spared out of the property for this class of people, the testator should at least state in the will that they should be treated with kindness and he himself should also say kind words to them. The injunction laid down in the verse does not concern orphans particularly, but forms a part of the law of inheritance in general. As death leaves behind orphans, therefore injunctions pertaining to orphans have been coupled with those pertaining to the disposal of a deceased person's property.

492. Commentary :

The verse contains a strong and highly forceful appeal in favour of orphans. Those to

11. Surely, ^athey who devour the property of orphans unjustly, only swallow fire into their bellies, and they shall burn in a blazing fire.⁴⁹³

اِنَّ الَّذِيْنَ يَاْكُلُوْنَ اَمْوَالَ الْيَتٰمٰى ظُلْمًا اِنَّمَا يَاْكُلُوْنَ فِيْ بُطُوْنِهِمْ نَارًا ۖ وَسَيَصْلَوْنَ سَعِيْرًا ۝

12. Allah commands you concerning your children : a ^bmale shall have as much as the share of two females ; but if there be females *only, numbering* more than two, then they shall have two-thirds of what the *deceased* leaves ; and if there be one, she shall have the half. And his parents shall have each of them a sixth of the inheritance, if he have a child ; but if he have no child and his parents be his heirs, then his mother shall have a third ; and if he have brothers and sisters, then his mother shall have a sixth, after the payment of any bequests he may have bequeathed or of debt. Your fathers and your children : you know not which of them is nearest to you in benefit. *This* fixing *of portions* is from Allah. Surely, Allah is All-Knowing, Wise.⁴⁹⁴

يُوْصِيْكُمُ اللّٰهُ فِيْ اَوْلَادِكُمْ لِلذَّكَرِ مِثْلُ حَظِّ الْاُنْثَيَيْنِ ۚ فَاِنْ كُنَّ نِسَاءً فَوْقَ اثْنَتَيْنِ فَلَهُنَّ ثُلُثَا مَا تَرَكَ ۚ وَاِنْ كَانَتْ وَاحِدَةً فَلَهَا النِّصْفُ ۚ وَلِاَبَوَيْهِ لِكُلِّ وَاحِدٍ مِّنْهُمَا السُّدُسُ مِمَّا تَرَكَ اِنْ كَانَ لَهُ وَلَدٌ ۚ فَاِنْ لَّمْ يَكُنْ لَّهُ وَلَدٌ وَّوَرِثَهُ اَبَوَاهُ فَلِاُمِّهِ الثُّلُثُ ۚ فَاِنْ كَانَ لَهُ اِخْوَةٌ فَلِاُمِّهِ السُّدُسُ مِنْ بَعْدِ وَصِيَّةٍ يُّوْصِيْ بِهَا اَوْ دَيْنٍ ۗ اٰبَاؤُكُمْ وَاَبْنَاؤُكُمْ لَا تَدْرُوْنَ اَيُّهُمْ اَقْرَبُ لَكُمْ نَفْعًا ۚ فَرِيْضَةً مِّنَ اللّٰهِ ۗ اِنَّ اللّٰهَ كَانَ عَلِيْمًا حَكِيْمًا ۝

---

^aSee 4 : 3.   ^b4 : 177.

whom the guardianship of orphans is entrusted are told to imagine just how they would feel if they knew that they were to die leaving behind little children and no one to take care of them. The implication is that they should treat their wards as kindly as they would like their own little children to be treated in case of their own death.

493. Important Words :

يصلون (burn) is derived from صلى. They say صلى اللحم i.e. he roasted the meat. صلى الشيئ means, he threw the thing into the fire to be burned. صلى النار means, he felt the burning heat of the fire, or he entered the fire and was burnt (Aqrab).

Commentary :

The words, *into their bellies*, in the clause, (they) *only swallow fire into their bellies*, though seemingly superfluous are not really so. They have been added to point out that the fire which they swallow will, as it were, become a part of their bodies and continue as a constant source of burning.

494. Important Words :

ابويه (his parents) is really ابوينه, the letter ن being dropped owing to اضافة. The word ابوين is the genitive of ابوان which is the dual form of اب which is originally ابو meaning, father or grandfather or any male ancestor or paternal uncle. ابوان literally meaning " two fathers " signifies " father and mother " (Lane).

ولد (child) is very general in its significance meaning : (1) a child, son, daughter or a young one ; (2) children, sons, daughters, offspring or young ones. Thus the word is used both as singular and plural, feminine and masculine (Lane).

Commentary :

This and the succeeding verse combined with the last verse of the *Sūra* give the Islamic law of inheritance in a nutshell.

Islam prescribes suitable shares for all near relatives in the property of a deceased person without distinction of sex or order of birth. Children, parents, husbands and wives are the principal heirs who, if alive, get suitable shares in all circumstances, other relations having a title only in special cases. A male has been given double the share of a female because he has been made responsible for the maintenance of the family (Ma'ānī, ii. 32).

The Islamic law of inheritance is perfect and it safeguards against all evils that result from laws prescribed by, or in vogue in, other faiths and communities. It aims at a fair distribution of wealth and equal chances of progress for all. To give the property of a deceased parent to the first-born son only or to exclude the female members from inheritance or to disinherit parents in the presence of children has proved a veritable curse for society in many ways—moral, social and economic. The Islamic law of inheritance, reinforced by the system of *Zakāt* (prescribed alms) and by the injunction prohibiting the giving and taking of interest, provides a golden mean between capitalism and communism—the two evil extremes of present-day economic system.

The verse begins by laying down a general rule as to the proportion of shares between sons and daughters. A son is to have as much as two daughters. So wherever there are both sons and daughters, this rule will come in force. When, however, there are only daughters and no son, the verse allots two-thirds of the legacy to the daughters, if there are more than two of them, and one-half if there is only one. The share of daughters in case there are two, is not expressly stated. But the use of the conjunction فا (but) in the clause, *but if there be females only, numbering more than two,* clearly points to the fact that the share of two females has been referred to in the preceding words " two females." Moreover, the share of two females can be gathered from what has already been said in the beginning of the verse about the ratio between the shares of the males and the females. According to that ratio, a son is to get as much as two daughters. Thus, if there be one son and one daughter, the son will have two-thirds. But as the share of one son has been made equal to that of " two daughters," the latter, in case there is no son, will have two-thirds, *viz.,* the same share as has been expressly fixed for three daughters. Thus, the very construction of the verse shows that if there be two daughters and no son, they too, as in the case of three daughters, will get two-thirds. If it had not been the object of the Quran to point to the share of two daughters in the clause, it would have been something like this, " a male shall have twice as much as a female ", and not as it is now.

The above meaning is corroborated by a saying of the Holy Prophet himself. It is related that when a Companion of the Holy Prophet named Sa'd bin Rabī'a died in the Battle of Uḥud, leaving two daughters and one widow, his brother took away the whole property, leaving nothing for the two daughters. Thereupon the widow of Sa'd went to the Holy Prophet and said, " Here are the two daughters af Sa'd. Their uncle has taken the whole of his property and has left nothing for them." The Holy Prophet told her to wait till God should decide

13. And you shall have half of that which your wives leave, if they have no child ; but if they have a child, then you shall have a fourth of that which they leave, after the payment of any bequests they may have bequeathed or of debt. And they shall have a fourth of that which you leave, if you have no child ; but if you have a child, then they shall have an eighth of that which you leave, after the payment of any bequests you may have bequeathed or of debt. ^aAnd if there be a man or a woman whose heritage is to be divided and he *or she* has neither parent nor child, and he *or she* has a brother and a sister, then each one of them shall have a sixth. But if they be more than that, then they shall be *equal* sharers in one-third, after the payment of any bequests which may have been bequeathed or of debt, without prejudice *to the debt*. *This is* an injunction from Allah and Allah is Wise, Forbearing.⁴⁹⁵

^a4 : 177

the matter. Then this verse was revealed and the Prophet called upon Saʿd's brother to give two-thirds of Saʿd's property to his two daughters and one-eighth to their mother and keep the rest for himself (Tirmidhī & Dāwūd).

The verse speaks of three cases as regards the share of the parents : (1) If a person dies leaving one or more children, then each of his parents shall have one-sixth ; (2) If a person dies issueless and his parents are the sole heirs (there being no wife or husband of the deceased person), then the mother will have one-third of the property and the remaining two-thirds will go to the father ; (3) There is a third case, which is really an exception to the second case. A man dies without issue and his parents are

his sole heirs, but he has brothers or sisters. Then, although his brothers or sisters will not inherit from him, yet their presence will affect the share of the parents, for, in this case, the mother will have one-sixth (instead of one-third, as in the second case) and the remaining five-sixths will go to the father. The reason why the father is awarded a larger share in this case is that the father has also to support the brothers or sisters of the deceased. The subject of inheritance is continued in the succeeding verse.

495. Important Words :

كلالة (one who has neither parent nor child) is derived from كلّ *i.e.* he was or became fatigued, tired or wearied and could proceed no further ; he was or became one having no child and no parent, the latter meaning being based on the former, as a person having no child or parent becomes, as it were, too fatigued for the racial march. كلالة is (1) a person who leaves behind neither father nor child, male or female; or (2) a person who leaves behind neither father nor son. According to Ibn 'Abbās كلالة is a person who leaves no son irrespective of the fact whether his father is living or not. This would thus be the third meaning of كلالة (Lane, Aqrab & Mufradāt).

Commentary :

The first part of this verse determines the share of the husband and the wife in inheritance and needs no comment. The latter part deals with the case of a *Kalāla* i.e. one who leaves neither parent nor child and whose property is inherited by his or her brother and sister. Now, if there is only one brother and one sister, each of them will get one-sixth. But if they are more than that, they will be sharers in one-third.

It should, however, be noted that in this respect brothers and sisters fall under three heads; firstly, real brothers or sisters, offspring of the same parents (such brothers or sisters are technically known as اعيانى, *a'yānī*); secondly, brothers and sisters on the side of the father only (these are technically known as علّى, *'allātī*); thirdly, brothers and sisters on the side of the mother only, their father being not the same as that of the deceased (such brothers and sisters being technically called اخيافى, *akhyāfī*). It is to the last-mentioned class that the commandment given in the present verse pertains; the law with regard to the first two classes of brothers and sisters being given in the last verse of this *Sūra*.

The reader will further note that the shares allotted to the brothers and sisters of the last-mentioned class are smaller than those allotted to the brothers and sisters of the first two

classes, the reason being that the brothers and sisters of this class are on the side of the mother only, while the brothers and the sisters of the other two classes are the children of the same father as the deceased.

It is also noteworthy that in the property of a person who dies as a *Kalāla*, as mentioned in the present verse, both brothers and sisters have equal shares, the usual ratio of two to one being not observed in their case.

The words, "without prejudice to the debt," are important. They mean that the payment of debts should not suffer by the payment of bequests. In other words, debts are to be paid prior to the payment of bequests. It was in compliance with this Quranic injunction that the Holy Prophet used to have the debts paid before the payment of bequests. The rights of other people must be safeguarded before any bequest made by the deceased is complied with. So strict was the Holy Prophet in these matters that he refused to perform the funeral service of the man whose debts were likely to remain unpaid.

It may incidentally be noted here that heirs are divided into two main groups :—

1. ذو والفرائض (*Dhawū'l-Farā'iḍ*) i.e. persons to whom Islam allots a fixed and definite share ($\frac{1}{2}$, $\frac{1}{4}$, $\frac{1}{8}$, $\frac{2}{3}$, $\frac{1}{3}$ or $\frac{1}{6}$) in the estate of a deceased person.

2. عصبات ('*Aṣabāt*) i.e. the heirs who receive the residue after the *Dhawū'l Farā'iḍ* have received their allotted shares.

It is, however, not necessary that a member of the first group should always remain a *Dhū'l Farīḍa*. In certain cases, he may be both a *Dhū'l Farīḍa* (sharer) and an '*Aṣaba* (residuary) and in other cases he may be simply an '*Aṣaba*.

The *Dhawū'l-Farā'iḍ* (sharers) are 12 in number, four males and eight females. The males are 1. father, 2. paternal grandfather, 3. husband and 4. half-brother on the maternal side. The females are (1) daughter, (2) son's daughter,

14. These are the limits set by Allah; and *whoso obeys Allah and His Messenger, *He will make him enter gardens through which streams flow; therein shall they abide; and that is a great triumph.

تِلْكَ حُدُوْدُ اللّٰهِ وَمَنْ يُّطِعِ اللّٰهَ وَرَسُوْلَهٗ يُدْخِلْهُ جَنّٰتٍ تَجْرِيْ مِنْ تَحْتِهَا الْاَنْهٰرُ خٰلِدِيْنَ فِيْهَا ۚ وَذٰلِكَ الْفَوْزُ الْعَظِيْمُ ۝

15. *And whoso disobeys Allah and His Messenger and transgresses His commandments, He will make him enter into Fire; therein he shall abide; and he shall have an humiliating punishment.

وَمَنْ يَّعْصِ اللّٰهَ وَرَسُوْلَهٗ وَيَتَعَدَّ حُدُوْدَهٗ يُدْخِلْهُ نَارًا خَالِدًا فِيْهَا ۚ وَلَهٗ عَذَابٌ مُّهِيْنٌ ۝

16. *And those of your women who are guilty of lewdness—call to witness four of you against them; and if they bear witness, then confine them to the houses until death overtake them or Allah open for them a way.⁴⁹⁶

وَالّٰتِيْ يَاْتِيْنَ الْفَاحِشَةَ مِنْ نِّسَآئِكُمْ فَاسْتَشْهِدُوْا عَلَيْهِنَّ اَرْبَعَةً مِّنْكُمْ ۚ فَاِنْ شَهِدُوْا فَاَمْسِكُوْهُنَّ فِي الْبُيُوْتِ حَتّٰى يَتَوَفّٰهُنَّ الْمَوْتُ اَوْ يَجْعَلَ اللّٰهُ لَهُنَّ سَبِيْلًا ۝

---

*3 : 133 ; 8 : 21 ; 33 : 72.   *See 2 : 26.   *72 : 24.   *4 : 20, 26 ; 24 : 20.

---

(3) mother, (4) wife, (5) full sister, (6) half-sister on paternal side, (7) half-sister on maternal side, and (8) grandmother whether paternal or maternal.

The 'Aṣabāt (residuaries) are of four kinds, (1) ascendants of the deceased *i.e.* father, paternal grandfather, etc. (2) descendants of the deceased *i.e.* son, son's son, etc. (3) descendants of the father of the deceased *i.e.* full brother, brother's son, etc. (4) descendants of the grandfather *i.e.* full paternal uncle, paternal uncle's son, etc.

496. Important Words:

الْفَاحِشَة (lewdness) is derived from فحش. They say فحش الامر *i.e.* the matter or the affair or the thing was or became foul, evil, immodest or lewd; or it became excessively foul, etc. فحشت المرأة means, the woman became foul or ugly. فاحشه means, he vied with him or strove to surpass him in foul or obscene speech or language, etc. فاحشة therefore means, an excess or enormity or anything exceeding the bounds of rectitude; or a thing excessively and enormously foul, evil, immoral, lewd or obscene; a sin or crime which is excessively foul; adultery or fornication. فحشاء besides giving the same meaning as فاحشة also signifies avarice or niggardliness in the payment of Zakāt or the poor-rate (Lane).

Commentary:

The women referred to in this verse are those guilty of foul or immoral conduct short of adultery. Abū Muslim and Mujāhid, among others, have also held this view.

The words, *confine them to the houses until death overtake them or Allah open for them a way*, mean that they should be prevented from

17. And if two men from among you are guilty of it, punish them both. And if they repent and amend, then leave them alone; surely, Allah is Oft-Returning *with compassion and Merciful.*[497]

وَالَّذَانِ يَأْتِيٰنِهَا مِنْكُمْ فَاٰذُوْهُمَا ۚ فَاِنْ تَابَا وَاَصْلَحَا فَاَعْرِضُوْا عَنْهُمَا ۗ اِنَّ اللّٰهَ كَانَ تَوَّابًا رَّحِيْمًا ۝

mixing with other women until they reform themselves or get married, marriage being an effective means of weaning people from immoral practices. As the offence mentioned is a serious one, four witnesses are considered necessary in order to prevent injustice being done to women.

Some scholars have sought to interpret the verse in the light of a saying of the Holy Prophet which runs as follows: "Learn from me, Allah has indeed opened for them a way, which is that if an unmarried couple commit fornication with each other, they should receive a hundred stripes and should be banished for one year. But if a married man commits adultery with a married woman, then they should receive a hundred stripes each and be stoned to death" (Jarīr, iv. 182). These scholars hold that the word فاحشة (*fāhisha*) mentioned in the verse means "adultery" and that this verse prescribed that the women who committed adultery were to be detained in their houses till their death or till the time when God should open a way for them *i.e.* reveal the law concerning them; and that the law which was afterwards revealed was to the effect that an unmarried woman committing fornication should receive a hundred stripes and one year's banishment, while a married woman guilty of adultery should be stoned to death after she had received a hundred stripes. This interpretation, however, is open to many objections :—

1. If the words, *confine them to the houses until death overtake them or Allah open for them a way,* mean that they were to be detained in their houses until God gave His law concerning

them, the question is, what hindered God from giving His law at the very time of the revelation of the verse under comment ? There is no hint here that the time was not yet ripe for such a law to be revealed. In this case, the only inference will be that God hesitated to give the necessary law at the time when this verse was revealed because He was not yet decided, the matter being still under His consideration. Such a supposition cannot be made about God.

2. The law mentioned in the above-quoted ḥadīth is not found in the Quran.

3. The Holy Prophet's own practice was against this ḥadīth. No less than four persons were stoned to death for adultery in his life-time, but none of them was given the punishment of a hundred stripes before being stoned as the above-mentioned ḥadīth prescribes.

It may also be pointed out here that according to the usage of the Quran, the word فاحشة (*fāhisha*) does not always mean "adultery" but as shown under Important Words above it is also applied to all sorts of excesses or sins or crimes or acts exceeding the bounds of rectitude. For this meaning of the word the reader is referred to 33:31 which says: *O wives of the Prophet, if any of you be guilty of* فاحشة مبينة (*manifestly dishonourable conduct*) ; and 65:2 which says: *unless they commit* فاحشة مبينة (*an act which is manifestly foul*) ; and 7:29 which says: *and when they commit* فاحشة (*a foul deed*). In none of these verses does the word فاحشة mean adultery.

497. Commentary :

The verse refers to two males who are guilty

18. Verily, *Allah undertakes to accept the repentance of only those who do evil ignorantly and then repent soon after. These are they to whom Allah turns with mercy ; and Allah is All-Knowing, Wise.498

اِنَّمَا التَّوْبَةُ عَلَى اللّٰهِ لِلَّذِيْنَ يَعْمَلُوْنَ السُّوْٓءَ بِجَهَالَةٍ ثُمَّ يَتُوْبُوْنَ مِنْ قَرِيْبٍ فَاُولٰٓئِكَ يَتُوْبُ اللّٰهُ عَلَيْهِمْ ۗ وَكَانَ اللّٰهُ عَلِيْمًا حَكِيْمًا ۝

19. There is no *acceptance of* repentance for those who *continue to* do evil until, when death faces one of them, he says, ' I do repent now ; ' *nor for those who die disbelievers. It is these for whom We have prepared a painful punishment.

وَلَيْسَتِ التَّوْبَةُ لِلَّذِيْنَ يَعْمَلُوْنَ السَّيِّاٰتِ ۚ حَتّٰى اِذَا حَضَرَ اَحَدَهُمُ الْمَوْتُ قَالَ اِنِّيْ تُبْتُ الْـٰٔنَ وَلَا الَّذِيْنَ يَمُوْتُوْنَ وَهُمْ كُفَّارٌ ۗ اُولٰٓئِكَ اَعْتَدْنَا لَهُمْ عَذَابًا اَلِيْمًا ۝

---

*6:55; 16:120; 24:6.   *2:62; 3:92; 47:35.

---

of an unnatural offence or something approaching it. What particular form the punishment mentioned here should take has been left to the discretion of the authorities concerned.

Both this verse and the preceding one refer to offences for which no حد شرعى (punishment definitely fixed by the Law) has been prescribed, the matter having been left to the discretion of the authorities to be decided according to circumstances.

498. Commentary :

The expression بجهالة (ignorantly) does not mean that the offenders do evil without knowing that it is evil. In fact, every evil deed which a man does is an act of ignorance, born of lack of true knowledge. The Holy Prophet is reported to have said, " There are some kinds

of ' knowledge' which are really ' ignorance ' " *i.e.* the learning of which is injurious to man (Biḥār). So the expression بجهالة (ignorantly) has been added to point to the philosophy of sin and to exhort people to acquire true knowledge with a view to avoiding sin.

The words من قريب (soon after) here mean " before death " which may come at any time and is thus always near. The Holy Prophet is reported to have said : " Allah accepts the repentance of man till the agonies of death " (Muslim, ch. on *Tauba*). This explanation is corroborated by what is said in the next verse (4 : 19), *viz.*, *who continue to do evil until when death faces one of them, he says, I do repent now.* This shows that repentance may be accepted of any person, if he sincerely repents before death actually overtakes him.

20. O ye who believe, it is not lawful for you to inherit women against their will; nor should you detain them wrongfully that you may take away part of that which you have given them, except that *they be guilty of a flagrant evil; and consort with them in kindness; and *if you dislike them, it may be that you dislike a thing wherein Allah has placed much good.[499]

يَٰٓأَيُّهَا الَّذِينَ اٰمَنُوا لَا يَحِلُّ لَكُمْ اَنْ تَرِثُوا النِّسَآءَ كَرْهًا ۖ وَلَا تَعْضُلُوهُنَّ لِتَذْهَبُوا بِبَعْضِ مَآ اٰتَيْتُمُوهُنَّ اِلَّآ اَنْ يَّأْتِيْنَ بِفَاحِشَةٍ مُّبَيِّنَةٍ ۚ وَعَاشِرُوهُنَّ بِالْمَعْرُوفِ ۚ فَاِنْ كَرِهْتُمُوهُنَّ فَعَسَىٰٓ اَنْ تَكْرَهُوا شَيْئًا وَّيَجْعَلَ اللّٰهُ فِيْهِ خَيْرًا كَثِيْرًا ۝

*See 4:16.   *2:217.

499. Commentary:

Men become heirs of women against their will in various ways : (1) A man does not like his wife and does not treat her well, yet he does not divorce her, hoping to possess her property after her death ; (2) He treats his wife harshly and compels her by ill-treatment to obtain separation (*Khul'*) from him by giving him a part or whole of her property, or by surrendering her dowry; (3) The relations of the deceased husband of a widow prevent her from marrying another husband in order to get possession of her property after her death ; (4) They force her to marry some one from among themselves against her will, treating her virtually as a part of the property left by her dead husband; (5) The husband takes by force the property of his wife, as if it were his by legal right ; (6) The relatives of the deceased husband take away by force the property of his widow, depriving her of her right of inheritance.

The deceased person's relatives cannot prevent his widow from contracting a new marriage so that they may get hold of her property; but they can prevent her from doing so, if she intends to marry a person of manifestly objectionable character.

If the address is to the husbands, the verse would mean that if the wives do not want to live with their husbands and seek separation from them, which they can do by means of *Khul'*, the husbands should not prevent them from doing so out of greed for their money. But they can do so, if the wives are going to be guilty of a manifestly foul act.

The words, *consort with them in kindness*, embody the pith of the Islamic teachings about the treatment of wives. They are not to be treated in a dry, business-like way but with love and kindness. The Holy Prophet is reported to have said : خيركم خيركم لاهله *i.e.* "the best among you is he who is best in his treatment of his wife" (Tirmidhī). But as a one-sided affair can never be truly successful, the Quran uses the expression عاشروهن (consort with them) which being of the measure مفاعلة denotes reciprocity. So husbands and wives are both enjoined to live amicably with each other and reciprocate each other's love and kindness.

Woman cannot adequately appreciate and acknowledge the great debt she owes to the Quran. No other scripture has given to her the high status that the Quran gives her. It not only lays down her inalienable rights but also exhorts men to overlook the weaknesses and shortcomings of their wives and treat them with kindness and benevolence, even if they do not like them. The memorable words

21. And if you desire to take one wife in place of another and you have given one of them a treasure, take not aught therefrom. Will you take it by lying and with manifest sinfulness?[500]

وَاِنۡ اَرَدۡتُّمُ اسۡتِبۡدَالَ زَوۡجٍ مَّكَانَ زَوۡجٍ لَّا وَّاٰتَيۡتُمۡ اِحۡدٰىهُنَّ قِنۡطَارًا فَلَا تَاۡخُذُوۡا مِنۡهُ شَيۡـًٔا ؕ اَتَاۡخُذُوۡنَهٗ بُهۡتَانًا وَّاِثۡمًا مُّبِيۡنًا ۝

22. And how can you take it when one of you has been alone with the other, and they (the women) have taken from you a strong covenant?[501]

وَكَيۡفَ تَاۡخُذُوۡنَهٗ وَقَدۡ اَفۡضٰى بَعۡضُكُمۡ اِلٰى بَعۡضٍ وَّاَخَذۡنَ مِنۡكُمۡ مِّيۡثَاقًا غَلِيۡظًا ۝

---

of the Holy Prophet quoted above *i.e.* "the best of you is he who is best in his treatment of his wife" (Tirmidhī), are only an echo of the noble teachings of the Quran with regard to women.

500. Important Words :

بهتان (lying) is the noun-infinitive from بهت. They say بهته *i.e.* he slandered him or accused him falsely; or he did so in such a manner as to make him confounded at the falsity of the charge. بهتان therefore means, a calumny, slander or false accusation ; falsehood by reason of which one is perplexed or confounded and is rendered unable to see his right course; a false accusation of adultery against a woman (Lane & Aqrab).

Commentary :

The verse does not mean that man can divorce his wife at will. Anas, a Companion of the Holy Prophet, relates that once Abū Ayyūb and Abū Ṭalḥa wanted to divorce their wives (without valid reason) and asked the Holy Prophet about it. He counselled them not to do so, characterizing their act as an act of injustice. Thereupon, they abandoned their intention of divorcing their wives and retained them. This does not mean that a husband cannot divorce his wife without obtaining the permission of the authorities ; he can do so, if he so desires ; but he will certainly be accountable before God if

he does so without valid reason. Elsewhere the Holy Prophet is reported to have said, "Surely of the things sanctioned by the Law of Islam the most hateful in the sight of God is divorce" (Dāwūd ch. on *Talāq*).

If for some special reason a man wishes to divorce one wife and marry another, he is not allowed to take back from the former what he has already given her, no matter however big the sum may be. If he does so, he will be guilty of infidelity and sin.

501. Important Words :

افضى (has been alone) is formed from فضا meaning, it was or became empty or vacant, or void ; it was or became wide or spacious. افضيت الى الشيئ means, I came to or reached a thing. افضى الى امرأته means, he went in unto his wife ; or he came in contact with his wife, skin to skin ; he was with her alone in private (Lane).

Commentary :

The words, *one of you has been alone with the other*, do not necessarily imply sexual intercourse. They only mean living with each other and meeting each other in private on terms of extreme intimacy. According to this verse, a man cannot take back from his wife any property or sum of money he may have given her, even though he may not have gone in unto her.

The expression, *and they (the women) have*

23. And marry not those women whom your fathers married, except what has already passed. It is a thing foul and hateful, and an evil way.[502]

وَلَا تَنْكِحُوْا مَا نَكَحَ اٰبَآؤُكُمْ مِّنَ النِّسَآءِ اِلَّا مَا قَدْ سَلَفَ ۚ اِنَّهٗ كَانَ فَاحِشَةً ۭ وَّمَقْتًا ۭ وَسَآءَ سَبِيْلًا ۞

R. 4   24. Forbidden to you are your mothers, and your daughters, and your sisters, and your fathers' sisters, and your mothers' sisters, and brother's daughters, and sister's daughters, and your *foster*-mothers that have given you suck, and your foster-sisters, and the mothers of your wives, and your step-daughters, who are your wards, by your wives to whom you have gone in—but if you have not gone in unto them, there shall be no sin upon you —and the wives of your sons that are from your loins ; and *it is forbidden to you* to have two sisters together in marriage, except what has already passed ; surely, Allah is Most Forgiving, Merciful.[503]

حُرِّمَتْ عَلَيْكُمْ اُمَّهٰتُكُمْ وَبَنٰتُكُمْ وَاَخَوٰتُكُمْ وَعَمّٰتُكُمْ وَخٰلٰتُكُمْ وَبَنٰتُ الْاَخِ وَبَنٰتُ الْاُخْتِ وَاُمَّهٰتُكُمُ الّٰتِىْٓ اَرْضَعْنَكُمْ وَاَخَوٰتُكُمْ مِّنَ الرَّضَاعَةِ وَاُمَّهٰتُ نِسَآئِكُمْ وَرَبَآئِبُكُمُ الّٰتِىْ فِىْ حُجُوْرِكُمْ مِّنْ نِّسَآئِكُمُ الّٰتِىْ دَخَلْتُمْ بِهِنَّ ۫ فَاِنْ لَّمْ تَكُوْنُوْا دَخَلْتُمْ بِهِنَّ فَلَا جُنَاحَ عَلَيْكُمْ ۫ وَحَلَآئِلُ اَبْنَآئِكُمُ الَّذِيْنَ مِنْ اَصْلَابِكُمْ ۙ وَاَنْ تَجْمَعُوْا بَيْنَ الْاُخْتَيْنِ اِلَّا مَا قَدْ سَلَفَ ۭ اِنَّ اللّٰهَ كَانَ غَفُوْرًا رَّحِيْمًا ۞

---

taken from you a strong covenant, shows that women are not the slaves of the whim or caprice of men. Both are bound by a sacred contract and men owe to their wives obligations which they must respect and faithfully discharge, because, as regards social rights, both are on much the same level. Men are warned here not to treat light-heartedly the covenant they have made with their wives, the very tie of marriage having the force of a covenant.

502. Important Words :

مَقْتًا (hateful). مَقَتَ means, he hated him on account of a foul or evil action committed by him ; he hated him with a violent hatred on account of a foul or evil action. مَقْت therefore, means, violent hatred based on some foul or evil action ; contracting marriage with the former wife of one's father which is considered to be a most hateful act (Aqrab).

Commentary :

The clause, *except what has already passed,* does not mean that step-mothers taken as wives before this verse was revealed could be retained. What the words mean is, simply, that if such men repent and amend, no harm will come to them for what unlawful acts they might have committed in the past. The past will certainly be forgiven but the women whom it was unlawful to marry were to be divorced at once after this verse was revealed. In fact, the position of women in pre-Islamic Arabia was so degraded that men looked upon their step-mothers as part of the chattels, left by their fathers, with whom they did what they liked. Islam accorded to women inviolable rights which could not be infringed with impunity.

503. Important Words :

رَبَآئِب (step-daughters) is derived from رَبّ

and is the plural of ربيبة meaning, the daughter of a woman's husband by another wife or the daughter of a man's wife by another husband, because he or she rears her in spite of her being not a real daughter; or it means the wife of a man having child by another wife; also a woman who has the charge of a child, who rears or fosters it (Lane & Aqrab).

حجور (wards) is the plural of حجر which is derived from حجر meaning, he prevented or hindered it. حجر means, bosom or breast or the part beneath the armpit; custody, care or guardianship. They say, نشأ زيد فى حجر عمرو *i.e.* Zaid grew up in the care and protection of 'Amr. The expression التى فى حجوركم would, therefore, mean, those who are under your care or guardianship *i.e.* your wards (Lane, Aqrab & Mufradāt).

حلائل (wives) is the plural of حليل and حليلة which are both derived from حل *i.e.* he alighted or took up his abode; or he or it became lawful; or he untied a knot, etc. حليل means, husband and حليلة wife. حليل also means, a fellow-lodger or fellow-resident of another in one house (Aqrab). It also means a neighbour and a guest (Lane).

ارضعنكم (have given you suck) is derived from رضع . They say رضع امه *i.e.* he sucked the breast of his mother. هذا اخى من الرضاعة means, he is my foster-brother, we both having sucked the breast of the same woman. ارضعته امه means, his mother suckled him; and استرضعت المرأة ولدى means, I sought or demanded of the woman that she should suckle my child (Lane).

Commentary :

The prohibition about marrying mothers, sisters and daughters may look superfluous; but there are certain people (*e.g.* certain sects among the Hindus) who regard such marriages as not only permissible but even meritorious. The Quran, being a perfect code of Law, contains everything essential for man's physical, moral and spiritual well-being. The Quranic laws are in perfect harmony with human nature; in fact, they only remind us of what is writ large on the book of human nature by God's own hand. Human nature responds to what is taught by the Quran and the Quran commands that which human nature demands, and it prohibits what human nature revolts against. The Holy Prophet is reported to have said that the relatives of foster-mothers are as forbidden as those within prohibited degree of relationship of real mothers. It is not lawful to marry foster-sisters and foster-daughters and so on. There exists, however, a difference of opinion among Muslim theologians as to what amount of suckling makes the marriage of foster-mothers and foster-sisters and their relations (within prohibited degree of marriage) unlawful. Some hold the view that the prohibition comes into operation in all cases even when a woman has given suck to a child only once. According to others who derive their authority from a saying of the Holy Prophet reported by 'Ā'isha, *viz.* لا تحرم المصة ولا المصتان *i.e.* " a suck or two do not make marriage unlawful " (Tirmidhi, ch. on *Riḍā'*), the least number of sucks to render marriage unlawful is three. But there is yet another saying of the Holy Prophet, also reported by 'Ā'isha, that mentions خمس رضعات معلومات (five distinctly known sucks) as necessary to make marriage unlawful (Muslim), and this appears to be the correct view. One suck amounts to the quantity taken by a child at one stretch *i.e.* when for the time being it should leave off sucking of its own accord and before returning to it. The age of the child must be within two years at the time of sucking.

The qualifying clause, *who are your wards*, is only added to draw our attention to the fact that we should bring up our wards with the same care and tenderness that we bestow upon our own children; otherwise marriage with the daughters of women with whom conjugal

25. And *forbidden to you are* married women, except such as your right hands possess. This has Allah enjoined on you. And allowed to you are those beyond that, that you seek *them* by means of your property, [a]marrying them properly and not committing fornication. And for the benefit you receive from them, [b]give them their dowries, as fixed, and there shall be no sin for you in anything you mutually agree upon, after the fixing *of the dowry.* Surely, Allah is All-Knowing, Wise.[504]

وَّالْمُحْصَنٰتُ مِنَ النِّسَآءِ اِلَّا مَا مَلَكَتْ اَيْمَانُكُمْ ۚ كِتٰبَ اللّٰهِ عَلَيْكُمْ ۚ وَ اُحِلَّ لَكُمْ مَّا وَرَآءَ ذٰلِكُمْ اَنْ تَبْتَغُوْا بِاَمْوَالِكُمْ مُّحْصِنِيْنَ غَيْرَ مُسٰفِحِيْنَ ۚ فَمَا اسْتَمْتَعْتُمْ بِهٖ مِنْهُنَّ فَاٰتُوْهُنَّ اُجُوْرَهُنَّ فَرِيْضَةً ۚ وَلَا جُنَاحَ عَلَيْكُمْ فِيْمَا تَرَاضَيْتُمْ بِهٖ مِنْۢ بَعْدِ الْفَرِيْضَةِ ۚ اِنَّ اللّٰهَ كَانَ عَلِيْمًا حَكِيْمًا ۝

[a]4 : 26 ; 5 : 6.   [b]4 : 5 ; 60 : 11.

relations have been established is unlawful, whether or not they are brought up as wards. The daughters of those women with whom such relations have not been established can be taken into marriage and this is the meaning of the words, *but if you have not gone in unto them, there shall be no sin upon you.*

The expression, *of your sons that are from your loins,* is added to exclude wife's sons as well as adopted ones. Islam does not recognize the system of adoption. It wants us to look upon all Muslims as brothers ; and as the adoption of certain individuals as sons conflicts with this principle of universal brotherhood, it has been prohibited by Islam. The system of adoption also leads to contention and litigation.

In conformity with the command contained in the words, *it is forbidden to you to have two sisters together in marriage,* the Holy Prophet is reported to have ordered one of the two sisters who were together the wives of one man to be divorced by him after this injunction was revealed (Tirmidhi, ch. on *Nikāh*). The injunction is based on sentiments of deference to near relationship and is meant to exclude possibility of dissensions in the close family circle.

For similar reasons the Holy Prophet has forbidden to unite in marriage a maternal aunt and her sister's daughter or a paternal aunt and her brother's daughter.

504. Important Words :

المحصنات (married) is the plural of محصنة and is derived from حصن meaning, he or it was or became inaccessible, fortified or protected against attack. حصن المرأة means, the woman was chaste *i.e.* protected against moral or sexual sinfulness. احصنت المرأة means, the woman got married. محصنة therefore, means a married woman ; a chaste woman who abstains from what is unlawful ; a free or noble woman as opposed to a bondwoman. Similarly محصن means, a married man ; a chaste man who abstains from what is unlawful ; a free or noble man. حصن means, a fort or a fortress. The word محصنات would, therefore, mean, women who have protected themselves by entering, as it were, the fortress of marriage. The word has been used in the Quran in all the different senses *i.e.* (1) married women, (2) chaste women and (3) free women ; but in the present verse it has been used in the sense of married women (Lane & Aqrab).

مسافحين (committing fornication) is the active participle from سافح which is derived from سفح. They say سفح الدم *i.e.* he shed blood or made it flow. سفح الدمع means, tears began to flow. Thus the word is both transitive and intransitive. سافح means, he vied with the other party in shedding blood; he committed fornication. مسافح means, a fornicator and مسافحة means, a fornicatress (Lane & Aqrab).

اجور (dowries) is the plural of اجر which means, reward or wages. اجر المرأة means, dowry of a woman (Tāj). In 33 : 51, also the word has been used in the sense of dowry.

استمتعتم (the benefit you receive) is formed from متع. They say متعها بكذا *i.e.* he gave her (his wife) such a thing. تمتع بالمرأة means, he benefited by the woman temporarily. استمتع بكذا means, he benefited by it for a long time. The Arabic idiom does not countenance the use of استمتاع with regard to a woman in the sense of temporary connection (Lisān). It must also be noted that whenever the noun تمتع (*tamattu'*) is used to denote temporary connection with a woman, it is followed by the preposition بـ (*bā*) put before the word standing for the woman, as in the above example. But in the expression فما استمتعتم به منهن the pronoun هن referring to women is preceded by the preposition من.

ما ملكت ايمانكم (what your right hands possess). The Arabs say هذا ملك يمينى *i.e.* he or it is in the possession of my right hand, meaning, he or it is in my possession and I can deal with him or it as I like (Lisān & Aqrab). The expression ما ملكت ايمانكم generally signifies, men or women taken prisoner in war and being in the custody and control of their Muslim captors. In this verse, the expression means women prisoners only. The term has been used by the Quran in preference to عباد or اماء (slaves and bondwomen) to point to just and rightful possession, the word ايمان (right hands) also pointing to the same fact.

Commentary :

The expression, *such as your right hands possess*, has been used in the Quran with regard to those men or women who took part in aggressive wars against Islam and fell prisoners into the hands of Muslims. The context, however, shows that the expression used in the present verse means female prisoners of war. Islam does not allow women taken prisoner in ordinary wars to be taken as wives. This exceptional injunction becomes operative only when a hostile nation wages a religious war against Islam with a view to extirpating it and compelling Muslims to abandon their religion, at the point of the sword, and treats their prisoners as slaves, as was done in the days of the Holy Prophet when the enemy took away Muslim women as prisoners and treated them as slaves. The Islamic injunction was thus only a retaliatory measure and also served the additional purpose of protecting the morals of captive women who were generally in large numbers and whom war separated from their kith and kin. A people who seek to compel others to forsake their religion at the point of the sword and reduce them to slavery are mere brutes and not respectable human beings. They must be paid back in their own coin in order to bring them to their senses. For a fuller exposition of this subject see General Introduction.

It may be noted that it is not permitted to take into marriage such female relations of a bondwoman who is treated as wife, as correspond to the relations of a free woman within the prohibited degree. For instance, the mothers, sisters, daughters etc. of such bondwomen cannot be taken in marriage.

The advocates of *Mut'a* (temporary marriage) have endeavoured in vain to infer its legality from this verse. The Quran and the Arabic language both contradict this manifestly unfounded inference. The misunderstanding

26. And whoso of you cannot afford to marry free, believing women, *let him* marry what your right hands possess, namely, your believing hand-maids. And Allah knows your faith best; you are *all* one from another ; so marry them with the leave of their masters and give them their dowries according to what is fair, they being chaste, not committing fornication, nor taking secret paramours. And if, after they are married, *they are guilty of lewdness, they shall have half the punishment prescribed for free women. This is for him among you who fears lest he should commit sin. And that you restrain yourselves is better for you ; and Allah is Most Forgiving, Merciful.505

وَمَنْ لَّمْ يَسْتَطِعْ مِنْكُمْ طَوْلًا اَنْ يَّنْكِحَ الْمُحْصَنٰتِ الْمُؤْمِنٰتِ فَمِنْ مَّا مَلَكَتْ اَيْمَانُكُمْ مِّنْ فَتَيٰتِكُمُ الْمُؤْمِنٰتِ وَ اللّٰهُ اَعْلَمُ بِاِيْمَانِكُمْ بَعْضُكُمْ مِّنْ بَعْضٍ فَانْكِحُوْهُنَّ بِاِذْنِ اَهْلِهِنَّ وَ اٰتُوْهُنَّ اُجُوْرَهُنَّ بِالْمَعْرُوْفِ مُحْصَنٰتٍ غَيْرَ مُسٰفِحٰتٍ وَّلَا مُتَّخِذٰتِ اَخْدَانٍ فَاِذَآ اُحْصِنَّ فَاِنْ اَتَيْنَ بِفَاحِشَةٍ فَعَلَيْهِنَّ نِصْفُ مَا عَلَى الْمُحْصَنٰتِ مِنَ الْعَذَابِ ذٰلِكَ لِمَنْ خَشِيَ الْعَنَتَ مِنْكُمْ وَ اَنْ تَصْبِرُوْا خَيْرٌ لَّكُمْ وَ اللّٰهُ غَفُوْرٌ رَّحِيْمٌ ۞

---

*a*4 : 16, 20 ; 24 : 20.

---

about *Mut'a* seems to have arisen from the failure to understand the difference between the meanings of تَمَتَّعَ and اِسْتَمْتَعَ given under Important Words. The author of Lisān al-'Arab quotes Zajjāj as saying : " This is a verse in the interpretation of which some men have committed a great blunder, owing to their ignorance of the Arabic language. They have inferred from it the legality of *Mut'a*, which, by the consensus of opinion among Muslim theologians, has been declared to be unlawful, whereas the words simply mean marriage performed in accordance with the conditions mentioned above."

According to Arabic usage, the legality of *Mut'a*, as asserted by some people, cannot, therefore, be inferred from this verse. If there had been any reference to *Mut'a*, the preposition used ought to have been بِ (*bā*) and not مِنْ *min*). Moreover, the expression used here is not تَمَتَّعَ but اِسْتَمْتَعَ which possesses a sense

different from that of the former word.

Nor can any inference in favour of *Mut'a* be drawn from the expression اُجُوْرَهُنَّ which, as explained under Important Words, means " their dowries," in which sense it has been used in the Quran elsewhere also (33 : 51).

On principle, the dowry must be paid immediately at marriage ; but with the wife's consent the payment can be suitably deferred. The husband can increase the amount of the dowry later, if he so desires ; but he cannot decrease it except with the permission of the wife or the *Qāḍi*.

505. **Important Words :**

طَوْلًا (to afford) is noun from طَالَ *i.e.* he or it was or became long, tall or high. طَوْل means, bounty or gift ; ampleness of means ; excellence ; excess or increase ; power or ability ; wealth or competence. It may also mean,

27. ^aAllah desires to make clear to you, and guide you to, the paths of those before you, and to turn to you in mercy. And Allah is All-Knowing, Wise.

يُرِيْدُ اللّٰهُ لِيُبَيِّنَ لَكُمْ وَ يَهْدِيَكُمْ سُنَنَ الَّذِيْنَ مِنْ قَبْلِكُمْ وَيَتُوْبَ عَلَيْكُمْ وَ اللّٰهُ عَلِيْمٌ حَكِيْمٌ ۝

28. And ^bAllah wishes to turn to you in mercy, but those who follow *their low* desires wish that you should stray far away.⁵⁰⁶

وَ اللّٰهُ يُرِيْدُ اَنْ يَّتُوْبَ عَلَيْكُمْ وَ يُرِيْدُ الَّذِيْنَ يَتَّبِعُوْنَ الشَّهَوٰتِ اَنْ تَمِيْلُوْا مَيْلًا عَظِيْمًا ۝

---

^a4 : 177.   ^b9 : 104 ; 33 : 74 ; 42 : 26.

---

dowry or expenses of marriage (Lane, Aqrab & Mufradāt).

اخدان (secret paramours) is the plural of خدن . They say خادنه *i.e.* he was or became his friend or companion ; or he was or became his secret or private friend. اخدان means friends or secret friends ; amorous companions or associates ; companions or associates affected with sensual appetency (Lane & Mufradāt).

العنت (sins) is the noun-infinitive from عنت *i.e.* he fell into a difficulty ; or he committed a sin or a crime or an act of disobedience ; or he committed fornication or adultery. عنت therefore, means, severe difficulty or hardship; a state of perdition ; a corrupt or evil state or conduct ; a sin or crime or an act of disobedience deserving punishment; a wrong action (intentional or unintentional) ; fornication or adultery (Lane & Aqrab). See also 3 : 119 & 2 : 221.

Commentary :

As God attaches great value to the faith of a Muslim, He does not like it to become impaired by his marrying disbelieving women. Hence the condition that even the bondwoman a Muslim may marry should be a believer.

The words, *you are all one from another,* are meant to raise believing bondwomen in the estimation of Muslims, who are hereby required not to despise them or treat them with contempt on account of their so-called lower status.

The words, *half the punishment,* mean 50 stripes, the punishment for (unmarried) free women being 100 stripes. See also 24 : 3. The word *half* shows that the verse refers to a punishment which can be halved, and not to stoning to death, which was inflicted on married free women. The punishment definitely prescribed in the Quran (24 : 3) for a fornicator and a fornicatress is only a hundred stripes, but as the Holy Prophet differentiated between married and unmarried persons, inflicting on the former the punishment of stoning to death, the aforesaid verse has been taken as applying to unmarried persons only.

The expression, *this is for him among you who fears lest he should commit sin,* shows that Muslims are enjoined to avoid, as far as possible, contracting conjugal relations with bondwomen taken prisoner from belligerent disbelievers. This is to be done only if, on the one hand, one is not able to marry a free woman and, on the other, by remaining unmarried, one fears to fall into sin. The Muslim Empire of Baghdad fell to pieces because the *Khalīfas* took to contracting conjugal relations with bondwomen. The incompetent princes born of them ruined the State. In most cases marital relations with bondwomen are calculated to have a demoralizing effect on both husbands and children.

506. Commentary :

In the matter of bondwomen, the Quran wants

29. Allah desires to lighten your burden, for man has been created weak.[507]

يُرِيدُ اللهُ اَنْ يُّخَفِّفَ عَنْكُمْ وَخُلِقَ الْاِنْسَانُ ضَعِيْفًا ۝

30. O ye who believe! [a]devour not your property among yourselves by unlawful means, except that *you earn* by trade with mutual consent. And kill not yourselves. Surely, Allah is Merciful towards you.[508]

يٰٓاَيُّهَا الَّذِيْنَ اٰمَنُوْا لَا تَاْكُلُوْٓا اَمْوَالَكُمْ بَيْنَكُمْ بِالْبَاطِلِ اِلَّآ اَنْ تَكُوْنَ تِجَارَةً عَنْ تَرَاضٍ مِّنْكُمْ ۗ وَلَا تَقْتُلُوْٓا اَنْفُسَكُمْ ۗ اِنَّ اللهَ كَانَ بِكُمْ رَحِيْمًا ۝

31. And whosoever does that by way of transgression and injustice, We shall cast him into Fire; and that is easy with Allah.

وَمَنْ يَّفْعَلْ ذٰلِكَ عُدْوَانًا وَّظُلْمًا فَسَوْفَ نُصْلِيْهِ نَارًا ۗ وَكَانَ ذٰلِكَ عَلَى اللهِ يَسِيْرًا ۝

32. If you [b]keep away from the more grievous of the things which you are forbidden, We will remove from you your *minor* evils and admit you to a place of great honour.[509]

اِنْ تَجْتَنِبُوْا كَبَآئِرَ مَا تُنْهَوْنَ عَنْهُ نُكَفِّرْ عَنْكُمْ سَيِّاٰتِكُمْ وَنُدْخِلْكُمْ مُّدْخَلًا كَرِيْمًا ۝

---

[a]2 : 189.   [b]42 : 38 ; 53 : 33.

Muslims to exercise self-control, without which it is feared they may deviate from the path of moral rectitude.

507. Commentary:

The reason why the Law is revealed is that man is by nature weak and cannot himself find out the ways of spiritual advancement. So God has taken this burden from him. It was far from God to entrust man with a work which he could not discharge.

The verse also constitutes refutation of the Christian doctrine of Atonement which rejects the Law (*Sharīʻat*) on the ground of human weakness. As a matter of fact, Islam declares human weakness to be the very reason for the revelation of the Law, so that it may help man to fulfil his high destiny. The Law is not, therefore, a curse but a help and a blessing.

508. Commentary:

By *unlawful means* are meant all those means and methods which are forbidden by the Law.

The verse declares all commercial transactions without the mutual consent of seller and buyer to be null and void.

The clause, *kill not yourselves*, makes it clear that the devouring of other persons' property by unlawful means or carrying on transactions without the free consent of the parties concerned brings about the moral death of the guilty party.

The words, *kill not yourselves*, also imply interdiction of suicide. The Holy Prophet is reported to have said, " Whosoever kills himself with a weapon, will be brought on the Day of Judgement with the said weapon in his hand and will be thrown into the Fire wherein he will abide. And whosoever kills himself with a poison will be thrown into the Fire, with that poison in his hand, where he will continue to take it " (Kathīr).

509. Commentary:

Truly speaking, there is no classification of

33. And covet not that whereby [a]Allah has made some of you excel others. Men shall have a share of that which they have earned, and women a share of that which they have earned. And ask Allah of His bounty. Surely, Allah has perfect knowledge of all things.[510]

وَلَا تَتَمَنَّوْا مَا فَضَّلَ اللهُ بِهِ بَعْضَكُمْ عَلٰى بَعْضٍ لِلرِّجَالِ نَصِيْبٌ مِّمَّا اكْتَسَبُوْا وَلِلنِّسَآءِ نَصِيْبٌ مِّمَّا اكْتَسَبْنَ وَاسْئَلُوا اللهَ مِنْ فَضْلِهِ إِنَّ اللهَ كَانَ بِكُلِّ شَيْءٍ عَلِيْمًا ۝

34. And [b]to every one We have appointed heirs to what the parents and the relations leave, and also those with whom your oaths have ratified a contract. So give them their portion. Surely, Allah watches all things.[511]

وَلِكُلٍّ جَعَلْنَا مَوَالِيَ مِمَّا تَرَكَ الْوَالِدَانِ وَالْأَقْرَبُوْنَ وَالَّذِيْنَ عَقَدَتْ أَيْمَانُكُمْ فَاٰتُوْهُمْ نَصِيْبَهُمْ إِنَّ اللهَ كَانَ عَلٰى كُلِّ شَيْءٍ شَهِيْدًا ۝

*a*4 : 35.　　*b*4 : 8.

---

more grievous and less grievous sins in the Quran. The term is rather a relative one. The commission of anything forbidden by God is a sin and the commission of all sins which one finds difficult to shun is grievous. The meaning of the verse, therefore, is that if you avoid doing those things the giving up of which seems difficult and burdensome to you, the result will be that you will be enabled to get rid of other sins as well. Some scholars interpret the word كبائر (grievous sins) as signifying the last stage of each act of sin. For instance, a person contemplates committing a theft. Now, whereas the actual commitment of theft is "grievous," the preliminary acts leading up to it would be "minor evils." If one restrains oneself from committing the final act, the preliminary ones will be forgiven him.

510. Commentary:

The first part of the verse means that: (1) One should not pray that God may give one the very thing which another man possesses; (2) One may, however, pray that God may bestow on one "the like of that" which has

been given to another man; (3) That while praying, one should not keep in view any particular favoured person, wishing that God may make one like that particular person, for it may be the will of God to bestow His favours upon one in even a greater measure. One should only pray to God generally for His bounty and grace, for Allah's bounty and grace are unbounded.

The words, *Men shall have a share of that which they have earned*, etc., contain the key to national progress and advance. Both men and women get what they earn and deserve. So we should not wish evil for others but should work and pray. This is the way to succeed in life and to win the pleasure of God. The words also reveal the equality of men and women so far as their work and reward are concerned.

511. Important Words:

موالي (heirs) is derived from ولي and is the plural of مولى which means, lord or chief; master or owner; son of a paternal uncle; or a relation such as a son of a paternal uncle and the like; a freedman whom the emancipator

R. 6

35. ^aMen are guardians over women because ^bAllah has made the one of them to excel the other, and because they (men) spend of their wealth. So virtuous women are those who are obedient, and guard the secrets *of their husbands* with Allah's protection. And *as for* those on whose part you fear disobedience, admonish them and leave them alone in their beds, and chastise them. Then if they obey you, seek not a way against them. Surely, Allah is High *and* Great.[512]

اَلرِّجَالُ قَوَّامُوْنَ عَلَى النِّسَآءِ بِمَا فَضَّلَ اللهُ بَعْضَهُمْ عَلَى بَعْضٍ وَّ بِمَآ اَنْفَقُوْا مِنْ اَمْوَالِهِمْ فَالصّٰلِحٰتُ قٰنِتٰتٌ حٰفِظٰتٌ لِّلْغَيْبِ بِمَا حَفِظَ اللهُ وَالّٰتِيْ تَخَافُوْنَ نُشُوْزَهُنَّ فَعِظُوْهُنَّ وَاهْجُرُوْهُنَّ فِى الْمَضَاجِعِ وَاضْرِبُوْهُنَّ فَاِنْ اَطَعْنَكُمْ فَلَا تَبْغُوْا عَلَيْهِنَّ سَبِيْلًا اِنَّ اللهَ كَانَ عَلِيًّا كَبِيْرًا ۝

---

^a2 : 229.   ^b2 : 238 ; 4 : 33.

---

is bound to aid and whose property he inherits if he dies leaving no heir ; a slave ; emancipator of a slave ; a neighbour ; an ally ; a friend or helper ; a follower ; a partner ; an heir, etc. (Lane & Lisân).

Commentary :

The verse may also be rendered thus : " To every one We have appointed heirs to what he leaves. They are the parents, the relations and those with whom your oaths have ratified a contract. So give them their portion." Again, the verse may also be rendered as : " To everything which parents and relations leave we have appointed heirs, etc."

The words, *with whom your oaths have ratified a contract*, signify " spouses ", embracing both husbands and wives. The pronoun " them " in the clause, *so give them their portion*, refers to, and stands for, the noun " heirs " in the opening clause.

512. Important Words :

قوّامون (guardians) is derived from قام *i.e.* he stood. They say قام عليه *i.e.* he tended or took care of it or him. قام باليتيم means, he maintained the orphan. قام على المرأة means, he undertook the maintenance of the woman ;

he undertook or managed her affairs ; he protected her, or became her guardian. قوّم الشيئ (qawwama) means, he set the thing right, or made it straight or even. قوّام therefore means, one who manages affairs well ; a ruler or governor ; one in a position to issue orders (Lane & Aqrab).

قانتات (obedient) is the plural of قانتة being the active participle from قنت . They say قنت لله *i.e.* he was obedient to God. امرأة قنوت means, a woman humble, submissive and obedient to her husband (Lane). See also 2 : 117.

نشوز (disobedience) is the noun-infinitive from نشز *i.e.* he rose or raised himself. نشزت المرأة على زوجها means, the woman rose against, or was disobedient to, her husband and exalted herself against him and resisted him and was an evil companion to him. نشز المرء على زوجته means, the husband treated his wife unjustly and was unkind to her or forsook her or hated her and was an evil companion to her (Lane & Aqrab).

اهجروهن (leave them alone). هجره means, he cut him off from friendly or loving communion or intercourse ; he forsook or abandoned him ; he " cut " him *i.e.* he boycotted him and ceased to speak to him or to associate with him. مجر الشيئ means, he forsook, or abandoned the thing; he shunned or avoided it. مجر زوجته means, he separated himself from his wife or kept away from her (Lane & Mufradāt).

اضربوهن (chastise them) is derived from ضرب. They say ضربه i.e. he beat, struck, smote or hit him (with hand, stick, etc.); hence, he chastised him.

علا (High) is derived from علا i.e. he or it was or became high, elevated, lofty or exalted. تعالى means, he was or became high, elevated, exalted or supremely exalted or extolled. على means high, elevated or lofty in rank, condition or state. العلى which is one of the attributive names of God (e.g. 2 : 256) means, the High; the Most High; He above Whom is nothing. المتعال is also an attributive name of God (e.g. 13 :10) meaning, He Who is great or supremely great, the High or the Most High; One Higher than every other high one. تعال means, come thou, as if said by a man in a high place when calling upon a man in a low place, but is also used generally (Lane).

Commentary :

The verse gives two reasons why man has been made the head of the family : (a) his superior mental and physical powers ; (b) his being bread-earner and maintainer of the family. It is natural and fair that he who earns and supplies the money should have the final say in the disposal of affairs.

The word قانتات (obedient) spoken of wives may mean either obedient to God, or to husbands.

The expression, *guard the secrets of their husbands*, means that when the husbands are at home, they are obedient to them and guard their secrets ; and when they are away, they not only guard their secrets but take care of their property and guard their own chastity.

The clause, *leave them alone in their beds*, may mean : (a) abstention from conjugal relations with them; (b) sleeping in separate beds ; or (c) ceasing to talk to them. The use of the word " beds " also incidentally implies that the disobedient wives are to stay at home and are not to be allowed to leave or be turned out of their homes.

The measures mentioned in the verse are not to remain in force for an indefinite period, for wives are not to be left *like a thing suspended* (4 : 130). Four months, according to the Quran, is the utmost limit for abstention from conjugal relations *i.e.* for practical separation (2 : 227).

If the husband deems the affair to be sufficiently grave, he will have to observe the conditions mentioned in 4 : 16.

Regarding " chastisement " mentioned as a last resort in the verse under comment a Companion reports the Holy Prophet to have said that if at all a Muslim has to beat his wife, the beating should not be such as to leave any mark on her body (Tirmidhī ch. on *Riḍā'*). According to Abū Dāwūd and Nasā'ī the Holy Prophet forbade the beating of women at all, but when 'Umar complained that they had become refractory, he gave the permission with the afore-mentioned condition; but on complaint of ill-treatment of women by their husbands he indignantly said that the husbands who beat their wives were not the best among men (Kathīr, iii). On another occasion the Holy Prophet is reported to have said : " The best among you is he who treats his wife best and I am the best of you in this respect " (Tirmidhī).

The divine attributes of " High and Great " mentioned at the end of the verse are also intended to warn husbands that the chastisement of their wives, if at all resorted to,

36. And *if you fear a breach between them, then appoint an arbiter from his folk and an arbiter from her folk. If they (the arbiters) desire reconciliation, Allah will effect it between them. Surely, Allah is All-Knowing, All-Aware.[513]

وَاِنْ خِفْتُمْ شِقَاقَ بَيْنِهِمَا فَابْعَثُوْا حَكَمًا مِّنْ اَهْلِهٖ وَحَكَمًا مِّنْ اَهْلِهَا ۚ اِنْ يُّرِيْدَاۤ اِصْلَاحًا يُّوَفِّقِ اللّٰهُ بَيْنَهُمَا ؕ اِنَّ اللّٰهَ كَانَ عَلِيْمًا خَبِيْرًا ۞

37. And *worship Allah and associate naught with Him, and *show* kindness to parents, and to kindred, and orphans, and the needy, and to the neighbour that is a kinsman and the neighbour that is a stranger, and the companion by *your* side, and the wayfarer, and those whom your right hands possess. Surely, Allah loves not the proud *and* the boastful ;[514]

وَاعْبُدُوا اللّٰهَ وَلَا تُشْرِكُوْا بِهٖ شَيْئًا ۚ وَّ بِالْوَالِدَيْنِ اِحْسَانًا وَّبِذِى الْقُرْبٰى وَالْيَتٰمٰى وَالْمَسٰكِيْنِ وَالْجَارِ ذِى الْقُرْبٰى وَالْجَارِ الْجُنُبِ وَالصَّاحِبِ بِالْجَنْبِ وَ ابْنِ السَّبِيْلِ ۙ وَمَا مَلَكَتْ اَيْمَانُكُمْ ؕ اِنَّ اللّٰهَ لَا يُحِبُّ مَنْ كَانَ مُخْتَالًا فَخُوْرَا ۞

---

*a*4 : 129.   *b*6 : 152 ;   7 : 34 ;   17 : 24 ;   23 : 60.

---

should not be unjust or vindictive or high-handed ; for if they are high and great above their wives, there is One Who is High and Great above all and He shall call husbands to account for any improper use of the qualified authority given to them over their wives.

513. Important Words :

حَكَم (arbiter) is from حَكَمَ. They say حَكَمَهُ *i.e.* he made him judge. حَاكِم or حَكَم means, one who judges, a judge, an arbiter, arbitrator or umpire between people ; a ruler or governor (Lane).

Commentary :

The pronoun, used in the plural number, in the expression اِنْ خِفْتُمْ (*if you fear*) refers to the Muslim State or to the community or the people generally. The arbiters should preferably be chosen from the relations of the contending parties, because they are expected to be acquainted with the real cause of differences and it is easier also for both parties to put their

case before them. The verse makes it clear that Islam leaves no avenue unexplored to bring about reconciliation between husband and wife before it allows them to sever the tie of marriage.

514. Important Words :

جَارُ الْجُنُبِ (neighbour that is a stranger) is a compound word made up of جَار (neighbour) and جُنُب (stranger or one distant). The compound word thus means, a neighbour who is not from one's own tribe or community ; a distant neighbour (Aqrab & Mufradāt).

صَاحِبُ الْجَنْبِ (companion by your side) is also a compound word made up of صَاحِب (companion) and جَنْب (one's side). The compound word thus means, the immediate neighbour or the near neighbour; or simply companion or co-worker or colleague (Aqrab, Lisān & Mufradāt).

Commentary :

After laying down in the preceding verses that one should be kind to one's wife, in the

38. *Who are niggardly and enjoin people to be niggardly, and conceal that which Allah has given them of His bounty. And We have prepared for the disbelievers an humiliating punishment;[515]

اِلَّذِیۡنَ یَبۡخَلُوۡنَ وَ یَاۡمُرُوۡنَ النَّاسَ بِالۡبُخۡلِ وَیَکۡتُمُوۡنَ مَاۤ اٰتٰىهُمُ اللّٰهُ مِنۡ فَضۡلِهٖ ؕ وَ اَعۡتَدۡنَا لِلۡکٰفِرِیۡنَ عَذَابًا مُّهِیۡنًا ﴿ۙ

39. And for *those who spend their wealth to be seen of men, and believe not in Allah nor the Last Day. And *whoso has Satan for his companion, *let him remember that* an evil companion is he.[516]

وَ الَّذِیۡنَ یُنۡفِقُوۡنَ اَمۡوَالَهُمۡ رِئَآءَ النَّاسِ وَلَا یُؤۡمِنُوۡنَ بِاللّٰهِ وَ لَا بِالۡیَوۡمِ الۡاٰخِرِ ؕ وَ مَنۡ یَّکُنِ الشَّیۡطٰنُ لَهٗ قَرِیۡنًا فَسَآءَ قَرِیۡنًا ﴿

---

*3 : 181 ; 17 : 30 ; 25 : 68.   *2 : 265.   *43 : 37, 39.

present verse the Quran enjoins a Muslim to make his kindness so comprehensive as to include in its scope the whole of mankind, from parents who are the nearest, to strangers who are the farthest removed.

The Arabic expression rendered as, *neighbour that is a kinsman*, may also mean : (1) the neighbour that lives near ; (2) the neighbour that is kindly.

Similarly the words, *neighbour that is a stranger*, may also include : (1) the neighbour that lives at a distance ; (2) the neighbour that is not kindly.

The expression, *companion by your side,* may mean : (1) wife or husband ; (2) comrade on a journey ; (3) fellow-partner in a trade or a co-worker ; (4) associate ; (5) immediate neighbour.

The words, *those whom your right hands possess,* may refer to slaves, bondwomen, servants and even subordinates.

A person who does not carry out the divine commandments contained in this verse is condemned as " proud and boastful " because, instead of doing good to others and being kind to them, he looks down upon them and behaves arrogantly. The very act of abstaining from

being kind to one's fellow-beings, whether relations or neighbours or strangers, is an act of pride condemned by Islam.

515. **Commentary :**

Some persons are so niggardly that, far from spending their wealth for the benefit of others, they do not spend it even upon themselves, lest people should come to know of it. These, as it were, conceal Allah's bounty. They are not only deprived of the rewards and good results of charity but also become guilty of concealing God's bounty which He has bestowed upon them for the good of mankind. Elsewhere the Quran says, *Acknowledge the bounty of thy Lord in word and deed* (93 : 12).

516. **Important Words :**

قَرِیۡنًا (companion) is the verbal adjective from قرن . They say قرن شیئا بشیئی *i.e.* he connected, coupled or conjoined a thing with another. قرین means, an associate ; a comrade ; a companion ; also a husband (Lane & Aqrab).

Commentary :

Some people spend their money while they have no faith in God or in the Last Day. They

40. And what *harm* would have befallen them, if they had believed in Allah and the Last Day and spent out of what Allah has given them ? And Allah knows them full well.

وَمَاذَا عَلَيْهِمْ لَوْ اٰمَنُوْا بِاللّٰهِ وَالْيَوْمِ الْاٰخِرِ وَاَنْفَقُوْا مِمَّا رَزَقَهُمُ اللّٰهُ ۚ وَكَانَ اللّٰهُ بِهِمْ عَلِيْمًا ۞

41. Surely, [a]Allah wrongs not *any one even* by the weight of an atom. And if there be a good deed, He multiplies it and gives from Himself a great reward.[517]

اِنَّ اللّٰهَ لَا يَظْلِمُ مِثْقَالَ ذَرَّةٍ ۚ وَاِنْ تَكُ حَسَنَةً يُّضٰعِفْهَا وَيُؤْتِ مِنْ لَّدُنْهُ اَجْرًا عَظِيْمًا ۞

42. And how *will it fare with them* [b]when We shall bring a witness from every people, and shall bring thee as a witness against these ![518]

فَكَيْفَ اِذَا جِئْنَا مِنْ كُلِّ اُمَّةٍ بِشَهِيْدٍ وَّجِئْنَا بِكَ عَلٰى هٰۤؤُلَآءِ شَهِيْدًا ۞

---

[a]10 : 45 ; 18 : 50 ; 28 : 85.   [b]16 : 90.

---

do it to win the applause of men and not the pleasure of God. So, instead of winning reward, they earn God's displeasure. Sometimes, however, money is spent openly in the cause of God with the object of inducing others to do the same. This display of charity belongs to an altogether different category and is commendable.

517. Important Words :

مِثْقَال (weight) is derived from ثقل meaning, it was or became heavy, weighty or ponderous. مِثْقَال means, the weight of a thing whether great or small ; a thing with which one weighs ; a certain weight of which the quantity is well-known ; a *dirhem* ; a *dīnār* (Lane).

ذَرَّة (atom) is derived from ذَرّ meaning, he sprinkled or scattered. ذَرّ of which ذَرَّة is the singular means, the young of ants ; ant's eggs ; small red ants ; the smallest of ants ; the motes that are seen in a ray of the sun that enters through an aperture (Lane).

Commentary :

No good deed, done even by a disbeliever, goes unrewarded. If the good deeds of disbelievers do not make them deserving of salvation, they at least serve to mitigate the severity, and lessen the duration, of their punishment. In fact, wherever the Quran says that the deeds of disbelievers will not avail them, it means either that they will not succeed in their efforts against the truth or that their deeds will be of no help to them in securing for them admission into Heaven.

The reward promised in this verse is of two kinds : *firstly*, the direct result of one's good acts ; and *secondly*, their indirect consequence in the form of God's pleasure.

518. Commentary :

Every Prophet will bear witness on the Day of Judgement against or concerning those to whom he was sent as a Messenger. The word هٰؤُلَاء (these) includes both believers and disbelievers, the nature of evidence being different in different cases.

43. On that day [a]those who disbelieved and disobeyed the Messenger will wish that the earth were made level with them, and they shall not *be able to* conceal anything from Allah.[519]

44. O ye who believe! approach not Prayer when you are not in *full possession of your senses*, until you know what you say, nor when you are unclean, except when you are travelling along a way, until you have bathed. And if you are ill or *you are* on a journey *while unclean*, or *if* one of you comes from the privy or you have touched women and you find no water, then betake yourselves to pure dust and wipe therewith your faces and your hands. Surely, Allah is Most Indulgent, Most Forgiving.[520]

يَوۡمَئِذٍ يَّوَدُّ الَّذِيۡنَ كَفَرُوۡا وَعَصَوُا الرَّسُوۡلَ لَوۡ تُسَوّٰى بِهِمُ الۡاَرۡضُ ؕ وَلَا يَكۡتُمُوۡنَ اللّٰهَ حَدِيۡثًا ۟ ۪

يٰۤاَيُّهَا الَّذِيۡنَ اٰمَنُوۡا لَا تَقۡرَبُوا الصَّلٰوةَ وَاَنۡتُمۡ سُكٰرٰى حَتّٰى تَعۡلَمُوۡا مَا تَقُوۡلُوۡنَ وَلَا جُنُبًا اِلَّا عَابِرِىۡ سَبِيۡلٍ حَتّٰى تَغۡتَسِلُوۡا ؕ وَاِنۡ كُنۡتُمۡ مَّرۡضٰۤى اَوۡ عَلٰى سَفَرٍ اَوۡ جَآءَ اَحَدٌ مِّنۡكُمۡ مِّنَ الۡغَآئِطِ اَوۡ لٰمَسۡتُمُ النِّسَآءَ فَلَمۡ تَجِدُوۡا مَآءً فَتَيَمَّمُوۡا صَعِيۡدًا طَيِّبًا فَامۡسَحُوۡا بِوُجُوۡهِكُمۡ وَاَيۡدِيۡكُمۡ ؕ اِنَّ اللّٰهَ كَانَ عَفُوًّا غَفُوۡرًا ۟

---

[a]78 : 41.

---

519. Important Words :

حَدِيۡثًا (anything) is derived from حدث meaning, it came into existence, not having been before. حدث (*haddatha*) means, he talked or related or narrated, etc. حديث means, a piece of information ; an announcement ; news or tidings ; an account ; a narration or story ; a tradition ; a thing or matter that is talked of or narrated or transmitted ; any talk or discourse that one hears. The word also means, new or recent or brought into existence newly (Lane & Aqrab).

Commentary :

The expression, *will wish that the earth were made level with them*, shows that the words 'earth and heaven' as mentioned in the Quran, do not always signify the physical earth and heaven but may represent one's existing moral and spiritual condition. On the day when men will stand before God, this earth will have ceased to exist for them.

520. Important Words :

سكارى (not in full possession of your senses) is the plural of سكران which is derived from سكر *i.e.* he was or became intoxicated, inebriated or drunken. They say سكر على فلان *i.e.* such a one became angry or violently angry with him. سكرت الريح means, the wind became still after blowing. سكر الباب means, he closed or stopped up the door. سكرة الموت means, the intoxication or agony of death which causes confusion of intellect and deprives the sufferer of reason. سكرة الهم والنوم means, the oppressive sensation, etc. attendant upon anxiety and upon sleep. سكر (*sukrun*) which is the noun-infinitive from the verb سكر means, the state of intoxication, inebriation or drunkenness ; a state that intervenes as an obstruction between a man and his intellect, mostly used in relation to intoxicating drinks but sometimes as meaning such a state arising from anger or from the passion of love, etc. (Lane). **For further** explanation see 15 : 73 ; 22 : 3. In view of the different meanings of this word a person would be called سکران (intoxicated) when he is drunk; or is in a fit of anger; or in raptures of love ; or has received a great and sudden shock; or is stricken with fear; or is over-powered by sleep or some other disturbing element which may distract his attention or obscure his reason, etc.

جنبا (unclean) is derived from جنب . They say جنبه i.e. he led him or it by his side; he put him or it at a distance. جنب اليه means, he was or became disquieted by a vehement desire to see or meet him. جنابة means, distance ; the state of being unclean owing to sexual intercourse or discharge of semen, when it becomes obligatory for one to perform a total ablution by bathing. جنب means, a stranger ; one who is distant and remote ; one who is under the obligation of performing a total ablution (bathing) by reason of sexual inter-course or discharge of semen. The word is used both as masculine and feminine, singular and plural (Lane).

عابرى سبيل (are travelling along a way) is really عابرى which is the plural of عابر which is derived from عبر . They say عبره i.e. he crossed it, went across it, or passed over it from one side to another. عبر السبيل means, he travelled or passed along the way or road. عبر also means, he died, as though he had travelled the road of life (Lane). The expression عابرى سبيل signifies one who is actually travelling. Every person away from home cannot be called عابرى سبيل . Again, if a person is away from home on a journey but halts at a place or decides to stay in a town or village for a few days, he will not be reckoned as one of the عابرى سبيل (those travelling along a way) ; but if, while travelling, he halts for a night on the roadside, for example in a *serai* or at a rest-house or at a railway station, etc., he will be regarded as one.

غائط (privy) is derived from غاط which means,

he or it became hidden in the ground ; he dug, excavated or hollowed out in the earth ; it sank or became depressed in the ground ; it descended or sloped downwards in the ground. غائط therefore means : (1) a wide and depressed piece of ground having acclivities bordering it ; (2) a place in which one satisfies one's want of nature, the custom being to do so in a depressed place where one may remain hidden ; (3) human excrement or ordure because it is cast away in a غائط (a depressed place). The expression اتى الغائط means, he responded to the call of nature ; he satisfied the want of nature ; he voided excrement or ordure (Lane).

تيمموا (betake yourselves to) is derived from يمه . They say يمه i.e. he aimed at it or desired it, or he betook himself to it. تيم المريض means, the sick man, instead of performing the usual ablution for Prayer, betook himself to pure dust and wiped his face and hands therewith. تيم (*tayammum*) is technically the process of striking the palms of the hands on the surface of pure earth and then wiping or passing them over the face, etc. in the prescribed manner (Tāj).

Commentary :

According to this verse, Prayer cannot be considered to have been properly performed if the devotee simply repeats the words of Prayer without understanding what he says. It is also implicit in the verse that a non-Arab Muslim, besides praying in the prescribed Arabic words, should also pray to God and supplicate Him in his own tongue, in the language which he usually speaks and in which he can best express his thoughts and feelings.

The word سکارى though primarily meaning "intoxicated" is, as shown under Important Words, much wider in its significance. Any state or condition in which one is not in full possession of oneself, either through anger or love or hunger or sleep, etc. is included in this expression. The Holy Prophet is reported to have said : "If a man is sleepy, then he should not say his Prayers till the state of sleepiness has left him" (Bukhārī, ch. on *Wuḍū*). Again : "A man should not say his Prayers when he is hungry and the food has been placed before him (Bukhārī, ch. on *Ṣalāt*) ; or when the call of nature demands his attention" (Dāwūd, ch. on *Ṭahārat*).

The expression, *nor when you are unclean*, means that just as a man cannot perform Prayers when he is in a state of سکر (not in full possession of his senses), similarly he cannot perform Prayers in a state of being جنبا (for the meaning of which see Important Words above) until he performs total ablution by bathing. Sexual intercourse creates a sort of uncleanness in the body which must be removed by bathing in order to ensure proper state of purity, cheerfulness and vivacity necessary for worship.

The clause, *except when you are travelling along a way*, means that though ordinarily a person who is in a state of "uncleanness" cannot perform his Prayers except after properly bathing, yet if he becomes "unclean" when he is actually travelling on the way, bathing is not obligatory on him for the performance of Prayers. He can in this case perform *tayammum* as ordered in the concluding part of the verse.

The sentence, *if you are ill or you are on a journey (while unclean) or if one of you comes from the privy or you have touched women and you find no water, then betake yourselves to pure dust*, mentions four classes of persons on whom وضو (ablution) or غسل (total ablution) is not obligatory for the performance of Prayer, they being required to perform what is known as *tayammum i.e.* betaking to pure dust and wiping therewith the face and the hands, as detailed in Ḥadīth and Sunna. These four classes are : (1) the sick ; (2) those on a journey ; (3) those coming from the privy ; (4) those touching women (*i.e.* having carnal

knowledge of them). Out of these only the last two are such as proc of uncleanness, necessitating the p of وضو (ablution) or غسل (total ... .ion), as the case may be. So the clause, *and you find no water*, relates to them only. The verse thus purports to say that if the last-mentioned two classes of men do not find water, they can perform *tayammum i.e.* wipe their faces and hands with pure dust before saying their Prayers.

In the case of the former two clauses no condition as to water is necessary. These two classes of men may resort to تیمم (*tayammum*) even if they find water. This is why the words, "and you are unclean" have been supplied after the words, *if you are ill or you are on a journey*. It must be noted that the expression على سفر (on a journey) is, in the present verse, the same as the expression عابری سبیل (travelling along a way), both signifying the state of actual travelling when one is, as it were, on the wing.

Finally it must be noted that dust has been chosen as a substitute for water because, just as water reminds a person of his origin (77 : 21), thus creating in him a sense of humility, similarly, dust calls to his mind the other humble substance from which he was created (*He created you from dust*, 30 : 21). But the dust used must be pure, which is a necessary condition for the performance of Prayers. Any excess should be blown away before it is used in order to ensure just the minimum quantity for the performance of تیمم.

From the verse it is clear that though performing proper ablution is ordinarily necessary for Prayers, yet Islam being a perfect religion, one is allowed to substitute *tayammum* in place of ablution in certain exceptional cases.

45. Dost thou not know of those who were given a portion of the Book? [a]They buy error and desire that you *too* may lose the way.

الَمْ تَرَ اِلَى الَّذِيْنَ اُوْتُوْا نَصِيْبًا مِّنَ الْكِتٰبِ يَشْتَرُوْنَ الضَّلٰلَةَ وَيُرِيْدُوْنَ اَنْ تَضِلُّوا السَّبِيْلَ ۞

46. And Allah knows your enemies full well. And [b]sufficient is Allah as a Friend, and sufficient is Allah as a Helper.

وَاللّٰهُ اَعْلَمُ بِاَعْدَآئِكُمْ ۗ وَكَفٰى بِاللّٰهِ وَلِيًّا ۗ وَّكَفٰى بِاللّٰهِ نَصِيْرًا ۞

47. There are some among the Jews who [c]pervert words from their *proper* places. And they say, 'We hear and we disobey' and 'hear *thou* without being heard,' and [d]'Rā‘inā', screening with their tongues *what is in their minds* and *seeking* to injure the Faith. And if they had said, 'We hear and we obey,' and 'hear *thou*,' and 'Unẓurnā,' it would have been better for them and more upright. But Allah has cursed them for their disbelief; so they believe but little.[521]

مِنَ الَّذِيْنَ هَادُوْا يُحَرِّفُوْنَ الْكَلِمَ عَنْ مَّوَاضِعِهٖ وَيَقُوْلُوْنَ سَمِعْنَا وَعَصَيْنَا وَاسْمَعْ غَيْرَ مُسْمَعٍ وَّرَاعِنَا لَيًّا بِاَلْسِنَتِهِمْ وَطَعْنًا فِى الدِّيْنِ ۗ وَلَوْ اَنَّهُمْ قَالُوْا سَمِعْنَا وَاَطَعْنَا وَاسْمَعْ وَانْظُرْنَا لَكَانَ خَيْرًا لَّهُمْ وَاَقْوَمَ ۙ وَلٰكِنْ لَّعَنَهُمُ اللّٰهُ بِكُفْرِهِمْ فَلَا يُؤْمِنُوْنَ اِلَّا قَلِيْلًا ۞

---

[a]4 : 90.   [b]4 : 174 ; 33 : 18, 66.   [c]2 : 76 ; 3 : 79 ; 5 : 42.   [d]2 : 105.

521. Commentary :

The verb يقولون (they say) is used in Arabic both for words of mouth, and for what one expresses by one's condition or conduct (see 2 : 31). In this verse the expression has been used of the Jews in both these senses, *viz.*, "they say with their tongues that they have heard and obeyed but their conduct shows that instead of obeying they disobey and defy." The expression غير مسمع (without being heard) gives a number of meanings : (1) mayest thou not be made to hear *i.e.* mayest thou not hear by reason of deafness ; (2) mayest thou not hear any speech or news which thou wouldst like or which may please thee ; (3) may not what thou sayest be accepted, or may not thy invitation be accepted and thy call responded to ; (4) mayest thou not be obeyed ;

or (5) the expression may mean, though it was not certainly intended by the Jews, mayest thou not hear anything offensive or unpleasant.

For the expression راعنا (rā‘inā) see note on 2 : 105.

The Jews used the aforesaid ambiguous expressions in order (1) to conceal what evil thoughts they entertained about the Holy Prophet ; (2) to make Muslims imitate them and use analogous expressions while addressing the Holy Prophet ; and (3) to taunt Muslims with regard to matters affecting their religion, saying to them in effect, "We speak to your Prophet jestingly and abuse him in ambiguous words ; if he had been a true Prophet of God, he would have certainly come to know of this."

48. O ye People of the Book ! believe in what We have sent down, fulfilling that which is with you, *a*before We destroy *some of* the leaders and turn them on their backs or curse them as *b*We cursed the people of the Sabbath. And the decree of Allah is *bound* to be carried out.[522]

يَٰٓأَيُّهَا الَّذِينَ أُوتُوا الْكِتَٰبَ ءَامِنُوا بِمَا نَزَّلْنَا مُصَدِّقًا لِّمَا مَعَكُم مِّن قَبْلِ أَن نَّطْمِسَ وُجُوهًا فَنَرُدَّهَا عَلَىٰٓ أَدْبَارِهَآ أَوْ نَلْعَنَهُمْ كَمَا لَعَنَّآ أَصْحَٰبَ السَّبْتِ ۚ وَكَانَ أَمْرُ اللَّهِ مَفْعُولًا ۝

49. Surely, *c*Allah will not forgive that any partner be associated with Him ; but He will forgive whatever is short of that to whomsoever He pleases. And whoso associates partners with Allah has indeed devised a very great sin.[523]

إِنَّ اللَّهَ لَا يَغْفِرُ أَن يُشْرَكَ بِهِۦ وَيَغْفِرُ مَا دُونَ ذَٰلِكَ لِمَن يَشَآءُ ۚ وَمَن يُشْرِكْ بِاللَّهِ فَقَدِ افْتَرَىٰٓ إِثْمًا عَظِيمًا ۝

*a*10 : 89.   *b*2 : 66 ; 4 : 155 ; 7 : 164 ; 16 : 125.   *c*4 : 117.

---

522. Important Words :

وجوها (leaders) is the plural of وجه which gives a number of meanings : face ; the outward appearance of a person or thing ; the front or the side that confronts the eyes of the looker ; the first part of a thing ; the leader or chief of a people ; motive or intention, etc. (Aqrab).

Commentary :

This verse contains two prophecies concerning the Jews : (1) God will destroy their leaders, and they will be vanquished and " turned on their backs " *i.e.* banished from and turned out of their country ; (2) God will curse them as He had cursed the people who profaned the Sabbath. The words embodying the two prophecies are joined together by the conjunction او (or) not to express doubt but to show that either of the two punishments was to befall the Jews ; or that some of them were to be visited with one kind of punishment and others with the other. The expression, *We will turn them on their backs,* does not mean, as some Commentators have thought, " We

will physically disfigure them and put their faces on their backs." This meaning, besides being against Arabic idiom, is entirely uncorroborated by history. If the word وجوه is taken in the sense of " faces ", then the whole sentence will be taken in a figurative sense, signifying total transformation or ruin.

The verse also makes it clear that when speaking of the profaners of the Sabbath as having been turned into apes (2 : 66 ; 5 : 61 ; 7 : 164—169), the verses referred to do not mean that they were actually and physically transformed into apes ; for, as the present verse shows, the same prophecy was made concerning the Jews who opposed the Holy Prophet and they were never actually transformed into apes.

523. Important Words :

يشرك (associates partners) is derived from شرك . They say شرك فيه *i.e.* he shared or participated with him in it ; he was or became his co-partner in it. اشرك بالله means, he attributed to God or associated with Him a

50. Dost thou not know of those who hold themselves to be pure ? Nay, it is Allah Who purifies whomsoever He pleases, and [a]they will not be wronged a whit.[524]

51. Behold, how [b]they forge a lie against Allah ! And sufficient is that as a manifest sin.[525]

اَلَمۡ تَرَ اِلَی الَّذِیۡنَ یُزَکُّوۡنَ اَنۡفُسَهُمۡ ؕ بَلِ اللّٰهُ یُزَکِّیۡ مَنۡ یَّشَآءُ وَ لَا یُظۡلَمُوۡنَ فَتِیۡلًا ۝

اُنۡظُرۡ کَیۡفَ یَفۡتَرُوۡنَ عَلَی اللّٰهِ الۡکَذِبَ ؕ وَ کَفٰی بِهٖۤ اِثۡمًا مُّبِیۡنًا ۝

---

[a]4 : 78, 125 ; 17 : 72.   [b]5 : 104 ; 10 : 70 ; 16 : 117.

---

partner or co-partner, whether in His person or attributes or dominion, etc. شرك means : (1) participation or co-partnership ; (2) the attribution of a co-partner to, or associating a partner with, God i.e. belief in the plurality of Gods (Lane & Aqrab). شرك in its wider sense is not confined to worshipping idols or looking upon certain beings or things as partners with God or possessing His attributes or sharing in His dominion, etc. It extends to loving a thing or a being as one should love God or trusting in a thing or a being as one should trust in God, and so on. This latter kind of شرك is known as شرك خفی i.e. the hidden شرك being not easily discernible.

Commentary :

The reference in the verse is not only to idol-worship but also to such idolatrous practices as are in vogue among common people, even among present-day Muslims, such as the adoration of saints and offering prayers and oblations to them. All such abominable practices are *shirk* in the sight of God. But شرك خفی (hidden *shirk*) i.e. loving or trusting in a thing or being as one should love and trust in God, may be forgiven, if done in ignorance and through lack of proper care, provided one is a sincere believer in God and His Prophet and strives to do good works.

The expression, *Allah will not forgive*, does not mean that an idolatrous person can never repent or that his repentance cannot be accepted even in the present life. The expression relates to the time after death i.e. one who dies in a state of *shirk* will not be forgiven.

524. Important Words :

فَتِیۡلًا (a whit) is derived from فتل. They say فتله i.e. he twisted it, as one twists a rope or a wick. One would say رجل محکم الفتل i.e. a man firm or compact, in respect of make, as though firmly twisted. فتیل means, (1) a twisted rope ; (2) a small thread in the cleft of a date-stone ; also the fine thread of dirt formed between two fingers or the palms of two hands when they are rubbed together ; hence a thing of no worth or significance. They say ما اغنی عنك فتیلا meaning, I do not or cannot avail or profit thee a whit (Lane).

Commentary :

What led the Jews to *shirk*, or associating partners with God, was the erroneous idea that they were quite pure and needed no more divine Reformers. Present-day Muslims, too, have fallen a victim to similar deceptive notions. When a people become impure from the religious point of view, it is only God Who can bring about their reform by raising divinely inspired Reformers.

525. Commentary :

It was tantamount to forging a lie on the part

52. Dost thou not know of those who were given a portion of the Book ? They believe in evil things and *follow* those who transgress, and they say of the disbelievers, 'These are better guided in religion than those who believe.'[526]

53. These are those [a]whom Allah has cursed ; and he whom Allah curses, thou shalt not find for him a helper.[527]

54. Have they a share in the Kingdom ? Then would they not give men *even so much as* the little hollow in the back of a date-stone.[528]

اَلَمۡ تَرَ اِلَى الَّذِيۡنَ اُوۡتُوۡا نَصِيۡبًا مِّنَ الۡكِتٰبِ يُؤۡمِنُوۡنَ بِالۡجِبۡتِ وَالطَّاغُوۡتِ وَيَقُوۡلُوۡنَ لِلَّذِيۡنَ كَفَرُوۡا هٰۤؤُلَآءِ اَهۡدٰى مِنَ الَّذِيۡنَ اٰمَنُوۡا سَبِيۡلًا ۝

اُولٰٓئِكَ الَّذِيۡنَ لَعَنَهُمُ اللّٰهُ ؕ وَمَنۡ يَّلۡعَنِ اللّٰهُ فَلَنۡ تَجِدَ لَهٗ نَصِيۡرًا ۝

اَمۡ لَهُمۡ نَصِيۡبٌ مِّنَ الۡمُلۡكِ فَاِذًا لَّا يُؤۡتُوۡنَ النَّاسَ نَقِيۡرًا ۝

---

[a]2 : 160 ; 3 : 87-88.

---

of the Jews to say that God would raise no more Prophets because they needed none. If the people had become corrupt, a Prophet was sure to appear and he did appear in the person of the Holy Prophet of Islam.

526. Important Words :

الجبت (evil things) means : (1) an idol or idols ; or the name of a certain idol belonging to the Quraish ; (2) that which is worshipped instead of God, whatever it be ; (3) that wherein there is no good ; (4) a diviner or an enchanter or the like ; (5) the Devil or Satan ; (6) enchantment or magic (Lane & Aqrab).

Commentary :

The Muslims believed in all the Prophets mentioned in the Bible and also in the divine origin of the Law that was given to Moses, yet so great was the hatred of Jews for them that they declared the idol-worshippers of Arabia, who rejected their Prophets as well as their scriptures, to be better guided than Muslims. It is regrettable that some present-day Muslims also have the hardihood to say that it is better

to renounce Islam than to accept Ahmad, the Promised Messiah, than whom there is no greater champion of Islam.

527. Commentary :

God cursed the Jews in consequence of their perversity in declaring idolaters to be better guided than Muslims, although the former reject and abuse the Prophets of God.

The words, *thou shalt not find for him a helper*, contain a prophecy regarding the miserable condition to which the Jews were to be reduced. The whole world has witnessed how remarkably this prophecy has been fulfilled during the ages.

528. Important Words :

نقيرا (the little hollow in the back of a date-stone) is derived from نقر meaning, it (a bird) pecked at or picked up a grain from this place or that with its beak ; he (a person) hit the butt with an arrow without making his arrow pass through it wholly or partly ; he struck a thing with a pointed instrument ; he engraved a writing upon a stone ; he struck

55. Or do they envy men for what Allah has given them out of His bounty ? *If that is so,* surely, We gave the Book and Wisdom to the children of Abraham *also* and We *also* gave them a great kingdom.[529]

56. And *a*of them were some who believed in him ; and of them were others who turned away from him. And sufficient is Hell as a blazing fire.

57. Those who disbelieve in Our Signs, We shall soon cause them to enter Fire. As often as their skins are burnt up, We shall give them in exchange other skins that they may taste the punishment. Surely, Allah is Mighty *and* Wise.[530]

*a*2 : 254 ; 10 : 41 ; 61 : 15.

a lute or a tambourine with his finger ; he bored, perforated or made a hole in a thing ; he hollowed or excavated a piece of wood, etc. نقير means, (1) what is bored or perforated ; and what is hollowed out or excavated ; (2) a piece of wood ; or a block of wood, or a stump or the lower part of a palm-tree which is hollowed out ; (3) the little hollow in the back of a date-stone (Lane & Aqrab). The word is figuratively used to denote the smallest quantity.

529. Commentary :

Jews, who are the children of Abraham, were given the Book and Wisdom and a great kingdom. Now if God has bestowed the same boons upon another people who are similarly descended from Abraham, as the Arabs are, the Jews should have no cause to begrudge them.

At the time when this verse was revealed, Muslims had received only a part of the " great kingdom " and the rest was yet to follow, but the Quran speaks of the giving of a great kingdom as an accomplished fact, because the promises of God are as good as fulfilled.

530. Commentary :

Medical science has now established the fact that the skin is much more sensitive to pain than the flesh, there being a larger number of nerves in the former. The Quran revealed this great truth about fourteen hundred years ago by saying that the skin and not the flesh of the inmates of Hell would be renewed after being burnt up.

58. And ªthose who believe and do good works, We shall make them enter gardens through which streams flow, to abide therein for ever ; therein shall they have pure spouses ; and We shall admit them to a *place of* pleasant and ᵇplenteous shade.⁵³¹

59. Verily, Allah commands you to ᶜgive over the trusts to those entitled to them, and that, when you judge between men, you judge with justice. And surely excellent is what Allah admonishes you with ! Allah is All-Hearing, All-Seeing.⁵³²

وَالَّذِيْنَ اٰمَنُوْا وَعَمِلُوا الصّٰلِحٰتِ سَنُدْخِلُهُمْ جَنّٰتٍ تَجْرِيْ مِنْ تَحْتِهَا الْاَنْهٰرُ خٰلِدِيْنَ فِيْهَآ اَبَدًا ۖ لَهُمْ فِيْهَآ اَزْوَاجٌ مُّطَهَّرَةٌ ۖ وَّنُدْخِلُهُمْ ظِلًّا ظَلِيْلًا ۝

اِنَّ اللّٰهَ يَأْمُرُكُمْ اَنْ تُؤَدُّوا الْاَمٰنٰتِ اِلٰۤى اَهْلِهَا ۙ وَاِذَا حَكَمْتُمْ بَيْنَ النَّاسِ اَنْ تَحْكُمُوْا بِالْعَدْلِ ۚ اِنَّ اللّٰهَ نِعِمَّا يَعِظُكُمْ بِهٖ ۗ اِنَّ اللّٰهَ كَانَ سَمِيْعًۢا بَصِيْرًا ۝

ª4 : 123 ; 13 : 30 ; 14 : 24 ; 22 : 24 ; see also 2 : 26.   ᵇ13 : 36 ; 56 : 31.   ᶜ8 : 28.

---

531. Commentary :

The word مطهرة (pure) does not literally mean "pure" but "made pure", signifying that the spouses whom pious believers will have in Heaven will be made as highly pure as the environment of Heaven demands.

The expression, *pleasant and plenteous shade,* signifies an atmosphere of peace and calm, free from all pain-giving element. Elsewhere the Quran says : *They will know there (in Heaven) neither extreme heat nor extreme cold* (76 : 14).

532. Important Words :

امانات (trusts) is the plural of امانة which is derived from امن. They say امنه *i.e.* he trusted in him ; he entrusted him with power and authority, control or a charge ; he gave him a charge over a thing or person. امانة means, trustiness or faithfulness or fidelity ; a thing committed to the care or trust of a person ; a trust or deposit ; a duty or task allotted to a person; the commandment of God given to His servants ; a man's family or household (Lane). The Holy Prophet is reported to have said that a position or office of authority is also an امانة or a trust (Muslim, ch. on *Imārat*).

Commentary :

As in the previous verses authority and dominion were promised to Muslims, the Quran in the present verse proceeds to bid them entrust authority to such persons as possess the necessary qualifications to rule. Authority or power to rule has been here described as a "trust" of the people in order to point out that, truly speaking, it belongs to the people and is not the birthright of any particular individual or dynasty.

The verse also draws the attention of the Muslim people to their heavy responsibility in respect of the very important matter of electing their Chief or *Khalīfa*. They are warned that if in electing a *Khalīfa* or a Chief they allowed considerations of personal liking or nepotism to prevail against the interests of the State or the community or those of religion and displayed lack of conscientiousness, they would be called to account like one false to his trust. The verse also condemns dynastic or hereditary rule and institutes instead a representative form of government. The *Khalīfa* or the ruler is to be elected ; and in electing him, the people are bidden to vote for one best fitted for the office. The *Khalīfa* or the ruler in his turn

60. O ye who believe! obey Allah, and obey *His* Messenger and *a*those who are in authority among you. And *b*if you differ in anything among yourselves, refer it to Allah and *His* Messenger if you are believers in Allah and the Last Day. That is best and most commendable in the end.[533]

يَا۟يُّهَا الَّذِيۡنَ اٰمَنُوۡۤا اَطِيۡعُوا اللّٰهَ وَاَطِيۡعُوا الرَّسُوۡلَ وَ اُولِى الۡاَمۡرِ مِنۡكُمۡ ۚ فَاِنۡ تَنَازَعۡتُمۡ فِىۡ شَىۡءٍ فَرُدُّوۡهُ اِلَى اللّٰهِ وَالرَّسُوۡلِ اِنۡ كُنۡتُمۡ تُؤۡمِنُوۡنَ بِاللّٰهِ وَالۡيَوۡمِ الۡاٰخِرِ ؕ ذٰلِكَ خَيۡرٌ وَّاَحۡسَنُ تَاۡوِيۡلًا ۞

---

*a*4 : 84.   *b*4 : 66.

---

is bidden to be fair and just in his administration —fair to individuals, fair to communities and fair to the State as a whole.

The words, *that you judge with justice*, apply both to the Head of the Muslim State and to all those persons who are entrusted with the work of administration. They are all enjoined to use their authority equitably and well.

The addition of the divine attributes of "All-Hearing and All-Seeing" at the end of the verse is meant to remind Muslims that if at any time they find it difficult to carry out his commandment, then instead of violating it they should pray to God and He will hear their prayer and will see to it that they get their rights. (See General Introduction for the detailed discussion of the institution of *Khilāfat*).

533. Important Words :

اولى الامر (those in authority) is made up of two words : (1) اولى which is originally اولوا meaning, possessors of or possessing or having ; and (2) امر meaning, rule, authority, command, affair or matter, etc. اولى الامر means: (1) those who possess or hold authority, command or rule ; and (2) the learned men who, as it were, possess authority in knowledge (Tāj & Aqrab).

Commentary :

The word "obey" which has been repeated before the words "Allah" and "Messenger" has been omitted before the words, *those who are in authority*, in order to point out that obedience to the authority properly constituted by Law is in reality obedience to God and His Messenger.

The clause, *refer it to Allah and His Messenger*, means that in case of difference the matter should be referred to the Quran and the authentic *Sunna* and Ḥadīth of the Holy Prophet. The injunction may either relate to differences between the rulers and the ruled or to those among the ruled themselves. In the former case the significance is that if there is a matter on which disagreement arises between the rulers and the ruled, it should be decided in the light of the Quranic teaching, or failing that, in that of the authentic *Sunna* and Ḥadīth. If, however, the Quran, the *Sunna* and Ḥadīth are silent on the question, it should be left in the hands of those in whom is vested the authority to manage the affairs of Muslims ; and the latter are enjoined to abide by their decision even if they do not see eye to eye with them, because true obedience consists in obeying against one's will and judgement. The words, *refer it to Allah and His Messenger*, may also mean that in case of a difference between the people and those in authority, the former are enjoined to do as Allah and His Messenger have bidden them do on such occasions, *i.e.*, that in such a case they should obey those in authority.

61. Dost thou not know of those who pretend that they believe in what has been revealed to thee and what has been revealed before thee ? They desire to seek judgement from the rebellious, although they were commanded not to obey them. And Satan desires to lead them astray far away *from the right path.*[534]

اَلَمْ تَرَ اِلَى الَّذِيْنَ يَزْعُمُوْنَ اَنَّهُمْ اٰمَنُوْا بِمَا اُنْزِلَ اِلَيْكَ وَمَا اُنْزِلَ مِنْ قَبْلِكَ يُرِيْدُوْنَ اَنْ يَّتَحَاكَمُوْا اِلَى الطَّاغُوْتِ وَقَدْ اُمِرُوْۤا اَنْ يَّكْفُرُوْا بِهٖ وَيُرِيْدُ الشَّيْطٰنُ اَنْ يُّضِلَّهُمْ ضَلٰلًۢا بَعِيْدًا ۝

62. And [a]when it is said to them, 'Come ye to what Allah has sent down and to *His* Messenger,' thou seest the hypocrites turn away from thee with aversion.

وَاِذَا قِيْلَ لَهُمْ تَعَالَوْا اِلٰى مَاۤ اَنْزَلَ اللّٰهُ وَاِلَى الرَّسُوْلِ رَاَيْتَ الْمُنٰفِقِيْنَ يَصُدُّوْنَ عَنْكَ صُدُوْدًا ۝

63. Then how is it that when an affliction befalls them because of what their hands have sent on before them, they come to thee swearing by Allah, *saying,* 'We meant nothing but the doing of good and reconciliation.'[535]

فَكَيْفَ اِذَاۤ اَصَابَتْهُمْ مُّصِيْبَةٌۢ بِمَا قَدَّمَتْ اَيْدِيْهِمْ ثُمَّ جَآءُوْكَ يَحْلِفُوْنَ ۛ بِاللّٰهِ اِنْ اَرَدْنَاۤ اِلَّاۤ اِحْسَانًا وَّتَوْفِيْقًا ۝

---

[a]63 : 6.

Primarily, however, the words, *if you differ,* do not refer to any differences between the rulers and the ruled but to disagreements arising among the ruled themselves. In this case the injunction embodied in the verse is that in matters pertaining to discipline and administration Muslims should obey those in authority, but in disputes and differences regarding social matters, etc. they should be guided by the Law of Islam and not by other laws. This is the interpretation which Ibn Kathīr (iii. 130-31) has adopted and which is in keeping with the context. The next verse also refers only to disputes among the ruled, and not to those between rulers and ruled.

The words, *those in authority,* in their wider significance include even such non-Muslims as may happen to be in authority over Muslims. In this case the additional words منكم would

not mean "from among you" but simply "among you" *i.e.* "over you." The practice of the Holy Prophet as well as his sayings make it clear that in secular matters Muslims should obey even such of their rulers as are not Muslims.

534. Commentary :

The words, *They desire to seek judgement from the rebellious,* need not be taken as referring to any particular incident ; they speak of a general tendency among hypocrites.

535. Important Words :

تَوْفِيقًا (reconciliation) is derived from وفق (*waffaqa*) which is derived from وفق (*Wafiqa*). They say وفق امره *i.e.* his affair or case was right or agreeable with what was desired. وفقه لامر means, he disposed or adapted him to a thing or made him fit for it. وفق بين الشيئين means, he effected an agreement or harmony

64. These are they, the secrets of whose hearts Allah knows *well*. So turn away from them and admonish them and speak to them an effective word concerning their own selves.[536]

أُولَٰئِكَ الَّذِينَ يَعْلَمُ اللَّهُ مَا فِي قُلُوبِهِمْ فَأَعْرِضْ عَنْهُمْ وَعِظْهُمْ وَقُلْ لَهُمْ فِي أَنْفُسِهِمْ قَوْلًا بَلِيغًا ۝

---

or reconciliation or adjustment between the two things. وفقت بين القوم means, I effected an agreement or harmony between the people ; made peace between them (Lane).

Commentary :

This verse may also be taken as applying to the case of hypocrites generally. An incident, however, is related in traditions in connection with this verse which, though not reliable, may be mentioned here. There was some dispute between a Jew and one who hypocritically professed to be a Muslim. The latter, thinking that the Holy Prophet would decide the case in his favour, proposed to the Jew that they should go to him for decision. The Holy Prophet, however, contrary to the expectation of the hypocrite, decided the case in favour of the Jew who happened to be in the right. Being disappointed there, the hypocrite proposed to the Jew that they should go to Abū Bakr, hoping that though the Holy Prophet had shown him no favour, Abū Bakr at least would favour him. But Abū Bakr also decided in favour of the Jew. Being disappointed a second time, the hypocrite thought that 'Umar, who was a jealous Muslim, would never decide iu favour of a Jew. So he proposed to his rival that they should go to 'Umar for decision.

But 'Umar, says the tradition, on learning from the Jew that the case had already been decided in his favour by the Holy Prophet, cut off the head of the hypocrite, because he professed Islam and yet would not accept the Prophet's verdict. Thereupon the hypocrites gathered together and went to the Holy Prophet and told him that in going to 'Umar their object was only to bring about a compromise and reconciliation (Muhīṭ, iii. 279).

The words, *We meant nothing but the doing of good and reconciliation*, reported to have been uttered by the hypocrites, show that there was an intrigue. The incident, however, is highly improbable and lacks proper authority.

536. Commentary :

In the words, *speak to them an effective word*, the Prophet is enjoined to deal kindly with hypocrites. The injunction is to the effect that God knows that the hearts of hypocrites are afflicted with the disease of hypocrisy but He gives them respite that they may repent and mend their ways. The Prophet was also to treat them leniently and not punish them for their secret doings against Islam. They were not yet beyond redemption. It was possible they might one day see the error of their ways and become sincere and true Muslims.

65. And We have sent no Messenger but that he should be obeyed by the command of Allah. And if they had come to thee, when they had wronged their ^asouls, and asked forgiveness of Allah, and *if* the Messenger *also* had asked forgiveness for them, they would have surely found Allah Oft-Returning *with compassion, and* Merciful.⁵³⁷

وَمَآ اَرْسَلْنَا مِنْ رَّسُوْلٍ اِلَّا لِيُطَاعَ بِاِذْنِ اللّٰهِ ۗ وَلَوْ اَنَّهُمْ اِذْ ظَّلَمُوْۤا اَنْفُسَهُمْ جَآءُوْكَ فَاسْتَغْفَرُوا اللّٰهَ وَاسْتَغْفَرَ لَهُمُ الرَّسُوْلُ لَوَجَدُوا اللّٰهَ تَوَّابًا رَّحِيْمًا ۝

66. But no, by thy Lord, ^bthey are not believers until they make thee judge in all that is in dispute between them and then find not in their hearts any demur concerning that which thou decidest and submit with full submission.⁵³⁹

فَلَا وَرَبِّكَ لَا يُؤْمِنُوْنَ حَتّٰى يُحَكِّمُوْكَ فِيْمَا شَجَرَ بَيْنَهُمْ ثُمَّ لَا يَجِدُوْا فِيْۤ اَنْفُسِهِمْ حَرَجًا مِّمَّا قَضَيْتَ وَيُسَلِّمُوْا تَسْلِيْمًا ۝

---

^a4 : 111. ^b4 : 60.

---

537. Commentary :

It is sometimes sought to be inferred from the words, *We have sent no Messenger but that he should be obeyed by the command of Allah*, that though a Prophet is to be always obeyed by the people to whom he preaches his message, yet he himself gives allegiance to no other Prophet nor can he be subject to the Law of any other Prophet. This is evidently a very wrong inference. The simple and straightforward meaning of the words is only this that when God sends a Prophet, He means that those to whom he is sent should obey him. But the fact that a Prophet is the object of other people's obedience cannot preclude the possibility of his being himself subordinate to, and a follower of, another Prophet. A governor is sent to a province to be obeyed but that does not mean that he is not subordinate to the governor-general, if any, or to the king. According to the Quran, Aaron was a subordinate Prophet to Moses. This is why, when Moses went up to the Mount leaving Aaron behind him to look after the Israelites, and the Israelites took to worshipping the calf, Moses severely reprimanded him on his return, saying "*Hast thou then disobeyed my command*" (20 : 94). In this connection see also 5 : 45.

538. Important Words :

حَرَجًا (demur) is the noun-infinitive from حرج meaning, it was or became narrow ; or he became disquieted and contracted in his bosom ; he doubted, because doubt disquiets the mind ; he became straitened or in difficulty, particularly owing to the commission of a sin or crime for which he deserved punishment ; حرج therefore means, straitness ; difficulty ; a sin or crime or an act of disobedience for which one deserves punishment (Lane & Aqrab).

Commentary :

It should be noted that the injunction contained in this verse does not refer to the Holy Prophet alone. The verse speaks of the settlement of disputes, and so the injunction contained in it should be taken to pertain not to the person of the Holy Prophet but to him as Head of the Muslim State and is, therefore, applicable to his Successors as well. Muslims should not only have their disputes settled

67. And if We had commanded them, *a* 'Kill your people or leave your homes,' they would not have done it except a few of them; and if they had done what they are exhorted to do, it would surely have been better for them and conducive to greater strength.[539]

وَلَوْ اَنَّا كَتَبْنَا عَلَيْهِمْ اَنِ اقْتُلُوْۤا اَنْفُسَكُمْ اَوِ اخْرُجُوْا مِنْ دِيَارِكُمْ مَّا فَعَلُوْهُ اِلَّا قَلِيْلٌ مِّنْهُمْ ۖ وَلَوْ اَنَّهُمْ فَعَلُوْا مَا يُوْعَظُوْنَ بِهٖ لَكَانَ خَيْرًا لَّهُمْ وَاَشَدَّ تَثْبِيْتًا ۟

68. And then We would have surely given them a great reward from Ourself;

وَّاِذًا لَّاٰتَيْنٰهُمْ مِّنْ لَّدُنَّاۤ اَجْرًا عَظِيْمًا ۟

69. And *b*We would surely have guided them in the right path.[540]

وَّلَهَدَيْنٰهُمْ صِرَاطًا مُّسْتَقِيْمًا ۟

70. And *c*whoso obeys Allah and this Messenger *of His* shall be among those *d*on whom Allah has bestowed His blessings, namely, the Prophets, the Truthful, the Martyrs, and the Righteous. And excellent companions are these.[541]

وَمَنْ يُّطِعِ اللّٰهَ وَالرَّسُوْلَ فَاُولٰٓئِكَ مَعَ الَّذِيْنَ اَنْعَمَ اللّٰهُ عَلَيْهِمْ مِّنَ النَّبِيّٖنَ وَالصِّدِّيْقِيْنَ وَالشُّهَدَاۤءِ وَالصّٰلِحِيْنَ ۚ وَحَسُنَ اُولٰٓئِكَ رَفِيْقًا ۟

---

*a*4 : 78.   *b*19 : 37 ; 36 : 62 ; 42 : 53-54.   *c*4 : 14 ; 8 : 25.   *d*1 : 7 ; 5 : 21 ; 19 : 59 ; 57 : 20.

in accordance with the Law of Islam but should submit to the awards of those in authority with cheerfulness. The injunction is most essential for the maintenance of solidarity among the Muslim community. In fact, the chief cause of discord in a community is that people should regard their own judgement as right and should refuse to give to those in authority their due. The verse requires the Faithful not only to refer their differences to the Holy Prophet, and for that matter to his Successors, deputies and representatives, but to submit to their decisions cheerfully and without demur.

539. Commentary :

This verse refers to the hypocrites of Medina. The words اقتلوا انفسكم (kill your people) do not mean "kill yourselves" because suicide has been declared in Islam to be unlawful.

The expression انفسكم simply means "your people" (see note on 2 : 55). The Refugees had to leave their hearths and homes and had to kill their own disbelieving kith and kin in the war that had been forced upon them by the latter.

540. Commentary :

The next verse explains what is meant here by being guided in the right path.

541. Important Words :

مع (among) is a common word of the Arabic language denoting concomitance. It means 'with' or 'among', etc., signifying the being together of two or more persons both literally and figuratively. The word مع thus denotes (1) concomitance of two or more persons in one place ; or (2) concomitance of two or more persons at one time ; or (3) concomitance of two or more persons in position, rank or status.

The word also implies the sense of assistance, as in the verse ان الله معنا *i.e.* Allah is with us, which means, God is our Helper (Mufradāt).

Commentary :

The verse is important inasmuch as it describes the avenues of spiritual progress open to Muslims. The four spiritual ranks : (1) the Prophets (2) the Truthful (3) the Martyrs and (4) the Righteous can be attained only by following the Holy Prophet. This is an honour reserved for the Holy Prophet alone. No other Prophet shares it with him. The inference is further supported by the verse which speaks of Prophets generally and says, *And those who believe in Allah and His Messengers, they are the Truthful and the Martyrs in the presence of their Lord* (57 : 20). When read together these two verses purport to mean that whereas the followers of other Prophets could only rise to the rank of the Truthful and the Martyrs, and no higher, the followers of the Holy Prophet can achieve even higher ranks ; *viz.* they can rise to the rank of a Prophet also.

Some critics take exception to the particle ع rendered as " among " but generally taken to mean " with " and allege that a follower of the Holy Prophet will only be placed " with " the Prophets and not " among " them. Apart from what has been said under Important Words, if the particle ع be taken to denote that a follower of the Holy Prophet is merely joined to and placed with these four classes of men, without actually becoming one of them and without attaining their rank, it will follow from the construction of the verse that not only no person, by following in the footsteps of the Holy Prophet, can attain to the rank of a Prophet but also that he cannot even attain the rank of a *Ṣiddīq* (Truthful) or a *Shahīd* (Martyr) or a *Ṣāliḥ* (Righteous) but that he can only be joined to and placed with the people holding these ranks without himself attaining to their spiritual status, which is simply absurd. It is evident that the preposition ع rendered

as " among " governs all the four nouns equally *viz.* the *Ṣāliḥīn*, the *Shuhadā'*, the *Ṣiddīqīn* and the *Nabiyyīn*, the four having been linked together in one chain. So what holds good in one case should hold good in the other cases as well. Hence, if according to this verse a person can attain the rank of a *Ṣāliḥ* (Righteous) by following the Holy Prophet of Islam, he can also attain the rank of a Prophet. If we deny the rank of a Prophet to the followers of the Holy Prophet, we will have to deny to them the rank of the Righteous also.

Besides, as shown under Important Words, it is wrong to say that the preposition ع always denotes merely being joined to or placed with a class of people physically without attaining to their position or rank. The word has been used at several places in the Quran in the sense of فى *i.e.* " among " or " from among " (see 3 : 194 and 4 : 147). In the latter verse *i.e.* 4 : 147, God says that those of the hypocrites who repent and amend will be مع المؤمنين *i.e.* "among the believers." Now by no stretch of imagination can it be presumed that these people will only " be placed with the believers " and will not form part of them. The verse thus definitely proves that the word ع has been used here in the sense of فى or " among " and in no other sense. So is the case with 3 : 194. It is exactly in this sense that it has been used in the present verse. If, in the above-mentioned verses in which the word ع occurs, it is taken to give the sense of mere companionship, these verses would become meaningless. Certainly, it can give no comfort to a believer to be told that as a reward of his submission to God and the Holy Prophet, he would be merely made to sit in the company of the Prophets, the Truthful, the Martyrs and the Righteous, without attaining the spiritual rank they attained. That the preposition ع is not always used in the sense of companionship finds a further illustration in the words which the Holy Prophet

71. This grace is from Allah, and sufficient is Allah, the All-Knowing.[542]

ذٰلِكَ الْفَضْلُ مِنَ اللّٰهِ ۗ وَكَفٰى بِاللّٰهِ عَلِيمًا ۞

is reported to have uttered just before his death viz. الحفى بالرفيق الاعلى i.e. "O God, join me with the exalted companions" (meaning the class of the Prophets in Heaven). Now does this prayer of the Holy Prophet offered at the time of his death mean that he only wished to live in the company of these exalted personages and that he himself was not a Prophet of God ?

Support for the above-mentioned wrong inference is sometimes sought from the words, *this grace is from Allah*, occurring in the succeeding verse. The word "grace," it is alleged, indicates that what these people will get will be purely through God's grace and not as any reward or result of their own works and deeds. But the question is : Did the Prophets, the Truthful, the Martyrs and the Righteous attain to their high spiritual stations independently of the "grace" of God ? Did not the Holy Prophet himself, when asked whether he would get salvation by his deeds, say that he too would get it through the "grace" of God ? (Bukhāri, ch. on *Marḍā*). Does this reply of the Prophet mean that he did not "deserve" salvation ? In fact, the truth is that every blessing that one receives is a "grace" of God, in spite of the fact that it is the actions of man that draw this grace.

It may here be pointed out that the interpretation we have put on the verse under comment is not a new one. Abū Ḥayyān, the well-known author of Baḥr al-Muḥīṭ and Al-Rāghib, the great lexicographer, agree with this view. The Baḥr al-Muḥīṭ (vol. iii, p. 287) quotes Al-Rāghib as saying : "God has divided the believers into four classes in this verse, and has appointed for them four stages, some of which are lower than the others, and He has exhorted true believers not to remain behind any of these stages." This explanation shows that both these Commentators of the Quran held that, as hinted in this verse, the rank of prophethood was attainable by following the Holy Prophet. Similarly, the author of the well-known commentary Rūḥ al-Ma‘ānī in explanation of this verse, writes as follows : "Prophethood is of two kinds, *general*, and *special*. The *special* prophethood, viz., the Law-bearing prophethood is now unattainable; but the *general* prophethood, still continues." In fact, it is only the prophethood with a new Law that has now ceased, the Quran being the final Law of God, but prophethood without a new Law continues and is certainly attainable by the followers of the Holy Prophet who has himself said : "If my son Ibrāhīm had lived, he would have become a Prophet" (Mājah, ch. on *Janā‘iz*).

It may also be noted that even if the word مع is rendered as "with" and not as "among", it will not make much difference, for the word "with" very often gives the sense of being one of the party. When you are with a people, you are one of them. Even in English the word "with" is used in that sense. For fuller discussion of the subject of prophethood see 33 : 41.

Finally, the word "companions" occurring at the end of the verse should not be construed to mean that mere companionship is meant here ; for the expression has been used to hint at an additional significance, viz., that those who sincerely and truly follow God and His Messenger will not only rank among the Prophets, etc., but will also form a sort of company or brotherhood with them.

542. **Commentary :**

See note on the preceding verse.

72. O ye who believe! take your precautions; then either go forth in separate parties or go forth all together.[543]

يَٰٓأَيُّهَا الَّذِينَ اٰمَنُوا خُذُوا حِذْرَكُمْ فَانْفِرُوا ثُبَاتٍ اَوِ انْفِرُوا جَمِيعًا ۞

73. And among you there is he who will tarry behind, and if a misfortune befall you, he says, 'Surely, Allah has been gracious to me, since I was not present with them.'[544]

وَاِنَّ مِنْكُمْ لَمَنْ لَّيُبَطِّئَنَّ ۚ فَاِنْ اَصَابَتْكُمْ مُّصِيبَةٌ قَالَ قَدْ اَنْعَمَ اللّٰهُ عَلَيَّ اِذْ لَمْ اَكُنْ مَّعَهُمْ شَهِيدًا ۞

543. Important Words :

ثُبَاتٍ (separate parties) is derived from ثبى and not from ثبت as some wrongly suppose. They say ثبى الشيى *i.e.* he collected the thing and added to it. ثبوت له خيرا means, I mentioned his qualities one after the other. ثبة of which ثبات is plural means, a company or body of men; a distinct body or company of men; a troop of horsemen; the place where water collects in a valley or ground (Lane & Aqrab).

حذر (precautions). The verb حذر means, he was cautious or vigilant or on his guard; he took care; he prepared himself against; he feared. حذر means, caution or precaution; vigilance; guard; state of preparation; or of fear (Lane). The word extends to all kinds of precautions and preparations necessary for defence, and has been taken to include the putting on of weapons of defence.

Commentary :

The Muslims are warned to be always vigilant and on their guard and in a perfect state of preparation even when they march out in force. The verse may also be taken in the figurative sense, applying to missionary and cultural activities.

544. Important Words :

ليبطئن (tarries behind) is derived from بطؤ meaning, he was or became slow, late or backward. بطأ means, it made him slow, late or backward. But بطأ is also used intransitively, as in the tradition من بطأ به عمله *i.e.* he whom his evil deeds hold back (lit. he whose evil deeds keep back along with him). So بطأ would mean, (1) he held back or tarried behind, and (2) he made others hold back and tarry behind (Aqrab, Lane, Mufradāt & Kashshāf).

Commentary :

This verse refers to the internal enemies of Islam. It gives two characteristics of hypocrites : (1) they fail to march out with Muslims and are glad to do so ; (2) they do not share with Muslims their joys and sorrows. They are more anxious about their own selves than about the success of Islam. If Muslims meet with trouble, they rejoice that they themselves escaped it by remaining behind, and exultingly remind Muslims of the advice which they gave them and by acting against which the Muslims came to grief, as they did after the Battle of Uḥud.

It is worthy of note here that though in connection with the Battle of Uḥud, the Holy Prophet himself was at first in favour of fighting the enemy by staying in Medina, he did not rebuke the Muslims when they suffered a reverse by telling them that they had met with a disaster by going against his wish. But the hypocrites did taunt the Muslims that they had suffered defeat by defying their advice. It is for this taunting that the hypocrites have

74. But if there comes to you some good fortune from Allah, he says, as if there were no love between you and him, 'Would that I had been with them, then should I have *indeed* achieved a great success !'

وَلَئِنْ اَصَابَكُمْ فَضْلٌ مِّنَ اللّٰهِ لَيَقُوْلَنَّ كَاَنْ لَّمْ تَكُنْ بَيْنَكُمْ وَبَيْنَهٗ مَوَدَّةٌ يّٰلَيْتَنِيْ كُنْتُ مَعَهُمْ فَاَفُوْزَ فَوْزًا عَظِيْمًا ۞

75. Let those then fight in the cause of Allah ᵃwho would sell the present life for the Hereafter. And whoso fights in the cause of Allah, ᵇbe he slain or be he victorious, We shall soon give him a great reward.

فَلْيُقَاتِلْ فِيْ سَبِيْلِ اللّٰهِ الَّذِيْنَ يَشْرُوْنَ الْحَيٰوةَ الدُّنْيَا بِالْاٰخِرَةِ ۚ وَمَنْ يُّقَاتِلْ فِيْ سَبِيْلِ اللّٰهِ فَيُقْتَلْ اَوْ يَغْلِبْ فَسَوْفَ نُؤْتِيْهِ اَجْرًا عَظِيْمًا ۞

76. And what is the matter with you *that* you fight not in the cause of Allah and of ᶜthe weak—men, women and children—who say, 'Our Lord, take us out of this town, whose people are oppressors, and make for us some friend from Thyself, and make for us from Thyself some helper.'⁵⁴⁵

وَمَا لَكُمْ لَا تُقَاتِلُوْنَ فِيْ سَبِيْلِ اللّٰهِ وَالْمُسْتَضْعَفِيْنَ مِنَ الرِّجَالِ وَالنِّسَآءِ وَالْوِلْدَانِ الَّذِيْنَ يَقُوْلُوْنَ رَبَّنَآ اَخْرِجْنَا مِنْ هٰذِهِ الْقَرْيَةِ الظَّالِمِ اَهْلُهَا ۚ وَاجْعَلْ لَّنَا مِنْ لَّدُنْكَ وَلِيًّا ۙ وَّاجْعَلْ لَّنَا مِنْ لَّدُنْكَ نَصِيْرًا ۞

77. Those who believe fight in the cause of Allah, and those who disbelieve fight in the cause of the Evil One. Fight ye therefore against the friends of Satan ; surely, Satan's strategy is weak !

اَلَّذِيْنَ اٰمَنُوْا يُقَاتِلُوْنَ فِيْ سَبِيْلِ اللّٰهِ ۚ وَالَّذِيْنَ كَفَرُوْا يُقَاتِلُوْنَ فِيْ سَبِيْلِ الطَّاغُوْتِ فَقَاتِلُوْا اَوْلِيَآءَ الشَّيْطٰنِ ۚ اِنَّ كَيْدَ الشَّيْطٰنِ كَانَ ضَعِيْفًا ۞

ᵃ9 : 111.   ᵇ9 : 52.   ᶜ4 : 99.

been reprimanded in this verse, because such a course, if allowed, is calculated to prove detrimental to the cause of communal unity and concord.

Muslims were not the first to open hostilities. They only fought a war of defence with a view to protecting their religion and saving their weaker co-religionists.

545. Commentary :
The verse is a clear proof of the fact that

Important Words :
الطاغوت (the Evil One). See 2 : 257.

78. Dost thou not know of those to whom it was said: 'Restrain your hands, observe Prayer and pay the Zakat.' And ^awhen fighting has been prescribed for them, behold ! a section of them fear men as they should fear Allah, or with still greater fear ; and they say, 'Our Lord, why hast Thou prescribed fighting for us ? ^bWouldst Thou not grant us respite yet a while ?' Say, ^c'The benefit of this world is little and the Hereafter will be better for him who fears *God*; and ^dyou shall not be wronged a whit.'⁵⁴⁶

79. Wheresoever you may be, ^edeath will overtake you, even if you be in strongly built towers. And if some good befalls them, they say, ' This is from Allah ; ' and if evil befalls them, they say, ' This is from thee.' Say, 'All is from Allah.' What has happened to these people that they come not near understanding anything ?⁵⁴⁷

اَلَمْ تَرَ اِلَى الَّذِيْنَ قِيْلَ لَهُمْ كُفُّوْا اَيْدِيَكُمْ وَاَقِيْمُوا الصَّلٰوةَ وَاٰتُوا الزَّكٰوةَ ۚ فَلَمَّا كُتِبَ عَلَيْهِمُ الْقِتَالُ اِذَا فَرِيْقٌ مِّنْهُمْ يَخْشَوْنَ النَّاسَ كَخَشْيَةِ اللّٰهِ اَوْ اَشَدَّ خَشْيَةً ۚ وَقَالُوْا رَبَّنَا لِمَ كَتَبْتَ عَلَيْنَا الْقِتَالَ ۚ لَوْ لَاۤ اَخَّرْتَنَاۤ اِلٰۤى اَجَلٍ قَرِيْبٍ ۚ قُلْ مَتَاعُ الدُّنْيَا قَلِيْلٌ ۚ وَالْاٰخِرَةُ خَيْرٌ لِّمَنِ اتَّقٰى ۚ وَلَا تُظْلَمُوْنَ فَتِيْلًا ۴۸

اَيْنَ مَا تَكُوْنُوْا يُدْرِكْكُّمُ الْمَوْتُ وَلَوْ كُنْتُمْ فِيْ بُرُوْجٍ مُّشَيَّدَةٍ ۚ وَاِنْ تُصِبْهُمْ حَسَنَةٌ يَّقُوْلُوْا هٰذِهٖ مِنْ عِنْدِ اللّٰهِ ۚ وَاِنْ تُصِبْهُمْ سَيِّئَةٌ يَّقُوْلُوْا هٰذِهٖ مِنْ عِنْدِكَ ۚ قُلْ كُلٌّ مِّنْ عِنْدِ اللّٰهِ ۚ فَمَالِ هٰۤؤُلَاۤءِ الْقَوْمِ لَا يَكَادُوْنَ يَفْقَهُوْنَ حَدِيْثًا ۴۹

---

^a2 : 247 ; 4 : 67. ^b14 : 45 ; 63 : 11. ^c9 : 38 ; 57 : 21. ^dSee 4 : 50. ^e62 : 9.

---

546. Commentary :

This verse refers to a class of men who show eagerness to fight when they are told not to fight, but when the actual time for fighting arrives, they refuse to fight or try to avoid it by various pretexts, thus showing that their former eagerness for fighting was either insincere or was only due to a temporary excitement.

The verse may also be regarded as referring to انصار (Helpers) of Medina who, before the advent of Islam to that city were constantly at war among themselves. But when they accepted Islam, they were asked to cease fighting. When, however, they were called upon to take up arms to defend Islam, a section of them, who were always fighting among themselves before they embraced Islam, became afraid of fighting in the cause of God.

547. Important Words :

مشيدة (strongly built) is derived from شاد meaning, he plastered (a wall, etc.) with the requisite material. شاد البناء means, he raised the building high. شادوا الدين means, they strengthened and exalted the religion. شيده means, he raised it high, namely, a

80. Whatever of good comes to thee is from Allah; and whatever of evil befalls thee is from thyself. And We have sent thee as a Messenger to mankind. And sufficient is Allah as a Witness.[548]

مَاۤ اَصَابَكَ مِنۡ حَسَنَةٍ فَمِنَ اللّٰهِ ۫ وَمَاۤ اَصَابَكَ مِنۡ سَيِّئَةٍ فَمِنۡ نَّفۡسِكَ ؕ وَاَرۡسَلۡنٰكَ لِلنَّاسِ رَسُوۡلًا ؕ وَكَفٰی بِاللّٰهِ شَهِيۡدًا ۝

place or a building; or he built it firmly and strongly and raised it high (Lane & Aqrab).

Commentary :

The words, *Wheresoever you may be, death will overtake you,* may either refer to the general physical law about the inevitability of death, meaning that when one must die sooner or later, there is no reason why one should be so afraid of death as to refuse to fight in a just cause; or they may be taken as particularly addressed to the hypocrites, who disobeyed the divine command to fight, thinking that in this way they would be able to avoid death. The verse purports to say that God had decreed that they should suffer death and destruction, however well protected they might be.

It was customary with the hypocrites that when Muslims achieved a success, they attributed it to God, saying that since Islam was a divine religion, it was bound to prosper and succeed. But when a misfortune overtook Muslims, they declared that it was due to mistakes committed by the Prophet. The Quran says that from the view-point from which they ascribe success to God, failures are also ascribable to Him. By attributing success to God and failure to the Prophet the hypocrites sought to discredit the Prophet and to lower him in the estimation of Muslims.

The words, *Say, All is from Allah,* point to the fact that both successes and misfortunes were foretold by the Holy Prophet (*e.g.* see 2 : 156—158). So even the failures which the hypocrites attributed to the Holy Prophet really constituted a proof of his truth. The expression, *All is from Allah,* is also true in this sense that God is the final controlling power in the universe and whatever good or evil befalls man is attributable either to the general law of nature ordained by God or to one or other of His special decrees.

548. Commentary :

The verse appears to run counter to what has been said in the preceding verse but it is not really so. God has endowed man with natural powers and faculties by making a right use of which he can achieve success; but when he makes a wrong use of them, he is involved in trouble. Hence, from this point of view, all good is ascribable to God, and all evil to man.

As the verse embodies a general law applicable to all men, therefore the address is made to the Holy Prophet, this being a particular Quranic way of addressing mankind in general. But that it is not the person of the Holy Prophet but mankind collectively to whom the address is made in this verse, is clear from the fact that the Holy Prophet has been addressed distinctly and separately in the latter part of the verse, and also in the verse that follows.

81. Whoso obeys the Messenger obeys Allah indeed : and whoso turns away, then We have not sent thee to be a keeper over them.[549]

مَنْ يُّطِعِ الرَّسُوْلَ فَقَدْ اَطَاعَ اللّٰهَ وَمَنْ تَوَلّٰى فَمَآ اَرْسَلْنٰكَ عَلَيْهِمْ حَفِيْظًا ۞

82. And they say : 'Obedience *is our guiding principle;*' but when they go forth from thy presence, a section of them *a*spends the night scheming against what thou sayest. Allah records whatever they scheme by night. So turn away from them, and put thy trust in Allah. And sufficient is Allah as a Disposer of affairs.[550]

وَيَقُوْلُوْنَ طَاعَةٌ فَاِذَا بَرَزُوْا مِنْ عِنْدِكَ بَيَّتَ طَآئِفَةٌ مِّنْهُمْ غَيْرَ الَّذِيْ تَقُوْلُ ۗ وَاللّٰهُ يَكْتُبُ مَا يُبَيِّتُوْنَ فَاَعْرِضْ عَنْهُمْ وَتَوَكَّلْ عَلَى اللّٰهِ ۗ وَكَفٰى بِاللّٰهِ وَكِيْلًا ۞

*a*4 : 109.

---

549. Important Words :

حَفِيْظًا (keeper) is derived from حفظ . They say حفظ الشیئ *i.e.* he kept the thing or preserved it or guarded it or protected it or took care of it ; he prevented it from becoming lost. حافظ or حفیظ (the latter having more intensive meaning) means, keeper, preserver or guardian. When used about God, the attributive name حفیظ besides giving the above meanings, also means, the Preserver of all things ; One Who preserves the good and evil works of His creatures (Lane).

Commentary :

The words, *Whoso obeys the Messenger obeys Allah indeed,* further explain the meaning of the expression, *Say, All is from Allah,* occurring in 4 : 79 above. The verse purports to say that obedience to the Prophet is really obedience to God, and if Muslims get into trouble by obeying the Prophet, it is all subject to God's own will and must not be attributed to the Prophet ; and such trouble can never result in evil. God's dealings with the Prophet come under His special providence, and therefore he who finds fault with him really finds fault with God.

550. Important Words :

يبيت (spends the night scheming) is derived from بات meaning, he passed or spent the night. بات زید نائمًا means, Zaid passed the night sleeping. يبت الامر means, he did or designed or schemed the thing at night. يبت رايه means, he thought upon his opinion, and concealed it, or he conceived it in his mind. يبت العدو means, he attacked the enemy, and took him by surprise, by night (Lane & Aqrab).

Commentary :

The word " night " or " scheming by night " should not be taken too literally. The reference is to secret plotting, whether by night or during the day time. As generally secret plotting is done at night, the word يبت has been used, the night time affording a sort of cover and secrecy.

83. ^aWill they not, then, meditate upon the Quran ? Had it been from anyone other than Allah, they would surely have found therein much disagreement.⁵⁵¹

اَفَلَا يَتَدَبَّرُوْنَ الْقُرْاٰنَ ۚ وَلَوْ كَانَ مِنْ عِنْدِ غَيْرِ اللّٰهِ لَوَجَدُوْا فِيْهِ اخْتِلَافًا كَثِيْرًا ۞

84. And when there comes to them any tidings *whether* of peace or of fear, they spread it about ; whereas if they had referred it to the Messenger and to ^bthose in authority among them, surely those of them, who can elicit *the truth from* it, would have understood it. And had it not been for the grace of Allah upon you and His mercy, you would have followed Satan, save a few.⁵⁵²

وَاِذَا جَآءَهُمْ اَمْرٌ مِّنَ الْاَمْنِ اَوِ الْخَوْفِ اَذَاعُوْا بِهٖ ۚ وَلَوْ رَدُّوْهُ اِلَى الرَّسُوْلِ وَاِلٰۤى اُولِى الْاَمْرِ مِنْهُمْ لَعَلِمَهُ الَّذِيْنَ يَسْتَنْۢبِطُوْنَهٗ مِنْهُمْ ۗ وَلَوْلَا فَضْلُ اللّٰهِ عَلَيْكُمْ وَرَحْمَتُهٗ لَاتَّبَعْتُمُ الشَّيْطٰنَ اِلَّا قَلِيْلًا ۞

---

^a47 : 25.   ^b4 : 60.

---

551. Commentary :

The word اختلاف (disagreement) may have two meanings : (1) either it may refer to contradictions in the text of the Quran and the teachings contained therein ; or (2) it may refer to the non-agreement between the Quranic announcements in the form of prophecies and their result or fulfilment. The Quran is free from اختلاف (disagreement) in both these respects. In spite of covering an extremely vast field of reform—spiritual, moral, social, economic, political, legal, etc.—its teachings are perfectly harmonious, no part clashing in letter or spirit with another, no section nourished at the cost of another.

Taken in the second sense, the verse means that all the different announcements and prophecies made by the Quran are proving, and will prove, to be true ; and there can be no disagreement in this respect either. If the Quran had not been the word of God, but the fabrication of man, most of the prophecies and promises made by it under extremely adverse conditions would have failed to materialize.

So the fact that the prophecies made in the Quran have been, and are being, fulfilled against all calculations and all expectations and in a most wonderful manner is a proof positive of the fact that it is the revealed word of God.

The word, *much*, qualifying the word disagreement should not be construed to mean that *some* disagreement in the Quran is possible. The expression is simply intended to mean that, whereas otherwise there would have been *much disagreement*, the Quran being the word of God there is, in fact, none.

552. Commentary :

The reason why tidings or matters relating to peace have been mentioned before those relating to fear is that the Quran is here speaking of war, and during war it is sometimes more dangerous to give publicity to matters likely to lead to happy results than to matters of fear. For instance, if any information comes that the forces of the enemy are about to attack, the publication of this news among the people may not prove so dangerous as disclosure of, for example, the news that the Muslim army was

85. Fight, therefore, in the cause of Allah—thou art not made responsible except for thyself—and *urge on the believers. It may be that Allah will restrain the might of those that disbelieve; and Allah is stronger in might and stronger in inflicting punishment.[553]

86. Whoso makes a righteous intercession shall have a share thereof, and whoso makes an evil intercession, shall have a like portion thereof; and Allah is powerful over everything.[554]

فَقَاتِلْ فِيْ سَبِيْلِ اللّٰهِ لَا تُكَلَّفُ اِلَّا نَفْسَكَ وَ حَرِّضِ الْمُؤْمِنِيْنَ ۚ عَسَى اللّٰهُ اَنْ يَّكُفَّ بَاْسَ الَّذِيْنَ كَفَرُوْا ۚ وَاللّٰهُ اَشَدُّ بَاْسًا وَّاَشَدُّ تَنْكِيْلًا ۝

مَنْ يَّشْفَعْ شَفَاعَةً حَسَنَةً يَّكُنْ لَّهٗ نَصِيْبٌ مِّنْهَا ۚ وَمَنْ يَّشْفَعْ شَفَاعَةً سَيِّئَةً يَّكُنْ لَّهٗ كِفْلٌ مِّنْهَا ۚ وَكَانَ اللّٰهُ عَلٰى كُلِّ شَيْءٍ مُّقِيْتًا ۝

*8 : 66.

going to attack the enemy at a certain weak point of the latter. The latter class of news would disclose the intentions of the Muslim army to the enemy and he would take immediate steps to strengthen his position at the threatened point. Under normal conditions too the injunction is very important, exercising direct influence on the discipline and well-being of society.

The words, *those in authority*, refer to the Holy Prophet or his Successors or the Chiefs appointed by both.

553. Commentary :

The words, *Fight therefore in the cause of Allah*, do not mean that the command to fight related to the Holy Prophet alone. If that had been the case, the second clause in the verse would have read as لَا تُكَلَّفُ اِلَّا نَفْسَكَ (*illā nafsuka*) i.e. none is made responsible except thyself, and not as لَا تُكَلَّفُ اِلَّا نَفْسَكَ (*illā nafsaka*) i.e. *Thou art not made responsible except for thyself*, as in the verse. What the verse means is that every Muslim, not excluding the Prophet, was individually answerable to God. But the duty of the Holy Prophet was twofold: (1) to fight, and (2) to urge his followers to fight. He was, however,

not answerable for them. He was only to communicate to them the divine behests, and if they disobeyed, they themselves were answerable for it. The commandment making *Jihād* obligatory on Muslims had already been revealed (4 : 78).

The clause, *It may be that Allah will restrain the might of those that disbelieve*, means that God will bring into existence such circumstances as will make war cease of itself, or that the enemy will fail to exert his power to the full and will finally collapse. Thus we see that at the Battle of the Ditch and at the fall of Mecca providential circumstances helped the Muslims.

554. Important Words :

For the significance of the words شَفَعَ and شَفَاعَة see under 2 : 49.

Commentary :

Read in the light of the context the words, *Whoso makes a righteous intercession. . . .* may mean that a person who persuades others to fight in the cause of God shall have an ample reward, while he who dissuades them from fighting shall suffer punishment for doing so. The verse also signifies that people should not

87. And when you are greeted with a prayer, greet ye with a better prayer or *at least* return it. Surely, Allah takes account of all things.[555]

وَاِذَا حُيِّيْتُمْ بِتَحِيَّةٍ فَحَيُّوْا بِاَحْسَنَ مِنْهَاۤ اَوْرُدُّوْهَاۤ اِنَّ اللّٰهَ كَانَ عَلٰى كُلِّ شَيْءٍ حَسِيْبًا ۝

---

look upon the subject of intercession or recommendation lightly; for the person who intercedes on behalf of, or recommends, another is answerable for his act. If the intercession or recommendation is right and just, he will have a suitable reward; otherwise he will share and be responsible for the evil consequence thereof.

Taking the word شفاعة in the sense of connection, the verse may also be rendered as "whoso forms a good connection shall have a share thereof and whoso forms a bad connection shall have a like portion thereof", thus emphasizing the importance of forming a good connection whether with God or with His Prophets or with other people. Whereas a good connection may be the cause of rise and progress, a bad one may result in downfall and ruin. For a full discussion of the subject of شفاعة (intercession) see detailed note under 2 : 49.

It is noteworthy that in connection with "righteous intercession" the word used is نصيب (share or fixed share) whereas in connection with "evil intercession" the word used is كفل (like portion). This is to point out that, whereas the punishment of an evil intercession will only be the like thereof, the good reward of a righteous intercession will have no such restriction but will be as large as God has fixed it *i.e.* ten times greater.

555. Important Words :

حُيِّيْتُمْ (when you are greeted) and تحية (prayer) and حيوا (greet) are all derived from حى *i.e.* he lived or he had life; or he was or became in good condition. حياه means, he greeted him with a prayer for long and good life; or he prayed for his life; or simply he

prayed for him. حياك الله means, may God prolong thy life or preserve thy life; or may He make thy life free from harm and evil; or may He honour thee and bestow favours on thee; or may He grant thee dominion and kingship. حياه بتحية المؤمن means, he greeted him with the usual greetings of a believer *i.e.* said السلام عليك to him *viz.*, peace be on you. تحية means, greeting or salutation or benediction; endless or everlasting life; freedom and security from all evils; also dominion and kingship (Lane & Aqrab).

Commentary :

The verse, besides being general in its significance, also draws the attention of Muslims to the great boons and blessings that have come to them through the Holy Prophet and tells them that they are now morally bound to return the good they have received, by helping him to the best of their power in the furtherance of the cause he holds so dear. This would be a token of gratitude for the numerous and manifold divine favours received by them through him. The Prophet's message of life was a greeting on his part, so let the Faithful respond to it in a befitting manner.

The verse also enjoins on Muslims that they should greet and return each other's greeting in a most becoming manner when they meet. This is a social and moral duty the neglect of which will render one guilty of it accountable before God, as the concluding words of the verse point out.

The usual formula of greeting prescribed by Islam is السلام عليكم *i.e.* "peace be on you," to which are often added the words ورحمة الله و بركاته "and God's mercy and His blessings." Pious Muslims would often add to

88. Allah is He besides Whom there is none worthy of worship. He will certainly *continue to* assemble you till the Day of Resurrection, about which there is no doubt. And who is more truthful in his word than Allah ?556

89. What has happened to you that you are divided into two parties regarding the hypocrites ? And Allah has overthrown them because of what they earned. Desire ye to guide him whom Allah has caused to perish ? And for him whom Allah causes to perish thou shalt not find a way.557

اَللّٰهُ لَاۤ اِلٰهَ اِلَّا هُوَ ۚ لَيَجْمَعَنَّكُمْ اِلٰى يَوْمِ الْقِيٰمَةِ لَا رَيْبَ فِيْهِ ۗ وَمَنْ اَصْدَقُ مِنَ اللّٰهِ حَدِيْثًا ۟۠ ۝

فَمَا لَكُمْ فِى الْمُنٰفِقِيْنَ فِئَتَيْنِ وَاللّٰهُ اَرْكَسَهُمْ بِمَا كَسَبُوْا ۗ اَتُرِيْدُوْنَ اَنْ تَهْدُوْا مَنْ اَضَلَّ اللّٰهُ ۗ وَمَنْ يُّضْلِلِ اللّٰهُ فَلَنْ تَجِدَ لَهٗ سَبِيْلًا ۝

---

the formula some additional prayer in compliance with the injunction, *greet ye with a better prayer or at least return it.* But the verse is much more general in its significance and extends to all forms of greetings, wishes, prayers, etc.

The words, *return it,* signify that if one cannot respond with a better greeting, one should at least respond with a similar one.

556. Commentary :

Taking the particle الى (till) in the sense of فى (*in* or *on* for which see Lane), the clause لِيَجْمَعَنَّكُمْ الى يوم القيامة may also be rendered as, 'He will certainly assemble you on the Day of Resurrection" but the more correct rendering is that given in the text *i.e. He will certainly (continue to) assemble you till the Day of Resurrection.* The difference in meaning is obvious. People are born and die and will go on doing so till the Last Day. Thus the process of assembling is always going on and will continue till the Day of Resurrection, when God will call all to account.

557. Important Words :

اركسهم (has overthrown them). See 4 : 92.

Commentary :

Believers disagreed among themselves as to how the hypocrites living in the suburbs of Medina *i.e.* the Bedouin tribes of the countryside, were to be treated. Some sympathized with them and recommended leniency towards them, hoping that in this way they might gradually reform themselves, while others looked upon them as a serious menace to Islam and Muslims and advocated severity towards them. As this disagreement was likely to cause a split among Muslims and divide them into two parties, the Quran here expresses its disapproval of such a course. Muslims, it says, should beware of becoming divided among themselves for the sake of the hypocrites. They should remember that a split in their own ranks was a much more serious affair than a danger from outside. The hypocrites were the enemies of God, and believers should not allow themselves to be divided on their account.

90. ^aThey wish that you should disbelieve as they have disbelieved, so that you may become all alike. Take not, therefore, friends from among them, until they emigrate in the way of Allah. And if they turn away, then seize them and kill them wherever you find them; and take no friend nor helper from among them;⁵⁵⁸

وَدُّوْا لَوْ تَكْفُرُوْنَ كَمَا كَفَرُوْا فَتَكُوْنُوْنَ سَوَآءً فَلَا تَتَّخِذُوْا مِنْهُمْ اَوْلِيَآءَ حَتّٰى يُهَاجِرُوْا فِىْ سَبِيْلِ اللّٰهِ فَاِنْ تَوَلَّوْا فَخُذُوْهُمْ وَاقْتُلُوْهُمْ حَيْثُ وَجَدْتُّمُوْهُمْ وَلَا تَتَّخِذُوْا مِنْهُمْ وَلِيًّا وَّلَا نَصِيْرًا ۞

91. Except those who are connected with a people between whom and you there is a pact, or those who come to you, while their hearts shrink from fighting you or fighting their own people. And if Allah had so pleased, He could have given them power against you, then they would have surely fought you. So, if they keep aloof from you and fight you not, and make you an offer of peace, then *remember that* Allah has allowed you no way *of aggression* against them.⁵⁵⁹

اِلَّا الَّذِيْنَ يَصِلُوْنَ اِلٰى قَوْمٍ بَيْنَكُمْ وَبَيْنَهُمْ مِّيْثَاقٌ اَوْ جَآءُوْكُمْ حَصِرَتْ صُدُوْرُهُمْ اَنْ يُّقَاتِلُوْكُمْ اَوْ يُقَاتِلُوْا قَوْمَهُمْ وَلَوْ شَآءَ اللّٰهُ لَسَلَّطَهُمْ عَلَيْكُمْ فَلَقَاتَلُوْكُمْ فَاِنِ اعْتَزَلُوْكُمْ فَلَمْ يُقَاتِلُوْكُمْ وَالْقَوْا اِلَيْكُمُ السَّلَمَ فَمَا جَعَلَ اللّٰهُ لَكُمْ عَلَيْهِمْ سَبِيْلًا ۞

---

^a2 : 110; 4 : 45; 14 : 14.

558. Commentary :

The word كفر (disbelief) as used in this verse stands for hypocrisy, as a hypocrite is none but a disbeliever at heart. The hypocrites belonging to the Bedouin tribes of the desert, referred to in the preceding verse, claimed to be believers but rendered no help to Islam. Believers are enjoined to have nothing to do with them.

The words, *until they emigrate in the way of Allah*, show that the hypocrites referred to in this verse did not belong to the town of Medina but to outside territory. They attached no value to faith and through cowardice wished that all should become like themselves, making friends with the enemies of Islam and mixing with them as they liked. The Quran forbids Muslims to take such men as friends, or to seek help from them, unless they emigrate in the way of God and sever all connection with the enemy.

As the word قتل is also used in the sense of boycotting (see 2 : 62), the words اقتلوهم (kill them) may also mean boycott them, *i.e.*, have nothing to do with them, treating them in the same manner in which you treat those with whom they have made common cause. This meaning finds support in the fact that the expression اقتلوهم (kill them) is followed by the words, *take no friend nor helper from among them.*

559. Important Words :

يصلون (are connected) is derived from وصل. They say وصل الشيئ باشيئ *i.e.* he joined or connected this thing with that; he brought the two things together. وصله means, he had

92. You will find others who desire to be secure from you and to be secure from their own people. Whenever they are made to revert to hostility, ᵃthey fall headlong into it. Therefore, if they do not keep aloof from you nor offer you peace nor restrain their hands, ᵇthen seize them and kill them, wherever you find them. Against these We have given you clear authority.⁵⁶⁰

سَنَجِدُوۡنَ اٰخَرِیۡنَ یُرِیۡدُوۡنَ اَنۡ یَّاۡمَنُوۡکُمۡ وَ یَاۡمَنُوۡا قَوۡمَهُمۡ ؕ کُلَّمَا رُدُّوۡۤا اِلَی الۡفِتۡنَۃِ اُرۡکِسُوۡا فِیۡهَا ۚ فَاِنۡ لَّمۡ یَعۡتَزِلُوۡکُمۡ وَ یُلۡقُوۡۤا اِلَیۡکُمُ السَّلَمَ وَ یَکُفُّوۡۤا اَیۡدِیَهُمۡ فَخُذُوۡهُمۡ وَ اقۡتُلُوۡهُمۡ حَیۡثُ ثَقِفۡتُمُوۡهُمۡ ؕ وَ اُولٰٓئِکُمۡ جَعَلۡنَا لَکُمۡ عَلَیۡهِمۡ سُلۡطٰنًا مُّبِیۡنًا ۠

ᵃ33 : 15.   ᵇ9 : 5.

close and friendly relations with him. وصل اليه means, he or it arrived at, or came to, or reached him or it. اتصل الى بنى فلان means, he belonged to, or was connected with, that tribe (Aqrab).

سلطهم عليهم (given them power against you). سلط (sallaṭa) is derived from سلط (salaṭa) for which see the succeeding verse. سلط عليه (sallaṭa) means, he made him to overcome him or to prevail over him or to have power or force over him, etc. They also say سلط عليه الكلاب i.e. he set the dogs upon him (Lane).

Commentary :

The preceding verses enjoined the taking of disciplinary action against the Bedouin hypocrites of the countryside round Medina. This verse makes exceptions in the case of : (1) those who went over to, or were connected with, some tribe having an alliance with the Muslims ; and (2) those who came over to Medina and had leanings towards Islam, though their attitude was still one of hesitancy and vacillation. In fact, Islam attaches great importance to pacts, express or implied, and would in no case tolerate their breach. Incidentally, the verse also shows that جهاد (Jihād) is permitted only against those who first make war upon the Muslims or their allies or from whom an attack is apprehended.

560. Important Words :

ارکسوا (fall headlong) is in the passive voice and the right translation of it would be, " are made to fall headlong," or " are overthrown " etc. but for the sake of clearness the word has been translated here in the active voice. ارکسوا is formed from رکس. They say رکس الشیئ i.e. he turned the thing over or upside down. ارکس الشیئ means, he turned the thing to its former state ; he turned or threw it over upon its head ; he reversed it or turned it back ; he made the first part of it to be the last. ارکس الله عدوك means, may God turn thine enemy upon his head ; or may He overthrow him or change or reverse his condition (Lane & Aqrab).

الفتنة (hostility) generally meaning, (1) persecution, (2) mischief, (3) discord and dissension, (4) civil war, etc., also means war i.e. hostility (Lane). See also 2 : 192.

سلطان (authority) is the noun-infinitive from سلط which means, he or it overcame, prevailed or predominated ; he became firm or established in superior power ; he possessed power or dominion or sovereignty ; he was or became sharp ; it was or became hard or strong ; he was or became chaste or perspicuous in speech, or eloquent and sharp in tongue. They say قد جعلت لك سلطانا على اخذ حقى من فلان i.e.

R. 13 **93.** It does not become a believer to kill a believer unless it be by mistake. And he who kills a believer by mistake shall free a believing slave, and *pay* blood-money to be handed over to his heirs, unless they remit it as charity. But if *the person slain* be of a people hostile to you, and be a believer, then *the offender* shall free a believing slave; and if he be of a people between whom and you is a pact, then *the offender* shall pay blood-money to be handed over to his heirs, and free a believing slave. But whoso finds not *one*, then [a]he shall fast for two consecutive months—a mercy from Allah. And Allah is All-Knowing, Wise.[561]

وَمَا كَانَ لِمُؤْمِنٍ اَنْ يَّقْتُلَ مُؤْمِنًا اِلَّا خَطَئًا وَمَنْ قَتَلَ مُؤْمِنًا خَطَئًا فَتَحْرِيرُ رَقَبَةٍ مُّؤْمِنَةٍ وَّدِيَةٌ مُّسَلَّمَةٌ اِلٰٓى اَهْلِهٖٓ اِلَّآ اَنْ يَّصَّدَّقُوْا فَاِنْ كَانَ مِنْ قَوْمٍ عَدُوٍّ لَّكُمْ وَهُوَ مُؤْمِنٌ فَتَحْرِيرُ رَقَبَةٍ مُّؤْمِنَةٍ وَاِنْ كَانَ مِنْ قَوْمٍ بَيْنَكُمْ وَبَيْنَهُمْ مِّيْثَاقٌ فَدِيَةٌ مُّسَلَّمَةٌ اِلٰٓى اَهْلِهٖ وَتَحْرِيرُ رَقَبَةٍ مُّؤْمِنَةٍ فَمَنْ لَّمْ يَجِدْ فَصِيَامُ شَهْرَيْنِ مُتَتَابِعَيْنِ تَوْبَةً مِّنَ اللّٰهِ وَكَانَ اللّٰهُ عَلِيْمًا حَكِيْمًا ۞

---

[a]58 : 5.

I have given you the power or authority to take my due from such a one. سلطان means, strength, might, force or power; predominance; power or authority; the sovereign or ruling power; king or ruler; sharpness; hardness; proof or argument; evidence; plea (Lane & Aqrab).

Commentary :

The reference in this verse is to those people who had no alliance with Muslims or any tribe having an alliance with them. They were time-servers who awaited their opportunity. The difference between these people and those mentioned in the previous verse is that the latter had some sort of alliance with this or that party though they did not possess the strength to assert themselves, while the former only sought security by deceitful means and hastened to make common cause with the enemies of Islam whenever invited to do so. Fighting was enjoined against this class of people, unless they entered into a treaty of peace with Muslims and loyally observed its terms.

561. Commentary :

As the preceding verses contained injunctions which, if misconstrued or misapplied, were likely to lead to a Muslim being killed by a Muslim, the present verse gives a timely warning against such an eventuality.

The words, *It does not become a believer to kill a believer*, have been used to make a touching appeal to believers to abstain from killing each other, since they are like brothers. It in no case behoves a brother to kill a brother. The words thus contain an important injunction which forms a fitting sequence to the one contained in the preceding verses concerning the hypocrites. The verse cautions a Muslim to be always on his guard lest in carelessness he should happen to kill a brother Muslim.

In case the slain person is a believer but happens to belong to a hostile people, then the offender shall only free a believing slave and no blood-money shall be levied on him, because money paid to a hostile people would go to strengthen their military power against Islam

94. And ^awhoso kills a believer intentionally, his reward shall be Hell wherein he shall abide. And Allah shall be wroth with him and shall curse him and shall prepare for him a great punishment.⁵⁶²

وَمَنْ يَّقْتُلْ مُؤْمِنًا مُّتَعَمِّدًا فَجَزَآؤُهُ جَهَنَّمُ خَالِدًا فِيْهَا وَغَضِبَ اللّٰهُ عَلَيْهِ وَلَعَنَهُ وَاَعَدَّ لَهُ عَذَابًا عَظِيْمًا ۝

95. O ye who believe! when you go forth in the cause of Allah, ^bmake proper investigation and say not to any one who greets you with the greeting of peace, 'Thou art not a believer.' You seek the goods of this life, but with Allah are good things in plenty. Such were you before this, but Allah conferred His favour on you; so do make proper investigation. Surely, Allah is well aware of what you do.⁵⁶³

يٰٓاَيُّهَا الَّذِيْنَ اٰمَنُوْٓا اِذَا ضَرَبْتُمْ فِيْ سَبِيْلِ اللّٰهِ فَتَبَيَّنُوْا وَلَا تَقُوْلُوْا لِمَنْ اَلْقٰٓى اِلَيْكُمُ السَّلَمَ لَسْتَ مُؤْمِنًا تَبْتَغُوْنَ عَرَضَ الْحَيٰوةِ الدُّنْيَا فَعِنْدَ اللّٰهِ مَغَانِمُ كَثِيْرَةٌ كَذٰلِكَ كُنْتُمْ مِّنْ قَبْلُ فَمَنَّ اللّٰهُ عَلَيْكُمْ فَتَبَيَّنُوْا اِنَّ اللّٰهَ كَانَ بِمَا تَعْمَلُوْنَ خَبِيْرًا ۝

---

^a25 : 69-70.   ^b49 : 7.

---

which can in no case be allowed.

In the expression, *and if he be of a people between whom and you is a pact*, the words, *and he be a believer*, have not been repeated, in order to point out that the law with regard to the *dhimmis* (disbelievers under the protection of Muslims), or *Mu'āhid* (disbelievers belonging to a people in alliance with Muslims) is the same as for Muslims.

It is worthy of note here that disbelievers who are in alliance with Muslims have not only been placed on a par with the latter, but even a distinction has been made in favour of the former. In case a Muslim is slain, the command relating to the payment of fine has been placed after the injunction to free a slave; while in case one belonging to a people in alliance with Muslims is slain, the order has been reversed, the injunction to pay the fine to his heirs being put before the injunction to free a slave. This has been done to impress upon Muslims the need of showing special regard for treaties and

pacts. The payment of fine was an obligation which Muslims owed to disbelievers with whom they had made a pact, and in order to bring home to Muslims the lesson that they should have particular regard for their pacts and treaties, the injunction to pay the fine has in their case been placed before the injunction to free a slave.

562. Commentary :

The solidarity of Islam and the tie of brotherhood among believers have been made absolutely inviolable. One who knowingly kills a fellow-Muslim is like one who kills a son of his own father under the very eyes of the latter. The father would have nothing to do with such a man.

563. Important Words :

السلام (peace) means the Islamic salutation of *salām*; peace; security; submission, etc. (Aqrab & Lane). See also 2 : 113, 209 ; 3 : 20. مغانم (good things) is derived from غنم

551

96. *Those of the believers who sit *still*, excepting the disabled ones, and those who strive in the cause of Allah with their wealth and their persons, are not equal. Allah has exalted in rank those who strive with their wealth and their persons above those who sit *still*. And to each Allah has promised good. And Allah has exalted those who strive above those who sit *still*, by a great reward.[564]

لَا يَسْتَوِى الْقَاعِدُوْنَ مِنَ الْمُؤْمِنِيْنَ غَيْرُ اُولِى الضَّرَرِ وَالْمُجَاهِدُوْنَ فِىْ سَبِيْلِ اللّٰهِ بِاَمْوَالِهِمْ وَاَنْفُسِهِمْ ۗ فَضَّلَ اللّٰهُ الْمُجَاهِدِيْنَ بِاَمْوَالِهِمْ وَاَنْفُسِهِمْ عَلَى الْقَاعِدِيْنَ دَرَجَةً ۗ وَكُلًّا وَّعَدَ اللّٰهُ الْحُسْنٰى ۗ وَفَضَّلَ اللّٰهُ الْمُجَاهِدِيْنَ عَلَى الْقَاعِدِيْنَ اَجْرًا عَظِيْمًا ۝

***

*a*9 : 19-20 ; 57 : 11.

***

meaning, he got or took spoil, or got a thing as spoil ; he acquired or gained a thing without difficulty or inconvenience. غنيمة or مغنم means, spoil, booty or plunder ; the acquisition of a thing without difficulty or inconvenience ; the thing so acquired ; what is obtained from disbelievers in war (Lane & Aqrab)

Commentary :

This verse does not mean that if any person greets a Muslim with the Islamic formula of salutation, he should be regarded as a believer. Many non-Muslims nowadays, and many Jews in the days of the Holy Prophet, greeted Muslims with the prescribed salutation, but they cannot be, and indeed never were, regarded as Muslims merely on that ground. What the verse means is that when a people offers peace or shows a peaceful attitude towards Muslims, the latter should respect that attitude and refrain from hostility. The word سلام (peace) may also mean submission or security. Similarly, the word مومن (believer) may also be rendered as giver of security or offerer or afforder of peace.

The word مغانم (good things) does not mean only the spoils of war. It also means the good things of the world. In Bukhārī (ch. on *Tafsīr*) we have لقى ناس من المسلمين رجلا معه غنيمة له *i.e.* "some of the Muslims met a man who had with him some good things belonging to him".

As explained under Important Words, anything acquired without difficulty is also غنيمة .

The words كذالك كنتم (such were you) embody a very strong appeal to both sentiment and reason. The expression signifies that, like disbelievers, Muslims too were disbelievers at first, but God gave them time and opportunity and they were at last able to see the truth. So they should be patient with, and lenient to, others and give them time, so that they too may ponder over the truth and accept it if they choose.

564. Commentary :

The verse speaks of the different classes of believers only and not of hypocrites. Believers are of two classes : (1) Those who sincerely accept the truth and try to live up to the teachings of Islam but take no part in the struggle to defend and propagate the faith. These are, as it were, passive believers— " sitters " as the verse names them. (2) Those who not only live up to the teachings of Islam but also vigorously participate in the work of its propagation. These are active believers— the " strivers " or *Mujāhid* as they are called. The latter are far superior to the former in the sight of God. There is, however, a class of believers who, even though they do not join their brethren in actually fighting disbelievers get an equal reward with those who take part

97. *Namely*, by degrees of excellence *bestowed* by Him, and *by special* forgiveness and mercy. And Allah is Most Forgiving, Merciful.[565]

98. Verily, [a]those whom the angels cause to die while they are wronging their own souls, they (the angels) will say *to them* : 'What were you after?' They will reply : 'We were treated as weak in the land.' They will say, 'Was not Allah's earth vast enough for you to emigrate therein?' It is these whose abode shall be Hell, and an evil destination it is;[566]

---

[a]16 : 29.

---

in the actual struggle. These are referred to in the words "excepting the disabled ones." Their inability to take part in actual fighting is due to circumstances over which they have no control. They are heart and soul with the Muslims who are *Mujāhid*, wherever the latter go to fight in the cause of God; but their particular circumstances—disease, poverty, etc.—do not allow them to join the expeditions in person. Of these the Holy Prophet once told his Companions in one of his expeditions that there were men in Medina who were with them in every march they made and in every valley they traversed and who were getting the same reward. The Companions asked the Holy Prophet in surprise how that could be possible and who were those fortunate ones. "They are those of your brethren", replied the Holy Prophet, "who were eager to join us but were prevented from doing so by circumstances beyond their control." These are the ones in whose case the verse makes an exception in the words, *excepting the disabled ones*. But the actual "sitters," though entitled to good reward if true and sincere in their faith, were

in no case on a par with the "strivers," neither in rank nor in reward.

565. **Commentary :**

This verse further explains and emphasizes the distinction between the "sitters" at home without valid excuse and the "strivers" in the cause of God. The latter are not only superior to the former by "many degrees" but are much more entitled to God's mercy and forgiveness.

566. **Commentary :**

The words فتهاجروا (for you to emigrate) show that the people referred to here were not so weak as not to be able to emigrate from their homes. They were thus not truly "disabled ones" as mentioned in 4:96 above. The present verse therefore strongly condemns them. Islam would not be satisfied with a weak or passive belief, for it is neither good for the believer nor for the community. If the environment of a believer is not suitable for him, he should shift to a different environment more congenial to his faith; and if he does not do so, he is not sincere in his faith.

99. Except *such weak ones among men, women, and children, as are incapable of adopting any plan or of finding any way.[567]

اِلَّا الْمُسْتَضْعَفِيْنَ مِنَ الرِّجَالِ وَالنِّسَآءِ وَالْوِلْدَانِ لَا يَسْتَطِيْعُوْنَ حِيْلَةً وَّلَا يَهْتَدُوْنَ سَبِيْلًا ۝

100. As to these, may-be Allah will efface their sins; for Allah is the Effacer of sins, the Most Forgiving.[568]

فَاُولٰٓئِكَ عَسَى اللّٰهُ اَنْ يَّعْفُوَ عَنْهُمْ ۖ وَكَانَ اللّٰهُ عَفُوًّا غَفُوْرًا ۝

*4 : 76.

---

567. Important Words :

حِيْلَة (plan) is derived from حَال *i.e.* it became changed or altered; it revolved and passed; it became complete, etc. حِيْلَة means, mode or manner of changing from one state to another; a mode or means of evading a thing; a mode or means of attaining an object; a contrivance, device, artifice or plan (Lane).

Commentary :

There may be cases in which a person is really unable to emigrate. For such this verse provides an exception to the class mentioned in the preceding one; for God is just and never overlooks extenuating circumstances.

The verse also shows that the word يهتدون (here translated as "finding any way" but generally rendered as "being rightly guided") is sometimes used in the sense of being saved, whether from the hardships of this world or from those of the next.

568. Important Words :

عَفُوًّا (Effacer of sins) is derived from عفا meaning, it was or became effaced, erased or obliterated; it perished or came to naught or came to an end. They say عفت الريح الدار *i.e.* the wind effaced the traces of the house. سلوا الله العافية means, ask ye of God the effacement of your sins or pray for forgiveness. The word عفا also means, it was or became much in quantity or many in number. An Arab would say اعفيت شعر البعير *i.e.* I left the hair of the camel to become abundant and long. عَفُوًّا which is one of the attributes of God, means, One Who forgives much; the Very Forgiving; the Effacer of sins (Lane & Aqrab). See also 2 : 110, 188, 220, 238 ; 3 : 135.

Commentary :

The words, *Allah will efface their sins*, mean not only that Allah will forgive them their weaknesses but that He will also put an end to their hardships by giving victory to Muslims and making them masters of those places where the weak among them were being oppressed and tormented by cruel disbelievers. The expression عسى (may-be) does not indicate doubt on the part of God but is used to keep the believers referred to here in a state of suspense—between hope and fear—so that they may not become lax in prayer and good deeds. The expression is designed to hold out hope without creating a sense of security or a state of complete complacency.

101. And whoso emigrates from his country in the cause of Allah will find in the earth an abundant place of refuge and plentifulness. And whoso goes forth from his home, emigrating in the cause of Allah and His Messenger, and death overtakes him, his reward lies on Allah, and Allah is Most Forgiving, Merciful.[569]

15 102. And when you journey in the land, ᵃit shall be no sin on you to shorten the Prayer, if you fear that those who disbelieve may give you trouble. Verily, the disbelievers are an open enemy to you.[570]

وَمَنْ يُّهَاجِرْ فِيْ سَبِيْلِ اللّٰهِ يَجِدْ فِي الْاَرْضِ مُرٰغَمًا كَثِيْرًا وَّسَعَةً ۚ وَمَنْ يَّخْرُجْ مِنْ بَيْتِهٖ مُهَاجِرًا اِلَى اللّٰهِ وَرَسُوْلِهٖ ثُمَّ يُدْرِكْهُ الْمَوْتُ فَقَدْ وَقَعَ اَجْرُهٗ عَلَى اللّٰهِ ۗ وَكَانَ اللّٰهُ غَفُوْرًا رَّحِيْمًا ۝

وَاِذَا ضَرَبْتُمْ فِي الْاَرْضِ فَلَيْسَ عَلَيْكُمْ جُنَاحٌ اَنْ تَقْصُرُوْا مِنَ الصَّلٰوةِ ۖ اِنْ خِفْتُمْ اَنْ يَّفْتِنَكُمُ الَّذِيْنَ كَفَرُوْا ۗ اِنَّ الْكٰفِرِيْنَ كَانُوْا لَكُمْ عَدُوًّا مُّبِيْنًا ۝

ᵃ2 : 240.

569. Important Words :

مُرٰغَمًا (place of refuge) is the plural of مُرْغَم which is derived from رَغِمَ. They say رَغِمَ اَنْفُهُ meaning, his nose clove to the dust i.e. he became abased and humbled. رَغِمَهُ means, he disliked it. رَاغَمَ اَهْلَهُ or اَرْغَمَ اَهْلَهُ means, he forsook or deserted his family against their wish. رَغَام means, earth or dust. مُرْغَم or مُرٰغَم means, a road by travelling on which a man separates himself from his people against their wish or so as to displease them ; a place to which one emigrates ; a place of refuge ; a safe and fortified place (Lane & Aqrab).

Commentary :

The verse promises those sincere believers who are forced by circumstances to emigrate from their homes in the cause of God *abundant place of refuge and plentifulness*. There is, therefore, no excuse for the people to stay at home surrounded by hostile disbelievers. But the motive must be good and the emigration sincere.

The Holy Prophet is reported to have said : " Whoso emigrates from his home for the sake of God and His Messenger, his emigration will be regarded as having been performed for the sake of God and His Messenger and will be rewarded as such. But whoso leaves his home for the sake of a worldly gain which he wishes to get or for a woman whom he wishes to marry, will be considered to have emigrated for the sake of the object for which he emigrated and his emigration will not be considered as having been performed in the cause of God " (Bukhārī, ch. on *Bad'ul Waḥy*).

570. Commentary :

The subject how Prayers are to be performed when one is on a journey or when there is fear of an attack from the enemy has been incidentally introduced here in connection with the subject of emigration dealt with in the previous verses. At the conclusion of this subject which has been incidentally brought in, the Quran will again refer to the main theme dealing with hypocrites and the weak of faith.

The subject of Prayers in time of fear has been dealt with in the Quran in three separate verses *viz.* (1) in 2 : 240 which deals with Prayers performed in times of extreme fear when no formal Prayer is possible; (2) in 4 : 102 *i.e.* the present verse which deals with Prayers performed individually in times of ordinary fear; and (3) in 4 : 103 *i.e.* the following verse which deals with Prayers performed in congregation.

The "shortening of Prayer" as mentioned in the present verse, which relates to the saying of Prayers individually, does not here signify the lessening of the number of *rak'ats* which has from the very beginning been fixed at two in a state of journey. It signifies the saying of the prescribed Prayers quickly and hurriedly when there is danger of an attack from the enemy. Ordinarily, a Muslim is enjoined to say his Prayers slowly and attentively, but he may say them quickly and hurriedly when an attack from the enemy is apprehended. The number of *rak'ats* to be said when a man is on a journey has ever been two, in the case of those Prayers which are ordinarily performed in four *rak'ats*; but in time of danger when one has to say one's Prayers individually, even these two *rak'ats* may be gone through quickly. This is what is meant by the "shortening of Prayer" in the verse under comment. Ibn Kathír says : "Some of the learned theologians hold that by the "shortening of Prayer" here is meant not the shortening of the quantity *i.e.* the number of *rak'ats*, but of the quality *i.e.* time passed in Prayer, which, in other words, means saying the Prayers quickly without lessening the number of *rak'ats* or reducing the additional prayers which one ordinarily offers in the prescribed Prayers in one's own words." This view is endorsed by Mujáhid, Dahhák, and other authorities; and

Imám Muhammad bin Ismá'íl also expresses the same view, for in Bukhárí he couples this verse with the next one, which deals with the subject of congregational Prayers in time of fear, under the common heading of Ṣalát al-Khauf (*i.e.* Prayer in time of fear).

The above view is further supported by the following traditions : 'Â'isha is reported to have said, "At first the number of *rak'ats* enjoined was two, whether one was on a journey or at home. Later on, however, the number was increased to four for those staying at home, but the number of *rak'ats* said on a journey continued to be the same as before " (Bukhárí, ch. on Ṣalát). Again 'Umar says, "The Prayer to be said on a journey is two *rak'ats*; the Prayer of the two *'Íds* is also two *rak'ats* each; similarly the Friday Prayer is two *rak'ats*; this is the full number of *rak'ats* without having undergone any curtailment. We learnt this from the very lips of the Holy Prophet " (Musnad, Nasa'í, & Májah).

The number of *rak'ats* whether the Prayer is performed in a state of fear or when one is on a journey is not expressly dealt with in the Quran. It is found detailed in *Sunna* or Hadíth which confines the number of *rak'ats* to two in the case of those Prayers which ordinarily have four *rak'ats*. For instance, there is a saying to the effect that Khálid bin Sa'íd once asked Ibn 'Umar where was صلوة المسافر (Prayer of the way-farer) mentioned in the Quran which prescribes only the صلوة الخوف (Prayer in time of fear). To this Ibn 'Umar replied that in this respect they did what they saw the Holy Prophet doing *i.e.* saying two *rak'ats* of Prayer while on a journey (Jarír, v. 144, also see Nasa'í ch. on Ṣalát).

103. And when thou art among them, and leadest the Prayer for them, let a party of them stand with thee and let them take their arms. And when they have performed their prostrations, let them go to your rear, and let another party, who have not yet prayed, come forward and pray with thee; and let them take their means of defence and their arms. The disbelievers wish that you be neglectful of your arms and your baggage that they may fall upon you at once. And it shall be no sin on you, if you are in trouble on account of rain or if you are sick, that you lay aside your arms. But you should *always* take your means of defence. Surely, Allah has prepared an humiliating punishment for the disbelievers.[571]

وَاِذَا كُنْتَ فِيْهِمْ فَاَقَمْتَ لَهُمُ الصَّلٰوةَ فَلْتَقُمْ طَآئِفَةٌ مِّنْهُمْ مَّعَكَ وَلْيَاْخُذُوْٓا اَسْلِحَتَهُمْ ۟ فَاِذَا سَجَدُوْا فَلْيَكُوْنُوْا مِنْ وَّرَآئِكُمْ ۖ وَلْتَاْتِ طَآئِفَةٌ اُخْرٰى لَمْ يُصَلُّوْا فَلْيُصَلُّوْا مَعَكَ وَلْيَاْخُذُوْا حِذْرَهُمْ وَاَسْلِحَتَهُمْ ۚ وَدَّ الَّذِيْنَ كَفَرُوْا لَوْ تَغْفُلُوْنَ عَنْ اَسْلِحَتِكُمْ وَاَمْتِعَتِكُمْ فَيَمِيْلُوْنَ عَلَيْكُمْ مَّيْلَةً وَّاحِدَةً ۚ وَلَا جُنَاحَ عَلَيْكُمْ اِنْ كَانَ بِكُمْ اَذًى مِّنْ مَّطَرٍ اَوْ كُنْتُمْ مَّرْضٰٓى اَنْ تَضَعُوْٓا اَسْلِحَتَكُمْ ۚ وَخُذُوْا حِذْرَكُمْ ۗ اِنَّ اللّٰهَ اَعَدَّ لِلْكٰفِرِيْنَ عَذَابًا مُّهِيْنًا ۝

---

571. Commentary:

Whereas the preceding verse spoke of the Prayer in time of fear in the case of individuals, the present one gives the details of the manner of its performance when the Faithful are in the form of a company or group and the Prayer is to be performed in congregation. Apparently the Holy Prophet alone seems to have been addressed here, but really the verse possesses general application. When a Muslim army is about to say their Prayer in congregation, half of them should say the Prayer with the *Imām*, carrying their arms, and the other half should stand facing the enemy, to fight him or repulse his attack, as the case may be. When the first half have finished one *rak'at*, they should retire to take the place of those who are facing the enemy. The latter should then come forward and say one *rak'at* with the *Imām*.

As many as eleven different ways in which these Prayers were said on different occasions

are described in the Ḥadīth (for details see **Al-Baḥr al-Muḥīṭ**). In some cases, each of the two parties said only one *rak'at* of Prayer, while the *Imām* said two. In other cases, each of the parties said two *rak'ats*, one *rak'at* with the *Imām* and the other alone, thus all saying two *rak'ats*. On yet other occasions each of the two parties said two *rak'ats* of Prayer with the *Imām*, the *Imām* himself having said four *rak'ats*—two *rak'ats* with each party. These different methods were observed in different circumstances. If the danger was great, each of the parties said only one *rak'at* of Prayer with the *Imām* while the *Imām* himself said two; but if the danger was not so great, each party said two *rak'ats* while the *Imām* said four. Again, methods varied with the varying position of the army. If the enemy, for instance, was in front of the *Imām*, the congregation followed a method different from that which they followed on other occasions.

104. And when you have finished the Prayer, [a]remember Allah, standing, and sitting, and *lying* on your sides. And [b]when you are secure *from danger*, then observe Prayer *in the prescribed form*; verily Prayer is enjoined on the believers *to be performed* at fixed hours.[572]

فَإِذَا قَضَيْتُمُ الصَّلٰوةَ فَاذْكُرُوا اللّٰهَ قِيَامًا وَّقُعُوْدًا وَّعَلٰى جُنُوْبِكُمْ ۚ فَإِذَا اطْمَاْنَنْتُمْ فَأَقِيمُوا الصَّلٰوةَ ۚ إِنَّ الصَّلٰوةَ كَانَتْ عَلَى الْمُؤْمِنِيْنَ كِتٰبًا مَّوْقُوْتًا ۝

105. And [c]slacken not in seeking these people. If you suffer, they too suffer even as you suffer. But you hope from Allah what they do not hope. And Allah is All-Knowing, Wise.[573]

وَلَا تَهِنُوْا فِي ابْتِغَاءِ الْقَوْمِ ۚ إِنْ تَكُوْنُوْا تَأْلَمُوْنَ فَإِنَّهُمْ يَأْلَمُوْنَ كَمَا تَأْلَمُوْنَ ۚ وَتَرْجُوْنَ مِنَ اللّٰهِ مَا لَا يَرْجُوْنَ ۚ وَكَانَ اللّٰهُ عَلِيْمًا حَكِيْمًا ۝

---

[a]3 : 192.　　　[b]2 : 240.　　　[c]3 : 147.

To sum up, whereas Prayer in a state of simple journey consists of two *rak'ats* in such Prayers as ordinarily consist of four *rak'ats*, the Prayer in time of fear may assume different forms, the more important being :—

(a) Splitting up the worshippers into two parties, each party either saying one part of its Prayer with the *Imām* and then retiring, or saying one part of its Prayer with the *Imām* and the other part separately, the number of *rak'ats* performed by the worshippers being either one or two as the case may be (the presens verse) ;

(b) Shortening the duration of Prayers only (the preceding verse) ;

(c) Doing away with all form and repeating the words of Prayer while walking, running or riding (2 : 240).

The verse observes a difference between اسلحة (arms) and حذر (means of defence or simply precautions). Whereas the former may be put aside in moments of comparative security, the latter should always be adhered to and never neglected. See also 4 : 72.

572. **Commentary:**

As in the midst of a battle formal Prayers

are either said in haste, or performed in the form of one *rak'at* only, Muslims are enjoined in this verse, with a view to making up the deficiency, to continue remembering God and praying to Him in an informal manner after the obligatory service is over. This was to compensate, on the one hand, for the shortening of Prayer and, on the other, to serve as a means of drawing the special aid and help of God in a time of great danger.

The expression, *And when you are secure (from danger), then observe Prayer (in the prescribed form)*, very clearly brings out the difference between the words اقضوا الصلوة or صلوا (pray or offer Prayer) and the words اقيموا الصلوة (observe Prayer). The latter expression signifies observing Prayer attentively with all its necessary conditions. The verse thus clearly shows that Islam does not look upon the hasty performance of Prayer as coming under the injunction, اقيموا الصلوة (observe Prayer). See also 2 : 4.

573. **Commentary:**

The expression, *you hope from Allah*, does

106. We have surely sent down to thee the Book comprising the truth, *a*that thou mayest judge between men by that which Allah has taught thee. And be not thou a disputer for the faithless ;574

107. And ask forgiveness of Allah. Surely, Allah is Most Forgiving, Merciful.575

108. And plead not on behalf of those who are dishonest to themselves. Surely, *b*Allah loves not one who is perfidious *and* a great sinner.576

*a*5 : 49.   *b*8 : 59 ; 22 : 39.

not merely signify " hoping to get a reward or recompense " but also includes " hoping to win the pleasure of God and attain His nearness." There can be no bigger incentive for making sacrifices in the cause of religion than the hope that one will thereby win the pleasure and nearness of one's Lord and Master.

574. Commentary :

The Quran being the repository of all truth, all questions should be referred to it for decision and settlement. But no favour is to be shown, and no support given, to those who act dishonestly and faithlessly.

The address in this verse is not to the Holy Prophet, in particular, but to every Muslim who accepts and studies the Quran.

575. Commentary :

استغفار (asking forgiveness) is the keystone of all spiritual progress. The word does not merely mean verbal asking for forgiveness but also extends to acts leading to the covering up of one's sins and shortcomings ; and this covering-up, implied in the root meaning of *Istighfār* (see 2 : 200), may be of diverse nature :

(1) the covering-up of evil propensities in man; (2) the covering-up of evil thoughts and their being restrained from being converted into actions ; (3) the covering-up of sins actually committed and preventing them from being exposed ; and (4) finally the covering-up of the sins, as it were, from the sight of God Himself *i.e.* complete and absolute forgiveness and their being treated as non-existent. What a vista of bliss for a true believer !

576. Commentary :

The expression انفسهم (themselves) may also mean " their brethren " (see 2 : 85, 86 and 4 : 67), in which case the clause would mean " those who act dishonestly with regard to their brethren." The verse further emphasizes the fact, stated in 4 : 106 above, that those who act unfaithfully and dishonestly should not be supported. They do not deserve support not only because they are dishonest with regard to their own souls or those of their brethren and because the good name of their community suffers on their account, but also because they are encouraged in this way to persist in their evil practices. Here, too, the address is general as in 4 : 106.

109. They seek to hide from men, but they cannot hide from Allah; and *a*He is with them when they spend the night plotting about matters which He does not approve. And Allah encompasses what they do.

110. Behold! you are they who pleaded for them in the present life. But who will plead with Allah for them on the Day of Resurrection, or who will be a guardian over them?[577]

111. And whoso does evil or wrongs his soul, and then *b*asks forgiveness of Allah, will find Allah Most Forgiving *and* Merciful.[578]

112. And *c*whoso commits a sin commits it only against his own soul. And Allah is All-Knowing, Wise.

113. And whoso commits a fault or a sin, then *d*imputes it to an innocent person, certainly bears the *burden of* a calumny and a manifest sin.[579]

---

*a*4 : 82.   *b*4 : 65.   *c*2 : 287 ; 99 : 9.   *d*24 : 2, 24 ; 33 : 59.

577. Commentary :

The use in the present verse of the word انتم (you) which is in the plural number clearly shows that in the previous verses it was not the Holy Prophet but Muslims in general who were addressed. The Holy Prophet could not be expected to dispute on behalf of dishonest people. The Quran addresses him merely because he is the recipient of the Word of God and it is through him that people receive divine commands.

578. Commentary :

The God of Islam is a God of mercy and is never revengeful. Whenever a servant of His commits a sin or does an evil act and then sincerely repents and asks His forgiveness, he always finds Him most Forgiving and Merciful. Ah, what a loving God! Truly has the Holy Prophet said that the joy of God at the repentance of a sinful servant of His is greater than the joy of a lonely wayfarer who, while travelling in the desert, loses his camel laden with provisions and despairs of life but then suddenly finds it (Bukhārī ch. on *Da'wāt*).

579. Important Words :

The difference between خطيئة (fault) and اثم (sin) mentioned side by side in this verse is that the former can be both intentional and

17   114. And but for the grace of Allah upon thee and His mercy, ^aa party of them had resolved to bring about thy ruin. And they ruin none but themselves and they cannot harm thee at all. And Allah has sent down to thee the Book and Wisdom and ^bhas taught thee what thou knewest not, and great is Allah's grace on thee.⁵⁸⁰

وَلَوْلَا فَضْلُ اللّٰهِ عَلَيْكَ وَرَحْمَتُهُ لَهَمَّتْ طَّآئِفَةٌ مِّنْهُمْ أَنْ يُّضِلُّوكَ وَمَا يُضِلُّونَ إِلَّا أَنْفُسَهُمْ وَمَا يَضُرُّونَكَ مِنْ شَيْءٍ وَأَنْزَلَ اللّٰهُ عَلَيْكَ الْكِتٰبَ وَالْحِكْمَةَ وَعَلَّمَكَ مَا لَمْ تَكُنْ تَعْلَمُ وَكَانَ فَضْلُ اللّٰهِ عَلَيْكَ عَظِيْمًا ۝

115. There is no good in many of their conferences except *the conferences of* such as enjoin charity, or goodness, or ^cthe making of peace among men. And whoso does that, seeking the pleasure of Allah, We shall soon bestow on him a great reward.⁵⁸¹

لَا خَيْرَ فِيْ كَثِيْرٍ مِّنْ نَّجْوٰىهُمْ إِلَّا مَنْ أَمَرَ بِصَدَقَةٍ أَوْ مَعْرُوْفٍ أَوْ إِصْلَاحٍ بَيْنَ النَّاسِ وَمَنْ يَّفْعَلْ ذٰلِكَ ابْتِغَآءَ مَرْضَاتِ اللّٰهِ فَسَوْفَ نُؤْتِيْهِ أَجْرًا عَظِيْمًا ۝

^a17 : 74.   ^b42 : 52 ; 96 : 6.   ^c2 : 225.

unintentional and is often confined to the doer ; while the latter is intentional and its scope may extend to other people as well. Moreover, the former may be a dereliction of duty due to God ; while the latter is often an offence against both God and man and is therefore more serious and deserving of greater punishment than the former. See also 2 : 82 and 2 : 174.

Commentary :

The commission of a fault or sin makes it doubly grave, if he who commits it tries to fix it on an innocent person. This is why such an attempt has not only been termed بهتان (calumny) but also إثم مبين (manifest sin). As the word مبين (manifest) also means "that which cuts asunder" (2 : 169), the expression إثمًا مبينًا may also signify that a double sin (*i.e.* committing a sin and then imputing it to an innocent person) is that which is likely to cut asunder the connection of the sinner with his Maker.

580. Important Words :

يضلوك (bring about thy ruin). See 2 : 27.

Commentary :

Various were the ways the hypocrites adopted to bring the Holy Prophet to grief. They would try to mislead him into coming to a wrong decision on a matter of vital importance. But their evil designs were always frustrated because the Holy Prophet was invariably led by God to the right course concerning matters affecting the future of Islam.

The words فضل (grace) and رحمة (mercy), though also general in their significance, sometimes denote " worldly good " and " spiritual blessings " respectively (see 2 : 65). In this case the verse would mean that the Holy Prophet enjoyed God's protection in temporal as well as spiritual matters.

581. Important Words :

نجوى (conference) is derived from نجا

116. And *as to* him who opposes the Messenger after guidance has become clear to him, and ^afollows a way other than that of the believers, We shall let him pursue the way he is pursuing and shall cast him into Hell; and an evil destination it is.⁵⁸²

وَمَنْ يُّشَاقِقِ الرَّسُوْلَ مِنْ بَعْدِ مَا تَبَيَّنَ لَهُ الْهُدٰى وَيَتَّبِعْ غَيْرَ سَبِيْلِ الْمُؤْمِنِيْنَ نُوَلِّهٖ مَا تَوَلّٰى وَنُصْلِهٖ جَهَنَّمَ ۚ وَسَآءَتْ مَصِيْرًا ۝

---

*a*7 : 4.

---

which means, he became safe; he escaped. نجا الجلد عن الذبيحة means, he removed the skin of the slaughtered animal, laying bare the interior. نجا الرجل means, he discoursed secrets with the man, or simply he discoursed with him. ناجا الرجل means, he talked with him in private, or he discoursed secretly with him. نجوى therefore means, a secret between two or more persons; a person or persons discoursing or talking secretly, or holding secret talks, or telling secrets to one another, or talking confidentially, or holding confidential conference; the act of talking or discussing secrets with one another or holding confidential conferences (Aqrab & Tāj). According to some authorities, the word نجوى is not restricted to secret conferences but signifies all conferences whether secret or otherwise in which some people meet at a place and discuss matters or talk together (Lisān). Zajjāj also endorses the same view, saying that secrecy is not essential to نجوى which is applied to all conferences, whether open or secret (Muḥīṭ). The word thus extends to those conferences which though not secret are attended only by regular members or specially invited persons.

Commentary :

The verse is important inasmuch as it differentiates between good and bad conferences. The verse teaches that only three kinds of conferences or societies or meetings can be productive of good: Firstly, من امر بصدقة *i.e.* those that are founded or held with the object of promoting the welfare of the poor, the needy, etc. Secondly, من امر بمعروف *i.e.* those the object of which is to promote the spread and propagation of, or investigation and research into, sciences, law, education, learning, the arts, etc. Thirdly, من امر باصلاح بين الناس *i.e.* those established for the purpose of settling disputes and removing causes of friction in domestic, social, national, or international matters. This would include associations for the purpose of conducting the political affairs of a nation or a country, for their object also is to promote peace among mankind. This teaching, if faithfully acted upon, should go a long way to establish peace and harmony in the world.

582. Commentary :

The verse means that people who oppose the Prophet openly or secretly and seek for themselves a way other than that of believers, in spite of the fact that the divine guidance has become clear to them, will be deprived of the means of guidance, and God will let them follow the wrong course they are pursuing *i.e.* they will increase in their hypocrisy and disbelief.

117. *ᵃAllah shall not forgive that anything be associated with Him as partner, but He will forgive what is short of that to whomsoever He pleases. And ᵇwhoso associates anything with Allah has indeed strayed far away.**583**

اِنَّ اللّٰهَ لَا يَغْفِرُ اَنْ يُّشْرَكَ بِهٖ وَ يَغْفِرُ مَا دُوْنَ ذٰلِكَ لِمَنْ يَّشَآءُ وَ مَنْ يُّشْرِكْ بِاللّٰهِ فَقَدْ ضَلَّ ضَلٰلًۢا بَعِيْدًا ۝

118. They invoke beside Him none but lifeless objects ; and they invoke none but Satan, the rebellious,**584**

اِنْ يَّدْعُوْنَ مِنْ دُوْنِهٖۤ اِلَّاۤ اِنَاثًا وَ اِنْ يَّدْعُوْنَ اِلَّا شَيْطٰنًا مَّرِيْدًا ۝

119. Whom Allah has cursed. And he said, ᶜ“I will assuredly take a fixed portion from Thy servants ;**585**

لَّعَنَهُ اللّٰهُ وَ قَالَ لَاَتَّخِذَنَّ مِنْ عِبَادِكَ نَصِيْبًا مَّفْرُوْضًا ۝

ᵃ4 : 49.   ᵇ4 : 137.   ᶜ14 : 23 ; 17 : 65.

---

583. Commentary :

See note on 4 : 49.

584. Important Words :

اناث (lifeless objects) is the plural of انثى which is derived from انث which means, it was or became female or feminine ; or it (iron, etc.) was or became soft. انثى means, female ; feminine ; of the female sex or feminine gender. اناث , which is the plural of انثى , also means, inanimate or lifeless things ; small stars (Lane).

مريد (rebellious) is derived from مرد i.e. he was or became rebellious and transgressed proper limits. مارد means, one who rebels and transgresses proper limits. مريد means, mischievous, haughty and rebellious (Aqrab).

Commentary :

The word اناث (lifeless objects) explained above includes all false deities, whether living or dead. The word has been used to point to the utter weakness and helplessness of the false deities.

The use of the word "Satan" in the verse signifies that idolaters, while invoking their deities, in reality invoke Satan, because it is at his bidding that they invoke false gods.

The verse provides two reasons for the statement made in the previous verse : (1) the worship of false gods does the idolaters no good ; (2) it positively does them harm, because it strengthens their relation with Satan, who is the avowed enemy of man and a rebel against the true God.

585. Commentary :

The opening part of the verse refers to Satan as mentioned in the preceding verse. When cursed by God, he vowed to mislead men ; but he can lead astray only a "fixed portion" of them i.e. those who themselves choose to accept his lead. The words "fixed portion" thus mean portion determined under the eternal laws of God.

120. 'And assuredly I will lead them astray and assuredly I will excite in them vain desires, and assuredly I will incite them and they will cut the ears of cattle ; and assuredly I will incite them and they will alter Allah's creation. And he, who takes Satan for a friend beside Allah, has certainly suffered a manifest loss.[586]

وَلَاُضِلَّنَّهُمْ وَلَاُمَنِّيَنَّهُمْ وَلَاٰمُرَنَّهُمْ فَلَيُبَتِّكُنَّ اٰذَانَ الْاَنْعَامِ وَلَاٰمُرَنَّهُمْ فَلَيُغَيِّرُنَّ خَلْقَ اللّٰهِ ۗ وَمَنْ يَّتَّخِذِ الشَّيْطٰنَ وَلِيًّا مِّنْ دُوْنِ اللّٰهِ فَقَدْ خَسِرَ خُسْرَانًا مُّبِيْنًا ۞

121. [a]He holds out promises to them and raises vain desires in them, and Satan promises them nothing but vain things.[587]

يَعِدُهُمْ وَيُمَنِّيْهِمْ ۗ وَمَا يَعِدُهُمُ الشَّيْطٰنُ اِلَّا غُرُوْرًا ۞

*a*14 : 23; 17 : 65.

---

586. Important Words :

فَلَيُبَتِّكُنَّ (will cut) is derived from بتك . They say بَتَكَ *i.e.* he cut it or severed it, or slit it, or cut it off entirely, or plucked it out (Lane).

Commentary :

The opening part of the verse is a continuation of the speech of Satan begun in the last verse, and the latter part embodies a pronouncement of the judgement of God.

As a mark of their dedication to false deities, the Arabs used to cut the ears of dedicated animals in order to distinguish them from other animals. This foolish practice persists even to this day among some ignorant people in India and elsewhere.

The "alteration of God's creation" can be, and is, generally done in four ways : (1) by deifying God's creation ; (2) by changing and corrupting the religion of God; (3) by deforming or disfiguring the body of a new-born child ; (4) by turning to an evil use that which God

has created for a good purpose. For instance, God has endowed man with many faculties by making a right use of which he can make great progress in all departments of life, but not unoften he seeks to alter God's creation by making an evil use of them and as a result thereof "suffers a manifest loss."

587. Important Words :

غُرُوْرًا (vain things) is derived from غر . They say غَرَّهُ *i.e.* he deceived him; he beguiled him; he made him desire what was vain or false. غُرُوْر (*ghurūr*) means, false or vain thing; vanity or what is false or vain ; a deception ; a thing by which one is deceived. غَرُوْر (*gharūr*) (*e.g.* 31 : 34), with different vowel point, means, very deceitful, or what deceives one, the Devil; also the present world (Lane).

Commentary :

The promises made by Satan and the desires raised by him in the hearts of his votaries, as against the works and decrees of God, never materialize.

122. These are they whose abode shall be Hell and ^athey shall find no way of escape from it.[588]

اُولٰٓئِكَ مَاۡوٰىهُمۡ جَهَنَّمُ ۫ وَ لَا یَجِدُوۡنَ عَنۡهَا مَحِیۡصًا ۞

123. But *as to* ^bthose who believe and do good works, We will admit them into gardens, beneath which streams flow, abiding therein for ever. *It is* Allah's unfailing promise; and who can be more truthful than Allah in word?

وَ الَّذِیۡنَ اٰمَنُوۡا وَ عَمِلُوا الصّٰلِحٰتِ سَنُدۡخِلُهُمۡ جَنّٰتٍ تَجۡرِیۡ مِنۡ تَحۡتِهَا الۡاَنۡهٰرُ خٰلِدِیۡنَ فِیۡهَاۤ اَبَدًا ؕ وَعۡدَ اللّٰهِ حَقًّا ؕ وَ مَنۡ اَصۡدَقُ مِنَ اللّٰهِ قِیۡلًا ۞

124. It shall not be according to your desires, nor according to the desires of the People of the Book. Whoso does evil shall be rewarded for it; and ^che shall find for himself no friend or helper beside Allah.[589]

لَیۡسَ بِاَمَانِیِّکُمۡ وَ لَاۤ اَمَانِیِّ اَهۡلِ الۡکِتٰبِ ؕ مَنۡ یَّعۡمَلۡ سُوۡٓءًا یُّجۡزَ بِهٖ ۙ وَ لَا یَجِدۡ لَهٗ مِنۡ دُوۡنِ اللّٰهِ وَلِیًّا وَّ لَا نَصِیۡرًا ۞

125. But ^dwhoso does good works, whether male or female, and is a believer, such shall enter heaven, and shall not be wronged even *as much as* the little hollow in the back of a date-stone.[590]

وَ مَنۡ یَّعۡمَلۡ مِنَ الصّٰلِحٰتِ مِنۡ ذَکَرٍ اَوۡ اُنۡثٰی وَ هُوَ مُؤۡمِنٌ فَاُولٰٓئِکَ یَدۡخُلُوۡنَ الۡجَنَّةَ وَ لَا یُظۡلَمُوۡنَ نَقِیۡرًا ۞

---

^a14 : 22.   ^bSee 2 : 26.   ^c4 : 46 ; 33 : 18, 66.   ^d40 : 41.

---

588. Important Words:

محیص (way of escape) is derived from حاص. They say حاص عنه *i.e.* he turned away from, and escaped it. محیص therefore means, a way or place of escape; a place of refuge; a place to which one turns or flees (Aqrab & Lane).

589. Commentary:

The expression, *It shall not be according to your desires*, does not mean that the desires of the Faithful will not materialize. The verse purports to lay down a general principle that it is only the will of God which prevails. As the desires of true believers must coincide with the will of God, they are bound to materialize.

590. Commentary:

The verse is important inasmuch as it clearly places men and women on the same level so far as works and their rewards are concerned. Both alike are servants of the Lord and both are equally entitled to a good reward, if they do good works. It is indeed strange that in spite of such explicit teaching some Christian missionaries should have the hardihood to bring against Islam the charge that according to it women, unlike men, are devoid of souls.

It should also be noted that true belief is a necessary condition for salvation, as the words, *and is a believer*, clearly indicate.

126. And who is better in faith than *he who submits himself to Allah, and he is a doer of good, and follows the religion of Abraham, the upright ? And Allah took Abraham for a special friend.[591]

وَمَنْ اَحْسَنُ دِيْنًا مِّمَّنْ اَسْلَمَ وَجْهَهٗ لِلّٰهِ وَهُوَ مُحْسِنٌ وَّاتَّبَعَ مِلَّةَ اِبْرٰهِيْمَ حَنِيْفًا ۗ وَاتَّخَذَ اللّٰهُ اِبْرٰهِيْمَ خَلِيْلًا ۝

127. And *to Allah belongs all that is in the heavens and all that is in the earth ; and *Allah encompasses all things.[592]

وَلِلّٰهِ مَا فِى السَّمٰوٰتِ وَمَا فِى الْاَرْضِ ۗ وَكَانَ اللّٰهُ بِكُلِّ شَىْءٍ مُّحِيْطًا ۝

---

*2 : 132.   *2 : 285 ; 4 : 132 ; 10 : 56 ; 16 : 53 ; 24 : 65.   *41 : 55 ; 85 : 21.

---

591. Important Words :

خَلِيْل (special friend) is derived from خَلَّ. They say خَلَّ الشَّىْءَ *i.e.* he bored a hole into the thing. خَلَّ فِى دُعَائِهٖ means, he was particular in his prayer. خَلِيْل means, a special and particular friend whose love penetrates your inner parts (Aqrab & Lane). See also 2 : 255.

Commentary :

This verse gives the essence of Islam which signifies submission to the will of God and the devotion of one's faculties and powers to His service (see also note on 2 : 113). Abraham has been held out to the People of the Book who revere him as a patriarch and to the Arabs who were proud of being descended from him, as an example who embodied in his person the essence of Islam by his full submission to the will of God; and both these people are herein told that it is only the true observance of the teachings of Islam that can make one like Abraham—beloved of God and His special friend.

There is an ḥadīth in which the Holy Prophet is reported to have said : "If I had taken anyone from among men as my خَلِيْل (special friend whose love penetrates one's heart), I would have certainly taken Abū Bakr as such. But such friendship is permissible with God alone Who is my خَلِيْل" (Bukhārī, ch. on *Faḍā'il* of the holy Companions).

592. Commentary :

The word مُحِيْط (One Who encompasses) signifies two things : (1) that God encompasses every thing with His knowledge; and (2) that He encompasses all with His power. There is nothing that He does not know and nothing that He does not hold in His power.

19 128. And they seek of thee the decision *of the Law* with regard to women. Say, Allah gives you His decision regarding them. And so does *a*that which is recited to you in the Book concerning the orphan girls whom you give not what is prescribed for them and whom you desire to marry, and *concerning* the weak among children. And *He enjoins you to* observe equity towards the orphans. And whatever good you do, surely Allah knows it well.[593]

وَيَسْتَفْتُوْنَكَ فِى النِّسَآءِ ۚ قُلِ اللّٰهُ يُفْتِيْكُمْ فِيْهِنَّ ۙ وَ مَا يُتْلٰى عَلَيْكُمْ فِى الْكِتٰبِ فِى يَتٰمَى النِّسَآءِ الّٰتِىْ لَا تُؤْتُوْنَهُنَّ مَا كُتِبَ لَهُنَّ وَتَرْغَبُوْنَ اَنْ تَنْكِحُوْهُنَّ وَالْمُسْتَضْعَفِيْنَ مِنَ الْوِلْدَانِ ۙ وَاَنْ تَقُوْمُوْا لِلْيَتٰمٰى بِالْقِسْطِ ۚ وَمَا تَفْعَلُوْا مِنْ خَيْرٍ فَاِنَّ اللّٰهَ كَانَ بِهٖ عَلِيْمًا ۝١٢٨

*a*4 : 4.

---

593. Important Words :

يَسْتَفْتُوْنَكَ (they seek of thee the decision of the Law) and يُفْتِيْكُم (gives you His decision) are both derived from فتو or فتى *i.e.* he was or became youthful or he was in the prime of life. فَتَا الرَّجُلَ means, he surpassed the man in فَتْوَة *i.e.* in generosity. اَفْتَاهُ فِى الْاَمْرِ means, he made known or explained to him the decision of the *Sharī'at* respecting the matter; or he gave him an answer stating the decision of the Law respecting a question. اِسْتَفْتَيْتُ الْفَقِيْهَ فِى الْاَمْرِ means, I asked or sought of the jurist or the lawyer or the learned man the decision of the *Sharī'at* respecting the matter. فَتْوَى therefore means, an explanation or notification or pronouncement of the decision of the Law in some dubious or difficult matter given by a jurist or a lawyer or a man learned in religious Law. اِسْتِفْتَاء means, asking or seeking of a jurist or a lawyer or a learned man the decision of the Law (*Sharī'at*) in a certain dubious or difficult matter (Lane & Aqrab). The expression اَفْتَانَا rendered in the verse as gives you the decision, is also sometimes used in the sense of permitting or giving permission, as in the well-known ḥadīth الْاِثْمُ مَا حَاكَ فِى صَدْرِكَ وَاَنْ اَفْتَاكَ النَّاسُ *i.e.* a sin is that which pricks in thy mind even if people should say that it is permissible (Lisān). In this case the Quranic clause يُفْتِيْكُم اللّٰه rendered as, *Allah gives you His decision*, may also be translated as "Allah gives you permission".

Commentary :

The verse which has been differently translated is considered to be a rather difficult one. The *decision* spoken of in the clause, *Allah gives you His decision*, refers to what follows in the succeeding verses *i.e.* 4 : 129—131.

The allusion in the words, *that which is recited to you in the Book*, is to verse 4 : 4 in the beginning of the present *Sūra*. It was prohibited to Muslims to marry those orphan girls whose rights they could not adequately discharge. 'Umar, the Holy Prophet's Second Successor, would not allow the guardians of wealthy and handsome orphan girls to marry them but would insist on better husbands being found for them. On the other hand, if they were not so wealthy or handsome, he recommended them to their guardians for marriage so that, being acquainted with their defects and weaknesses, they might overlook them and deal kindly with them. For further instructions about good treatment of orphans see 4 : 6,7.

129. And ^aif a woman fear ill-treatment or indifference on the part of her husband, it shall be no sin on them that they be suitably reconciled to each other ; and reconciliation is best. And people are prone to covetousness. And if you do good and are righteous, surely Allah is aware of what you do.⁵⁹⁴

وَاِنِ امْرَاَةٌ خَافَتْ مِنْۢ بَعْلِهَا نُشُوْزًا اَوْاِعْرَاضًا فَلَا جُنَاحَ عَلَيْهِمَآ اَنْ يُّصْلِحَا بَيْنَهُمَا صُلْحًا ۭ وَالصُّلْحُ خَيْرٌ ۭ وَاُحْضِرَتِ الْاَنْفُسُ الشُّحَّ ۭ وَاِنْ تُحْسِنُوْا وَتَتَّقُوْا فَاِنَّ اللّٰهَ كَانَ بِمَا تَعْمَلُوْنَ خَبِيْرًا ۧ ۝

130. And ^byou cannot keep *perfect* balance between wives, however much you may desire it. But incline not wholly *to one* so ^cthat you leave the other like a thing suspended. And if you amend and act righteously, surely Allah is Most Forgiving *and* Merciful.⁵⁹⁵

وَلَنْ تَسْتَطِيْعُوْٓا اَنْ تَعْدِلُوْا بَيْنَ النِّسَآءِ وَلَوْحَرَصْتُمْ فَلَا تَمِيْلُوْا كُلَّ الْمَيْلِ فَتَذَرُوْهَا كَالْمُعَلَّقَةِ ۭ وَاِنْ تُصْلِحُوْا وَتَتَّقُوْا فَاِنَّ اللّٰهَ كَانَ غَفُوْرًا رَّحِيْمًا ۝

---

^a4 : 35.   ^b4 : 4.   ^c2 : 232.

Generally speaking the clause, *Allah gives you His decision regarding them* (women) *and so does that which is recited to you in the Book concerning the orphan girls*, means that some instructions about women have already been given in the Quran and other instructions follow.

594. Commentary :

The words, *it shall be no sin on them that they be suitably reconciled to each other*, constitute a peculiar Quranic expression denoting both exhortation and rebuke. They may be interpreted as something like this : " Do the contending parties think that they would be committing a sin if they became reconciled to each other ? It is no sin to do so. On the contrary, it is a commendable thing."

The words احضرت الانفس الشح (people are prone to covetousness) literally mean, " souls have been put face to face with covetousness." These words thus give the real cause that often leads to estrangement between husband and wife. It may be expressed as niggardliness on the part of the husband and covetousness

on the part of the wife. When the husband does not like his wife, he thinks it a burden to support her. On the other hand, the wife sometimes makes excessive demands on her husband. The verse exhorts both to treat each other equitably and fairly.

The words, *and reconciliation is best*, embody an appeal to the married couple to live amicably and avoid disagreements ; for that is in their own interest in all respects.

595. Important Words :

معلقة (a thing suspended) is derived from علق. They say علقه *i.e.* he hung it up or suspended it. علق الامر means, he left the affair suspended *i.e.* undecided. معلقة is, therefore, a woman whose husband neither keeps her properly as a wife nor divorces her so that she might marry another man (Lane & Aqrab).

Commentary :

The words, *And you cannot keep perfect balance between wives, however much you may desire it*, mean that it is not humanly possible for a man to keep perfect balance between his

131. And if they separate, Allah will make both independent out of His abundance; and Allah is Bountiful, Wise.⁵⁹⁶

132. And ᵃto Allah belongs whatever is in the heavens and whatever is in the earth. And ᵇWe have assuredly commanded those who were given the Book before you, and *commanded* you also, to fear Allah. But if you disbelieve, then *remember that* to Allah belongs whatever is in the heavens and whatever is in the earth, and Allah is Self-Sufficient, Praiseworthy.⁵⁹⁷

وَاِنْ يَّتَفَرَّقَا يُغْنِ اللّٰهُ كُلًّا مِّنْ سَعَتِهٖ ۚ وَكَانَ اللّٰهُ وَاسِعًا حَكِيْمًا ۞

وَلِلّٰهِ مَا فِى السَّمٰوٰتِ وَمَا فِى الْاَرْضِ ۚ وَلَقَدْ وَصَّيْنَا الَّذِيْنَ اُوْتُوا الْكِتٰبَ مِنْ قَبْلِكُمْ وَاِيَّاكُمْ اَنِ اتَّقُوا اللّٰهَ ۚ وَاِنْ تَكْفُرُوْا فَاِنَّ لِلّٰهِ مَا فِى السَّمٰوٰتِ وَمَا فِى الْاَرْضِ ۚ وَكَانَ اللّٰهُ غَنِيًّا حَمِيْدًا ۞

ᵃSee 4 : 127.   ᵇ42 : 14.

---

different wives in every respect. For instance, love being an affair of the heart over which man has no control, a husband cannot be expected to have equal love for all his wives. But he can certainly deal by them with equity in matters of money, time, etc., and this he must do. So acting equitably between the different wives, which has been laid down by Islam as an essential condition for polygamy, pertains only to such overt acts over which man has control. This is the interpretation which the Holy Prophet himself has put on this verse, both by his words and example. 'A'isha reports that the Holy Prophet used to deal by his wives with equity in all matters over which man can have control, and having done this, he used to pray to God, saying, " My Lord, these are my dealings in matters over which I have control; so blame me not for that which is in Thy power and not mine," meaning the feelings of the heart (Dāwūd, ch. *al-Nikāh*). The Holy Prophet is also reported to have said: " If a man has two wives and he is inclined to one of them (neglecting the other), he will rise on the Day of Resurrection with one of his sides having been torn off (Dāwūd, ch. on *al-Nikāh*). Thus both the example and the

sayings of the Holy Prophet show that though a husband cannot love his wives equally, he should in his outward treatment *i.e.* allotment of time, money, etc. be equally just and fair to all of them. In this connection see also 4 : 4.

596. Commentary :

If, in spite of the husband and the wife having done their best to live amicably, they find that they cannot pull on together, and separation takes place, then God promises to provide for both parties out of His beneficence *i.e.* they may find other and more suitable matches. How Islam looks upon divorce is vividly portrayed in a well-known ḥadīth of the Holy Prophet, *viz.*, " Of all permissible things divorce is most hateful in the eyes of God" (Dāwūd, ch. on *Talāq*).

597. Important Words :

حَمِيْد (Praiseworthy) is derived from حَمِدَ which means, he praised or eulogized him; or he praised him for something depending on the latter's will. Thus the describing of a pearl as lustrous is not حَمِدَ but مَدَحَ (see also 1 : 2). حَمِيْد or مَحْمُود with which it is almost synonymous, means, praised, eulogized or commended;

133. And ^ato Allah belongs whatever is in the heavens and whatever is in the earth, and sufficient is Allah as a Guardian.⁵⁹⁸

وَلِلّٰهِ مَا فِى السَّمٰوٰتِ وَمَا فِى الْاَرْضِ ۪ وَكَفٰى بِاللّٰهِ وَكِيْلًا ۝

134. If He please, He can take you away, O people, and bring others *in your stead;* and Allah has full power to do that.

اِنْ يَّشَاْ يُذْهِبْكُمْ اَيُّهَا النَّاسُ وَيَاْتِ بِاٰخَرِيْنَ ۪ وَكَانَ اللّٰهُ عَلٰى ذٰلِكَ قَدِيْرًا ۝

135. ^bWhoso desires the reward of this world, then *let him remember that* with Allah is the reward of this world and of the next; and Allah is All-Hearing, All-Seeing.⁵⁹⁹

مَنْ كَانَ يُرِيْدُ ثَوَابَ الدُّنْيَا فَعِنْدَ اللّٰهِ ثَوَابُ الدُّنْيَا وَالْاٰخِرَةِ ۪ وَكَانَ اللّٰهُ سَمِيْعًا بَصِيْرًا ۝

---

^aSee 4 : 127.   ^b2 : 201, 202 ; 42 : 21.

---

praiseworthy or laudable. الحميد which is one of the names of God, means, He Who is praised or is praiseworthy in every case (Lane).

Commentary:

See the next verse.

598. Commentary:

The expression, *And to Allah belongs whatever is in the heavens and whatever is in the earth,* is repeated thrice in this and the preceding verse to emphasize the fact that God will amply reward and protect from all harm and loss those who sincerely obey His commandments, because He is the Lord and Master of all that is in the heavens and the earth and because He is the Guardian over everything, so that He is in a position to help and reward those who act

righteously and punish those who defy and break His laws.

599. Commentary:

The verse contains a beautiful exhortation to the people to seek after the good things of the world to come, along with those of the present. When God can bestow on man in an ample measure both the good things of this world and the blessings of the life to come, why should man neglect to strive after both, particularly the good things of the next world which are far superior and are ever-lasting. Being All-Hearing, God hears our prayers and we can get what we desire by praying to Him; and being All-Seeing, He knows our needs and requirements and He can satisfy them even without our asking for them, in case we are not aware of any of our needs.

20 136. O ye who believe! *be strict in observing justice, *and be* witnesses for Allah, even though it be against yourselves or *against* parents and kindred. Whether he be rich or poor, Allah is more regardful of them both *than you are.* Therefore follow not low desires so that you may be able to act equitably. And if you conceal *the truth* or evade *it,* then *remember that* Allah is well aware of what you do.[600]

يَآأَيُّهَا الَّذِيْنَ اٰمَنُوْا كُوْنُوْا قَوَّامِيْنَ بِالْقِسْطِ شُهَدَآءَ لِلّٰهِ وَلَوْ عَلٰۤى اَنْفُسِكُمْ اَوِ الْوَالِدَيْنِ وَالْاَقْرَبِيْنَ ۚ اِنْ يَّكُنْ غَنِيًّا اَوْ فَقِيْرًا فَاللّٰهُ اَوْلٰى بِهِمَا ۖ فَلَا تَتَّبِعُوا الْهَوٰۤى اَنْ تَعْدِلُوْا ۚ وَاِنْ تَلْوٗۤا اَوْ تُعْرِضُوْا فَاِنَّ اللّٰهَ كَانَ بِمَا تَعْمَلُوْنَ خَبِيْرًا ۝

*a*5 : 9.

600. Important Words :

اوْلٰى (more regardful) is derived from وَلَى. They say وَلِيَهُ i.e. he was or became near unto him ; he loved him and was a friend to him. وَلِى الشَّيْئَ means, he managed and looked after the thing. الْوَلِى means, friend ; one who loves ; helper ; one who looks after your affairs. اَوْلٰى means, more entitled, having a better right (Aqrab). They say فُلَان اَوْلٰى بِكَذَا i.e. such a one is more entitled to such a thing ; or has a better right or better title or claim to it ; or is more deserving or worthy of it ; or is more competent or fit for it (Lane). اَوْلٰى also means, more regardful or more thoughtful or more considerate (Kashshāf & Muḥīṭ).

Commentary :

As in the settlement of differences between husband and wife, a subject dealt with in the preceding verses, witnesses have often to be called in, therefore the Quran here fittingly turns to that subject.

The expression, *be witnesses for Allah,* means that one should bear witness truly for the sake of God and in strict accordance with His injunctions. The words عَلٰى اَنْفُسِكُمْ rendered as " against yourselves " may also be rendered as " against your people or against your kith and kin," signifying that one should give true evidence in all cases, even against the members of one's own community or one's near relations or even when one's own honour or property is at stake.

The words, *parents or kindred,* have been added to increase the force of the injunction, *i.e.,* you should give true evidence not only against the members of your own community, but even against those who are closely related to you by blood—your own parents and others near and dear. As one has more often to bear witness against other people than against near relatives, therefore the former class of persons has been put before the latter.

571

137. O ye who believe! believe in Allah and His Messenger, and in the Book which He has revealed to His Messenger, and *a*the Book which He revealed before *it*. And *b*whoso disbelieves in Allah and His angels, and His Books, and His Messengers, and the Last Day, *c*has surely strayed far away.[601]

138. *d*Those who believe, then disbelieve, then *again* believe, then disbelieve, *and* then increase in disbelief, Allah will never forgive them nor will He guide them to the way.[602]

139. *e*Give to the hypocrites the tidings that for them is a grievous punishment;

يَاَيُّهَا الَّذِيْنَ اٰمَنُوْۤا اٰمِنُوْا بِاللّٰهِ وَرَسُوْلِهٖ وَالْكِتٰبِ الَّذِيْ نَزَّلَ عَلٰى رَسُوْلِهٖ وَالْكِتٰبِ الَّذِيْۤ اَنْزَلَ مِنْ قَبْلُ ۚ وَمَنْ يَّكْفُرْ بِاللّٰهِ وَمَلٰٓئِكَتِهٖ وَكُتُبِهٖ وَرُسُلِهٖ وَالْيَوْمِ الْاٰخِرِ فَقَدْ ضَلَّ ضَلٰلًۢا بَعِيْدًا ۞

اِنَّ الَّذِيْنَ اٰمَنُوْا ثُمَّ كَفَرُوْا ثُمَّ اٰمَنُوْا ثُمَّ كَفَرُوْا ثُمَّ ازْدَادُوْا كُفْرًا لَّمْ يَكُنِ اللّٰهُ لِيَغْفِرَ لَهُمْ وَلَا لِيَهْدِيَهُمْ سَبِيْلًا ۞

بَشِّرِ الْمُنٰفِقِيْنَ بِاَنَّ لَهُمْ عَذَابًا اَلِيْمًا ۞

---

*a*2 : 5, 137 ; 4 : 163 ; 5 : 60.   *b*4 : 151.   *c*4 : 117.   *d*3 : 91 ; 63 : 4.   *e*9 : 3.

601. Commentary :

In the clause, *O ye who believe, believe in Allah and His Messenger . . .* the first-mentioned belief refers to lip-profession and the second to true and genuine belief which really matters. The words thus show that sometimes expressions like "O ye who believe" or "believers" may be used for those who profess to be believers in Islam but do not live up to its teachings by carrying out faithfully its precepts into practice. Their assertion is a mere lip-profession that carries no weight.

602. Commentary :

This verse incidentally refutes the allegation that apostasy in Islam is punishable with death.

If such had been the law of Islam, apostates would have had no opportunity of apostatizing from Islam again and again, as appears from this verse. For an exposition of the teachings of Islam about apostasy see "Islam and the Law relating to Apostasy" (published from Qadian).

The verse does not signify that after so many successive acts of apostasy the repentance of an apostate is not accepted. Rather it is intended to point out that even after repeated acts of apostasy the door of repentance remains open. That door is closed only when after apostatizing, an apostate goes on "increasing in disbelief" as the verse clearly puts it.

140. ^aThose who take disbelievers for friends rather than believers. Do they seek honour at their hands? Then *let them remember that* ^ball honour belongs to Allah.⁶⁰³

اَلَّذِيْنَ يَتَّخِذُوْنَ الْكٰفِرِيْنَ اَوْلِيَآءَ مِنْ دُوْنِ الْمُؤْمِنِيْنَ ۚ اَيَبْتَغُوْنَ عِنْدَهُمُ الْعِزَّةَ فَاِنَّ الْعِزَّةَ لِلّٰهِ جَمِيْعًا ۞

141. And He has already revealed to you in the Book that, when you hear the Signs of God being denied and mocked at, sit not with them ^cuntil they engage in a talk other than that; for in that case you would be like them. Surely, Allah will assemble the hypocrites and the disbelievers in Hell, all together;⁶⁰⁴

وَقَدْ نَزَّلَ عَلَيْكُمْ فِى الْكِتٰبِ اَنْ اِذَا سَمِعْتُمْ اٰيٰتِ اللّٰهِ يُكْفَرُ بِهَا وَ يُسْتَهْزَاُ بِهَا فَلَا تَقْعُدُوْا مَعَهُمْ حَتّٰى يَخُوْضُوْا فِىْ حَدِيْثٍ غَيْرِهٖ ۖ اِنَّكُمْ اِذًا مِّثْلُهُمْ ۗ اِنَّ اللّٰهَ جَامِعُ الْمُنٰفِقِيْنَ وَ الْكٰفِرِيْنَ فِىْ جَهَنَّمَ جَمِيْعًا ۞

^a3 : 29, 119 ; 4 : 145.   ^b10 : 66 ; 35 : 11.   ^c6 : 69.

603. Commentary:

The verse gives a most graphic and painful portrait of many present-day Muslims.

604. Commentary:

The reference in the words, *has already revealed to you*, is to 6 : 69 where we read, *And when thou seest those who engage in vain discourse concerning Our Signs, then turn thou away from them until they enter into a discourse other than that : and if Satan cause thee to forget, then sit not, after recollection, with the unjust people.*

The *Sūra* in which the above-quoted verse occurs was revealed at Mecca *i.e.* before the present *Sūra* which is a Medinite one. This clearly shows that the present order of the verses and the *Sūras* of the Quran is not the same as that in which they were revealed. The reference in the words, *He has already revealed to you in the Book*, is, as stated above, to 6 : 69 which was revealed prior to the verse under comment; yet the former has been placed after the latter in the existing arrangement of the Quran.

It is also worthy of note here that while referring to a verse already revealed the verse under comment uses the words نزّل عليكم (has revealed to you) and not يُتل عليكم (is recited to you). The latter expression *i.e.* " is recited to you " has been used in 4 : 128 with reference to 4 : 4 which had not only been already revealed but has also been placed before the former, *i.e.* 4 : 128, in the existing order of the Quran. Again 6 : 146 makes an allusion to 16 : 116 in the words اوحى الى (has been revealed to me). Thus the fact that the Quran uses the words نزّل and اوحى for alluding to verses that were revealed earlier but were to be placed later and the word يُتل for alluding to those verses that were not only revealed earlier but were also to be placed earlier, clearly shows that the present order was not devised by the Holy Prophet but was devised and revealed by God Himself.

Another noteworthy point that emerges from

142. *aThose who wait *for news* concerning you. If you have a victory from Allah, they say, ' Were we not with you ? ' And if the disbelievers have a share *of it,* they say *to them,* ' Did we not get the better of you, and protect you against the believers ? ' Allah will judge between you on the Day of Resurrection ; and Allah will not grant the disbelievers a way *to prevail* against the believers.605

اِلَّذِيۡنَ يَتَرَبَّصُوۡنَ بِكُمۡ فَاِنۡ كَانَ لَكُمۡ فَتۡحٌ مِّنَ اللّٰهِ قَالُوۡۤا اَلَمۡ نَكُنۡ مَّعَكُمۡ ۖ وَاِنۡ كَانَ لِلۡكٰفِرِيۡنَ نَصِيۡبٌ ۙ قَالُوۡۤا اَلَمۡ نَسۡتَحۡوِذۡ عَلَيۡكُمۡ وَنَمۡنَعۡكُمۡ مِّنَ الۡمُؤۡمِنِيۡنَ ؕ فَاللّٰهُ يَحۡكُمُ بَيۡنَكُمۡ يَوۡمَ الۡقِيٰمَةِ ؕ وَلَنۡ يَّجۡعَلَ اللّٰهُ لِلۡكٰفِرِيۡنَ عَلَى الۡمُؤۡمِنِيۡنَ سَبِيۡلًا ۞

*a*9 : 98 ; 57 : 15.

this verse is that when an address is made to the Holy Prophet, it is not always meant for him personally but is often meant for his followers *i.e.* Muslims in general. In 6 : 69 the commandment appears to have been addressed to the Holy Prophet, because in that verse all the pronouns and verbs have been used in the second person singular number ; but the verse under comment, while referring to the commandment contained in 6:69, clearly addresses Muslims generally, for the words used are, *He has already revealed to you in the Book that, when you hear the Signs of God being denied and mocked at, sit not with them,* which establishes the fact that the addressees in the commandment embodied in both these verses are the same *i.e.* Muslims. If the pronoun "thou" in 6 : 69 was meant for the Holy Prophet himself, the present verse, while referring to the self-same commandment, could not address Muslims generally by using the pronoun "you", particularly when besides 6:69 there is no verse in the Quran to which the verse under comment can possibly refer.

The substitution in the present verse of the words لا تقعدوا (sit not with them) for the words اعرض (turn away from them) occurring in 6 : 69 indicates that the latter expression as used at some places in the Quran is meant to convey the sense of "severing connection with."

The underlying principle in the injunction contained in the present verse is threefold : (1) to emphasize the seriousness and importance of religious matters ; (2) to protect the Faithful against the demoralizing influences of disbelievers ; and (3) to engender and promote feelings of pious jealousy for religion in the hearts of Muslims.

605. Important Words :

نَسۡتَحۡوِذۡ عَلَيۡكُمۡ (get the better of you). is derived from حاذ. They say حاذه *i.e.* he guarded or protected it and took care of it. حاذ الابل means, he drove the camels quickly or he gained mastery over the camels and collected them together. استحوذ عليه means, he overcame or mastered or gained mastery of him or it ; he got the better of him or it (Tâj).

نَمۡنَعۡكُم (protected you) is derived from منع *i.e.* (1) he prevented or hindered ; (2) he denied or refused ; (3) he protected or guarded (Lane).

Commentary :

The words, *did we not get the better of you,* are addressed by the hypocrites to the disbelievers and mean "we had you in our power but we spared you." Similarly, the words, *and protect you against the believers,* may be interpreted something like this : "we separated ourselves from the Muslims with the result that they became weak

143. ^aThe hypocrites seek to deceive Allah, but He will punish them for their deception. And when they stand up for Prayer, ^bthey stand lazily *and* to be seen of men, and they remember Allah but little;[606]

اِنَّ الْمُنٰفِقِيْنَ يُخٰدِعُوْنَ اللّٰهَ وَهُوَ خَادِعُهُمْ ۚ وَاِذَا قَامُوْۤا اِلَى الصَّلٰوةِ قَامُوْا كُسَالٰى ۙ يُرَآءُوْنَ النَّاسَ وَلَا يَذْكُرُوْنَ اللّٰهَ اِلَّا قَلِيْلًا ۙ

144. Wavering between *this and* that, belonging neither to these nor to those. And he whom Allah causes to perish, for him thou shalt not find a way[607].

مُّذَبْذَبِيْنَ بَيْنَ ذٰلِكَ ۖ لَاۤ اِلٰى هٰۤؤُلَآءِ وَلَاۤ اِلٰى هٰۤؤُلَآءِ ۚ وَمَنْ يُّضْلِلِ اللّٰهُ فَلَنْ تَجِدَ لَهٗ سَبِيْلًا ۞

*a*2 : 10. *b*9 : 54.

---

and you were thus saved from them." Or the words may mean, "some of the faint-hearted among you wished to make peace with the Muslims, but we prevented them from doing so, and now the result is that you are victorious." In the latter case the clause عنكم من المؤمنين would be translated as "we prevented you from making peace with the believers."

The last sentence of the verse means that the hypocrites will never be able to bring a valid objection against Muslims.

606. Important Words :

For the meaning of the word يُخٰدِعُون and خَادِعُهُم see 2 : 10. The latter expression, though similar in root and construction, means "will punish them for their deception" and not "will deceive them." See also 2 : 16.

Commentary :

It is not the Holy Prophet but God Himself Whom in reality the hypocrites seek to deceive because the Prophet is only an agent of God and all plots hatched against him are really so many plots hatched to frustrate the purpose of God. Therefore He Himself will punish them for their deceitful conduct.

Laziness and slowness are the characteristics of a hypocrite. The Holy Prophet is reported to have said, "The most burdensome of Prayers

for the hypocrites are the late-evening and morning Prayers"; and "A hypocrite waits until the sun is about to set; then he gets up and hurriedly performs four *rak'ats* of late-afternoon Prayer, and remembers God but little" (Muslim). It is only true faith and certainty that can engender in man the spirit of eagerness to live up to one's conviction.

607. Important Words :

مذبذبين (wavering) which is the plural of مذبذب is derived from ذب. They say ذبّ عنه meaning, he repelled from him *i.e.* he defended him. ذبذب الشيئ means, he made the thing move to and fro; he put it in a state of motion, commotion or agitation. ذبذبه means, he or it made him confounded or perplexed so that he could not know his right course; he left him wavering, vacillating, going to and fro. تذبذب الشيئ means, the thing dangled or moved to and fro; or was in a state of motion or commotion. مذبذب means, driven away or repelled from this side and that; wavering or vacillating between two persons or parties or things; not attaching oneself steadily to either (Lane & Aqrab). Another قرأة (reading) of مذبذبين is متذبذبين and yet another (*mudhabdhibīn*) with different vowel point at the second ذ (Kashshāf).

The expression بين ذلك (between this

145. O ye who believe, *a*take not disbelievers for friends, in preference to believers. Do you mean to give Allah a manifest proof against yourselves ?[608]

يَا۫يُّهَا الَّذِيۡنَ اٰمَنُوۡا لَا تَتَّخِذُوا الۡكٰفِرِيۡنَ اَوۡلِيَآءَ مِنۡ دُوۡنِ الۡمُؤۡمِنِيۡنَ اَتُرِيۡدُوۡنَ اَنۡ تَجۡعَلُوۡا لِلّٰهِ عَلَيۡكُمۡ سُلۡطٰنًا مُّبِيۡنًا ﴿۱۴۵﴾

146. The hypocrites shall surely be in the lowest depth of the Fire ; and thou shalt find no helper for them.[609]

اِنَّ الۡمُنٰفِقِيۡنَ فِى الدَّرۡكِ الۡاَسۡفَلِ مِنَ النَّارِ وَلَنۡ تَجِدَ لَهُمۡ نَصِيۡرًا ﴿۱۴۶﴾

---

*a*3 : 29, 119 ; 4 : 140.

---

and that) means, between belief and disbelief or between believers and disbelievers.

Commentary :

The verse very aptly describes the condition of the hypocrites. **To quote a well-known** Indian maxim, they have their feet in two separate boats. A hypocrite thinks himself to be acting wisely (2 : 14) but his action is really the height of folly.

608. Commentary :

He who makes friends with disbelievers when believers are engaged in a life-and-death struggle with them, helps the cause of disbelief against Islam and is thus sure to draw upon himself the wrath of God.

The expression, *in preference to believers,* is added to heighten the folly of the act.

609. Important Words :

درك (depth). They say, درك المطر *i.e.* the rain fell in close consecutiveness. ادرك الشيئ means, he attained, reached or overtook the thing ; he sought or pursued and attained it. درك means, the act of attaining, or overtaking ; the attainment or acquisition of an object ; a consequence ; an evil consequence ;

the bottom or lowest depth of a thing or of anything deep as of a well or sea. درك signifies, a stage counting downwards whereas درج is a stage upwards (Lane & Aqrab).

الاسفل (lowest) is both comparative and superlative degree from سافل meaning, low or base or vile. اسفل means, lower or lowest, both physically and in rank (Lane & Aqrab).

Commentary :

The Quran's strong denunciation of the hypocrites is a clear refutation of the charge brought against it that it exhorts its followers to spread Islam by means of the sword. If a man is forced to accept Islam against his will, he can never make a sincere believer. In other words, such a one will be a hypocrite and the last thing that can be alleged against the Quran is that it enjoins its followers to augment their numbers by admitting hypocrites into their fold.

The hypocrites will be placed in the lowest depth of Hell, because they combine the sin of disbelief with that of hypocrisy. The lowest depth does not necessarily signify a depth which is the lowest physically but a depth which is the hardest in torment and is meant for offenders of the lowest type.

147. ᵃExcept those who repent and amend and ᵇhold fast to Allah and are sincere in their obedience to Allah. These are among the believers. And Allah will soon bestow a great reward upon the believers.⁶¹⁰

اِلَّا الَّذِيْنَ تَابُوْا وَ اَصْلَحُوْا وَ اعْتَصَمُوْا بِاللّٰهِ وَ اَخْلَصُوْا دِيْنَهُمْ لِلّٰهِ فَاُولٰٓئِكَ مَعَ الْمُؤْمِنِيْنَ وَ سَوْفَ يُؤْتِ اللّٰهُ الْمُؤْمِنِيْنَ اَجْرًا عَظِيْمًا ۝

148. Why should Allah punish you, if you are thankful and *if* you believe ? And ᶜAllah is Appreciating, All-Knowing.⁶¹¹

مَا يَفْعَلُ اللّٰهُ بِعَذَابِكُمْ اِنْ شَكَرْتُمْ وَ اٰمَنْتُمْ ۚ وَ كَانَ اللّٰهُ شَاكِرًا عَلِيْمًا ۝

149. Allah likes not the uttering of unseemly speech in public, except on the part of one who is *being* wronged. Verily, Allah is All-Hearing, All-Knowing.⁶¹²

لَا يُحِبُّ اللّٰهُ الْجَهْرَ بِالسُّوْٓءِ مِنَ الْقَوْلِ اِلَّا مَنْ ظُلِمَ ۚ وَ كَانَ اللّٰهُ سَمِيْعًا عَلِيْمًا ۝

ᵃSee 2 : 161.　　ᵇ3 : 102.　　ᶜ2 : 159.

610. Important Words :

For the meaning of مع see note on 4 : 70.

Commentary :

The verse is important inasmuch as it helps definitely to determine the meaning of the word مع (among) which does not, and indeed cannot, convey here the sense of "with," for the obvious reason that the penitent from among the hypocrites are not only to be reckoned "with the believers as mere companions" but are to become members and, as it were, part and parcel, of the Muslim community, being definitely reckoned among them. The verse also hints that the door of repentance is open even for the hypocrites who have been so strongly condemned in the foregoing verse.

611. Commentary :

شكر (gratitude) on the part of man is to have a due sense of the favours of God and render thanks for them both by words of mouth and by action ; and on the part of God, it is to give proper rewards to men for their obedience and righteousness. See also 1 : 2.

612. Commentary :

Islam does not allow Muslims to speak ill of a man in public, but he who is wronged may cry aloud when he is actually being transgressed against, so that other men may come to his help. He may as well seek redress in a law-court. But he should not go about complaining to all and sundry, because that is calculated to create ill-will and bad blood and may disturb public peace which the Quran in no case countenances.

The words, *Allah is All-Hearing, All-Knowing,* have been added to point out that even for a man who is wronged it is better to act patiently and refrain from speaking ill of any one. He may either go to a law-court or pray to God and seek justice and solace from Him.

150. Whether you make public a good deed or conceal it, or pardon an evil, Allah is certainly the Effacer of sins, All-Powerful.[613]

اِنۡ تُبۡدُوۡا خَیۡرًا اَوۡ تُخۡفُوۡهُ اَوۡ تَعۡفُوۡا عَنۡ سُوۡٓءٍ فَاِنَّ اللّٰهَ كَانَ عَفُوًّا قَدِیۡرًا ۝

151. Surely, [a]those who disbelieve in Allah and His Messengers and desire to make a distinction between Allah and His Messengers, and say, 'We believe in some and disbelieve in others,' and desire to take a way in between,[614]

اِنَّ الَّذِیۡنَ یَكۡفُرُوۡنَ بِاللّٰهِ وَ رُسُلِهٖ وَ یُرِیۡدُوۡنَ اَنۡ یُّفَرِّقُوۡا بَیۡنَ اللّٰهِ وَ رُسُلِهٖ وَ یَقُوۡلُوۡنَ نُؤۡمِنُ بِبَعۡضٍ وَّ نَكۡفُرُ بِبَعۡضٍ وَّ یُرِیۡدُوۡنَ اَنۡ یَّتَّخِذُوۡا بَیۡنَ ذٰلِكَ سَبِیۡلًا ۝

[a]4 : 137.

613. Commentary:

The verse further enlarges on the idea contained in the preceding verse, at the same time hinting that as far as possible man should try to pardon the wrongs done him by his brethren; for is not God, before Whom all of us will one day stand, the great Pardoner and the Effacer of sins?

614. Commentary:

This verse provides clear proof of the fact that belief in all the Messengers of God is essential. The expression رسله (His Messengers) comprehends all Messengers of God and admits of no exception, demanding belief in all Prophets, whether old or new.

The words, *We believe in some and disbelieve in others*, condemn those people who would believe in some Messengers of God and reject others. The idea is further explained by 4 : 153 below which says, *those who believe in Allah and all of His Messengers, and make no distinction between any of them.* Here the expression, *any of them,* clearly refers to "the Messengers" and not to God and the Messengers combined, which shows that the present clause, *We believe in some and disbelieve in others,* refers to the distinction some people seek to

make between the different Messengers, and not to the distinction they make between God and His Messengers, which has already been referred to in the preceding clause of the present verse *i.e. make a distinction between Allah and His Messengers.*

Ibn Kathīr, the famous expositor of the Quran, explains this verse as follows: "What is meant here is that he who rejects any of the Prophets of God really rejects all of them, for God has made it obligatory on man to believe in every Prophet whom He has raised for any people at any time on the earth" (vol. iii. 224). In fact, if a people reject a Prophet of God out of envy or bigotry or self-will, it becomes clear that their faith in the Prophet in whom they profess to believe is also not sincere and true but is mere make-belief. For, if they had really believed in him as a Messenger of God, they would have believed in that other one also who was his like and whose claim was supported by similar arguments.

The expression, *desire to take a way in between*, means that such people "seek a middle course between faith and disbelief" *i.e.* they accept God and reject His Prophets or accept some Prophets and reject others, or accept some

152. These indeed are veritable disbelievers, and We have prepared for the disbelievers an humiliating punishment.[615]

اُولٰٓئِكَ هُمُ الْكٰفِرُوۡنَ حَقًّا ۚ وَ اَعۡتَدۡنَا لِلۡكٰفِرِيۡنَ عَذَابًا مُّهِيۡنًا ۞

153. And as for *a*those who believe in Allah and *in all of* His Messengers and make no distinction between any of them, these are they whom He will soon give their rewards. And Allah is Most Forgiving, Merciful.[616]

وَ الَّذِيۡنَ اٰمَنُوۡا بِاللّٰهِ وَ رُسُلِهٖ وَ لَمۡ يُفَرِّقُوۡا بَيۡنَ اَحَدٍ مِّنۡهُمۡ اُولٰٓئِكَ سَوۡفَ يُؤۡتِيۡهِمۡ اُجُوۡرَهُمۡ ۚ وَ كَانَ اللّٰهُ غَفُوۡرًا رَّحِيۡمًا ۞

---

*a*2 : 137 ; 2 : 286 ; 3 : 85.

---

claims of a Prophet and reject others or regard the claims of a Prophet to be true but do not consider themselves bound to join his fold. True faith lies in total submission, accepting God and all His Messengers with all their claims. No middle course is permissible. See also the two succeeding verses.

615. Commentary :

Those who seek to take a middle course, as explained in the previous verse, are "veritable disbelievers" in the sight of God and shall be awarded "an humiliating punishment."

616. Commentary :

The verse 4 : 151 above dealt with four classes of disbelievers : (1) those who disbelieve both in Allah and His Messengers ; (2) those who profess to believe in Allah but reject His Messengers, *i.e.*, those who believe that there is indeed a God but that He sends no Messengers, or those who think they are bound to accept only that which God sends down by His revelation but do not look upon the behests and precepts of the Prophet as binding on them ; (3) those who accept some of the Messengers of God and reject others ; and (4) those who accept some claims of a divine Messenger and reject others, or those who, though declaring a claimant to prophethood to be true in his claims, do not think it to be binding on them to enter his fold. In continuation of the above the verse under comment says that only those people can hope for reward from God who spurn all the above different forms of disbelief and whose faith in God and in all His Prophets is full and unqualified.

R. 22 **154.** The People of the Book ask thee to cause a book to descend on them from heaven. *ᵃ*They asked Moses a greater thing than this : they said, *ᵇ*' Show us Allah openly.' Then a destructive punishment overtook them because of their transgression. Then *ᶜ*they took the calf *for worship* after clear Signs had come to them, but We pardoned *even* that. And We gave Moses manifest authority.⁶¹⁷

يَسْـَٔلُكَ اَهْلُ الْكِتٰبِ اَنْ تُنَزِّلَ عَلَيْهِمْ كِتٰبًا مِّنَ السَّمَآءِ فَقَدْ سَاَلُوْا مُوْسٰۤى اَكْبَرَ مِنْ ذٰلِكَ فَقَالُوْۤا اَرِنَا اللّٰهَ جَهْرَةً فَاَخَذَتْهُمُ الصّٰعِقَةُ بِظُلْمِهِمْ ثُمَّ اتَّخَذُوا الْعِجْلَ مِنْۢ بَعْدِ مَا جَآءَتْهُمُ الْبَيِّنٰتُ فَعَفَوْنَا عَنْ ذٰلِكَ ۚ وَ اٰتَيْنَا مُوْسٰى سُلْطٰنًا مُّبِيْنًا ۞

155. And *ᵈ*We raised high above them the Mount while making a covenant with them, and We said to them, *ᵉ*' Enter the gate submissively,' and We said to them, *ᶠ*'Transgress not in the matter of the Sabbath.' And We took from them a firm covenant.⁶¹⁸

وَ رَفَعْنَا فَوْقَهُمُ الطُّوْرَ بِمِيْثَاقِهِمْ وَ قُلْنَا لَهُمُ ادْخُلُوا الْبَابَ سُجَّدًا وَّ قُلْنَا لَهُمْ لَا تَعْدُوْا فِى السَّبْتِ وَ اَخَذْنَا مِنْهُمْ مِّيْثَاقًا غَلِيْظًا ۞

156. Then *ᵍ*because of their breaking of their covenant, and their denial of the Signs of Allah, and *ʰ*their seeking to kill the Prophets unjustly, and their saying : *ⁱ*' Our hearts are wrapped in covers,'—nay, but *ʲ*Allah has sealed them because of their disbelief, so they believe not but little—⁶¹⁹

فَبِمَا نَقْضِهِمْ مِّيْثَاقَهُمْ وَ كُفْرِهِمْ بِاٰيٰتِ اللّٰهِ وَ قَتْلِهِمُ الْاَنْۢبِيَآءَ بِغَيْرِ حَقٍّ وَّ قَوْلِهِمْ قُلُوْبُنَا غُلْفٌ ۚ بَلْ طَبَعَ اللّٰهُ عَلَيْهَا بِكُفْرِهِمْ فَلَا يُؤْمِنُوْنَ اِلَّا قَلِيْلًا ۞

---

*ᵃ*2:109.   *ᵇ*2:56.   *ᶜ*2:52,93 ; 7:149, 153.   *ᵈ*2 ; 64, 94.   *ᵉ*2:59 ; 7:162.   *ᶠ*2:66 ; 4:48 ;
7 : 164 ; 16 : 125.   *ᵍ*5 : 14.   *ʰ*3 : 182.   *ⁱ*2 : 89.   *ʲ*2 : 89 ; 16 : 109 ; 83 : 15.

---

617. Important Words :

For the meaning of صاعقة (destructive punishment) see 2 : 56.

Commentary :

For an explanation of the words " show us Allah openly " see 2 : 56.

618. Commentary :

See and compare 2 : 59, 64, 66 & 4 : 48.

619. Important Words :

طبع (sealed) is similar to ختم for which see 2 : 8. طبع means, he sealed, stamped, imprinted or impressed (Lane).

غلف (wrapped in covers). See 2 : 89.

Commentary :

See 2 : 8 ; 2 : 62 & 2 : 89.

157. And because of their disbelief and their uttering against Mary a grievous calumny,[620]

وَّبِكُفْرِهِمْ وَقَوْلِهِمْ عَلٰى مَرْيَمَ بُهْتَانًا عَظِيمًا ۟

158. And their saying, 'We did kill the Messiah, Jesus, son of Mary, the Messenger of Allah;' whereas they slew him not, nor crucified him, but he was made to appear to them like *one crucified*; and those who differ therein are certainly in *a state of* doubt about it: [a]they have no *definite* knowledge thereof, but only follow a conjecture; and they did not convert this *conjecture* into a certainty[621]—

وَّقَوْلِهِمْ اِنَّا قَتَلْنَا الْمَسِيْحَ عِيْسَى ابْنَ مَرْيَمَ رَسُوْلَ اللّٰهِ ۚ وَمَا قَتَلُوْهُ وَمَا صَلَبُوْهُ وَلٰكِنْ شُبِّهَ لَهُمْ ۚ وَاِنَّ الَّذِيْنَ اخْتَلَفُوْا فِيْهِ لَفِيْ شَكٍّ مِّنْهُ ۚ مَا لَهُمْ بِهٖ مِنْ عِلْمٍ اِلَّا اتِّبَاعَ الظَّنِّ ۚ وَمَا قَتَلُوْهُ يَقِيْنًا ۙ ۟

---

[a]10 : 37 ; 53 : 29.

620. Commentary:

The fact that the Jews uttered "a calumny" against Mary constitutes a clear evidence of the fatherless birth of Jesus. For if Jesus had a father, what " calumny " was it that the Jews uttered against Mary? Merely taunting her for the claims made by Jesus could in no sense be called a calumny. Elsewhere the Quran says that the mother of Jesus was a righteous woman and that Satan had no share in his birth (3 : 37 ; 5 : 76).

621. Important Words:

ما قتلوه (they slew him not). قتله means, he slew him by striking him with a sword or with a stone or by poison or by any other means. See also 2 : 62 & 4 : 158.

ما قتلوه يقينا (they did not convert this *conjecture* into certainty) is a peculiar Arabic idiom. The Arabs say قتل الشىء خبرا (lit. he killed the thing with certainty of knowledge and proper examination) *i.e.* he acquired full and thorough knowledge of the thing so as to dispel all possibility of doubt. So the words ما قتلوه يقينا would mean, their knowledge regarding it was not comprehensive, or they did not know it for certain that he had been killed, or they did not convert this (conjecture of theirs) into certainty, meaning that they were not sure and they did not make sure whether Jesus died on the Cross or not. In this case, the pronoun in قتلوه would refer to the noun ظن (a conjecture) immediately preceding it (Lane, Aqrab, Mufradāt & Lisān).

In plain English the words would mean that their knowledge about the death of Jesus on the Cross was not so full and comprehensive as to have attained the stage of certainty. The expression may also mean that they certainly did not slay him or that they did not kill him as a certainty *i.e.* they did not execute him in such a way as to definitely assure themselves that life had indeed become extinct in him.

ما صلبوه (nor crucified him). The word صلبوا is from the root صلب. They say صلب الشىء *i.e.* he burned the thing. صلب العظام means, he extracted the marrow out of the bones. صلب اللص means, he crucified the thief *i.e.* he put him to death in a certain well-known manner (Lane & Aqrab).

In crucifixion one was nailed to a framework made in the form of a cross and, being kept without food and drink, slowly died of pain, hunger, fatigue and exposure.

شبه لهم (he was made to appear to them like one crucified). شبهه ایاه means, he made it or him to be like it or him, or he made it or him to resemble it or him. شبه علیه الامر means, the matter was rendered confused, obscure or dubious to him. شبه علیه الامر means, he rendered the matter confused to him (by making it to appear like some other thing); he rendered it confused, obscure or dubious to him (Lane & Aqrab).

Commentary :

This and the preceding verse mention two main objections of the Jews against Jesus : (1) his alleged illegitimate birth, and (2) his supposed death on the Cross which, according to Jewish Law, was an accursed death (Deut. 21 : 23). The words, *We did kill the Messiah, Jesus, son of Mary, the Messenger of Allah*, are spoken ironically and tauntingly, meaning, " we have killed Jesus who posed as the Messiah and a Messenger of God."

The argument of the Jews was that because Jesus died on the Cross, he could not be a true Prophet according to Jewish Law. The inference was based on their sacred scriptures ; for, according to the Bible, he who is hanged is accursed of God, and a false Prophet shall meet with destruction. Says the Bible : " His body shall not remain all night upon the tree, but thou shalt in any wise bury him that day ; (for he that is hanged is accursed of God) that thy land be not defiled, which the Lord thy God giveth thee for an inheritance " (Deut. 21 : 23). Again : " My hand shall be upon false prophets that see vanity, and that divine lies " (Ezek. 13 : 9). Again : " Therefore thus saith the Lord concerning the prophets that prophesy in My name, and I sent them not, yet they say, Sword and famine shall not be in this land ; by sword and famine shall those prophets be consumed " (Jer. 14 : 15).

On the strength of such verses of the Bible the Jews claimed that, as Jesus had been crucified and met with destruction, he could not be a true Prophet of God, but was a false claimant and an accursed one.

Regarding the charge about the alleged death of Jesus by crucifixion, the Quran says that the act of crucifixion having not been completed, and Jesus having been taken down alive from the Cross, the charge carries no weight. It should, however, be noted that the Quran does not deny the mere hanging of Jesus on the Cross ; it only denies his death on it.

Two different views prevail among the Jews regarding Jesus' alleged death by crucifixion. Some of them hold that Jesus was first killed and then his dead body was hung on the Cross, while others are of the view that he was put to death by being fixed to the Cross. The former view is reflected in Acts 5 : 30 where we read " which ye slew and hanged on a tree." The Quran refutes both these views by saying, *they slew him not, nor crucified him.* The words may also signify that the Quran first rejects the slaying of Jesus in any form, and then proceeds to deny the particular way of killing by hanging on the Cross.

The verb شبه (in the passive voice) means, he was made to appear like, or was made to resemble. Now the question arises, who is the person who was made to appear "like one crucified." Clearly it was Jesus whom the Jews tried to crucify or slay. Nobody else can be meant here, for there is absolutely no reference to any other person in the context. Hence, the theory invented by certain Commentators that Judas or somebody else was made to appear like Jesus and was then crucified in his place is simply absurd. The context cannot be so twisted as to make room for somebody else of whom no mention at all is made in the verse.

To what then was Jesus made like ? The context provides a clear answer to that question. The Jews did not kill him by crucifixion, but he was made to appear to them like "one crucified", and thus it was that they wrongly took him for dead. It was thus Jesus who was made to resemble "one crucified". This interpretation is not only in perfect harmony with the context but is also clearly borne out by all relevant facts of history.

The second meaning of the expression شبه لهم is, as explained under Important Words, that "the matter became confused to them". This interpretation is also clearly borne out by history; for, although the Jews asserted that they had put Jesus to death by suspending him on the Cross, they were not sure of it and the circumstances being obscure the matter had certainly become confused to them. The fact that the Jews themselves were not sure whether Jesus had actually died on the Cross is supported by the Bible and by all authentic historical facts.

The statements made in this verse are clearly substantiated by the following facts narrated in the Gospels :—

(1) Jesus had himself predicted his escape from death on the Cross, saying, "As Jonah was three days and three nights in the whale's belly, so shall the son of man be three days and three nights in the heart of the earth" (Matt. 12 : 40). Now it is an accepted fact that Jonah had entered the whale's belly alive and had come out alive ; so, according to his own prophecy, Jesus was to enter the heart of the earth (i.e. his tomb) alive and was to come out of it alive.

(2) The trying magistrate (Pilate) believed Jesus to be innocent and, being sympathetic, was anxious to save his life (Matt. 27 : 17, 18 ; Mark 15 : 9, 10, 14 ; Luke 23 : 4, 14, 15, 20, 22 ; John 18 : 38, 39) ; and he must have secretly tried to save him or at least connived at the attempt of others to do so.

(3) Pilate's wife had seen a vision concerning the innocence of Jesus : "When he (Pilate) was set down on the judgement seat, his wife sent unto him, saying, 'Have thou nothing to do with that just man, for I have suffered many things this day in a dream because of him'" (Matt. 27 : 19). This message must certainly have influenced Pilate, and his wife must have also done her best to save Jesus.

(4) Pilate held the killing of Jesus in such horror that he actually washed his hands with water, saying that he was innocent of the blood of that just man (Matt. 27 : 24).

(5) Pilate did all he could to help Jesus ; and the soldiers in charge also treated Jesus with kindness, apparently under Pilate's directions. The following are some of the special favours shown to Jesus : (a) Every malefactor carried his own cross but another man was made to carry that of Jesus (Matt. 27 : 32 ; Mark 15 : 21); (b) Jesus was given wine or vinegar mingled with myrrh. This was intended to render him less sensible to pain. The two thieves who were crucified with him were not given this drink. When after some time the effects of the drink were wearing off and Jesus cried with pain, the drink was administered again to render him unconscious of pain (Matt. 27 : 34, 48, Mark 15 : 23, 36 ; John 19 : 29, 30).

(6) The unconsciousness which followed the administration of vinegar was mistaken for death (John 19 : 30).

(7) Jesus remained on the Cross for only about three hours (John 19 : 14. cf. Matt. 27 : 46) and according to Mark only for six hours (Mark 15 : 25, 33), and either of these periods was by no means sufficient to kill a young man like Jesus on the Cross.

(8) When Joseph of Arimathaea came and craved the body of Jesus, Pilate "marvelled if he were already dead," and calling to him the centurion asked him whether he had been any while dead (Mark, 15 : 44).

(9) The soldiers did not break the legs of Jesus, but the legs of the two malefactors who had been crucified with him were broken (John 19: 32, 33).

(10) Jesus was not buried in the earth with the two malefactors but was laid separately in a spacious sepulchre hewn out of a rock and situated in a garden which was private property (Mark 15 : 46, John 19 : 41, 42).

(11) The Jews themselves were not sure that Jesus was dead; for they came to Pilate and besought him that his legs be broken (John 19:31).

(12) The doubt that Jesus was alive and might, with the aid of his sympathizers, escape from the sepulchre rankled in the minds of the Jews. They remembered also the prophecy of Jesus that he would show them the miracle of Jonah and would come out of the heart of the earth alive. So, influenced by such misgivings, the chief priests and pharisees went together to Pilate, saying, " Sir, we remember that the deceiver said, while he was yet alive— ' After three days I will rise again.'—Command therefore that the sepulchre be made sure until the third day." Pilate told them to make their own arrangements; "so they went, and made the sepulchre sure, sealing the stone and setting a watch " (Matt. 27 : 62-66).

(13) In spite of the watch and despite the sealing of the stone, Jesus had left the sepulchre before the third day had dawned, when Mary Magdalene and Mary, mother of James, came to see the sepulchre and found the stone rolled away and the sepulchre empty (Matt. 28 : 1— 6 ; Mark 16 : 1— 6), which shows that the men set to watch were also in league with, and won over by, the friends of Jesus.

(14) After leaving the sepulchre Jesus moved about secretly, lest the Jews should have him arrested again (Mark 16 : 12, John 20 : 19, 26 ; 21 : 4).

(15) Mary Magdalene and other disciple actually saw Jesus in this body of clay (Mark 16 : 9, 12).

(16) Jesus showed them his wounds to assure them that he was not a spirit but a man of flesh and blood and that the body they saw before them was the same physical body that had been nailed to the Cross (Luke 24 : 39, 40 ; John 20 : 27).

(17) After leaving the sepulchre Jesus felt hungry and partook of food with his disciples (John 21 : 5, 13 ; Luke 24 : 41, 42, 43).

The above references among others make it abundantly clear that Jesus did not die on the Cross, that he was alive when he was taken down from the Cross, and also when he was laid in the sepulchre, and that he came out of it alive on the third day at early morn, as he had himself prophesied, and that later he appeared to his disciples in secret and assured them that he was not dead.

(18) Jesus had said, " And other sheep I have which are not of this fold, them also I must bring, and they shall hear my voice and there shall be one fold and one shepherd" (John 10 : 16). In these words he was obviously referring to the lost ten tribes of Israel who had scattered in Afghanistan, Kashmir, etc. In search of these Jesus came to the East after his miraculous escape from an accursed death on the Cross, and among these he now lies buried in Khan Yar Street in Srinagar, Kashmir. Conclusive historical evidence has established the fact that the holy occupant of the tomb in the Khan Yar Street in Srinagar is no other than Jesus, son of Mary. For further discussion of this important subject, see *Masīḥ Hindustān Men* (Jesus in India) by the Promised Messiah, and R. Rel. Vol. II Nos. 1, 2, 5, 6, 10 published from Qadian, and the " Tomb of Jesus " by Dr. M. M. Ṣādiq of Qadian.

159. ^aOn the contrary, Allah exalted him to Himself. And Allah is Mighty, Wise;[622]

بَلْ رَّفَعَهُ اللّٰهُ اِلَيْهِ ۚ وَكَانَ اللّٰهُ عَزِيْزًا حَكِيْمًا ۝

160. And there is none among the People of the Book but will believe in it before his death ; and on the Day of Resurrection, ^bhe (Jesus) shall be a witness against them,—[623]

وَاِنْ مِّنْ اَهْلِ الْكِتٰبِ اِلَّا لَيُؤْمِنَنَّ بِهٖ قَبْلَ مَوْتِهٖ ۚ وَيَوْمَ الْقِيٰمَةِ يَكُوْنُ عَلَيْهِمْ شَهِيْدًا ۝

---

^a2 : 254 ; 3 : 56 ; 7 : 177 ; 58 : 12.   ^b5 : 118.

---

622. Important Words :

رفعه (exalted him). See 2 : 64.

Commentary :

The words, *On the contrary, Allah exalted him to Himself*, constitute a reply to the taunt embodied in the words of the Jews : *We did kill the Messiah, Jesus, son of Mary, the Messenger of Allah* (4 : 158). The verse thus purports to say that he whom the Jews so exultingly claimed to have killed on the Cross was never so killed but was exalted to God Himself and granted His nearness. There is no reference here whatever to the supposed physical ascension of Jesus to the skies. The verse only contains a refutation of the allegation of the Jews that, having become accursed by crucifixion, Jesus had become spiritually fallen and degraded, and was, as it were, driven away from the presence of God. In refutation of this charge the verse clears him of the insinuated blemish by speaking of his spiritual exaltation.

It should also be noted that the Quran does not say here that Allah raised Jesus *towards the skies*, but only that He exalted him *towards Himself*, which clearly signifies not a physical but a spiritual exaltation, because no fixed abode can be, or has ever been, assigned to God. It is a pity that such an ennobled and holy spiritual significance of the verse should be distorted and debased to prove the utterly unfounded notion that Jesus was taken up to the heavens alive. The Quran would not accept the idea of a human being being physically taken up into the skies even if it were the Holy Prophet himself (17 : 94). See also note on 3 : 56.

623. Important Words :

The pronoun " it " in the clause, *believe in it*, stands for the false belief (referred to in the preceding verses) that Jesus met his death on the Cross. So the verse signifies that both Jews and Christians will continue to believe in the supposed crucifixion of Jesus till the time of their death, when the veil will be lifted and everything will become clear. They are indeed bound to believe in the alleged death of Jesus on the Cross. If the Jews do not do so, his truth becomes established and their whole position becomes indefensible. Similarly if the Christians do not believe in it, the doctrine of Atonement becomes untenable and the entire fabric of Christianity crashes to pieces. So both these peoples go on sticking to this absurd and unfounded belief in the face of all reason and all established facts of history.

The attempt to make the words لَيُؤْمِنَنَّ بِهٖ قَبْلَ مَوْتِهٖ (will believe in it before his death) mean " will believe in him (Jesus) before his (Jesus') death " is simply ridiculous. The context spurns the idea, as does the second reading of the expression موته (his death) *viz.* موتهم (their death) reported by Ubayy (Jarīr, vi. 13).

161. So, because of the transgression of the Jews, ^aWe forbade them pure things which had been allowed to them, and *also* because of their hindering many *men* from Allah's way,[624]

162. And *because of* ^btheir taking interest, although they had been forbidden it, and *because of* ^ctheir devouring people's wealth wrongfully. And We have prepared for those of them who disbelieve a painful punishment.[625]

163. But ^dthose among them who are firmly grounded in knowledge, and ^ethe believers, believe in what has been sent down to thee and what was sent down before thee, and *especially* those who observe Prayer and those who pay the Zakāt and those who believe in Allah and the Last Day. To these will We surely give a great reward.[626]

فَبِظُلْمٍ مِّنَ الَّذِيْنَ هَادُوْا حَرَّمْنَا عَلَيْهِمْ طَيِّبٰتٍ اُحِلَّتْ لَهُمْ وَبِصَدِّهِمْ عَنْ سَبِيْلِ اللّٰهِ كَثِيْرًا ۞

وَّاَخْذِهِمُ الرِّبٰوا وَقَدْ نُهُوْا عَنْهُ وَاَكْلِهِمْ اَمْوَالَ النَّاسِ بِالْبَاطِلِ ؕ وَاَعْتَدْنَا لِلْكٰفِرِيْنَ مِنْهُمْ عَذَابًا اَلِيْمًا ۞

لٰكِنِ الرّٰسِخُوْنَ فِى الْعِلْمِ مِنْهُمْ وَالْمُؤْمِنُوْنَ يُؤْمِنُوْنَ بِمَا اُنْزِلَ اِلَيْكَ وَمَا اُنْزِلَ مِنْ قَبْلِكَ وَالْمُقِيْمِيْنَ الصَّلٰوةَ وَالْمُؤْتُوْنَ الزَّكٰوةَ وَالْمُؤْمِنُوْنَ بِاللّٰهِ وَ الْيَوْمِ الْاٰخِرِ ؕ اُولٰٓئِكَ سَنُؤْتِيْهِمْ اَجْرًا عَظِيْمًا ۞

---

^a6 : 147.   ^b2 : 276, 277 ; 3 : 131 ; 30 : 40.   ^c9 : 34.   ^d3 : 8.   ^e2 : 5, 137 ; 3 : 200 ; 4 : 137 ; 5 : 60.

---

624. Commentary :

The expression, *We forbade them pure things which had been allowed to them*, refers to the blessings and favours of God of which the Jews had become deprived by reason of their transgressions. The verse does not refer to any material thing which was forbidden to them after being allowed before, because no Law-giving Prophet appeared among the Israelites after Moses to forbid them things that had been allowed to them by the Torah. It was also to the spiritual blessings which the Jews had lost that Jesus referred when he said, (*I come*) to *allow you some of that which had been forbidden to you* (3:51) *i.e.* I come to restore to you some of the divine blessings of which you have been deprived on account of your misdeeds.

625. Commentary :

The Jews were forbidden to lend money on interest to other Jews, but they were permitted to take interest from non-Jews (Exod. 22 : 25; Lev. 25 : 36, 37; Deut. 23 : 19, 20). But they broke the Law and began to exact interest even from Jews (Neh. 5 : 7). Later they promised Nehemiah to give up taking interest from Jews (Neh. 5 : 12). But they again broke their word; and so, in accordance with the prophecy of Ezekiel (Ezek. 18 : 13), they suffered national death and were scattered over the earth to suffer persecution at the hands of their enemies.

626. Important Words :

مقيمين (who observe Prayer) is the active participle from اقام which is derived from

23 164. Surely, *We have sent revelation to thee, as We sent revelation to Noah and the Prophets after him; and We sent revelation to Abraham and Ishmael and Isaac and Jacob and *his* children and Jesus and Job and Jonah and Aaron and Solomon, and *b*We gave David a Book.[627]

إِنَّآ أَوْحَيْنَآ إِلَيْكَ كَمَآ أَوْحَيْنَآ إِلٰى نُوحٍ وَّالنَّبِيّٖنَ مِنْۢ بَعْدِهٖ ۚ وَاَوْحَيْنَآ إِلٰٓى اِبْرٰهِيْمَ وَاِسْمٰعِيْلَ وَاِسْحٰقَ وَيَعْقُوْبَ وَالْاَسْبَاطِ وَعِيْسٰى وَاَيُّوْبَ وَيُوْنُسَ وَهٰرُوْنَ وَسُلَيْمٰنَ ۚ وَاٰتَيْنَا دَاوٗدَ زَبُوْرًا ۟

165. *And We sent some* °Messengers whom We have already mentioned to thee and *some* Messengers whom We have not mentioned to thee; and Allah spoke to Moses particularly.[628]

وَرُسُلًا قَدْ قَصَصْنٰهُمْ عَلَيْكَ مِنْ قَبْلُ وَرُسُلًا لَّمْ نَقْصُصْهُمْ عَلَيْكَ ۚ وَكَلَّمَ اللّٰهُ مُوْسٰى تَكْلِيْمًا ۟

*a*2 : 137; 3 : 85; 6 : 85—88.   *b*17 : 56.   °40 : 79.

قام *i.e.* he stood up or he stood still. اقام الامر means, he put the affair in a right state or condition. اقام الصلوة means, he said or observed Prayer constantly, regularly and with all the conditions attached to it (Lane & Aqrab). According to ordinary rules of grammar, this word ought to have been المقيمون and not المقيمين. But the اعراب of the word has been varied from that of the preceding or succeeding words *e.g.* المؤمنون and الراسخون in order to arrest the attention of the reader and thus to impress upon his mind the importance of the matter. The rules of the Arabic language sanction that variation for the purpose of emphasis (Jarīr, vi. 16; Kashshāf, i. 336).

Commentary:

The words, *But those among them who are firmly grounded in knowledge,* refer to those learned Jews who embraced Islam. The word "believers" has been added to indicate that only those Jews are meant here who turned Muslim.

627. Commentary:

زبورا (a Book) signifies any writing or book; or a book that is confined to intellectual science exclusive of legal statutes or ordinances. الزبور signifies particularly the Book of the Psalms of David (Lane & Aqrab). See also 3 : 185.

Commentary:

Typical Prophets have been mentioned here and in the succeeding verse to point out that the mission of the Prophet of Islam was not a new thing, the specific mention of زبور, the Book of wisdom given to David, in the present verse and of the Law-bearing revelation vouchsafed to Moses in the succeeding one, being made to hint that Islam combines in itself both " Law " and " Wisdom."

628. Commentary:

The Quran mentions by name only 24 Prophets whereas a saying of the Holy Prophet states that as many as 1,24,000 Prophets have appeared in the world (Musnad, v. 266). Elsewhere the Quran says : *There is not a people to whom a warner has not been sent* (35 : 25).

For an explanation of the clause, *and Allah spoke to Moses particularly,* see the preceding verse.

166. Messengers, ^abearers of glad tidings and warners, so that people may have no plea against Allah, after *the coming of* the Messengers. And Allah is Mighty, Wise.⁶²⁹

رُسُلًا مُّبَشِّرِيْنَ وَمُنْذِرِيْنَ لِئَلَّا يَكُوْنَ لِلنَّاسِ عَلَى اللّٰهِ حُجَّةٌ ۢ بَعْدَ الرُّسُلِ ۚ وَكَانَ اللّٰهُ عَزِيْزًا حَكِيْمًا ۝

167. But ^bAllah bears witness by means of *the revelation* which He has sent down to thee that He has sent it down *pregnant* with His knowledge; and the angels *also* bear witness; and sufficient is Allah as a Witness.⁶³⁰

لٰكِنِ اللّٰهُ يَشْهَدُ بِمَاۤ اَنْزَلَ اِلَيْكَ اَنْزَلَهٗ بِعِلْمِهٖ ۚ وَالْمَلٰٓئِكَةُ يَشْهَدُوْنَ ۚ وَكَفٰى بِاللّٰهِ شَهِيْدًا ۝

168. ^cThose who disbelieve and hinder others from the way of Allah, have certainly strayed far away.⁶³¹

اِنَّ الَّذِيْنَ كَفَرُوْا وَصَدُّوْا عَنْ سَبِيْلِ اللّٰهِ قَدْ ضَلُّوْا ضَلٰلًۢا بَعِيْدًا ۝

---

^a2 : 214 ; 6 : 49 ; 17 : 106 ; 18 : 57.   ^b3 : 19 ; 11 : 15.   ^c4 : 138.

629. Commentary :

The words, *bearers of glad tidings and warners,* point to two essential functions of God's Messengers. They are bearers of glad tidings for those who accept them, promising them prosperity in this world and blissful felicity in the life to come, and they are warners of impending misery and afflictions for those who reject them. When the people of the world are sunk deep in iniquity, God raises among them a Messenger who warns them of the impending punishment and calls upon them to repent because "We never punish until We have sent a Messenger" (17 : 16).

God sends His Messengers so that the people, on being punished, might have no excuse to say that no warner was sent to them to point out to them their evil deeds and warn them of the impending visitation—an excuse depicted in the words : *Our Lord, wherefore didst Thou*

not send to us a Messenger that we might have followed Thy commandments (20 : 135).

630. Commentary :

God has placed in the Quran such vast treasures of eternal truth and spiritual knowledge as bear witness to its being the word of God. The manifold qualities of the Quran for such as ponder over it furnish an irrefutable evidence of its divine origin.

The angels testify to the truth of the Quran by appearing in dreams and visions to righteous men, telling them that the Quran is the word of God. They also bear witness by suggesting suitable ideas to the minds of men, leading them to the acceptance of Islam. See also 3 : 19.

631. Commentary :

The Quran being such a treasure of spiritual knowledge, those who reject it are indeed great losers.

169. Surely *a*those who have disbelieved and have acted unjustly, Allah is not going to forgive them, nor will He show them any way,[632]

اِنَّ الَّذِيْنَ كَفَرُوْا وَ ظَلَمُوْا لَمْ يَكُنِ اللّٰهُ لِيَغْفِرَ لَهُمْ وَ لَا لِيَهْدِيَهُمْ طَرِيْقًا ۙ

170. Except the way of Hell, wherein they shall abide for a long, long period. And *b*that is easy for Allah.[633]

اِلَّا طَرِيْقَ جَهَنَّمَ خٰلِدِيْنَ فِيْهَآ اَبَدًا ؕ وَ كَانَ ذٰلِكَ عَلَى اللّٰهِ يَسِيْرًا ۝

171. O mankind, the Messenger has indeed come to you with Truth from your Lord ; believe therefore, it will be better for you. But if you disbelieve, verily, to Allah belongs whatever is in the heavens and in the earth. And Allah is All-Knowing, Wise.[634]

يٰٓاَيُّهَا النَّاسُ قَدْ جَآءَكُمُ الرَّسُوْلُ بِالْحَقِّ مِنْ رَّبِّكُمْ فَاٰمِنُوْا خَيْرًا لَّكُمْ ؕ وَ اِنْ تَكْفُرُوْا فَاِنَّ لِلّٰهِ مَا فِى السَّمٰوٰتِ وَ الْاَرْضِ ؕ وَ كَانَ اللّٰهُ عَلِيْمًا حَكِيْمًا ۝

---

*a*4 : 138.   *b*33 : 31 ; 64 : 8.

---

632. Commentary :

The expression, *Allah is not going to forgive them nor will He show them any way*, means, that it does not stand to reason that Allah should forgive or lead to Himself such people as reject His Prophets and His Signs and act unjustly. See also 4 : 138.

633. Commentary :

The natural destination of those people who are mentioned in the preceding verse is Hell. A bad man must come to a bad end.

634. Commentary :

The words, *to Allah belongs whatever is in the heavens and in the earth*, have been added to point out that in case of disbelief the disbelievers cannot harm God or His religion. It is only themselves that they would harm.

172. ^aO People of the Book, exceed not the limits in your religion, and say not of Allah anything but the truth. Verily, the Messiah, Jesus, son of Mary, was only a Messenger of God, and *a fulfilment of* His word which He sent down to Mary, and ^ba mercy from Him. *So* believe in Allah and His Messengers, and ^csay not 'They are three.' Desist, *it will be* better for you. Verily, Allah is the only One God. ^dFar is it from His Holiness that He should have a son. To Him belongs whatever is in the heavens and whatever is in the earth. And sufficient is Allah as a Guardian !⁶³⁵

يَآ اَهْلَ الْكِتٰبِ لَا تَغْلُوْا فِيْ دِيْنِكُمْ وَ لَا تَقُوْلُوْا عَلَى اللّٰهِ اِلَّا الْحَقَّ ؕ اِنَّمَا الْمَسِيْحُ عِيْسَى ابْنُ مَرْيَمَ رَسُوْلُ اللّٰهِ وَ كَلِمَتُهٗ ۚ اَلْقٰهَآ اِلٰى مَرْيَمَ وَ رُوْحٌ مِّنْهُ ۫ فَاٰمِنُوْا بِاللّٰهِ وَ رُسُلِهٖ ۚ وَ لَا تَقُوْلُوْا ثَلٰثَةٌ ؕ اِنْتَهُوْا خَيْرًا لَّكُمْ ؕ اِنَّمَا اللّٰهُ اِلٰهٌ وَّاحِدٌ ؕ سُبْحٰنَهٗٓ اَنْ يَّكُوْنَ لَهٗ وَلَدٌ ۘ لَهٗ مَا فِى السَّمٰوٰتِ وَ مَا فِى الْاَرْضِ ؕ وَ كَفٰى بِاللّٰهِ وَكِيْلًا ۧ ﴿۱۷۲﴾

---

^a5 : 78.   ^b58 : 23.   ^c5 : 74.   ^d2 : 117 ;   10 : 69 ;   17 : 112 ;   18 : 5 ;   112 : 4, 5.

---

635. Important Words:

كَلِمَتُهٗ (His word). كَلِمَة has been used in the Quran in different senses : (1) good tidings (*e.g.* 37 : 171, 172) ; (2) warning of coming punishment (*e.g.* 39 : 20) ; (3) a thing or being created without the instrumentality of any physical means, *i.e.*, by the will of God expressed by saying "Be" (*e.g.* 3 : 46—48) ; (4) a Sign (*e.g.* 18 : 110) ; (5) a message (*e.g.* 3 : 65) ; (6) a design ; (*e.g.* 9 : 40) ; (7) a word or saying (*e.g.* 23 : 101). See also 3 : 46.

رُوْح (mercy) is derived from رَاح *i.e.* it became cool and pleasant ; he was brisk, lively, active, prompt or quick. رُوْح means, soul or spirit ; the subtle substance in man which is the principle of vitality and of sensation and of voluntary motion ; the breath which a man breathes and which pervades the whole body, after the exit of which he ceases to breathe ; divine revelation or inspiration ; the Quran ; angel ; joy and happiness ; mercy (Lane).

Commentary :

From the above-mentioned different meanings of رُوْح and كَلِمَة it becomes clear that no higher spiritual status can be assigned to Jesus

than to the other Prophets, on account of the word رُوْح or كَلِمَة having been used about him in the Quran. These and similar expressions have been used in the Quran about other Prophets also and even about persons who were not Prophets, such as Mary and the children of Adam (see 58 : 23 ; 15 : 30 ; 32 : 10 ; 21 : 92). It may be noted here that the words رُوْح مِّنْهُ (mercy from Him) do not mean that the رُوْح formed a part of the divine Being but that it was only a gift of God. The expression مِنْهُ (from Him) has been used in the Quran in this sense in 45 : 14.

In fact, the Quran uses these words about Jesus because foul charges were brought against him and his mother, Mary, by the Jews. These words are thus meant to exculpate and exonerate him from those charges and not to deify him. The Quran lends no support whatsoever to the absurd and unfounded view that Jesus was anything higher than a human being. He was human and of the earth, and yet a Messenger of God (*e.g.* 43 : 60 ; 19 : 31).

The verse refers to the three alleged persons of the Trinity *i.e.* the Father, the Son and the

173. Surely, [a]the Messiah will never disdain to be a servant of Allah, nor will the angels near *unto God*; and whoso disdains to worship Him and feels proud, He will gather them all to Himself.[636]

لَنْ يَّسْتَنْكِفَ الْمَسِيْحُ اَنْ يَّكُوْنَ عَبْدًا لِّلّٰهِ وَلَا الْمَلٰٓئِكَةُ الْمُقَرَّبُوْنَ ۭ وَمَنْ يَّسْتَنْكِفْ عَنْ عِبَادَتِهٖ وَيَسْتَكْبِرْ فَسَيَحْشُرُهُمْ اِلَيْهِ جَمِيْعًا ۝

174. Then as for those who believed and did good works, [b]He will give them their rewards in full and will give them more out of His bounty; but as for those who disdained and were proud, He will punish them with a painful punishment. And [c]they shall find for themselves beside Allah no friend nor helper.

فَاَمَّا الَّذِيْنَ اٰمَنُوْا وَعَمِلُوا الصّٰلِحٰتِ فَيُوَفِّيْهِمْ اُجُوْرَهُمْ وَيَزِيْدُهُمْ مِّنْ فَضْلِهٖ ۚ وَاَمَّا الَّذِيْنَ اسْتَنْكَفُوْا وَاسْتَكْبَرُوْا فَيُعَذِّبُهُمْ عَذَابًا اَلِيْمًا ۙ وَّلَا يَجِدُوْنَ لَهُمْ مِّنْ دُوْنِ اللّٰهِ وَلِيًّا وَّلَا نَصِيْرًا ۝

175. O ye people, a manifest proof has indeed come to you from your Lord, [d]and We have sent down to you a clear light.[637]

يٰٓاَيُّهَا النَّاسُ قَدْ جَآءَكُمْ بُرْهَانٌ مِّنْ رَّبِّكُمْ وَاَنْزَلْنَآ اِلَيْكُمْ نُوْرًا مُّبِيْنًا ۝

---

[a]5 : 117, 118.   [b]3 : 58 ; 16 : 97 ; 39 : 11.   [c]4 : 46 ; 32 : 18, 66.   [d]7 : 158 ; 64 : 9.

Holy Ghost and condemns Trinity, declaring Allah alone to be the one true God, and the Messiah and the Holy Spirit as only the servants of God and in no way sharers in Godhead.

636. Important Words:

يَسْتَنْكِف (will disdain) is derived from اِسْتَنْكَف which is derived from نَكَف . They say نَكَف عَنه *i.e.* he disdained it and turned away from it. اِسْتَنْكَف الرَّجل means, the man was or became proud and vain, disdaining others. اِسْتَنْكَف مِن كذا means, he kept back or turned away from it, or he disdained it by way of pride, vanity or haughtiness (Aqrab).

637. Commentary:

The word بُرْهَان (manifest proof) may either refer to the Quran with its great and manifest Signs, or to the person of the Holy Prophet who, by his personal example, demonstrated to the world that the Quranic teachings were a great blessing for mankind.

The words نُوْرًا مُّبِيْنًا (a clear light) may also either refer to the Holy Prophet or to the Quran which supplies the clearest of light for all spiritual wayfarers. The verse thus also incidentally constitutes a repudiation of the Christian dictum that *Sharī'at* is a curse.

176. So, as for those who believe in Allah and ^ahold fast to Him, He will surely admit them to His mercy and grace and will guide them on a straight path *leading* to Himself.[638]

177. They ask thee for instruction. ^bSay, Allah gives His instructions concerning 'Kalāla': If a man dies leaving no child and he has a sister, then she shall have half of what he leaves; and he shall inherit her if she has no child. But if there be two sisters, then they shall have two-thirds of what he leaves. And if the *heirs* be brethren—*both* men and women —^cthen the male shall have as much as the portion of two females. ^dAllah explains *this* to you lest you go astray and Allah knows all things well."[639]

*a*3 : 102 ; 4 : 147.   *b*4 : 13.   *c*4 : 12.   *d*4 : 27.

638. Commentary :

The words, *hold fast to Him*, imply a forceful exhortation to Christians not to take Jesus as a deity but to look upon, and hold fast to, God alone as the means of their salvation and advancement.

639. Important Words :

For the meaning of the word كلالة see 4 : 13.

Commentary :

ولد (child) means, child or children whether male or female, but as كلالة (*Kalāla*) means, one having no child and no parent, the words ولا والد (and neither parent) may be taken as being understood after the words ليس له ولد . The word اثنتين (lit. two) here means two or more sisters. This meaning is supported by a verdict of the Holy Prophet in which he applied this verse to the case of Jābir who died, leaving

seven sisters (Jarīr, vi. 24). The word اخوة (brethren) here includes sisters and brothers both, as the words رجالا و نساء (both men and women) forming case in apposition with اخوة indicate.

This verse, placed as it is in between the verses dealing with the Christians and their false doctrines, appears to be rather misplaced. But as the following note will show, it is very fittingly placed here, furnishing a striking proof of the Quran as well as its present arrangement being the work of God.

In 4 : 13 mention was made of one kind of *Kalāla* (one who leaves behind neither a parent nor an offspring) who had brothers and sisters from the side of his mother only. The present verse refers to a *Kalāla* who has brothers and sisters from both his parents, or from the side of his father only. By comparing the verse under comment with 4 : 13 it becomes clear that for obvious reasons the share allotted to the former class of brothers and sisters is less than that allotted to those of the latter class.

This part of the law of inheritance has been purposely treated separately from the main portion of the law dealt with in 4 : 12, 13 in the beginning of the *Sûra*. The object in doing so is not far to seek. After dealing at some length with the charges levelled against Jesus by the Jews and clearing his position, the Quran reverts to the subject of *Kalâla*, at the end of the *Sûra*, thus seeking (beside completing the law relating to *Kalâla*) to draw, by a most fitting parable, our attention to the spiritual heirlessness of Jesus who, in a sense, was also a

Kalâla. He was born without the agency of a father, and he left behind no spiritual successor to succeed him in his prophetic office, which was, after his death, inherited by the Ishmaelites. In this case the words, *If a man dies, leaving no child,* may also signify that Jesus was a *Kalâla,* not in the sense that spiritually speaking he had neither parents nor child, but in the restricted sense that he had no child. See 4 : 13 under Important Words where Ibn 'Abbâs defines a *Kalâla* as simply one who leaves no child. Thus Jesus was spiritually a *Kalâla* in the sense that he left behind no spiritual successor. Compare also the prophecy, "I will raise them a prophet from among their brethren" (Deut. 18 : 18).

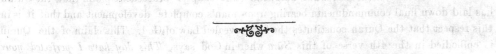

CHAPTER 5
AL-MĀ'IDA
(*Revealed after Hijra*)

Title and Date of Revelation

This *Sūra* derives its title from the prayer which, at the request of his "helpers," Jesus offered about the material progress and prosperity of the Christian faith, and which is referred to in the verses 113—116 of this chapter.

According to different Commentators the whole of this chapter belongs to the Medinite period. 'Ā'isha is reported by Ḥākim and Imām Aḥmad to have related that this is the last *Sūra* which was revealed to the Holy Prophet. This may not be strictly true but, considering together all the different traditions, one is led to the conclusion that the chapter was certainly revealed in the last years of the Prophet's ministry and some of its verses are among the latest to be revealed. Though Imām Aḥmad says on the authority of Asmā', daughter of Yazīd, that the whole of this *Sūra* was revealed together, it seems that as the major portion of it was revealed at one time, the whole of it came to be regarded as having been revealed at the same time.

Subject-Matter

This *Sūra*, like its predecessors, *Sūras* Āl 'Imrān and Al-Nisā, deals mainly with Christianity and particularly denounces the Christian doctrine that the Law is a curse. It opens with the injunction that all covenants must be kept and fulfilled and that it is necessary to lay down laws as to what is lawful and what unlawful. The chapter proceeds to claim that the Quran has laid down final commandments bearing upon man's complete development and that it is in this respect that the Quran constitutes the final revealed Law of God. This claim of the Quran is embodied in the 4th verse of this *Sūra* wherein God says, *This day have I perfected your religion for you and completed My favour upon you and have chosen for you Islam as religion.* This verse epitomizes the above-mentioned claim and constitutes a general proclamation to the effect that Islam as a religion is perfect in all respects and is the complete manifestation of God's favour and, as a code of laws, is beyond reproach and above criticism. This claim of Islam also implies the inference that it is wrong to regard the Law as a curse because the Law is meant to help man in his moral and spiritual development and only that Law can be condemned as a curse which, instead of fulfilling this purpose, leads to bad morals and the degradation of man. The verse also hints that when the eating of meats offered to idols and of blood and of strangled animals was forbidden to Christians and this commandment constituted an ordinance of the Law (Acts 13:20, 29), they could not take exception to the Law and condemn it as a curse.

The fifth verse lays down an Islamic commandment with regard to eatables and enjoins that only pure things are to be used, meaning that such things should be used as are not only lawful but are also pure *i.e.* their eating should not in any way injure man's physical or moral

health. Subject to this commandment, all those things
though constituting lawful food, offend against the feeling
culated to injure health. For instance, the eating of cucu
to cause cholera, it becomes forbidden, being غير طيب .
is subject to two vital conditions : (1) it should be حلال i.
طيب or pure *i.e.* its use should in no way contravene or off
and regulations. Islam alone of all religions has, while lay
and unlawful things, pointed out the nice distinction bet
both lawful and pure. These ordinances extend to the 9t
four verses (10—13), while referring to the previous favours
that good results are sure to follow if these ordinances are faith
are warned that the followers of previous religions broke God's
parts of His word. This led to their condemnation and disgrac   ..... the
right path and become corrupt and suffer humiliation because .... Law was a curse but because
they consigned the Law to oblivion. So now there was no door left open to them but to follow
the Holy Prophet and through him re-inherit God's favours (14—17).

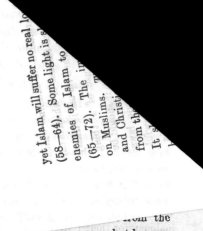

The *Sūra* then proceeds to warn Christians that at first by deifying Jesus they kindled the
wrath of God upon them and now they have begun to be jealous of the Holy Prophet because God
has chosen him for His favours. This jealous attitude of theirs towards the Holy Prophet resembles
that of Cain towards Abel—the two sons of Adam (18—37). The 38th verse contains a prophecy
that Christians will hatch plots against Islam and that some weak of faith from among
Muslims would also become implicated in these plots. But the Faithful are enjoined to trust
in God and fear none but Him. As the hatchers of these secret plots would work clandestinely
like thieves, ordinances dealing with theft have been laid down in the next few verses
(39—45).

Then the attention of the Muslims is drawn to the fact that, when on account of opposition
by Christians the hypocrites would again be inclined to create mischief, Jews would make common
cause with them. It is stated that while Jews and Christians lose no opportunity to oppose
Islam, they themselves have become so depraved that they have ceased to act upon their own
religious scriptures and are increasingly becoming ignorant of their own religions. They have
become so corrupt that when they find that there is a likelihood of their securing a favourable
decision regarding a dispute in accordance with the Islamic Law, they do not hesitate to refer
it to the Holy Prophet for settlement and seek his judgement. They are told that so long as they
do not accept Islam, they must follow their own scriptures and abide by their own Law ; but
that if, bowing to the political supremacy of Islam, they sometimes seek the judgement of the
Islamic Government, it must be according to the Quranic Law (46—57).

The *Sūra* proceeds to draw the attention of the Muslims to the great change that has
come over Islamic politics and they are told that as the power of the infidels has been finally
broken and, instead of infidels, Christians are now to be their principal enemies, and Jews, in
spite of their enmity towards Christianity, are to side with Christians, Muslims should be on
their guard against them. Jews will try to turn some of the Muslims into hypocrites and, though
they may succeed in their endeavours and some Muslims may fall victim to their machinations,

...ss on that account and eventually Muslims will conquer and prevail ...ned on the strategems and machinations that will be employed by the ...urn Muslims away from their faith and to lower it in their estimation ...portance of the preaching of Islam is impressed on the Holy Prophet and ...hey are told that the one real method effectively to defeat the activities of Jews ...ns is to preach the message of Islam to them and to bring home to them the truth ...ir own scriptures that they can reject Islam only by denying and belying those scriptures. ...nould also be made clear to them that their salvation, too, lies in Islam. Their idolatrous ...eliefs should also be proved to be baseless from their own scriptures, particularly the doctrine of the sonship of Jesus, who should be shown to be only a Prophet of God (73—78).

Similarly, mention is made of Jews who, by opposing and persecuting the two great Prophets of God, David and Jesus, have incurred the displeasure of the Almighty and excited His wrath against them which has led to the disappearance from among them of all feeling of jealousy for their religion. Muslims are told to draw the attention of these people to their past faults and failings but are warned that by experience they will learn that Christians are more amenable to accepting the truth than Jews (79—87). (The experience of the past thirteen centuries bears ample testimony to the fact that far more Christians than Jews have accepted Islam during this period. Perhaps the time for the reformation of the Jews may also be drawing near).

Thereafter commandments have been laid down which particularly concern Christian peoples and countries; *viz.*, commandments about what is lawful and what is unlawful; commandments about oaths; commandments about the use of wine and games of hazard; commandments about hunting; commandments regarding the criticism of religion, and ordinances about rites and ceremonies and about evidence (88—109).

Last of all a somewhat detailed mention is made of the particular circumstances of Jesus and it is shown that they only resemble those of other Prophets of God. It is mentioned that there was nothing of Godhead about him and that all material progress of Christians is due to a prayer of his. But they have made an improper use of that progress and, as a result, instead of believing in the Oneness of God, have succumbed to polytheistic beliefs and practices. God will, on the Day of Judgement, establish their guilt and put them to shame from the mouth of Jesus himself, who will confess that he never preached any polytheistic doctrine or asked them to regard him as God or His equal. He will also confess that these people deviated from the right path and became corrupt only after his death (110—120). The *Sūra* ends with the declaration that to God belongs the kingdom of the heavens and the earth and He has power over all things, which implies the beautiful hint that the belief that the kingdom of God is only on heaven and is not on earth is false and that to Him alone belongs the dominion both of heaven and earth and that as a proof of it He will now grant Islam, His true religion, predominance and victory over the Christian peoples. And so it actually came to pass.

سُوۡرَةُ الۡمَآئِدَةِ مَدَنِیَّةٌ

1. *a*In the name of Allah, the Gracious, the Merciful.[640]

بِسۡمِ اللّٰہِ الرَّحۡمٰنِ الرَّحِیۡمِ ۚ﴿۱﴾

2. O ye who believe! fulfil *your* compacts. Lawful are made to you quadrupeds *of the class* of cattle other than *b*those which are being announced to you, except that you should not hold game to be lawful while you are in a state of pilgrimage : verily, Allah decrees what He wills.[641]

یٰۤاَیُّہَا الَّذِیۡنَ اٰمَنُوۡۤا اَوۡفُوۡا بِالۡعُقُوۡدِ ۬ؕ اُحِلَّتۡ لَکُمۡ بَہِیۡمَۃُ الۡاَنۡعَامِ اِلَّا مَا یُتۡلٰی عَلَیۡکُمۡ غَیۡرَ مُحِلِّی الصَّیۡدِ وَ اَنۡتُمۡ حُرُمٌ ؕ اِنَّ اللّٰہَ یَحۡکُمُ مَا یُرِیۡدُ ﴿۲﴾

---

*a*See 1 : 1.　*b*2 : 174 ; 5 : 4 ; 6 : 146.

---

640. Commentary:

See 1 : 1.

641 Important Words:

عقود (compacts) is the plural of عقد ('aqdun), being derived from the verb عقد ('aqada). They say عقد الحبل *i.e.* he tied the rope ; or he tied it firmly and fast ; or he tied it into a knot or knots. عقد means, a compact ; a covenant ; an agreement ; a responsibility ; an obligation ; a treaty ; an ordinance of God (Lane & Aqrab).

بهیمة (quadrupeds) of which the plural is بهائم is derived from بهم. They say بهم الرجل *i.e.* the man continued looking at a thing without his being relieved by doing so *i.e.* he looked vacantly ; he was silent and perplexed or was confounded when asked respecting a thing. ابهم الامر means, the affair became vague or dubious or confused. ابهم الباب means, he closed the door. استبهم علیه الامر means, the affair was as though it were closed against him so that he knew not how to engage in it or execute it. بهیمة means, a beast or a brute ; any quadruped whether of the land or of the sea ; any animal that does not discriminate or does not possess the power of expression ; all animals except beasts of prey and birds (Lane & Aqrab).

انعام (cattle) is the plural of نعم (an animal of the class of cattle). They say نعم عیشه *i.e.* his life was or became easy, good or pleasant. نعم of which the plural is انعام means, pasturing cattle consisting of camels or sheep or goats ; or all these ; or camels alone (Lane & Aqrab).

The phrase بهیمة الانعام (quadrupeds of the class of cattle) which is made up of two words : بهیمة (quadrupeds) and انعام (cattle) is of rather peculiar construction. The phrase does not mean quadrupeds from among cattle, for the obvious reason that quadrupeds form a class wider than cattle. In fact, the اضافة in the phrase بهیمة الانعام is of the kind which may be called اضافة تشبیهیة or اضافة بیانیة. According to the former, the words بهیمة الانعام would mean, the بهیمة (quadrupeds) which belong to the class of انعام (cattle) ; and according to the latter, they would mean بهیمة (quadrupeds) which resemble انعام (cattle). This construction has been used by the Quran to signify that whereas all بهیمة (quadrupeds) do not make lawful food, those of them that form the counterparts of انعام (cattle) are allowed. Thus the expression is intended to comprise not only cattle but also

597

such beasts of the forest as correspond to cattle *i.e.* wild goat, wild cow, *nilgāi*, wild buffalo, etc.

Commentary :

In this verse the word عقود (compacts) signifies compacts made by man with God or the obligations due to Him. The word, literally meaning "knots," has acquired this meaning because in ancient times knots were tied on strings or ropes as symbols of solemn compacts. The fulfilling of compacts or obligations due to God, referred to in the present verse which primarily deals with the subject of food, contains a veiled hint that a time was coming when Muslims would have to face trials and suffer hardships in order to avoid forbidden food. It is then that they would have to be particularly regardful of God's commandments in this respect. That time has already come and Muslims who go to Europe or America experience great difficulty in getting clean and lawful food, and they have to take special care in procuring it, if they want to avoid forbidden food.

The word صيد (game), here used in connection with *ihrām*, means the animal hunted and not

the act of hunting itself, for the commandment with regard to hunting has been given separately in 5 : 97. In the present verse it is only the eating of game killed by a pilgrim that is mentioned, because not only is the hunting of a land animal by a pilgrim forbidden, but even the eating of it is for him unlawful. If, however, a land animal has been killed by a pilgrim who has not yet entered into the state of *ihrām*, the eating of it is not forbidden to those who are in a state of *ihrām*, provided they render no help to the man who kills the game.

The words, *other than those which are being announced to you*, refer to the flesh of the animals mentioned in 5 : 4 below, viz., *that which has been strangled, and that which has been beaten to death, and that which has been killed by a fall, and that which has been gored to death*, etc. The words, however, do not refer to the first part of 5 : 4, viz, *the flesh of an animal which dies of itself, and blood, and the flesh of swine*, because "swine" is not included among cattle and the exception here made is from among the cattle and not from among all animals, and also because this portion had already been revealed in 2 : 174.

3.　O ye who believe ! profane not the Signs of Allah, nor the Sacred Month, nor the animals brought as an offering, nor the *animals of sacrifice wearing collars*, nor those repairing to the Sacred House, ᵃseeking grace from their Lord, and *His* pleasure. And when you put off the pilgrims' garb *and are clear of the Sacred Territory*, you may hunt. And ᵇlet not the enmity of a people that they hindered you from the Sacred Mosque incite you to transgress. And help one another in righteousness and piety ; but help not one another in sin and transgression. And fear Allah ; surely, Allah is severe in punishment.⁶⁴²

يَاۤيُّهَا الَّذِيۡنَ اٰمَنُوۡا لَا تُحِلُّوۡا شَعَآئِرَ اللّٰهِ وَلَا الشَّهۡرَ الۡحَرَامَ وَلَا الۡهَدۡىَ وَلَا الۡقَلَآئِدَ وَلَاۤ اٰمِّيۡنَ الۡبَيۡتَ الۡحَرَامَ يَبۡتَغُوۡنَ فَضۡلًا مِّنۡ رَّبِّهِمۡ وَرِضۡوَانًا ۚ وَاِذَا حَلَلۡتُمۡ فَاصۡطَادُوۡا ۚ وَلَا يَجۡرِمَنَّكُمۡ شَنَاٰنُ قَوۡمٍ اَنۡ صَدُّوۡكُمۡ عَنِ الۡمَسۡجِدِ الۡحَرَامِ اَنۡ تَعۡتَدُوۡا ۘ وَتَعَاوَنُوۡا عَلَى الۡبِرِّ وَالتَّقۡوٰى ۚ وَلَا تَعَاوَنُوۡا عَلَى الۡاِثۡمِ وَالۡعُدۡوَانِ ۚ وَاتَّقُوا اللّٰهَ ؕ اِنَّ اللّٰهَ شَدِيۡدُ الۡعِقَابِ ۞

ᵃ59 : 9.　　ᵇ5 : 9 ; 11 : 90.

---

642 Important Words :

الهدى (the animal brought as an offering) is the noun-infinitive from هدى meaning, he directed ; or he showed the way. هدية means, a present *i.e.* a thing sent or offered to another as a token of love, courtesy or honour. هدى means (1) mode or manner of acting ; conduct or character ; (2) what one brings as an offering to the Ka'ba, consisting of camels or kine or sheep or goats to be sacrificed ; or the goods or commodities so brought ; (3) camels absolutely (Aqrab & Lane).

القلائد (collars) is the plural of قلادة which is the noun-infinitive from قلد meaning, he twisted or wound or wreathed a thing upon another. قلدها (*qallada-hā*) means, he put a necklace upon her neck. قلد البدنة means, he hung upon the neck of the camel or cow, etc., brought as an offering to Mecca, a collar, to show that it was meant for sacrifice as an offering. قلادة means, a necklace ; a collar or the like ; that which is hung, as a sign or mark, upon the neck of a camel or cow, etc., brought to Mecca for sacrifice (Lane &

Aqrab). The word قلائد (collars) may also mean " collared animals " (Muḥīt). The words هدى and قلائد as used in this verse both signify animals that are taken to Mecca for sacrifice during the Pilgrimage, قلائد particularly meaning such animals as have collars round their necks, and هدى all animals without distinction that are brought to Mecca for sacrifice.

اٰمِّيۡن (who repair) is the plural of اٰمّ which is the active participle from اٰمّ . They say امه *i.e.* he repaired or directed his course to it ; he aimed at or sought after it ; he endeavoured to reach or attain it (Lane). See also 3 : 8 ; 3 : 21 ; 3 : 114.

Commentary :

The words شعائر الله (Signs of Allah, for which see 2 : 159) signify anything that leads to the knowledge and realization of God. The offerings made to God, or the animals of sacrifice brought to the Ka'ba, are " Signs of God," in the sense that they teach us to be ever ready to sacrifice all that belongs to us for the sake of God.

The words الشهر الحرام (Sacred Month) may signify each one of the four Sacred Months, viz., *Shawwāl, Dhū'l-Qa'da Dhū'l Ḥijja* and *Rajab*. Some theologians, however, hold the view that here the "Sacred Month" means only *Dhū'l Ḥijja i.e.* the month of حج (Greater Pilgrimage), to which a special reference has been made on account of the great gathering of pilgrims that takes place at Mecca in that month. Others are of the opinion that the word here refers to *Rajab*, the usual month of عمرة (Lesser Pilgrimage), to which no respect was paid by certain Arab tribes. Abstaining from profaning the Sacred Month may also mean paying due respect to the works performed therein.

All manner of fighting must cease during the four Sacred Months. As pilgrims have to travel to and from Mecca during these months, not only are pilgrims and animals of sacrifice not to be molested on the way, but all hostilities must cease and there should be perfect peace so that pilgrims may perform both their inward and outward journeys in complete security. The hunting of land animals has also been forbidden for a similar reason.

The words, *nor those repairing to the Sacred House,* refer particularly to the pilgrims who go to Mecca for the Greater or the Lesser Pilgrimage. But they may also refer to such travellers as may proceed to Mecca for any valid purpose, including such non-Muslims as may visit the Sacred House with the permission of its custodians to gain religious knowledge.

The expression, *help not one another in sin and transgression,* constitutes an effective reply to the malicious charge that Islam is a militant religion, encouraging aggressive warfare against the infidels. How can a Book which gives such clear injunctions to its followers as are contained in the above words, be expected to command them to take up arms against innocent and unoffending people and to kill them wherever they are found on the sole ground that they do not profess Islam.

The verse clearly forbids Muslims to fight their enemies in the four Sacred Months even when a state of war exists. The Holy Prophet himself was the first to carry out this injunction. He would not fight the idolatrous Meccans when, at Ḥudaibiya, they refused to allow him and his 1,400 followers to perform عمرة (Lesser Pilgrimage) for which he had undertaken such a long and arduous journey. He went back to Medina after signing a treaty, the terms of which at that time appeared to be very humiliating, in spite of the fact that his followers were prepared to fight. The Holy Prophet, however, paid no heed to the outraged feelings of his followers and did what righteousness and piety demanded. But when non-Muslims are the first to attack Muslims during a Sacred Month, the latter are allowed to defend themselves (2 : 195, 218).

4. *a*Forbidden to you is *the flesh of an animal* which dies of itself, and blood and the flesh of swine; and that on which is invoked the name of one other than Allah; and that which has been strangled; and that which has been beaten to death; and that which has been killed by a fall; and that which has been gored to death; and that of which a wild animal has eaten, except that which you have properly slaughtered; and that which has been slaughtered at an altar *as an offering to idols. And *b*forbidden is also this* that you seek to know your lot by the divining arrows. That is *an act of* disobedience. This day have those who disbelieve despaired of *harming* your religion. So fear them not, but fear Me. This day have I perfected your religion for you and completed My favour upon you and *c*have chosen for you Islam as religion. But *d*whoso is forced by hunger, without being wilfully inclined to sin, then, surely Allah is Most Forgiving *and* Merciful.[643]

حُرِّمَتْ عَلَيْكُمُ الْمَيْتَةُ وَالدَّمُ وَلَحْمُ الْخِنْزِيرِ وَ مَآ أُهِلَّ لِغَيْرِ اللهِ بِهِ وَالْمُنْخَنِقَةُ وَالْمَوْقُوذَةُ وَالْمُتَرَدِّيَةُ وَالنَّطِيحَةُ وَمَآ أَكَلَ السَّبُعُ إِلَّا مَا ذَكَّيْتُمْ وَمَا ذُبِحَ عَلَى النُّصُبِ وَأَنْ تَسْتَقْسِمُوا بِالْأَزْلَامِ ذَلِكُمْ فِسْقٌ اَلْيَوْمَ يَئِسَ الَّذِينَ كَفَرُوا مِنْ دِينِكُمْ فَلَا تَخْشَوْهُمْ وَاخْشَوْنِ اَلْيَوْمَ أَكْمَلْتُ لَكُمْ دِينَكُمْ وَأَتْمَمْتُ عَلَيْكُمْ نِعْمَتِي وَرَضِيتُ لَكُمُ الْإِسْلَامَ دِيناً فَمَنِ اضْطُرَّ فِي مَخْمَصَةٍ غَيْرَ مُتَجَانِفٍ لِإِثْمٍ فَإِنَّ اللهَ غَفُورٌ رَحِيمٌ ۝

---

*a*2 : 174 ; 6 : 146.   *b*5 : 91.   *c*3 : 20, 86.   *d*2 : 174 ; 6 : 146 ; 16 : 116.

---

643. Important Words :

الْمَيْتَةُ (an animal which dies of itself). Though generally speaking everything that is dead is مَيْتَة, in its specific sense, the word signifies an animal that has died of itself without being properly slaughtered (Lane). See also 2 : 174.

الْمُنْخَنِقَةُ (that which has been strangled) is derived from خَنَق. They say خَنَقَهُ *i.e.* he squeezed his or its throat that he or it might die; he squeezed his or its throat so that he or it died; he strangled or throttled or choked him or it. اخْتَنَقَ or انْخَنَقَ means, he or it became throttled or strangled or choked. شَاةٌ مُنْخَنِقَةٌ means, a goat or sheep strangled or

throttled (Lane).

الْمَوْقُوذَةُ (that which has been beaten to death) is derived from وَقَذَ. They say وَقَذَهُ *i.e.* he beat or struck him or it violently till he or it became relaxed and was at the point of death; he broke his or its skull, wounding the brain; he beat him or it till he or it died. شَاةٌ مَوْقُوذَةٌ means, a goat or sheep beaten to death either with a stick or staff or stones, etc. (Lane).

الْمُتَرَدِّيَةُ (that which has been killed by a fall) is derived from رَدِى. They say رَدِى الرَّجُلُ *i.e.* the man perished. رَدَاهُ بِحَجَرٍ means, he threw stones at him and hit him. تَرَدَّى means, he or it fell or tumbled down into a well or a pit. It also means, he or it fell down from a mountain, or a height and died. المتردية means, that (a goat, etc.) which falls from a mountain or a height, or falls down a well, or a pit and dies (Lane).

النطيحة (that which has been gored to death) is derived from نطح. They say نطحه i.e. he (a ram, etc.) smote him or it with his horn. النطيحة means, a sheep or goat smitten with the horn and so killed (Lane).

ما ذكيتم (that which you have properly slaughtered). ذكى (dhakkā) is derived from ذكى (dhakā). They say ذكت النار i.e. the fire blazed or burned brightly. ذكت الارض means, the land was or became clean and pure. ذكى النار (dhakkā) means, he made the fire blaze or burn brightly. ذكى العقل means, it (medicine, etc.) sharpened the intellect. ذكى الشاة means, he slaughtered the goat in the manner prescribed by the Law of Islam (Lane).

النصب (idols) is derived from نصب which means, he set up or he fixed. النصب according to some, is singular, the plural of which is انصاب; and according to others, it is plural, of which the singular is نصاب. The word means, signs or marks set up to show the way; stones set up and worshipped to the exclusion of, or in preference to, God; anything that is so worshipped; stones which the pagan Arabs set up to sacrifice or slay animals before them, the name of some deity being pronounced in the killing of such animals; idol or idols; but whereas idols were generally carved and had some form or shape, النصب were simple uncarved stones (Lane & Aqrab).

ازلام (divining arrows) is the plural of زلم and is derived from the verb زلم (zalama), meaning, he cut off the protruding part of a thing, such as the nose; he made his gift, small in quantity as though he had cut off something from it. زلم السهم means, he cut or pared the arrow to make it proportionate and good-looking. زلم means, an arrow without a head and

without feathers. ازلام (the plural of زلم) were those divining arrows by means of which pre-Islamic Arabs sought to know what was allotted to them. On some of these arrows the word "command" and on others "prohibition" were written, while others were left blank, and all these were kept together in a suitable vessel. When any one wanted to do a certain thing or go on a journey, he would take out one of the arrows without looking at them and then act according to the instruction of "command" or "prohibition" as the case might be. If the blank arrow came out, the experiment was repeated, till an arrow bearing the word "command" or "prohibition" was taken out (Lane).

اليوم (this day) here really signifies "now." See 1 : 4.

مخمصة (hunger) is derived from خمص. They say خمص البطن i.e. the belly was or became empty i.e. hungry. خمصت القدم means, the foot rose from the ground or was hollow in the middle of the sole, so that it did not touch it. خمصه الجوع means, hunger rendered him lank in the belly. مخمصة therefore, means, emptiness of the belly; hunger (Lane & Aqrab).

Commentary :

This verse shows that the Quran does not consider the prosperity and predominance of Islam to be dependent on territorial conquest and the extension of material power, but on its being a perfect and complete religion. It draws the attention of Muslims to the fact that now that all the teachings needed for the moral and spiritual regeneration of man have been embodied in the Quran, it is up to them to win the premier place in the comity of nations by acting upon them and holding fast to them.

The words ikmāl (perfecting) and itmām (completing) which are noun-infinitives from اكملت (have I perfected) and تممت (completed) occurring in the clause, *This day have I perfected your religion for you and completed My favour upon you*, are full of meaning and convey two different and distinct senses. The former (*i.e.* perfection) relates to *quality*, and the latter (*i.e.* completion) to *quantity*. The use of the word كملت (I have perfected) with regard to the teaching of the Quran thus shows that doctrines and commandments affecting the physical, moral and spiritual development of man have been embodied in the Quran in their most perfect form; while the word أتمت (I have completed) shows that nothing which was needed by man has been left out. Again, the former *i.e.* perfection, pertains to commandments relating to the physical side of man or his external self, while the latter *i.e.* completion, relates to his spiritual side or his inner self, *viz.*, the completion of the spiritual blessings which follow the observance of the outward Law.

Thus the verse hints that as the divine Law has been perfected and completed in the Quran, it shall not be superseded by any other Law. The Laws that preceded the Quran were meant for particular peoples and limited periods, being suited to their special requirements only. Similarly, the Prophets that preceded the Holy Prophet of Islam were sent to particular nations only. This was quite in the fitness of things. The means of communication between different countries were then in a very undeveloped state and people living in one country knew little or nothing of the countries that lay far off from them. Moreover, nations of the earth were then in different stages of development, some being very backward and others only partially developed and the mind of man had not attained its full growth and development. Hence, the circumstances then obtaining required that separate Messengers be sent to separate nations who should give them such teachings as suited their particular needs and requirements. This state of things, however, was not to last for ever. The Oneness of God

presupposed oneness of mankind and it was quite natural that, when the God-given faculties of man became fully developed and the means of communication also improved so that intercourse between different nations became easier and more common, God should raise a Prophet for the whole of mankind and give him a perfect Law which should fulfil all the needs and meet all the problems of humanity.

But the mere existence of a perfect Law cannot prevent the moral degeneration of humanity. So in spite of the presence of the Quran, it was necessary that heavenly Reformers should continue to appear in the world in times of degeneration, and, being inspired of God, should give new life to corrupt and degenerate humanity. In fact, the promise about the appearance of such Reformers is implied even in the words, (*this day*) *have I completed My favour upon you*, for if religion has been completed, it does not stand to reason that when mankind should consign God to oblivion and forget the object of their creation, God should make no provision for their regeneration. In that case, His favour upon them cannot be said to have been "completed." Thus, the very completion of God's favour upon Muslims requires that He should raise among them such Reformers as should breathe a new life into them, whenever their spiritual and moral degeneration demands it. Says the Holy Prophet, "God will raise among the Muslims at the head of each century a Reformer who would regenerate their religion for them" (Dāwūd, ch. on *Malāḥim*).

It may also be noted here that the perfection and completion of God's religion and favour has been mentioned side by side with the law relating to eatables in order to point out that the use of lawful food forms one of the most important bases of good morals which in time provide a pedestal for spiritual progress,

5. They ask thee what is made lawful for them. Say, 'All good things have been made lawful for you; and what you have taught the beasts and birds of prey *to catch for you*, training *them* for hunting *and* teaching them of what Allah has taught you. So eat of that which they catch for you, and ^apronounce thereon the name of Allah. And fear Allah, surely Allah is quick in reckoning.' [644]

يَسْـَٔلُوْنَكَ مَاذَآ اُحِلَّ لَهُمْ ۗ قُلْ اُحِلَّ لَكُمُ الطَّيِّبٰتُ ۙ وَمَا عَلَّمْتُمْ مِّنَ الْجَوَارِحِ مُكَلِّبِيْنَ تُعَلِّمُوْنَهُنَّ مِمَّا عَلَّمَكُمُ اللّٰهُ ۫ فَكُلُوْا مِمَّآ اَمْسَكْنَ عَلَيْكُمْ وَاذْكُرُوا اسْمَ اللّٰهِ عَلَيْهِ ۪ وَاتَّقُوا اللّٰهَ ۗ اِنَّ اللّٰهَ سَرِيْعُ الْحِسَابِ ۞

^a6 : 119.

644. Important Words:

جَوَارِح (animals of prey) is the plural of جَارِحَة which is derived from جَرَحَ . They say جَرَحَهُ *i.e.* he wounded him; or he cut him; or he clove or rent his body. It also means, he gained, acquired or earned. جَوَارِح means, beasts and birds of prey that catch game. The word also means, the limbs of a human being with which things are gained or earned (Lane).

مُكَلِّبِيْن (training them for hunting) is the plural of مُكَلِّب which is the active participle from كَلَّبَ (*kallaba*) which is the transitive form of كَلِبَ (*kaliba*) meaning, he thirsted; he ate voraciously; he was seized with the disease of dogs; he barked. كَلَّبَ (*kallaba*) means, he trained (a dog) to hunt; he trained any beast or bird of prey to take game. مُكَلِّب means, one who trains dogs to hunt; or one who trains any beast or bird of prey to take game. مُكَلِّب also means, one who possesses dogs trained to hunt and hunts with them. كَلْب means, a dog or any animal of prey (Lane).

Commentary:

The forbidden things having been described in the preceding verse, the rest are here declared lawful, provided they are طَيِّبات *i.e.* good and pure, it being left to each individual to decide what is good for him and what is not, in view of his particular circumstances and the condition of his health. The Holy Prophet has definitely excluded beasts of prey and birds having claws from the category of lawful food. See also 2 : 174.

The training of animals or birds of prey for catching game has been made lawful. As for the eating of the flesh of the game so hunted the injunction varies according to circumstances. The more accepted view is as follows : (1) If the hunter finds the game alive, the eating of its flesh is lawful in all circumstances, provided the hunter slaughters the game in the prescribed manner. (2) If the hunter finds the game dead, the eating of its flesh is lawful only in case (*a*) the animal of prey is trained, and (*b*) it does not itself eat of the game, and (*c*) the hunter sends the animal of prey after reciting thereon the name of Allah. (3) If the game dies of sheer fear, before the animal of prey has actually caught and wounded it, the eating of its flesh is unlawful.

6. This day all good things have been made lawful for you. And the food of the People of the Book is lawful for you, and your food is lawful for them. And *lawful for you are* chaste believing women and chaste women from among those who were given the Book before you, when you give them their dowries, contracting valid marriage and not committing fornication nor taking secret paramours. And whoever rejects the faith, his work has doubtless come to naught, and in the Hereafter he will be among the losers.[645]

645. Important Words :

For the meaning of the word محصنين (contracting valid marriage) and مسافحين (committing fornication) and اخدان (secret paramours) see 4 : 25, 26.

Commentary :

The verse declares that if a person from among the People of the Book invites a Muslim to dinner, it is lawful for the latter to accept the invitation and partake of the food of the former, provided, of course, the food does not include anything forbidden by Islam. Similarly, a Muslim is allowed to invite the People of the Book to dinner.

Some Commentators have taken the word طعام (food) in the clause, *the food of the People of the Book is lawful for you*, in the sense of "flesh of animals used as food." In this sense, the verse would signify that Muslims are allowed to partake of the flesh of an animal slaughtered by one from among the People of the Book, provided, of course, the name of God has been pronounced on the slaughtered animal.

The words, *And lawful for you are chaste believing women and chaste women from among those who were given the Book before you*, are intended to hint that whereas Islam permits marriage of Muslim men with non-Muslim women from among the People of the Book, it certainly prefers that Muslim men should ordinarily marry only Muslim women.

The words يكفر بالإيمان rendered as "rejects the faith" may either mean "turns apostate" which is its primary significance ; or it may mean "is ungrateful respecting faith." For the meaning of the particle ب see 1 : 1.

R. 2   7.   O ye who believe ! when you stand up for Prayer, wash your faces, and your hands up to the elbows, and pass your *wet* hands over your heads, and *wash* your feet to the ankles. And if you be unclean, purify yourselves *by bathing*. And if you are ill or *you are* on a journey *while unclean*, or one of you comes from the privy or you have touched women, and you find not water, betake yourselves to pure dust and wipe therewith your faces and your hands. *a*Allah desires not that He should place you in a difficulty but He desires to purify you and to complete His favour upon you, so that you may be grateful.⁶⁴⁶

يَٰٓأَيُّهَا الَّذِينَ آمَنُوٓا إِذَا قُمْتُمْ إِلَى الصَّلَوٰةِ فَاغْسِلُوا وُجُوهَكُمْ وَأَيْدِيَكُمْ إِلَى الْمَرَافِقِ وَامْسَحُوا بِرُءُوسِكُمْ وَأَرْجُلَكُمْ إِلَى الْكَعْبَيْنِ وَإِن كُنتُمْ جُنُبًا فَاطَّهَّرُوا وَإِن كُنتُم مَّرْضَىٰٓ أَوْ عَلَىٰ سَفَرٍ أَوْ جَآءَ أَحَدٌ مِّنكُم مِّنَ الْغَآئِطِ أَوْ لَٰمَسْتُمُ النِّسَآءَ فَلَمْ تَجِدُوا مَآءً فَتَيَمَّمُوا صَعِيدًا طَيِّبًا فَامْسَحُوا بِوُجُوهِكُمْ وَأَيْدِيكُم مِّنْهُ مَا يُرِيدُ اللَّهُ لِيَجْعَلَ عَلَيْكُم مِّنْ حَرَجٍ وَلَٰكِن يُرِيدُ لِيُطَهِّرَكُمْ وَلِيُتِمَّ نِعْمَتَهُ عَلَيْكُمْ لَعَلَّكُمْ تَشْكُرُونَ ۝

*a*2 : 186.

646. Important Words :

جُنُبًا (unclean) for which see 4 : 44.

Commentary :

After the questions of food and marriage comes the question of cleanliness on which Islam lays so much emphasis, specially on cleanliness necessary for the proper performance of worship. The feet are here mentioned after the head, not because they are intended, as alleged by the *Shias*, to be only wiped like the head, but because they come last in the process of ablution. This is apparent from the fact that the word ارجل (feet) has been put in the accusative case in the standard text, like the words وجوه (faces) and ايدى (hands), thus showing that, like the latter, the word "feet" is also governed in the accusative case by the verb اغسلوا (wash) and not by the particle ا (over) which governs the word رؤس (heads) only. Hence the addition of the verb "wash" before it in the translation. It is true that a solitary reading gives the word ارجل (*arjula*)

as ارجل *arjuli* (in the genitive case). But even this does not necessarily mean that the word is not governed by the verb اغسلوا (wash) ; for, according to the rules of Arabic grammar, nouns in the accusative case may sometimes be put in the genitive case owing to their proximity to a noun in the genitive case. According to this rule, ارجل (feet) would be taken to have been put in this reading in the genitive case owing to its proximity to the word رؤس (heads), but really it is governed not by the preposition ا but by the verb اغسلوا . In fact, the word ارجل (feet) has been put after رؤس (heads) to point out the order which is to be observed in the performance of ablution. The authentic sayings of the Holy Prophet also make it clear that in performing an ablution the feet should be washed and not merely wiped. These sayings are also supported by the practice of the Holy Prophet.

There are, however, cases when the feet are not to be washed but simply "wiped" like

8. And remember Allah's favour upon you and the covenant which He made with you, when you said, ^a' We hear and we obey.' And fear Allah. Surely, Allah knows well what is in the minds.⁶⁴⁷

وَاذْكُرُوْا نِعْمَةَ اللّٰهِ عَلَيْكُمْ وَمِيْثَاقَهُ الَّذِیْ وَاثَقَكُمْ بِهٖ ۙ اِذْ قُلْتُمْ سَمِعْنَا وَاَطَعْنَا ۫ وَاتَّقُوا اللّٰهَ ۚ اِنَّ اللّٰهَ عَلِيْمٌۢ بِذَاتِ الصُّدُوْرِ ۝

a2 : 286.

the head, e.g., when one is wearing socks or stockings. So it may be that the common reading ارجل arjula (in the accusative case) applies to the general rule of " washing " the feet when performing وضوء (ablution), while the exceptional reading ارجل arjuli (in the genitive case) applies to the exceptional cases when the feet are to be " wiped " like the head.

The words, you have touched women, embody a chaste and graceful expression and mean " you have had sexual intercourse with them." The sense of the verse may be summed up as follows : (1) Before offering his Prayers, a Muslim should perform the prescribed ablution i.e. washing of the face and the hands, wiping of the head, and washing of the feet. (2) If a man is جنب (unclean) i.e. he has had sexual intercourse with his wife or, for that matter, has had a nocturnal discharge, he should have a complete bath in order to purify himself for Prayers. (3) If, however, a man is sick and the process of ablution or bathing is likely to do him harm, or if he is on a journey and cannot find water, then even after answering the call of nature or becoming "unclean" by having sexual intercourse with his wife,

he is allowed to forego the process of ablution or bathing and to perform instead the تيمم with pure dust. See also 4 : 44.

647. Commentary :

It is Muslims, and not the People of the Book, that are addressed here. As, however, no special covenant is known to have ever been made with Muslims, the "covenant" mentioned here must be taken to refer to the process of بيعت (oath of allegiance) taken from every new convert to Islam ; or the word may refer to the Law revealed in the Quran and accepted by Muslims. The words, We hear and we obey, obviously refer to the acceptance of Islam by the Faithful.

The words, Allah knows well what is in the minds, have been added to point out that mere lip-profession is not acceptable to God. He who would accept Islam should accept it from the depths of his heart and willingly act up to its teachings. The words thus incidentally provide a strong refutation of the charge so wrongfully brought against Islam that it sanctions conversion at the point of the sword. The sword can only govern the tongue but not the heart.

607

9. O ye who believe ! *a*be steadfast in the cause of Allah, bearing witness in equity; and *b*let not a people's enmity incite you to act otherwise than with justice. Be *always* just, that is nearer to righteousness. And fear Allah. Surely, Allah is aware of what you do.⁶⁴⁸

يَـٰٓأَيُّهَا الَّذِينَ اٰمَنُوا كُوْنُوْا قَوَّامِيْنَ لِلّٰهِ شُهَدَآءَ بِالْقِسْطِ ۖ وَلَا يَجْرِمَنَّكُمْ شَنَاٰنُ قَوْمٍ عَلَىٰٓ اَلَّا تَعْدِلُوْا ۚ اِعْدِلُوْا هُوَ اَقْرَبُ لِلتَّقْوٰى ۖ وَاتَّقُوا اللّٰهَ ۚ اِنَّ اللّٰهَ خَبِيْرٌۢ بِمَا تَعْمَلُوْنَ ۝

10. *c*Allah has promised those who believe and do good deeds that they shall have forgiveness and a great reward.

وَعَدَ اللّٰهُ الَّذِينَ اٰمَنُوْا وَعَمِلُوا الصّٰلِحٰتِ ۙ لَهُمْ مَّغْفِرَةٌ وَّاَجْرٌ عَظِيْمٌ ۝

11. And *as for* *d*those who disbelieve and reject Our Signs, they are the people of Hell.

وَالَّذِينَ كَفَرُوْا وَكَذَّبُوْا بِاٰيٰتِنَآ اُولٰٓئِكَ اَصْحٰبُ الْجَحِيْمِ ۝

*a*4 : 136. *b*5 : 3 ; 11 : 90. *c*22 : 57 ; 24 : 56 ; 48 : 30. *d*5 : 87 ; 6 : 50 ; 7 : 37, 41 ; 22 : 58.

648. Commentary :

As the word قوّام (for which see 4 : 35), means one who performs his work thoroughly and ceaselessly, the expression, *be steadfast in the cause of Allah*, would mean that Muslims should take a firm hold of the commandments of God and carry them out completely and thoroughly and should never become lax or negligent.

The words, *bearing witness in equity*, mean that the Faithful should bear practical witness to the truth of Islam by becoming good Muslims and leading good lives in order to become examples for others. They also signify that the Muslims should convey the message of Islam to others and thus become witnesses for them. As, however, propagation of Islam implies contact with other peoples, the verse fittingly ends with the commandment, *let not a people's enmity incite you to act otherwise than with justice. Be always just, that is nearer to righteousness.* Surely no other religion gives such fair and just teachings about its enemies as does Islam. A true Muslim should act justly not only to other Muslims but also to all non-Muslims—even to those who are enemies of Islam.

The words, *And fear Allah, surely Allah is aware of what you do*, contain a stern warning that the just and equitable treatment of the enemy enjoined above should not be by way of show but should proceed from the heart and be based on the fear of God, from Whom nothing is hidden.

12. O ye who believe ! remember
Allah's favour upon you when a people
intended to stretch out their hands
against you, but *He withheld their
hands from you ; and fear Allah. And
on Allah should the believers rely.[649]

يَا۠اَيُّهَا الَّذِيْنَ اٰمَنُوا اذْكُرُوْا نِعْمَتَ اللّٰهِ عَلَيْكُمْ اِذْ هَمَّ قَوْمٌ اَنْ يَّبْسُطُوْٓا اِلَيْكُمْ اَيْدِيَهُمْ فَكَفَّ اَيْدِيَهُمْ عَنْكُمْ ۚ وَاتَّقُوا اللّٰهَ ۗ وَعَلَى اللّٰهِ فَلْيَتَوَكَّلِ الْمُؤْمِنُوْنَ ۞

13. And indeed *Allah did take a
covenant from the children of Israel ;
and *We raised among them twelve
leaders. And Allah said, ' Surely, I
am with you. If you observe Prayer,
and pay the Zakāt, and believe in My
Messengers and support them, and lend
to Allah a goodly loan, I will remove
your evils from you and *admit you
into gardens beneath which streams
flow. But *whoso from among you
disbelieves thereafter does indeed
stray away from the right path.' [650]

وَلَقَدْ اَخَذَ اللّٰهُ مِيْثَاقَ بَنِيْٓ اِسْرَآءِيْلَ ۚ وَبَعَثْنَا مِنْهُمُ اثْنَيْ عَشَرَ نَقِيْبًا ۚ وَقَالَ اللّٰهُ اِنِّيْ مَعَكُمْ ۗ لَئِنْ اَقَمْتُمُ الصَّلٰوةَ وَاٰتَيْتُمُ الزَّكٰوةَ وَاٰمَنْتُمْ بِرُسُلِيْ وَعَزَّرْتُمُوْهُمْ وَاَقْرَضْتُمُ اللّٰهَ قَرْضًا حَسَنًا لَّاُكَفِّرَنَّ عَنْكُمْ سَيِّاٰتِكُمْ وَلَاُدْخِلَنَّكُمْ جَنّٰتٍ تَجْرِيْ مِنْ تَحْتِهَا الْاَنْهٰرُ ۚ فَمَنْ كَفَرَ بَعْدَ ذٰلِكَ مِنْكُمْ فَقَدْ ضَلَّ سَوَآءَ السَّبِيْلِ ۞

---

*a*5 : 111.　　*b*2 : 41, 84.　　*c*2 : 61 ; 7 : 161.　　*d*See 2 : 26.　　*e*2 : 109.

649. Commentary :

The verse is considered by some Commentators
to refer to an incident which took place when
the Holy Prophet was returning from Tabūk.
It is said that on this occasion six hypocrites
lay in ambush to kill him, but God saved him
by disclosing the plot to him. The verse may,
however, not necessarily be applied to any
particular incident. It may be taken to refer
generally to the protection which God vouchsafed to Muslims from the aggressive attacks
of their enemies. By " a people " is here
primarily meant the disbelievers of Mecca,
who spared no pains to extirpate Islam and
the Muslims, but the word is also general in
its application.

650. Important Words :

نقيبا (leaders) is the verbal adjective from
نقب. They say نقبه i.e. he perforated or
made a hole through it. نقب فى الارض means,

he went through the land. نقب عن الاخبار
means, he scrutinized or examined the news.
نقب على قومه means, he acted as نقيب (leader
or supervisor) over his people. نقيب means, a
thing perforated or pierced through ; a musical
reed or pipe ; the head or chief of a people who
investigates and superintends their affairs,
takes notice of their actions and is responsible
for them (Lane).

عزرتموهم (you support them) is derived
from عزر. عزره means, he censured him ;
he helped him. They say عزره عن كذا i.e. he
prevented or hindered him or turned him
away from such a thing. عزره ('azzara-hū)
means: (1) (he chastised or punished or
censured or corrected him, in order to turn
him away from evil ; (2) he aided and assisted
him ; he strengthened him ; he aided him against
his enemy by repelling the latter ; (3) he treated
him with reverence, respect or honour (Lane).

609

14. So, *because of their breaking their covenant, We have cursed them, and have hardened their hearts. *They pervert the words from their proper places and have forgotten a *good* part of that with which they were exhorted. And thou wilt not cease to discover treachery on their part, except *in a few* of them. So pardon them and turn away *from them*. Surely, Allah loves those who do good.⁶⁵¹

فَبِمَا نَقْضِهِمْ مِّيْثَاقَهُمْ لَعَنّٰهُمْ وَجَعَلْنَا قُلُوبَهُمْ قَاسِيَةً ۚ يُحَرِّفُوْنَ الْكَلِمَ عَنْ مَّوَاضِعِهٖ ۙ وَنَسُوْا حَظًّا مِّمَّا ذُكِّرُوْا بِهٖ ۚ وَلَا تَزَالُ تَطَّلِعُ عَلٰى خَآئِنَةٍ مِّنْهُمْ اِلَّا قَلِيْلًا مِّنْهُمْ فَاعْفُ عَنْهُمْ وَاصْفَحْ ۚ اِنَّ اللّٰهَ يُحِبُّ الْمُحْسِنِيْنَ ۝

*a*4 : 156.   *b*2 : 76 ; 3 : 79 ; 4 : 47 ; 5 : 42.

Commentary :

The verse contains a veiled warning to Muslims that they can expect the help of God only so long as they adhere to their covenant with Him and obey His behests.

By the words " twelve leaders " are meant the twelve Prophets of Israel who came after Moses. According to some authorities, these were the twelve " Princes " said to have been appointed by Moses (Num. 1 : 4—16).

The words قرضا حسنا (goodly loan) may either mean good deeds for which a reward is expected from God, or voluntary contributions to help the cause of religion. The verse is addressed to the Israelites.

651. Important Words :

قَاسِيَة (hardened) is derived from قسا which means : (1) it was or became hardened ; (2) it became darkened (Aqrab). Thus the words جعلنا قلوبهم قاسية rendered as, *We have hardened their hearts*, may also mean, We have made their hearts devoid of light.

نسوا (have forgotten) is derived from نسى meaning, he forgot, or he abandoned or ceased acting on (Aqrab).

خائنة (treachery) is both the noun-infinitive and the active participle from خان *i.e.*, he acted unfaithfully or treacherously.

They say خان *i.e.* he was unfaithful to the confidence or trust that he (the other party) reposed in him; he was treacherous or perfidious to him. خائنة means : (1) treachery, perfidiousness or unfaithfulness ; (2) one who is very treacherous, unfaithful or perfidious. In the latter sense the word خائنة is the intensive form of خائن . The expression خائنة الاعين used elsewhere in the Quran (40 : 20) means, a surreptitious or intentional look at a thing at which it is not allowable to look ; or the looking with a look that induces suspicion or evil opinion ; or the making of a sign with the eye to indicate a thing that one conceals in the mind ; or as some say, the contracting of the eye by way of making an obscure indication (Lane). The word خائنة may also be taken to have been used as an adjective qualifying the noun امة (people or party) which may be taken to be understood before it.

Commentary :

The words, *They pervert the words from their proper places*, may mean : (1) they tamper with the text of the Book ; or (2) they distort the true meaning of the text.

The words نسوا حظا rendered as *they have forgotten a good part*, may also be translated as, " they have abandoned and ceased to act on a goodly part."

15. And from those *also* who say, 'We are Christians,' We took a covenant, but they too have forgotten a *good* part of that with which they were exhorted. So ^aWe have caused enmity and hatred among them till the Day of Resurrection. And Allah will soon let them know what they have been doing.[652]

16. O People of the Book! there has come to you Our Messenger ^bwho unfolds to you much of what you had kept hidden of the Book and passes over much. There has come to you indeed from Allah a Light and a clear Book.[653]

وَ مِنَ الَّذِيۡنَ قَالُوۡۤا اِنَّا نَصٰرٰۤی اَخَذۡنَا مِیۡثَاقَهُمۡ فَنَسُوۡا حَظًّا مِّمَّا ذُكِّرُوۡا بِهٖ ۪ فَاَغۡرَیۡنَا بَیۡنَهُمُ الۡعَدَاوَةَ وَالۡبَغۡضَآءَ اِلٰی یَوۡمِ الۡقِیٰمَةِ ؕ وَ سَوۡفَ یُنَبِّئُهُمُ اللّٰهُ بِمَا کَانُوۡا یَصۡنَعُوۡنَ ۝

یٰۤاَهۡلَ الۡکِتٰبِ قَدۡ جَآءَکُمۡ رَسُوۡلُنَا یُبَیِّنُ لَکُمۡ کَثِیۡرًا مِّمَّا کُنۡتُمۡ تُخۡفُوۡنَ مِنَ الۡکِتٰبِ وَ یَعۡفُوۡا عَنۡ کَثِیۡرٍ ؕ قَدۡ جَآءَکُمۡ مِّنَ اللّٰهِ نُوۡرٌ وَّ کِتٰبٌ مُّبِیۡنٌ ۝

^a3 : 56 ; 5 : 65.   ^b5 : 20.

---

652. Commentary :

After referring to the Jews in the preceding verses, the Quran here refers to the Christians, who had also fallen low owing to their ceasing to act on the commandments of God.

The words, *We have caused enmity and hatred among them*, either refer to the Christians and the Jews spoken of in the preceding verse or they refer to the Christians alone as understood by the present verse. In any case they embody a great prophecy to the truth of which the whole world is a witness. Unappeasable animosity, hatred and rivalry exist not only between Christians and Jews but also between the different sections of Christians themselves. This enmity and discord are a natural result of their rejection of Islam. The Holy Prophet, who had a universal mission, brought the message of the oneness of all mankind. All nations of the world were invited to assemble under his banner and thus become welded into one nation and one people. But the People of the Book refused to accept him. So not only will Jews and Christians as

well as the sections thereof continue to remain at loggerheads with each other, but the phantom of world-peace will also continue to elude humanity till men come to render allegiance to that Great and Noble Prophet whom God sent as " a mercy for all mankind."

The Arabic word یصنعون (have been doing) is generally used concerning works of art. The allusion is thus primarily to the works of art in which Christian nations were to excel and take pride.

653. Important Words :

یعفو (passes over) is derived from عفا which gives a number of meanings for which see 2 : 110. Among others the word عفا means, it became effaced or obliterated ; or He (God) effaced or obliterated (a sin, etc.) *i.e.* forgave and pardoned. عفوت عن الحق means, I have relinquished or given up my right or what was due to me. The word العفو is also used in the sense of الترك *i.e.* the act of giving up or abandoning or leaving off or passing over (Tāj).

Commentary :

The verse refers to the suppression of many

17. Thereby does Allah guide those who seek His pleasure on the paths of peace, and [a]leads them out of darkness into light by His will, and guides them to the right path.[654]

يَهْدِىْ بِهِ اللّٰهُ مَنِ اتَّبَعَ رِضْوَانَهٗ سُبُلَ السَّلٰمِ وَيُخْرِجُهُمْ مِّنَ الظُّلُمٰتِ اِلَى النُّوْرِ بِاِذْنِهٖ وَيَهْدِيْهِمْ اِلٰى صِرَاطٍ مُّسْتَقِيْمٍ ۝

---

[a]2 : 258 ; 14 : 2 ; 33 : 44 ; 57 : 10 ; 65 : 12.

---

noble teachings and great truths by the People of the Book and draws their attention to the fact that not only are many of the truths contained in the older Books being re-taught by the Holy Prophet of Islam but also many more are being revealed and new and wider avenues of guidance have been opened, though at the same time some laws and ordinances which proved burdensome to the previous peoples or were meant only for a specific period have not been embodied in the teachings of the New Faith.

The word "Light" at the end of the verse refers to the Holy Prophet, who elsewhere in the Quran has been called "a Bright Lamp" (33 : 47), because from him later Reformers were to receive the light of divine knowledge. It may also contain a reference to the fact that the Holy Prophet was the "Seal of the Prophets" (33 : 41) in the sense that he who followed him in the most perfect manner could receive even the gift of prophethood from God—a great truth laid bare by the Holy Founder of the Ahmadiyya Movement. The Holy Prophet was, thus, a great spiritual light that could kindle other similar lights. But it must be clearly understood that since the Law of Islam is perfect in all respects and is meant for all ages to come, no other Book of Law can come after the Quran.

654. Commentary:

The pronoun in يهدى به (thereby does Allah guide) may refer either to the "Book" or the "Light" spoken of in the previous verse. The use of the word سبل (paths) in the plural number indicates that just as there are diverse kinds of difficulties and obstacles that beset the path of a spiritual wayfarer, so God has also provided for him many ways and means of deliverance and safe arrival at his destination. السلام (peace) being also one of the names of God (see 50 : 24), the words سبل السلام may mean, "the paths leading to God."

The clause, and guides them to the right path, is added to show that the God of Islam not only leads men out of darkness into light but also does so by the shortest and the straightest path, the word مستقيم (right) also meaning "straight." See 2 : 6.

18. ^aThey have indeed disbelieved who say, ' Surely, Allah is none but the Messiah, son of Mary.' Say, ' Who then has any power against Allah, if He desire to bring to naught the Messiah, son of Mary, and his mother and all those that are in the earth?' And ^bto Allah belongs the kingdom of the heavens and the earth and what is between them. He creates what He pleases ; and Allah has power to do all things.⁶⁵⁵

لَقَدْ كَفَرَ الَّذِيْنَ قَالُوْۤا اِنَّ اللّٰهَ هُوَ الْمَسِيْحُ ابْنُ مَرْيَمَ ۗ قُلْ فَمَنْ يَّمْلِكُ مِنَ اللّٰهِ شَيْئًا اِنْ اَرَادَ اَنْ يُّهْلِكَ الْمَسِيْحَ ابْنَ مَرْيَمَ وَاُمَّهٗ وَمَنْ فِى الْاَرْضِ جَمِيْعًا ۗ وَلِلّٰهِ مُلْكُ السَّمٰوٰتِ وَالْاَرْضِ وَمَا بَيْنَهُمَا ۗ يَخْلُقُ مَا يَشَآءُ ۗ وَاللّٰهُ عَلٰى كُلِّ شَىْءٍ قَدِيْرٌ ۞

---

^a5 : 73, 74.   ^bSee 3 : 190.

---

655. Important Words :

هلك (bring to naught) is derived from اهلك which is the causative form of هلك which means, he or it perished or came to naught ; or he or it came to an end and became non-existent. اهلكه means, he caused him or it to perish, or he destroyed him or it, or he brought him or it to naught (Lane). اهلكه also means, he punished him (Mufradāt). The Holy Prophet is reported to have said : اذا قال الرجل هلك الناس فهو اهلكهم *i.e.* "When a man says, such and such people have perished (*viz.*, they have become morally and spiritually ruined and their state is past recovery), it is he himself who causes them to perish by saying so, for he makes them despair of recovery and of salvation " (Muslim, ch. on *al-Birr wa'l-Ṣila.*) The word is used in this sense also elsewhere in the Quran (67 : 29 ; 8 : 43).

Commentary :

The expression هلك (bring to naught) is used here not simply in the sense of destroying but in that of destroying by punishment. It is indeed a jealous and indignant God that speaks in this verse. He condemns Christians in a tone of strong indignation and vehement reproach at their preposterous claims about the Godhead of Jesus ; and as Jesus and his mother, Mary, have become the means and object of this highly sinful doctrine, the verse fittingly refers to the divine power of punishing them also if God should so desire. It will be noted that a section of Christians looks upon Mary also as divine and superhuman.

The words, *those that are in the earth*, obviously refer to those who deify Jesus. God's purpose in using such strong language is to expose the monstrosity of the doctrine that Jesus was God or the Son of God. Elsewhere also in the Quran strong language has been used about those who hold such blasphemous beliefs and they are threatened with exemplary punishment (19 : 89—92).

The words, *what is between them*, corroborate and add force and strength to the argument given in the earlier part of the verse, at the same time hinting at the final dissolution of Christian empires as a result of the most blasphemous doctrine of the divinity of Jesus. See also 3 : 27.

What the Christians say is, " The Messiah, son of Mary, is God," and not " God is none but the Messiah " as the verse puts it. The assertion has been inverted in order to bring home to Christians their great error ; for, to say that " The Messiah is God " is really tantamount to saying that " God is none but

19. The Jews and the Christians say, *a*'We are sons of Allah and His loved ones .' Say, 'Why then does He punish you for your sins ? Nay, you are *only* human beings among those He has created.' *b*He forgives whom He pleases and punishes whom He pleases. And to Allah belongs the kingdom of the heavens and the earth and what is between them, and to Him shall be the return.656

20. O ye People of the Book ! there has come to you Our Messenger, after a break in the series of Messengers, *c*who makes *things* clear to you lest you say, 'There has come to us no bearer of glad tidings and no warner'. So a bearer of glad tidings and a warner has indeed come to you. And Allah has power to do all things.657

وَ قَالَتِ الْيَهُوْدُ وَ النَّصٰرٰى نَحْنُ اَبْنٰٓؤُا اللّٰهِ وَ اَحِبَّآؤُهٗ قُلْ فَلِمَ يُعَذِّبُكُمْ بِذُنُوْبِكُمْ بَلْ اَنْتُمْ بَشَرٌ مِّمَّنْ خَلَقَ يَغْفِرُ لِمَنْ يَّشَآءُ وَ يُعَذِّبُ مَنْ يَّشَآءُ وَ لِلّٰهِ مُلْكُ السَّمٰوٰتِ وَ الْاَرْضِ وَ مَا بَيْنَهُمَا وَ اِلَيْهِ الْمَصِيْرُ ۝

يٰٓاَهْلَ الْكِتٰبِ قَدْ جَآءَكُمْ رَسُوْلُنَا يُبَيِّنُ لَكُمْ عَلٰى فَتْرَةٍ مِّنَ الرُّسُلِ اَنْ تَقُوْلُوْا مَا جَآءَنَا مِنْ بَشِيْرٍ وَّ لَا نَذِيْرٍ فَقَدْ جَآءَكُمْ بَشِيْرٌ وَّ نَذِيْرٌ وَ اللّٰهُ عَلٰى كُلِّ شَيْءٍ قَدِيْرٌ ۝

---

*a*62 : 7.   *b*2 : 285 ; 3 : 130 ; 5 : 41.   *c*5 : 16.

---

the Messiah," But Christians, being too conscious of the weaknesses of their Messiah, dare not accept the latter proposition, which thus goes to prove the hollowness of their claim that the Messiah, son of Mary, is God.

656. Commentary :

The claim of Jews and Christians to be " the sons of God and His beloved ones " is found in 2 : 81, 112 ; 3 : 25 ; 62 : 7.

The clause, *Why then does He punish you for your sins*, contains a double argument against the preposterous claim of the People of the Book. If they are truly the sons of God and His beloved ones, why do they commit sins which is a sign of filth and uncleanness ? One springing from God and beloved of Him must certainly be above this, for God loves not those who are filthy and commit sins. Again, if they are really the sons of God and His beloved ones, why do they suffer torment and punishment while a divine being must be

above such weakness ?

657. Important Words :

فَتْرَة (interval) is the noun-infinitive from فَتَر. They say فَتَرَ الشَّيْئُ *i.e.* the thing remitted or became allayed or abated or still after vehemence ; or it became gentle after violence. They say فَتَرَ عَنْ عَمَلِهٖ *i.e.* he flagged or became remiss or languid in his work. فَتَرَ الْحَرُّ means, the heat abated or flagged after being intense and vehement. فَتْرَة means, langour or remissness ; weakness or feebleness ; an interval of time between two things ; an interval of time between two Prophets during which there is a cessation of prophetic revelation (Aqrab & Lane).

Commentary :

As generally believed, no Prophet appeared among Jews and Christians after Jesus. According to some historians, however, three Prophets did appear after Jesus, and according

21. And *remember* when Moses said to his people, 'O my people, call to mind *a*Allah's favour upon you when He appointed Prophets among you and made you kings, and gave you what He gave not to any other among the peoples.[658]

22. 'O my people, enter the Holy Land which Allah has ordained for you and do not turn back, for then you will turn losers.'

وَ اِذْ قَالَ مُوْسٰى لِقَوْمِهٖ يٰقَوْمِ اذْكُرُوْا نِعْمَةَ اللّٰهِ عَلَيْكُمْ اِذْ جَعَلَ فِيْكُمْ اَنْۢبِيَآءَ وَ جَعَلَكُمْ مُّلُوْكًا ۗ وَّ اٰتٰىكُمْ مَّا لَمْ يُؤْتِ اَحَدًا مِّنَ الْعٰلَمِيْنَ ۞

يٰقَوْمِ ادْخُلُوا الْاَرْضَ الْمُقَدَّسَةَ الَّتِيْ كَتَبَ اللّٰهُ لَكُمْ وَ لَا تَرْتَدُّوْا عَلٰۤى اَدْبَارِكُمْ فَتَنْقَلِبُوْا خٰسِرِيْنَ ۞

*a*1 : 7 ; 4 : 70 ; 19 : 59.

---

to Kalbī, Jesus was followed by four Prophets, one of them, Khālid bin Salām, appearing in Arabia. It was with regard to Khālid bin Salām that the Holy Prophet is reported to have said, "He was a Prophet to whose message his people paid no heed" (Muḥīṭ). Whatever the truth, the Holy Prophet was preceded by a period of فَتْرَة or cessation of prophethood, no Prophet of God having appeared immediately before him.

The expression, *lest you say, there has come to us no bearer of glad tidings and no warner*, points to the important truth that God never visits a people with punishment unless He first sends a Messenger to them (17 : 16), because if punishment overtakes men without the appearance of a Messenger, they can justifiably say that they are being punished without being told what their offence is and without being given the opportunity to repent and mend their ways. In the present age too the world has been visited with calamities of diverse kinds on an extraordinary scale. A Messenger, therefore, must have come. He has indeed come in the fulness of time in the person of Ahmad, the Holy Founder of the Ahmadiyya Movement.

658. Commentary :

When speaking about the raising of the

Prophets, the verse uses the word "among" which is omitted when the making of kings is mentioned. This is so because the mission of a Prophet was in those days confined to his own people to whom he was sent. Prophets have therefore been spoken of as being raised "among" them. But kings have to rule over foreign nations as well. In their case, therefore, the word has been dropped. Moreover, in the substitution of the word كُمْ (you) instead of فِيْكُمْ (among you) the allusion is to the fact that whereas each and every member of the nation to which a ruling monarch belongs possesses, as it were, dominion and sovereignty, it is not so in the case of a Prophet.

It may be noted that the word عالمين (the peoples) as used in this verse does not mean "peoples of all times", but only the people of that particular age. See also 2 : 48.

Commentary :

The expression, *ordained for you*, contains a veiled promise to the effect that God would help them and make them victorious, if the Israelites only showed the courage to step forward and enter the Holy Land. But they did not possess the requisite faith and the requisite courage and so "turned losers." See vv. 25 & 27 below.

23. They said, 'O Moses, there is in that *land* a haughty and powerful people, and we shall not enter it until they go forth from it. But if they go forth from it, then we will enter it.'⁶⁵⁹

قَالُوْا يٰمُوْسٰۤى اِنَّ فِيْهَا قَوْمًا جَبَّارِيْنَ ۖ وَاِنَّا لَنْ نَّدْخُلَهَا حَتّٰى يَخْرُجُوْا مِنْهَا ۚ فَاِنْ يَّخْرُجُوْا مِنْهَا فَاِنَّا دٰخِلُوْنَ ۩

24. Thereupon two men from among those who feared *their Lord*, on whom Allah had conferred His favour, said, 'Enter the gate, *advancing* against them; when *once* you have entered it, then surely you will be victorious. And ªput your trust in Allah, if you are believers.'⁶⁶⁰

قَالَ رَجُلَانِ مِنَ الَّذِيْنَ يَخَافُوْنَ اَنْعَمَ اللّٰهُ عَلَيْهِمَا ادْخُلُوْا عَلَيْهِمُ الْبَابَ ۚ فَاِذَا دَخَلْتُمُوْهُ فَاِنَّكُمْ غٰلِبُوْنَ ۙ وَعَلَى اللّٰهِ فَتَوَكَّلُوْۤا اِنْ كُنْتُمْ مُّؤْمِنِيْنَ ۩

ª3 : 161; 5 : 12; 9 : 51.

659. Important Words:

جَبَّارِيْن (haughty and powerful) is the plural of جَبَّار which is derived from جَبَرَ. They say جَبَرَ الْعَظْمَ (*jabar al-'aẓma*) or (*jabbar al-'aẓma*) i.e. he set the bone; he reduced it from the fractured state. جَبَرَ الرَّجُلَ (*jabar al-rajula*) or (*jabbar al-rajula*) means, he restored the man from the state of poverty and weakness to that of wealth and strength. جَبَرْتُ الْيَتِيْمَ means, I put the affairs of the orphan into good order. جَبَرَهُ means, he compelled and forced him against his will. جَبَّار means, one who magnifies himself and behaves proudly, haughtily and insolently; one who slays when in anger or one who slays unjustly; one who domineers over others by absolute force and power; one extravagant in acts of wrong-doing, disobedience and rebellion; one huge, tall and strong; a giant. When used about God الْجَبَّار means, One Who can force His creatures to obey His commands; the Supreme, the Unattainable, the High above His creatures; the Restorer of the poor and the weak to wealth and power; the Reformer of the people by raising them from a low state to a high one (Lane & Aqrab).

Commentary:

Compare this insolent and cowardly attitude of the companions of Moses to the willing and almost unbelievable sacrifices of the Companions of the Holy Prophet, who were ever eager to jump into the very jaws of death at the bidding of their Master.

660. Important Words:

عَلَيْهِم (against them). The word عَلَى as a particle has several meanings. Here it gives the meaning of "against" (Lane). The Quran says وَلَهُمْ عَلَيَّ ذَنْب i.e. and they have a crime or offence standing against me (26 : 15). In his *Arabic Grammar*, Wright says that the particle عَلَى is sometimes used in "a hostile sense in which case it can be generally rendered as 'against' or 'upon,' as in خَرَجَ عَلَيْه i.e. he went out against him or he rebelled against him."

Commentary:

The two "men" spoken of here are generally supposed to be Joshua, the son of Nun, and Caleb, the son of Jephunneh (Num. 14:6). But from the context Moses and Aaron appear more likely to be the two "men" here referred to.

The word رَجُل (man) is thus here expressive of manliness and courage. By using this word, the Quran means to say that of that big host of cowardly people there were only two men who were truly brave and courageous. That these two brave men were Moses and Aaron themselves may also be inferred from the fact that when these two " men " spoke to their people, and urged them to " enter " the land, the latter, in reply, addressed none other but Moses, saying, *O Moses, we will never enter it so long as they remain in it* (5:25), thus making it clear that it was Moses himself who had spoken to them the words contained in this verse. Again, when the people refused to obey Moses, he is reported to have prayed to God, saying, *My Lord, I have power over none but myself and my brother, therefore make Thou a distinction between us and the rebellious people* (5:26). Now, if the two " men " had been other than Moses and Aaron, they should have certainly been included in his prayer by Moses, because they had deserved it by boldly offering to enter the land in spite of resistance, exhorting others also to do so. But Moses prayed only for himself and his brother, which shows that the two men whom God praises as "men" (*i.e.* brave men) and of whom He speaks as His favoured ones were Moses and Aaron themselves. God does not name them but simply speaks of them as رَجُلاَن. *i.e.* " two brave men " in order to praise their manliness and courage and at the same time to condemn by implication the cowardice of the other Israelites who were with them.

The expression, *enter the gate advancing against them*, possesses a spiritual connotation as well. For every person there is a " holy land," which is his goal and paradise. Allah has " ordained " this " holy land " for man

(5 : 22) because he has been created for it. But the cowardly and the low-spirited are always afraid of entering it. They are too timorous to face " the rebellious ones" *i.e.* the evil ones and their own evil inclinations. They desire to enter Heaven without deserving it, without any exertion on their part, without facing and fighting their evil passions and without fighting those who stand in their way. They tremble and quail before the trials and tribulations that confront them. But here too God has created for every person " two men " *i.e.* two wise counsellors who encourage him and exhort him not to be afraid of difficulties and to follow undauntedly the path that leads to eternal happiness and everlasting bliss. These two counsellors are (1) human reason and (2) man's pure and unsullied nature. These two go on telling man and urging him that he need only be up and doing and God will help him. He should boldly face trials and God will make everything easy for him, and he will come out of the struggle victorious and triumphant. Most men, however, wish that the power of their enemies should break of itself, but it cannot break without their using the weapon of self-sacrifice. " Forty years," as hinted in 5 : 27 below, is the time required by man to attain to perfect manhood. This is a sufficiently long time. If he does not mend his ways during this period and defies the dictates of reason and conscience, he is lost and there is little hope for him. But if he makes up his mind boldly to meet the evil influences, he may be saved. He need only take heart and make bold to enter the struggle, and what appears to him to be a thick jungle of difficulties will turn out to be a garden, the seeming " Hell " assuming the form of a veritable " Heaven."

25. They said, 'O Moses, we will never enter it so long as they remain in it. Therefore, go thou and thy Lord and fight, *and* here we sit.'[661]

قَالُوْا يٰمُوْسٰۤى اِنَّا لَنْ نَّدْخُلَهَاۤ اَبَدًا مَّا دَامُوْا فِيْهَا فَاذْهَبْ اَنْتَ وَرَبُّكَ فَقَاتِلَاۤ اِنَّا هٰهُنَا قٰعِدُوْنَ ۟

26. He said, 'My Lord, I have power over none but myself and my brother; therefore make thou a distinction between us and the rebellious people.'[661A]

قَالَ رَبِّ اِنِّىْ لَاۤ اَمْلِكُ اِلَّا نَفْسِىْ وَاَخِىْ فَافْرُقْ بَيْنَنَا وَبَيْنَ الْقَوْمِ الْفٰسِقِيْنَ ۟

27. *God* said: [a]'Verily, it shall be forbidden them for forty years; in distraction shall they wander through the land. So grieve not over the rebellious people.'[662]

قَالَ فَاِنَّهَا مُحَرَّمَةٌ عَلَيْهِمْ اَرْبَعِيْنَ سَنَةً يَتِيْهُوْنَ فِى الْاَرْضِ فَلَا تَاْسَ عَلَى الْقَوْمِ الْفٰسِقِيْنَ ۟

[a]2 : 244.

---

661. Commentary :

The companions of Moses perhaps never fell so low as on the present occasion. They were cowardly, faithless and slothful. Compare with this the noble example of the Companions of the Holy Prophet of Islam. There is a report to the effect that when the Holy Prophet, with a handful of his ill-equipped Companions, intended to go forth to meet the vastly superior and much better-equipped Meccan force at Badr, he consulted them about it. Thereupon one of the Companions stood up and addressed the Holy Prophet in the following memorable words, " We would not say to thee, O Prophet of God ! as said the companions of Moses, 'go thou and thy Lord and fight and here we sit '. On the contrary, O Prophet of the Lord ! we are ever with thee and we will go with thee whither thou goest. We will fight the enemy on thy right and on thy left and in thy front and behind thy back ; and we trust God that thou wilt see from us what will comfort thine eyes." The tradition says that when the Holy Prophet heard these words, his face beamed with delight ; and no wonder (Bukhārī & Hishām).

661A. Commentary :

Even if, as the Bible says, " the two men " referred to in 5 : 24 above were Joshua and Caleb, the present prayer of Moses remains true ; for Aaron being a Prophet of God was the only one truly entitled to the guarantee expressed by Moses.

662. Important Words :

يَتِيْهُوْنَ (they shall wander in distraction) is derived from تَاهَ meaning : (1) he lost his way in the desert ; (2) he was or became confounded or perplexed ; (3) he went away in the land confounded or perplexed and was unable to see his right course ; (4) his intellect or mind was or became disordered and confused and he perished ; (5) he magnified himself or behaved proudly or insolently (Aqrab & Lane).

Commentary :

When the Israelites behaved in a cowardly manner, God decreed that they should remain in the desert for a period of 40 years so that the life of the desert should invigorate them and strengthen their morals. In the meantime, the old generation became practically extinct and the younger generation grew brave

5 28. And relate to them truly the story of the two sons of Adam, when they *each* offered an offering, and it was accepted from one of them and was not accepted from the other. The latter said, 'I will surely kill thee.' The former replied, 'Allah accepts only from the righteous.[663]

وَاتْلُ عَلَيْهِمْ نَبَاَ ابْنَىْ اٰدَمَ بِالْحَقِّ اِذْ قَرَّبَا قُرْبَانًا فَتُقُبِّلَ مِنْ اَحَدِهِمَا وَلَمْ يُتَقَبَّلْ مِنَ الْاٰخَرِ قَالَ لَاَقْتُلَنَّكَ قَالَ اِنَّمَا يَتَقَبَّلُ اللّٰهُ مِنَ الْمُتَّقِيْنَ ۝

29. 'If thou stretch out thy hand against me to kill me, I am not going to stretch out my hand against thee to kill thee. I do fear Allah, the Lord of the Universe.[664]

لَئِنْۢ بَسَطْتَ اِلَىَّ يَدَكَ لِتَقْتُلَنِىْ مَآ اَنَا بِبَاسِطٍ يَّدِىَ اِلَيْكَ لِاَقْتُلَكَ اِنِّىْۤ اَخَافُ اللّٰهَ رَبَّ الْعٰلَمِيْنَ ۝

---

and strong enough to conquer the Promised Land. See also note on 5 : 24 above. For the relevant portion of the Bible see Num. ch. 14.

663. Important Words :

قَرَّبَا (they offered) and قُرْبَانًا (offering) are both derived from قَرُبَ (*qaruba*) which means, he or it was or became near, either in place or in station or grade or rank. قَرَّبَهُ (*qarraba-hū*) means, he caused or made him to become near; he made him to be a near associate; or he made him an object of favour or honour. قَرَّبَ اللّٰه قُرْبَانًا means, he offered or presented to God an offering or oblation. Hence قُرْبَانٌ means, an offering or oblation; a sacrifice; anything by means of which one seeks nearness to God; a near or particular or favourite associate or companion (Lane).

Commentary :

As sacrifice is at the root of all success, whether individual or national, the Quran here fittingly turns to the subject of sacrifice, the lack of which proved the fall of the followers of Moses. "The two sons of Adam" may be taken in the figurative sense as well, meaning any two individuals from among mankind.

The words, *Allah accepts only from the righteous*, addressed by Abel to his brother Cain (both sons of Adam) are intended to mean that the

latter would gain nothing by slaying the former, except that he would become all the more removed from righteousness—a quality essential for the acceptance of an offering.

The concluding words of the verse point to the important truth that in sacrifice mere outward form is nothing. It is only the underlying spirit that makes it acceptable and fruitful. The story is continued in the following verses.

664. Commentary :

The expression, *I am not going to stretch out my hand against thee to kill thee*, does not mean that Abel did not even desire to defend himself. These words only mean that if he were forced to stretch forth his hand towards his brother, it would not be with the intention of slaying him, but only in self-defence. The declaration was necessary, for there are cases in which both the slayer and the slain become equally guilty. The Holy Prophet is reported to have said that not unoften "both the slayer and the slain go to Hell." This ḥadīth obviously refers to such slain persons as engage in a fight with the intention of killing their opponents, but it so happens that the latter get the better of them and kill them. In such cases, the intention of both parties

30. ' I wish that thou shouldst bear my sin as well as thy sin, and thus be among the inmates of the Fire, and that is the reward of those who do wrong.'[665]

اِنِّیْۤ اُرِیْدُ اَنْ تَبُوْٓاَ بِاِثْمِیْ وَاِثْمِكَ فَتَكُوْنَ مِنْ اَصْحٰبِ النَّارِ وَذٰلِكَ جَزٰٓؤُا الظّٰلِمِیْنَ ۝

31. But his mind induced him to kill his brother, so he killed him and became one of the losers.[666]

فَطَوَّعَتْ لَهٗ نَفْسُهٗ قَتْلَ اَخِیْهِ فَقَتَلَهٗ فَاَصْبَحَ مِنَ الْخٰسِرِیْنَ ۝

being equally criminal, both are guilty and both deserve to be cast into Hell. But Abel, who desired to live righteously and die righteously, would not stain his conduct even in a moment of extreme danger and wanted to take good care that he did not overstep the limits of the right of self-defence.

665. Important Words :

اُرِیْد (I wish) is derived from رَاد i.e. he or it went to and fro ; or he desired or sought (a thing). اَرَاد means, he intended or willed or wished or desired or sought. But sometimes the word does not express an actual will or wish but simply a practical state or condition likely to develop in a certain manner. The Arabs say of a seriously sick person یُرِیْد اَنْ یَّمُوْت (lit. he wishes to die) meaning, he is about to die or his condition bespeaks of nearness of death. The Quran says یُرِیْد اَنْ یَّنْقَضَّ viz. the wall intended to fall down i.e. it was about or ready to fall down (18 : 78) (Aqrab & Lane).

Commentary :

The verse does not mean, as some may be led to think, that Abel desired his brother, Cain, to be cast into Hell. What he meant by the word اُرِیْد (I wish), as explained under Important Words above, was simply that the natural and inevitable consequence of his own non-aggressive attitude would be that his brother would go to Hell. In fact, by using

this expression Abel desired to dissuade Cain from perpetration of the horrible crime of fratricide by picturing to him its awful consequences. He told his brother that, as for himself, he would rather die the death of one sinned against than raise his hand to kill him. The result of this would be that he (Cain) would take upon himself the burden of his (Abel's) sin (i.e. that of slaying him) as well as that of other sins of his own.

The expression may be explained in another way also. The Holy Prophet is reported to have said that on the Day of Judgement the good deeds of transgressors would be transferred to the account of the persons whom they had wronged and if transgressors had no good deeds to their account, the sins of the persons transgressed against would be transferred to them and thus wrongdoers would bear not only their own sins but also those of the persons whom they had wronged (Muslim, ch. on al-Birr wa'l-Ṣila).

666. Commentary :

Instead of directly and briefly saying that " he killed his brother," the verse expresses the same idea in a somewhat longer sentence, viz., his mind induced him to kill his brother, so he killed him. This is done to point to the great truth that it is man's own نَفْس or mind, or more properly his own " self", which often becomes the source of evil for him.

32. Then Allah sent a raven which scratched in the ground, that He might show him how to hide the corpse of his brother. He said, ' Woe is me ! Am I not able to be even like this raven so that I may hide the corpse of my brother ? ' And then he became regretful.⁶⁶⁷

فَبَعَثَ اللّٰهُ غُرَابًا يَّبْحَثُ فِي الْاَرْضِ لِيُرِيَهُ كَيْفَ يُوَارِيْ سَوْءَةَ اَخِيْهِ ۚ قَالَ يٰوَيْلَتٰۤى اَعَجَزْتُ اَنْ اَكُوْنَ مِثْلَ هٰذَا الْغُرَابِ فَاُوَارِيَ سَوْءَةَ اَخِيْ ۚ فَاَصْبَحَ مِنَ النّٰدِمِيْنَ ۝

33. On account of this, We prescribed for the children of Israel that whosoever killed a person—unless it be for *killing* a person or for creating disorder in the land—it shall be as if he had killed all mankind ; and whoso gave life to one, it shall be as if he had given life to all mankind. And ᵃOur Messengers came to them with clear Signs, yet even after that, many of them commit excesses in the land.⁶⁶⁸

مِنْ اَجْلِ ذٰلِكَ ۚۛ كَتَبْنَا عَلٰى بَنِيْۤ اِسْرَآءِيْلَ اَنَّهٗ مَنْ قَتَلَ نَفْسًۢا بِغَيْرِ نَفْسٍ اَوْ فَسَادٍ فِي الْاَرْضِ فَكَاَنَّمَا قَتَلَ النَّاسَ جَمِيْعًا ۚ وَمَنْ اَحْيَاهَا فَكَاَنَّمَاۤ اَحْيَا النَّاسَ جَمِيْعًا ۚ وَلَقَدْ جَآءَتْهُمْ رُسُلُنَا بِالْبَيِّنٰتِ ثُمَّ اِنَّ كَثِيْرًا مِّنْهُمْ بَعْدَ ذٰلِكَ فِي الْاَرْضِ لَمُسْرِفُوْنَ ۝

ᵃ7 : 102 ; 9 : 70 ; 14 : 10 ; 40 : 23.

---

667. Commentary :

Commentators differ as to whether the incident of the raven mentioned in the present verse was an actual fact or whether it is merely meant as a parable. It is not at all improbable that an incident of this nature might have actually occurred. The study of the ways and habits of birds has led to many useful discoveries. For the Biblical story of the two sons of Adam see Gen. 4 : 1—15 ; also the Jerusalem Targum.

668. Commentary :

This verse draws a great moral from the simple incident related in the foregoing verses. The incident of the two sons of Adam had a parallel in the history of nations, as hinted in the words, *On account of this We prescribed for the children of Israel, etc.* If the incident simply related to " the two sons of Adam " it had obviously no direct bearing on the Israelites.

As a matter of fact, what is hinted at is that an incident similar to that of the two sons of Adam mentioned here but of much greater import was to take place later. There was to appear among the brethren of the Israelites a Prophet whose offering God was to favour with acceptance, while that of his brethren, the Israelites, was to be rejected owing to their impiety and lack of righteousness. This was to enrage the Israelites against that Prophet and they were to become thirsty for his blood on account of envy, even as Cain had become thirsty for the blood of his brother Abel. The story of Cain and Abel was, therefore, intended, as hinted in the opening words of this verse, to serve as a warning for the Israelites. The Prophet meant to be raised from among the brethren of the Israelites was to be no ordinary soul. He was to be a World-Reformer, ordained to bring the eternal Law for mankind whose entire future depended on him and

34. The reward of *those who wage war against Allah and His Messenger and strive to create disorder in the land is only this that they be slain or crucified or their hands and their feet be cut off on alternate sides, or they be expelled from the land. That shall be a disgrace for them in this world, and in the Hereafter they shall have a great punishment;[669]

اِنَّمَا جَزٰٓؤُا الَّذِيۡنَ يُحَارِبُوۡنَ اللّٰهَ وَرَسُوۡلَهٗ وَيَسۡعَوۡنَ فِى الۡاَرۡضِ فَسَادًا اَنۡ يُّقَتَّلُوۡۤا اَوۡ يُصَلَّبُوۡۤا اَوۡ تُقَطَّعَ اَيۡدِيۡهِمۡ وَاَرۡجُلُهُمۡ مِّنۡ خِلَافٍ اَوۡ يُنۡفَوۡا مِنَ الۡاَرۡضِ ذٰلِكَ لَهُمۡ خِزۡيٌ فِى الدُّنۡيَا وَلَهُمۡ فِى الۡاٰخِرَةِ عَذَابٌ عَظِيۡمٌ ۙ

35. Except those *who repent before you have them in your power. So know that Allah is Most Forgiving *and* Merciful.[670]

اِلَّا الَّذِيۡنَ تَابُوۡا مِنۡ قَبۡلِ اَنۡ تَقۡدِرُوۡا عَلَيۡهِمۡ ۚ فَاعۡلَمُوۡۤا اَنَّ اللّٰهَ غَفُوۡرٌ رَّحِيۡمٌ ۟

---

*9 : 107.   *4 : 18.

---

therefore his slaying was equivalent to the slaying of the whole of mankind, and the preservation of his life was, as it were, the preservation of the life of the whole of mankind. This great soul had *killed no person, nor had it created disorder in the land.*

The advent of this Prophet was foretold in the Bible (Deut. 18 : 18—22), and therein it was also announced that God would demand requital of those who did not hearken to this Prophet.

669. Commentary :

The verse has two applications. Figuratively it applies to the People of the Book who, by rejecting the Prophet from among their brethren (see the preceding verse), were, as it were, waging war against God. The punishment which the verse prescribes for them finds a fitting illustration in their history. Taken in its apparent sense, the verse lays down the different forms of punishment that may be meted out to those who wage war against innocent Muslims, killing and slaying them and creating disorder in the land.

The object underlying the injunction embodied in the words, *their hands and their feet be cut off on alternate sides,* is, on the one hand, to disable the culprit from carrying on a war of aggression, and on the other, to leave him fit enough to earn his living by doing some work. The cutting off of the hand and the foot on the same side would leave the victim utterly helpless. The verse also shows that Islam does not hesitate to take extreme measures to uproot an evil when the interests of society or the State demand it. Islam is not a religion of false sentiments but of sound judgement and true reason. See also the next verse.

670. Commentary :

This and the preceding verse refer, not to ordinary dacoits and robbers, as is wrongly assumed by some, but to rebels and those miscreants who make aggressive war upon the Muslim State, as is clear from the words, *who wage war against Allah and His Messenger.* This inference finds further support from the fact that the present verse promises amnesty

36. O ye who believe fear Allah and *seek the way of approach unto Him and *strive in His way that you may prosper.⁶⁷¹

يَآَيُّهَا الَّذِيْنَ اٰمَنُوا اتَّقُوا اللّٰهَ وَ ابْتَغُوْۤا اِلَيْهِ الْوَسِيْلَةَ وَ جَاهِدُوْا فِيْ سَبِيْلِهٖ لَعَلَّكُمْ تُفْلِحُوْنَ ۝

37. Surely, if *those who disbelieve had all that is in the earth and as much over again, to ransom themselves there-with from the punishment of the Day of Resurrection, it would not be accept-ed from them ; and they shall have a painful punishment.

اِنَّ الَّذِيْنَ كَفَرُوْا لَوْ اَنَّ لَهُمْ مَّا فِي الْاَرْضِ جَمِيْعًا وَّ مِثْلَهٗ مَعَهٗ لِيَفْتَدُوْا بِهٖ مِنْ عَذَابِ يَوْمِ الْقِيٰمَةِ مَا تُقُبِّلَ مِنْهُمْ ۚ وَ لَهُمْ عَذَابٌ اَلِيْمٌ ۝

*17:58.   *9:41 ; 22:79.   *13:19 ; 39:48.

---

to offenders if they repent. But obviously those who commit heinous offences against individuals or against society, such as dacoits, robbers and thieves, cannot, in ordinary circumstances, be pardoned by the State even if they repent. They must suffer the penalty of their wicked deeds as prescribed by the Law. Surely, repentance may secure for them pardon from God, but the powers of the State are limited in this respect. Political offenders, however, may be forgiven if they repent and desist from further acts of rebellion and other offences against the State.

671. Important Words :

الْوَسِيْلَة (way of approach) is the noun-infinitive from وسل . They say وسل الى الله بعمل i.e. he did a deed by which he became near to God. وسل اليه بكذا means, he sought to bring himself near to him, or to approach or gain access to him, or to advance himself in his favour. وسيلة, therefore, signifies, a means of access to a thing; a means of becoming near to, or intimate with, a thing or person; honourable rank with a king : degree ; affinity ; a tie or connection (Lane).

Commentary :

It is wrong to interpret the word وسيلة as meaning " an intermediary between man and God "; such an interpretation is not only unsupported by the usage of the Arabic language, but is also opposed to the teachings of the Quran and the sayings of the Holy Prophet. The Quran says that those whom people invoke beside God and whom they desire to make intermediaries between them-selves and God in order to attain His nearness are themselves in need of attaining His nearness (17 : 58). The Holy Prophet is also reported to have said : " Ask for وسيلة (nearness of God) for me," i.e. pray to God that He may grant me His special nearness. The prayer after the usual call to Prayer includes the words, " O God ! give Muhammad *waṣila*," meaning that God may vouchsafe to the Prophet increasingly greater nearness to Himself, and not that he may have someone to act as intermediary between him and God.

The words that follow, viz., *strive in His way*, also point to the same interpretation; for they describe the means by which the nearness of God may be attained.

38. They will wish to come out of the Fire, but they will not be able to come out of it, and they shall have a lasting punishment.[671A]

يُرِيْدُوْنَ اَنْ يَّخْرُجُوْا مِنَ النَّارِ وَمَاهُمْ بِخٰرِجِيْنَ مِنْهَا وَلَهُمْ عَذَابٌ مُّقِيْمٌ ۝

39. And *as for* the man who steals and the woman who steals, cut off their hands in retribution of their offence as an exemplary punishment from Allah. And Allah is Mighty, Wise.[672]

وَالسَّارِقُ وَالسَّارِقَةُ فَاقْطَعُوْٓا اَيْدِيَهُمَا جَزَآءً بِمَا كَسَبَا نَكَالًا مِّنَ اللّٰهِ وَاللّٰهُ عَزِيْزٌ حَكِيْمٌ ۝

40. But [a]whoso repents after his transgression and amends, then will Allah surely turn to him in mercy; verily, Allah is Most Forgiving *and* Merciful.

فَمَنْ تَابَ مِنْ بَعْدِ ظُلْمِهٖ وَاَصْلَحَ فَاِنَّ اللّٰهَ يَتُوْبُ عَلَيْهِ اِنَّ اللّٰهَ غَفُوْرٌ رَّحِيْمٌ ۝

---

[a]6 : 55; 20 : 83; 25 : 72.

671A. Commentary :

The word مُقِيْم rendered here as "lasting" does not mean "never ending" but simply very long and not merely transitory. See also 11 : 108, 199.

672. Commentary :

In this verse the words, *the man who steals*, have been put before the words, *the woman who steals*, because stealing is more common among men than among women, while in 24 : 3 the word *fornicatress* precedes the word *fornicator* because the guilt of fornication is generally more easily proved against women than against men. This arrangement of words shows that there exists not only an intelligent order in the verses of the Quran, as shown elsewhere, but also an intelligent order in its words as well.

The punishment prescribed for a thief in this verse may appear to be too severe in the sight of those who are swayed by false sentiments. But the experience of the world shows that punishment, if it is to be deterrent, should be severe and exemplary. It is better to be severe to one and save a thousand than to be indulgent to all and ruin many. The God of Islam would not make Muslims spoilt children. When Islam was in power, there were very few cases of the cutting-off of the hands of thieves for the obvious reason that in view of the deterrent punishment prescribed by Islam there were very few cases of theft. Nowadays, however, when false sentiment prevails, thieves are given a light punishment, with the result that cases of theft are appallingly on the increase. He is certainly not a good surgeon who hesitates to amputate a rotten limb and thereby destroys the whole body.

As for the definition of the word يد (hand) 'Alī, Son-in-law and Fourth Successor of the Holy Prophet, holds that only the fingers of a thief are to be cut off (Ma'ānī, ii. 304); while most scholars are of the view that the hand is to be cut off at the wrist.

Theologians differ as to the least amount of money or property stolen for which the prescribed punishment is to be inflicted. Imām Abū Ḥanīfa held it to be ten *dirhems*, while Imām Mālik and Imām Shāfi'ī considered three *dirhems* or a quarter of a *dīnār* to be the

41. Dost thou not know that ªAllah is He to Whom belongs the kingdom of the heavens and the earth ? He punishes whom He pleases and forgives whom He pleases ; and Allah has power to do all things.672A

42. O Messenger *of Ours*, let not those grieve thee who hastily fall into disbelief—those who say with their mouths, 'We believe,' but their hearts believe not. And among the Jews *too* are those who would fondly listen to any lie—ᵇwho listen for *conveying it to* another people who have not come to thee. ᶜThey pervert words after their being put in their right places ; and say, ' If you are given this, then accept it, but if you are not given this, then beware ! ' And as for him whom Allah desires to try, thou shalt not avail him aught against Allah. These are they whose hearts Allah has not been pleased to purify ; they shall have disgrace in this world, and in the Hereafter they shall have a severe punishment.673

ª5 : 19 ; 48 : 15.   ᵇ9 : 47.   ᶜ2 : 76 ; 3 : 79 ; 4 : 47.

---

least amount, *dirhem* and *dīnār* being old silver and gold coins respectively. Both the above views are based on different interpretations of the sayings of the Holy Prophet. A *dirhem* or a drachm (dram) is believed to be one-sixteenth part of an oz. in avoirdupois weight or one-eighth part of an oz. in apothecaries weight, while a *dīnār* is equal to 71 barley-corns and a half (Lane and New Standard Dictionary).

672A **Commentary :**

Expressions like, *He punishes whom He pleases and forgives whom He pleases*, do not mean that the divine government of the universe is arbitrary and is based on no system or law.

Such expressions are only intended to point out that, God being the final authority in the universe, His word is the law, there being no appeal against His orders. So man should be extremely careful in following His wish and carrying out His commandments. But, as God has Himself ordained, " His mercy surpasses or outweighs His anger " (Bukhārī), and the universe is governed by " set laws of good and evil " (Muslim, ch. on *Imān*).

673. Commentary :

The expression سمّاعون للكذب (who would fondly listen to any lie) is capable of bearing two meanings : (1) they listen to you in order

43. They are habitual listeners to falsehood, ^adevourers of things forbidden. If, then, they come to thee for judgement, judge between them or turn aside from them. And if thou turn aside from them, they cannot harm thee at all. And if thou judge, judge between them with justice. Surely, Allah loves those who are just.⁶⁷⁴

44. And how will they make thee *their* judge when they have with them the Torah, wherein is Allah's judgement? Yet, in spite of that they turn their backs; and certainly they will not believe.⁶⁷⁵

سَمِعُوْنَ لِلْكَذِبِ اَكّٰلُوْنَ لِلسُّحْتِ فَاِنْ جَآءُوْكَ فَاحْكُمْ بَيْنَهُمْ اَوْ اَعْرِضْ عَنْهُمْ وَاِنْ تُعْرِضْ عَنْهُمْ فَلَنْ يَّضُرُّوْكَ شَيْئًا وَاِنْ حَكَمْتَ فَاحْكُمْ بَيْنَهُمْ بِالْقِسْطِ اِنَّ اللّٰهَ يُحِبُّ الْمُقْسِطِيْنَ ۝

وَكَيْفَ يُحَكِّمُوْنَكَ وَعِنْدَهُمُ التَّوْرٰىةُ فِيْهَا حُكْمُ اللّٰهِ ثُمَّ يَتَوَلَّوْنَ مِنْ بَعْدِ ذٰلِكَ وَمَآ اُولٰٓئِكَ بِالْمُؤْمِنِيْنَ ۝

---

^a5 : 63, 64.

to lie, *i.e.*, they come to you so that they may listen to your words, and then go out and distort and twist your words and their meanings before their own people and ascribe to you things which you did not say or mean; (2) they hearken to lies and accept them, *i.e.*, they believe the lies which others utter about you and accept them as true. Similarly, the clause معاعون لقوم آخرين (who listen for *conveying it to* another people) means: (1) they listen (to you) for the sake of another people; *i.e.* they come and listen to what you say in order to report it to another people; (2) they believe what others say about you and take it as true.

674. Important Words:

سحت (things forbidden) is the noun-infinitive from سحت. They say سحته *i.e.* he extirpated or destroyed it utterly. سحت شعره means, he removed his hair utterly (in shaving and cutting). سحت فى تجارته means, he earned foul or unlawful gain in his trade. An Arab would say ماله سحت *i.e.* his property may be destroyed with impunity. سحت therefore means, a thing which is forbidden or

unlawful; that which is foul and of bad repute; a bribe that is given to a judge or the like; anything little or small in quantity or number; or anything paltry, mean and inconsiderable (Lane).

Commentary:

The words اكّالون للسحت mean: (1) that the Jews devour things that are forbidden and unlawful; or (2) they devour things the result of which is spiritual ruin and national destruction; or (3) they do not hesitate to take paltry and mean things unlawfully; or (4) they accept bribes. For an explanation of the words سماعون للكذب see the previous verse.

675. Commentary:

The verse means to say that when the Jews do not accept the verdict of their own Book which they believe to be the word of God, how can they be expected to accept the decision of the Holy Prophet which they do not believe as such. Their coming to the Prophet and seeking his judgement in their disputes in the presence of their own Book exposes the wickedness of their motives.

45. Surely We sent down *the Torah wherein was guidance and light. By it did the Prophets, who were obedient *to Us*, judge for the Jews, as did the godly people and those learned *in the Law ;* for they were required to preserve the Book of Allah, and *because* they were guardians over it. Therefore fear not men but fear Me; and *barter not My Signs for a paltry price. And *whoso judges not by that which Allah has sent down, these it is who are the disbelievers.[676]

اِنَّآ اَنْزَلْنَا التَّوْرٰىةَ فِيْهَا هُدًى وَّنُوْرٌ ۚ يَحْكُمُ بِهَا النَّبِيُّوْنَ الَّذِيْنَ اَسْلَمُوْا لِلَّذِيْنَ هَادُوْا وَالرَّبَّانِيُّوْنَ وَالْاَحْبَارُ بِمَا اسْتُحْفِظُوْا مِنْ كِتٰبِ اللّٰهِ وَكَانُوْا عَلَيْهِ شُهَدَآءَ ۚ فَلَا تَخْشَوُا النَّاسَ وَاخْشَوْنِ وَلَا تَشْتَرُوْا بِاٰيٰتِيْ ثَمَنًا قَلِيْلًا ۚ وَمَنْ لَّمْ يَحْكُمْ بِمَآ اَنْزَلَ اللّٰهُ فَاُولٰٓئِكَ هُمُ الْكٰفِرُوْنَ ۝

---

*6 : 92 ; 7 : 155.   *2 : 42.   *5 : 46, 48.

The words, *wherein is Allah's judgement*, do not mean that the Quran regarded the Torah as it existed at the time of the Holy Prophet to be God's judgement on matters of dispute. The words have simply been used to express the attitude of the Jews towards the Torah. But at the same time it must not be understood that the Quran regards the Torah in its present form as devoid of all truth. In spite of its text having been tampered with, it does contain certain ordinances, laws and truths in their original, pure form.

676. Important Words :

ربانيون (godly people). See 3 : 80.

احبار (learned men) is the plural of حبر. They say حبر *i.e.* he made it beautiful; or he made him happy; or he treated him with honour. حبر (*hibr*) or حبر (*habr*) means, a learned man of the Jews; or any learned man; a good or righteous man (Lane & Aqrab).

استحفظوا (were required to preserve) is in the passive voice being formed from حفظ. They say حفظه *i.e.* he kept it or preserved it or guarded it or protected it; or he prevented it from perishing or becoming lost. استحفظه

(in the active voice) means, he asked him to keep or guard or preserve it from perishing or becoming lost; or he asked him to be careful of, or attentive to, it; or he placed it with him to preserve or guard or take care of it; or he entrusted him with it or gave it to him in trust (Lane).

Commentary :

In this verse the Quran brings home to the Jews the charge mentioned in the previous verse. When even the Prophets of God who followed Moses were required to judge according to the Torah, who are they to refuse to refer their disputes to it ?

The words, *Therefore fear not men but fear Me, and barter not My Signs for a paltry price*, mean that the referring by the Jews of their disputes to the Holy Prophet meant that they no longer looked upon the Torah as the revealed word of God, and also that they had complete faith in the honesty, truthfulness and justice of the Holy Prophet. If such was the case, and there were also clear prophecies in their scriptures bearing witness to his truth, then their refusal to believe in him showed that they feared men more than they feared God. Moreover, the rejection of the Holy

46. And therein We prescribed for them : A life for a life, and an eye for an eye, and a nose for a nose, and an ear for an ear, and a tooth for a tooth, and for *other* injuries equitable retaliation. And whoso waives the right thereto, it shall be an expiation for his *own* sins; and *a*whoso judges not by what Allah has sent down, these it is who are wrongdoers.⁶⁷⁷

47. And *b*We caused Jesus, son of Mary, to follow in their footsteps, *c*fulfilling that which was *revealed* before him in the Torah; and We gave him the Gospel which contained guidance and light, fulfilling that which was *revealed* before it in the Torah, and a guidance and an admonition for the God-fearing.⁶⁷⁸

---

*a*5 : 45, 48.   *b*2 : 88; 57 : 28.   *c*3 : 51; 61 : 7.

Prophet meant not only the rejection of those prophecies but of Moses himself, who brought the Book which contains those prophecies.

It is also clear from this verse that it is not necessary for every Prophet to bring a new Law and not to be the follower of another Prophet or Book. The Prophets that appeared among the Jews after Moses, including Jesus, brought no new Law but followed Moses and acted upon the Law that was revealed to him. Says the verse, *By it did the Prophets, who were obedient to Us, judge for the Jews.* The Prophets who judged the Jews by the Torah were obviously subject to the Law of the Torah and had no Law of their own.

677. Commentary :

As the law mentioned in this verse is clearly stated to have belonged to the Torah, though

it is not to be found in the Bible as we now have it, the words, *And whoso waives the right thereto,* constitute clear evidence of the fact that the teaching about forgiveness of which Christians boast so much was no monopoly of the Gospels. It was contained in the Torah also, though at the same time there can be no denying the fact that the teachings of Moses lay extra stress on retaliation, as do those of Jesus on forgiveness and non-resistance.

678. Commentary :

The words, *We caused Jesus, son of Mary, to follow in their footsteps,* show that, like the Prophets who preceded him, Jesus also was a follower of the Law of Moses, the Gospels being only an exposition of selected teachings of the Torah suited to those times.

48. And let the People of the Gospel judge according to what Allah has revealed therein, and *a*whoso judges not by what Allah has revealed, these it is who are the rebellious.[679]

وَلْيَحْكُمْ اَهْلُ الْاِنْجِيلِ بِمَا اَنْزَلَ اللّٰهُ فِيْهِ ۖ وَمَنْ لَّمْ يَحْكُمْ بِمَا اَنْزَلَ اللّٰهُ فَاُولٰٓئِكَ هُمُ الْفٰسِقُوْنَ ۝

49. And *b*We have revealed unto thee the Book comprising the truth *and* fulfilling that which was *revealed* before it in the Book, and as a guardian over it. *c*Judge, therefore, between them by what Allah has revealed, and follow not their evil inclinations, *turning* away from the truth which has come to thee. For each of you We prescribed a clear spiritual Law and a manifest way *in secular matters.* And *d*if Allah had enforced *His* will, He would have made you *all* one people, but *He wishes to* try you by that which He has given you. *e*Vie, then, with one another in good works. To Allah shall you all return ; then will He inform you of that wherein you differed.[680]

وَاَنْزَلْنَآ اِلَيْكَ الْكِتٰبَ بِالْحَقِّ مُصَدِّقًا لِّمَا بَيْنَ يَدَيْهِ مِنَ الْكِتٰبِ وَمُهَيْمِنًا عَلَيْهِ فَاحْكُمْ بَيْنَهُمْ بِمَا اَنْزَلَ اللّٰهُ وَلَا تَتَّبِعْ اَهْوَآءَهُمْ عَمَّا جَآءَكَ مِنَ الْحَقِّ لِكُلٍّ جَعَلْنَا مِنْكُمْ شِرْعَةً وَّمِنْهَاجًا ۚ وَلَوْ شَآءَ اللّٰهُ لَجَعَلَكُمْ اُمَّةً وَّاحِدَةً وَّلٰكِنْ لِّيَبْلُوَكُمْ فِيْ مَآ اٰتٰىكُمْ فَاسْتَبِقُوا الْخَيْرٰتِ ۚ اِلَى اللّٰهِ مَرْجِعُكُمْ جَمِيْعًا فَيُنَبِّئُكُمْ بِمَا كُنْتُمْ فِيْهِ تَخْتَلِفُوْنَ ۝

---

*a*5 : 45-46. *b*6 : 106 ; 39 : 3. *c*5 : 50. *d*10 : 100 ; 11 : 119 ; 16 : 10. *e*3 : 134 ; 35 : 33 ; 57 : 22.

679. Commentary :

The words, *And let the People of the Gospel judge according to what Allah has revealed therein,* do not mean that the Gospel is a Book of Law and that Christians should act upon the Law revealed in it, for the obvious reason that the Gospel is not a Book of Law, Jesus himself having followed the Law of Moses from which not a jot or tittle was to pass away till there had come the revelation of the perfect Law embodied in the Quran.

In fact, these words, like the similar ones contained in 5 : 45, do not enjoin obedience to any Law of Moses or Jesus but refer to the prophecies contained in the Torah and the Gospel about the Holy Prophet of Islam. Thus the present verse as well as 5 : 45 warns Jews and Christians that if they defied these prophecies and rejected the Holy Prophet, they would be regarded as " wrongdoers " and " rebellious " in the sight of God. For the Biblical prophecies about the Holy Prophet of Islam see note on 2 : 42, 90 ; and also John 16 : 7—13.

680. Important Words :

مُهَيْمِنًا (guardian) is derived from هَيْمَنَ. They say هَيْمَنَ الرَّجُلُ *i.e.* the man said, Amen. هَيْمَنَ الطَّائِرُ عَلَى فِرَاخِهِ means, the bird fluttered its wings over its young. هَيْمَنَ فُلَانٌ عَلَى كَذَا means, such a one became a protector and guardian over it. الْمُهَيْمِنُ when used about God means, He Who affords security and protection to His creatures when they are in a state of fear and danger (Aqrab). According to Lisān, the word مُهَيْمِن is derived from هَمَنَ which is originally اَمَنَ, the active participle مهيمن being really مؤامن. The word مهيمن means, witness; afforder of security and peace; controller and super-intendent of the affairs of men; guardian and protector (Lisān).

شرعة (clear spiritual Law) is derived from شرع. They say شرع فى الامر *i.e.* he entered into the affair; or he entered upon or commenced the affair. شرع المال means, he brought the cattle to the watering place so that they might drink water. شرع الله لنا كذا means, God made it apparent or manifest to us; or God prescribed it for us as a religious Law. شرعة means, a custom; the religious Law of God consisting of such ordinances as those of Fasting, Prayer and Pilgrimage and other acts of piety; a way of belief and conduct which is manifest and right. شريعة means, a watering place such as is permanent and apparent to the eye, like the water of rivers, to which men and beasts resort; a way to water; religion or way of belief and practice (Lane).

منهاجا (manifest way in secular matters) is derived from نهج *i.e.* it (a road or way) became manifest, plainly apparent or open; or he rendered (a road or an affair) manifest, plainly apparent or open. النهج or المنهاج means, a manifest, plainly apparent and open road or way (Lane). Al-Mubarrad says that شرعة signifies the beginning of a way and منهاج signifies the well-trodden body

of it (Qadīr). Thus شرعة would be mostly law relating to spiritual matters and منهاج law relating to secular matters.

Commentary :

The Quran is spoken of as a guardian over the previous scriptures in the sense that it has preserved all that was true and permanent in them by embodying the same in itself, and has left out what lacked the element of per-manence and failed to meet the needs of all mankind at all times. Again, it is called a guardian over scriptures because it enjoys divine protection against being tampered with, a blessing denied to other revealed scriptures. All that is of permanent use in the previous scriptures has been preserved in the Quran.

The words, *for each of you*, mean that not only for every nation but for every individual also God has appointed two clear ways, one per-taining to spiritual and the other to secular matters.

This verse also supplies an answer to the question, why God did not raise one Prophet for the whole of mankind in the beginning of the world, so that all peoples might have become one. The verse says that God has done so to "try" men and find out their fitness for the final Law. It is like appointing different stages of examinations to test the ability of students and thus raise them gradually to the final and topmost class.

50.   And *We have revealed the Book to thee bidding thee* to *a*judge between them by that which Allah has revealed and not to follow their evil inclinations, and to be on thy guard against them, *b*lest they cause thee to fall into affliction on account of part of what Allah has revealed to thee. But if they turn away, then know that Allah intends to smite them for some of their sins. And indeed a large number of men are disobedient.[681]

51.   Do they then seek the judgement of *the days of* Ignorance ? And who is better than Allah as a Judge for a people who have firm faith ?[682]

52.   O ye who believe! *c*take not the Jews and the Christians for friends. They are friends one to another. And whoso among you takes them for friends is indeed one of them. Verily, Allah guides not the unjust people.[683]

---

*a*5 : 49.   *b*17 : 74.   *c*3 : 29, 119 ; 4 : 145 ; 5 : 58 ; 60 : 10.

---

681. Important Words :

يَفْتِنُوكَ (cause thee to fall into affliction). يَفْتِنُونَ is derived from فَتَنَ. They say فَتَنَهُ *i.e.* he burnt it ; he or it caused him to fall into trial, affliction, trouble or distress ; he made him turn from or quit the position in which he was ; or he made him turn from the right course (Lane & Aqrab). See also 2 : 103, 192 ; 4 : 92.

عَنْ (on account of) is a particle used to give a number of meanings. Here it signifies "because of" or "on account of" (Lane).

Commentary :

The words, *they cause thee to fall into affliction on account of part of what Allah has revealed to thee,* mean that the cause of the enmity and hatred of the disbelievers for the Holy Prophet is the revelation which God has sent down to him. His enemies hatch plots against him and seek to involve him in trouble because some parts of his teachings are particularly repugnant to them, running counter to their most cherished views.

682. Important Words :

حُكْم (judgement) gives a number of meanings including judgement, rule, jurisdiction, dominion, government, ordinance, decree, law ; also predicament (Lane). See also 2 : 130 ; 3 : 8 ; 4 : 36.

683. Commentary :

The verse should not be construed to prohibit or discourage just or benevolent treatment of Jews, Christians and other disbelievers. Elsewhere, the Quran says : *Allah forbids you not*

53. And thou wilt see those in whose hearts is a disease, hastening towards them, saying, 'We fear lest a misfortune befall us.' Maybe, [a]Allah will bring about victory or some *other* event from Himself. Then will they become regretful of what they concealed in their minds.[684]

فَتَرَى الَّذِينَ فِي قُلُوبِهِمْ مَرَضٌ يُسَارِعُونَ فِيهِمْ يَقُولُونَ نَخْشَى اَنْ تُصِيبَنَا دَآئِرَةٌ ۚ فَعَسَى اللهُ اَنْ يَّأْتِيَ بِالْفَتْحِ اَوْ اَمْرٍ مِّنْ عِنْدِهِ فَيُصْبِحُوا عَلٰى مَآ اَسَرُّوْا فِيْ اَنْفُسِهِمْ نٰدِمِيْنَ ۟

54. And those who believe will say, 'Are these they who swore by Allah with their most solemn oaths that they were surely with you?' Their works are vain and they have become the losers.

وَيَقُولُ الَّذِينَ اٰمَنُوْا اَهٰؤُلَآءِ الَّذِينَ اَقْسَمُوْا بِاللهِ جَهْدَ اَيْمَانِهِمْ اِنَّهُمْ لَمَعَكُمْ ۚ حَبِطَتْ اَعْمَالُهُمْ فَاَصْبَحُوْا خٰسِرِيْنَ ۟

[a]32 : 30, 31.

---

respecting those who have not fought against you on account of your religion and who have not driven you forth from your homes, that you be kind to them and act equitably towards them; surely Allah loves those who are equitable (60 : 9). Thus it is only those Jews or Christians who are at war with Muslims whom the Quran forbids to be taken for friends.

Moreover, the word اولياء (friends) signifies not only friends but helpers and protectors also, and may thus be rendered as "protecting friends"; and surely Muslims cannot take Jews and Christians as their protecting friends. Their only protecting friends are God and His Prophet as well as their own brethren in faith. See also 5 : 56 below.

The expression, *They are friends one to another*, means that Jews and Christians forget their own differences and become united in their opposition to Islam and the Holy Prophet. Truly has the Prophet said الكفر ملة واحدة i.e., "all disbelief forms one community" viz. all disbelievers, however inimical to one another, are like one community when opposed to Islam.

684. **Important Words :**

دَائِرَة (misfortune) is derived from دار meaning, he or it went or moved round; or he or it circled or revolved or returned to the place from which he or it began to move. دار بالبيت means, he went round about the house; or he surrounded or encompassed it. They say دارت الايام meaning, the days came round in their turn i.e. repeated themselves. The expression دارت به دوائر الزمان means, the revolutions of fortune or time made him turn round from one state or condition to another. They say : دارت عليهم الدوائر meaning, calamities befell them. دَائِرَة therefore, means : (1) the circuit, ambit or circumference of a thing ; (2) a ring, a circle ; (3) a turn of fortune, especially an evil accident ; a misfortune ; a calamity ; defeat or rout ; slaughter or death (Lane & Aqrab).

Commentary :

The verb سارع (he hastened) from which يسارعون (hastening) has been formed is generally followed by the preposition الى ; but according to Arabic usage sometimes a verb takes after it a preposition which properly

55. O ye who believe! *a*whoso among you turns back from his religion, then *let it be known that in his stead* Allah will soon bring a people whom He will love and who will love Him, *and who will be* kind and humble towards believers, hard and firm against disbelievers. They will strive in the cause of Allah and will not fear the reproach of a fault-finder. That is Allah's grace; He bestows it upon whomsoever He pleases; and Allah is Bountiful, All-Knowing.[685]

يَآيُّهَا الَّذِيْنَ اٰمَنُوْا مَنْ يَّرْتَدَّ مِنْكُمْ عَنْ دِيْنِهٖ فَسَوْفَ يَأْتِى اللّٰهُ بِقَوْمٍ يُّحِبُّهُمْ وَيُحِبُّوْنَهٗٓ اَذِلَّةٍ عَلَى الْمُؤْمِنِيْنَ اَعِزَّةٍ عَلَى الْكٰفِرِيْنَ يُجَاهِدُوْنَ فِيْ سَبِيْلِ اللّٰهِ وَلَا يَخَافُوْنَ لَوْمَةَ لَآئِمٍ ذٰلِكَ فَضْلُ اللّٰهِ يُؤْتِيْهِ مَنْ يَّشَآءُ وَاللّٰهُ وَاسِعٌ عَلِيْمٌ ۝

---

*a*3 : 145.

---

belongs to another verb mentioned or understood before it, thus retaining not only its own sense but also acquiring that of the verb whose preposition it takes. In the present verse the verb يسارعون (hastening) has been followed not by the preposition الى meaning, to or toward, but by the preposition فى which means in, among or into, thus adding to its own sense the further significance of the verb يدخلون (they enter). Hence the expression يسارعون فيهم (hastening towards them) would really mean "hastening towards them they enter among them."

The word "victory" mentioned in the verse may either refer to the fall of Mecca or to victory in general. The word امر (event) coming after victory evidently refers to something greater than victory. Obviously it refers to the entry into Islam of the whole Arabian peninsula and the establishment of the power of Islam in it.

685. Important Words:

اذلة (kind and humble) is derived from ذل *i.e.* he or it was or became low, base, paltry, humble or weak. ذات الدابة means, the beast became easy, submissive and manageable. ذل الطريق means, the road became beaten and trodden and easy to be travelled. اذله means, he rendered him low, base, humble or weak. ذل (dhillun) or (dhullun) means, submissiveness or manageableness; also gentleness and mercy. ذليل which is the singular of اذلة means low, base, mean, paltry, humble or weak; easy and smooth; also gentle and merciful (Lane).

اعزة (hard and firm) is the plural of عزيز which is verbal adjective from عز meaning, he was or became mighty, potent, powerful or strong, or high and elevated; he magnified or exalted himself; he resisted or withstood; he was indomitable and invincible; it (a thing) was or became rare, scarce, hard to find; or he or it was or became dear, highly esteemed and greatly valued; or it became difficult and hard. عزيز of which the plural is اعزة means, mighty and powerful; high and elevated; resisting and invincible; hard and difficult; rough in manners; rare or scarce or highly esteemed (Lane & Aqrab). See also 2 : 130.

واسع (Bountiful) is derived from وسع *i.e.* it (place, vessel, etc.) was sufficient or sufficiently large or capacious or ample or abundant. السعة means, width or extent; ampleness or plentifulness; capacity or power. واسع means, possessing ample power or ability; powerful,

56. ^aYour friend is only Allah and His Messenger and the believers who observe Prayer and pay the Zakāt and worship God alone.⁶⁸⁶

اِنَّمَا وَلِیُّکُمُ اللهُ وَرَسُوْلُهٗ وَالَّذِیْنَ اٰمَنُوا الَّذِیْنَ یُقِیْمُوْنَ الصَّلٰوۃَ وَیُؤْتُوْنَ الزَّکٰوۃَ وَهُمْ رَاکِعُوْنَ ۞

57. And those who take Allah and His Messenger and the believers for friends *should rest assured* that ^bit is the party of Allah that must triumph.⁶⁸⁷

وَمَنْ یَّتَوَلَّ اللهَ وَرَسُوْلَهٗ وَالَّذِیْنَ اٰمَنُوْا فَاِنَّ حِزْبَ اللهِ هُمُ الْغٰلِبُوْنَ ۞

R. 9　58. O ye who believe! ^ctake not those for friends ^dwho make a jest and sport of your religion from among those who were given the Book before you, and the disbelievers. And fear Allah if you are believers ; ⁶⁸⁸

یٰۤاَیُّهَا الَّذِیْنَ اٰمَنُوْا لَا تَتَّخِذُوا الَّذِیْنَ اتَّخَذُوْا دِیْنَکُمْ هُزُوًا وَّلَعِبًا مِّنَ الَّذِیْنَ اُوْتُوا الْکِتٰبَ مِنْ قَبْلِکُمْ وَالْکُفَّارَ اَوْلِیَآءَ وَاتَّقُوا اللهَ اِنْ کُنْتُمْ مُّؤْمِنِیْنَ ۞

---

^a2 : 258 ; 3 : 69.　　^b58 : 23.　　^c3 : 29, 119 ; 4 : 145 ; 5 : 52 ; 60 : 10.　　^d6 : 71 ; 7 : 52.

---

bountiful; One Who gives to all; One Who encompasses all things (Lane & Aqrab).

Commentary :

The verse lays down an infallible sign of a true and living religion which is that the number of its followers is never allowed to fall or decrease permanently. If one individual goes out of its pale, God brings in a number to take his place. If the followers of a religion are found to be steadily and perpetually decreasing with no arrangement for recovery, that religion must be dead and truth must have departed from it.

The words اذلة على المؤمنين (kind and humble toward believers) mean that true believers whom God will bring in place of apostates will be susceptible to the influence of brother believers, will be lenient in their dealings with them, will connive at their shortcomings, will be ready to forgive and forget their faults and will love and be kind to them. And the expression اعزة على الكافرين (hard and firm toward disbelievers) means that they will not be afraid of disbelievers nor will they be susceptible to their baneful influence. In

fact, the above are the two main characteristic qualities of a rising people who love God.

The words, *They will strive in the cause of Allah*, mean that, unlike the weak of faith who are ever ready to *turn back from their religion* and stumble at every trial, the newcomers will be zealous Muslims, eager to bring others into the fold of Islam.

We are further told in the verse that a true believer is never afraid of laying down his life in the cause of Allah. He does not fear the reproaches of fault-finders or scoffers. He fears neither the sword nor the censure of the enemy.

686. Important Words :

راکعون (who worship God alone). See 2 : 44.

687. Commentary :

People seek the friendship of great men in order to succeed in life. But, asks the verse who is greater than God and His Messenger and the true believers, and how can those who make friends with them fail in life ?

688. Commentary :

This verse further explains the previous verse

59. And *who*, when you call *people* to Prayer, take it as jest and sport. That is because they are a people who do not understand.[689]

وَإِذَا نَادَيْتُمْ إِلَى الصَّلٰوةِ اتَّخَذُوْهَا هُزُوًا وَّ لَعِبًا ۙ ذٰلِكَ بِأَنَّهُمْ قَوْمٌ لَّا يَعْقِلُوْنَ ۞

60. Say, 'O People of the Book! do [a]you find fault with us because we believe in Allah and what has been sent down to us and what was sent down previously? Or is *it* because most of you are disobedient *to God?*'[690]

قُلْ يٰۤاَهْلَ الْكِتٰبِ هَلْ تَنْقِمُوْنَ مِنَّاۤ اِلَّاۤ اَنْ اٰمَنَّا بِاللّٰهِ وَمَاۤ اُنْزِلَ اِلَيْنَا وَمَاۤ اُنْزِلَ مِنْ قَبْلُ ۙ وَاَنَّ اَكْثَرَكُمْ فٰسِقُوْنَ ۞

---

[a]7 : 127 ; 60 : 2.

---

about the principle underlying the befriending of disbelievers. Muslims are not allowed to have friendly relations with people who scoff at their religion and mock at their Prophet. It would kill a Muslim's self-respect if he were to do so, and who can be more jealous and more self-respecting than a true Muslim? In 5 : 52 Muslims are forbidden to make friends with disbelievers because of their hostile and belligerent attitude towards them; in the present verse they are forbidden to do so because they scoff at their religion. This, however, does not mean that they are prevented from having dealings of any kind with disbelievers or from doing good to them and treating them kindly. In this connection see also 60 : 9, 10.

The word كفّار (disbelievers) when used in contrast to the People of the Book means "disbelievers from among idolaters"; but when used generally, it is applied both to the People of the Book and the idolaters. Here it refers to idolaters.

689. Commentary:

The verse cites an instance of how the People of the Book and idolaters made a jest of the religion of Islam.

690. Important Words:

هل (do you?) is an interrogative particle which, when followed by إلا (except or but), may be translated in the form of a negative statement. Thus the words هل تنقمون منّا الا ان آمنا may also be rendered as, "you do not find fault with us but because we believe." Sometimes it is used in the sense of قد (verily) to express a positive statement as هل اتى على الانسان حين من الدهر *i.e. Surely, there has come upon man a period of time*, etc.

تنقمون (you find fault with) is formed from نقم. They say نقم منه *i.e.* he punished or exacted vengeance on him. نقم منه كذا means, He criticized him, found fault with him and severely disliked him for such an evil deed of his. ما تنقم منّا means, what fault do you find with us, or what blame do you bring against us while we have committed no offence? (Aqrab). See also 3 : 5.

Commentary:

The verse drives home to Jews and Christians their folly in persecuting Muslims and finding fault with them. It seems, in effect, to say to them that the only offence which has made Muslims deserving of their persecution and criticism is that they believe in all the Prophets and all the Books of God; while before the advent of Islam they disbelieved in all these things. A Muslim not only believes in the Holy Prophet and the Quran but also in Moses and Jesus and all other Prophets, and looks upon what was revealed to each one of

61. Say, 'Shall I inform you of those whose reward with Allah is worse than that? *They are* those whom Allah has cursed and on *a*whom His wrath has fallen and of whom He has made apes and swine and *b*who worship the Evil One. *c*These indeed are in a worse plight, and farther astray from the right path.[691]

قُلْ هَلْ اُنَبِّئُكُمْ بِشَرٍّ مِّنْ ذٰلِكَ مَثُوْبَةً عِنْدَ اللّٰهِ مَنْ لَّعَنَهُ اللّٰهُ وَغَضِبَ عَلَيْهِ وَجَعَلَ مِنْهُمُ الْقِرَدَةَ وَالْخَنَازِيْرَ وَعَبَدَ الطَّاغُوْتَ اُولٰٓئِكَ شَرٌّ مَّكَانًا وَّاَضَلُّ عَنْ سَوَآءِ السَّبِيْلِ ۞

---

*a*2 : 66 ; 7 : 167.   *b*2 : 258 ; 4 : 52.   *c*12 : 78 ; 25 : 35.

---

them as of divine origin. Thus the verse administers a subtle but very effective rebuke to Christians and Jews, whose Prophets Islam calls upon its followers to respect and honour as true Messengers of God. The verse may equally apply to the opponents of every other Prophet, because the attitude of the rejectors of all Prophets of God and the reason for their persecuting believers are invariably the same.

691. Commentary:

The word ذالك (that) may refer either to the persecution of Muslims by the People of the Book hinted in the words, *do you find fault with us?* occurring in the previous verse, or it may refer to the party of believers whom they persecuted. In the former case, the first clause of the present verse would be rendered as "Shall I inform you of those whose reward with God is worse than the pain and misery they are inflicting upon Muslims?" In the latter case, the clause would be rendered as "Shall I inform you of those whose reward with God is worse than that of those people whom they persecute?" Those whose reward with God is worse are, of course, the Jews themselves. They are warned that they will suffer much greater torment than that which they can inflict on Muslims.

The words "apes" and "swine" have been used here in a figurative sense. Certain traits are peculiar to particular animals, and these cannot be fully described unless the animal to which they are known to belong is expressly named. For instance, in order to express the unluckiness or inauspiciousness of a person, an Arab would say, "Such a one is more inauspicious than the owl." Similarly the words "apes" and "swine" have been used in the present verse not by way of abuse, for the Quran does not use abusive language, nor was the Holy Prophet an abuser, but to point to the typical traits of the Jewish character. The peculiar characteristic of the ape is expressed in the well-known Arabic saying: "Such a one is more adulterous than the ape" (an epithet also used by Jesus about the Jews of his time). The ape is also noted for its mimicry (see 2 : 66). The swine is characterized by filthy and shameless habits and also by its foolishness. See also 2 : 174.

Though the Holy Prophet himself never used these words about the Jews, yet the Quran does so, because God as Judge and Master is justified and entitled to do so. A judge is often called upon to use expressions that may be necessary fully to describe the guilt of the condemned party. In fact, he would be failing in his duty if he did not do so. Jesus used similar expressions with regard to the Jews of his day. He did not abuse them; but only condemned them as a judge and vicegerent of God. See also note on 2 : 66.

62. And when they come to you, they say, ' We believe ', while they enter with unbelief and go out therewith ; and Allah best knows what they conceal.[692]

وَاِذَا جَآءُوْكُمْ قَالُوْۤا اٰمَنَّا وَقَدْ دَّخَلُوْا بِالْكُفْرِ وَهُمْ قَدْ خَرَجُوْا بِهٖ ؕ وَاللّٰهُ اَعْلَمُ بِمَا كَانُوْا يَكْتُمُوْنَ ۝

63. And thou seest many of them hastening towards sin and transgression and [a]the eating of things forbidden. Evil indeed is that which they practise.[693]

وَتَرٰى كَثِيْرًا مِّنْهُمْ يُسَارِعُوْنَ فِى الْاِثْمِ وَالْعُدْوَانِ وَ اَكْلِهِمُ السُّحْتَ ؕ لَبِئْسَ مَا كَانُوْا يَعْمَلُوْنَ ۝

64. [b]Why do not the divines and those learned in the Law prohibit them from uttering falsehood and eating things forbidden ? Evil indeed is that which they do.[694]

لَوْ لَا يَنْهٰىهُمُ الرَّبَّانِيُّوْنَ وَالْاَحْبَارُ عَنْ قَوْلِهِمُ الْاِثْمَ وَاَكْلِهِمُ السُّحْتَ ؕ لَبِئْسَ مَا كَانُوْا يَصْنَعُوْنَ ۝

---

[a]5 : 43.   [b]5 : 80.

---

692. Commentary :

By hypocritically uttering the words, *We believe*, the Jews merely copied the believers' mode of expressing their belief without understanding and realizing the real import of these words ; and thus they displayed (as hinted in the foregoing verse) the mimicking characteristic of the ape. See also the next verse.

693. Commentary :

This and the preceding verse give the reasons why the Jews have been called apes and swine in 5 : 61. Whereas the ape imitates and mimics, the swine eats filth and is aggressive in attack, beside being extra filthy in some of its habits.

694. Commentary :

The words قولهم الاثم (uttering falsehood) literally mean " their uttering of sin." As اثم (sin), in spite of including a sinful utterance, is generally committed and not uttered, some Commentators have suggested that the word قول has been used here in the sense of " doing." But it is more probable that the word قول has been joined to the word اثم (sin) in order to express the combined idea of both " uttering " and " doing." As will be noted, the present verse is preceded both by a saying of the Jews, *viz.* " we believe " (5 : 62), which being a false utterance is a sin, and by a " deed " of theirs, *viz.*, "hastening towards sin and transgression " (5 : 63), which are obviously sinful acts. Thus, by joining the word قول (uttering) to the word اثم (sin), the Quran aims at combining both sinful words and deeds.

Mention of the second wicked deed of the Jews referred to in 5 : 63, *viz.*, " their eating of forbidden things," is repeated in the present verse in order to point out that not only the common folk but the leaders of the Jewish community also were steeped in sin.

65. And *a*the Jews say, 'The hand of Allah is tied up.' Their *own* hands shall be tied up and they shall be cursed for what they say. Nay, both His hands are wide open; He spends how He pleases. And *b*what has been sent down to thee from thy Lord will most surely increase many of them in rebellion and disbelief. And *c*We have cast among them enmity and hatred till the Day of Resurrection. Whenever *d*they kindle a fire for war, Allah extinguishes it. And they strive to create disorder in the earth, and Allah loves not those who create disorder.[695]

وَقَالَتِ الۡيَهُوۡدُ يَدُ اللّٰهِ مَغۡلُوۡلَةٌ ؕ غُلَّتۡ اَيۡدِيۡهِمۡ وَلُعِنُوۡا بِمَا قَالُوۡا ؕ بَلۡ يَدَاهُ مَبۡسُوۡطَتٰنِ ۙ يُنۡفِقُ كَيۡفَ يَشَآءُ ؕ وَلَيَزِيۡدَنَّ كَثِيۡرًا مِّنۡهُمۡ مَّاۤ اُنۡزِلَ اِلَيۡكَ مِنۡ رَّبِّكَ طُغۡيَانًا وَّكُفۡرًا ؕ وَاَلۡقَيۡنَا بَيۡنَهُمُ الۡعَدَاوَةَ وَالۡبَغۡضَآءَ اِلٰى يَوۡمِ الۡقِيٰمَةِ ؕ كُلَّمَاۤ اَوۡقَدُوۡا نَارًا لِّلۡحَرۡبِ اَطۡفَاَهَا اللّٰهُ ۙ وَيَسۡعَوۡنَ فِى الۡاَرۡضِ فَسَادًا ؕ وَاللّٰهُ لَا يُحِبُّ الۡمُفۡسِدِيۡنَ ۝

---

*a*3 : 182 ; 36 : 48.   *b*5 : 69.   *c*3 : 56 ; 5 : 15.   *d*2 : 18.

---

695. Important Words :

یداه (both His hands). The word ید (hand or arm) is derived from یدی (*yadyun*) and, besides its literal meaning, gives a number of figurative meanings *e.g.*, (1) favour, benefit, bounty or generosity ; (2) power, dominion, control, authority or superiority (Aqrab & Lane).

Commentary :

The expression, *Their own hands shall be tied up*, signifies that the Jews shall be suitably punished for their insolent saying expressed in the words, *The hand of Allah is tied up*. The sentence may also be taken as optative, meaning, "may their hands be tied up." But as what Allah wills must come to pass, therefore the expression may be better rendered in the form of a positive statement, meaning that the Jews shall become miserly and stingy.

The clause, *Nay, both His hands are wide open*, constitutes a crushing reply to the taunt of the Jews, that the hand of Allah is tied up. The

Quran says that not only is the hand of God not tied up but that both His hands are wide open—the one to give to the believers in plenty and the other to punish the Jews for their insolence. The sentences which follow the clause, *Nay, both His hands are wide open*, refer respectively to the work of the two hands of God, namely (1) the bestowal of special bounties upon believers, and (2) the exemplary punishment of Jews for their sins. It will be noted that the hand is used both as an instrument for bestowing a favour or bounty and as a symbol of power and dominion for seizing and punishing an offender.

The *enmity and hatred* referred to in the verse are to exist and continue not only among Jews themselves but also among Christians, as well as between Jews and Christians.

The expression, *Whenever they kindle a fire for war*, refers to the attempts of Jews to incite the idolaters of Arabia to wage war against Muslims, as well as to their own hostile activities against Islam.

66. And *a*if the People of the Book had believed and been righteous, We would surely have removed from them their evils and We would surely have admitted them into gardens of bliss.⁶⁹⁶

وَلَوْ اَنَّ اَهْلَ الْكِتٰبِ اٰمَنُوْا وَاتَّقَوْا لَكَفَّرْنَا عَنْهُمْ سَيِّاٰتِهِمْ وَلَاَدْخَلْنٰهُمْ جَنّٰتِ النَّعِيْمِ ۝

67. And if *b*they had observed the Torah and the Gospel and what has been *now* sent down to them from their Lord, they would, surely, have eaten *of good things* from above them and from under their feet. Among them are a people who are moderate; but many of them—evil indeed is that which they do.⁶⁹⁷

وَلَوْ اَنَّهُمْ اَقَامُوا التَّوْرٰىةَ وَالْاِنْجِيْلَ وَمَا اُنْزِلَ اِلَيْهِمْ مِّنْ رَّبِّهِمْ لَاَكَلُوْا مِنْ فَوْقِهِمْ وَمِنْ تَحْتِ اَرْجُلِهِمْ مِنْهُمْ اُمَّةٌ مُّقْتَصِدَةٌ وَكَثِيْرٌ مِّنْهُمْ سَاٰءَ مَا يَعْمَلُوْنَ ۝

---

*a*7 : 97.   *b*5 : 48.

696. Important Words:

النَّعِيْم (bliss) is derived from نعم. They say عيشه نعم *i.e.* his life was or became plentiful and easy; or it was or became good or pleasant. نعمة (*na'mat*) means, ease and plenty; pleasantness and softness of life; enjoyment of a life of ease; comfort and affluence; tenderness, bloom, or freshness. نعمة (*ni'mat*) means, a benefit; favour; boon; blessing; bounty; grace or what God bestows on man. نعيم means, grace of God; ease and plenty; welfare; well-being; delight and pleasure; blessing (Lane).

Commentary:

The verse makes it absolutely clear that in order to get salvation and enter Heaven, it is necessary that the People of the Book should believe in the Holy Prophet and the Quran and that their believing in past Prophets and past Books is not sufficient. In this connection see also 2 : 63.

The expression, *gardens of bliss*, denotes a perfect state of spiritual pleasure as well as an abode of bliss. It may be noted here that while qualifying the word جنة (garden or Heaven) the Quran uses four distinct expressions :—

(1) جنات النعيم *i.e.* gardens of bliss, as in the present verse; (2) جنات المأوى *i.e.* gardens of refuge, as in 32 : 20; (3) جنات عدن *i.e.* gardens of eternity, as in 9 : 72; and (4) جنات الفردوس *i.e.* gardens of Paradise, as in 18 : 108. These names represent different aspects as well as different grades and sections of Heaven.

697. Commentary:

If Jews and Christians had given due consideration to the prophecies in their scriptures, they would certainly have believed in the Quran, which had come in fulfilment of those prophecies.

The words, *they would surely have eaten of good things from above them and from under their feet*, mean: (1) they would have received both heavenly blessings, such as divine revelation and communion with God, as well as worldly prosperity; (2) they would have had not only timely and abundant rains from above but the earth below their feet would also have yielded to them its produce in abundance; and (3) God would have provided them with both heavenly and earthly means of progress.

R. 10   68.   O Messenger! *a*convey *to the people* what has been revealed to thee from thy Lord ; and if thou do it not, thou hast not conveyed His message *at all.* And Allah will protect thee from men. Surely, Allah guides not the disbelieving people.[698]

يَـٰٓأَيُّهَا الرَّسُولُ بَلِّغْ مَآ أُنزِلَ إِلَيْكَ مِن رَّبِّكَ وَإِن لَّمْ تَفْعَلْ فَمَا بَلَّغْتَ رِسَالَتَهُ وَاللّٰهُ يَعْصِمُكَ مِنَ النَّاسِ إِنَّ اللّٰهَ لَا يَهْدِى الْقَوْمَ الْكَـٰفِرِينَ ۝

69.   Say, 'O People of the Book, you stand on nothing until you observe the Torah and the Gospel and what has *now* been sent down to you from your Lord.' And surely *b*what has been sent down to thee from thy Lord will increase many of them in rebellion and disbelief ; so grieve not for the disbelieving people.[699]

قُلْ يَـٰٓأَهْلَ الْكِتَابِ لَسْتُمْ عَلَىٰ شَىْءٍ حَتَّىٰ تُقِيمُوا التَّوْرَىٰةَ وَالْإِنجِيلَ وَمَآ أُنزِلَ إِلَيْكُم مِّن رَّبِّكُمْ وَلَيَزِيدَنَّ كَثِيرًا مِّنْهُم مَّآ أُنزِلَ إِلَيْكَ مِن رَّبِّكَ طُغْيَانًا وَكُفْرًا فَلَا تَأْسَ عَلَى الْقَوْمِ الْكَـٰفِرِينَ ۝

*a*6 : 20.   *b*5 : 65.

698. Commentary :

There is much difference of opinion about the time when this verse, containing a promise of God to protect the Holy Prophet against his enemies, was revealed. Ibn Jarīr, Ibn Kathīr, Durri Manthūr and Al-Baḥr al-Muḥiṭ mention a large number of narrators who report that the verse was revealed at Mecca. There are certain others, however, according to whom the verse was revealed at Medina. The author of the Rūḥ al-Ma'ānī says, the verse was first revealed at Mecca, and was revealed again at Medina, and this seems to be the correct view. In fact, it appears to have been revealed four or five times.

The words, *if thou do it not, thou hast not con-veyed His message,* do not signify apprehension that the Holy Prophet was going to be remiss in his duty. They have been simply used to express the general principle that he who fails to convey part of his message in fact fails to deliver the message at all.

The expression لا يهدى (guides not) is not used here in the sense of " not showing he way to truth," for occurring directly after the command to deliver the message of God to the people it cannot mean that God will not guide disbelievers to truth. If they were not to be guided to the right path, what was the sense in commanding the Prophet to deliver God's message to them ? The expression is therefore used here not in the spiritual but in the physical sense. Occurring immediately after the divine promise of protec-tion to the Holy Prophet the expression لا يهدى means that God will not suffer disbelievers to devise means of successfully harming him ; they will not be guided to come near him and kill him. It must, however, be remembered that the divine promise regarding the protection of the Holy Prophet did not mean that his enemies would not be allowed to do him any physical harm whatsoever. It only means that they would not be permitted to take his life or disable him permanently so as to render him unfit for his work.

699. Commentary :

It may be objected here that in 2 : 114 Jews and Christians were rebuked for saying of one

70. Surely, *a*those who have believed, and the Jews, and the Sabians, and the Christians—whoso believes in Allah and the Last Day and does good deeds, *b*on them shall come no fear, nor shall they grieve.[700]

اِنَّ الَّذِيۡنَ اٰمَنُوۡا وَالَّذِيۡنَ هَادُوۡا وَالصّٰبِئُوۡنَ وَالنَّصٰرٰی مَنۡ اٰمَنَ بِاللّٰهِ وَالۡیَوۡمِ الۡاٰخِرِ وَعَمِلَ صَالِحًا فَلَا خَوۡفٌ عَلَیۡهِمۡ وَلَا هُمۡ یَحۡزَنُوۡنَ ۞

71. Surely, We took a covenant from the children of Israel, and We sent Messengers to them. But *c*every time there came to them a Messenger with what their hearts desired not, they treated some as liars, and some they sought to kill.[701]

لَقَدۡ اَخَذۡنَا مِیۡثَاقَ بَنِیۡۤ اِسۡرَآءِیۡلَ وَاَرۡسَلۡنَاۤ اِلَیۡهِمۡ رُسُلًا ؕ كُلَّمَا جَآءَهُمۡ رَسُوۡلٌۢ بِمَا لَا تَهۡوٰۤی اَنۡفُسُهُمۡ ۙ فَرِیۡقًا كَذَّبُوۡا وَفَرِیۡقًا یَّقۡتُلُوۡنَ ۞

72. And they thought there would be no punishment, so they became blind and deaf. But Allah turned to them in mercy; yet again many of them became blind and deaf; and Allah is Watchful of what they do.[702]

وَحَسِبُوۡۤا اَلَّا تَكُوۡنَ فِتۡنَةٌ فَعَمُوۡا وَصَمُّوۡا ثُمَّ تَابَ اللّٰهُ عَلَیۡهِمۡ ثُمَّ عَمُوۡا وَصَمُّوۡا كَثِیۡرٌ مِّنۡهُمۡ ؕ وَاللّٰهُ بَصِیۡرٌۢ بِمَا یَعۡمَلُوۡنَ ۞

---

*a*2 : 63; 22 : 18.   *b*See 2 : 63.   *c*2 : 88.

another that they stood on nothing, and in the present verse the Quran itself uses an identical expression about the People of the Book. But on deeper thinking one should concede that there is an obvious difference between the two statements. The statement referred to in 2 : 114 was unqualified, but the statement in the present verse is qualified by the clause, "unless you observe the Torah," etc.

700. Commentary:

See notes on 2 : 63 and 5 : 66.

701. Commentary:

By comparing this verse with 5 : 13, it appears that "the leaders" mentioned in the latter verse are none but the "Messengers" mentioned in the present verse.

702. Important Words:

فِتۡنَة (punishment) is the noun-infinitive from فتن and means a sin; an act of disobedience for which one deserves punishment; punishment itself; disgrace, shame or ignominy, etc. (Lane & Aqrab). See also 2 : 192 & 4 : 92.

Commentary:

The Jews thought that their rejection of, and opposition to, the Prophets would bring no punishment upon them. But they were mistaken. Misery and affliction continued to dog their footsteps till God turned to them in mercy by raising the Holy Prophet that they might believe in him and escape divine punishment; but they rejected him also and thus lost their spiritual sight and hearing.

73. Indeed, ^athey are disbelievers who say, ' Surely, Allah is none but the Messiah, son of Mary,' whereas the Messiah *himself* said, ' O children of Israel, ^bworship Allah Who is my Lord and your Lord.' Surely, whoso associates partners with Allah, him has Allah forbidden Heaven, and the Fire will be his resort. And the wrongdoers shall have no helpers.[703]

لَقَدْ كَفَرَ الَّذِيْنَ قَالُوْٓا اِنَّ اللّٰهَ هُوَ الْمَسِيْحُ ابْنُ مَرْيَمَ ۚ وَقَالَ الْمَسِيْحُ يٰبَنِيْٓ اِسْرَآءِيْلَ اعْبُدُوا اللّٰهَ رَبِّيْ وَرَبَّكُمْ ؕ اِنَّهٗ مَنْ يُّشْرِكْ بِاللّٰهِ فَقَدْ حَرَّمَ اللّٰهُ عَلَيْهِ الْجَنَّةَ وَمَأْوٰىهُ النَّارُ ؕ وَمَا لِلظّٰلِمِيْنَ مِنْ اَنْصَارٍ ۞

74. ^cThey are surely disbelievers who say, ' Allah is the third of three '; there is no god but the One God. And if they do not desist from what they say, a grievous punishment shall surely befall those of them that disbelieve.[704]

لَقَدْ كَفَرَ الَّذِيْنَ قَالُوْٓا اِنَّ اللّٰهَ ثَالِثُ ثَلٰثَةٍ ۘ وَمَا مِنْ اِلٰهٍ اِلَّآ اِلٰهٌ وَّاحِدٌ ؕ وَاِنْ لَّمْ يَنْتَهُوْا عَمَّا يَقُوْلُوْنَ لَيَمَسَّنَّ الَّذِيْنَ كَفَرُوْا مِنْهُمْ عَذَابٌ اَلِيْمٌ ۞

75. Will they not then turn to Allah and beg His forgiveness, while Allah is Most Forgiving *and* Merciful ?[705]

اَفَلَا يَتُوْبُوْنَ اِلَى اللّٰهِ وَيَسْتَغْفِرُوْنَهٗ ؕ وَاللّٰهُ غَفُوْرٌ رَّحِيْمٌ ۞

---

^a4 : 172; 5 : 18; 9 : 30.   ^b5 : 118; 19 : 37.   ^c4 : 172.

703. Commentary :

That Jesus taught the Israelites to worship God alone is apparent even from the Gospels in their present distorted form (*e.g.* Matt. 4 : 10; Luke 4 : 8). Also see 5 : 18.

704. Commentary :

The reference in this verse is to the doctrine of Trinity, that mysterious and abstruse dogma of the three persons of Godhead— Father, Son and Holy Ghost—co-existing and co-equal in all respects, combining to make one God and yet remaining three. It was the Nicene Council and especially the Athenasian Creed that first gave the dogma its definite shape. The doctrine forms the basic Article of the Christian faith. What a fall for the enlightened West !

705. Commentary :

No vicarious sacrifice is needed for the salvation of man. God himself can forgive all sins. Only a truly penitent and contrite heart is required to attract His forgiveness. Why then do not Christians turn to God and entreat Him to pardon their sins ? What need is there to resort to, and depend on, an unintelligible doctrine that Jesus, "son of God", was crucified to atone for the sins of men and that those who wish to have their sins forgiven should believe in this atonement. The verse points out that, as God possesses full power to forgive, so those who sincerely repent of their sins and turn to Him with truly penitent hearts can always hope to find Him Forgiving and Merciful.

76. The Messiah, son of Mary, was only a Messenger; surely, Messengers *like unto him* had passed away before him. And his mother was a truthful woman. ^aThey both used to eat food. See how We explain the Signs for their good, and see how they are turned away.[706]

مَا الْمَسِيحُ ابْنُ مَرْيَمَ اِلَّا رَسُوْلٌ قَدْ خَلَتْ مِنْ قَبْلِهِ الرُّسُلُ وَاُمُّهُ صِدِّيْقَةٌ كَانَا يَاْكُلَانِ الطَّعَامَ اُنْظُرْ كَيْفَ نُبَيِّنُ لَهُمُ الْاٰيٰتِ ثُمَّ انْظُرْ اَنّٰى يُؤْفَكُوْنَ ۝

77. Say, ^bWill you worship beside Allah that which has no power to do you harm or good? And it is Allah Who is All-Hearing, All-Knowing.[707]

قُلْ اَتَعْبُدُوْنَ مِنْ دُوْنِ اللّٰهِ مَا لَا يَمْلِكُ لَكُمْ ضَرًّا وَّلَا نَفْعًا ۚ وَاللّٰهُ هُوَ السَّمِيْعُ الْعَلِيْمُ ۝

---

^a21 : 9.   ^b6 : 72 ; 10 : 107 ; 21 : 67 ; 22 : 13.

---

706. Important Words :

يُؤْفَكُوْنَ (they are turned away) is derived from اَفَكَ (afaka). They say اَفَكَهُ i.e. he changed his or its state or condition or manner of being ; he turned him or it away or back from a thing ; he turned him away or back by lying ; he changed or perverted his judgement or opinion ; or he deceived or beguiled him. They say اَفَكَ الرَّجُلَ عَنِ الْخَيْرِ i.e. the man was turned away or turned back from good by deceit or guile. اَفَكَ (afaka) or اَفَّكَ (affaka) also means, he told a lie or uttered a falsehood which, in essence, is the same as changing the state of a thing (Lane).

Commentary :

The verse advances a number of arguments against the alleged divinity of Jesus. Firstly, it points out that Jesus was no better than other Messengers of God in any way. He enjoyed no higher status. He showed no miracles the like of which were not shown by other Prophets. In fact, the greatest miracle ascribed to him by his followers is that of the alleged raising of the dead. But the Bible ascribes similar miracles to other Prophets also (see 2 Kings 4 : 16, 17, 34, 35 ; 13 : 21).

The second argument mentioned by the verse against his alleged divinity is that he was born of a woman. Being born of a human being, he could not be divine. Moreover, a child is known to inherit some of the prominent traits of the physical and moral make-up of its parent. Jesus, being born of a woman, must have inherited her nature and her qualities and so he could not be God.

Again, being human, he was, like other human beings, subject to the natural laws of hunger and of satisfying it by taking food and he was subject also to the natural phenomena that ensue.

[By describing the mother of Jesus as " a truthful woman " the Quran has incidentally refuted the Jewish allegations concerning the birth of Jesus.

707. Commentary :

Jesus, who is looked upon as God, had no power to do either harm or good to any person. He could not, rather cannot, hear prayers nor does he know the needs of men that he may satisfy them ; for it is Allah alone Who is All-Hearing, All-Knowing.

78. Say, ^aO People of the Book, exceed not the limits in *the matter of* your religion unjustly, nor follow the evil inclinations of a people who went astray before and caused many to go astray, and *who* have strayed away from the right path.[708]

R. 11

79. ^bThose amongst the children of Israel who disbelieved were cursed by the tongue of David, and of Jesus, son of Mary. That was because they disobeyed and used to transgress.[709]

قُلْ يَا أَهْلَ الْكِتَابِ لَا تَغْلُوْا فِىْ دِيْنِكُمْ غَيْرَ الْحَقِّ وَلَا تَتَّبِعُوْا اَهْوَآءَ قَوْمٍ قَدْ ضَلُّوْا مِنْ قَبْلُ وَاَضَلُّوْا كَثِيْرًا وَّضَلُّوْا عَنْ سَوَآءِ السَّبِيْلِ ۝

لُعِنَ الَّذِيْنَ كَفَرُوْا مِنْ بَنِىْ اِسْرَآءِيْلَ عَلٰى لِسَانِ دَاوُدَ وَعِيْسَى ابْنِ مَرْيَمَ ذٰلِكَ بِمَا عَصَوْا وَّكَانُوْا يَعْتَدُوْنَ ۝

---

^a4 : 172.   ^b3 : 87-88 ; 4 : 48.

---

708. Commentary :

The words ولا تقولوا (and say not or speak not) may be taken to be understood before the words غير الحق (which have been translated in the text as "unjustly" but which also mean an untruth), for it is the false doctrines of Christians that, more than their actions, have contributed to the corruption of their faith and their spiritual degradation. In this case the verse would read thus : "Say, O People of the Book, exceed not the limits in *the matter of* your religion *and speak not* an untruth."

The words, *nor follow the evil inclinations of a people who went astray before,* indicate that the doctrines of Trinity, Atonement and Sonship are really borrowed doctrines. Having borrowed them from the nations that "went astray before," early Christian religious leaders made such alterations in their own doctrines as made them acceptable to the heathen nations with whom they came in contact. Modern research into the sources of Christianity goes to establish the truth of this Quranic statement made more than thirteen hundred years ago (Enc. Bib., col. 4695 ; Enc. R. Eth., vol. ii, p. 143 ; vol. vii, p. 436).

709. Commentary :

Of all the Israelite Prophets, David and Jesus suffered most at the hands of the Jews. Jewish persecution of Jesus culminated in his being hung on the Cross, and the hardships and privations to which David was subjected by these ungrateful people are reflected in the deep pathos of his Psalms. From the agony of their hearts did David and Jesus both curse them. The curse of David resulted in the Israelites being smitten by Nebuchadnezzar, who destroyed Jerusalem and carried the Israelites into captivity in 586 B.C. ; while, as a result of the curse of Jesus, they were visited by terrible afflictions by Titus, who captured Jerusalem in about 70 A.D., devastated the city and profaned the Temple by causing swine to be slaughtered there—an animal hated and abhorred by Jews.

80. ^aThey did not prohibit one another from the iniquity which they committed. Evil indeed was that which they used to do. ⁷¹⁰

كَانُوْا لَا يَتَنَاهَوْنَ عَنْ مُّنْكَرٍ فَعَلُوْهُ لَبِئْسَ مَا كَانُوْا يَفْعَلُوْنَ ۞

81. ^bThou shalt see many of them taking the disbelievers as *their* friends. Surely, evil is that which they themselves have sent on before for themselves ; *with the result* that ^bAllah is displeased with them ; and in *this* punishment they shall abide.⁷¹¹

تَرٰى كَثِيْرًا مِّنْهُمْ يَتَوَلَّوْنَ الَّذِيْنَ كَفَرُوْا لَبِئْسَ مَا قَدَّمَتْ لَهُمْ أَنْفُسُهُمْ أَنْ سَخِطَ اللهُ عَلَيْهِمْ وَفِى الْعَذَابِ هُمْ خٰلِدُوْنَ ۞

82. And if they had believed in Allah and this Prophet, and *in* that which has been revealed to him, they would not have taken them as *their* friends, but many of them are disobedient.⁷¹²

وَلَوْ كَانُوْا يُؤْمِنُوْنَ بِاللهِ وَالنَّبِيِّ وَمَا أُنْزِلَ إِلَيْهِ مَا اتَّخَذُوْهُمْ أَوْلِيَاءَ وَلٰكِنَّ كَثِيْرًا مِّنْهُمْ فٰسِقُوْنَ ۞

^a5 : 64 : 4.   ^b3 : 163.

---

710. Commentary :

One of the great sins which drew the wrath of God upon the Jewish people was that they did not prohibit one another from the evil practices which were so rife among them. While some simply connived at these evil practices, others actually encouraged them. Unfortunately, Muslim scholars and priests of the present day are also guilty of this deadly sin. They will not preach against the evils to which the wealthier and the more powerful Muslims are addicted.

711. Important Words :

سخط (is displeased). The word سخط means, he was or became displeased or discontented ; he was or became angry. They say سخط عليه *i.e.* he was or became displeased or discontented or angry with him. سخط الشيئ means, he disliked or became discontented with the thing (Lane & Aqrab).

Commentary :

In this verse the word " disbelievers " stands for " idolaters." See note on 5 : 58. The clause بئس ما قدمت لهم انفسهم (*evil is that which they themselves have sent on before for themselves*) may also be rendered as " evil is that which their souls have brought forward, or brought to the forefront, for them " *i.e.* that which their souls have made to appear fair in their sight is really evil and foul.

712. Commentary :

The Prophet referred to in this verse is the Holy Prophet of Islam and not Moses ; for wherever the Quran uses the word النبى (the Prophet), it invariably refers to the Holy Prophet. Even the Jews referred to him as " that Prophet " (see John 1 : 21, 25) *i.e.*, the Prophet whose advent had been foretold in Deut. 18 : 18.

The verse means to say that if Jews had accepted the Holy Prophet and acted upon the Quranic principle that when making friends with others those who are nearer in faith should be given preference over those who are not, they would never have preferred idolaters to Muslims as friends ; for, while the latter have

83. Thou shalt certainly find the Jews and those who associate partners with God to be the most vehement of men in enmity against the Believers. And thou shalt assuredly find those who say, ' We are Christians ', to be the nearest of them in love to the Believers. That is because amongst them are savants and monks and because they are not proud.⁷¹³

لَتَجِدَنَّ اَشَدَّ النَّاسِ عَدَاوَةً لِّلَّذِيۡنَ اٰمَنُوا الۡيَهُوۡدَ وَالَّذِيۡنَ اَشۡرَكُوۡا ۚ وَلَتَجِدَنَّ اَقۡرَبَهُمۡ مَّوَدَّةً لِّلَّذِيۡنَ اٰمَنُوا الَّذِيۡنَ قَالُوۡٓا اِنَّا نَصٰرٰى ؕ ذٰلِكَ بِاَنَّ مِنۡهُمۡ قِسِّيۡسِيۡنَ وَرُهۡبَانًا وَّاَنَّهُمۡ لَا يَسۡتَكۡبِرُوۡنَ ۞

---

most things in common with them and believe in all their Prophets, the former do not. In contravention of this great principle, however, Jews, to their own detriment, not only chose to make friends with idolaters in preference to Muslims, but even declared the former to be better guided than the latter (4 : 52).

713. Important Words :

قِسِّيۡسِيۡن (savants) is the plural of قِسِّيۡس which is formed from قَس . They say قَسَّه i.e. he sought after or pursued it ; or he sought after or pursued it leisurely or repeatedly or by degrees. The word also means, he became a قِسِّيۡس which means, the head or chief of the Christians in knowledge or science, or one of their heads or chiefs ; a learned man of the Christians who has sought after and acquired great knowledge ; an intelligent and learned man (Lane).

رُهۡبَانًا (monks) is the plural of رَاهِب which is derived from رَهِب which means, he feared, or he feared with caution. رَاهِب means, a fearer or a cautious fearer ; a fearer of God ; an ascetic, because he fears God much ; a Christian devotee or monk ; a religious recluse ; one who devotes himself to religious services or exercises in a cell or monastery. رَهَبَانِيَّة means the state of a رَاهِب (monk) and signifies, excess in religious exercises and discipline and detaching oneself from mankind ; monkery ; asceticism (Lane).

Commentary :

As a rule, the followers of a new Prophet meet with greater opposition from the followers of the Prophet immediately preceding him than from the followers of those Prophets who had appeared in the remote past. But, contrary to this general practice, Jews, who should have been less inimically disposed towards the Muslims than Christians, proved at least in the Holy Prophet's time to be bitterer enemies of Islam than Christians, who were comparatively less inimical. This state of affairs, however, was not to last for ever. The Quran elsewhere warns Muslims that they were destined to suffer most grievously at the hands of Christians, who would attack them from all directions (21 : 97). In the Ḥadith also there are prophecies to this effect. So the verse under comment may not be taken to apply to Christians of all times but only to those of the Holy Prophet's time who lived round about him ; and history bears out this inference. Najāshi, the Christian King of Abyssinia, gave shelter to Muslim refugees ; and Muqauqas, the Christian ruler of Egypt, sent presents to the Holy Prophet.

It appears that humility formed one of the chief characteristics of early Christians, and the teachings of Jesus about turning the other cheek to the striker seems to have exercised its influence on their lives for some centuries. This is evident from the different ways in which

84. And when they hear what has been revealed to this Messenger, thou seest their eyes overflow with tears, because of the truth which they have recognized. They say, *a*'Our Lord, we believe, so write us down among those who bear witness.[714]

وَإِذَا سَمِعُوا مَا أُنزِلَ إِلَى الرَّسُولِ تَرَىٰ أَعْيُنَهُمْ تَفِيضُ مِنَ الدَّمْعِ مِمَّا عَرَفُوا مِنَ الْحَقِّ يَقُولُونَ رَبَّنَا آمَنَّا فَاكْتُبْنَا مَعَ الشَّاهِدِينَ ۝

85. 'And why should we not believe in Allah and in the truth which has come to us, while *b*we earnestly wish that our Lord should include us among the righteous people?'[715]

وَمَا لَنَا لَا نُؤْمِنُ بِاللَّهِ وَمَا جَاءَنَا مِنَ الْحَقِّ وَنَطْمَعُ أَن يُدْخِلَنَا رَبُّنَا مَعَ الْقَوْمِ الصَّالِحِينَ ۝

---

*a*3 : 54, 194.   *b*26 : 52.

---

the epistles of the Holy Prophet were treated by the King of Persia, who was a heathen, and by Heraclius, Emperor of the Eastern Roman Empire, who was a Christian. The former tore the letter to pieces, while the latter received it respectfully and even evinced some inclination towards Islām.

So long as the above qualities formed distinctive features of the Christian character, Muslims generally met with fairer treatment at their hands. But as time passed, these qualities gradually took leave of them and now there are very few among Christian divines and religious leaders who are engaged in real and honest religious research, withdrawing from the cares of the world and taking an active and living interest in spiritual matters. Christian scholars began to meddle in politics in the 13th or 14th century, with the result that they became hostile to Islam.

714. Commentary:

The description given in this verse of some of the Christians of the time of the Holy Prophet applies to all those who have a real hankering after truth and are ready to accept it wherever they find it. The verse has also been applied

to Najāshī in particular. When Ja'far, a cousin of the Holy Prophet and the spokesman of Muslim refugees to Abyssinia, tried to make clear their attitude towards Jesus and to dispel the suspicion caused by the Meccan emissaries about the alleged derogatory language used by the Quran concerning Jesus and read to Najāshī the opening verses of the chapter *Maryam*, the latter, along with such of his companions as feared God, was visibly moved and tears rolled down his cheeks and he said in a voice full of pathos that that exactly was his belief about Jesus, and that he did not look upon him by even a twig more than that (Hishām, i. 305, 306).

715. Commentary:

The verse may be regarded as constituting the substance of the words, referred to in the preceding verse, which Najāshī spoke to those of his courtiers who remonstrated with him, saying that Jesus was God, and not a human being as represented in the Quran, and urged him to deliver the Muslim refugees to the Meccans. At this Najāshī is reported to have said that nothing could prevent him from accepting the truth.

86. So ^aAllah rewarded them, for what they said, with gardens beneath which streams flow. Therein shall they abide ; and that is the reward of those who do good.

فَاَثَابَهُمُ اللّٰهُ بِمَا قَالُوْا جَنّٰتٍ تَجْرِیْ مِنْ تَحْتِهَا الْاَنْهٰرُ خٰلِدِیْنَ فِیْهَا ۚ وَذٰلِكَ جَزَآءُ الْمُحْسِنِیْنَ ۝

87. And ^bthose who have disbelieved and rejected Our Signs, these are they who are the inmates of Hell.

وَالَّذِیْنَ كَفَرُوْا وَكَذَّبُوْا بِاٰیٰتِنَاۤ اُولٰٓئِكَ اَصْحٰبُ الْجَحِیْمِ ۝

R. 12

88. O ye who believe ! ^cmake not unlawful the good things which Allah has made lawful for you, and do not transgress. Surely, Allah loves not the transgressors.⁷¹⁶

یٰۤاَیُّهَا الَّذِیْنَ اٰمَنُوْا لَا تُحَرِّمُوْا طَیِّبٰتِ مَاۤ اَحَلَّ اللّٰهُ لَكُمْ وَلَا تَعْتَدُوْا ۚ اِنَّ اللّٰهَ لَا یُحِبُّ الْمُعْتَدِیْنَ ۝

89. And ^deat of that which Allah has provided for you of what is lawful and good. And fear Allah in whom you believe.

وَكُلُوْا مِمَّا رَزَقَكُمُ اللّٰهُ حَلٰلًا طَیِّبًا ۫ وَّاتَّقُوا اللّٰهَ الَّذِیْۤ اَنْتُمْ بِهٖ مُؤْمِنُوْنَ ۝

90. ^eAllah will not call you to account for such of your oaths as are vain, but He will call you to account for the oaths which you take in earnest. Its expiation, then, is the feeding of ten poor persons with such average food as you feed your families with, or the clothing of them or the freeing of a neck. But whoso finds not the means shall fast for three days. That is the expiation of your oaths when you have sworn them. And do keep your oaths. Thus does Allah explain to you His Signs that you may be grateful.⁷¹⁷

لَا یُؤَاخِذُكُمُ اللّٰهُ بِاللَّغْوِ فِیْۤ اَیْمَانِكُمْ وَلٰكِنْ یُّؤَاخِذُكُمْ بِمَا عَقَّدْتُّمُ الْاَیْمَانَ ۚ فَكَفَّارَتُهٗۤ اِطْعَامُ عَشَرَةِ مَسٰكِیْنَ مِنْ اَوْسَطِ مَا تُطْعِمُوْنَ اَهْلِیْكُمْ اَوْ كِسْوَتُهُمْ اَوْ تَحْرِیْرُ رَقَبَةٍ ۚ فَمَنْ لَّمْ یَجِدْ فَصِیَامُ ثَلٰثَةِ اَیَّامٍ ۚ ذٰلِكَ كَفَّارَةُ اَیْمَانِكُمْ اِذَا حَلَفْتُمْ ۚ وَاحْفَظُوْۤا اَیْمَانَكُمْ ۚ كَذٰلِكَ یُبَیِّنُ اللّٰهُ لَكُمْ اٰیٰتِهٖ لَعَلَّكُمْ تَشْكُرُوْنَ ۝

---

^asee 2 : 26.   ^b5 : 87; 6 : 50; 7 : 37; 22 : 58.   ^c10 : 60.   ^d2 : 169; 8 : 70; 16 : 115.   ^e2 : 226.

---

716. Commentary :

Just as the making of a forbidden thing lawful is an act of excess and transgression, similarly the declaring of a good and lawful thing to be unlawful, or practically treating it as such, is an act of sin. Both these acts are acts of transgression. The verse may have a figurative sense also. In this case the expression,

make not unlawful the good things which Allah has made lawful for you, would mean " do not shut the door of God's favours on yourselves by rejecting the Prophet of Islam."

717. Commentary :

The verb عقّد ('aqqada) is the intensive form of عقد ('aqada) for which see 5 : 2. It conveys

91.   O ye who believe ! ^awine and the game of hazard and idols and ^bdivining arrows are only an abomination of Satan's handiwork. So shun each one of them that you may prosper.⁷¹⁸

يَآاَيُّهَا الَّذِيْنَ اٰمَنُوْٓا اِنَّمَا الْخَمْرُ وَالْمَيْسِرُ وَالْاَنْصَابُ وَالْاَزْلَامُ رِجْسٌ مِّنْ عَمَلِ الشَّيْطٰنِ فَاجْتَنِبُوْهُ لَعَلَّكُمْ تُفْلِحُوْنَ ۹۱

^a2 : 220 ; 5 : 92.   ^b5 : 4.

---

the idea of greater deliberation and solemnity. Hence the expression ما عقدتم الايمان (oaths which you take in earnest) would really mean, oaths which you swear solemnly and deliberately.

The use of the word اوسط (average) means both ' middle ' (*i.e.* average) and ' best ' (see 2 : 144) and is thus meant to imply that an oath may be regarded as expiated if ten poor men are fed with food the expiator ordinarily provides for his family, but that it is better to feed them with the best food with which he feeds his own family.

The pronoun هم (their) in كسوتهم (their clothing) may refer either to families or to poor persons. In the former case, the sentence would read, "the clothing (of ten poor men) with the average (or the best) kind of clothing which you provide for your families." In the latter case, it would simply mean, "the clothing of ten poor men."

The verse should not be taken as describing three different ways by which a person can expiate a broken oath. The different ways are intended to represent three progressive stages of expiation, the third alternative being better than the second, and the second better than the first.

The injunction to expiate oaths does not mean that they may be broken with impunity and then expiated. The prescription of penalties is merely meant to meet a possible eventuality. But oaths contrary to Islamic Law are no

oaths. They must be broken. Then there are oaths that pertain to the rights of individuals. These cannot be expiated even by adopting any of the above-mentioned three courses. If, for instance, a man promises on oath to give to a person a certain sum of money, and then breaks his oath, and makes the prescribed expiation, the expiation will not absolve him from his obligation to make the promised payment. He must pay the man the promised sum, notwithstanding the expiation. The expiation will only atone for the sin he committed against God by breaking his oath.

718. Important Words :

الخمر والميسر (wine and games of hazard). See note on 2 : 220.

انصاب والازلام (idols and divining arrows). See note on 5 : 4.

رجس (abomination) is derived from رجس which means, it was or became unclean or dirty or filthy or disliked or hated ; he performed a bad or evil or abominable action. رجس means, it made a sound or noise. رجس means, dirt or filth ; or a dirty or filthy thing; anything or any action that is disliked or hated for its uncleanness or filthiness ; a sin or crime ; **an** action that leads to punishment; punishment ; unbelief and infidelity; suggestion of the devil (Lane & Aqrab).

Commentary :

See 2 : 220 & 5 : 4. Almost all the meanings of رجس are applicable here.

92. Satan desires only to create enmity and hatred among you by means of wine and the game of hazard, and to keep you back from the remembrance of Allah and from Prayer. But will you keep back?[719]

اِنَّمَا يُرِيدُ الشَّيْطَانُ اَنْ يُّوْقِعَ بَيْنَكُمُ الْعَدَاوَةَ وَالْبَغْضَاءَ فِي الْخَمْرِ وَالْمَيْسِرِ وَيَصُدَّكُمْ عَنْ ذِكْرِ اللّٰهِ وَعَنِ الصَّلٰوةِ فَهَلْ اَنْتُمْ مُّنْتَهُوْنَ ۝

93. And *a*obey Allah and obey the Messenger, and be on *your* guard. But if you turn away, then know that *b*on Our Messenger lies only the clear conveyance of the message.[720]

وَاَطِيْعُوا اللّٰهَ وَاَطِيْعُوا الرَّسُوْلَ وَاحْذَرُوْا فَاِنْ تَوَلَّيْتُمْ فَاعْلَمُوْۤا اَنَّمَا عَلٰى رَسُوْلِنَا الْبَلٰغُ الْمُبِيْنُ ۝

---

*a*3 : 133 ; 4 : 70 ; 64 : 13.   *b*5 : 100 ; 16 : 83 ; 36 : 18 ; 64 : 13.

---

719. Commentary :

After stating that the four things mentioned in the previous verse are all رجس (abomination) in one sense or another, the present verse confines itself to two of the four mentioned things—wine and games of hazard—and gives additional reasons against them. These reasons are, as stated in the verse, four in number and rest on political, social, spiritual and socio-religious grounds, this being hinted in the words "enmity and hatred and keeping back from the remembrance of Allah and from Prayer." The interrogation in the clause, *But will you keep back?*, embodies a strong admonition not to do the thing, the use of the interrogative form being the most effective form of exhortation. See also 2 : 220.

720. Commentary :

The words, *be on your guard*, may either mean, "you should be on your guard against evils" or they may signify that if you obey Allah and obey the Prophet, the result will be that you will be able to guard yourselves against evil.

The concluding part of the verse means that the duty of a Messenger of God is only to convey to men His commandments. It forms no part of his work to force them to follow him. This exposes the absurdity of the objection that Islam enjoins the use of force for its propagation. Elsewhere the Quran says: *There should be no compulsion in religion* (2 : 257). Both these verses and many similar others were revealed at Medina when a state of war existed between disbelievers and believers, which clearly shows that the Holy Prophet took up arms only to defend himself and his followers and not to propagate his religion at the point of the sword, as is often maliciously alleged by the opponents of Islam.

94. On those who believe and do good works there shall be no sin for what they eat, provided they fear *God* and believe and do good works, *and* again fear *God* and believe, yet again fear *God* and do good. And Allah loves those who do good.[721]

بَيْسَ عَلَى الَّذِيْنَ اٰمَنُوْا وَعَمِلُوا الصّٰلِحٰتِ جُنَاحٌ
فِيْمَا طَعِمُوْا اِذَا مَا اتَّقَوْا وَّاٰمَنُوْا وَعَمِلُوا الصّٰلِحٰتِ
ثُمَّ اتَّقَوْا وَّاٰمَنُوْا ثُمَّ اتَّقَوْا وَّاَحْسَنُوْا وَاللّٰهُ يُحِبُّ
الْمُحْسِنِيْنَ ۞

721. Commentary :

The verse does not mean, as may be wrongly inferred, that if a person believes and does good works, he can take any food. On the contrary, it purports to lay down a condition the observance of which can secure a person against using a forbidden food, *i.e.*, a food which is calculated to do him physical or spiritual harm. The condition is that he should *fear God and believe and do good works*; and it is evident that those who really fear God and believe in Him and do good works can never think of eating forbidden food. Indeed, a person may eat anything, if his partaking of it leads to his becoming pious and God-fearing; and it is clear that such food, the eating of which makes a person pious and God-fearing, cannot but be pure and clean, for it is only clean food which can bring about such a result.

Two important principles emerge from this verse: (*a*) that the things of this world having been made for the use and benefit of man are, as a rule, pure and clean; the forbidden things being only exceptions; (*b*) that clean and pure food exercises a beneficial influence on man's spiritual development, while unclean and impure food produces an adverse effect upon it.

Moreover, the verse lays down three stages of spiritual progress for believers. In the first stage, believers fear God and believe and do good works, while in the second stage they fear God and believe, their belief being at this stage so strong as to become a natural and constant source of good works which become as it were part and parcel of their belief, and in the third and final stage they fear God and do good to others which is not possible without perfect belief and good works, the mention of both of which has consequently been here left out as being understood. Thus the words " and do good works " have been omitted in the description of the second stage, while the words " and believe " have been replaced with the words " and do good " in the description of the third stage.

It should be noted that the expression اتَّقَوْا (fear God) which has been repeated three times in the verse under comment is peculiar to the Arabic language and gives a very vast meaning, the root idea underlying the word being "to be ever watchful and to be ever taking God for shelter " (see 2 : 3). Similarly the expression اَحْسَنُوْا (do good) is very vast in its significance for which see 2 ; 113.

R. 13

95. O ye who believe! Allah will surely try you in a little matter: the game which your hands and your lances can reach, so that [a]Allah may distinguish those who fear Him in secret. Whoso, therefore, will transgress after this shall have a grievous punishment.[722]

يَاۤ اَيُّهَا الَّذِيۡنَ اٰمَنُوۡا لَيَبۡلُوَنَّكُمُ اللّٰهُ بِشَيۡءٍ مِّنَ الصَّيۡدِ تَنَالُهٗۤ اَيۡدِيۡكُمۡ وَرِمَاحُكُمۡ لِيَعۡلَمَ اللّٰهُ مَنۡ يَّخَافُهٗ بِالۡغَيۡبِ ۚ فَمَنِ اعۡتَدٰى بَعۡدَ ذٰلِكَ فَلَهٗ عَذَابٌ اَلِيۡمٌ ۝

96. O ye who believe! [b]kill not game while you are in a state of pilgrimage. And whoso amongst you kills it intentionally, its compensation is a quadruped like unto that which he has killed, as determined by two just men from among you, the same to be brought as an offering to the Ka'ba; or as an expiation he shall have to feed *a number of* poor persons, or fast an equivalent number *of days*, so that he may taste the penalty of his deed. [c]*As for* the past, Allah forgives *it*; but whoso reverts to it, Allah will punish him *for his offence*. And Allah is Mighty, Lord of retribution.[723]

يَاۤ اَيُّهَا الَّذِيۡنَ اٰمَنُوۡا لَا تَقۡتُلُوا الصَّيۡدَ وَاَنۡتُمۡ حُرُمٌ ؕ وَمَنۡ قَتَلَهٗ مِنۡكُمۡ مُّتَعَمِّدًا فَجَزَآءٌ مِّثۡلُ مَا قَتَلَ مِنَ النَّعَمِ يَحۡكُمُ بِهٖ ذَوَا عَدۡلٍ مِّنۡكُمۡ هَدۡيًاۢ بٰلِغَ الۡكَعۡبَةِ اَوۡ كَفَّارَةٌ طَعَامُ مَسٰكِيۡنَ اَوۡ عَدۡلُ ذٰلِكَ صِيَامًا لِّيَذُوۡقَ وَبَالَ اَمۡرِهٖ ؕ عَفَا اللّٰهُ عَمَّا سَلَفَ ؕ وَمَنۡ عَادَ فَيَنۡتَقِمُ اللّٰهُ مِنۡهُ ؕ وَاللّٰهُ عَزِيۡزٌ ذُو انۡتِقَامٍ ۝

[a]57 : 26. [b]5 : 2, 97. [c]2 : 276.

---

722. Commentary:

As hunting is ordinarily done in a jungle where one is generally alone and where there is none beside God to observe one's breaking divine commandments, the verse fittingly mentions hunting to illustrate تقوى or God-fearingness. While engaged in hunting, man's abstention from violating divine commandments would show that he has really done so out of the fear of God. It is thus that, by an outward act, the inner condition of a man's heart may become revealed.

The verse also serves as an introduction to the commandment that follows in the next verse and prepares believers for the acceptance of an injunction which ran counter to the prevalent practice.

723. Important Words:

انتقام (retribution) is derived from نقم . They say نقم عليه *i.e.* he exacted vengeance upon him; he punished him. انتقمت منه means, I took vengeance on him; I inflicted penal retribution on him or I punished him. انتقام thus means, vengeance, punishment or penal retribution (Lane & Aqrab). See also 3 : 5 and 5 : 60.

Commentary:

If a man kills game, when he is in the state of احرام (pilgrimage), he should give as compensation a like animal to be taken to Mecca for sacrifice. For instance, if the game killed by him is a deer, he should offer a goat. If the like of the game killed cannot be found

97. The game of the sea and the eating thereof have been made lawful for you as a provision for you and the travellers; but *forbidden to you is the game of the land as long as you are in a state of pilgrimage. And fear Allah to whom you shall be gathered.⁷²⁴

أُحِلَّ لَكُمْ صَيْدُ الْبَحْرِ وَطَعَامُهُ مَتَاعًا لَّكُمْ وَلِلسَّيَّارَةِ وَحُرِّمَ عَلَيْكُمْ صَيْدُ الْبَرِّ مَا دُمْتُمْ حُرُمًا وَاتَّقُوا اللّٰهَ الَّذِيۤ إِلَيْهِ تُحْشَرُوْنَ ۟

98. *Allah has made the Ka'ba, the inviolable House, as a means of support and uplift for mankind, as also the Sacred Month and the offerings and the *animals with collars. That is so that you may know that Allah knows what is in the heavens and what is in the earth, and that Allah knows all things well.⁷²⁵

جَعَلَ اللّٰهُ الْكَعْبَةَ الْبَيْتَ الْحَرَامَ قِيَامًا لِّلنَّاسِ وَالشَّهْرَ الْحَرَامَ وَالْهَدْيَ وَالْقَلَائِدَ ذٰلِكَ لِتَعْلَمُوۤا أَنَّ اللّٰهَ يَعْلَمُ مَا فِي السَّمٰوٰتِ وَمَا فِي الْأَرْضِ وَأَنَّ اللّٰهَ بِكُلِّ شَيْءٍ عَلِيمٌ ۟

*5 : 2, 96.   *2 : 126; 3 : 97-98.   *5 : 3.

then an animal costing approximately as much as the game killed should be offered, or failing that, the pilgrim should spend the estimated price of the game in feeding the poor, which is two مد per head according to some theologians and one صاع according to others, a مد being roughly two handfuls of corn while a صاع is four times as much as a مد. If, however, the pilgrim is unable to do even that, he should fast for as many days as the number of the poor he could feed with the estimated price of the game killed. The fasting and the feeding of the poor, as the case may be, should preferably be done at Mecca.

724. Commentary :

The word بحر (sea) here includes rivers, streams, lakes, ponds, etc. See 7 : 139.

As, during the time of Pilgrimage, hunting on land is likely to prove inconvenient and even dangerous to pilgrims visiting the Ka'ba, whereas the catching of sea-game does not interfere with traffic, so the former has been prohibited and the latter allowed.

725. Important Words :

قياما (means of support and uplift) is the noun-infinitive from قام meaning, he stood up, or he stood still. They say قام المرأة i.e. he (the husband) supported or maintained the woman. قام به قياما تاما means, he managed it (an affair, etc.) perfectly. قياما therefore signifies, means of support and uplift (Lane, Aqrab & Zamakhsharī). See also 4 : 6.

Commentary :

God has made Pilgrimage to the Ka'ba a sign for the progress and prosperity of Muslims. So long as they will continue to perform Pilgrimage, God's grace will continue to attend them. But it is regrettable that wealthy Muslims have now generally grown negligent in this respect, with the result that their glory has departed.

Pilgrimage is a means of support for men in a material sense also. Muslims from all parts of the world visit the Ka'ba and this serves as a means of support for the people of Mecca. Abraham left his wife Hagar and his son

99. *a*Know that Allah is severe in punishment and that Allah is *also* Most Forgiving *and* Merciful.726

اِعْلَمُوْۤا اَنَّ اللّٰهَ شَدِیْدُ الْعِقَابِ وَ اَنَّ اللّٰهَ غَفُوْرٌ رَّحِیْمٌ ۟

100. *b*On the Messenger lies only the conveying of the message. And *c*Allah knows what you reveal and what you hide.727

مَا عَلَی الرَّسُوْلِ اِلَّا الْبَلٰغُ ۫ وَ اللّٰهُ یَعْلَمُ مَا تُبْدُوْنَ وَ مَا تَکْتُمُوْنَ ۟

---

*a*15 : 50-51.   *b*16 : 83 ; 36 : 18 ; 64 : 13.   *c*2 : 78 ; 6 : 4 ; 11 : 6 ; 16 : 20.

Ishmael in the wilderness of Paran near Mecca, apparently to die from starvation. But God made provision not only for Hagar and Ishmael in that barren and bleak desert but also for their posterity for all time to come. See also ch. 106. But to say that the promise that the Pilgrimage will continue to prove a means of subsistence for Meccans only is to limit its vast scope and application. It certainly is not confined to the people of Mecca but encompasses all mankind. It is clear from the verse that not only will the Pilgrimage to Mecca with its attendant rites continue till the end of time, but that the world itself will last only so long as the Pilgrimage to the Ka'ba continues and that it will come to an end when the Pilgrimage ceases to be performed. This is indeed a great prophecy ; for there have been many places in the world which were the resorts of pilgrims in their own time but which have long ceased to be so and are now deserted and forgotten. But the Ka'ba is meant to remain for all time " an inviolable house and a means of support and uplift for mankind."

726. **Commentary :**

The divine attributes of Forgiveness and Mercy are given great prominence in the Quran. *My mercy encompasses all things*, says the Holy Book (7 : 157). Therefore, whenever God warns people of His punishment in the Quran, He makes it a point to remind them of His attributes of Forgiveness and Mercy also, thus showing that these attributes predominate over His other attributes and only await a gesture of goodness on the part of man to show themselves.

727. **Commentary :**

This verse sheds some light on the responsibility and duty of a Prophet. With the deliverance of the message entrusted to a Prophet his duty ends, and he is not responsible if, in spite of his clear warnings, the people reject his mission. He has not been given the power to force them to believe. In fact, each divine message serves as a guidance for the people to whom it is given. If they live up to it and repent of their evil ways, they find God Forgiving and Merciful ; but if they persist in their wicked practices, they are punished and God makes another people take their place.

101. Say, 'The bad and the good are not alike', even though the abundance of the bad may cause thee to wonder. So fear Allah, O men of understanding, that you may prosper.⁷²⁸

قُلْ لَّا يَسْتَوِى الْخَبِيثُ وَ الطَّيِّبُ وَلَوْ اَعْجَبَكَ كَثْرَةُ الْخَبِيثِ فَاتَّقُوا اللّٰهَ يَآ اُولِى الْاَلْبَابِ لَعَلَّكُمْ تُفْلِحُوْنَ ۞

4 102. O ye who believe! ask not about things which, if revealed to you, would cause you trouble; though if you ask about them while the Quran is being sent down, they will be revealed to you. Allah has left them out. And Allah is Most Forgiving and Forbearing.⁷²⁹

يٰٓاَيُّهَا الَّذِيْنَ اٰمَنُوْا لَا تَسْـَٔلُوْا عَنْ اَشْيَآءَ اِنْ تُبْدَ لَكُمْ تَسُؤْكُمْ وَ اِنْ تَسْـَٔلُوْا عَنْهَا حِيْنَ يُنَزَّلُ الْقُرْاٰنُ تُبْدَ لَكُمْ عَفَا اللّٰهُ عَنْهَا وَ اللّٰهُ غَفُوْرٌ حَلِيْمٌ ۞

ᵃ2 : 268.   ᵇ2 : 109.

728. Commentary :

Being naturally influenced by his environment, man is prone to follow and imitate what others do, particularly when they happen to be in the majority. This verse, however, is a warning against unthinking and blind following of the majority. The real criterion by which the worth of a thing is to be judged is not how many people do it but what good it contains ; and, God being the source of all good, the only true and unfailing test is, as the verse puts it, تقوى or God-fearingness.

729. Commentary :

The verse is important, as it sheds light on the principle underlying the Sharī'at i.e. the code of divine laws. The bases of the Islamic Sharī'at are threefold : (1) the Law embodied in the Quran, (2) Sunnah or the practice of the Holy Prophet, and (3) the injunctions and precepts contained in his sayings. These three sources of Islamic Law deal with all the fundamental problems of man, but minor details are left to be thought out by man himself in the light of the above three torch-bearers of guidance, aided and

assisted by his own God-given intellectual powers and faculties. It is to matters relating to minor details that the present verse refers and God warns the Faithful that the habit of asking questions about such matters will do them more harm than good.

As a matter of fact, God, in His infinite wisdom, leaves sufficient room for individuals to exercise and develop their power of judgement and their reasoning faculty. When man is confronted with situations and circumstances about which he finds no definite and clear-cut guidance in the Quran, or in the practice or sayings of the Holy Prophet, he has to find a way for himsef in order to meet them as best be can, keeping always in view the guiding and unalterable principle that nothing is to be done which runs counter to any Quranic injunction or to the established practice and the authentic sayings of the Holy Prophet. Islam is thus not a hard and fast code of laws, for it does not lay down rigid injunctions regarding minor and ever-changing details. On the contrary, it affords sufficient scope for individuals to exercise their judgement in order to adapt an injunction of

103. ^aA people before you asked about such *things, but* then they became disbelievers therein.⁷³⁰

قَدْ سَاَلَهَا قَوْمٌ مِّنْ قَبْلِكُمْ ثُمَّ اَصْبَحُوْا بِهَا كٰفِرِيْنَ ۝

104. ^bAllah has not ordained any 'Baḥīra' or 'Sā'iba' or 'Waṣīla' or 'Ḥāmī'; but those who disbelieve forge a lie against Allah, and most of them do not make use of their understanding.⁷³¹

مَا جَعَلَ اللّٰهُ مِنْ بَحِيْرَةٍ وَّلَا سَآئِبَةٍ وَّلَا وَصِيْلَةٍ وَّلَا حَامٍ وَّلٰكِنَّ الَّذِيْنَ كَفَرُوْا يَفْتَرُوْنَ عَلَى اللّٰهِ الْكَذِبَ وَ اَكْثَرُهُمْ لَا يَعْقِلُوْنَ ۝

^a2 : 109.   ^b6 : 137.

a general nature to meet a new and changed situation. The basic principles, however, are unchangeable. But as details continue to change, Islam has not resorted to rigid legislation with regard to minor details and has forbidden Muslims to ask for legislation regarding them. Indeed, it was about filling up these very details to meet new and altered conditions that the Holy Prophet said اختلاف امتى رحمة *i.e.* "the difference of opinion among my followers is, indeed, a source of mercy." This ḥadīth meant that as it had been left to Muslims to chalk out a way for themselves with regard to such minor details about which no definite pronouncement is to be found in the *Sharī'at*, there was bound to be a difference of opinion among Muslim theologians about them, but that this difference would prove a blessing for them, because it would afford opportunities for the exercise and cultivation of their reasoning faculties as well as a suitable and flexible law about ever-changing details.

The reader will see that this verse also incidentally refutes the allegations of those who say that the laws of Islam, being rigid and unchangeable, afford no room for the exercise of individual judgement, and that they fetter humanity for all time to hard and fast rules and are thus calculated to impede the intellectual advancement of man rather than help it.

The expression, *which if revealed to you would cause you trouble*, means that if God or His Prophet had legislated about minor details and had not left such matters to individual discretion so that people might formulate laws concerning them according to their own judgement and their own circumstances, they would have found it troublesome and the development of man's intellect would have become seriously hampered.

730. Commentary :

Unnecessary questioning about minor details and seeking legislation on them is always to the detriment of the questioner himself. It limits his discretion and fetters his judgement, besides binding him and his co-religionists to unnecessary and irksome legislation. The Israelites are reported in the Quran to have put unnecessary questions to Moses in regard to minor details with the result that they created difficulties for themselves and became more and more perplexed and confounded and ended with breaking the commandments of God and drawing His displeasure on themselves (*e.g.* 2 : 109).

731. Important Words :

بَحِيْرَة (Baḥīra) is derived from بحر which means, he cut or slit lengthwise; he split or clave. *Baḥīra* was a name given by the pagan Arabs to a camel (or a goat) which they let loose to feed, after slitting its ears. The word may be applied both to males and females, but in practice it was only the females that were thus let loose to pasture where they liked. They were dedicated to some god and their milk was not used, nor their back. The description of *Baḥira* varied among different tribes.

سائبة (*Sā'iba*) is derived from ساب which means, it or he went away at random or went wherever it or he liked. سائبة was a name given to a she-camel set free to go wherever she pleased. She was generally let loose as an offering to the gods when one recovered from a sickness or returned safe from a journey. Often a she-camel having given birth to 10 female young ones was let loose to pasture where she would, and she was not ridden nor was her milk drunk except by her young.

وصيلة (*Waṣila*) is derived from وصل which means, he connected or joined. وصيلة was the name given to a she-camel that was let loose in the name of a god after she had given birth to seven female young ones consecutively. If, at the seventh birth, she bore a pair, male and female, each of the latter was also let loose.

حام (*Ḥāmi*) is derived from حمى. They say احمى الشيئ *i.e.* he prohibited the thing; or he protected it; or defended it against encroachment, invasion or attack. حام which is really حامى therefore, means a stallion camel that has his back prohibited or interdicted to be used for bearing a rider or carrying a burden; such camel was neither ridden nor shorn of his fur; he was left at liberty and was not debarred from pasturage or from water. The word is also used about a stallion camel whose offspring's offspring has conceived (Lane).

Commentary :

After having said that minor matters and details should be left to man to legislate as he thinks proper, the Quran, in the present verse, fittingly draws our attention to the fact that such freedom and discretion cannot be allowed to man in fundamentals and things of importance, because in such matters unanimity is essential and divergence of opinion may prove immensely harmful. The verse under comment gives an illustration to show that human intellect cannot be trusted with the making of laws on fundamental matters, for, if left to itself, it is likely to make laws that would lead man to perdition. An instance of such laws is given in this verse. It is really Christians for whom the address in this verse is meant; but instead of drawing attention to the laws devised and invented by Christians, the Quran very wisely refers here to certain practices of the pagan Arabs, for one can more easily see a mote in another man's eye than a beam in one's own. The Arabs used to let loose the animals mentioned in the verse in honour of their idols. Besides being based on disbelief and superstition, the practice was also highly foolish. The animals thus let loose wrought great havoc wherever they went. They devastated field crops and gardens and killed children. The Quran refers to the letting loose of these animals as an example of man-made laws and warns Christians who question the wisdom and blessing of a revealed Law to learn a lesson from the degrading practices to which the pagan Arabs had fallen victim because they had no revealed Law to guide them.

105. And *when it is said to them 'Come to what Allah has revealed, and to the Messenger,' they say, 'Sufficient for us is that wherein we found our fathers.' What! even though their fathers had no knowledge and no guidance ?[732]

وَاِذَا قِيْلَ لَهُمْ تَعَالَوْا اِلٰى مَآ اَنْزَلَ اللّٰهُ وَاِلَى الرَّسُوْلِ قَالُوْا حَسْبُنَا مَا وَجَدْنَا عَلَيْهِ اٰبَآءَنَا اَوَلَوْ كَانَ اٰبَآؤُهُمْ لَا يَعْلَمُوْنَ شَيْئًا وَّلَا يَهْتَدُوْنَ ۞

106. O ye who believe! be heedful of your own selves. *He who goes astray cannot harm you when you *yourselves* are rightly guided. To Allah will you all return; then will He disclose to you what you used to do.[733]

يٰٓاَيُّهَا الَّذِيْنَ اٰمَنُوْا عَلَيْكُمْ اَنْفُسَكُمْ لَا يَضُرُّكُمْ مَّنْ ضَلَّ اِذَا اهْتَدَيْتُمْ طاِلَى اللّٰهِ مَرْجِعُكُمْ جَمِيْعًا فَيُنَبِّئُكُمْ بِمَا كُنْتُمْ تَعْمَلُوْنَ ۞

---

*2 : 171 ; 31 : 22.   *2 : 138.

---

732. Commentary :

It is indeed strange that when science and knowledge advance and new discoveries and new inventions are made, people are quick to throw overboard worn-out ideas and theories tenaciously held by their forefathers and hasten to accept and benefit by the new inventions and discoveries ; but when a Prophet brings to them a new guidance from God, they refuse to accept it on the ground that it does not agree with the beliefs and ideas held by their ancestors and with their own time-honoured notions and theories. How foolish is this attitude and how lame and absurd the excuse for the rejection of divine truths ! This is how the Quran exposes the untenability of the position of the rejectors of truth.

733. Commentary :

This verse tells us that though man can sacrifice his worldly interests for the sake of others, yet he cannot so sacrifice his beliefs and religious principles. In religious matters our duty is only to show people the right path and exhort them to follow it ; but we should not ruin or wrong our souls for their sake. It cannot profit mankind nor ourselves if we lose our own soul in trying to save others. The body

may be sacrificed but not the soul. Christians abandoned some of the fundamental principles of their religion, hoping to win over certain heathen nations to Christianity. But in doing so they lost the truth and struck a very bad bargain.

The verse, however, should not be understood to mean that we should not preach the truth to others, and should confine our attention to saving our own souls only and have no thought for others. In fact, the Quran enjoins upon every Muslim to try his utmost to make others see the truth, because *firstly*, it is our duty to propagate the truth ; and *secondly*, placed as we are, we cannot properly save ourselves unless we also save those among whom we live. What the verse, therefore, means is that our duty is only to preach the truth to others. If they accept it, well and good ; but if in spite of our efforts, they refuse to be weaned from their evil course, their rejection of the truth will do us no harm. But in no circumstances should we compromise our principles in order to win others over to our way of thinking. That would be ruining our own souls to save others.

There is an hadīth to the effect that once the

107. O ye who believe ! the *right* evidence among you, when death presents tself to one of you, at the time of making a bequest, is of two just men from among you; or of two others not from among you, if you be journeying in the land and the calamity of death befall you. You shall detain them both after Prayer *for giving evidence;* and, if you doubt, they shall both swear by Allah, *saying:* ' We take not in exchange for this any price, even though he be a near relation, and "we conceal not the testimony *enjoined* by Allah ; surely, in that case, we shall be among the sinners.'⁷³⁴

يَاَيُّهَا الَّذِيْنَ اٰمَنُوْا شَهَادَةُ بَيْنِكُمْ اِذَا حَضَرَ اَحَدَكُمُ الْمَوْتُ حِيْنَ الْوَصِيَّةِ اثْنٰنِ ذَوَا عَدْلٍ مِّنْكُمْ اَوْ اٰخَرٰنِ مِنْ غَيْرِكُمْ اِنْ اَنْتُمْ ضَرَبْتُمْ فِى الْاَرْضِ فَاَصَابَتْكُمْ مُّصِيْبَةُ الْمَوْتِ تَحْبِسُوْنَهُمَا مِنْۢ بَعْدِ الصَّلٰوةِ فَيُقْسِمٰنِ بِاللّٰهِ اِنِ ارْتَبْتُمْ لَا نَشْتَرِيْ بِهٖ ثَمَنًا وَّلَوْ كَانَ ذَا قُرْبٰى وَلَا نَكْتُمُ شَهَادَةَ اللّٰهِ اِنَّا اِذًا لَّمِنَ الْاٰثِمِيْنَ ۞

ᵃ2 : 141, 284.

Holy Prophet explained this verse as meaning that you should preach the truth under all circumstances but when you see that the person to whom you preach the truth persists in following his own evil inclinations and does not listen to you, then your duty will have ended by your having duly preached to him the truth, and in this case his evil practices would do you no harm, if only you yourselves scrupulously follow the truth (Tirmidhī, ch. on *Tafsīr*).

The words, *He who goes astray cannot harm you when you yourselves are rightly guided*, may also

mean that if you do the right sort of preaching and try to find the right way of approach to a person and even then he does not accept the truth, then his going astray will not harm you and you will not be held responsible for it. In this case the words, *when you yourselves are rightly guided*, would mean, "if you succeed in finding out the right way of preaching and put in the right sort of effort."

734. Commentary :

See collective note on 5 : 109 below.

108. But if it be discovered that the two *witnesses* are guilty of sin, then two others shall take their place from among those against whom the *former* two *witnesses*—who were in a better position *to give true evidence*—*sinfully* deposed, and the two *latter witnesses* shall swear by Allah, *saying,* ' Surely, our testimony is truer than the testimony of the *former* two, and we have not been unfair *in any way* ; for then, indeed, we should be of the unjust.'735

فَإِنْ عُثِرَ عَلَىٰٓ أَنَّهُمَا اسْتَحَقَّآ إِثْمًا فَٱخَرَانِ يَقُومَانِ مَقَامَهُمَا مِنَ الَّذِينَ اسْتَحَقَّ عَلَيْهِمُ الْأَوْلَيَانِ فَيُقْسِمَانِ بِاللَّهِ لَشَهَادَتُنَآ أَحَقُّ مِن شَهَادَتِهِمَا وَمَا اعْتَدَيْنَآ إِنَّآ إِذًا لَّمِنَ الظَّالِمِينَ ﴿١٠٨﴾

109. Thus it is more likely that they will give evidence according to facts or that they will fear that other oaths will be taken after their oaths. And fear Allah and hearken. And Allah guides not the disobedient people.736

ذَٰلِكَ أَدْنَىٰٓ أَن يَأْتُوا بِالشَّهَادَةِ عَلَىٰ وَجْهِهَآ أَوْ يَخَافُوٓا أَن تُرَدَّ أَيْمَانٌۢ بَعْدَ أَيْمَانِهِمْ وَاتَّقُوا اللَّهَ وَاسْمَعُوا وَاللَّهُ لَا يَهْدِي الْقَوْمَ الْفَاسِقِينَ ﴿١٠٩﴾

735. Important Words:

أَوْلَيَان (the two who were in a better position) is derived from ولى being the dual of أولى which means, one more worthy or more competent or more entitled or more deserving or better fitted or having a better claim to do a thing, etc. (Lane). See also 4 : 136.

استحقا اثما (the two are guilty of sin) and استحق عليهم (against whom they sinfully deposed). The word استحق is derived from حق which means, it was or became suitable to the requirements of wisdom, justice, right and truth ; it was or became right, proper, correct or true ; it became established as a truth. استحقه means, he demanded it as his right or due ; he had a right or title or claim to it ; he deserved or merited it. They say استحق اثما i.e. he did what necessitated sin ; or he was guilty of a sin and deserved it being said of him that he was a sinner. The expression عليهم added to the word استحق means " against them," the particle على sometimes

meaning "against." استحقها على المشترى means, he has a right to it in preference to the purchaser, i.e., he has a better claim to it as against the buyer. The words استحق عليهم therefore, would mean, they (the two witnesses who were in a better position to give true evidence) gave false evidence against their just rights, seeking to deprive them (heirs of the deceased) of their rights by giving false evidence against them.

Commentary :

See collective note on 5 : 109 below.

736. Commentary :

The Arabic words ترد ايمان بعد ايمانهم rendered as " other oaths will be taken after their oaths " literally mean: (1) " oaths will be repeated i.e. taken again, after their oaths " ; or (2) " their oaths will be rejected after their (other witnesses') oaths," the significance in both cases being practically the same, i.e., the oaths of the first two witnesses will be rejected and two other witnesses called in to give true evidence on oath.

The purport of this and the preceding two verses is that when a person is about to make his will at the time of his death, he should have as witnesses to his statement two just men, who should testify to the validity of his will after his death. But if death comes upon a person suddenly when he is away from home and no Muslim witnesses are at hand, then two trustworthy non-Muslims may be asked to serve as witnesses. If, however, the veracity of the witnesses is called into question by the heirs of the deceased, the former should be asked to prove their truthfulness by a statement on oath made after the time of Prayer. But if the persons in whose favour the will was made have good reason to believe that the witnesses have been guilty of perjury, then they can state on oath that their statement is truer than that of the two witnesses, and in that case the Qāḍī or judge, if satisfied, will give his decree in their favour.

An incident is reported to have occurred in the days of the Holy Prophet which throws some light on the verses under comment. A Muslim who died away from home entrusted his goods to two men before his death and asked them to deliver the same to his heirs at Medina. On receiving the goods the heirs found that a silver bowl was missing. The two men were thereupon called upon to explain the loss of the bowl, but they denied all knowledge of it on oath. Later, the heirs of the deceased person happened to see the bowl with some persons at Mecca who told them that it had been sold to them by the two men to whom the deceased had entrusted his property. Thereupon the two men were again summoned, and in their presence the heirs of the deceased

stated on oath that the bowl was theirs, whereupon it was handed over to them (Manthūr).

The Prayer mentioned in 5 : 107 above may be any Prayer but preferably it should be the 'Aṣr or late afternoon Prayer, because it was after this Prayer that the Holy Prophet summoned the two witnesses to whom reference has been made above and who were believed to have stolen the silver bowl. The time after Prayer has been chosen with a view to inspiring witnesses with ideas of piety and God-fearingness and inclining their minds to truthfulness. If the witnesses be non-Muslims, then they may be called upon to swear after the time of their own worship, so that the solemnity of the hour may incline them to make a true statement, because the worship of God is calculated to exercise a purifying influence on the human mind and men fresh from Prayer are expected to fear God and make a true statement.

The word أوليان (the two who were in a better position) occurring in 5 : 108 above is the dual of اولى which means more competent or more worthy. It refers to the first two witnesses and signifies that these two were in a better position to give true evidence, being the persons who were with the deceased at the time of his death and in whose presence the will was made and to whom the property was entrusted to be handed over to the heirs of the deceased. The expression also serves as a sort of veiled reproach to them that, in spite of being in a better position and more competent to give true evidence, they stumbled and drifted away from truth.

The second two witnesses should be from among the deceased person's heirs whom the first two witnesses deprived of their right by bearing false witness regarding the will of the deceased.

R. 15   110. *Think of* the day when ^aAllah will assemble the Messengers and say, ' What reply was made to you ? ' They will say, ' We have no knowledge, it is only Thou Who art the Knower of hidden things ' ;[737]

يَوْمَ يَجْمَعُ اللّٰهُ الرُّسُلَ فَيَقُوْلُ مَاذَآ اُجِبْتُمْ ۚ قَالُوْا لَا عِلْمَ لَنَا ۗ اِنَّكَ اَنْتَ عَلَّامُ الْغُيُوْبِ ۝

^a7 : 7 ; 28 : 66.

737. Commentary :

The words, *We have no knowledge ; it is only Thou Who art the Knower of hidden things*, constitute both a sort of veiled recommendation and a glorification of God. The Prophets will, in effect, say, " The people did indeed reject us ; but Thou art the Knower of secrets. We do not know what was in their minds and whether they rejected us from their hearts or only expressed disbelief out of the fear of others. It is, therefore, for Thee to decide what their real attitude was and what treatment should be meted out to them." This recommendation seems to run counter to 4 : 42, which shows that the Prophets will bear witness against their people. The study of the relevant verses, however, shows that the occasions are different. The above-mentioned reply of the Prophets will be made when in the beginning God will question them in a general way ; whereas the tendering of evidence will come at a later stage when God will call upon them definitely to come forward and give the required evidence about those who rejected them. There

is, thus, no real conflict between the two verses.

The answer given by the Prophets is also in harmony with the dignity of God and constitutes an act of His glorification on the part of the Prophets. God perfectly knows what reply the people made to the Prophets, but, in spite of this, He will ask the Prophets to say what answer they were given by the people, as if He Himself was not aware of that answer. The Prophets, therefore, will very appropriately remove this apparent implication of ignorance on the part of God, by attributing all knowledge to Him.

The answer of the Prophets also implies that the object of God's question was not to elicit information from them or to supplement His own knowledge, for He knew what answer they were given. In fact, there was some other purpose behind His question which was that they should give their testimony against the disbelievers, as is clear from 4 : 42, and thus carry out the divine command referred to in the latter verse.

111. When Allah will say, "O Jesus, son of Mary, remember My favour upon thee and upon thy mother; when *a*I strengthened thee with the spirit of holiness *so that* *b*thou didst speak to the people in the cradle and when of middle age; and when *c*I taught thee the Book and Wisdom and the Torah and the Gospel; and when *d*thou didst fashion out *a creation* out of clay, in the likeness of a bird, by My command; then thou didst breathe into it *a new spirit* and it became a soaring being by My command; and thou didst heal the night-blind and the leprous by My command; and when thou didst raise the dead by My command; and when *e*I restrained the children of Israel from *putting* thee *to death* when thou didst come to them with clear Signs; and those who disbelieved from among them said, 'This is nothing but clear deception;'"738

اِذۡ قَالَ اللّٰهُ يٰعِیۡسَی ابۡنَ مَرۡیَمَ اذۡکُرۡ نِعۡمَتِیۡ عَلَیۡکَ وَ عَلٰی وَالِدَتِکَ اِذۡ اَیَّدۡتُّکَ بِرُوۡحِ الۡقُدُسِ تُکَلِّمُ النَّاسَ فِی الۡمَهۡدِ وَ کَهۡلًا وَ اِذۡ عَلَّمۡتُکَ الۡکِتٰبَ وَ الۡحِکۡمَةَ وَ التَّوۡرٰةَ وَ الۡاِنۡجِیۡلَ وَ اِذۡ تَخۡلُقُ مِنَ الطِّیۡنِ کَهَیۡئَةِ الطَّیۡرِ بِاِذۡنِیۡ فَتَنۡفُخُ فِیۡهَا فَتَکُوۡنُ طَیۡرًا بِاِذۡنِیۡ وَ تُبۡرِیُٔ الۡاَکۡمَهَ وَ الۡاَبۡرَصَ بِاِذۡنِیۡ وَ اِذۡ تُخۡرِجُ الۡمَوۡتٰی بِاِذۡنِیۡ وَ اِذۡ کَفَفۡتُ بَنِیۡۤ اِسۡرَآءِیۡلَ عَنۡکَ اِذۡ جِئۡتَهُمۡ بِالۡبَیِّنٰتِ فَقَالَ الَّذِیۡنَ کَفَرُوۡا مِنۡهُمۡ اِنۡ هٰذَاۤ اِلَّا سِحۡرٌ مُّبِیۡنٌ ۝

---

*a*2 : 88; 2 : 254.   *b*3 : 47.   *c*3 : 49.   *d*3 : 50.   *e*5 : 12.

---

738. Commentary :

In the clause, *thou didst speak to the people in the cradle and when of middle age*, the act of speaking in the cradle signifies speaking words of wisdom and piety in childhood. This sort of speaking on the part of Jesus reflected great credit on his mother, who, herself being wise and pious, brought him up as a wise and pious child. And the speaking of good words in middle age shows that not only was Mary a pious woman, but Jesus too was a righteous man so that even when he was of middle age and was no longer under the direct influence of his mother, he spoke words of piety and wisdom to men. See also 3 : 47 & 3 : 49, 50, where similar works of Jesus *i.e.* the creation of birds and the quickening of the dead, etc. have been discussed.

Protection similar to that alluded to in the latter part of this verse in the words, *I restrained the children of Israel from putting thee to death,* was promised to the Holy Prophet as well (5 : 68). This promise met with a remarkable fulfilment. Though even at Mecca his life was in constant danger, at Medina that danger very much increased. The Holy Prophet led many expeditions in person and several attempts were made on his life. At Uhud he was severely wounded and at Hunain he was left alone among a large host of blood-thirsty archers. Yet amidst all these dangers he remained safe, and after having triumphed over his enemies passed away peacefully in his house at Medina. The reference in the present verse is to the attempts of the Jews to kill Jesus on the Cross, from which accursed death God delivered him. The words, *I restrained the children of Israel,*

112. And when *a*I inspired the disciples *of Jesus* to believe in Me and in My Messenger, they said, ' We believe and bear Thou witness that we have submitted.'739

وَاِذْ اَوْحَيْتُ اِلَى الْحَوَارِيّنَ اَنْ اٰمِنُوْا بِىْ وَبِرَسُوْلِىْ قَالُوْا اٰمَنَّا وَاشْهَدْ بِاَنَّنَا مُسْلِمُوْنَ ۝

113. When the disciples said, ' O Jesus, son of Mary, is thy Lord able to send down to us a table spread with food from heaven ? ', he said, ' Fear Allah, if you are believers ' ;740

اِذْ قَالَ الْحَوَارِيُّوْنَ يٰعِيْسَى ابْنَ مَرْيَمَ هَلْ يَسْتَطِيْعُ رَبُّكَ اَنْ يُّنَزِّلَ عَلَيْنَا مَآئِدَةً مِّنَ السَّمَآءِ قَالَ اتَّقُوا اللهَ اِنْ كُنْتُمْ مُّؤْمِنِيْنَ ۝

114. They said, ' We desire that we may eat of it, and that our hearts be at rest and that we may know that thou hast spoken truth to us, and that we may be witnesses thereto.'741

قَالُوْا نُرِيْدُ اَنْ نَّاْكُلَ مِنْهَا وَتَطْمَئِنَّ قُلُوْبُنَا وَنَعْلَمَ اَنْ قَدْ صَدَقْتَنَا وَنَكُوْنَ عَلَيْهَا مِنَ الشَّاهِدِيْنَ ۝

---

*a*3 : 53-54 ; 61 : 15.

---

should not, however, be understood to mean that Jesus suffered even no persecution at the hands of his enemies. A similar expression has been used with regard to early Muslims in the Quran (5 : 12) but it is a well-known fact that they had to pass through grievous trials and tribulations. The expression thus only means that the enemy will fail to kill Jesus, whom God will protect from being destroyed.

739. Important Words :

The verb اوحى (inspired) does not always mean verbal revelation. It sometimes simply means to inspire a person with an idea, or to suggest it to him ; and it is in this sense that the word is used here. The word has also been used with reference to the bee (16 : 69).

الحوارين (disciples). See 3 : 53.

740. Commentary :

The words, *send down to us a table spread with food from heaven*, show that it was not a single meal that the disciples of Jesus asked for, but a permanent provision of sustenance which

might be had without any trouble or hardship. The words " from heaven " denote a thing that is obtained without trouble and is sure and lasting.

741. Commentary :

The disciples of Jesus have, in this verse, mentioned four objects which the fulfilment of the prayer of Jesus about the food asked for was meant to serve : (1) that they might eat thereof and their hunger might be satisfied ; (2) that their minds might be at rest. This also shows that they desired a permanent provision of sustenance because a single meal could not put their minds at rest or relieve them of anxiety about their livelihood in future so that they might be able to preach the message of God free from all care and devote themselves fully to the service of religion ; (3) that the prophecy of Jesus contained in 3 : 50 might be fulfilled ; and (4) that they might become witnesses to the fulfilment of his prayer and of the truth of their religion, and people might know that God helps and favours those who

115. Said Jesus, son of Mary, 'O Allah, our Lord, send down to us a table from heaven spread with food that it may be to us a festival, to the first of us and to the last of us, and a Sign from Thee; and provide sustenance for us, for Thou art the best of sustainers.'[742]

قَالَ عِيْسَى ابْنُ مَرْيَمَ اللّٰهُمَّ رَبَّنَآ اَنْزِلْ عَلَيْنَا مَآئِدَةً مِّنَ السَّمَآءِ تَكُوْنُ لَنَا عِيْدًا لِّاَوَّلِنَا وَاٰخِرِنَا وَاٰيَةً مِّنْكَ وَارْزُقْنَا وَاَنْتَ خَيْرُ الرّٰزِقِيْنَ ۝

116. Allah said, 'Surely, I will send it down to you; but whosoever of you disbelieves afterwards,—I will surely punish them with a punishment wherewith I will not punish any other of the peoples.'[743]

قَالَ اللّٰهُ اِنِّىْ مُنَزِّلُهَا عَلَيْكُمْ فَمَنْ يَّكْفُرْ بَعْدُ مِنْكُمْ فَاِنِّىْ اُعَذِّبُهٗ عَذَابًا لَّا اُعَذِّبُهٗ اَحَدًا مِّنَ الْعٰلَمِيْنَ ۝

---

are devoted to the service of His religion. The history of the early Christian Church shows that God did actually make extraordinary provision for the sustenance of those who devoted their lives to the preaching of the message of Jesus. Nay, even now Christians, though they have drifted far away from the truth, are enjoying an extra good table spread with food.

742. Commentary :

This verse shows that Jesus approved of the wish of his disciples and therefore, while praying, he included himself among them.

The words, *that it may be to us a festival, to the first of us and to the last of us*, embody a great prophecy. There were to be two periods of prosperity and progress for the Christian peoples, as the word عيد (festival) literally meaning "a day which returns," shows. The first was to be in the time immediately after Jesus, while the second was to be in the Latter Days; and the period between these two was to be marked by decay and decline. And this is exactly what is more clearly referred to in the words, *to the first of us and to the last of us*. Christian peoples were granted worldly good in abundance in the early ages *i.e.* before the rise of Islam, and now in the Latter Days *i.e.* after the decline of Islam, they have had material

prosperity and grandeur in such measure as has no parallel in the history of any other religion. But with the advent of the like of Jesus in the person of Ahmad, the Promised Messiah, in Islam, the sun is indeed nearing its setting on "the last of the Christians," who can now save themselves only by identifying themselves with him who has come in the spirit and power of their Master.

743. Commentary :

This verse also makes it clear that the مائدة (the table spread with food) did not mean a meal that was actually to descend from heaven, for such miracles are never shown, it being impossible to disbelieve after one has witnessed the wonderful phenomenon of a table set out with food actually descending from on high.

The punishment referred to in the verse is the same as is mentioned in 19 : 91.

Christians did "disbelieve afterwards" and the threatened punishment has already made its appearance. The last and the present World War, along with their repercussions, constitute one phase of the fulfilment of this prophecy, and God knows what dreadful forms the fulfilment of this great prophecy is decreed to take in future and what dire visitations are yet in store for Christians in this world and in the next.

R. 16   **117.** And when Allah will say, "O Jesus, son of Mary, didst thou say to men, ' Take me and my mother for two gods beside Allah,' " he will answer, " Holy art Thou. I could never say that to which I had no right. If I had said it, Thou wouldst have surely known it. Thou knowest what is in my mind, and I know not what is in Thy mind. *a*It is only Thou Who art the Knower of hidden things.[744]

وَاِذْ قَالَ اللّٰهُ يٰعِيْسَى ابْنَ مَرْيَمَ ءَاَنْتَ قُلْتَ لِلنَّاسِ اتَّخِذُوْنِيْ وَاُمِّيَ اِلٰهَيْنِ مِنْ دُوْنِ اللّٰهِ ۙ قَالَ سُبْحٰنَكَ مَا يَكُوْنُ لِيْ اَنْ اَقُوْلَ مَا لَيْسَ لِيْ بِحَقٍّ ۚ اِنْ كُنْتُ قُلْتُهٗ فَقَدْ عَلِمْتَهٗ ۗ تَعْلَمُ مَا فِيْ نَفْسِيْ وَلَآ اَعْلَمُ مَا فِيْ نَفْسِكَ ۗ اِنَّكَ اَنْتَ عَلَّامُ الْغُيُوْبِ ۝

---

*a*5 : 110 ; 9 : 78 ; 34 : 49.

---

744. Important Words :

The words ما يكون لى (I could not) may be interpreted in various ways, such as, it was not fitting or proper for me to do so ; or it did not behove me ; or it was beyond my power or position ; or it was impossible for me ; or I had no right to do so, etc. See also 3 : 80.

نفس (mind) means, among other things, knowledge ; purpose or intention (Lane). See also 3 : 29.

Commentary :

The expression, *Holy art Thou*, besides hinting that it is only God Who is free from error, embodies a beautiful reply on the part of Jesus to the question put to him by God in the words, *didst thou say to men, Take me and my mother for two gods*, which seemed to imply a sort of reproach and an expression of displeasure. The reply of Jesus appears to be something like this : " I was only Thy humble Messenger, O God, therefore I could not ask

men to take me and my mother as gods beside Thee, for if I had done so, that would have been a reflection on Thee that Thou didst choose as Thy Messenger a person who turned faithless to Thee and asked his followers to take him and his mother as gods beside Thee. But Thy choice, O God, cannot be wrong ; hence it was impossible that I, a Messenger of Thine, should have bidden men take me and my mother as gods, and Thine own all-embracing knowledge, O God, is a testimony of my innocence."

The word نفس (mind) when used about God implies " intention." Thus the last sentence of the verse would mean, " I do not know what Thou meanest by this question. Thou, being All-Knowing, well knowest that I did not say so ; hence, I fail to understand the object or purpose of Thy question." This reply of Jesus shows that in his heart he was afraid that some shortcoming in the execution of his duty might have displeased the Almighty.

118. "I said nothing to them except that which Thou didst command me— *a*'Worship Allah, my Lord and your Lord.' And I was a witness over them as long as I remained among them, but since *b*Thou didst cause me to die, Thou hast been the watcher over them ; and Thou art witness over all things.745

مَا قُلْتُ لَهُمْ إِلَّا مَا أَمَرْتَنِي بِهِ أَنِ اعْبُدُوا اللهَ رَبِّي وَرَبَّكُمْ وَكُنْتُ عَلَيْهِمْ شَهِيدًا مَا دُمْتُ فِيهِمْ فَلَمَّا تَوَفَّيْتَنِي كُنْتَ أَنْتَ الرَّقِيبَ عَلَيْهِمْ وَأَنْتَ عَلَى كُلِّ شَيْءٍ شَهِيدٌ ۝

119. "If Thou punish them, they are Thy servants ; and if Thou forgive them, Thou surely art the Mighty, the Wise."746

إِنْ تُعَذِّبْهُمْ فَإِنَّهُمْ عِبَادُكَ وَإِنْ تَغْفِرْ لَهُمْ فَإِنَّكَ أَنْتَ الْعَزِيزُ الْحَكِيمُ ۝

---

*a*5 : 73 ; 19 : 37.   *b*3 : 56 ; 19 : 16.

---

745. Important Words:

تَوَفَّيْتَنِي (Thou didst cause me to die). See 2 : 235 & 3 : 56.

Commentary :

For the corroboration of the first sentence of this verse *i.e.* the teaching of Jesus about the worship of God alone see Matt. 4 : 10 & Luke 4 : 8.

The latter portion of the verse conclusively proves two things : (1) that Jesus is dead and not alive, as supposed by most of present-day Muslims ; (2) that he is not to return to this earth a second time in his own person. The inference is beyond any shadow of doubt. From the verse it is clear that no interval intervened between Jesus' life on this earth and his death. As long as he was alive, he kept a careful watch over his followers and saw to it that they did not deviate from the right path, but he did not know what occurred to them after his death. This shows : (1) that it was by death and not by his supposed ascension to heaven that Jesus became separated from his people, and (2) that it was only after his death that his people deified him. Now, as his followers have already gone

astray, it definitely follows that Jesus is dead, for, as the verse points out, it was after his death that he began to be worshipped as God.

Similarly, the fact that this verse speaks of Jesus as expressing ignorance of his followers having taken him and his mother for gods after he had left them, proves that he is not to come back to this earth. For, if he were to come back to this earth and see with his own eyes the corruption of his followers, he could not express ignorance of his deification by his people. In that case the answer of Jesus pleading his ignorance would amount to a veritable lie. Thus the verse definitely and clearly proves that Jesus is dead and that he will never come back to this world. For detailed discussion of the question of the death of Jesus and his non-ascension to heavens with his physical body see 3 : 56 & 4 : 159.

746. Commentary :

This verse constitutes a most pathetic appeal by Jesus to God on behalf of his followers ; and the succeeding verse provides the divine answer to that appeal.

120. Allah will say, ' This is a day when *only* the truthful shall profit by their truthfulness. For them are Gardens beneath which streams flow; therein shall they abide for ever. *a*Allah is well pleased with them, and they are well pleased with Him; that indeed is the great triumph.'747

قَالَ اللهُ هٰذَا يَوْمُ يَنْفَعُ الصّٰدِقِيْنَ صِدْقُهُمْ لَهُمْ جَنّٰتٌ تَجْرِىْ مِنْ تَحْتِهَا الْاَنْهٰرُ خٰلِدِيْنَ فِيْهَاۤ اَبَدًا رَضِىَ اللهُ عَنْهُمْ وَرَضُوْا عَنْهُ ذٰلِكَ الْفَوْزُ الْعَظِيْمُ ۝

121. *b*To Allah belongs the kingdom of the heavens and the earth and whatever is in them; and He has power over all things.748

لِلّٰهِ مُلْكُ السَّمٰوٰتِ وَالْاَرْضِ وَمَا فِيْهِنَّ وَهُوَ عَلٰى كُلِّ شَىْءٍ قَدِيْرٌ ۝

---

*a*9 : 100 ; 58 : 23 ; 98 : 9.   *b*5 : 18, 41 ; 42 : 50 ; 48 : 15.

---

747. Commentary :

The words, *This is a day*, refer to the Day of Judgement, which shows that the question mentioned in 5 : 117 above will be put to Jesus on the Day of Judgement *i.e.* after he will have paid his supposed second visit to the earth, as is alleged by those who believe in his ascension to, and descent from, heaven.

The word " truthful " used in the verse hints that as the followers of Jesus did not prove truthful they could not hope to benefit by divine mercy. The word really refers to Muslims, who were true to the teachings of their Prophet. They believed as he taught them to believe, and acted as he taught them to act, and were true to their God. The word may also refer to the followers of Ahmad,

the Promised Messiah, who was raised as the مِثِيل or like of Jesus. God, as it were, says, " We sent two Messiahs, the followers of the one drifted away from his teachings and began to look upon him as God, but the followers of the other Messiah were true to his teachings. So this day only the truth of the truthful shall profit them."

748. Commentary :

The verse forms a fitting sequel to a *Sūra* in which the errors of the Christian people are effectively exposed and demolished. It also contains a veiled declaration that as Christians will set a very bad example of " belief " and " action," so their glory will not last and God will finally transfer His " kingdom " to those who are more deserving of it.

CHAPTER 6

AL-AN'ĀM

(Revealed before Hijra)

Title and Date of Revelation

This *Sūra* belongs to the Meccan period. According to most accounts, the whole of it was revealed in one portion ; and as reported by some traditionists, as many as 70,000 angels stood guard when it was being revealed, which points to the high position it holds among the Quranic *Sūras* and the special protection which was afforded to its subject-matter. The *Sūra* probably derives its title from the subject dealt with in vv. 137—139 where cattle (the word *An'ām* meaning cattle) have been condemned as one of the main causes of idolatry. At another place the Quran says that idolatry makes idolaters sink so low as to render them, as it were, like mere cattle (25 : 45).

Subject-Matter

In this *Sūra* there is a change in the treatment of the subject-matter from that of the previous *Sūras*. It contains a refutation of religions other than the Israelite. It starts with the refutation of the Zoroastrian faith, which believes in the duality of godhead—in two separate gods of good and evil. The Quran exposes this doctrine by declaring that both the powers of doing good and evil are in reality two links of the same chain, one remaining incomplete without the other ; so they cannot be said to have been created by two different gods. Light and darkness are indeed the creation of the same God and, instead of pointing to the duality of the godhead, they really constitute a strong argument in favour of its oneness and possess a peculiar affinity with the creation of man and his natural powers and faculties.

The *Sūra* proceeds to discuss the important subject that evil is born of the wrong use of God-given faculties; and whenever men cease to make a right use of them, God raises a Prophet to teach them their right use. But, instead of receiving a patient and reverent hearing, he receives mockery and derision, in spite of the fact that such mockery has always led to disastrous results.

Further on, in the second section (*Rukū'*), the *Sūra* says that delay in divine punishment overtaking disbelievers often makes them all the more intrepid, though this delay is always due to God's mercy and not to His inability to call them to account as and when He likes. Then it proceeds to say that the severe persecution to which the Prophet and his followers are subjected can never result in a weakening of their connection with God, because their belief in God is based on true realization of His attributes which they impart to others by means of the Signs that God shows at their hands. In view of these Signs, how can those gifted with sight follow those who are deprived of it ? In the third *Rukū'* it is said that disbelievers should not worry as to whether the Prophet is true or false, because God has taken it upon Himself to destroy a false prophet. The patent fact, however, is that whereas the faith of believers is

669

unflinching and steadfast, disbelievers never hesitate to disown their idolatrous beliefs whenever they are overtaken by misfortunes. The absurdity of their position is further exposed when it is noticed that while they say to the Prophet that they cannot give up the ways and usages of their forefathers, they base their own rejection of the Prophets on the plea that the latter merely imitate their forefathers, forgetting the plain logic that if idolatry is the result of following in the footsteps of forefathers, belief in the Oneness of God cannot be the result of similar imitation.

In the fourth *Rukū'* light is thrown on the subject that irreligiousness is born of lack of faith in life after death or in the possibility of the establishment of real connection with God. This dual lack of faith makes the disbeliever bold in his rejection of truth. But believers are admonished not to be disheartened by this attitude of disbelievers, because all Prophets of God have been treated like that. The opposition to the Prophets on the part of disbelievers is in fact but natural, because only those people seek God who possess some natural kinship with spiritual matters, for the deaf in spirit cannot hear the voice of God. These people witness Sign after Sign and yet disbelieve and reject them and continue to repeat, parrot-like, that no Sign has been shown to them. Such disbelievers are warned that now only the Sign of punishment remains for them to witness and when that Sign comes, they will forget all their boastful rejection of truth. In the fifth *Rukū'* it is stated that in the time of the former Prophets disbelievers adopted a similar attitude till punishment overtook them. But God is not quick in sending punishment. Disbelievers were granted respite in the past; similarly respite is being granted to them now. Messengers of God are both bearers of glad tidings and warners. They first seek to bring the people to the right path by giving them glad tidings. It is only when the latter wilfully shut the door of guidance upon themselves that warning comes into operation.

The *Sūra* further proceeds to say in the 6th *Rukū'* that only those who have fear of God in their hearts can accept the truth, and the Prophet is told to address his appeal to them. For the others, it is necessary that fear of God be first created in their hearts so that arguments and reasons may benefit them. Further, it is most essential for the progress of Islam that special attention be paid to the spiritual training of believers, whether rich or poor, because since the Prophet is mortal and must die, only the community of the believers remains behind to preach and propagate the divine message. In the 7th and 8th *Rukū's* the Holy Prophet is asked to tell disbelievers that they are foolish to find fault with him merely because the promised punishment does not speedily overtake them. The sending of punishment is outside his province and lies entirely in the hand of God Who sends it whenever He thinks fit and opportune. Moreover, the sender of the punishment should also be the knower of the unseen. He should know fully the future of man, because he who does not possess the knowledge of what the future holds in its bosom is likely to punish a person who, being at present the enemy of truth, may be deserving of punishment today, but may be destined to effect a true reformation in himself tomorrow. So the sending of the punishment or the deferring thereof is God's own work. Towards the end of the *Rukū'* it is stated that when God alone knows the unseen, it is unwise not to preach the truth to a person who may appear to be an enemy of truth, because in the unlimited knowledge of God he may be destined to accept the truth at some future time.

In the ninth *Rukū'* the falsity of ploytheistic doctrines has been exposed by means of an rgument which the Patriarch Abraham had with his people and which has been dealt with at some length in this *Rukū'*. The next two sections describe how God bestowed favours and blessings on Abraham and his descendants because they believed in God's Oneness and strove hard to establish it in the world. In the twelfth *Rukū'* we are told that the mission of God's Messengers never fails. Like rain-water, it gives fertility and freshness to a soil spiritually bleak and barren. The thirteenth *Rukū'* deals with the supreme subject that it is impossible to attain to God and have His true realization unless He reveals Himself to men. It is therefore necessary that divine Messengers should appear time after time, because it is through them that God reveals Himself to the world. Believers are further admonished that though the beliefs and ideals of idolaters are false, they should have due regard for their susceptibilities when holding a discourse with them about their beliefs and doctrines. In the 14th *Rukū'*, however, we are told that for the attainment of true faith, a corresponding wholesome change of heart is a *sine qua non*. Without such a change, even Signs and miracles prove of no avail. In this connection some objections of disbelievers have been mentioned and refuted. The same subject is continued and developed in the next four sections (15—18) and the attention of believers is drawn to yet more foolish objections of disbelievers. In the 19th section a contrast is drawn between Islamic teaching, which answers and satisfies the demands of reason and justice, and the doctrines and practices of idolaters, which are based on neither reason nor argument. The latter are told that, in view of this contrast, they cannot legitimately deny the necessity of divine revelation.

In the last section we are told that the Quran has been revealed to raise and honour even those nations to whom no revealed Book has so far been sent so that they may not feel low and debased before the People of the Book. The Message of the Quran, unlike that of former revealed Scriptures, is for the whole of mankind and it seeks to establish a real and permanent peace between different sections of humanity as well as between man and his Creator.

سُوْرَةُ الْاَنْعَامِ مَكِّيَةٌ

1. ^aIn the name of Allah, the Gracious, the Merciful.⁷⁴⁹

بِسْمِ اللّٰهِ الرَّحْمٰنِ الرَّحِيْمِ ۝

2. All praise belongs to Allah Who created the heavens and the earth and brought into being darkness and light; yet ^bthose who disbelieve set up equals to their Lord.^{749A}

اَلْحَمْدُ لِلّٰهِ الَّذِيْ خَلَقَ السَّمٰوٰتِ وَ الْاَرْضَ وَجَعَلَ الظُّلُمٰتِ وَ النُّوْرَ ثُمَّ الَّذِيْنَ كَفَرُوْا بِرَبِّهِمْ يَعْدِلُوْنَ ۝

---

^aSee 1 : 1.   ^b6 : 151 ; 27 : 61.

---

749. Commentary :

See under 1 : 1.

749A. Important Words :

جَعَل (brought into being) is sometimes used synonymously with خَلَق i.e. he created, but whereas خَلَق gives the sense of creating a thing after measuring and designing it, جَعَل signifies the making of a thing in a particular state or condition, or constituting or appointing it for a definite purpose (Lane).

Commentary :

The practice of attributing co-partners to God is based on two different theories. One class of people hold that God has delegated His powers to certain beings. Among the people of this class the most prominent are the Hindus. Another class of men who ascribe co-partners to God think that evil cannot proceed from God and, therefore, there must be some other source of evil. So they seek a separate god whom they look upon as a source of evil or of darkness. This class of people is represented by Zoroastrians, who believe in a spirit of evil or darkness called Ahriman, a deity regarded as the equal of the creator Ormuzd, the spirit of good or light. The verse refutes both these doctrines.

By saying, *All praise belongs to Allah Who created the heavens and the earth*, the Quran refutes the first-mentioned class of men. When God has created all things and when He Himself can do everything and to Him belongs all praise, what need is there for Him to entrust part of His work to other beings ? One entrusts one's work to others when one cannot do it single-handed or when one desires to pass one's time in idleness, which is an act of dispraise. But God, being above all this, has no need of transferring His powers to other beings. These words also refute the Christian doctrine of Trinity ; for if each of the three persons of Trinity is equally omnipotent and worthy of perfect praise, what need is there for the other two ? On the contrary, if only all the three combined can do the work and none can do it singly, God cannot be considered to be worthy of all praise.

By saying, *and brought into being darkness and light*, the Quran refutes the second class of men. The words, *All praise belongs to Allah*, must be read with this part of the verse also, thus hinting that even "darkness," *i.e.*, things which are generally looked upon as evil, such as death, disease, misery and affliction, are also things for which praise is due to God. In fact, every kind of "darkness" has its uses. Directly or indirectly it is meant for the good of man and for his general advancement. Now when even apparently evil things are meant for the

3. ^aHe it is Who created you from clay, and then He decreed a term. And there is ^banother term fixed with Him. Yet you doubt !⁷⁵⁰

هُوَ الَّذِى خَلَقَكُمْ مِّنْ طِيْنٍ ثُمَّ قَضَى أَجَلًا وَأَجَلٌ مُّسَمًّى عِنْدَهُ ثُمَّ أَنْتُمْ تَمْتَرُوْنَ ۝

4. And ^cHe is Allah, *the God, both* in the heavens and in the earth. He knows your inside and your outside. And He knows what you earn.⁷⁵¹

وَهُوَ اللّٰهُ فِى السَّمٰوٰتِ وَفِى الْأَرْضِ يَعْلَمُ سِرَّكُمْ وَجَهْرَكُمْ وَيَعْلَمُ مَا تَكْسِبُوْنَ ۝

---

^a15 : 27 ; 23 : 13 ; 32 : 8 ; 37 : 12 ; 38 : 72.   ^b71 : 5.   ^c43 : 85.

---

ultimate good of man, the natural conclusion would be that half of the things meant for the good of men are created by one god and the other half by another, which is simply absurd.

As for the good underlying apparently evil things, it may be hinted that the difficulties and troubles which beset man serve as a means of turning him to virtue, and of his attaining divine favours and bounties. Take death for instance. If a man should not die but should remain alive for ever, he could not achieve the blessings of Heaven, which embody the most perfect favours of God. On the other hand, these favours cannot be given to man in this life ; for, if they were given to him here, they would become apparent to all ; in that case there would remain no veil and no secrecy and consequently there would remain no merit in faith. A person deserves credit for his faith only when there is some secrecy about the thing in which he is called upon to believe.

750. Commentary :

The creation of man referred to in the words, *Who created you,* is meant as an illustration of the light mentioned in the previous verse, while the decreeing of a term, *i.e.,* the ordaining of death, is meant as an illustration of " darkness." The verse ascribes both these acts to God, as acts of mercy, thus refuting those who believe in two separate gods, one of evil and the other of good.

The words, *there is another term fixed with Him,* refer to the Day of Judgement or of Resurrection when men, after passing through the gate of death, will receive their rewards from their Lord.

751. Commentary :

The words, *both in the heavens and in the earth,* do not mean that God's person pervades the heavens and the earth. What is meant is that the knowledge and power of God comprehend the entire universe. The Quran itself explains this by the words that follow *i.e., He knows your inside and your outside.*

The latter part of the verse points out that a being cannot be looked upon as perfect if his knowledge or power is defective. But such is not the case with God. Both His knowledge and power are perfect. This is what is hinted in the words, *He knows what you earn,* which convey a twofold idea : (1) that God is All-Knowing, and (2) that He will requite men according to their deeds which, in other words, means that He is All-Powerful. Hence, as both the knowledge and power of God are perfect, it follows that God is perfect, knowing everything and possessing the power of doing everything. So He does not stand in need of entrusting any part of His work to other beings and taking them as His helpers or co-partners.

Again, the above-quoted words also show that it is God Who punishes evil. Now, when the punishment of evil is from God, it is foolish to

5. And ^athere comes not to them any Sign of the Signs of their Lord, but they turn away from it.⁷⁵²

وَمَا تَأْتِيْهِمْ مِّنْ اٰيَةٍ مِّنْ اٰيٰتِ رَبِّهِمْ اِلَّا كَانُوْا عَنْهَا مُعْرِضِيْنَ ۝

6. So ^bthey rejected the truth when it came to them ; but soon shall come to them the tidings of that at which they mocked.⁷⁵³

فَقَدْ كَذَّبُوْا بِالْحَقِّ لَمَّا جَآءَهُمْ ۚ فَسَوْفَ يَأْتِيْهِمْ اَنْۢبٰٓؤُا مَا كَانُوْا بِهٖ يَسْتَهْزِءُوْنَ ۝

7. See they not how many a generation We have destroyed before them? ^cWe had established them in the earth as We have established you not, and ^dWe sent the clouds over them, pouring down abundant rain ; and We caused streams to flow beneath them ; then did We destroy them because of their sins and raised up after them another generation.⁷⁵⁴

اَلَمْ يَرَوْا كَمْ اَهْلَكْنَا مِنْ قَبْلِهِمْ مِّنْ قَرْنٍ مَّكَّنّٰهُمْ فِى الْاَرْضِ مَا لَمْ نُمَكِّنْ لَّكُمْ وَاَرْسَلْنَا السَّمَآءَ عَلَيْهِمْ مِّدْرَارًا ۖ وَّجَعَلْنَا الْاَنْهٰرَ تَجْرِيْ مِنْ تَحْتِهِمْ فَاَهْلَكْنٰهُمْ بِذُنُوْبِهِمْ وَاَنْشَأْنَا مِنْۢ بَعْدِهِمْ قَرْنًا اٰخَرِيْنَ ۝

---

^a21 : 3; 26 : 6; 36 : 47.   ^b26 : 7.   ^c46 : 27.   ^d11 : 53; 71 : 12.

---

think that the god of evil must be some other being.

752. Commentary :

An important evidence of the knowledge and power of God are the prophecies which He reveals to His Messengers and the aid and help which He vouchsafes them against overwhelming odds. These are called Signs here. Thus, in order to prove the perfect knowledge and power of God, the verse refers to the powerful Signs which God was showing to demonstrate the truth of the Holy Prophet and the wonderful way in which He was helping him.

753. Important Words :

اِنْبَاء (tidings) is the plural of نَبَأ which means, news or tidings. The word is generally used in the Quran about important news relating to some great event (Aqrab & Kulliyāt).

Commentary :

The words, *shall come*, imply that the important "tidings" referred to in the verse were ordained to come to the Meccans from outside. The words, which were revealed at Mecca, thus contain a veiled prophecy to the effect that the Holy Prophet will have to flee from Mecca and that, after his flight, the Meccans will go out and fight him but that they will be routed, and the news of the great success of the Holy Prophet or, to quote the expression of the Quran, *the tidings of that at which they mocked*, will reach the Meccans from outside. This prophecy was fulfilled in a wonderful way at the famous Battle of Badr, thus showing that God possesses both perfect knowledge and perfect power.

754. Important Words :

قَرْن (generation). The verb form of the word, *i.e.*, قَرَن (qarana) means, he connected or linked or coupled or joined. قِرْن means, one's equal in age, *i.e.*, connected with the same age ; a generation of men succeeding or preceding another generation, as if both were conjoined ; people of one time ; people of a time among

8. And if We had sent down to thee a writing upon parchment and they had felt it with their hands, *even then* the disbelievers would have surely said, 'This is nothing but manifest sorcery.'[755]

9. And they say, [a]'Why has not an angel been sent down to him?' And if We had sent down an angel, the matter would have been settled, *and* then they would not have been granted a respite.[756]

وَلَوْ نَزَّلْنَا عَلَيْكَ كِتَابًا فِى قِرْطَاسٍ فَلَمَسُوهُ بِأَيْدِيهِمْ لَقَالَ الَّذِينَ كَفَرُوٓا اِنْ هٰذَآ اِلَّا سِحْرٌ مُّبِيْنٌ ۝

وَقَالُوْا لَوْلَآ اُنْزِلَ عَلَيْهِ مَلَكٌ ۚ وَلَوْ اَنْزَلْنَا مَلَكًا لَّقُضِىَ الْاَمْرُ ثُمَّ لَا يُنْظَرُوْنَ ۝

---

[a]2 : 211 ; 25 : 8.

---

whom there appears a Prophet. قرين means an associate, comrade or companion (Lane & Aqrab).

Commentary :

The verse predicts that the enemies of the Holy Prophet shall be destroyed like the enemies of the former Prophets. Even within the confines of Arabia there had been people who were visited with divine punishment in consequence of their opposition to their respective Prophets who appeared in by-gone times. Among them were the tribes, *Tubba‘*, *‘Ād*, *Thamūd* and others whose stories were current among the Arabs.

The words, *as We have established you not*, do not mean that the world is retrogressing. The fact is that although the world is progressing as a whole, yet some of the older nations which rose to the heights of civilization in their time were so advanced in certain branches of art and science that in these specific branches they have so far not been equalled by the generations that followed. Take, for instance, the ancient Egyptians. The modern age, in spite of the marvels it has wrought in the domain of science, still gazes with wonder at some of the works of ancient Egyptian civilization. Similarly, there were people among the Arabs who carved wonderful

fortresses out of rocks. Thus every people that ever attained to the heights of civilization enjoyed a certain distinction which is not shared by other nations. By using this expression, the Quran means to say : When these powerful people were destroyed in spite of their mastery of certain branches of knowledge, how can your arts save you from destruction ?

755. Important Words :

قرطاس (parchment) means, paper ; a roll or scroll of paper ; anything one writes upon ; a writing or book ; a butt or target (Lane).

Commentary :

The words, *and they had felt it with their hands*, mean, " and they had made sure that it was a heavenly thing and not an earthly one." The words also embody a beautiful allusion to the spiritual blindness of the people. Being blind, they cannot see ; so they have to feel with their hands.

The verse signifies that when a man gives himself up to doubting, nothing, however clear and manifest, can convince him.

756. Commentary :

The question, *Why has not an angel been sent down to him*, implies a desire on the part of the

10. And if We had appointed *as Messenger* an angel, We would have made him *appear as* a man ; and *thus* We would have made confused to them that which they are *themselves* making confused.[757]

وَلَوْ جَعَلْنٰهُ مَلَكًا لَّجَعَلْنٰهُ رَجُلًا وَّ لَّلَبَسْنَا عَلَيْهِمْ مَّا يَلْبِسُوْنَ ۝

11. And surely [a]have the Messengers been mocked at before thee, but that which they mocked at encompassed those of them who scoffed.[758]

وَلَقَدِ اسْتُهْزِئَ بِرُسُلٍ مِّنْ قَبْلِكَ فَحَاقَ بِالَّذِيْنَ سَخِرُوْا مِنْهُمْ مَّا كَانُوْا بِهٖ يَسْتَهْزِءُوْنَ ۝

R. 2   12. Say, [b]'Go about in the earth, and see what was the end of those who treated *the Prophets* as liars.'[759]

قُلْ سِيْرُوْا فِي الْاَرْضِ ثُمَّ انْظُرُوْا كَيْفَ كَانَ عَاقِبَةُ الْمُكَذِّبِيْنَ ۝

---

[a]21 : 42.   [b]3 : 138 ; 22 : 47 ; 27 : 70.

disbelievers to be visited by an angel whom they might see and be thus convinced of the divine mission of the Prophet. The Quran exposes their folly by replying that although the angels of God do come to the Prophet, yet when they visit disbelievers and are seen by them, they invariably come with divine punishment. Such angels appeared at the Battle of Badr, when, to quote the expression of the Quran, *the matter was decided* (2 : 211). See also the succeeding verse.

757. Commentary :

Another possible form of the appearance of an angel is that he be sent to this world as a Messenger. But this could not improve things ; for in that case, to make his mission to mankind worth anything, he should appear in the form of a man ; but if he were to appear to them in the form of a man, then the people would entertain the same doubts about his heavenly mission as they were now doing about that of the Holy Prophet.

758. Commentary :

The words, *And surely have the Messengers been mocked at before thee*, imply a hint that the demand of disbelievers regarding the coming of an angel is really nothing but a mockery. The verse also contains a prophecy about the destruction of the enemies of the Holy Prophet. The enemies of the former Prophets laughed them to scorn and were consequently punished by God, the very object of their mockery becoming the means of their destruction. The enemies of the Holy Prophet were also scoffing at him and so they too would meet with the same fate which befell their predecessors.

759. Commentary :

When the disbelievers were told, in reply to their demand for the coming of an angel, that disbelievers saw angels only when they came with punishment from God, the disbelievers arrogantly said, " Let them come with it then." The verse tells them that such foolhardy demands were made by their predecessors also ; so let them go about in the land and see what was the end of such people.

13. Say, 'To whom belongs what is in the heavens and the earth?' Say, 'To Allah.' [a]He has taken upon Himself *to show* mercy. [b]He will certainly *continue to* assemble you till the Day of Resurrection. There is no doubt in it. Those who ruin their souls will not believe.[760]

قُلْ لِّمَنْ مَّا فِى السَّمٰوٰتِ وَالْاَرْضِ قُلْ لِّلّٰهِ كَتَبَ عَلٰى نَفْسِهِ الرَّحْمَةَ لَيَجْمَعَنَّكُمْ اِلٰى يَوْمِ الْقِيٰمَةِ لَا رَيْبَ فِيْهِ اَلَّذِيْنَ خَسِرُوْا اَنْفُسَهُمْ فَهُمْ لَا يُؤْمِنُوْنَ ۝

14. To Him belongs whatever dwells in the night and the day. And He is the All-Hearing, the All-Knowing.[761]

وَلَهُ مَا سَكَنَ فِى الَّيْلِ وَالنَّهَارِ وَهُوَ السَّمِيْعُ الْعَلِيْمُ ۝

---

[a]6 : 55 ; 7 : 157.   [b]3 : 10 ; 4 : 88 ; 45 : 27.

---

760. Important Words :

خَسِرُوْا اَنْفُسَهُمْ (who ruin their souls). خَسِرُوْا is derived from خَسِرَ which means, he lost ; he suffered a loss ; he went astray ; he became lost ; he perished (Lane). From the above it is clear that the word خَسِرَ is really intransitive. The transitive use of the word in the verse is merely apparent. In fact when the Quran says خَسِرُوْا اَنْفُسَهُمْ it does not mean, they made their souls suffer, but, that they suffered with regard to themselves, *i.e.*, they themselves suffered. The correct transitive form of the word is خَسَرَ (khasara), *i.e.*, he caused to perish, and not خَسِرَ (khasira), *i.e.*, he suffered or he was lost, which the Quran has used. This peculiar use of the word is intended to intensify the meaning. Thus the words الَّذِيْنَ خَسِرُوْا اَنْفُسَهُمْ would really read الَّذِيْنَ خَسِرُوْا وَ خَسَرُوْا اَنْفُسَهُمْ, *i.e.*, those who suffered a loss and caused their souls to perish. For the sake of convenience, however, the expression has been rendered in the text as, *those who ruin their souls*. For a somewhat similar expression, *i.e.*, سَفِهَ نَفْسَهُ see Lisān where that expression has been fully dealt with.

Commentary :

Here God first puts a question, and then Himself answers it. This form has also been employed elsewhere in the Quran. It is meant to bring out the disbelievers' extreme weakness of faith and make them realize it.

All that is in the heavens and the earth belongs to Allah ; so the enemies of Faith also belong to God. No one would like to destroy that which belongs to him, much less would God like to do so, for He is Merciful and has made mercy binding on Himself. So He is giving the enemies of the Holy Prophet time to repent. He is putting off punishment so that they may turn to Him and repent of their sins. Hence, instead of demanding punishment, let them ask forgiveness and benefit by His mercy.

It should be noted that disbelief alone does not bring punishment upon men in this life. So far as simple disbelief is concerned, the case of the believers and the disbelievers will be decided on the Day of Judgement when all will be assembled together and God's judgement will be pronounced. It is only the extreme wickedness of men and their active opposition to the Prophets of God that hastens punishment for them in this life. So the verse exhorts disbelievers not to demand punishment but rather to repent, so that God may have mercy on them.

761. Commentary :

Not only have darkness and light been made

15. Say, 'Shall I take any protector other than Allah, [a]the Maker of the heavens and the earth, [b]Who feeds and is not fed?' Say, [c]'I have been commanded to be the first of those who submit'. And be thou not of those who associate partners *with* God.[762]

قُلْ أَغَيْرَ اللهِ اَتَّخِذُ وَلِيًّا فَاطِرِ السَّمٰوٰتِ وَالْأَرْضِ وَهُوَ يُطْعِمُ وَلَا يُطْعَمُ ۚ قُلْ اِنِّيْ أُمِرْتُ اَنْ اَكُوْنَ اَوَّلَ مَنْ اَسْلَمَ وَلَا تَكُوْنَنَّ مِنَ الْمُشْرِكِيْنَ ۝

16. Say, 'Of a truth, [d]I fear, if I disobey my Lord, the punishment of an awful day.'[763]

قُلْ اِنِّيْ اَخَافُ اِنْ عَصَيْتُ رَبِّيْ عَذَابَ يَوْمٍ عَظِيْمٍ ۝

---

[a]12:102; 14:11; 35:2; 39:47.   [b]20:133; 51:58-59.   [c]6:164; 39:13.
[d]10:16; 39:14.

---

by God (6:2), but, as the present verse puts it, all that dwells in them also belongs to Him. This shows that both darkness and light have been made with a purpose. Now when God is the Master of all that dwells in darkness and light, how could He entrust His own possessions to other beings?

As pointed out under 6:2 above, even darkness and afflictions have their advantages. God involves men in darkness and sends down afflictions so that their character may be perfected and they may pray to God and He may hear them, for He is All-Hearing. And if there is no time for men to pray or they do not know or do not realize the danger and consequently do not pray, even then God is All-Knowing and may come to their help without their praying for it.

762. Important Words :

فَاطِر (Maker) is derived from فَطَر. They say فَطَرَهُ, *i.e.*, he clove or split or rent it; he created it or brought it into existence; or he originated it. فَطَرَ الْعَجِين means, he made the dough into bread without leavening it. أَفْطَرَ means, he broke the fast. تَفَطَّرَ and اِنْفَطَرَ mean, it became cleft or split or rent. الْفِطْرَة means, the natural constitution with which a child is created. فَاطِر when used about

God, means the Originator or the Creator or the Maker (Tāj).

Commentary :

The question in the first part of the verse implies that, as God alone is the Maker of the heavens and the earth and as it is He alone Who feeds all without being fed by anybody, therefore there is none worthy of being taken as protector but He. None else is worthy of being worshipped as God.

The words, *Who feeds*, refute the godhead of those lifeless objects which men have taken for gods. They admittedly feed none, but God feeds all; hence these objects are not worthy of being taken as gods.

The words, *is not fed*, negative the godhead of those living beings who have been deified by men. They stand in need of food, but God needs no food; hence they cannot be gods.

763. Commentary :

This verse is an expression of the supreme independence of God. The Holy Prophet is made to say, " O men, it is indeed strange that you should not fear the punishment of God while I, who am a Prophet of God, fear His punishment if I disobey Him." This is an emphatic way of exhorting men to avoid

17. He from whom it is averted on that day, God indeed has had mercy on him. And that indeed is a manifest triumph.[764]

مَنْ يُصْرَفْ عَنْهُ يَوْمَئِذٍ فَقَدْ رَحِمَهُ ۚ وَذَٰلِكَ الْفَوْزُ الْمُبِينُ ۝

18. And [a]if Allah touch thee with affliction, there is none that can remove it but He; and if He touch thee with happiness, then He has power to do all that He wills.[765]

وَإِنْ يَمْسَسْكَ اللّٰهُ بِضُرٍّ فَلَا كَاشِفَ لَهُ إِلَّا هُوَ ۖ وَإِنْ يَمْسَسْكَ بِخَيْرٍ فَهُوَ عَلَىٰ كُلِّ شَيْءٍ قَدِيرٌ ۝

19. And [b]He is Supreme over His servants; and He is the Wise, the All-Aware.[766]

وَهُوَ الْقَاهِرُ فَوْقَ عِبَادِهِ ۚ وَهُوَ الْحَكِيمُ الْخَبِيرُ ۝

---

[a]10 : 108.   [b]6 : 62.

---

disobedience of God. The expression does not imply that the Holy Prophet is likely to disobey God or even that it is possible for him to do so. It is simply meant to convince disbelievers that God is above all and none can dare disobey Him with impunity.

764. Commentary:

The word ذَٰلِكَ (that) may either refer to the " averting of punishment " or to "mercy", for both "mercy" and the "averting of punishment" are manifest triumphs.

765. Commentary:

It is his own actions that are the cause of all harm that befalls a man. The words, *if Allah touch thee with affliction,* therefore do not mean that God is the cause of affliction. They are meant to convey the idea that God being the first cause of all things, everything that happens in the universe is in a way attributable to Him. The expression is also intended to hint that it is God alone Who can remove man's afflictions.

Happiness indeed comes from God, Who is the real source of all good. This is why, when speaking of happiness coming to man, the Quran uses the expression, *He has power to do all that He wills.*

766. Important Words:

قَاهِر (Supreme) is derived from قَهَرَ. They say قَهَرَهُ, *i.e.,* he overcame, conquered or subjected him; or he became superior in power or force to him. It also means, he oppressed him; or he forced or compelled him. So قَاهِر means, one who overcomes, conquers or subdues. الْقَاهِر and الْقَهَّار are attributes of God, meaning, the Subduer of His creatures by His sovereign authority and power, and the Disposer of them as He pleases (Lane).

Commentary:

The attribute الْقَاهِر (Supreme) does not imply any injustice on the part of God. All things being His servants, He does not subdue anything which does not belong to Him and is not His creation. This refutes those who allege that matter and soul are co-existent with God and are not His creation. If they were not the creation of God, He had no right to subdue or rule over them. Hence, those who allege that matter and soul are not the creation of God, attribute to Him an act of injustice; for in that case we would have to assume that God has subdued such things as are not His creation.

20. Say, 'What thing is most weighty as a witness.' Say, ^a'Allah is a witness between me and you. And this Quran has been revealed to me so that with it I may warn you and whomsoever it reaches. What! do you really bear witness that there are other gods beside Allah?' Say, 'I bear not witness *thereto*.' Say, 'He is the One God, and certainly I am far removed from that which you associate *with Him*.'⁷⁶⁷

21. ^bThose to whom We gave the Book recognize him as they recognize their sons. But those who ruin their souls will not believe.⁷⁶⁸

قُلْ اَیُّ شَیْءٍ اَکْبَرُ شَهَادَةً قُلِ اللهُ شَهِیدٌ بَیْنِیْ وَ بَیْنَکُمْ وَ اُوْحِیَ اِلَیَّ هٰذَا الْقُرْاٰنُ لِاُنْذِرَکُمْ بِهٖ وَ مَنْ بَلَغَ اَئِنَّکُمْ لَتَشْهَدُوْنَ اَنَّ مَعَ اللهِ اٰلِهَةً اُخْرٰی قُلْ لَّا اَشْهَدُ قُلْ اِنَّمَا هُوَ اِلٰهٌ وَّاحِدٌ وَّ اِنَّنِیْ بَرِیْءٌ مِّمَّا تُشْرِکُوْنَ ۝

اَلَّذِیْنَ اٰتَیْنٰهُمُ الْکِتٰبَ یَعْرِفُوْنَهٗ کَمَا یَعْرِفُوْنَ اَبْنَآءَهُمُ الَّذِیْنَ خَسِرُوْۤا اَنْفُسَهُمْ فَهُمْ لَا یُؤْمِنُوْنَ ۝

---

^a4:167; 13:44; 29:53. ^b2:147.

767. Commentary:

God Himself answers the question which He has put in the beginning of the verse; for the disbelievers did not know how to answer. They could not think that God also could bear witness. The answer has been given by God in order to instruct and teach believers.

Now the question is, how does God bear witness? This verse and the next two mention three ways by which God bears witness to the truth of the Holy Prophet. The first is by means of the Quran. *This Quran has been revealed to me*, the verse calls upon the Holy Prophet to say, *so that with it I may warn you and whomsoever it reaches*. These words signify that whosoever opposes the Quran and obstructs it will be visited by divine punishment. This punishment will constitute God's testimony to the truth of the Holy Prophet. The second and the third ways by which God bears witness are mentioned in the verses that follow.

768. Commentary:

This verse describes the second way by which

God bears testimony to the truth of the Holy Prophet, *i.e.*, through the previous Scriptures. The previous Books contain prophecies which clearly apply to the Holy Prophet and definitely point him out as the Promised One, and it is by means of these prophecies that God bears witness to the truth of the Holy Prophet. It may be asked, if the People of the Book recognize the Holy Prophet as having come in fulfilment of the prophecies contained in their Scriptures, why do they not accept him? This question the Quran answers in the words, *But those who ruin their souls will not believe*, meaning that the People of the Book will not believe because their souls are lost and they have no sense of honesty and faith left in them.

The words, *Those to whom We gave the Book recognize him as they recognize their sons*, are based on a very deep spiritual truth. A Prophet, or for that matter any object of faith, is not recognized in the beginning, as one recognizes the sun or the moon. He is recognized only as a father recognizes his son—with great probability but not with dead

3　22.　And ^awho is more unjust than he who forges a lie against Allah or gives the lie to His Signs ? Surely the unjust shall not prosper.⁷⁶⁹

وَمَنْ اَظْلَمُ مِمَّنِ افْتَرٰى عَلَى اللّٰهِ كَذِبًا اَوْ كَذَّبَ بِاٰيٰتِهٖ ؕ اِنَّهٗ لَا يُفْلِحُ الظّٰلِمُوْنَ ۟

23.　And ^bthink of the day when We shall gather them all together; then shall We say to those who associated partners with God, 'Where are the partners you spoke of, those whom you used to assert ?'⁷⁷⁰

وَ يَوْمَ نَحْشُرُهُمْ جَمِيْعًا ثُمَّ نَقُوْلُ لِلَّذِيْنَ اَشْرَكُوْٓا اَيْنَ شُرَكَآؤُكُمُ الَّذِيْنَ كُنْتُمْ تَزْعُمُوْنَ ۟

24.　Then the end of their mischief will be naught save that they shall say, ' By Allah, our Lord, we were not idolaters.'⁷⁷¹

ثُمَّ لَمْ تَكُنْ فِتْنَتُهُمْ اِلَّآ اَنْ قَالُوْا وَاللّٰهِ رَبِّنَا مَا كُنَّا مُشْرِكِيْنَ ۟

---

^a6 : 94 ; 7 : 38 ; 10 : 18 ; 11 : 19 ; 61 : 8.　^b10 : 29.

---

certainty. Faith must always begin in the region of the unseen.

769. Commentary :

This verse mentions the third way by means of which God bears witness. This kind of testimony is based on human reason. Every sane man will testify that if a person claims to speak in the name of God while God has not spoken to him, and he forges lies against Him, such a person is one of the greatest culprits and God must bring him to naught ; for if impostors are allowed to prosper like true Prophets, there will remain no criterion to distinguish the true from the false, and the truth will be lost. So, in order to distinguish between the true and the false, God must bring to naught the false claimant. Thus the hard fact that God is helping the Prophet of Islam and causing him to prosper in the teeth of all opposition and against heavy odds is a clear testimony from God to his being a true Prophet.

On the other hand, those who reject true Prophets and treat them as impostors are also among the greatest culprits who, by reason of their opposing God's Messengers and leaving no stone unturned to bring to naught the movement set on foot by them, must incur God's anger ; and, instead of being permitted to destroy the heavenly movement, must themselves be destroyed. Thus, not only by granting success to the Holy Prophet but also by bringing about the destruction of his enemies God is bearing witness to his truth.

770. Commentary :

The verb تَزْعُمُوْن (you used to assert) has always been used in the Quran with regard to falsehood. It signifies an assertion of which one is not sure. Thus كُنْتُمْ تَزْعُمُوْن (you used to assert) would mean, " you asserted with your tongues, while you had doubts in your minds."

771. Commentary :

The verse means that on the Day of Judgement all the mischief which disbelievers worked in their life on earth will end and nothing will be left to them save to deny their having ever attributed partners to God. This denial will really be a confession of their helplessness and a form of petition for divine mercy.

25. See how they lie against themselves. And *that which they fabricated has failed them.[772]

انْظُرْ كَيْفَ كَذَبُوا عَلَى أَنْفُسِهِمْ وَضَلَّ عَنْهُمْ مَّا كَانُوا يَفْتَرُونَ ۝

26. And among them are some *who give ear to thee ; but *We have put veils on their hearts, that they should not understand, and deafness in their ears. And *even* if they see every Sign, they would not believe therein, so much so that when they come to thee, disputing with thee, those who disbelieve say, ' This is nothing but fables of the ancients.'[773]

وَمِنْهُمْ مَّنْ يَّسْتَمِعُ إِلَيْكَ وَجَعَلْنَا عَلَى قُلُوبِهِمْ أَكِنَّةً أَنْ يَّفْقَهُوهُ وَفِيْ آذَانِهِمْ وَقْرًا وَإِنْ يَّرَوْا كُلَّ آيَةٍ لَّا يُؤْمِنُوا بِهَا حَتَّى إِذَا جَاءُوكَ يُجَادِلُونَكَ يَقُولُ الَّذِينَ كَفَرُوا إِنْ هَذَا إِلَّا أَسَاطِيرُ الْأَوَّلِينَ ۝

27. And they forbid *others* to *believe* it and *themselves* too they keep away from it. And they ruin none but their own selves ; only they perceive not.[774]

وَهُمْ يَنْهَوْنَ عَنْهُ وَيَنْأَوْنَ عَنْهُ وَإِنْ يُّهْلِكُونَ إِلَّا أَنْفُسَهُمْ وَمَا يَشْعُرُونَ ۝

---

*7 : 54 ; 11 : 22. *10 : 43 ; 17 : 48. *17 : 47 ; 41 : 6.

772. Commentary :

The words, *they lie against themselves*, mean that by denying that they ascribed co-partners to God they will utter a lie which will prove their guilt. By making this statement they will, in other words, admit that ascribing co-partners to God is an evil deed. Thus their very denial will be a confession of their guilt.

The words, *see how*, express astonishment at the way in which they, while trying to deny the charge, will be led into a confession of guilt.

773. Commentary :

For an explanation of "veils" and "deafness" see 2 : 8.

What the Quran calls "Signs" are described by disbelievers as mere "fables of the ancients," which saying of theirs is condemned by God. This shows that in the sight of God the stories of past Prophets and past nations given in the

Quran are not meant as "tales" or "stories" but as "Signs," being prophecies of future events which, when fulfilled, will serve as "Signs."

774. Commentary :

The order in which the words have been put in this verse is worth noting. Disbelievers' forbidding others to listen to the Quran or to the words of the Holy Prophet implied that they too were keeping away from the Holy Prophet and the Quran. In spite of this, their own keeping away has been expressly and separately mentioned in the verse in order to show that they were afraid of being influenced by the words of the Quran or the discourses of the Holy Prophet. So great was their fear that they not only forbade others to go near the Holy Prophet but themselves took special care to remain aloof from him, lest his words should captivate their hearts. This shows that they were aware of the great influence which the

28. And if thou couldst only see ^awhen they are made to stand before the Fire! ^bThey will say, 'Oh, would that we might be sent back! And *then* we would not treat the Signs of our Lord as lies and we would be of the believers.'[775]

وَلَوْ تَرٰٓى اِذْ وُقِفُوْا عَلَى النَّارِ فَقَالُوْا يٰلَيْتَنَا نُرَدُّ وَلَا نُكَذِّبَ بِاٰيٰتِ رَبِّنَا وَنَكُوْنَ مِنَ الْمُؤْمِنِيْنَ ۝

29. Nay, that which they used to conceal before has *now* become clear to them. And if they were sent back, they would surely return to that which they are forbidden. And they are certainly liars.[776]

بَلْ بَدَا لَهُمْ مَّا كَانُوْا يُخْفُوْنَ مِنْ قَبْلُ ۚ وَلَوْ رُدُّوْا لَعَادُوْا لِمَا نُهُوْا عَنْهُ وَاِنَّهُمْ لَكٰذِبُوْنَ ۝

---

^a46 : 35.   ^b2 : 168 ; 23 : 100-101 ; 26 : 103 ;   39 : 59.

Quran and the discourses of the Holy Prophet exercised on the minds of hearers. No wonder that the disbelievers looked upon the Quran as a "manifest magic" (34 : 44).

775. Important Words :

وُقِفُوْا (made to stand) is derived from وقف which is both transitive and intransitive, meaning, he or it paused or stood still or became stationary ; or he made him or it pause or stand still or become stationary. وقف عليه means, he comprehended or understood it. وقفته على ذنبه means, I made him know or made him acquainted with his offence or sin. وقف الدار means, he dedicated the house in the cause of Allah ; or he set it apart inalienably for a definite purpose. وقف عليه (in the passive voice) means, he was made to pause or stand at or before it ; he was introduced into it and knew what was in it ; he was made to know it surely and definitely (Tāj).

Commentary :

The words اذ وقفوا على النار (when they are made to stand before the Fire) may also mean, "when they will be made to enter the

Fire to abide therein for long, or when they will be made to know or realize the nature of the Fire."

776. Commentary :

The words, *has now become clear to them*, signify that even the enemies of God's Prophets have in their minds a certain consciousness of the truth of the divine Messengers ; but owing to their bigotry, they try to suppress such thoughts and do not make them known to anyone. On the Day of Judgement, however, these latent thoughts which they tried to conceal would become apparent, and the truthfulness of the Prophets, of which they had dim consciousness, would become manifest.

The word "liars" at the end of the verse implies that, although disbelievers would desire to be sent back to this world so that they might believe in the Prophets and not reject them, yet if they were actually sent back to it, and the same circumstances in which they lived before were created again, even then they would again act as they had acted before, rejecting the Prophets as they had rejected them before.

30. And they say, ^a"There is nothing except *this* our present life, and we shall not be raised *again*.'⁷⁷⁷

وَقَالُوٓا اِنْ هِىَ اِلَّا حَيَاتُنَا الدُّنْيَا وَمَا نَحْنُ بِمَبْعُوثِيْنَ ۝

31. And if thou couldst only see when they are made to stand before their Lord ! ^bHe will say, ' Is not this *second life* the truth ?' They will say, ' Yea, by our Lord.' He will say, ' Then taste the punishment because you disbelieved.'⁷⁷⁸

وَلَوْ تَرٰىٓ اِذْ وُقِفُوْا عَلٰى رَبِّهِمْ قَالَ اَلَيْسَ هٰذَا بِالْحَقِّ قَالُوْا بَلٰى وَرَبِّنَا قَالَ فَذُوْقُوا الْعَذَابَ بِمَا كُنْتُمْ تَكْفُرُوْنَ ۝

R. 4   32. ^cThose indeed are the losers who deny the meeting with Allah, so much so, that when the Hour shall come on them unawares, they will say, ^d'O our grief for our neglecting this *Hour*!' And they shall bear their burdens on their backs. Surely, evil is that which they bear.⁷⁷⁹

قَدْ خَسِرَ الَّذِيْنَ كَذَّبُوْا بِلِقَآءِ اللّٰهِ حَتّٰى اِذَا جَآءَتْهُمُ السَّاعَةُ بَغْتَةً قَالُوْا يٰحَسْرَتَنَا عَلٰى مَا فَرَّطْنَا فِيْهَا وَهُمْ يَحْمِلُوْنَ اَوْزَارَهُمْ عَلٰى ظُهُوْرِهِمْ اَلَا سَآءَ مَا يَزِرُوْنَ ۝

---

^a23 : 38 ; 44 : 36 ; 45 : 25.   ^b46 : 35.   ^c10 : 46.   ^d2 : 168.

777. Commentary :

The things of this world and the enjoyments of the present life are, in the sight of most men, so engrossing that they never pause to think of death or of the Hereafter. Would that man could realize the object of his creation and see the everlasting life beyond the grave !

778. Commentary :

The words بلٰى و ربنا (Yea, by our Lord) speak of deeply stirred feelings and embody a pathetic, though veiled, appeal for mercy. But the time for mercy is past and nothing but the grim reality of God's judgement now awaits them.

779. Important Words :

فرطنا (our neglecting) is derived from فرط (*farraṭa*) which again is derived from فرط (*faraṭa*) which means, he went before or preceded. فرط منه الكلام means, the speech or the words issued from him hastily before

reflection. فرط عليه means, he acted hastily and unjustly towards him. فرطه (*farraṭa-hū*) means, he made him to precede ; or he made him to be before, or beforehand or first or foremost. فرطه also means, he sent it before, himself remaining behind it. فرط عنه means, he left or forsook him ; or he abstained or desisted from it. فرط فيه means, he neglected it or he was remiss with respect to it ; or he preferred backwardness in it ; or he failed to do, or fell short of doing, what he ought to have done with respect to it. افرط فى الامر means, he exceeded due bounds or just limits in the matter. Thus تفريط (from فرط) has generally come to mean, "falling short of" and افراط (from افرط) "exceeding proper limits" (Lane & Aqrab).

الا (surely) originally denotes an interrogation respecting a negative, or a wish or reproof, or the asking for or requiring a thing. It is also used as an inceptive particle giving

33. And *a*worldly life is nothing but a sport and a pastime. And surely *b*the abode of the Hereafter is better for those who are righteous. Will you not then understand?[780]

و َ مَا الْحَيْوةُ الدُّنْيَا إِلَّا لَعِبٌ وَّلَهْوٌ وَلَلدَّارُ الْاخِرَةُ خَيْرٌ لِّلَّذِيْنَ يَتَّقُوْنَ اَفَلَا تَعْقِلُوْنَ ۝

34. We know full well that verily *c*what they say grieves thee; for surely it is not thee that they charge with falsehood but it is the Signs of Allah that the evil-doers reject.[781]

قَدْ نَعْلَمُ اِنَّهٗ لَيَحْزُنُكَ الَّذِيْ يَقُوْلُوْنَ فَاِنَّهُمْ لَا يُكَذِّبُوْنَكَ وَلٰكِنَّ الظّٰلِمِيْنَ بِاٰيٰتِ اللهِ يَجْحَدُوْنَ ۝

---

*a*29 : 65 ; 47 : 37 ; 57 : 21.   *b*7 : 170 ; 12 : 110.   *c*15 : 98 ; 16 : 104.

---

the sense of "now" or "why." It also means, verily, truly or surely (Lane).

Commentary :

The pronoun in فيها (this) may refer to the "Hour" mentioned above. In that case "neglecting this Hour" would mean that disbelievers never believed that the Hour would come and never gave it a thought ; or it may refer to الدنيا (the earth) or to حياتنا الدنيا (our present life) occurring in 6 : 30 above. In this case the sentence would mean that they acted negligently during their life on this earth.

The words, *they shall bear their burdens on their backs*, are intended to hint that their burdens would be exceedingly heavy.

780. Important Words :

لعب (sport). The verb form لعب means he played, sported or jested ; or he did an act with the object of amusement or recreation or by way of jesting. It is often the opposite of جد which means, he was serious or in earnest. So لعب means, play, sport or jest ; amusement or recreation (Aqrab & Lane).

لهو (pastime) is derived from لها . They say لها عنه *i.e.*, he became diverted from it so as to forget it. لهت المرأة الى حديث الرجل means, the woman became cheered with, and was diverted by, the discourse of the man.

So لهو means, diversion, pastime or sport ; what occupies a man so as to divert him from that which would render him sad or serious ; relief of the mind by such means as wisdom does not require (Lane & Lisān).

Commentary :

The words, *And worldly life is nothing but a sport and a pastime*, do not mean that life on this earth is only a sport. What is meant is that worldly life, *i.e.*, life engrossed in the things of this world and passed in neglect of the Hereafter is nothing but a sport. Elsewhere (21 : 17, 18) the Quran says that God has not created this world as لعب (sport) or لهو (pastime). Both announcements are equally correct. The words, *And worldly life is nothing but a sport and a pastime*, may also mean that the environments of this world are such that, unless one is particularly watchful, one is liable to become negligent about the next world, just as sports and pastimes often make man negligent of his duties on earth.

781. Commentary :

The verse signifies that the Holy Prophet was grieved at the attitude of disbelievers, not because they accused him of falsehood but because their denial of him meant the denial of the Signs of God. Thus the grief of the Holy Prophet was not personal, the cause of his grief being that God was being denied. It

35. And Messengers indeed have been rejected before thee; but notwith-standing their rejection and persecution they remained patient until *a*Our help came to them. *b*There is none that can change the words of Allah. And there have already come to thee tidings of *past* Messengers.⁷⁸²

36. And if their aversion is grievous to thee, then, if thou art able to seek a passage into the earth or a ladder unto heaven and bring them a Sign, *thou canst do so.* And *c*had Allah enforced *His* will, He could surely have brought them together into the guidance. So be thou not of those who lack knowledge.⁷⁸³

وَلَقَدْ كُذِّبَتْ رُسُلٌ مِّنْ قَبْلِكَ فَصَبَرُوا عَلٰى مَا كُذِّبُوا وَأُوذُوا حَتّٰى أَتٰهُمْ نَصْرُنَا ۚ وَلَا مُبَدِّلَ لِكَلِمٰتِ اللّٰهِ ۚ وَلَقَدْ جَآءَكَ مِنْ نَّبَإِ الْمُرْسَلِينَ ۝

وَإِنْ كَانَ كَبُرَ عَلَيْكَ إِعْرَاضُهُمْ فَإِنِ اسْتَطَعْتَ أَنْ تَبْتَغِيَ نَفَقًا فِي الْأَرْضِ أَوْ سُلَّمًا فِي السَّمَآءِ فَتَأْتِيَهُمْ بِآيَةٍ ۚ وَلَوْ شَآءَ اللّٰهُ لَجَمَعَهُمْ عَلَى الْهُدٰى فَلَا تَكُونَنَّ مِنَ الْجَاهِلِينَ ۝

---

*a*2 : 215; 40 : 52.   *b*6 : 116.   *c*5 : 49; 6 : 150; 11 : 119; 13 : 32; 16 : 10.

---

pained him to see people denying God. He did not mind denial of himself, but he could not bear to see men rejecting God and His Signs.

782. Commentary :

In this verse God lovingly addresses the Holy Prophet with words of comfort and solace, as if saying : " We know that thou art indeed pained to see people denying God, but the law of God cannot be changed. We never compel men to become believers." The words, *There is none that can change the words of Allah*, refer to this very law of God, which is unalterable. The law is twofold : *firstly*, that whenever a Prophet of God appears, there are always men who deny and oppose him; *secondly*, that God never compels such men to accept the truth. See 2 : 257 ; 3 : 21 ; 36 : 31.

783. Important Words :

نفقا (passage). نفق means, a hole or a passage bored into or through the earth and having an opening at the other end (Aqrab). See also 9 : 67.

سلّم (ladder) is derived from سلم (*sallama*). They say سلّمه, *i.e.*, he made him safe and secure. سلّمه اليه means, he gave or delivered it to him. سلّم (*sullam*) means, a ladder or series of stairs or steps meant for ascending. It is so called because it delivers one to the place to which one desires to go. The word also signifies, a means to a thing (Lane).

Commentary :

The words, *to seek a passage into the earth,* signify using worldly means, *i.e.*, preaching and propagating the truth in the earth in order to strengthen the Faith ; and the words, *a ladder unto heaven,* imply using spiritual means, *i.e.,* offering up prayers to God for the guidance of disbelievers, etc. Prayer is indeed the ladder by which a man can mount to heaven.

The Holy Prophet has been told here that God is not going to compel men to embrace Islam ; if he desires their wholesale conversion he should assiduously follow the two prescribed courses, one earthly and the other heavenly. He should, on the one hand, devote himself

37. Only those can accept who listen. And as for the dead, Allah will raise them *to life*, then to Him shall they be brought back.[784]

اِنَّمَا يَسْتَجِيبُ الَّذِينَ يَسْمَعُونَ ۘ وَالْمَوْتٰى يَبْعَثُهُمُ اللّٰهُ ثُمَّ اِلَيْهِ يُرْجَعُونَ ۝

38. And they say, [a]'Why has not a Sign been sent down to him from his Lord?' Say, 'Surely, Allah has power to send down a Sign, but most of them do not know.'[785]

وَ قَالُوا لَوْلَا نُزِّلَ عَلَيْهِ اٰيَةٌ مِّنْ رَّبِّهٖ ۚ قُلْ اِنَّ اللّٰهَ قَادِرٌ عَلٰى اَنْ يُّنَزِّلَ اٰيَةً وَّ لٰكِنَّ اَكْثَرَهُمْ لَا يَعْلَمُونَ ۝

---

[a]10 : 21 ; 29 : 51.

vigorously to preaching and propagating the truth; and, on the other, he should fervently pray to God that He may guide mankind and help the cause of Islam.

It goes without saying that the Holy Prophet acted upon both these methods to the fullest extent, as a result of which God helped the cause of Islam, so much so that within a small space of time the whole of Arabia was converted.

The word جاهل (one lacking knowledge) is here used only in the sense of one not knowing or unacquainted, and not in the stronger sense of ignorant. It has been used in this sense in other verses of the Quran also. For instance, we read in 2 : 274 : " One who does not know them (the needy) thinks them to be free from want ", *i.e.*, those who are unacquainted with the real condition of the poor think them to be well off. In the verse under comment the Holy Prophet has been exhorted not to remain unacquainted with the law of God in this respect.

It should also be noted that it was not by way of rebuke, as some have thought, that the Holy Prophet was asked to seek a passage into the earth or a ladder into the sky. The words become meaningless, if taken in that light. What is meant is simply the suggestion of two

ways of success which, when acted upon, proved wonderfully effective.

784. Commentary :

The verse signifies that those who are good of heart and are willing to listen will readily accept the truth as the result of preaching. As for those who are potentially dead but are fit for rejuvenation, God will quicken them with a Sign and then they will listen and embrace Islam. Thus it was that when God showed His Sign at the fall of Mecca, the whole of Arabia embraced Islam, and the word of God was fulfilled.

785. Commentary :

The words, *Allah has power to send down a Sign*, do not mean that though God has the power to send down a Sign, yet He will not actually do so. The word قادر (having power) used as active participle is intended to denote readiness to show the required power and the closing words of the verse support that inference.

The word قادر also embodies the sense of measuring and determining (Lane). In this sense the clause would mean that God is devising means for the success of Islam, for people are already joining Islam and swelling the number of Muslims. This is a clear

39. ªThere is not an animal *that crawls* in the earth, nor a bird that flies on its two wings, but they are communities like you. ᵇWe have left out nothing in the Book. Then to their Lord shall they be gathered together.[786]

وَمَا مِنْ دَآبَّةٍ فِى الْاَرْضِ وَلَا طٰٓئِرٍ يَّطِيْرُ بِجَنَاحَيْهِ اِلَّاۤ اُمَمٌ اَمْثَالُكُمْ مَا فَرَّطْنَا فِى الْكِتٰبِ مِنْ شَىْءٍ ثُمَّ اِلٰى رَبِّهِمْ يُحْشَرُوْنَ ۞

ª11 : 7, 57.   ᵇ16 : 90.

indication of the will of God, but disbelievers would not ponder over it. The Quran makes this point clear by suitable illustrations in the following verse.

786. Important Words :

امم (communities), which is derived from امّ *i.e.,* he betook himself to or aimed at or sought, is the plural of امّة which means, a way, course or manner of acting or of conduct or of life ; religion, which is a course that men follow ; the followers of a religion ; or a people to whom a Prophet is sent, whether unbelievers or believers ; a generation ; a nation, a people, a race, a tribe or a family ; a collective body of men or of other living beings ; a kind, genus or generical class ; creatures of God. It also means, a righteous man who is an object of imitation, being a model for others ; or one who follows the true religion ; or a learned man who has no equal in his time (Lane).

امثال (like) is the plural of مثل (*mathal*) and مثل (*mithl*), both being derived from the verb مثل for which see 2 : 107. مثل (*mathal*) means, description, condition, state or case ; a description by way of comparison ; similitude ; argument or sign, etc. The word is also used in the sense of مثل (*mithl*) which means, a like ; one similar to ; the thing itself *i.e.,* the same as (Aqrab & Lane).

Commentary :

The Quran draws the attention of disbelievers to the animals that move on the earth and to the birds that fly in the air. Even animals and birds can understand by means of signs that a change has taken place in the season, but disbelievers are worse than these ; for they do not see the signs which indicate that Islam is triumphing while disbelief is beating a retreat. Even a dog can see whether its master is angry or pleased ; but disbelievers cannot see whether their Lord is displeased with them. Thus both the birds that fly in the air and the animals that move on the earth are in this respect better than disbelievers.

Incidentally, the verse also hints that even birds and animals will be resurrected and requited for their actions like men. The resemblance between the requital of men and animals may not be perfect, but it is still there. Some of the sayings of the Holy Prophet also lend support to this conclusion ; for it is said in a ḥadīth that the horned goat shall be made to pay penalty to the goat without horns which it kills or injures (Muslim, ch. on *Taḥrīm al-ẓulm*).

The last words of the verse *i.e., We have left out nothing in the Book. Then to their Lord shall they be gathered together,* may also refer to disbelievers. In that case, this part of the verse would mean that all the works of disbelievers will be preserved and nothing will be left out, and that they will finally be requited for their actions on the Day of Resurrection.

40. ^aThose who have rejected Our Signs are deaf and dumb, in utter darkness. Whom Allah wills He causes to perish and whom He wills He places on the right path.

وَ الَّذِيْنَ كَذَّبُوْا بِاٰيٰتِنَا صُمٌّ وَّ بُكْمٌ فِی الظُّلُمٰتِ ؕ مَنْ يَّشَاِ اللّٰهُ يُضْلِلْهُ ؕ وَ مَنْ يَّشَأْ يَجْعَلْهُ عَلٰی صِرَاطٍ مُّسْتَقِيْمٍ ۝

41. Say, ^b'What think ye? If the punishment of Allah come upon you or there come upon you the Hour, will you call upon any other than Allah, if you are truthful?'⁷⁸⁷

قُلْ اَرَءَيْتَكُمْ اِنْ اَتٰكُمْ عَذَابُ اللّٰهِ اَوْ اَتَتْكُمُ السَّاعَةُ اَغَيْرَ اللّٰهِ تَدْعُوْنَ ۚ اِنْ كُنْتُمْ صٰدِقِيْنَ ۝

42. Nay, ^cbut on Him alone will you call; then will He remove that which you call on Him to remove, if He please, and you will forget what you associate with Him.⁷⁸⁸

بَلْ اِيَّاهُ تَدْعُوْنَ فَيَكْشِفُ مَا تَدْعُوْنَ اِلَيْهِ اِنْ شَآءَ وَ تَنْسَوْنَ مَا تُشْرِكُوْنَ ۝

5 43. And indeed We sent Messengers to peoples before thee; then ^dWe afflicted them with poverty and adversity that they might humble themselves.⁷⁸⁹

وَ لَقَدْ اَرْسَلْنَآ اِلٰٓی اُمَمٍ مِّنْ قَبْلِكَ فَاَخَذْنٰهُمْ بِالْبَأْسَآءِ وَ الضَّرَّآءِ لَعَلَّهُمْ يَتَضَرَّعُوْنَ ۝

---

^a2:19, 172; 27:81-82; 30:53-54. ^b6:48; 12:108; 43:67. ^c10:23-24. ^d7:95.

787. Commentary:

The word "Hour" refers to the Hour of the decisive victory of Islam, or, in other words, the fall of Mecca. Thus whereas "punishment" refers to ordinary afflictions, "Hour" refers to the final and decisive event of the struggle. The question put in this verse is answered in the next.

788. Commentary:

The opening words of the verse contain the answer to the question put in the previous verse. The words, *then will He remove that which you call on Him to remove,* were fulfilled by the general pardon which the Holy Prophet granted to disbelievers at the fall of Mecca. The memorable words spoken by him on that occasion were: "Go, I forgive you all. Go,

you are free" (Zurqānī, ii. 328).

The words, *you will forget what you associate with Him,* were also signally fulfilled on that day. At the fall of Mecca, the Meccans lost all faith in their gods, as Abū Sufyān and his wife, Hind, and others frankly admitted in the presence of the Holy Prophet. Ultimately, idolatry disappeared from Arabia.

789. Commentary:

The previous verses referred to divine punishment in general. In this verse its various forms have been mentioned. Many have an erroneous idea of divine punishment, which not unoften comes veiled in the form of ordinary afflictions. In fact, all financial and bodily misfortunes, *e.g.,* poverty, disease, etc. are in one sense or

44. Why, then, when Our punishment came upon them, did they not grow humble ? But ^atheir hearts were hardened and ^bSatan made all that they did seem fair to them.⁷⁹⁰

فَلَوْلَآ اِذْ جَآءَهُمْ بَأْسُنَا تَضَرَّعُوْا وَلٰكِنْ قَسَتْ قُلُوْبُهُمْ وَزَيَّنَ لَهُمُ الشَّيْطٰنُ مَا كَانُوْا يَعْمَلُوْنَ ۝

45. Then, when ^cthey forgot that with which they had been admonished, We opened unto them the gates of all things, until, when they became exultant at what they were given, ^dWe seized them suddenly, and lo ! they were plunged in despair.⁷⁹¹

فَلَمَّا نَسُوْا مَا ذُكِّرُوْا بِهٖ فَتَحْنَا عَلَيْهِمْ اَبْوَابَ كُلِّ شَىْءٍ حَتّٰى اِذَا فَرِحُوْا بِمَآ اُوْتُوْا اَخَذْنٰهُمْ بَغْتَةً فَاِذَا هُمْ مُبْلِسُوْنَ ۝

46. ^eSo the last remnant of the people who did wrong was cut off ; and all praise belongs to Allah, the Lord of all the worlds.⁷⁹²

فَقُطِعَ دَابِرُ الْقَوْمِ الَّذِيْنَ ظَلَمُوْا وَالْحَمْدُ لِلّٰهِ رَبِّ الْعٰلَمِيْنَ ۝

---

^a2 : 75 ; 57 : 17. ^b6 : 123 ; 8 : 49 ; 16 : 64 ; 29 : 39. ^c5 : 14 ; 7 : 166. ^d7 : 96 ; 39 : 56.
^e7 : 73 ; 15 : 67.

---

another, punishments from God. They are not generally meant to destroy men but to make them reform themselves and turn to God.

790. Commentary :

The words لولا (why not) are here used not to express mere interrogation but also to express feelings of pity. Thus the verse signifies, "They ought to have humbled themselves before God; but it is a pity that they did not."

The afflictions were really a mercy from God, but, instead of turning to God, the people became hard-hearted. When misfortunes befell them, they ascribed them not to their own iniquities but to the Prophets.

The words, *all that they did*, refer to the hostile activities of disbelievers.

791. Commentary :

When disbelievers became hardened and treated divine admonition as a thing forgotten, God let them wander in their blind trans-

gression. The words, *We opened unto them the gates of all things*, signify that God let them stray away and advance further and further into the evil deeds in which they were engaged. Sometimes the afflictions were removed from them for a time and they rejoiced to think that they were right in thinking that the afflictions were not due to their sins. Then the punishment of God suddenly seized them, and they gave themselves up to despair. Thus there are two kinds of afflictions that visit disbelieving people in the days of divine Messengers : (1) temporary afflictions that come as warnings and then pass away; (2) general disaster which finally overtakes and destroys the wicked.

792. Important Words:

دَابِر (last remnant) is derived from دبر. They say دبره, *i.e.*, he followed behind his back; or he followed him with respect to place, time or rank. ادبر means, he went turning his back, or he turned back. دُبُر means, the back or the hinder part ; latter or the last part.

47. Say, 'What think ye ? *a*If Allah should take away your hearing and your sight, and seal up your hearts, who is the god other than Allah who could bring it back to you'? See how We vary the Signs, yet they turn away.[793]

قُلْ اَرَءَيْتُمْ اِنْ اَخَذَ اللهُ سَمْعَكُمْ وَاَبْصَارَكُمْ وَخَتَمَ عَلٰى قُلُوبِكُمْ مَّنْ اِلٰهٌ غَيْرُ اللهِ يَاْتِيْكُمْ بِهٖ ۚ اُنْظُرْ كَيْفَ نُصَرِّفُ الْاٰيٰتِ ثُمَّ هُمْ يَصْدِفُوْنَ ۝

*a*2 : 8; 16 : 109 ; 45 : 24.

دابِر means, person or thing following behind the back ; last remains of a people; the root, stock, race, or the like (Lane).

Commentary :

The words قَطَعَ دَابِرَ الْقَوْمِ (the last remnant of the people was cut off) mean: (1) the people were cut off to the last man, *i.e.*, the whole people were cut off ; (2) the leaders of the people were cut off just as a tree is cut down to its roots, the leaders occupying the position of the roots ; (3) the leaders' followers were cut off, *i.e.*, the leaders were deprived of their political power, for it is on the strength of their followers that the political power of the leaders depends.

Apparently, there is no occasion here for saying, *All praise belongs to Allah,* for these words are spoken on an occasion when one receives a favour from God and is thankful to Him. When, however, one is afflicted with a misfortune, then the words which suit the occasion and which Muslims are bidden to recite are اِنَّا لِلّٰهِ وَاِنَّا اِلَيْهِ رَاجِعُوْنَ *i.e. Surely to Allah we belong and to Him shall we return* (2 : 157). The apparent incongruity is, however, easily explained. The words الْحَمْدُ لِلّٰهِ (all praise belongs to Allah) have been used here in order to point out that the cutting-off of what is injurious is in fact a thing to feel grateful for, and not a matter of regret. When a limb becomes diseased and is incurable, we get it amputated and cheerfully pay the fee to the surgeon for the operation, and also express our thanks to him. Just as a diseased limb is amputated to save the rest of the body, it sometimes becomes necessary to cut off that section of mankind which has become corrupt, so that the infection may not spoil entire humanity.

793. Commentary :

The preceding verse spoke of the punishment that cuts at the root. But there is a stage when only a part is affected, or even if the whole body is affected the disease is not deep-rooted and there is yet time to prevent the total loss of the body. In its early stages a disease is generally curable; but if it is not attended to in time, it may be aggravated and become incurable. It is against such negligence that men are warned in the present verse. Some men delay acceptance of divine Messengers. They wait for more and more Signs, and go on postponing the tendering of allegiance to the heavenly Messengers until it is too late. The punishment of God descends on the enemies of the Prophets; and those who do not make use of their inward light and prefer to wait for more and more evidence of the truth of the divine Messengers also perish with their enemies. So this verse warns those who are in the habit of delaying and postponing, and exhorts them to use their inward light for the recognition of the divine Messenger, and expedite their acceptance of him lest delay should result in the total extinction of their God-given faculties and they should perish with the rest. They should be prompt to make use of their hearing, and their eyes, and their hearts; for if they fail to

48. Say, 'What think ye ? ^aIf the punishment of Allah come upon you suddenly or openly, will any be destroyed save the wrongdoing people ?'⁷⁹⁴

قُلْ اَرَءَيْتَكُمْ اِنْ اَتٰكُمْ عَذَابُ اللّٰهِ بَغْتَةً اَوْ جَهْرَةً هَلْ يُهْلَكُ اِلَّا الْقَوْمُ الظّٰلِمُوْنَ ۝

49. And ^bWe send not the Messengers but as bearers of glad tidings and as warners. So ^cthose who believe and reform *themselves*, on them shall come no fear nor shall they grieve.⁷⁹⁵

وَ مَا نُرْسِلُ الْمُرْسَلِيْنَ اِلَّا مُبَشِّرِيْنَ وَ مُنْذِرِيْنَ فَمَنْ اٰمَنَ وَ اَصْلَحَ فَلَا خَوْفٌ عَلَيْهِمْ وَ لَا هُمْ يَحْزَنُوْنَ ۝

50. And ^dthose who reject Our Signs, punishment will touch them, because they disobeyed.

وَ الَّذِيْنَ كَذَّبُوْا بِاٰيٰتِنَا يَمَسُّهُمُ الْعَذَابُ بِمَا كَانُوْا يَفْسُقُوْنَ ۝

---

^a6: 41; 10: 51; 12: 108; 43: 67.   ^b4: 166; 5: 20; 18: 57.   ^c5: 70; 7: 36.
^d3: 12; 5: 11; 7: 37, 73; 10: 74; 22: 58.

---

make use of these faculties in time, they will gradually become impaired and will finally be lost; then no power will be able to restore these faculties to them after they have been completely lost.

The words, *how We vary the Signs*, signify that in order to make things perfectly clear, God brings the different aspects of Signs before the people, sometimes showing one kind of Sign and sometimes another, so that all kinds of people may be satisfied.

794. Commentary:

The word "suddenly" signifies the coming of the divine punishment without warning or previous indication. The fall of Mecca belonged to this class of Signs.

The word "openly" implies giving a warning

beforehand so that such people as still retain inward light and have a desire to follow the guidance may become warned and may accept the truth without further delay, lest they should also perish along with the wrongdoers.

795. Commentary:

All divine Messengers have a sort of dual personality—a twofold mission. They bring glad tidings for one class of men and warnings for others. Those who accept them receive tidings of blessings and those who reject them receive warnings of punishments. Those who are weak should hasten to join the class of men for whom glad tidings are meant. They have no reason to fear; for, as the verse makes it clear, if they accept the Prophets, "no fear shall come on them, nor shall they grieve !"

51. Say: *"I do not say to you: 'I possess the treasures of Allah,' nor do I know the unseen; nor do I say to you: 'I am an angel,' *I follow only that which is revealed to me." Say: 'Can a blind man and one who sees be alike?' Will you not then reflect?⁷⁹⁶

قُلْ لَّا أَقُوْلُ لَكُمْ عِنْدِىْ خَزَآئِنُ اللّٰهِ وَلَآ أَعْلَمُ الْغَيْبَ وَلَآ أَقُوْلُ لَكُمْ إِنِّىْ مَلَكٌ ۚ إِنْ أَتَّبِعُ إِلَّا مَا يُوْحٰٓى إِلَىَّ ۚ قُلْ هَلْ يَسْتَوِى الْأَعْمٰى وَالْبَصِيْرُ ۚ أَفَلَا تَتَفَكَّرُوْنَ ۝

52. And warn thereby those who fear that they shall be gathered to their Lord that they shall have no friend nor intercessor beside Him, so that they may become righteous.⁷⁹⁷

وَأَنْذِرْ بِهِ الَّذِيْنَ يَخَافُوْنَ أَنْ يُّحْشَرُوْٓا إِلٰى رَبِّهِمْ لَيْسَ لَهُمْ مِّنْ دُوْنِهٖ وَلِيٌّ وَّلَا شَفِيْعٌ لَّعَلَّهُمْ يَتَّقُوْنَ ۝

---

*11 : 32. *10 : 16 ; 46 : 10.

796. **Commentary :**

The words, *I do not say to you, I possess the treasures of Allah*, imply that when the Quran says that the Messengers of God are the announcers of glad tidings, this should not be construed to mean that as soon as a person believes in a Prophet of God, he acquires wealth. He will have to wait for the favours of God to come at their appointed time.

The words, *nor do I say to you, I am an angel*, here imply that it is not in the power of the Prophet to bring down punishment, for he is not "an angel of punishment."

After the above declarations it might be asked what good there was in following the Prophet when worldly favours took time in coming and when the Prophet was so powerless against his enemies. The Quran answers this implied question by saying that the getting of a treasure was not the only boon which one could desire. The perfect guidance which was received through the Prophet was a great blessing in itself; for those who accepted the guidance were like one who possessed eyes, while those who rejected it were like one who had no eyes and the blind and the seeing could never be alike. These are matters to be reflected upon and pondered over.

797. **Commentary :**

A warning can benefit only those who believe in the danger they are warned against. If a people do not believe in the existence of that which they are asked to guard against, the exhortation will do no good. Hence, in this verse, where the warning relates to the dangers of the Day of Resurrection, the Holy Prophet is bidden to warn not all mankind but only those who believe in the Day of Resurrection that they will have no friend or intercessor on that awful day. As for those who do not believe in Resurrection, the way of preaching will be different—they will be first convinced of Resurrection and then warned against its dangers. Thus incidentally the verse also teaches us how to preach. We should always base our arguments on things which the persons addressed believe to be true so that our preaching may have the desired effect,

53. And ^adrive not away those who call upon their Lord morning and evening, ^bseeking His countenance. Thou art not at all accountable for them nor are they at all accountable for thee, that thou shouldst drive them away and be of the unjust.⁷⁹⁸

وَلَا تَطْرُدِ الَّذِيْنَ يَدْعُوْنَ رَبَّهُمْ بِالْغَدٰوةِ وَالْعَشِيِّ يُرِيْدُوْنَ وَجْهَهٗ ۖ مَا عَلَيْكَ مِنْ حِسَابِهِمْ مِّنْ شَيْءٍ وَّمَا مِنْ حِسَابِكَ عَلَيْهِمْ مِّنْ شَيْءٍ فَتَطْرُدَهُمْ فَتَكُوْنَ مِنَ الظّٰلِمِيْنَ ۞

^a11 : 30.   ^b18 : 29.

---

798. Important Words :

الغدٰوة (morning), which is often written as غداة the letter (و) being silent, is derived from غدا which means, he went forth or went away in the early part of the morning, i.e., between daybreak and sunrise. So. غدٰاة or غدٰة or غدوة or غدية means, early part of the morning; the period between daybreak and sunrise ; morning; first part of the day; forenoon (Lane).

العشى (evening) is derived from عشا which means, he ate the evening meal ; he repaired to (him, etc.) at night. عشى means, late part of the evening; evening; afternoon ; time between sunset and nightfall. It also means the time between the declining of the sun and sunset; also the time from the declining of the sun to morning; night (Lane).

وجهه (His countenance). The word وجه also means نفس الشيئى i.e. the thing itself (see 2 : 113).

Commentary :

The words بالغدٰاة والعشى (morning and evening) taken in their wider significance cover, as shown under Important Words, practically all the 24 hours, excluding only the time in which the offering of Prayers is prohibited. Thus in one sense the two words taken together comprise both day and night, and in another they indicate only morning and evening.

The words يريدون وجهه (seeking His countenance) may also mean, "seeking God Himself," for the expression وجه also means, "the thing itself". In that case, the clause would mean "they seek nothing but God, i.e. they seek God alone."

The words, *thou shouldst be of the unjust*, hint that there are some men who look upon themselves as being too great and disdain to join a movement set on foot by a Prophet, because its adherents are mostly poor and do not belong to what is called higher society. They would join it only if the poorer adherents were expelled. So, in order to demolish such hopes on their part, God bids the Holy Prophet declare that he would not drive away his poor followers so that the so-called great might join his fold. The prohibition does not mean that the Holy Prophet actually used to drive away his poorer followers. It is only meant as a reply and a rebuff to the desires of the proud and the haughty. They are told that the humble followers of the Holy Prophet who remember God morning and evening or day and night cannot be turned out for their sake. The Quran has already made the Holy Prophet say, *I follow only that which is revealed to me* (6 : 51). So now when the prohibition, *drive not away those who call upon their Lord morning and evening*, has so forcibly been revealed, the so-called great should despair of the humble being driven away. So these words were revealed not as a reflection on the Holy Prophet whose kindness

54. And in like manner have We tried some of them by others, that they may say, ^a'Is it these whom Allah has favoured from among us?' Does not Allah know best those who are grateful?⁷⁹⁹

وَكَذٰلِكَ فَتَنَّا بَعْضَهُمْ بِبَعْضٍ لِّيَقُوْلُوْۤا اَهٰۤؤُلَآءِ مَنَّ اللّٰهُ عَلَيْهِمْ مِّنْ بَيْنِنَا ۗ اَلَيْسَ اللّٰهُ بِاَعْلَمَ بِالشّٰكِرِيْنَ ۝

55. And when those who believe in Our Signs come to thee, say: 'Peace be unto you! ^bYour Lord has taken it upon Himself to show mercy, so that ^cwhoso among you does evil ignorantly, and repents thereafter and amends, then He is Most Forgiving and Merciful.'⁸⁰⁰

وَاِذَا جَآءَكَ الَّذِيْنَ يُؤْمِنُوْنَ بِاٰيٰتِنَا فَقُلْ سَلٰمٌ عَلَيْكُمْ كَتَبَ رَبُّكُمْ عَلٰى نَفْسِهِ الرَّحْمَةَ ۙ اَنَّهٗ مَنْ عَمِلَ مِنْكُمْ سُوْٓءًۢا بِجَهَالَةٍ ثُمَّ تَابَ مِنْ بَعْدِهٖ وَاَصْلَحَ فَاَنَّهٗ غَفُوْرٌ رَّحِيْمٌ ۝

---

^a11 : 28.   ^b6 : 13 ; 7 : 157.   ^c4 : 18 ; 16 : 120.

---

to the poor is so well-known but in order to shatter the hopes of the proud.

The words, *Thou art not at all accountable for them nor are they at all accountable for thee*, are also meant to point to the same great truth. Though the Prophet could not turn the poor out on account of the humbleness of their position yet it might be thought that he might turn them out on account of some weakness on their part in respect of actions, but, besides the fact that in this respect the poor and the rich stand on the same footing, the Law does not hold the Prophet responsible for their actions, hence he cannot turn them out on this score either, unless of course when some serious offence is committed by them.

799. Commentary :

The words, *We have tried some of them by others*, refer to God's trying the rich and the great by admitting the poor and the humble into the society of the followers of the Holy Prophet. The presence of the poor in the community of the believers served as a stumbling-block in the way of the rich and

hindered the more haughty among them from entering into the fellowship of Islam.

The rich and the great ask whether God had chosen those poor men for His favours, as if saying, "We are wealthy and rich, but God has preferred the poor to us and has bestowed His favour upon them rather than upon us." God answers the question by saying, "I gave them little but they have been thankful to Me even for that and have accepted My Messenger. I gave you much, but you have not been grateful and have rejected My Messenger. Do not the poor then deserve to be chosen for My favour in preference to you?" See also the preceding verse.

800. Commentary :

The message conveyed in the words, *Peace be unto you*, is the message of God which the Holy Prophet is bidden to convey to believers ; the "peace" spoken of is to come from God Himself. It is with reference to this "peace" promised to believers in the present verse that they are enjoined to greet one another with the words السلام عليكم *i.e.*, "may the

56. And thus do We expound the Signs *that you may seek forgiveness* and that the way of the sinners may become manifest.[801]

وَكَذٰلِكَ نُفَصِّلُ الْاٰيٰتِ وَلِتَسْتَبِيْنَ سَبِيْلُ الْمُجْرِمِيْنَ ۞

R. 7   57. Say: 'I am forbidden to worship those on whom you call beside Allah.' Say: [a]'I will not follow your evil inclinations. In that case, I shall become lost and I shall not be of the guided.'[802]

قُلْ اِنِّیْ نُهِیْتُ اَنْ اَعْبُدَ الَّذِیْنَ تَدْعُوْنَ مِنْ دُوْنِ اللّٰهِ ۚ قُلْ لَّا اَتَّبِعُ اَهْوَآءَكُمْ ۙ قَدْ ضَلَلْتُ اِذًا وَّ مَاۤ اَنَا مِنَ الْمُهْتَدِیْنَ ۞

58. Say: [b]'I *take my stand* on a clear evidence from my Lord and you reject it. That which you desire to be hastened is not in my power. [c]The decision rests with none but Allah. He explains the truth, and He is Best of judges.'[803]

قُلْ اِنِّیْ عَلٰی بَیِّنَةٍ مِّنْ رَّبِّیْ وَكَذَّبْتُمْ بِهٖ ۚ مَا عِنْدِیْ مَا تَسْتَعْجِلُوْنَ بِهٖ ۚ اِنِ الْحُكْمُ اِلَّا لِلّٰهِ ۚ یَقُصُّ الْحَقَّ وَ هُوَ خَیْرُ الْفٰصِلِیْنَ ۞

---

[a]5:50; 42:16   [b]11:64; 12:109.   [c]12:41, 68.

(promised) peace be on you." The reader will have noted that whereas the verse uses the word *salām* (peace), the word used in the formula of mutual greeting is *al-salām* (the peace). This is to point out that the greeting of peace offered is in conformity with the peace promised in the verse under comment.

801. Commentary :

There is an ellipsis here, the words لِتَسْتَغْفِرُوا (that you may seek forgiveness) or the words لِتُؤْمِنُوا (that you may believe) may be taken to be understood before the words وَلِتَسْتَبِیْنَ (and may become manifest).

802. Commentary :

This verse is connected with 6 : 53 above. The Holy Prophet is here bidden to say to disbelievers what may be described as follows: "I have nothing to do with your gods and I therefore cannot, for your sake, drive away my poor followers. They believe in One God, while you are idolaters. How can I then drive away the believers in One God for the sake of those who disbelieve! You say that if you

join Islam, it will receive strength and support from you. But the truth is that if I follow your wishes, the result will be that I shall become lost and my movement will be ruined rather than strengthened. Again, my mission is that men may accept and follow guidance ; but if I act upon your wishes, the result will be that I myself will go astray. Then there will be no Islam and no guidance. What then shall I gain from your support ?"

803. Commentary :

The verse calls upon the Holy Prophet to say to disbelievers what may be expressed as follows: "You are perversely sticking to your errors while I have clear evidence with me. You say, 'If we are in error, why does not God visit us with punishment?' You must remember that it does not lie in my power to bring down punishment. It is God alone Who sends down punishment on whomsoever and at whatever time He wills and He is the Best of judges. He will justly decide the matter between you and me."

59. Say : ^a'If that which you desire to be hastened were in my power, surely the matter would be decided between me and you. And Allah knows best the unjust.'[804]

60. And with Him are the keys of the unseen ; none knows them but He. And He knows whatsoever is in the land and *in* the sea. And there falls not a leaf but He knows it ; nor is there a grain in the darkness of the earth, nor anything green or dry, but is recorded in a clear Book.[805]

قُلْ لَّوْ اَنَّ عِنْدِىْ مَا تَسْتَعْجِلُوْنَ بِهِ لَقُضِىَ الْاَمْرُ بَيْنِىْ وَ بَيْنَكُمْ وَ اللّٰهُ اَعْلَمُ بِالظّٰلِمِيْنَ ۝

وَ عِنْدَهٗ مَفَاتِحُ الْغَيْبِ لَا يَعْلَمُهَآ اِلَّا هُوَ وَيَعْلَمُ مَا فِى الْبَرِّ وَ الْبَحْرِ وَ مَا تَسْقُطُ مِنْ وَّرَقَةٍ اِلَّا يَعْلَمُهَا وَ لَا حَبَّةٍ فِىْ ظُلُمٰتِ الْاَرْضِ وَ لَا رَطْبٍ وَّ لَا يَابِسٍ اِلَّا فِىْ كِتٰبٍ مُّبِيْنٍ ۝

---

^a6 : 9 ; 10 : 12.

---

804. Commentary :

This verse gives one of the reasons why it has not been placed in the power of Prophets to bring down punishment. The reason lies in the fact that God alone knows who are just and who are unjust. Therefore, if the work of punishment be entrusted to human beings, who do not know the inner secrets of the heart, they may punish many who are not really unjust. 'Umar, for instance, was in the beginning bitterly opposed to the Holy Prophet. But God knew that he would one day become a zealous champion of Islam, so much so that he would finally become the Second Successor of the Holy Prophet. Now, if the work of punishment had been entrusted to the Holy Prophet, he might have selected 'Umar for punishment during the period of his bitter opposition to the new Faith, to the great loss to Islam. So only a Being Who knows the hidden secrets of man's heart can award punishment, for He alone knows who is really deserving of punishment and who not. There are many men who are outwardly very meek, but in their hearts they are not better than ravenous wolves. Similarly, there are many who are outwardly very harsh and stubborn, but they are good at heart. If

it had been left to the Prophets to punish their enemies, they might have punished them much sooner than God punishes them.

805. Commentary :

This verse gives a further reason why the work of punishment must remain in the hands of God ; it is God alone with Whom are the keys of the unseen, *i.e.*, it is He alone Who knows the unseen. None but He knows the secrets of men's hearts and therefore He alone is in a position to punish.

The expressions " land," " sea", " falling of a leaf ", " grain in the darkness of the earth," and " green or dry " are all descriptive of the various conditions of man. The " sea", according to the Arab conception, is typical of hardships, whereas " land " symbolizes ease and comfort. Similarly, " the falling of a leaf " represents the actions of man that are rendered vain and fruitless ; whereas the " grain in the darkness of the earth," if left unprotected, may become lost just as virtue, if left uncared for, may become lost. Again, " the green or the dry " is also known to God. A tree appears to us to be dry, but when it is watered by rain, it becomes green.

61. And ^aHe it is Who takes your souls by night and knows that which you do by day; then He raises you up again therein, that the appointed term may be completed. Then to Him is your return. Then will He inform you of what you used to do.⁸⁰⁶

وَهُوَ الَّذِیْ یَتَوَفّٰکُمۡ بِالَّیۡلِ وَ یَعۡلَمُ مَا جَرَحۡتُمۡ بِالنَّهَارِ ثُمَّ یَبۡعَثُکُمۡ فِیۡهِ لِیُقۡضٰۤی اَجَلٌ مُّسَمًّی ثُمَّ اِلَیۡهِ مَرۡجِعُکُمۡ ثُمَّ یُنَبِّئُکُمۡ بِمَا کُنۡتُمۡ تَعۡمَلُوۡنَ ۝

^a39 : 43.

Similarly, a man sometimes appears to us to be devoid of all spirituality, but when he is watered with the water of divine mercy, he becomes full of spiritual life.

The word کتاب (Book) also signifies knowledge. Other instances of this use may be seen in 30 : 57 and 68 : 48 where the words کتاب (lit. book) and یکتبون (lit. they write) respectively mean "knowledge" and "they know". The Holy Prophet is also reported to have written to the people of Yemen, saying, قد بعثت الیکم کاتبا من اصحابی : I "have sent to you a writer, *i.e.*, a man of knowledge, from among my Companions" (Biḥār, iii. 193). So the Arabic words rendered as "is recorded in a clear Book" may also be translated as "is preserved in sure divine knowledge."

Thus, as God alone possesses the keys of the unseen and as all the conditions and actions of man are known to Him alone, it is He only Who can punish him. No one who is devoid of perfect knowledge is qualified to punish. Again, God alone knows how far hardship or ease influences the actions of a man. He alone knows whether or not the good works done by a man have been rendered null and void through the operation of other causes. He alone knows the grains of virtue that lie embedded in the heart of man and whether or not these grains will sprout forth and grow and thrive and bring forth fruit. He alone can tell whether a person who, to all appearances, is "dry" and devoid of all spiritual life, will turn " green " when

supplied with heavenly water or whether he is dead beyond revival. In short, God alone has true knowledge of all things and all conditions and all possibilities and all potentialities, and therefore He alone can say whether a man deserves to be punished or not.

806. Important Words:

یتوفّاکم (who takes your souls). The learned author of the *Al-Baḥr al-Muḥīṭ* says : "The word توفّی (*tawaffī*), as is well known, means, to cause to die,' but in this verse it has been metaphorically used in the sense of 'causing to sleep' on account of the close resemblance between sleep and death." See also 2 : 235 & 3 : 56.

جرحتم (you do) is derived from جرح. They say جرحه *i.e.* he wounded him. جرح also means, he acquired, earned, worked or did (Lane).

Commentary :

The subject that none but God is entitled to punish is continued in this verse, which says that God alone knows the condition of man by night and his actions by day, and all times are subject to His control, and therefore it is He alone Who knows the true character of the pious and the wicked, and consequently none but He is in a position to punish. Again, it is He alone Who knows the time most suited for the death of a person and therefore He has not entrusted the work of punishment to others.

The words, *that the appointed term may be completed,* do not refer to any term arbitrarily

8   62. And ᵃHe is Supreme over His servants, and ᵇHe sends guardians to *watch* over you, until, when death comes to anyone of you, Our messengers take his soul, and they fail not.⁸⁰⁷

وَهُوَ الْقَاهِرُ فَوْقَ عِبَادِهِ وَيُرْسِلُ عَلَيْكُمْ حَفَظَةً حَتّٰى اِذَا جَآءَ اَحَدَكُمُ الْمَوْتُ تَوَفَّتْهُ رُسُلُنَا وَهُمْ لَا يُفَرِّطُوْنَ ۝

63. Then are they returned to Allah, their true Lord. Surely, His is the judgement. And He is the quickest of reckoners.⁸⁰⁸

ثُمَّ رُدُّوْۤا اِلَى اللّٰهِ مَوْلٰىهُمُ الْحَقِّ اَلَا لَهُ الْحُكْمُ وَهُوَ اَسْرَعُ الْحٰسِبِيْنَ ۝

64. Say, ᶜ"Who delivers you from the calamities of the land and the sea, *when* you call upon Him in humility and in secret, *saying,* 'If He deliver us from this, we will surely be of those who are grateful'?"⁸⁰⁹

قُلْ مَنْ يُّنَجِّيْكُمْ مِّنْ ظُلُمٰتِ الْبَرِّ وَالْبَحْرِ تَدْعُوْنَهٗ تَضَرُّعًا وَّخُفْيَةً ۚ لَئِنْ اَنْجٰنَا مِنْ هٰذِهٖ لَنَكُوْنَنَّ مِنَ الشّٰكِرِيْنَ ۝

ᵃ6 : 19 ; 13 : 17.   ᵇ13 : 12 ; 82 : 11.   ᶜ10 : 23 ; 17 : 68 ; 29 : 66 ; 31 : 33.

---

fixed by God. The "term" spoken of here is determined by the faculties and powers with which man is endowed from the time of his birth, and is liable to be increased or decreased according as a right or wrong use is made of the faculties granted to him. There is no reference here to the eternal knowledge of God.

807. Commentary:

This verse provides another reason why God alone is entitled to punish. He is قَاهِر (Supreme), *i.e.*, Powerful and Mighty over all, therefore He can punish any of His creatures whenever He thinks it proper. The powerful are never in a hurry to punish, for they know that they can punish whenever they will. Again, it is God Himself Who guards His creatures and supports them, and it is through His grace that they enjoy security. So destruction can befall them only when He withdraws His grace, and He does so when He thinks it proper.

The words, *they fail not,* signify that when

God finally issues a decree, nothing can delay it or set it aside.

808. Commentary:

The reader should note that when speaking of death, the Quran uses the expression " When death comes to anyone of you" (see the preceding verse which uses the singular number), while in the present verse it refers to the Resurrection of all men together by saying, "Then are they returned to Allah." This is because whereas death comes to men individually and not to all men together, the Resurrection of mankind will be simultaneous and universal.

809. Commentary:

تَضَرُّعًا (in humility) is derived from ضَرُع which means, he was or became lowly, humble or submissive ; or he lowered, humbled or abased himself and petitioned for a gift ; or he was weak, slender or emaciated. ضَرُع also means, it (a kid, etc.) took with its mouth the teat or dug of its mother. تَضَرَّع means, he

65. Say, 'Allah delivers you from them and from every distress, yet you associate partners *with Him.*'[810]

قُلِ اللّٰهُ يُنَجِّيكُمۡ مِّنۡهَا وَ مِنۡ كُلِّ كَرۡبٍ ثُمَّ اَنۡتُمۡ تُشۡرِكُوۡنَ ۝

66. Say, 'He has power to send punishment upon you from above you or from beneath your feet, or to confound you by *splitting you into* sects and make you taste the violence of one another.' See how We expound the Signs in various ways that they may understand ![811]

قُلۡ هُوَ الۡقَادِرُ عَلٰۤى اَنۡ يَّبۡعَثَ عَلَيۡكُمۡ عَذَابًا مِّنۡ فَوۡقِكُمۡ اَوۡ مِنۡ تَحۡتِ اَرۡجُلِكُمۡ اَوۡ يَلۡبِسَكُمۡ شِيَعًا وَّيُذِيۡقَ بَعۡضَكُمۡ بَاۡسَ بَعۡضٍ اُنۡظُرۡ كَيۡفَ نُصَرِّفُ الۡاٰيٰتِ لَعَلَّهُمۡ يَفۡقَهُوۡنَ ۝

---

lowered, humbled or abased himself; or he addressed himself with earnest or energetic supplication. It also means, he writhed and called for aid (Lane).

خفية (secretly) is derived from خفى which means, it was or became unperceived, concealed, hidden, low or faint. They say قتل خفية *i.e.* he was slain secretly (Lane).

Commentary :

The word ظلمات (calamities), literally meaning "darkness," here signifies afflictions, calamities and misfortunes; for, with the Arabs, darkness is a symbol of misfortune. Thus, a day of great misfortune is called "a starry day," because it is considered so dark as to make even stars visible in the firmament.

The reader should note that instead of saying "openly" and "secretly", the Quran here uses the words "humbly" and "secretly", substituting the word "humbly" for "openly", thus indicating that a prayer said openly is useful only when it is offered in humility. "Open" prayers may sometimes be offered from a motive of display and show. Such prayers are of no value. Prayers are efficacious only when offered with due humility.

810. Commentary :

The words, *from every distress*, signify that Allah may deliver you not only from the afflictions from which you pray to be rescued but also from other troubles for the removal of which you do not pray.

This and the preceding verse give the third reason why none beside God is in a position to send down punishment. We are told that none but God hears the prayers of men and delivers them from the afflictions which befall them. Now the Being Who hears prayers and removes afflictions should also be the Being Who can send down punishment; for if there be two different beings, then there is sure to be opposition and conflict between them.

811. Commentary :

This verse gives the fourth reason why no mortal possesses the power to bring down punishment upon men for their sins, and that it is God alone Who possesses that power. This reason consists in the fact that the punishments which mortals inflict upon others are merely external and are limited in their character; while the punishments that come from God are varied and far-extending. For instance, man can at most kill another man and end his life, but the punishment which God inflicts sometimes grows in the very heart of man and causes him great heart-burning and uneasiness of

67. And [a]thy people have rejected it, though it is the truth. Say, [b]'I am not a guardian over you.'[812]

وَكَذَّبَ بِهٖ قَوْمُكَ وَهُوَ الْحَقُّ ۚ قُلْ لَسْتُ عَلَيْكُمْ بِوَكِيْلٍ ۝

68. For every prophecy there is a fixed time; and soon will you come to know.[813]

لِكُلِّ نَبَإٍ مُّسْتَقَرٌّ وَّسَوْفَ تَعْلَمُوْنَ ۝

69. And [c]when thou seest those who engage in *vain discourse concerning* Our Signs, then turn thou away from them until they engage in a discourse other than that. And if Satan cause thee to forget, then sit not, after recollection, with the unjust people.[814]

وَاِذَا رَاَيْتَ الَّذِيْنَ يَخُوْضُوْنَ فِيْٓ اٰيٰتِنَا فَاَعْرِضْ عَنْهُمْ حَتّٰى يَخُوْضُوْا فِيْ حَدِيْثٍ غَيْرِهٖ ۗ وَاِمَّا يُنْسِيَنَّكَ الشَّيْطٰنُ فَلَا تَقْعُدْ بَعْدَ الذِّكْرٰى مَعَ الْقَوْمِ الظّٰلِمِيْنَ ۝

---

[a]6:6.   [b]39:42; 42:7.   [c]4:141.

---

mind. Such punishments, which are often greater than mere killing, cannot be inflicted by man. The Quran here refers to some of the kinds of punishment which God may send down on men.

Punishments "from above" signify famines, earthquakes, floods, hurricanes, the oppression of the weak by the powerful, mental agony, etc. And punishments "from beneath" signify diseases, pestilences, revolt by subject peoples, etc. Then there is the punishment of discord, disunity and dissension which sometimes end in civil war. This is hinted in the words, *make you taste the violence of one another.*

All these different forms of punishment are under the control of God and none other; hence it is God alone Who has the real power of sending down punishment upon men.

812. Commentary :

The pronoun "it" in the words "*rejected it*" refers either (1) to the matter under discussion *i.e.* it is God alone Who can send down punishment, or (2) to the Quran, or (3) to punishment. Taking the last meaning, the words "it is the truth" would mean that the promised punishment is sure to come.

The words, *I am not a guardian over you,* imply that if now, when I have conveyed to you the divine Message, the punishment of God comes, I cannot help it. I will not be able to protect you from it. It is worthy of note that whereas disbelievers are demanding punishment, the Holy Prophet is expressing sympathy for them.

813. Commentary :

The verse signifies that God, in His infinite wisdom, has fixed a time for the fulfilment of every prophecy. So the punishment that has been promised to the rejectors of truth will also come to pass in due time. Then will they know that it was not a false prophecy. Disbelievers demand that the divine punishment should come upon them at once. That cannot be; for nothing that has a fixed time can come before its time.

814. Important Words :

ذكرى (recollection) is the noun-infinitive

701

70. And *a*those who are righteous are not at all accountable for them, but *their duty is* to admonish them, that they may fear God.[815]

وَمَا عَلَى الَّذِينَ يَتَّقُونَ مِنْ حِسَابِهِمْ مِّنْ شَيْءٍ وَّلَٰكِنْ ذِكْرَىٰ لَعَلَّهُمْ يَتَّقُونَ ۝

*a*6 : 53.

from ذكر *i.e.* "he remembered, etc." for which see 2 : 41, 153, 201. ذكرى means, remembering or recollecting; remembrance; the presence of a thing in the mind; mentioning or relating a thing; accepting of an exhortation; reminding or causing to remember; admonition. Thus the word is used both intransitively and transitively (Lane & Aqrab).

Commentary :

When the disbelievers, in reply to their demand for punishment, were told that there was a time fixed for every prophecy and that the punishment of God could not come before its time, they began to laugh at the prophecy. So the Quran calls upon the Holy Prophet and, through him, the believers to *turn away from them, i.e.,* to quit their company and depart from the place, so that they might not provoke the further wrath of God by indulging in their vain and insolent discourse. Believers are told not to afford disbelievers an occasion to commit further excesses by sitting in their company but to leave them at once on such occasions, so that they may be induced to turn to other talk.

The words, *turn thou away from them,* may also be taken figuratively, signifying that you should overlook and treat as unnoticed their action of ridiculing and should not dispute with them about it, so that they might drop the subject and turn to some other topic.

"Satan," for which see 2 : 15, does not always mean the Evil Spirit; the word is also applied to other harmful things.

It has even been applied to "anger" and "jealousy" in some of the sayings of the Holy Prophet. Here also it is used in the sense of "anger" and the sentence would thus mean, "if anger or wrath should cause you to forget the injunction to leave the company of such persons and to quit the place . . . ." This interpretation, however, will hold good only in the case of men who stand on a high level of righteousness. In the case of ordinary men, the word would be taken to mean "evil suggestion" or "negligence."

The word ذكرى (recollection), as shown under Important Words, means both "recollection", *i.e.* remembering, and "reminding." Taking it in the intransitive sense, the sentence would mean that when you recollect the injunction to quit the place, you should do so forthwith. Taking the word ذكرى in the sense of "reminding," the sentence would mean that before quitting the place, you should remind the scoffers of their mischievous conduct and tell them that it is an evil and dishonourable course which they follow and that it is calculated to excite against them the wrath of God.

It should also be remembered that really it is not the Holy Prophet but every believer that is addressed in this verse.

815. Important Words :

ذكرى (to admonish). See the preceding verse.

71. And let alone *a*those who take their religion to be a sport and a pastime, and whom worldly life has beguiled. And admonish *people* thereby lest a soul be consigned to perdition for what it has wrought. It shall have no helper nor intercessor beside Allah; and even if it offer every ransom, it shall not be accepted from it. These are they who have been delivered over to destruction for their own acts. *b*They will have a drink of boiling water and a grievous punishment, because they disbelieved.816

وَذَرِ الَّذِيْنَ اتَّخَذُوْا دِيْنَهُمْ لَعِبًا وَّلَهْوًا وَّغَرَّتْهُمُ الْحَيٰوةُ الدُّنْيَا وَذَكِّرْ بِهٖٓ اَنْ تُبْسَلَ نَفْسٌۢ بِمَا كَسَبَتْ ۖ لَيْسَ لَهَا مِنْ دُوْنِ اللّٰهِ وَلِيٌّ وَّلَا شَفِيْعٌ ۚ وَاِنْ تَعْدِلْ كُلَّ عَدْلٍ لَّا يُؤْخَذْ مِنْهَا ۗ اُولٰٓئِكَ الَّذِيْنَ اُبْسِلُوْا بِمَا كَسَبُوْا ۚ لَهُمْ شَرَابٌ مِّنْ حَمِيْمٍ وَّعَذَابٌ اَلِيْمٌۢ بِمَا كَانُوْا يَكْفُرُوْنَ ۧ

---

*a*5 : 58 ; 7 : 52 ; 8 : 36.   *b*10 : 5.

---

816. Important Words :

تُبْسَل (be consigned to perdition) is derived from بَسَل *i.e.* he prevented or prohibited or debarred. ابسل besides giving the above-mentioned meaning, also means, he gave in pledge ; or gave in exchange. ابسله also means, he gave him up to or he delivered him over to or he consigned him to destruction or perdition or punishment (Lane & Aqrab).

شراب(drink) is derived from شرب *i.e.* he drank. شراب means, a drink or beverage ; any liquid which is drunk and not eaten or chewed. This is the original significance. Post-classical writers, however, sometimes use the word in the sense of خمر (wine) also (Lane).

حميم (boiling water) is derived from حمّ *i.e.* it (water, etc.) became hot or very hot. The word is also used transitively, meaning, he heated water, etc., or he heated it fully. حمّ الشحمة means, he melted the fat. حمّه means, he washed him with hot water or, conversely, with cold water. حميم means, hot water or, conversely, cold water ; sweat or perspiration. The word also means a friend or a beloved person (Lane). The last significance is probably based on warmth of feeling.

Commentary :

The context and the sense of the passage required the use of the words "thy religion," but the Quran uses the words "their religion" instead of "thy religion". This is to point out that it was for their own good that the religion of Islam had been sent and that they were injuring themselves by rejecting it.

The words, *admonish people thereby*, signify that if disbelievers are in a state of excitement and it is found that admonition will provoke them all the more, then one should "let them alone"; but if there is no fear of their being provoked, then one should first admonish them and then quit their company. The pronoun in بهٖ (thereby) refers to the Quran.

The verse also contains an exhortation to believers not to get enraged at the scornful remarks of disbelievers. As it is the duty of believers to admonish and warn disbelievers, therefore the former should patiently endure the taunts of the latter.

As shown under Important Words, the word تُبْسَل (consigned to perdition) may also mean, "be given up or surrendered." Taking the word in the latter sense, the

703

R. 9   72. Say: ^a"Shall we call, beside Allah, upon that which can neither profit us nor harm us, and shall we be turned back on our heels after Allah has guided us, like one whom the evil ones entice away *leaving him* bewildered in the land, *and* who has companions who call him to guidance, *saying,* 'Come to us'?" Say: 'Surely, the guidance of Allah is the only guidance and we have been commanded to submit to the Lord of all the worlds.⁸¹⁷

قُلْ اَنَدْعُوا مِنْ دُونِ اللّٰهِ مَا لَا يَنْفَعُنَا وَلَا يَضُرُّنَا وَنُرَدُّ عَلٰٓى اَعْقَابِنَا بَعْدَ اِذْ هَدٰىنَا اللّٰهُ كَالَّذِى اسْتَهْوَتْهُ الشَّيٰطِيْنُ فِى الْاَرْضِ حَيْرَانَ لَهٗٓ اَصْحٰبٌ يَّدْعُوْنَهٗٓ اِلَى الْهُدَى ائْتِنَا قُلْ اِنَّ هُدَى اللّٰهِ هُوَ الْهُدٰى وَاُمِرْنَا لِنُسْلِمَ لِرَبِّ الْعٰلَمِيْنَ ۟ۙ

---

^a21 : 67 ; 22 : 74.

---

sentence would mean, "admonish the people lest a soul be surrendered to what it has wrought," *i.e.,* admonish them lest they be given over to the evil works they are now engaged in, *viz.,* lest they continue in their evil condition. See also 2 : 16. Taking the word in the former sense, *i.e.,* as rendered in the text, the sentence would mean, "admonish them lest they be consigned to destruction or punishment on account of the evil deeds which they have wrought."

The verse is addressed to believers and points out to them the urgent need of preaching the truth to disbelievers. It calls upon believers to picture to themselves the dire consequences of their failure to preach the truth to disbelieving people. If they do not show disbelievers the right path, the result will be that the latter will continue in their error and will be delivered over to destruction on account of their sins, being reduced to a condition when they will have no helper and no intercessor and when no compensation or ransom will be accepted from them.

The "boiling water" mentioned in the verse will serve as a medicine to bring about a cure, while the "grievous punishment" will be in the nature of an operation.

817. Important Words :

اسْتَهْوَتْهُ (entice away) is derived from هَوَى . They say هَوَى الشَّيْءُ *i.e.* the thing fell down or came down (from a higher to a lower place). Conversely هَوَى الرَّجُلُ الْجَبَلَ means, the man climbed the hill. هَوَتِ الرِّيحُ means, the wind blew. هَوِيَهُ means, he loved and desired it. الْهَوَى means, love of good or evil ; desire ; inclination ; evil inclination or desire. اسْتَهْوَاهُ means, he took away all his desire and reason leaving him confounded ; he made his evil desires look fair in his eyes (Aqrab). الْهَوَى also means, inclination of the soul or the mind to a thing ; an object of love ; the inclination of the soul to that in which the animal appetites take delight, without any lawful invitation thereto ; opinion swerving from the right way or from the truth (Lane).

حَيْرَان (bewildered) is derived from حَار which means, he was or became dazzled by a thing at which he looked so that he turned away his eyes from it ; he was or became confounded or perplexed and unable to see his right course ; he erred or lost his way. حَيْرَان means, in a state of confusion or perplexity, being unable to see his right course ; erring ; having lost his way (Lane).

73. "And *we have been given the command :* ᵃ'Observe Prayer and fear Him ; ' and He it is to Whom you shall be gathered."⁸¹⁸

وَ اَنْ اَقِيْمُوا الصَّلٰوةَ وَ اتَّقُوْهُ وَ هُوَ الَّذِىْ اِلَيْهِ تُحْشَرُوْنَ ۞

74. And ᵇHe it is Who created the heavens and the earth in accordance with the requirements of wisdom ; and the day He says, ' Be,' it will be. His word is the truth, and His will be the kingdom on the day ᶜwhen the trumpet will be blown. *He is* ᵈthe Knower of the unseen and the seen. And He is the Wise, the All-Aware.⁸¹⁹

وَ هُوَ الَّذِىْ خَلَقَ السَّمٰوٰتِ وَ الْاَرْضَ بِالْحَقِّ وَ يَوْمَ يَقُوْلُ كُنْ فَيَكُوْنُ ۬ قَوْلُهُ الْحَقُّ وَ لَهُ الْمُلْكُ يَوْمَ يُنْفَخُ فِى الصُّوْرِ عٰلِمُ الْغَيْبِ وَ الشَّهَادَةِ وَ هُوَ الْحَكِيْمُ الْخَبِيْرُ ۞

ᵃ4 : 78 ; 22 : 79 ; 24 : 57.   ᵇ14 : 20 ; 16 : 4 ; 29 : 45.   ᶜ27 : 88 ; 39 : 69.
ᵈ9 : 94 ; 13 : 10 ; 23 : 93 ; 39 : 17 ; 59 : 23.

Commentary :

The opening clause of the verse teaches by means of an example how to preach the truth. It points out that the best way to preach is to begin by exposing the errors of the opposing party as hinted in the words, *neither profit us nor harm us*, and then to proceed to point out the truth as hinted in the words, *after Allah has guided us*.

The verse then gives an apt illustration to expose the futility of شرك *i.e.* attributing co-partners to God. It compares the case of an idol-worshipper to that of a distracted person who has no fixed course to pursue. Such a person first goes to one idol or to the tomb of one saint and then to another and has no certainty or conviction. But a true believer has a fixed purpose and a fixed goal. He always prays to the One God with a deep-rooted conviction and does not wander about distracted like an idolater.

The reader will note that, true to its own principle, the verse first exposes the error of idolaters and then gives the teachings of Islam.

818. Commentary :

The concluding theme of the preceding verse has been continued in the present one.

819. Commentary :

The word كُنْ (be) really denotes a simple command intended to bring about a change. When the word is used concerning a thing which does not exist, it naturally signifies the bringing into being something which God has willed. When, however, the word is used concerning a thing which already exists, then it generally means that the thing will come to nought when God so wills. Thus the sentence, *He it is Who created . . . . . and the day He says, 'Be', it will be,* signifies that everything is in the power of God ; so when God issues a command concerning the breaking-up of the power of disbelievers, it will surely come to nought.

The expression, *His word is the truth*, means that the prophecy mentioned above is a true one and must come to pass and nothing can stop it. See the meaning of حق under 2 : 148 & 3 : 4

The words, *His will be the kingdom on the day when the trumpet will be blown*, mean that the visible kingdom of God will be established when Islam triumphs and false and idolatrous

75. And *remember the time* ᵃwhen Abraham said to his father, Āzar : 'Dost thou take idols for gods? Surely, I see thee and thy people in manifest error.'⁸²⁰

وَاِذْ قَالَ اِبْرٰهِيْمُ لِاَبِيْهِ اٰزَرَ اَتَتَّخِذُ اَصْنَامًا اٰلِهَةً ۚ اِنِّيْ اَرٰىكَ وَقَوْمَكَ فِيْ ضَلٰلٍ مُّبِيْنٍ ۞

ᵃ19 : 43.

beliefs and practices vanish. A Prophet of God is indeed a trumpet, through whom the voice of God is heard, and the sounding of the trumpet is a symbol for the wide publication and establishment of the teachings brought by him. Thus the verse means that when the teachings of the Holy Prophet are widely published and accepted in the world and when Islam flourishes and triumphs, then the kingdom of God will be visibly established on the earth and on that day will idols be broken to pieces.

820. **Important Words :**

اب (father) which is originally ابو givse the following meanings: a father; an ancestor; a paternal uncle. ابو المرأة means, the woman's husband. ابو المثوى means, master or owner of the dwelling (Lane). See also 4 : 12. اٰزر (Āzar). For the discussion of the word and the relationship of Āzar with Abraham see under Commentary below. The word is considered by some to be of non-Arabic origin, though in Arabic too it has a root. Thus اٰزر النبات means, the vegetation grew thick and strong. اٰزر فلانا means, he strengthened such and such a person. اٰزره means, he sympathized with and helped him (Aqrab). The name, which thus appears to be attributive, was given to Āzar probably because he helped his people in establishing idol-worship. According to Mujāhid, اٰزر was originally the name of an idol (Qadīr).

Commentary :

With this verse the Quran turns to an account of Abraham, which is given here for two reasons : Firstly, because it is the idolatrous Quraish that are chiefly addressed in these verses and they revered Abraham as their progenitor and patriarch. Hence, by giving an account of Abraham, God wants to tell the Quraish that their great ancestor Abraham was also, like the Holy Prophet, opposed to idolatry, which shows that idol-worship is a later innovation. Secondly, by means of this account, God wants to impress upon idolaters the hollow and unsound foundation on which stands the belief and practice of idol-worship and the absurd ideas which give rise to idolatry.

In the present verse Abraham is represented as arguing with his اب (father) on the subject of idolatry. This اب (father) is here named Āzar. Now we have to see in what relation this man stood to Abraham and what was his true name. Christian writers have criticized the Quran on the ground that it calls Abraham's father by the name Āzar while his true name was *Terah.* It is true that in Gen. 11:26 Abraham's father is named *Terah.* But it is equally true that in Luke 3:34 Abraham is called the son of *Thara* and not *Terah.* The reader should note the change not only in the first consonant but also in the vowel that follows. The Talmud also gives the name of Abraham's father as *Thara.* Eusebius, the great Church historian, who has been rightly styled the Father of Ecclesiastical History, gives, in spite of Gen. 11:26 and Luke : 3:34, which could not be unknown to him, *Athar* as the name of Abraham's father (Sale). This clearly shows that even among the Jews there existed no unanimity as to the name of Abraham's father. The fact that Eusebius

76. And thus did We show Abraham the kingdom of the heavens and the earth *that he might be rightly guided* and that he might be of those who have certainty of faith.[821]

وَكَذٰلِكَ نُرِىٓ اِبْرٰهِيۡمَ مَلَكُوۡتَ السَّمٰوٰتِ وَالۡاَرۡضِ وَ لِيَكُوۡنَ مِنَ الۡمُوۡقِنِيۡنَ ۞

---

followed neither Gen. 11 : 26, nor Luke 3 : 34 shows that he had strong reasons to differ from these two well-known sources. The correct form thus appears to be *Athar*, which later became changed into *Thara* or *Terah*. Now the form adopted by Eusebius is almost, if not exactly, the same as given by the Quran. If there is any difference, it is only that of pronunciation; otherwise both forms, *i.e.* Āzar and *Athar*, are identical. Christians have therefore no reason to quarrel with the Quran for calling Abraham's father by the name Āzar. It may also be noted that Abraham's father is also called Zarah in the Talmud (Sale) and Zarah is approximately the same as Āzar. All this goes to prove not only that the Quran is not wrong in calling the father of Abraham by the name Āzar but also that the Quranic version is much more reliable than that of the Bible.

The next question we have to consider is that of the relationship in which Āzar stood to Abraham. In the Quran he has been called Abraham's اب (*ab*), a word applied, as shown under Important Words, not only to father but also to uncle, grandfather, etc. who stand in the position of a father. From the Quran it appears that Āzar, though called the اب (*ab*) of Abraham, was not really his father. In 9 : 114 we are told that Abraham had made a promise to Āzar, his اب (*ab*), to pray to God for his forgiveness but when he came to know that he was an enemy of God, he abstained from praying for him and was actually forbidden to do so (see also 26 : 87 where again Āzar is spoken as the اب of Abraham). Elsewhere, however, the Quran itself records a prayer of Abraham which

he offered in the last days of his life, after he had built the Ka'ba in company with his son, Ishmael. In this prayer, Abraham prays for his father and is not forbidden to pray for him; but here Abraham does not use for him the word اب *ab* but والد (14 : 42). Now, as has already been stated, the word اب *ab* may be applied to a person other than the real father, but the word والد (*wālid*) which means "the begetter" is applied to none but the actual father. This clearly shows that Āzar who has been called the اب (*ab*) of Abraham was a different person from the والد (*wālid*) of Abraham. He was probably his uncle.

Some passages of the Bible also support this conclusion. We are told that Abraham married Sarah, the daughter of Terah (Gen. 20 : 12). This shows that Terah was not his real father, for in that case he could not marry Terah's daughter, his own sister. It appears that his father being dead, he was brought up by his uncle, Āzar or *Athar*, who gave him his daughter Sarah in marriage. As Āzar brought up Abraham and was in the position of a father to him, the latter came to be ascribed to him as a son, and this led to the error of Āzar or *Athar* being taken as the real father of Abraham. Again, from the Talmud it appears that Āzar prosecuted Abraham and presented him before the king for the offence of breaking idols. If Āzar had been the real father of Abraham, he would not have followed such a course against his own son.

821. **Important Words :**

مَلَكُوۡت (kingdom) is derived from مَلَك *i.e.* he possessed complete ownership of, and power

77. And when the night darkened upon him, he saw a star. He said: 'This is my Lord!' But when it set, he said: 'I like not those that set.'822

فَلَمَّا جَنَّ عَلَيْهِ الَّيْلُ رَاٰ كَوْكَبًا قَالَ هٰذَا رَبِّيْ فَلَمَّآ اَفَلَ قَالَ لَاۤ اُحِبُّ الْاٰفِلِيْنَ ۝

78. And when he saw the moon rise with spreading light, he said, 'This is my Lord.' But when it set, he said, 'If my Lord guide me not, I shall surely be of the people who go astray.'823

فَلَمَّا رَاَ الْقَمَرَ بَازِغًا قَالَ هٰذَا رَبِّيْ فَلَمَّآ اَفَلَ قَالَ لَئِنْ لَّمْ يَهْدِنِيْ رَبِّيْ لَاَكُوْنَنَّ مِنَ الْقَوْمِ الضَّآلِّيْنَ ۝

79. And when he saw the sun rise with spreading light, he said: 'This is my Lord, this is the greatest.' But when it set, he said, 'O my people, surely I am clear of that which you associate with God.824

فَلَمَّا رَاَ الشَّمْسَ بَازِغَةً قَالَ هٰذَا رَبِّيْ هٰذَاۤ اَكْبَرُ فَلَمَّآ اَفَلَتْ قَالَ يٰقَوْمِ اِنِّيْ بَرِيْٓءٌ مِّمَّا تُشْرِكُوْنَ ۝

---

over. ملكوت means, sovereignty; dominion; great kingdom; power to deal with a thing as one likes; the place of holy spirits in the heavens (Aqrab). The word ملكوت is specifically used about the kingdom or dominion of God (Mufradāt). See also 1 : 4.

Commentary :

The word ملكوت (kingdom), as shown above, is peculiar to the dominion of God. Thus the words, *And thus did We show Abraham the kingdom of the heavens and the earth*, mean, We showed Abraham the power and control which We exercise over every part of the universe. Shihāb al-Dīn Suhrwardī, a great Muslim divine, says in his famous work, the *'Awārif al-Ma'ārif*, that when a spiritual wayfarer reaches this stage, *i.e.*, when he is made to witness the sovereignty of God, he is, as it were, spiritually re-born and that no person can be admitted into the presence

of God until he has attained this stage. When, however, a man has attained this stage of certainty and conviction, doubt cannot enter his mind, for then he lives in the very presence of God.

822. Important Words :

جن (darkened) means, it covered up. They say جن الليل على الشئ or جن الليل الشئ *i.e.* the night covered the thing up; or the night threw its covering of darkness over the thing. جن الليل means, the night grew dark. See also 2 : 26 & 6 : 129.

Commentary :

See collective note under 6 : 80 below.

823. Commentary :

See collective note under 6 : 80 below.

824. Commentary :

See collective note under 6 : 80 below.

80. ^{a'} I have turned my face toward Him Who created the heavens and the earth, being ever inclined *to God*, and I am not of those who associate gods *with God*.'[825]

اِنِّیْ وَجَّهْتُ وَجْهِیَ لِلَّذِیْ فَطَرَ السَّمٰوٰتِ وَالْاَرْضَ حَنِیْفًا وَّمَآ اَنَا مِنَ الْمُشْرِكِیْنَ ۝

---

*a*3 : 21.

---

825. Commentary :

Verses 77 to 80 contain an argument which Abraham employed to bring home to his idolatrous people the absurdity of their belief in the godhead of the sun, the moon and the stars, which they worshipped (Jew. Enc.). It is an error to infer from these verses that Abraham was himself groping in the dark and did not know who his God was, that he took the evening star, the moon, and the sun for God one after another and, when each of them set in its turn, he gave up his belief in their divinity and turned to the One God, the Creator of heavens and earth. The passage contains no less than eleven clear evidences to show that Abraham was not really taking these heavenly bodies for gods, but that his object was to demonstrate to his people the vanity of their beliefs, step by step. Some of these evidences may be summed up as below:—

Firstly, the opening part of this passage, *i.e.* the first part of 6 : 77 is connected with the previous verses with the double particle فلما (and when) which denotes close sequence *i.e.* that which has been said in this passage is connected with, and occurred immediately after, what is related in the preceding verses. Now the preceding verses, *i.e.* vv. 75 and 76, clearly show Abraham as having attained certainty and conviction of faith and as being a firm believer in one God and being advanced in spirituality. Thus placed and protected, he cannot be considered as groping in the dark like a blind man and wandering from one deity to another.

Secondly, there is no sense in supposing Abraham to have seen the star or the moon for the first time that night. He belonged to a community which used to worship stars and he must have seen the stars many times before. If he was really a star-worshipper, he ought to have first imbibed the idea from what he had heard from his father and others and not by seeing a star himself, and reflecting over it. Star-worship was not at all a new idea discovered by him by looking at a star. Thus there is no doubt that Abraham's words, *This is my Lord*, were not meant as an expression of faith but simply as an argument against star-worship. He assumed the star he saw to be his Lord merely to expose its lordship afterwards on the basis of its setting and thereby to tell his people that they were wrong in taking the star for their Lord.

Thirdly, when the star disappeared, Abraham is reported to have said, *I like not those that set*. Now Abraham certainly knew already that the star must set ; he must have already seen it disappear times without number. So the argument, *I like not those that set*, must have already been familiar to his mind and he could not take to worshipping the star in view of this argument. In fact, what he wanted was to use the argument against star-worshippers in a way that might prove effective. So he first assumed or supposed the star to be his Lord and, when it disappeared, he hastened to declare, *I like not those that set*. Similar was the case with the setting of the moon and the sun. Of the sun he spoke the word " greater " or " greatest " ironically in order to taunt his people for their folly. It should be incidentally

81. And his people argued with him. He said, 'Do you argue with me concerning Allah when He has guided me aright? And I fear not that which you associate with Him, unless my Lord wills anything. *My Lord comprehends all things in His knowledge. Will you not then be admonished?[826]

وَحَآجَّهٗ قَوْمُهٗ ۖ قَالَ اَتُحَآجُّوٓنِّیْ فِی اللّٰهِ وَ قَدْ هَدٰىنِ ۖ وَلَاۤ اَخَافُ مَا تُشْرِكُوْنَ بِهٖۤ اِلَّاۤ اَنْ یَّشَآءَ رَبِّیْ شَیْئًا ۖ وَسِعَ رَبِّیْ كُلَّ شَیْءٍ عِلْمًا ۖ اَفَلَا تَتَذَكَّرُوْنَ ۝

82. 'And why should I fear that which you associate *with God*, when you fear not *b*to associate with Allah that for which He has sent down to you no authority?' Which, then, of the two parties has greater right to security, if indeed you know?

وَكَیْفَ اَخَافُ مَاۤ اَشْرَكْتُمْ وَلَا تَخَافُوْنَ اَنَّكُمْ اَشْرَكْتُمْ بِاللّٰهِ مَا لَمْ یُنَزِّلْ بِهٖ عَلَیْكُمْ سُلْطٰنًا ۖ فَاَیُّ الْفَرِیْقَیْنِ اَحَقُّ بِالْاَمْنِ ۚ اِنْ كُنْتُمْ تَعْلَمُوْنَ ۝

83. Those who believe and *c*mix not up their belief with injustice—it is they who shall have peace, and who are rightly guided.

اَلَّذِیْنَ اٰمَنُوْا وَلَمْ یَلْبِسُوٓا اِیْمَانَهُمْ بِظُلْمٍ اُولٰٓئِكَ لَهُمُ الْاَمْنُ وَهُمْ مُّهْتَدُوْنَ ۝

---

*a*7:90.   *b*7:34; 22:72.   *c*31:14.

---

noted here that Abraham did not use the word اكبر (greater or greatest) for the moon which was also greater than the evening star. The omission is significant, as it clearly shows, that he was already intending to refer to the sun after disposing of the case of the moon.

Fourthly, if Abraham was really searching for God and had sincerely taken the star, the moon and the sun, in turn, for his Lord, then the conclusion at which he ought to have naturally arrived, after gradually rejecting the godhead of these three heavenly bodies, should have been that there was no God at all, but instead of declaring that there was no God, Abraham forthwith turned to his people saying, *O my people, surely I am clear of that which you associate with God. I have turned my face toward*

Him Who created the heavens and the earth, being ever inclined to God. This shows that Abraham already knew the true God and believed in Him and was simply trying gradually to draw his people towards Him. Let the reader only read the whole reply of Abraham (vv. 81—83) and it will become crystal clear to him that Abraham was not only familiar with the name of Allah and believed in Him but also possessed a deep knowledge of His attributes.

826. **Commentary:**

This and the following two verses definitely show that the incident related in vv. 77—80 above was purposely used by Abraham by way of argument; otherwise he himself was a staunch monotheist and had dived deep into the depths of divine love and knowledge.

10   84.   And that is Our argument which We gave to Abraham against his people. ^aWe exalt in degrees of rank whomso We please. Thy Lord is indeed Wise, All-Knowing.⁸²⁷

وَ تِلْكَ حُجَّتُنَآ اٰتَيْنٰهَآ اِبْرٰهِيْمَ عَلٰى قَوْمِهٖ ؕ نَرْفَعُ دَرَجٰتٍ مَّنْ نَّشَآءُ ؕ اِنَّ رَبَّكَ حَكِيْمٌ عَلِيْمٌۭ ۞

85.   And ^bWe gave him Isaac and Jacob; each did We guide aright, and Noah did We guide aright aforetime, and of his progeny, David and Solomon and Job and Joseph and Moses and Aaron. Thus do We reward those who do good.⁸²⁸

وَ وَهَبْنَا لَهٗۤ اِسْحٰقَ وَ يَعْقُوْبَ ؕ كُلًّا هَدَيْنَا ۚ وَ نُوْحًا هَدَيْنَا مِنْ قَبْلُ وَ مِنْ ذُرِّيَّتِهٖ دَاوٗدَ وَ سُلَيْمٰنَ وَ اَيُّوْبَ وَ يُوْسُفَ وَ مُوْسٰى وَ هٰرُوْنَ ؕ وَ كَذٰلِكَ نَجْزِى الْمُحْسِنِيْنَۙ ۞

^a12 : 77.   ^b29 : 28.

827. Commentary :

This verse forms the concluding portion of the passage (beginning with 6 : 77 above) containing Abraham's argument with his people. It definitely settles the question whether Abraham gradually came to have a faith in God by taking one heavenly body after another for his Lord or whether it was a skilfully graduated argument by means of which he sought to demonstrate the error of his people in worshipping these heavenly bodies as gods. Says God, *That is Our argument which We gave to Abraham against his people.* Thus, the Quran refers to what has gone above as an "argument" which God Himself taught Abraham and which Abraham used with such great effect against his people. This declaration by the Quran leaves not the slightest doubt that Abraham was not wandering about after false gods but was trying to convince his people of their error by means of a very effective process of reasoning. This is why it is referred to in the present verse in the light of a favour by the Wise and All-knowing God.

This verse, though put in *Rukū'* 10, really forms part of the preceding passage. It must be remembered that the division of the Quran

into 30 *Paras* (parts) and the division of the *Sūras* (Chapters) into *Rukū's* (sections) was not made by the Holy Prophet nor by his Companions, but was effected long afterwards by Muslim scribes for providing facility in reading, and for the convenience of reference. In the time of the Holy Prophet there were only *Sūras* and verses and nothing else.

828. Important Words :

ايوب (Ayyūb or Job), who is the hero of the Book of Job, is mentioned in the Bible as living in the land of Uz. Some authorities say that this is Idumea or Arabia Deserta; others fix Mesopotamia as his country. It appears that Uz was somewhere in the north of Arabia. It is said that Job lived there before the departure of the Israelites from Egypt. He thus lived before Moses or, as some say, he was a compatriot of Moses, having received his prophetic mission about 20 years before him. Job was not an Israelite, having been descended from Esau, the elder brother of Israel. He had a very chequered career, being " tried " by God in diverse ways; but he proved most faithful and righteous and was patient and steadfast in the extreme. He still lives in the memory of mankind as a paragon of patience

(Jew. Enc. & Encyclopaedia of Islam).

داود (David or Dāwūd) has been taken to mean : (1) beloved or friend ; or (2) paternal uncle; or (3) best of all. King of Judah and Israel, David, who was of Israelite origin being from the tribe of Judah, was founder of the Judean dynasty at Jerusalem. The date of his reign is generally fixed at about 1010-970 B.C. He was a great warrior and a great statesman. His importance as the real builder of the Hebrew Kingdom can hardly be over-estimated. Through him all the tribes of Israel from Dan to Beersheba became united and organized into a powerful nation whose kingdom extended from the Euphrates to the Nile. Towards the end of his life David had to suffer much at the hands of scheming slanderers, which deeply grieved him. He has poured out his grief in his celebrated Psalms (Enc. Brit. & Enc. Bib.). The Quran, however, absolves him from the charges imputed to him in the Bible (38 : 19-26).

سليمان (Solomon) was the second son of David & Bath-Sheba and the third king of Israel. He reigned from about 971 to 931 B.C. He was called Jedidiah (beloved of Yehovah) by Nathan, the Prophet. But David was told by Yehovah that his son's name should be Solomon (peaceful). These two names are predictive of the character of his reign, which was both highly prosperous and peaceful. Besides his principal names, Jedidiah and Solomon, various others are assigned to him such as *Agur* (he who girt his loins), *Bin* (he who built the temple), *Jakeh* (he who reigned over the world), *Ithiel* (he who understood the signs of God), and *Ucal* (he who could withstand them). The word سليمان may have been derived from the root سلم which means, he was or became safe, secure or in peace, or free from evils of any kind. The fact that he ruled for the long period of forty years shows that he must have consolidated firmly the kingdom he inherited from his father. He was a great monarch and a wise judge. He greatly extended and developed the trade and commerce of his country and contracted friendly alliances with foreign rulers. He was the master-builder among the Israelite kings and is best known for his building of the Temple at Jerusalem, which is known as the Temple of Solomon and which became the *Qibla* of the Israelites for all time. In spite of the prosperity of his kingdom, Solomon's reign was not altogether happy. Plots were hatched against him by secret societies to bring about his downfall. The Society of the Free Masons is also believed to have dated from his reign. He was followed by a worthless son (Enc. Bri. ; Enc. Bib. & Jew. Enc.). Like his father, David, Solomon was the victim of much calumny and slander from which the Quran has exonerated him (2 : 103).

هارون (Aaron) who belonged to the tribe of Levi, was the son of Amram and the elder brother of Moses, who was three years younger than him, their sister Miriam being the eldest of the three. Aaron was the traditional founder and head of the Jewish priesthood and, in company with Moses, he led the Israelites out of Egypt. Aaron and Moses were jointly commissioned to deliver the Israelites from the clutches of Pharaoh and to preach to them the message of the Oneness of God, though Moses was the senior Prophet and Aaron subordinate to him. While Moses was both the religious and secular head, Aaron represented only the priestly functions of his tribe. His duties were generally ministerial and not directive. Aaron was known for his eloquence and persuasive speech and was of a mild, amiable disposition (Enc. Bib.; Enc. Bri. & Jew. Enc.).

Commentary :

This and the succeeding verses tell us that not

86. And *We guided* Zachariah and John and Jesus and Elias; each *one of them* was of the virtuous.[829]

وَزَكَرِيَّا وَيَحْيَى وَعِيسَى وَإِلْيَاسَ كُلٌّ مِّنَ الصَّالِحِينَ ۞

---

only Abraham but other Prophets also preached against شرك *i.e.* setting up associates with God.

The present verse mentions the descendants of Abraham to the second generation, naming a son (Isaac) and a grandson (Jacob or Israel). The name of Ishmael, the eldest son of Abraham, has been included in a separate group (6 : 87 below), and not in a subordinate position under Abraham.

The reader should note that the Prophets descended from Noah have been divided in the present and the succeeding two verses into three different groups and to each group has been added a separate description. The first group referred to in the present verse comprises David, Solomon, Job, Joseph, Moses and Aaron—Prophets who were given power and prosperity, and who consequently were able to do good to human beings. Hence members of this group have been designated as المحسنين or doers of good, for through their temporal power and prosperity they were able to do material good to humanity. David and Solomon were kings; Joseph and Job were blessed with prosperity after they had been tried with afflictions which they both bore with extraordinary patience. Moses and Aaron enjoyed supreme authority among their people.

The second group (for which see 6 : 86) consists of Zachariah, John, Jesus and Elias. None of these possessed temporal power or worldly goods; each lived a humble and lowly life, so much so that of Elias it is said that he was rarely seen and generally lived in the woods. Hence they have been differentiated in 6 : 86 as الصالحين *i.e.* virtuous. The first

three comprising the second group were contemporaries; while Elias, though not a contemporary, bore a striking resemblance to John, who came in his spirit and power; so he also has been classed with this group.

The third group (mentioned in 6 : 87) consists of Ishmael, Elisha, Jonah and Lot. They had no worldly power, but God granted them grace and excellence. It has been alleged about them that they coveted power and riches. Of Ishmael, we read in the Bible: "He will be a wild man; his hand will be against every man, and every man's hand against him" (Gen. 16 : 12). In the Talmud, Ishmael is represented as having followed his father Abraham when the latter took Isaac out for sacrifice, rejoicing at the thought that he would inherit all the lands and herds. Of Elisha it is said that he caused a king, who did not obey him, to be slain so that he might thus gain political power. Jonah was displeased with God, because he was disgraced by the non-fulfilment of his prophecy, which, it is alleged, showed that he sought power for himself. Of Lot it is alleged that he coveted fertile pasture-lands and was always quarrelling with his kinsman, Abraham. Thus all these Prophets have been accused of coveting wealth and power. But the Quran declares all these charges to be false. These Prophets were a group of heavenly people enjoying spiritual communion with God. They had no need to be covetous or seekers of power; for, as stated in 6 : 87, God had "exalted" them above the people.

829. Important Words :

الياس (Elias or Elijah) who lived about 900 B.C. was a native of Gilead, a country on the eastern bank of the Jordan. According to the Bible,

87. And *We also guided* Ishmael and Elisha and Jonah and Lot : and "each one did We exalt above the people.830

وَاِسْمٰعِيلَ وَالْيَسَعَ وَيُوْنُسَ وَلُوْطًا ۚ وَكُلًّا فَضَّلْنَا عَلَى الْعٰلَمِيْنَ ۙ

88. And *We exalted* some of their fathers and their children and their brethren, and We chose them and We guided them in the straight path.

وَمِنْ اٰبَآئِهِمْ وَذُرِّيّٰتِهِمْ وَاِخْوَانِهِمْ ۚ وَاجْتَبَيْنٰهُمْ وَهَدَيْنٰهُمْ اِلٰى صِرَاطٍ مُّسْتَقِيْمٍ ۝

"2 : 48 ; 3 : 34-35 ; 45 : 17.

he was translated to heaven (II Kings 2). We read in Malachi : "Behold, I will send you Elijah, the Prophet, before the coming of the great and dreadful day of the Lord " (4 : 5). This prophecy, as interpreted by Jesus (Matt. 11 : 14), was fulfilled in the person of John the Baptist, who was his forerunner and who came " in the spirit and power of Elijah." Similarly, the prophecy about the second advent of Jesus himself has been fulfilled in the person of Ahmad of Qadian, the Promised Messiah, who came in the spirit and power of Jesus.

Commentary :

See 6 : 85 above.

830. Important Words :

اليسع (Elisha) was the son of Shaphat, the disciple and successor of Elijah. He was a native of Abelmeholah, a village in Galilee. He was taken from the plough and anointed by Elijah to be his successor. Directed by God, Elijah found him in the field and threw his mantle over him. Many miracles are attributed to Elisha. But neither the sanctity of his life nor the miracles he wrought had the effect of reforming the nation at large. At length, worn out by his public and private labour, he breathed his last at the age of ninety in 838 B.C.

يونس (Jonah), son of Amittai, was born in Gath-hepher, in the tribe of Zebulun. He lived either before or during the reign of Jeroboam II or in the reign of Jehoahaz about 850 B.C. He was an Israelite Prophet with a mission to the people of Nineveh. Jonah prophesied the destruction of his people within 40 days. But they repented and turned to God with humble supplication, whereupon they were saved. This, however, upset Jonah who, being ashamed to face his people, ran away and, while crossing a sea, was thrown into the water and swallowed by a fish (Jonah 1 : 17). Jonah remained in the belly of the fish for three days and was then disgorged by it and saved. It is to this incident that Jesus referred when he said that no miracle would be shown to his people except that of Jonah (Matt. 16 : 4), meaning that he would be put on the Cross but would be taken down alive and would then be placed in the womb of the earth for three days after which he would escape therefrom, just as Jonah had escaped from the belly of the fish.

Commentary :

See 6 : 85 above. The verse speaks of Lot as being " exalted above the people." Now if the word العالمين (lit. the peoples) be taken to signify " all the peoples," it would be evidently wrong ; for Lot lived in the time of Abraham and was admittedly not superior to the Patriarch. Thus the word العالمين cannot here signify even " the people of the age " as

89. That is the guidance of Allah. He guides thereby those of His servants whom He pleases. And [a]if they had worshipped aught beside Him, surely all they did would have been of no avail to them.[831]

90. It is these to [b]whom We gave the Book and dominion and prophethood. But if these *people* are ungrateful for them, *it matters not*, for We have now entrusted them to a people who are not ungrateful for them.[832]

ذٰلِكَ هُدَى اللّٰهِ يَهْدِىْ بِهٖ مَنْ يَّشَآءُ مِنْ عِبَادِهٖ ۚ وَلَوْ اَشْرَكُوْا لَحَبِطَ عَنْهُمْ مَّا كَانُوْا يَعْمَلُوْنَ ۞

اُولٰٓئِكَ الَّذِيْنَ اٰتَيْنٰهُمُ الْكِتٰبَ وَالْحُكْمَ وَالنُّبُوَّةَ ۚ فَاِنْ يَّكْفُرْ بِهَا هٰٓؤُلَآءِ فَقَدْ وَكَّلْنَا بِهَا قَوْمًا لَّيْسُوْا بِهَا بِكٰفِرِيْنَ ۞

---

[a]39 : 66. [b]45 : 17.

it has been rendered elsewhere but simply "the people," *i.e.* a section thereof. In fact, the exaltation spoken of here refers only to the people to whom the Prophets mentioned in the verse were sent.

831. Commentary :

The verse signifies that real and true guidance is that which was given to the Prophets named in the above verses; they all preached against شرك (idol-worship). The latter part of the verse hints that these Prophets did not associate anything with God even before they were sent as Prophets; otherwise they would not have been raised to that high spiritual rank.

832. Commentary :

The giving of a Book by God generally occurs in two ways : Firstly, directly, as in the case of Moses and the Holy Prophet of Islam. Secondly, indirectly, as in the case of those Prophets to whom no new Book was revealed and who only followed a Book that had been revealed to a previous Prophet. Thus of the Torah we are told in the Quran, *Surely, We sent down the Torah wherein was guidance and light. By it did the Prophets who were obedient to Us judge for the Jews* (5 : 45). The above

quoted verse proves that there appeared many Prophets among the Israelites to whom no new Book was revealed and who only followed the Torah. This statement of the Quran is also borne out by history, which tells us that there were many Prophets among the Israelites to whom no Book was revealed. Hence, when the verse under comment says : *It is these to whom We gave the Book*, it does not mean that a Book was given to every Prophet separately but only that every Prophet received knowledge of the divine Book. Another consideration which lends support to the above conclusion is that the word "these" put in the beginning of the verse not only refers to the Prophets named in the foregoing verses, but also to *some of their fathers and their children and their brethren* (6 : 88), and it is evident that the latter did not receive any new Book.

There are also other verses of the Quran in which the expression, "We gave the Book" has been used in the sense of giving the Book indirectly. Among others the reader is referred to 2 : 122 ; 2 : 147 ; 29 : 48 & 45 : 17. It is of interest that in the last-mentioned verse, *i.e.* 45 : 17, not only the Book but all the three things mentioned in the verse under comment have been spoken of as having been given to

91. These it is whom Allah guided aright, so follow thou their guidance. Say: 'I ask not of you any reward for it. This is naught but an admonition for all mankind.'833

اُولٰٓئِكَ الَّذِيۡنَ هَدَى اللّٰهُ فَبِهُدٰىهُمُ اقۡتَدِهۡ قُلۡ لَّاۤ اَسۡـَٔلُكُمۡ عَلَيۡهِ اَجۡرًا اِنۡ هُوَ اِلَّا ذِكۡرٰى لِلۡعٰلَمِيۡنَ ۞

R. 11 92. And ^athey do not make a just estimate of Allah, when ^bthey say: 'Allah has not revealed anything to any man.' Say: 'Who revealed the Book which Moses brought, a light and guidance for the people—though you treat it as scraps of paper which you show while you conceal much; and you have been taught that which neither you nor your fathers knew?'—Say: 'Allah'. Then leave them to amuse themselves with their vain discourse.834

وَمَا قَدَرُوا اللّٰهَ حَقَّ قَدۡرِهٖۤ اِذۡ قَالُوۡا مَاۤ اَنۡزَلَ اللّٰهُ عَلٰى بَشَرٍ مِّنۡ شَيۡءٍ ؕ قُلۡ مَنۡ اَنۡزَلَ الۡكِتٰبَ الَّذِيۡ جَآءَ بِهٖ مُوۡسٰى نُوۡرًا وَّهُدًى لِّلنَّاسِ تَجۡعَلُوۡنَهٗ قَرَاطِيۡسَ تُبۡدُوۡنَهَا وَتُخۡفُوۡنَ كَثِيۡرًا ۚ وَعُلِّمۡتُمۡ مَّا لَمۡ تَعۡلَمُوۡۤا اَنۡتُمۡ وَلَاۤ اٰبَآؤُكُمۡ ؕ قُلِ اللّٰهُ ۙ ثُمَّ ذَرۡهُمۡ فِيۡ خَوۡضِهِمۡ يَلۡعَبُوۡنَ ۞

---

^a22 : 75 ; 39 : 68. ^b36 : 16 ; 67 : 10.

---

the children of Israel. The verse runs thus: *And We gave the children of Israel the Book, and sovereignty, and prophethood, and We provided them with good things, and exalted them over the people of the time* (45 : 17).

In short, when on the one hand we learn not only from the Quran but also from history that there have been many Prophets who did not receive any new Book directly, and on the other hand, we see that the expression, "We gave the Book" has also been used in the Quran in the sense of giving a Book indirectly, the verse under comment cannot be interpreted to mean that every Prophet was given a Book directly from God. Muslim Commentators are agreed in holding that every Prophet was not given a Book directly by God, and that in the case of those Prophets to whom no Book was given directly, the words, "We gave the Book", simply mean, "We gave them knowledge or understanding of the Book", or "We made them inherit the Book."

The word "people" in the latter portion of the verse refers to Muslims; and the pronoun "them" at the end refers to the Book, dominion and prophethood mentioned in the opening clause of the verse.

833. Commentary :

The words, *so follow thou their guidance*, may be taken to be addressed either to the Holy Prophet or to every Muslim. The fundamental teaching of all Prophets is the same.

834. Commentary :

In this verse the Quran gives the reason why there are differences in religion. Differences spring from ignorance, from a lack of true estimation or true understanding, as indicated by the words, *they do not make a just estimate of Allah*. Indeed, those who say that *Allah has not revealed anything to any man* make a very poor estimate of His attributes. To hold such a view about God is highly derogatory to His glory and most inconsistent with His attributes.

93. And ^athis is a Book which We have revealed, full of blessings, to fulfil that which preceded it, and to enable thee ^bto warn the Mother of towns and those around her. And those who believe in the Hereafter believe therein and ^cthey strictly observe their Prayers.[835]

وَهَـٰذَا كِتَابٌ اَنْزَلْنَاهُ مُبَارَكٌ مُّصَدِّقُ الَّذِىْ بَيْنَ يَدَيْهِ وَلِتُنْذِرَ اُمَّ الْقُرَىٰ وَمَنْ حَوْلَهَا ۚ وَالَّذِيْنَ يُؤْمِنُوْنَ بِالْاٰخِرَةِ يُؤْمِنُوْنَ بِهٖ ۖ وَهُمْ عَلَىٰ صَلَاتِهِمْ يُحَافِظُوْنَ ۞

---

^a6 : 156 ; 21 : 51 ; 38 : 30.   ^b42 : 8.   ^c23-10 ; 70 : 24.

As regards religious beliefs, there were two classes of men in the days of the Holy Prophet. Firstly, there were those who denied revelation *in toto.* According to them, there had never been any revelation in any age. Secondly, there were those who believed that there had been revelation in the past, but that God had sent no revelation in their own age. To the first-mentioned class belonged the مشركين (Idolaters) *i.e.* those who ascribed co-partners to God and worshipped idols. To the second class belonged the People of the Book. As the words, *Allah has not revealed anything to any man,* may mean, (1) that God has never revealed anything to any man; or (2) that He has not revealed anything to any man in the present age, so they may be ascribed to both idol-worshippers and the People of the Book. In the foregoing verses only the former were addressed, but now the latter have also been included in the address.

As regards the People of the Book, the Quran specifically states : *Say, Who revealed the Book which Moses brought, a light and guidance for the people, though you treat it as scraps of paper which you show while you conceal much, i.e.,* you have split up the Book of Moses into parts, disclosing one part and concealing the other which contains prophecies and signs of the advent of the Holy Prophet. You deny the Quranic revelation, but your own Book contains evidence of its truth which you suppress.

The above reply, however, could not satisfy the idol-worshippers who did not believe in the Book of Moses or, for that matter, in any revealed Book. The Quran, therefore, gives them a rational answer. It says, *And you have been taught that which neither you nor your fathers knew.* This is an argument which is meant to prove the divine origin of the Quran rationally and is meant not merely for the People of the Book but also for idol-worshippers. The argument may be put thus : " If this Book (the Quran) has not been revealed by God, then who embodied in it such wise and comprehensive teachings as were known neither to you nor to your forefathers—teachings which it was beyond your power to produce ? Such teachings could not proceed from a man. Only God could give such teachings. "

The last words of the verse, *i.e., leave them to amuse themselves with their vain discourse,* do not mean that you should abandon preaching to disbelievers. The meaning is, " Tell them and make clear to them that the Quran is the word of God, for it is superhuman and full of wisdom ; but if they still persist in ridiculing it, then leave them alone while they thus amuse themselves. " This injunction is similar to the one given in 6 : 69 above.

835. **Important Words :**

مُبَارَك (full of blessings) is derived from برك They say برك الجمل *i.e.* the camel kneeled and lay down on his chest with his legs folded. برك also means, he or it was or became firm, steady or steadfast. برك على فلان (barraka) means, he prayed that such a one might be blessed. بارك عليه means, he kept or applied himself constantly to it. بارك الله فيك or بارك الله عليك means, may God bless thee and make thee prosperous, or may He continue to shower blessings on thee. تبارك الله means, blessed is God; or hallowed is He; or far removed is He from every imperfection; or highly exalted is He. بركة (barakat) means, a blessing; any good bestowed by God, particularly that which continues and goes on increasing. It also means, increase, abundance or plenty. بركة (birka) means, a tank dug in the ground; a lake or pond; a place where water remains and collects. مبارك means, blessed; gifted with blessing; abounding in good (Lane).

ام (mother), apart from its primary meaning, also signifies: source, origin, foundation or basis; support or cause of subsistence; the main or chief part of a thing; anything to which other things are collected together or joined; place of collection or comprehension or combination of a thing. The word is also applied to inanimate things, as the Arabs say ام الشجرة i.e. the mother of the tree; or ام النجوم i.e. the Milky Way, viz. the place where the stars are collected together in a great multitude. ام القرى signifies, the mother of the towns; the metropolis; Mecca, because, being the Qibla, it is the gathering-place of men, or because of all towns it possesses the greatest dignity. In fact, every city is the ام of the smaller towns around it (Lane). Mecca is called ام القرى also because it is the source of spiritual food for mankind.

Commentary :

This verse further explains the rational argument contained in the words, *you have been* taught that which neither you nor your fathers knew (see note on the preceding verse), and makes it clear that it is the Quran that the words quoted above refer to. The present verse mentions four features of the Quran : (1) it has been sent by God ; (2) it is full of blessings as the word مبارك indicates, *i.e.*, it is a Book in which, like a بركة (a place where water collects), are collected all the blessings of God ; (3) it fulfils that which preceded it, *i.e.*, it fulfils the prophecies contained in the previous Scriptures ; and (4) it has been revealed so that the Holy Prophet may warn thereby *the Mother of towns and those around her.* The place where a Prophet of God appears is called " the mother of towns," for it is out of it that men drink spiritual milk, even as a child sucks milk from the breast of its mother. The words, *those around her,* are intended to include the whole earth. The earth being round, all parts of it lie around the place where the Holy Prophet made his appearance *i.e.* Mecca. Thus this verse also proves the universal mission of the Holy Prophet.

The words, *those who believe in the Hereafter believe therein,* signify that a true believer in the life to come cannot but believe in the Quranic teaching. In fact, he who has real faith in the life to come will always be anxious to find out the truth in order to ensure his salvation, and he who earnestly seeks after truth will necessarily be led to believe in the Quran, for as the Quran says : *those who strive in Our cause—We will surely guide them in Our ways* (29 : 70). Thus belief in the Quran is really a criterion of true faith in the Day of Resurrection. Again, when a man comes to have faith in the Quran, he will naturally try to mould his actions according to its teachings and will be constant in his Prayers.

94. And *who is more unjust than he who forges a lie against Allah, or says, 'It has been revealed to me,' while nothing has been revealed to him; and who says, 'I will send down the like of that which Allah has sent down?' And if thou couldst only see, when the wrongdoers are in the agonies of death, and the angels stretch forth their hands, *saying,* 'Yield up your souls. *This day shall you be awarded the punishment of disgrace, because of that which you spoke against Allah falsely and *because* you turned away from His Signs with disdain.'836

وَمَنْ أَظْلَمُ مِمَّنِ افْتَرَى عَلَى اللّٰهِ كَذِبًا أَوْ قَالَ أُوحِيَ إِلَيَّ وَلَمْ يُوحَ إِلَيْهِ شَيْءٌ وَمَنْ قَالَ سَأُنْزِلُ مِثْلَ مَا أَنْزَلَ اللّٰهُ وَلَوْ تَرَى إِذِ الظَّالِمُونَ فِي غَمَرَاتِ الْمَوْتِ وَالْمَلَائِكَةُ بَاسِطُوا أَيْدِيهِمْ أَخْرِجُوا أَنْفُسَكُمُ الْيَوْمَ تُجْزَوْنَ عَذَابَ الْهُونِ بِمَا كُنْتُمْ تَقُولُونَ عَلَى اللّٰهِ غَيْرَ الْحَقِّ وَكُنْتُمْ عَنْ آيَاتِهِ تَسْتَكْبِرُونَ ۝

*6 : 22; 7 : 38; 10 : 18; 11 : 19; 61 : 8.   *46 : 21.

---

836. **Commentary:**

This verse gives another reason of the fact that the Quran is the revealed word of God. If this Book, says the verse, is not the word of God, then he who has forged this lie against God is the most guilty of men and cannot escape divine punishment. But the verse also reminds deniers or rejectors that if the Quran is not a forged Book but the word of God, as it actually is, then they are as great offenders as the one who forges a lie against God. In this case, it will be they who will be visited with divine punishment.

The second sentence, *i.e., or says, It has been revealed to me while nothing has been revealed to him,* may be taken as an explanation or elaboration of the first sentence, *i.e. who forges a lie against Allah;* or the first sentence is general, while the second is particular. For instance, falsely to ascribe any teaching to God will come under the first category, and to claim falsely that God has spoken to him particular words will come under the second.

By saying, *I will send down the like of that which Allah has sent down,* a disbeliever only borrows the phraseology of those whom he addresses, *viz.,* believers. Being a disbeliever in divine revelation, he does not believe that God sends down anything, so he only quotes the expression made use of by believers concerning divine revelation. Another instance of such usage is to be met with in 5 : 44.

The words, *if thou couldst only see,* signify that if anyone should witness the torment which the deniers of Prophets undergo when their souls leave their bodies, he would at once realize how severe is the torment of those who reject a divine Messenger. This torment is not to be identified with the ordinary agonies of death, which are shared, under the general law of nature, by righteous and unrighteous alike, but to the specific punishment that clings to the rejectors of Prophets from the very moment of their death. The "punishment of disgrace" mentioned in the latter part of the verse refers, as the words "this day" indicate, not to the punishment of Hell but to the punishment which sinners begin to undergo immediately after death and before the Day of Resurrection. This is known as عذاب القبر ('Adhāb al-Qabr) *i.e.* punishment in the grave, in Islamic religious terminology,

95. And now *a*you come to Us one by one even as We created you at first, and you have left behind you that which We bestowed upon you, and We see not with you your intercessors of whom you asserted that they were partners *with God* in your affairs. Now you have been cut off from one another and that which you presumed has failed you.[837]

R. 12 96. Verily, it is Allah Who causes the grain and the date-stones to sprout. *b*He brings forth the living from the dead, and *He* is the bringer forth of the dead from the living. That is Allah; wherefore, then, are you turned back?[838]

وَلَقَدْ جِئْتُمُوْنَا فُرَادٰى كَمَا خَلَقْنٰكُمْ اَوَّلَ مَرَّةٍ وَّتَرَكْتُمْ مَّا خَوَّلْنٰكُمْ وَرَآءَ ظُهُوْرِكُمْ ۚ وَمَا نَرٰى مَعَكُمْ شُفَعَآءَكُمُ الَّذِيْنَ زَعَمْتُمْ اَنَّهُمْ فِيْكُمْ شُرَكٰٓؤُا ۭ لَقَدْ تَّقَطَّعَ بَيْنَكُمْ وَضَلَّ عَنْكُمْ مَّا كُنْتُمْ تَزْعُمُوْنَ ۩

اِنَّ اللّٰهَ فَالِقُ الْحَبِّ وَالنَّوٰى ۭ يُخْرِجُ الْحَيَّ مِنَ الْمَيِّتِ وَمُخْرِجُ الْمَيِّتِ مِنَ الْحَيِّ ۭ ذٰلِكُمُ اللّٰهُ فَاَنّٰى تُؤْفَكُوْنَ ۞

---

*a*18 : 49.   *b*3 : 28 ; 10 : 32 ; 30 : 20.

قبر or grave being the name given to the place where souls are kept after death but before Resurrection. Says the Holy Prophet : " When any one dies, a window is opened out for him in the grave facing Heaven or Hell as the case may be " (Mājah, ch. on *Qabr*). This is of course not the final retribution but only preparatory to it.

837. Important Words :

خَوَّلْنٰكُمْ (bestowed on you) is derived from خَال which means, he became possessed of servants, slaves and other dependents as well as gifts, after having been without them. خَوَّلَهُ اللهُ مَالًا means, God conferred upon him property as a favour. The noun الخَوَل means, slaves, servants and other dependents, or cattle, camels, etc. given to one by God; a gift or gifts (Lane). The word signifies the bestowal of things meant for the betterment and progress of the person receiving them (Mufradāt).

Commentary :

As shown under Important Words, خَوَل (bestowal) implies the giving of a thing for the purpose of setting things right or bettering the condition of the recipient. Thus, the sentence, *you have left behind you that which We bestowed upon you*, means, " We gave you certain things so that you might thereby improve your spiritual condition, but you have left them behind, *i.e.* you made no use of them, and now the time for their use has passed away."

The words, *We see not with you your intercessors*, imply that your hope lay in your mediators, whom you supposed to be co-partners with God and who, you imagined, would help you; but your connection with them is now completely cut off and they are not here with you to render you any help; they have failed you and become entirely lost to you.

838. Commentary :

The Quran now proceeds to give arguments from nature to prove the need of revelation and divine guidance. Firstly, the attention of man is drawn to the seeds and stones from which trees sprout. How insignificant is the seed, but how it grows and develops

97. ᵃHe causes the break of day; and ᵇHe made the night for rest and ᶜthe sun and the moon for reckoning *time*. That is the decree of the Mighty, the Wise.[839]

فَالِقُ الْإِصْبَاحِ وَجَعَلَ الَّيْلَ سَكَنًا وَّالشَّمْسَ وَالْقَمَرَ حُسْبَانًا ذَلِكَ تَقْدِيرُ الْعَزِيزِ الْعَلِيمِ ۞

98. And He it is ᵈWho has made the stars for you that you may follow the right direction with their help amid the darknesses of the land and the sea. We have explained the Signs in detail for a people who possess knowledge.[840]

وَهُوَ الَّذِيْ جَعَلَ لَكُمُ النُّجُوْمَ لِتَهْتَدُوْا بِهَا فِيْ ظُلُمَاتِ الْبَرِّ وَالْبَحْرِ قَدْ فَصَّلْنَا الْآيَاتِ لِقَوْمٍ يَّعْلَمُوْنَ ۞

ᵃ113:2;   ᵇ25:48; 78:11;   ᶜ36:39-40;   55:6.   ᵈ16:17.

---

into a big tree. Similarly, you look upon man as a contemptible thing and say, *Allah has not revealed anything to any man* (6:92). But man also, whom you imagine to be so despicable, is like a seed and is capable of growing into something great.

The words, *He brings forth the living from the dead*, signify that not unoften noble and great men are born of low and ill-bred parents. Why then do you wonder and think it impossible that a righteous man should rise spiritually and become recipient of divine favours? Your God has made man after the manner of a seed. He has endowed him with many faculties and has made him capable of great progress. Why do you not then understand and see the truth?

839. Important Words:

حُسْبَانًا (reckoning) is the noun-infinitive from حَسَبَ. They say حَسَبَ *i.e.* he numbered or counted or reckoned it. حُسْبَان means, numbering, counting or reckoning; also punishment, calamity or affliction with which a man is tried; the revolving firmament (Lane).

Commentary:

The words, *He causes the break of day*, signify that just as God causes the dawn to break *i.e.* the night to change into day, similarly He

brings men from spiritual darkness into light. He takes them out of the darkness of disbelief and sin into the light of faith and virtue.

The words, *He made the night for rest*, signify that just as a man who works during the day gets tired and goes to sleep at night and then gets refreshed, similarly the people among whom the Holy Prophet made his appearance had had a long night of rest, and so their powers had been renewed. The Holy Prophet had made his appearance when the time was ripe for it and when the people, with their powers refreshed, were best fitted for work and could benefit most by his advent. They were now full of energy and well able to ascend the heights of spirituality under his lead; and so it actually happened.

By referring to the sun and the moon in this verse, the Quran draws the attention of the deniers of revelation to the fact that, just as in the physical world the sun and the moon are indispensable, being measures of time and sources of light, so are the Prophets of God indispensable in the spiritual world.

840. Commentary:

The argument embodied in this verse runs like this: "When God has made stars for guidance during the hours of night in the

99.   And He it is *Who has produced you from a single person and there is *for you* *a home and a lodging. We have explained the Signs in detail for a people who understand.[841]

وَهُوَ الَّذِىٓ اَنْشَاَكُمْ مِنْ نَّفْسٍ وَّاحِدَةٍ فَمُسْتَقَرٌّ وَّمُسْتَوْدَعٌ ۗ قَدْ فَصَّلْنَا الْاٰيٰتِ لِقَوْمٍ يَّفْقَهُوْنَ ۝

*a*4 : 3 ; 7 : 190 ; 39 : 7 ;   *b*11 : 7.

physical world, would He make no stars for the guidance of man in the spiritual world ? The spiritual welfare of man is much more important than his physical welfare ; so when God has created means of guidance for the temporal welfare of man, does it not stand to reason that He should have also provided means for the spiritual guidance of erring humanity ? "

841. Important Words :

اَنْشَاَكُمْ (has produced you). The word is derived from نَشَأَ which means, he lived ; he rose or became high or elevated ; he grew up ; it became produced or originated. اَنْشَأَ means, he created, produced or originated ; he raised or lifted (Lane).

مُسْتَقَرٌّ (home) is derived from قَرَّ which means, he or it settled or became firm or fixed or established ; or he or it remained or continued in a place ; or he or it rested ; or he or it became still or quiet or stationary. اِسْتَقَرَّ gives the same meaning as above. It also means, it subsisted. مُسْتَقَرٌّ means, place or time of settledness ; or of permanence and continuance *i.e.* home ; also a resting place (Lane).

مُسْتَوْدَعٌ (lodging) is derived from ودع (*wada'a*) or ودع (*wadu'a*) which means, he or it became still, quiet or at rest. ودع الشىئ (*wada'a*) means, he left off the thing. ودع عنده مالا means, he left the property with him as a deposit. ودّعه (*wadda'a-hū*) means, he bade him farewell ; he forsook or deserted him. استودعه مالا means, he entrusted him with property for safe custody. مُسْتَوْدَعٌ means, a depository ; a place of safety or security ; womb or the part of the body in which the child lies before its birth (Lane & Aqrab).

Commentary :

The expressions مُسْتَقَرٌّ (home) and مُسْتَوْدَعٌ (lodging) besides giving distinct and independent meanings are also sometimes used to give identical meanings, being interchangeable. The Quran says *i.e.* ونقر فى الارحام مانشاء *And We cause what We will to remain in the wombs* (22 : 6). Again it says ولكم فى الارض مستقر *i.e. and for you there is an abode in the earth* (2 : 37). From these two verses it appears that according to the Quran, "the womb" of the mother and "the earth," though places of temporary residence, are each a مُسْتَقَرٌّ *i.e.* a resting-place or a home for men. Corresponding to these, "the womb" may be called a مُسْتَوْدَعٌ *i.e.* a lodging or a depository. The next world is truly a مُسْتَقَرٌّ *i.e.* a home for man. In fact these are really relative terms, the same place being both a مُسْتَقَرٌّ and a مُسْتَوْدَعٌ in reference to different things. Again, a place may be called a مُسْتَقَرٌّ (home) because one stays therein, and it may be called a مُسْتَقَرٌّ (lodging) because it provides security.

The verse signifies that when God has multiplied humanity out of one individual, it could not be without a purpose. The great object for which He has created and multiplied human beings is that He has appointed for them not only a period of residence on this earth but also an everlasting life beyond the grave where the righteous will meet the Lord—a lofty goal to which they can rise under the guidance of divine Messengers.

100. And it is [a]He Who sends down water from the cloud; and We bring forth therewith every kind of growth; then We bring forth with that green foliage wherefrom We produce clustered grain. And from the date-palm. out of its sheaths, *come forth* bunches hanging low. And *We produce therewith* [b]gardens of grapes, and the olive and the pomegranate—similar and dissimilar. Look at the fruit thereof when it bears fruit, and the ripening thereof. Surely, in this are Signs for a people who believe.[842]

وَهُوَ الَّذِىْ اَنْزَلَ مِنَ السَّمَآءِ مَآءً ۚ فَاَخْرَجْنَا بِهٖ نَبَاتَ كُلِّ شَىْءٍ فَاَخْرَجْنَا مِنْهُ خَضِرًا نُّخْرِجُ مِنْهُ حَبًّا مُّتَرَاكِبًا ۚ وَمِنَ النَّخْلِ مِنْ طَلْعِهَا قِنْوَانٌ دَانِيَةٌ وَّجَنّٰتٍ مِّنْ اَعْنَابٍ وَّالزَّيْتُوْنَ وَالرُّمَّانَ مُشْتَبِهًا وَّغَيْرَ مُتَشَابِهٍ ۚ اُنْظُرُوْا اِلٰى ثَمَرِهٖ اِذَآ اَثْمَرَ وَيَنْعِهٖ ۚ اِنَّ فِىْ ذٰلِكُمْ لَاٰيٰتٍ لِّقَوْمٍ يُّؤْمِنُوْنَ ۞

---

[a]14 : 33; 16 : 11; 22 : 64; 35 : 28.   [b]6 : 142; 13 : 5.

842. Important Words :

مُتَرَاكِبًا (clustered) is derived from رکب. They say رکبه i.e. he rode it or mounted it; it got upon it or it became superincumbent upon it. تراكب means, it lay one part upon another; it was or became heaped or piled up. So مُتَراكب means, piled or clustered together one above another (Aqrab).

طلع (sheaths) is from the verb طلع (*tala‘a*) i.e. he or it rose or appeared or came forth. طلع is what comes forth from the palm tree and becomes dates; the spathe or flowers of the palm tree (Lane).

قِنْوَان (bunches) is the plural of قنو which is derived from قنا. They say قنا المال i.e. he acquired and amassed property for himself. قنو means, a bunch of dates (Aqrab).

ينعه (the ripening thereof). ينع is from the verb ينع (*yana‘a*). They say ينع الثمر i.e. the fruit became ripened and fit for gathering; it (fruit, etc.) became red. يانع means, the ripe fruit. ينع is both the noun-infinitive from the verb ينع (*yana‘a*) in which case it means the ripening of a fruit, and the plural of يانع in which case it means the ripe fruits (Aqrab).

Commentary :

In this verse revelation is likened to rain-water, and the verse answers the question why there is discord and strife at the advent of Prophets, if revelation is indeed a blessing. The verse says that just as by rain-water all kinds of vegetation grow up, both bad and good, according to the seeds lying concealed in the earth, similarly at the advent of divine revelation, men, so far remaining mixed up, become divided into good and bad. The good ones accept the Messenger of God, help him and become pious and holy, like trees which bear good fruit or like shrubs which bring forth beautiful flowers or like herbs which give out a sweet odour; but there are others—the bad ones—who oppose the Prophet, persecute his followers and act corruptly in the earth. These are like trees which bear bitter fruit or like flowerless and thorny bushes or like plants and herbs which give out a bad smell.

The words مشتبها و غير متشابه (similar and dissimilar) imply that whereas some fruits resemble each other, some differ from others. This may apply either to fruits of different kinds, which resemble one another in certain respects and differ in others, or to fruits of the

723

101. And *"they hold the Jinn to be partners with Allah, although He created them ; and they falsely ascribe to Him sons and daughters without any knowledge. Holy is He and exalted *far* above what they attribute to Him !*[843]

وَجَعَلُوْا لِلّٰهِ شُرَكَآءَ الْجِنَّ وَخَلَقَهُمْ وَخَرَقُوْا لَهٗ بَنِيْنَ وَبَنَاتٍ بِغَيْرِ عِلْمٍ ۖ سُبْحٰنَهٗ وَتَعٰلٰى عَمَّا يَصِفُوْنَ ۞

---

*a*2 : 117 ; 9 : 31 ; 10 : 19.

---

same kind which, although resembling one another in the main points, differ from one another in minor details, some tasting sweeter than others and some varying in colour or size. The same is the case with those who believe in the Prophets and follow divine guidance. Although they bear great resemblance to one another, yet there are differences between them, some being morally and spiritually more advanced than others. Again, some are advanced in one phase of spiritual growth, while others are advanced in another. Among the Companions of the Holy Prophet, too, we see that one became an Abū Bakr, another an 'Umar, and another an 'Uthmān and yet another an 'Alī and so on. They attained to different stages of spirituality and developed different phases, according to their respective natural capacities and dispositions.

The words, *the ripening thereof*, refer to an implied objection that might be raised by the deniers of revelation—namely, that even those who accept divine revelation do not all become pure and holy. The above-quoted words answer this objection by pointing to the analogy of the ripening of fruit. The people are asked first to note the condition of fruits when they are yet unripe and then see how sweet and delicious they become after becoming ripe. Just as it is unfair to judge a fruit by an unripe specimen, similarly, it is unfair to find fault with the fruits of revelation on the basis of such individuals as are yet in the process of development and have not attained to perfection. The

verse points out that in the beginning there are bound to be weaknesses and shortcomings even in believers just as there is bound to be sourness in the taste of an unripe or undeveloped fruit. So it is not just to deny the usefulness of revelation on the basis of weaknesses that are to be met with in believers whose spiritual condition is not yet fully developed.

The verse most beautifully draws attention to three important points that can be deduced from the analogy of the various kinds of vegetation that grow as a result of rain : (1) that rain brings forth both good and bad vegetation (believers and disbelievers) ; (2) that even in good fruits (believers) some variety is to be found *i.e.* points of similarity and dis-similarity ; and (3) that in the early stage of development even good fruits are not sweet and may even be sour.

843. Important Words :

الجن (the *Jinn*) is derived from the verb جن *i.e.* he covered up or concealed. The word here signifies such beings as remain aloof from the people, as if remaining concealed, *e.g.,* kings and other potentates. In its wider significance the word extends to angels and other hidden creatures. See also 2 : 26 ; 6 : 77 & 6 : 129.

خرقوا (they falsely ascribe) is derived from خرق. They say خرقه *i.e.* he made a hole in it, or he cut it or tore it. خرق الارض means, he traversed or crossed the land by journeying so as to reach the furthest part thereof.

13   102.   ᵃThe Originator of the heavens and the earth! How can He have a son when He has no consort, and *when* He has created everything and has knowledge of all things?[844]

103.   ᵇSuch is Allah, your Lord. There is no god but He, ᶜthe Creator of all things, so worship Him. And He is Guardian over everything.[845]

ᵃ2:118.   ᵇ40:63.   ᶜ13:17; 39:63.

خرق الكذب means, he forged the lie. Sometimes the word خرق even when used without a qualifying word means, he forged a lie, or he lied, or he falsely ascribed something to somebody (Tāj).

Commentary :

This verse draws attention to the way in which man stumbles when he rejects divine revelation and follows his own judgement and reason. It calls upon the reader to mark the difference between divine and man-made teachings. Men, unguided by divine light and following their own reason, have strayed so far away from the path of rectitude that some suppose the *Jinn* (kings, etc.) to be co-partners with God, as did the Egyptians in the time of Moses; while others attribute sons and daughters to Him, as do the Christians, who have deified Jesus and believe him to be the son of God. A comparison of these man-made teachings with those revealed by God definitely proves the need of divine revelation.

844. Important Words :

ولد (son) is from the verb ولد meaning, he or she begot or brought forth a child or a young one. The word ولد (*waladun*) or ولد (*wuldun*) or ولد (*waldun*) is very comprehensive in its meaning. It not only signifies male and female but is also used as singular or plural, extending even to remote offspring. Thus the word means, a child, a son, a daughter, or any young one; children, sons, daughters, or young ones; also offspring (Lane).

Commentary :

After making a reference to man-made teachings, the Quran proceeds to give divine teachings.

There are only two ways by which one can have a son, either by a wife or by adoption. As for the first way, God has no spouse, so He cannot have a son. Christians call Jesus the son of God, but they do not call Mary the consort of God. If, however, Jesus was the son of God by adoption, then that does not entitle him to a higher spiritual status than other human beings, for any other man might as well have been adopted by God as His son. Again, as God is the Creator of everything and possesses perfect knowledge, He does not stand in need of a son.

845. Commentary :

God, being the Creator of all things and being Guardian over them, can alone be the true Deity. If there is anything which He has not created or of which He is not the guardian, then He cannot be perfect.

725

104. Eyes can not reach Him but He reaches the eyes. And ^aHe is the Incomprehensible, the All-Aware.⁸⁴⁶

لَا تُدْرِكُهُ الْأَبْصَارُ وَهُوَ يُدْرِكُ الْأَبْصَارَ وَهُوَ اللَّطِيفُ الْخَبِيرُ ۞

^a22 : 64 : 67 : 15.

---

846. **Important Words :**

لَا تُدْرِكُهُ (cannot reach Him). تُدْرِك is derived from ادرك which again is derived from درك . They say ادركه *i.e.* he or it attained, reached or overtook it. It also means, he perceived it ; or he attained knowledge of it ; or he attained perfect knowledge of it ; or he comprehended it. The word also means, he or it attained puberty or maturity or ripeness (Lane).

ابصار (eyes) is the plural of بصر which means, eye or sight, or understanding or perspicacity ('Aqrab).

لطيف (Incomprehensible) is derived from لطف . They say لطف الشيئ (*latufa*) *i.e.*, the thing was or became small, thin or fine. لطف به *i.e. latafa* (with different vowel point on the central letter) means, he was kind, gentle and affectionate to him. لطيف means : (1) gentle, gracious, and kind ; (2) subtle, abstruse or recondite ; (3) knower of the subtleties and obscurities of things. It is one of the attributes of God (Tāj, Lisān & Aqrab).

Commentary :

Some persons may claim that they can know or reach God by means of reason or understanding alone. The Quran forcefully refutes this idea by saying, *Eyes cannot reach Him*, *i.e.*, human reason alone, unaided by divine help, is incapable of knowing or reaching God. It is God Himself Who reaches the eyes (*viz.* human understanding) and reveals Himself to man, *i.e.*, God has, on the one hand, placed in human mind a power to search after and know Him, and, on the other, He sends down revelation to man, thereby making Himself known to him. Revelation also helps to kindle in human reason a light by means of which man is enabled to know God.

The two divine attributes اللطيف (Incomprehensible) and الخبير (All-Aware) furnish in a most beautiful manner the reason of the two claims made in the opening words of the verse. The first claim is that *Eyes cannot reach Him*, the corresponding reason being stated to be that *He is Subtle and Incomprehensible* and, being so, He cannot be comprehended by human reason alone. The second claim is that *He reaches the eyes*, the corresponding reason being stated to be that *He is All-Aware* and, being so, He knows that mankind stands in need of knowing Him without which there can be no spiritual life, so He Himself approaches man and reveals Himself to him. The two claims have thus been followed, in a perfect natural order, by two corresponding reasons. The reader should note what wise order governs the arrangement of the words of the Quran. They have not been put together at random, but each word has been put in the most appropriate place and is meant to fulfil a great purpose.

105. ^aProofs have indeed come to you from your Lord ; so whoever sees, it is for his own good ; and whoever becomes blind, it is to his own harm. And I am not a guardian over you.⁸⁴⁷

106. And ^bthus do We vary the Signs *that the truth may become established,* but *the result is* that they say, 'Thou hast learnt *well*;' and *We vary the Signs* that We may explain it to a people who have knowledge.⁸⁴⁸

107. ^cFollow that which has been revealed to thee from thy Lord ; there is no god but He ; and turn aside from the idolaters.

قَدْ جَآءَكُمْ بَصَآئِرُ مِنْ رَّبِّكُمْ فَمَنْ اَبْصَرَ فَلِنَفْسِهِ وَمَنْ عَمِيَ فَعَلَيْهَا ۚ وَمَآ اَنَا عَلَيْكُمْ بِحَفِيظٍ ۞

وَكَذٰلِكَ نُصَرِّفُ الْاٰيٰتِ وَلِيَقُوْلُوْا دَرَسْتَ وَلِنُبَيِّنَهٗ لِقَوْمٍ يَّعْلَمُوْنَ ۞

اِتَّبِعْ مَآ اُوْحِيَ اِلَيْكَ مِنْ رَّبِّكَ ۚ لَآ اِلٰهَ اِلَّا هُوَ ۚ وَاَعْرِضْ عَنِ الْمُشْرِكِيْنَ ۞

^a7 : 204.   ^b7 : 59.   ^c10 : 110 ; 33 : 3.

847. Commentary :

The word بَصَائِر (proofs) also helps to explain the words, *He reaches the eyes*, occurring in the preceding verse and signifies that God reveals proofs by means of which man becomes able to know Him. By "proofs" is here meant the divine Signs and evidences sent by God.

The words, *whoever sees*, mean, whoever makes use of his reason after proofs have been revealed to him by God. Similarly the words, *whoever becomes blind*, refer to such persons as shut their eyes to all truth and virtually make themselves blind.

The duty of the Holy Prophet described in the words, *I am not a guardian over you*, is only to convey what is revealed by God ; it is not his business to compel people to believe in God. Thus the verse also provides a refutation of the baseless charge that Islam countenances compulsion in the propagation of religion.

848. Important Words :

دَرَسْتَ (thou hast learnt well) is derived from دَرَسَ which means, it became effaced, erased or obliterated; or transitively, it effaced, erased or obliterated. دَرَسَ الثَّوْبُ means, the cloth became old and worn out. Similarly, دَرَسَ الثَّوْبُ means, he rendered the cloth old and worn out. دَرَسَ الْكِتَابَ means, he read the book or he read it repeatedly so as to remember it ; or he made it easy to remember by much reading ; or he learnt or studied it (Lane).

Commentary :

The verse purports to say, " We have explained Our teachings in various ways with the result that believers have acquired perfect belief in them, while disbelievers have rejected them, saying, 'You have learnt these teachings from Jews and Christians and are now repeating them to us.'" The verb دَرَسْتَ (thou hast learnt well) has thus been used here ironically. Taking the transitive meaning of دَرَسْتَ the clause would mean that disbelievers reject the teachings, saying, "You have read or recited the Signs and teachings you claim to have brought to us and we have heard them. That is enough ; do not bother us any more."

In fact, whereas the teachings of the Quran benefit those who accept them, they serve

108. And if Allah had enforced *His* will, they would not have set up gods *with God*. And *ᵃ*We have not made thee a keeper over them nor art thou over them a guardian.⁸⁴⁹

وَ لَوْ شَآءَ اللّٰهُ مَاۤ اَشْرَكُوْا ۭ وَ مَا جَعَلْنٰكَ عَلَيْهِمْ حَفِيْظًا ۚ وَ مَاۤ اَنْتَ عَلَيْهِمْ بِوَكِيْلٍ ۞

109. And revile not those whom they call upon beside Allah, lest they, out of spite, revile Allah in their ignorance. Thus *ᵇ*unto every people have We caused their doing to seem fair. Then unto their Lord is their return ; and He will inform them of what they used to do.⁸⁵⁰

وَ لَا تَسُبُّوا الَّذِيْنَ يَدْعُوْنَ مِنْ دُوْنِ اللّٰهِ فَيَسُبُّوا اللّٰهَ عَدْوًۢا بِغَيْرِ عِلْمٍ ۭ كَذٰلِكَ زَيَّنَّا لِكُلِّ اُمَّةٍ عَمَلَهُمْ ثُمَّ اِلٰى رَبِّهِمْ مَّرْجِعُهُمْ فَيُنَبِّئُهُمْ بِمَا كَانُوْا يَعْمَلُوْنَ ۞

---

*ᵃ*39 : 42 ; 42 : 7 ; 88 : 23. *ᵇ*6 : 123 ; 9 : 37 ; 10 : 13 ; 27 : 5 ; 40 : 38 ; 49 : 8.

---

the purpose of establishing the guilt of those who reject them so that they become answerable to God for their rejection.

849. Commentary :

The Arabic words rendered as, *if Allah had enforced His will, they would not have set up gods with God*, do not, and indeed cannot, mean, as some may suppose, that the idolaters commit sins because God so wills. They only mean that God has made man a free agent in matters of faith and has not forced His will on him. If He had enforced His will and compelled man to believe and act rightly, man could not have gone against His will. But in His infinite wisdom, He has made man a free agent in this respect. The verse thus makes it clear that Allah does not compel any person to accept the truth but leaves it to his option. If He had thought of compelling the people, He would certainly have compelled them to follow the truth ; but in the interests of man himself it has not pleased God to use compulsion.

The concluding words, *We have not made thee a keeper over them, nor art thou over them a guardian*, are also intended to echo the same truth, *i.e.*, just as God does not compel man to

accept the truth, the Holy Prophet also cannot compel anybody, for he is only a Messenger of God. The words حَفِيظ (keeper) and وَكِيل (guardian or disposer of affairs) are intended to signify that the Prophet is neither responsible for the actions of disbelievers nor is he the disposer of their affairs. For a fuller discussion of the words حَفِيظ and وَكِيل see 3 : 174 & 11 : 58.

850. Commentary :

In the foregoing verses, the Quran has spoken rather contemptuously of the utter helplessness of the false deities whom people associate with God. This might lead some Muslims to revile the false deities of the polytheists ; the present verse warns them against following such a course. God has denounced the idols in His capacity as a judge, and the denunciation of a judge is not considered as abuse, but as a necessary expression of opinion. This does not give others the right to abuse the persons condemned by the Heavenly Judge and thereby offend their feelings, or the feelings of those who love and respect them.

The verse provides yet another reason for this noble teaching. It purports to say, if you, O Muslims, revile disbelievers' false gods whom they treat with love and reverence, the result will be that they

110. And they swear their strongest oaths by Allah that if there came to them a Sign, they would surely believe therein. Say, ' Surely, Signs are with Allah. But what should make you understand that when the Signs come, they will not believe ? '851

وَاَقْسَمُوْا بِاللّٰهِ جَهْدَ اَيْمَانِهِمْ لَئِنْ جَآءَتْهُمْ اٰيَةٌ لَّيُؤْمِنُنَّ بِهَا قُلْ اِنَّمَا الْاٰيٰتُ عِنْدَ اللّٰهِ وَمَا يُشْعِرُكُمْ اَنَّهَآ اِذَا جَآءَتْ لَا يُؤْمِنُوْنَ ۝

111. And We shall confound their hearts and their eyes, as they believed not therein at the first time, and "We shall leave them in their transgression to wander in distraction.852

وَنُقَلِّبُ اَفْئِدَتَهُمْ وَاَبْصَارَهُمْ كَمَا لَمْ يُؤْمِنُوْا بِهٖٓ اَوَّلَ مَرَّةٍ وَّنَذَرُهُمْ فِيْ طُغْيَانِهِمْ يَعْمَهُوْنَ ۝

---

*a*2 : 16.

will be excited by your abuse and will retaliate by reviling God in return. The verse thus not only inculcates respect for the feelings of others but also assures amity between nations and communities.

The expression زَيَّنَ (have We caused to seem fair) signifies not that God has actually beautified evil actions but that He has so created the nature of man (and in this law of God lies the secret of man's progress) that when he goes on doing a thing for some length of time, he acquires a liking for it, and his action begins to appear good in his sight. So, in accordance with this general law of God, idolaters have also come to like their worship of idols, which appears to them to be good and meritorious.

851. Important Words :

اِنَّمَا (surely) is considered to be a compound of اِنَّ and مَا . It imports restriction of that which it precedes to that which follows it, giving the sense of "only." The Quran says: اِنَّمَا الصَّدَقَاتُ لِلْفُقَرَاءِ i.e. the ṣadaqāt (the alms) are meant only for the poor, etc. But the word does not always import restriction but sometimes only corroboration of an affirmation, giving the sense of " verily " or " surely," as in the tradition اِنَّمَا الرِّبَا فِى النَّسِيئَةِ i.e. verily, (one form of) usury is in the delay of payment (Lane & Aqrab).

Commentary :

The latter part of the verse may also be rendered thus : Say, "Surely, Signs are with Allah, and that (too is with Allah) which will make you know that when it comes, they will not believe." In this rendering, the particle مَا rendered in the text as "what" would be taken as a relative pronoun, in the sense of الَّذِى i.e. "that" and not as an interrogative pronoun. According to this rendering, the words " and that (too is with Allah) which will make you know that when it comes, they will not believe " would refer to the punishment of God and the clause would mean that not only are other Signs with God, but the Sign of punishment is also with Him and that when that Sign comes, you will see that it will do them no good.

852. Commentary :

The verse signifies that when the Signs of God come, they will do the disbelievers no good; God will turn away their hearts and their eyes from the Signs so that they will not believe. This turning away of their hearts and their eyes from the Signs of God will be the result of their hasty denial of the Signs of God at the very outset, which will have hardened their hearts and deprived them of the power

R. 14   **112.** And even if We send down unto them angels, and ^athe dead speak to them, and We gather to them all things face to face, they would not believe, unless God enforced *His* will. But most of them behave ignorantly.⁸⁵³

وَلَوْ اَنَّنَا نَزَّلْنَا اِلَيْهِمُ الْمَلَائِكَةَ وَكَلَّمَهُمُ الْمَوْتٰى وَحَشَرْنَا عَلَيْهِمْ كُلَّ شَيْءٍ قُبُلًا مَّا كَانُوْا لِيُؤْمِنُوْا اِلَّا اَنْ يَّشَاءَ اللّٰهُ وَلٰكِنَّ اَكْثَرَهُمْ يَجْهَلُوْنَ ۝

---

^a13 : 32.

---

of benefiting by the Signs of God. It is a law of God that those who deny His Prophets at the very outset, without pausing to think over their claims and without pondering over the signs and evidences of their truth, deprive themselves of the blessings of being rightly guided ; but those who do not hasten to deny them and are ready to think over their claims with an open mind and in the fear of God and entertain a genuine desire to know the truth are ultimately guided to it.

853. Commentary :

The subject of the previous verse is continued in this one. One of the functions of the angels is to suggest good ideas to men and to invite them to virtue (2 : 32). They sometimes perform this function through the medium of dreams and visions. The opening words of the verse refer to this very function.

The words, *the dead speak to them,* refer to the testimony of pious men of the past to the truth of a divine Messenger either by means of prophecies which are handed down to posterity in writing or orally, or by their appearing to men in dreams and visions.

There is another way also in which the dead may speak to men. This happens when a person who is spiritually dead or a nation which is devoid of spiritual life is quickened to life by seeing the truth of their Prophet and then testifies to his truth before other persons or nations.

The words, *and We gather to them all things*

face to face, refer to the testimony of the different objects of nature to the truth of a Prophet before his enemies. The different objects of nature bear testimony in the form of earthquakes, pestilences, storms, floods, famines and other visitations. These things come upon the enemies of a Prophet as punishments from heaven. Nature itself appears to be angry with them ; the very elements are up in arms against them. All things that are God's (and what is there that is not God's ?) stand up in opposition to the enemies of a divine Messenger. Thus it is that both heaven and earth bear testimony to a Prophet's truth.

It should be noted that all these Signs were actually shown in the time of the Holy Prophet. As for the angels, they appeared at the Battle of Badr and were even seen by some of the disbelievers (Jarīr, iv. 47), but those who were hard-hearted did not believe. They knew the Holy Prophet to be a truthful and upright man but, surrounded by evil associates and swayed by evil passions, they denied his claims. In the beginning even men like Abū Jahl were impressed by the truth and honesty of the Holy Prophet ; for it is recorded that when the verses of the Quran were recited to Abū Jahl for the first time, he admitted that it was the truth. In spite of this, however, he exclaimed, "When did we follow the children of 'Abd Manāf ? " (an ancestor of the Holy Prophet), meaning that he could not accept the leadership of the Prophet. Thereafter he gradually increased in perversity,

113. And ^ain like manner have We made for every Prophet an enemy, evil ones from among men and Jinn. They suggest one to another gilded speech in order to deceive—and if thy Lord had enforced *His* will, they would not have done it ; so leave them alone with that which they fabricate—[854]

وَكَذٰلِكَ جَعَلْنَا لِكُلِّ نَبِيٍّ عَدُوًّا شَيٰطِيْنَ الْاِنْسِ وَ الْجِنِّ يُوْحِىْ بَعْضُهُمْ اِلٰى بَعْضٍ زُخْرُفَ الْقَوْلِ غُرُوْرًا ۚ وَلَوْ شَآءَ رَبُّكَ مَا فَعَلُوْهُ فَذَرْهُمْ وَمَا يَفْتَرُوْنَ ۝

---

^a25 : 32.

---

so much so that at the Battle of Badr he actually prayed to God to destroy whichever of them (meaning himself and the Holy Prophet) had created mischief and discord among his people. The prayer was heard, but he himself was its victim. His case is a typical instance of how the hearts of men were hardened because they rejected the Holy Prophet at the very outset, in spite of knowing him to be sincere and truthful.

The words, *most of them behave ignorantly,* imply that they will not believe unless God forces His will on them and compels them to accept the truth ; but God will not do that, and these people are so foolhardy that they would not change their hostile attitude unless compelled to do so.

854. Important Words :

زُخْرُف (gilded). They say زخرف البيت *i.e.,* he adorned, decorated or embellished the house. زخرف الكلام means, he arranged or put into a right state the speech or language ; he embellished it with lies, etc. زخرف means, gold ; any ornament or decoration or embellishment ; also anything adorned, decorated or embellished ; anything embellished with false colouring or with lies (Aqrab).

For غرورا (in order to deceive) see 4 : 121.

Commentary :

The words, *men and Jinn,* which occur in many verses of the Quran do not refer to two different species of God's creatures, but only to two classes of human beings *i.e.* " men " denoting the masses or the common folk, and *Jinn* standing for the big people who often remain aloof from the common people and do not mix with them, practically remaining concealed from public gaze. See also 6 : 101.

Those of the common people and the big people who lead the opposition to the Prophets of God have been styled *Shayāṭīn* (evil ones), for an explanation of which see note on 2 : 15. This word shows that those who lead lives of sin before the advent of a Prophet generally increase in sinfulness as a punishment for their evil deeds, so that when a Prophet makes his appearance, they assume the role of arch-enemies to him and become leaders of opposition. It is a law of God, in both the physical and spiritual worlds, that the powers of man develop in the direction in which they are exercised. So, as such men employ their powers in the wrong way, the result is that at the advent of a Prophet they become still greater sinners and become leaders of men in opposing the truth. Again, in order to augment their mischief, these leaders suggest, as hinted in the words, *gilded speech,* such arguments to one another as appear to be sound and true but are really false and hollow, and their object in suggesting such things is to deceive the weak-minded.

114. And in order that the hearts of those who believe not in the Hereafter may incline thereto and that they may be pleased therewith and that they may *continue to* earn what they are earning.[855]

وَلِتَصْغَىٰ إِلَيْهِ أَفْئِدَةُ الَّذِينَ لَا يُؤْمِنُونَ بِالْآخِرَةِ وَ لِيَرْضَوْهُ وَلِيَقْتَرِفُوا مَا هُمْ مُقْتَرِفُونَ ۝

115. Shall I seek for judge other than Allah, when [a]He it is Who has sent down to you the Book, clearly explained ? And [b]those to whom We gave the Book know that it has been sent down from thy Lord with truth ; so be thou not of those who doubt.[856]

أَفَغَيْرَ اللَّهِ أَبْتَغِي حَكَمًا وَهُوَ الَّذِي أَنْزَلَ إِلَيْكُمُ الْكِتَابَ مُفَصَّلًا وَالَّذِينَ آتَيْنَاهُمُ الْكِتَابَ يَعْلَمُونَ أَنَّهُ مُنَزَّلٌ مِنْ رَبِّكَ بِالْحَقِّ فَلَا تَكُونَنَّ مِنَ الْمُمْتَرِينَ ۝

---

[a]7 : 53 ; 12 : 112 ; 16 : 90.   [b]2 : 147 ; 6 : 21.

---

855. Important Words :

يَقْتَرِفُوا (they may earn) is derived from اقترف which again is derived from قرف . They say قرف لعياله *i.e.* he earned for his family. قرف على القوم means, he transgressed against the people and lied. قرف الرجل means, the man lied and mixed truth with falsehood. قرف الشئ means, he peeled the skin or bark (of a tree, etc.). اقترف الرجل means, the man earned, especially an evil. اقترف الذنب means, he committed the sin (Aqrab).

Commentary :

The subject of the previous verse is continued here. Wicked leaders from among the common people and from among the big people suggest to one another gilded speech and fallacious reasoning in order to deceive the weak-minded and in order to attract towards themselves the hearts of disbelievers with a view to winning their applause and making them persist in their evil course against the Prophets.

856. Commentary :

The words, *Shall I seek for judge other than Allah,* illustrate how wicked leaders bring forward gilded speech and fallacious reasoning against the Prophets. They try to turn away the attention of men from the revealed Scriptures which bear testimony to the truth of a Prophet and bring forward doubtful traditions and quotations from religious writings of human authors in support of their false notions. Or, as sometimes happens, they propose the names of certain persons to act as judges and to give their verdict after hearing the arguments of both sides. As the Prophets of God have to expose the errors of all parties, therefore wicked leaders are sure that the judges, influenced by the general opposition to the Prophets, will give their verdict against them. So the Quran makes the Holy Prophet emphatically declare, *Shall I seek for judge other than Allah ?* i.e. in religious matters none beside Allah can be taken as judge. The writings of theologians cannot make us dispense with the revealed word of God, nor can any human being act as judge in matters pertaining to faith. Allah alone can act as judge and His word alone can guide to the truth.

Now the question arises, How does Allah or His word act as judge ? This question is answered by the verse in the words : *And those to whom We gave the Book know that it has been*

116. And the word of thy Lord has been fulfilled in truth and justice. *None can change His words; and He is the All-Hearing, the All-Knowing.857

وَتَمَّتْ كَلِمَتُ رَبِّكَ صِدْقًا وَّعَدْلًا ۚ لَا مُبَدِّلَ لِكَلِمٰتِهٖ ۚ وَهُوَ السَّمِيْعُ الْعَلِيْمُ ۝

---

a6 : 35.

sent down from thy Lord with truth. This means that the Quran has come in accordance with, and in fulfilment of the prophecies contained in the previous Scriptures and, as none knows the secrets of the future save God, so the Quran must be accepted as proceeding from Him. The previous Scriptures contain clear prophecies concerning the Holy Prophet and these prophecies bear testimony to his truth and the truth of the Quran; hence, those who have been given a knowledge of the Book and consequently of the prophecies contained therein should know that the Holy Prophet of Islam is a true Prophet and that the revelation that has been sent down to him is a true revelation. It is thus that God acts as judge.

The word "Book" in the clause, *those to whom We gave the Book,* may also refer to the Quran; for not only the previous word of God, but also the Quran itself, bears testimony to the Holy Prophet. The Quran contains teachings which run counter to the views and beliefs current among the nations of the world; yet every opponent before whom these teachings are rehearsed and explained is compelled to acknowledge their great reasonableness and superiority. Again, not only were these teachings accepted by thousands in the lifetime of the Holy Prophet but those who believed in them were so convinced of their truth that they were prepared to lay down their lives rather than give up these teachings. So the very lives of the Companions of the Holy Prophet bore witness to the truth of the Quran. A Book which is possessed of such spiritual power cannot be rejected as false.

The last words of the verse *i.e. be thou not of those who doubt,* refer to the reader, and not to the Holy Prophet. When the previous Scriptures as well as the Quran bear unmistakable testimony to the truth of the Holy Prophet and of the revelation that has been sent down to him, then no one is justified in entertaining doubt concerning them.

857. Commentary :

The verb تَمَّ (has been fulfilled) though grammatically in the past tense is here used in the future tense, meaning, shall be fulfilled, for in prophecies often a preterite is used to express the future tense. This is done in order to show that the event predicted is, in the sight of God, as good as fulfilled. The words thus contain a prophecy and mean that what God has said about the future triumph of Islam shall certainly come to pass. It is reported that when Mecca fell and the Holy Prophet entered the Ka'ba, which was at that time full of idols, and struck the idols one after another with his stick, he recited the very words of this prophecy: *the word of thy Lord has been fulfilled in truth and justice,* in allusion to the fact that with the fall of Mecca the word of God had indeed been fulfilled (Manthūr, under 6 : 116).

The words, *None can change His words,* refer to the prophecies or to the ways or usage of God. With regard to the سنة or usage of God, it must be remembered that it is not for us to determine what the usage or the law of God is. Generally speaking, it is that which has been expressly mentioned as such

117. And if thou obey the majority of those on earth, they will lead thee astray from Allah's way. *They follow nothing but *mere* conjecture, and they do nothing but lie.858

وَاِنۡ تُطِعۡ اَكۡثَرَ مَنۡ فِی الۡاَرۡضِ یُضِلُّوۡکَ عَنۡ سَبِیۡلِ اللّٰهِ ؕ اِنۡ یَّتَّبِعُوۡنَ اِلَّا الظَّنَّ وَاِنۡ هُمۡ اِلَّا یَخۡرُصُوۡنَ ۝

118. Surely, *b*thy Lord knows best those who go astray from His way; and He knows best those who are rightly guided.859

اِنَّ رَبَّکَ هُوَ اَعۡلَمُ مَنۡ یَّضِلُّ عَنۡ سَبِیۡلِهٖ ۚ وَهُوَ اَعۡلَمُ بِالۡمُهۡتَدِیۡنَ ۝

---

*a*10 : 37 ; 53 : 29.   *b*16 : 126.

in the Quran. Thus, one of the laws of God specified in the Quran is that His Messengers triumph and their enemies are brought to naught. Such laws have been spoken of as سنن الله (the ways or usages of God) and are not to be confounded with the laws of nature.

By the words, *the All-Hearing, the All-Knowing,* is meant that God hears not only the prayers of believers but also what the enemies of the Holy Prophet say against him. Similarly, He knows not only the sufferings and sacrifices of believers but also what the enemies of Islam are doing to harm and ruin it. So He will decide between the two parties.

858. Important Words :

یخرصون (lie) is derived from خرص which means, he computed the quantity or number of a thing by conjecture ; he conjectured ; he opined while he was not certain. It also means, he spoke falsely, or he lied, or he said what was untrue. خراص means, a liar ; or one who only conjectures or opines and does not make sure of a thing by ascertaining the truth (Lane & Aqrab).

Commentary :

The verse purports to say that the question of the truth or otherwise of Islam should not be decided according to the verdict of the majority,

for the majority of mankind are ignorant. Therefore matters of faith cannot be decided by the verdict of the majority. There has never been a people the majority of whom are wise or learned. Even in wordly legislatures, it is only a limited number of persons whose opinion matters. Again, even in so-called advanced countries the masses have their leaders, and it is these leaders whose opinion they follow. Thus in reality it is always a limited number whose opinion matters.

The verse refers particularly to the people of Arabia in the time of the Holy Prophet, the majority of whom were undoubtedly ignorant.

859. Commentary :

The verse signifies that, apart from the fact stated in the preceding verse that the majority of men often possess less knowledge than the minority, neither the majority nor the minority can be trusted in matters of faith. Sometimes the minority are in the right and sometimes the majority. Hence it is necessary that God should decide as to which party follows the right path. In fact, God alone can be the judge. He gives His decision by showing heavenly Signs and by helping the party which pursues the path of truth.

119. ªEat, then, of that over which the name of Allah has been pronounced, if you are believers in His Signs.[860]

فَكُلُوْا مِمَّا ذُكِرَ اسْمُ اللّٰهِ عَلَيْهِ اِنْ كُنْتُمْ بِاٰيٰتِهٖ مُؤْمِنِيْنَ ۝

---

a5 : 5.

---

860. Commentary :

The commandment to eat of that over which the name of Allah has been pronounced may appear to some to have no connection with the subject-matter of the previous verses. But it is really not so. The very fact that this verse is preceded by the particle فَ (then) shows that this commandment has come as a sequence of what has gone before. Again, the verb كُلُوْا (eat) is plural and as this commandment is given in continuation of the preceding commandments, it follows that the previous commandments, although given in the singular number, are general in their application and are not addressed to the Holy Prophet personally. Thus the commandment, *be thou not of those who doubt* (6 : 115 above), is also addressed to really each and every reader.

As regards the connection between the present commandment and the preceding ones, it may be noted that elsewhere the Quran says : *O ye who believe, eat of the good things We have provided for you, and render thanks to Allah* (2 : 173). Again, *O ye Messengers, eat of the things that are pure, and do good works* (23 : 52). These verses clearly show that the eating of good and pure things has a direct bearing on the actions of man, who is thereby enabled to feel grateful to God and do good works. As the weak among the Faithful sometimes gave way to doubt when they heard the objections of disbelievers referred to in the previous verses, the Quran here bids them to partake of pure and holy food. The result will be that they themselves will become pure and their faith will become strengthened and thus they will become proof against the doubts which

disbelievers seek to create in their minds by raising objections.

It may be objected that present-day Muslims pronounce the name of God on the animals they slaughter, and yet their minds are not free from doubt. The reason is that they pronounce the name of God only as a cold formality without sincerity or earnestness.

It should also be remembered that the injunction to eat of that on which the name of God has been pronounced applies not only to the flesh of animals but to all kinds of food. The verse enjoins Muslims to pronounce the name of God on all food of which they partake so that they may be constantly reminded of God and their lives may be sanctified.

The verse also shows how those who follow reason only, independently of divine revelation, commit blunders. One of the objections raised by disbelievers against Muslims was that, although they professed to be devoted to God, yet they did not partake of the flesh of the animal that was killed by God (meaning the animal that died of itself), while they cheerfully partook of the flesh of animals which they themselves killed (*i.e.* slaughtered animals). This is the kind of objection which is sometimes raised by men who depend merely on reason and think themselves to be independent of divine revelation. The verse incidentally answers this objection by hinting that it is not a question of who kills the animal. The question is, who follows the commandment of God and who partakes of his food in His name. Certainly only he who acts upon the commandment of God and eats in His name will win His pleasure.

120. And what reason have you that you should not eat of that over which the name of Allah has been pronounced, when ^aHe has already explained to you that which He has forbidden unto you,—save that which you are forced to ? And surely many mislead *others* by their evil desires through lack of knowledge. Assuredly, thy Lord knows best the transgressors.[861]

121. And ^beschew open sins as well as secret ones. Surely, those who earn sin will be rewarded for that which they have earned.[862]

^a2 : 174 ; 5 : 4-5 ; 6 : 146 ; 16 : 116.   ^b6 : 152 ; 7 : 34.

861. Commentary :

In this verse the objection of disbelievers has been answered in the very words in which it was made. Their objection was that Muslims profess to be devoted to the name of Allah, yet they do not eat of the flesh of the animal killed by God *i.e.* the animal that dies of itself. The answer given in the present verse is, "when we are devoted to Allah, why should we not eat of the food on which the name of our Lord is pronounced ?" But the name of God is not pronounced on an animal that dies of itself. Its death takes place under the general law of nature.

The words, *He has already explained*, refer to 16 : 116, which was revealed earlier.

The word "mislead" signifies that man-made teachings, which are given by most men in opposition to the teachings of God, only lead people astray.

The word "transgressors" at the end of the verse indicates that the objections raised against the teachings of God have their source in malice and enmity and those who bring forward such objections are indeed transgressors.

862. Commentary :

There are certain things which are manifestly evil and there are others which appear to be good but are really evil ; or even if they do not appear to be good, their evil nature lies concealed and is not apparent. The Quran enjoins Muslims here to abstain from both, for such is the requirement of true piety.

The verse beautifully explains why it is forbidden to eat such animals as die of themselves or such as are not duly slaughtered by pronouncing thereupon the name of God. The pronouncing of the name of God exercises only a subtle influence. It brings about no physical change in the flesh, but it does produce a sanctifying effect on the heart. The killing of an animal is likely to harden the heart. But when a man pronounces the name of God at the time of slaughter, he, as it were, says : "I have no right to kill this animal of my own accord, but Allah Whose creation and property it is has granted me permission to do so." This mental attitude will insure the heart against becoming hardened. Moreover, the pronouncing of the name of God is meant to be a guarantee that the animal is being

122. And *eat not of that on which the name of Allah has not been pronounced, for surely that is disobedience. And certainly the evil ones inspire their friends that they may dispute with you. And if you obey them, you will indeed be setting up gods *with God.*[863]

وَلَا تَأْكُلُوْا مِمَّا لَمْ يُذْكَرِ اسْمُ اللّٰهِ عَلَيْهِ وَاِنَّهٗ لَفِسْقٌ ۗ وَاِنَّ الشَّيٰطِيْنَ لَيُوْحُوْنَ اِلٰۤى اَوْلِيٰٓـِٕهِمْ لِيُجَادِلُوْكُمْ ۚ وَاِنْ اَطَعْتُمُوْهُمْ اِنَّكُمْ لَمُشْرِكُوْنَ ۟

15. 123. Can *he, who was dead and We gave him life and made for him a light whereby he walks among men, be like him whose condition is *that he is* in utter darkness whence he cannot come forth? *Thus have the doings of the disbelievers been made *to seem* fair to them.[864]

اَوَمَنْ كَانَ مَيْتًا فَاَحْيَيْنٰهُ وَجَعَلْنَا لَهٗ نُوْرًا يَّمْشِيْ بِهٖ فِى النَّاسِ كَمَنْ مَّثَلُهٗ فِى الظُّلُمٰتِ لَيْسَ بِخَارِجٍ مِّنْهَا ۗ كَذٰلِكَ زُيِّنَ لِلْكٰفِرِيْنَ مَا كَانُوْا يَعْمَلُوْنَ ۟

---

*5 : 4; 6 : 146.   *8 : 25.   *6 : 109; 10 : 13; 27 : 5.

---

slaughtered in the name of the Lord and Master of the universe and not in that of any other.

It was on a similar principle that 'Umar, Second Successor of the Holy Prophet, acted when, while kissing the Blackstone at the time of performing the طواف or circuit of the Ka'ba, he addressed it in the memorable words: "I know thou art only a stone, but I kiss thee because I saw the Prophet of God kiss thee" (Bukhārī, ch. on *Hajj*). By so saying, he pointed to the great truth that devotion to God should make man averse from paying homage to anything beside Him and that all actions of man should be performed for God.

863. Commentary:

The verse points out that if believers eat of the flesh of those animals on which the name of God has not been pronounced, it will be an act of disobedience and transgression.

One sin leads to another. If a believer fails to pronounce the name of God on his food, his heart becomes devoid of reverence for Him and this gradually leads to شرك *i.e.*

associating partners with God.

864. Commentary:

In the foregoing verses it was pointed out that man-made teachings are always defective. Now the Quran proceeds to show that man-made teachings cannot stand against divine teachings.

The verse purports to put the question: "If there is a teaching which is really from God, will it not be better than that devised by man?" Now, this is a question which every man, even a disbeliever, will have to reply in the affirmative. Indeed, human reason cannot have the boldness to deny it. The question has thus been put to make disbelievers conscious of a great truth.

The expression, *he is in utter darkness whence he cannot come forth,* refers to the man who devises laws with the aid of reason alone— reason that is fettered by numberless limitations to which man is subject. The laws made by men are always subject to change owing to their intrinsic defectiveness. A law

124. And thus ^ahave We made in every town the great ones from among its sinners *such as are in utter darkness* with the result that they plot therein; and they plot not except against their own souls; but they perceive not.[865]

وَكَذٰلِكَ جَعَلْنَا فِيْ كُلِّ قَرْيَةٍ اَكٰبِرَ مُجْرِمِيْهَا لِيَمْكُرُوْا فِيْهَا ۖ وَمَا يَمْكُرُوْنَ اِلَّا بِاَنْفُسِهِمْ وَمَا يَشْعُرُوْنَ ۝

125. And when there comes to them a Sign, they say, ^b'We will not believe until we are given the like of that which Allah's Messengers have been given.' Allah knows best where to place His message. Surely, humiliation before Allah and a severe punishment shall smite the offenders because of their plotting.[866]

وَاِذَا جَآءَتْهُمْ اٰيَةٌ قَالُوْا لَنْ نُّؤْمِنَ حَتّٰى نُؤْتٰى مِثْلَ مَآ اُوْتِيَ رُسُلُ اللّٰهِ ۘ اَللّٰهُ اَعْلَمُ حَيْثُ يَجْعَلُ رِسَالَتَهٗ ۗ سَيُصِيْبُ الَّذِيْنَ اَجْرَمُوْا صَغَارٌ عِنْدَ اللّٰهِ وَعَذَابٌ شَدِيْدٌ ۢبِمَا كَانُوْا يَمْكُرُوْنَ ۝

---

*a*17 : 17.   *b*28 : 49.

---

is made today but it has to be changed tomorrow on account of the defects which by experience are found in it. Then the new law is again changed for the same reason, and this process goes on indefinitely and sometimes even a sort of a circle comes into being. Thus the case of such men as devise their laws with the aid of human reason alone is like one who is in darkness from which he will never come out.

The words, *made to seem fair*, imply that Satan and his associates adorn the evil doings of men. In the beginning it is Satan who misleads men by inciting them to evil. But when a man goes on doing evil deeds, his evil deeds gradually begin to appear good to him. This is the law of God meant as a punishment. It is to this later adornment of deeds under the law of God that the Quran refers in 6 : 109 above.

865. Commentary :

The verse is rather difficult to translate. Some translators make the word اكٰبر (great ones) the first object of the verb جعلنا (have We made) and the word مجرميها (its sinners) the second object. But the better rendering and

one more befitting the context is to treat the words اكٰبر and مجرميها as مضاف and مضاف اليه making them jointly the first object of جعلنا and supplying the second object from the expression "in utter darkness" occurring in the preceding verse. Similarly the لام in ليمكروا is not لام تعليل but لام عاقبة.

We are told in 6 : 113 above that it is the law of God that wicked leaders from among the common people and from among the big ones are always hostile to the Prophets of God. It is to these wicked leaders that the verse under comment refers. They are surrounded by utter darkness from which they never emerge (see the preceding verse).

866. Commentary :

The verse embodies the last argument or the last excuse of disbelievers in the present discussion. They say, "We will never believe in divine revelation until we also receive revelation like unto the revelation of the Messengers of God. If God speaks to them, let Him speak to us also."

God answers this foolish objection by saying, "It is not to every man that God speaks; He

126. So, whomsoever Allah wishes to guide, He expands his bosom for *the acceptance* of Islam; and as to him whom He wishes to *let* go astray, He makes his bosom narrow *and* close, as though he were mounting up into the skies. Thus does [a]Allah inflict punishment on those who do not believe.[867]

فَمَنْ يُّرِدِ اللهُ اَنْ يَّهْدِيَهُ يَشْرَحْ صَدْرَهُ لِلْاِسْلَامِ ۚ وَمَنْ يُّرِدْ اَنْ يُّضِلَّهُ يَجْعَلْ صَدْرَهُ ضَيِّقًا حَرَجًا كَاَنَّمَا يَصَّعَّدُ فِى السَّمَاءِ ۚ كَذٰلِكَ يَجْعَلُ اللهُ الرِّجْسَ عَلَى الَّذِيْنَ لَا يُؤْمِنُوْنَ ۝

127. And [b]this is the path of thy Lord *leading* straight *to Him*. We have, indeed, explained the Signs in detail for a people who would be admonished.

وَهٰذَا صِرَاطُ رَبِّكَ مُسْتَقِيْمًا ۗ قَدْ فَصَّلْنَا الْاٰيٰتِ لِقَوْمٍ يَّذَّكَّرُوْنَ ۝

---

[a]10:101.   [b]6:154.

---

speaks only to him whom He finds worthy of it and whom He selects for the purpose." As for those who make themselves deserving of humiliation and abasement, they cannot be honoured with messages from God. Their doom is only " humiliation and a severe punishment."

867. Important Words :

حرجا (close) means, close, strait or narrow (Lane). See also 4:66.

رجس (punishment). See 5:91.

Commentary :

The desire of Allah mentioned in the words, *whomsoever Allah wishes to guide,* follows the actions of man. It is the result of man's own good deeds, and not arbitrary.

The words, *He expands his bosom for the acceptance of Islam,* signify that such a one is cheerfully willing to accept and obey every command of God. He feels pleasure in obeying God's behests. If a man is always ready and willing to obey the commandments of God, it shows that he is progressing spiritually. But if a man feels divine commandments to be a burden, it is an indication of the fact that

he is spiritually retrogressing.

The " wish " of Allah to make a man go astray also comes as a sequence to man's own evil deeds. When a man becomes a sinner and does wicked deeds the result is that he is led astray from the right path. Such a one feels the commandments of God to be burdensome, and perceives difficulty and mental trouble in carrying them out. His bosom becomes narrow and close. His case is like that of a person who is asked to climb up a steep height.

It may be noted here in passing that the verse hints that to ascend into heaven with the physical body is a sort of punishment and not a boon.

The verse tells us that God helps those who practise virtue and willingly obey His commandments and He causes them to progress spiritually, while those who do not believe and lead sinful lives continue to advance in sin and wickedness.

The verse further teaches us that we cannot progress spiritually unless we render obedience to God with willing and cheerful hearts.

128. For them is *the abode of peace with their Lord, and He is their Friend because of their works.**868**

129. And *b*on the day when He will gather them all together, *He will say,* 'O company of Jinn! you sought *to make subservient to yourselves* a great many from among men!' And their friends from among men will say, ' Our Lord ! we profited from one another but now we have reached our term which Thou didst appoint for us.' He will say, ' The Fire is your abode, wherein you shall abide, save what Allah may will.' Surely, thy Lord is Wise, All-Knowing.**869**

لَهُمْ دَارُ السَّلَامِ عِنْدَ رَبِّهِمْ وَهُوَ وَلِيُّهُمْ بِمَا كَانُوا يَعْمَلُونَ ۞

وَيَوْمَ يَحْشُرُهُمْ جَمِيعًا يَا مَعْشَرَ الْجِنِّ قَدِ اسْتَكْثَرْتُمْ مِنَ الْإِنْسِ وَقَالَ أَوْلِيَاؤُهُمْ مِنَ الْإِنْسِ رَبَّنَا اسْتَمْتَعَ بَعْضُنَا بِبَعْضٍ وَبَلَغْنَا أَجَلَنَا الَّذِي أَجَّلْتَ لَنَا قَالَ النَّارُ مَثْوَاكُمْ خَالِدِينَ فِيهَا إِلَّا مَا شَاءَ اللَّهُ إِنَّ رَبَّكَ حَكِيمٌ عَلِيمٌ ۞

---

*a*10 : 26. *b*7 : 39-40 ; 10 : 29 ; 34 : 32.

---

868. Commentary :

As سلام (peace) is also one of the names of God, the expression دار السلام may also be rendered as the abode of God *i.e.* the presence of God. The virtuous are thus promised the reward of God's nearness.

869. Important Words :

معشر (company) is derived from عشر. They say عشر المال *i.e.*, he took one tenth of the property. عشرهم means, he took one from among them, they being ten. عشرة and عشر mean, ten. معشر means, a company ; a collective body ; a community ; a family. It is so called because a company or community consists of many individuals, the word عشرة (ten) being that large and perfect number after which there is no number but what is composed of the units comprised in it (Lane).

الجن (Jinn) is derived from جن (janna). They say جنه *i.e.* he veiled, concealed, hid, covered or protected him or it. That is the primary significance which is retained in all the derivations of the word. Thus a garden is known as جنة (jannat) because its trees cover or conceal the ground. A child in its mother's womb is known as جنين because it lies concealed in the womb. The heart is known as جنان because it lies concealed in the bosom. A grave is known as جفن because it conceals the dead body. The piece of cloth worn by a woman is known as جنة (junna) because it covers her head and bosom. A shield is known as مجنة because it covers and protects the fighter. Madness or insanity is known as جنون because it obscures and, as it were, veils the faculty of reason. A serpent is known as جان because it generally lies concealed in holes or dark corners. Similarly, جن (Jinn) are so called because they are considered to be invisible bodies concealed from human sight. جن also means the prime or first part of a thing, probably because it covers or conceals the main body that follows (Lisān & Tāj). For a fuller discussion of the word and an explanation of the Jinn see note on 15 : 28. See also 6 : 101.

استكثرتم (you sought to make subservient to yourselves a great many) is derived from كثر.

which means, it was or became much or abundant or many or numerous. استكثر من الشيئ means, he desired or wished much of the thing; or he reckoned it much, abundant or many (Lane). استكثرتم منهم signifies, you have misled many of them; or you have made many of them follow you; or you have made them subservient to yourselves (Kashshāf).

مثوى (abode) is derived from ثوى. They say ثوى بالمكان i.e. he remained, stayed, or abode in the place; or he stayed or dwelt long in it; he settled in the place; he alighted at the place. So مثوى means, a place where one remains, stays, dwells or abides; an abode or a dwelling; a place of alighting (Lane).

Commentary :

The verse definitely proves that at least here the Quran does not use the word *Jinn* to signify a species other than mankind. The very words and the only possible signification of the verse contradict that sense. The word as used in this verse, which thus holds a sort of key position, cannot but mean great and powerful men as opposed to the weak and poor classes. The word جن as shown under Important Words is derived from a root which means to hide or conceal. As the beings properly known as *Jinn* are hidden from the eyes of men, therefore they have been called جن. The great men have also been called *Jinn* because they very rarely mix with the general public and remain, as it were, hidden from them.

The sentence قد استكثرتم من الانس (you have sought to make subservient to yourselves a great many from among men) has two meanings: (1) you have taken to yourselves many from among the masses, *i.e.*, you have won them over to your side and made them follow you and have thus misled them; (2) you have

reckoned the masses to be many (as against God), *i.e.*, you have attached more importance to the masses than to God; you did not accept the truth out of fear of the masses, lest they should desert you and cease to hold you in honour. It is indeed strange that just as the weak do not sometimes accept the truth out of fear of the great, lest they should inflict loss or pain on them, similarly the great are sometimes afraid of their humbler followers and do not accept the truth, fearing lest the latter should turn away from them and desert them. Heraclius, for instance, was convinced of the truth of the Holy Prophet but did not openly acknowledge it out of the fear of his subjects who, he thought, were bitterly opposed to Islam and would rebel against him, if he declared his faith (Bukhārī).

The words, *we profited from one another*, imply that the friendships of disbelievers are also transitory and that they will fall out among themselves on the Day of Judgement. The poor will say : " We led lives of humiliation in subjection to the big ones who derived profit from us. So, O Lord, inflict upon them a double punishment." This also shows that the word *Jinn*, here, does not refer to any creatures separate from human beings, but to a special class of men ; for if taken in that sense the above-quoted words cannot apply to them, for human beings do not profit from the genii nor the genii from human beings. It is only one class of man that profits by the other, *i.e.* the great profit by the poor and *vice versa*.

The words, *The Fire is your abode*, are addressed to the humble class of people who pleaded that they were merely tools in the hands of the great. They are told that no pleading can do them any good now, and that they must enter the Fire and remain there until God is pleased to deliver them therefrom. Both the big and the poor are alike guilty.

130. And in like manner do We set some of the wrongdoers over the others because of what they earned.[870]

وَكَذٰلِكَ نُوَلِّيْ بَعْضَ الظّٰلِمِيْنَ بَعْضًۢا بِمَا كَانُوْا يَكْسِبُوْنَ ۝

R. 16. 131. [a]'O company of Jinn and men! did not Messengers come to you from among yourselves who related to you My Signs and who warned you of the meeting of this your day!' They will say, 'We bear witness against ourselves.' And the worldly life deceived them. And [b]they will bear witness against themselves that they were disbelievers.[871]

يٰمَعْشَرَ الْجِنِّ وَالْاِنْسِ اَلَمْ يَاْتِكُمْ رُسُلٌ مِّنْكُمْ يَقُصُّوْنَ عَلَيْكُمْ اٰيٰتِيْ وَيُنْذِرُوْنَكُمْ لِقَآءَ يَوْمِكُمْ هٰذَا ۚ قَالُوْا شَهِدْنَا عَلٰٓى اَنْفُسِنَا وَغَرَّتْهُمُ الْحَيٰوةُ الدُّنْيَا وَشَهِدُوْا عَلٰٓى اَنْفُسِهِمْ اَنَّهُمْ كَانُوْا كٰفِرِيْنَ ۝

132. That is because [c]thy Lord would not destroy the towns unjustly while their people were unwarned.[872]

ذٰلِكَ اَنْ لَّمْ يَكُنْ رَّبُّكَ مُهْلِكَ الْقُرٰى بِظُلْمٍ وَّاَهْلُهَا غٰفِلُوْنَ ۝

---

[a]39 : 72 ; 40 : 51 ; 67 : 9-10.   [b]7 : 38.   [c]11 : 118 ; 20 : 135 ; 26 : 209 ; 28 : 60.

---

870. Commentary :

The verse signifies that actually both the poor and the great are wrongdoers and it is on account of their sins that the poor become tools in the hands of the great.

This verse provides another proof of the fact that by the word جنّ (*Jinn*) is here meant only a class of human beings, viz., the great and the powerful, for it is only one class of men that is set over the other. *Jinn* as beings different from men have never been set over men, nor men over *Jinn*.

871. Commentary :

The words, *Messengers from among yourselves,* supply further evidence of the fact that the word *Jinn* does not here refer to a separate creation but to only a section of human beings. We learn from the Quran that Moses and the Holy Prophet were sent as Messengers to *Jinn* also (46 : 30-33 ; 72 : 2-16.) and we find no trace of any separate Messengers having ever

been raised from among *Jinn*, which shows that the word *Jinn* here refers only to a special class of men. It may also be noted here that this word when applied to the great and powerful persons from among men is generally used in a bad sense, being applied to the wicked among them.

872. Commentary :

The word القرى (towns) refers to all those cities, towns and villages to which a Prophet of God is sent. As the Holy Prophet was raised for all mankind, the word would, in his case, apply to the whole world.

The expression بظلم (unjustly) also means, "by reason of their iniquity." The verse would then be translated : "That is because thy Lord would not destroy the towns on account of their iniquity, while their people were unwarned."

The verse gives an important law of God—that He never sends general calamities upon

133. And for all are degrees *of rank* according to what they do, and thy Lord is not unmindful of what they do.

وَلِكُلٍّ دَرَجَاتٌ مِّمَّا عَمِلُوا ۚ وَمَا رَبُّكَ بِغَافِلٍ عَمَّا يَعْمَلُونَ ۝

134. And thy Lord is Self-Sufficient, ᵃfull of mercy. If He please, ᵇHe can do away with you and cause to succeed you what He pleases, even as He raised you from the offspring of other people.⁸⁷³

وَرَبُّكَ الْغَنِيُّ ذُو الرَّحْمَةِ ۚ إِن يَشَأْ يُذْهِبْكُمْ وَيَسْتَخْلِفْ مِنْ بَعْدِكُمْ مَّا يَشَاءُ كَمَا أَنشَأَكُم مِّن ذُرِّيَّةِ قَوْمٍ آخَرِينَ ۝

135. Surely, ᶜthat which you are promised shall come to pass and you cannot frustrate *it*.⁸⁷⁴

إِنَّ مَا تُوعَدُونَ لَآتٍ ۖ وَّمَا أَنتُم بِمُعْجِزِينَ ۝

ᵃ6 : 148; 18 : 59.   ᵇ4 : 134; 14 : 20; 35 : 17.   ᶜ11 : 34; 42 : 32.

---

cities on account of their iniquities, unless He first warns them of the impending punishment by sending a warner.

If God had destroyed cities without first raising a Messenger, the people might have excused themselves by saying that, being unwarned, they were following their own reason. After receiving a warner, however, they have no excuse left to them. The world has been visited with widespread calamities in the present age, and in accordance with the law enunciated in the verse under comment, there must have appeared a warner in this age too. There has indeed come a great warner in the person of Ahmad of Qadian, the Promised Messiah, Founder of the Ahmadiyya Movement, who has warned the world of impending disasters and called it to repentance. Let the God-fearing ponder over it.

The verse also shows that the calamities here referred to are not calamities which overtake individuals only, but general calamities which smite whole peoples and nations, as has been the case in the present age.

873. Commentary :

The divine attribute of الغني (Self-Sufficient) means, " one able to do without others " (see 2 : 264). As God is Self-Sufficient, He can punish rejectors as and when He desires; but He is also full of mercy, therefore He delays the hour of punishment.

The words مايشاء (what He pleases) have been used in preference to من يشاء (whom He pleases) in order to combine the idea of " any other people " with that of " in any other state or condition."

874. Important Words :

معجزين (frustrate) is derived from اعجز which again is derived from عجز which means, he lacked strength, power or ability; he was or became powerless. اعجزه means, he found him to be without strength, power or ability; or he made him to be without strength, power or ability; or he disabled or incapacitated him; or he rendered him unable to accomplish or attain his object; or he frustrated his endeavours; or he escaped him (Lane).

136. Say, *a*' O my people, act as best you can. I, too, am acting. Soon will you know whose will be the ultimate reward of the abode.' Surely, the wrongdoers shall not prosper.[875]

قُلْ يٰقَوْمِ اعْمَلُوا عَلٰى مَكَانَتِكُمْ اِنِّیْ عَامِلٌ فَسَوْفَ تَعْلَمُوْنَ مَنْ تَكُوْنُ لَهٗ عَاقِبَةُ الدَّارِ اِنَّهٗ لَا يُفْلِحُ الظّٰلِمُوْنَ ۱۳۶

*a*11 : 94, 122 ; 39 : 40-41.

Commentary :

The words, *that which you are promised*, refer to the promise of destruction contained in the previous verse. The chapter was revealed at Mecca, when Muslims were few and weak while their enemies were strong and numerous and were subjecting them to bitter persecution with a view to annihilating Islam. In these circumstances the prophecy relating to the destruction of the enemy in such forceful words and in such tones of certainty could not be made by the helpless man that the Holy Prophet at that time was. It could proceed from none but the Almighty God, Who alone could bring about its fulfilment ; and it is writ large on the pages of history how the prophecy was fulfilled. The same prophecy or challenge is continued in the next verse in equally forceful words.

875. Important Words :

مَكَانَتِكُمْ (as best you can). The word مَكَان is considered by some to have been derived from كَانَ which means, he or it was, or he or it came into existence. مَكَان means, place of being or existence. مَكَانَة means, place of being or existence ; state or condition. The Arabs say مَكَانَكَ و زَيْدًا *i.e.*, keep where

thou art and approach not Zaid (Lane & Aqrab). The expression مَكَانَتِكُمْ means, do what you can ; or act as best you can ; or remain where you are and do your worst (Kashshāf). Some authorities, however, consider the word to have been derived from مَكُنَ in which case it signifies greatness ; or high rank or standing ; or honourable place or position, especially with a king or potentate (Aqrab & Lane). In this sense the expression would mean, you look upon yourselves to be great or high in rank. Now come and exert your full power against Islam and then see what the result will be.

Commentary :

As explained under Important Words, the expression اعْمَلُوا عَلٰى مَكَانَتِكُمْ means, you may do your worst and exert yourselves to the utmost of your power and resources to extirpate Islam and destroy the small Muslim community, but you will never succeed.

The words, *Soon will you know whose will be the ultimate reward*, signify, " you will soon see which of the two parties will succeed in the end." The word الدَّار (abode) may refer either to this world or to the next. In both cases the ultimate reward is reserved for the truthful.

137. And ^athey have assigned Allah a portion of the crops and cattle which He has produced, and they say, ' This is for Allah,' as they imagine, ' and this is for our idols.' But that which is for their idols reaches not Allah, while that which is for Allah reaches their idols. Evil is what they judge.[876]

وَجَعَلُوْا لِلّٰهِ مِمَّا ذَرَاَ مِنَ الْحَرْثِ وَالْاَنْعَامِ نَصِيْبًا فَقَالُوْا هٰذَا لِلّٰهِ بِزَعْمِهِمْ وَ هٰذَا لِشُرَكَآئِنَا ۚ فَمَا كَانَ لِشُرَكَآئِهِمْ فَلَا يَصِلُ اِلَى اللّٰهِ ۚ وَ مَا كَانَ لِلّٰهِ فَهُوَ يَصِلُ اِلٰى شُرَكَآئِهِمْ ۗ سَآءَ مَا يَحْكُمُوْنَ ۝

138. And in like manner have their associate-gods made the killing of their children appear beautiful to many of the idolaters that they may ruin them and cause them confusion in their religion. And if Allah had enforced *His* will, they would not have done this ; so leave them alone with that which they invent.[877]

وَكَذٰلِكَ زَيَّنَ لِكَثِيْرٍ مِّنَ الْمُشْرِكِيْنَ قَتْلَ اَوْلَادِهِمْ شُرَكَآؤُهُمْ لِيُرْدُوْهُمْ وَلِيَلْبِسُوْا عَلَيْهِمْ دِيْنَهُمْ ۗ وَلَوْ شَآءَ اللّٰهُ مَا فَعَلُوْهُ فَذَرْهُمْ وَمَا يَفْتَرُوْنَ ۝

---

*a*16 : 57.

---

876. Commentary :

Note the point and the force in the words, *He has produced.* By using these words, the Quran exposes the folly of disbelievers, who are presumptuous enough to divide the produce of the earth and cattle between their deities and God, as if they were the owners ; while the fact is that God is the owner of all these things and it is He Who has brought them into existence. They are God's things, and it is strange that disbelievers should presume to divide God's things according to their own choice, setting apart only a portion for God, the true owner, and allotting the rest to their false deities.

Disbelievers gave two kinds of alms ; firstly, in the name of God, and secondly, in the name of their deities. If the portion which they set apart for their deities was spent for other purposes, then the portion which they had reserved for God was also given away as charity in the name of their deities, but if the portion set apart for God was spent for other ends, then the portion set aside for the deities

was not transferred to God. That is what is meant by the words, *that which is for their idols reaches not Allah, while that which is for Allah reaches their idols.* This is another instance of how men blunder, making laws with the sole aid of reason.

The expression, *as they imagine,* signifies that God does not accept a charity which false gods are made to share with Him. Disbelievers suppose that they have set apart a portion for God, but that is not really the portion of God, for the jealous God disdainfully rejects such allotment.

877. Commentary :

The " associate-gods " here referred to are diviners, soothsayers and others. The " killing of children " happened in three ways : (1) some of the Arabs killed their female children and preserved the male ones ; (2) some took the vow that if they had a certain number of children, whether male or female, one of them would be slaughtered in the name of God or in

139. And they say, ' Such and such cattle and crops are forbidden. None shall eat thereof save whom we please ' —so they allege—and there are cattle whose backs are forbidden, and there are cattle over which they pronounce not the name of Allah, forging a lie against Him. Soon will He requite them for that which they have fabricated.[878]

وَقَالُوا هٰذِهٖ أَنْعَامٌ وَّحَرْثٌ حِجْرٌ ۤ لَّا يَطْعَمُهَآ إِلَّا مَنْ نَّشَآءُ بِزَعْمِهِمْ وَ أَنْعَامٌ حُرِّمَتْ ظُهُورُهَا وَأَنْعَامٌ لَّا يَذْكُرُونَ اسْمَ اللّٰهِ عَلَيْهَا افْتِرَآءً عَلَيْهِ ۚ سَيَجْزِيهِمْ بِمَا كَانُوْا يَفْتَرُوْنَ ۝

140. And they say, ' That which is in the wombs of such and such cattle is exclusively reserved for our males and is forbidden to our wives ; but if it be born dead, then they are all partakers thereof. He will reward them for their assertion. Surely, He is Wise, All-Knowing.[879]

وَقَالُوا مَا فِيْ بُطُونِ هٰذِهِ الْأَنْعَامِ خَالِصَةٌ لِّذُكُورِنَا وَمُحَرَّمٌ عَلٰۤى أَزْوَاجِنَا ۚ وَإِنْ يَّكُنْ مَّيْتَةً فَهُمْ فِيْهِ شُرَكَآءُ ۚ سَيَجْزِيهِمْ وَصْفَهُمْ ۚ إِنَّهُ حَكِيمٌ عَلِيمٌ ۝

---

the name of one of their deities ; and (3) sometimes they sacrificed their children to avert a calamity.

The word كثير (many) in the expression, *to many of the idolaters*, shows that all Arabs did not indulge in this practice, nor even most of them, but only a considerable number. But, whatever the number, the practice provides one more instance of how men go astray when they begin to make laws for themselves with the sole aid of reason.

The particle ل (that) in ليردوهم (that they may ruin them) is here used to express عاقبة (the result) and not the cause or motive. Thus the sentence would mean that the result of the action of the associate-gods was that men who followed them were spiritually ruined. When a man goes so far as even to sacrifice his son in obedience to another person's bidding, then he is entirely under the latter's control and is thus completely ruined in respect of religion.

878. Important Words :

حجر (forbidden). حجره (*hajara-hū*) means, he

prevented or prohibited or forbade or interdicted him ; or he deprived him. حجر (*hijr*) means, forbidden or prohibited or unlawful ; the faculty of reason or understanding, because it prevents one from doing improper acts. The word also means custody or guardianship (Aqrab).

Commentary :

This verse gives another instance of the absurdity of man-made laws.

By "forbidden crops" are meant such cultivated fields as were dedicated to idols. These could be used only by the priests that attended upon the idols. The cattle might eat of all crops except those that were dedicated to idols.

The cattle whose backs were forbidden are those mentioned in 5 : 104. Nobody was allowed to ride them or use them as beasts of burden.

The *cattle over which they pronounce not the name of Allah* are the cattle which they dedicated to their associate-gods. There is no reference here to the mentioning of God's name at the time of slaughtering.

879. Commentary :

The verse refers to another absurd custom

141. Losers indeed are they who kill their children foolishly for lack of knowledge, and make unlawful what Allah has provided for them, forging a lie against Allah. They have indeed gone astray and are not rightly guided.[880]

قَدْ خَسِرَ الَّذِينَ قَتَلُوا اَوْلَادَهُمْ سَفَهًا بِغَيْرِ عِلْمٍ وَّحَرَّمُوا مَا رَزَقَهُمُ اللّٰهُ افْتِرَاءً عَلَى اللّٰهِ ۚ قَدْ ضَلُّوا وَمَا كَانُوا مُهْتَدِينَ ۞

17 142. And [a]He it is Who brings into being gardens, trellised and untrellised, and the date-palm and cornfields whose fruits are of diverse kinds, and the olive and the pomegranate, alike and unlike. Eat of the fruit of each when it bears fruit, but pay His due on the day of harvest and exceed not the bounds. Surely, Allah loves not those who exceed the bounds.[881]

وَهُوَ الَّذِيۤ اَنْشَاَ جَنّٰتٍ مَّعْرُوشٰتٍ وَّغَيْرَ مَعْرُوشٰتٍ وَّالنَّخْلَ وَالزَّرْعَ مُخْتَلِفًا اُكُلُهُ وَالزَّيْتُونَ وَالرُّمَّانَ مُتَشَابِهًا وَّغَيْرَ مُتَشَابِهٍ ۚ كُلُوا مِنْ ثَمَرِهِ اِذَاۤ اَثْمَرَ وَاٰتُوا حَقَّهُ يَوْمَ حَصَادِهٖ ۖ وَلَا تُسْرِفُوا ۚ اِنَّهُ لَا يُحِبُّ الْمُسْرِفِينَ ۞

---

[a]6 : 100 ; 13 : 5 ; 16 : 12 ; 35 : 28 ; 36 : 35-36.

---

of the Arabs. The divine attributes "Wise" and "All-Knowing" have been mentioned here to point out that the people got entangled in these foolish beliefs and practices because they turned away from the Wise and Knowing God and followed false deities and their foolish devotees.

880. Commentary :

This verse recapitulates what has been said above about man-made laws. For the killing of children see 6 : 138 above. The words, *for lack of knowledge,* signify that they do so because they do not possess revealed knowledge, which is the only source of true guidance.

881. Important Words :

مَعْرُوشٰت (trellised) is the plural of مَعْرُوشَة and is derived from عرش which means, he built or constructed a framework or a trellis for supporting grape-vines ; or he built a shed or an enclosure, etc. So مَعْرُوشَة means, furnished with or trained on trellises. They say كُرُوم مَعْرُوشٰت *i.e.,* grape-vines furnished

with or trained on trellises which are a framework for supporting the vines. عريش means, structure or trellis made for supporting grape-vines ; an enclosure made for beasts to protect them from cold. عرش means, a shed or booth, etc. constructed for shade ; a hut ; a house or a dwelling ; the roof of a house ; a throne (Lane).

حَصَاد (harvest) is derived from حصد *i.e.* he reaped or cut a seed-produce or herbage, etc. حصيد means, reaped produce. حِصَاد means time or season of reaping ; also fruit or produce (Lane).

Commentary :

In the foregoing verses the Quran referred to some of the laws which pagan Arabs, unaided by divine revelation, had devised for themselves. Now the Quran proceeds to give some of its own laws, so that the reader may contrast them with the man-made laws alluded to above. One of the man-made laws pertained to the fruits of the earth (6 : 141 above) ; the Quran,

143. And of the cattle, *He created* some for burden and some for slaughter. Eat of that which Allah has provided for you, and *a*follow not the footsteps of Satan.. Surely, he is to you an open foe.882

وَ مِنَ الْاَنْعَامِ حَمُوْلَةً وَّ فَرْشًا ۖ كُلُوْا مِمَّا رَزَقَكُمُ اللّٰهُ وَ لَا تَتَّبِعُوْا خُطُوٰتِ الشَّيْطٰنِ ؕ اِنَّهٗ لَكُمْ عَدُوٌّ مُّبِيْنٌ ۟ ﴿١٤٣﴾

---

*a*See 2 : 209.

---

therefore, here gives its laws about these. It declares them to be lawful and pure, subject only to the condition that in eating them we should " not exceed the bounds " *i.e.* we should only eat as much of them as is not injurious to our health and morals.

The pronoun in the words حَقَّهٗ (His due) may either refer to God, or to ثَمَرٌ (fruit). In the former case, the sentence would mean that on the day of reaping we should give as alms what is due to God. In the latter case, it would mean that on the day of reaping we should give as charity a portion of the fruit which is in the nature of something due against it in order to make it pure.

It may be noted here that there are two kinds of charity in Islam—obligatory and optional. But as, according to the practice and sayings of the Holy Prophet, زَكٰوة *i.e.* obligatory charity or legal alms, is not due from all the fruits named in the verse but only from the fruit of the palm tree, so if it is the obligatory charity that is meant here, then the commandment to " pay His due " will apply only to the fruit of palm trees. It is, however, better to take the verse as referring to optional

charity which may be given from all kinds of fruits. The use of the imperative mood in the words " pay His due " does not necessarily make it an obligatory command, for this form of the verb is also freely used in the Quran for the purpose of exhortation. This interpretation is in keeping with the practice of the Holy Prophet's Companions who were in the habit of setting apart a portion of their produce for the poor, and such is also the practice of pious Muslims today.

882. Important Words :

فَرْشًا (for slaughter) is derived from فَرْش. They say فَرْشَهُ *i.e.* he spread it or expanded it ; or he prostrated it ; or he threw it down (for slaughter). فَرْش means, what is spread on the ground, etc. ; a plain tract of land ; a depressed tract of land ; shrubs or small trees ; such animals as are fit for slaughter, or such as are thrown down for slaughter (Lane).

Commentary :

Apart from its primary meaning the verse also hints that the eating of lawful things is a means of ensuring one against the attacks of Satan.

144. *And* ^a*of the cattle He has created* eight mates : of the sheep two, and of the goats two ;—say, Is it the two males that He has forbidden or the two females or that which the wombs of the two females contain ? Inform me with knowledge, if you are truthful.⁸⁸³

ثَمٰنِيَةَ اَزۡوَاجٍ مِنَ الضَّاۡنِ اثۡنَيۡنِ وَمِنَ الۡمَعۡزِ اثۡنَيۡنِ قُلۡ ءٰٓالذَّكَرَيۡنِ حَرَّمَ اَمِ الۡاُنۡثَيَيۡنِ اَمَّا اشۡتَمَلَتۡ عَلَيۡهِ اَرۡحَامُ الۡاُنۡثَيَيۡنِ نَبِّـُٔوۡنِیۡ بِعِلۡمٍ اِنۡ كُنۡتُمۡ صٰدِقِيۡنَ ۝

145. And of the camels two, and of the oxen two. Say, Is it the two males that He has forbidden or the two females or that which the wombs of the two females contain ? Were you present when Allah enjoined this on you ? ^bWho is then more unjust than he who forges a lie against Allah that he may lead men astray without knowledge. Surely Allah guides not the unjust people.⁸⁸⁴

وَمِنَ الۡاِبِلِ اثۡنَيۡنِ وَمِنَ الۡبَقَرِ اثۡنَيۡنِ قُلۡ ءٰٓالذَّكَرَيۡنِ حَرَّمَ اَمِ الۡاُنۡثَيَيۡنِ اَمَّا اشۡتَمَلَتۡ عَلَيۡهِ اَرۡحَامُ الۡاُنۡثَيَيۡنِ اَمۡ كُنۡتُمۡ شُهَدَآءَ اِذۡ وَصّٰىكُمُ اللّٰهُ بِهٰذَا فَمَنۡ اَظۡلَمُ مِمَّنِ افۡتَرٰی عَلَی اللّٰهِ كَذِبًا لِّيُضِلَّ النَّاسَ بِغَيۡرِ عِلۡمٍ اِنَّ اللّٰهَ لَا يَهۡدِی الۡقَوۡمَ الظّٰلِمِيۡنَ ۝

---

^a39 : 7.   ^b6 : 22 ; 7 : 38 ; 11 : 19.

883. Important Words :

اَزۡوَاج (mates) is the plural of زَوۡج (a mate). The word is used to signify, one of the pair, whether male or female and whether among human beings or among animals, or whether among plants or among any class of things.

الضَّاۡن (sheep) is the plural of الضَّاۡئِن (one sheep). The word is applied to all animals of the class of غَنَم (which covers both sheep and goats) having wool (Aqrab & Lane).

الۡمَعۡز (goats) is the generic plural of الۡمَاعِز (one goat). The word is applied to all animals of the class of غَنَم (for which see above) having hair (not wool) and small tails (Aqrab & Lane).

Commentary :

See note under the following verse.

884. Commentary :

Speaking of the laws devised by man, the Quran had referred to some pagan customs with regard to animals (6 : 140, 141). Now it gives its own laws with regard to them.

While speaking of sheep and goats in 6 : 144 above, the Holy Prophet is made here to ask the idolaters to inform him if these animals were unlawful *i.e.* not fit for eating, and to bring forward (as hinted in the words نَبِّـُٔوۡنِی بِعِلۡمٍ *i.e.* inform me with knowledge) some rational argument or scientific reason to show that they should not be eaten. When, however, it speaks of oxen and camels in the present verse, the Quran asks idolaters whether they were witnesses when Allah forbade the eating of these animals. In other words, the verse here calls upon them to produce a religious authority showing that the cow and the camel were really forbidden. This is so because the

R. 18   146. Say, *a*'I find not in what has been revealed to me aught forbidden to an eater *who wishes* to eat it, except it be that which dies of itself or blood poured forth, or the flesh of swine,—for *all* that is unclean—or *b*what is profane, on which is invoked the name of other than Allah. But whoso is driven by necessity, being neither disobedient nor exceeding the limit, then surely thy Lord is Most Forgiving, Merciful.'885

قُلْ لَّا أَجِدُ فِى مَآ أُوحِىَ إِلَىَّ مُحَرَّمًا عَلَى طَاعِمٍ يَطْعَمُهُ إِلَّا أَن يَّكُونَ مَيْتَةً أَوْ دَمًا مَّسْفُوحًا أَوْ لَحْمَ خِنْزِيرٍ فَإِنَّهُ رِجْسٌ أَوْ فِسْقًا أُهِلَّ لِغَيْرِ اللّٰهِ بِهِ ۚ فَمَنِ اضْطُرَّ غَيْرَ بَاغٍ وَّلَا عَادٍ فَإِنَّ رَبَّكَ غَفُورٌ رَّحِيمٌ ۝

---

*a*2 : 174 ; 5 : 4 ; 16 : 116.   *b*6 : 122.

---

cow and the camel are looked upon as forbidden by some on religious authority. For instance, the Hindus think it unlawful to eat beef for religious reasons and the Jews look upon the camel as forbidden by their Scriptures.

This restriction is, however, unjustified ; for as regards beef, it is clearly allowed by the Vedas and was freely used in ancient India not only as ordinary food but also as an essential part of many religious ceremonies (*Indo-Aryans* by R. Mitra LL.D., C.I.E. Rev. Rel. for 1923). As regards the camel, it is indeed forbidden by the Bible, but that prohibition is not meant for all time, for the Bible announces the advent of another Law-giver whose Law was to abrogate the Law of the Bible (Deut. 18 : 18).

The words, *Were you present when Allah enjoined*, signify that when pagans do not believe in any revelation, they cannot possibly know that anything was forbidden by God.

885. **Commentary :**

The verse points out that the laws made by pagan Arabs with regard to permissible and forbidden foods were arbitrary, without any wisdom underlying them ; while the food-laws made by Islam were based on reason and deep wisdom. Fundamentally speaking, Islam forbids four things—three on the basis of their being رجس *i.e.* unclean and impure, and one on the basis of its being فسق *i.e.* profane and irreligious. The three first-mentioned things are (1) carrion, (2) the blood which pours out when an animal is slaughtered or wounded and (3) the flesh of swine. All these are, as the verse says, رجس *i.e.* unclean and impure *i.e.* they are harmful to the physical and moral health of man. The word رجس it must be noted, is to be read with each of the three first-mentioned forbidden things.

The fourth thing forbidden is that on which the name of one other than Allah is pronounced. The reason for the prohibition of this kind of food lies in the fact that such food is, as the verse calls it, فسق *i.e.* profane, *viz.,* a source of disobedience or rebellion against God. The eating of such food will injure the spiritual health of man and will crush his feelings of love and jealousy for God. See also 2 : 174.

147. And ^ato those who are Jews We forbade all animals having claws; and of the oxen and the sheep and goats did We forbid them their fats, save that which their backs bear or the intestines, or that which is mixed with a bone. That is the reward We gave them for their rebellion. And most surely We are truthful.[886]

وَعَلَى الَّذِيْنَ هَادُوْا حَرَّمْنَا كُلَّ ذِيْ ظُفُرٍ ۚ وَمِنَ الْبَقَرِ وَالْغَنَمِ حَرَّمْنَا عَلَيْهِمْ شُحُوْمَهُمَا إِلَّا مَا حَمَلَتْ ظُهُوْرُهُمَا أَوِ الْحَوَايَا أَوْ مَا اخْتَلَطَ بِعَظْمٍ ۚ ذٰلِكَ جَزَيْنٰهُمْ بِبَغْيِهِمْ ۖ وَإِنَّا لَصٰدِقُوْنَ ۝

148. But if they accuse thee of falsehood, say, ^b'Your Lord is possessed of all-embracing mercy, and His wrath shall not be turned back from the guilty people.'[887]

فَإِنْ كَذَّبُوْكَ فَقُلْ رَّبُّكُمْ ذُوْ رَحْمَةٍ وَّاسِعَةٍ ۚ وَلَا يُرَدُّ بَأْسُهُ عَنِ الْقَوْمِ الْمُجْرِمِيْنَ ۝

^a16 : 119.   ^b6 : 134; 7 : 157.

886. Commentary :

The reader is referred to the Bible (Lev. 3 : 17) where it is said, "Ye eat neither fat nor blood." Again, in Lev. 7 : 23 it is said "Ye shall eat no manner of fat of ox or of sheep or of goat." In the Talmud, exception is made of the fat that sticks to the ribs. Similarly, the Jews regard as lawful any fat that cannot be separated from the intestines and the flesh (Enc. Bib. cols. 1544-45). This corroborates the Quran which says, *and of the oxen and the sheep and goats did We forbid them their fats, save that which their backs bear or the intestines, or that which is mixed with a bone.*

It is declared in the previous verse that the only things forbidden in Islam are (1) carrion, (2) blood poured forth, (3) flesh of swine, and (4) the slaughtered animal on which the name of any one other than God is pronounced. The Jews might, however, say that there are other things beside the above which are also forbidden

them by God. The Quran therefore adds that it is true that there are other foods which are forbidden to Jews, but they have not been included in the prohibited things here enumerated, for these things had been forbidden them not because they were unclean but as a punishment for their transgression. So the declaration of the previous verse still remains true.

887. Commentary :

The verse answers an implied objection of the Jews, *viz*, if God had forbidden them certain extra things, why was not the prohibition continued in Islam? The verse answers this objection by saying that whereas the divine law of punishment demanded that Jews should be punished, the law of mercy demanded that Muslims should be shown mercy. It was unfair to continue a special prohibition that had been imposed by way of punishment under a new dispensation.

149. *a*Those who join gods with God will say, 'If Allah had pleased, we could not have joined gods with Him, nor could our fathers ; nor could we have made anything unlawful.' In like manner did those who were before them accuse *God's Messengers* of falsehood, until they tasted of Our wrath. Say, 'Have you any knowledge ? Then produce it for us. You follow nothing but *mere* conjecture. And you do nothing but lie.'888

سَيَقُوْلُ الَّذِيْنَ اَشْرَكُوْا لَوْ شَاۤءَ اللهُ مَاۤ اَشْرَكْنَا وَ لَاۤ اٰبَاۤؤُنَا وَ لَا حَرَّمْنَا مِنْ شَيْءٍ ۚ كَذٰلِكَ كَذَّبَ الَّذِيْنَ مِنْ قَبْلِهِمْ حَتّٰى ذَاقُوْا بَأْسَنَا ۚ قُلْ هَلْ عِنْدَكُمْ مِّنْ عِلْمٍ فَتُخْرِجُوْهُ لَنَا ۚ اِنْ تَتَّبِعُوْنَ اِلَّا الظَّنَّ وَ اِنْ اَنْتُمْ اِلَّا تَخْرُصُوْنَ ۝

150. Say, ' Allah's is the argument that reaches *home*. *b*If He had enforced *His* will, He could have surely guided you all.'889

قُلْ فَلِلّٰهِ الْحُجَّةُ الْبَالِغَةُ ۚ فَلَوْ شَاۤءَ لَهَدٰىكُمْ اَجْمَعِيْنَ ۝

---

*a*16 : 36 ; 43 : 21   *b*5 : 49 ; 11 : 119 ; 13 : 32 ; 16 : 10.

888. Commentary :

Being unable to answer the arguments given against idolatry and man-made laws in the foregoing passages, idolatrous Arabs had recourse to the trite plea in support of idol-worship: *if Allah had pleased, we could not have joined gods with Him.* From this they inferred that attributing co-partners to God was in accordance with God's will. The Quran gives four answers to this plea, two in the present verse and two in the next. The first answer is contained in the words: *In like manner did those who were before them accuse God's Messengers of falsehood, until they tasted of Our wrath.* These words signify that this plea of theirs is not a new one. The same plea was brought forward by those gone before. If this plea was true, and the act of setting up associates with God was in accordance with God's will, why should He have punished the previous peoples? The very fact that God punished them for their associating gods with Him shows that this act of theirs was not in accordance with His will. The second answer is contained in the words: *Have you any knowledge ? Then produce it for us. You follow nothing but mere conjecture. And you do nothing but lie,* i.e., you possess no argument based on true knowledge to support your assertion ; what you say is mere conjecture. The remaining two answers are given in the next verse.

889. Commentary :

The third answer to the objection mentioned in the preceding verse is given here. The words contained in the previous verse, *i.e.,* If *Allah had pleased, we could not have joined gods with Him* (6 : 149), implied that it was under a sort of compulsion that they had set up associates with God ; it was God's own will and they could not go against His will ; they were helpless against Him. So in the present verse the Quran says that God has no need to resort to compulsion, for *Allah's is the argument that reaches home.* He has arguments which reach the hearts of men. He can bring home to men the wisdom of His commandments ; so He is not under the necessity of forcing

151. Say, 'Bring forward your witnesses who testify that Allah has forbidden this.' If they bear witness, bear thou not witness with them, *a*nor follow thou the evil inclinations of those who treat Our Signs as lies and those who believe not in the Hereafter and *b*who set up equals to their Lord.[890]

قُلْ هَلُمَّ شُهَدَاءَكُمُ الَّذِيْنَ يَشْهَدُوْنَ اَنَّ اللّٰهَ حَرَّمَ هٰذَا ۚ فَاِنْ شَهِدُوْا فَلَا تَشْهَدْ مَعَهُمْ ۚ وَلَا تَتَّبِعْ اَهْوَاءَ الَّذِيْنَ كَذَّبُوْا بِاٰيٰتِنَا وَالَّذِيْنَ لَا يُؤْمِنُوْنَ بِالْاٰخِرَةِ وَهُمْ بِرَبِّهِمْ يَعْدِلُوْنَ ۞

---

*a*5:49; 45:19.   *b*6:2; 27:61.

---

men to do His will. The fourth answer is contained in the words: *if He had enforced His will, He could have surely guided you all.* The words mean that if God had resorted to compulsion and had decided to force men to do His will, He would certainly have made them do things that are right and not the things that are wrong. But in His infinite wisdom He has made man a free agent. He has explained to him what is right and what is wrong, and then has left him free to follow whichever course he may choose; and everyone will reap as he sows.

890. Important Words :

هَلُمَّ (bring forward) is both intransitive and transitive, meaning (1) come ; or (2) cause to come *i.e.* bring forth or produce (Lane). هَلُمَّ (halumma) is, according to the people of the Ḥijāz, one of the words known as اسماء الفعل and is thus used by them in the fixed form whether the number is singular or plural and whether the gender is masculine or feminine ; but others differ from this view (Aqrab).

Commentary :

The Quran now returns to the subject of man-made laws about prohibitions. The verse signifies that disbelievers should declare that they do not agree with the Quran and find its teachings inferior to their own and then God Himself will decide between the two parties. Indirectly the words also hint that everybody should express his opinion freely when he disagrees with others and should refrain from dissimulation.

R. 19   152. Say, 'Come, I will rehearse to you what your Lord has forbidden: [a]that you associate not anything as partner with Him and that you do good to parents, and [b]that you kill not your children for *fear of* poverty,— it is We Who provide for you and for them—and [c]that you approach not foul deeds, whether open or secret; and that you kill not the life which Allah has made sacred, save by right. That is what He has enjoined upon you, that you may understand.'[891]

قُلْ تَعَالَوْا اَتْلُ مَا حَرَّمَ رَبُّكُمْ عَلَيْكُمْ اَلَّا تُشْرِكُوْا بِهٖ شَيْئًا وَّ بِالْوَالِدَيْنِ اِحْسَانًا وَّ لَا تَقْتُلُوْا اَوْلَادَكُمْ مِّنْ اِمْلَاقٍ نَحْنُ نَرْزُقُكُمْ وَ اِيَّاهُمْ وَ لَا تَقْرَبُوا الْفَوَاحِشَ مَا ظَهَرَ مِنْهَا وَ مَا بَطَنَ وَ لَا تَقْتُلُوا النَّفْسَ الَّتِيْ حَرَّمَ اللّٰهُ اِلَّا بِالْحَقِّ ذٰلِكُمْ وَصّٰكُمْ بِهٖ لَعَلَّكُمْ تَعْقِلُوْنَ ۝

[a]4 : 37; 17 : 24.   [b]17 : 32.   [c]6 : 121; 7 : 34.

891. Important Words :

اِمْلَاق (poverty) is derived from ملق. They say ملق الشيئ *i.e.* he erased the thing. ملقه بالعصا means, he beat him with a stick. ملق الولد امه means, the child sucked from the breasts of his mother. املق الرجل means, the man spent all his money and became poor. اِمْلَاق means, poverty or destitution (Aqrab).

Commentary :

The Quran has already given the commandments and prohibitions of the Islamic Law with regard to the fruits of the earth and the flesh of animals, in opposition to the laws devised by men. Now it gives general commandments and prohibitions.

It should be noted that the injunctions which follow the word "forbidden" are what God requires us to do and not what He forbids us to do. Thus it is the contrary of the injunctions given in the verse that is forbidden. The injunctions have been expressly mentioned and the converse of them which is forbidden is implied. Thus, on the one hand, by using the word "forbidden" and, on the other, by following it up with positive commandments, the verse combines in itself both the direct injunctions and their converse, and the attention of the reader has been drawn to both.

The verse may be construed in another way also. The first sentence should be taken as having finished with the words ما حرم ربكم *i.e. what your Lord has forbidden*, and the next sentence should be taken as beginning with the words عليكم which would in this case mean, "it is enjoined upon you or it is incumbent on you." The verse will then read as follows: "Come, I will rehearse to you what your Lord has forbidden. It is incumbent on you that you associate not anything as partner with Him. . . . "

The order in which the injunctions are given in this verse is noteworthy. The injunctions begin with the words, *Come, I will rehearse to you what your Lord has forbidden.* The Arabic word for "Lord" is رب which means "Creator, Sustainer, and Nourisher" (see 1 : 2), and it is the very idea of "sustaining and nourishing" that governs the order of the injunctions here given. The first injunction i.e. *associate not anything as partner with Him,* pertains to the Great Nourisher, Allah. The second injunction pertains to the lesser nourishers, *viz.*, parents. The word احسان

(doing good) expresses the idea that the service of the parents enjoined in the words, *do good to parents,* is to be performed in the best way possible, for احسان literally signifies "doing a thing very well." Next come those who are nourished and sustained by the "lesser nourishers", *viz.,* children. Parents are bidden to nourish and bring up their children well, as implied in the words, *kill not your children for fear of poverty.* Indeed, he who neglects to bring up his children properly for fear of poverty virtually "kills" them. If it is the duty of the children to serve their parents well, it is equally the duty of the parents to bring up their children well.

The pronoun "you" in the clause, *it is We Who provide for you and for them,* refers to parents and the pronoun "them" refers to children, the former being put before the latter in order to draw our attention to the fact that God's providing for the parents is a proof of the fact that He will provide for the children also.

The next injunction is contained in the words, *approach not foul deeds.* The word فواحش (foul deeds) is the plural of فاحشة one meaning of which is "fornication or adultery" (see 4 : 16), which is another form of killing one's children; for the man who forms immoral connection with a woman other than his wife, not only destroys his seed but also neglects his own wife, which

cannot but affect his begetting children in lawful wedlock. Similarly, illegitimate children born of a woman other than one's wife are not one's own children, nor are they properly looked after.

The words, *whether open or secret,* used in connection with فواحش (foul deeds) refer respectively to openly going in to prostitutes and to forming secret connections with women other than one's wife.

Next to the relations between parents and children come brotherly and friendly relations which are referred to in the words, *kill not the life which Allah has made sacred.* This injunction requires us to treat our brethren and friends as well as members of our society with fairness and justice. The word "killing", it will be noted, pertains not only to actually killing but to an attempt at killing as well as causing serious injury and boycotting, etc. (see meaning of قتل *i.e. killing* under 2 : 62 ; 3 : 155 & 4 : 158). The expression, *save by right,* used with regard to "killing" means "except when a man has made himself deserving of the treatment to be meted out to him." For instance, in case of murder a person will be put to death only by order of proper authority. Similarly in case of "boycotting" a person will be boycotted only under the orders of the person or the body that possesses that power. It will not be right for any man to take the law in his own hands.

153.　And ^aapproach not the property of the orphan, except in *a way* which is best, till he attains his maturity. And ^bgive full measure and weight with equity. ^cWe task not any soul except according to its capacity. And when you speak, observe justice, even if a relation be concerned, and ^dfulfil the covenant of Allah. That is what He enjoins upon you, that you may remember.⁸⁹²

وَلَا تَقۡرَبُوۡا مَالَ الۡيَتِيۡمِ اِلَّا بِالَّتِىۡ هِىَ اَحۡسَنُ حَتّٰى يَبۡلُغَ اَشُدَّهٗ ۚ وَاَوۡفُوا الۡكَيۡلَ وَالۡمِيۡزَانَ بِالۡقِسۡطِ ۚ لَا نُكَلِّفُ نَفۡسًا اِلَّا وُسۡعَهَا ۚ وَاِذَا قُلۡتُمۡ فَاعۡدِلُوۡا وَلَوۡ كَانَ ذَا قُرۡبٰى ۚ وَبِعَهۡدِ اللّٰهِ اَوۡفُوۡا ۚ ذٰلِكُمۡ وَصّٰكُمۡ بِهٖ لَعَلَّكُمۡ تَذَكَّرُوۡنَ ۞

***

^a4 : 11 ; 17 : 35.　^b17 : 36 ; 26 : 182-183 ; 55 : 10.　^c2 : 287 ; 7 : 43.　^d5 : 2 ; 16 : 92 ; 17 : 35.

892. Commentary :

Next to the injunction to protect the lives of our brethren (see preceding verse) comes the injunction to protect their property. Of these the Quran takes first those who cannot take care of their own property, viz., orphans. The verse says : *And approach not the property of the orphan, except in a way which is best.* In these words we are bidden to take due care of the property of those whose parents are dead and who are too young to take care of their property. We are to act as trustees for their property and we are strongly forbidden to misappropriate it. The injunction not to "approach" the property, however, does not mean that we should not even make such use of their property as may be to the advantage of the orphans themselves, *e.g.,* investing it in some profitable business which may bring gain to our wards. The Quran allows such profitable investment by saying, *except in a way which is best.* Again by using the words, *till he attains his maturity,* the Quran reminds us that we are to be the custodians of the property of orphans not for a month or a year but until the time when they are old enough to take charge of it and look after their own affairs.

Next to orphans come those of our brethren who, though able to take care of their property,

may sometimes become the dupes of others. So the next injunction is of general application and is to the effect : *And give full measure and weight with equity.* In these words we are bidden not to cheat or defraud others of their property in any way, even if the other party is not intelligent or watchful enough to look after his or her interests.

After the injunctions pertaining to the protecting of property, comes the injunction to guard our tongues. Says the Quran : *And when you speak, observe justice even if a relation be concerned.* This signifies that when we are called upon to bear witness, we should speak the truth, even if our testimony may prove harmful to one near and dear to us. On the other hand, we should not unjustly harm our relations either. We must be true to them also, for they too are our brethren and come under the general injunction.

After the injunction to guard the tongue comes the injunction to guard the heart. Says the verse, *and fulfil the covenant of Allah.* Obviously this injunction pertains to the heart, for whereas the previous injunctions pertained to the covenant with men, the present one relates to the covenant with God.

It should also be noted that the injunctions contained in 6 : 152 pertained to outward

154. And *say*, *a*this is My path *leading* straight. So follow it; and follow not *other* ways, lest they lead you away from His way. That is what He enjoins upon you, that you may *become able to* guard *against evils*.[893]

155. Again, *b*We gave Moses the Book —completing the favour upon him who did good, and *c*an explanation of all *necessary* things, and a guidance and a mercy—that they might believe in the meeting with their Lord.[894]

وَاَنَّ هٰذَا صِرَاطِىْ مُسْتَقِيْمًا فَاتَّبِعُوْهُ ۚ وَلَا تَتَّبِعُوا السُّبُلَ فَتَفَرَّقَ بِكُمْ عَنْ سَبِيْلِهٖ ۚ ذٰلِكُمْ وَصّٰىكُمْ بِهٖ لَعَلَّكُمْ تَتَّقُوْنَ ۝

ثُمَّ اٰتَيْنَا مُوْسَى الْكِتٰبَ تَمَامًا عَلَى الَّذِىْٓ اَحْسَنَ وَ تَفْصِيْلًا لِّكُلِّ شَىْءٍ وَّ هُدًى وَّ رَحْمَةً لَّعَلَّهُمْ بِلِقَآءِ رَبِّهِمْ يُؤْمِنُوْنَ ۝

---

*a*6 : 127.   *b*2 : 54; 5 : 45.   *c*7 : 146.

evils, hence they were followed by the words, *that you may understand i.e.* if you will act upon these injunctions, your power of understanding will be strengthened. But the injunction contained in the latter portion of the present verse pertains to the heart; it has therefore been aptly followed by the words, *that you may remember.*

893. Commentary :

All the above injunctions have been jointly referred to here and we are told that if we act upon these teachings, we shall come under the protection of God, Who will enable us to guard ourselves against all evil.

894. Important Words :

تَمَامًا (completing) is the noun-infinitive from تَمَّ. They say تَمَّ الشَّىْءُ *i.e.* the thing was or became complete or entire or full or perfect or free from deficiency. تَمَّ اِلٰى كَذَا means, he reached or repaired to or came to such a thing. تَمَّ عَلَيْهِ means, he performed or executed it; or he accomplished it. اَتَمَّ from which the infinitive is اِتْمَام means, he made (a thing) complete or entire or full, etc. (Lane). For the sake of convenience the word

تَمَامًا has been rendered in the verse as "completing."

Commentary :

In some of the previous verses the Quran referred to the diverse paths which, when followed, lead away from God's way. Here we are told that when there come into existence diverse paths, then God sends a Messenger to remove differences and appoints one way for all. Then it becomes incumbent on all to follow that path. This is what is meant by the words, *We gave Moses the Book.*

The expression الَّذِىْ اَحْسَنَ (him who did good) refers to Moses. Thus the sentence means that the Book was revealed to Moses to complete divine favours upon him. The words الَّذِىْ اَحْسَنَ (him who did good) may also be taken in the general sense, meaning "any person who did good." In that case the sentence would mean that the Book was revealed so that those who were righteous and did good might have divine favours completed upon them.

The words كُلِّ شَىْءٍ (all things) are not absolute but refer to the things the explanation of which was needed in the days of Moses, the

R. 20   156. And ^athis is a Book which We have sent down; *it is* full of blessings. So follow it, and guard against *sin* that you may be shown mercy;[895]

وَهٰذَا كِتٰبٌ اَنْزَلْنٰهُ مُبٰرَكٌ فَاتَّبِعُوْهُ وَاتَّقُوْا لَعَلَّكُمْ تُرْحَمُوْنَ ۞

157. Lest you should say, ' The Book was sent down only to two peoples before us, and we were indeed unaware of their reading ';[896]

اَنْ تَقُوْلُوْۤا اِنَّمَاۤ اُنْزِلَ الْكِتٰبُ عَلٰى طَآئِفَتَيْنِ مِنْ قَبْلِنَا ۪ وَاِنْ كُنَّا عَنْ دِرَاسَتِهِمْ لَغٰفِلِيْنَ ۞

---

^a6:93; 21:51.

---

words meaning that the Book given to Moses fulfilled all the needs of the time.

The verse mentions four things as the objects of a revealed Book: (1) That God desires to complete His favour by means of it. (2) That it embodies all the commandments that are needed for the period of time for which it is meant. (3) That it contains the means for guiding men to the right path. (4) That it is a mercy *i.e.* those who follow it receive blessings from God.

895. Commentary :

The words, *this is a Book,* refer to the Quran. Before giving the command to follow the Quran, this verse gives the reasons thereof. The first reason is that it is a revealed Book, being sent down by God. The second reason is that it is مبارك (full of blessings) which, as the root meaning of the word implies, shows that it comprises in itself the blissful teachings of all the other Scriptures (for an explanation of the word مبارك see note on 6:93 above).

The verse purports to say (1) that as the Quran is a revealed Book, so you should accept it and thereby become recipients of all the favours attached to revealed Books ; (2) that as it comprises in itself the teachings of all other revealed Scriptures, so you should leave all other Books and follow it alone.

896. Important Words :

غافلين (unaware) is the plural of غافل which also means, wanting in requisite knowledge (Lane).

Commentary :

This and the succeeding verses are addressed to the pagan tribes of Arabia and give the reason why the Quran has been revealed to a Prophet of that country. If the Quran had not been sent down to the pagan Arabs, they might have justly offered the excuse that Books had been sent down to two other peoples (explained below) in tongues which the Arabs could not understand, and that if a Book had been sent down to them, they would have acted upon its teachings more faithfully. To meet this excuse the Quran has been revealed to a Prophet from among the Arabs in their own tongue ; so now they cannot offer that excuse.

The " two peoples " mentioned in the verse are (1) the Jews to whom was given the Book of Moses and whose religion originated in the north of Arabia ; and (2) the Zoroastrians to whom was given the Zend-Avesta and who lived on the east side of Arabia. The Christians were given no separate Law, for both Jesus and his disciples followed the Law of Moses ; hence, so far as religious Laws are concerned, they do not form a separate people but must be classed with the Jews.

158. *a*Or lest you should say, ' Had the Book been sent down to us, we should surely have been better guided than they.' There has now come to you a clear evidence from your Lord, and a guidance and a mercy. *b*Who, then, is more unjust than he who rejects the Signs of Allah and turns away from them? We will requite those who turn away from Our Signs with an evil punishment because of their turning away.[897]

اَوۡ تَقُوۡلُوۡا لَوۡ اَنَّاۤ اُنۡزِلَ عَلَیۡنَا الۡکِتٰبُ لَکُنَّاۤ اَهۡدٰی مِنۡهُمۡ ۚ فَقَدۡ جَآءَکُمۡ بَیِّنَةٌ مِّنۡ رَّبِّکُمۡ وَ هُدًی وَّ رَحۡمَةٌ ۚ فَمَنۡ اَظۡلَمُ مِمَّنۡ کَذَّبَ بِاٰیٰتِ اللّٰهِ وَ صَدَفَ عَنۡهَا ؕ سَنَجۡزِی الَّذِیۡنَ یَصۡدِفُوۡنَ عَنۡ اٰیٰتِنَا سُوۡٓءَ الۡعَذَابِ بِمَا کَانُوۡا یَصۡدِفُوۡنَ ۝

159. *c*Do they expect aught but that angels should come to them or that thy Lord should come or that some of the Signs of thy Lord should come? The day when some of the Signs of thy Lord shall come, to believe in them shall not profit a soul which believed not before, nor earned any good by its faith. Say, ' Wait ye, we *too* are waiting.'[898]

هَلۡ یَنۡظُرُوۡنَ اِلَّاۤ اَنۡ تَاۡتِیَهُمُ الۡمَلٰٓئِکَةُ اَوۡ یَاۡتِیَ رَبُّکَ اَوۡ یَاۡتِیَ بَعۡضُ اٰیٰتِ رَبِّکَ ؕ یَوۡمَ یَاۡتِیۡ بَعۡضُ اٰیٰتِ رَبِّکَ لَا یَنۡفَعُ نَفۡسًا اِیۡمَانُهَا لَمۡ تَکُنۡ اٰمَنَتۡ مِنۡ قَبۡلُ اَوۡ کَسَبَتۡ فِیۡۤ اِیۡمَانِهَا خَیۡرًا ؕ قُلِ انۡتَظِرُوۡۤا اِنَّا مُنۡتَظِرُوۡنَ ۝

---

*a*35 : 43.　　*b*6 : 22; 7 : 38; 10 : 18.　　*c*2 : 211; 16 : 34.

897. Commentary :

The words, *better guided,* are either intended to express a possible idea on the part of the Arabs that the " two peoples " mentioned above did not faithfully act on divine teachings or they merely express a possible feeling of regret that whereas others were granted divine guidance, they were not. It must be said to the credit of the Arabs that when the Quran was revealed to the Holy Prophet, those of them that accepted it did follow it much more faithfully than the " two peoples " referred to above or for that matter any other people. Thus, when the Holy Prophet was attacked by the Quraish of Mecca at Badr and he summoned a council of his followers to consult them, the latter told him without demur that they would not, like the companions

of Moses, say to him, *Go thou and thy Lord and fight and here we sit* (5 : 25), but would fight in his front and fight at his back and fight on his right and fight on his left, meaning that the enemy would not be permitted to reach him except over their dead bodies (Bukhārī, ch. on *Maghāzī*).

898. Commentary :

The " coming of angels " here refers to the punishment of the people through wars; for in the Quran the coming of angels has been mentioned in connection with the battles that took place between Muslims and their enemies (3 : 125, 126 & 8 : 10).

The term " coming of the Lord " with regard to disbelievers has been used in the Quran to express death and destruction (2 : 211). The

160. *As for* ᵃthose who split up their religion and became *divided into* sects, thou hast no concern at all with them. Surely their case will come before Allah, then shall He inform them of what they used to do.⁸⁹⁹

إِنَّ الَّذِيْنَ فَرَّقُوْا دِيْنَهُمْ وَكَانُوْا شِيَعًا لَّسْتَ مِنْهُمْ فِيْ شَيْءٍ ۚ اِنَّمَاۤ اَمْرُهُمْ اِلَى اللهِ ثُمَّ يُنَبِّئُهُمْ بِمَا كَانُوْا يَفْعَلُوْنَ ۝

161. ᵇWhoso does a good deed shall have ten times as much; but he who does an evil deed, shall have only a like reward; and they shall not be wronged.⁹⁰⁰

مَنْ جَآءَ بِالْحَسَنَةِ فَلَهٗ عَشْرُ اَمْثَالِهَا ۚ وَمَنْ جَآءَ بِالسَّيِّئَةِ فَلَا يُجْزٰۤى اِلَّا مِثْلَهَا وَهُمْ لَا يُظْلَمُوْنَ ۝

ᵃ30:33. ᵇ4:41; 27:90; 28:85.

words thus refer to the punishment of death that was to overtake the enemies of Islam in other ways than by war. In fact, when an offender is spoken of as having been summoned before God, it is only for punishment.

The "coming of the Signs" refers to punishments such as famines, pestilences, etc.

Finally, the verse makes it clear that believing at the time when a man is visited by punishment can do him no good. The verse mentions two conditions under which faith is of no avail: *firstly,* the faith of the man who believes at the time when he is overtaken by punishment; *secondly,* the faith of the man who has earned no good by his faith *i.e.* he whose faith is not accompanied by good works and righteous deeds. The verse does not mean that faith will benefit nobody when the Signs of God come. What it means is that at the time when the Sign of punishment comes, faith will not avail those for whom this punishment is meant.

899. Important Words:

شِيَعًا (sects) is the plural of شِيعَة which means, a separate or distinct party or sect of men; any people that have combined in or for an affair. The word is derived from شاع which means, it became spread, published,

divulged or made known; it became scattered or dispersed. شاع also means, he or it followed (him). شيع ابله means, he called out to his (straying or lingering) camels, whereupon they went along and followed one another. شيعه also means, he encouraged and strengthened him. تشايعت الابل means, the camels became separate parties; or they went together (Lane).

Commentary:

The words, *split up their religion,* signify that when all and sundry begin to follow their own judgement, there are sure to be differences among them and there remains no unity of opinion.

900. Commentary:

The verse beautifully illustrates how the mercy of God transcends and predominates over His wrath or punishment. A good deed is like a good seed that brings forth a produce ten times its number and even more (2:262; 4:41; 10:27, 28; also Tirmidhī, ch. on *Fasting*) whereas an evil deed is counted as only one deed. The verse also throws light on the fact that where there are to be rewards and punishments, there must be a law and a system. There can be no rewarding or punishing without a law.

162. Say, ' As for me, my Lord has guided me unto a straight path—a right religion, *the religion of Abraham, the upright. And he was not of those who join gods *with* God.'901

قُلْ اِنَّنِىْ هَدٰىنِىْ رَبِّىْ اِلٰى صِرَاطٍ مُّسْتَقِيْمٍ دِيْنًا قِيَمًا مِّلَّةَ اِبْرٰهِيْمَ حَنِيْفًا ۚ وَمَا كَانَ مِنَ الْمُشْرِكِيْنَ ۝

163. Say, ' My Prayer and my sacrifice and my life and my death are *all* for Allah, the Lord of the worlds.902

قُلْ اِنَّ صَلَاتِىْ وَنُسُكِىْ وَمَحْيَاىَ وَمَمَاتِىْ لِلّٰهِ رَبِّ الْعٰلَمِيْنَ ۝

---

*a*3 : 96 ; 16 : 124.

901. Important Words :

قِيَم (right) is derived from قَام which means, he stood still or he stood up. قَام بِالْامْر means, he undertook the affair ; he managed or conducted it. قِيَم means, right, correct or true. قِيَم الْامْر means, manager, conductor or superintendent of the affair (Lane). See also 4 : 6, 35, 163.

Commentary :

The previous verse proved the need of a revealed religion. In the present verse we are told that now the revealed religion was the one which the Holy Prophet of Islam was following and which in principle was also the religion of Abraham, the upright. The word حَنِيْف means (1) upright and (2) one who is ever inclined to God ; and such a one can only be he who believes in all the Prophets of God.

902. Important Words :

نُسُك (sacrifice) is derived from نَسَك . They say نَسَك الثَّوب i.e. he washed the cloth and rendered it clear and pure. نَسَك الذَّبِيحة means, he slaughtered and sacrificed the animal. نَسَك البَيت means, he repaired to the Ka'ba for Pilgrimage. نَسَك الرَّجل means, the man worshipped God and devoted himself to His service. نَسَك لله means, he offered a sacrifice to win the pleasure of God and attain His nearness. So نُسُك means, sacrifice ; worship ; a right

due to God ; blood of an animal shed by way of sacrifice or in fulfilment of a vow ; animal of sacrifice (Aqrab).

Commentary :

This and the following verse beautifully describe the Holy Prophet's religion, to which reference was made in the preceding verse.

The two latter mentioned expressions, *viz.,* " my life " and " my death " correspond respectively to the two former expressions *viz.* " my Prayer " and " my sacrifice." As Prayer imparts life to the worshipper, so it has been followed by the words, " my life." On the contrary, " sacrifice " kills the self of man, so it has been followed by the words, " my death." These four words *i.e.* Prayer, sacrifice, life and death, thus cover the entire field of man's actions, and the Holy Prophet has been asked to declare that all phases of his life were devoted to God alone. All his prayers were offered to God ; all his sacrifices were made to Him ; all his life was devoted to His service ; and if in the cause of religion he sought death, that was also to win His pleasure. He lived for God and would not die but in harness.

With regard to Prayer particularly, the Holy Prophet is reported to have said جُعِلَتْ قُرَّة عَيْنِى فِى الصَّلوة i.e. " the coolness or delight of my eyes lies in Prayer " (Nasa'ī).

164. *a*'He has no partner. And so am I commanded, and I am the first of those who submit.'[903]

لَا شَرِيكَ لَهُ ۚ وَبِذَٰلِكَ أُمِرْتُ وَأَنَا أَوَّلُ الْمُسْلِمِينَ ۝

165. Say, *b*'Shall I seek a lord other than Allah, while He is the Lord of all things?' And no soul acts but only against itself; *c*nor does any bearer of burden bear the burden of another. Then to your Lord will be your return, and He will inform you of that wherein you used to differ.[904]

قُلْ أَغَيْرَ اللَّهِ أَبْغِي رَبًّا وَهُوَ رَبُّ كُلِّ شَيْءٍ ۚ وَلَا تَكْسِبُ كُلُّ نَفْسٍ إِلَّا عَلَيْهَا ۚ وَلَا تَزِرُ وَازِرَةٌ وِزْرَ أُخْرَىٰ ۚ ثُمَّ إِلَىٰ رَبِّكُمْ مَرْجِعُكُمْ فَيُنَبِّئُكُمْ بِمَا كُنْتُمْ فِيهِ تَخْتَلِفُونَ ۝

166. And He it is Who has made you successors *of others* on the earth and has exalted some of you over the others in degrees of rank, *d*that He may try you by that which He has given you. Surely, thy Lord is quick in punishment; and surely He is Most Forgiving, Merciful.[905]

وَهُوَ الَّذِي جَعَلَكُمْ خَلَائِفَ الْأَرْضِ وَرَفَعَ بَعْضَكُمْ فَوْقَ بَعْضٍ دَرَجَاتٍ لِيَبْلُوَكُمْ فِي مَا آتَاكُمْ ۗ إِنَّ رَبَّكَ سَرِيعُ الْعِقَابِ ۖ وَإِنَّهُ لَغَفُورٌ رَحِيمٌ ۝

---

*a*6:15; 39:12-13.   *b*7:141.   *c*17:16; 35:19; 53:39.   *d*5:49; 11:8; 67:3.

---

903. Commentary:

Not only were all the energies of the Holy Prophet devoted to God, but he believed in no other deity and his eyes were shut to every thing but his Lord and Maker, to Whom alone he submitted. The Holy Prophet was indeed the First Muslim.

904. Commentary:

The verse supplies the reason why one should be devoted to God, for He alone is "the Lord of all things." The verse also makes it clear that on the day when man will be presented before God and will render an account of his deeds, nobody will be able to take upon himself a part of his burden. The word "burden" here signifies "sin." In the words, *bearer of burden*, it is also hinted that this principle applies only to human beings who are the bearers of burdens; but that if God so willed, He could Himself remove the

burden of a soul *i.e.* pardon it.

905. Commentary:

This *Sūra* began with a reference to "darkness" and "light," and in its concluding verse also reference has been made to the same subject, though in different words. The verse purports to say that the people of darkness and the people of light will get their respective rewards at the hands of God. The words, *quick in punishment*, refer to the punishment of those who are in darkness, while the words, *Most Forgiving, Merciful*, refer to the good reward of those who are endowed with light. The words, *that He may try you by that which He has given you*, are intended to point to the great purpose for which "darkness" and "light" have been created, the expression, *given you*, hinting that both light and darkness have been created for the ultimate good of man. Indeed if there had been no darkness, there would have been no progress. See also 6:2.

people", which is their correct rendering he has translated them as, "O ye people of Mecca." He has done his utmost to lend support and emphasis to his view that by the word الناس in the Quran's والناس Sale always meant the people of Mecca, in spite of the fact that the word الناس does not so to this expression. Where has based his commentary of the Quran on ... ... be found no fault with Sale for taking such a liberty with the text ... ... but even on his own justification to Sale al-Baydawi he has declared that ... ... can prefer. It is a pity that bias and prejudice render a person incapable of justice and fairness. For these very Orientalists have declared ... ... as of Moslems period in spite of the fact that the word ... ... "... O ye people) occur in them. This means that whenever there is the least likelihood of Islam being exposed to criticism ...

CHAPTER 7

AL-A'RĀF

(*Revealed before Hijra*)

Place of Revelation

According to Ibn 'Abbās, Ibn Zubair, Ḥasan, Mujāhid 'Ikrima, 'Aṭā and Jābir bin Zaid, this *Sūra* belongs to the Meccan period with the exception of vv. 165-172. It has 207 verses including *Bismillah*. Qatāda says that v. 165 was revealed at Medina. The Rev. E. M. Wherry also considers this *Sūra* to be of Meccan origin with the exception of the above-mentioned eight verses, *i.e.*, vv. 165-172 and also vv. 159-161. It is strange that the reverend gentleman has assigned the revelation of vv. 159-161 to Medina without valid reason or reliable historical evidence. No traditionist nor even any Orientalist supports him in his contention, which seems to be based on the verses which contain a reference to the Jews and to some of the prophecies of the Bible which were fulfilled in the person of the Holy Prophet. He seems to have apprehended lest a perusal of these prophecies might convince the reader of the truth of the Quran and the Holy Prophet. In order to obviate this possibility, he took it upon himself, against all historical evidence and against the considered opinion of the Orientalists, to assign these verses to the Medinite period. He did so in the hope that in this way the Holy Prophet would be considered to have inserted the above-mentioned prophecies in the Quran after having heard them from the Jews. Blind prejudice alone can be held responsible for this baseless inference on his part. Even a person of ordinary intelligence can understand that the fact that a particular prophecy has been mentioned in a certain Book cannot bring about its fulfilment. If a particular prophecy truly applied to the Holy Prophet, how could it be said that he had copied it from some other Book ? But if it did not apply to him, how could the mere fact that it has been inserted in the Quran benefit him ? On the contrary, its very subject-matter, whether it was inserted in the Quran at Mecca or after having been heard from the Jews at Medina, would have sufficed to establish the falsity of his claim. What is stranger still is the fact that Mr. Wherry, in his eagerness to show that the prophecy referred to has not been fulfilled in the person of the Holy Prophet, has consigned to oblivion all the rules and principles devised by himself and the Orientalists to determine whether a particular verse was revealed at Mecca or at Medina. Orientalists hold the view that all Quranic verses which contain the words يَا اَيُّهَا النَّاس (O ye people) must belong to the Meccan period and that "the people" so addressed are the Meccans. This idea has taken such a strong hold of them that, without pausing to consider any other reason, the mere fact that a certain verse contains the words "O ye people" is a sufficient reason for them to ascribe that verse to the Meccan period. Sale is so obsessed with this view that, instead of translating the words يَا اَيُّهَا النَّاس that occur in 2:22 as, "O ye people," which is their correct rendering, he has translated them as "O ye people of Mecca." He has done this obviously to lend support and emphasis to his view that by the word الناس in the Quranic expression يا ايها الناس is always meant the people of Mecca, in spite of the fact that the word مكة is not to be found anywhere in the above expression. Wherry has based his Commentary of the Quran on Sale's translation. Not only has he found no fault with Sale for his taking such liberty with the text of the Quran, but even in his own Introduction to *Sūra* Al-Baqara he has declared this verse to belong to the Meccan period. It is a pity that bias and prejudice render a person insensible to all dictates of justice and fairness, for these very Orientalists have declared vv. 159-161 of the present *Sūra* as of Medinite period in spite of the fact that the words يا ايها الناس (O ye people) occur in them. This means that whenever there is the least likelihood of Islam being exposed to criticism if a particular verse of the Quran in which the expression يا ايها الناس (O ye people) occurs were proved to belong to the Meccan period, they will confidently declare it to belong to the Meccan period; but when Islam is considered to be open to attack by proving that another verse which comprises the same expression is of Medinite origin, these scholars complacently assign it to the Medinite period. May God open their hearts that they may see the truth, so that they may not make Jesus feel ashamed of them on the Day of Judgement.

Noeldeke, however, has refused to ascribe vv. 165-172 to the Medinite period. This refusal is based only on a mere conjecture, unsubstantiated by any reliable historical evidence, and therefore cannot be accepted. Historical evidence can be rejected only on the basis of established facts of history or irrefutable internal evidence.

Title of the Sūra

The *Sūra* is known as *Al-A'rāf* and this name is supposed to have been given to it on the basis of this word having occurred in its 47th verse. But the contention that the *Sūra* has been given this name only because the word اعراف (*A'rāf*) has happened to occur in it is inadmissible unless this word is shown to possess some real connection with the subject-matter of the *Sūra* itself. Orientalists and Commentators have not succeeded in finding out any such connection between this word and the subject-matter of the *Sūra*. This is because they have assigned a wrong meaning to the word اعراف. They think that اعراف (*A'rāf*) is the name of an intervening spiritual stage between Paradise and Hell and that the dwellers in this stage will appear distinct from the inmates of Hell but will not as yet have entered Paradise. The Quran, however, rejects this meaning of the word because it mentions only two groups of people, *viz.*, the dwellers of Paradise and the inmates of Hell. There is no mention of any third group or class of people. The Quran thus lends no support to the interpretation of the word اعراف as the place for a people of a middling spiritual status, nor can any internal evidence of the verses in which this word occurs be adduced in support of this interpretation. The Quran depicts the people of اعراف (*A'rāf*) as at one time addressing the dwellers of Paradise and at another time talking to the inmates of Hell, and their spiritual knowledge has been declared to be so great that they can recognize the dwellers of Paradise by their special marks and also the inmates of Hell by the latter's particular signs. They rebuke and upbraid the inmates of Hell and pray for the inmates of Paradise (7 : 47, 49, 50). Can a person who himself is hanging, as it were, in a state of uncertainty between Paradise and Hell, be so presumptuous as to assume an air of superiority as the people of A'rāf have been shown to do. The fact is that the people of اعراف (A'rāf) are the Prophets of God, who will occupy a very high spiritual stage on the Day of Judgement and will pray for the dwellers of Paradise and rebuke and reprimand the inmates of Hell. And because the present Sūra is the first among the Quranic Sūras in which the life-stories of the Prophets have been dealt with at some length, it has been given the name اعراف in consideration of the very high spiritual station of God's Messengers.

Moreover, the very construction of the word supports this inference. اعراف is the plural of عرف ('urf) which means a high and elevated place (Lane). Similarly عرف ('urf) means that spiritual realization which a man has through his unsullied nature, acquiring it by the help of God-given intellect and the testimony of his inner self. So اعراف means those teachings of which the truth is established by rational arguments and the testimony of human nature ; and, as the teachings of Prophets possess all these qualities, they (the Prophets) alone deserve this spiritually high position, and thus be rightly called اصحاب الاعراف i.e. the people of اعراف (elevated places). Their high spiritual station signifies that, apart from the special favours of God, they take their stand on the solid rock of the testimony of human nature and intellect. Such a lofty position is indeed beyond the attainment of ordinary men.

In short, the Chapter A'rāf is so called because in it illustrations have been given from the lives of those eminent men of very high spiritual status who in the past have taught mankind eternal truths in accordance with the demands of human nature and human intellect, whom the men of this world resisted and sought to bring low, but whom the jealous God did not allow to be debased but, on the contrary, raised to a very exalted position.

Subject-Matter

Spiritually this Sūra serves as a kind of برزخ (intervening link) between the Sūras that precede it and those that follow it, which means that the subject-matter of the preceding Sūras has been developed into a new theme in this Sūra. In the preceding Sūras the main theme consisted of a refutation of Judaism and Christianity and also a refutation of other Faiths which profess to derive their authority mainly from Philosophy and reason. In the present Sūra both these themes have been jointly treated and the falsity of the positions of both these sets of religions has been established and the truth of Islam demonstrated to their followers. First of all, it has been stated that since the Quran is the revealed word of God, there is no possibility of its meeting with destruction or failing to achieve its object. Then in vv. 4-10 the followers of the Holy Prophet are warned that they should not, in a fit of despondency, come to a hasty compromise with the followers of other religions, because the opponents of a true religion have always suffered disgrace and humiliation in the end. Verse 11 states that God has created man for the attainment of a most sublime object but most men forget this noble purpose of their life.

In vv. 12-27 the paradisaical life of Adam and his expulsion from it have been cited as an illustration of this subject and it is stated how, from the very beginning of the world, God created man and provided the means necessary for his attainment of a high spiritual status ; but he gave no heed to God's plans for him and obeyed and followed Satan. In vv. 28-30 we are told that Satan had made Adam spiritually naked and now God has sent the Holy Prophet of Islam to clothe him with the raiment of righteousness and he is the Prophet who has come to deliver man from the punishment of his sins and to make him regain that heavenly life of which he had become deprived. So the Faithful should beware lest their deeds keep them deprived of that heavenly life. In vv. 31-35 it has been hinted that, unlike former Faiths which aimed at individual development, Islam seeks to bring about a reformation among whole communities. Whereas former Prophets sought to make individuals enter Paradise, Islam aims that whole communities and nations should attain bliss. But, as every effort at reformation has to encounter many obstacles and vicissitudes before it reaches its consummation, vv. 36-38 tell us that when the Muslim community deviates from Islamic principles and teachings, God will raise for their reformation divinely-inspired Reformers from among the followers of the Holy Prophet so that men may not lose this newly-gained Paradise by deviating from the path of national progress and development. In vv. 39-48 rules and principles have been laid down for the recognition of these promised Reformers and light has also been shed on the ultimate doom of their opponents. In vv. 49-52 we are told that it is the Prophets of God who alone can arouse into action the latent powers and qualities of human nature and can lead men to progress and prosperity. In the next two verses the Meccans are exhorted to accept and benefit by the light of prophethood of which they have had an ample share and not to make themselves the object of divine punishment by rejecting it.

In vv. 55-59 it is said that all divine plans work gradually. As in the material world, so in the realm of the spirit, all progress is subject to the law of evolution and it is by a process of progressive evolution that the spiritual development of man has taken place from the time of Adam to that of the Holy Prophet of Islam, and the new mission that has come into force through the Holy Prophet, in which greater attention has been given to the betterment and organization of the community than to that of the individual, will also find its consummation after going through a process of evolution. Muslims should, therefore, conform to the divine will and purpose and should strive to fulfil this great mission. They should always keep in mind that from small seeds grow big trees and that even great objects seem very insignificant in the beginning and remain hidden from the eyes of the people. So it behoves them to keep their eyes open and not let this grand object remain hidden from their sight because, if once it were allowed to become hidden, it would remain hidden for ever.

With v. 60 begins a brief account of the life-history of some Prophets of antiquity whose mission it was to take man as an individual back to the blissful heavenly existence from which he was expelled. This account extends to v. 172. In vv. 173-178 it is stated that good is ingrained in human nature and constitutes an integral part of it while evil comes later and is the result of external influences. In vv. 179-184 we are told that, in spite of the instinctive goodness of man, he cannot attain perfection without the help of divine revelation. By rejecting divine guidance he becomes deprived of his instinctive goodness and is ruined.

In vv. 185-187 reference has again been made to the mission of the Holy Prophet, and his opponents are admonished not to ignore the patent fact that his intellect is sound and motives pure and that his teachings are in perfect harmony with human nature and natural law and that the testimony of the time also is in his favour. In vv. 188-199 some misgivings and doubts of disbelievers have been removed, and it is stated that disbelievers will put up a very strong opposition to the Holy Prophet but God will protect him from all harm. The idols of idolaters will not be able to help them. In vv. 200-203, however, Muslims are admonished not only to endure patiently the opposition of disbelievers (because all this opposition is the result of lack of true knowledge) but also to pray for them. Then in v. 204 the Holy Prophet is told that, like the opponents of former Prophets, his opponents also will continue to demand Signs, but he should tell them that the showing of Signs lies entirely in God's own hand. He will show them when in His infallible wisdom He thinks it opportune. But does not the Quran itself (the Prophet is enjoined to say to disbelievers) which fulfils the real object and purpose of prophethood, constitute a sufficient Sign ? Towards the end of the *Sūra* Muslims are exhorted to give to the miracle of the Quran that great measure of true appreciation which it richly deserves, because the more heavenly light is vouchsafed to man, the truer should be his appreciation of it.

In his Introduction to this *Sūra*, Mr. Wherry has made, as is his wont, a fantastic charge against the Holy Prophet. He says that the accounts of the life-histories of former Prophets which this *Sūra* contains are only a reflection of the Holy Prophet's own experiences in life. Here are his actual words :

"Even the most careless reader can hardly fail to see that all these Prophets are facsimiles of Muhammad himself. Their character and authority, their message and accompanying claims to inspiration, the incredulity and hardness of heart shown by the tribes to whom they were sent, the consequent rejection of the Prophets, and threatenings of the sudden and dreadful judgements of God upon unbelievers, all these correspond to the experience of Muhammad, and the inference suggested by each story is that the rejection of the Prophet of Makkah would bring with it judgements on the Quraish similar to and dreadful as those which befell those tribes who rejected the former Prophets."

Mr. Wherry means to suggest that no incidents mentioned in this *Sūra* as having happened to the Prophets ever took place ; the Holy Prophet has only ascribed his own experiences to them. But can the reverend gentleman have the courage to deny that the incidents, attributed in the Quran to former Prophets, are also mentioned in the Bible as having happened to them ? Did there ever live a Prophet of whose life the Bible contains some account who did not claim to have received revelation from God ? We find that every Prophet mentioned in the Bible definitely laid claim to divine revelation ; and how can any intelligent man possibly conceive that any person could lay claim to prophethood without claiming at the same time that he received revelation from God. Moreover, there is no cause or occasion for surprise at the fact that the opposition and cruel treatment, which the Quran says former Prophets met at the hands of their opponents, resembled the treatment and opposition which the Holy Prophet received from his opponents. What is there in the mutual resemblance of the conditions and circumstances of the Holy Prophet and those of former Prophets which

767

can cause surprise ? Every Prophet of God brings a new message which contradicts and demolishes the accepted views of his people. They naturally oppose him. This was the experience of every Prophet. They all resemble each other in this respect. If this resemblance seems strange to Mr. Wherry, he alone must have known Prophets who did not receive cruel treatment from their people. If such is the case, then what would he say about him who said : " O Jerusalem, Jerusalem, which killeth the Prophets, and stoneth them that are sent unto her!" (Matt. 23 : 37). And, "That the blood of all the Prophets, which was shed from the foundation of the world, may be required of this generation" (Luke 11 : 50). Would Mr. Wherry and those who subscribe to his view tell us that the man who uttered the above words was also ascribing his own experiences to former Prophets and that in reality they received no such treatment ? Did he (Jesus) tell a lie or is it a fact that the Prophets from the beginning of the world were really rejected and opposed ? If Mr. Wherry has the hardihood to accuse even Jesus of falsehood, then we have no complaint against him. But if what Jesus said was true, and it was certainly true, then there is no denying the fact that the Prophets of God have always received opposition and maltreatment from their opponents. Enmity and blind prejudice alone have impelled Mr. Wherry to make this most unjust charge against the Holy Prophet.

Similarly, if the objection of Mr. Wherry is true that the claim of the Quran that the former Prophets had warned their opponents of divine punishment was a reflection of the Holy Prophet's own mind and nothing of the kind ever happened, then what would he say about the Bible, which is full of prophecies containing warnings for the Prophets' opponents. Did not Noah and Moses and Jeremiah and Hezekiah and Daniel warn their opponents of divine punishment ? Did not Jesus himself threaten his opponents with impending doom ? If such is the case, then is it not merely blind prejudice to take exception to the Quranic statement that all the Prophets warned their opponents of their ultimate destruction and that destruction actually befell them ? Let Mr. Wherry and those of his way of thinking remember that all Prophets of God bear a close resemblance to one another just as their opponents resemble each other. This is why perhaps the objections of Mr. Wherry bear a striking resemblance to the objections of the Scribes and the Pharisees; and the answers of the Holy Prophet resemble those given by Moses and Jesus to their opponents.

سُوْرَةُ الْاَعْرَافِ مَكِّيَّةٌ

1. In the name of Allah, the Gracious, the Merciful.⁹⁰⁶

بِسْمِ اللّٰهِ الرَّحْمٰنِ الرَّحِيْمِ ۟

2. ᵃAlif Lām Mīm Ṣād.⁹⁰⁶ᴬ

الٓمّٓصٓ ۟

3. ᵇThis is a Book revealed unto thee—so let there be no straitness in thy bosom concerning it—that thou mayest warn thereby, and that it be an exhortation to the believers.⁹⁰⁷

كِتٰبٌ اُنْزِلَ اِلَيْكَ فَلَا يَكُنْ فِىْ صَدْرِكَ حَرَجٌ مِّنْهُ لِتُنْذِرَ بِهٖ وَذِكْرٰى لِلْمُؤْمِنِيْنَ ۟

4. ᶜFollow that which has been sent down to you from your Lord, and follow no protectors other than Him. How little do you remember!⁹⁰⁸

اِتَّبِعُوْا مَآ اُنْزِلَ اِلَيْكُمْ مِّنْ رَّبِّكُمْ وَلَا تَتَّبِعُوْا مِنْ دُوْنِهٖۤ اَوْلِيَآءَ ؕ قَلِيْلًا مَّا تَذَكَّرُوْنَ ۟

5. ᵈHow many a town have We destroyed! and Our punishment came upon it by night or while they slept at noon.⁹⁰⁹

وَكَمْ مِّنْ قَرْيَةٍ اَهْلَكْنٰهَا فَجَآءَهَا بَاْسُنَا بَيَاتًا اَوْ هُمْ قَآئِلُوْنَ ۟

ᵃ2:2; 3:2; 29:2; 30:2; 31:2; 32:2.   ᵇ6:52; 19:98; 25:2.   ᶜ33:3; 39:56.
ᵈ7:98; 21:12; 28:59.

---

906. Commentary:

See under **1:1.**

906ᴀ. Commentary:

According to Ibn 'Abbās, the combined four letters المص are the abbreviations of the words انا الله اعلم وافصل i.e. "I am Allah, I know and I explain." The contents of this *Sūra* justify this interpretation, because the *Sūra* not only embodies divine knowledge but "explains" at greater length and with a greater wealth of illustrations the subject dealt with in the previous *Sūra*. See also note on الم in 2:2.

907. Commentary:

This verse is addressed to each and every believer, and not to the Holy Prophet particularly. The believers are told that the Quran is God's own revelation and not the outcome of

the Prophet's mind, and since it is the revealed word of the All-Knowing God, they should feel no straitness or hesitance in acting upon its injunctions and preaching them to others.

908. Commentary:

No patronage or help from any quarter can be of avail to a people in opposition to God and His Messengers. This is a lesson writ large on the pages of history and is well worth remembering.

909. Important Words:

بَيَاتًا (by night) is the noun-infinitive from بَاتَ i.e. he passed the night. بَاتَ فَعَلَ كَذَا means, he did such a thing by or at night; or he passed the night doing such a thing; or he entered upon the night doing such a thing. تَامَ الامر بياتا means, the thing or event

6. So when Our punishment came upon them, their cry was nothing but this that they said : *a*'We were indeed wrongdoers !'910

فَمَا كَانَ دَعْوَىٰهُمْ إِذْ جَاءَهُمْ بَأْسُنَا إِلَّا أَن قَالُوا إِنَّا كُنَّا ظَالِمِينَ ۝

7. And *b*We will certainly question those to whom the *Messengers* were sent, and *c*We will certainly question the Messengers.911

فَلَنَسْأَلَنَّ الَّذِينَ أُرْسِلَ إِلَيْهِمْ وَلَنَسْأَلَنَّ الْمُرْسَلِينَ ۝

8. Then will We certainly relate to them *their deeds* with knowledge, for We were never absent.912

فَلَنَقُصَّنَّ عَلَيْهِم بِعِلْمٍ وَمَا كُنَّا غَائِبِينَ ۝

---

*a*21 : 15.   *b*28 : 66.   *c*5 : 110.

happened to them at night, or in the latter part of the night (Aqrab). See also 4 : 82. قَائِلُونَ (slept at noon) is derived from قَالَ (of which the aorist is يَقِيلُ and not يَقُولُ) *i.e.* he slept or rested during mid-day ; or he drank water, etc. at mid-day. So قَائِل means, one sleeping or resting during mid-day. قَيْلُولَة means, the act of sleeping or resting during mid-day. قَائِلَة means, mid-day (Aqrab).

Commentary :

The particle فَا in فَجَاءَهَا here means "and". If, however, it be taken to mean "then" and the words that follow be translated as "then Our punishment came upon them," then the verb اهْلَكْنَا (have We destroyed) will have to be rendered as "We had decreed to destroy." Two separate and distinct hours, *viz.*, (1) the latter part of the night and (2) mid-day are here mentioned as the two times when divine visitations generally come upon men. These are the times when people are often in a state of sleep or negligence.

910. Commentary :

The reason why even confirmed atheists have been found to cry to God for help when divine punishment overtakes them, is that at such a dreadful time, man becomes not only conscious of his own utter helplessness but also of the might and power of a Higher Being.

911. Commentary :

The verse embodies the important principle that in one way or another all are responsible to God. The people will be questioned as to how they received God's Messengers, and the Messengers will be questioned as to how they delivered the divine message and what response the people gave them.

912. Commentary :

God's purpose in questioning the Messengers and the people (7 : 7 above) would not be to gain information or supplement His knowledge, —for He is All-Knowing—but, on the contrary, to impress upon both parties the extent and perfection of His own knowledge. After the people and the Prophets will have said what they will have to say, God Himself will tell them in detail what they did and what they should have done but failed to do, and thus the all-comprehensiveness of God's knowledge will be fully brought home to them.

9. And ªthe weighing on that day will be true. Then as for those whose scales are heavy, it is they who shall prosper.913

وَالْوَزْنُ يَوْمَئِذٍ الْحَقُّ فَمَنْ ثَقُلَتْ مَوَازِينُهُ فَأُولَٰئِكَ هُمُ الْمُفْلِحُونَ ۹

10. And as for those ᵇwhose scales are light, it is they who shall have ruined their souls because of their being unjust to Our Signs.914

وَمَنْ خَفَّتْ مَوَازِينُهُ فَأُولَٰئِكَ الَّذِينَ خَسِرُوا أَنْفُسَهُمْ بِمَا كَانُوا بِآيَاتِنَا يَظْلِمُونَ ۱۰

11. And ᶜWe have established you in the earth and provided for you therein the means of subsistence. How little thanks you give !915

وَلَقَدْ مَكَّنَّاكُمْ فِي الْأَرْضِ وَجَعَلْنَا لَكُمْ فِيهَا مَعَايِشَ قَلِيلًا مَا تَشْكُرُونَ ۱۱

ª21 : 48; 23 : 103; 101 : 9-10.   ᵇ23 : 104; 101 : 9-10.   ᶜ15 : 21; 46 : 27.

913. Important Words :

موازينه (whose scales). موازين is the plural of ميزان which is derived from وزن. They say وزن الشيء i.e. he weighed the thing, or he determined or estimated the weight of the thing. وزن الشعر means, he composed verses according to the fixed measure. وزن الشيء (with different vowel point at the central root letter) means, the thing became heavy and weighty. وزن which is noun-infinitive means, the act of weighing; or the weight of a thing; or weightiness. وزن الرجل means, he was a person of weighty opinion. ميزان means, a weighing instrument; a balance; a pair of scales; the weight of a thing; the measure of a verse (Lane & Aqrab).

Commentary :

The verse does not mean that pairs of scales will actually be set up and human actions and deeds weighed like material things. The language used is figurative. Material things are indeed weighed in scales made of metal or wood, but the weighing of things which are not material means determining their real value or worth or importance.

The verse also throws interesting side-light on the fact that on the Day of Reckoning it is only good works that will carry weight. In the following verse the Quran makes the point further clear by saying, *those whose scales are light* (i.e. those who have no good works to their credit or who have only evil works which carry no weight), *it is they who shall have ruined their souls.*

914. Commentary :

The words, *whose scales are light,* mean, those whose good deeds are few and evil deeds many. The word ظلم (rendered as being unjust to) literally means, to put a thing in the wrong place, and is here used to signify that the disbelievers did not treat the Signs of God in the manner in which they should have been treated. They were meant to instil fear of God and humility in the minds of the people; but, on the contrary, disbelievers became all the more arrogant and insolent and received the Signs of God with mockery and derision.

915. Commentary :

The verse purports to tell the people that in spite of the fact that God has given them

771

R. 2   12.   And We did create you *and* then
^aWe gave you shape ; then ^bsaid We to
the angels, 'Submit to Adam' ; and they
all submitted.   But Iblis *did not*; he
would not be of those who submit.⁹¹⁶

وَلَقَدْ خَلَقْنٰكُمْ ثُمَّ صَوَّرْنٰكُمْ ثُمَّ قُلْنَا لِلْمَلٰٓئِكَةِ اسْجُدُوْا لِاٰدَمَ ۚ فَسَجَدُوْۤا اِلَّاۤ اِبْلِيْسَ ؕ لَمْ يَكُنْ مِّنَ السّٰجِدِيْنَ ۝

---

^a23 : 15 ; 39 : 7 ; 40 : 65.   ^b2 : 35 ; 15 : 30-31 ; 17 : 62 ; 18 : 51 ; 20 : 117 ; 38 : 73-75.

---

all necessary things, yet they are not grateful to Him. This is intended to warn men to be prepared to reap the fruits of their evil actions.

916. Commentary:

The story of Adam has already been partly related in 2 : 31—40. Another part of the same story with some additional details is given here with a different purpose. In the former *Sūra*, the narration was meant to show that God had been sending down revelation from the beginning of the world and so the revelation sent to the Holy Prophet of Islam was not an innovation. Here it is given to show that there have always been enemies of the Prophets of God and so the hostility of the people towards the Holy Prophet was in fact a sign of his truth. The story of Adam is incapable of being fully understood without our first being acquainted with the scene of its occurrence. Was Adam first placed in Paradise and was it in Paradise that the scene described in this and the following few verses was enacted? All doubts on this score are set at rest by the plain words of the Quran, *I am about to place a vicegerent in the earth* (2 : 31). It was indeed in this very earth that the creation of Adam and all that followed it took place. The Bible as well as Zoroastrian and Hindu religious writings also lend support to this view. The Holy Prophet is reported to have described the Nile and the Euphrates as the two rivers of جنّة (the garden), referring to the place where Adam lived ; (Muslim, ch. on *Jannat*) ; and the Ḥadīth,

too, places Adam in Mesopotamia which is watered by the waters of the Tigris and the Euphrates. It was, therefore, here that the garden of Adam was situated and all the different incidents mentioned about him in the Quran also took place here ; and if there be any incident which cannot be proved to have literally occurred on this earth, then that incident will have to be taken in a figurative sense.

Another fact worth remembering is that 2 : 31, according to which Adam was created on this earth, also tells us that he was not the first man to live on this planet, and that other men lived even before he was brought into existence. In 2 : 31 Adam has been called *Khalīfa* which word, meaning a successor, shows that he had predecessors whom he succeeded. The verse under comment also clearly points to the same conclusion. Addressing the people, it says, *And We did create you and then We gave you shape ; then said We to the angels, Submit to Adam.* The plural pronoun " you " in the clause, *We did create you,* having preceded the words containing the command to angels to submit to Adam, which is preceded by the conjunction " then " shows that it was after the creation of men, and not only Adam, that God ordered angels to submit to Adam and that therefore human beings were already living on this earth when angels received this command. It is, thus, wrong to conclude that the human race began with Adam, that its whole life is only a little more than six thousand years and that the different races now living on this earth are all necessarily descended from Adam.

The aborigines of Australia or the Red Indians of America or the Negroes of Africa may not be the descendants of the Adam about whom the Quran speaks in the verse under comment. See also 2 : 31.

As already pointed out, events which cannot be literally shown to have occurred on this earth must be regarded as having taken place in a figurative sense. That figurative language has actually been used in this narrative is clear from the following facts :—

1. The angels were bidden to perform سجدة (falling prostrate before Adam) which is not permissible for any being other than God. So God could not command the angels to fall prostrate before Adam in the literal sense of the words. These words must therefore be taken only in the figurative sense *i.e.* that of submitting and rendering every kind of help. This is why the Arabic expression اسجدوا has here been translated as "submit to," which is a perfectly correct rendering according to the figurative idiom of the Arabic language.

2. The command to fall prostrate before Adam was given to the angels only ; but *Iblis* who is not an angel, is also apparently included in it ; which proves this inclusion also to be a figurative one.

3. *Iblis* is represented in the Quran as having been created from fire (7 : 13), and he is also described as being one of the جن (*Jinn*) which signifies an invisible creation (18 : 51). So he must have been invisible to Adam who was in all respects like other human beings. But he is here represented as having appeared to Adam in a visible form and having talked to him face to face. This shows that the word شيطان (Satan) has been used in the following verses in a figurative sense, and that it does not refer to the Evil Spirit which tempts men.

4. It is said that when Adam and his wife tasted of the forbidden tree, their nakedness became manifest to them. But we know of no tree on this earth the tasting of which has the property of making a person realize his nakedness. So we will have to take ' the tree ' and ' the nakedness ' also in a figurative sense.

5. We are told in 20 : 119 that when God placed Adam in the garden, He told him that he would not become naked therein. But in 7 : 23 we are told that he did in fact become naked. So one of the two statements will have to be taken figuratively.

The straight and simple meaning of the verse is only this : the angels are bidden to submit to Adam and to help him in his work. This commandment was given to the angels when Adam was made a Prophet. As one of the functions of the angels is to exhort men to do virtuous deeds, they were commanded to help Adam by instilling good ideas into the minds of men and exhorting them to accept Adam as a Messenger of God. The chief angel is Gabriel. Similarly, there are evil spirits whose chief is *Iblis*. The evil spirits make evil suggestions to men and incite them to disobey God. So, while the angels in obedience to God's command submitted to Adam, *Iblis*, chief of the evil spirits, refused to submit to him and to help him in his work.

It should be remembered that the incident mentioned here is in no way connected with the first progenitor of the human race, who may be called the first Adam. It is only with the later Adam (who lived on this earth about six thousand years ago and from whom Noah and Abraham and their posterity were directly descended) that the present story is connected. See also notes on 2 : 31 & 2 : 35

773

13. ^aGod said, ' What prevented thee from submitting when I commanded thee ? ' He said, ' I am better than he. Thou hast created me of fire while him hast Thou created of clay.'⁹¹⁷

قَالَ مَا مَنَعَكَ اَلَّا تَسْجُدَ اِذْ اَمَرْتُكَ ۚ قَالَ اَنَا خَيْرٌ مِّنْهُ ۚ خَلَقْتَنِيْ مِنْ نَّارٍ وَّخَلَقْتَهٗ مِنْ طِيْنٍ ۞

14. God said, ^b' Then go down hence ; it is not for thee to be arrogant here. Get out ; thou art certainly of those who are abased.⁹¹⁸

قَالَ فَاهْبِطْ مِنْهَا فَمَا يَكُوْنُ لَكَ اَنْ تَتَكَبَّرَ فِيْهَا فَاخْرُجْ اِنَّكَ مِنَ الصّٰغِرِيْنَ ۞

15. ^cHe said, ' Grant me respite till the day when they will be raised up.'⁹¹⁹

قَالَ اَنْظِرْنِيْ اِلٰى يَوْمِ يُبْعَثُوْنَ ۞

16. God said, ' Thou shalt be of those who are given respite.'

قَالَ اِنَّكَ مِنَ الْمُنْظَرِيْنَ ۞

17. ^dHe said : ' Now, since Thou hast adjudged me as lost, I will assuredly lie in wait for them on Thy straight path.'⁹²⁰

قَالَ فَبِمَا اَغْوَيْتَنِيْ لَاَقْعُدَنَّ لَهُمْ صِرَاطَكَ الْمُسْتَقِيْمَ ۞

---

^a15 : 33-34 ; 38 : 76-77.   ^b15 : 35 ; 38 : 78.   ^c15 : 37 ; 38 : 80.   ^d15 : 40 ; 38 : 83.

---

917. Commentary :

What is represented in the present verse as a dialogue between God and *Iblīs* does not necessarily show that an exchange of words actually took place between the two. The words may only depict a state of things, a picture of the conditions that came into existence as a result of the refusal of *Iblīs* to submit to Adam. The verb قال (said) as shown under 2 : 31 and 2 : 34 does not always signify the actual uttering of words, being sometimes used to represent only a state of affairs.

For an explanation of the words " fire " and " clay " see 2 : 81 and 3 : 50.

918. Commentary :

There being no noun mentioned in the verse to which the pronoun ها (it) implied in the expression منها (hence) refers, it may be taken to denote the condition or state or position in which *Iblīs* was, before he refused to submit to Adam. Thus the expression, *go down*

hence, signifies, " be thou degraded from thy present position."

919. Commentary :

The resurrection to which the words, *when they will be raised up*, refer is not the general resurrection of mankind decreed for the Here-after but the spiritual resurrection of man that comes into being whenever a Prophet is raised. *Iblīs* can lead man astray only so long as he is not spiritually resurrected. But once a man attains the spiritual stage which is designated by the term بقا (*rebirth*), *Iblīs* can do him no harm. It is indeed a similar spiritual stage which is mentioned in the words, *As to My servants, thou (Satan) shalt certainly have no power over them* (17 : 66).

920. Important Words :

اغويتني (Thou hast adjudged me as lost). اغويت is derived from اغوى which again is derived from غوى which means, he erred ;

18. 'Then will I surely come upon them from before them and from behind them and from their right and from their left, and Thou wilt not find most of them to be grateful.'⁹²¹

ثُمَّ لَاٰتِيَنَّهُمۡ مِّنۢ بَيۡنِ اَيۡدِيۡهِمۡ وَمِنۡ خَلۡفِهِمۡ وَعَنۡ اَيۡمَانِهِمۡ وَعَنۡ شَمَآئِلِهِمۡ وَلَا تَجِدُ اَكۡثَرَهُمۡ شٰكِرِيۡنَ ۝

19. God said: 'Get out hence, despised and banished. ᵃWhosoever of them shall follow thee, I will surely fill Hell with you all.'⁹²²

قَالَ اخۡرُجۡ مِنۡهَا مَذۡءُوۡمًا مَّدۡحُوۡرًا ؕ لَّمَنۡ تَبِعَكَ مِنۡهُمۡ لَاَمۡلَئَنَّ جَهَنَّمَ مِنۡكُمۡ اَجۡمَعِيۡنَ ۝

20. 'And ᵇO Adam, dwell thou and thy wife in the Garden and eat therefrom wherever you will, but approach not this tree lest you be among the wrongdoers.'⁹²²ᴬ

وَيٰۤاٰدَمُ اسۡكُنۡ اَنۡتَ وَزَوۡجُكَ الۡجَنَّةَ فَكُلَا مِنۡ حَيۡثُ شِئۡتُمَا وَلَا تَقۡرَبَا هٰذِهِ الشَّجَرَةَ فَتَكُوۡنَا مِنَ الظّٰلِمِيۡنَ ۝

ᵃ11:20; 15:43-44; 32:14; 38:86.   ᵇ2:38; 20:118.

he deviated from the right way; he acted ignorantly; he failed in his object and was disappointed; he was lost; he perished; his life became unpleasant. اغوا means, he caused him to err; or he caused him to deviate from the right course; he caused him to be disappointed, or to fail in attaining his desire; he seduced him, or misled him; or he caused him to be lost or to perish; he declared or adjudged him to be lost; he destroyed him; or he punished him for erring; or he called upon him to do a thing as a result of which he deviated from the right course and was lost (Lane, Lisān, Aqrab & Mufradāt).

Commentary:

Iblīs here declares that as God had adjudged him as lost, he would now tempt and waylay men and cause them to be lost even as he himself was lost. This work becomes his life's function. See also 2:35.

The particle ٻ (since) in the clause فبما اغویتنی may also be taken in the sense of

"swearing", in which case the clause would mean, "I swear by Thy having adjudged me as lost."

921. Commentary:

Note the network of seductions threatened by Satan. But the great truth still stands and shall ever stand: *As to My servants, thou (Satan) shalt certainly have no power over them* (17:66). The refuge certainly lies in God only, the Lord of man and the Lord of Satan and indeed the Lord of the worlds.

922. Commentary:

The verse makes it clear that *Iblīs* will not be allowed to waylay those chosen servants of God who would have attained to the exalted stage of spiritual re-birth. He will not also be able to force men to disobey God; for, as the verse clearly points out, only those will come under his influence who themselves choose to 'follow' him.

922ᴬ. Commentary:

See 2:36.

21. But ^aSatan whispered evil suggestions to them so that he might make known to them what was hidden from them of their shame, and said, 'Your Lord has only forbidden you this tree, lest you should become angels or such *beings* as live for ever.'⁹²³

فَوَسْوَسَ لَهُمَا الشَّيْطٰنُ لِيُبْدِيَ لَهُمَا مَا وٗرِيَ عَنْهُمَا مِنْ سَوْاٰتِهِمَا وَقَالَ مَا نَهٰكُمَا رَبُّكُمَا عَنْ هٰذِهِ الشَّجَرَةِ اِلَّآ اَنْ تَكُوْنَا مَلَكَيْنِ اَوْ تَكُوْنَا مِنَ الْخٰلِدِيْنَ ۝

22. And He swore to them, *saying*, 'Surely I am a sincere counsellor unto you.'

وَقَاسَمَهُمَآ اِنِّیْ لَكُمَا لَمِنَ النّٰصِحِیْنَ ۝

---

^a2 : 37 ; 20 : 121.

---

923. Important Words :

وسوس (whispered evil suggestions) literally means, he spoke in a low voice ; he whispered. They say وسوس له الشيطان *i.e.* Satan spoke to him something evil in which there is no good. وسوس الرجل means, the man's reason was affected and he spoke in a disorderly manner. وسواس (*wiswās*) means, the act of whispering ; evil suggestion. وسواس (*waswās*) with different vowel point means, melancholia ; Satan (Aqrab).

سوآتهما (their shame). سوآت is the plural of سوءة which is derived from ساء which means, it was or became evil, foul or abominable. سوءة means, any evil, foul, unseemly or abominable saying or action or habit or practice ; any saying or action of which one is ashamed when it appears, and which one would like to hide ; any disgracing action or thing ; the external portion of the organs of generation of a man or of a woman ; the anus ; corpse or dead body ; nakedness (Lane & Aqrab). The word is also sometimes figuratively applied to such weaknesses of a man as lie concealed within him.

Commentary :

As the place where Adam was made to reside has been metaphorically described in the Quran as a garden, therefore in the description that follows the metaphor is continued and Adam is represented as forbidden to approach a certain 'tree', which was not a tree in its literal sense but a certain family or tribe from which he was bidden to keep aloof, because the members of that family were his enemies and they would have spared no pains to do him harm. For the meaning of the word شجرة (tree) see 2 : 36.

Another reading of the word ملكين (*malakain*) *i.e.* two angels, is ملكين (*malikain*) *i.e.* two kings or rulers. This reading is corroborated by 20 : 121 *i.e. Shall I lead thee to the tree of eternity, and to a kingdom which shall never become decayed.*

The wicked man who is here represented as Satan worked his mischievous plan as follows : He came to Adam and said that the reason why God had forbidden him to have anything to do with the family referred to was none other than this that its members were inimically disposed to him and that they would have conspired to bring about his downfall, if he had then contracted intimate relations with them. But as the family had subsequently become friendly towards him, the danger no longer existed ; nay, the family would now even prove a source of strength for him. God's

23. So he caused them to fall *into disobedience* by deceit. And *^awhen they tasted of the tree, their shame became manifest to them and they began to stick the leaves of the Garden *together* over themselves. And their Lord called them, saying, 'Did I not forbid you that tree and tell you : *^bverily Satan is to you an open foe.'*?'⁹²⁴

فَدَلَّٮهُمَا بِغُرُوْرٍ ۚ فَلَمَّا ذَاقَا الشَّجَرَةَ بَدَتْ لَهُمَا سَوْاٰتُهُمَا وَطَفِقَا يَخْصِفٰنِ عَلَيْهِمَا مِنْ وَّرَقِ الْجَنَّةِ ۖ وَنَادٰىهُمَا رَبُّهُمَا اَلَمْ اَنْهَكُمَا عَنْ تِلْكُمَا الشَّجَرَةِ وَاَقُلْ لَّكُمَا اِنَّ الشَّيْطٰنَ لَكُمَا عَدُوٌّ مُّبِيْنٌ ۝

---

^a2:37; 20:122.   ^b2:169, 209; 6:143; 12:6; 20:118; 28:16; 35:7; 36:61.

---

prohibition, he pleaded, was not meant for all time, and the condition attached to it having come to an end, the prohibition also ceased to operate. In this way this Satan succeeded in deceiving Adam and he assured him on oath that he was his well-wisher (7:22.). Adam wavered and was led into thinking that as the reasons for the prohibition had indeed ceased to exist, the prohibition itself was no longer operative. That was an error of judgement on Adam's part. He did not wilfully disobey God's commandment. Elsewhere the Quran says, *He (Adam) forgot to observe Our commandment and We found in him no determination to do evil* (20:116).

924. Important Words :

دَلَّاهُمَا (caused them to fall into disobedience) is derived from دَلَّى or دَلَا. They say دَلَا الدَّلْوَ *i.e.* he pulled or drew the bucket (of water) out of the well. دَلَا حَاجَتَهُ means, he sought or demanded the object of his want. اَدْلَى الدَّلْوَ means, he let down the bucket into the well to draw out water with it. دَلَّى الشَّيْءَ means, he let down the thing or he let it fall or he made it hang down. It also means, he brought or drew the thing near to another. دَلَّاهُ بِغُرُوْرٍ means, he caused him to fall into disobedience by deceit; or he excited his cupidity with deceit and guile; or he caused him to fall into that which he desired without

his knowledge and so exposed him to loss or injury (Lane). The expression, as used in this verse, shows that Satan deceived Adam and drew him and his wife to himself or to the forbidden tree by deceitful talk and thus caused them to fall into disobedience, while they knew not.

وَرَق (leaves) is both singular and plural and is noun from the verb وَرَقَ. They say وَرَقَ الشَّجَرُ *i.e.* the tree put forth its leaves. اَوْرَقَ الرَّجُلُ means, the man became rich; his wealth and money increased. وَرَق, therefore, means, leaves, foliage, parchment; sheet of paper; thin plate of metal; minted silver coins; the prime and freshness of a thing; the young lads of a community; any animal having life (Aqrab, Lane & Lisān).

Commentary :

Every person has certain weaknesses which are hidden even from himself but which become exposed at a time of strain and stress or when he is tempted and tried. For instance, some men are cowardly, but they are not generally conscious of their cowardice. When, however, they encounter a danger, and their heart fails them, they realize their weakness. So it was when Adam was tempted and deceived by Satan that he became aware of his natural weaknesses. The Quran does not

24. They said, ^a'Our Lord, we have wronged ourselves; and if Thou forgive us not and have not mercy on us, we shall surely be of the lost.'925

قَالَا رَبَّنَا ظَلَمْنَا اَنْفُسَنَا وَاِنْ لَّمْ تَغْفِرْ لَنَا وَتَرْحَمْنَا لَنَكُوْنَنَّ مِنَ الْخٰسِرِيْنَ ۩

*a*2 : 38.

say that the weaknesses of Adam and his wife became known to other people, but that they became known to themselves.

The word سَوْأَة (treated under 7 : 21 above) is not used here in the sense of "nakedness" but rather of "objects of shame" or "weakness," because no man's nakedness is hidden from him. Some of Adam's weaknesses were indeed hidden from him and he came to realize them when his enemy lured him away from his position of security. Before this he did his work, aided and helped by divine grace which kept covered his failings and weaknesses; but when he allied himself with the family against which he had been warned, he was exposed and he realized, to his sorrow, how weak he was.

As Satan had succeeded in causing a split in the community and some of the weaker members had gone out of its fold, Adam gathered together the اوراق (leaves) of the garden *i.e.* the youth of the community and began to re-unite and re-organize his people with their help. It is generally the young men who, being mostly free from bias and regardless of dangers, follow and help the Prophets of God. Speaking of Moses, the Quran says : *And none obeyed Moses, save some youths from among his people, because of the fear of Pharaoh and their chiefs* (10 : 84).

It must be noted here that the being whom the Quran has represented as having refused to submit to Adam is called *Iblīs*, while the person who tempted him is called Satan. This distinction is observed not only in the verse under comment, but in all the relevant verses throughout the Quran. This shows that, so far as this narrative is concerned, Satan and *Iblīs* were two different persons. In fact, the word *Shaiṭān* (Satan) is applied not only to evil spirits but to certain human beings also who, on account of their evil nature and wicked deeds, become, as it were, fiends incarnate. Just as a man can advance in virtue and piety so as to become like an angel, similarly he may become morally so depraved and degenerate as to be called a devil. Thus the *Shaiṭān* who tempted Adam and caused him to slip was not an invisible evil spirit but a wicked man of flesh and blood, a devil from among human beings, a manifestation of Satan, and an agent of *Iblīs*. He was a member of the family which Adam had been bidden to avoid. The Holy Prophet tells us that his name was Ḥārith, literally meaning a farmer (Tirmidhī, ch. on *Tafsīr*) which is further evidence of his being a human being and not an evil spirit. See also 2 : 15 & 2 : 37.

Adam's error lay in taking this man-devil for a well-wisher, although God had warned him against having anything to do with him.

925. **Commentary :**

Adam did not long remain in error. He soon realized his mistake and hastened to turn to God in repentance.

25. He said, *a*'Go forth, some of you being enemies of others. And for you there is an abode on the earth and a provision for a time.'926

قَالَ اهْبِطُوْا بَعْضُكُمْ لِبَعْضٍ عَدُوٌّ ۚ وَ لَكُمْ فِي الْاَرْضِ مُسْتَقَرٌّ وَّ مَتَاعٌ اِلٰى حِيْنٍ ۞

26. He said, *b*'Therein shall you live, and therein shall you die, and therefrom shall you be brought forth.'927

قَالَ فِيْهَا تَحْيَوْنَ وَ فِيْهَا تَمُوْتُوْنَ وَ مِنْهَا تُخْرَجُوْنَ ۞

27. O children of Adam, We have indeed sent down to you raiment to cover your shame, and to be an elegant dress; but the raiment of righteousness—that is the best. That is *one* of the Signs of Allah, that they may remember.928

يٰبَنِيْ اٰدَمَ قَدْ اَنْزَلْنَا عَلَيْكُمْ لِبَاسًا يُّوَارِيْ سَوْاٰتِكُمْ وَ رِيْشًا ۚ وَ لِبَاسُ التَّقْوٰى ذٰلِكَ خَيْرٌ ۚ ذٰلِكَ مِنْ اٰيٰتِ اللّٰهِ لَعَلَّهُمْ يَذَّكَّرُوْنَ ۞

*a*2 : 37, 39 : 20 : 124.   *b*20 : 56 ; 71 : 18-19.

926. Commentary :

The verse shows that Adam was commanded to emigrate from the land of his birth because enmity and hatred had sprung up between different members of his community. This constitutes a further evidence of the fact that "the garden" which Adam was bidden to leave was not the Heaven or Paradise of the Quran, because, as the Quran itself tells us, Paradise is a place from which nobody is ever turned out (15 : 49), nor can Satan deceive or even approach any one there. It appears that Adam emigrated from Mesopotamia, the land of his birth, to a neighbouring land. The emigration was perhaps a temporary one, and Adam may have returned to his native land not long after. Indeed, the words, *a provision for a time,* contain a veiled hint at the emigration being a temporary one.

927. Commentary :

Adam is warned in this verse to be careful in future; for it was in his native land that he was now to live for ever.

Taken in the general sense, the verse also hints that no human being can ascend into the heavens with his physical body. Man must live and die on the earth.

928. Important Words :

رِيْش (elegant dress) is the substantive from رَاشَ. They say رَاشَهُ *i.e.* he feathered it, namely an arrow ; he fed him and gave him drink and clad him ; he strengthened and aided him ; he helped him to obtain his subsistence ; He (God) restored him from a state of poverty to a state of wealth or competence ; he did good to him. رِيْش means, feathers ; plumage of birds ; clothing ; or superb or fine clothing ; wealth ; the means of subsistence ; household goods or furniture (Lane & Aqrab).

Commentary :

This verse mentions two objects which our dress is meant to serve, *viz.*, (1) to cover our nakedness and (2) to serve as a decoration and embellishment and make us look elegant. With these two objects of clothing before us it is indeed regrettable that clothing has continued

28. O children of Adam, let not Satan seduce you, even as he turned your parents out of the Garden, stripping them of their raiment that he might show them their shame. Truly he sees you, he and his tribe, from where you see them not. Surely, *We have made satans friends for those who believe not.*929

يَـٰبَنِىٓ اٰدَمَ لَا يَفْتِنَنَّكُمُ الشَّيْطٰنُ كَمَآ اَخْرَجَ اَبَوَيْكُمْ مِّنَ الْجَنَّةِ يَنْزِعُ عَنْهُمَا لِبَاسَهُمَا لِيُرِيَهُمَا سَوْاٰتِهِمَا اِنَّهٗ يَرٰىكُمْ هُوَ وَقَبِيْلُهٗ مِنْ حَيْثُ لَا تَرَوْنَهُمْ اِنَّا جَعَلْنَا الشَّيٰطِيْنَ اَوْلِيَآءَ لِلَّذِيْنَ لَا يُؤْمِنُوْنَ ۝

29. And when they commit a foul deed, they say : 'We found our fathers doing it, and Allah has enjoined it upon us ?' Say, *Allah never enjoins foul deeds.* Do you say of Allah that which you know not ?'930

وَاِذَا فَعَلُوْا فَاحِشَةً قَالُوْا وَجَدْنَا عَلَيْهَآ اٰبَآءَنَا وَاللّٰهُ اَمَرَنَا بِهَا ۚ قُلْ اِنَّ اللّٰهَ لَا يَأْمُرُ بِالْفَحْشَآءِ ۚ اَتَقُوْلُوْنَ عَلَى اللّٰهِ مَا لَا تَعْلَمُوْنَ ۝

---

*a*2 : 258 ; 3 : 176 ; 16 : 101. *b*16 : 91.

to be progressively discarded by women in the West and this moral disease is now fast spreading in the East as well.

The words, *the raiment of righteousness,* explain the real significance of the word ریش (elegant dress). We are told that the apparel of piety is, in fact, the really fine raiment for man. Ordinary dress covers our physical nakedness, while the apparel of piety covers our spiritual and moral nakedness, and it was with this very apparel of piety that Adam covered his "nakedness" in the garden. He prayed to God Who heard his supplication and turned to him with mercy and forgiveness (7 : 24).

The verse beautifully reminds us that when we consider it to be so necessary to have good clothing to cover our physical nakedness and use elegant dress to look graceful, we should all the more be anxious to cover our moral and spiritual nakedness, which can only be done by prayer and by asking God's forgiveness and mercy as Adam did.

929. Commentary :

The Evil Spirit called شیطان (*Shaiṭān*) and those of his kind, are generally invisible to the human eye. They exercise their influence imperceptibly and search for the hidden weaknesses of man in order to expose him and confirm him in his evil ways. *Shaiṭān* is a descriptive name, meaning "one who has become removed from God." It is only by being removed away from God that one perishes. For a detailed explanation of the word see 2 : 37.

The expression, *We have made satans friends for those who believe not,* shows that Satan and his associates exercise their pernicious influence only on those who are already evilly disposed.

930. Commentary :

This verse, applied generally, gives an apposite description of those who follow Satan as stated in the preceding verse. It may also particularly apply to Christians who allege that Adam sinned and that it is from him that sin came as a heritage to his posterity who, therefore,

30. Say, *a* 'My Lord has enjoined justice. And fix your attention aright at every *time and* place of worship, and call upon Him, making yourselves sincere towards Him in religion. As He brought you into being, so shall you return.' 931

31. *b*Some has He guided, and *as for* others error has become their desert. They have taken evil ones for friends to the exclusion of Allah, and they think that they are rightly guided.

قُلْ اَمَرَ رَبِّيْ بِالْقِسْطِ وَاَقِيْمُوْا وُجُوْهَكُمْ عِنْدَ كُلِّ مَسْجِدٍ وَّادْعُوْهُ مُخْلِصِيْنَ لَهُ الدِّيْنَ ۦ كَمَا بَدَاَكُمْ تَعُوْدُوْنَ ۝

فَرِيْقًا هَدٰى وَفَرِيْقًا حَقَّ عَلَيْهِمُ الضَّلٰلَةُ ۣ اِنَّهُمُ اتَّخَذُوا الشَّيٰطِيْنَ اَوْلِيَآءَ مِنْ دُوْنِ اللّٰهِ وَيَحْسَبُوْنَ اَنَّهُمْ مُّهْتَدُوْنَ ۝

---

*a*4 : 59 ; 16 : 91 ; 57 : 26.   *b*16 : 37 ; 22 : 19.

---

cannot get rid of it. The Quran condemns this doctrine most forcibly; *firstly* because it is simply absurd and foolish, and *secondly* because the Quran exonerates Adam from the charge of having committed a sin.

By saying, *Allah has enjoined it upon us*, disbelievers mean that it is God Who has given them the power to commit sins or that He it is Who has created Satan that leads them astray. They thus seek to absolve themselves of the responsibility of their evil deeds. The latter part of the verse embodies an effective answer to this lame excuse. God never enjoins foul deeds, says the verse. As for Satan, the people do not understand the object of his creation. Satan is only a trial for men. He serves the purpose of a hurdle in a hurdle race. The hurdles are placed there not to block our progress but to make us vigilant and to cause us to increase our efforts. The careless and negligent person who stumbles over a hurdle and thus loses the race should blame himself and not the person who puts it in his way in order to try and prove his mettle.

931. Important Words :

مَسْجِد (time and place of worship) is derived from سَجَد *i.e.* he prostrated himself; or he bent himself down towards the ground and put his forehead on it; he lowered his head and bent himself; he was lowly, humble or submissive. مَسْجِد means, a place in which one performs the act of سَجْدَة *i.e.* the act of prostrating before God; a place in which one performs acts of worship or devotion; a place in which a person says his Prayers; a house of Prayer; a mosque or a Muslim temple (Lane). Being اسم ظرف the word may also mean, time of worship.

Commentary :

We are told in this verse that when the time of Prayer approaches and we are about to go to a mosque, we should fix our attention aright, setting our face to God and taking our minds away from the cares and thoughts of the world. The ablution performed before every Prayer also serves the useful purpose of turning our thoughts towards God and putting us in the right state for Prayers.

The words, *As He brought you into being, so shall you return*, are important because they point to the great truth that just as our bodies gradually develop in the wombs of our mothers, so will our souls pass through a similar process of development after our death. We should, therefore, be very careful about our souls.

32. O children of Adam, look to your adornment at every *time and* place of worship, and eat and drink but *a*exceed not the bounds ; surely, He does not love those who exceed the bounds.**932**

يٰبَنِيْۤ اٰدَمَ خُذُوْا زِيْنَتَكُمْ عِنْدَ كُلِّ مَسْجِدٍ وَّ كُلُوْا وَاشْرَبُوْا وَلَا تُسْرِفُوْا ۚ اِنَّهٗ لَا يُحِبُّ الْمُسْرِفِيْنَ ۞

R. 4   33. Say, 'Who has forbidden the adornment of Allah which He has produced for His servants, and *b*the good things of *His* providing ? ' Say 'They are for the believers in the present life *and* exclusively *for them* on the Day of Resurrection. Thus do We explain the Signs for a people who have knowledge.'**933**

قُلْ مَنْ حَرَّمَ زِيْنَةَ اللّٰهِ الَّتِيْۤ اَخْرَجَ لِعِبَادِهٖ وَالطَّيِّبٰتِ مِنَ الرِّزْقِ ۚ قُلْ هِيَ لِلَّذِيْنَ اٰمَنُوْا فِي الْحَيٰوةِ الدُّنْيَا خَالِصَةً يَّوْمَ الْقِيٰمَةِ ۗ كَذٰلِكَ نُفَصِّلُ الْاٰيٰتِ لِقَوْمٍ يَّعْلَمُوْنَ ۞

*a*17 : 28 ; 25 : 68.   *b*2 : 169, 173 ; 23 : 52.

---

932. Commentary :

The adornment mentioned in the verse may either be physical or spiritual. Taking it in the physical sense, the verse enjoins believers to go to a place of worship, as far as possible, in a clean and decent dress, free from physical impurities and evil smell. The Holy Prophet is reported to have forbidden Muslims to go to a mosque after having eaten onions, garlic, etc., as the bad smell of these things causes discomfort to others. He is also reported to have enjoined the Faithful to take frequent baths, especially before the great congregational Prayer on Friday. Taken in the spiritual sense, the verse would mean that Prayers should be offered with a pure and sincere heart free from distracting thoughts.

The latter part of the verse embodies a basic commandment about eating and drinking. It has been joined to the commandment relating to "adornment at a place of worship," *firstly* because clothing and eating are allied subjects, and *secondly* to indicate that while issuing a commandment about Prayers, which is a spiritual matter, Islam does not overlook man's physical requirements.

The words, *exceed not the bounds,* signify: (1) that one should not over-eat oneself and (2) that one should not always use the same kind of food, but should vary it from time to time. Animal foods, vegetables, fruits, etc. should all be eaten in proper quantity and proper proportion. In this connection see *The Teachings of Islam* by Ahmad, the Promised Messiah.

933. Commentary :

Islam being not a religion of monasticism, the verse implies a rebuke for those who forbid the use of pure and good things.

The good and pure things of God's provision, which are really meant for, and deserved by, believers only are also shared by disbelievers in this life ; but in the life to come they will be enjoyed by believers only, to the exclusion of disbelievers.

34. Say, *a*‘ My Lord has only forbidden foul deeds, whether open or secret, and sin and wrongful transgression, and that *b*you associate with Allah that for which He has sent down no authority, and that you say of Allah that of which you have no knowledge.’934

قُلْ اِنَّمَا حَرَّمَ رَبِّيَ الْفَوَاحِشَ مَا ظَهَرَ مِنْهَا وَمَا بَطَنَ وَالْاِثْمَ وَالْبَغْيَ بِغَيْرِ الْحَقِّ وَاَنْ تُشْرِكُوْا بِاللّٰهِ مَا لَمْ يُنَزِّلْ بِهٖ سُلْطٰنًا وَّاَنْ تَقُوْلُوْا عَلَى اللّٰهِ مَا لَا تَعْلَمُوْنَ ۝

35. And *c*for every people there is a term, and when their term is come, they cannot remain behind a single moment, nor can they get ahead *of it.*935

وَلِكُلِّ اُمَّةٍ اَجَلٌ ۚ فَاِذَا جَآءَ اَجَلُهُمْ لَا يَسْتَأْخِرُوْنَ سَاعَةً وَّلَا يَسْتَقْدِمُوْنَ ۝

---

*a*6 : 152.   *b*3 : 152 ; 7 : 72 ; 22 : 72.   *c*10 : 50 ; 15 : 6 ; 16 : 62 ; 35 : 46.

---

934. Commentary :

The verse draws our attention to the purity of divine teachings by pointing out that all evil things are forbidden by Islam. But at the same time it reminds the reader that there are certain things the evil of which is generally hidden from men. These, too, are forbidden and most of them have been mentioned by the Holy Prophet.

The verse next proceeds to explain what it means by فواحش (foul deeds). It divides them into three classes : (1) اثم (the sin of disobedience or of falling short in the performance of a duty), and بغى (transgression *i.e.* exceeding the proper bounds). (2) شرك (associating with God that for which He has sent down no authority). The فواحش (foul deeds) of this class mean idolatrous beliefs and polytheistic ideals. (3) "That you say against Allah what you do not know." By the فواحش of this class are meant the false and evil words we utter. Thus we are enjoined to be pure not only in thought but also in word and deed.

935. Important Words :

يستقدمون (get ahead) is derived from قدم *i.e.* he preceded ; or he came before ; or he headed (someone else). استقدم القوم means, he preceded the people, or he went ahead of the people, or he went before them (Lane & Aqrab). As one who gets ahead of a thing virtually leaves it behind, therefore the idea in يستقدمون (get ahead) is that of escaping.

يستأخرون (remain behind) is derived from اخر. They say استأخر القوم *i.e.* he remained behind the people. استأخر also means, he or it was put behind or put off or delayed (Lane & Aqrab). As one who remains behind a thing virtually puts the thing off, therefore the idea in يستأخرون (remain behind) is that of putting off.

Commentary :

The verse means that when the time fixed for the punishment of a people comes, it cannot be averted. Disbelievers, who have incurred it, can neither escape it nor put it off by a single moment.

36. O children of Adam, ^aif Messengers come to you from among yourselves, rehearsing My Signs unto you, then whoso shall fear God and do good deeds, on them shall come no fear nor shall they grieve.[936]

يٰبَنِیۡۤ اٰدَمَ اِمَّا یَاۡتِیَنَّکُمۡ رُسُلٌ مِّنۡکُمۡ یَقُصُّوۡنَ عَلَیۡکُمۡ اٰیٰتِیۡ فَمَنِ اتَّقٰی وَ اَصۡلَحَ فَلَا خَوۡفٌ عَلَیۡهِمۡ وَ لَا هُمۡ یَحۡزَنُوۡنَ ۞

37. But ^bthose who reject Our Signs and turn away from them with disdain,—these shall be the inmates of the Fire; they shall abide therein.[937]

وَ الَّذِیۡنَ کَذَّبُوۡا بِاٰیٰتِنَا وَ اسۡتَکۡبَرُوۡا عَنۡهَاۤ اُولٰٓئِکَ اَصۡحٰبُ النَّارِ ۚ هُمۡ فِیۡهَا خٰلِدُوۡنَ ۞

---

^a2:39; 20:124.   ^b2:40; 5:11, 87; 6:50; 7:41; 22:58.

936. Commentary :

The point is worthy of special note that, like some previous verses (e.g. 7:27, 28 & 32), the address in the words, *O children of Adam*, is here made to the people of the Holy Prophet's time and to the generations that are yet to be born and not to the people who lived in the distant past and followed Adam immediately. This form of address has been employed with a view to introducing an important subject which was to be conveyed to future generations of mankind. This is to the effect that Messengers of God will continue to appear as long as the children of Adam live upon this earth and that the opposition of the Holy Prophet's enemies would not bring about his downfall nor the cessation of prophethood. The great promise which was held out to the progeny of Adam in the time of Adam (2:39) and according to which Messengers of God appeared among different peoples in different countries at different times will continue to be fulfilled till the end of time.

The words, *if Messengers come to you from among yourselves*, do not mean that Messengers of God may or may not come, just as the words, *If there comes to you guidance from Me* (2:39), do not mean that guidance might or might not come. Indeed, the word اما (if) is intended to mean that if you happen to live at a time when a Messenger of God appears, you should not fail to accept him. Thus the word is simply meant to leave the time unfixed; the Messenger of God may appear in one generation or another but whenever he appears, he must be accepted.

The words, *rehearsing My Signs unto you*, hint at the fact that the Messengers who were to come after the Holy Prophet were to bring no new Law but were to follow the Law of Islam; they were simply to "rehearse" or recite the verses already revealed in the Quran.

937. Commentary :

This verse serves as a particular warning for Muslims that they should not make light of the Messengers who would appear among them and should not reject them. The Law has indeed been made perfect in the Quran; but that does not mean that later Messengers of God may be rejected with impunity.

38. ^aWho is, then, more unjust than he who forges a lie against Allah or gives the lie to His Signs ? It is these who shall have their lot as ordained till when Our messengers shall visit them to take away their souls, they shall say, ^b'Where is that which you used to call upon beside Allah ?' They will answer, 'We cannot find them;' and ^cthey will bear witness against themselves that they were disbelievers.[938]

39. He will say, 'Enter ye into the Fire among the nations of Jinn and men who passed away before you.' Every time a people enters, it shall curse its sister (people) until, when they have all successively arrived therein, the last of them will say of the first of them, ^d' Our Lord, these led us astray, so give them a double punishment of the Fire.' He will say, ' For each *preceding party* there shall be double *punishment*, but you do not know.'[939]

فَمَنْ اَظْلَمُ مِمَّنِ افْتَرٰى عَلَى اللّٰهِ كَذِبًا اَوْ كَذَّبَ بِاٰيٰتِهٖ ۚ اُولٰٓئِكَ يَنَالُهُمْ نَصِيْبُهُمْ مِّنَ الْكِتٰبِ ۚ حَتّٰى اِذَا جَآءَتْهُمْ رُسُلُنَا يَتَوَفَّوْنَهُمْ ۙ قَالُوْۤا اَيْنَ مَا كُنْتُمْ تَدْعُوْنَ مِنْ دُوْنِ اللّٰهِ ۗ قَالُوْا ضَلُّوْا عَنَّا وَشَهِدُوْا عَلٰۤى اَنْفُسِهِمْ اَنَّهُمْ كَانُوْا كٰفِرِيْنَ ۝

قَالَ ادْخُلُوْا فِيْۤ اُمَمٍ قَدْ خَلَتْ مِنْ قَبْلِكُمْ مِّنَ الْجِنِّ وَالْاِنْسِ فِي النَّارِ ۗ كُلَّمَا دَخَلَتْ اُمَّةٌ لَّعَنَتْ اُخْتَهَا ۗ حَتّٰۤى اِذَا ادَّارَكُوْا فِيْهَا جَمِيْعًا ۙ قَالَتْ اُخْرٰىهُمْ لِاُوْلٰىهُمْ رَبَّنَا هٰٓؤُلَآءِ اَضَلُّوْنَا فَاٰتِهِمْ عَذَابًا ضِعْفًا مِّنَ النَّارِ ۗ قَالَ لِكُلٍّ ضِعْفٌ وَّلٰكِنْ لَّا تَعْلَمُوْنَ ۝

---

^a6 : 22 ; 10 : 18 ; 11 : 19 ; 61 : 8.   ^b6 : 23 ; 40 : 74-75.   ^c6 : 131   ^d38 : 62.

---

938. Commentary :

The verse gives the reasons why the rejectors of divine Messengers deserve severe punishment. People incur the wrath of God because they treat His Messenger as a liar and reject the heavenly Signs he brings with him. Indeed, impostors and the rejectors of true Messengers are equally doomed and can never escape the punishment ordained for them.

The words, *who shall have their lot as ordained*, mean that the rejectors of God's Messengers will see before their very eyes the fulfilment of the prophecies foretelling their defeat and discomfiture and shall taste of the punishment promised to them for opposing God's Messengers.

939. Important Words :

اداركوا (successively arrived) is derived from درك. They say درك المطر *i.e.* the rain dropped with close consecutiveness. ادركه means, he attained, reached or overtook him. اداركوا which is the same as تداركوا means, they attained, reached, overtook or came up with one another ; or the last of them attained, reached, overtook or came up with the first of them. The expression حتى اذا اداركوا فيها جميعا means, until when they have overtaken one another ; or until they have successively arrived therein all together (Lane).

Commentary :

The words, *For each preceding party there*

40. And the first of them will say to the last of them : ' You have then no superiority over us ; taste therefore the punishment for all that you did.'

وَقَالَتْ أُولَاهُمْ لِأُخْرَاهُمْ فَمَا كَانَ لَكُمْ عَلَيْنَا مِن فَضْلٍ فَذُوقُوا الْعَذَابَ بِمَا كُنتُمْ تَكْسِبُونَ ﴿٣٩﴾

R. 5　41. ^aThose who reject Our Signs and turn away from them with disdain, the gates of the *spiritual* firmament will not be opened for them, nor will they enter Heaven until a camel goes through the eye of a needle. And thus do We requite the offenders.⁹⁴⁰

إِنَّ الَّذِينَ كَذَّبُوا بِآيَاتِنَا وَاسْتَكْبَرُوا عَنْهَا لَا تُفَتَّحُ لَهُمْ أَبْوَابُ السَّمَاءِ وَلَا يَدْخُلُونَ الْجَنَّةَ حَتَّى يَلِجَ الْجَمَلُ فِي سَمِّ الْخِيَاطِ وَكَذَلِكَ نَجْزِى الْمُجْرِمِينَ ﴿٤٠﴾

---

^aSee 7 : 37.

---

shall be double punishment, are explained in a saying of the Holy Prophet which is to the effect that he who starts a good practice, *i.e.*, he who does a good deed in such a manner that others copy and follow him, shall have a double reward, and he who starts a bad practice shall have a double punishment. In fact, a person who does a good or a bad deed not only benefits or suffers by it himself but leaves it as an example to follow for those who come after him. He, therefore, deserves a double reward or punishment as the case may be. The above-quoted words of the verse are also intended to point to the fact that each party that follows another also precedes the one that follows it. So there is no question of awarding double punishment to one and letting the other go with only single punishment.

940. Important Words :

الْجَمَلُ (camel) is the noun-infinitive from جمل They say جمل الشيء *i.e.* he collected the thing. جمل الشهم means, he melted the fat. جميل (*jamila*) or جمل (*jamula*) with different vowel points at the central root letter, means, he was or became beautiful, goodly or pleasing in person or behaviour. جمل means, a he-camel ; a full grown he-camel ; a camel ; palm-trees as being likened to the he-camel in respect of their tallness and bigness ; a large sea fish or whale (Lane.) It also means a cable or a ship's rope (Aqrab).

Commentary :

With this verse begins a description of the life after death, a brief reference to which was made in the three preceding verses.

Heaven is the lofty abode of true believers. The Holy Prophet used to say that it is the souls of the righteous that shall reside in the garden of Heaven, while those of the wicked shall descend into the pit of Hell.

The words, *the gates of the spiritual firmament will not be opened for them,* signify that rejectors of God's Signs are never vouchsafed the spiritual knowledge and the nearness of God granted to believers.

Though in the translation the word جمل has been rendered as ' camel ' following a parallel expression in the New Testament (Matt. 19 : 24), yet the Arabic sentence may be better explained by using the word ' rope ', for a rope rather than a camel bears a resemblance to the thread which is passed through the eye of a needle. The expression, *until a camel (or a rope) goes through the eye of a needle*, signifies that it will be impossible for rejectors of God's Signs to enter Heaven.

42. ^aThey shall have a bed of Hell, and over them coverings *of the same.* And thus do We requite the unjust.⁹⁴¹

لَهُمْ مِّنْ جَهَنَّمَ مِهَادٌ وَّمِنْ فَوْقِهِمْ غَوَاشٍ ۚ وَ كَذٰلِكَ نَجْزِى الظّٰلِمِيْنَ ۞

43. But *as to* those who believe and do good works,—*and* ^bWe task not any soul beyond its capacity—these are the inmates of Heaven; they shall abide therein.⁹⁴²

وَالَّذِيْنَ اٰمَنُوْا وَعَمِلُوا الصّٰلِحٰتِ لَا نُكَلِّفُ نَفْسًا اِلَّا وُسْعَهَآ اُولٰٓئِكَ اَصْحٰبُ الْجَنَّةِ هُمْ فِيْهَا خٰلِدُوْنَ ۞

44. And ^cWe shall remove whatever rancour may be in their hearts. ^dBeneath them shall flow rivers. And they shall say, ^e'All praise belongs to Allah Who has guided us to this. And we could not have found guidance, if Allah had not guided us. The Messengers of our Lord did indeed bring the truth.' And it shall be proclaimed unto them : 'This is the Heaven which you have been given for an inheritance as a reward for what you used to do.'⁹⁴³

وَنَزَعْنَا مَا فِيْ صُدُوْرِهِمْ مِّنْ غِلٍّ تَجْرِيْ مِنْ تَحْتِهِمُ الْاَنْهٰرُ ۚ وَقَالُوا الْحَمْدُ لِلّٰهِ الَّذِيْ هَدٰىنَا لِهٰذَا وَمَا كُنَّا لِنَهْتَدِيَ لَوْلَا اَنْ هَدٰىنَا اللّٰهُ ۚ لَقَدْ جَآءَتْ رُسُلُ رَبِّنَا بِالْحَقِّ ۖ وَنُوْدُوْا اَنْ تِلْكُمُ الْجَنَّةُ اُوْرِثْتُمُوْهَا بِمَا كُنْتُمْ تَعْمَلُوْنَ ۞

---

^a39 : 17. ^b2 : 234, 287 ; 6 : 153 ; 7 : 43 ; 23 : 63. ^c15 : 48. ^dSee 2 : 26. ^e10 : 11 ; 39 : 75.

---

941. Important Words :

غَوَاشٍ (coverings) is the plural of غَاشِيَة which is derived from غَشِى. They say غَشِيَهُ *i.e.* it covered or concealed him ; or it overcame or overwhelmed him. غَشِيَهُ also means, he came to him. غِشَاوَة (of which غَوَاشٍ is the plural) means, a covering ; a calamity or misfortune ; punishment ; fire of Hell ; a man's resorters such as hangers-on, seekers of favours, servants and dependants ; also visitors, guests and friends (Lane).

Commentary :

The word غَوَاشٍ rendered as "coverings" also means "servants," and "dependants." Taking the word in the latter sense, the sentence may mean that disbelievers will have their believing "servants" and "dependants" above them on the Day of Judgement.

942. Commentary :

The parenthetical clause, *We task not any soul beyond its capacity,* contradicts the Christian dogma that sin being ingrained in human nature, it is beyond the power of man to get rid of it, and that this natural disability of man is remedied only by belief in the atonement of Jesus. The word 'task' shows that by 'good works' are meant such good works as are in the power of man to do.

943. Important Words :

غِل (rancour) is from the verb غَلَّ which means, it entered (into a thing) or it caused to enter. Thus it is both transitive and intransitive. غَلَّ also means, it entered and became mixed up or confused with a thing. غَلَّ فُلَانٌ كَذَا means, such a one took that thing secretly and concealed it. غَلَّ بَصَرَهُ

45. And the inmates of Heaven will call out to the inmates of Hell, *saying*: ' We have indeed found what our Lord promised us to be true. Have you too found what your Lord promised you to be true ? ' They shall say : ' Yes '. Then a proclaimer shall proclaim between them, *saying*, ' The curse of Allah is on the wrongdoers—[944]

46. [a] ' Who turn *men* away from the path of Allah and seek to make it crooked, and who are disbelievers in the Hereafter.'[945]

وَنَادَى أَصْحَابُ الْجَنَّةِ أَصْحَابَ النَّارِ أَنْ قَدْ وَجَدْنَا مَا وَعَدَنَا رَبُّنَا حَقًّا فَهَلْ وَجَدْتُمْ مَا وَعَدَ رَبُّكُمْ حَقًّا قَالُوا نَعَمْ فَأَذَّنَ مُؤَذِّنٌ بَيْنَهُمْ أَنْ لَعْنَةُ اللَّهِ عَلَى الظَّالِمِينَ ۝

الَّذِينَ يَصُدُّونَ عَنْ سَبِيلِ اللَّهِ وَيَبْغُونَهَا عِوَجًا وَهُمْ بِالْآخِرَةِ كَافِرُونَ ۝

---

[a]7 : 87; 11 : 20; 14 : 4; 16 : 89.

---

means, his eye-sight deviated from the right course. غل الرجل means, the man acted unfaithfully and dishonestly. غل means, rancour or latent rancour; malevolence; malice; spite; enmity; insincerity and dishonesty (Lane & Aqrab).

Commentary :

The freedom of the heart from feelings of rancour and malice is indeed one of the great blessings of Heaven promised to the believers ; and as true heavenly life should begin in this very world, a Muslim should always try to purge his heart of such feelings as are nothing but a source of disquiet for one who is a prey to them.

The question implied in the words, *we could not have found guidance, if Allah had not guided us*, is answered in the words that follow which may be expanded thus : " If Allah had not sent His Messengers, we could not have been rightly guided; for it was not possible for us to devise a Law for ourselves and without a Law we could not perform good works. Law is therefore not a curse but a blessing, for it enables us to reach Heaven."

The word تلكم (this) in the clause, *This is*

the Heaven, is used to point to a thing. Heaven is here pointed out to believers, as they have not yet entered it. But they have at the same time been declared to be "the inmates of Heaven," because they have already earned it by their good works. Moreover, true heavenly life begins in this very world, although the full manifestation thereof will be in the next. See 2 : 26 & 55 : 47.

944. Commentary :

A highly significant dialogue between the inmates of Heaven and of Hell begins from this verse.

The word الظالمين (wrongdoers) may also be rendered as "idolaters" or "worshippers of false deities." See 31 : 14.

945. Commentary :

This verse defines and qualifies the " wrongdoers " mentioned in the preceding verse. The expression, *and seek to make it crooked*, means that the wrongdoers desire to corrupt true religion. They are not only themselves wicked but also try to make others so, and even seek to corrupt the religion sent for their good. They also disbelieve in the Hereafter.

47. And between the two there shall be a partition, and on the elevated places there shall be men who will know all by their marks. And they will call out to the people of Heaven. 'Peace be on you.' These will not have *yet* entered it although they will be hoping *to do so.*946

وَبَيْنَهُمَا حِجَابٌ ۚ وَعَلَى الْأَعْرَافِ رِجَالٌ يَعْرِفُونَ كُلًّا بِسِيمَاهُمْ ۚ وَنَادَوْا أَصْحَابَ الْجَنَّةِ أَنْ سَلَامٌ عَلَيْكُمْ ۗ لَمْ يَدْخُلُوهَا وَهُمْ يَطْمَعُونَ ۝

48. And when their eyes are turned towards the people of the Fire, they will say, *a*'Our Lord, put us not with the unjust people.' 947

وَإِذَا صُرِفَتْ أَبْصَارُهُمْ تِلْقَاءَ أَصْحَابِ النَّارِ قَالُوا رَبَّنَا لَا تَجْعَلْنَا مَعَ الْقَوْمِ الظَّالِمِينَ ۝

---

*a*23 : 95.

946. Important Words :

اعراف (elevated places) is the plural of عرف 'urf (an elevated place) which is substantive from عرف. They say عرف الشيئ *i.e.* he knew the thing; he was or became acquainted with the thing; he knew it by means of the five senses; or he knew it by mental perception or reflection. They say عرف على القوم *i.e.* he was or became manager or superintendent of the affairs of the people, being acquainted with their circumstances. عرف ('urf) means, goodness, favour, bounty and a thing freely given; good fellowship with others; an elevated sand; an elevated place; an elevated or overtopping back of anything high (Lane & Aqrab).

Commentary :

It is generally men of high dignity and distinguished position that are seated on elevated places. According to Ḥasan and Mujāhid, the men on the elevated places will be the *elite* among the believers or the most learned among them; according to Kirmānī, they will be the Martyrs. Some others think that they will be the Prophets and this appears to be the most correct view. The men seated on elevated places will not only command a better view, but, on account of their high rank and position, will also be better informed. They will know the rank and station of every person from his very appearance.

The words, *These will not have yet entered it*, refer to those would-be dwellers of Heaven who will not have yet entered it, but will be hoping to do so soon. The people on the elevated places will recognize them as dwellers of Heaven, even though they will not have yet entered it.

It is a commonly held, but nevertheless a wrong, view that the men on the A'rāf (elevated places) will be those middling persons whose case will not have yet been decided, it being, as it were, still under consideration. But if such had been the case, they could not have rebuked the inmates of the Fire in the manner in which they are represented to be doing in 7 : 49 below. There is also no sense in placing middling persons on elevated places while the true believers, including Martyrs, Prophets, etc., occupy lower ones.

947. Commentary :

The passive voice used in the words, *when their eyes are turned*, shows that the eyes of the men on the elevated places will be made to turn towards the inmates of Hell by some higher power *i.e.* God, with some definite purpose which was to provide occasion for making certain announcements.

R. 6　49. And the occupants of the elevated places will call out to men whom they will know by their marks, *and* say, "Your multitude availed you not, nor your arrogance.⁹⁴⁸

وَنَادٰٓى اَصْحٰبُ الْاَعْرَافِ رِجَالًا يَّعْرِفُوْنَهُمْ بِسِيْمٰهُمْ قَالُوْا مَآ اَغْنٰى عَنْكُمْ جَمْعُكُمْ وَمَا كُنْتُمْ تَسْتَكْبِرُوْنَ ۝

50. *a*"Are these the men about whom you swore that Allah would not extend mercy to them ? *To them it has been said,* 'Enter Paradise ; no fear shall come upon you, nor shall you grieve.'"⁹⁴⁹

اَهٰٓؤُلَآءِ الَّذِيْنَ اَقْسَمْتُمْ لَا يَنَالُهُمُ اللّٰهُ بِرَحْمَةٍ اُدْخُلُوا الْجَنَّةَ لَا خَوْفٌ عَلَيْكُمْ وَلَآ اَنْتُمْ تَحْزَنُوْنَ ۝

51. And the inmates of the Fire will call out to the inmates of Heaven, 'Pour out on us some water or some of that which Allah has provided for you.' They will say, 'Verily, Allah has forbidden them both to disbelievers—⁹⁵⁰

وَنَادٰٓى اَصْحٰبُ النَّارِ اَصْحٰبَ الْجَنَّةِ اَنْ اَفِيْضُوْا عَلَيْنَا مِنَ الْمَآءِ اَوْ مِمَّا رَزَقَكُمُ اللّٰهُ قَالُوْٓا اِنَّ اللّٰهَ حَرَّمَهُمَا عَلَى الْكٰفِرِيْنَ ۝

---

*a*23 : 111.

The last sentence of the verse spoken by the men on the elevated places, *i.e., Our Lord, put us not with the unjust people,* does not show that those who will utter these words will yet be in a state of uncertainty and that their case will not yet have been decided. They are mere words of piety or of God-fearingness that even a Prophet would utter when he sees an object of God's punishment.

948. Commentary :

The occupants of the elevated places, *i.e.,* the Prophets, shall call out to certain persons from among the people, to whom they had been sent and whom they will recognize by their marks, telling them to see the end of their opposition.

The particle ما (not) may also be taken in the interrogative sense, meaning "what". In that case the sentence would be rendered as "of what avail was your multitude to you and your arrogance ? " In this sense the sentence

would constitute a very pointed rebuke by the Prophets to the dwellers of Hell.

949. Commentary :

The reference in the word هٰؤُلَاء (these) is to the would-be inmates of Heaven. The Prophets will address the inmates of Hell, telling them to look at the inmates of Heaven and then will ask them, "Are these the men about whom you swore that Allah would not extend mercy to them ?" And then without waiting for an answer the Prophets would turn to the would-be inmates of Heaven and ask them to come forward and enter Paradise.

The words, *Enter Paradise,* show that the would-be inmates of Heaven had not yet entered Paradise but hoped to do so soon.

950. Important Words :

اَفِيْضُوْا (pour) is derived from اَفَاضَ which again is derived from فَاضَ which means, it (water, etc.) overflowed, or poured forth from fulness. اَفَاضَ means, he filled (a vessel) so

52. ^a'Those who took their religion for a pastime and a sport, and whom the life of the world beguiled.' This day, ^bthen, shall We forget them as they forgot the meeting of this day of theirs, and as they used to deny Our Signs.⁹⁵¹

53. And surely ^cWe have brought them a Book which We have expounded with knowledge, a guidance and a mercy for a people who believe.⁹⁵²

الَّذِيْنَ اتَّخَذُوْا دِيْنَهُمْ لَهْوًا وَّ لَعِبًا وَّ غَرَّتْهُمُ الْحَيَوةُ الدُّنْيَا ۚ فَالْيَوْمَ نَنْسٰهُمْ كَمَا نَسُوْا لِقَآءَ يَوْمِهِمْ هٰذَا ۙ وَمَا كَانُوْا بِاٰيٰتِنَا يَجْحَدُوْنَ ۝

وَلَقَدْ جِئْنٰهُمْ بِكِتٰبٍ فَصَّلْنٰهُ عَلٰى عِلْمٍ هُدًى وَّ رَحْمَةً لِّقَوْمٍ يُّؤْمِنُوْنَ ۝

---

^a5:58; 6:71.   ^b45:35.   ^c6:115; 10:58; 12:112; 16:90; 29:52.

---

that it overflowed; he made it (water, etc.) to flow or run; he poured out water, etc. (Lane).

Commentary:

The use of the words افيضوا علينا (pour on us) by the inmates of Hell implies that they would in a way flatter the inmates of Heaven by saying to them that they had enjoyed God's blessings (which were virtually overflowing) to their heart's content, and would then beg of them to give them a little of the abundant good that God had bestowed upon them. This condition of the inmates of Hell is well illustrated by the parable of Abraham and Lazarus in Luke 16:23-24.

951. Commentary:

This verse qualifies the word "disbelievers" occurring in the preceding verse. The dis-

believers spoken of at the end of that verse were convinced in their hearts of the truth of Islam but, as they took their religion as a pastime, they refused to listen to the dictates of reason and the voice of their conscience. So God forgot them even as they had forgotten the meeting of their Lord.

952. Commentary:

The Book referred to in this verse is the Quran. It embodies three distinct things:—

(1) "Knowledge" essential for recognizing and knowing God;

(2) "Guidance" properly to discharge the duties due to God and to observe the rights of man; and

(3) "God's mercy" descending on the Faithful.

54. *a*Do they wait only for the fulfilment *of warnings* thereof ? On the day when the fulfilment thereof shall come, those who had forgotten it before shall say, ' The Messengers of our Lord did indeed bring the truth. Have we then any intercessors to intercede for us ? Or *b*could we be sent back so that we might do other than that which we used to do ?' They have indeed ruined their souls and that which they used to fabricate has failed them.[953]

هَلْ يَنْظُرُوْنَ اِلَّا تَأْوِيْلَهٗ يَوْمَ يَأْتِيْ تَأْوِيْلُهٗ يَقُوْلُ الَّذِيْنَ نَسُوْهُ مِنْ قَبْلُ قَدْ جَآءَتْ رُسُلُ رَبِّنَا بِالْحَقِّ فَهَلْ لَّنَا مِنْ شُفَعَآءَ فَيَشْفَعُوْا لَنَآ اَوْ نُرَدُّ فَنَعْمَلَ غَيْرَ الَّذِيْ كُنَّا نَعْمَلُ قَدْ خَسِرُوْا اَنْفُسَهُمْ وَضَلَّ عَنْهُمْ مَّا كَانُوْا يَفْتَرُوْنَ ۝

7   55. Surely, *c*your Lord is Allah, Who created the heavens and the earth in six days ; then He settled Himself on the Throne. *d*He makes the night cover the day, which pursues it swiftly. *And He created* the sun and the moon and the stars, *all* made subservient by His command. Verily, His is the creation and the command. Blessed is Allah, the Lord of the worlds.[954]

اِنَّ رَبَّكُمُ اللّٰهُ الَّذِيْ خَلَقَ السَّمٰوٰتِ وَالْاَرْضَ فِيْ سِتَّةِ اَيَّامٍ ثُمَّ اسْتَوٰى عَلَى الْعَرْشِ يُغْشِى الَّيْلَ النَّهَارَ يَطْلُبُهٗ حَثِيْثًا وَّالشَّمْسَ وَالْقَمَرَ وَالنُّجُوْمَ مُسَخَّرٰتٍ بِاَمْرِهٖ اَلَا لَهُ الْخَلْقُ وَالْاَمْرُ تَبٰرَكَ اللّٰهُ رَبُّ الْعٰلَمِيْنَ ۝

---

*a*2 : 211 ; 6 : 159.   *b*26 : 103 ; 35 : 38 ; 39 : 59.   *c*10 : 4 ; 11 : 8 ; 25 : 60 ; 32 : 5 ; 41 : 10—13 ;
                 50 : 39 ; 57 : 5.   *d*13 : 4 ; 36 : 38.

---

953. Important Words :

تَأْوِيْل (fulfilment) means, revealing, disclosing, or expounding ; interpretation ; and issue, result or final sequel. The words هل ينظرون الا تاويله mean, do they wait for aught save the result to which their case will come by the appearance of the promises and threats which it (the Book) has foretold (Lane). See also 3 : 8. For the sake of convenience the word has been rendered here as " fulfilment of warnings."

Commentary :

The verse constitutes at once a rebuke and a warning to the disbelievers. What are they waiting for, asks the verse, after they have been given such a perfect Book as the Quran and such a perfect exemplar as the Holy Prophet, except that God's promised punishment should overtake them ?

954. Important Words :

عرش (Throne) is substantive from the verb which means, he constructed or built a shed or a building, etc. عرش البيت means, he built or constructed the house. عرش بالمكان means, he put up, or lodged, in the house. The saying من العرش الى الفرش means, from the highest sphere to the lowness of the earth. عرش means, a shed or building constructed for shade ; a house in an absolute sense ; a dwelling or a place of abode ; the wood upon which one stands when drawing water ; the roof of a house or the like ; the throne or the seat of a king ; the means of support of a thing or an affair ; might or power ; regal power ; sovereignty ; dominion. The expression استوى على العرش means, He (God) reigned as King ; He settled Himself on the Throne ; He was or became established on the Throne of Power and Majesty (Lane & Aqrab). See also 2 : 30 & 6 : 142.

Commentary :

The word يوم (day) also means "time" absolutely (1 : 4) ; and it is in this sense that the word has been used in the present verse. It is difficult to say how long these six periods of time were in which, according to this verse, the heavens and the earth were created. They may have extended over hundreds of thousands of years. The word ايام (days) evidently is not used here in the sense of ordinary days of 24 hours, because such days are determined by the rising and setting of the sun and the sun itself being a part of this universe came into existence simultaneously with it.

The word ثم (then) shows that after completing the creation of the heavens and the earth in six "days" or six "periods," God settled Himself on the Throne on the seventh day. As the Arabic word سبع (seven) is generally used as a symbol of perfection, the expression would signify that on the seventh day when God became established on the Throne of His Power and Majesty, the universe became in perfect working order.

The "night and day" mentioned in the clause, *He makes the night cover the day*, have been mentioned here as symbolizing sin and virtue. In fact, the phenomenon of sin in a perfectly ordered universe is explainable only by the phenomenon of night. Just as that part of the earth which is hidden from the sun is covered by darkness ; similarly when a man turns away from God, he becomes involved in the darkness of sin ; but when he turns his face towards God, the day dawns for him and he basks in the light of truth and righteousness.

The words, *He makes the night cover the day, which pursues it swiftly*, are explained in 2 : 165 by the expression "the alternation of night and day." The clause may also imply that it is God's سنة or practice that after a period of darkness He brings a period of light so that mankind may not suffer.

By using the word مسخرات (all made subservient) with respect to the sun, the moon and the stars, the verse reminds us that it was not in the power of man to make all these planets serve him and that it is God alone Who has placed them at his service. Therefore if, in spite of these great favours, he would not listen to God's voice, he would be marked as a transgressor and consequently merit His punishment.

The distinction between خلق (the creation) and امر (the command) is that while the former generally means, the measuring out or evolving of a thing out of pre-existing matter, the latter means, bringing into being without matter by uttering the simple command "Be." The clause, *His is the creation and the command*, may also mean that God has not only created the universe but also exercises authority and command over it.

For the words, *He settled Himself on the Throne*, see under 10 : 4 where the expressions "divine throne", and "God's settling on it" have been fully dealt with.

56. ᵃCall upon your Lord in humility and in secret. Surely, He does not love the transgressors.⁹⁵⁵

اُدْعُوْا رَبَّكُمْ تَضَرُّعًا وَّخُفْيَةً ؕ اِنَّهٗ لَا يُحِبُّ الْمُعْتَدِيْنَ ۝

57. And create not disorder in the earth after it has been set in order, and ᵇcall upon Him in fear and hope. Surely, the mercy of Allah is nigh unto those who do good.⁹⁵⁶

وَلَا تُفْسِدُوْا فِى الْاَرْضِ بَعْدَ اِصْلَاحِهَا وَادْعُوْهُ خَوْفًا وَّطَمَعًا ؕ اِنَّ رَحْمَتَ اللّٰهِ قَرِيْبٌ مِّنَ الْمُحْسِنِيْنَ ۝

ᵃ6 : 64 ; 7 : 206.   ᵇ21 : 91 ; 32 : 17.

---

955. Commentary :

For an explanation of the words, in humility and in secret, see 6 : 64.

956. Commentary :

The expression, after it has been set in order, means that before the revelation of the Quran the disbelievers had some excuse for leading an unrighteous life ; but now that a perfect guidance has come to them, they will not be allowed to go on making mischief and grovelling in sin and iniquity and leading unrighteous lives with impunity. The word اصلاح (order) refers to the good and ordered life that has come into being on account of the revelation of the Quran and the advent of the Holy Prophet.

The words, call upon Him in fear and hope, strike a golden mean. Some religions lay undue stress on fear, while others dangle before man the false hope of getting salvation and everlasting life through belief in a vicarious atonement. The Quran follows the middle course and teaches its followers to be both fearing and hopeful. A true Muslim is the most cautious and heedful of men. He walks in humility and constant fear of God, lest one false word, one irresponsible act should deprive him of God's mercy. But at the same time he is full of hope. He has faith in the all-embracing mercy of God. Thus it is a true Muslim alone who can keep the right balance between fear and hope which are the two important component parts of perfect faith necessary for perfect actions.

The words, the mercy of Allah is nigh unto those who do good, point out the way which leads to the acceptance of prayers. It is through the mercy of God that prayers are accepted, and the mercy of God comes only to the محسنين (those who do good). A believer, therefore, should try to become a Muhsin in the true sense of the word, so that his prayers may be accepted. But it should be remembered that a محسن is not an ordinary doer of good. The word signifies " one who strives to be perfect in his deeds." A saying of the Holy Prophet describes a محسن as one who does a good deed as if he were actually seeing God or that at least God was seeing him.

58. And ^aHe it is Who sends the winds as glad tidings before His mercy, till, when they bear a heavy cloud, We drive it to a dead land, then We send down water therefrom, and We bring forth therewith fruits of every kind. In like manner do We bring forth the dead that you may remember.[957]

وَهُوَ الَّذِىْ يُرْسِلُ الرِّيْحَ بُشْرًۢا بَيْنَ يَدَىْ رَحْمَتِهٖ ۚ حَتّٰۤى اِذَاۤ اَقَلَّتْ سَحَابًا ثِقَالًا سُقْنٰهُ لِبَلَدٍ مَّيِّتٍ فَاَنْزَلْنَا بِهِ الْمَآءَ فَاَخْرَجْنَا بِهٖ مِنْ كُلِّ الثَّمَرٰتِ ۚ كَذٰلِكَ نُخْرِجُ الْمَوْتٰى لَعَلَّكُمْ تَذَكَّرُوْنَ ۝

59. And <i>as for</i> the good land, its vegetation comes forth <i>plentifully</i> by the command of its Lord; and that which is bad, <i>its vegetation</i> does not come forth but scantily. In like manner do We vary the Signs for a people who are grateful.[958]

وَالْبَلَدُ الطَّيِّبُ يَخْرُجُ نَبَاتُهٗ بِاِذْنِ رَبِّهٖ ۚ وَالَّذِىْ خَبُثَ لَا يَخْرُجُ اِلَّا نَكِدًا ۚ كَذٰلِكَ نُصَرِّفُ الْاٰيٰتِ لِقَوْمٍ يَّشْكُرُوْنَ ۝

---

^a15:23; 24:44; 25:49; 27:64; 30:47; 35:10.

---

957. Important Words :

اَقَلَّتْ (bear) is derived from قل . They say قل الشىئ <i>i.e.</i> the thing was or became few, small or scanty. اقل الشىئ means, he lifted, raised, bore or carried the thing (Aqrab).

Commentary :

The word رحمة (mercy) in this verse refers to rain. Just as in the physical world rain is preceded by cool breezes which serve as its harbingers, similarly before a Prophet of God is to make his appearance, there is a sort of general religious awakening among men. This religious awakening was witnessed among the Arabs before the appearance of the Holy Prophet. There appeared among them certain individuals called <i>Ḥanīfs</i> who rejected idolatry and believed in and preached the Oneness of God. In the present time also, the advent of Ahmad, the Promised Messiah, was preceded by a general religious awakening among the nations of the world.

The words, <i>a dead land</i>, literally mean, physically dead, but metaphorically the words also signify a spiritually dead land. Just as rain-water puts new life into a dead land and causes fruits, vegetables and corn to grow from it, similarly, the heavenly water of revelation breathes a new life into a people devoid of spiritual life. The verse thus holds out the promise that the bleak, arid and barren land of Arabia would soon blossom forth into a garden full of trees laden with fruit, and plants bearing fragrant flowers in consequence of the heavenly water that had descended on it. No wonder, indeed, that the Arabs, who had hitherto been regarded as the dregs and scum of humanity, suddenly emerged as teachers and leaders thereof.

958. Commentary :

Rain produces different effects upon different plots of land according to their nature and quality; so does divine revelation affect different men in different ways. The Holy Prophet is reported to have said that there are three kinds of land: (<i>a</i>) the good level land which, when watered by rain, absorbs the rain water and yields good vegetation and brings forth abundant fruit; (<i>b</i>) the land which, being

R. 8   60.   ^aWe sent Noah to his people and he said, ' O my people, worship Allah, you have no other god but Him. Indeed, I fear for you the punishment of the great day.'⁹⁵⁹

لَقَدْ اَرْسَلْنَا نُوْحًا اِلٰى قَوْمِهٖ فَقَالَ يٰقَوْمِ اعْبُدُوا اللّٰهَ مَا لَكُمْ مِّنْ اِلٰهٍ غَيْرُهٗ ۚ اِنِّىْ اَخَافُ عَلَيْكُمْ عَذَابَ يَوْمٍ عَظِيْمٍ ۞

---

^a11 : 26-27 ; 23 : 24.

---

low-lying and rocky, only collects the water of rain but does not absorb it and so brings forth no vegetation but provides drinking water for man and beast; (c) the high stony ground which neither collects the water of rain nor absorbs it, being useless both for the purpose of vegetation and as a storage for rain-water. Similarly, men are of three kinds : (1) Those who not only accept but also profit by divine revelation. They are like the good level land which receives rain and yields good produce. (2) Those who do not themselves profit by the divine revelation, but receive it and keep it stored up for others to benefit thereby. They are like that piece of land which yields no produce, but from which men and beasts benefit by the water collected during the rain. (3) Those who neither derive any benefit from the divine revelation themselves nor keep it stored for the use of others. They are like that piece of land which neither yields any produce nor hoards up water so that men and beasts may drink from it.

959. Important Words :

نوح (Noah) a very ancient Prophet who, as the Bible tells us, lived nine generations after Adam and eleven generations before Abraham. (Gen. 5 : 3—32 ; Luke 3 : 34—38). His native land was Mesopotamia. He is believed to be the progenitor of the greater part of mankind. The word نوح (Noah) may, in Arabic, be considered to have been derived from ناح which means, he bewailed or mourned. They say ناحت على زوجها i.e. the woman bewailed or mourned her dead husband.

ناحت الحمامة نوحا means, the pigeon cooed in a plaintive manner. The Prophet Noah is particularly known for the Flood that overtook his people as the result of his bewailings and lamentations before God for the persecution he had to suffer at the hands of his wicked people, most of whom perished in the Flood. His three sons, Shem, Ham, and Japheth, are generally believed to be the ancestors of the three principal races of mankind. See also 11 : 26.

Commentary :

After having briefly described the great moral and spiritual reformation that the appearance of a Prophet brings about among a people, and the evil consequences to which opposition to him leads, the present verse proceeds to give illustrations of some of the nations of antiquity, beginning with the people of Noah, to show that those who oppose God's Prophets meet with nothing but destruction. Most of the different races now living on this earth are believed to be descended from Noah. His descendants seem to have spread in all directions, as may be seen from the story of the Deluge which is known to the people of Europe, Asia, Africa and even America.

The words, *We sent Noah to his people*, shows that the Deluge overtook only the people to whom Noah was sent. It was not a universal phenomenon, but the descendants of Noah may have carried the tale to distant lands.

The words يوم عظيم literally meaning "a great day," have been used to signify a day of heavy punishment which was too dreadful to be forgotten.

61. ^aThe chiefs of his people said ' Surely, we see thee to be in manifest error.'⁹⁶⁰

قَالَ الْمَلَأُ مِنْ قَوْمِهٖٓ اِنَّا لَنَرٰىكَ فِيْ ضَلٰلٍ مُّبِيْنٍ ۝

62. He said, ^b' O my people, there is no error in me, but I am a Messenger from the Lord of the worlds.⁹⁶¹

قَالَ يٰقَوْمِ لَيْسَ بِيْ ضَلٰلَةٌ وَّ لٰكِنِّيْ رَسُوْلٌ مِّنْ رَّبِّ الْعٰلَمِيْنَ ۝

63. ^c' I deliver to you the messages of my Lord and give you sincere advice, and I know from Allah what you do not know.

اُبَلِّغُكُمْ رِسٰلٰتِ رَبِّيْ وَ اَنْصَحُ لَكُمْ وَاَعْلَمُ مِنَ اللّٰهِ مَا لَا تَعْلَمُوْنَ ۝

64. ^d' Do you wonder that an exhortation has come to you from your Lord through a man from among yourselves, that he may warn you and that you may become righteous and that you may be shown mercy ? '⁹⁶²

اَوَ عَجِبْتُمْ اَنْ جَآءَكُمْ ذِكْرٌ مِّنْ رَّبِّكُمْ عَلٰى رَجُلٍ مِّنْكُمْ لِيُنْذِرَكُمْ وَ لِتَتَّقُوْا وَ لَعَلَّكُمْ تُرْحَمُوْنَ ۝

---

^a11 : 28 ; 23 : 25-26.   ^b7 : 68.   ^c7 : 69, 80 ; 46 : 24.   ^d7 : 70 ; 10 : 3 ; 38 : 5 ; 50 : 3.

---

960. Commentary :

It is worth noting that Noah's people do not here accuse him of imposture. They attribute to him merely an error of judgement and not fabrication or deliberate falsehood. This shows that they looked upon him as an upright man. Indeed, all Prophets, before they receive their mission from God, are looked upon as upright and virtuous men. It is only after they announce their heavenly mission that they are dubbed liars.

961. Commentary :

The words, *but I am a Messenger from the Lord of the worlds*, rebut the charge of error on Noah's part in a most beautiful and convincing manner. The rejectors of Noah claimed that he was in error or that he had lost his way. The argument given by Noah in refutation of this charge is to the effect that a person who is proceeding to a place may indeed be said to be unacquainted with the way or to have lost it owing to his having never trodden it before,

but how can a person who is returning from a certain place be said not to know the way to that place and how can he possibly lose the way in leading others to it? So Noah could not be in error, for he was actually coming from God, and therefore there was no possibility of his wandering away from the path that leads to Him.

962. Commentary :

The reason why people so readily reject the Prophets of God is that they cannot persuade themselves to believe that divine revelation can come to a human being or that such an exalted spiritual rank as that of the bearer of a divine message can be conferred upon an ordinary person from among themselves. The verse under comment sets at rest this feeling of surprise and wonder in the disbelievers in a very appealing manner. It asks them, why do they wonder if an admonition has come to them from their Lord (*Rabb*), Who is not only their Creator but Who also nourishes

65. But [a]they accused him of falsehood, so We saved him and those with him in the Ark, and We drowned those who rejected Our Signs. They were indeed a blind people.[963]

R. 9   66. And [b]unto 'Ād *We sent* their brother Hūd. He said, ' O my people, worship Allah ; you have no other deity but Him. Will you not then be God-fearing ? '[964]

فَكَذَّبُوهُ فَاَنْجَيْنٰهُ وَالَّذِيْنَ مَعَهُ فِى الْفُلْكِ وَاَغْرَقْنَا الَّذِيْنَ كَذَّبُوْا بِاٰيٰتِنَا ۖ اِنَّهُمْ كَانُوْا قَوْمًا عَمِيْنَ ۝

وَاِلٰى عَادٍ اَخَاهُمْ هُوْدًا ۗ قَالَ يٰقَوْمِ اعْبُدُوا اللّٰهَ مَا لَكُمْ مِّنْ اِلٰهٍ غَيْرُهٗ ۗ اَفَلَا تَتَّقُوْنَ ۝

---

[a]7 : 73 ; 26 : 120-121.   [b]11 : 51 ; 46 : 22.

---

them and looks after their physical and spiritual needs, and Who by sending down a new revelation has only satisfied a spiritual want which was long felt. Nor is there any cause for wonder that divine revelation should come to a man from among them. Do they think that they have become so degraded that none of them could become the recipient of divine revelation ?

963. Important Words :

عَمِيْن (blind) or عَمُوْن is the plural of اَعْمٰى meaning a blind man. The word is derived from عَمِى meaning, he was or became blind in both eyes ; or, figuratively, he was blind in respect of the mind ; he erred and did not find the right way. اَعْمٰى means, blind in both eyes ; blind in respect of the mind ; erring (Lane).

Commentary :

In spite of all his arguments and appeals, the people rejected the Prophet Noah and began to treat him as a liar, for they were a "blind people" and could not see and understand the evidence and proofs of his truth. The Flood engulfed them all.

964. Important Words :

عَاد ('Ād) was the name of a tribe who lived in the distant past in a part of Arabia. In Arabic the verb عَاد means, he returned. For further description see 11 : 51.

هُوْد (Hūd) was the name of the Prophet who was sent to 'Ād. He lived after Noah, being seventh in descent from him. In Arabic the word هُوْد takes its derivation from هَاد i.e. he returned from evil to good ; he repented and returned to truth ; he became a Jew. The name هُوْد is also applied to the Jewish people collectively in which case it is the plural of هَائِد . See also 2 : 112.

Commentary :

After making mention of Noah, whose story is found in the lore of almost all nations, the Quran proceeds to deal with the Prophets that appeared in the Arabian peninsula particularly. These Prophets find mention in the Quran only. No reference to them is to be found in the Bible or in the general books of history, although they were well known to the Arabs through their national traditions.

The tribe of 'Ād, at one time, ruled over most of the fertile parts of greater Arabia, particularly Yemen, Syria and Mesopotamia. They were the first people to exercise dominion over practically the whole of Arabia. They are known as *'Ādanil 'Ūlā* or the former *'Ād*.

The verse under comment shows that throughout the ages all the Prophets of God have brought identical teachings so far as the fundamental principles of religion are concerned.

67. The disbelieving chiefs of his people said, *a*' We surely see thee *lost* in foolishness, and we surely think thee to be *one* of the liars.'⁹⁶⁵

قَالَ الۡمَلَاُ الَّذِیۡنَ کَفَرُوۡا مِنۡ قَوۡمِهٖۤ اِنَّا لَنَرٰىکَ فِیۡ سَفَاهَةٍ وَّ اِنَّا لَنَظُنُّکَ مِنَ الۡکٰذِبِیۡنَ ۝

68. He replied, *b*' O my people, there is no foolishness in me, but I am a Messenger from the Lord of the worlds.⁹⁶⁶

قَالَ یٰقَوۡمِ لَیۡسَ بِیۡ سَفَاهَةٌ وَّ لٰکِنِّیۡ رَسُوۡلٌ مِّنۡ رَّبِّ الۡعٰلَمِیۡنَ ۝

69. *c*' I deliver to you the messages of my Lord and I am to you a sincere and faithful counsellor.⁹⁶⁷

اُبَلِّغُکُمۡ رِسٰلٰتِ رَبِّیۡ وَ اَنَا لَکُمۡ نَاصِحٌ اَمِیۡنٌ ۝

70. *d*' Do you wonder that an exhortation has come to you from your Lord through a man from among yourselves that he may warn you? And remember the time when *e*He made you inheritors *of His favours* after the people of Noah, and increased you abundantly in constitution. Remember, then, the favours of Allah, that you may prosper.'⁹⁶⁸

اَوَعَجِبۡتُمۡ اَنۡ جَآءَکُمۡ ذِکۡرٌ مِّنۡ رَّبِّکُمۡ عَلٰی رَجُلٍ مِّنۡکُمۡ لِیُنۡذِرَکُمۡ وَ اذۡکُرُوۡۤا اِذۡ جَعَلَکُمۡ خُلَفَآءَ مِنۡۢ بَعۡدِ قَوۡمِ نُوۡحٍ وَّ زَادَکُمۡ فِی الۡخَلۡقِ بَصۜۡطَةً فَاذۡکُرُوۡۤا اٰلَآءَ اللّٰهِ لَعَلَّکُمۡ تُفۡلِحُوۡنَ ۝

---

*a*41 : 16.   *b*7 : 62.   *c*7 : 63, 80; 46 : 24.   *d*7 : 64; 10 : 3; 38 : 5; 50 : 3.
*e*6 : 166; 7 : 75, 130; 10 : 15.

---

965. Commentary :

By ascribing folly to Hūd, his people meant that he laboured under a misunderstanding as regards his mission. The word سفاهة (foolishness) is used to express almost the same idea as is expressed by the word ضلالة (error) used in 7 : 61 above. It appears from this verse that the enemies of Hūd brought two charges against him, *viz.*, of being in error and of lying.

966. Commentary :

The Prophet Hūd here refutes the charge of being in error by the same argument by which Noah refuted a similar charge (see 7 : 62 above). God being the fountain-head of all wisdom, he who comes from Him cannot be looked upon as foolish. The other charge is refuted in the next verse.

967. Commentary :

This verse contains the answer to the charge of lying brought against Hūd in 7 : 67 above. A person resorts to lying either because (1) he seeks thereby to gain some advantage, or (2) to do another person some harm or (3) because lying is a habit with him. Now Hūd refutes the charge by saying, *I am to you a sincere and faithful counsellor, i.e.* being sincere I have no selfish motive, nor do I wish evil to any one ; on the contrary, I am solicitous of doing you good ; and being faithful *i.e.,* possessing faith, I am not in the habit of lying.

968. Important Words :

خلفاء (inheritors of God's favours) is the plural of خليفة which is verbal adjective from خلف meaning, he came after, followed,

71. They said, *a* ' Hast thou come to us that we may worship Allah alone and forsake what our fathers used to worship. Bring us, then, that which thou threatenest us with, if thou art of the truthful.'⁹⁶⁹

قَالُوٓا اَجِئۡتَنَا لِنَعۡبُدَ اللّٰهَ وَحۡدَهٗ وَنَذَرَ مَا كَانَ يَعۡبُدُ اٰبَآؤُنَا فَاۡتِنَا بِمَا تَعِدُنَآ اِنۡ كُنۡتَ مِنَ الصّٰدِقِيۡنَ ۞

72. He replied, ' Indeed there have *already* fallen on you punishment and wrath from your Lord. *b*Do you dispute with me about names which you have named,—you and your fathers,—for which Allah has sent down no authority ? Wait then, *c*I am with you among those who wait.'⁹⁷⁰

قَالَ قَدۡ وَقَعَ عَلَيۡكُمۡ مِّنۡ رَّبِّكُمۡ رِجۡسٌ وَّغَضَبٌ اَتُجَادِلُوۡنَنِيۡ فِيۡٓ اَسۡمَآءٍ سَمَّيۡتُمُوۡهَآ اَنۡتُمۡ وَ اٰبَآؤُكُمۡ مَّا نَزَّلَ اللّٰهُ بِهَا مِنۡ سُلۡطٰنٍ فَانۡتَظِرُوۡٓا اِنِّيۡ مَعَكُمۡ مِّنَ الۡمُنۡتَظِرِيۡنَ ۞

---

*a*10 : 79 ; 11 : 63, 88.   *b*3 : 152 ; 7 : 34 ; 22 : 72 ; 53 : 24.   *c*10 : 21, 103 ; 11 : 123.

succeeded another, or remained after another. خلفه also means, he was or became his successor, vicegerent or substitute. خلف الرجل means, he lived after the man and took his place. خليفة means, a successor; vicegerent; lieutenant; substitute; deputy; one who has been appointed to take the place of him who has been before him; the supreme ruler or sovereign who supplies the place of him who has been before him; the Successor of a Prophet (Lane & Aqrab). In the text the word خلفاء has been rendered as "inheritors of His favours," signifying that just as Noah and his people inherited God's favours in their time, Hūd and his people, who came after them, were also inheritors of God's favours. See also 2 : 31.

بسطة (abundantly) is the same as بسطة which is the noun-infinitive from بسط. They say بسطة *i.e.* he spread it or spread it out; he expanded it; he extended it; he made it wide or ample. بسطة or بصطة means, width or ampleness; length or height; increase or excess; excellence or perfection in body; knowledge or mental powers (Lane & Aqrab).

Commentary :

See note on 7:64 above.

The 'Ādites were a ruling nation. They were a mighty and powerful people. Their rule extended over vast territories. They were the first Arab nation to wield temporal power in Arabia.

969. Commentary :

Being unable to meet the arguments of Hūd, disbelievers took a new line and declared that they would rather die than give up the faith of their fathers. That it was the threatened punishment of God that they challenged Hūd to bring upon them is clear from the reply which he gave them and which is contained in the words : *Indeed there have already fallen on you punishment and wrath from your Lord,* occurring in the following verse.

970. Commentary :

This verse shows that one may follow one's fore-fathers only if one has the support of reason and not otherwise. Blind and unthinking following is condemned.

73. And ^aWe saved him and those who were with him, by Our mercy, and We cut off the last remnant of those who rejected Our Signs. And they were not believers.⁹⁷¹

فَأَنْجَيْنَهُ وَ الَّذِيْنَ مَعَهٗ بِرَحْمَةٍ مِّنَّا وَ قَطَعْنَا دَابِرَ الَّذِيْنَ كَذَّبُوْا بِاٰيٰتِنَا وَ مَا كَانُوْا مُؤْمِنِيْنَ ۞

10 74. And ^bto Thamūd We sent their brother Ṣāliḥ. He said, 'O my people, worship Allah; you have no other deity but Him. Verily there has come to you a clear evidence from your Lord—^cthis she-camel of Allah, a Sign for you. So leave her that she may feed in Allah's earth, and do her no harm, lest a painful punishment seize you.'⁹⁷²

وَ اِلٰى ثَمُوْدَ اَخَاهُمْ صٰلِحًا قَالَ يٰقَوْمِ اعْبُدُوا اللّٰهَ مَا لَكُمْ مِّنْ اِلٰهٍ غَيْرُهٗ قَدْ جَآءَتْكُمْ بَيِّنَةٌ مِّنْ رَّبِّكُمْ هٰذِهٖ نَاقَةُ اللّٰهِ لَكُمْ اٰيَةً فَذَرُوْهَا تَأْكُلْ فِيْ اَرْضِ اللّٰهِ وَ لَا تَمَسُّوْهَا بِسُوْٓءٍ فَيَأْخُذَكُمْ عَذَابٌ اَلِيْمٌ ۞

---

^a7:165; 26:120-121.   ^b11:62; 27:46.   ^c7:78; 11:65; 17:60; 26:156; 24:28; 91:14.

---

971. Commentary:

The word دابر (last remnant) also means "root" (see 6:46), in which case it may be taken to signify leaders of a community i.e. those who lead and organize opposition to a Prophet and devise plans to compass his ruin. The tribe of 'Ād was destroyed by a furious wind, (see 69:7).

972. Important Words:

ثَمُوْد (Thamūd) was the name of a tribe that lived after 'Ād. The name may have been derived from the Arabic root ثمد. They say ثمده i.e. he dug out a hole in the earth so that water might collect in it (Aqrab). The tribe Thamūd lived in the western parts of Arabia, having spread from Aden northward to Syria. They lived shortly before the time of Ishmael. Their territory was adjacent to that of 'Ād, but they lived mostly in the hills. For a fuller note on the subject see 11:62.

صالح (Ṣāliḥ) is an Arabic word being derived from صلح i.e. he was or became good or righteous. صالح means, a righteous person. See 2:12, 161. The Prophet Ṣāliḥ lived after Hūd and was probably a contemporary of Abraham.

Commentary:

The camel formed the chief means of conveyance in Arabia, and it was on his she-camel that the Prophet Ṣāliḥ used to travel from place to place to preach his message. So he told his people that placing obstruction in the way of the free movements of the she-camel or doing harm to it would be tantamount to obstructing the work with which God had entrusted him, and that if they did not stand out of her way, God's punishment would surely descend upon them. Thus it was that the she-camel was meant as a Sign for the tribe of Thamūd. There was nothing unusual about the camel itself. It was an ordinary animal. The sanctity that attached to it was that God had declared it to be a sign and a symbol of the sanctity and inviolability of the person of the Prophet Ṣāliḥ and doing an injury to it was declared to be tantamount to doing an injury to Ṣāliḥ himself and to hampering his work.

75. And remember *the time* *a*when He made you inheritors *of His favours* after 'Ād, and assigned you an abode in the land; you build palaces in its plains, and *b*you hew the mountains into houses. Remember, therefore, the favours of Allah and commit not iniquity in the earth causing disorder.[973]

وَاذْكُرُوْٓا اِذْ جَعَلَكُمْ خُلَفَآءَ مِنْۢ بَعْدِ عَادٍ وَّبَوَّاَكُمْ فِى الْاَرْضِ تَتَّخِذُوْنَ مِنْ سُهُوْلِهَا قُصُوْرًا وَّتَنْحِتُوْنَ الْجِبَالَ بُيُوْتًا ۚ فَاذْكُرُوْٓا اٰلَآءَ اللّٰهِ وَلَا تَعْثَوْا فِى الْاَرْضِ مُفْسِدِيْنَ ۝

76. The chief men of his people who were arrogant said to those who were reckoned weak—those among them who believed—'Do you know *for certain* that Ṣāliḥ is one sent by his Lord?' They answered, 'Surely, we believe in that with which he has been sent.'[974]

قَالَ الْمَلَاُ الَّذِيْنَ اسْتَكْبَرُوْا مِنْ قَوْمِهٖ لِلَّذِيْنَ اسْتُضْعِفُوْا لِمَنْ اٰمَنَ مِنْهُمْ اَتَعْلَمُوْنَ اَنَّ صٰلِحًا مُّرْسَلٌ مِّنْ رَّبِّهٖ ۚ قَالُوْٓا اِنَّا بِمَآ اُرْسِلَ بِهٖ مُؤْمِنُوْنَ ۝

77. Those who were arrogant said, 'Verily, we do disbelieve in that in which you believe.'[975]

قَالَ الَّذِيْنَ اسْتَكْبَرُوْٓا اِنَّا بِالَّذِيْٓ اٰمَنْتُمْ بِهٖ كٰفِرُوْنَ ۝

---

*a*6 : 166; 7 : 70, 130; 10 : 15.   *b*15 : 83; 26 : 150;

The words, *leave her that she may feed in Allah's earth,* do not mean that she was to be allowed to graze in any field she pleased. What is meant is only that no obstruction was to be put in her way, and that she was to be permitted to proceed to any place to which Ṣāliḥ might choose to go. The declaration by Ṣāliḥ about the free movement of his she-camel was also in harmony with a time-honoured Arab custom.

973. Important Words:

بَوَّاَكُمْ (assigned you an abode). بَوَّا is derived from بَاءَ which means, he returned. بَوَّاهُ مَنْزِلًا means, he lodged him in an abode. بَوَّا لَهُ مَنْزِلًا means, he prepared for him an abode and assigned or gave him a place therein (Lane).

Commentary:

The words, *you build palaces in its plains,* refer to the winter residences of the tribe, while the expression, *and you hew the mountains into houses,* allude to their summer residences in the hills. The tribe of Thamūd were a cultured people—industrious, wealthy and resourceful. Judged by the standards of that time, they led a luxurious and comfortable life, going up the hills in the hot season and spending their winters in the plains.

974. Important Words:

الْمَلَاُ (chief men). See 2 : 247.

Commentary:

When the so-called leaders of his tribe found, to their mortification, that Ṣāliḥ stood firm as a rock in his convictions and no amount of persuasion could make him swerve from his purpose, they began to harass his followers, but these too they found bold and firm.

975. Commentary:

The words, *Verily, we do disbelieve in that in*

78. Then ^athey hamstrung the she-camel and rebelled against the command of their Lord, and said, ' O Ṣāliḥ, bring us that which thou threatenest us with, if thou art *indeed one* of the Messengers.'⁹⁷⁶

فَعَقَرُوا النَّاقَةَ وَعَتَوْا عَنْ اَمْرِ رَبِّهِمْ وَقَالُوْا يٰصٰلِحُ ائْتِنَا بِمَا تَعِدُنَآ اِنْ كُنْتَ مِنَ الْمُرْسَلِيْنَ ۝

79. So ^bthe earthquake seized them and in their homes they lay prostrate upon the ground.⁹⁷⁷

فَاَخَذَتْهُمُ الرَّجْفَةُ فَاَصْبَحُوْا فِيْ دَارِهِمْ جٰثِمِيْنَ ۝

^aSee 7 : 74.   ^b7 : 92 ; 11 : 68 ; 15 : 84 ; 26 : 159.

---

which you believe, in popular parlance signify a typical form of arrogant but veiled threat generally held out by rich and powerful people to the weaker and poorer section of society. The words may be interpreted as : " How dare you, weak and poor as you are, accept a teaching which we, your betters and superiors, have thought fit to reject ? "

976. Important Words :

عقروا (hamstrung) is derived from عقر . They say عقره *i.e.* he wounded him, or he wounded him much ; he hacked or hamstrung it (a beast) ; he struck or cut its (an animal's) leg with a sword, etc. ; he stabbed an animal, etc ; he killed, slew or destroyed. عقرنى means, he detained or restrained me. عقر and عقرت mean, he or she was barren and produced no issue (Lane).

Commentary :

The reference in the pronoun "that" in the clause, *bring us that*, is to the punishment mentioned in 7 : 74 above. The she-camel was held out as a Sign, and that Sign was to be witnessed on her being obstructed by disbelievers. They not only hindered the free movement of the she-camel but even wounded and killed her which amounted to an open challenge to Ṣāliḥ to do his worst, —to call upon his God to send down the threatened punishment upon them.

977. Important Words :

الرجفة (earthquake) is derived from رجف which means, it was or became in a state of motion, commotion, convulsion or disturbance ; or in a state of violent motion, etc. رجفة means, commotion or convulsion, particularly an earthquake ; a violent earthquake ; a vehement cry from heaven ; any punishment that befalls a people (Lane).

اصبحوا (lay) is derived from اصبح which again is derived from صبح . They say صبح القوم *i.e.* he came to the people in the morning. اصبح means : (1) he entered upon the time of morning ; (2) he became ; or he entered upon a certain state. اصبح زيد عالما means, Zaid became learned. So اصبحوا جاثمين means, they became prostrate *i.e.* they lay prostrate ; or they entered upon the time of morning, while they lay prostrate (Lane & Aqrab).

جاثمين (prostrate on the ground) is the plural of جاثم which is the active participle from جثم which means, he clove to the ground, or he fell upon his breast ; or he kept to his place, not quitting it. So جاثم means, one who, or that which, cleaves to the ground or falls upon his or its breast. It also means, motionless or dead (Lane & Aqrab).

Commentary :

According to the different meanings of the word جثم given under Important Words, the verse would mean that (1) they were

80. Then *Ṣāliḥ* turned away from them and said, [a]' O my people, I did deliver the message of my Lord unto you and offered you sincere counsel, but you love not sincere counsellors.'[978]

فَتَوَلّٰى عَنْهُمْ وَقَالَ يٰقَوْمِ لَقَدْ اَبْلَغْتُكُمْ رِسَالَةَ رَبِّيْ وَنَصَحْتُ لَكُمْ وَلٰكِنْ لَّا تُحِبُّوْنَ النّٰصِحِيْنَ ۝

81. And [b]*We sent* Lot—when he said to his people ' Do you commit an abomination such as no one in the world ever did before you ? [979]

وَلُوْطًا اِذْ قَالَ لِقَوْمِهٖٓ اَتَاْتُوْنَ الْفَاحِشَةَ مَا سَبَقَكُمْ بِهَا مِنْ اَحَدٍ مِّنَ الْعٰلَمِيْنَ ۝

82. [c]' You approach men with lust instead of women. Nay, you are a people who exceed *all bounds*.'[980]

اِنَّكُمْ لَتَاْتُوْنَ الرِّجَالَ شَهْوَةً مِّنْ دُوْنِ النِّسَآءِ ؕ بَلْ اَنْتُمْ قَوْمٌ مُّسْرِفُوْنَ ۝

---

[a]7 : 63, 69 ; 46 : 24.   [b]27 : 55 ; 29 : 29.   [c]26 : 166 ; 27 : 56 ; 29 : 30.

crushed to death by the earthquake and lay prostrate ; (2) when the earthquake overtook them, they were terrified and fell prostrate on the ground, praying to God for deliverance.

978. Commentary :

Ṣāliḥ left the stricken city in grief, as he could no longer bear to see the appalling sight, uttering the pathetic words mentioned in the verse with a sad and sorrowful heart, as did the Holy Prophet of Islam at Badr.

979. Important Words :

لوط (Lot) was a nephew and contemporary of Abraham (Gen. 11 : 27, 31). See also 6 : 87.

Commentary :

This verse throws some light on the fact that the perfect Law could not be revealed in the beginning of the world, because laws are meant to meet and remedy evils, and so religious Laws were gradually revealed as evils grew and spread. If a perfect Law had been revealed in the very beginning, detailing all the evils, it would, in a way, have proved the means of

teaching men evils of which they were yet ignorant. Hence, a perfect Law could be revealed only at a time when all or most of the evils, particularly those known as root evils, had made their appearance and become established. Such was the case when the Quran was revealed. To this fact the Quran alludes in the words, *Corruption has appeared (and become established) on land and sea*, (30 : 42), which means that at the advent of the Holy Prophet, all the diverse root evils had become manifest and established.

The " abomination " mentioned in the present verse is explained in the next. The words, *as no one in the world ever did before you*, imply that it was a new kind of evil which was unknown before, or that its present extent had had no parallel before.

980. Commentary :

Lot rebuked his people for having not only innovated the extremely foul practice of sodomy but for having also excelled in other evil practices.

83. And *the answer of his people was no other than that they said, 'Turn them out of your town, for they are men who would keep pure.'⁹⁸¹

وَمَا كَانَ جَوَابَ قَوْمِهٖ اِلَّا اَنْ قَالُوْا اَخْرِجُوْهُمْ مِّنْ قَرْيَتِكُمْ اِنَّهُمْ اُنَاسٌ يَّتَطَهَّرُوْنَ ۝

84. And ᵇWe saved him and his family, except his wife; she was of those who stayed behind.⁹⁸²

فَاَنْجَيْنٰهُ وَاَهْلَهٗ اِلَّا امْرَاَتَهٗ ۫ كَانَتْ مِنَ الْغٰبِرِيْنَ ۝

85. And ᶜWe rained upon them a rain. Now see, what was the end of the sinners.⁹⁸³

وَاَمْطَرْنَا عَلَيْهِمْ مَّطَرًا ۫ فَانْظُرْ كَيْفَ كَانَ عَاقِبَةُ الْمُجْرِمِيْنَ ۝

ᵃ27:57.   ᵇ26:171-172; 27:58; 29:34; 37:135-136.   ᶜ26:174; 27:59.

---

981. Commentary:

The word يتطهرون (who would keep pure) may also signify "who affect to be pure"; because the باب (form) of تفعل is not unoften used to imply affectation. The word was used by the opponents of Lot about his followers by way of taunt, signifying that they posed and paraded as extra-righteous and holy persons.

982. Important Words:

الغابرين (who stayed behind) is derived from غبر i.e. he or it remained, lasted or continued; he stayed, tarried or waited; or contrarily, he or it passed away or went away; or it (a wound) was or became in a bad state, especially after once being healed; or it healed externally while it was in a withering state internally; he (a man) hid enmity or hatred in his heart. So غابر is one who remains or stays or tarries behind or waits, etc. (Lane & Aqrab).

Commentary:

The verse does not necessarily imply that the wife of Lot was a disbeliever. The fact that she tarried to inform her relatives

of the impending punishment shows that she probably possessed some faith. As, however, she disregarded the command that no warning of the coming calamity was to be given to any disbeliever, she was punished. The word غابرين (who stayed behind) treated under Important Words above throws some interesting light on the real condition of Lot's wife. Most probably she outwardly believed in her husband but was like a withering wound within and stayed or lingered behind, while Lot and his companions hurriedly left the doomed place.

There exists some difference of opinion among students of history as to the situation of the place where the people of Lot lived. According to some the Dead Sea is the site of the ruined cities. The Quran, however, appears to place it on the route from Medina to Syria (15:80).

983. Commentary:

It appears that there was a violent eruption, and burning matter was thrown out of the ground and buried the disbelieving people underneath it.

R. 11 86. ^aAnd to Midian *We sent* their brother Shu'aib. He said, 'O my people, worship Allah; you have no other deity but Him. A clear Sign has indeed come to you from your Lord. So ^bgive full measure and full weight, and diminish not unto people their things, and create not disorder in the earth after it has been set in order. This is better for you, if you are believers.⁹⁸⁴

87. And sit not on every path, threatening and ^cturning away from the path of Allah those who believe in Him, and seeking to make it crooked. And ^dremember when you were few and He multiplied you. And behold, what was the end of those who created disorder !⁹⁸⁵

---

^a11:85; 29:37.   ^b6:153; 11:86.   ^c7:46; 11:20; 14:4; 16:89.   ^d3:124; 8:27.

---

984. Important Words :

مدين (Midian) was Abraham's son from Keturah (Gen. 25:1, 2). His descendants dwelt in the north of the Ḥijāz. Midian was also the name of a town near the Red Sea, opposite to Sinai on the Arabian shore. The town was so called because it was inhabited by the descendants of Midian. Some have referred to it as a sea-port on account of its proximity to the sea, being situated only at a distance of eight miles from it; others have spoken of it as an inland town.

شعيب (Shu'aib) was the name of a non-Israelite Prophet who lived before Moses. He is generally looked upon as the father-in-law of Moses, though the Bible makes no mention of the name. According to the story of the Bible, the name of the father-in-law of Moses was Jethro, who is not spoken of as a Prophet. The Quran speaks of Moses as having been

raised after Shu'aib, so he could not be a contemporary (7:104). As Shu'aib has been mentioned in this verse as the "brother" of Midian, the inference is inevitable that he was a descendant of Abraham, Midian being a son of the Patriarch by his bond-maid Keturah. For fuller discussion of Shu'aib see 11:85.

The word اصلاح (being set in order) refers here to the coming down of divine revelation and the advent of the Prophet Shu'aib (see 7:57). According to the verse under comment, the most prominent evil of the Midian people was their unfair practice in measuring and weighing.

985. Commentary :

The tribe of Shu'aib appears to resemble very much the Arabs in their ways and customs, for the Meccans did with the Holy Prophet exactly what the people of Shu'aib's did with

88. And if there is a party among you who believes in that with which I have been sent, and a party who does not believe, then have patience until Allah judges between us. And He is the best of judges'[986]

89. [a]The chief men of his people who were arrogant said, 'Assuredly, we will drive thee out, O Shu'aib, and the believers *that are* with thee, from our town, or you shall have to return to our religion.' He said : 'Even though we be unwilling?'[987]

وَاِنْ كَانَ طَآئِفَةٌ مِّنْكُمْ اٰمَنُوْا بِالَّذِیْۤ اُرْسِلْتُ بِهٖ وَطَآئِفَةٌ لَّمْ یُؤْمِنُوْا فَاصْبِرُوْا حَتّٰی یَحْكُمَ اللّٰهُ بَیْنَنَا ۚ وَهُوَ خَیْرُ الْحٰكِمِیْنَ ۸۸

قَالَ الْمَلَاُ الَّذِیْنَ اسْتَكْبَرُوْا مِنْ قَوْمِهٖ لَنُخْرِجَنَّكَ یٰشُعَیْبُ وَالَّذِیْنَ اٰمَنُوْا مَعَكَ مِنْ قَرْیَتِنَاۤ اَوْ لَتَعُوْدُنَّ فِیْ مِلَّتِنَا ؕ قَالَ اَوَلَوْ كُنَّا كٰرِهِیْنَ ۸۹

_____

[a]14 : 14.

_____

him. Both of them hindered the outsiders from approaching their respective Prophets.

The words, لَا تَقْعُدُوْا بِكُلِّ صِرَاطٍ besides the meaning given in the text, may also be interpreted as " have not recourse to every means," and taken in this sense, the prohibition shows that the people of Shu'aib tried all means in their power to dissuade men from accepting the truth.

The children of Abraham from Keturah, who was a bondwoman, were despised by both Israelites and Ishmaelites. They were looked down upon as weak and despicable, but God increased their number and gave them wealth and power. They are therefore asked to remember this favour of God and be grateful to Him.

986. Commentary :

The verse refers to the last course that a Prophet adopts after the failure of all his efforts to make his people see the error of their ways and accept the truth. He leaves

the whole matter in the hand of God and asks them to wait till God should show a decisive Sign which would clearly distinguish between right and wrong.

987. Commentary :

Disbelievers, complacently conscious of their power and wealth, listen to no request however reasonable, and in the words of the opponents of Shu'aib always say : "There is no need for anyone to judge between us. We ourselves can judge, and our verdict is that only he who follows our religion will be allowed to live with us." On the other hand, the followers of every Prophet, like the followers of Shu'aib, have always made a pathetic, though un-availing, appeal to their persecutors in the words : "Will you compel us to adopt your religion, even if it offends our reason and goes against our conscience ?" The concluding words of the verse also show that throughout history good and intelligent men have always believed that force should not be used in matters relating to conscience.

90. 'We have indeed been forging a lie against Allah, if we *now* return to your religion after Allah has saved us therefrom. And it behoves us not to return thereto except that Allah, our Lord, should *so* will. ªOur Lord comprehends all things in *His* knowledge. In Allah have we put our trust. *So* O our Lord, decide Thou between us and between our people with truth, and Thou art the best of those who decide.'⁹⁸⁸

قَدِ افْتَرَيْنَا عَلَى اللّٰهِ كَذِبًا اِنْ عُدْنَا فِىْ مِلَّتِكُمْ بَعْدَ اِذْ نَجّٰىنَا اللّٰهُ مِنْهَا ۚ وَمَا يَكُوْنُ لَنَا اَنْ نَّعُوْدَ فِيْهَا اِلَّا اَنْ يَّشَاءَ اللّٰهُ رَبُّنَا ۚ وَسِعَ رَبُّنَا كُلَّ شَىْءٍ عِلْمًا ۚ عَلَى اللّٰهِ تَوَكَّلْنَا ۗ رَبَّنَا افْتَحْ بَيْنَنَا وَبَيْنَ قَوْمِنَا بِالْحَقِّ وَاَنْتَ خَيْرُ الْفٰتِحِيْنَ ۝

91. And the chief men of his people who disbelieved said, 'If you follow Shu'aib, you shall then certainly be the losers.'

وَقَالَ الْمَلَاُ الَّذِيْنَ كَفَرُوْا مِنْ قَوْمِهٖ لَئِنِ اتَّبَعْتُمْ شُعَيْبًا اِنَّكُمْ اِذًا لَّخٰسِرُوْنَ ۝

92. So ᵇthe earthquake seized them and in their homes they lay prostrate upon the ground;⁹⁸⁸ᴬ

فَاَخَذَتْهُمُ الرَّجْفَةُ فَاَصْبَحُوْا فِىْ دَارِهِمْ جٰثِمِيْنَ ۝

ª2 : 256 ; 40 : 8.   ᵇ7 : 79 ; 11 : 68 ; 15 : 84 ; 26 : 159.

988. Commentary :

The argument of the followers of Shu'aib for not renouncing their religion is continued in this verse. There could be only two reasons, they said, for giving up their faith ; *firstly*, if they had been false and insincere in their profession of faith ; *secondly*, if their religion itself had been false. But as neither of these two things was true, therefore, it was impossible for them to give up their faith. They further reinforce their argument by the words, *Our Lord comprehends all things in His knowledge*, meaning that when they are fully convinced of their religion being the religion of God and of God being always in the right, it is impossible for them to recant their faith. There is only one possibility of their doing so *i.e. that Allah, our Lord, should so will, viz.*, that some hidden weakness or sin of theirs may move God to cut them asunder like a diseased limb. But they have faith in their Lord and trust in Him Who has given them the opportunity and the power to accept the truth. He would not let them go astray because His permitting them to forsake the path of rectitude would be inconsistent with His attribute of being their رب or Lord.

The words, *In Allah have we put our trust*, are also intended to imply that, as the votaries of truth have perfect faith in God, so no amount of persecution can intimidate them into giving it up. They are encouraged and strengthened by constantly praying to God to protect them from the plots and machinations of their enemies.

988ᴬ. Important Words :

الرجفة (earthquake). See 7 : 79 above.

Commentary :

The people of Shu'aib were destroyed by an earthquake probably in the early morning.

93. Those who accused Shuʻaib of lying became as if they had never dwelt therein. Those who accused Shuʻaib of lying—it was they who were the losers.⁹⁸⁹

اَلَّذِيۡنَ كَذَّبُوۡا شُعَيۡبًا كَاَنۡ لَّمۡ يَغۡنَوۡا فِيۡهَا ۚ اَلَّذِيۡنَ كَذَّبُوۡا شُعَيۡبًا كَانُوۡا هُمُ الۡخٰسِرِيۡنَ ۝

94. Then he turned away from them and said, ᵃ' O my people, indeed, I delivered to you the message of my Lord and gave you sincere counsel. How then should I sorrow for a disbelieving people ? '⁹⁹⁰

فَتَوَلّٰى عَنۡهُمۡ وَقَالَ يٰقَوۡمِ لَقَدۡ اَبۡلَغۡتُكُمۡ رِسٰلٰتِ رَبِّيۡ وَنَصَحۡتُ لَكُمۡ ۚ فَكَيۡفَ اٰسٰى عَلٰى قَوۡمٍ كٰفِرِيۡنَ ۝

12 95. And never did We send a Prophet to any town but ᵇWe seized the people thereof with adversity and suffering, that they might become humble.⁹⁹¹

وَمَاۤ اَرۡسَلۡنَا فِيۡ قَرۡيَةٍ مِّنۡ نَّبِيٍّ اِلَّاۤ اَخَذۡنَاۤ اَهۡلَهَا بِالۡبَاۡسَاءِ وَالضَّرَّاءِ لَعَلَّهُمۡ يَضَّرَّعُوۡنَ ۝

ᵃ7 : 69, 80 ; 46 : 24.　　ᵇ6 : 43.

---

989. Commentary :

The disbelievers had threatened Shuʻaib with expulsion from their town, if he did not return to their religion (7 : 89). They forgot that it was not their but God's town and He would allow whomsoever He pleased to dwell therein. So, in order to demonstrate that it was not they but God Who was the Master of the land, He so utterly destroyed them, and all signs of their habitations and dwellings were so completely effaced that it appeared as if they had never dwelt therein. That was indeed a fitting punishment for those who proudly called God's land their own and threatened to drive God's Messenger away therefrom.

The words, *Those who accused Shuʻaib of lying*, have been repeated in the second part of the verse to add further emphasis to the exemplary destruction of the rejectors of Shuʻaib. The concluding words of the verse *i.e. it was they who were the losers*, contain a dreadful allusion to the words of the disbelieving chiefs who spoke of the followers of Shuʻaib as the losers (7 : 91 above), and point out that it is they, and not the followers of Shuʻaib, who are lost.

990. Commentary :

The words put in the mouth of Shuʻaib in this verse are full of pathos. Shuʻaib, like every true Prophet, feels deep grief and distress for his people, but then he tries to console his distressed heart by saying, *How then should I sorrow for a disbelieving people*, *i.e.* "These ungrateful people persistently refused to accept the truth from their Lord. They defied and disobeyed God's Prophet and rejected His Signs and thus drew upon themselves His wrath and brought about their ruin with their own hand. In spite of this my heart sorrows for them. Would that they had believed !"

991. Commentary :

This verse refers to a general law of God which invariably comes into operation whenever a Prophet of God makes his appearance. The advent of every Prophet is attended in an extraordinary manner with calamities and miseries of diverse kinds that afflict mankind in order to serve as an eye-opener for the people.

96. Then We changed *their* evil condition into good until they grew *in affluence and number* and said, 'Suffering and happiness betided our fathers *also.*' Then We seized them suddenly, while they perceived not.⁹⁹²

97. And ᵃif the people of *those* towns had believed and been righteous, We would have surely opened for them blessings from heaven and earth; but they disbelieved, so We seized them because of that which they used to earn.⁹⁹³

ثُمَّ بَدَّلْنَا مَكَانَ السَّيِّئَةِ الْحَسَنَةَ حَتّٰى عَفَوْا وَّ قَالُوْا قَدْ مَسَّ اٰبَآءَنَا الضَّرَّآءُ وَ السَّرَّآءُ فَاَخَذْنٰهُمْ بَغْتَةً وَّهُمْ لَا يَشْعُرُوْنَ ۞

وَ لَوْ اَنَّ اَهْلَ الْقُرٰۤى اٰمَنُوْا وَ اتَّقَوْا لَفَتَحْنَا عَلَيْهِمْ بَرَكٰتٍ مِّنَ السَّمَآءِ وَ الْاَرْضِ وَ لٰكِنْ كَذَّبُوْا فَاَخَذْنٰهُمْ بِمَا كَانُوْا يَكْسِبُوْنَ ۞

ᵃ2 : 104 ; 5 : 66.

If the Messenger of God is raised for a particular people, then only that people are made to suffer, but if he is raised for the whole world, then the whole world is visited by afflictions and disasters. These afflictions are meant as warnings and are intended to awaken the people. Two things may be inferred from this verse : (1) that general disasters do not overtake a people unless a Prophet of God has first been raised; (2) that it never happens that the advent of a Prophet of God is not accompanied by calamities of a general nature.

992. Important Words :

عَفَوْا (they grew) is derived from عَفَا which gives a number of meanings : (1) it was or became effaced or obliterated; (2) transitively, he or it effaced or obliterated something; (3) he forgave or pardoned; (4) it was or became much in quantity or many in number; or (5) transitively, he made it much in quantity or many in number, etc. (Lane).

Commentary :

The words حَسَنَة (good condition) and سَيِّئَة (evil condition) are not used here in their moral sense, but in the sense of straitness and plenty.

It is invariably the case that when the afflictions and miseries which come upon a disbelieving people as a result of their rejection of a Prophet of God pass away and ease and comfort take their place, then, instead of improving their condition and turning to God in repentance, they refuse to recognize past afflictions as heavenly visitations and as signs of the truth of their Prophet, but, on the contrary, begin to say that they were merely normal occurrences of nature which even their forefathers experienced in their time but which then passed away.

993. Commentary :

In this verse the words, *the people of those towns,* refer to all the different peoples mentioned in the fore-going verses. The verse is thus intended to sum up the given narration with a view to introducing the case of the people of the Holy Prophet's time.

The words فَتَحْنَا الخ rendered as, *We would have surely opened for them blessings from heaven and earth,* may signify : "We would have taught them wisdom or granted them knowledge from heaven as well as from earth." By earthly wisdom or knowledge is meant that wisdom or knowledge which a person acquires

98. Are the people of *these* towns, then, secure from *a* the coming of Our punishment upon them by night while they are asleep ? [994]

اَفَاَمِنَ اَهۡلُ الۡقُرٰۤی اَنۡ یَّاۡتِیَهُمۡ بَاۡسُنَا بَیَاتًا وَّهُمۡ نَآئِمُوۡنَ ۹۸

99. And are the people of *these* towns secure from *b* the coming of Our punishment upon them in the early part of the forenoon while they are engaged in play ? [995]

اَوَ اَمِنَ اَهۡلُ الۡقُرٰۤی اَنۡ یَّاۡتِیَهُمۡ بَاۡسُنَا ضُحًی وَّهُمۡ یَلۡعَبُوۡنَ ۹۹

100. Are they then secure from the design of Allah ? And none feels secure from the design of Allah save the people that perish. [996]

اَفَاَمِنُوۡا مَکۡرَ اللّٰهِ ۚ فَلَا یَاۡمَنُ مَکۡرَ اللّٰهِ اِلَّا الۡقَوۡمُ الۡخٰسِرُوۡنَ ۱۰۰

---

*a*7 : 5.   *b*7 : 5.

---

from personal observation or from his fellowmen; but the wisdom or knowledge from Heaven is that wisdom or knowledge which comes directly from God. The word "blessings" may also be taken in the physical sense. In this case blessings from heaven would mean, for example, timely rains, extraordinary success, the removal of diseases, etc., while blessings from the earth would signify, for example, abundant produce of land, peace and order, etc.

994. Commentary :

In this and the following verse the words اهل القرى (people of *these* towns) refer to the people of the time of the Holy Prophet to whom the Quran now turns as a fitting sequel to the story of by-gone peoples who were destroyed by God for rejecting their Prophets. The verse thus purports to warn the people of Mecca and other towns of Arabia that their turn is fast approaching and that the punishment of God may overtake them at any moment of negligence.

995. Commentary :

Whereas the preceding verse mentioned the time of night and sleep, the present one refers to the time of forenoon and play—both times of extreme negligence and forgetfulness.

996. Commentary :

As stated under 7 : 98 above, the Quran mentioned the fate of peoples that had opposed the Prophets of God in times gone by in order to warn opponents of the Holy Prophet that they also could not expect to escape a similar fate if they persisted in their opposition. The Prophets who have been mentioned in the preceding verses lived either in Arabia itself or in the neighbouring countries, and stories of the fate that befell their opponents were still current among the contemporaries of the Holy Prophet.

The home of the 'Ādites was in Yemen, but their conquests extended over the whole of Arabia. Arab tradition represents them as conquerors of the whole world—of Persia, India and China, but history furnishes no proof of this claim.

The territory of the tribe of Thamūd lay between Medina and Syria. The Holy Prophet passed through the ruins of their dwelling places during his expedition to Tabūk. The tribe of Thamūd were worshippers of idols, among them being the Lāt and the 'Uzza.

R. 13 101. *a*Does it not afford guidance to those who have inherited the earth in succession to its *former* inhabitants, that if We please, We can smite them for their sins and *b*seal up their hearts, so that they should not understand.[997]

أَوَلَمْ يَهْدِ لِلَّذِينَ يَرِثُونَ الْأَرْضَ مِنْ بَعْدِ أَهْلِهَآ أَنْ لَّوْ نَشَآءُ أَصَبْنَهُمْ بِذُنُوْبِهِمْ وَنَطْبَعُ عَلٰى قُلُوْبِهِمْ فَهُمْ لَا يَسْمَعُوْنَ ۝

102. Such were the towns some of whose news We have related to thee. And *c*their Messengers did indeed come to them with clear Signs. But they would not believe what they had disbelieved before. In this manner does Allah seal up the hearts of the disbelievers.[998]

تِلْكَ الْقُرٰى نَقُصُّ عَلَيْكَ مِنْ أَنْبَآئِهَا ۚ وَلَقَدْ جَآءَتْهُمْ رُسُلُهُمْ بِالْبَيِّنٰتِ ۚ فَمَا كَانُوْا لِيُؤْمِنُوْا بِمَا كَذَّبُوْا مِنْ قَبْلُ ۚ كَذٰلِكَ يَطْبَعُ اللّٰهُ عَلٰى قُلُوْبِ الْكٰفِرِيْنَ ۝

103. And We found not in most of them any *observance of* covenant and surely We found most of them to be evil-doers.

وَمَا وَجَدْنَا لِأَكْثَرِهِمْ مِنْ عَهْدٍ ۚ وَإِنْ وَّجَدْنَآ أَكْثَرَهُمْ لَفٰسِقِيْنَ ۝

---

*a*20 : 129; 32 : 27.   *b*10 : 75; 16 : 109; 45 : 24.   *c*3 : 185; 5 : 33.

The Midianites also lived in the north of Arabia, near the coast of the Red Sea. The history of all these peoples was current among the Arabs who were well-informed of their power, designs and machinations as well as of their subsequent destruction as a result of the opposition offered by them to their Prophets. The reference in the verse to *the people that perish* is, therefore, straight and pointed.

997. Commentary :

The veiled threat in the preceding verse is openly made in the present one. The enemies of Islam should either take lesson from the sad end of those gone before them and give up offering opposition to it or be prepared for a similar doom. The word يسمعون (understand) here signifies not listening but understanding (Lane).

998. Commentary :

The word القرى (the towns) again refers here to ancient towns fallen into ruin. The Quran reverts to their mention in order to emphasize

the seriousness of a Prophet's rejection and to introduce the narration of yet another by-gone people, the rejectors of Moses.

By using the words, *some of whose news*, the verse makes it clear that the Quran has not given the entire history of by-gone peoples but only the relevant parts of it. Nevertheless, no book of history contains more reliable information about the peoples of 'Ād and Thamūd than does the Quran, and students of history have admitted that what the Quran tells us is the only authentic and reliable knowledge that we possess about these ancient peoples, and all other stories current about them may be only so many myths. As regards Lot, later Jewish writers have admitted that he was a Prophet of God, as the Quran represents him to be, though the Bible does not seem to accord him this rank.

The verse hints that as the Holy Prophet represents in his person all the Prophets that

104. Then, after them, ^aWe sent Moses with Our Signs to Pharaoh and his chiefs, but they unjustly *rejected* them. Behold, then, what was the end of those who created disorder !⁹⁹⁹

ثُمَّ بَعَثْنَا مِنْ بَعْدِهِمْ مُّوْسٰى بِاٰيٰتِنَاۤ اِلٰى فِرْعَوْنَ وَمَلَائِهٖ فَظَلَمُوْا بِهَا ۚ فَانْظُرْ كَيْفَ كَانَ عَاقِبَةُ الْمُفْسِدِيْنَ ۞

105. And ^bMoses said, ' O Pharaoh, truly, I am a Messenger from the Lord of the worlds,

وَقَالَ مُوْسٰى يٰفِرْعَوْنُ اِنِّيْ رَسُوْلٌ مِّنْ رَّبِّ الْعٰلَمِيْنَ ۞

106. ' It is not meet that I should say anything of God except the truth. I have come to you with a clear Sign from your Lord ; therefore, ^clet the children of Israel go with me.'¹⁰⁰⁰

حَقِيْقٌ عَلٰٓى اَنْ لَّاۤ اَقُوْلَ عَلَى اللّٰهِ اِلَّا الْحَقَّ قَدْ جِئْتُكُمْ بِبَيِّنَةٍ مِّنْ رَّبِّكُمْ فَاَرْسِلْ مَعِيَ بَنِيْۤ اِسْرَآءِيْلَ ۞

---

^a17 : 102 ; 28 : 37 ; 43 : 47.   ^b26 : 17 ; 20 : 48 ; 43 : 47.   ^c20 : 48 ; 26 : 18.

---

have gone before him, therefore his rejectors will be visited with all the various forms of punishment that befell the rejectors of former Prophets.

The opponents of God's Prophets are in the habit of rejecting their claims on the basis of mere hearsay and make-believe. The result of such a hasty rejection is that the hearts of the rejectors become sealed and they become deprived of the power to understand the arguments and Signs which God shows to establish the truth of His Messengers. The verse thus throws light on how the hearts or minds of disbelievers are sealed. They are sealed only when disbelievers refuse to make use of their God-given power of reasoning and understanding.

999. Commentary :

The clause, *Then after them We sent Moses*, does not mean that Moses appeared directly or immediately after the Prophets mentioned in the preceding verses. Other Messengers may have intervened between Moses and these Prophets, of whom Shu'aib appears to be the nearest in time to Moses. In fact, the use of

the words, *Then after them,* in the above clause only means that Moses appeared and lived some time after them. The expression also contradicts the popular view that Shu'aib was a contemporary and the father-in-law of Moses.

The words ظَلَمُوْا بِهَا (they unjustly rejected them) literally meaning "they did wrong by means of the Signs, or did them wrong," really signify that "they rejected the Signs and treated them as lies, or they made them the means of doing wrong to men by ridiculing them and in this way deceiving the people."

The word ظُلْم also means, "to put a thing in the wrong place, or to make a wrong use of a thing " (Lane). Taking the word in this sense, the clause would mean, "they made a wrong use of the Signs " *i.e.* though the Signs were meant to engender fear of God in the hearts of men, the disbelievers, instead of profiting by them, jeered and mocked at them.

1000. Important Words :

حَقِيْق (it is meet) is derived from حَقّ meaning, it was or became suitable to the requirements of wisdom, justice, truth and

107. *Pharaoh* replied, ' *a*If thou hast indeed come with a Sign, then produce it, if thou art of the truthful.'

قَالَ اِنْ كُنْتَ جِئْتَ بِاٰيَةٍ فَاْتِ بِهَاۤ اِنْ كُنْتَ مِنَ الصّٰدِقِيْنَ ۝

108. So *b*he flung down his rod and behold, it was a serpent plainly visible.[1001]

فَاَلْقٰى عَصَاهُ فَاِذَا هِىَ ثُعْبَانٌ مُّبِيْنٌ ۝

---

*a*26 : 32.   *b*20 : 21 ; 26 : 33 ; 27 : 11 ; 28 : 32.

---

right ; or it was or became just, proper, correct, valid, established or confirmed as a truth or fact ; or it became necessary, unavoidable, obligatory or due. They say يَحِقُّ عَلَيْكَ اَنْ تَفْعَلَ كَذَا *i.e.* it is incumbent upon thee, or it behoves thee, or it is meet for thee, that thou shouldst do such a thing. Thus حَقِيْق means, adapted, disposed, apt, meet, fit or worthy. The expression حَقِيْق اَنْ لَا اَقُوْل would thus mean, I am disposed not to say ; or it is binding or obligatory or incumbent on me that I should not say ; or, as some render the expression, I am vehemently desirous that I should not say (Lane & Aqrab).

Commentary :

Taking the word حَقِيْق in the sense of "desirous", the opening sentence of the verse would mean "I am desirous that I should speak of God nothing but the truth." These words are put in the mouth of Moses as a reply also to those who accused the Holy Prophet of lying. The Prophets of God are, as it were, represented as saying that, far from speaking a lie, they are but too anxious, and desire nothing but, to speak pure and unadulterated truth. Other meanings of حَقِيْق are also equally applicable here.

When Moses went to Pharaoh, his object was not so much the preaching of his message to him as to call upon him to let the Israelites go with him, though ordinarily he would preach to him also. As a matter of fact, the message of Moses was meant primarily for the Israelites, but as long as the Israelites remained mixed up with the natives of Egypt, Moses had to preach to them both. When the Israelites left the land, he had no concern with the Egyptians and confined his attention to his own kith and kin to whom he had been sent.

1001. Important Words :

ثُعْبَان (serpent) is derived from ثَعَبَ. They say ثَعَبَهُ *i.e.* he gave vent to it ; or he made it (water, etc.) to flow or run or stream. ثُعْبَان means, a kind of long serpent ; a great serpent, whether male or female, but particularly the male ; or the serpent in general whether male or female, great or small ; also applied to an enormous fabulous serpent (Lane).

Commentary :

The Quran has used three different words for describing the turning of the rod of Moses into a serpent : (1) ثُعْبَان as in the verse under comment and in 26 : 33 ; (2) حَيَّة as in 20 : 21, and (3) جَانّ as in 28 : 32 and 27 : 11. The words حَيَّة and ثُعْبَان are applied both to a large or a small serpent, while the word جَانّ signifies only a small serpent. Thus there is no conflict or contradiction in using these three different words for the same thing, as all of them may be used to give the same meaning *i.e.* a small serpent.

Moreover, on carefully pondering over the verses in which these words occur, we find that different words have been used to suit different occasions. The word جَانّ has been used on the occasion when the rod is made to appear as a serpent to Moses alone (27 : 11) while the words ثعبان and حية have been used in connection with the occasion when the miracle was wrought in public. This shows that to Moses the rod appeared as only a small serpent, while in the presence of Pharaoh and other men, it was made to appear like a big serpent. Thus the use of three different words for different occasions was not haphazard and casual but deliberate and evidently intended to serve a definite purpose.

Moreover, in the verses in which the word جان is used, it is not said that the rod actually turned into a جان (small serpent) but that it moved as though it were a جان. This does not mean that the rod necessarily turned into a small serpent but that it only moved quickly like a small serpent, though it may have been a large serpent. So the different words used by the Quran do not conflict with each other, whether the rod be taken as turning into a small serpent or a large one.

It should also be noted here that this miracle did not really contradict any law of nature. If the existence of a thing is proved beyond doubt, it must be admitted, even if we are unable to explain it in the light of the laws of nature, as we know them. Our knowledge of the laws of nature is evidently very limited and so we cannot deny a fact on the basis of our limited and imperfect knowledge. Moreover, the said miracle did not take place in the manner in which it is popularly understood to have occurred. Indeed, miracles shown by God's Prophets are not like the performances of jugglers. They are meant to serve some great moral or spiritual purpose. One of their primary objects is to bring about certainty of faith and engender feelings of piety and fear of God in the minds of those who witness them. If the rod had actually turned into a serpent, the whole performance must have looked more like the hand-tricks of a juggler than the miracle of a Prophet. In spite of what the Bible might say about this miracle, the Quran lends no support whatever to the view that the rod actually turned into a real and living serpent. No such thing ever took place. The rod only *appeared* like a moving serpent. It was a sort of a vision in which God either exercised special control over the sight of the onlookers in order to make them see the rod in the form of a serpent or the rod itself was made to appear like a serpent; and this vision was shared by Pharaoh and his courtiers and the enchanters along with Moses. The rod remained a rod, only it appeared to Moses and others as a serpent. It is a spiritual phenomenon of common occurrence that in a vision when man rises above the encumbrances of the flesh and becomes temporarily transported to a spiritual sphere, he can see things taking place which are beyond his ken and are quite invisible to his physical eyes. The miracle of the rod turning into a serpent was one such spiritual experience.

A similar spiritual phenomenon took place when in the time of the Holy Prophet the moon was seen as rent asunder not only by the Holy Prophet but by some of his followers and opponents as well (Bukhārī, ch. on *Tafsīr*). Such visions, which constitute a peculiar state between sleep and wakefulness, are a common spiritual experience of God's Prophets and His Elect, but sometimes they are shared by ordinary men and by even disbelievers. Tradition tells us that Gabriel whom the Holy Prophet often saw in his visions, was also once seen by his Companions, who were sitting with him (Bukhārī, ch. on *Imān*). Similarly, some angels were seen even by some of the disbelievers at the Battle of Badr (Jarīr, vi. 47). Another instance of this kind occurred when a Muslim army under the well-known Muslim general, Sāriya, was fighting the enemy in Iraq at a distance of hundreds of miles from Medina. 'Umar, the Second *Khalīfa*,

109. And ^aHe drew forth his hand, and lo ! it was white for the beholders.[1002]

وَّنَزَعَ يَدَهُ فَاِذَا هِىَ بَيْضَآءُ لِلنّٰظِرِيْنَ ۧ

^a26 : 34 ; 27 : 13 ; 28 : 33.

while delivering his Friday sermon at Medina, saw in a vision that the Muslim army was being overwhelmed by the superior numbers of the enemy and that a disastrous defeat was imminent. Thereupon 'Umar suddenly discontinued his sermon and cried out from the pulpit, saying, " O Sāriya, take to the mountain, take to the mountain." Sāriya, hundreds of miles away and surrounded by the deafening noise of the battlefield, heard the voice of 'Umar and obeyed it ; and the Muslim army was saved from destruction (Khamīs, ii. 270).

The miracle of Moses mentioned in the verse under comment possessed a special significance. It may be interpreted something like this. God told Moses to throw down his rod which then appeared to him like a serpent ; and when subsequently on God's bidding he took it up, lo ! the rod was a mere piece of wood. Now a serpent, in the language of visions and dreams, is a symbol of the enemy, while a rod is emblematic of one's community (Tā'tīr al-Anām). Thus, by means of this vision, God made Moses understand that if He cast away his people from him, they would become veritable serpents. But if he kept them under his care, they would grow into a strong and well-knit community of righteous and God-fearing men. Moses had in the beginning begged to be excused from being entrusted with the onerous task of reclaiming a morally depraved people, but God told him by means of this vision that the well-being of his people depended upon his taking them in his charge, failing which they would turn into veritable serpents.

Abū Jahl, the arch-enemy of Islam, was also once made to see a similar vision. It is reported

that the Holy Prophet one day went to him and asked him to pay a certain sum of money which he owed to a poor man, a stranger in Mecca, but which he had so far declined to pay. On the Holy Prophet's demand, Abū Jahl, in spite of his great enmity to the Prophet, made the payment at once, and when asked by his friends the reason for his doing so, he said he saw two enraged camels on both sides of Muhammad about to tear him to pieces if he refused to comply with his demand (Hishām). Arabia is a land of camels, so Abū Jahl was made to see camels, while Egypt being a land of magic serpents, Pharaoh was made to see a serpent.

1002. Commentary :

The miracle of the white hand has also been mentioned in the Bible (Exod. 4 : 6), with the difference that whereas in the Bible the hand is represented as "leprous", the Quran represents it as being "without disease" (28 : 33). Another difference between the two accounts is that the Quran represents Moses as having shown both Signs to Pharaoh, while according to the Bible, although Moses is bidden to show this Sign to Pharaoh (Exod. 4 : 8), it does not mention that Moses did actually show the latter Sign to him. The Quranic version clearly seems to be the more correct, not only because Moses could not omit to show the Sign of the white hand to Pharaoh as he was commanded by God, as admitted by the Bible itself, but also because Pharaoh having failed to profit by the first Sign, Moses must have shown him the second Sign also, after the rejection of the first.

The bodies of highly spiritual men are known to emit invisible rays of various colours

110. ᵃThe chiefs of Pharaoh's people said, 'This is most surely a skilful magician.¹⁰⁰³

قَالَ الْمَلَأُ مِنْ قَوْمِ فِرْعَوْنَ اِنَّ هٰذَا لَسٰحِرٌ عَلِيْمٌ ۙ﴿۱۱۰﴾

111. ᵇ'He desires to turn you out from your land. Now what do you advise?'¹⁰⁰⁴

يُّرِيْدُ اَنْ يُّخْرِجَكُمْ مِّنْ اَرْضِكُمْ ۚ فَمَاذَا تَأْمُرُوْنَ ﴿۱۱۱﴾

112. ᶜThey said, 'Put him off and his brother awhile, and send into the cities summoners,

قَالُوْۤا اَرْجِهْ وَاَخَاهُ وَاَرْسِلْ فِى الْمَدَآئِنِ حٰشِرِيْنَ ۙ﴿۱۱۲﴾

113. ᵈ'Who should bring to thee every skilful magician.'

يَأْتُوْكَ بِكُلِّ سٰحِرٍ عَلِيْمٍ ﴿۱۱۳﴾

ᵃ20 : 64 ; 26 : 35.   ᵇ20 : 64 ; 26 : 36.   ᶜ26 : 37.   ᵈ26 : 38.

---

according to the degree or nature of their spiritual development. The rays that emerge from the bodies of perfectly holy men, such as Prophets, are of pure white colour. So the rays that issued from the hand of Moses must have been of that colour, and when these rays were made visible, his hand naturally appeared white to the beholders. Men are known to have had such spiritual experience in the times of other Prophets of God as well. For instance, authentic instances of such spiritual experiences having been felt by certain individuals in the time of Ahmad, the Promised Messiah, are on record (Al-Fazl, vol. 32, No. 217).

Elsewhere the Quran says, God said to Moses : *Thrust thy hand into thy bosom ; it will come forth white without disease* (28 : 33). This constituted, in symbolic language, a clear hint to Moses that if he kept his followers close to him and under his fostering care, they would not only become men of light themselves but would also impart light to others, otherwise they would become not only black but also diseased. The miracle was not, there-fore, the performance of a magician but a Sign full of deep spiritual significance.

1003. Important Words :

The word سَاحِر (magician) does not necessarily mean a magician. It also means, an enchanter ; fascinator ; one knowing, or one skilful and intelligent ; one able to make a thing look other than what it is ; a deceiver, deluder or beguiler, etc. (Lane). See also 2 : 103.

1004. Important Words :

تَأْمُرُوْن (you advise) is derived from أمر. They say أمره i.e. he commanded, ordered or enjoined him. The word also means, he counselled or advised him (Lane).

Commentary :

The words, *He desires to turn you out*, are intended to work up the feelings of the people against Moses, whereas the truth was that Moses had no desire of turning out the Egyptians. On the contrary, he only desired to take his own people away and leave the Egyptians in Egypt.

114. And *a*the magicians came to Pharaoh *and* said : ' We shall, of course, have a reward, if we prevail.'[1005]

وَجَآءَ السَّحَرَةُ فِرْعَوْنَ قَالُوۤا اِنَّ لَنَا لَاَجْرًا اِنْ كُنَّا نَحْنُ الْغٰلِبِيْنَ ۝

115. *b*He said, ' Yes, and you shall *also* be of those who are placed near me.'[1006]

قَالَ نَعَمْ وَاِنَّكُمْ لَمِنَ الْمُقَرَّبِيْنَ ۝

116. *c*They said, ' O Moses, either throw thou *first*, or we shall be the *first* throwers.'[1007]

قَالُوْا يٰمُوْسٰۤى اِمَّاۤ اَنْ تُلْقِىَ وَاِمَّاۤ اَنْ نَّكُوْنَ نَحْنُ الْمُلْقِيْنَ ۝

117. He replied, ' Throw ye.' And *d*when they threw, they enchanted the eyes of the people, and struck them with awe and brought forth a great magic.[1008]

قَالَ اَلْقُوْا ۚ فَلَمَّاۤ اَلْقَوْا سَحَرُوْۤا اَعْيُنَ النَّاسِ وَاسْتَرْهَبُوْهُمْ وَجَآءُوْ بِسِحْرٍ عَظِيْمٍ ۝

118. And We inspired Moses, *saying*, '*e*Throw thy rod,' and lo! it swallowed up whatever they feigned.[1009]

وَاَوْحَيْنَاۤ اِلٰى مُوْسٰۤى اَنْ اَلْقِ عَصَاكَ ۚ فَاِذَا هِىَ تَلْقَفُ مَا يَأْفِكُوْنَ ۝

---

*a*26 : 42.   *b*26 : 43.   *c*20 : 66.   *d*20 : 67 ; 26 : 45.   *e*20 : 70 ; 26 : 46.

1005. Commentary :

The words, *We shall, of course, have a reward, if we prevail*, were probably spoken by the magicians to one another and not addressed to Pharaoh who, however, overheard them.

1006. Commentary :

When Pharaoh heard, or rather overheard, the magicians saying to one another the words contained in the previous verse, he told them that they would not only get the reward they rightly expected, but that they would also become his favourite courtiers.

1007. Commentary :

Mark the intensity of the scene—both parties arrayed before one another ready to come to grips in a decisive struggle.

1008. Important Words :

سِحْر عَظِيْم (a great magic). For the meaning of the word سِحْر see 2 : 103 & 7 : 110.

Commentary :

Moses was not slow in availing himself of the opportunity offered and at once replied that they should throw first. The Prophets of God generally wait for an attack on the part of their opponents, for they prefer to defend and then look to God for succour.

1009. Important Words :

تَلْقَفُ (it swallowed up) is derived from لَقِفَ. They say لَقِفَ الشَّىْءَ *i.e.* he took or seized the thing quickly ; or he took or seized the thing quickly when it was thrown to him. تَلْقَفُ الطَّعَام or لَقِفَ الطَّعَام means, he swallowed up the food (Aqrab).

Commentary :

It was certainly not the " serpent " made out of the rod, but the rod itself which undid

119. So was the Truth established, and their works proved vain.

فَوَقَعَ الْحَقُّ وَبَطَلَ مَا كَانُوْا يَعْمَلُوْنَ ۚ

120. Thus were they vanquished there, and they returned humiliated.[1010]

فَغُلِبُوْا هُنَالِكَ وَانْقَلَبُوْا صٰغِرِيْنَ ۚ

121. And *the magicians were impelled to fall down prostrate.[1011]

وَاُلْقِىَ السَّحَرَةُ سٰجِدِيْنَ ۚ

122. And *they said, ‘We believe in the Lord of the worlds,[1012]

قَالُوْۤا اٰمَنَّا بِرَبِّ الْعٰلَمِيْنَ ۙ

123. *‘The Lord of Moses and Aaron.’

رَبِّ مُوْسٰى وَهٰرُوْنَ ۚ

---

*20 : 71 ; 26 : 47.   *20 : 71 ; 26 : 48.   *20 : 71 ; 26 : 49.

---

the magic of the magicians. The rod of Moses wielded with the spiritual force of a great Prophet and thrown at the command of God exposed the deception they had wrought on the spectators by breaking to pieces the things which, by their magic, they had made the people take for real serpents. The words تَلْقَفُ مَا يَأْفِكُوْنَ literally meaning "it swallowed up whatever they feigned" really signify that the rod quickly exposed the deception wrought by the magicians.

1010. Commentary :

This verse refers to Pharaoh's party and not to the magicians. The latter have been spoken of in the next verse. So the words, *and they returned humiliated*, do not evidently apply to them. Moreover, the word صٰغِرِيْن (humiliated) could not have been used about men who had evinced such regard for truth as to have accepted it without even waiting to see what Pharaoh had to say about it. The word, "humiliated" has also been elsewhere used in the Quran about the disbelievers (9 : 29).

The word انْقَلَبُوْا (they returned) does not simply mean, "they became." The expression becomes much more powerful if taken in its literal sense, the meaning being that those who a few moments before had come to the scene of combat with a most proud and arrogant attitude and confident of success, now *returned* to their places humbled and crest-fallen.

1011. Commentary :

The passive voice in the words, *were impelled to fall down prostrate*, is full of meaning. The discomfiture of the magicians was so complete that it appeared that some hidden power had taken the ground from under their feet. They were, as it were, made to fall down prostrate on the ground in an attitude of prayer and humility before God.

1012. Commentary :

Their discomfiture proved to the magicians that the Lord of the worlds was on the side of Moses ; so they hastened to believe in Him.

124. ^aPharaoh said, 'You have believed in him before I gave you leave. Surley, this is a plot that you have plotted in the city, that you may turn out therefrom its inhabitants, but you shall soon know *the consequences*.[1013]

قَالَ فِرْعَوْنُ اٰمَنْتُمْ بِهٖ قَبْلَ اَنْ اٰذَنَ لَكُمْ ۚ اِنَّ هٰذَا لَمَكْرٌ مَّكَرْتُمُوْهُ فِى الْمَدِيْنَةِ لِتُخْرِجُوْا مِنْهَاۤ اَهْلَهَا ۚ فَسَوْفَ تَعْلَمُوْنَ ۝

125. ^b'Most surely, will I cut off your hands and your feet on alternate sides. Then will I surely crucify you all together.[1014]

لَاُقَطِّعَنَّ اَيْدِيَكُمْ وَاَرْجُلَكُمْ مِّنْ خِلَافٍ ثُمَّ لَاُصَلِّبَنَّكُمْ اَجْمَعِيْنَ ۝

126. ^cThey answered, 'To our Lord *then* shall we return.[1015]

قَالُوْۤا اِنَّاۤ اِلٰى رَبِّنَا مُنْقَلِبُوْنَ ۚ ۝

*a*20:72; 26:50.   *b*20:72; 26:50.   *c*20:73; 26:51.

1013. Commentary :

The sudden change in the magicians, brought about by the powerful hand of God, gave rise to doubts and misgivings in the mind of Pharaoh ; or it may be he simply used it as an excuse to hide his own discomfiture.

By the words "its inhabitants" are here meant Pharaoh's people, who, however, were not the real inhabitants of Egypt, having wrested the country from the sons of the soil.

The Bible also agrees with the Quran in saying that the magicians became believers in Moses (Exod. 8 : 19), with the difference that whereas, according to the Quran, the magicians became believers on the spot immediately after witnessing this miracle of Moses, according to the Bible, they believed in Moses some time later. The Quranic account is certainly more natural.

1014. Commentary :

Although crucifixion meant painful death, the punishment of cutting off the hands and feet was added to make the infliction all the more exemplary and death all the more painful. Incidentally, the verse shows that even as early as the time of Moses the punishment of death by crucifixion was in vogue.

1015. Commentary :

The magicians are not frightened by the threat of Pharaoh. On the contrary, they throw out a challenge to him saying, as it were : "If you crucify us, it will do us no harm ; on the other hand, it will only make us return to our Lord all the more quickly and we will have the pleasure of meeting Him earlier." Just note the change that true faith had brought about in these hitherto worldly-minded men. A few moments before they talked of reward in the form of money and wealth, and now they were prepared to spurn all the pleasures of the world for the sake of God and were eager to meet Him as early as possible. Faith indeed is a great power and works wonders.

127. 'And *a*thou dost not wreak vengeance on us but because we have believed in the Signs of our Lord, when they came to us. Our Lord, pour forth upon us steadfastness and cause us to die resigned *unto Thee.*'[1016]

15 **128.** And the chiefs of Pharaoh's people said, 'Wilt thou leave Moses and his people to create disorder in the land, and forsake thee and thy gods?' He answered, *b*'We will *ruthlessly* slay their sons and let their women live. And surely we are dominant over them.'[1017]

*a*20:74. *b*2:50; 7:142; 14:7; 28:5.

1016. Important Words:

افرغ (pour forth) is derived from فرغ *i.e.* it was or became empty, vacant, devoid or unoccupied; or he was or became devoid of, or free from business, occupation or employment. فرغ الماء means, the water poured forth. افرغه means, he poured out or poured forth water, etc. So the clause ربنا افرغ علينا صبرا would mean, O our Lord, pour forth upon us patience (or steadfastness) just as water from a bucket is poured forth; or send down upon us such patience as may envelop us (Lane).

Commentary:

As shown under Important Words above, the words, *pour forth upon us,* are intended to express the idea of abundance. The magicians prayed to God that He might grant them patience in abundance that they might become, as it were, covered with, and enveloped by, patience and might bear the trials without flinching. They were already unusually patient, but still they pray for more and yet more help from God to keep them firm and steadfast. That indeed is the true spiritual station.

1017. Important Words:

قاهرون (dominant). For the full meaning of this word see 6:19.

Commentary:

It was the chiefs themselves who had counselled Pharaoh to give respite to Moses and his brother (7:112); but now the same chiefs blame him for the delay he had allowed Moses and Aaron in accordance with their own advice. This is how a deterioration takes place in the morals of those who meet with disgrace and humiliation.

Pharaoh himself was worshipped as a god by his people (28:39) and he in turn worshipped other deities. Hence the chief men accused Moses and Aaron of having denounced the worship of Pharaoh and his gods.

The verb نقتل (we will *ruthlessly* slay) is in the intensified form and expresses the sense of ruthlessness and a slow and gradual process.

129. ^aMoses said to his people, 'Seek help from Allah and be steadfast. Verily the earth is Allah's; He gives it as a heritage to whomsoever He pleases of His servants, and the end is for the God-fearing.'[1018]

قَالَ مُوْسٰى لِقَوْمِهِ اسْتَعِيْنُوْا بِاللّٰهِ وَاصْبِرُوْا ۚ اِنَّ الْاَرْضَ لِلّٰهِ ۚ يُوْرِثُهَا مَنْ يَّشَآءُ مِنْ عِبَادِهٖ ۚ وَ الْعَاقِبَةُ لِلْمُتَّقِيْنَ ۝

130. They replied, 'We were persecuted before thou camest to us and *even* after thou camest to us.' He said, ^b'Your Lord is about to destroy your enemy and make you rulers in the land, *that* He may then see how you act.'[1019]

قَالُوْۤا اُوْذِيْنَا مِنْ قَبْلِ اَنْ تَأْتِيَنَا وَمِنْ بَعْدِ مَا جِئْتَنَا ۚ قَالَ عَسٰى رَبُّكُمْ اَنْ يُّهْلِكَ عَدُوَّكُمْ وَ يَسْتَخْلِفَكُمْ فِى الْاَرْضِ فَيَنْظُرَ كَيْفَ تَعْمَلُوْنَ ۝

---

^a2 : 46, 154.   ^b10 : 14, 15.

This expression is thus intended to signify the hardships and privations which Pharaoh inflicted on the Israelites and by means of which he sought to bring about their gradual but sure and ruthless destruction. The Quran therefore cannot be accused of anachronism on the ground that Pharaoh did not slay the children of the Israelites after Moses went to him as a Messenger of God, for it is an authentic fact of history that both before and after Moses went to Pharaoh with his message, the latter had put into execution schemes against the Israelites with a view to bringing about their gradual but inevitable ruin. This is the reason why the Israelites said to Moses and Aaron, "Ye have made our savour to be abhorred in the eyes of Pharaoh and in the eyes of his servants, to put a sword in their hand to slay us" (Exod. 5 : 10—21). Reference to this is to be found in 7 : 130. Moreover, the verse does not say that Pharaoh actually caused the Israelite children to be slain on this occasion. It only mentions a threat and not an accomplished fact.

1018. Commentary :

Pharaoh was proud of his power and dominion and was tyrannical in the extreme; so the Israelites are here comforted by Moses with an assurance that they need not be afraid of him, as his power shall be broken and his kingdom taken away from him.

The expression, *He gives it as a heritage to whomsoever He pleases of His servants*, does not necessarily mean that the Israelites were to be made to inherit Egypt after the destruction of Pharaoh. It only means that Pharaoh's power was to be broken and others were to take possession of his kingdom. History tells us that after the destruction of Pharaoh and the break-up of his kingdom, another dynasty, who were friendly to the Israelites, took possession of the land.

1019. Commentary :

It appears from the Bible that, like the followers of other Prophets of God, the followers of Moses were made to bear additional burdens of which they complained to Moses. (Exod. 5 : 10—21). To that complaint a reference is made in this verse.

The word "land" mentioned in the verse refers not to Egypt but to the Hoy Land which had been promised to the Israelites and which they inherited in accordance with the promise. The word may also mean "the earth" generally.

16 **131.** And ^aWe punished Pharaoh's people with drought and scarcity of fruits, that they might be admonished. [1020]

وَلَقَدۡ اَخَذۡنَاۤ اٰلَ فِرۡعَوۡنَ بِالسِّنِیۡنَ وَنَقۡصٍ مِّنَ الثَّمَرٰتِ لَعَلَّهُمۡ یَذَّکَّرُوۡنَ ۞

132. But when there came to them good, they said, ' This is for us.' And ^bif evil befell them, they ascribed the evil fortune to Moses and those with him. Now, surely, *the cause of* their evil fortune is with Allah. But most of them do not know. [1021]

فَاِذَا جَآءَتۡهُمُ الۡحَسَنَةُ قَالُوۡا لَنَا هٰذِهٖ ۚ وَاِنۡ تُصِبۡهُمۡ سَیِّئَةٌ یَّطَّیَّرُوۡا بِمُوۡسٰی وَمَنۡ مَّعَهٗ ؕ اَلَاۤ اِنَّمَا طٰٓئِرُهُمۡ عِنۡدَ اللّٰهِ وَلٰکِنَّ اَکۡثَرَهُمۡ لَا یَعۡلَمُوۡنَ ۞

---

^a17 : 102.   ^b27 : 48; 36 : 19.

Though primarily the address in the words, *that He may then see how you act*, is to the Israelites of the time of Moses, the words possess a much wider application. They apply with equal force to succeeding generations as well.

It is noteworthy that similar words have been used with regard to Muslims also (10 : 15) and, like the Israelites, they have been told that God would make them successors in the land and would bestow upon them *Khilāfat* and dominion, and then He would see whether they acted righteously in the earth. This resemblance also shows that Muslim dispensation is a counterpart of the Mosaic dispensation and that a time was to come when Muslims also were to become corrupt like the Jews. It is to this tragic fact that a reference has been made in the prayer, " make us not of those upon whom Thy wrath has descended" (see note on 1 : 7).

1020. Important Words :

سنین (drought) is the plural of سنة which is derived, according to different authorities, either from سنه or سنی or سنو. They say سنه الطعام *i.e.* the food became bad or foul or became altered (for the worse) by the lapse of years. سنا السحاب الارض means, the cloud watered the earth. سنا البعیر means, the camel turned round about the well to draw

water. سنی الرجل means, the man became high and exalted in rank. سنة means, a year; a single revolution of the sun *i.e.* a single revolution of the earth round the sun; a solar year; hence it is generally considered longer than عام which is mostly applied to a lunar year; a year of drought or famine; drought or barrenness or intense drought (Lane & Aqrab). See also 2 : 260

Commentary :

This verse speaks of two kinds of punishment which overtook Pharaoh's people—loss of property and loss of life the word ثمرات (fruits) meaning both fruits and children or offspring. The details of these punishments follow in 7 : 134.

1021. Important Words :

یطیروا (ascribed the evil fortune) is really یتطیروا which is derived from طار, from which also the word طائر (evil fortune) is derived. They say, طار الطائر *i.e.* the bird flew or moved in the air by means of its wings. تطیر بالشیٔ means, he augured evil from the thing, because it was the custom among the Arabs to take augury from the flight of birds, طائر meaning a bird. An Arab would say جری له الطائر بامر کذا *i.e.* the bird viz. fortune brought to him such an event. طائر

133. And they said, ' Whatever Sign thou mayest bring us to bewitch us with, ^awe will not submit to thee.'[1022]

وَقَالُوْا مَهْمَا تَأْتِنَا بِهٖ مِنْ اٰيَةٍ لِّتَسْحَرَنَا بِهَا فَمَا نَحْنُ لَكَ بِمُؤْمِنِيْنَ ۝

134. ^bThen We sent upon them the storm and the locusts, and the lice, and the frogs, and the blood—clear Signs : but they behaved proudly and were a sinful people.[1023]

فَأَرْسَلْنَا عَلَيْهِمُ الطُّوْفَانَ وَالْجَرَادَ وَالْقُمَّلَ وَالضَّفَادِعَ وَالدَّمَ اٰيٰتٍ مُّفَصَّلٰتٍ فَاسْتَكْبَرُوْا وَكَانُوْا قَوْمًا مُّجْرِمِيْنَ ۝

---

*a*10 : 79.   *b*17 : 102 ; 43 : 49.

---

therefore, means, a bird ; a thing from which one augurs either good or evil ; an omen, a bodement of good or of evil ; an evil fortune or ill-luck ; actions ; the means of subsistence ; the brain. The words اغا طائرهم عند الله mean, their evil fortune is with God ; or the cause of their good and evil is with God ; or the cause of their evil fortune is with God *i.e.* their actions which are the real cause of their evil fortune have reached God and lie in store there (Lane & Lisān). See also 3 : 50.

Commentary :

The people of Pharaoh ascribed to Moses the evils and misfortunes that befell them. They pretended to think that the miseries with which they had been afflicted were due to the inauspicious advent of Moses. Such has always been the practice of disbelievers. When, at the advent of a heavenly Messenger, misfortunes befall the people in consequence of their misdeeds, they, instead of repenting of their sins, ascribe them to the inauspicious advent of the heavenly Messenger.

Since the word طائر (lit. a bird) signifies an action or evil fortune, the verse constitutes a severe rebuke administered to the people of Pharaoh. They are told that the misfortunes which had befallen them were due not to what

they called the "inauspicious" advent of Moses, but to their own sins and iniquitous deeds. Thus the expression, *the cause of their evil fortune is with Allah*, means that the evil and malicious words which they uttered concerning Moses would be preserved with God and they would be duly punished for their insolence.

1022. Commentary :

Pharaoh's people proudly said to Moses that however great and powerful the Signs he might show, they would never submit to him and would never allow the Israelites to go with him.

1023. Important Words :

القمل (lice) is derived from قمل . They say قمل رأسه *i.e.* his head became infected with lice or the lice abounded in his head. قمل القوم means, the people multiplied and increased in number (like unto lice). قمل فلان means, such a one became corpulent and big-bellied. So القمل (*al-qaml*) means, lice, etc., that infect the head or body of a person as a result of uncleanliness and filth. القمل (*al-qummal*) means, small ants ; small insects like flies or mosquitoes having small wings and infesting vegetation and animals and men ; the word has also been taken to mean lice, etc. (Aqrab & Lisān).

مفصلات (clear) also means, separate, distinct, etc.

135. And ^awhen there fell upon them the punishment, they said, 'O Moses, pray for us to thy Lord according to that which He has promised to thee. If thou remove from us the punishment, we will surely believe thee and we will surely send with thee the children of Israel.'[1024]

وَلَمَّا وَقَعَ عَلَيْهِمُ الرِّجْزُ قَالُوْا يٰمُوْسَى ادْعُ لَنَا رَبَّكَ بِمَا عَهِدَ عِنْدَكَ ۚ لَئِنْ كَشَفْتَ عَنَّا الرِّجْزَ لَنُؤْمِنَنَّ لَكَ وَلَنُرْسِلَنَّ مَعَكَ بَنِيْ اِسْرَآءِيْلَ ۞

136. But ^bwhen We removed from them the punishment for a term which they were to reach, lo! they broke their promise.[1025]

فَلَمَّا كَشَفْنَا عَنْهُمُ الرِّجْزَ اِلٰى اَجَلٍ هُمْ بٰلِغُوْهُ اِذَا هُمْ يَنْكُثُوْنَ ۞

---

^a43 : 50.   ^b43 : 51.

Commentary :

This verse explains the two kinds of punishment mentioned in 7 : 131 above. Locusts and storms bring about famine, whereas lice and frogs and blood may cause disease resulting in loss of life.

The Bible mentions 10 Signs, besides the Signs of the rod and of the white hand: (1) the turning of the water of the river into blood; (2) frogs; (3) lice; (4) swarms of flies; (5) the murrain of beasts; (6) the plague of boils and blains; (7) the plague of hail; (8) locusts; (9) the plague of darkness; and (10) the death of the first-born (Exod. Chaps. 7—11). All these Signs are included in the Signs mentioned in the verse under comment. Thus the word طوفان (storm) comprises the plague of hail and the plague of darkness; جراد (locusts) expresses the plague of locusts; قمل (lice) comprises lice, the swarms of flies, the murrain of beasts and the death of the first-born, because all these may be caused by infection carried through lice, flies, mosquitoes, etc. The Sign of الدم (the blood) comprises the turning of the water of the river into blood as well as boils and blains. The Sign of blood may also comprise the death of the first-born. The turning of the water of the river into blood may also mean that the water of the river became vitiated so that it spoiled the blood of those who drank of it. That the river was actually turned into blood is negatived by the Bible itself, for we read there that the water only became blood when it was sprinkled on the land (Exod. 4 : 9). This only means that the water of the river became unfit for drinking purposes and it vitiated the blood of those who drank it. Similarly, the storms raised dust which in turn gave rise to lice. These Signs seem to have been greatly exaggerated in the Bible.

1024. Commentary :

The words, *according to that which He has promised to thee,* may refer either to the promise which God made to Moses that He would listen to his prayers, or to the promise of God to forgive those who repented. The people of Pharaoh reminded Moses of these promises of God and asked him to pray to God in their behalf so that He might pardon them their sins and remove from them the punishment which had befallen them. The sentence may also mean, "pray for us to thy Lord with the prayers which He has taught thee, or in the way He has taught thee to pray."

1025. Important Words :

اجل (term) means both " term " and " end

825

137. ^aSo We took vengeance upon them and drowned them in the sea, because they treated Our Signs as lies and were heedless of them.¹⁰²⁶

فَانْتَقَمْنَا مِنْهُمْ فَاَغْرَقْنٰهُمْ فِى الْيَمِّ بِاَنَّهُمْ كَذَّبُوْا بِاٰيٰتِنَا وَكَانُوْا عَنْهَا غٰفِلِيْنَ ۝

138. And ^bWe caused the people who were considered weak to inherit the eastern parts of the land and the western parts thereof, which We blessed. And ^cthe gracious word of thy Lord was fulfilled for the children of Israel because they were steadfast; and We destroyed all that Pharaoh and his people had built and all that they had erected.¹⁰²⁷

وَاَوْرَثْنَا الْقَوْمَ الَّذِيْنَ كَانُوْا يُسْتَضْعَفُوْنَ مَشَارِقَ الْاَرْضِ وَمَغَارِبَهَا الَّتِىْ بٰرَكْنَا فِيْهَا ۚ وَتَمَّتْ كَلِمَتُ رَبِّكَ الْحُسْنٰى عَلٰى بَنِىْ اِسْرَآءِيْلَ ۙ بِمَا صَبَرُوْا ۚ وَدَمَّرْنَا مَا كَانَ يَصْنَعُ فِرْعَوْنُ وَقَوْمُهٗ وَمَا كَانُوْا يَعْرِشُوْنَ ۝

---

^a43:56.   ^b28:6.   ^c32:25.

---

term." See 2:232. The punishment was removed only for a time to grant Pharaoh an opportunity to repent and comply with the demand of Moses.

1026. Important Words:

اليم (sea) is substantive from يم or يمم. The Arabs say يم الرجل i.e. the man was thrown into the sea; or he was drowned in the sea. يم الساحل means, the water of the sea or the water of the river overflowed its banks. اليم means, the sea; or the sea of unknown or unreached depth; a great body of water either salt or sweet (Lisān). The Quran uses the word يم both in the sense of sea (as in the present verse) and in the sense of a great river as in 20:40. See also 7:139 below.

1027. Important Words:

يعرشون (they erect) is formed from عرش i.e. he constructed or erected a structure for grape-vines to rise and spread upon; or he erected or built a shed or an enclosure or a house, etc. (Lane). See also 2:260; 6:142.

Commentary:

The words, *the eastern parts of the land and the western parts thereof*, signify, according to Arabic idiom, the entire country.

The words, *which We blessed*, refer to the Holy Land which had been promised to the descendants of Abraham and Jacob (5:22). It was blessed because it was the land where the Israelites were to thrive and prosper and grow into a great nation. The words, *And the gracious word of thy Lord was fulfilled*, mean that the promise which God had made to Abraham and Jacob came to pass.

The words, *We destroyed all that Pharaoh and his people had built*, mean that the great buildings and memorials erected by Pharaoh by unjustly exacting hard labour from the children of Israel fell into ruin in the time of the dynasty that ruled Egypt after him.

139. And We brought the children of Israel across the sea, and they came to a people who were devoted to their idols. They said, 'O Moses, make for us a god just as they have gods.' He said, 'Surely, you are an ignorant people.'[1028]

140. 'As to these, surely destroyed shall be all that they are engaged in, and vain shall be all that they do.[1029]

وَجَاوَزْنَا بِبَنِيٓ اِسْرَآءِيْلَ الْبَحْرَ فَاَتَوْا عَلٰى قَوْمٍ يَّعْكُفُوْنَ عَلٰٓى اَصْنَامٍ لَّهُمْ ۚ قَالُوْا يٰمُوْسَى اجْعَلْ لَّنَآ اِلٰهًا كَمَا لَهُمْ اٰلِهَةٌ ۚ قَالَ اِنَّكُمْ قَوْمٌ تَجْهَلُوْنَ ۝

اِنَّ هٰٓؤُلَآءِ مُتَبَّرٌ مَّا هُمْ فِيْهِ وَبٰطِلٌ مَّا كَانُوْا يَعْمَلُوْنَ ۝

1028. Important Words :

البحر (sea) is derived from بحر i.e. he cut open a thing ; or he enlarged and made it wide. بحر means, it became wide and spacious (Lane). Most probably the word البحر is used of the sea on account of its great spaciousness, and the word اليم (see 7 : 137 above) is used about it on account of its great depth.

Commentary :

Though the words البحر and اليم are generally considered synonymous, yet it is significant that the Quran uses the word اليم when speaking of the drowning of the people of Pharaoh (7 : 137) and البحر (as in the present verse) when speaking of the escape of the Israelites across it. This confirms the inference that generally the word البحر denotes spaciousness and the word اليم depth.

The request of the Israelites to Moses embodied in the words, *make for us a god just as they have gods*, does not show that they really wished to worship idols. As they were yet new in faith, so when they happened to see the idols of an idol-worshipping people, they simply wished to have an image of their God. The idols of the people thus suggested to them the idea of having an image of their God on which to fix their attention. The words, *This is your God, and the God of Moses*, used elsewhere in the Quran (20 : 89), also show that what the Israelites wanted was simply a representation of the God of Moses and that they did not want to abandon Him or set up equals to Him.

The expression, *Surely you are an ignorant people*, contains the answer to their request. They were told that it was foolish on their part to think that they could fix their attention on God better by concentrating on an idol, because *firstly*, there was really nothing like Him and *secondly*, the practice was sure subsequently to develop into real idol-worship. The right way to fix attention on God is to ponder and meditate upon His attributes. To bow down before a lifeless image cannot but degrade a man both morally and spiritually.

1029. Commentary :

The word "these" refers to the idol-worshippers whom the Israelites wished to copy. Moses explains to his men that the people they desired to imitate were a people doomed to perdition.

141. ^aHe said, 'Shall I seek for you a god other than Allah, ^bwhile He has exalted you above all peoples?'¹⁰³⁰

قَالَ اَغَيْرَ اللّٰهِ اَبْغِيْكُمْ اِلٰهًا وَّ هُوَ فَضَّلَكُمْ عَلَى الْعٰلَمِيْنَ ۝

142. And *remember the time* when We delivered you from Pharaoh's people who afflicted you with grievous torment, slaughtering your sons and sparing your women. And therein was a great trial for you from your Lord.¹⁰³¹

وَ اِذْ اَنْجَيْنٰكُمْ مِّنْ اٰلِ فِرْعَوْنَ يَسُوْمُوْنَكُمْ سُوْٓءَ الْعَذَابِ يُقَتِّلُوْنَ اَبْنَآءَكُمْ وَ يَسْتَحْيُوْنَ نِسَآءَكُمْ وَ فِيْ ذٰلِكُمْ بَلَآءٌ مِّنْ رَّبِّكُمْ عَظِيْمٌ ۝

143. And ^dWe made Moses a promise of thirty nights and supplemented them with ten. Thus the period appointed by his Lord was completed—forty nights. And Moses said to his brother, Aaron, 'Act for me among my people in my absence, and manage *them* well, and follow not the way of those who cause disorder.'¹⁰³²

وَ وٰعَدْنَا مُوْسٰى ثَلٰثِيْنَ لَيْلَةً وَّ اَتْمَمْنٰهَا بِعَشْرٍ فَتَمَّ مِيْقَاتُ رَبِّهٖٓ اَرْبَعِيْنَ لَيْلَةً ۚ وَ قَالَ مُوْسٰى لِاَخِيْهِ هٰرُوْنَ اخْلُفْنِيْ فِيْ قَوْمِيْ وَ اَصْلِحْ وَ لَا تَتَّبِعْ سَبِيْلَ الْمُفْسِدِيْنَ ۝

---

^a6 : 15, 165.   ^b2 : 48; 3 : 34.   ^c2 : 50; 7 : 128; 14 : 7; 28 : 5.   ^d2 : 52.

1030. Commentary :

The error of the Israelites in desiring to have an image of God like the idols of other peoples (7:139) has been brought home to them by three cogent reasons. Firstly, they are told that the works of the people whose example had prompted them to wish for an image of God would be brought to nought and their image-worship would prove of no avail to them (7 : 140). The second argument is given in the present verse. The idea that by having a representation of God they would not be guilty of idolatry is rebutted by saying that the image thus made would be, and cannot but be, something *other than Allah*, and it is inconceivable that one should make an image of God and then think that he is not worshipping anything beside Him. The third argument is contained in the words, *He has exalted you above all peoples*, which are intended to point out that he, who makes an image with his own hand and then proceeds to worship it, degrades himself and brings himself lower than God has intended him to be.

1031. Commentary :

If the verse be taken as referring to the time of Moses and not the time that preceded his ministry, the words, *your sons*, would mean " your grown up sons " on whom heavy tasks were laid with a view to weakening and annihilating them. The children of Israel complained to Moses, saying, "The Lord look upon you and judge ; because ye have made our savour to be abhorred in the eyes of Pharaoh and in the eyes of his servants, to put a sword in their hand to slay us" (Exod. 5 : 21). See also 7 : 128 above.

1032. Commentary :

The promised nights were only thirty, and ten

144. And ^awhen Moses came at Our appointed time and his Lord spoke to him, he said, 'My Lord, show *Thyself* to me that I may look at Thee.' He replied, 'Thou shalt not see Me, but look at the mountain; and if it remain in its place, then shalt thou see Me.' And when his Lord manifested Himself on the mountain, He broke it into pieces and Moses fell down unconscious. And when he recovered, he said, 'Holy art Thou, I turn towards Thee, and I am the first to believe.'[1033]

وَلَمَّا جَآءَ مُوسٰى لِمِيقَاتِنَا وَكَلَّمَهٗ رَبُّهٗ قَالَ رَبِّ اَرِنِیۡۤ اَنۡظُرۡ اِلَیۡكَ قَالَ لَنۡ تَرٰىنِیۡ وَلٰكِنِ انۡظُرۡ اِلَی الۡجَبَلِ فَاِنِ اسۡتَقَرَّ مَكَانَهٗ فَسَوۡفَ تَرٰىنِیۡ فَلَمَّا تَجَلّٰی رَبُّهٗ لِلۡجَبَلِ جَعَلَهٗ دَكًّا وَّخَرَّ مُوسٰى صَعِقًا ۚ فَلَمَّاۤ اَفَاقَ قَالَ سُبۡحٰنَكَ تُبۡتُ اِلَیۡكَ وَاَنَا اَوَّلُ الۡمُؤۡمِنِیۡنَ ۝

---

^a2:254; 4:165.

were added subsequently to increase the favour. In fact, God's communion with Moses was completed in the promised thirty nights, as hinted in the next verse. So the prolongation of the period by ten nights, which was due to the request of Moses to God to manifest Himself to him, did not form part of the promise but was something additional.

The words, *Act for me among my people in my absence*, clearly indicate that Aaron's position was subordinate to that of Moses. Moses called the Israelites "my people" and directed Aaron to act for him *i.e.* officiate in his place during his absence, which shows that Aaron occupied no independent position but was only a subordinate Prophet to Moses.

The words, *and follow not the ways of those who cause disorder*, are intended as a warning to Aaron to beware of the mischief-makers and adopt a strong policy.

The use of the word "nights" is significant. As this period was meant to be passed in meditation and devotion for which the quiet and calmness of the night is much more suitable than the day, so God used the word "nights."

1033. Important Words:

تجلّى (manifested Himself) is derived from

جلا. They say جلا الامر *i.e.* the affair was or became clear, manifest, displayed, uncovered or laid open. تجلّى الشیئ *i.e.* the thing became manifest or apparent. تجلّى الشیئ used transitively means, he looked at the thing standing upon a higher position. The Quranic expression فلمّا تجلّى ربه للجبل means, when his Lord became manifest to the mountain *i.e.* when He manifested Himself on the mountain (Lane & Aqrab).

دكّا (pieces) is the noun-infinitive from دكّ *i.e.* he broke or crushed or pounded a thing. They say دكّ الارض *i.e.* he made even the elevations and depressions of the earth. دكّه الحمى means, fever weakened him. دكّ, therefore, means, an even or level place; a land broken and made even; a crumbled mountain; a mound or hill or dust or earth such as is a sand-hill. The Quranic words جعله دكّا mean, He made it even or level; or He made it crumbled (Lane).

Commentary:

This verse sheds light on one of the most important religious subjects—whether it is possible for one to see God with the physical eyes. The verse lends no support to the view that God is visible to the physical eyes. Let alone seeing Him, the human eye cannot even see angels. Says the Quran: *If God had appointed as Messenger an angel, He would have made him appear a man* (6 : 10). As we cannot see angels but only a manifestation of them, similarly we can see only a manifestation of God, and not God Himself. It is therefore inconceivable that a great Prophet of God like Moses with all his knowledge of the attributes of God, should have desired an impossibility. Moses knew that he could see only a manifestation of God and not God Himself. But he had already seen a manifestation of God in "the fire" when travelling from Midian to Egypt (28 : 30). What then did Moses mean by his request to see God, contained in the words, *My Lord, show Thyself to me that I may look at Thee?* The request seems to refer to the perfect manifestation of God that was not granted to Moses but was to take place at the time of the Holy Prophet of Islam who was to be a مثيل or like of Moses. Indeed, Moses had already been given the promise that there was to appear, from among the brethren of the Israelites, a Prophet in whose mouth God was to put His word (Deut. 18 : 18—22). The words in which the promise was given implied a greater manifestation of God than had been vouchsafed to Moses. So Moses was naturally anxious to see what sort of God's Glory and Majesty the promised Manifestation would be. He, therefore, wished that something of that Glory and Majesty might be shown to him. But a manifestation of that Glory was beyond the capacity of Moses to bear; it could not take place in or upon his heart. He was, therefore, asked to see a manifestation of it taking place at the Mount. But this should not be understood to mean that the Mount was to serve as a receptacle for the Great Glory; for, according to the Quran (33 : 73), the heart of Moses was certainly more capable of enduring it than the Mount. The Mount thus served only as the site or locality where

that great manifestation was to take place. But even this proved too much for the Mount which shook violently.

The effect on the Mount was similar in nature to that produced on a Companion of the Holy Prophet when the latter's head happened to be resting on his thigh at a time when a revelation descended on the Prophet. He felt such a heavy weight on his thigh that he feared that it would be crushed under it. Moses, too, could not bear to see the manifestation of divine Power and Majesty and fell down unconscious, in spite of the fact that he had been warned beforehand of the terrible quaking that was to overtake the Mount. Thus it was that Moses realized that he did not possess the capacity for that powerful manifestation of divine Glory which was to take place later through the Holy Prophet of Islam. This is why when he recovered his senses, Moses cried, *Holy art Thou, I turn towards Thee, and I am the first to believe.* These words meant that he had realized that he did not possess the capacity for that perfect manifestation of divine Glory which was to take place through the Promised Prophet and that he was the first believer in the great spiritual eminence which that Prophet was destined to attain. This belief of Moses in the Holy Prophet has also been referred to in 46 : 11.

The words, *He broke it into pieces*, should not be taken literally, for the Mount was not actually broken into pieces. The words are used figuratively to express the great severity of the earthquake.

It may be also noted here that Moses was told to look at the mountain, and he was also told that he would see God, if it remained in its place. The laying down of this condition shows that Moses had not asked for an impossible thing; for the laying down of a condition for an impossible thing is evidently meaningless.

145. *God* said, 'O Moses, I have chosen thee above the people *of thy time* by My messages and by My word. So take hold of that which I have given thee and be of the grateful.'[1034]

قَالَ يٰمُوْسَى اِنِّى اصْطَفَيْتُكَ عَلَى النَّاسِ بِرِسٰلٰتِى وَ بِكَلَامِى ۖ فَخُذْ مَاۤ اٰتَيْتُكَ وَكُنْ مِّنَ الشّٰكِرِيْنَ ۞

146. And ^aWe wrote for him, upon the tablets about everything—an admonition and an explanation of all things. So hold them fast and bid thy people follow the best thereof. Soon shall I show you the abode of the transgressors.[1035]

وَكَتَبْنَا لَهٗ فِى الْاَلْوَاحِ مِنْ كُلِّ شَىْءٍ مَّوْعِظَةً وَّتَفْصِيْلًا لِّكُلِّ شَىْءٍ ۚ فَخُذْهَا بِقُوَّةٍ وَّأْمُرْ قَوْمَكَ يَأْخُذُوْا بِاَحْسَنِهَا ۚ سَاُورِيْكُمْ دَارَ الْفٰسِقِيْنَ ۞

---

*a*6 : 155.

The words, *look at the mountain,* implied that he should look outside himself because the manifestation could not take place within him. The fact that Moses fell down in a swoon shows that he did witness some manifestation though only partly and imperfectly. The manifestation that takes place in the heart is permanent and lasting, while that which takes place outside is only temporary and passing.

A reference to this request of Moses to see God is to be found in Exod. 33 : 18.

1034. Commentary :

The words of this verse were addressed to Moses by way of consolation after God had made him realize that he could not attain to that high spiritual rank to which the Great Prophet of the House of Ishmael was destined to attain. He was asked not to covet the high dignity which was reserved for "that Prophet" but to remain content with, and be grateful for, the rank that God had bestowed upon him. The words, *So take hold of that which I have given thee and be of the grateful,* definitely prove that it was not the seeing of God Himself that Moses desired but only a manifestation of God higher than the one granted to him.

1035. Commentary :

The word "wrote" here does not mean that God actually wrote the commandments upon the tablets with His own hand. The same word has been used elsewhere with regard to the Psalms (21 : 106). It was indeed Moses and not God who wrote on the tablets the commandments that were revealed to him on the Mount; but as the commandments were revealed by God, the act of writing has been ascribed to Him. It is also possible that the word كَتَبْنَا does not here mean "We wrote" but "We enjoined" or "We made binding."

The words "everything" and "all things" used in this verse are not absolute but mean respectively "everything" concerning which an admonition was needed at the time of Moses, and "all things" that required to be explained to the Israelites.

The words, *follow the best thereof,* point to a golden principle of individual and national advancement. The teachings of God's Prophets are of different grades. Some are meant for the weak of faith, others for those whose faith is firm and strong and from whom a high standard of virtue is expected. Moses is asked here to exhort his people to try to practise the higher form of virtue and not to remain content

147. I shall soon turn away from My Signs those who behave proudly in the land in an unjust manner; and even *a*if they see all the Signs, they will not believe therein; and if they see the way of righteousness, they will not adopt it as *their* way; but if they see the way of error, they will adopt it as *their* way. That is because they treated Our Signs as lies and were heedless of them.[1036]

148. And *b*those who disbelieve in Our Signs and the meeting of the Hereafter—their works are vain. Can they *expect to* be rewarded *for anything* except for what they do?[1037]

R. 18   **149.** And *c*the people of Moses made, in his absence, out of their ornaments, a calf—a *lifeless* body producing a lowing sound. *d*Did they not see that it spoke not to them, nor guided them to any way? They took it *for worship* and they were transgressors.[1038]

---

*a*6:26.   *b*3:12; 5:11; 7:37; 21:78.   *c*2:52, 93; 4:154; 7:153; 20:89.   *d*20:90.

---

with merely acting upon the injunctions that are meant for the weak of faith.

The words, *Soon shall I show you the abode of the transgressors*, mean that soon the obedient shall be distinguished and separated from the disobedient. At the time of the flight of the Israelites from Egypt, it was a medley host of all sorts of people that had fled from fear of Pharaoh. But when the Law was revealed to Moses, it served to distinguish the true from the false. Those who were sincere obeyed the Law, while those who had no faith in their hearts rejected and defied it. Thus true believers became distinguished and separated from the transgressors. The word دار (abode) here signifies "station or position."

1036. Commentary:

This verse explains the true significance of the word دار (abode) occurring in the sentence, *I shall show you the abode of the transgressors*, contained in the preceding verse.

1037. Commentary:

The verse serves as a great warning for all men. One should not live on pious hopes. Only good works count when rewards are meted out.

1038. Commentary:

The calf is discarded and condemned as a deity, because it does not speak to its votaries nor guide them to any way. This shows that God can remain a true deity only as long as

150. And when they were smitten with remorse and saw that they had indeed gone astray, they said, ' If our Lord do not have mercy on us and forgive us, we shall surely be among the losers.'[1039]

وَلَمَّا سُقِطَ فِیۤ اَیۡدِیۡہِمۡ وَرَاَوۡا اَنَّہُمۡ قَدۡ ضَلُّوۡا ۙ قَالُوۡا لَئِنۡ لَّمۡ یَرۡحَمۡنَا رَبُّنَا وَیَغۡفِرۡ لَنَا لَنَکُوۡنَنَّ مِنَ الۡخٰسِرِیۡنَ ۟

He speaks to His servants and provides for their guidance. So those are manifestly in the wrong who think that, whereas God used to speak and reveal Himself in the past, He has ceased to do so now. It is foolish to say that there is no harm, if God has ceased to speak now when He spoke to His chosen servants in times gone by. If this argument possessed weight, worshippers of the calf could also advance a similar argument with regard to it. The fact is that no attribute of God can be supposed to have ceased to operate or become extinct. The gift of divine revelation is attainable even now as it was attainable in the past, and those who look upon it as a thing of the past are grievously mistaken. God speaks at all times, and those, who possess the capacity and quality to hear His voice, can and do hear it even now. Take away the power of speech from God and you leave Him no better than a calf. It is absurd to argue that as the Law of Islam has been made perfect, so no revelation is needed after the Holy Prophet. Revelation does not come merely to bring a new Law. It is primarily meant to grant freshness of spiritual life to man and bring him near unto his Lord and Master.

1039. Important Words :

سُقِطَ فِی اَیۡدِیۡہِمۡ—*suqiṭa* (they were smitten with remorse). The word سَقَطَ (*saqaṭa*) means, he or it fell down ; or dropped down from a higher to a lower place. They say سَقَطَ فِی کَلَامِہٖ *i.e.* he committed a mistake in his speech. سَقَطَ فُلَانٌ عَنۡ عَیۡنِی means, such a one fell from the place he held in my regard. سَقَطَ فِی یَدِہٖ means, he repented of what he had done ; or he grieved for, and regretted, an act of inadvertence done by him ; or he became confounded or perplexed and unable to see his right course. So فَلَمَّا سُقِطَ فِی اَیۡدِیۡہِمۡ means, when they repented ; or when they struck their hands upon their hands by reason of repentance ; or when they repented greatly. The expression has also been read as سَقَطَ فِی اَیۡدِیۡہِمۡ (*saqaṭa*) meaning, سَقَطَ النَّدَمُ فِی اَیۡدِیۡہِمۡ *i.e.* shame and repentance fell into their hands (*viz.* their shame and repentance became apparent). The word سَقَطَ is intransitive but it is used in the verse as if it were transitive. Such apparently transitive use of the word is permissible in rare cases as in the expression تَمۡرَۃٌ مَسۡقُوۡطَۃٌ *i.e.* a fallen date (Lane & Aqrab).

Commentary :

A party of those who had taken the calf for worship repented and felt ashamed of their deed before Moses returned, and therefore they were saved. The other party did not repent and therefore perished. They are here spoken of as " losers."

151. And ^awhen Moses returned to his people, indignant and grieved, he said, 'Evil is that which you did in my place in my absence. Did you hasten *to devise a way for yourselves* without *waiting for* the command of your Lord?' And he put down the tablets, and ^bcaught hold of his brother's head, dragging him towards himself. He (Aaron) said, 'Son of my mother, the people indeed deemed me weak, and were about to kill me. Therefore make not the enemies rejoice over me, and place me not with the unjust people.'[1040]

وَلَمَّا رَجَعَ مُوسَى إِلَى قَوْمِهِ غَضْبَانَ أَسِفًا قَالَ بِئْسَمَا خَلَفْتُمُونِى مِنْ بَعْدِى أَعَجِلْتُمْ أَمْرَ رَبِّكُمْ وَأَلْقَى الْأَلْوَاحَ وَأَخَذَ بِرَأْسِ أَخِيهِ يَجُرُّهُ إِلَيْهِ قَالَ ابْنَ أُمَّ إِنَّ الْقَوْمَ اسْتَضْعَفُونِى وَكَادُوا يَقْتُلُونَنِى فَلَا تُشْمِتْ بِىَ الْأَعْدَاءَ وَلَا تَجْعَلْنِى مَعَ الْقَوْمِ الظَّالِمِينَ ۝

^a20 : 87.   ^b20 : 95.

1040. Important Words:

فَلَا تُشْمِتْ (make not rejoice). تَشْمَتْ is formed from اشمت which is derived from شمت. They say شمت or شمت به *i.e.* he (an enemy) rejoiced; or he (some one) rejoiced at his enemy's affliction. اشمته الله به means, God made him (the enemy) rejoice at his affliction. شمت على العاطس means, he prayed for the sneezer that he might not be in a state in which his enemy might rejoice at his affliction (Lane).

Commentary:

When the return of Moses was delayed owing to the ten additional nights, his followers became impatient and thought that he was lost. They expressed their impatience in the words "we wot not what is become of him" (Exod. 32 : 1).

According to the Bible, Moses cast the tablets out of his hands and broke them beneath the Mount, so that they had to be renewed (Exod. 32 : 19 ; 34 : 1). But this is not borne out by the Quran which simply states, *And he put down the tablets* and this is more in harmony with the dignity of a Prophet.

Moses caught hold of Aaron's head, not because the latter had abetted calf-worship, as he is represented to have done in the Bible (Exod. 32 : 2—4), but because he did not successfully prevent the people from worshipping the calf. As Moses' representative, he should have effectively prevented the people from idol-worship, but he failed to do so. So the display of anger on the part of Moses was due, not to any religious or legal offence committed by Aaron, but to his failure to manage affairs properly in the absence of Moses. Aaron had hoped that Moses would set things right on his return. That was only an error of judgement or lack of proper control, not a legal or religious offence.

The way in which Moses treated Aaron also shows that the latter was subordinate to the former. The treatment, however, should not be taken as a display of rough manners on the part of Moses. The anger of Moses was justified because a great sacrilege had been committed and the very work of his life was jeopardized ; and Aaron being subordinate to Moses, the latter was entitled to take disciplinary action.

The words, *Son of my mother*, were used by

152. He (Moses) said, 'My Lord, forgive me and my brother, and admit us to Thy mercy, and Thou art the most merciful of those who show mercy.'[1041]

قَالَ رَبِّ اغْفِرْ لِيْ وَلِاَخِيْ وَاَدْخِلْنَا فِيْ رَحْمَتِكَ ۖ وَاَنْتَ اَرْحَمُ الرّٰحِمِيْنَ ۞

19 153. As to *those who took the calf for worship*, wrath from their Lord shall overtake them and abasement in the present life. And thus do We reward those who invent lies.[1042]

اِنَّ الَّذِيْنَ اتَّخَذُوا الْعِجْلَ سَيَنَالُهُمْ غَضَبٌ مِّنْ رَّبِّهِمْ وَذِلَّةٌ فِي الْحَيٰوةِ الدُّنْيَا ۖ وَكَذٰلِكَ نَجْزِي الْمُفْتَرِيْنَ ۞

154. But *those who did evil deeds and repented after that and believed, surely thy Lord is thereafter Most Forgiving, Merciful.[1043]

وَالَّذِيْنَ عَمِلُوا السَّيِّاٰتِ ثُمَّ تَابُوْا مِنْ بَعْدِهَا وَاٰمَنُوْا ۖ اِنَّ رَبَّكَ مِنْ بَعْدِهَا لَغَفُوْرٌ رَّحِيْمٌ ۞

---

*a*2:52, 93; 4:154; 7:149; 20:89.   *b*5:40; 16:120.

Aaron not because Moses was a half-brother to him but because he wished to make an effective appeal to his feelings of tenderness and affection, and in this he succeeded.

The meaning of the particle مع (with) in the clause, *and place me not with the unjust people*, helps to explain its real sense in 4:70. Here as well as there the particle gives the meaning of "among."

1041. Commentary:

Moses soon saw the innocence of Aaron, so he included him with himself in his prayer for God's mercy.

1042. Commentary:

As it was not Aaron who took the calf for worship, so he was excluded when the offenders were punished. This absolves Aaron of all complicity in calf-worship. The account of the Bible in this connection is certainly misleading, as admitted by Encyclopaedia Biblica (vol. 1. col, 2).

As a matter of fact, only those who took the leading part in making the image of the calf and taking it for worship were punished. The rest who were misled by the ring-leaders and who afterwards repented were granted pardon, as hinted in the following verse.

1043. Commentary:

The addition in this verse of the word 'believed' to the word 'repented' is significant, because the Israelites had already believed, and so the addition of the word "believed" appears to be rather misplaced. This doubt is easily explained. Those who had taken part in calf-worship had, in fact, acted against their "belief." So they were asked not only to repent but to renew and strengthen their belief as well, for true belief alone is the source of all good actions. The words, *repented* and *believed*, are thus intended to show that only those, who not only feel sorry for their evil deeds but also make proper amends and inculcate true belief in God, can be forgiven by Him.

155. And when the anger of Moses was appeased, he took the tablets, and *in their writing there was guidance and mercy for those who fear their Lord.[1044]

وَلَمَّا سَكَتَ عَنْ مُّوْسَى الْغَضَبُ أَخَذَ الْأَلْوَاحَ ۚ وَفِيْ نُسْخَتِهَا هُدًى وَّرَحْمَةٌ لِّلَّذِيْنَ هُمْ لِرَبِّهِمْ يَرْهَبُوْنَ ۝

156. And Moses chose *of* his people seventy men for Our appointment. But when the earthquake overtook them, he said, ' My Lord, if Thou hadst pleased, *b*Thou couldst have destroyed them before *this*, and me *also*. Wilt Thou destroy us for that which the foolish among us have done ? This is nothing but a trial from Thee. Thou causest to perish thereby whom Thou pleasest and Thou guidest whom Thou pleasest. Thou art our Protector ; forgive us then and have mercy on us, and Thou art the best of those who forgive.[1045]

وَاخْتَارَ مُوْسَى قَوْمَهُ سَبْعِيْنَ رَجُلًا لِّمِيْقَاتِنَا ۚ فَلَمَّا أَخَذَتْهُمُ الرَّجْفَةُ قَالَ رَبِّ لَوْ شِئْتَ أَهْلَكْتَهُمْ مِّنْ قَبْلُ وَإِيَّايَ ۖ أَتُهْلِكُنَا بِمَا فَعَلَ السُّفَهَاءُ مِنَّا ۖ إِنْ هِيَ إِلَّا فِتْنَتُكَ ۚ تُضِلُّ بِهَا مَنْ تَشَاءُ وَتَهْدِيْ مَنْ تَشَاءُ ۚ أَنْتَ وَلِيُّنَا فَاغْفِرْ لَنَا وَارْحَمْنَا وَأَنْتَ خَيْرُ الْغَافِرِيْنَ ۝

---

*5:45; 6:92.   *b*13:28.

1044. Important Words :

سكت (was appeased) means, he was or became silent, mute or, speechless ; he was or became still and quiet ; he died. سكت غضبه means, his anger became appeased, allayed or stilled. سكت عنه الغضب means, his anger became stilled or appeased so that it departed from him (Lane).

نسختها (its writing). نسخة is derived from نسخ which means : (1) he or it annulled or superseded or cancelled or abrogated or changed or altered (something) ; (2) he copied or transferred a writing, letter for letter. So نسخة means, copy or transcript, so called because it supplies the place of the original ; also a copy or an original from which a transcript is made (Lane). Thus the word نسخة does not exactly mean a " writing ", though, for the sake of convenience, it has been translated as such.

1045. Commentary :

This verse shows that the tablets were not broken as alleged by the Bible ; for if they were broken, how could the very tablets have been taken up again. The word نسخة (writing) explained above also hints that Moses did not receive any written tablets from God but that he himself wrote them under divine inspiration.

The word سفهاء (the foolish) is used here not in the general sense but in the specific sense of the foolish in the ways of God *i.e.* "ignorant ", for every act of disobedience is born of ignorance, even if it is committed intentionally. Those who were clever enough to render Aaron helpless could not be called fools in the ordinary sense of the word. They are called سفهاء (fools) because they did not possess the sense and intelligence to understand the word of God.

157. 'And *a*ordain for us good in this world, as well as in the next; we have turned to Thee with repentance.' *God* replied, *b*'I will inflict My punishment on whom I will; but *c*My mercy encompasses all things; so I will ordain it for those who act righteously, and pay the Zakāt and those who believe in Our Signs—[1046]

وَاكْتُبْ لَنَا فِيْ هٰذِهِ الدُّنْيَا حَسَنَةً وَّفِي الْاٰخِرَةِ اِنَّا هُدْنَا اِلَيْكَ ۚ قَالَ عَذَابِيْ اُصِيْبُ بِهٖ مَنْ اَشَآءُ وَرَحْمَتِيْ وَسِعَتْ كُلَّ شَيْءٍ ۚ فَسَاَكْتُبُهَا لِلَّذِيْنَ يَتَّقُوْنَ وَيُؤْتُوْنَ الزَّكٰوةَ وَالَّذِيْنَ هُمْ بِاٰيٰتِنَا يُؤْمِنُوْنَ ۞

158. 'Those who follow the Messenger, *d*the Prophet, the Immaculate One, *e*whom they find mentioned in the Torah and the Gospel *which are* with them. *f*He enjoins on them good and forbids them evil, and makes lawful for them the good things and forbids them the bad, and removes from them their burden and the shackles that were upon them. So those who shall believe in him, and honour and support him, and help him, and follow the light that has been sent down with him,—these shall prosper.'[1047]

اَلَّذِيْنَ يَتَّبِعُوْنَ الرَّسُوْلَ النَّبِيَّ الْاُمِّيَّ الَّذِيْ يَجِدُوْنَهٗ مَكْتُوْبًا عِنْدَهُمْ فِي التَّوْرٰىةِ وَالْاِنْجِيْلِ ۖ يَأْمُرُهُمْ بِالْمَعْرُوْفِ وَيَنْهٰىهُمْ عَنِ الْمُنْكَرِ وَيُحِلُّ لَهُمُ الطَّيِّبٰتِ وَيُحَرِّمُ عَلَيْهِمُ الْخَبٰٓئِثَ وَيَضَعُ عَنْهُمْ اِصْرَهُمْ وَالْاَغْلٰلَ الَّتِيْ كَانَتْ عَلَيْهِمْ ۚ فَالَّذِيْنَ اٰمَنُوْا بِهٖ وَعَزَّرُوْهُ وَنَصَرُوْهُ وَاتَّبَعُوا النُّوْرَ الَّذِيْ اُنْزِلَ مَعَهٗ ۙ اُولٰٓئِكَ هُمُ الْمُفْلِحُوْنَ ۞

---

*a*2:202.   *b*2:285; 5:41.   *c*40:8.   *d*29:49; 42:53; 62:3.   *e*18:30.   *f*See 3:105.

The incident of the calf proved to be the first occasion when the transgressors among the Israelites became distinguished from true believers, and the prophecy, *Soon shall I show you the abode of the transgressors* (7:146), was fulfilled.

1046. Commentary:

The sentence, *so I will ordain it for those who act righteously and pay the Zakāt and those who believe in Our Signs*, consists of two parts. The first part *i.e. those who act righteously and pay the Zakāt* refers to those of the Israelites who sincerely believed in Moses and acted righteously, while the second part, *i.e., and those who believe in Our Signs*, refers to the believers in the

Prophets that were yet to come, particularly the Holy Prophet of Islam, as the following verse points out.

1047. Important Words:

امى (Immaculate One) is derived from ام. They say امه i.e. he repaired to it; or he aimed at or sought after it; or he endeavoured to get it. ما كنت اما ولقد امت means, thou wast not a mother, but thou hast come to be sought like a mother. امى means, belonging to or pertaining to the mother, *i.e.,* as innocent as a child at the breast of its mother. The word also means, one not having a revealed Scripture, particularly an Arab; one who does not know the art of reading or writing; one belonging to

Mecca which was known as ام القرى i.e. the mother of towns. See also 3 : 21.

اغلال (shackles) is the plural of غل (ghullun) which is derived from غل (ghalla). They say غل فلانا i.e. he put upon the neck or the hand of such a one a collar or a manacle, etc. غل , therefore, means, a ring or collar of iron put upon the neck ; a shackle for the neck or the hand ; a pinion or manacle for the hand ; a shackle of iron collecting together the two hands to the neck ; a difficult and fatiguing work. The Arabs say هذا غل ى عنقك , i.e., this is tied to your neck, meaning, it is inseparable from you and the punishment of it will stick to you (Lane & Aqrab).

Commentary :

This verse qualifies and explains the last sentence of the previous verse, viz., those who believe in Our Signs.

The verse puts the words " Messenger " and " Prophet " side by side which may lead some to think that one may be a Messenger without being a Prophet or vice versa. But this is not so. A رسول (Messenger) of God is also a نبى (Prophet) of God. The former epithet is applied to him in his relation to God from Whom he brings a message, while the latter is applied to him in his relation to men to whom he conveys that message, the word نبى (Prophet) meaning, one who prophesies, or makes known hidden secrets.

The word امى (Ummī) literally means " belonging to the mother " i.e. as innocent as a new-born child. The Promised Prophet, who is none other than the Holy Prophet of Islam, has been called امى because he was to be innocent like a child at the breast of its mother. The word has also been translated as " illiterate " or " one belonging to Mecca " or " an Arab ", but " innocent " or " immaculate'' is a preferable rendering, inasmuch as it is in keeping with the sense of the prophecy contained in Deut. 18 : 18 — 22 to which this

verse particularly refers and wherein truthfulness has been mentioned as a distinctive feature of the Promised Prophet. For some of the prophecies of the Bible about the Holy Prophet see under 2 : 42 and also Matt. 23 : 39 ; John 14 : 16, 26 ; 16 : 7—14 ; Acts 3 : 21—24.

If the word امى be taken in the sense of " unlettered," the verse would signify that although the Prophet had received no education whatever and was quite unread and illiterate, yet God vouchsafed to him such knowledge as can impart light and guidance even to those who are considered to be most advanced in learning and enlightenment.

The illiteracy (امية) of the Holy Prophet mentioned in this verse and believed to have also been hinted at in 10 : 17 has been subjected to much hostile criticism. George Sale, a well-known Christian Commentator of the Quran, writes as follows : " For so old was Muhammad before he took upon him to be a Prophet, during which time his fellow-citizens well knew that he had not applied himself to learning of any sort, nor frequented learned men, nor had ever exercised himself in composing verses or orations, whereby he might acquire the art of rhetoric or elegance of speech " (Prelim. Disc, Section II).

Referring to this view of Sale, another Christian Commentator of the Quran, the Rev. E. M. Wherry, says :—

" This view, however, does not agree with what is recorded of his previous career. Is it likely that he should have been trained in the same household with 'Alī, who knew both how to read and write, and not have received similar instruction ? Could he have conducted an important mercantile business for years without some knowledge of letters ? That he could read and write in later years is certain. Tradition tells us, he said to Mu'āwiya, one of his secretaries : ' Draw the ب straight, divide the س properly ', etc., and that in his last moments he called for writing materials. The question arises, when did he acquire this art? The Commentators say that God gave him the power, as he did his inspiration, and they quote chap. xcvi. 4, one of the earliest verses of the Quran, in proof. Certainly that verse seems to teach clearly that he could write as well as read, though it by no means teaches that he had not received the knowledge of both before-hand, or that he did not receive it in the ordinary way. His use of amanuenses does not militate against his knowledge of the art of writing, for such use of amanuenses was common in that age, even among the most learned. But still there remains the testimony of many traditions and the almost universal belief of Muhammadans. How account for this? I am inclined to think it originated with a misunder-standing of Muhammad's repeated claim that he was the " Illiterate Prophet," or rather the " Prophet of the Illiterate," the term " illiterate " being generally applied by the Jews to the Arabs. See notes on chap. v. 85, 86. This misunderstanding turned out to the furtherance of Muhammad's claims, in-asmuch as the miracle of the matchless style of the Quran was enhanced by the consideration that the Prophet was illiterate. On the whole, we think there is very good reason for believing Muhammad to have been acquainted with the art of both reading and writing from an early period in his life " (Commentary of the Quran, ii. 326).

The above constitutes the gist of Wherry's criticism of the generally accepted view that the Holy Prophet was اُمِّي or illiterate. But this contention seems to possess no substance. It is indeed a poor argument to say that because the Prophet " had been trained in the same house with 'Alī, who knew both how to read and write," therefore he should also have learnt reading and writing. It only betrays ignorance of elementary facts of the Holy Prophet's life on the part of the reverend

gentleman. Even a desultory acquaintance with the life-history of the Holy Prophet should make one know that 'Alī and the Holy Prophet could not be brought up together. There was a great difference between the ages of the two. The Prophet was no less than 29 years older than 'Alī; therefore it was impossible for the two to be trained and brought up together.

Those whom prejudice against the Holy Prophet has not blinded to the patent facts of history know that, let alone the Prophet being educated and trained together with 'Alī, which the great disparity in their ages evidently obviated, it was 'Alī who got his training in the house and under the fostering care of the Holy Prophet (Hishām). Abū Ṭālib in whose house the Holy Prophet was brought up was a man of very meagre means. He did not know the value of learning and knowledge nor was their possession regarded as an asset and acquisition in his time. The Holy Prophet therefore remained illiterate in his house. But 'Alī was brought up in the house of the Holy Prophet himself, whose marriage with Khadīja, a wealthy lady of great repute, had placed ample means at his disposal. The Prophet also fully realized how priceless a thing good education was. So under his benign care and ennobling influence 'Alī, judged by the standards of that time, naturally grew up to be a young man of good education.

Wherry's second objection is that if the Holy Prophet had been illiterate and did not know how to read and write, he could not have proved such a successful business man as he actually was. This objection is born of the mistaken concept of a good and successful Arab business man of the Prophet's time. Judging by the present European standards of a successful business man, Wherry thought that lack of education and success in business could not go together. He would not have made this objection, if he had known that in Asia even in the present twentieth century highly successful business men are to be found who have not received even elementary education. In Mecca, in the Holy Prophet's time, education was not much in favour. There were very few persons there who could read and write, though hundreds carried on most successful and flourishing businesses. Education was not at that time regarded in Arabia as the *sine qua non* of a good business man. Moreover, the fact that Khadīja had given the Prophet, a slave named Maisara who knew reading and writing and who always accompanied him on his trade journeys, knocks the bottom out of Wherry's objection.

The tradition which says that the Holy Prophet had once asked Mu'āwiya to write correctly the letters ب and س does not seem to be quite reliable. In the 'Abbaside period many traditions derogatory to the Umayyads were forged. This tradition seeks to show off Mu'āwiya, a prominent member of the distinguished House of Umayya, as a man of very poor education who could not even write properly such simple letters as ب and س. Even, however, if this tradition be proved to be reliable, it does not show that the Holy Prophet was literate, because, he had become so used to dictating the Quran that it was not impossible for him to have become familiar with the general form of letters and to give instruction regarding an improperly written word. It is also possible that some one, while rehearsing some portion of the Quran to the Prophet, might have stopped at a certain place, not being able to decipher the writing, and the Holy Prophet having asked the cause of stopping, the reader might have replied that the delay was due to the letters ب and س not having been written properly or legibly. This might have led the Holy Prophet to instruct Mu'āwiya to see that the letters were written correctly.

The fact that the Holy Prophet sent for pen and paper in the last moments of his life also lends no support to Wherry's assumption. It is an established fact of history that whenever any verse was revealed, the Holy Prophet used to send for pen and paper and dictate to one of his scribes what had been revealed to him. The mere sending for pen and paper cannot, therefore, prove that the Holy Prophet himself knew how to read and write.

Nor do the words referred to by Wherry in support of his contention *viz.*, "read in the name of thy Lord," prove anything. The Arabic word اقرء (read) used in the verse referred to above not only means the reading of a written thing but also repeating and rehearsing what one hears from another person. Again, the words هو يحسن القراءة (*i.e.* he recites well) occurring in a tradition can be spoken of even of a blind man who can recite the Quran properly and well. Moreover, the Ḥadīth establishes the fact that when at the time of the first revelation the angel, Gabriel, said to the Prophet اقرء (read), no writing was actually placed before him to read. He was simply asked to repeat orally what the angel was reciting to him. The word قراءة not only means to read a writing but to repeat orally or recite or rehearse what another man has uttered.

Wherry's inference that the idea that the Holy Prophet could not read or write originated with a misunderstanding of his repeated claim that he was the "Illiterate Prophet," is as strange as it is ill-based. It is really very surprising to say that those with whom he had lived day and night for years could not find out that he was illiterate but were misled into this belief only by his own repeated claim that he was امى (illiterate). Only a man of Wherry's hostile attitude could come to such a conclusion. The question is, whether it was the Prophet's own contemporaries who suffered from this misunderstanding or those who came afterwards. If it were the former, then the question would naturally arise, how those who saw him daily with their own eyes reading and writing could possibly fall victims to the glaring misunderstanding that he was illiterate. If it were the latter class, even then the whole theory of misunderstanding advanced by Wherry looks frivolous, because the argument put forward by him is that because the Holy Prophet was considered to be illiterate, therefore the matchless style of the Quran was regarded as a miracle. This inference is both foolish and flimsy, inasmuch as Muslims and other contemporaries of the Prophet, who were fully aware that he knew quite well how to read and write, could never believe in such a miracle.

Wherry's last argument in support of his contention that "his (the Holy Prophet's) use of amanuenses does not militate against his knowledge of the art of writing, for such use of amanuenses was common in that age, even among the most learned," betrays his ignorance of Arab and Islamic history. The fact is that there were no *ulema* or learned men among the Arabs in the time of the Holy Prophet in the sense in which this word is understood now, nor were they used to keeping amanuenses and scribes. There is no instance on record of an amanuensis having been kept by an Arab. We know of only one learned man among the Meccans in the Prophet's time *viz*, Waraqa bin Naufal, and he was his own secretary. It is a pity that in their zeal for misrepresenting Islam, some Christian writers do not even hesitate to invent historical facts.

The words, *and removes from then their burden and shackles*, occurring in the latter part of the verse contain a hint that by accepting the Promised Prophet Christians will get rid of the curse of the original sin of Adam and Eve and of the punishment thereof which, according to them, has dogged their footsteps through no fault of theirs.

R. 20   **159.** Say, 'O mankind, *a*truly I am a Messenger to you all from Allah to Whom belongs the kingdom of the heavens and the earth. There is no God but He. *b*He gives life, and He causes death. So believe in Allah and His Messenger, the Prophet, the Immaculate One, who believes in Allah and His words ; and follow him that you may be rightly guided.[1048]

160. And *c*of the people of Moses there is a party that exhorts *people* to truth and does justice therewith.' [1049]

قُلْ يٰٓاَيُّهَا النَّاسُ اِنِّىْ رَسُوْلُ اللّٰهِ اِلَيْكُمْ جَمِيْعَا ِالَّذِىْ لَهٗ مُلْكُ السَّمٰوٰتِ وَالْاَرْضِ لَاۤ اِلٰهَ اِلَّا هُوَ يُحْى وَ يُمِيْتُ فَاٰمِنُوْا بِاللّٰهِ وَرَسُوْلِهِ النَّبِىِّ الْاُمِّىِّ الَّذِىْ يُؤْمِنُ بِاللّٰهِ وَكَلِمٰتِهٖ وَاتَّبِعُوْهُ لَعَلَّكُمْ تَهْتَدُوْنَ ۞

وَمِنْ قَوْمِ مُوْسٰۤى اُمَّةٌ يَّهْدُوْنَ بِالْحَقِّ وَبِهٖ يَعْدِلُوْنَ ۞

---

*a*21 : 108 ; 25 : 2 ; 34 : 29.   *b*2 : 259 ; 23 : 81 ; 44 : 9 ; 57 : 3.   *c*7 : 182.

1048. Commentary :

This verse beautifully declares that the prophecies of the Old and New Testaments concerning the Promised Prophet have been fulfilled in the Holy Prophet.

The reference in the words, *to Whom belongs the kingdom of the heavens and the earth,* is to the fact that just as there is one kingdom in the heavens, so, as a result of the advent of the Holy Prophet, there will in future be only one spiritual kingdom on earth. It is to this kingdom that the prayer of Jesus (Matt. 6 : 10) refers. This prayer embodied a prophecy about the advent of the Holy Prophet.

The establishment of one spiritual kingdom on earth points to the fact that the Promised Prophet will be a Messenger of God to all

mankind, and that by his advent all distinctions of race, nationality and colour will cease.

1049. Commentary :

This verse makes it clear that all followers of Moses were not corrupt. There were some among them who guided men to truth and acted justly. The Quran never condemns a people wholesale. Its condemnation is confined only to such sections of a people as are corrupt and therefore deserve to be condemned. Whenever the Quran mentions the evil practices of a people, it never fails to refer also to the good qualities that some of its members are found to possess. Truly has the Quran said : *And let not a people's enmity incite you to act otherwise than with justice. Be always just ; that is nearer to righteousness, and fear Allah. Surely Allah is aware of what you do* (5 : 9).

161. And *We divided them into twelve tribes, *distinct* peoples. And, We revealed to Moses, *when his people asked drink of him, *saying,* 'Strike the rock with thy rod;' and from it there gushed forth twelve springs; every tribe knew their drinking place. And *We caused the clouds to overshadow them, and We sent down for them Manna and Salwa. 'Eat of the good things We have provided for you.' And they wronged Us not, but it was themselves that they wronged.¹⁰⁵⁰

162. And *when it was said to them, "Dwell in this town and eat therefrom wherever you will, and say '*God!* Lighten our burden', and enter the gate in humility, We shall forgive you your sins, *and* surely We shall give increase to those who do good."¹⁰⁵¹

163. *But the transgressors among them changed *it* for a word other than that which was said to them. So We sent upon them a punishment from heaven, because of their wrongdoing.¹⁰⁵²

---

*5 : 13. *2 : 61. *2 : 58 ; 20 : 81. *2 : 59. *2 : 60.

1050. **Commentary :**

See notes on 2 : 58 & 61.

The words, *And they wronged Us not,* mean that they did not harm the cause of the religion revealed by God.

1051. **Commentary :**

See note on 2 : 59.

1052. **Commentary :**

See note on 2 : 60.

R. 21 164. And ask them concerning the town which stood by the sea. [a]When they profaned the Sabbath; when their fish came to them on their Sabbath day appearing on the surface *of the water,* but on the day when they did not keep Sabbath, they came not to them. Thus [b]did We try them because they were rebellious.[1053]

وَسْـَٔلْهُمْ عَنِ الْقَرْيَةِ الَّتِي كَانَتْ حَاضِرَةَ الْبَحْرِ اِذْ يَعْدُوْنَ فِى السَّبْتِ اِذْ تَأْتِيْهِمْ حِيْتَانُهُمْ يَوْمَ سَبْتِهِمْ شُرَّعًا وَّيَوْمَ لَا يَسْبِتُوْنَ لَا تَأْتِيْهِمْ كَذٰلِكَ نَبْلُوْهُمْ بِمَا كَانُوْا يَفْسُقُوْنَ ۝

---

[a]2 : 66 ; 4 : 148, 155.   [b]7 : 169.

1053. Important Words :

شرعا (appearing on the surface) is the plural of شارع which is active participle from شرع. They say شرع فى الامر *i.e.* he entered upon or began or commenced the affair. شرع المنزل means, the dwelling had its door opening upon a thoroughfare, or the door of the house opened on the road. شرع الشيئ means, he raised or elevated the thing much. شارع of which the plural is شرع (*shurra'un*) means, entering into water or entering into an affair; appearing on the surface of water; situated on a main road; having its door opening on a road; a main road or thoroughfare; a legislator or announcer of the law. حيتان شرع means, fishes raising their heads above water; or fishes directing themselves from the deep water to the bank; or fishes appearing upon the surface of the water (Lane & Aqrab).

Commentary :

The قرية (town) referred to in this verse is said to be Aila (Elath) on the Red Sea. It was situated on the N. E. arm of the Red Sea, in the Aelanitic Gulf (which has derived its name from the place itself) and is mentioned as one of the last stages of the Israelites during their wanderings. It is mentioned also in 1 Kings 9 : 26 and 2 Chron. 8 : 17. In Solomon's time the city came into the possession of the Israelites but afterward it was probably taken from them. Later Uzziah reconquered it, but under Ahaz it was again lost (Enc. Bib. and Jew. Enc.).

As no fish were caught on the Sabbath day, they had instinctively come to know the time when they were safe and therefore this instinctive feeling of security made them appear on the surface or approach near the coast in great numbers on the Sabbath day. This fact proved too strong a temptation for the Jews, and they began to make arrangements to catch them on the Sabbath day. The cause of evasion was not far to seek. The Israelites had the fish caught by the non-Israelite people and then purchased them from the latter and in this way sought to evade the commandment, although it was forbidden to them even to make purchases on that day. It was to stop this mean practice that Nehemiah stationed his servants at the gates of Jerusalem to see that no loads were brought in on the Sabbath day (Neh. 13 : 19).

165. And when a party among them said, ' Wherefore do you preach to a people whom Allah is going to destroy or punish with a severe punishment ?' They said, ' As an excuse before your Lord, and that they may become righteous.'[1054]

وَاِذْ قَالَتْ اُمَّةٌ مِّنْهُمْ لِمَ تَعِظُوْنَ قَوْمَا ۙ اللّٰهُ مُهْلِكُهُمْ اَوْ مُعَذِّبُهُمْ عَذَابًا شَدِيْدًا ۚ قَالُوْا مَعْذِرَةً اِلٰى رَبِّكُمْ وَلَعَلَّهُمْ يَتَّقُوْنَ ۝

166. And [a]when they forgot all that with which they had been admonished, We saved those who forbade evil, and We seized the transgressors with a severe punishment because they were rebellious.[1055]

فَلَمَّا نَسُوْا مَا ذُكِّرُوْا بِهٖۤ اَنْجَيْنَا الَّذِيْنَ يَنْهَوْنَ عَنِ السُّوْٓءِ وَاَخَذْنَا الَّذِيْنَ ظَلَمُوْا بِعَذَابٍۭ بَيِٕيْسٍۭ بِمَا كَانُوْا يَفْسُقُوْنَ ۝

---

[a]6 : 45.

1054. Commentary :

This verse shows how necessary it is to preach the truth to others. We must not fail to tell our brethren what is good for them and what is not. The thought that those in whom we inculcate the doing of good will not benefit by our advice should not deter us from doing our duty. Our preaching may or may not produce any good result, but we will have done our duty and will not be held answerable before God for neglecting to do what we should have done. The verse mentions two possible results of preaching and both are equally meritorious : (1) either our preaching will take effect and the people preached to will become righteous, or (2) we will at least have done our duty to God.

1055. Important Words :

بَيِٕيْس (severe) is verbal adjective from بَؤُسَ which means, he was or became mighty or strong in war or fight ; or courageous or valiant. بَأْس is infinitive-noun from this root and means, might or strength in war or fight ; courage and valour ; war or fight ; fear ; harm or injury ; punishment, or a severe punishment. بَئِيْس means, mighty or strong ;

courageous or valiant. عَذَاب بَئِيْس means, a vehement or severe punishment (Lane). See also 2 : 178.

Commentary :

In the preceding two verses three classes of men have been mentioned : (1) those who profaned the Sabbath ; (2) those who, while themselves refraining from profaning the Sabbath, did not prohibit others from violating it ; and (3) those who not only themselves refrained from profaning the Sabbath but also urged the profaners to abstain from this evil. Of these three classes, the present verse declares only those as saved who not only themselves abstained from doing evil but also exhorted others to abstain from it, and the rest have been represented as " transgressors " and these were visited with divine punishment. This shows that the second party who, though they themselves refrained from profaning the Sabbath yet did not prevent their brethren from violating it, were also condemned as transgressors and shared the punishment with those who actually broke the commandment of God. This constitutes a great warning to us that we can be classed with the righteous only when we not only ourselves eschew evil

167. And when they insolently rebelled against that which they had been forbidden, ^aWe said to them, ' Be ye apes despised.'¹⁰⁵⁶

فَلَمَّا عَتَوْا عَنْ مَّا نُهُوْا عَنْهُ قُلْنَا لَهُمْ كُوْنُوْا قِرَدَةً خٰسِئِيْنَ ۝

168. And *remember the time* when thy Lord proclaimed that ^bHe would truly raise against them, till the Day of Resurrection, those who would afflict them with grievous torment. Surely thy Lord is quick in retribution, and surely He is *also* Most Forgiving, Merciful.¹⁰⁵⁷

وَاِذْ تَاَذَّنَ رَبُّكَ لَيَبْعَثَنَّ عَلَيْهِمْ اِلٰى يَوْمِ الْقِيٰمَةِ مَنْ يَّسُوْمُهُمْ سُوْءَ الْعَذَابِ ۗ اِنَّ رَبَّكَ لَسَرِيْعُ الْعِقَابِ ۖ وَاِنَّهٗ لَغَفُوْرٌ رَّحِيْمٌ ۝

169. And We broke them up into *separate* peoples in the earth. Among them are those that are righteous and among them are those that are otherwise. And ^cWe tried them with good things and bad things that they might return.¹⁰⁵⁸

وَقَطَّعْنٰهُمْ فِى الْاَرْضِ اُمَمًا مِّنْهُمُ الصّٰلِحُوْنَ وَمِنْهُمْ دُوْنَ ذٰلِكَ وَبَلَوْنٰهُمْ بِالْحَسَنٰتِ وَالسَّيِّاٰتِ لَعَلَّهُمْ يَرْجِعُوْنَ ۝

---

*a*2 : 66 ; 5 : 61.   *b*2 : 62 ; 3 : 113.   *c*7 : 164.

---

but exhort our brethren also to do the same. We should do our duty both to God and man, the one being as important as the other.

1056. Commentary :

The expression, *Be ye apes despised*, explains the " severe punishment " mentioned in the previous verse. See also 2 : 66.

1057. Commentary :

The reference in the memorable words, *those who would afflict them with grievous torment*, is to those people who throughout the ages have persecuted and tormented the Jews. The degradation of the Jews holds a lesson for us. Those who neither act righteously nor try to reform their environment gradually drift more and more into evil practices, with the result

that finally they lose their independence and are subjugated by other nations who trample them under their feet.

This and the following verses also show that the people who are spoken of as " apes despised " in the preceding verse were not actually transformed into apes but continued as human beings, though they led a miserable existence and were looked down upon by others. See also 2 : 66

1058. Commentary :

The prophecy contained in this verse has met with a remarkable fulfilment. No people has been so much harassed and so widely dispersed over the face of the earth as the Jews have been.

170. ^aThen there has come an *evil* generation after them who inherited the Book. They take the paltry goods of this low *world* and say, ' It will be forgiven us.' But if there came to them similar goods *again*, they would take them. Was not the covenant of the Book taken from them, that they would not say of Allah *anything* but the truth ? And they have studied what is therein. And ^bthe abode of the Hereafter is better for those who are righteous. Will you not then understand ?[1059]

171. And *as to* those ^cwho hold fast by the Book, and observe Prayer, surely We suffer not the reward of *such* righteous *people* to perish.

فَخَلَفَ مِنْ بَعْدِهِمْ خَلْفٌ وَّرِثُوا الْكِتٰبَ يَأْخُذُوْنَ عَرَضَ هٰذَا الْاَدْنٰى وَيَقُوْلُوْنَ سَيُغْفَرُ لَنَا وَاِنْ يَّأْتِهِمْ عَرَضٌ مِّثْلُهٗ يَأْخُذُوهُ اَلَمْ يُؤْخَذْ عَلَيْهِمْ مِّيْثَاقُ الْكِتٰبِ اَنْ لَّا يَقُوْلُوْا عَلَى اللهِ اِلَّا الْحَقَّ وَدَرَسُوْا مَا فِيْهِ وَالدَّارُ الْاٰخِرَةُ خَيْرٌ لِّلَّذِيْنَ يَتَّقُوْنَ اَفَلَا تَعْقِلُوْنَ ۱۴

وَالَّذِيْنَ يُمَسِّكُوْنَ بِالْكِتٰبِ وَاَقَامُوا الصَّلٰوةَ اِنَّا لَا نُضِيْعُ اَجْرَ الْمُصْلِحِيْنَ ۱۴۱

---

^a19 : 60.   ^b6 : 33 ; 12 : 110.   ^c31 : 23.

1059. Important Words :

خلف (an evil generation) is a substantive from خلف (*khalafa*) meaning, he came after, succeeded or remained after another. خلف means, the location or quarter that is behind ; the time past ; the side corresponding to the front ; one who remains after another, or persons remaining after others ; a remnant of people ; a generation after a generation ; a bad son ; an evil generation ; one or more persons in whom there is no good ; a thing in which there is no good (Lane & Aqrab). See also 2 : 31 ; 7 : 70.

عرض (paltry goods) is derived from عرض. They say عرض له الشيئى *i.e.* he presented, showed or offered the thing to him. عرض means, a thing that befalls or happens to a man, such as disease, misfortune and the like ; a thing that is not permanent ; the paltry goods of the present world ; worldly goods or commodities ; booty or spoil ; an object of desire ; an eager desire or covetousness (Lane & Aqrab).

درسوا (they have studied) is from درس *i.e.* (1) he read or studied a book ; (2) it became effaced, erased or obliterated ; (3) he effaced, erased or obliterated something (Lane). See also 6 : 106.

Commentary :

The Book spoken of in this verse is the Bible and the expression, *who inherited the Book,* means who received the Book as a sacred trust from God through the Prophets, or through those gone before them.

The words درسوا ما فيه (they have studied what is therein) may also be rendered as " they have obliterated or effaced what is therein ", meaning that they were taught the divine Book but they forgot it and rendered it as something effaced and obliterated.

172. And [a]when We shook the mountain over them as though it were a covering, and they thought it was going to fall on them, *We said,* 'Hold fast that which We have given you, and remember what is therein that you may be saved.'[1060]

R. 22   173. And when thy Lord brings forth from Adam's children—out of their loins—their offspring and makes them witnesses against their ownselves *by saying* : [b]' Am I not your Lord ?' they say, ' Yea, we do bear witness.' *This He does* lest you should say on the Day of Resurrection, 'We were surely unaware of this.'[1061]

وَإِذْ نَتَقْنَا الْجَبَلَ فَوْقَهُمْ كَأَنَّهُ ظُلَّةٌ وَظَنُّوٓا اَنَّهُ وَاقِعٌ بِهِمْ خُذُوْا مَآ اٰتَيْنٰكُمْ بِقُوَّةٍ وَّاذْكُرُوْا مَا فِيْهِ لَعَلَّكُمْ تَتَّقُوْنَ ۝

وَإِذْ اَخَذَ رَبُّكَ مِنْۢ بَنِيْٓ اٰدَمَ مِنْ ظُهُوْرِهِمْ ذُرِّيَّتَهُمْ وَاَشْهَدَهُمْ عَلٰٓى اَنْفُسِهِمْ اَلَسْتُ بِرَبِّكُمْ قَالُوْا بَلٰى شَهِدْنَآ اَنْ تَقُوْلُوْا يَوْمَ الْقِيٰمَةِ اِنَّا كُنَّا عَنْ هٰذَا غٰفِلِيْنَ ۝

---

[a]2 : 64.   [b]43 : 38.

1060. Important Words :

نَتَقْنَا (We shook) is formed from نَتَق . They say نَتَقَهُ *i.e.* (1) he shook it ; (2) he raised it ; or (3) he spread it. An Arab would say نَتَق اللهُ فوقهم الجبل *i.e.* God raised the mountain shaking above them (Aqrab).

ظُلَّة (covering). See 2 : 211.

Commentary :

Owing to the violent shaking, the Mount looked like being suspended over the heads of the Israelites as though it were a covering. See also 2 : 64, 94 & 4 : 155.

1061. Important Words :

ظُهُور (loins) is the plural of ظَهْر (back) which is derived from ظَهَر which means, it was or became apparent, open, plain or evident. ظَهْر means, among other things, the back ; the part extending from the lower portion of the neck to the nearest part of the buttocks. Elsewhere the Quran uses the more familiar word اصلاب (4 : 24) *i.e.* loins. So in the text the word has been rightly translated as "loins".

Commentary :

The verse may be interpreted in two ways. It may either be taken to refer to the inborn idea in man about the existence of a Supreme Being Who has created and Who governs the Universe. God has embedded this idea in the very nature of man so that he may be admonished thereby and seek a way towards his Maker. The expression, *out of their loins,* supports this interpretation. It should not, however, be supposed that the dialogue actually took place. The words are simply meant to express a state of affairs.

The second interpretation relates to the appearance of Prophets whom God sends to show people His way. In this case it is worthy of note that when speaking about "making them witnesses against their ownselves" the verse does not mention Adam but the children of Adam, which points to the fact that the expression, "offspring from the children of Adam", means the people of every new age or era to whom a Messenger of God is sent. It is, in fact, the advent of every new Messenger that prompts the divine query, *Am I not your*

174. Or *lest* you should say, *a*'It was only our fathers who attributed co-partners *to God* in the past and we were *merely* a generation after them. Wilt Thou then destroy us for what was done by those who lied ?'1062

175. And thus do We make clear the Signs, *that they may be admonished* and that they may return *to Us*.

176. And relate to them the story of him to whom we gave Our Signs, but he stepped away from them ; so Satan followed him up, and he became *one* of those who go astray.1063

او تَقُوْلُوْٓا اِنَّمَآ اَشْرَكَ اٰبَآؤُنَا مِنْ قَبْلُ وَكُنَّا ذُرِّيَّةً مِّنْۢ بَعْدِهِمْ ۚ اَفَتُهْلِكُنَا بِمَا فَعَلَ الْمُبْطِلُوْنَ ۝

وَكَذٰلِكَ نُفَصِّلُ الْاٰيٰتِ وَلَعَلَّهُمْ يَرْجِعُوْنَ ۝

وَاتْلُ عَلَيْهِمْ نَبَاَ الَّذِيْٓ اٰتَيْنٰهُ اٰيٰتِنَا فَانْسَلَخَ مِنْهَا فَاَتْبَعَهُ الشَّيْطٰنُ فَكَانَ مِنَ الْغٰوِيْنَ ۝

---

*a*7 : 39.

Lord ? The query asserts that when God has made a provision for the physical sustenance of mankind as well as for their moral and spiritual development, they cannot deny His lordship. To this question the only possible reply can be, *Yea, we do bear witness*. It is indeed only through the rejection of their Prophet that the people of an age become witnesses against themselves ; for in that case they cannot take shelter behind the excuse that they did not know God or His Law or the Day of Judgement.

1062. Commentary :

The appearance of a Prophet also debars the people of his time from urging the plea mentioned in the present verse, for then the truth is made manifest from falsehood and idolatry stands publicly condemned.

1063. Important Words :

انسلخ (stepped away) is derived from سلخ. They say سلخ جلدها *i.e.* he stripped off its skin. سلخت عنها قميصها means, I pulled off or stripped off her shirt. سلخنا الشهر means, we passed the month, or passed forth from the month. One would say سلخ النبات *i.e.* the plant shed its foliage and became leafless

and then became green again. انسلخ means, he or it became stripped, or he or it passed, or he quitted a thing entirely. They say انسلخت الحية من قشرها *i.e.* the serpent cast off, or divested itself of, its slough. انسلخ منه means, he or it became altogether separated from it ; or he or it quitted it entirely (Lane & Aqrab).

اتبعه (followed him up). اتبع is derived from تبع. They say تبعه *i.e.* he followed him or it, or he went or walked after him or it. اتبع besides giving the causative sense is also used like تبع in the sense of following. They say اتبعه *i.e.* he followed his footsteps ; he sought him ; also he overtook him (Lane).

Commentary :

The verse does not refer to any particular individual but may apply to all persons to whom God shows Signs through a Prophet and who reject them. Similar expressions which do not refer to any particular individual but are of general application also occur elsewhere in the Quran (*e.g.*, 2 : 18). The verse under comment has been applied to one Bal'am bin Ba'ūra who, it is related, lived in the time of Moses. He is reported to have been a virtuous

177. And if We had pleased, We could have exalted him thereby; but he inclined to the earth and followed his evil inclination. His case therefore is like the case of a *thirsty* dog; if thou drive him away, he hangs out his tongue; and if thou leave him, he hangs out his tongue. Such is the case of the people who disbelieve in Our Signs. So give *them* the description that they may ponder.[1064]

وَلَوْ شِئْنَا لَرَفَعْنَهُ بِهَا وَلَكِنَّهُ اَخْلَدَ اِلَى الْاَرْضِ وَاتَّبَعَ هَوَاهُ فَمَثَلُهُ كَمَثَلِ الْكَلْبِ اِنْ تَحْمِلْ عَلَيْهِ يَلْهَثْ اَوْ تَتْرُكْهُ يَلْهَثْ ذٰلِكَ مَثَلُ الْقَوْمِ الَّذِيْنَ كَذَّبُوْا بِاٰيٰتِنَا فَاقْصُصِ الْقَصَصَ لَعَلَّهُمْ يَتَفَكَّرُوْنَ ۞

178. Evil is the case of *a*the people who treat Our Signs as lies. And it was their ownselves that they wronged.

سَآءَ مَثَلَا ۨالْقَوْمُ الَّذِيْنَ كَذَّبُوْا بِاٰيٰتِنَا وَاَنْفُسَهُمْ كَانُوْا يَظْلِمُوْنَ ۞

*a*3 : 12 ; 7 : 183 ; 8 : 55.

man, but pride turned his head and he ended in disgrace. But the verse aptly describes also the case of Abū Jahl who had clearly seen and even admitted the truth of the Holy Prophet but proudly and scornfully remarked that his people had never owed allegiance to the house of 'Abd Manāf, a progenitor of the Holy Prophet. The verse may equally apply to 'Abdullah bin Ubayy bin Salūl, the arch-hypocrite, who witnessed many Signs establishing the truth of the Holy Prophet and even apparently professed his faith in him, but at heart ever remained his implacable enemy.

1064. Important Words:

تَحْمِل عَلَيْهِ (thou drive him away). is derived from حمل . They say حَمَلَهُ *i.e.* he bore or carried or conveyed it. حمل عليه الشيئ means, he loaded him with the thing, or he put the thing on him as a load; or he imposed on him the thing as a burden. حمل عليه means, he charged or assaulted or attacked him (Lane). It is in the last mentioned sense that the word has been rendered here as "drive him away."

يلهث (hangs out his tongue) is formed from لهث meaning, he thirsted; or thirst heated his body. They say لهث الكلب *i.e.* the dog put forth his tongue on account of thirst or fatigue or weariness. لهث الرجل means, the breath of the man rose on account of fatigue or weariness; or he was fatigued or weary (Lane & Aqrab).

قصص (description) is the noun-infinitive from قص . They say قص أثره *i.e.* he followed his footsteps; or he followed his track in pursuit. قص الشعر means, he cut or clipped the hair. قص عليه الخبر means, he related to him the news or the narrative or the story. قصص therefore, means, description or explanation; a narrative or story; following someone or something in his or its footsteps or track (Lane & Aqrab). See also 3 : 63.

Commentary:

The verse continues the description of the similitude begun in the previous verse. When a man becomes wholly engrossed in worldly affairs and begins to follow his evil desires and inclinations and rejects truth, he becomes degraded, as it were, to the position of a dog. His thirst for money becomes insatiable. He

179. *a*He whom Allah guides is on the right path. And they whom He adjudges astray, these it is who shall be the losers.[1065]

180. Verily, We have created many of the Jinn and men whose end shall be Hell! *b*They have hearts *but* they understand not therewith, and they have eyes *but* they see not therewith, and they have ears *but* they hear not therewith. *c*They are like cattle; nay, they are *even* more astray. They are indeed *quite* heedless.[1066]

مَنْ يَّهْدِ اللهُ فَهُوَ الْمُهْتَدِيْ وَمَنْ يُّضْلِلْ فَاُولٰٓئِكَ هُمُ الْخٰسِرُوْنَ ۝

وَلَقَدْ ذَرَأْنَا لِجَهَنَّمَ كَثِيْرًا مِّنَ الْجِنِّ وَالْاِنْسِ ۖ لَهُمْ قُلُوْبٌ لَّا يَفْقَهُوْنَ بِهَا وَلَهُمْ اَعْيُنٌ لَّا يُبْصِرُوْنَ بِهَا وَلَهُمْ اٰذَانٌ لَّا يَسْمَعُوْنَ بِهَا اُولٰٓئِكَ كَالْاَنْعَامِ بَلْ هُمْ اَضَلُّ اُولٰٓئِكَ هُمُ الْغٰفِلُوْنَ ۝

---

*a*17 : 98 ; 18 : 18.   *b*2 : 8 ; 22 : 47 ; 45 : 24.   *c*25 : 45.

continues to hanker after the paltry goods of this world. This description quite fits in with an hypocrite or one weak in faith. Whether or not he is made to undergo sacrifices in the cause of religion, he seems to be always panting like a thirsty dog, as if the ever-increasing burden of sacrifices is leaving him exhausted. The above interpretation is in accord with the meaning of the expression حمل عليه in the sense of "putting a load on". If, however, the expression is taken in the sense of "attacking or charging" or for that matter "driving", then the words would mean that the weak of faith belonging to the class of people mentioned here always feel fatigued and weary in the way of God, whether they are smitten with afflictions and trials or not.

1065. Commentary :

See 2 : 27.

1066. Important Words :

The particle ل in the expression لجهنم is used to denote "end or result" and not "object" of the creation of the *Jinn* and men. Such use is in perfect conformity with the idiom of the Arabic language, the لام in such a case being known as لام عاقبة (Lane).

Commentary :

The verse does not at all mean that men and *Jinn* were created to be thrown into Hell. The use of the word "many" also belies that inference. Their creation, in fact, is intended to serve a great purpose (see 51 : 57). The present verse has thus nothing to do with the object of man's creation but only mentions the regrettable end of the life of many a man and *Jinn*, the latter word also meaning a special class of men *i.e.* rulers or chiefs or great men. They lead an evil life, the inevitable result of which is Hell. But from the way in which they spend their days in sin and iniquity it seems as if they were only created for Hell. The verse gives a brief but perfect description of those destined for Hell. They are the people whom God had endowed with understanding and with the faculty of perception and sight. They were blessed with all the necessary means by which they could find out and follow the right path and attain nearness to their Maker ; but out of their perversity and waywardness they did not avail themselves of those means, with the result that they wandered away from the truth and fell into error. It was not, therefore, for Hell but for

181. And [a]to Allah *alone* belong *all* perfect attributes. So call on Him by these. And leave alone those who deviate from the right way with respect to His attributes. They shall be repaid for what they do. [1067]

وَ لِلّٰهِ الْاَسْمَآءُ الْحُسْنٰى فَادْعُوْهُ بِهَا وَ ذَرُوا الَّذِيْنَ يُلْحِدُوْنَ فِيْ اَسْمَآئِهٖ سَيُجْزَوْنَ مَا كَانُوْا يَعْمَلُوْنَ ۱۸۱

---

[a]17 : 111.

Heaven that God created them, but they themselves forsook the path of Heaven and chose the path of Hell.

The condition of such men is indeed worse than that of "cattle", because in spite of the fact that they possess understanding and the power to rise, they do not avail themselves of their understanding and, instead of rising (for which they are meant) ever go on falling lower and lower.

1067. Important Words:

الْاَسْمَآءُ الْحُسْنٰى (perfect attributes). The word اَسْمَآء is the plural of اِسْم (for which see 1 : 1 & 2 : 32), meaning, (1) name ; and (2) attribute. الْحُسْنٰى which is the feminine of الْاَحْسَن means, that which is better or that which is best ; the final good state or condition. So الْاَسْمَآء الْحُسْنٰى means, best names, or best attributes, or perfect attributes. The term is specifically used to denote the attributes of God.

يُلْحِدُوْن (deviate from the right way) is derived from لَحَدَ which means, he or it declined or deviated from the right course, or he or it inclined. اَلْحَدَ also means the same. اَلْحَدَ فِى الدِّيْن means, he deviated or swerved from the right way with respect to religion ; he impugned religion. اَلْحَدَ also means, he disputed or wrangled. اَلْحَدَ بِهٖ means, he brought a reproach upon him ; or he held him in light estimation ; or he despised him ; or he said of him what was false (Lane & Aqrab).

Commentary :

The proper name of God is only Allah, all the rest being, strictly speaking, not His names

but attributes. The verse tells us the secret as to how our prayers can be readily accepted. While praying, we should invoke such attributes of God as are directly related to the object of our prayer. This will make our prayer more susceptible of acceptance, because, by so doing, we would excite the jealousy of God with regard to the relevant attribute of His, with the result that the prayer, if otherwise acceptable, will not be suffered to go in vain. The Quran specifically mentions as many as 69 divine attributes but there are others which may be inferred and yet others which are found mentioned in the Ḥadīth.

The verse next proceeds to enjoin the believers to have nothing to do with those who devise for God attributes which are not attributable to Him. Says the verse : *Leave alone those who deviate from the right way with respect to His attributes.* When God possesses all the best attributes mentioned in the Quran or the Ḥadīth, what need is there to devise other attributes for Him ? Such attributes cannot be free from error. An instance of such an ill-devised attribute is عادل (Just) which Christians attribute to God. The Quran says that God certainly is not unjust but at the same time it scrupulously avoids the ascription of the attribute of عادل (Just) to Him, for the ascription of this attribute to God would imply that His justice should demand that He must always punish sinners. But He is not bound to do so, because He is Forgiving and Merciful and He can pardon any sinner. In fact, God is not like a judge bound by

182. And *of those We have created there are a people that guide *men* with truth and do justice therewith. [1068]

وَمِمَّنْ خَلَقْنَآ اُمَّةٌ يَّهْدُوْنَ بِالْحَقِّ وَبِهٖ يَعْدِلُوْنَ ۝

183. And *b*those who reject Our Signs, We will draw them *to destruction* step by step in a manner which they do not know. [1069]

وَالَّذِيْنَ كَذَّبُوْا بِاٰيٰتِنَا سَنَسْتَدْرِجُهُمْ مِّنْ حَيْثُ لَا يَعْلَمُوْنَ ۝

184. And *c*I give them the rein; surely My plan is mighty. [1070]

وَاُمْلِيْ لَهُمْ ؕ اِنَّ كَيْدِيْ مَتِيْنٌ ۝

185. *d*Have they not considered *that* there is no insanity about their companion? He is only a plain warner. [1071]

اَوَلَمْ يَتَفَكَّرُوْا ۣ مَا بِصَاحِبِهِمْ مِّنْ جِنَّةٍ ؕ اِنْ هُوَ اِلَّا نَذِيْرٌ مُّبِيْنٌ ۝

---

*a*7 : 160.   *b*3 : 12; 7 : 183; 8 : 55.   *c*3 : 179; 68 : 46.   *d*23 : 26; 34 : 47; 52 : 30; 81 : 23.

---

the Law to deal by men according to their deeds. But He is مالك or Master of His creatures and Master of His law as well. He can forgive the sins of His servants as and when He pleases. By calling God "just", the Christian Church had to enlist the aid of a so-called redeemer who, by his supposed death on the Cross, should atone for the sins of men to satisfy God's attribute of justice.

1068. Commentary :

The verse does not mean that among the opponents of the Holy Prophet there were "people who guided men with truth and did justice therewith." What it means is that among God's creatures there are men who not only themselves are rightly guided and practise justice but also enjoin others to do the same ; and the verse hints that it behoves other people to follow their example. The reference obviously is to those who accepted the Holy Prophet ; or the verse may refer to God-fearing people who lived before Islam.

1069. Commentary :

This verse speaks of the opponents of Islam. The Battle of Badr provided a good illustration of the detsruction promised to them in this verse. Neither the Muslims nor the Meccans knew that a battle was about to take place. The disaster came to the Meccans as a bolt from the blue, so that when the news of the overwhelming defeat reached Mecca, the people were simply stunned to hear it. Other disasters also followed.

1070. Important Words :

مَتِيْن (mighty) is derived from مَتَن . They say مَتَن الشَّيْ *i.e.* the thing became strong, firm or hard. مَتِيْن means, strong, stout, firm or hard ; possessing any quality in a strong degree Lane). مَتِيْن is also one of the attributes of God meaning, Strong and Mighty ; He Whom fatigue or weariness touches not (Aqrab).

Commentary :

God's delay in punishing disbelievers does not mean that He is weak ; on the contrary, being All-Powerful and having them completely in His grasp, He is never in a hurry to punish. He punishes when in His infinite wisdom He thinks fit to do so.

1071. Important Words :

صَاحِب (companion) is derived from صَحِب which means, he was or became his companion,

186. ^aAnd have they not looked into the kingdom of the heavens and the earth, and all things that Allah has created ?　And *do they not see* that, it may be, their *own* term has already drawn near ?　^bThen in what thing will they believe thereafter ? [1072]

187. ^cWhomsoever Allah adjudges astray, there can be no guide for him. And ^dHe leaves such in their transgression wandering in distraction. [1073]

اَوَلَمْ يَنْظُرُوْا فِيْ مَلَكُوْتِ السَّمٰوٰتِ وَالْاَرْضِ وَمَا خَلَقَ اللّٰهُ مِنْ شَيْءٍ ۙ وَّاَنْ عَسٰۤى اَنْ يَّكُوْنَ قَدِ اقْتَرَبَ اَجَلُهُمْ ۚ فَبِاَيِّ حَدِيْثٍ بَعْدَهٗ يُؤْمِنُوْنَ ۝

مَنْ يُّضْلِلِ اللّٰهُ فَلَا هَادِيَ لَهٗ ۚ وَيَذَرُهُمْ فِيْ طُغْيَانِهِمْ يَعْمَهُوْنَ ۝

---

^a6 : 76 ; 10 : 102.　　^b45 : 7 ; 77 : 51.　　^c7 : 179 ; 17 : 98 ; 18 : 18.　　^d2 : 16 ; 6 : 111.

---

associate, comrade, fellow or friend. صاحب of which the plural is اصحاب or صحابة means, a companion, associate, comrade, fellow or friend ; owner or master ; possessor ; inmate ; manager or disposer ; one who keeps or adheres to a thing (Lane). Figuratively the word is also used in the sense of helper.

Commentary :

The word صاحب (companion) meaning both a companion and an helper is not intended as a plain reference to the Holy Prophet. The word has been specially chosen to imply a refutation of the charge of insanity brought by some of his enemies against the Holy Prophet, as well as a veiled rebuke to the Meccans. They are told that the Prophet was their companion and associate. He lived and moved among them and they knew him perfectly well and therefore they could easily see, and indeed in their heart of hearts they knew that there was nothing of insanity about him. He was also their helper and was constantly working for their good which constituted further proof of the fact that he was not insane. That he was نذير مبين (a plain warner) and issued his warnings in a clear and reasoned manner also pointed to the same conclusion— that he was in full possession of his senses.

1072. Commentary :

The verse draws the attention of the Meccans to the great and numerous changes that were taking place around them, which pointed to the approach of a new era. All signs pointed to the fact that idolatry was going to disappear from the country, giving place to Islam. The word ملكوت (kingdom) refers to the control which God exercises over heaven and earth. See also 6 : 76.

The words بأى حديث (in what thing) may also be rendered as " by means of what thing." In this case, the last sentence of the verse would mean that when disbelievers had reached their term, they would have no time left to believe and repent. The sentence thus constitutes a sort of exhortation to them to make haste and avail themselves of the present opportunity, before it is too late.

In the former sense of the words (*i.e.* as rendered in the text), the sentence would mean : when the disbelievers are rejecting the Quran which is such a perfect and complete Law what else is left for them to believe in ?

1073. Commentary :

See 2 : 27.

188. [a]They ask thee respecting the Hour: when will it come to pass? Say, [b]"The knowledge thereof is only with my Lord. None can manifest it at its time but He. It lies heavy on the heavens and the earth. [c]It shall not come upon you but of a sudden.' They ask thee as if thou wert well acquainted therewith. Say, ' The knowledge thereof is only with Allah; but most men do not know.'[1074]

بِسْمِ اللّٰهِ الرَّحْمٰنِ الرَّحِيْمِ

---

[a]33 : 64; 78 : 2; 79 : 43.   [b]31 : 35; 43 : 86.   [c]16 : 78; 54 : 51.

1074. Important Words:

ايان مرساها (when will it come to pass?). مرسى is derived from رسا . They say رسا الجبل i.e. the mountain was firmly based or fixed upon the ground. رست السفينة means, the ship cast anchor and became stationary. مرسى is the noun-infinitive or a noun of time or a noun of place, meaning, the act of anchoring or the time or place of anchorage ; or the time and place of becoming stationary; or of coming to pass. The expression ايان مرساها means, when will it come to pass, or what is the time of its taking place ; or when will it occur or happen ? (Lane & Aqrab).

حفى (well-acquainted) is derived from حفى which means, he walked bare-footed; or his feet became chafed by walking much. حفى به means, he showed him much honour and kindness and affection ; or he behaved towards him with solicitude and manifested joy and pleasure. حفى عنه means, he asked or inquired much respecting him; he exceeded the usual bounds in making much inquiry respecting him. So حفى means, showing much honour and solicitude and manifesting joy or pleasure at meeting another; asking or inquiring much respecting another's state or condition ; going to the utmost in asking or inquiring ; or knowing in the utmost degree (Lane & Aqrab).

Commentary:

The reference in the opening sentence of the verse is to 7 : 186. When the opponents of Islam were told that their hour had already drawn near, they inquired of the Prophet the exact time when the promised hour would come. The awarding of punishment is as painful to God as the receiving of it is to men, and this is the meaning of the words, *It lies heavy on the heavens and the earth.* The word " heavens " here represents God and angels, while the word " earth " represents human beings.

The word حفى signifies (1) importunate in inquiring ; or (2) well-acquainted. The sentence would thus mean : (1) They ask thee concerning the exact time when the hour of their punishment will come to pass, as if thou wert repeatedly inquiring of God as to its time of occurrence. Or (2) they ask thee about the time of the " Hour ", as if thou wert well-acquainted with it. In both these cases the clause would imply that the Holy Prophet neither knew when the " Hour " would come to pass nor was he very solicitous about it.

189. ᵃSay, 'I have no power to do good or harm to myself, save as Allah pleases. And if I had knowledge of the unseen, I should have secured abundance of good; and evil should not have touched me. ᵇI am only a warner and a bearer of good tidings to a people who believe.' 1075

قُلْ لَّا أَمْلِكُ لِنَفْسِى نَفْعًا وَّلَا ضَرًّا إِلَّا مَا شَاءَ اللّٰهُ وَلَوْ كُنْتُ أَعْلَمُ الْغَيْبَ لَا سْتَكْثَرْتُ مِنَ الْخَيْرِ وَمَا مَسَّنِىَ السُّوءُ إِنْ أَنَا إِلَّا نَذِيْرٌ وَّبَشِيْرٌ لِّقَوْمٍ يُّؤْمِنُوْنَ ۝

R. 24 190. ᶜHe it is Who has created you from a single soul, and made therefrom its mate, ᵈthat he might find comfort in her. And when he knows her, she bears a light burden, and goes about with it. And when she grows heavy, they both pray to Allah, their Lord, *saying:* 'If Thou give us a good *child*, we will surely be of the thankful.' 1076

هُوَ الَّذِىْ خَلَقَكُمْ مِّنْ نَّفْسٍ وَّاحِدَةٍ وَّجَعَلَ مِنْهَا زَوْجَهَا لِيَسْكُنَ إِلَيْهَا فَلَمَّا تَغَشّٰهَا حَمَلَتْ حَمْلًا خَفِيْفًا فَمَرَّتْ بِهٖ فَلَمَّا أَثْقَلَتْ دَّعَوَا اللّٰهَ رَبَّهُمَا لَئِنْ آتَيْتَنَا صَالِحًا لَّنَكُوْنَنَّ مِنَ الشّٰكِرِيْنَ ۝

ᵃ10:50; 72:22. ᵇ2:120; 5:20; 11:3. ᶜ4:2; 16:73; 39:7. ᵈ30:22.

1075. Commentary:

By the word "good" in the sentence, *I should have secured abundance of good*, is meant no material good, but spiritual good. As for material good, it is well known that it did come to the Holy Prophet, but he discarded it, praying to God in the words اللهم احيني مسكينا و امتني مسكينا *i.e.* "My God, make me live the life of a poor man and let death come to me when I am poor" (Tirmidhī). So by the word "good" is here meant, not worldly good or riches but spiritual good or the good of Islam, which the Holy Prophet so ardently desired.

The word "unseen" in the clause, *If I had knowledge of the unseen*, means the secret ways of purifying men's hearts which are known to God alone (16:10). The Holy Prophet is thus represented as saying: 'If I had known the secret and hidden ways by which men's hearts are turned to truth, I would have certainly used them and would have made

all of you accept the true Faith."

The expression, *and evil should not have touched me*, means that in the event of my having won over all men to Islam, there would have been no war.

1076. Commentary:

By the words, *a single soul*, is here meant the father. The verse does not refer to Adam or for that matter to any particular man but speaks of men generally. See also 4:2.

The verse describes one of the objects of marriage, which is that man and woman may be a source of comfort and solace to each other. Man is highly social by nature, and it is his natural craving for a close companion that is supplied by marriage. Without the institution of marriage man, in most cases, would have vainly spent his whole life in search of a true and loyal companion.

191. But when He gives them a good *child*, they attribute to Him partners in respect of that which He has given them. But exalted is Allah above what they associate *with Him*.[1077]

فَلَمَّآ اٰتٰىهُمَا صَالِحًا جَعَلَا لَهٗ شُرَكَآءَ فِيْمَآ اٰتٰىهُمَا ۚ فَتَعٰلَى اللّٰهُ عَمَّا يُشْرِكُوْنَ ۝

192. Do [a]they associate *with Him* as partners those who create nothing, and are themselves created? [1078]

اَيُشْرِكُوْنَ مَا لَا يَخْلُقُ شَيْئًا وَّهُمْ يُخْلَقُوْنَ ۝

193. And [b]they can give them no help, nor can they help themselves.

وَلَا يَسْتَطِيْعُوْنَ لَهُمْ نَصْرًا وَّلَآ اَنْفُسَهُمْ يَنْصُرُوْنَ ۝

194. And [c]if you call them to guidance, they will not follow you. It is the same to you whether you call them or you remain silent. [1079]

وَاِنْ تَدْعُوْهُمْ اِلَى الْهُدٰى لَا يَتَّبِعُوْكُمْ ۚ سَوَآءٌ عَلَيْكُمْ اَدَعَوْتُمُوْهُمْ اَمْ اَنْتُمْ صَامِتُوْنَ ۝

195. Surely, those whom you call on beside Allah are *mere* servants like you. Then [d]call on them and let them answer you, if you are truthful. [1080]

اِنَّ الَّذِيْنَ تَدْعُوْنَ مِنْ دُوْنِ اللّٰهِ عِبَادٌ اَمْثَالُكُمْ فَادْعُوْهُمْ فَلْيَسْتَجِيْبُوْا لَكُمْ اِنْ كُنْتُمْ صٰدِقِيْنَ ۝

---

[a]16 : 21; 25 : 4.   [b]7 : 198; 21 : 44; 36 : 76.   [c]7 : 199.   [d]35 : 15.

1077. Commentary :

The words, *they attribute to Him partners*, mean that when the parents have begotten a good child, they begin to think that the child was the gift of some one other than Allah.

1078. Commentary :

This and the next verse speak of such human beings as are looked upon and worshipped as God.

1079. Commentary :

This verse refers to inanimate things such as idols and images which some people, out of their ignorance, take as gods.

1080. Commentary :

The verse constitutes an open challenge to the idol-worshippers or believers in the plurality of gods that all animate and inanimate things that they call on beside Allah will never answer their prayers, because they do not possess the power to do so.

196. Have they feet wherewith they walk, or *have they hands wherewith they hold, or have they eyes wherewith they see, or have they ears wherewith they hear? Say, 'Call upon the partners you associate *with God*, then *contrive *you all* against me, and give me no time.'[1081]

اَلَهُمۡ اَرۡجُلٌ يَّمۡشُوۡنَ بِهَاۤ اَمۡ لَهُمۡ اَيۡدٍ يَّبۡطِشُوۡنَ بِهَاۤ اَمۡ لَهُمۡ اَعۡيُنٌ يُّبۡصِرُوۡنَ بِهَاۤ اَمۡ لَهُمۡ اٰذَانٌ يَّسۡمَعُوۡنَ بِهَاۤ قُلِ ادۡعُوۡا شُرَكَآءَكُمۡ ثُمَّ كِيۡدُوۡنِ فَلَا تُنۡظِرُوۡنِ ۟

197. Truly, *my protector is Allah Who revealed the Book. And He protects the righteous.

اِنَّ وَلِيِّ اللّٰهُ الَّذِیۡ نَزَّلَ الۡكِتٰبَ وَهُوَ يَتَوَلَّی الصّٰلِحِيۡنَ ۟

198. And *they whom you call on beside Him have no power to help you, nor can they help themselves.[1082]

وَالَّذِيۡنَ تَدۡعُوۡنَ مِنۡ دُوۡنِهٖ لَا يَسۡتَطِيۡعُوۡنَ نَصۡرَكُمۡ وَلَاۤ اَنۡفُسَهُمۡ يَنۡصُرُوۡنَ ۟

---

*a*2 : 8 ; 22 : 47 ; 45 : 24.   *b*10 : 72 ; 11 : 56.   *c*45 : 20.   *d*7 : 193 ; 21 : 44 ; 36 : 76.

1081. Commentary :

This and the next verse are an amplification of the challenge held out in the previous one. Disbelievers are challenged to call upon their gods to help them in their campaign against Islam, to make use of their entire resources and to muster all their forces to attack it, combining their feet, hands, eyes and ears (symbolic of different classes of men) and leaving no stone unturned to bring it to naught and to waste no time in attacking the Holy Prophet and then see what harm their combined and determined efforts do to him. God has promised to help His Prophet and to make his cause prosper and triumph (5 : 68 & 58 : 22).

The above challenge was made at Mecca, when Islam, being yet in its infancy, was very weak and the Holy Prophet and his followers seemed to be entirely at the mercy of their cruel and powerful foe. Such a challenge under such conditions, could not but be issued by a true Messenger of God. The challenge was also meant to demonstrate to the Meccans the helplessness of their gods ; for it invited them to enlist their help against Islam.

1082. Commentary :

The words, *And they ... have no power to help you, nor can they help themselves*, embody the dual prophecy which foretold the discomfiture of the idolaters in their struggle against the Holy Prophet on the one hand, and the disappearance of idolatry from Arabia on the other. The prophecy was fulfilled in a very remarkable way when Mecca fell and the Ka'ba was cleared of the idols which had been worshipped there for centuries by the Arabs as their national deities. That day the idolaters clearly realized the futility of idol-worship and embraced Islam in large numbers.

199. ^aAnd if you invite them to guidance, they hear not. And ^bthou seest them looking towards thee, but they see not.¹⁰⁸³

وَاِنْ تَدْعُوْهُمْ اِلَى الْهُدٰى لَا يَسْمَعُوْا ۖ وَتَرٰىهُمْ يَنْظُرُوْنَ اِلَيْكَ وَهُمْ لَا يُبْصِرُوْنَ ۝

200. ^cTake to forgiveness, and enjoin kindness, and turn away from the ignorant.¹⁰⁸⁴

خُذِ الْعَفْوَ وَأْمُرْ بِالْعُرْفِ وَأَعْرِضْ عَنِ الْجٰهِلِيْنَ ۝

201. And ^dif an evil suggestion from Satan incite thee, then seek refuge in Allah ; surely, He is All-Hearing, All-Knowing.¹⁰⁸⁵

وَاِمَّا يَنْزَغَنَّكَ مِنَ الشَّيْطٰنِ نَزْغٌ فَاسْتَعِذْ بِاللّٰهِ ۚ اِنَّهُ سَمِيْعٌ عَلِيْمٌ ۝

---

^a7 : 194.   ^b10 : 44.   ^c3 : 160 ; 31 : 18.   ^d41 : 37.

1083. Commentary :

A person steeped in error refuses to accept the truth, however clear and unmistakable the Signs shown to him to establish the untenability of his position. The verse means to say that disbelievers see the cause of Islam making progress by rapid strides before their own eyes, yet they pretend not to see it and refuse to acknowledge it.

1084. Commentary :

Mark the beauty of the verse in its extra-ordinary setting. Surrounded all round by blood-thirsty enemies, Islam would not give up its great principle of toleration and mercy. The Holy Prophet is here bidden to bear with patience the persecution of his enemies and to see that his followers also do the same. He indeed set an unparalleled example of patience and fortitude. But when the mischief of the Meccans exceeded all bounds and the very existence of Islam was in danger, it was then, and not till then, that the Muslims were permitted to take up arms in self-defence (see 22 : 40).

1085. Important Words :

نَزْغٌ (evil suggestion). They say نَزَغَهُ نَزْغًا i.e. he found fault with, and spoke evil of, him. نَزَغَ بَيْنَ الْقَوْمِ means, he incited or excited the people one against another and thus created disorder. نَزَغَهُ الشَّيْطٰنُ اِلَى الْمَعَاصِى means, Satan incited him to commit sins. النَّزْغُ means, an evil speech or evil suggestion meant to incite people against one another (Aqrab).

Commentary :

The address in this verse is to the readers in general and to the Holy Prophet in particular. The first clause of the verse may mean : (1) if Satan incites you to anger or makes an evil suggestion to you ; or (2) if some wicked person incites you against your enemies or stirs up mischief.

The words, *then seek refuge in Allah*, mean that in such a case you should control yourself and pray to God for help.

202. *As to* [a]those who are righteous, when a suggestion from Satan assails them, they remember *God* : and behold ! they begin to see *things rightly*. [1086]

اِنَّ الَّذِیْنَ اتَّقَوْا اِذَا مَسَّهُمْ طَآئِفٌ مِّنَ الشَّیْطٰنِ تَذَکَّرُوْا فَاِذَا هُمْ مُّبْصِرُوْنَ ۝

203. And their brethren make them continue in error and then they relax not. [1087]

وَاِخْوَانُهُمْ یَمُدُّوْنَهُمْ فِی الْغَیِّ ثُمَّ لَا یُقْصِرُوْنَ ۝

204. And when thou bringest not to them a Sign, they say, 'Wherefore dost thou not forge it ?' Say, [b]'I follow only that which is revealed to me from my Lord. [c]These are evidences from your Lord, and guidance and mercy for a people that believe.' [1988]

وَاِذَا لَمْ تَأْتِهِمْ بِاٰیَةٍ قَالُوْا لَوْلَا اجْتَبَیْتَهَا قُلْ اِنَّمَاۤ اَتَّبِعُ مَا یُوْحٰۤی اِلَیَّ مِنْ رَّبِّیْ هٰذَا بَصَآئِرُ مِنْ رَّبِّکُمْ وَهُدًی وَّرَحْمَةٌ لِّقَوْمٍ یُّؤْمِنُوْنَ ۝

---

[a]3 : 136.   [b]3 : 51.   [c]6 : 105 ; 17 : 103.

1086. Important Words :

طَآئِف (suggestion) is derived from طَافَ (with the letter ی as the central letter of the infinitive). They say طَافَ بِهِ الْخَیَال *i.e.* the apparition, etc. came to him or visited him. in sleep. طِیف or طَآئِف means, an apparition or phantom or imaginary form ; anything that obscures the sight, arising from a suggestion of Satan or a human being (generally in sleep) ; a thing that comes to one or visits one ; Satan's visitation by touch or suggestion or vain prompting ; anger, etc. (Lane).

Commentary :

The expression, *when a suggestion from Satan assails them*, means : (1) when righteous people are incited to anger by Satan ; or (2) when some mischief is stirred up against them by wicked men. The words, *they remember God*, mean : (1) they pray to God ; or (2) they call to mind the commandment of God to control their anger. The verse means that if in a fit of anger a Muslim should become, as it were, blind and lose self-control or if some mischief be stirred up against him by his enemies and he becomes involved in a difficulty,

he should pray to God so that with His help he may regain self-control and begin to see his way out of the difficulty.

1087. Commentary :

The verse may be rendered in two ways : (1) wicked men cause their comrades to increase in error and they continue to aid and abet one another in their evil practices ; or (2) wicked men strive to entice the pious into error. According to the latter rendering, the pronoun "them" in the words, *make them continue in error*, will refer to pious and righteous Muslims. By implication Muslims are exhorted in this verse to be always on their guard against the evil suggestions and evil machinations of wicked and mischievous men.

1088. Important Words :

اجْتَبَیْتَهَا (dost thou forge it). The word اجْتَبَیْتَهَا is derived from جَبٰی . They say, جَبَی الْمَالَ *i.e.* he collected wealth or property. اجْتَبَاہ means, he chose it or selected it. اجْتَبَاہ also means, he forged it ; he extemporised it.

205. And [a]when the Quran is recited, give ear to it and keep silence, that you may be shown mercy.[1089]

وَ اِذَا قُرِئَ الْقُرْاٰنُ فَاسْتَمِعُوْا لَهٗ وَ اَنْصِتُوْا لَعَلَّكُمْ تُرْحَمُوْنَ ۝

[a]17 : 107.

The expression اولا اجتبيتها would, therefore, mean, wherefore hast thou not forged it, or produced it, or invented it ; or wherefore hast thou not demanded it of God (Lane & Aqrab).

بصائر (evidences) is the plural of بصيرة which is derived from بصر which means, he saw ; he was or became endowed with mental perception or belief or knowledge or understanding or intelligence or skill. ابصر الطريق means, the way became manifest. You say انا على بصيرة i.e. I am certain ; or I possess certain knowledge. بصيرة means, mental perception ; the perceptive faculty of the mind ; understanding ; intelligence or skill ; firm belief of the heart ; constancy or firmness in religion ; an evidence, testimony, proof or argument ; a witness ; an example by which one is admonished ; a shield (Lane & Aqrab).

Commentary :

The word آية means " a Sign." The verses of the Quran are also called آيات (Signs) because every one of them by itself constitutes a divine Sign, an evidence of the divine origin of the Quran, and of the truth of the Holy Prophet. The purport of the verse is that although the word of God is being revealed as occasion demands, and successive Signs of God are being shown to men, yet whenever there is some delay in the coming of divine revelation or the occurrence of Signs, disbelievers ignore the word of God already revealed and the Signs already shown and shamelessly begin to ask of the Prophet, "Why do you not bring any revelation or show any Sign in your support," as if no Sign had so far been shown and no revelation had come. To this impudent demand of disbelievers, the Holy Prophet is instructed to reply that the sending down of revelation or the showing of Signs lies entirely in the hands of God and that he himself possesses no power to produce them at will. But why do they demand a fresh revelation or a new Sign, asks the Quran. Are not the revelations that have already come and the Signs that have already appeared enough to establish the truth of Islam? Why do they not ponder over them and profit by them ?

It should be remembered that God seldom shows Signs at the demand of disbelievers. Moreover, the demand for a fresh Sign on their part implies that the Signs already shown were no Signs and furnished no evidence of the Prophet's truth. Thus to accede to their demand means a reflection on the Signs already shown and detracts from their value. It is, therefore, very rare that God shows fresh Signs or miracles as demanded by disbelievers. He requires them rather to consider past Signs and profit by them.

1089. Commentary :

In answer to their demand for fresh Signs disbelievers are here told to listen to the Quran carefully, because it contains Signs and evidences enough and to spare. This will make them realize the error of their demand and they will see the truth and will as a result become deserving of the mercy of God.

206. And ^aremember thy Lord in thy mind with humility and fear, and without loudness of speech, in the mornings and evenings ; and be not of the neglectful.[1090]

وَاذْكُرْ رَّبَّكَ فِيْ نَفْسِكَ تَضَرُّعًا وَّخِيْفَةً وَّدُوْنَ الْجَهْرِ مِنَ الْقَوْلِ بِالْغُدُوِّ وَالْاٰصَالِ وَلَا تَكُنْ مِّنَ الْغٰفِلِيْنَ ۞

207. Truly, ^bthose who are near to thy Lord, turn not away with pride from His worship, but they glorify Him and prostrate themselves before Him.[1091]

اِنَّ الَّذِيْنَ عِنْدَ رَبِّكَ لَا يَسْتَكْبِرُوْنَ عَنْ عِبَادَتِهٖ وَيُسَبِّحُوْنَهٗ وَلَهٗ يَسْجُدُوْنَ ۩ ۞

---

^a3 : 64 ; 7 : 56.   ^b21 : 20-21 ; 41 : 39.

1090. Commentary :

Remembering God does not here mean the performance of the prescribed Prayers but prayers generally. The Holy Prophet has been enjoined to pray to God morning and evening for the guidance of disbelievers. Thus on the one hand, disbelievers have been told to listen to the Quran attentively (the preceding verse) and, on the other, the Holy Prophet has been enjoined to pray for their guidance. The verse may also be taken to be addressed to disbelievers, suggesting to them that in order to know the truth they should listen to the Quran attentively and pray to God in humility.

Though Islam permits prayers, both aloud and in secret, yet in the present verse suppressed prayers are emphasized in order to create in the heart feelings of humility, sincerity and fear.

1091. Commentary :

This is the last verse of the present *Sūra*. Disbelievers are told that they should pray to God for their guidance because even such righteous servants of God as have attained His nearness and are far superior to them in all respects do not disdain to worship and glorify Him.

The verse mentions three signs of those who attain nearness to God : (1) they turn not away with pride from His worship, meaning that they not only worship God but worship Him in all humility ; (2) they glorify God *i.e.* they not only silently worship God but even declare their faith openly and propagate the truth and try to establish the kingdom of God on earth ; (3) they prostrate themselves before God *i.e.* they submit to Him and their lives are devoted to His service.

It should be noted that it was the practice with the Holy Prophet that wherever a Quranic verse spoke of believers prostrating themselves before God, he used to perform a سجدة (act of prostration) and also enjoined his followers to do the same. This constitutes a great lesson for us—that we should not only be ever ready to obey God when a direct command is addressed to us but should also be eager to copy the good acts of others, even if we are not directly commanded to do so. The present verse embodies the first سجدة of the Quran.

CHAPTERS 8 & 9

ANFĀL & TAUBA

(*Revealed after Hijra*)

Title and Connection between the Two Sūrās

Though, as commonly known, it is only the first of these two *Sūrās* that is known by the name of *Anfāl*, but truly speaking the Chapter *Anfāl* comprises both the parts—the one which is known as *Anfāl* and the other which is known as *Tauba*. This means that *Tauba* is really no separate *Sūra* but is a part of *Anfāl*. This is the solitary instance where a *Sūra* has been split into parts, all the other *Sūrās* being compact wholes. The proof of the fact that *Tauba* is no separate *Sūra* but is a part of *Anfāl* is that the portion which is known as *Tauba* (Repentance) or *Barā'at* (Declaration of Absolution), is not prefixed by *Bismillah* (In the name of Allah), while, as divinely directed, the Holy Prophet invariably instructed that *Bismillah* be written at the head of every *Sūra*. Tirmidhī reports Ibn 'Abbās as saying, " I asked 'Uthmān, ' why did you amalgamate *Anfāl* which is a smaller *Sūra* with *Barā'at* or *Tauba* which is a larger one and did not write *Bismillah* in the beginning of the latter *Sūra* ? ' To this 'Uthmān replied that *Anfāl* was the first Medinite *Sūra* to be revealed and *Tauba* or *Barā'at* the last, and there existed such a deep and striking similarity between the subject-matter of the two as to make them appear as one *Sūra*, and since there was no instruction from the Holy Prophet as to these being two separate *Sūrās*, I combined them into one."

The above statement makes one thing clear. It is that there is very great resemblance between the subject-matter of these two *Sūrās* and that because, unlike other *Sūrās*, *Bismillah* was not revealed in the beginning of *Barā'at*, therefore it must form part of some other *Sūra*. The assumption, however, that it was 'Uthmān who placed this *Sūra* with *Anfāl* possesses no traditional basis, and one of the intermediate *Rāvīs* or reporters of the above tradition seems to have erred here, because, as established by incontrovertible historical evidence, the arrangement of the Quran in its present form was effected neither by 'Uthmān nor by anybody else, but by the Holy Prophet himself, and even those who ascribe the present arrangement to the Companions of the Prophet do not ascribe it to 'Uthmān but to Abū Bakr. 'Uthmān did only this—that having satisfied himself by taking evidence from Companions of unimpeachable integrity that the copy of the Quran existing in his time was the same which had been reduced to writing and transcribed in the form of a book by the orders of Abū Bakr, he added his testimony to it and disallowed all other forms of reading of the Quran except the one in the dialect of the Ḥijāz. The question which naturally arises here is that when the Quran was reduced to writing in the form of a book in the time of Abū Bakr, what was the arrangement of these *Sūrās* in that copy. If, because of the smallness of its size, *Anfāl* was placed by Abū Bakr among the later *Sūrās* which are generally small in size, and Abū Bakr also wrote *Bismillah* in the beginning of *Tauba,* and it was 'Uthmān who changed the arrangement decided upon by Abū Bakr and who dropped the *Bismillah,* this important fact should have certainly been mentioned by Ibn 'Abbās. Nay, he should have surely raised his voice against the omission of *Bismillah* in the beginning of *Tauba* and against the discrepancy in the arrangement of the *Sūrās.* But he did nothing of the kind. This shows that the above statement, as quoted by Tirmidhī, has been attributed to Ibn 'Abbās either owing to some misunderstanding on the part of one of the intermediary narrators or is a later interpolation. The truth is, as stated above, that *Anfāl* and *Tauba* or *Barā'at* both make one *Sūra* and *Tauba* is called a *Sūra,* which literally means a piece, because it has been treated as a distinct portion of *Anfāl,* otherwise it is not a *Sūra* in the sense in which other *Sūrās* are known by this name.

Date of Revelation

Both *Anfāl* and *Tauba* or *Barā'at* are Medinite *Sūrās. Anfāl* was revealed about the time of the Battle of Badr, in the first or second year after Hijra. As, however, mention has been made in seven verses of this *Sūra* of the machinations of the disbelievers which they hatched at the time of the *Hijrat* (Flight), some Commentators have regarded those verses as of Meccan origin. But this is evidently a wrong inference, because the Quran has in similar words mentioned events in the lives of Adam, Abraham and Moses. If a particular verse can be taken to have been revealed at Mecca because it mentions some incident that occurred at Mecca, the verses which describe the events that occurred in the time of Adam or Abraham or Moses will then have to be regarded as having been revealed in the times of these Prophets, which is evidently wrong. According to Imām Bukhārī Chapter *Tauba* or *Barā'at* was among the last portions of the Quran to be revealed as against Chapter *Anfāl* which was among the first to be revealed after Hijra.

A Collective Note on both Sūrās

In *Anfāl* the prophecy was made that God would give to Muslims a great victory and the possessions of their enemies would fall into their hands. This prophecy continued to prove for disbelievers a constant source of mockery at the expense of the Faithful, because God, out of His infallible wisdom and in conformity with His eternal law, delayed its fulfilment along with the revelation of that portion of Chapter *Anfāl* which contained a mention of it. When Mecca fell and the aforesaid prophecy was fulfilled, the remaining portion of the *Sūra* was revealed and it began with " *a declaration of complete absolution on the part of Allah and His Messenger from all obligations to the idolaters with whom you made promises. So go about in the land for four months, and know that you cannot frustrate the plan of Allah and that Allah will humiliate the disbelievers.*" Incidentally it may be noted here that some Commentators have taken the above declaration to mean that a period of four months was granted to those idolaters with whom Muslims had treaty engagements and that it was intended as a notice, after which all treaties and agreements with them were to be considered as having terminated. This interpretation of the Declaration is evidently wrong; because if only a notice for the denunciation of the treaties was meant, there was no sense in combining the Declaration with the injunction that they should go about the land and see for themselves that God's purpose had prevailed. He who is granted a limited respite naturally makes hasty preparation to depart for a place of safety and does not go about the land seeing sights. Again, if the verse be understood to give notice of termination of existing treaties and to grant a limited respite to those idolatrous tribes who had these treaties of alliance with Muslims, how would the very next verse be explained which says that such people as have entered into treaties with Muslims are not to be expelled till the termination of their treaties. It is thus clear that the Quranic words الذين عاهدتم as used in the first verse of Chapter *Tauba* allude to no political treaty or agreement but only to such declarations which Muslims and disbelievers had made against each other. On the side of Islam it was declared in Chapter *Anfāl* that the possessions of the disbelievers would fall in the hands of Muslims, and the disbelievers on their side had declared that Islam would be exterminated and they would capture the belongings of the Muslims. It is these opposite declarations that have been metaphorically termed as عهد or agreement in the verse referred to above and the idolaters are told to go about in the country and see for themselves whether or not the declaration which was made in Chapter *Anfāl* about their eventual destruction had proved true. So truly speaking Chapter *Barā'at* constitutes only a declaration of the fulfilment of the great prophecy made in *Anfāl* and is no separate *Sūra*. In short, there exists a very real connection between these two *Sūras* which really constitute one Chapter, for, as stated above, Chapter *Anfāl* was revealed at the time of the first battle of Islam *i.e.* the Battle of Badr and in this Chapter a clear prophecy was made of the ultimate destruction of the disbelievers. Then after the last encounter with the idolaters of Mecca, Chapter *Barā'at* was revealed to announce the fulfilment of that prophecy and the ushering in of a new era.

Subject-Matter

Chapter *Anfāl* opens with a description of the Battle of Badr and in vv. 1-15 Muslims are told that they will win a great victory over the disbelievers and the latter's possessions will fall into their hands, but this success and acquisition of wealth should not make them greedy of material things. These wars are the Signs of God and should not be made the means of seeking worldly gains. In vv. 16-20, Muslims are told that they should fight courageously in the cause of God and should not be proud of their strength or organization, neither should they be afraid of the numbers and military prowess of their enemies, because the outcome of these wars rests solely in the hand of God. In vv. 21-28 obedience to authority is emphasized and Muslims are warned that the weakness of a few among them might injure the whole cause of Islam. In v. 29 it is pointed out that undue love of wealth and progeny is a source of weakness for the community, so Muslims should keep their love of these things within proper bounds. In vv. 30 and 31, it is explained that obedience to God's commands will open for the Muslims the avenues to success and prosperity and will protect them against the machinations and intrigues of their enemies even as God protected the Holy Prophet against the secret plots of the Meccans. In vv. 32-35 we are told that the enemy on his part is proud of his numbers and military power and believes himself to be in the right and even invokes the wrath of God upon the liar. Such a determined enemy would not easily admit defeat. The next four verses (*viz.* 36-39) expose the false pretensions of the disbelievers which their actions belie. This discrepancy between the words and deeds of the disbelievers shows that their faith is a mere slave of their intellect and has found no place in their heart. The next verse impresses upon Muslims the necessity of preaching the message of Islam even in time of war. In vv. 41-46 Muslims are further encouraged with the promise that the war in which they are now engaged will not end in stalemate but will be fought to a finish. Even more wars will be fought and success will continue to attend Muslims. In vv. 47-51 obedience to authority and endurance and unity of action are enjoined on the Muslims who are warned not to get disheartened by the mischievous activities of the hypocrites.

The next ten verses deal with the sanctity of treaty obligations and Muslims are told that disbelievers will repeatedly violate their agreements during the wars but this should not incite them to a breach of their obligations, and that they should disabuse their minds of the misconception that they would, in any way, suffer by not avenging a breach of agreement by disbelievers by a corresponding violation of an obligation on their part, because if they continue to observe good morals, they are sure to win ultimately. But the observance of good morals should also be accompanied by suitable preparation for war, because this also is in accordance with the divine law. The next two verses i.e. vv. 62 and 63 contain the injunction that if, during hostilities, disbelievers sue for peace, their offer should not be rejected. Then if they violate the terms of peace mutually agreed upon and re-start hostilities, it will be to the advantage of Muslims who will not, in any way, suffer on account of this fresh breach of trust on the part of the disbelievers. This injunction implies a hint to the Truce of Ḥudaibiya when a breach of treaty obligations by the disbelievers led to the fall of Mecca. In vv. 64-67 it is said that God has created love and unity in the hearts of Muslims for one another. This is a divine favour which helps the believers to win victory against heavy odds. Muslims should not therefore become discouraged by the smallness of their numbers. In the next five verses i.e. vv. 68-72 Muslims are told that in their wars captives will fall into their hands ; they should treat them with kindness. In vv. 73-76 they are advised to behave all the more affectionately towards one another in time of war and disturbance as do the disbelievers ; for whereas they are under divine grace the disbelievers are deprived of it.

The promises of victory given to Muslims in *Anfāl* are declared to have been fulfilled in vv. 1-6 of *Barā'at* where it is stated that Muslims have become masters of the whole of Arabia ; so the idolaters should go about the land and see for themselves whether or not the whole country has come under Muslim domination. In vv. 7-29 disbelievers are reprimanded for their repeated breach of treaties and agreements and Muslims are warned not to enter into any new treaty with them and also not to be afraid that their departure from Arabia would, in any way, adversely affect the prosperity of the country, because God Himself would provide for Muslims.

In vv. 30-37 mention is made of the Israelites, and Muslims are told that they should not think that after the conquest of Arabia wars have come to an end and that they would now be allowed to live in peace. They are told that on account of the intrigues and secret plots of Jews and Christians, a new series of wars is about to start. These people are really given to idolatry and cannot bear to see true and perfect Unity of God established in the earth. Moreover, they have become morally depraved. Islam will establish true equality and freedom. How can then a Christian government view with equanimity the establishment by its side of a government based on equality and freedom, whose proximity would make its subjects inclined to rebellion against it ? So having proper regard for the things which God has declared sacred, Muslims should make suitable preparations for the impending war.

As there was an interval between the revelation of the first 37 verses of the *Sūra* and those that follow, mention has been made in the latter verses about the fulfilment of the prophecy made in the former. In connection with this a brief description is given of the expedition to Tabūk and of the circumstances in which the prophecy referred to above was fulfilled. The hypocrites and those weak of faith among Muslims who were seized with the fear of the powerful kingdom of Kaiser are reprimanded. Their moral weakness is exposed, and Muslims are bidden not to accept their help, for even without their help God will grant victory to them over the kingdom of the Kaiser (this subject has been dealt with in fuller detail in Chapters *Rūm* and *Fath*). In this connection mention is made of the intrigues of the hypocrites to injure Muslims. Towards the close of the *Sūra*, it is emphasized that the Holy Prophet will succeed not by human aid but by the help of God, "the Lord of the Mighty Throne."

سُوْرَةُ الْاَنْفَالِ مَدَنِيَّةٌ (٨)

1. ^aIn the name of Allah, the Gracious, the Merciful.[1092]

بِسْمِ اللّٰهِ الرَّحْمٰنِ الرَّحِيْمِ ۝

2. They ask thee concerning the spoils. Say, 'The spoils *of war* belong to Allah and the Messenger. So fear Allah, and set things right among yourselves, and ^bobey Allah and His Messenger, if you are believers.'[1092A]

يَسْـَٔلُوْنَكَ عَنِ الْاَنْفَالِ قُلِ الْاَنْفَالُ لِلّٰهِ وَالرَّسُوْلِ فَاتَّقُوا اللّٰهَ وَاَصْلِحُوْا ذَاتَ بَيْنِكُمْ وَاَطِيْعُوا اللّٰهَ وَرَسُوْلَهٗۤ اِنْ كُنْتُمْ مُّؤْمِنِيْنَ ۝

---

^aSee 1 : 1.   ^b3 : 33 ; 4 : 60 ; 8 : 47 ; 9 : 71 ; 24 : 55.

1092. Commentary :

See 1 : 1.

1092A. Important Words :

انفال (spoils) is the plural of النفل which is derived from نفل . They say نفل الرجل فلانا *i.e.* the man gave to such a one a gift for which he expected no return. نفل الامام الجند means, the leader allotted the spoils to the soldiers. انفله النفل or نفله النفل means, he gave him the spoils of war. نفله also means, he gave him more than his portion or more than his due. النافلة (of which the plural is النوافل) means, spoils of war ; gift or a voluntary gift ; something done or recommended to be done voluntarily without its being obligatory ; a grand child, because he or she is over and above one's own children. نفل—*nafal* (of which the plural is انفال) means, spoils of war ; a free gift ; something extra or additional or in excess. النفل—*nafl* (of which the plural is النوافل) means, an act performed voluntarily, without its being obligatory (Aqrab). النفل (plural انفال) also means, such spoil or gain as comes in the form of God's favour without one having laboured for it or deserved it (Mufradāt).

Commentary :

This verse does not relate to the division of spoils. The law with regard to that is to be found in 8 : 42 below. The present verse relates only to the attainment of gains and spoils and not to their division. It was revealed after the Battle of Badr. Before that battle, God had promised the Muslims victory over one of the two parties of idolaters, either the caravan which was returning from Syria under the leadership of Abū Sufyān, or the Meccan army that had, under the leadership of Abū Jahl, marched out of Mecca to fight the Muslims. The Muslims were very weak at that time ; and, considering their extreme weakness, they naturally asked whether, in spite of the great disparity in numbers and resources between them and their enemy, they were to gain victory over the enemy and win spoils. The question was similar to that of Zachariah who, when given the glad tidings of a son, asked : *My Lord, how shall I have a son, when old age has overtaken me, and my wife is barren ?* (3 : 41). The question asked by Muslims in the verse under comment pertained not only to the encounter which took place at Badr but also to subsequent encounters which were sure to take place between the two parties. The Quran answers the question by saying, *The spoils belong to Allah and the Messenger,* meaning that God has decreed that Muslims

3. *aTrue* believers are only those whose hearts tremble when *the name of Allah* is mentioned, and who, *bwhen* His Signs are recited to them, have their faith increased thereby, and who put their trust in their Lord.[1093]

اِنَّمَا الْمُؤْمِنُوْنَ الَّذِيْنَ اِذَا ذُكِرَ اللّٰهُ وَجِلَتْ قُلُوْبُهُمْ وَاِذَا تُلِيَتْ عَلَيْهِمْ اٰيٰتُهٗ زَادَتْهُمْ اِيْمَانًا وَّعَلٰى رَبِّهِمْ يَتَوَكَّلُوْنَ ۝

4. *cWho* observe Prayer and *dspend* out of that which We have provided for them.[1094]

الَّذِيْنَ يُقِيْمُوْنَ الصَّلٰوةَ وَمِمَّا رَزَقْنٰهُمْ يُنْفِقُوْنَ ۝

5. *eThese* it is who are true believers. They have grades *of rank* with their Lord, as well as forgiveness and an honourable provision.[1095]

اُولٰٓئِكَ هُمُ الْمُؤْمِنُوْنَ حَقًّا ۚ لَهُمْ دَرَجٰتٌ عِنْدَ رَبِّهِمْ وَمَغْفِرَةٌ وَّرِزْقٌ كَرِيْمٌ ۝

---

*a*22 : 36.   *b*9 : 124.   *c*5 : 56 ; 9 : 71 ; 27 : 4 ; 31 : 5 ; 73 : 21.   *d*See 2 : 4.   *e*8 : 75.

---

should secure victories against their enemy and nothing can stop it.

The words : *So fear Allah and set things right among yourselves and obey Allah and His Messenger,* signify that though victories and spoils will come, yet there are three conditions for the fulfilment of this promise of victory. The first condition requires Muslims to be God-fearing ; the second lays down that their mutual relations should be cordial and they should live at peace and amity with one another; the third calls upon them to obey God and follow the instructions of the Holy Prophet. If Muslims fulfilled these three conditions, God would undoubtedly fulfil His promise of victory.

1093. Commentary :

The preceding verse ended with the words, *if you are believers,* and the present fittingly describes a sure sign of true belief necessary for the fulfilment of the promise of victory contained in the previous verse. If a person claims to be a believer in God but in practical life the name of God means nothing to him and quickens no chords in his heart, his belief is not a true one. Belief should be something real and living.

1094. Commentary :

This and the previous verse mention some of the qualities of true believers, to whom God has promised victory in 8 : 2 above. God will grant them victories, provided they, on their part, answer the description given in these verses. See also 2 : 4.

1095. Commentary :

The verse declares that only those who possess the qualities mentioned in the foregoing two verses are true believers in the sight of God, and then proceeds to say that true believers never go unrewarded. They will surely attain three things : (1) grades of rank with their Lord ; (2) forgiveness of sins; and (3) an honourable provision.

The verse also hints that the booty obtained during the war need not be consigned to flames, as the Law of Moses enjoined, but may be gladly consumed, for spoils lawfully obtained form " an honourable provision."

6. As *it was* thy Lord *Who* rightfully brought thee forth from thy house, while a party of the believers were averse, *therefore He helped thee against thy enemy.*[1096]

كَمَآ اَخْرَجَكَ رَبُّكَ مِنْۢ بَيْتِكَ بِالْحَقِّ وَاِنَّ فَرِيْقًا مِّنَ الْمُؤْمِنِيْنَ لَكٰرِهُوْنَ ۙ

7. They dispute with thee concerning the truth after it has become manifest, as though they are being driven to death while they actually see *it*.[1097]

يُجَادِلُوْنَكَ فِى الْحَقِّ بَعْدَ مَا تَبَيَّنَ كَاَنَّمَا يُسَاقُوْنَ اِلَى الْمَوْتِ وَهُمْ يَنْظُرُوْنَ ؕ

1096. Important Words:

The particle كَ (as) ordinarily meaning " just as " or " like unto " is also sometimes used in the sense of " as " or " since " or " because." The Arabs say كَمَا تُطِيعُ اللهُ يُدْخِلْكَ الْجَنَّةَ *i.e.* as you obey Allah, so He will make you enter Heaven (Muḥīṭ).

Commentary:

There has been much difference of opinion about the significance of the word كَمَا (as) occurring in the beginning of this verse and briefly treated under Important Words above. Preferably the word has been used here in the sense of " as " or " since " in which case the words نَصْرُكَ عَلَى اعدائك (therefore He helped thee against thy enemies) would be taken to be understood at the end of the verse, as shown in the text. If, however, the word كَ is taken in its ordinary sense of " just as, " then the verse would be interpreted as providing an illustration of how God grants victories to His servants and bestows spoils and honourable provision on them (see the promises contained in 8 : 2, 5 above). In this case the verse could be rendered as : " God grants victories and spoils to His servants and bestows on them honourable provision just as He did when He brought thee forth from thy house, etc."

The expression بالحق (rightfully) refers to the fact that it was by divine command, and under divine revelation, that the Holy Prophet went forth from Medina to meet the enemy.

The verse thus signifies that, as the Holy Prophet had come forth by God's own command, and under His special revelation, therefore God could not forsake him ; so He helped him against the enemy.

The verse relates to the Battle of Badr. When Muslims came forth from Medina, they did not know that they would have to fight a Meccan army. So they did not come fully prepared for battle. Hence, when on the way the Holy Prophet revealed to them the fact that they would have to fight the Meccan army, they asked him why he had not told them so at Medina, so that they might have come prepared to meet the enemy. Their anxiety was not for themselves but for the Holy Prophet whom they loved more than their lives. Hence, in their condition of unpreparedness, they were unwilling to expose him to danger. That the Muslims were anxious for the sake of the Holy Prophet and not for themselves and that it was his going forth that they did not like is clear from the verse itself which uses the words " brought thee forth " and not " brought you forth." The verse thus implies that when the Companions of the Holy Prophet were so anxious about their beloved Master, God, Whose Messenger he was, could not leave him unprotected ; His love for him was certainly greater than that of his Companions.

1097. Commentary:

This verse refers not to the Companions of the Holy Prophet, as wrongly understood by

8. And *a*remember *the time* when Allah promised you one of the two parties that it should be yours, and you wished that the one without sting should be yours, but Allah desired to establish the truth by His words and to cut off the root of the disbelievers,[1098]

وَاِذْ يَعِدُكُمُ اللّٰهُ اِحْدَى الطَّآئِفَتَيْنِ اَنَّهَا لَكُمْ وَ تَوَدُّوْنَ اَنَّ غَيْرَ ذَاتِ الشَّوْكَةِ تَكُوْنُ لَكُمْ وَيُرِيْدُ اللّٰهُ اَنْ يُّحِقَّ الْحَقَّ بِكَلِمٰتِهٖ وَيَقْطَعَ دَابِرَ الْكٰفِرِيْنَ ۝

*a*8 : 43.

some Commentators, but to his enemies. There is absolutely no evidence in history to show that the Holy Prophet's Companions disputed with him with regard to fighting the enemy. On the contrary, it is expressly related that when before the Battle of Badr, he consulted them, they all expressed their readiness and even eagerness to accompany him and fight the enemy wherever he might take them (Hishām, ii. 13). Even the disbelievers who came out to fight the Muslims admitted that the latter looked like so many " seekers of death " on the field of battle (Ṭabarī). What the verse, therefore, means is simply this that as the enemies of Islam abhorred the truth as one abhors death, so, as a result of this, they were going to be punished with death itself.

1098. Important Words:

الشَّوْكَة (sting) is derived from شَاك . They say شَاكَنِى الشَّوْك *i.e.* the thorn hurt or wounded me or it pierced my body. الشَّوْكَة is both the noun-infinitive from شَاك and the singular of الشَّوْك (thorns, spines, etc.). الشَّوْكَة means, thorn ; sting ; point of a spear, etc. ; any weapon or weapons ; sharpness of weapons ; strength or might or vehemence thereof in war and fighting (Lane & Aqrab).

Commentary :

The "two parties " mentioned in the verse refer to (1) the Meccan army that had come forth to fight the Muslims, and (2) the Meccan caravan that was returning from the north and proceeding home. The former, besides being much larger in number, was heavily armed and very well-equipped ; while the caravan was only lightly armed. Both belonged to Mecca and were equally hostile to Islam.

The verse signifies that as Allah had already made a promise to the Holy Prophet that He would give victory to Muslims over one of the two Meccan parties, *viz.*, the caravan or the army, so against all hope He granted them victory in fulfilment of His promise. This shows that while yet at Medina, the Holy Prophet had been informed by God of the possible attack by the Meccan army, for without this Allah could not refer to " one of the two parties," but that the Holy Prophet kept the matter secret. The words, *thy Lord Who rightfully brought thee forth from thy house, while a party of the believers were averse* (8 : 6 above), also show that at Medina the Holy Prophet had undoubtedly received divine revelation informing him of the coming attack by the enemy and that it was God Who had ordered the Holy Prophet to come forth. The above-quoted words also hint that the Holy Prophet kept this information secret, revealing it to only a few of his chosen comrades.

The words غَيْرَ ذَاتِ الشَّوْكَة (without sting) imply that the Muslims wanted to meet the party that was without sting (*i.e.* the caravan) which they could easily overcome but that God desired to bring about an encounter with the army which could not be easily conquered, and His object in doing so was *to establish the truth by His words and to cut off*

9. ᵃThat He might establish the truth and bring to naught that which is false, although the guilty might dislike it.¹⁰⁹⁹

لِيُحِقَّ الْحَقَّ وَيُبْطِلَ الْبَاطِلَ وَلَوْ كَرِهَ الْمُجْرِمُوْنَ ۝

10. ᵇWhen you implored the assistance of your Lord, and He answered you, *saying*, 'I will assist you with a thousand of the angels, following one another.'¹¹⁰⁰

اِذْ تَسْتَغِيْثُوْنَ رَبَّكُمْ فَاسْتَجَابَ لَكُمْ اَنِّیْ مُمِدُّكُمْ بِاَلْفٍ مِّنَ الْمَلَئِكَةِ مُرْدِفِيْنَ ۝

11. And ᶜAllah made it only as glad tidings, and that your hearts might thereby be set at rest. But help comes from Allah alone; surely, Allah is Mighty, Wise.¹¹⁰¹

وَمَا جَعَلَهُ اللّٰهُ اِلَّا بُشْرٰی وَلِتَطْمَئِنَّ بِهٖ قُلُوْبُكُمْ وَمَا النَّصْرُ اِلَّا مِنْ عِنْدِ اللّٰهِ اِنَّ اللّٰهَ عَزِيْزٌ حَكِيْمٌ ۝

ᵃ10 : 83.   ᵇ3 : 124.   ᶜ3 : 127.

---

the root of the disbelievers, so that the prophecies with regard to the destruction of the enemy might be fulfilled that day, and their fulfilment against all hope might become the means of establishing the truth of Islam. For a more detailed account of the Battle of Badr see notes on 3 : 14 & 8 : 42-45.

1099. Commentary:

The words, *establish the truth,* used in the preceding verse have been repeated here for the sake of emphasis and for vividly contrasting the idea contained in these words with that of those that follow, *i.e., bring to naught that which is false.*

1100. Important Words:

تَسْتَغِيْثُوْنَ (you implored the assistance) is derived from غَاثَ. They say غَاثَهُ or اَغَاثَهُ *i.e.* he helped, assisted or succoured him; He God) removed from him trouble or affliction. غَوْثٌ or غَوَاثٌ means, a cry for aid or succour. غِيَاثٌ means, aid or succour; deliverance from difficulty or distress. اِسْتَغَاثَهُ means, he sought or desired aid or succour of him; or he called for his aid or succour or assistance (Lane & Aqrab).

مُرْدِفِيْنَ (following one another) is derived from اِرْدَفَ which is derived from رَدَفَ. They say رَدَفَهُ *i.e.* he rode behind him on the same beast; or he or it followed or came after him or it. اِرْدَفَ signifies the same as رَدَفَ. They say اِرْدَفَهُ اَمْرٌ *i.e.* an event happened to him afterwards; or an event came upon him suddenly and unexpectedly so as to overwhelm him. اِرْدَفَ الشَّیْءَ بِشَیْئٍ means, he made the thing follow another thing. رَدِيْف means, one who rides behind another on the same beast; a star which is rising when its opposite star is setting or *vice versa.* رِدْف means, sequence or consequence of a thing or event; followers or assistants or auxiliaries; night and day following each other; the star that follows another star. So مُرْدِفِيْنَ means, following one another (Lane & Aqrab).

Commentary:

For the advent of angels, see 3 : 125—127 and 6 : 159. Also see 2 : 31.

1101. Commentary:

See note on 3 : 127. As an intermediary means is sometimes likely to be confused with the real source of help which is Almighty God,

2   12. ^aWhen He caused sleep to come upon you as a *sign of* security from Him, and He sent down water upon you from the clouds, that thereby He might purify you, and remove from you the filth of Satan, and that He might strengthen your hearts and make *your* steps firm therewith.¹¹⁰²

اِذْ يُغَشِّيْكُمُ النُّعَاسَ اَمَنَةً مِّنْهُ وَيُنَزِّلُ عَلَيْكُمْ مِّنَ السَّمَآءِ مَآءً لِّيُطَهِّرَكُمْ بِهِ وَيُذْهِبَ عَنْكُمْ رِجْزَ الشَّيْطٰنِ وَلِيَرْبِطَ عَلٰى قُلُوْبِكُمْ وَيُثَبِّتَ بِهِ الْاَقْدَامَ ۝

---

*a*3 : 155.

---

the Quran takes particular care to remind Muslims that the real source of all help and all power is God alone.

1102. Important Words:

رِجْز (filth) is derived from رَجَزَ. They say رَجَزَ النَّاقَةُ *i.e.* the she-camel had the disease of convulsive motion in the legs or thighs. رَجَزَتِ الرِّيحُ means, the wind was continuous or lasting. رِجْز means, commotion or agitation or convulsion ; consecutiveness of motions ; punishment that agitates by its vehemence and occasions vehement consecutive commotions ; conduct that leads to punishment ; sin ; uncleanness or filth ; polytheism or worship of idols ; the Devil and his suggestions ; plague or pestilence (Lane).

Commentary :

Before a battle, especially an important one, begins, there is generally great uneasiness and disquietude among the contestants; their hearts throb with anxiety, and sleep vanishes. So the verse mentions the coming of sleep on the battle-field of Badr as a sign of God's favour. God caused sleep to come upon Muslims with the result that their anxiety was removed, that they were inspired with a feeling of confidence and security and that it had a soothing effect on their minds. This mental state proved highly helpful and materially contributed to their success.

The second favour mentioned in the verse pertains to the falling of rain. God caused rain to fall, which, as the verse points out, served *four* useful purposes : Firstly, it purified the Muslims because, seeing this token of God's help, their faith in God was strengthened, with the result that their hearts, being filled with faith, were purified. Secondly, it dispelled from them the filth of Satan *i.e.* thirst. In the Quran, thirst has been figuratively described as a pang due to Satan or the Devil ; for instance, it is related that when Job was stricken with the pangs of thirst, he prayed to God, saying: *Satan has smitten me with affliction and torment* (38 : 42), whereupon God accepted his prayer, saying: *Strike thy riding beast with thy foot. Here is cool water to wash with and a drink* (38 : 43). So the removal of "the filth of Satan" signifies removal of thirst or the pangs of extreme thirst. The word "Satan" may also signify " those who are of Satan, " *i.e.*, the friends or associates of Satan. Taken in this sense, the clause would mean : " God dispelled from you the attack of the wicked people," the hint being that the rain proved a means of dispelling the attack of the Quraish, inasmuch as it rendered the hard ground occupied by the Meccan army slippery, thus preventing the enemy from making a successful attack on the Muslims. Thirdly, the rain strengthened the hearts of the Faithful. This was due to their faith being reinforced by witnessing signs of God's special assistance. Fourthly, the rain helped to make the steps of the Muslims firm for, as mentioned in books of history, the ground occupied by the

13. When thy Lord revealed to the angels, *saying,* ' I am with you ; so give firmness to those who believe. I will cast terror into the hearts of those who disbelieve. Smite, then, the upper parts of *their* necks, and smite off all finger-tips.' [1103]

اِذۡ یُوۡحِیۡ رَبُّکَ اِلَی الۡمَلٰٓئِکَۃِ اَنِّیۡ مَعَکُمۡ فَثَبِّتُوا الَّذِیۡنَ اٰمَنُوۡا ؕ سَاُلۡقِیۡ فِیۡ قُلُوۡبِ الَّذِیۡنَ کَفَرُوا الرُّعۡبَ فَاضۡرِبُوۡا فَوۡقَ الۡاَعۡنَاقِ وَاضۡرِبُوۡا مِنۡہُمۡ کُلَّ بَنَانٍ ﴿۱۲﴾

14. [a]That is because they have opposed Allah and His Messenger. And whoso opposes Allah and His Messenger, then Allah is surely severe in retribution.

ذٰلِکَ بِاَنَّہُمۡ شَآقُّوا اللّٰہَ وَرَسُوۡلَہٗ ۚ وَمَنۡ یُّشَاقِقِ اللّٰہَ وَرَسُوۡلَہٗ فَاِنَّ اللّٰہَ شَدِیۡدُ الۡعِقَابِ ﴿۱۳﴾

---

[a]6 : 116 ; 47 : 33 ; 59 : 5.

Muslims was sandy, so the rain made it hard, and the Muslims were able to tread it with firm steps. All these factors contributed to the success of the Muslims.

The reader should note the beautiful order in the words of this verse. It begins with the purification of the heart (the first purpose served by the rain) and ends with the establishing of the steps and making them firm (the fourth purpose served by the rain) *i.e.* the favour of God descended on the *heart* and then, as it were, travelled down to the *feet.*

1103. **Important Words :**

فَوۡق (upper part) is derived from فَاق. They say فَاقَهُمۡ *i.e.* he was or became above them. So فَوۡق means, the location or place that is above or over a person or a thing. They say فَوۡقَهٗ رَاسَهٗ *i.e.* his upper part is his head (Lane).

Commentary :

This verse shows that the angels are, as it were, intermediaries between God and men. It is through them that God's assistance comes to men.

The verse also hints that there are some angels whose function is to strengthen the hearts of good men and make them firm, while there are others who are deputed to cast terror into the hearts of wicked men. So God bade the former class of angels to strengthen the hearts of the believers and told them that He would cast terror into the hearts of the disbelievers through the other class of angels.

God instructed the believers to strike the disbelievers at " the upper parts of their necks" because the upper part of the neck, *i.e.,* that which is just below the head, is considered to be the best point for dealing an effective blow with the sword. This order related to such of the enemy as deserved to be killed and without killing whom the Muslims could not defend themselves. The striking on the " finger-tips " was meant to incapacitate the enemy and make them unfit for fighting. This order thus related to those of the enemy who, so far as possible, were to be spared with the infliction of minimum injury. Both these orders were faithfully carried out, for although the Muslims were very weak at Badr, they were able to kill 70 of the disbelievers, mostly leaders, and take as many prisoners, while the enemy could kill only 14 of them.

15. ^aThat *is your punishment*, taste it then ; and *know* that for disbelievers there is the punishment of the Fire.' 1104

16. O ye who believe ! ^bwhen you meet those who disbelieve, advancing in force, turn not *your* backs to them. 1105

17. And whoso turns his back to them on such a day, unless manœuvring for battle or turning to *join another* company, he indeed draws upon himself the wrath of Allah, and Hell shall be his abode. And an evil resort it is. 1106

ذٰلِكُمْ فَذُوْقُوْهُ وَاَنَّ لِلْكٰفِرِيْنَ عَذَابَ النَّارِ ۞

يٰٓاَيُّهَا الَّذِيْنَ اٰمَنُوْۤا اِذَا لَقِيْتُمُ الَّذِيْنَ كَفَرُوْا زَحْفًا فَلَا تُوَلُّوْهُمُ الْاَدْبَارَ ۞

وَمَنْ يُّوَلِّهِمْ يَوْمَئِذٍ دُبُرَهٗۤ اِلَّا مُتَحَرِّفًا لِّقِتَالٍ اَوْ مُتَحَيِّزًا اِلٰى فِئَةٍ فَقَدْ بَآءَ بِغَضَبٍ مِّنَ اللهِ وَمَأْوٰىهُ جَهَنَّمُ ۥ وَبِئْسَ الْمَصِيْرُ ۞

---

^a22 : 23 ; 34 : 43.   ^b8 : 46 ; 47 : 5.

1104. Commentary :

In this verse God refers to two punishments for disbelievers, one in this life, and the other in the life to come. When the threat with regard to the punishment of this life had come to pass, it was quite reasonable to expect that the threat with regard to the punishment in the next life would also come to pass. Similarly, God had made two promises to believers : *firstly*, the promise of victory and success in this life ; *secondly*, the promise of bliss in the life to come. When the former had been fulfilled in a most amazing manner, the latter would also be similarly fulfilled.

1105. Important Words :

زحفا (advancing in force) is derived from زحف *i.e.* he walked, marched or went on foot little by little ; he crept or crawled along ; or he went leisurely or heavily ; or he walked or moved with an effort ; or he dragged himself along upon the ground. They say زحف العسكر meaning, the army moved heavily on account of its great numbers. زحف means, an army or military force marching slowly or heavily by reason of their multitude ; a numerous

army (Lane & Aqrab).

Commentary :

The word زحفا (advancing in force) qualifies and refers to the believers and not the disbelievers, as supposed by some Commentators. The following verse, as well as the wording of the present one, makes the reference positively clear.

When a Muslim army (not a small detachment) meets the enemy, they are strictly forbidden to flee from the field of battle. They must fight and go on fighting till they win or die ; there is no third course open to them. This command constitutes a great secret of success, besides being a sure source of self-discipline.

1106. Important Words :

متحيزا (turning) is derived from تحيز which is derived from حاز. They say حازه *i.e.* he drew, collected or gathered it together. حاز الابل means, he drove the camels. تحيز or تحوز means, he or it writhed or twisted about and turned over and over ; or he or it was restless, not remaining still on the ground ; or he withdrew or retired to a distance ; or he drew back. تحيز اليهم means, he turned or

18. So you killed them not, but it was Allah Who killed them. And thou threwest not when thou didst throw, but it was Allah Who threw, *that ᵃHe might overthrow the disbelievers* and that He might confer on the believers a great favour from Himself. Surely, Allah is All-Hearing, All-Knowing.¹¹⁰⁷

فَلَمْ تَقْتُلُوهُمْ وَلَكِنَّ اللهَ قَتَلَهُمْ ۚ وَمَا رَمَيْتَ اِذْ رَمَيْتَ وَلَكِنَّ اللهَ رَمٰى ۚ وَلِيُبْلِيَ الْمُؤْمِنِيْنَ مِنْهُ بَلَاءً حَسَنًا ۚ اِنَّ اللهَ سَمِيْعٌ عَلِيْمٌ ۝

19. That *is what happened*; and *know* that Allah is He Who weakens the design of the disbelievers.

ذٰلِكُمْ وَاَنَّ اللهَ مُوْهِنُ كَيْدِ الْكٰفِرِيْنَ ۝

ᵃ33 : 12.

---

withdrew or retired or joined himself to them (company of men). حيز also means, he turned aside or withdrew to his place or his proper place. حيز means, a place in which a thing is; the proper or natural place of a thing; the container or receptacle of anything (Lane).

فئة (company) is derived either from فاو *i.e.* he struck or smote or clove, or from فاء *i.e.* he returned, or he returned to a good state or condition. The word فئة means, a party, division or distinct body; or a company or congregated body of men; or a party or division of men; or a company of soldiers who fight in the rear of another party or company and to whom the latter has recourse in the case of fear or defeat; or a company of men who (in war) have recourse for aid, one to another (Lane).

Commentary:

The verse is important inasmuch as it defines and describes the circumstances in which an apparent retreat or withdrawal of a Muslim force against an enemy force is allowable. Such a retreat is allowed only on two distinct conditions: *firstly* as a war strategy or a battle manœuvre when a fighting force shifts its position not to fly but to hoodwink the enemy or to occupy a better position; *secondly*, when a force decides to fall back to join the main army or another Muslim force before giving battle to the enemy. No other retreat or withdrawal is allowed. Muslims must either win or die. Those who turn their backs incur the wrath of God and "Hell shall be their abode."

The words, *and Hell shall be his abode*, have a double significance: (1) that those who turn back from the battle-field, except in the circumstances stated above, shall be awarded the punishment of Hell-fire in the Hereafter; (2) that although such run-aways think that by turning back from the field of battle they will find security from danger, the truth is that they will thereby be running into the very jaws of fire, for such ignominious defeat will embolden the enemy against them and will open the doors of their persecution wider still.

A fight that begins with a single individual (a divine Messenger) arrayed against the entire forces of the world cannot possibly allow at a later stage the retreat of a believing party against a disbelieving host on the basis of disparity in numbers. Where true faith comes in, numbers do not and indeed cannot count. It must be a fight to the finish, for what does a believer await except one of the two good things—victory or martyrdom, (9 : 52)?

1107. Important Words:

ليبلي (that He might confer). يبلي is

derived from بلاء which is derived from بلا. They say بلاه or ابلاه *i.e.* he tried, proved or tested him with something good or evil. ابلاه الله بلاء حسنا means, God did to him a good deed. ابليته معروفا means, I conferred upon him a favour or benefit. بلاء means, the act of trying or testing; a trial or a test; an affliction of any kind by which one's patience or any other virtue is tried or proved or tested; a benefit, favour or blessing; grief; imposition of a difficult or troublesome thing. بلاء حسن means, a great benefit or favour or blessing of God or a good gift of God. الابلاء signifies trying, proving or testing with something; seeking and desiring; choosing or selecting (Lane).

Commentary :

The words, *So you killed them not, but it was Allah Who killed them,* signify that the victory at Badr was not due to any effort on the part of the Muslims; it was purely an act of God. Thus, as enjoined in the preceding verse, there is no justification for Muslims to flee from a battle-field.

The Battle of Badr, fought in the second year of Hijra, began with single combats; then there was a general attack. At this juncture the Holy Prophet took a handful of pebbles and cast them towards the enemy. That was a token for the help of God to come, just as striking the waters of the sea with the rod by Moses was a signal for God's aid to arrive. When the Holy Prophet cast the pebbles, there rose a strong gale which, blowing directly in the direction of the enemy, blinded their eyes with sand and thus contributed to their discomfiture and the victory of the Muslims. It is to this incident that the words, *it was Allah Who threw,* refer, hinting that really it was the hand of God, and not the hand of the Prophet, which cast the pebbles,

and that the victory was due to God coming to the help of the Muslims.

The reader should note that while speaking of the Companions of the Holy Prophet in the words, *you killed them not,* the verse ascribes no act to the Companions, but simply denies their having killed the enemy, whereas in the case of the throwing of the pebbles by the Holy Prophet the verse says, *thou threwest not when thou didst throw, but it was Allah Who threw,* thus hinting that although victory came from God, yet the Holy Prophet also had a share in the affair. He contributed his share in the form of earnest prayers which drew the help of God.

The throwing of a handful of pebbles and sand by the Holy Prophet bears a remarkable resemblance to the striking of the waters by Moses with the rod. Just as in the latter case the act of Moses was a signal for the wind to blow, which led to the drowning of Pharaoh and his hosts in the sea, similarly, the throwing of a handful of pebbles by the Holy Prophet was a signal for a strong wind to blow which led to the destruction of Abū Jahl (of whom the Holy Prophet spoke as the Pharaoh of his people) and his host in the desert. Again, after the Battle of Badr, the bodies of Abū Jahl and other leaders of the Quraish were cast into the bottom of a pit or an old well, and thus the similarity of the fate of Abū Jahl with that of Pharaoh was completed; for just as the latter together with his host was drowned into the depths of the sea, so was the former with his comrades cast into the bottom of a well.

The reference in the words, *Allah is All-Hearing, All-Knowing,* is to the prayers of the Holy Prophet which God heard and accepted and in response to which He conferred such a signal victory on the Muslims.

20. ᵃIf you sought a judgement, then judgement has indeed come to you. And if you desist, it will be better for you ; but if you return *to hostility*, We *too* will return. And your party shall be of no avail at all to you, however numerous it be, and *know* that Allah is with the believers.¹¹⁰⁸

R. 3   21. O ye who believe ! obey ᵇAllah and His Messenger, and do not turn away from him while you hear *him speak*.¹¹⁰⁹

اِنْ تَسْتَفْتِحُوْا فَقَدْ جَآءَكُمُ الْفَتْحُ ۚ وَاِنْ تَنْتَهُوْا فَهُوَ خَيْرٌ لَّكُمْ ۚ وَاِنْ تَعُوْدُوْا نَعُدْ ۚ وَلَنْ تُغْنِيَ عَنْكُمْ فِئَتُكُمْ شَيْئًا وَّلَوْ كَثُرَتْ ۙ وَاَنَّ اللّٰهَ مَعَ الْمُؤْمِنِيْنَ ۝

يٰٓاَيُّهَا الَّذِيْنَ اٰمَنُوْٓا اَطِيْعُوا اللّٰهَ وَرَسُوْلَهٗ وَلَا تَوَلَّوْا عَنْهُ وَاَنْتُمْ تَسْمَعُوْنَ ۝

ᵃ32 : 29.   ᵇ3 : 33 ; 4 : 60 ; 8 : 47 ; 24 : 55.

1108. Important Words :

تَسْتَفْتِحُوْا (you sought a judgement) is derived from اِسْتَفْتَحَ which again is derived from فَتَحَ which means, he opened or he unlocked : فَتَحَ الْحَاكِمُ بَيْنَ النَّاسِ means, the judge or magistrate judged between the people. اِسْتَفْتَحَ means, he asked or sought or demanded victory ; or he asked or sought or demanded judgement (Lane & Aqrab).

Commentary :

The verse is addressed to the disbelievers who demanded the Sign of victory or God's judgement from the Holy Prophet. They said, "If you are a true Messenger of God, why does He not help you and grant you victory ? " They are here told that God's judgement in the form of victory has indeed come and that if they now desist from fighting, it will be well for them ; but if they return to war, God will show them further Signs of victory and they shall be defeated and brought low in spite of their great superiority in numbers and resources, for *Allah is with the believers.*

1109. Commentary :

As God was the source of all strength and the Prophet was a means thereof, so the Faithful are here enjoined to obey God and His Messenger. Muslims had by this time witnessed many Signs of God ; they had only just witnessed a mighty Sign in the Battle of Badr. Having witnessed so many Signs, it was incumbent on them to be obedient to God and His Messenger. Those who had taken part in the Battle of Badr were all true Muslims ; there was no hypocrite among them except perhaps one. But in future battles, there were to be hypocrites also ; hence there was the greater need for Muslims to be on their guard and to be more careful in the matter of obedience. The fact is that until the Battle of Badr, 'Abdullah bin Ubayy, the arch-hypocrite, and his confederates had been under the delusion that Islam was only a passing show and that the little group of Muslims would soon disappear. The victory at Badr therefore came to them as a severe shock, and their false hopes were shattered. So from this time onward, they became increasingly more active in their machinations against Islam and the Holy Prophet. Hence the need of an exhortation to Muslims to be ever obedient to God and His Messenger, for it was in obedience and in unity that lay the secret of their future success and prosperity.

22. And be not like those *who say, ' We hear ', but they hear not. [1110]

وَلَا تَكُوْنُوْا كَالَّذِيْنَ قَالُوْا سَمِعْنَا وَهُمْ لَا يَسْمَعُوْنَ ۛ

23. Surely, *the worst of beasts in the sight of Allah are the deaf *and the* dumb, who have no sense. [1111]

اِنَّ شَرَّ الدَّوَآبِّ عِنْدَ اللهِ الصُّمُّ الْبُكْمُ الَّذِيْنَ لَا يَعْقِلُوْنَ ۛ

24. And if Allah had known any good in them, He would certainly have made them hear. And if He *now* makes them hear, they will turn away, in aversion. [1112]

وَلَوْ عَلِمَ اللهُ فِيْهِمْ خَيْرًا لَّاَسْمَعَهُمْ ۖ وَلَوْ اَسْمَعَهُمْ لَتَوَلَّوْا وَّهُمْ مُّعْرِضُوْنَ ۛ

25. O ye who believe! *respond to Allah, and the Messenger when he calls you that he may give you life, and know that Allah comes in between a man and his heart, and that He it is unto Whom you will be gathered. [1113]

يٰٓاَيُّهَا الَّذِيْنَ اٰمَنُوا اسْتَجِيْبُوْا لِلهِ وَلِلرَّسُوْلِ اِذَا دَعَاكُمْ لِمَا يُحْيِيْكُمْ ۖ وَاعْلَمُوْٓا اَنَّ اللهَ يَحُوْلُ بَيْنَ الْمَرْءِ وَقَلْبِهٖ وَاَنَّهٗٓ اِلَيْهِ تُحْشَرُوْنَ ۛ

---

*2 : 94 ; 4 : 47.   *8 : 56 ; 98 : 7.   *3 : 33 ; 4 : 60 ; 8 : 47 ; 24 : 55.

1110. Commentary :

True Muslims are here warned against following the example of hypocrites, who say they listen but they listen not.

1111. Commentary :

The verse primarily refers to the hypocrites. They have ears but they listen not to the word of God, so truly speaking they are deaf ; they have tongues, but they do not seek after and inquire about the truth, so they are dumb ; they have hearts, but they do not ponder over the truth, so they have no sense and do not understand. Indeed, if the gifts of hearing and of speaking and of thinking are taken away from man, he is left no better than a beast. Nay, he virtually becomes "the worst of beasts" for, in spite of possessing the faculty and power of hearing and speaking and thinking, he does not use these powers.

1112. Commentary :

The expression اسمعهم (made them hear) in the first place mean that if God had known any good in them, He would have made them hear and accept the truth. The verse thus shows that it is only those whose hearts are wholly corrupt that are caused or allowed to go astray by God. Those in whose hearts there is any good are always led by God to the acceptance of the truth.

The second clause of the verse indicates that while Allah makes good men accept and follow guidance, He never forces anyone to go astray. The expression اسمعهم (makes them hear) in the second place, therefore, means that if in their present condition God should force them to accept the truth, the result would be that their hearts would remain unconverted and they would never become true Muslims.

1113. Commentary :

Though the verse enjoins the Faithful to respond to both Allah and His Messenger, it does not say "when they (Allah and His Messenger) call you" but simply "when he

26. And *beware of an affliction which will surely not smite those among you exclusively who have done wrong. And know that Allah is severe in requiting.[1114]

وَاتَّقُوْا فِتْنَةً لَّا تُصِيْبَنَّ الَّذِيْنَ ظَلَمُوْا مِنْكُمْ خَآصَّةً ۚ وَاعْلَمُوْا اَنَّ اللّٰهَ شَدِيْدُ الْعِقَابِ ۝

---

*11 : 114.

---

calls you." The pronoun "he" obviously refers to the Messenger, for it is the Messenger who actually calls. Calling by God is also through His Messenger. Or the singular pronoun "he" may be taken to refer to both Allah and the Messenger taken separately, *i.e.*, when Allah calls you or when the Messenger calls you.

The words, *that he may give you life*, embody a great truth. The calling of the Messenger is always for the purpose of giving life to those who believe. It must, however, be remembered that when the quickening of, or the giving of life to, the dead is ascribed to a Prophet of God, the words should be taken not in their physical but in their spiritual sense.

The words, *know that Allah comes in between a man and his heart*, are important. There are two powers in men, *firstly*, the will-power of the "I". This power has its seat in the mind and has, therefore, been referred to in the verse as "man." The second power lies in the heart. The "I" or the will-power, or in other words "the man," issues its command and it is for the heart to obey it. But an unpurified heart does not always obey the command emanating from the mind. The words, *Allah comes in between a man and his heart*, therefore signify that God has His position between the "I" and the heart. Man has not the power to purify his heart, *i.e.* he cannot make it obey the dictates of the "I", for he has no control over it. But God controls the heart and can purify it. So we should obey God that He

may purify our heart and make it follow the will of the "I". The expression is figurative and means that it is God alone Who can make the dictates of the "I" have the desired effect on the heart.

The verse also hints that one should always hasten to hear and obey a good call; for if one delays doing so, the law of God meant for those who hesitate to accept the truth and keep back from it is likely to come in, and make the heart rusty, with the result that it becomes all the more disinclined to accept the truth.

1114. Important Words:

فِتْنَة (affliction). See 2 : 192.

Commentary :

The verse embodies a great and important truth. It is not enough that you should become good yourselves. If you are surrounded by wicked and ungodly persons, you cannot escape the contagion and its consequences. Thus, even a good man may sometimes be overtaken by divine punishment, if he is living among wicked people and does not shun their society. Hence we should not only try to lead righteous lives ourselves, but should also endeavour to make others do the same. We should not only reform ourselves but try to reform the society in which we move and the people among whom we live. We cannot long enjoy safety if the houses surrounding ours are on fire.

27. And *a*remember *the time* when you were few *and* deemed weak in the land, *and* were in fear lest people should snatch you away, but He sheltered you and strengthened you with His help, and provided you with good things that you might be thankful.[1115]

28. O ye who believe! prove not false to Allah and the Messenger, nor prove false to your trusts knowingly.[1116]

29. And know that *b*your possessions and your children are but a trial and that it is Allah with Whom is a great reward.[1117]

وَاذْكُرُوۡۤا اِذْ اَنْتُمۡ قَلِيۡلٌ مُّسْتَضْعَفُوۡنَ فِى الۡاَرْضِ تَخَافُوۡنَ اَنۡ يَّتَخَطَّفَكُمُ النَّاسُ فَاٰوٰىكُمۡ وَاَيَّدَكُمۡ بِنَصْرِهٖ وَرَزَقَكُمۡ مِّنَ الطَّيِّبٰتِ لَعَلَّكُمۡ تَشْكُرُوۡنَ ۞

يٰۤاَيُّهَا الَّذِيۡنَ اٰمَنُوۡا لَا تَخُوۡنُوا اللّٰهَ وَالرَّسُوۡلَ وَتَخُوۡنُوۡۤا اَمٰنٰتِكُمۡ وَاَنْتُمۡ تَعْلَمُوۡنَ ۞

وَاعْلَمُوۡۤا اَنَّمَاۤ اَمْوَالُكُمۡ وَاَوْلَادُكُمۡ فِتْنَةٌ ۙ وَّ اَنَّ اللّٰهَ عِنْدَهٗۤ اَجْرٌ عَظِيۡمٌ ۞

---

*a*7 : 87.   *b*3 : 124; 64 : 16.

1115. Commentary:

Muslims are here told that as God saved them when they were weak in the land and were surrounded by wicked and mischievous people, so they should strive to save those who are weak and surrounded by dangers. The verse also hints that as Muslims will soon prosper and attain power; they should never forget the days of hardships through which they have passed *i.e.*, in the days of their power, they should never oppress the weak creatures of God but should always treat them with justice and mercy.

1116. Commentary:

The verse enjoins Muslims not to act faithlessly with regard to either the commandments of God or the rights of one another. Indeed, a Muslim should always be true to God and true to his fellow-beings.

It is significant that when speaking of being true to God, the verse directly says, *prove not false to Allah*, but when speaking of men the words used are, *prove not false to your trusts*.

This is to point out that whereas faithfulness to God is absolute and eternal, being based on the very creation of man, faithfulness to man springs from the trusts and obligations that one may form or enter into.

1117. Important Words:

فِتْنَةٌ (trial) is derived from فَتَنَ. They say فَتَنَهُ *i.e.* he tried or proved or tested him. So فِتْنَةٌ means, a trial meant to separate the good from the bad. See also 2 : 103, 192; 4 : 92 & 5 : 50, 72. Thus فِتْنَةٌ is anything that is a means of purification and advancement for the good and a means of exposure and downfall for the wicked.

Commentary:

As فِتْنَةٌ (trial) is a means of purification, our possessions and our children are called a "trial," because they are a means of our spiritual purification. It is by means of them that we are able to make sacrifices in the cause of religion and humanity. If we have no wealth, we cannot give it away in the service of God or of our fellow-creatures. If we have no

R. 4   30. O ye who believe ! *a*if you fear Allah, He will grant you a distinction and will remove your evils from you and will forgive you ; and Allah is *Lord* of great bounty.[1118]

يَاۤيُّهَا الَّذِيْنَ اٰمَنُوْۤا اِنْ تَتَّقُوا اللّٰهَ يَجْعَلْ لَّكُمْ فُرْقَانًا وَّيُكَفِّرْ عَنْكُمْ سَيِّاٰتِكُمْ وَيَغْفِرْ لَكُمْ ۚ وَاللّٰهُ ذُو الْفَضْلِ الْعَظِيْمِ ۝

31. And *remember the time* when the disbelievers plotted against thee that they might imprison thee or kill thee or expel thee. And *b*they planned and Allah *also* planned, and Allah is the best of planners.[1119]

وَاِذْ يَمْكُرُ بِكَ الَّذِيْنَ كَفَرُوْا لِيُثْبِتُوْكَ اَوْ يَقْتُلُوْكَ اَوْ يُخْرِجُوْكَ ۚ وَيَمْكُرُوْنَ وَيَمْكُرُ اللّٰهُ ۚ وَاللّٰهُ خَيْرُ الْمَاكِرِيْنَ ۝

---

*a*18 : 6 ; 64 : 10 ; 66 : 9.   *b*3 : 55 ; 27 : 51.

---

children, we will not be in a position to train them as good and pious men for the service of God and mankind. Moreover, if we have no children, we shall be free and shall have no obstacle to overcome ; and therefore our spending money in the cause of God will, in that case, not give us as much credit as it would do if we spent it while we had children. Thus, both our possessions and our children enable us to make sacrifices in the cause of God and our fellow-beings ; they are, therefore, a blessing, not a curse. But they may become a curse for the wicked, for whom the love of wealth and children proves a great stumbling-block.

The words, " a great reward ", signify that when God has conferred on us blessings like wealth and children without any endeavour on our part, He can bestow on us far greater rewards, if we strive in His cause and try to win His favour. But if the word فتنة (trial) is taken in a bad sense *i.e.* a stumbling block, then the words " a great reward " would signify that if our wealth and children prove a stumbling block for us, we should not allow them to stand in our way but should turn to God with Whom we will find a great reward for this sacrifice of ours.

1118. Important Words :

فُرْقَان (distinction) means : (1) that which enables one to distinguish between truth and falsehood and right and wrong ; (2) proof or evidence or argument ; (3) aid or victory ; (4) dawn (Lane). See also 2 : 54.

Commentary :

The word فُرْقَان (distinction) may be taken here in all the four senses mentioned under Important Words above. Firstly, if a man becomes God-fearing, he is given a light by means of which he is able to distinguish between right and wrong. Secondly, the righteous and the God-fearing are taught and vouchsafed proofs and arguments by God. They do not blindly believe in the truth of their religion but they are granted proofs and arguments for what they believe. Thirdly, God-fearing men receive aid and victory from God. Fourthly God removes from them the darkness of hardships and there dawns upon them the day of happiness and bliss.

1119. Important Words :

يُثْبِتُوْكَ (imprison thee). يُثْبِتُوْا is derived from اثبت which is derived from ثبت which means, it continued or subsisted or endured ;

or it remained fixed or stationary ; or it was or became constant, fast or established. اثبه means, he made it to continue or subsist or endure ; or he made it to remain fixed or stationary. They say اثبه جراحة i.e. a wound rendered him unable to move. ضربوه حتى اثبته means, they beat him so as to render him motionless. اثبه بوثاق means, he made him fast with a bond so that he could not move. So ليثبتوك (li-yuthbitū-ka) or ليثبتوك (li-yuthabbitū-ka), which is another reading of the word, means, that they might inflict upon thee a wound by reason of which thou shouldst not be able to rise or move about ; or that they might confine thee to thy place, i.e., imprison thee and prevent thy moving about (Lane).

Commentary :

The Holy Prophet bore resemblance to all the Prophets of God. At the Battle of Badr, God showed a miracle, similar to the miracle of Moses (see 8 : 18 above) while the present verse refers to a Sign which was like the Signs of Jonah and Jesus. At Mecca, the Quraish had a council-room called Dār al-Nadwa. There they used to hold their consultations against the Holy Prophet. When they learnt that Islam had spread to Medina, where converts to the New Faith were fleeing for refuge, Abū Jahl and other leaders of the Quraish held a meeting at Dār al-Nadwa in order to consider some decisive step to put an end to the New Movement. Various proposals were made at the meeting. One was that the Holy Prophet should be put under confinement i.e. imprisoned; another was that he should be expelled from the city ; yet another was that suitable men belonging to all the different tribes of the Quraish should be selected, and these should make a joint attack on the Holy Prophet and slay him. This last proposal was finally agreed upon, and the Holy Prophet's house was surrounded one dark night with the object of attacking him as soon as he came forth. But, being apprised by God of the coming danger,

the Holy Prophet had already made arrangements with Abū Bakr to flee from Mecca that very night. He, therefore, caused his nephew 'Alī to lie in his bed and himself prepared to leave. Those who had laid siege to the house occasionally peeped into the house and, mistaking 'Alī for the Holy Prophet, waited patiently for him outside. While thus waiting, it so happened that the watchers were overpowered by sleep, and the Holy Prophet, availing himself of the opportunity, departed from the house unnoticed. Abū Bakr was already waiting for him at some distance, and the two, bidding farewell to their beloved city, repaired, according to a pre-arranged plan, to a cave in a difficult mountain-top outside Mecca, where they took shelter. When the bloodthirsty Meccans knew of his escape, they quickly prepared to pursue him. They actually followed him, tracing his steps, till they reached the very cave where the Holy Prophet and Abū Bakr were in hiding ; but, as the report says, already a spider had spun its cobweb across the mouth of the cave. Thus confronted, it never occurred to them that the Holy Prophet had taken shelter in that out-of-the-way cave whose entrance looked as if it had not been used for a long time. They argued that the tracer who had brought them to the mouth of the cave was at fault and it so happened that none of them so much as glanced into the cave to make sure whether or not anybody was inside. Thus it was that God saved His beloved servant from the clutches of the ravenous wolves that so savagely pursued him. Being unable to find any further trace of him, they returned to Mecca. As, however, a heavy price was set on his head, and it was announced that whoever brought him, dead or alive, would have a reward of 100 camels, people pursued him in all directions ; but here too God came to his help and none could lay hands on him. After remaining hidden in the cave for three days, the Holy Prophet and his devoted Companion resumed

32. And ^awhen Our verses are recited to them, they say, 'We have heard. If we wished we could certainly utter the like of this. This is nothing but *mere* tales of the ancients.'[1120]

وَإِذَا تُتْلَىٰ عَلَيْهِمْ آيَاتُنَا قَالُوا قَدْ سَمِعْنَا لَوْ نَشَآءُ لَقُلْنَا مِثْلَ هَٰذَا إِنْ هَٰذَا إِلَّا أَسَاطِيرُ الْأَوَّلِينَ ٣٢

---

^a6 : 26 ; 68 : 16 ; 83 : 41.

---

their flight to Medina and, avoiding the better-known tracks, hastened to their destination where the Muslim community of the *Anṣār* and such of the *Muhājirīn* as had already reached there accorded them a most cordial welcome.

Thus, the Quraish practically resorted to all the three plans that have been mentioned in the verse under comment: (1) they confined the Holy Prophet when they laid siege to his house at night ; (2) they drove him from his native city ; and (3) they attempted to carry out their resolution of *Dār al-Nadwa* to put him to death. But God baffled every attempt of theirs, and he who had fled from their town as a helpless fugitive returned to them eight years later as an illustrious victor, at whose hands they cringingly sought, and readily obtained, pardon. They planned and plotted against him, as the verse says ; but their plans and intrigues led to their own ruin. They drove him from their city, but his very flight led him to power and prosperity and proved the cause of their destruction. Some time after the flight a Meccan army proudly issued forth from Mecca and proceeded to Badr, a place near Medina, little dreaming that it was going to its own ruin. All this was arranged and decreed by God, Who is " the best of planners." He so arranged that the army which had come forth with such pomp and display of power returned from Badr an utterly routed and disorderly rabble, leaving its proud leaders either dead on the battlefield or captives in the hands of those whom they hated and despised.

It should be noted that the word مكر (plan) used in this verse does not necessarily mean an evil plot. It is general in its significance, comprising both good and evil planning, according to the purpose for which it is contrived. The plots of the enemies of truth were, of course, evil ; but God never has recourse to evil design. He planned things in such a way as to frustrate the evil designs of the enemy and make the cause of Islam triumph. The very fact that the Quran prefixes the word خير (best) to the word ماكرين (planners) shows that the word has been used in a good sense with respect to God ; for the word خير (meaning good, better or best) is invariably prefixed to words which are used in a good sense. See also 3 : 55.

The present verse has been placed most fittingly between the verses relating to the Battle of Badr ; for after speaking of that great battle, the Quran reminds the Holy Prophet and his Companions of the plots of the enemy against him and draws his attention to the wonderful way in which God had helped him at the time of his flight, frustrating the designs of the enemy and turning them to the advantage of Islam. He would do it again when needed and the Battle of Badr was another instance of the kind.

1120. Commentary :

The disbelievers alleged that they could produce a composition like that of the Quran. It was, however, nothing but an empty boast on their part, which they never attempted to carry into effect ; and the challenge of the Quran, which declared that they would never be able to produce even a short Chapter like any Chapter of the Quran, has ever remained

33. And *remember the time* when they said, ' O Allah, if this be indeed the truth from Thee, then rain down upon us stones from heaven or bring down upon us a grievous punishment.' 1121

وَإِذْ قَالُوا اللّٰهُمَّ إِنْ كَانَ هٰذَا هُوَ الْحَقَّ مِنْ عِنْدِكَ فَأَمْطِرْ عَلَيْنَا حِجَارَةً مِّنَ السَّمَاءِ أَوِ ائْتِنَا بِعَذَابٍ أَلِيمٍ ۝

34. But Allah would not punish them while thou wast among them, and ^aAllah would not punish them while they sought forgiveness. 1122

وَمَا كَانَ اللّٰهُ لِيُعَذِّبَهُمْ وَأَنْتَ فِيهِمْ وَمَا كَانَ اللّٰهُ مُعَذِّبَهُمْ وَهُمْ يَسْتَغْفِرُونَ ۝

^a11 : 4.

---

unanswered. The disbelievers also thought that the Quran contained nothing but the tales of the ancients. The verse under comment contradicts this assertion by drawing their attention to the powerful prophecies contained in the Quran which unmistakably prove it to be the word of God, it being beyond the power of man to produce a composition containing such powerful prophecies. The Battle of Badr, for instance, fulfilled many a mighty prophecy, foretold by the Quran (*e.g.* 54 : 45—47 ; 34 : 30, 31)—a fact which rendered it impossible for man to imitate a production like it, and which fully exposed the absurdity of the assertion that the Quran was nothing but tales of the ancients.

1121. Commentary :

This was the prayer which Abū Jahl, the leader of the disbelievers, offered to God at Badr and it was accepted. He prayed on that memorable day that God might destroy him and his party if the Prophet was in the right (Bukhārī, ch. on *Tafsīr*). Strange to say, not only were Abū Jahl and his companions punished at Badr by God but, as prayed for by Abū Jahl, even stones were rained down upon them ; for, when at the throwing of a handful of pebbles by the Holy Prophet (8 : 18), there arose a strong wind, it literally rained upon the disbelieving host hard pebbles from the desert.

1122. Commentary :

The verse embodies two basic protections against divine punishment : (1) a people are not punished when they have a God's Messenger living among them ; and (2) they are not punished when they are seeking forgiveness of God. At the Battle of Badr, the Holy Prophet was not " among " the disbelievers, for there the believers and the disbelievers formed two distinct and opposite parties. At Mecca, however, he was " among " them, for both he and his opponents lived under the same conditions and the same laws. Nor did the Quraish of Mecca enjoy the second protection at the Battle of Badr for, instead of asking forgiveness of God, they prayed that if Islam was a true religion, God might destroy them with a grievous punishment. The verse, therefore, hints that the Battle of Badr was the proper occasion for punishing the enemies of Islam.

35. And ^awhat excuse have they *now* that Allah should not punish them, when they hinder *men* from the Sacred Mosque, and they are not its *true* guardians ? ^bIts *true* guardians are only those who are righteous, but most of them know not.¹¹²³

وَمَا لَهُمْ اَلَّا يُعَذِّبَهُمُ اللّٰهُ وَهُمْ يَصُدُّوْنَ عَنِ الْمَسْجِدِ الْحَرَامِ وَمَا كَانُوْۤا اَوْلِيَآءَهٗ ۚ اِنْ اَوْلِيَآؤُهٗۤ اِلَّا الْمُتَّقُوْنَ وَلٰكِنَّ اَكْثَرَهُمْ لَا يَعْلَمُوْنَ ۝

36. And their prayer at the House is nothing but whistling and clapping of hands. ' Taste then the punishment because you disbelieved.'¹¹²⁴

وَمَا كَانَ صَلَاتُهُمْ عِنْدَ الْبَيْتِ اِلَّا مُكَآءً وَّتَصْدِيَةً ۚ فَذُوْقُوا الْعَذَابَ بِمَا كُنْتُمْ تَكْفُرُوْنَ ۝

^a22 : 26.   ^b10 : 63, 64.

1123. Commentary :

The verse purports to say that when the Quraish did not enjoy either of the two basic protections against divine punishment (see preceding verse), they were being rightly punished for their false beliefs and wicked deeds. The verse also says that the Quraish have no right to act as guardians of the Sacred Mosque. As guardians thereof, they ought to have been worshippers of the One True God ; but they have put idols even in the Sacred Mosque ; hence, far from having any right to act as its guardians, they deserve to be expelled therefrom and punished for the sacrilege.

The words, *Its true guardians are only those who are righteous*, contain a prophecy to the effect that soon Muslims would become guardians of the Sacred Mosque, the words, *most of them know not*, signifying that although most of the disbelievers do not at present think this announcement to be true, yet it would surely come to pass.

1124. Important Words :

مُكَآء (whistling) is the noun-infinitive from مَكَا (with واو as the last root letter). They say مَكَا الرَّجُل *i.e.* the man whistled with his

mouth ; or he brought together his fingers and blew through them, producing a whistling sound (Aqrab).

تَصْدِيَة (clapping of hands) is derived from صَدَّ (ṣaddā). They say صَدَّى يَدَيْه *i.e.* he clapped with his hands. So تَصْدِيَة means, clapping with the hands. الصَّدَى means, the sound or cry returned by a mountain, etc., when one shouts at it ; echo (Lane under صَدَى). Some authorities derive the word تَصْدِيَة from the root صَدَّ (he turned away), the word الصَّدّ signifying the face or front of the hand (Lane under صَدّ).

Commentary :

The verse describes the sacrilegious use of the Sacred Mosque by idolaters. Instead of using it for worship and devotion, they used it for talking and gossiping and for whistling and the clapping of hands.

The words, *And their prayer at the House is nothing but whistling*, etc. mean : (1) that even their acts of worship consisted of nothing but whistling, etc. ; or (2) instead of praying and performing acts of devotion, they passed their time in whistling, etc.

37. Surely, those who disbelieve, spend their wealth to turn *men* from the way of Allah. They will surely continue to spend it ; *but* then shall it become a *source of* regret for them, *and* ᵃthen shall they be overcome. And the disbelievers shall be gathered unto Hell ;¹¹²⁵

اِنَّ الَّذِيْنَ كَفَرُوْا يُنْفِقُوْنَ اَمْوَالَهُمْ لِيَصُدُّوْا عَنْ سَبِيْلِ اللّٰهِ فَسَيُنْفِقُوْنَهَا ثُمَّ تَكُوْنُ عَلَيْهِمْ حَسْرَةً ثُمَّ يُغْلَبُوْنَ ۢ وَالَّذِيْنَ كَفَرُوْا اِلٰى جَهَنَّمَ يُحْشَرُوْنَ ۟

38. ᵇThat God may separate the bad from the good, and put the bad, one upon another, and heap them up all together, *and* then cast them into Hell. These indeed are the losers.¹¹²⁶

لِيَمِيْزَ اللّٰهُ الْخَبِيْثَ مِنَ الطَّيِّبِ وَيَجْعَلَ الْخَبِيْثَ بَعْضَهٗ عَلٰى بَعْضٍ فَيَرْكُمَهٗ جَمِيْعًا فَيَجْعَلَهٗ فِيْ جَهَنَّمَ ۚ اُولٰٓئِكَ هُمُ الْخٰسِرُوْنَ ۟

39. Say to those who disbelieve, if they desist, that which is past will be forgiven them ; and if they return *thereto*, then verily the example of the former peoples has already gone *before them.*¹¹²⁷

قُلْ لِّلَّذِيْنَ كَفَرُوْٓا اِنْ يَّنْتَهُوْا يُغْفَرْ لَهُمْ مَّا قَدْ سَلَفَ ۚ وَاِنْ يَّعُوْدُوْا فَقَدْ مَضَتْ سُنَّتُ الْاَوَّلِيْنَ ۟

ᵃ3 : 13.   ᵇ3 : 180.

1125. Commentary :

The verse embodies two prophecies concerning disbelievers, *firstly*, that the wealth which the disbelievers were spending in their war against Islam would prove of no avail and would become a source of grief for them and they would suffer defeat ; *secondly*, that in the life to come they would be put in Hell as a result of their evil deeds. The first prophecy which related to the present life was clearly fulfilled, thus serving as evidence of the fact that the second prophecy, *i.e.*, the one with regard to the life to come, would also similarly come true.

1126. Commentary :

The words, *separate the bad from the good*, refer to the first part of the previous verse, giving the reason for the defeat and failure of the disbelievers. God would cause their war against

Islam to end in their defeat so that He migh distinguish the righteous from the unrighteou: Similarly, the latter part of this verse, *viz put the bad, one upon another, and heap them up all together, and then cast them into Hel* corresponds to the latter part of the previou verse, *viz., that the disbelievers shall be gathere unto Hell.* The words, *heap them up all togethe:* imply that as the disbelievers made a commo: cause against Islam, they would, as it were all be heaped up into a bundle and then throw: into the fire of Hell as one huge piece of fuel.

1127. Commentary :

After the Battle of Badr, in which the opponent of Islam suffered a crushing defeat, they ar once more invited to desist from fighting, an it is promised to them that if they ceas hostilities against Islam, their past offence will be forgiven them. But they are at th

40. And ^afight them until there is no persecution and religion is wholly for Allah. But if they desist, then surely Allah is Watchful of what they do.[1128]

وَقَاتِلُوهُمْ حَتّٰى لَا تَكُونَ فِتْنَةٌ وَّيَكُونَ الدِّيْنُ كُلُّهُ لِلّٰهِ ۚ فَاِنِ انْتَهَوْا فَاِنَّ اللّٰهَ بِمَا يَعْمَلُوْنَ بَصِيْرٌ ۝

41. ^bAnd if they turn their backs, then know that Allah is your Protector. What an excellent Protector and what an excellent Helper![1129]

وَاِنْ تَوَلَّوْا فَاعْلَمُوْۤا اَنَّ اللّٰهَ مَوْلٰىكُمْ ۚ نِعْمَ الْمَوْلٰى وَنِعْمَ النَّصِيْرُ ۝

---

^a2 : 194.   ^b3 : 151 ; 22 : 79 ; 47 : 12.

---

same time warned that if they return to war, they will meet with the same fate which the former opponents of truth met with. See also 8 : 20 above.

1128. Commentary :

The verse shows that fighting was to be continued only so long as there was persecution and men were not free to profess the religion they liked. If the opponents of Islam desisted from fighting, Muslims were also to desist. Islam fought only to defend itself and to establish freedom of conscience. See also 2 : 194.

The words, *Allah is Watchful*, imply that Muslims should not feel afraid that the disbelievers may desist only ostensibly and temporarily, and that they may attack the

Muslims again when a favourable opportunity offered itself. God was Watchful of all that they do, and He would surely help Muslims, if the disbelievers acted faithlessly towards them.

1129. Commentary :

The words, *if they turn their backs*, mean, "if they turn their backs and refuse to accept the offer that was being made to them," *i.e.*, if they return to hostilities. Thus God here promises to help Muslims if the enemy should again resort to war. Such promises (which always proved true) could only be given by the All-Powerful God, and they served as unmistakable evidence of the fact that the Quran was the word of God and not the fabrication of man.

42. And know that *whatever you take as spoil *in war*, a fifth thereof shall go to Allah and to the Messenger and to the kindred and orphans and the needy and the wayfarer, if you believe in Allah and in what We sent down to Our servant on the Day of Distinction,— *the day when the two armies met—and Allah has the power to do all things.[1130]

وَاعْلَمُوْٓا اَنَّمَا غَنِمْتُمْ مِّنْ شَىْءٍ فَاَنَّ لِلّٰهِ خُمُسَهٗ وَلِلرَّسُوْلِ وَلِذِى الْقُرْبٰى وَالْيَتٰمٰى وَالْمَسٰكِيْنِ وَابْنِ السَّبِيْلِ اِنْ كُنْتُمْ اٰمَنْتُمْ بِاللّٰهِ وَمَاۤ اَنْزَلْنَا عَلٰى عَبْدِنَا يَوْمَ الْفُرْقَانِ يَوْمَ الْتَقَى الْجَمْعٰنِ ۚ وَاللّٰهُ عَلٰى كُلِّ شَىْءٍ قَدِيْرٌ ۝

*8 : 70.   *3 : 14, 167.

1130. Commentary :

This verse (see also 8:2) relates to the division of the spoils of war. One *fifth* of such property was to be set apart, and the remainder was to be divided among the soldiers (who received no pay). In pre-Islamic Arabia, the practice was that first of all the commander chose from the booty any thing he liked. This was known as صفية *i.e.* the thing chosen. Of the remainder he took خمس (one fifth) in addition to صفية (the chosen thing). Islam abolished the practice of صفية (*ṣafiyya*) and the fifth part also was not to go entirely to the commander, but was to be shared by others. In the life-time of the Holy Prophet the practice was that of the خمس *i.e.*, the fifth part, the Prophet took only a portion, and divided the remainder among his kinsmen, the orphans, the poor and the wayfarers. By 'kinsmen' were meant the descendants of Hāshim and 'Abd al-Muṭṭalib, the two near ancestors of the Holy Prophet. After the death of the Holy Prophet, the fifth part went to the *Khalīfa* or *Imām* who was to divide it among himself, the kinsmen of the Holy Prophet, the orphans, the poor and the wayfarers. According to Imām Mālik, the division need not necessarily be made into equal portions, but is to be left to the discretion of the *Imām*, who is to divide it as circumstances and the need of the hour demand. Such was also the practice of the Holy Prophet and his four rightly-guided Successors.

The words, *if you believe in Allah*, are meant for the *Imām* or the commanders, and serve as a reminder to them that they are not to appropriate the whole خمس (fifth portion) for themselves but should also give to other classes of men their due, as directed in the verse.

The words, *if you believe in Allah and in what We sent down to Our servant on the Day of Distinction*, serve a two-fold purpose. *Firstly* they are meant to show that the qualification implied in the words, *if you believe*, does not relate to the Holy Prophet. *Secondly*, they serve to remind Muslims that since God helped them against disbelievers at Badr, when all material factors were against them, they should trust in His help and accept all His commandments regarding the distribution of spoils, etc. willingly and cheerfully.

The Battle of Badr is called يوم الفرقان (Day of Distinction) because on that day God brought into being extraordinary circumstances to give victory to His Prophet, and to make it clear which party was fighting in the cause of God and which in the cause of Satan. Thus the words يوم الفرقان (Day of Distinction) are here intended to hint that when a Muslim commander or an *Imām* gains a victory over his enemies, he should bear in mind that it is due to God's assistance and therefore he should not hesitate to divide the booty in accordance with His command.

43. When you were on the nearer bank of the valley, and they were on the farther bank, and the caravan was below you. And if you had to make a mutual appointment, you would have certainly differed with regard to the appointment. But *the encounter was brought about* that Allah might accomplish the thing that was decreed; so that he who had *already* perished through a clear Sign might perish, and he who had *already* come to life through a clear Sign might live. And certainly Allah is All-Hearing, All-Knowing.[1131]

44. *a*When Allah showed them to thee in thy dream as few; and if He had shown them to thee as many, you would have surely faltered and would have disagreed with one another about the matter; but Allah saved *you*. Surely, He has full knowledge of what is in *your* breasts.[1132]

اِذْ اَنْتُمْ بِالْعُدْوَةِ الدُّنْيَا وَهُمْ بِالْعُدْوَةِ الْقُصْوٰى وَالرَّكْبُ اَسْفَلَ مِنْكُمْ وَلَوْ تَوَاعَدْتُّمْ لَاخْتَلَفْتُمْ فِى الْمِيْعٰدِ وَلٰكِنْ لِّيَقْضِىَ اللّٰهُ اَمْرًا كَانَ مَفْعُوْلًا لِّيَهْلِكَ مَنْ هَلَكَ عَنْ بَيِّنَةٍ وَّيَحْيٰى مَنْ حَىَّ عَنْ بَيِّنَةٍ وَاِنَّ اللّٰهَ لَسَمِيْعٌ عَلِيْمٌ ۟

اِذْ يُرِيْكَهُمُ اللّٰهُ فِىْ مَنَامِكَ قَلِيْلًا وَّلَوْ اَرٰكَهُمْ كَثِيْرًا لَّفَشِلْتُمْ وَلَتَنَازَعْتُمْ فِى الْاَمْرِ وَلٰكِنَّ اللّٰهَ سَلَّمَ اِنَّهُ عَلِيْمٌ بِذَاتِ الصُّدُوْرِ ۟

*a*3 : 14.

1131. Commentary :

In this verse and those that follow, the Quran describes how God arranged and planned to bring about an encounter at Badr between believers and disbelievers, so that He might thereby crush the power of the enemy and show a Sign in support of Islam.

The verse begins with a graphic picture of the situation of the different parties at Badr and then proceeds to say that, if it had been left to the Muslims to appoint the time of the encounter, they would certainly have differed with regard to it and would have preferred to postpone the date of the first clash, for at that time they did not feel strong enough to meet their much more powerful and far better-equipped enemy in a field of battle. As, however, God's object was to show a powerful Sign, so He brought about the encounter

at a time when the Muslims were still very weak and the enemy very strong. This was done so that the party which had been proved to be in error and to be spiritually dead by means of clear reasons and arguments might perish and the party which had been proved to be spiritually alive and established on the firm basis of truth might survive and live.

The Quran has mentioned, more than once, the divine attribute of "All-Hearing" in connection with the Battle of Badr, in order to allude to the fact that prayers had played a great part in bringing about the victory and that they can play a similar part again.

1132. Important Words :

مَنَام (dream) is derived from نَام *i.e.* he slept. مَنَام means, sleep ; place where one sleeps ; dream (Aqrab).

45. And *when at the time of your meeting *in battle*, He made them appear to you as few in your eyes, and made you appear as few in their eyes, that Allah might bring about the thing that was decreed. And *b*to Allah are all affairs referred *for final decision*.[1133]

وَاِذْ يُرِيْكُمُوْهُمْ اِذِ الْتَقَيْتُمْ فِىْ اَعْيُنِكُمْ قَلِيْلًا وَّ يُقَلِّلُكُمْ فِىْ اَعْيُنِهِمْ لِيَقْضِىَ اللّٰهُ اَمْرًا كَانَ مَفْعُوْلًا ۭ وَاِلَى اللّٰهِ تُرْجَعُ الْاُمُوْرُ ۝

46. *c*O ye who believe! when you encounter an army, remain firm, and *d*remember Allah much that you may prosper.[1134]

يٰٓاَيُّهَا الَّذِيْنَ اٰمَنُوْٓا اِذَا لَقِيْتُمْ فِئَةً فَاثْبُتُوْا وَاذْكُرُوا اللّٰهَ كَثِيْرًا لَّعَلَّكُمْ تُفْلِحُوْنَ ۝

---

*a*3 : 14.   *b*2 : 211 ; 3 : 110 ; 35 : 5.   *c*8 : 16 ; 47 : 5.   *d*33 : 42 ; 62 : 11.

Commentary :

While on his way to Badr, the Holy Prophet was shown the Meccan army in a dream to be less in number than they actually were (Jarīr, x. 9). In the language of dreams, this meant that the Meccan force, in spite of their superior numbers and equipment, would be overcome by the Muslims. On the other hand, if the enemy had been shown in a dream to be in large numbers, the interpretation of the dream would have been that the party to which the dreamer belonged would lose heart and would be overpowered by the enemy.

1133. Commentary :

Whereas the preceding verse referred to the appearance of the enemy in a dream, the present verse refers to its actual appearance on the battle-field. What happened was that the enemy had kept one-third of their number behind mounds so that, when both parties came face to face, Muslims saw only two-thirds of their army. The Meccan army, about 1,000 strong, was more than three times the number of the Muslims who were only 313, but it so happened that the latter saw them to be only twice their own number. This naturally made the Faithful more hopeful. As hinted above, the enemy had concealed one-third of their number from the Muslims so that (as they

thought) the latter might not be overawed and flee from the battle-field. This ruse was meant by them as an enticement to the Muslims so that the latter might be encouraged to give them battle and consequently be annihilated. Indeed, the Muslims were so weak at that time that the Meccans were anxious to get them within their grip, so that they might wipe them out of existence and thus extirpate Islam. The weakness of the Muslims became all the more apparent when the Meccans actually saw them, for they saw them smaller than their actual number, and both these impressions helped to encourage either party to come to grips with the opposing party, with the result that the " thing decreed " was miraculously brought about.

1134. Commentary :

Muslims are here told that they should not think that war with disbelievers had ended with the attle of Badr. The enemy was to return to the attack repeatedly and with larger and still larger forces. So Muslims are exhorted to remain firm and not to waver before the repeated onslaughts of the enemy.

The words, *remember Allah much*, imply that as the enemy will call his allies to his aid, so the Faithful too should call God to their help by constantly praying to Him.

47. And ^aobey Allah and His Messenger and dispute not with one another, lest you falter and your power depart *from you.* And be steadfast; surely, Allah is with those who are steadfast.[1135]

وَاَطِيْعُوا اللّٰهَ وَرَسُوْلَهٗ وَلَا تَنَازَعُوْا فَتَفْشَلُوْا وَتَذْهَبَ رِيْحُكُمْ وَاصْبِرُوْا ۚ اِنَّ اللّٰهَ مَعَ الصّٰبِرِيْنَ ۞

48. And be not like those who came forth from their homes boastfully, and to be seen of men, and who turn *men* away from the path of Allah, and Allah encompasses all that they do.[1136]

وَلَا تَكُوْنُوْا كَالَّذِيْنَ خَرَجُوْا مِنْ دِيَارِهِمْ بَطَرًا وَّرِئَآءَ النَّاسِ وَيَصُدُّوْنَ عَنْ سَبِيْلِ اللّٰهِ ۚ وَاللّٰهُ بِمَا يَعْمَلُوْنَ مُحِيْطٌ ۞

---

^a3 : 33 ; 4 : 60 ; 8 : 21 ; 24 : 55.

The secret of success is stated here to lie in two things : (1) that Muslims should never feel secure from the attacks of the enemy and should always be prepared for them, and (2) that they should be always invoking God's help.

1135. Important Words :

ريح (power) is derived from راح *i.e.* it (a day) was violently windy ; or it was or became cool and pleasant by means of the wind. راح الشجر means, the tree felt the wind. راح also means, he was or became brisk, lively, active or quick (as though he felt the wind and was refreshed by it). ريح means wind *i.e.* the air that is between heaven and earth ; the breath of the air, or, in like manner, of anything (said to be so called because it generally brings rest or ease) ; puff or gust of wind ; also predominance or prevalence ; power or force ; aid against an enemy ; victory or conquest ; a turn of good fortune. One would say ذهبت ريحهم *i.e.* their turn of good fortune had departed تذهب ريحكم means, your predominance and power would depart (Lane).

Commentary :

The verse mentions three ways by following which Muslims could remain firm and become successful. *Firstly,* they are bidden to obey the commandments of God and His Messenger. *Secondly,* they are enjoined not to dispute with one another but to remain united. *Thirdly,* they are commanded to remain patient and steadfast.

1136. Important Words :

بطرا (boastfully). بطر الرجل means, the man exulted or exulted excessively ; or he behaved insolently and ungratefully ; or he behaved with pride and boastfulness ; or he became stupefied and confounded with his wealth (and power), bearing it in an evil manner and turning it to a wrong purpose ; or he regarded a thing with hatred and dislike, without its deserving to be so regarded ; or he walked with a proud and conceited gait (Lane).

Commentary :

Boastfulness and the desire to be seen of, and praised by others have always been a source of weakness in man, and the verse condemns them in the strongest terms. Again, in the field of religion, true service lies in opposing the enemy not only with fervour and zeal but with a view to helping and advancing

49. And when *satan made their deeds seem fair to them and said, *‘None among men shall prevail against you this day, and I am your protector.’ But when the two armies came in sight of each other, he turned on his heels, and said, ‘ Surely, I have nothing to do with you ; surely, I see what you see not. Surely, I fear Allah ; and Allah is severe in punishing.’[1137]

وَاِذْ زَيَّنَ لَهُمُ الشَّيْطٰنُ اَعْمَالَهُمْ وَقَالَ لَا غَالِبَ لَكُمُ الْيَوْمَ مِنَ النَّاسِ وَاِنِّيْ جَارٌ لَّكُمْ فَلَمَّا تَرَآءَتِ الْفِئَتٰنِ نَكَصَ عَلٰى عَقِبَيْهِ وَقَالَ اِنِّيْ بَرِيْٓءٌ مِّنْكُمْ اِنِّيْٓ اَرٰى مَا لَا تَرَوْنَ اِنِّيْٓ اَخَافُ اللّٰهَ وَاللّٰهُ شَدِيْدُ الْعِقَابِ ۞

---

*6 : 44 ; 16 : 64 ; 27 : 25 ; 29 : 49.   *14 : 23 ; 59 : 17.

---

the cause of truth. Those who are truly brave do nothing from motives of selfishness or self-display ; their only motive is to seek the pleasure of God. The verse gives a description of the Meccan army under Abū Jahl which came forth from Mecca in proud exultation, and the Muslims are warned against following their example.

1137. Important Words :

جَار (protector) is derived from جَار which means, he declined or deviated. جَاوَرَهُ means, he became his neighbour, or he lived in his neighbourhood. جَاوَرَهُ also means, he bound himself to him by a covenant to protect him. جَار means, a neighbour ; a person whom one protects ; one who seeks protection ; also a protector (Lane).

نَكَص (he turned). نَكَص عَنِ الاَمْرِ means, he receded or retired or drew back from the thing or the affair ; or he recoiled or shrank from it in fear. نَكَص عَلٰى عَقِبِهِ means, he turned back from a thing to which he had applied himself (Lane).

Commentary :

For the meaning of the word "satan" see 2 : 15. The word here means, one who misleads or gives evil advice. The person referred to in the verse is reported to be Surāqa bin Mālik bin Ju'sham who incited the Meccans against the Muslims but who afterwards embraced Islam.

The Meccan army was still at Mecca when some of the Quraishite leaders gave expression to the fear that Banū Bakr, a branch of Banū Kanāna, who were hostile to the Quraish, might surprise Mecca during their absence or attack the Meccan army from the rear. Their fears were allayed by Surāqa, a chief of Banū Kanāna, who assured them that his tribesmen would do them no harm (Jarīr, **x**. 13).

The words, *I see what you see not*, signify that when Surāqa saw the grim determination of the Muslims, fear took hold of him ; for on seeing them he was convinced that the Muslims would win or die. This was exactly what 'Utba and 'Umair also saw and felt when they told the Meccans that the Muslims looked like so many "seekers of death" (Ṭabarī). Surāqa uttered the words, *I fear Allah*, not because he really feared God at that time but because he wished to find an excuse to flee from the battlefield.

R. 7   50. ^aWhen the hypocrites and those in whose hearts is a disease said, 'Their religion has deluded these *men*'. And ^bwhoso puts his trust in Allah, then surely Allah is Mighty, Wise.¹¹³⁸

اِذْ يَقُوْلُ الْمُنٰفِقُوْنَ وَالَّذِيْنَ فِيْ قُلُوْبِهِمْ مَّرَضٌ غَرَّ هٰٓؤُلَآءِ دِيْنُهُمْ ۗ وَمَنْ يَّتَوَكَّلْ عَلَى اللّٰهِ فَاِنَّ اللّٰهَ عَزِيْزٌ حَكِيْمٌ ۝

51. And if thou couldst see, ^cwhen the angels take away the souls of those who disbelieve, smiting their faces and their backs and *saying* : ^d' Taste ye the punishment of burning,¹¹³⁹

وَلَوْ تَرٰٓى اِذْ يَتَوَفَّى الَّذِيْنَ كَفَرُوا الْمَلٰٓئِكَةُ يَضْرِبُوْنَ وُجُوْهَهُمْ وَاَدْبَارَهُمْ ۚ وَذُوْقُوْا عَذَابَ الْحَرِيْقِ ۝

52. 'That is because of that which your hands have sent on before *your-selves* and *know* that ^eAllah is not at all unjust to *His* servants.'¹¹⁴⁰

ذٰلِكَ بِمَا قَدَّمَتْ اَيْدِيْكُمْ وَاَنَّ اللّٰهَ لَيْسَ بِظَلَّامٍ لِّلْعَبِيْدِ ۝

---

^a33 : 13.   ^b9 : 51; 12 : 68; 14 : 12; 33 : 4; 65 : 4.   ^c47 : 28.   ^d3 : 182; 22 : 10.   ^e3 : 183; 22 : 11; 41 : 47.

1138. Commentary :

The words, *the hypocrites and those in whose hearts is a disease*, here refer to those men in the Meccan army who had embraced Islam in Mecca, but who, being weak, remained with disbelievers out of fear, and had now come forth with the Meccan army in order to fight the Muslims. There were four or five such men who, when they saw the small band of Muslims arrayed in battle-order against a well-equipped army of Meccan warriors, thought it foolhardy on the part of the former to take their stand against the overwhelming odds and made the remark mentioned in the verse. To this remark the verse gives the reply that the small band of Muslims faced the heavy odds not because their religion had deluded them but because they had put their trust in God Who was both Mighty and Wise and Who had promised to help them. The last words of the verse are thus also intended to reprimand the weak-hearted Muslims of Mecca and to remind them that their hypocritical policy resulted from the fact that they had no trust in the power and might of God.

1139. Commentary :

The verse signifies that angels will smite the *faces* and the *bac's* of disbelievers as a fitting punishment for their evil actions. The punishment corresponded with the actions of disbelievers, because the latter used to confront the believers and meet them *face to face* when fighting them. Again, they used to turn their *backs* disdainfully when truth was preached to them. So both faces and backs would receive punishment.

1140. Commentary :

This verse further explains and provides a reason for the idea expressed in the preceding verse.

53. ^a*Their case is* like the case of the people of Pharaoh and those before them : they disbelieved in the Signs of Allah ; so Allah punished them for their sins. Surely, Allah is Powerful *and* severe in punishing.¹¹⁴¹

كَدَأْبِ اٰلِ فِرْعَوْنَ وَالَّذِيْنَ مِنْ قَبْلِهِمْ كَفَرُوْا بِاٰيٰتِ اللّٰهِ فَاَخَذَهُمُ اللّٰهُ بِذُنُوْبِهِمْ اِنَّ اللّٰهَ قَوِيٌّ شَدِيْدُ الْعِقَابِ ۝

54. This is because ^bAllah would never change a favour that He has conferred upon a people until they change their own condition, and *know* that Allah is All-Hearing, All-Knowing.¹¹⁴²

ذٰلِكَ بِاَنَّ اللّٰهَ لَمْ يَكُ مُغَيِّرًا نِّعْمَةً اَنْعَمَهَا عَلٰى قَوْمٍ حَتّٰى يُغَيِّرُوْا مَا بِاَنْفُسِهِمْ وَاَنَّ اللّٰهَ سَمِيْعٌ عَلِيْمٌ ۝

55. ^c*Their case is* like the case of the people of Pharaoh and those before them ; they rejected the Signs of their Lord, so We destroyed them for their sins. And We drowned the people of Pharaoh, for they were all wrongdoers.¹¹⁴³

كَدَأْبِ اٰلِ فِرْعَوْنَ وَالَّذِيْنَ مِنْ قَبْلِهِمْ كَذَّبُوْا بِاٰيٰتِ رَبِّهِمْ فَاَهْلَكْنٰهُمْ بِذُنُوْبِهِمْ وَاَغْرَقْنَا اٰلَ فِرْعَوْنَ وَكُلٌّ كَانُوْا ظٰلِمِيْنَ ۝

---

^a3 : 12 ; 8 : 55.   ^b13 : 12.   ^c3 : 12 ; 8 : 53.

1141. Commentary :

The verse signifies that Allah has dealt with the opponents of Islam just as He dealt with the people of Pharaoh. The reference is to the Battle of Badr, where God destroyed Abū Jahl and his host as He destroyed Pharaoh and his people in the sea. The verse thus points to the similarity between the Holy Prophet and Moses (see Deut. 18 : 18).

1142. Commentary :

The word ذٰلِك (this) refers to the punishment spoken of in the previous verse. The disbelievers rejected the Signs of Allah, so Allah destroyed them for their rebellion and sins. God sent His punishment on the people because they had brought about a change in their hearts. The verse states a general law of God which is to the effect that God never deprives a people

of a favour which He had conferred upon them until there is first a change in their own hearts for the worse. For instance, if God grants a people dominion and power, He does not take it away from them until they lose their virtues and become wicked. The verse should also prove an eye-opener for present-day Muslims from whom God has definitely withdrawn His favour.

1143. Commentary :

The verse repeats the subject-matter of 8 : 53 above, with the change that here (1) the words اَخَذَهُمُ اللّٰه (Allah punished them, lit. Allah seized them) have been changed to اَهْلَكْنٰهُمْ (We destroyed them) ; and (2) the words, *We drowned the people of Pharaoh, etc.* have been added. This is to point to the severity of the punishment and the total destruction of the disbelievers.

56. Surely, *the worst of beasts in the sight of Allah are those who are ungrateful. So they will not believe,[1144]

اِنَّ شَرَّ الدَّوَابِّ عِنْدَ اللهِ الَّذِيْنَ كَفَرُوْا فَهُمْ لَا يُؤْمِنُوْنَ ۞

57. Those with whom thou didst make a covenant; then *they break their covenant every time, and they do not fear *God*.[1144A]

الَّذِيْنَ عَاهَدْتَّ مِنْهُمْ ثُمَّ يَنْقُضُوْنَ عَهْدَهُمْ فِيْ كُلِّ مَرَّةٍ وَّهُمْ لَا يَتَّقُوْنَ ۞

58. So, if thou catchest them in war, then by *routing* them strike fear in those that are behind them, that they may be admonished.[1145]

فَاِمَّا تَثْقَفَنَّهُمْ فِي الْحَرْبِ فَشَرِّدْ بِهِمْ مَّنْ خَلْفَهُمْ لَعَلَّهُمْ يَذَّكَّرُوْنَ ۞

---

*a*8 : 23; 98 : 7.   *b*2 : 28.

1144. Commentary :

This verse explains 6 : 39, which says that the animals that move on the earth and the birds that fly in the air are better than the disbelievers; for, whereas animals and birds do not understand, because they lack the power of understanding, the disbelievers possess the power to understand and yet they fail to do so. See also 8 : 23.

1144A. Commentary :

This verse qualifies and explains the one that precedes it.

1145. Important Words :

شرد (strike fear) is derived from شرد (sharada) which means, he (a horse, etc.) took fright and fled or ran away at random; or simply he fled or ran away. شرد به or شرده (sharrada) means, he made him take fright and flee or run away at random; or he drove him away. تشريد also signifies the act of dispersing or scattering. شرد به also means, he rendered him notorious by exposing his vices or faults. شرد به من خلفهم means, disperse or scatter by them or through them those who are or who shall come, after them; or terrify by or through them those who are, or who shall come, after them; or make them notorious to those who are, or who shall come, after them (Tāj).

Commentary :

The Quran uses the word تثقفنهم (for which see 2 : 192) meaning "thou catchest them" with a view to pointing to the fact that when a disbeliever meets a believer on a field of battle, the former is, as it were, in the very grip of the latter. Thus when believers have to fight, they are expected to fight like valiant men and the enemy who opposes them should be considered as having come within their grasp and should not be able to escape from their hands. The expression تشريد (striking fear) has also been used to point to the same truth. A believer is always slow to take up arms; but when he does so, he fights so valiantly that he not only takes the enemy in his iron grip but deals such blows to him as may strike terror in the hearts of those that are behind the enemy, as well as those that may come after him. A feebly-pursued and lingering war is never a good policy. If there is to be a war, it should be swift and exemplary. This is why the verse enjoins that, when forced to fight, Muslims should fight the enemy so valiantly that not

59. And if thou fearest treachery from a people, throw back to them *their covenant* with equity. Surely, [a]Allah loves not the treacherous.[1146]

وَاِمَّا تَخَافَنَّ مِنْ قَوْمٍ خِيَانَةً فَانْبِذْ اِلَيْهِمْ عَلٰى سَوَآءٍ ۚ اِنَّ اللّٰهَ لَا يُحِبُّ الْخَآئِنِيْنَ ۞

60. And [b]let not those who disbelieve think that they have outstripped *Us*. Surely, they cannot frustrate *God's purpose*.[1147]

وَلَا يَحْسَبَنَّ الَّذِيْنَ كَفَرُوْا سَبَقُوْا ۗ اِنَّهُمْ لَا يُعْجِزُوْنَ ۞

---

[a]4 : 108.   [b]3 : 179.

---

only those who are actually engaged in fighting should be routed, but even their supporters who are behind them should be struck with terror. In fact, Islam not only requires its followers to excel others in things moral and spiritual but also expects them to surpass others even in the physical sphere. They have to set the highest example in all matters. If they must fight, they should excel others in fighting as well.

1146. Commentary :

If a people with whom Muslims have entered into a covenant begin to commit acts of hostility towards them and it is feared that they are going to play false, then it should be openly and plainly declared to them that the covenant between them and the Muslims had come to an end.   Then if, after such a declaration, they should fight the Muslims, the latter should also fight them.   Thus Muslims are not allowed to make a surprise attack on any people without due notice.   The

Holy Prophet is reported to have said لَا تَقْرِطْ وَلَا تَفْجَأْ *i.e.* "Do not exceed the bounds in fighting, nor make a surprise attack on the enemy". Even in war Islam enjoins strict justice and mercy.

1147. Commentary :

This verse contains the great prophecy that the enemies of Islam who had waged war against the Muslims would never prevail. Such a prophecy could not be made by a human being in the circumstances in which it was made; for it is an established historical fact that at the time when this prophecy was made the Muslims were extremely weak both in number and equipment and no mortal could predict that such a weak and ill-equipped community could vanquish their numerous and powerful enemies. Only God, Who is Almighty and Omniscient, could predict victory for the Muslims in such circumstances; and the promised victory did actually come to pass.

61. And ^amake ready for them whatever you can of force and of mounted pickets at the frontier, whereby you may frighten the enemy of Allah and your enemy and others besides them whom you know not, *but* Allah knows them. And ^bwhatever you spend in the way of Allah, it shall be repaid to you in full and you shall not be wronged.[1148]

وَاَعِدُّوْا لَهُمْ مَّا اسْتَطَعْتُمْ مِّنْ قُوَّةٍ وَّمِنْ رِّبَاطِ الْخَيْلِ تُرْهِبُوْنَ بِهٖ عَدُوَّ اللّٰهِ وَعَدُوَّكُمْ وَاٰخَرِيْنَ مِنْ دُوْنِهِمْ ۚ لَا تَعْلَمُوْنَهُمْ ۚ اَللّٰهُ يَعْلَمُهُمْ ۚ وَمَا تُنْفِقُوْا مِنْ شَيْءٍ فِيْ سَبِيْلِ اللّٰهِ يُوَفَّ اِلَيْكُمْ وَاَنْتُمْ لَا تُظْلَمُوْنَ ۞

62. And if they incline towards peace, incline thou also towards it, and put thy trust in Allah. Surely, it is He Who is All-Hearing, All-Knowing.[1149]

وَاِنْ جَنَحُوْا لِلسَّلْمِ فَاجْنَحْ لَهَا وَتَوَكَّلْ عَلَى اللّٰهِ ۚ اِنَّهٗ هُوَ السَّمِيْعُ الْعَلِيْمُ ۞

---

^a3 : 201.   ^b2 : 273 ; 9 : 121 ; 64 : 18 ; 65 : 8.

1148. Important Words :

رِبَاطُ الْخَيْلِ (mounted pickets at the frontier). For رِبَاط see 3 : 201. خيل is derived from خال *i.e.* he thought or fancied. اختال means, he was proud and haughty. خيل means, horses collectively, so called because of the pride and conceit in their gait ; also horsemen (Lane).

Commentary :

This verse teaches Muslims that efficient preparation is the best means of preventing war. It teaches them that they should not only keep a sufficient fighting force in the country but also an adequate number of troops on the frontier so that the enemy might refrain from attack, thus enabling the Faithful to live in peace. The verse also points to the necessity of spending freely in war.

It is worthy of note that the verse does not simply say "your enemy" but *the enemy of Allah and your enemy*, thus hinting that disbelievers had become hostile to Muslims for the sole reason that the latter had accepted Islam, the religion of God. These words throw interesting light on the causes of early Islamic wars.

The verse further informs Muslims that the pagan Arabs were not the only enemies of Islam. There were other nations also which would attack Muslims in the future, as the Arabs had already done. So Muslims were told to keep their frontiers strong and well-protected and to spend freely in the cause of Allah. This prophecy referred to the Greeks and the Persians with whom Muslims came in contact soon after the death of the Holy Prophet.

1149. Commentary :

This verse, besides embodying an important principle about the formation of peace-treaties throws interesting light on the character of the wars undertaken by Islam. Muslims did not resort to war to force men to embrace Islam, but simply to maintain peace. Hence, if any people after making war against Muslims sued for peace, the latter were enjoined to desist from war and make peace with them, in spite of their being disbelievers. Even the consideration that the enemy might

63. And if they intend to deceive thee, then surely ^aAllah is sufficient for thee. He it is Who has strengthened thee with His help and with the believers;¹¹⁵⁰

وَاِنْ يُّرِيْدُوْٓا اَنْ يَّخْدَعُوْكَ فَاِنَّ حَسْبَكَ اللّٰهُ هُوَ الَّذِيْٓ اَيَّدَكَ بِنَصْرِهٖ وَبِالْمُؤْمِنِيْنَ ۙ ﴿٦٣﴾

64. And ^bHe has put affection between their hearts. If thou hadst expended all that is in the earth, thou couldst not have put affection between their hearts, but Allah has put affection between them. Surely, He is Mighty, Wise.¹¹⁵¹

وَاَلَّفَ بَيْنَ قُلُوْبِهِمْ ۗ لَوْ اَنْفَقْتَ مَا فِى الْاَرْضِ جَمِيْعًا مَّآ اَلَّفْتَ بَيْنَ قُلُوْبِهِمْ وَلٰكِنَّ اللّٰهَ اَلَّفَ بَيْنَهُمْ ۗ اِنَّهٗ عَزِيْزٌ حَكِيْمٌ ﴿٦٤﴾

65. O Prophet, ^cAllah is sufficient for thee and for those who follow thee of the believers.¹¹⁵²

يٰٓاَيُّهَا النَّبِيُّ حَسْبُكَ اللّٰهُ وَمَنِ اتَّبَعَكَ مِنَ الْمُؤْمِنِيْنَ ﴿٦٥﴾

9 66. O Prophet, ^durge the believers to fight. If there be of you twenty who are steadfast, they shall overcome two hundred; and if there be a hundred of you, they shall overcome a thousand of those who disbelieve, because they are a people who do not understand.¹¹⁵³

يٰٓاَيُّهَا النَّبِيُّ حَرِّضِ الْمُؤْمِنِيْنَ عَلَى الْقِتَالِ ۗ اِنْ يَّكُنْ مِّنْكُمْ عِشْرُوْنَ صٰبِرُوْنَ يَغْلِبُوْا مِائَتَيْنِ ۚ وَاِنْ يَّكُنْ مِّنْكُمْ مِّائَةٌ يَّغْلِبُوْٓا اَلْفًا مِّنَ الَّذِيْنَ كَفَرُوْا بِاَنَّهُمْ قَوْمٌ لَّا يَفْقَهُوْنَ ﴿٦٦﴾

---

^a8 : 65.   ^b3 : 104.   ^c8 : 63.   ^d4 : 85.

---

be suing for peace simply to deceive the Muslims and to gain time was not to deter them from making peace. This shows that what the Muslims desired was nothing but peace, and they were bidden to welcome it at all hazards. See also the verse that follows.

1150. Commentary :

An offer of peace by the enemy must be accepted, even if there is the risk of his playing false. See note on the preceding verse.

1151. Commentary :

The verse is intended to meet any possible demur on the part of believers in the matter of accepting a peace offer made by the enemy. It is no favour of the believers upon God or

His Messenger, if they have helped the Prophet; on the other hand, it is God's favour upon them that He has put affection "between their hearts," for before their acceptance of Islam they too were enemies of one another.

1152. Commentary :

The words مَنِ اتَّبَعَكَ (those who follow thee) are grammatically in apposition to the pronoun (thee) in حَسْبُكَ (sufficient for thee). It is thus wrong to translate the verse as " Allah is sufficient for thee and so are those who follow thee." The sufficing of God relates both to the Prophet and his followers.

1153. Commentary :

As disbelievers were not going to desist from

67. For the present Allah has lightened your burden, for He knows that there is weakness in you. So, if there be a hundred of you who are steadfast, they shall overcome two hundred; and if there be a thousand of you, they shall overcome two thousand by the command of Allah. And Allah is with those who are steadfast.[1154]

الْـٰٔنَ خَفَّفَ اللّٰهُ عَنْكُمْ وَعَلِمَ اَنَّ فِيْكُمْ ضَعْفًا ۚ فَاِنْ يَّكُنْ مِّنْكُمْ مِّائَةٌ صَابِرَةٌ يَّغْلِبُوْا مِائَتَيْنِ ۚ وَاِنْ يَّكُنْ مِّنْكُمْ اَلْفٌ يَّغْلِبُوْۤا اَلْفَيْنِ بِاِذْنِ اللّٰهِ ۭ وَاللّٰهُ مَعَ الصّٰبِرِيْنَ ۝

---

fighting, as they were invited to do (8 : 20, & 8 : 39 above), but were determined to carry on war of aggression against Islam, therefore the Holy Prophet has been asked in this verse to urge Muslims also to fight in self-defence.

The verse promises victory to Muslims over an enemy ten times their number *because they are a people who do not understand.* Fighters should understand the purpose of their fighting. They should look upon the war, they are engaged in, as their own. They should know the advantages which will accrue to their community if they win, and they should also know the losses which they will have to suffer if they are defeated. Mere hirelings or men, who are blindly led to war by their leaders but who do not understand its object and feel no personal interest in it, cannot win. The forces that fought against Islam were mostly composed of men who took part in the war merely because they were called upon to do so by their mischievous leaders—the wicked and avowed enemies of Islam. They felt no personal interest in the war against the new religion.

Religiously speaking also, they were a people who did not "understand", whereas Muslims did understand what faith meant. They were moved by a love for their God, their Prophet and their religion. Disbelievers, on the other hand, were not as devoted to their idols as the Faithful were to their God, in Whom they had a living faith.

The verse gives the number twenty as the minimum number for Muslims to win sure victory over their enemy because that was the least number that made a regular fighting party. If the number of men was less than twenty, it was not to be regarded as a fighting force and the laws relating to war did not apply to them.

Thus, a party of twenty persons, the minimum comprising a fighting unit, was bound to fight if they met an enemy as many as ten times their strength, and they were forbidden to flee. The question of retiring before the enemy is not to be decided by the men but by their officers, who may act as they may think best in the interest of war. See also 8 : 16.

1154. Commentary :

This verse does not abrogate the previous verse but only temporarily relieves Muslims in view of the then existing condition of their faith. Their faith, though sincere and true, was "weak" as compared with its future condition when it was to grow stronger by their witnessing more and more heavenly Signs and by their becoming more and more organized.

The words, *For the present Allah has lightened your burden,* show that the previous verse contains not a prophecy but a commandment. It does not announce by way of prophecy that Muslims will prevail over an enemy ten times their number; it simply gives the injunction that if twenty believers have to face two hundred disbelievers, they must fight them, and that

68. ^aIt does not behove a Prophet that he should have captives until he engages in a regular fighting in the land. ^bYou desire the goods of the world, while Allah desires *for you* the Hereafter. And Allah is Mighty, Wise.¹¹⁵⁵

مَا كَانَ لِنَبِيٍّ اَنْ يَّكُوْنَ لَهٗۤ اَسْرٰى حَتّٰى يُثْخِنَ فِى الْاَرْضِ ۖ تُرِيْدُوْنَ عَرَضَ الدُّنْيَا ۖ وَاللّٰهُ يُرِيْدُ الْاٰخِرَةَ ۖ وَاللّٰهُ عَزِيْزٌ حَكِيْمٌ ۝

---

^a47 : 5.   ^b4 : 95.

---

if they turn back in flight, they will be sinners. In the present verse, however, in view of the then weak condition of Muslims, the limit of disparity has been reduced to twice the number of the believers.

History tells us that in later times Muslims had sometimes to fight an enemy even more than ten times their number and still they were victorious. Thus at the Battle of Yarmūk the Muslim army numbered 30,000, according to the lowest calculation, while the enemy numbered at least 600,000 (the highest figures being respectively 60,000 and 1,000,000) and the battle ended in a decisive victory for the Muslims.

1155. Important Words :

اسرٰى (captives) is the plural of اسير (a captive) which is derived from اسر. They say اسره *i.e.* he bound or tied him, or he made him a captive or took him a prisoner. اسير means, one shackled or imprisoned ; a captive (Lane).

يثخن (he engages in a regular fighting) is derived from ثخن (*thakhuna*) or ثخن (*thakhana*) which means, it was thick or coarse or hard. اثخنه means, he rendered it thick ; or he rendered him heavy or languid or enervated ; or he overcame him and inflicted many wounds on him. اثخن فى العدو means, he made a great slaughter or a great wounding among the enemy. اثخن فى الارض means, he made much slaughter in the earth or the land ; or he fought vehemently in the earth (Lane). The expression حتى يثخن فى الارض

would thus mean, till he (the Prophet) has had a regular fighting in the land, inflicting wounds on the enemy.

Commentary :

It was a practice among pre-Islamic Arabs (and it is regrettable that the practice still continues in some parts of the world) to take men captives even if there was no war and no fighting, and then to make them slaves. The verse abolishes this evil custom and lays down in clear words that it is only in war and after regular fighting that enemy combatants can be taken prisoner and that it is not lawful to take any person captive when there is no war and there has been no fighting.

The verse has been very wrongly interpreted. It is said that when the Muslims took some men of the Meccan army captives at Badr, the Holy Prophet took counsel with his Companions as to what should be done with them. 'Umar suggested that they should be put to death, while Abū Bakr proposed that they should be released after accepting ransom from them. The Holy Prophet accepted the suggestion of Abū Bakr and the prisoners were released for ransom. But it is alleged that by revealing this verse, God expressed His disapproval of the Holy Prophet's action, declaring that the captives ought to have been put to death and no ransom should have been taken for them. This interpretation, however, is obviously wrong; *firstly*, because God had so far sent down no commandment forbidding the release of

69. Had there not been a decree from Allah which had gone before, great distress would have surely overtaken you in connection with that which you took.[1156]

70. So *a*eat, of that which you have won *in war*, as lawful and good, and fear Allah. Surely, Allah is Most Forgiving, Merciful.[1157]

*a*8 : 42.

---

prisoners for ransom and therefore He could not reprove the Holy Prophet for accepting ransom ; *secondly*, because the Holy Prophet had already accepted ransom for two persons taken captive at Nakhla prior to the Battle of Badr, and God had not disapproved of this action of his ; *thirdly*, because only two verses later God permits Muslims to *eat of that which you have won in war as lawful and good* (8 : 70). It is simply inconceivable that God should have reproved the Holy Prophet for having accepted ransom and then at the same time declared the money so taken to be lawful and good. This interpretation is, therefore, obviously wrong and the verse is only intended to lay down a general rule that captives should not be taken until there has been regular fighting and the enemy has been overpowered by the infliction of wounds.

1156. Commentary :

In the previous verse it was said that Muslims should not be hasty in taking captives from among the enemy. The verse under comment hints that kindness should be shown to prisoners and that they should be treated with mercy. The verse says that it is only through the assistance of God, which He had ordained for Muslims, that they have gained an easy victory and obtained much booty, and that if it had not been for the help which God had

promised them beforehand they would not have obtained the booty without being severely handled by the enemy and suffering great loss at his hands. The words, *a decree from Allah which had gone before*, obviously refer to the word of God which had already conveyed the promise of help to the Holy Prophet (see 8 : 6 above). The words "great distress" thus signify distress caused by the enemy and not affliction from God. The verse purports to say that when by the help of God the Muslims have gained so easy a victory, they should feel grateful for it and should show kindness to the prisoners who have fallen into their hands.

1157. Commentary :

The conjunction "so", placed in the beginning of the verse, indicates that the commandment that follows it, is connected with, and is the result of, what has been said in the previous verses. As the booty taken was obtained after regular fighting and the victory came as a result of God's help, so the booty taken in the battle and the ransom-money realized from the enemy-prisoners are both "lawful and good". God has been here spoken of as "Forgiving" because He covered up the weaknesses of Muslims and made them appear strong in the sight of the enemy ; and He has been spoken of as "Merciful" because He granted Muslims a decisive victory against overwhelming odds.

10   **71.** O Prophet, say to the captives who are in your hands, ' If Allah knows any good in your hearts, He will give you better than that which has been taken from you, and will forgive you. And Allah is Most Forgiving, Merciful'. [1158]

يَٰٓأَيُّهَا النَّبِيُّ قُل لِّمَن فِىٓ أَيْدِيكُم مِّنَ الْأَسْرَىٰٓ إِن يَعْلَمِ اللّٰهُ فِى قُلُوبِكُمْ خَيْرًا يُؤْتِكُمْ خَيْرًا مِّمَّآ أُخِذَ مِنكُمْ وَيَغْفِرْ لَكُمْ وَاللّٰهُ غَفُورٌ رَّحِيمٌ ۝

72. And if they intend to deal treacherously with thee, they have already dealt treacherously with Allah before, but He gave *thee* power over them. And Allah is All-Knowing, Wise.[1159]

وَإِن يُرِيدُوا۟ خِيَانَتَكَ فَقَدْ خَانُوا۟ اللّٰهَ مِن قَبْلُ فَأَمْكَنَ مِنْهُمْ وَاللّٰهُ عَلِيمٌ حَكِيمٌ ۝

1158. Commentary :

The words of this verse, addressed to the Meccan prisoners in the hands of the Muslims are meant by way of consolation. If they have been made to pay ransom for their release, they should not grieve, for if God sees some good in their hearts, He will not only forgive them their past errors but will also amply repay them for their financial loss. One of the prisoners taken at Badr was 'Abbās, an uncle of the Holy Prophet. Some Muslims recommended him to the Holy Prophet for free release in consideration of his near relationship to the Prophet and of his being a believer at heart, but the Holy Prophet refused to make any exception in his favour and declared that like other prisoners, he too should pay ransom for his release. When, however, he subsequently embraced Islam openly and came over to the Holy Prophet, he requested, on the basis of the verse under comment, that as God had promised to give the prisoners more than was taken from them as ransom, the promise may be fulfilled in his case, and the Holy Prophet granted his request (Jarīr, x. 31).

1159. Commentary :

The treacherous dealing mentioned here is that disbelievers should do evil in return for the kindness shown to them. As was the custom in Arabia, pre-Islamic Arabs used to slay their powerful enemies, whenever they fell into their hands. The verse therefore signifies that if the enemies of Islam proved treacherous, God would give Muslims power over them again ; so it is not necessary for Muslims to put their prisoners to death as pre-Islamic Arabs used to do.

God knew that the time was soon coming when the disbelievers would embrace Islam, hence the injunction to spare their lives and to treat them with kindness, for was not God " All-Knowing, Wise " ?

73. Surely, ^athose who have believed and fled from their homes and striven with their property and their persons for the cause of Allah, and those who have given *them* shelter and help—these are friends one of another. But as for those who have believed but have left not their homes, you are not at all responsible for their protection until they leave their homes. But if they seek your help in *the matter of* religion, then it is your duty to help them, except against a people between whom and yourselves there is a treaty. And Allah sees what you do.[1160]

اِنَّ الَّذِیْنَ اٰمَنُوْا وَهَاجَرُوْا وَجَاهَدُوْا بِاَمْوَالِهِمْ وَاَنْفُسِهِمْ فِیْ سَبِیْلِ اللّٰهِ وَالَّذِیْنَ اٰوَوْا وَّنَصَرُوْا اُولٰٓئِکَ بَعْضُهُمْ اَوْلِیَآءُ بَعْضٍ ؕ وَالَّذِیْنَ اٰمَنُوْا وَلَمْ یُهَاجِرُوْا مَا لَکُمْ مِّنْ وَّلَایَتِهِمْ مِّنْ شَیْءٍ حَتّٰی یُهَاجِرُوْا ۚ وَاِنِ اسْتَنْصَرُوْکُمْ فِی الدِّیْنِ فَعَلَیْکُمُ النَّصْرُ اِلَّا عَلٰی قَوْمٍ بَیْنَکُمْ وَبَیْنَهُمْ مِّیْثَاقٌ ؕ وَاللّٰهُ بِمَا تَعْمَلُوْنَ بَصِیْرٌ ۟

---

^a2 : 219 ; 9 : 20 ; 61 : 12.

1160. Important Words :

اٰوَوْا (gave shelter) is derived from اوی. They say اوی الیه *i.e.* he betook himself to it ; or he repaired to it for lodging, covert or refuge ; or simply he betook himself to it or repaired to it ; or he returned to it. اواه means, he gave or afforded him lodging, covert, refuge or asylum ; or he sheltered, protected or harboured him. اوی له means, he felt compassion or pity for him. اٰواه means, he gave or afforded him lodging, covert, refuge or asylum ; or he sheltered, protected or harboured him (Lane).

Commentary :

The verse enunciates a great principle which should govern the social relations of Muslims. It lays down that those Muslims who live in the same country and under the same administration, whether as immigrants or as original citizens, are bound to help one another

in the hour of need. If one of them is wronged the others must come to his help. But as regards those Muslims who have not emigrated to a Muslim country and prefer to live apart, they have no claim on the assistance of these Muslims in worldly matters. But if they seek their help in the matter of religion, *e.g.*, when they are persecuted for the sake of their religion, then they must be helped. If, however, they are living under a non-Muslim Government, with whom Muslims have entered into a treaty of peace, then no help should be rendered them even in matters of religion ; and in this case the only way open to them is to emigrate from the non-Muslim country. The reader should note what high regard for compacts and treaties the Quran inculcates in its followers. It is to warn Muslims against a violation of compacts that the verse fittingly ends with the words, *And Allah sees what you do.*

74. And those who disbelieve—they are friends one of another. If you do it not, there will be mischief in the land and great disorder.[1161]

وَالَّذِيْنَ كَفَرُوْا بَعْضُهُمْ اَوْلِيَآءُ بَعْضٍ اِلَّا تَفْعَلُوْهُ تَكُنْ فِتْنَةٌ فِى الْاَرْضِ وَفَسَادٌ كَبِيْرٌ ۞

75. And [a]those who have believed and left their homes and striven for the cause of Allah, and those who have given *them* shelter and help—these indeed are true believers. For them is forgiveness and an honourable provision.[1162]

وَالَّذِيْنَ اٰمَنُوْا وَهَاجَرُوْا وَجَاهَدُوْا فِىْ سَبِيْلِ اللهِ وَالَّذِيْنَ اٰوَوْا وَّنَصَرُوْٓا اُولٰٓئِكَ هُمُ الْمُؤْمِنُوْنَ حَقًّا لَهُمْ مَّغْفِرَةٌ وَّرِزْقٌ كَرِيْمٌ ۞

---

[a]2 : 219 ; 9 : 20 ; 61 : 12.

1161. Commentary :

The pronoun "it" in تفعلوه (you do it not) refers to what has been said in the previous verse *i.e.* helping oppressed Muslims as well as fulfilling compacts with non-Muslims. The verse purports to say that if this teaching is not observed by Muslims, the result will be oppression and disturbance in the earth.

1162. Commentary :

Two classes of believers have been commended here : *firstly*, those who being persecuted, flee from a country where they are not free to follow their faith ; *secondly*, those who give shelter to and help the immigrants. The Muslims of the former class are called *Muhājirīn* (Refugees), while those of the second class are known as *Anṣār* (Helpers). Both these classes have been called true believers, for both are active believers and make sacrifices for the cause of religion ; and the verse promises them forgiveness and honourable provision. This also shows that those who do not emigrate from their homes where they do not enjoy religious freedom and set worldly good above religion do not have an " honourable provision " *i.e.* their worldly gains are not honourable in the sight of God. Similarly, the verse hints that those who help and give shelter to the immigrants will, in spite of freely spending on their needy brethren, find their possessions ever increasing, and God will continue to grant them honourable provision.

76. And those who have believed since and left their homes and striven *for the cause of Allah* along with you,—these are of you ; and *a*as to blood relations, they are nearer one to another in the Book of Allah. Surely, Allah knows all things well.[1163]

وَالَّذِيْنَ اٰمَنُوْا مِنْ بَعْدُ وَهَاجَرُوْا وَجَاهَدُوْا مَعَكُمْ فَاُولٰٓئِكَ مِنْكُمْ ۚ وَاُولُوا الْاَرْحَامِ بَعْضُهُمْ اَوْلٰى بِبَعْضٍ فِيْ كِتٰبِ اللّٰهِ ۗ اِنَّ اللّٰهَ بِكُلِّ شَيْءٍ عَلِيْمٌ ۠

---

*a*33 : 7.

1163. Important Words :

اولٰى (nearer) means more entitled or having a better right or more deserving or more worthy. It also means, more regardful or more considerate. See 4 : 136.

Commentary :

The verse purports to say that the promise of " forgiveness and honourable provision " given to emigrants (see preceding verse) is not confined to the early emigrants only. It extends to the later emigrants also and is meant to continue while persecution or, for that matter, sincerity of faith continues.

The verse gives another injunction also. As all Muslims were declared to be brothers one to another (8 : 73), some persons might have been led to think that they might also inherit one another's property ; so the verse fittingly declares that only blood relations are entitled to inheritance and that other Muslims are only brothers in faith, but not heirs.

1. *This is* a declaration of *complete* absolution on the part of Allah and His Messenger *from all obligation* to the idolaters whom you had made promises.[1164]

بَرَاءَةٌ مِّنَ اللهِ وَرَسُوْلِهٖۤ اِلَى الَّذِيْنَ عٰهَدْتُّمۡ مِّنَ الْمُشْرِكِيْنَ ۙ

1164. Important Words :

بَرَاءَة (a declaration of absolution) is the noun-infinitive from بَرِىَ which means, he was or became clear or free from a thing ; or he was or became immune, secure or safe. بَرِىَ مِنَ الْمَرَض means, he became free from the disease or malady. بَرِىَ الْجُرْح means, the wound healed or was healing. بَرِىَ مِنَ الْاَمْر means, he was free from the thing or quit thereof ; or he was guiltless of it and was not responsible for it. They say بَرِىَ مِنَ الدَّيْن *i.e.* he became clear or quit of debt ; or he became exempt from the demand. بَرِىَ اِلَيْك مِنْ حَقِّك means, he was or became clear or quit to thee of thy claim or due or right ; or he was or became exempt from thy demand. بَرَاءَة being the noun-infinitive from بَرِىَ gives all the meanings derived from the verbal uses of the words given above. It particularly means, a declaration of granting or conferring or announcing immunity or exemption or absolution from a fault or responsibility ; freedom from blame ; exemption or absolution from a demand, etc. (Tāj & Aqrab). See also 3 : 50.

عٰهَدْتُّم (you made promises). عٰهَد is derived from عَهْد for which see 2 : 41. The word عٰهَد is here used not in the sense of entering into a treaty or a compact but making a promise, or making a solemn promise by which one binds oneself. They say عٰهَدْتُ اللهَ اَنْ لَا اَفْعَل كَذَا *i.e.* I

have made a promise to God that I will not do such a thing (Lisān).

Commentary :

This *Sūra* does not begin with the usual formula of بِسْمِ اللهِ (In the name of God) for the reason of which see Introductory Note to Chapter *Anfāl*.

The first verse of this *Sūra* refers to all the idolaters of Arabia including the *dhimmīs i.e.* those disbelievers who lived under the protection of Muslims as well as those non-Muslim Arab tribes with whom Muslims had treaty relations.

The verse declares the complete freedom of God and the Holy Prophet from all demand or blame, meaning thereby that all promises made by God and His Messenger had been fulfilled and their truthfulness fully established and therefore the idolaters to whatever class they belonged, could bring no charge against God and His Prophet. Prophecies about the defeat and discomfiture of infidels and the ultimate success and triumph of Islam had been repeatedly made, and, now that all these prophecies had been fulfilled, the infidels of Arabia could no longer say that the declarations of the Prophet about the final triumph of Islam were mere empty promises. By the fulfilment of these promises, the verse says, God and His Messenger had proved their absolute freedom from the charge of making false promises.

2. So go about in the land for four months, and ^aknow that you cannot frustrate *the plan of* Allah and that Allah will humiliate the disbelievers.[1165]

فَسِيحُوْا فِى الْاَرْضِ اَرْبَعَةَ اَشْهُرٍ وَّاعْلَمُوْٓا اَنَّكُمْ غَيْرُ مُعْجِزِى اللّٰهِ ۙ وَاَنَّ اللّٰهَ مُخْزِى الْكٰفِرِيْنَ ۝

3. And *this is* a proclamation from Allah and His Messenger to the people on the day of the Greater Pilgrimage, that Allah is clear of the idolaters, and so is His Messenger. So if you repent, it will be better for you; but if you turn away, then ^bknow that you cannot frustrate *the plan of* Allah. And ^cgive tidings of a painful punishment to those who disbelieve,[1166]

وَاَذَانٌ مِّنَ اللّٰهِ وَرَسُوْلِهٖٓ اِلَى النَّاسِ يَوْمَ الْحَجِّ الْاَكْبَرِ اَنَّ اللّٰهَ بَرِيْٓءٌ مِّنَ الْمُشْرِكِيْنَ ۙ وَرَسُوْلُهٗ ۚ فَاِنْ تُبْتُمْ فَهُوَ خَيْرٌ لَّكُمْ ۚ وَاِنْ تَوَلَّيْتُمْ فَاعْلَمُوْٓا اَنَّكُمْ غَيْرُ مُعْجِزِى اللّٰهِ ۗ وَبَشِّرِ الَّذِيْنَ كَفَرُوْا بِعَذَابٍ اَلِيْمٍ ۝

---

^a6 : 135 ; 11 : 21.   ^bSee 9 : 2.   ^c4 : 139.

1165. Commentary :

This verse particularly refers to the fulfilment of the prophecy contained in 54 : 2. Disbelievers are told to travel throughout the length and breadth of Arabia for four months (the period ordinarily required in the Prophet's time for such travel) and see whether there has remained any vestige of infidel rule and dominion in any part of the country. The infidels of Arabia opposed and persecuted the Prophet and his followers and spared no pains to crush and extirpate Islam. But Almighty God promised help to His Messenger with the result that the cause of Islam triumphed and all opposition was swept away.

1166. Important Words :

اَذَان (proclamation) is derived from اَذِنَ which means, he gave ear or listened ; he permitted or allowed ; he knew or he became informed, etc. اٰذَنَ means, he informed, or notified or announced. اَذَان means, notification, announcement or call.

بَرِئَ (clear) see 9 : 1 above. But whereas in that verse the word signifies absolution from obligations and from fulfilment of promises made

by Islam, in the present one it simply signifies being clear of a person or a thing *i.e.* having nothing to do with him or it (Lane).

Commentary :

The declaration, contained in this verse and the one that follows, is different from that embodied in 9:1 & 2 above, for whereas vv. 9:1 & 2 relate to absolution from the fulfilment of promises made to idolaters, the present verse pertains to the severance of connections with them. This severance, however, should not be taken to mean that the verse declares Islam to be free from all treaty obligations ; for, as the following verse makes it clear, treaties are to be respected in all cases and must not be violated.

It is related that on his return from Tabūk in the ninth year of the Hijra, the Holy Prophet sent Abū Bakr to Mecca to announce, on the occasion of the Greater Pilgrimage, that henceforward no one would be allowed to perform the circuit of the Ka‘ba naked or unclothed. Immediately afterwards the first portion of this *Sūra* was revealed. Upon

4. ^aExcepting those of the idolaters with whom you have entered into a treaty and who have not *subsequently* failed you in any thing nor aided anyone against you. So fulfil to these the treaty *you have* made with them till their term. Surely, Allah loves those who are righteous.[1167]

اِلَّا الَّذِيْنَ عَهَدْتُّمْ مِّنَ الْمُشْرِكِيْنَ ثُمَّ لَمْ يَنْقُصُوْكُمْ شَيْئًا وَّ لَمْ يُظَاهِرُوْا عَلَيْكُمْ اَحَدًا فَاَتِمُّوْۤا اِلَيْهِمْ عَهْدَهُمْ اِلٰى مُدَّتِهِمْ اِنَّ اللّٰهَ يُحِبُّ الْمُتَّقِيْنَ ۝

*a*9 : 7.

this the Holy Prophet sent 'Ali to Mecca, and he, as his cousin and representative, after reciting the opening verses of this *Sūra*, made a proclamation containing the following two announcements before the pilgrims who had gathered at Mecca from all parts of Arabia :—

1. No idolater shall approach the House of God after this year.

2. Treaties and engagements made by the Holy Prophet with idolatrous tribes shall stand and be faithfully respected till the end of their term. The idolaters of Arabia and the hypocrites of Medina had, by their plots and conspiracies against Muslims and by their persistent treacherous conduct, lost all claim to the clemency of the Holy Prophet. When he was absent on the expedition to Tabūk, they spread the false rumour that the whole Muslim army had been captured and the Prophet was dead. Moreover, Abū 'Āmir, a mischievous Arab leader, had gone to Syria to bring a Christian army to attack Muslims; and in Arabia itself secret preparations had begun for a general rising. But for the timely return of the Holy Prophet, these plots would have resulted in great disturbance and heavy loss of life. When, on his return, the Holy Prophet learnt of the great mischief set on foot in his absence and the plots hatched to deal a death-blow to Islam, he, with a view to preventing a recrudescence of such mischief,

ordered that henceforth no idolater could stay in the Ḥijāz with the exception of those with whom he had entered into a treaty, and these too were allowed to stay only till the expiry of the term of their treaty. The order was justified not only by the persistently treacherous conduct of the idolaters, but also by other political and cultural considerations which demanded its promulgation. The Ḥijāz had now become the religious as well as the political centre of Islam, and its interests demanded that it should be purged of all foreign and harmful elements likely to endanger its integrity and prove dangerous to the nascent Muslim community which had been brought into being to carry the message of the New Faith to the four corners of the earth.

1167. **Commentary :**

The verse makes an exception of such idolatrous tribes as had entered into a treaty with Muslims. These tribes were Banū Khuzā'a, Banū Mudlij, Banū Bakr, Banū Ḍumra and some of the Banū Sulaim tribes. The verse incidentally throws interesting light on the sanctity that Islam attaches to treaties and agreements. It requires its followers to respect their inviolability at all costs, and declares that faithfulness to the plighted word is an act of piety which earns the love of God.

5. And when the forbidden months have passed, kill the idolaters wherever you find them and take them *prisoners*, and beleaguer them, and lie in wait for them at every place of ambush. But ^aif they repent and observe Prayer and pay the Zakāt, then leave their way *free*. Surely, Allah is Most Forgiving, Merciful.[1168]

فَاِذَا انْسَلَخَ الْاَشْهُرُ الْحُرُمُ فَاقْتُلُوا الْمُشْرِكِيْنَ حَيْثُ وَجَدْتُمُوْهُمْ وَخُذُوْهُمْ وَاحْصُرُوْهُمْ وَاقْعُدُوْا لَهُمْ كُلَّ مَرْصَدٍ فَاِنْ تَابُوْا وَاَقَامُوا الصَّلٰوةَ وَاٰتُوا الزَّكٰوةَ فَخَلُّوْا سَبِيْلَهُمْ ۚ اِنَّ اللّٰهَ غَفُوْرٌ رَّحِيْمٌ ۥ

---

*a*7 : 154 ; 9 : 11.

1168. Commentary :

The term الاشهر الحرم is generally applied to the four sacred months of *Shawwāl, Dhū'l-Qa'da Dhū'l-Ḥijja* and *Rajab*, the first three being the months of the Greater Pilgrimage, while in the last the Arabs generally performed the Lesser Pilgrimage or *'Umra* (see notes on 2 : 195 and 2 : 218). In this verse, however, the words الاشهر الحرم signify not the "sacred months" but "forbidden months" and refer to the four months mentioned in 9 : 2 above. These were meant to grant a respite to idolaters to travel through the land in safety and see whether Islam had not triumphed and whether the word of God had not proved true. At the end of this period, during which all hostilities were to be suspended, war was to be resumed against the idolatrous Arabs with the exception, of course, of such as had entered into a treaty with Muslims, and the treacherous and faithless idolaters already at war with Muslims were to be captured and killed wherever found. It should, however, be remembered that the command to wage war after the expiry of the four forbidden months did not apply to all idolaters without discrimination but was directed only against such avowed enemies of Islam as had themselves started hostilities against Islam and had broken their plighted word and plotted to expel the Holy Prophet from the city. The reason for this ultimatum is given in the following few verses, *viz.* 9 : 8-13. As for those idolaters who had not

been guilty of faithlessness and treachery, they were to be protected (see 9 : 4, 7). It is highly regrettable, however, that, divorcing this commandment from its context, some critics have made this verse the basis for an attack against Islam, alleging that it inculcates the destruction of all non-Muslims. The Quran and history belie that baseless allegation.

The words, *and lie in wait for them at every place of ambush*, mean that a strict watch should be kept over the movements of the enemy that he may not be able to create mischief and carry on malicious propaganda against Muslims. The very words of the verse point to the existence of a great danger. These times were indeed very hard for Muslims. On the one hand, the Eastern Roman Empire was preparing to attack them and, on the other, the internal enemies of Islam were hatching plots to bring about its downfall.

The words, *But if they repent . . . ,* show that even those enemies of Islam at whose hands Muslims had suffered such grievous losses were to be forgiven if they repented and accepted Islam of their own free will. That no compulsion was to be used is clear from the very next verse, as also from the fundamental injunction laid down in 2 : 257. The truth is that there was a large number of men among the idolaters who, in their heart of hearts, believed in the truth of Islam, but who, either through pride or for fear of others or for other reasons, refrained from

6. And if any one of the idolaters ask protection of thee, grant him protection so that he may hear the word of Allah ; then convey him to his place of security. That is because they are a people who have no knowledge.[1169]

وَاِنْ اَحَدٌ مِّنَ الْمُشْرِكِيْنَ اسْتَجَارَكَ فَاَجِرْهُ حَتّٰى يَسْمَعَ كَلٰمَ اللّٰهِ ثُمَّ اَبْلِغْهُ مَاْمَنَهٗ ۚ ذٰلِكَ بِاَنَّهُمْ قَوْمٌ لَّا يَعْلَمُوْنَ ۞

making an open confession of faith. This verse was intended to convey to such people that, if any one of them declared his faith in Islam even during the war, his confession would not be taken as hypocritical or as made to save his skin. A conclusive proof of the fact that there were many among idolaters who were at heart inclined to Islam but were afraid to declare their faith openly owing to fear of persecution is that whenever war ceased, there was a rush for conversion to Islam. The two years of peace that followed the Treaty of Ḥudaibiya brought over a very large number of disbelievers to Islam. They could not have joined Islam in such large numbers, if they had not been believers in their hearts, having been held back only by fear of persecution. There are even cases on record of men accepting Islam in the thick of battle. Muslims did not at first spare such men, thinking that they had done so merely to save their lives. The Holy Prophet, however, took such Muslims severely to task, asking them if they had torn open the hearts of those people and had satisfied themselves that they were really devoid of sincerity. It is for this reason that the Quran directs Muslims not to harm such men from among the idolaters as profess their faith in

Islam and observe the commandments of God, for only God knows whether they are true Muslims or not.

The divine attributes of "Forgiving" and "Merciful" at the end of the verse show that the conduct of idolaters had been such as to make them deserving of the severest of punishments, and that to extend forgiveness to them even on their abandonment of idolatry was really an act of mercy.

1169. Commentary :

This verse clearly establishes the fact that war with idolaters was not undertaken to force them to embrace Islam, because, according to it, even when a state of war existed idolaters were to be permitted to come to the Muslim camp or the Muslim headquarters if they desired to investigate the truth. Then, after the truth had been preached to them and they had been acquainted with the teachings of Islam, they were to be safely conveyed to their place of security, if they did not feel inclined to embrace the New Faith. In the face of such clear teachings, it is the height of injustice to accuse Islam of intolerance or of allowing compulsion for the propagation of its teaching.

R. 2   7.   How can there be a treaty of these idolaters with Allah and His Messenger, *except those with whom you entered into a treaty at the Sacred Mosque? So, as long as they stand true to you, stand true to them. Surely, Allah loves those who are righteous.[1170]

كَيْفَ يَكُوْنُ لِلْمُشْرِكِيْنَ عَهْدٌ عِنْدَ اللهِ وَعِنْدَ رَسُوْلِهٖ اِلَّا الَّذِيْنَ عَاهَدْتُّمْ عِنْدَ الْمَسْجِدِ الْحَرَامِ فَمَا اسْتَقَامُوْا لَكُمْ فَاسْتَقِيْمُوْا لَهُمْ اِنَّ اللهَ يُحِبُّ الْمُتَّقِيْنَ ۞

8.   How *can it be* when, if they prevail against you, *they would not observe any tie of relationship or covenant in respect of you. They would please you with their mouths, while their hearts refuse, and most of them are perfidious.[1171]

كَيْفَ وَاِنْ يَّظْهَرُوْا عَلَيْكُمْ لَا يَرْقُبُوْا فِيْكُمْ اِلًّا وَّلَا ذِمَّةً ۖ يُرْضُوْنَكُمْ بِأَفْوَاهِهِمْ وَ تَأْبٰى قُلُوْبُهُمْ ۚ وَ اَكْثَرُهُمْ فٰسِقُوْنَ ۞

*a*9 : 4.   *b*9 : 10.

1170. Commentary :

The words, *So, as long as they stand true to you, stand true to them,* show that war was permissible only against such non-Muslims as were faithless to their covenants and attacked Muslims treacherously. As for the rest, Muslims have been bidden to observe their engagements strictly and faithfully with them. It will be noted that, like 9 : 4, this verse describes the observance of covenants and treaties as an act of piety and righteousness which is pleasing in the sight of God. No wonder that the Quran repeatedly exhorts Muslims to be faithful to their treaties.

1171. Important Words :

الّ (tie of relationship). الّه means, he pierced him with a bright javelin. They say الّ الفرس *i.e.* the horse went quickly, making itself prominent. الّ اللون means, the colour became clear and bright. الّ means, relationship, or nearness with respect to kindred; good origin; a compact or covenant; a promise or an assurance of safety or security; a neighbour; a visible state of relationship or of compact (Lane, Aqrab & Mufradāt).

ذمة (covenant) is the noun-infinitive from ذم. They say ذمه *i.e.* he blamed or found fault with him. اذم means, he did or said that for which he should be blamed or found fault with. اذمه also means, he protected him or granted him refuge or protection. اذم له means, he took or obtained a promise or an assurance of security or a covenant in his favour. ذمة means, a compact, covenant, treaty, engagement, obligation or responsibility; a right or due for the neglect of which one is to be blamed. The expression اهل الذمة is used for those non-Muslim people with whom the Muslim State has made a compact and who pay poll-tax to the State, in return for which the State is responsible for their security and freedom (Lane & Aqrab).

Commentary :

This verse makes it further clear that the commandment to wage war is meant only

9. *They barter the Signs of Allah for a paltry price and turn *men* away from His way. Evil indeed is that which they do.[1172]

اِشۡتَرَوۡا بِاٰیٰتِ اللّٰہِ ثَمَنًا قَلِیۡلًا فَصَدُّوۡا عَنۡ سَبِیۡلِہٖ اِنَّہُمۡ سَآءَ مَا کَانُوۡا یَعۡمَلُوۡنَ ۝

10. *They observe not any tie of relationship or covenant in respect of any one who trusts *them*. And it is they who are transgressors.[1173]

لَا یَرۡقُبُوۡنَ فِیۡ مُؤۡمِنٍ اِلًّا وَّلَا ذِمَّۃً ؕ وَاُولٰٓئِکَ ہُمُ الۡمُعۡتَدُوۡنَ ۝

11. *But if they repent, and observe Prayer and pay the Zakāt, then they are your brethren in faith. And We explain the Signs for a people who have knowledge.[1174]

فَاِنۡ تَابُوۡا وَاَقَامُوا الصَّلٰوۃَ وَاٰتَوُا الزَّکٰوۃَ فَاِخۡوَانُکُمۡ فِی الدِّیۡنِ ؕ وَنُفَصِّلُ الۡاٰیٰتِ لِقَوۡمٍ یَّعۡلَمُوۡنَ ۝

---

*2 : 175; 3 : 78, 188; 16 : 96.   *9 : 8.   *7 : 154; 9 : 5.

---

about such disbelievers as had not only been the first to open hostilities against Islam but were, at the same time, perfidious and treacherous, paying no respect either to ties of relationship or to compacts and covenants.

1172. Commentary :

See note on 2 : 42.

1173. Important Words :

مومن (one who trusts) is the active participle from آمن which is derived from امن which means, he was or became safe or secure or free from fear. امنه علی کذا means, he trusted him in respect of such a thing. آمنه means, he rendered him safe or secure or free from fear ; he trusted or confided in him. آمن به means, he believed in him. مؤمن therefore, means, a believer ; a faithful person ; a person who trusts or confides in others ; one who affords security and protection. المؤمن is also one of the attributes of God, meaning, He Who grants security and protection to His creatures (Lane).

Commentary :

This verse emphasizes the heinousness of the crime of disbelievers by adding the word مومن

(one who trusts). These disbelievers would not be true even to those who trusted them. Thus the present and the preceding two verses mention the reasons why Muslims were command-ed to wage war against these idolaters in 9 : 5. These reasons are : (1) they were treacherous and perfidious ; they professed to be friendly to Muslims, but as soon as they found an opportunity to injure them, they broke their plighted word and this inspite of the fact that Muslims trusted them (9 : 8 and the present verse); (2) they even disregarded the ties of relationship and killed their own kinsmen merely because the latter had embraced Islam (9 : 8); (3) their object in making war was to prevent men from embracing Islam (9 : 9); and (4) they were transgressors *i.e.* the first to attack Muslims (the present verse).

1174. Commentary :

The words, *they are your brethren in faith,* mean that not only should all hostilities cease against such disbelievers as repent but they are to be looked upon as brethren and treated as such. See also note on 9 : 5, above.

12. And if they break their oaths after their covenant, and attack your religion, then *a*fight *these* leaders of disbelief,—surely, they have no regard for their oaths—that they may desist.[1175]

وَاِنْ نَّكَثُوْۤا اَيْمَانَهُمْ مِّنْۢ بَعْدِ عَهْدِهِمْ وَطَعَنُوْا فِيْ دِيْنِكُمْ فَقَاتِلُوْۤا اَئِمَّةَ الْكُفْرِ ۙ اِنَّهُمْ لَاۤ اَيْمَانَ لَهُمْ لَعَلَّهُمْ يَنْتَهُوْنَ ۝

13. Will you not fight a people who have broken their oaths, and who plotted to turn out the Messenger, and they were the first to commence *hostilities* against you? Do you fear them? Nay, Allah is most worthy that you should fear Him, if you are believers.[1176]

اَلَا تُقَاتِلُوْنَ قَوْمًا نَّكَثُوْۤا اَيْمَانَهُمْ وَهَمُّوْا بِاِخْرَاجِ الرَّسُوْلِ وَهُمْ بَدَءُوْكُمْ اَوَّلَ مَرَّةٍ ۚ اَتَخْشَوْنَهُمْ ۚ فَاللّٰهُ اَحَقُّ اَنْ تَخْشَوْهُ اِنْ كُنْتُمْ مُّؤْمِنِيْنَ ۝

---

*a*2 : 191 ; 4 : 92.

1175. Commentary:

This verse leaves no doubt as to the fact that Muslims were bidden to fight disbelievers only if they broke their covenant and attacked Islam with a view to injuring it. It also makes it clear that the object in fighting disbelievers was to make them "desist" from transgression.

The words طعنوا فى دينكم (attack your religion) do not refer to mere verbal taunts and reproaches but to actual attacks meant to injure the vital interests of Islam ; the word طعن literally meaning "to pierce with a spear".

The epithet, *these leaders of disbelief*, is here applied not to a few leading individuals but to the whole people to whom this commandment to fight referred. They are called ائمة (leaders) because *firstly* they were among the first and the foremost to clash with Muslims and their example encouraged others ; and, *secondly*, their hostility towards Islam was so inveterate and implacable that they served, as it were, as evil models in this respect.

1176. Commentary:

The words, *who plotted to turn out the Messenger*, do not refer to the Meccans,

but to those who, when the Holy Prophet went on an expedition to the Syrian border, plotted to bring about his downfall by making the different tribes of Arabia stand up as one man against him on his return (see notes on 9 : 3,4 above). The Meccans did not merely plot to turn out the Holy Prophet but actually turned him out (see 47 : 14). Moreover, by the time these verses were revealed the Meccans had embraced Islam and all hostilities between Muslims and Meccans had ceased.

The words, *they were the first to commence hostilities against you*, also refer not to the Meccans but to those infidels, whether open or secret, who lived in and about Medina. The words provide conclusive proof of the fact that, far from being the transgressor, Islam was transgressed against. It was the infidels who first began hostilities against it. They acted most treacherously and resorted to all sorts of foul means to annihilate it. It was only such men that Muslims had been commanded to fight. Christian critics of Islam will do well to compare the wars of Islam with the wars of their great Law-giver, Moses, against a

14. Fight them, that Allah may punish them at your hands, and humiliate them, and help you *to victory* over them, and relieve the minds of a people who believe;[1177]

قَاتِلُوْهُمْ يُعَذِّبْهُمُ اللّٰهُ بِأَيْدِيْكُمْ وَيُخْزِهِمْ وَيَنْصُرْكُمْ عَلَيْهِمْ وَيَشْفِ صُدُوْرَ قَوْمٍ مُّؤْمِنِيْنَ ۞

15. And that He may take away the wrath of their hearts. And Allah turns *with mercy* to whomsoever He pleases. And Allah is All-Knowing, Wise.[1178]

وَيُذْهِبْ غَيْظَ قُلُوْبِهِمْ ۖ وَيَتُوْبُ اللّٰهُ عَلٰى مَنْ يَّشَآءُ ۗ وَاللّٰهُ عَلِيْمٌ حَكِيْمٌ ۞

---

people who had never taken up arms against him and had done nothing to offend him. Yet these people were ruthlessly butchered and even their women and children were not spared (Deut. 20:16, 17). As compared with this, the Holy Prophet took up arms only against those who first started hostilities, and even then he directed that their women and children and their religious devotees, as well as their churches, should be spared (Muslim, Ṭaḥāwī & Dāwūd). Those who regard the wars of Moses as holy have certainly no reason to criticize the wars of the Holy Prophet of Islam.

1177. Important Words :

يَشْفِ (relieve) is derived from شَفَا. They say شَفَاهُ مِنْ مَرَضِهِ *i.e.*, he cured him (of disease) and restored him to convalescence. شَفَيْتُهُ means, I relieved him from doubt. شَفَاهُ عَنِ المَسْأَلَةِ means, he relieved him from doubt respecting the question. يَشْفِيكَ اِنْ قَالَ means, he will please thee if he speaks *i.e.*, his speech will please thee (Lane).

Commentary :

The verse shows that the enemies of Islam

had made themselves deserving of divine punishment by their treacherous and wrongful conduct; and fighting was only a form of divine punishment that had been prescribed for them and it was inflicted on them after they had themselves started hostilities. It was most certainly not resorted to in order to compel them to embrace Islam.

1178. Commentary :

The pronoun "their" in the words, *the wrath of their hearts*, refers to disbelievers, and the sentence means that God may thereby do away with the wrath that had been kindled in the hearts of disbelievers against Muslims. This could be done in two ways: (1) by crushing their power completely and for ever; or (2) by making them accept Islam. Both of these means are intended here, for there were some who were destroyed and their power crushed and there were others who saw the light and voluntarily embraced Islam. The following words, *i.e.*, *And Allah turns with mercy to whomsoever He pleases*, obviously refer to the latter class.

16. ^aDo you think that you would be left alone, while Allah has not yet known those of you who strive *in the cause of Allah* and ^bdo not take *anyone* for an intimate friend besides Allah and His Messenger and the believers. And Allah is well aware of what you do.[1179]

R. 3   17. The idolaters cannot keep the Mosques of Allah in a good and flourishing condition while they bear witness against themselves to disbelief. It is they whose works shall be vain, and in the Fire shall they abide.[1180]

اَمْ حَسِبْتُمْ اَنْ تُتْرَكُوْا وَلَمَّا يَعْلَمِ اللهُ الَّذِيْنَ جَاهَدُوْا مِنْكُمْ وَلَمْ يَتَّخِذُوْا مِنْ دُوْنِ اللهِ وَلَا رَسُوْلِهٖ وَلَا الْمُؤْمِنِيْنَ وَلِيْجَةً ۚ وَاللهُ خَبِيْرٌۢ بِمَا تَعْمَلُوْنَ ۝

مَا كَانَ لِلْمُشْرِكِيْنَ اَنْ يَّعْمُرُوْا مَسٰجِدَ اللهِ شٰهِدِيْنَ عَلٰٓى اَنْفُسِهِمْ بِالْكُفْرِ ؕ اُولٰٓئِكَ حَبِطَتْ اَعْمَالُهُمْ ۚ وَفِي النَّارِ هُمْ خٰلِدُوْنَ ۝

^a3 : 143, 180 ; 29 : 3-4.   ^b3 : 29 ; 4 : 140, 145 ; 9 : 23.

1179. Important Words :

وَلِيْجَة (intimate friend) is derived from وَلَجَ. They say وَلَجَ الْبَيْتَ *i.e.* he entered the house. اَوْلَجَهُ means, he caused it or him to enter ; he inserted it. وَلِيْجَة means, anything that is introduced or inserted into another thing ; an intimate friend or associate ; one whom a person takes to rely upon, not being of his family (Lane).

Commentary :

This verse hints that the trials of Muslims were not yet over. They had still to face more grievous dangers and greater trials, and only those who were true and sincere believers would be able to stand them. The verse thus warns believers to be prepared for still severer tests and yet greater sacrifices. Muslims had indeed been already tried at Badr and Uḥud and at the Battle of the Ditch, and had stood the test. But as a new era was now dawning for them with the expedition to Tabūk on the border of Syria, the verse calls upon them to make yet greater preparations. The trials and tribulations through which Muslims had already passed were indeed little as compared with the ordeals they had yet to face. The later dangers were far more terrible and grievous than anything they had yet experienced.

The words, *and do not take anyone for an intimate friend besides Allah and His Messenger and the believers*, are also intended as a warning to Muslims to become yet more united and to allow no foreign element to split their ranks in the coming days of trial and sacrifice.

1180. Commentary :

This verse relates to idolatrous pilgrims and serves as an introduction to the announcement contained in 9 : 28 below. No idolater was henceforth to be allowed to approach the Ka‘ba, as announced by ‘Alī to the pilgrims assembled at Mecca on the occasion of the Greater Pilgrimage of the year 9 A. H. (see note on 9 : 3 above). The verse under comment gives the reason for that prohibition. The Ka‘ba being a temple dedicated to the worship of the One God, idolaters had nothing to do with it. They were declared enemies of God's Unity who bore witness to their own idolatrous beliefs and thus stood condemned by

18. He alone can keep the Mosques of Allah in a good and flourishing condition who believes in Allah, and the Last Day, and observes Prayer, and pays the Zakāt, and fears none but Allah; so these it is who may be among those who reach the goal.[1181]

إِنَّمَا يَعْمُرُ مَسَاجِدَ اللّٰهِ مَنْ اٰمَنَ بِاللّٰهِ وَالْيَوْمِ الْاٰخِرِ وَاَقَامَ الصَّلٰوةَ وَاٰتَى الزَّكٰوةَ وَلَمْ يَخْشَ اِلَّا اللّٰهَ فَعَسٰۤى اُولٰٓئِكَ اَنْ يَّكُوْنُوْا مِنَ الْمُهْتَدِيْنَ ۞

19. Do you hold the giving of drink to the pilgrims, and the maintenance of the Sacred Mosque as *equal to the works* of him who believes in Allah and the Last Day and strives in the path of Allah? They are not *at all* equal in the sight of Allah. And Allah guides not the unjust people.[1182]

اَجَعَلْتُمْ سِقَايَةَ الْحَاجِّ وَعِمَارَةَ الْمَسْجِدِ الْحَرَامِ كَمَنْ اٰمَنَ بِاللّٰهِ وَالْيَوْمِ الْاٰخِرِ وَجٰهَدَ فِىْ سَبِيْلِ اللّٰهِ لَا يَسْتَوٗنَ عِنْدَ اللّٰهِ وَاللّٰهُ لَا يَهْدِى الْقَوْمَ الظّٰلِمِيْنَ ۞

---

their own confession. Moreover, while performing the Pilgrimage, idolaters, instead of declaring God's Oneness, attributed co-partners to Him, for it is on record that, while reciting the prescribed formula "Here I am, O my Lord, here I am; Thou hast no co-partner", they used to add the words "except him whom Thou hast Thyself made Thy co-partner". The words, *while they bear witness against themselves to disbelief,* beside being general in their significance, may also refer to this practice of idolaters.

1181. Important Words:

عسى (may be) is meant to express desire or hope of obtaining something good or to express fear lest one should fall into an evil way (Aqrab). The word thus implies either desire or hope of good or fear of evil. They say عسى زيد ان يقوم *i.e.* Zaid is near to standing; or I eagerly desire or I hope that Zaid may be performing the act of standing; or it may be that Zaid is, or will be, standing. عسى may thus be explained as meaning, it may be that, or simply may be. When uttered by God, the word is expressive of an event of necessary occurrence (Lane). See also the meaning of the word لعل

under 2:22. Though desire or hope are not attributable to God, yet the words لعل and عسى are used by God to point to the fact that a certain thing is such that people may base their desire or hope on it (Mufradāt).

Commentary:

The prosperity of a Mosque of God, and for that matter of the Ka'ba itself, lies in the fulfilment of the noble object for which it is built. This object is the glorification and the remembrance of the name of God in it; and certainly this object is much the better realized by prohibiting those from visiting it who, instead of glorifying God, attribute co-partners to Him, and by encouraging and exhorting true believers to ferquent it.

The words, *these it is who may be among those who reach the goal,* signify that, since believers are destined to prosper, even the material prosperity of the Ka'ba will not suffer from the exclusion of infidels; for believers will go on pilgrimage to it in ever-increasing numbers.

1182. Commentary:

The outward and physical service of the Ka'ba, though in itself a meritorious act, is

20. ^aThose who believe and emigrate from their homes *for the sake of God* and strive in the cause of Allah with their property and their persons have the highest rank in the sight of Allah. And it is they who shall triumph.[1183]

اَلَّذِيْنَ اٰمَنُوْا وَهَاجَرُوْا وَجَهَدُوْا فِىْ سَبِيْلِ اللّٰهِ بِاَمْوَالِهِمْ وَاَنْفُسِهِمْ اَعْظَمُ دَرَجَةً عِنْدَ اللّٰهِ وَاُولٰٓئِكَ هُمُ الْفَآئِزُوْنَ ۟

21. ^bTheir Lord gives them glad tidings of mercy from Him, and of *His* pleasure, and of Gardens wherein there shall be lasting bliss for them ;

يُبَشِّرُهُمْ رَبُّهُمْ بِرَحْمَةٍ مِّنْهُ وَرِضْوَانٍ وَّجَنّٰتٍ لَّهُمْ فِيْهَا نَعِيْمٌ مُّقِيْمٌ ۟

22. They will abide therein for ever. Verily, with Allah there is a great reward.

خٰلِدِيْنَ فِيْهَآ اَبَدًا ۟ اِنَّ اللّٰهَ عِنْدَهٗٓ اَجْرٌ عَظِيْمٌ ۟

23. O ye who believe ! ^ctake not your fathers and your brothers for friends, if they prefer disbelief to faith. And whoso befriends them from among you, it is they that are wrongdoers.[1184]

يٰٓاَيُّهَا الَّذِيْنَ اٰمَنُوْا لَا تَتَّخِذُوْٓا اٰبَآءَكُمْ وَاِخْوَانَكُمْ اَوْلِيَآءَ اِنِ اسْتَحَبُّوا الْكُفْرَ عَلَى الْاِيْمَانِ وَمَنْ يَّتَوَلَّهُمْ مِّنْكُمْ فَاُولٰٓئِكَ هُمُ الظّٰلِمُوْنَ ۟

---

^a4 : 96 ; 57 : 11.   ^b3 : 16 ; 5 : 13 ; 9 : 72 ; 10 : 10 ; 57 : 21.   ^c3 : 29 ; 4 : 140, 145 ; 9 : 16 ; 58 : 23.

---

as nothing compared with the spiritual service thereof, which only a true Muslim can perform. If the preservation of the true faith were to involve the temporary destruction of the building of the Ka'ba, the Quran would unhesitatingly endorse such destruction, because it is the preservation of the faith and not the preservation of a house, however sacred it may be, which is the aim and object of Islam. The verse thus aslo implies an effective answer to the baseless view that Islam attaches greater importance to the outward form of its ordinances than to the spirit underlying them. It may also be noted here that, according to the teachings of Islam, even the life of a true believer has greater sanctity than the House of God. Says the Holy Prophet : ''A believer possesses greater sanctity than the Ka'ba'' (Mājah).

1183. **Commentary :**

In the previous verse it was pointed out that disbelievers could not be equal to believers, even if the former outwardly served the Ka'ba and aided pilgrims. In this verse it is added that believers are not all alike, some of them possessing a higher spiritual rank than others.

1184. **Commentary :**

This verse deals with that class of idolaters who were actively hostile to Islam and strove hard to exterminate it. They had declared war on innocent Muslims, and such was their hatred of Islam that they even disregarded the ties of relationship with a view to harming them. It was with such implacable enemies of Islam that Muslims were forbidden to make friends, for such an act on their part would have amounted to treachery to Islam and would

24. Say, if your fathers, and your sons, and your brethren, and your wives, and your kinsfolk, and the wealth you have acquired, and the trade whose dullness you fear, and the dwellings which you love are dearer to you than Allah and His Messenger and striving in His cause, then wait until Allah comes with His judgement; and Allah guides not the disobedient people.[1185]

قُلْ اِنْ كَانَ اٰبَآؤُكُمْ وَاَبْنَآؤُكُمْ وَاِخْوَانُكُمْ وَاَزْوَاجُكُمْ وَعَشِيْرَتُكُمْ وَاَمْوَالُ اقْتَرَفْتُمُوْهَا وَتِجَارَةٌ تَخْشَوْنَ كَسَادَهَا وَمَسٰكِنُ تَرْضَوْنَهَا اَحَبَّ اِلَيْكُمْ مِّنَ اللّٰهِ وَرَسُوْلِهٖ وَجِهَادٍ فِيْ سَبِيْلِهٖ فَتَرَبَّصُوْا حَتّٰى يَاْتِيَ اللّٰهُ بِاَمْرِهٖ وَاللّٰهُ لَا يَهْدِى الْقَوْمَ الْفٰسِقِيْنَ ۲۴

25. Surely, *a*Allah has helped you on many a battlefield, and on the day of Ḥunain, when your great numbers made you proud, but they availed you nought; and the earth, with *all* its vastness, became straitened for you, *and* then you turned your backs retreating.[1186]

لَقَدْ نَصَرَكُمُ اللّٰهُ فِيْ مَوَاطِنَ كَثِيْرَةٍ وَّيَوْمَ حُنَيْنٍ اِذْ اَعْجَبَتْكُمْ كَثْرَتُكُمْ فَلَمْ تُغْنِ عَنْكُمْ شَيْئًا وَّضَاقَتْ عَلَيْكُمُ الْاَرْضُ بِمَا رَحُبَتْ ثُمَّ وَلَّيْتُمْ مُّدْبِرِيْنَ ۲۵

---

*a*3 : 124.

---

certainly have done it incalculable harm. As for other disbelievers who were not at war with Muslims, the Quran exhorts Muslims to be benevolent and kind to them (see 60 : 9,10). As a matter of fact, Islam attaches greater importance to the spiritual welfare of man than to his material well-being, and it is evident that friendly relations with men who prefer disbelief to faith are bound to exercise a baneful influence on spiritual growth.

1185. Commentary :

The idolaters were closely connected with Muslims by ties of blood and relationship. Muslims are plainly told in this verse that these relationships and other worldly considerations of wealth, trade and property should not be allowed to stand in the way when a dearer relationship and a nobler cause and more vital considerations demanded their sacrifice. Love of kith and kin and worldly possessions should not be permitted

to hinder the Faithful from serving the cause of Islam. The judgement of God mentioned at the end of the verse came after the death of the Holy Prophet when "the disobedient people" *i.e.*, those who had joined the fold of Islam for worldly considerations, revolted and were punished by God through Abū Bakr, the First *Khalīfa.*

1186. Important Words :

مَوَاطِن (battle-fields) is the plural of مَوْطِن which is derived from وَطَن . They say وَطَنَ بِالْمَكَانِ *i.e.*, he dwelt or resided or settled in the place. الْوَطَن means, the place of one's abode or residence; place of permanent residence; home; place where cattle are tied or kept. مَوْطِن means, place of residence; a scene of battle or a battle-field (Aqrab).

حُنَيْن (Ḥunain), scene of an important battle between the Holy Prophet and certain pagan tribes of Arabia in A.H. 8. The place lies to the south east of Mecca about 18 miles from it.

26. Then ^aAllah sent down His peace upon His Messenger and upon the believers, and He sent down hosts which you did not see, and He punished those who disbelieved. And this is the reward of the disbelievers.[1187]

$$ثُمَّ اَنْزَلَ اللهُ سَكِيْنَتَهُ عَلٰى رَسُوْلِهٖ وَعَلَى الْمُؤْمِنِيْنَ وَاَنْزَلَ جُنُوْدًا لَّمْ تَرَوْهَا وَعَذَّبَ الَّذِيْنَ كَفَرُوْا وَذٰلِكَ جَزَآءُ الْكٰفِرِيْنَ ۝$$

*a*9 : 40 ; 48 : 27.

In this battle a number of the newly subdued disbelievers of Mecca took part on the side of the Muslims.

Commentary :

Muslims are here reminded of the great truth that mere numbers do not count much and that they should not think that the presence of disbelievers would contribute to their strength or prosperity. Their attention is drawn to their temporary reverse at the battle-field of Ḥunain which was due to the presence of 2,000 Meccans who, though professing to be Muslims, were but newly converted and were not yet well established in faith, 80 of them actually being idolaters. (Zurqānī, iii. 6).

After the fall of Mecca, the powerful tribes of Hawāzin and Tha īf, fearing lest Islam should become established in the Hijāz, joined forces and advanced to attack the Muslims. The Holy Prophet met them at Ḥunain, 18 miles from Mecca. He was accompanied by 12,000 men, among whom were 2,000 new converts mentioned above, who had joined the army at Mecca. Contrary to the practice of the Holy Prophet, these men hastened to attack the enemy, 20,000 strong, but were quickly repulsed and fled from the battle-field in great confusion, throwing into disorder the advancing Muslim force which was passing through a narrow gorge and which was consequently forced to fly. In the stampede that followed the Holy Prophet, who stuck to his place like a rock, was left on the battle-field with only 100 men around him. Arrows from the archers of the enemy fell thick and fast all round him. It was a moment of extreme danger but the Prophet, urging his mule towards the enemy, advanced undaunted, shouting at the top of his voice : انا النبي لا كذب انا ابن عبدالمطلب *i.e.* "I am indeed the Prophet of God. There is no untruth about it. I am a son of Abdul-Muṭṭalib". 'Abbās, an uncle of the Prophet, who possessed a stentorian voice, called out to the fleeing Muslims to stop and return to their Master who wanted them. This clarion call roused the Muslims as the trumpet call of the Day of Judgement will rouse the dead from their graves and, rallying with a giant effort they rushed back to their beloved Master and attacked the enemy with such vehemence as put terror in his heart and made him flee in utter confusion. Thus the scales were turned and the day ended in a signal victory for the Muslims, and no less than 6,000 disbelievers were taken prisoner (Ṭabarī & Hishām).

1187. Commentary :

It was only to the Holy Prophet and true believers that God vouchsafed peace and tranquillity. Thus those weak in faith became distinct from true believers ; and God soon sent down His special aid and the disbelievers were routed and suitably punished.

27. Then will Allah, after that, turn *with compassion* to whomsoever He pleases ; and Allah is Most Forgiving, Merciful.

ثُمَّ يَتُوبُ اللّٰهُ مِنۢ بَعْدِ ذٰلِكَ عَلٰى مَنْ يَّشَآءُ ۚ وَاللّٰهُ غَفُوْرٌ رَّحِيْمٌ ۝

28. O ye who believe ! surely, *the idolaters are unclean. So they shall not approach the Sacred Mosque after this year of theirs. And if you fear poverty, Allah will enrich you out of His bounty, if He pleases. ! Surely, Allah is All-Knowing, Wise.[1188]

يٰٓاَيُّهَا الَّذِيْنَ اٰمَنُوْٓا اِنَّمَا الْمُشْرِكُوْنَ نَجَسٌ فَلَا يَقْرَبُوا الْمَسْجِدَ الْحَرَامَ بَعْدَ عَامِهِمْ هٰذَا ۚ وَاِنْ خِفْتُمْ عَيْلَةً فَسَوْفَ يُغْنِيْكُمُ اللّٰهُ مِنْ فَضْلِهٖٓ اِنْ شَآءَ ۚ اِنَّ اللّٰهَ عَلِيْمٌ حَكِيْمٌ ۝

1188. Important Words :

نَجَس (unclean) is derived from نَجِس which means, it was or became unclean, filthy or impure. نَجَس therefore, means, unclean, filthy or impure ; it also signifies, a man having an incurable disease (Lane). نَجَاسَة (uncleanness) is of two kinds : one kind of نَجَاسَة is perceived by the physical senses and the other is perceived by the mind. In the present verse, it is the latter kind of uncleanness that is meant (Mufradāt).

سوف (will) is a particle denoting amplification because it changes the aorist from the strait time which is the present to the ample time which is the future and is used with respect to that which has not yet happened ; it is a word used to denote promising or threatening. According to some it is synonymous with سَ but according to others it has a larger meaning than that letter and is distinct from it by its sometimes having لـ prefixed to it. You say سَوْفَ اَفْعَل meaning, I *will* do such a thing (Lane).

Commentary :

The word نَجَس (unclean), as shown under Important Words, either means "one who is spiritually unclean" or "one having an incurable disease". Idolaters are thus here described as (1) being spiritually unclean or (2) having become so inured to idolatry that it is almost impossible for them to rid themselves of it. But since Mecca was the birthplace of Islam and a monument of Abraham's great faith in the One God, it was necessary that the place should be kept spiritually pure. Hence the prohibition to idolaters to approach the Sacred Mosque.

The coming of pilgrims to Mecca was a source of great income for Meccans and the prohibition might have given rise to fear in the hearts of some Muslims that their income would thereby be considerably lessened. They are, therefore, told here not to fear poverty, for God would make abundant provision for them out of His bounty.

29. ^aFight those from among the People of the Book, who believe not in Allah, nor in the Last Day, nor hold as unlawful what Allah and His Messenger have declared to be unlawful, nor follow the true religion, until they pay the tax with *their own* hand and acknowledge their subjection.[1189]

قَاتِلُوا الَّذِينَ لَا يُؤْمِنُونَ بِاللَّهِ وَلَا بِالْيَوْمِ الْآخِرِ وَلَا يُحَرِّمُونَ مَا حَرَّمَ اللَّهُ وَرَسُولُهُ وَلَا يَدِينُونَ دِينَ الْحَقِّ مِنَ الَّذِينَ أُوتُوا الْكِتَابَ حَتَّى يُعْطُوا الْجِزْيَةَ عَنْ يَدٍ وَهُمْ صَاغِرُونَ ۝

*a*2 : 191.

1189. Important Words :

جِزْيَة (tax) is derived from جَزَى meaning, he or it paid or gave satisfaction. They say جَزَيْتُ فُلَانًا حَقَّهُ *i.e.* I paid such a one his right or due. جَزَاهُ كَذَا means, he repaid, requited, or recompensed him for such a thing. جِزْيَة means, the tax that is taken from the free non-Muslim subjects of a Muslim State in lieu of the protection it ensures them (Lane & Aqrab).

يَد (hand) also means favour. See 5 : 65.

صَاغِرُونَ (acknowledge their subjection) is the plural of صَاغِر which is derived from صَغُرَ which means, he was or became small or little in body or in years or in estimation or in rank or dignity (Lane). صَاغِر which is the active participle from صَغُرَ signifies, one who agrees, and is satisfied, to occupy or remain in a subordinate position (Mufradāt).

Commentary :

War with idolaters having been dealt with in previous verses, fighting with the People of the Book is introduced with this verse. The verse refers to those People of the Book who lived in Arabia. Like the idolaters of that country, they too had been actively hostile to Islam and had tried to exterminate it. Muslims were, therefore, ordered to fight them unless they agreed to live as their loyal and peaceful subjects. The *Jizya*, referred to in the verse, was the tax which such non-Muslims had to pay as free subjects of the Muslim State in return for the protection they enjoyed under it. Islam has ordained that in Arabia, the birthplace of Islam and its headquarters, only the People of the Book, and not idolaters, could live as subjects by paying the *Jizya*, while outside Arabia all non-Muslims could live under a Muslim Government on payment of this tax. Arabia, being the cradle and centre of Islam and, as it were, the citadel thereof, was to be kept free from idolaters. It should also be noted that as against *Jizya* which was imposed on non-Muslims, the tax imposed on Muslims is called *Zakāt* which is a heavier tax than *Jizya*, and Muslims, in addition to this tax, had to perform military service which was very hard in those days and from which non-Muslims were exempt. Thus the latter in a way fared better, for they had to pay a lighter tax and were also free from military service.

The expression عَنْ يَدٍ (with their own hand) is used here in a figurative sense, signifying (1) that *Jizya* should not be forcibly taken from the People of the Book but that they should pay it with their own hand *i.e.* they should agree to pay it willingly and should acknowledge the superior power of the Muslims; or (2) that they should pay it out of hand *i.e.* in ready money and not in the form of deferred payment; or (3) that they should pay it considering it as a favour from Muslims, the word, يَد (hand) also meaning a favour.

30. And ^athe Jews say, Ezra is the son of Allah, and the Christians say, the Messiah is the son of Allah; that is what they say with their mouths. They imitate the saying of those who disbelieved before them. Allah's curse be on them! How are they turned away!¹¹⁹⁰

وَقَالَتِ الْيَهُودُ عُزَيْرُ ابْنُ اللّٰهِ وَقَالَتِ النَّصٰرَى الْمَسِيحُ ابْنُ اللّٰهِ ذٰلِكَ قَوْلُهُمْ بِاَفْوَاهِهِمْ يُضَاهِئُونَ قَوْلَ الَّذِيْنَ كَفَرُوْا مِنْ قَبْلُ قٰتَلَهُمُ اللّٰهُ اَنّٰى يُؤْفَكُوْنَ ۝

^a2 : 117 ; 5 : 18 ; 10 : 69.

The word صاغرون (acknowledge their subjection) is used here to express the subordinate political status of non-Muslims, i.e. they were to occupy the position of subjects in relation to Muslims. As regards the social relations of Muslims with the *dhimmīs*, as non-Muslim subjects of the Muslim State were called, these may be judged from the fact that the Holy Prophet himself used to stand up in reverence when the bier of a non-Muslim happened to pass by him (Dāwūd, ch. on *Janā'iz*), and 'Alī, the Fourth Caliph, bore on his own shoulders the bier of a Christian who happened to die in the time of his Caliphate.

1190. Important Words:

عزير (Uzair or Ezra) may be taken to have been derived in Arabic from عزر . They say عزره i.e. he prevented him or forbade him ; he taught him the obligatory statutes or ordinances of God ; he aided or assisted him ; he strengthened him ; he treated him with reverence or honour (Lane). Ezra (a Hebrew name), perhaps abbreviated from Azariah meaning " Yahwe (God) helps,'' was a descendant of Seraiah, the high priest, and, being himself a member of the priestly order, was known also as Ezra the Priest. He was one of the most important personages of his day and had far-reaching influence on the development of Judaism. He was especially honoured among the Prophets of Israel. In fact, he marks the spring time in the national history of Judaism and is regarded and quoted as the type of person most competent and learned in the Law. The Rabbis associate his name with several important institutions. Renan has remarked in the Preface to his *History of the People of Israel* that the definite constitution of Judaism may be dated only from the time of Ezra. In Rabbinical literature Ezra was considered worthy of being the vehicle of the Law, had it not been already given through Moses. According to tradition, he died at the age of 120 in Babylonia. He worked in close collaboration with Nehemiah. Ezra lived in the 5th century B.C. (Jew. Enc. & Enc. Bib.).

يضاهئون (they imitate) is derived from ضاهى which is derived from ضهى . They say ضاهاه or ضاهأه i.e. he resembled or conformed with him or it; he imitated him; he was or became gentle, tender or courteous to him. The well-known saying of the Holy Prophet اشد الناس عذابا يوم القيامة الذين يضاهئون خلق الله means, " the most severely punished of mankind on the Day of Judgement will be those who imitate (by what they make) the creation of God" e.g. sculptors, etc. (Lane).

قاتلهم الله (Allah's curse be on them). قاتل is from the root قتل . They say قتله i.e. he killed him; or he rendered him as one killed; or he attempted to kill him; or he cut off all connections with him. قاتله means, he fought or warred against him. قاتله الله means, may God curse him; or may He drive him from His mercy (Lisān & Aqrab). The expression also means, may God make war against him,

31. They have taken their learned men and their monks for lords beside Allah. And *so have they taken* the Messiah, son of Mary. And [a]they were not commanded but to worship the One God. There is no god but He. Too holy is He for what they associate *with Him!*[1191]

اِتَّخَذُوٓا اَحۡبَارَهُمۡ وَرُهۡبَانَهُمۡ اَرۡبَابًا مِّنۡ دُوۡنِ اللّٰهِ وَالۡمَسِیۡحَ ابۡنَ مَرۡیَمَ ۚ وَمَاۤ اُمِرُوۡۤا اِلَّا لِیَعۡبُدُوۡۤا اِلٰهًا وَّاحِدًا ۚ لَاۤ اِلٰهَ اِلَّا هُوَ ؕ سُبۡحٰنَهٗ عَمَّا یُشۡرِکُوۡنَ ﴿۳۱﴾

32. [b]They desire to extinguish the light of Allah with their mouths; but Allah will permit nothing except that He will perfect His light, though the disbelievers may dislike *it.*[1192]

یُرِیۡدُوۡنَ اَنۡ یُّطۡفِـُٔوۡا نُوۡرَ اللّٰهِ بِاَفۡوَاهِهِمۡ وَیَاۡبَی اللّٰهُ اِلَّاۤ اَنۡ یُّتِمَّ نُوۡرَهٗ وَلَوۡ کَرِهَ الۡکٰفِرُوۡنَ ﴿۳۲﴾

---

[a]12:41; 17:24; 98:6.   [b]61:9.

---

which cannot result except in such a one being destroyed (Mufradāt). See also 2:62.

Commentary:

After having dealt at some length with the idolatrous beliefs and practices of the pagans of Arabia, the Quran proceeds in this verse to deal with the polytheistic beliefs and practices of Jews and Christians. Those of the Jews who lived in Medina looked upon Ezra as the son of God. Similarly, a sect of Jews living at Ḥaḍramaut in the south of Arabia believed him to be the son of God. The remnants of this sect continued to linger till the end of the fourth century A.H. (Qasṭalānī & Dāwūd Ẓāhiri). As this doctrine of the Jews, which appears to be sectional, was a later innovation and did not subsist long, present Jewish sources make no mention of it but that does not affect the real situation. Elsewhere the Quran says that the Israelites were rather free in attributing sons to God (5:19).

This verse also shows that these blasphemous doctrines were not taught to Christians and Jews by their Prophets but were later borrowed by them from pagan sources. Incidentally, this claim of the Quran constitutes a proof of its divine origin, because here it states

a fact which was not known to the world even two centuries ago and has been only recently brought to light by modern research. A study of the origins of the Christian faith has now established the fact that Jews and Christians borrowed their later doctrines from Babylonian and Roman pagan sources.

The words, *Allah's curse be on them*, when spoken by man signify only an imprecation but, when spoken by God, they imply a prophecy of the destruction of the person or persons about whom they are uttered.

1191. **Important Words:**

For احبار (learned men) and رهبان (monks) see 5:45 and 5:83 respectively.

Commentary:

احبار (learned men) belonged to Jews and رهبان (monks) to Christians. Both these people virtually looked upon their religious leaders as so many gods besides the true God.

1192. **Commentary:**

The words, *They desire to extinguish the light of Allah with their mouths*, signify that they seek to injure the cause of Islam by making false propaganda against it and by inciting others to harm it. As borne out by history, the

33. *He it is Who sent His Messenger with guidance, and the religion of truth, that He may make it prevail over every *other* religion, even though the idolaters may dislike *it*.[1193]

هُوَ الَّذِىۤ أَرْسَلَ رَسُوْلَهٗ بِالْهُدٰى وَدِيْنِ الْحَقِّ لِيُظْهِرَهٗ عَلَى الدِّيْنِ كُلِّهٖ وَلَوْ كَرِهَ الْمُشْرِكُوْنَ ۝

---

*48 : 29 ; 61 : 10.

Christians of Arabia incited their powerful co-religionists in Syria and, by their help, sought to extinguish the light of Islam that God had kindled in Arabia. They are told in this verse that their plots and machinations would in no way succeed in injuring the cause of Islam. The Jews also had made a similar attempt by inciting the Persians against the Holy Prophet. See under 2 : 103.

1193. Commentary :

The previous verse ends with the word كافرون (disbelievers), while the present verse ends with the word مشركون (idolaters). Christians are كافر because they disbelieve in the Holy Prophet of Islam and they are مشرك because they associate co-partners with God. The difference is significant in another way also. The word كافرون (used in the preceding verse) is derived from كفر which literally means "to cover." The Quran has used this word to explain the fact that the "light" of God cannot be extinguished by those who try to cover it. In the present verse the word مشركون (idolaters) has been used to point to the fact that whereas in the case of God Christians do not refrain from associating co-partners with Him (thereby implying that His attributes can be shared by others), in their own case they cannot bear to see the favour of prophethood which they enjoy, shared by others. They cannot reconcile themselves to the idea that Prophets may be raised among any other people, as they have been raised among them. The verse thus tells them that God has caused others to share the gift of prophethood with them, whether they like it or not.

The promise that God would make Islam *prevail over every other religion* stands for all time. The promise was fulfilled when in its early history Islam triumphed over all peoples, including Christians ; and the fulfilment of this promise is going to be repeated in the present age, when God has raised the Promised Messiah, Holy Founder of the Ahmadiyya Movement, to serve and help the cause of Islam. This triumph is going to be complete and permanent. In fact, most Commentators (*e.g.*, Bayān). agree that the final and perfect fulfilment of this promise, as made in the present verse, is to take place at the time of the second advent of Jesus.

34. O ye who believe ! surely *a*many of the priests and monks devour the wealth of men by false means and *b*turn *men* away from the way of Allah. And those who hoard up gold and silver and spend it not in the way of Allah— give to them the tidings of a painful punishment.¹¹⁹⁴

يَا أَيُّهَا الَّذِيْنَ اٰمَنُوْٓا اِنَّ كَثِيْرًا مِّنَ الْاَحْبَارِ وَالرُّهْبَانِ لَيَأْكُلُوْنَ اَمْوَالَ النَّاسِ بِالْبَاطِلِ وَ يَصُدُّوْنَ عَنْ سَبِيْلِ اللّٰهِ ۗ وَالَّذِيْنَ يَكْنِزُوْنَ الذَّهَبَ وَالْفِضَّةَ وَلَا يُنْفِقُوْنَهَا فِيْ سَبِيْلِ اللّٰهِ ۙ فَبَشِّرْهُمْ بِعَذَابٍ اَلِيْمٍ ۩

35. On the day when it shall be made hot in the fire of Hell, and their fore-heads and their sides and their backs shall be branded therewith *and it shall be said to them:* 'This is what you treasured up for yourselves; so now taste what you used to treasure up.'¹¹⁹⁵

يَوْمَ يُحْمٰى عَلَيْهَا فِيْ نَارِ جَهَنَّمَ فَتُكْوٰى بِهَا جِبَاهُهُمْ وَ جُنُوْبُهُمْ وَظُهُوْرُهُمْ ۗ هٰذَا مَا كَنَزْتُمْ لِاَنْفُسِكُمْ فَذُوْقُوْا مَا كُنْتُمْ تَكْنِزُوْنَ ۩

*a*4 : 162.   *b*4 : 161.

1194. Commentary :

This verse sheds some light on the moral degradation of the Jewish and Christian religious leaders who were opposed to the Holy Prophet. Their moral depravity and spiritual degeneration was itself evidence of the truth of Islam, because when the leaders of a religion themselves become corrupt and depraved, reformation can come only through a heavenly Messenger. Jewish and Christian leaders opposed the Holy Prophet, but their own depravity testified to the fact that he had appeared at a time when his advent was urgently needed.

The words, *those who hoard up gold and silver and spend it not in the way of Allah—give to them the tidings of a painful punishment*, give a graphic picture of Jews and Christians. They hoard wealth and do not spend it in the cause of God, *i.e.*, in propagating truth and helping the poor and needy. They are threatened with a painful punishment.

1195. Important Words :

تُكْوٰى (branded) is formed from كَوَى. They say كَوَاهُ *i.e.* he cauterized him or it; he burned his or its skin with a piece of iron or the like (Lane). كَوَيْتُ الدَّابَةَ means, I cauterized or branded the beast with a piece of hot iron (Mufradāt). كَوَتِ الْعَقْرَبُ فُلَانًا means, the scorpion stung such a one. الْكَىُّ which is the noun-infinitive from كَوَى means, the act of cauterizing or branding with a piece of hot iron (whether for the purpose of putting a mark or for curing a disease). The Arabs say آخِرُ الدَّوَاءِ الْكَىُّ *i.e.* the last remedy (in certain diseases) is cauterizing (Aqrab).

Commentary :

The reward and punishment of the life to come will not be of a physical nature, but will be the spiritual representation of the actions of man in the present life. This is clear from the verse under comment, which states that only three parts of the body—the forehead, the side and the back—will be branded.

36. The reckoning of months with Allah has been twelve months by Allah's ordinance since the day when He created the heavens and the earth. Of these four are sacred. That is the right creed. So wrong not yourselves therein. And fight the idolaters all together as they fight you all together ; and know that Allah is with the righteous.[1196]

اِنَّ عِدَّةَ الشُّهُوۡرِ عِنۡدَ اللّٰهِ اثۡنَا عَشَرَ شَهۡرًا فِیۡ کِتٰبِ اللّٰهِ یَوۡمَ خَلَقَ السَّمٰوٰتِ وَالۡاَرۡضَ مِنۡهَاۤ اَرۡبَعَةٌ حُرُمٌ ذٰلِکَ الدِّیۡنُ الۡقَیِّمُ فَلَا تَظۡلِمُوۡا فِیۡهِنَّ اَنۡفُسَکُمۡ وَقَاتِلُوا الۡمُشۡرِکِیۡنَ کَآفَّةً کَمَا یُقَاتِلُوۡنَکُمۡ کَآفَّةً وَاعۡلَمُوۡۤا اَنَّ اللّٰهَ مَعَ الۡمُتَّقِیۡنَ ۝

The expression is clearly figurative. When a rich man, out of miserliness or pride, refuses to help a beggar, the first sign that appears on his person is that his forehead contracts into a frown. Then he turns on his side and finally he disdainfully shows his back to the man seeking his help. Fittingly, therefore, the forehead, the side and the back have been spoken of here as being branded i.e. in the after-life these parts will appear to be branded with a hot iron, as if bearing testimony against themselves.

The verse also signifies that even in the present life the hoarded treasures of Jews and Christians will become a source of grievous punishment for them. In this case, the threatened punishment might be taken to refer to devastating wars such as the present one, in which hot metal in various forms is destroying the western peoples. They receive it on their foreheads, sides and backs i.e. whether facing the enemy or making a flank movement or turning their backs; and, curiously enough, Jews are as much hit by these wars as are Christians.

1196. Important Words :

کِتٰب (ordinance) is derived from کَتَبَ i.e. (1) he wrote ; (2) he prescribed or ordained. کِتٰب means, a book or a writing ; divine prescript or ordinance or decree (Lane). See also 2 : 54 & 2 : 130.

Commentary :

The words فِیۡ کِتٰبِ اللّٰه (by Allah's ordinance) mean that God so ordained on the day when He created the heavens and the earth that the number of months should be twelve i.e. the law of nature determines that number, which holds true both in the solar and the lunar system.

The four sacred months are *Dhū'l-Qa‘da*, *Dhū'l-Ḥijja*, *Muḥarram* and *Rajab*. These months have been held sacred by the Arabs, who are mostly descended from Abraham, from time immemorial and Islam confirmed their sacredness. It is considered unlawful to wage war or, for that matter, to continue a state of war in these four months unless, as the Quran points out, the enemy is the first to violate their sanctity. See also note on 2 : 218.

927

37.   Surely, the postponement *of a Sacred Month* is an addition to disbelief. Those who disbelieve are led astray thereby. They allow it one year and forbid it another year, that they may agree in the number of *the months* which Allah has made sacred, and thus may make lawful what Allah has forbidden. *a*The evil of their deeds is made to seem fair to them. And Allah guides not the disbelieving people.[1197]

اِنَّمَا النَّسِیۡٓءُ زِیَادَۃٌ فِی الۡکُفۡرِ یُضَلُّ بِہِ الَّذِیۡنَ کَفَرُوۡا یُحِلُّوۡنَہٗ عَامًا وَّ یُحَرِّمُوۡنَہٗ عَامًا لِّیُوَاطِئُوۡا عِدَّۃَ مَا حَرَّمَ اللّٰہُ فَیُحِلُّوۡا مَا حَرَّمَ اللّٰہُ ؕ زُیِّنَ لَہُمۡ سُوۡٓءُ اَعۡمَالِہِمۡ ؕ وَ اللّٰہُ لَا یَہۡدِی الۡقَوۡمَ الۡکٰفِرِیۡنَ ۝

---

*a*6 : 44;   13 : 34;   16 : 64;   27 : 25;   29 : 49;   35 : 9.

1197. Important Words :

النَّسِیۡٓ (the postponement) is the noun-substantive from نَسَأَ meaning, he postponed or delayed a thing. They say انسأ الله اجله *i.e.* God postponed the end of his life, *viz.,* He prolonged his life. An Arab would say بايعه بنسيئة *i.e.* he sold it on credit *i.e.* the payment was to be made at a future period. نسى therefore means, postponement; or the postponement of a month *i.e.* the transfer of the sanctity of one month to a later month, a custom of the Arabs in the Days of Ignorance ; the month which the Arabs so postponed ; the postponement of the time of Pilgrimage, another custom of the Arabs ; a postponement of the time of payment of a debt or of the price of a thing sold (Lane & Aqrab).

لِیُوَاطِئُوۡا (that they may agree in) is derived from واطأ which is again derived from وطئ meaning, he trod upon it ; he trampled upon it. They say واطأه على الامر *i.e.* he agreed with him respecting the matter. تواطأ القوم على الامر means, the people agreed with each other respecting the affair (Lane & Aqrab).

Commentary :

The reference in this verse, as shown under Important Words, is to a long-standing Arab custom. The three successive sacred months of *Dhū'l-Qaʿda, Dhū'l-Ḥijja* and *Muḥarram* sometimes seemed to them too long a time to refrain from their predatory expeditions. In order, therefore, to free themselves from the restrictions of the Sacred Months, they sometimes treated a sacred month as an ordinary month and an ordinary month as sacred. This practice is denounced here because it involved fraud and interfered with the security of life guaranteed in these months. The procedure adopted for postponing the observance of a sacred month was generally something like this. When in the month of *Dhū'l-Ḥijja* the pilgrims returned from Minā, after having performed the ceremonies of *Ḥajj,* an influential man would arise from among the assembly and, according to Arab custom, would say, "I am he whose decree is not to be rejected." Thereupon, the assembly would request him to transfer the sanctity of the next month of *Muḥarram* to the following month (*Ṣafar*). Thus the sanctity of a month which God had made inviolable was violated with impunity. This artifice, however, was not resorted to every year, but only when it suited their interests or convenience. The Quran has condemned it as an impious innovation, and as evidence of the untrustworthiness of the pagan Arabs, implying that as they could not keep the ordinances of God, they could not be expected to remain true to their engagements with Muslims.

38. O ye who believe ! what is the matter with you that, when it is said to you, go forth in the way of Allah, you sink heavily towards the earth ? *a* Would you be contented with the present life in preference to the Hereafter ? *b* But the enjoyment of the present life is but little, as compared with the Hereafter.[1198]

يَا۟يُّهَا الَّذِيْنَ اٰمَنُوْا مَا لَكُمْ اِذَا قِيْلَ لَكُمُ انْفِرُوْا فِيْ سَبِيْلِ اللّٰهِ اثَّاقَلْتُمْ اِلَى الْاَرْضِ اَرَضِيْتُمْ بِالْحَيٰوةِ الدُّنْيَا مِنَ الْاٰخِرَةِ فَمَا مَتَاعُ الْحَيٰوةِ الدُّنْيَا فِى الْاٰخِرَةِ اِلَّا قَلِيْلٌ ۝

39. If you do not go forth *to fight*, He will punish you with a painful punishment, and will choose in your stead a people other than you, and you shall do Him no harm at all. And Allah has full power over all things.

اِلَّا تَنْفِرُوْا يُعَذِّبْكُمْ عَذَابًا اَلِيْمًا وَّيَسْتَبْدِلْ قَوْمًا غَيْرَكُمْ وَلَا تَضُرُّوْهُ شَيْئًا وَاللّٰهُ عَلٰى كُلِّ شَىْءٍ قَدِيْرٌ ۝

---

*a*13 : 27.   *b*See 3 : 15.

1198. Commentary :

Just as true Muslims should always be prepared to desist from war, whenever they are required to do so (see preceding verse), they should also be ever ready to march forth in the cause of Allah whenever called upon. It is to this great truth that the present verse draws our attention. Indeed, with this verse the Quran begins to throw light on such residents of Medina as were weak in faith, including the hypocrites, and exposes the attitude they adopted to evade the obligations that devolved on them as members of the Muslim community. The hypocrites are particularly addressed, the reference being to the expedition to Tabūk, a town situated about half-way between Medina and Damascus. News was brought to the Holy Prophet that the Greeks of the Eastern Roman Empire were assembling their forces on the Syrian frontier. As the Greeks, popularly known as Romans, possessed a regular and well-disciplined army, the Holy Prophet thought it necessary to make thorough preparations to meet them. Contrary to his usual practice, he even announced his objective, making no secret of his destination, so that those who took part in it should do so in full consciousness of the length and hardships of the journey. It was a time of great trial. The long and arduous journey through the desert was undertaken in the midst of the hot weather. The season promised drought and scarcity for those who took part in the expedition and the ripeness of the harvest for those who stayed behind. Pious Muslims, however, in their devotion to the cause of Islam, promptly responded to the Prophet's call. Of those who stayed behind without permission only three were true believers, the rest being all hypocrites. Thus at the head of an army about 30,000 strong the Holy Prophet left Medina in the 9th year of Hijra. On account of the great hardships the Muslim army had to suffer in the long journey, it came to be called جَيْشُ الْعُسْرَةِ *i.e.* the distressed army.

40. If you help him not, then *know that* Allah helped him *even* when the disbelievers drove him forth while he was one of the two when they were both in the cave, when he said to his companion, 'Grieve not, for Allah is with us.' Then [a]Allah sent down His peace on him, and strengthened him with hosts which you did not see, and humbled the word of those who disbelieved, and it is the word of Allah alone which is supreme. And Allah is Mighty, Wise.[1199]

اِلَّا تَنْصُرُوْهُ فَقَدْ نَصَرَهُ اللّٰهُ اِذْ اَخْرَجَهُ الَّذِيْنَ كَفَرُوْا ثَانِيَ اثْنَيْنِ اِذْ هُمَا فِى الْغَارِ اِذْ يَقُوْلُ لِصَاحِبِهٖ لَا تَحْزَنْ اِنَّ اللّٰهَ مَعَنَا ۚ فَاَنْزَلَ اللّٰهُ سَكِيْنَتَهٗ عَلَيْهِ وَاَيَّدَهٗ بِجُنُوْدٍ لَّمْ تَرَوْهَا وَجَعَلَ كَلِمَةَ الَّذِيْنَ كَفَرُوا السُّفْلٰى ۚ وَكَلِمَةُ اللّٰهِ هِىَ الْعُلْيَا ۚ وَاللّٰهُ عَزِيْزٌ حَكِيْمٌ ۝

---

[a]9 : 26 ; 48 : 27.

1199. Important Words :

كَلِمَة (word). See 2 : 38, 125 ; 3 : 46 & 4 : 172.

Commentary :

The reference in this verse is to the flight of the Holy Prophet from Mecca to Medina when, accompanied by Abū Bakr, he took shelter in a cave called *Thaur.* See note on 8 : 31. The Arabic words rendered as "one of the two" literally mean "the second of the two" and refer to the Holy Prophet and Abū Bakr. The Holy Prophet has been referred to as "the second" because in the Quranic idiom the more important member of the group is referred to as being the last part *i.e.* the final figure. For instance see 5 : 74 where God is referred to as being "the third of the trinity" according to the Christian doctrine.

The verse sheds important light on the high spiritual status of Abū Bakr, who accompanied the Holy Prophet in his flight from Mecca and was thus one of "the two" referred to in the verse. It is worthy of note that when at a time of danger, the Israelites anxiously addressed Moses, saying, *We are surely overtaken,* he replied, *nay, speak not thus, for my Lord is with me. He will direct me aright* (26 : 62, 63). In a similar situation, however, the Holy Prophet, when Abū Bakr expressed anxiety, calmly said : *Grieve not, for Allah is with us.* This speaks volumes for Abū Bakr's spiritual greatness, for the pronoun "us" signifies that God was not only with the Holy Prophet but with Abū Bakr as well. Again, it is on record that, while in the cave, Abū Bakr began to weep, and when asked by the Holy Prophet why he was weeping he replied, " I do not weep for my life, because if I die, it is only the question of a single life. But if you die, O Prophet of God, it will be the death of Islam and of the entire Muslim community" (Zurqānī).

The pronoun in the clause, *Allah sent down His peace on him,* stands for Abū Bakr and not the Holy Prophet, for the Holy Prophet had all along enjoyed peace. The succeeding pronoun in the clause, *strengthened him with hosts,* refers to the Holy Prophet. This divergence in the use of similar pronouns is permissible in Arabic, being known as انتشار ضمائر (see 2 : 75 ; 48 : 10).

The words, *and (God) humbled the word of those who disbelieved,* mean that God frustrated the designs of the disbelievers and they failed to accomplish what they desired. See also 8 : 31.

41. Go forth, light and heavy, and ^astrive with your property and your persons in the cause of Allah. That is better for you, if only you knew.[1200]

اِنْفِرُوْا خِفَافًا وَّثِقَالًا وَّجَاهِدُوْا بِاَمْوَالِكُمْ وَاَنْفُسِكُمْ فِيْ سَبِيْلِ اللّٰهِ ذٰلِكُمْ خَيْرٌ لَّكُمْ اِنْ كُنْتُمْ تَعْلَمُوْنَ ۝

42. If it had been an immediate gain and a short journey, they would certainly have followed thee, but the hard journey seemed too long to them. Yet they will swear by Allah, *saying*, 'If we had been able, we would surely have gone forth with you.' They ruin their souls; and Allah knows that they are liars.[1201]

لَوْ كَانَ عَرَضًا قَرِيْبًا وَّسَفَرًا قَاصِدًا لَّاتَّبَعُوْكَ وَلٰكِنْ بَعُدَتْ عَلَيْهِمُ الشُّقَّةُ ۚ وَسَيَحْلِفُوْنَ بِاللّٰهِ لَوِ اسْتَطَعْنَا لَخَرَجْنَا مَعَكُمْ ۚ يُهْلِكُوْنَ اَنْفُسَهُمْ ۚ وَاللّٰهُ يَعْلَمُ اِنَّهُمْ لَكٰذِبُوْنَ ۝

---

^a3 : 75 ; 9 : 88, 111 ; 61 : 12.

The verse also hints that even if none else had accompanied the Holy Prophet in the hazardous expedition to Tabūk, Abū Bakr would certainly have done so just as he did on the occasion of his flight from Mecca. The verse thus provides a great testimonial to the strength and sincerity of Abū Bakr's faith.

1200. Commentary :

Muslims are here commanded to march forth in the way of God, allowing no worldly consideration or impediment to prevent them from doing so. The words خِفَافًا وَثِقَالًا (light and heavy) have several meanings *i.e.* whether you are young or old; alone or in parties; on foot or on horseback; with sufficient arms and provisions or with insufficient equipment and scanty provisions, etc.

1201. Important Words :

عَرَضًا (gain) is derived from the verb عَرَض for which see 7 : 170. عَرَض means, anything that happens to a man; an accident of any kind; a thing that is not permanent; frail goods of the world; worldly goods of whatever kind; property or wealth whether little or much; booty or spoil; an object of desire; a gain; a gift (Lane & Aqrab).

قَاصِدًا (short) is the active participle from قصد. They say قَصَدَهُ *i.e.* he went to him or directed himself to him; or he made him or it his object; he sought or pursued him or it. قصد الطريق means, the way was direct or right. They say قصد الامر *i.e.* he pursued the right or direct course in the affair and did not exceed the due bounds therein; or he acted in a moderate manner. (*qaṣd*) قصد which is the noun-infinitive from قصد (*qaṣada*) means, the aim or course of a person; an object of desire; one's intention or meaning; a right way or course; a right thing. قَاصِد means, near. طريق قاصد means, a direct or right way or an even road. سفر قاصد means, an easy and short journey; a moderately easy and short journey (Lane & Aqrab).

الشُّقَّة (hard journey) is derived from شق. They say شقه *i.e.* he cut or rent or split or broke it. شق عليه means, it (an affair) affected him severely; it was hard and distressing to him. شقة means, a piece of a garment; a far or long journey; a difficult road; a region or quarter in the reaching of which one is taken by difficulty and distress; distance (Lane).

43. Allah remove thy *cares*. Why didst thou permit them *to stay behind* until those who spoke the truth had become known to thee and *until* thou hadst known the liars ? [1202]

عَفَا اللّٰهُ عَنْكَ لِمَ اَذِنْتَ لَهُمْ حَتّٰى يَتَبَيَّنَ لَكَ الَّذِيْنَ صَدَقُوْا وَتَعْلَمَ الْكٰذِبِيْنَ ۝

44. Those who believe in Allah and the Last Day will not ask leave of thee *to be exempted* from striving with their property and their persons. And Allah well knows the righteous.

لَا يَسْتَأْذِنُكَ الَّذِيْنَ يُؤْمِنُوْنَ بِاللّٰهِ وَالْيَوْمِ الْاٰخِرِ اَنْ يُّجَاهِدُوْا بِاَمْوَالِهِمْ وَاَنْفُسِهِمْ ۗ وَاللّٰهُ عَلِيْمٌۢ بِالْمُتَّقِيْنَ ۝

45. Only those will ask leave of thee *to be exempted* who do not believe in Allah and the Last Day, and whose hearts are full of doubt and in their doubt they waver.

اِنَّمَا يَسْتَأْذِنُكَ الَّذِيْنَ لَا يُؤْمِنُوْنَ بِاللّٰهِ وَالْيَوْمِ الْاٰخِرِ وَارْتَابَتْ قُلُوْبُهُمْ فَهُمْ فِيْ رَيْبِهِمْ يَتَرَدَّدُوْنَ ۝

46. And if they had intended to go forth, they would certainly have made some preparation for it ; but Allah was averse to their marching forth. So He kept them back, and it was said : 'Sit ye *at home* with those who sit.' [1203]

وَلَوْ اَرَادُوا الْخُرُوْجَ لَاَعَدُّوْا لَهٗ عُدَّةً وَّلٰكِنْ كَرِهَ اللّٰهُ انْۢبِعَاثَهُمْ فَثَبَّطَهُمْ وَقِيْلَ اقْعُدُوْا مَعَ الْقٰعِدِيْنَ ۝

1202. Important Words :

عَفَا اللّٰهُ عَنْكَ (Allah remove thy cares). عَفَا means, he or it effaced, erased or obliterated a trace, etc. They say عَفَا اللّٰهُ عَنْهُ *i.e.* may God efface from him his sin, fault, offence, etc. Sometimes the expression عَفَا اللّٰهُ عَنْكَ is used where no sin or fault has preceded and is not even conceivable. For instance, an Arab would say to one whom he holds in high esteem عَفَا اللّٰهُ عَنْكَ meaning, may God set thy affairs aright and bring honour and glory to thee (Aqrab). See also 2 : 110 ; 2 : 188 & 2 : 220.

Commentary :

As shown under Important Words, the word عفو does not necessarily imply the committing of a sin on the part of a person about whom it is used, for it is also used for a person who has committed no sin and even for him who

is incapable of committing a sin. In fact, the expression عَفَا اللّٰهُ عَنْكَ is sometimes used to express love or respect ; and here it implies a desire that the Prophet may be relieved of his cares and difficulties.

The expression, *Why didst thou permit them to stay behind*, is intended to hint that the refusal on the part of the Holy Prophet to give them leave would have served the useful purpose of unmasking the hypocrisy of the hypocrites. Of those who remained behind, only about half came to the Holy Prophet to ask his leave, while the majority stayed behind without asking his permission and without explaining their inability to accompany him.

1203. Important Words :

ثَبَّطَهُمْ (He kept them back) is derived from ثبط (*thabiṭa*) *i.e.* he was or became stupid or weak in

47. If they had gone forth with you, ^athey would have added to you nothing but trouble, and would have hurried to and fro in your midst, seeking to create discord among you. And there are among you those who would listen to them. And Allah well knows the wrongdoers.[1204]

لَوۡخَرَجُوۡا فِيۡكُمۡ مَّا زَادُوۡكُمۡ اِلَّا خَبَالًا وَّلَا اَوۡضَعُوۡا خِلٰلَكُمۡ يَبۡغُوۡنَكُمُ الۡفِتۡنَةَ ۚ وَفِيۡكُمۡ سَمّٰعُوۡنَ لَهُمۡ ؕ وَاللّٰهُ عَلِيۡمٌۢ بِالظّٰلِمِيۡنَ ۞

---

^a3 : 119.

---

his action; or he became heavy, sluggish or slow. بطّه عن الامر (*thabbaṭa-hū*) means, he hindered or withheld him from doing the affair; or he diverted him from it by occupying him otherwise; or he prevented him from doing it by making him cowardly and weak-hearted; or he intervened as an obstacle between him and the affair (Lane).

Commentary :

The verse exposes the hollowness of the excuses offered by the hypocrites. It purports to say that if the hypocrites had been really anxious to march out but had only been prevented from doing so by unforeseen obstacles over which they had no control and which had cropped up at the last moment, they should have made preparations for the expedition long before by providing themselves with arms and provision. But they did nothing of the sort. Thus the fact that they made no preparation and came with their excuses at the eleventh hour shows that from the very beginning they had no intention or desire to go and that the excuses they brought forward were only so many covers to veil their hypocrisy.

1204. Important Words :

خَبَالًا (trouble) is the noun-infinitive from خبل (*khabila*) i.e. he was or became corrupt, unsound or disordered in his reason or intellect or absolutely. خبّه (*khabala-hū*) of which the infinitive is خبل (*khablun*) means, it rendered him insane or it corrupted or disordered his

reason or intellect. خَبَال means, corruptness or unsoundness; or a disordered state in an absolute sense, or in reason or intellect; an affection in the heart resembling insanity or egregious stupidity; loss or a state of diminution; a state of perdition or destruction; distress, embarrassment, trouble or difficulty (Lane). See also 3 : 119.

خِلَالَكُمۡ (to and fro in your midst). خلال is derived from خل. They say خل الشيئ i.e. he or it perforated or pierced the thing through. خلال which is both singular and plural, means, inter-space or intervening space or a break or breach or gap between two things; looseness or want of compactness. They say دخلت بين خلال القوم i.e. I entered among the inter-spaces of the party. هو خلالهم means, he is amid them. جسنا خلال دور القوم means, we went to and fro or went about amid the houses of the people (Lane).

Commentary :

The verse declares that the defection of the hypocrites did no harm to the Muslims. On the contrary, it proved a blessing in disguise. For, if the hypocrites had gone forth with the Muslim army, they would only have caused trouble and mischief and tried to create discord and dissension.

The latter portion of the verse shows that some hypocrites or those weak of faith had actually gone forth with the Muslim army. These were ever ready to lend ear to the leaders among the hypocrites who generally remained behind.

48. They sought *to create* disorder even before *this*, and they devised plots against thee till the truth came and the purpose of Allah prevailed, though they did not like *it*.[1205]

لَقَدِ ابْتَغَوُا الْفِتْنَةَ مِنْ قَبْلُ وَقَلَّبُوْا لَكَ الْاُمُوْرَ حَتّٰى جَآءَ الْحَقُّ وَظَهَرَ اَمْرُ اللّٰهِ وَهُمْ كٰرِهُوْنَ ۝

49. And among them is he who says, 'Permit me *to stay behind* and put me not to trial.' Surely, they have already fallen into trial. And surely Hell shall encompass the disbelievers.[1206]

وَمِنْهُمْ مَّنْ يَّقُوْلُ ائْذَنْ لِّيْ وَلَا تَفْتِنِّيْ اَلَا فِي الْفِتْنَةِ سَقَطُوْا وَاِنَّ جَهَنَّمَ لَمُحِيْطَةٌۢ بِالْكٰفِرِيْنَ ۝

50. If good befall thee, it grieves them, but if a misfortune befall thee, they say, 'We had indeed taken our precaution beforehand.' And they turn away rejoicing.[1206A]

اِنْ تُصِبْكَ حَسَنَةٌ تَسُؤْهُمْ وَاِنْ تُصِبْكَ مُصِيْبَةٌ يَّقُوْلُوْا قَدْ اَخَذْنَا اَمْرَنَا مِنْ قَبْلُ وَيَتَوَلَّوْا وَّهُمْ فَرِحُوْنَ ۝

So if the latter too had accompanied the army, both would have joined hands to injure the cause of Islam.

1205. Important Words:

قلبوا لك الامور (devised plots against thee). قلبوا (qallabū) is the intensified form of قلب (qalaba). They say قلبه *i.e.* he turned it over or upside-down; he altered or changed its or his mode or manner of being. قلبته بيدى (qallabtu-hū) means, I turned it over and over with my hand. قلب الفكر فى امر means, he turned over and over or revolved repeatedly in his mind thoughts or considerations with a view to the attainment of some object in relation to an affair. قلب الامور means, he investigated, scrutinized or examined affairs and turned them over and over in his mind, meditating what he should do. So قلبو لك الامور means, they turned over and over in their minds affairs, meditating what they should do to thee; or they meditated or devised in relation to thee wiles, artifices, plots or stratagems; or they revolved ideas or opinions respecting the frustrating of thy affair (Lane).

Commentary:

This verse further explains what has been said in the previous verse, *viz.*, that the hypocrites would have plotted to injure the cause of Islam in the very midst of battle, if they had marched forth with the Muslims because they were always on the look-out to create mischief and had already been plotting to bring the Holy Prophet to grief.

1206. Commentary:

Some of the hypocrites sought to be excused on the plea that the Syrian women were exceptionally beautiful, and that if they went to that country they were likely so fall into temptation, meaning thereby that they wanted to stay behind only in order to save their morals and their faith. But faith, the verse tersely points out, they had already lost; for it was for God's sake that they had to undertake the journey, and since they declined to respond to the call of God, they could not be said to possess any faith. They destroyed the root to save the branch, if indeed they meant to save it.

1206A. Important Words:

امرنا (our precaution). The word امر gives a number of meanings *e.g.* command or decree;

51. Say, 'Nothing shall befall us save that which Allah has ordained for us. He is our Protector. And in Allah then should the believers put their trust.'[1207]

قُلْ لَّنْ يُّصِيْبَنَآ اِلَّا مَا كَتَبَ اللّٰهُ لَنَا ۚ هُوَ مَوْلٰىنَا ۚ وَعَلَى اللّٰهِ فَلْيَتَوَكَّلِ الْمُؤْمِنُوْنَ ۞

52. Say, 'You do not await for us anything except one of the two good things; while as regards you, we await that Allah will afflict you with a punishment either from Himself or at our hands. Wait then; we *also* are waiting with you.'[1208]

قُلْ هَلْ تَرَبَّصُوْنَ بِنَآ اِلَّا اِحْدَى الْحُسْنَيَيْنِ ۭ وَنَحْنُ نَتَرَبَّصُ بِكُمْ اَنْ يُّصِيْبَكُمُ اللّٰهُ بِعَذَابٍ مِّنْ عِنْدِهٖٓ اَوْ بِاَيْدِيْنَا ۫ فَتَرَبَّصُوْٓا اِنَّا مَعَكُمْ مُّتَرَبِّصُوْنَ ۞

53. Say, 'Spend willingly or unwillingly, it shall not be accepted from you. You are indeed a disobedient people.'[1209]

قُلْ اَنْفِقُوْا طَوْعًا اَوْ كَرْهًا لَّنْ يُّتَقَبَّلَ مِنْكُمْ ۭ اِنَّكُمْ كُنْتُمْ قَوْمًا فٰسِقِيْنَ ۞

---

thing, affair or matter; condition, case or state, etc. (Lane). Here it signifies precaution (Kashshāf).

1207. Commentary:

The expression, *save that which Allah has ordained for us*, means that victory as ordained by God will always be attained, however great the intervening difficulties. The words that follow, *viz. He is our Protector*, support this interpretation and also 58 : 22 which says, *Allah has decreed : Of a certainty I will prevail, and My Messengers*.

1208. Commentary:

The "two good things" referred to in this verse are martyrdom and victory. Only one of these two things can fall to the lot of believers in a war. Either they win and triumph or they die on the battle-field and become martyrs. Hence the evil desires which the disbelievers and hypocrites entertained concerning the Muslims could never be fulfilled. The verse thus purports to say that true believers can never

suffer a defeat; they either die fighting and thus win martyrdom or they return victorious from the field of battle.

1209. Commentary:

The expression, *it shall not be accepted from you*, means that if the hypocrites offered to pay the *Zakāt* or any other subscription, it should not be accepted from them in expiation of their non-participation in the expedition. The nature of the punishment meted out to the hypocrites is worthy of special notice. No fine was levied on them, nor were they imprisoned nor subjected to a punishment generally inflicted for offences of this nature. They were simply told that as, by disobeying the command of God and refusing to serve Islam at a time of great danger, they were doomed, *Zakāt*, which was a means of purification and therefore of winning salvation, would not be accepted from them. This shows that the dealings of the Holy Prophet with the hypocrites were not dictated by any monetary or mundane considerations.

54. And nothing has deprived them of the acceptance of their contributions save that they disbelieve in Allah and His Messenger. And *they come not to Prayer except lazily and they make no contribution save reluctantly.[1210]

وَمَا مَنَعَهُمْ اَنْ تُقْبَلَ مِنْهُمْ نَفَقَاتُهُمْ اِلَّا اَنَّهُمْ كَفَرُوْا بِاللّٰهِ وَبِرَسُوْلِهٖ وَلَا يَاْتُوْنَ الصَّلٰوةَ اِلَّا وَهُمْ كُسَالٰى وَلَا يُنْفِقُوْنَ اِلَّا وَهُمْ كٰرِهُوْنَ ۝

55. So *let not their wealth nor their children excite thy wonder. Allah only intends to punish them therewith in the present life and that their souls may depart while they are disbelievers.[1211]

فَلَا تُعْجِبْكَ اَمْوَالُهُمْ وَلَاۤ اَوْلَادُهُمْ ۚ اِنَّمَا يُرِيْدُ اللّٰهُ لِيُعَذِّبَهُمْ بِهَا فِى الْحَيٰوةِ الدُّنْيَا وَتَزْهَقَ اَنْفُسُهُمْ وَهُمْ كٰفِرُوْنَ ۝

56. And they swear by Allah that they are indeed of you, while they are not of you, but they are a people who are timorous.[1212]

وَيَحْلِفُوْنَ بِاللّٰهِ اِنَّهُمْ لَمِنْكُمْ ۚ وَمَا هُمْ مِّنْكُمْ وَلٰكِنَّهُمْ قَوْمٌ يَّفْرَقُوْنَ ۝

---

a4 : 143.   b9 : 85.

1210. Commentary :

Good works are of two kinds : (1) those done for the purification of one's own soul, of which Prayer is the most important, and (2) those done for the uplift of one's community, of which *Zakāt* or other similar subscriptions form an important part. Hypocrites, the verse points out, are lazy and reluctant in both these fields.

1211. Commentary :

The verse warns the hypocrites that their possessions and their children, for whose sake they refrained from going to battle, would become a source of torture for them. Their children would embrace the faith they hate and would become its devoted followers and thus their wealth would also be used in furthering and strengthening the very cause which they abhorred. Think of the shock which 'Abdulllah bin Ubayy, leader of the hypocrites at Medina, must have felt on learning that his own son had asked the Holy Prophet to allow him to kill his father when the latter, on one occasion, used highly insulting and threatening language regarding the Holy Prophet and tried to create discord among the Faithful.

1212. Important Words :

يَفْرَقُوْنَ (are timorous) is derived from فَرِقَ which means, he feared or was afraid or he became frightened. They say فَرِقْتُ مِنْكَ i.e. I feared thee or I was in fear of thee. فَرِقَ عَلَيْهِ means, he feared for him. فَرِقَ also means, he entered into a wave and dived therein (Lane).

Commentary :

As the Muslims predominated at Medina, the hypocrites who lacked moral courage had to conceal their infidelity and even outwardly became Muslims to secure worldly advantages. They had no faith in their hearts, but they did not possess the courage to give vent openly to their real feelings.

57. If they could find a place of refuge, or caves, or *even* a hole to enter, they would surely turn thereto, rushing uncontrollably.[1213]

58. And among them are those *a*who find fault with thee in the matter of alms. If they are given thereof, they are content; but if they are not given thereof, behold! they are discontented.[1214]

لَوْ يَجِدُوْنَ مَلْجَأً اَوْ مَغٰرٰتٍ اَوْ مُدَّخَلًا لَّوَلَّوْا اِلَيْهِ وَهُمْ يَجْمَحُوْنَ ۞

وَمِنْهُمْ مَّنْ يَّلْمِزُكَ فِى الصَّدَقٰتِ ۚ فَاِنْ اُعْطُوْا مِنْهَا رَضُوْا وَاِنْ لَّمْ يُعْطَوْا مِنْهَاۤ اِذَا هُمْ يَسْخَطُوْنَ ۞

*a*9 : 79.

1213. Important Words :

يَجْمَحُوْنَ (rushing uncontrollably) is derived from جَمَحَ. They say جَمَحَ الفرس *i.e.* the horse broke loose or ran way and went at random so as not to be turned by anything; or it ran so as to have the mastery over its rider. جَمَحَ الرجل means, the man went at random without consideration or aim and not obeying a guide to the right course. جَمَحَ مُرَادُه means, the object of his desire baffled his efforts to attain it. The words هُمْ يَجْمَحُوْنَ mean, they hasten or go quickly so that nothing turns them back, like horses that become ungovernable by their riders (Lane & Aqrab).

Commentary :

The preceding verse speaks of the extreme fear of the hypocrites. As one who is in a state of fear generally takes to one of the three possible places of rescue, the present verse refers to all those three places, whether real or supposed. These are (1) مَلْجَأ *i.e.* place of refuge ; (2) مَغٰرٰت *i.e.* caves ; and (3) مُدَّخَل *i.e.* a hole or a burrow. The first idea of a man in fright is to go to his friends and seek refuge with them. This is referred to in the word مَلْجَأ (place of refuge). If, however, one has no friends to go to, one seeks the shelter of nature in a cave, etc. This is spoken of in the word مَغٰرٰت (caves). But there may be occasions when even a cave is not available for shelter. In such a case, a frightened man tries to hide his head in any hole or burrow that may happen to be near, just as an animal in fright does. This is referred to in the word مُدَّخَل (hole). Thus the verse refers to the extreme fear of the hypocrites which they feel when confronted with an opportunity to fight in the way of God.

1214. Important Words :

يَلْمِزُكَ (find fault with thee) is derived from لَمَزَ. They say لَمَزَه *i.e.* he made a sign to him with the eye or the head, etc. ; he blamed or found fault with him ; he spoke evil of him. It also means, he pushed or impelled or repelled him. لُمَزَة occurring elsewhere in the Quran (104 : 2) means, one who blames or reproaches or finds fault with others much or habitually ; one who speaks evil of others and defames them ; a separator of companions and friends, who goes about with calumny (Lane).

Commentary :

As the hypocrites had joined Muslims to secure worldly advantages, therefore, if they were given something out of *Zakāt* or legal alms, they were pleased ; but if they failed to get anything, they grumbled and began to find fault with the Prophet. This is one of the unmistakable signs of a hypocrite.

937

R. 8

59. And if they had been content with what Allah and His Messenger had given them and said, 'Sufficient for us is Allah: Allah will give us of His bounty, and so will His Messenger. To Allah do we turn in supplication,' it would have been better for them.

60. The alms are only for the poor and the needy, and for those employed in connection therewith, and for those whose hearts are to be reconciled, and for the freeing of slaves, and for those in debt, and for the cause of Allah, and for the wayfarer—an ordinance from Allah. And Allah is All-Knowing, Wise.[1215]

[Arabic verse text]

1215. Important Words :

صدقات (alms) is the the plural of صدقة and here signifies Zakât. See also 4 : 5.

الفقراء (the poor) is the plural of فقیر which is derived from فقر (faqura) which means, he dug the ground or he dug a well to draw forth water; or ہ bored or perforated beads, etc. فقیر means, he made an incision in the nose of the camel to render it tractable. فقرہ also means, he broke the فقرہ or vertebrae of his back. فقر (faqura) or افتقر (faqira) means, he was or became poor or needy. فقر means, poverty, want or need; the state of a man when he became poor or needy. فقیر means, poor or needy; one having only what suffices for his household. مفقر means, one who has only what suffices for his household; one who is crippled by disease; one who has no trade or has only a mean trade. The word فقیر (one who possesses only what is barely sufficient) differs from مسکین (for which see below) which means, one who possesses nothing, altogether destitute. Some authorities however differ from this view (Lane). See also 2 : 269.

مساکین (the needy) is the plural of مسکین which is derived from سکن which means, he or it was or became still, motionless or stationary or quiet or calm; low, abject or in a state of humiliation; weak, subdued or suppressed; poor; destitute i.e. possessing nothing; or possessing somewhat; rendered by poverty to have little power of motion. Authorities differ as to who is in a worse condition—مسکین or فقیر (Lane).

Commentary :

In the previous verse reference was made to the displeasure of the hypocrites, if they were not given a share in the Zakât. The present verse defines the objects for which Zakât is to be spent and these, as the verse explains, are eight in number.

The first-mentioned class i.e. فقراء (the poor) signifies those broken or perforated with poverty or disease, whereas the second-mentioned class i.e. مساکین (the needy) signifies those rendered motionless through want of means e.g. the unemployed, or those possessing the ability to work but lacking the means thereof.

The words, those employed in connection therewith, signify those who are employed in collecting Zakât, or in keeping an account thereof or in the performance of any other duty connected therewith.

61. And among them are those who annoy the Prophet and say, 'He *gives* ear *to all.*' Say, 'His *giving* ear *to all* is good for you : he believes in Allah and believes the Faithful, and is [a]a mercy for those of you who believe.' And those who annoy the Messenger of Allah shall have a grievous punishment.[1216]

وَمِنْهُمُ الَّذِيْنَ يُؤْذُوْنَ النَّبِيَّ وَيَقُوْلُوْنَ هُوَ اُذُنٌ ۚ قُلْ اُذُنُ خَيْرٍ لَّكُمْ يُؤْمِنُ بِاللّٰهِ وَيُؤْمِنُ لِلْمُؤْمِنِيْنَ وَرَحْمَةٌ لِّلَّذِيْنَ اٰمَنُوْا مِنْكُمْ ۚ وَالَّذِيْنَ يُؤْذُوْنَ رَسُوْلَ اللّٰهِ لَهُمْ عَذَابٌ اَلِيْمٌ ۞

62. [b]They swear by Allah to you to please you ; but Allah and His Messenger are more worthy that they should please him *and God*, if they are believers.[1217]

يَحْلِفُوْنَ بِاللّٰهِ لَكُمْ لِيُرْضُوْكُمْ ۚ وَاللّٰهُ وَرَسُوْلُهٗ اَحَقُّ اَنْ يُّرْضُوْهُ اِنْ كَانُوْا مُؤْمِنِيْنَ ۞

---

[a]9 : 128 ; 21 : 108.   [b]9 : 96.

The words, *whose hearts are to be reconciled*, mean those whose hearts are sincerely inclined towards Islam but who, owing to their having become disconnected with their former society, stand in need of monetary help. The term extends to new converts also.

The word, *slaves*, signifies, besides actual slaves, captives and such persons as are called upon to pay blood-money to secure their freedom.

The expression, *for those in debt*, means those who are unable to pay their debts or those who have suffered an extraordinary loss in trade, etc.

The words, *for the cause of Allah*, imply every good or pious work commanded by God.

The term ابن السبيل (the wayfarer) includes those stranded on a journey for lack of money; or those who travel in search of knowledge or for promoting social relations. See also 2 : 178.

1216. Commentary :

The hypocrites, by using the words, هو اذن *i.e. he gives ear to all*, (lit. " he is all ear ") with regard to the Holy Prophet, meant to say that he was always listening to the reports of his reporters and thus, by reason of the excess of this practice, he had become, as it were, the very organ of hearing. The verse replies to this taunt of the hypocrites by saying that the Prophet did indeed receive reports but this practice was essential for good administration ; for if he who is in power does not keep himself well-informed, he cannot rule with justice.

Moreover, by using the words, *is good for you*, the verse hints that though the Prophet did listen to reports about the machinations of the hypocrites, he never punished them merely on the basis of these reports without first ascertaining whether they were true or false, and even when they proved to be true, he very often pardoned them. So it was not right for them to taunt him for keeping himself informed of what went on around him.

1217. Commentary :

The hypocrites used to try to please influential Muslims by making pious professions of good faith. The verse exposes their real motives by saying that if they were really sincere in their professions, they ought to have first

3. Have they not known that ^awhoso opposes Allah and His Messenger, for him is the fire of Hell, wherein he shall abide? That is the great humiliation.

اَلَمْ يَعْلَمُوْۤا اَنَّهٗ مَنْ يُّحَادِدِ اللّٰهَ وَرَسُوْلَهٗ فَاَنَّ لَهٗ نَارَ جَهَنَّمَ خَالِدًا فِيْهَا ذٰلِكَ الْخِزْىُ الْعَظِيْمُ ۞

64. The hypocrites fear lest a Sūra should be revealed against them, informing them of what is in their hearts. Say, ' Mock ye! surely, Allah will bring to light what you fear.'¹²¹⁸

يَحْذَرُ الْمُنٰفِقُوْنَ اَنْ تُنَزَّلَ عَلَيْهِمْ سُوْرَةٌ تُنَبِّئُهُمْ بِمَا فِيْ قُلُوْبِهِمْ ۚ قُلِ اسْتَهْزِءُوْا ۚ اِنَّ اللّٰهَ مُخْرِجٌ مَّا تَحْذَرُوْنَ ۞

65. And if thou question them, ^bthey will most surely say, ' We were only talking idly and jesting.' Say, ' Was it Allah and His Signs and His Messenger that you mocked at?¹²¹⁹

وَلَئِنْ سَاَلْتَهُمْ لَيَقُوْلُنَّ اِنَّمَا كُنَّا نَخُوْضُ وَنَلْعَبُ ۚ قُلْ اَبِاللّٰهِ وَاٰيٰتِهٖ وَرَسُوْلِهٖ كُنْتُمْ تَسْتَهْزِءُوْنَ ۞

---

^a58 : 6, 21.   ^b2 : 15.

---

tried to please the Prophet, who was their leader and master. As they had never done so, their dishonesty was established; and Muslims were, therefore, warned to be ever on their guard against the wiles of the hypocrites and not to allow themselves to be deceived by their flattery.

1218. Commentary :

The verse lifts the veil from the jokes the hypocrites used to indulge in at the cost of the Holy Prophet and the Muslims. When they sat together in private, they used to say jokingly to one another that they feared lest God should send down a *Sūra* to the Prophet informing him of what lay concealed in their minds. They did not actually believe that the Holy Prophet might indeed receive revelation about their secret thoughts from God, because they did not believe him to be the recipient of divine revelation. They only said this by way of ridicule, as the words that follow, *i.e.*, *Mock ye*, indicate.

The words, *Allah will bring to light what you fear* mean that whereas the hypocrites joked about the Holy Prophet in their secret meetings and affected to be afraid that he might be informed of those jokes by God, while in reality they entertained no such fears, the All-Knowing God would actually divulge their secrets to His Messenger and then the hypocrites would have real cause to experience their pretended apprehensions.

1219. Commentary :

The verse signifies that if and when the hypocrites are asked why they make insulting remarks about the Prophet in their private meetings, they naively reply that they only diverted themselves with idle and playful discourse. The verse proceeds to rebuke them by asking whether they could get hold of nothing else than God and His Messenger to make the butt of their jokes and scoffing.

66. ^a"Offer no excuse. You have certainly disbelieved after your believing. If We forgive a party from among you, a party shall We punish, for they have been guilty'.[1220]

67. The hypocrites, men and women, are *all* connected one with another. They enjoin evil and forbid good, and keep their hands closed. ^bThey neglected Allah, so He has neglected them. Surely, it is the hypocrites who are the disobedient.[1221]

لَا تَعْتَذِرُوْا قَدْ كَفَرْتُمْ بَعْدَ اِيْمَانِكُمْ ۚ اِنْ نَّعْفُ عَنْ طَآئِفَةٍ مِّنْكُمْ نُعَذِّبْ طَآئِفَةً ۢ بِاَنَّهُمْ كَانُوْا مُجْرِمِيْنَ ۞

اَلْمُنٰفِقُوْنَ وَ الْمُنٰفِقٰتُ بَعْضُهُمْ مِّنْۢ بَعْضٍ ۚ يَاْمُرُوْنَ بِالْمُنْكَرِ وَ يَنْهَوْنَ عَنِ الْمَعْرُوْفِ وَ يَقْبِضُوْنَ اَيْدِيَهُمْ ۚ نَسُوا اللّٰهَ فَنَسِيَهُمْ ۚ اِنَّ الْمُنٰفِقِيْنَ هُمُ الْفٰسِقُوْنَ ۞

---

^a66 : 8.   ^b59 : 20.

1220. Commentary :

The words, *You have certainly disbelieved after your believing*, mean, "you expressed belief in God and His Messenger but practically you remained disbelievers"; or "you possessed some light of faith in you in the beginning but you allowed that light to become gradually extinguished."

The verse also hints that the hypocrites may yet repent and their repentance would be accepted; and history tells us that some of the hypocrites did actually repent and became sincere Muslims.

1221. Important Words :

المُنافقون (the hypocrites) is derived from نافق which is derived from نفق. They say نفق الشيء *i.e.* the thing became diminished; or it became spent up and perished. نفقت السلعة means, the merchandise was in much demand. نفقت السوق means, the market became brisk, its goods selling quickly. نفق الرجل means, the man expired. نفق اليربوع means, the rat came out of its hole in the earth. انفق ماله means, he spent freely and constantly so as to reduce or exhaust his wealth. نافق في المحبة means, he acted hypocritically in respect of love. نافق الرجل في الدين means, the man concealed disbelief in the heart and

expressed belief with his tongue. نافق اليربوع means, the rat known as *yarbū* betook itself to its hole. النافقاء means, a hole in the earth having two open ends which the rat enters concealing one end and leaving the other exposed, so that in time of danger it may avail itself of the concealed end and escape through it النفق means, a hole or passage through earth leading up to some place through an opening at the other end. النفاق means, entering faith through one door and leaving it through another ; acting hypocritically. المنافق means, one who conceals disbelief in his heart and expresses belief with his tongue ; an hypocrite (Aqrab, Tāj & Mufradāt). Though hypocrites have been mentioned in the Quran as early as in 2 : 9, the word منافق (hypocrite) has been first used in 4 : 62.

نسيهم (He has neglected them). نسيان generally meaning "forgetfulness", does not always signify the act of forgetting. Truly speaking, نسيان means, one's ceasing to think of a person or a thing either owing to loss of memory or owing to negligence or deliberately. The Quran says لا تنسوا الفضل بينكم *i.e.* do not cease (lit. do not forget) to do good to one another. In fact, when the word نسيان is used about God, it never means "forgetting" but simply cutting off connection by way of punishment or ceasing

68. [a]Allah promises the hypocrites, men and women, and the disbelievers the fire of Hell, wherein they shall abide. It will suffice them. And Allah has cursed them. And they shall have a lasting punishment.[1222]

وَعَدَ اللّٰهُ الۡمُنٰفِقِیۡنَ وَ الۡمُنٰفِقٰتِ وَ الۡکُفَّارَ نَارَ جَهَنَّمَ خٰلِدِیۡنَ فِیۡہَا ؕ ہِیَ حَسۡبُہُمۡ ۚ وَ لَعَنَہُمُ اللّٰہُ ۚ وَ لَہُمۡ عَذَابٌ مُّقِیۡمٌ ﴿۶۸﴾

69. *Allah promises these hypocrites and disbelievers the fire of Hell* even as He promised those before you. They were mightier than you in power and richer in possessions and children. They enjoyed their lot for a short time, so have you enjoyed your lot as those before you enjoyed their lot. And you indulged in idle talk as they indulged in idle talk. [b]It is they whose works shall be of no avail in this world and the Hereafter. And it is they who are the losers.[1223]

کَالَّذِیۡنَ مِنۡ قَبۡلِکُمۡ کَانُوۡۤا اَشَدَّ مِنۡکُمۡ قُوَّۃً وَّ اَکۡثَرَ اَمۡوَالًا وَّ اَوۡلَادًا ۟ فَاسۡتَمۡتَعُوۡا بِخَلَاقِہِمۡ فَاسۡتَمۡتَعۡتُمۡ بِخَلَاقِکُمۡ کَمَا اسۡتَمۡتَعَ الَّذِیۡنَ مِنۡ قَبۡلِکُمۡ بِخَلَاقِہِمۡ وَ خُضۡتُمۡ کَالَّذِیۡ خَاضُوۡا ؕ اُولٰٓئِکَ حَبِطَتۡ اَعۡمَالُہُمۡ فِی الدُّنۡیَا وَ الۡاٰخِرَۃِ ۚ وَ اُولٰٓئِکَ ہُمُ الۡخٰسِرُوۡنَ ﴿۶۹﴾

---

[a]4 : 146.   [b]18 : 106.

---

to think of a person with feelings of love and affection (Mufradāt).

Commentary :

This verse mentions some of the signs by which hypocrites can be distinguished from true believers. These signs are : (1) that the hypocrites form a sort of inner society among themselves, shunning true believers and being inter-connected with one another ; (2) that they enjoin evil ; (3) that they forbid good ; (4) that they do not spend in the cause of God, keeping their hands closed ; (5) that they neglect Allah and His commandments ; (6) that, as a consequence, God too neglects them and they do not enjoy divine help in their works ; and (7) that they are disobedient to God, always seeking to evade His behests.

1222. Commentary :

The hypocrites will have, over and above the punishment of Hell, which in itself is a terrible punishment, the curse of God. This shows that the curse of God is even more dreadful than the punishment of Hell. Compare this with the " pleasure of Allah " promised to believers in 9 : 72 below, in addition to Heaven. Just as the curse of God is worse than Hell, so is the " pleasure of Allah " better than Heaven.

1223. Important Words :

The word الذی in the clause كالذی خاضوا (as they indulged in idle talk) has been variously explained. Either (1) it is in the sense of من or ما being used as a plural and giving the sense of الذین ; or (2) it has the word خوض understood before it, the full clause being كخوض الذی خاضوه *i.e.* like the idle talk in which they indulged ; or (3) it has the word فوج or some similar word understood before it, the full clause in this case being كالفوج الذی خاضوا *i.e.* like the party which indulged in idle talk, etc. (Kashshāf & Shaukānī).

70. aHas not the story reached them of those before them—the people of Noah, and 'Ād, and Thamūd, and the people of Abraham, and the dwellers of Midian, and the cities which were overthrown? Their Messengers came to them with clear Signs. So bAllah would not wrong them, but they wronged themselves.[1224]

71. And the believers, men and women, are friends one of another. cThey enjoin good and forbid evil and dobserve Prayer and epay the Zakāt and fobey Allah and His Messenger. It is these on whom Allah will have mercy. Surely, Allah is Mighty and Wise.[1225]

الَمۡ يَاۡتِهِمۡ نَبَاُ الَّذِيۡنَ مِنۡ قَبۡلِهِمۡ قَوۡمِ نُوۡحٍ وَّعَادٍ وَّثَمُوۡدَ وَقَوۡمِ اِبۡرٰهِيۡمَ وَاَصۡحٰبِ مَدۡيَنَ وَالۡمُؤۡتَفِكٰتِ ۚ اَتَتۡهُمۡ رُسُلُهُمۡ بِالۡبَيِّنٰتِ ۚ فَمَا كَانَ اللّٰهُ لِيَظۡلِمَهُمۡ وَلٰكِنۡ كَانُوۡۤا اَنۡفُسَهُمۡ يَظۡلِمُوۡنَ ۝

وَالۡمُؤۡمِنُوۡنَ وَالۡمُؤۡمِنٰتُ بَعۡضُهُمۡ اَوۡلِيَآءُ بَعۡضٍ ۚ يَاۡمُرُوۡنَ بِالۡمَعۡرُوۡفِ وَيَنۡهَوۡنَ عَنِ الۡمُنۡكَرِ وَيُقِيۡمُوۡنَ الصَّلٰوةَ وَيُؤۡتُوۡنَ الزَّكٰوةَ وَيُطِيۡعُوۡنَ اللّٰهَ وَرَسُوۡلَهٗ ؕ اُولٰٓئِكَ سَيَرۡحَمُهُمُ اللّٰهُ ؕ اِنَّ اللّٰهَ عَزِيۡزٌ حَكِيۡمٌ ۝

---

a14 : 10 ; 50 : 13-15.   b10 : 45 ; 29 : 41 ; 30 : 10.   c3 : 105, 111 ; 7 : 158 ; 9 : 112 ; 31 : 18. dSee 2 : 4.   eSee 2 : 44.   f See 8 : 2.

Commentary :

The reference in the pronoun "you" in the words, *before you,* may be either to the hypocrites in general or to 'Abdullah bin Ubayy (the leader of the hypocrites) and his close associates in particular. The words, *those before you,* are explained in the following verse.

1224. Important Words :

المُؤۡتَفِكَات (cities which were overthrown) is derived from أفك. They say أفكه *i.e.* he changed his or its manner of being or state ; he turned him or it away or back. They say اِئۡتَفَكَت البلدة باهلها *i.e.* the land or town was or became overturned or subverted with its inhabitants. مُؤۡتَفِكَات therefore means, towns or cities overthrown or subverted. It also means, the winds that turn over the surface of the earth, or the winds that blow from different quarters, now from this and now from that (Lane).

Commentary :

This verse explains the words, *those before you,* occurring in the preceding verse. The reference in words, *cities which were overthrown,* is to the towns to which Prophet Lot was sent and which were turned upside down on account of their transgression and depravity. The catastrophe was caused by a violent earthquake. The overthrown habitations were, according to the Bible, the two towns of Sodom and Gomorrah (Gen. 19 : 24 & 25). The site is believed to be that of the Dead Sea (Jew. Enc. under Sodom). The Quran speaks of the place as being situated on or near a "permanent way" (15 : 75-77).

1225. Commentary :

Compare this verse and the next with 9 : 67, 68 above. The present verse enumerates some of the signs of true believers. These signs are : (1) that they are friends to one another; (2) that

2. *a*Allah has promised to believers, men and women, Gardens beneath which rivers flow, wherein they will abide, and delightful dwelling-places in Gardens of eternity. And *b*the pleasure of Allah is the greatest of all. That is the supreme triumph.[1226]

وَعَدَ اللهُ الْمُؤْمِنِيْنَ وَالْمُؤْمِنٰتِ جَنّٰتٍ تَجْرِيْ مِنْ تَحْتِهَا الْاَنْهٰرُ خٰلِدِيْنَ فِيْهَا وَمَسٰكِنَ طَيِّبَةً فِيْ جَنّٰتِ عَدْنٍ وَرِضْوَانٌ مِّنَ اللهِ اَكْبَرُ ذٰلِكَ هُوَ الْفَوْزُ الْعَظِيْمُ ۞

R. 10　73. *c*O Prophet, strive against the disbelievers and the hypocrites. And be severe to them. Their abode is Hell, and a vile destination it is.[1227]

يٰۤاَيُّهَا النَّبِيُّ جَاهِدِ الْكُفَّارَ وَالْمُنٰفِقِيْنَ وَاغْلُظْ عَلَيْهِمْ وَمَأْوٰىهُمْ جَهَنَّمُ وَبِئْسَ الْمَصِيْرُ ۞

*a*See 2:26.　*b*3:16; 5:3; 9:22; 57:21.　*c*66:10.

they enjoin good; (3) that they forbid evil; (4) that they are steadfast in the performance of Prayers; (5) that they give the prescribed *Zakāt*; (6) that they obey God and His Messenger; and (7) that they are recipients of God's mercy.

1226. Important Words:

جنات عدن (Gardens of eternity). عدن is derived from عدن. They say عدن بالارض *i.e.* he remained, stayed, dwelt or abode in the land. عدنت البلد means, I took for myself the town or country as a home or a settled place of abode. An Arab would say عدنت الابل بمكان كذا *i.e.* the camels kept to such a place, not quitting it. جنات عدن would, therefore, mean Gardens of perpetual abode (Lane). See also 5:66.

Commentary:

The word طيبة translated as "delightful" in the text also means good, agreeable and clean. The use of this word thus hints that our houses and dwelling-places on this earth should also be clean and agreeable to live in. See also note on 9:68 above.

The expression, *Gardens of eternity*, hints that the permanent home of man is the Hereafter, the life of this world being only transient. Incidentally, it also implies that the blessings of Heaven are everlasting. See also 5:66.

1227. Commentary:

The words, *disbelievers and hypocrites*, do not here refer to two different classes of men, but only to hypocrites who are also disbelievers. As a matter of fact, the word "hypocrites" as used here explains the meaning of the word "disbelievers" which precedes it, hinting that the hypocrites referred to here are disbelievers at heart, though outwardly they profess to be believers. See also the succeeding verse.

The words, *be severe to them*, may mean "be strict in your dealings with the hypocrites" *i.e.* you should no longer be lenient to them or condone their offences, as you did formerly, but you should now call them to account for their misdeeds. The words do not signify cruel treatment or even harshness of language or demeanour but simply strictness of attitude and treatment.

74. They swear by Allah that they said nothing, but they did certainly use blasphemous language, and disbelieved after they had embraced Islam. And they meditated that which they could not attain. And they cherished hatred only because Allah and His Messenger had enriched them out of His bounty. So if they repent, it will be better for them; but if they turn away, Allah will punish them with a grievous punishment in this world and the Hereafter, and they shall have neither friend nor helper in the earth.[1228]

يَحْلِفُوْنَ بِاللّٰهِ مَا قَالُوْا ۖ وَلَقَدْ قَالُوْا كَلِمَةَ الْكُفْرِ وَ كَفَرُوْا بَعْدَ اِسْلَامِهِمْ وَهَمُّوْا بِمَا لَمْ يَنَالُوْا ۚ وَمَا نَقَمُوْا اِلَّا اَنْ اَغْنٰهُمُ اللّٰهُ وَرَسُوْلُهٗ مِنْ فَضْلِهٖ ۚ فَاِنْ يَّتُوْبُوْا يَكُ خَيْرًا لَّهُمْ ۚ وَاِنْ يَّتَوَلَّوْا يُعَذِّبْهُمُ اللّٰهُ عَذَابًا اَلِيْمًا ۙ فِي الدُّنْيَا وَالْاٰخِرَةِ ۚ وَمَا لَهُمْ فِي الْاَرْضِ مِنْ وَّلِيٍّ وَّلَا نَصِيْرٍ ۟

75. And among them there are those who made a covenant with Allah, *saying,* 'If He give us of His bounty, we would most surely give alms and be of the virtuous.'[1229]

وَمِنْهُمْ مَّنْ عَاهَدَ اللّٰهَ لَئِنْ اٰتٰىنَا مِنْ فَضْلِهٖ لَنَصَّدَّقَنَّ وَلَنَكُوْنَنَّ مِنَ الصّٰلِحِيْنَ ۟

76. But when He gave them of His bounty, they became niggardly of it, and they turned away in aversion.

فَلَمَّا اٰتٰهُمْ مِّنْ فَضْلِهٖ بَخِلُوْا بِهٖ وَتَوَلَّوْا وَّهُمْ مُّعْرِضُوْنَ ۟

1228. Commentary:

The words, *They swear by Allah that they said nothing,* also show that the preceding verse refers not to disbelievers and hypocrites jointly but to hypocrites only. As the verse points out, some of the men who later turned hypocrites were not insincere in the beginning; but as time went on and Islam made progress, they gradually drifted into disbelief and hypocrisy. For instance, 'Abdullah bin Ubayy, who afterwards became leader of the hypocrites, was at first a believer. But when he found that by giving his allegiance to the Holy Prophet his own prestige and importance had declined, he turned hostile and began to plot against Islam.

The expression, *because Allah and His Messenger had enriched them out of His bounty,* means that with the advent of the Holy Prophet to Medina, the prosperity of the town very much increased, its trade thrived and its inhabitants grew rich.

1229. Commentary:

The verse refers to the time when some of the men who later turned hypocrites retained some sincerity of faith. See the following verse.

77. So He requited them with hypocrisy *which shall last* in their hearts until the day when they shall meet Him, because they broke their promise to Allah, and because they lied.[1230]

فَأَعْقَبَهُمْ نِفَاقًا فِيْ قُلُوْبِهِمْ اِلٰى يَوْمِ يَلْقَوْنَهٗ بِمَآ اَخْلَفُوا اللّٰهَ مَا وَعَدُوْهُ وَبِمَا كَانُوْا يَكْذِبُوْنَ ۝

78. Know they not that *ᵃ*Allah knows their secrets as well as their private counsels and that Allah is the Best Knower of all unseen things?

اَلَمْ يَعْلَمُوْۤا اَنَّ اللّٰهَ يَعْلَمُ سِرَّهُمْ وَنَجْوٰىهُمْ وَاَنَّ اللّٰهَ عَلَّامُ الْغُيُوْبِ ۝

79. *ᵇ*Those who find fault with such of the believers as give alms of their own free will and with such as find nothing *to give* save *the earnings of* their toil. They thus deride them. Allah shall requite them for their derision, and for them is a grievous punishment.[1231]

اَلَّذِيْنَ يَلْمِزُوْنَ الْمُطَّوِّعِيْنَ مِنَ الْمُؤْمِنِيْنَ فِى الصَّدَقٰتِ وَالَّذِيْنَ لَا يَجِدُوْنَ اِلَّا جُهْدَهُمْ فَيَسْخَرُوْنَ مِنْهُمْ سَخِرَ اللّٰهُ مِنْهُمْ وَلَهُمْ عَذَابٌ اَلِيْمٌ ۝

---

*ᵃ*6:4; 11:6; 25:7; 28:70.   *ᵇ*9:58.

1230. Commentary:

The verse points to the great truth that sometimes one sin follows another as a natural consequence thereof. Hypocrisy took the place of faith in the hearts of those who did not keep the promise they had made with God. See also the preceding two verses.

1231. Commentary:

The verse purports to say that the hypocrites sought excuses to find fault with all classes of believers—both those who spent freely and those who could not do so. Particular reference is to the expedition to Tabūk. Before he started for Tabūk, the Holy Prophet invited the believers to make voluntary contributions to meet the expenses of this great expedition. 'Uthmān gave 300 camels and 10,000 *dinārs*; Abū Bakr parted with all that he possessed; while 'Umar gave as much as half of his entire property. The hypocrites attributed these and other similar liberal donations to a desire for show and display on the part of the donors. On the other hand, poor believers, who could make only small contributions, were also not spared. For instance, a poor Muslim, Abū 'Aqīl who gave only a small quantity of dates, his whole day's earnings, as his contribution, was scoffed at by the hypocrites for his scanty offering. It is to the taunting and scoffing of the hypocrites on this occasion that this verse particularly refers.

80. *Ask thou forgiveness for them, or ask thou not forgiveness for them ; even if thou ask forgiveness for them seventy times, Allah will never forgive them. That is because they disbelieved in Allah and His Messenger. And Allah guides not the perfidious people.[1232]

اِسْتَغْفِرْ لَهُمْ اَوْ لَا تَسْتَغْفِرْ لَهُمْ ۭ اِنْ تَسْتَغْفِرْ لَهُمْ سَبْعِيْنَ مَرَّةً فَلَنْ يَّغْفِرَ اللّٰهُ لَهُمْ ۭ ذٰلِكَ بِاَنَّهُمْ كَفَرُوْا بِاللّٰهِ وَرَسُوْلِهٖ ۭ وَاللّٰهُ لَا يَهْدِى الْقَوْمَ الْفٰسِقِيْنَ ۝

81. *Those who were left behind rejoiced in their sitting at home behind *the back of* the Messenger of Allah, and were averse to striving with their property and their persons in the cause of Allah. And they said, ' Go not forth in the heat.' Say, ' The fire of Hell is more intense in heat.' If only they could understand.[1233]

فَرِحَ الْمُخَلَّفُوْنَ بِمَقْعَدِهِمْ خِلٰفَ رَسُوْلِ اللّٰهِ وَ كَرِهُوْٓا اَنْ يُّجَاهِدُوْا بِاَمْوَالِهِمْ وَاَنْفُسِهِمْ فِيْ سَبِيْلِ اللّٰهِ وَقَالُوْا لَا تَنْفِرُوْا فِي الْحَرِّ ۭ قُلْ نَارُ جَهَنَّمَ اَشَدُّ حَرًّا ۭ لَوْ كَانُوْا يَفْقَهُوْنَ ۝

*63 : 7.   *9 : 87, 93.

1232. **Commentary :**

The verse refers to the offering of prayer for the hypocrites while they lived. It does not, however, refer to all hypocrites as a matter of principle but only to such as were doomed to perish and about whom God had revealed to His Prophet that they would die disbelievers (see 9 : 77 above). To pray for such hypocrites or disbelievers would virtually be contradicting the purpose of God. As for the injunction about funeral Prayer, it is contained in 9 : 84 below. It so happened that before the latter verse was revealed, 'Abdullah bin Ubayy, the leader of the hypocrites, died ; and the Holy Prophet, considering that he was outwardly a Muslim and that his son was a particularly devoted believer, prepared to offer funeral Prayer for him. Thereupon, 'Umar drew his attention to the verse under comment upon which the Holy Prophet said that the verse left it to him whether or not to say the funeral Prayer for a hypocrite and that he would ask forgiveness of God for 'Abdullah more than "seventy times".

It should be noted that the words, "seventy times," are not here meant literally but are simply intended to intensify the point that such hypocrites as are doomed to perish will never be forgiven ; but so great was the mercy of the Holy Prophet for those who professed faith in him that, taking advantage of the fact that God had not so far expressly commanded him to abstain from praying for the hypocrites at all, he interpreted the word "seventy" literally and offered to say funeral Prayer for 'Abdullah bin Ubayy, whose son was a very devoted Muslim.

1233. **Commentary :**

This and the following several verses speak of those who did not accompany the Holy Prophet on the expedition to Tabūk. The passive form in the word المخلّفون (those left behind) has been used in allusion to the words, *Allah was averse to their marching forth, so He kept them back, and it was said, 'Sit ye at home with those who sit',* occurring in 9 : 46 above.

These people not only stayed behind themselves but, as is usual with mischievous persons, also tried to dissuade others from joining the expedition.

82. They must laugh little and weep much as a reward for that which they used to earn.[1234]

فَلۡيَضۡحَكُوۡا قَلِيۡلًا وَّلۡيَبۡكُوۡا كَثِيۡرًا ۚ جَزَآءًۢ بِمَا كَانُوۡا يَكۡسِبُوۡنَ ۞

83. And if Allah return thee to a party of them, and they ask of thee leave to go forth to fight, say then, 'You shall never go forth with me, and shall never fight an enemy with me. You chose to sit *at home* the first time, so sit now with those who remain behind.'[1235]

فَاِنۡ رَّجَعَكَ اللّٰهُ اِلٰى طَآئِفَةٍ مِّنۡهُمۡ فَاسۡتَاۡذَنُوۡكَ لِلۡخُرُوۡجِ فَقُلۡ لَّنۡ تَخۡرُجُوۡا مَعِىَ اَبَدًا وَّلَنۡ تُقَاتِلُوۡا مَعِىَ عَدُوًّا ؕ اِنَّكُمۡ رَضِيۡتُمۡ بِالۡقُعُوۡدِ اَوَّلَ مَرَّةٍ فَاقۡعُدُوۡا مَعَ الۡخٰلِفِيۡنَ ۞

84. And never pray thou for any of them that dies, nor stand by his grave; for they disbelieved in Allah and His Messenger and died while they were disobedient.[1236]

وَلَا تُصَلِّ عَلٰٓى اَحَدٍ مِّنۡهُمۡ مَّاتَ اَبَدًا وَّلَا تَقُمۡ عَلٰى قَبۡرِهٖ ؕ اِنَّهُمۡ كَفَرُوۡا بِاللّٰهِ وَرَسُوۡلِهٖ وَمَاتُوۡا وَهُمۡ فٰسِقُوۡنَ ۞

1234. Commentary:

The verse obviously does not contain a commandment. It only embodies a prophecy that the time was soon coming when the hypocrites would *laugh little and weep much*. This was meant as retribution for their evil deeds.

1235. Commentary:

The verse was probably revealed when the Holy Prophet was away from Medina during his expedition to Tabūk. But if, as some Commentators think, it was revealed after his return to Medina, it would be taken to allude to what the hypocrites previously used to say regarding the said expedition. They thought that he would never return from the expedition alive. So the Quran, in this verse reminds them of what they used to say about the Holy Prophet, and of his safe return, contrary to their expectation.

The particle ان (if), it should be noted, does not always express doubt but is often used as simply a conditional particle. Moreover, it is sometimes used not from the point of view of the speaker, but from that of the person addressed. The word is here used by God and it is obvious that God had no doubt as to the safe return of the Prophet. So it must be taken to express the state of mind of the hypocrites.

1236. Commentary:

This verse prohibits Muslims from saying funeral Prayer for hypocrites who are disbelievers at heart. When 9 : 80 was revealed, the Holy Prophet thought that it was still open to him to perform the funeral service of a hypocrite if he should so choose; and when therefore 'Abdullah bin Ubayy died, he performed the service for him. By the present verse, however, God definitely forbade the performance of funeral service for disbelieving hypocrites. As a matter of principle, he who dies in a state of disbelief (whether he be an open disbeliever or a proved hypocrite) forfeits all claims on the prayers of the Faithful. His case is in the hands of God. He may punish or forgive him, as He may think fit. See also 9 : 80 above.

85. [a]And their possessions and their children should not excite thy wonder; Allah only intends to punish them therewith in this world and that their souls may depart while they are disbelievers.[1237]

وَلَا تُعْجِبْكَ اَمْوَالُهُمْ وَاَوْلَادُهُمْ اِنَّمَا يُرِيْدُ اللّٰهُ اَنْ يُّعَذِّبَهُمْ بِهَا فِى الدُّنْيَا وَتَزْهَقَ اَنْفُسُهُمْ وَهُمْ كٰفِرُوْنَ ۟

86. And when a Sūra is revealed, *enjoining*, ' Believe in Allah and strive *in the cause of Allah* in company with His Messenger,' those of them who possess affluence ask leave of thee and say, ' Leave us that we be with those who sit *at home*.'[1238]

وَاِذَآ اُنْزِلَتْ سُوْرَةٌ اَنْ اٰمِنُوْا بِاللّٰهِ وَجَاهِدُوْا مَعَ رَسُوْلِهِ اسْتَاْذَنَكَ اُولُوا الطَّوْلِ مِنْهُمْ وَقَالُوْا ذَرْنَا نَكُنْ مَّعَ الْقٰعِدِيْنَ ۟

87. [b]They are content to be with the womenfolk, and [c]their hearts are sealed so that they understand not.[1239]

رَضُوْا بِاَنْ يَّكُوْنُوْا مَعَ الْخَوَالِفِ وَطُبِعَ عَلٰى قُلُوْبِهِمْ فَهُمْ لَا يَفْقَهُوْنَ ۟

88. [d]But the Messenger and those who believe with him strive *in the cause of Allah* with their property and their persons, and it is they who shall have good things, and it is they who shall prosper.

لٰكِنِ الرَّسُوْلُ وَالَّذِيْنَ اٰمَنُوْا مَعَهُ جٰهَدُوْا بِاَمْوَالِهِمْ وَاَنْفُسِهِمْ وَاُولٰٓئِكَ لَهُمُ الْخَيْرٰتُ وَاُولٰٓئِكَ هُمُ الْمُفْلِحُوْنَ ۟

---

[a]9 : 55.   [b]9 : 81, 93.   [c]6 : 26 ; 63 : 4.   [d]8 : 75 ; 9 : 41, 111 ; 61 : 12.

1237. Commentary :

See note on 9 : 55 above.

1238. Commentary :

The words, *Leave us that we be with those who sit at home*, need not be taken to have been actually uttered by the hypocrites. They simply express a state of affairs implying that the hypocrites came to the Holy Prophet with various excuses, asking his leave to stay behind.

1239. Important Words :

خوالف (womenfolk) is the plural of both خالف

and خالفة which are active participles from the verb خلف which means, he remained or came after. خالف means, one who remains behind or after others, particularly in case of a war, the word خالفة being its feminine gender. So خوالف means, those who remain behind during war ; or the women (or children) remaining behind in houses or tents. The word also signifies, bad or corrupt persons (Lane). See also 7 : 70 & 170.

Commentary :

For the meaning of the words, *their hearts are sealed*, see 2 : 8 & 4 : 156.

89. ^aAllah has prepared for them Gardens underneath which flow rivers; therein they shall abide. That is the supreme triumph.

اَعَدَّ اللّٰهُ لَهُمْ جَنّٰتٍ تَجْرِیْ مِنْ تَحْتِهَا الْاَنْهٰرُ خٰلِدِیْنَ فِیْهَا ؕ ذٰلِكَ الْفَوْزُ الْعَظِیْمُ ۹

R. 12 90. And those who make excuses from among the desert Arabs came that exemption might be granted them. And those who were false to Allah and His Messenger stayed at home. A grievous punishment shall befall those of them who disbelieve.[1240]

وَ جَآءَ الْمُعَذِّرُوْنَ مِنَ الْاَعْرَابِ لِیُؤْذَنَ لَهُمْ وَقَعَدَ الَّذِیْنَ كَذَبُوا اللّٰهَ وَ رَسُوْلَهٗ ؕ سَیُصِیْبُ الَّذِیْنَ كَفَرُوْا مِنْهُمْ عَذَابٌ اَلِیْمٌ ۹

91. ^bNo blame lies on the weak, nor on the sick, nor on those who find naught to spend, if they are sincere to Allah and His Messenger. There is no cause of reproach against those who do good deeds; and Allah is Most Forgiving, Merciful.[1241]

لَیْسَ عَلَی الضُّعَفَآءِ وَ لَا عَلَی الْمَرْضٰی وَلَاعَلَی الَّذِیْنَ لَا یَجِدُوْنَ مَا یُنْفِقُوْنَ حَرَجٌ اِذَا نَصَحُوْا لِلّٰهِ وَ رَسُوْلِهٖ ؕ مَا عَلَی الْمُحْسِنِیْنَ مِنْ سَبِیْلٍ ؕ وَ اللّٰهُ غَفُوْرٌ رَّحِیْمٌ ۹

^aSee 2 : 26.   ^b48 : 18.

1240. Important Words :

المعذرون (those who make excuses) is the plural of معذر which is the active participle from عذر ('adhdhara) which again is derived from عذر ('adhara). They say عذره i.e. he excused him or he cleared him from blame, or he accepted his excuse. عذر ('adhdhara) means, he was without excuse; or he affected to excuse himself but had no excuse; or he excused himself but did not adduce a valid excuse for doing so; he was remiss or wanting or deficient in an affair, setting up an excuse for being so; he did not act vigorously in the affair, causing it to be imagined that he had an excuse when really he had none. Thus معذر is one who falls short of his duty and then excuses himself without having any real excuse; whereas معتذر is one who excuses himself whether he has a real excuse or not (Lane).

Commentary :

The verse speaks of the hypocrites as well as of those weak in faith who did not join the expedition to Tabūk. Some of them were disbelievers at heart, while others were only weak in Faith.

1241. Important Words :

نصحوا (are sincere) is derived from نصح . They say نصحه or له نصح i.e. he advised him or counselled him sincerely or faithfully; or he acted sincerely or honestly to him; or he deserved what was good for him, نصح الشیئی means, the thing became pure or unadulterated (Lane).

Commentary :

This and the succeeding verse speak of those who cannot join an expedition owing to some real inability. No blame lies on them. The verse also shows that those who have really nothing

92. Nor against those to whom, when they came to thee that thou shouldst mount them, thou didst say, ' I cannot find whereon I can mount you;' they turned back, their eyes overflowing with tears, out of grief that they could not find what they might spend.[1242]

وَلَا عَلَى الَّذِيْنَ اِذَا مَآ اَتَوْكَ لِتَحْمِلَهُمْ قُلْتَ لَآ اَجِدُ مَآ اَحْمِلُكُمْ عَلَيْهِ تَوَلَّوْا وَّاَعْيُنُهُمْ تَفِيْضُ مِنَ الدَّمْعِ حَزَنًا اَلَّا يَجِدُوْا مَا يُنْفِقُوْنَ ۝

93. The cause of reproach is only against those who ask leave of thee, while they are rich. *They are content to be with the womenfolk. And bAllah has set a seal upon their hearts so that they know not.[1243]

اِنَّمَا السَّبِيْلُ عَلَى الَّذِيْنَ يَسْتَأْذِنُوْنَكَ وَهُمْ اَغْنِيَآءُ رَضُوْا بِاَنْ يَّكُوْنُوْا مَعَ الْخَوَالِفِ وَطَبَعَ اللّٰهُ عَلٰى قُلُوْبِهِمْ فَهُمْ لَا يَعْلَمُوْنَ ۝

---

*a*9 : 79, 87.   *b*6 : 26 ; 9 : 87 ; 63 : 4.

---

to spend in the cause of God are also reckoned among those who actually strive in the cause of God, if they are sincere and faithful to God and His Messenger.

1242. Commentary :

The verse is general in its application but the persons particularly referred to were seven poor Muslims who were extremely desirous of going to *Jihād* but did not possess the means and the wherewithal to fulfil the wish of their hearts. These men came to the Holy Prophet, begging him to provide them with conveyance so that they might go forth with him. On being told by the Prophet that he was unable to grant their request, they were sorely grieved and went away with their eyes full of tears. It is said that after they had gone, the Holy Prophet was offered three camels by 'Uthmān and four by other Muslims and these he gave to the seven men. The Quran mentions this incident in order to contrast the faith and sincerity of these poor Muslims with the insincerity of those who proffered lame and false excuses and asked to be allowed to stay behind, although they possessed all the means to go. It also appears from this verse that all those who remained behind at Medina were not hypocrites but that among them there were also true and sincere Muslims who could not go because they did not possess the means to do so.

1243. Commentary :

For an explanation of the words, *Set a seal upon their hearts,* see 2 : 8 & 4 : 156.

94. They will make excuses to you when you return to them. Say, ' Make no excuses ; we shall not believe you. Allah has already informed us of the facts about you. And Allah will observe your conduct, and *also* His Messenger ; then you will be brought back to Him Who knows the unseen and the seen, and He will tell you all that you used to do.'[1244]

يَعْتَذِرُوْنَ اِلَيْكُمْ اِذَا رَجَعْتُمْ اِلَيْهِمْ قُلْ لَّا تَعْتَذِرُوْا لَنْ نُّؤْمِنَ لَكُمْ قَدْ نَبَّاَنَا اللّٰهُ مِنْ اَخْبَارِكُمْ وَسَيَرَى اللّٰهُ عَمَلَكُمْ وَرَسُوْلُهٗ ثُمَّ تُرَدُّوْنَ اِلٰى عٰلِمِ الْغَيْبِ وَالشَّهَادَةِ فَيُنَبِّئُكُمْ بِمَا كُنْتُمْ تَعْمَلُوْنَ ۝

95. They will swear to you by Allah, when you return to them, that you may leave them alone. So leave them alone. Surely, they are an abomination, and their abode is Hell—a *fit* recompense for that which they used to earn.[1245]

سَيَحْلِفُوْنَ بِاللّٰهِ لَكُمْ اِذَا انْقَلَبْتُمْ اِلَيْهِمْ لِتُعْرِضُوْا عَنْهُمْ فَاَعْرِضُوْا عَنْهُمْ اِنَّهُمْ رِجْسٌ وَّمَاْوٰىهُمْ جَهَنَّمُ جَزَاءً بِمَا كَانُوْا يَكْسِبُوْنَ ۝

1244. Commentary :

This verse was revealed when the Holy Prophet had not yet returned to Medina from his expedition to Tabūk.

1245. Commentary :

The words لِتُعْرِضُوْا عَنْهُمْ (that you may leave them alone) mean, that you may pardon them and not call them to account, whereas the expression فَاَعْرِضُوْا عَنْهُمْ (so leave them alone) means, turn yourselves away from them and have nothing to do with them. So the same word اعراض (leaving alone and turning away) has been used here in two different senses.

On his way back from Tabūk, one of those men who had remained behind met the Holy Prophet and offered excuses for not being able to go with him, but the Holy Prophet refused to listen to him. On the other hand, it is on record that in the case of some, he did accept their excuses on his return to Medina. This apparent disparity in the attitude of the Holy Prophet with regard to different persons may be explained by the fact that those who had stayed behind (hypocrites as well as believers) were of various types. The hypocrites were of three classes : (a) 'Abdullah bin Ubayy and his party ; (b) the hypocrites among the Arabs of the desert (9 : 90 above) ; and (c) the hypocrites who had built the *Masjid Ḍirār* with the intention of making it the centre of their activities against Islam (9 : 107 below). Similarly, the believers who had stayed behind were also of three classes : (1) those to whom the Quran has referred in 9 : 91 above *i.e.* the weak, the sick and the poor ; (2) those who were not wholly inexcusable but who possessed no excuse valid enough to justify their staying behind (9 : 102 below) ; and (3) those who possessed no excuse at all. As these stayers-behind belonged to different categories, therefore they were treated differently.

96. ^aThey will swear to you that you may be pleased with them. But *even* if you be pleased with them, Allah will not be pleased with the rebellious people.

يَحْلِفُوْنَ لَكُمْ لِتَرْضَوْا عَنْهُمْ فَاِنْ تَرْضَوْا عَنْهُمْ فَاِنَّ اللهَ لَا يَرْضٰى عَنِ الْقَوْمِ الْفٰسِقِيْنَ ۹۶

97. The Arabs of the desert are the worst in disbelief and hypocrisy, and most apt not to know the ordinances of *the Revelation* which Allah has sent down to His Messenger. And Allah is All-Knowing, Wise.[1246]

اَلْاَعْرَابُ اَشَدُّ كُفْرًا وَّنِفَاقًا وَّاَجْدَرُ اَلَّا يَعْلَمُوْا حُدُوْدَ مَآ اَنْزَلَ اللهُ عَلٰى رَسُوْلِهٖ ۖ وَاللهُ عَلِيْمٌ حَكِيْمٌ ۹۷

98. And among the Arabs of the desert are those who regard that which they spend *for God* as a fine and they wait for calamities to *befall* you. ^bOn themselves shall fall an evil calamity. And Allah is All-Hearing, All-Knowing.[1247]

وَمِنَ الْاَعْرَابِ مَنْ يَّتَّخِذُ مَا يُنْفِقُ مَغْرَمًا وَّيَتَرَبَّصُ بِكُمُ الدَّوَآئِرَ ۖ عَلَيْهِمْ دَآئِرَةُ السَّوْءِ ۖ وَاللهُ سَمِيْعٌ عَلِيْمٌ ۹۸

99. And among the Arabs of the desert are those who believe in Allah and the Last Day and regard that which they spend as means of drawing near to Allah and *of receiving* the blessings of the Prophet. Aye! it is for them certainly a means of drawing near *to God*. Allah will soon admit them to His mercy. Surely, Allah is Most Forgiving, Merciful.[1248]

وَمِنَ الْاَعْرَابِ مَنْ يُّؤْمِنُ بِاللهِ وَالْيَوْمِ الْاٰخِرِ وَيَتَّخِذُ مَا يُنْفِقُ قُرُبٰتٍ عِنْدَ اللهِ وَصَلَوٰتِ الرَّسُوْلِ ۚ اَلَآ اِنَّهَا قُرْبَةٌ لَّهُمْ ۚ سَيُدْخِلُهُمُ اللهُ فِيْ رَحْمَتِهٖ ۗ اِنَّ اللهَ غَفُوْرٌ رَّحِيْمٌ ۹۹

^a9 : 62.   ^b48 : 7.

1246. **Important Words :**

اَجْدَرُ (most apt) is derived from جَدَرَ which means, he or it was adapted, apt, suited, competent or worthy. They say جَدَرَهُ *i.e.* he made it or him adapted, apt, competent or worthy. One would say مَا اَجْدَرَهُ بِالْخَيْرِ *i.e.* how fit or suitable or adapted is he for what is good (Lane & Aqrab).

1247. **Important Words :**

مَغْرَمًا (fine) is the noun-infinitive from غَرِمَ which means, he paid or discharged a thing that had become obligatory upon him, *e.g.*, a blood-wit;

or he took upon himself to pay that which was not obligatory upon him ; or he took upon himself to pay a fine, etc. They say غَرِمَ الدَّيْنَ *i.e.* he paid or discharged the debt. غَرِمَ فِيْ تِجَارَةٍ means, he suffered a loss in his business. غَرَامَةٌ or مَغْرَمٌ or غُرْمٌ means, a thing that must be paid or discharged ; a damage or loss that befalls a man ; a debt ; a fine or mulct (Lane & Aqrab).

الدَّوَائِر (calamities) and دَائِرَة (calamity). See 5 : 53.

1248. **Important Words :**

قُرُبَات (means of drawing near) is the plural of

R. 13   100.   And *as for* the foremost *among the believers*, the first of the Emigrants and the Helpers, and those who followed them in the best possible manner, [a]Allah is well pleased with them and they are well pleased with Him; and He has prepared for them Gardens beneath which flow rivers. They will abide therein for ever. That is the supreme triumph.[1249]

وَالسّٰبِقُوۡنَ الۡاَوَّلُوۡنَ مِنَ الۡمُهٰجِرِيۡنَ وَالۡاَنۡصَارِ وَالَّذِيۡنَ اتَّبَعُوۡهُمۡ بِاِحۡسَانٍ رَّضِیَ اللّٰهُ عَنۡهُمۡ وَرَضُوۡا عَنۡهُ وَاَعَدَّ لَهُمۡ جَنّٰتٍ تَجۡرِیۡ تَحۡتَهَا الۡاَنۡهٰرُ خٰلِدِيۡنَ فِيۡهَاۤ اَبَدًا ؕ ذٰلِكَ الۡفَوۡزُ الۡعَظِيۡمُ ۞

101.   And of the desert Arabs around you some are hypocrites; and of the people of Medina *also*. They persist in hypocrisy. Thou knowest them not; We know them. We will punish them twice; then shall they be given over to a great punishment.[1250]

وَمِمَّنۡ حَوۡلَكُمۡ مِّنَ الۡاَعۡرَابِ مُنٰفِقُوۡنَ ۛؕ وَمِنۡ اَهۡلِ الۡمَدِيۡنَةِ ۟ؔ مَرَدُوۡا عَلَی النِّفَاقِ ۟ لَا تَعۡلَمُهُمۡ ؕ نَحۡنُ نَعۡلَمُهُمۡ ؕ سَنُعَذِّبُهُمۡ مَّرَّتَيۡنِ ثُمَّ يُرَدُّوۡنَ اِلٰی عَذَابٍ عَظِيۡمٍ ۞

---

[a]58 : 23 ; 98 : 9.

قِرۡبَة which is the noun-infinitive from قرب *i.e.* he or it was or became near in place, station or rank. قِرۡبَة therefore, means, nearness; a thing by which one seeks nearness to God or a thing by which one seeks to advance oneself in His favour (Lane).

Commentary :

The Quran is fair to all. As the Arabs of the desert were spoken of in 9 : 97, as being *the worst in disbelief and hypocrisy*, this verse points out that all Arabs of the desert are not alike. Even among them are sincere believers who are ever striving to attain nearness of God.

1249. Important Words :

السّابقون (foremost) is the plural of السابق being derived from سبق . They say سبقه *i.e.* he got or went or came before him or ahead of him; he outstripped him in a race, etc. So سابق is one who outstrips others in faith and actions (Lane).

الاولون (the first) is the plural of الاول which is derived from وأل being the opposite of الآخر *i.e.*

the last. اول means, the first; one preceding all others (Lane & Aqrab).

Commentary :

The verse mentions two distinctive qualifications of prominent believers: (1) السابقون *i.e.* those who are foremost in spiritual rank, outstripping others in faith and actions; and (2) الاولون *i.e.* those who are the first to believe, others only following them.

The Companions of the Holy Prophet are thus held up here as models for others, being both foremost in rank and the first to believe. Nay, even those who sincerely followed in their footsteps became the favoured ones of God. Incidentally, the verse also constitutes a forcible refutation of the Shia accusations against the first three Successors of the Holy Prophet and his prominent Companions.

1250. Important Words :

مردوا (persist) is from مرد (*marada*) which means, he exalted himself; he was insolent and

102. And there are others who have acknowledged their faults. They mixed a good work with another that was evil. It may be that Allah will turn to them with compassion. Surely, Allah is Most Forgiving, Merciful.[1251]

وَّاٰخَرُوۡنَ اعۡتَرَفُوۡا بِذُنُوۡبِهِمۡ خَلَطُوۡا عَمَلًا صَالِحًا وَّاٰخَرَ سَیِّئًا ؕ عَسَی اللّٰهُ اَنۡ یَّتُوۡبَ عَلَیۡهِمۡ ؕ اِنَّ اللّٰهَ غَفُوۡرٌ رَّحِیۡمٌ ۝

103. Take alms out of their wealth, so that thou mayest cleanse them and purify them thereby. And pray for them; thy prayer is indeed a *source of* tranquillity for them. And Allah is All-Hearing, All-Knowing.[1252]

خُذۡ مِنۡ اَمۡوَالِهِمۡ صَدَقَةً تُطَهِّرُهُمۡ وَتُزَکِّیۡهِمۡ بِهَا وَصَلِّ عَلَیۡهِمۡ ؕ اِنَّ صَلٰوتَكَ سَكَنٌ لَّهُمۡ ؕ وَاللّٰهُ سَمِیۡعٌ عَلِیۡمٌ ۝

---

audacious in pride and in acts of disobedience; he was excessively proud or disobedient or rebellious; he was refractory; or he outstripped others in pride or disobedience. They say مرد علی شیئی *i.e.* he became accustomed or inured to a thing and persisted in it. The expression مردوا علی النفاق means, they have become accustomed or inured to hypocrisy and persist in it; or they have become insolent and audacious in hypocrisy. مَرَد has about the same meaning. مرد (*marida*) with different vowel point at the central letter, means, it (a tree, etc.) was or became destitute of leaves (Lane & Aqrab)

Commentary:

The reference in the opening part of this verse is particularly to the five tribes of the desert living near Medina, viz., *Juhaina, Muzaina, Ashja', Aslam* and *Ghifār* (Ma'āni, iii. 361). After the death of the Holy Prophet the hypocrites from among the neighbouring tribes gathered together and made a raid on Medina (Khuldūn, ii. 66).

The word "twice" occurring in the sentence, *We will punish them twice*, does not refer to the form of punishment but to the period thereof which is explained in 9:126 below, where the Quran says, *do they not see that they are tried every year once or twice?* Thus the word

"twice" occurring in the present verse signifies that the hypocrites would be punished in a period ranging from one to two years *i.e.* if the punishment comes twice a year, they will have it in one year; if it comes once, they will have it in two years.

1251. Commentary:

The verse refers to those Muslims who did possess an excuse, but it was not strong enough to justify their staying behind (see note on 9:95 above). Their number, according to different reports, varied from seven to ten. As a self-inflicted punishment for their offence, these men bound themselves to the pillars of the Mosque at Medina, and when the Holy Prophet entered it to offer Prayers, they begged him to pardon them, to which he replied that he could not do it unless so commanded by God. When, however, this verse was revealed, they were ordered to be released.

1252. Commentary:

The persons referred to in the preceding verse brought a part of their property and begged the Holy Prophet to take the same as alms, but he told them that he had no instructions to accept anything from them, whereupon this verse was revealed, allowing him to accept their alms and to pray for them.

104. Know they not that ^aAllah is He Who accepts repentance from His servants and takes alms, and that Allah is He Who is Oft-Returning *with compassion, and* Merciful ?[1253]

ٱلَمۡ يَعۡلَمُوٓاۡ اَنَّ اللّٰهَ هُوَ يَقۡبَلُ التَّوۡبَةَ عَنۡ عِبَادِهٖ وَ يَأۡخُذُ الصَّدَقٰتِ وَاَنَّ اللّٰهَ هُوَ التَّوَّابُ الرَّحِيۡمُ ۝

105. And say, 'Work, and ^bAllah will surely see your work and *also* His Messenger and the believers. And you shall be brought back to Him Who knows the unseen and the seen; then He will tell you what you used to do.'[1254]

وَقُلِ اعۡمَلُوۡا فَسَيَرَى اللّٰهُ عَمَلَكُمۡ وَرَسُوۡلُهٗ وَالۡمُؤۡمِنُوۡنَ وَسَتُرَدُّوۡنَ اِلٰى عٰلِمِ الۡغَيۡبِ وَالشَّهَادَةِ فَيُنَبِّئُكُمۡ بِمَا كُنۡتُمۡ تَعۡمَلُوۡنَ ۝

106. And ^c*there are* others whose *case* has been postponed for the decree of Allah. He may punish them or He may turn to them with compassion. And Allah is All-Knowing, Wise.[1255]

وَاٰخَرُوۡنَ مُرۡجَوۡنَ لِاَمۡرِ اللّٰهِ اِمَّا يُعَذِّبُهُمۡ وَاِمَّا يَتُوۡبُ عَلَيۡهِمۡ وَاللّٰهُ عَلِيۡمٌ حَكِيۡمٌ ۝

---

^a42 : 26.   ^b9 : 94.   ^c9 : 118.

1253. Commentary :

The repentant Muslims are here told that the right course for them was to have become God's true worshippers, for it is only the righteous servants of God who are entitled to forgiveness and mercy.

1254. Commentary :

Though the party of Muslims referred to in the preceding verses repented and their repentance was accepted, yet they are here told that repentance cannot be complete unless one shows, by one's later actions, that one has really and truly reformed oneself. These men are therefore warned in this verse that their future actions would be particularly watched.

1255. Important Words :

مرجون (whose case has been postponed) is derived from ارجاء which again is derived from رجأ. They say ارجاء الامر *i.e.* he postponed, put off or delayed the affair. مرجون (which is really مرجئون) means, those who have been delayed or put off or postponed, *i.e.*, the consideration of whose case has been postponed or deferred (Lane & Aqrab).

Commentary :

The reference here is to yet another party which consisted of three Medinite Muslims, Hilāl, Murāra and Ka'b. The Holy Prophet deferred pronouncing his decision regarding them. This he did to keep them in a state of suspense for some time. The feeling of extreme uneasiness caused by the state of suspense served as a sort of atonement for their remissness and they were subsequently pardoned (see 9 : 118 below). In the meantime the Quran proceeds to speak of other people.

107. And *among the hypocrites are* those who have built a mosque in order to injure *Islam* and *help* disbelief and cause a division among the believers, and prepare an ambush for him who warred against Allah and His Messenger before *this*. And they will surely swear: ' We meant nothing but good '; but *a*Allah bears witness that they are certainly liars.[1256]

وَالَّذِيْنَ اتَّخَذُوْا مَسْجِدًا ضِرَارًا وَّكُفْرًا وَّتَفْرِيْقًا بَيْنَ الْمُؤْمِنِيْنَ وَاِرْصَادًا لِّمَنْ حَارَبَ اللّٰهَ وَرَسُوْلَهٗ مِنْ قَبْلُ ۚ وَلَيَحْلِفُنَّ اِنْ اَرَدْنَاۤ اِلَّا الْحُسْنٰى ۚ وَاللّٰهُ يَشْهَدُ اِنَّهُمْ لَكٰذِبُوْنَ ۝

---

*a*63 : 2.

1256. Important Words :

ارصادا (to prepare an ambush) is derived from ارصد which again is derived from رصد. They say رصده *i.e.* he sat or lay in wait for him in the way; or he watched or waited for him. ارصد له الامر means, he prepared for him the thing or affair. ارصده على كذا means, he charged him with the watching or guarding of such a thing. رصد or مرصاد or مرصد means, a place or way, etc. where one lies in wait, or watches, for an enemy. ارصاد therefore means, to prepare a place where one may wait, or lie in ambush, for the enemy (Lane & Aqrab).

Commentary :

The verse refers to a plot hatched by one Abū 'Āmir, a member of the Khazraj tribe of Medina and an arch-enemy of Islam. After the Battle of Badr, Abū 'Āmir fled to Mecca and there incited the Meccans and other Arabs to avenge the defeat of Badr. He was with the Meccan army at Uḥud. Learning that there were certain hypocrites in Medina, he entered into correspondence with them, with a view to plotting against Islam. It was his accomplices who built the so-called mosque at Qubā, a suburb of Medina, to carry on their secret and mischievous propaganda against Islam. The building was completed when the Holy Prophet was about to leave for Tabūk. The builders of the "mosque" requested him to consecrate it by saying Prayers therein. The Holy Prophet, who so far knew nothing of their evil designs, promised to do so on his return from the expedition. But in the meantime, the present verse was revealed to him, and on his return to Medina he ordered the "mosque" (which has come to be known as مسجد ضرار *i.e.* the harmful mosque) to be set on fire and razed to the ground.

The reference in the words, *and prepare an ambush for him who warred against Allah and His Messenger*, is to Abū 'Āmir, who, since the Battle of Badr, had been inciting the Arabs against the Muslims and had personally taken part in the Battle of Uḥud. He is also said to have been present at the Battle of the Ditch and of Ḥunain. At last, he fled to Syria, designing and hoping, to enlist the help of the Greeks against Islam, but he died at Kinnisrin, an exiled wretch. Abū 'Āmir is reported to have prayed for the death of the Holy Prophet in the words : امات الله الكاذب منا طريدا وحيدا غريبا *i.e.* " May God make him who is the liar of us two die, driven away, alone and in exile". When the Holy Prophet heard of this prayer of Abū 'Āmir, he calmly exclaimed, " Let it be so". The prayer met with wonderful acceptance, proving that it was Abū 'Āmir himself who was the liar and not the Holy Prophet (Khamīs, ii. 144).

108. Never stand *to pray* therein. A Mosque which was founded upon piety from the *very* first day is surely more worthy that thou shouldst stand *to pray* therein. In it are men who love to become purified, and Allah loves those who purify themselves.[1257]

لَا تَقُمْ فِيهِ اَبَدًا ۚ لَمَسْجِدٌ اُسِّسَ عَلَى التَّقْوٰى مِنْ اَوَّلِ يَوْمٍ اَحَقُّ اَنْ تَقُوْمَ فِيهِ ۚ فِيهِ رِجَالٌ يُّحِبُّوْنَ اَنْ يَّتَطَهَّرُوْا ۚ وَاللّٰهُ يُحِبُّ الْمُطَّهِّرِيْنَ ۝

109. Is he, then, who founded his building on fear of Allah and *His* pleasure better or he who founded his building on the brink of a tottering water-worn bank which tumbled down with him into the fire of Hell? And Allah guides not the wrongdoing people.[1258]

اَفَمَنْ اَسَّسَ بُنْيَانَهٗ عَلٰى تَقْوٰى مِنَ اللّٰهِ وَرِضْوَانٍ خَيْرٌ اَمْ مَّنْ اَسَّسَ بُنْيَانَهٗ عَلٰى شَفَا جُرُفٍ هَارٍ فَانْهَارَ بِهٖ فِيْ نَارِ جَهَنَّمَ ۚ وَاللّٰهُ لَا يَهْدِى الْقَوْمَ الظّٰلِمِيْنَ ۝

1257. Commentary:

According to some traditions the words, *A mosque which was founded upon piety from the very first day is surely more worthy*, refer to a mosque at Qubā which was built on the site where the Holy Prophet had alighted before entering Medina on the day of his arrival from Mecca; while, according to others, these words refer to the Mosque which the Holy Prophet himself built at Medina and which later came to be known as مسجد النبى *i.e.* "the Mosque of the Prophet". The wording of the verse seems to support the latter view.

1258. Important Words:

جرف (water-worn bank) is derived from جرف They say جرف الشىئ *i.e.* he carried away or removed the whole or greater part of the thing. The Arabs say جرفه الدهر *i.e.* time (fortune) destroyed his wealth and reduced him to poverty. جرف means, a bank of a valley, the lower part of which is excavated by water and hollowed out by torrents so that it remains unsound or weak

with its upper part overhanging; an abrupt water-worn bank or ridge; the side of the bank of a river that has been eaten by the water so that parts of it continually fall down (Lane & Aqrab).

هار (tottering) is the active participle from هار which is both transitive and intransitive and means, he demolished, or pulled down or pulled to pieces, a building; or it (building) fell to pieces or broke down and collapsed. هار which is originally هارى therefore, means, falling or tumbling down; or cracking without falling; or cracking in its hinder part, remaining yet in its place; tottering to fall (Lane & Aqrab).

Commentary:

The verse most vividly contrasts the two buildings, "the Mosque of the Prophet" and the "harmful mosque". Whereas the former is founded on the firm bed-rock of piety and of God's own pleasure, the other rests on the water-worn tottering bank of hypocrisy and disbelief.

110. *This* building of theirs, which they have built, will ever continue to be a *source of* disquiet to their hearts, unless their hearts be torn to pieces. And Allah is All-Knowing, Wise.[1259]

لَا يَزَالُ بُنْيَانُهُمُ الَّذِىْ بَنَوْا رِيْبَةً فِىْ قُلُوْبِهِمْ اِلَّا اَنْ تَقَطَّعَ قُلُوْبُهُمْ وَاللّٰهُ عَلِيْمٌ حَكِيْمٌ ۞

14

111. Surely, [a]Allah has purchased of the believers their persons and their property in return for the *Heavenly* Garden they shall have; [b]they fight in the cause of Allah, and they slay and are slain—an unfailing promise *that He has made* incumbent on Himself in the Torah, and the Gospel, and the Quran. And who is more faithful to his promise than Allah ? Rejoice, then, in your bargain which you have made with Him ; and that it is which is the supreme triumph.[1260]

اِنَّ اللّٰهَ اشْتَرٰى مِنَ الْمُؤْمِنِيْنَ اَنْفُسَهُمْ وَاَمْوَالَهُمْ بِاَنَّ لَهُمُ الْجَنَّةَ ۚ يُقَاتِلُوْنَ فِىْ سَبِيْلِ اللّٰهِ فَيَقْتُلُوْنَ وَيُقْتَلُوْنَ ۫ وَعْدًا عَلَيْهِ حَقًّا فِى التَّوْرٰىةِ وَالْاِنْجِيْلِ وَالْقُرْاٰنِ ۚ وَمَنْ اَوْفٰى بِعَهْدِهٖ مِنَ اللّٰهِ فَاسْتَبْشِرُوْا بِبَيْعِكُمُ الَّذِىْ بَايَعْتُمْ بِهٖ ۚ وَذٰلِكَ هُوَ الْفَوْزُ الْعَظِيْمُ ۞

---

[a]4 : 75 ; 61 : 11-12.   [b]3 : 196 ; 61 : 5.

1259. **Commentary :**

The words, *unless their hearts be torn to pieces,* are intended to hint that as the hearts of the hypocrites will never be cut into pieces, so the disquietude of their hearts will continue for ever. Or, the words signify that the disquietude of their hearts will cease only when they repent so deeply that their hearts are, as it were, torn up with regret and repentance.

1260. **Commentary :**

The words, *an unfailing promise that He has made incumbent on Himself in the Torah and the*

Gospel and the Quran, mean that the Torah, the Gospel and the Quran contain clear promises of divine favour and assistance for those who strive in the cause of God with their persons and property. The promise is general, but was to apply to Muslims alone after Islam had abrogated other religions. These words may also mean that the people of whom God purchased their lives and property in exchange for Heaven, *viz.,* the Companions of the Holy Prophet of Islam, have been spoken of and commended in all the three Books *i.e.* not only in the Quran, but in the Torah and the Gospels as well.

112. *They are* the ones who turn *to God in repentance,* ^awho worship *Him,* who praise *Him,* who go about in the land *serving Him,* who bow down *to God,* who prostrate themselves *in Prayer,* ^bwho enjoin good and forbid evil, and who watch the limits set by Allah. And give glad tidings to those who believe.[1261]

اَلتَّآئِبُوْنَ الْعٰبِدُوْنَ الْحٰمِدُوْنَ السَّآئِحُوْنَ الرّٰكِعُوْنَ السّٰجِدُوْنَ الْاٰمِرُوْنَ بِالْمَعْرُوْفِ وَ النَّاهُوْنَ عَنِ الْمُنْكَرِ وَ الْحٰفِظُوْنَ لِحُدُوْدِ اللّٰهِ وَبَشِّرِ الْمُؤْمِنِيْنَ ۝

---

^a33 : 36   ^b3 : 105, 111, 115 ; 7 : 158 ; 9 : 71 ; 31 : 18.

1261. Important Words :

سَآئِحُوْن (who go about in the land serving Him) is the plural of سَآئِح which is the active participle from سَاح which means, it flowed. They say سَاحَ الْمَاءُ عَلَى وَجْهِ الْارْضِ *i.e.* the water flowed or ran freely on the surface of the earth. سَاح فِى الْارْض means, he went or journeyed through the land for the purpose of devoting himself to the service of religion, etc. سَآئِح means, one who journeys through or goes about the land as a devotee or otherwise ; one who goes forth or journeys through the land to war against disbelievers or to seek knowledge ; one who fasts much and keeps to the mosques (Lane).

Commentary :

The present verse, which is a continuation of the previous one, shows that it is the Companions of the Holy Prophet and those who follow them righteously that are meant here.

The noble qualities of believers as mentioned in the verse under comment have been put in order of merit. The first stage of spiritual development is that of تَوْبَة *i.e.* repentance of one's sins. The second stage is that of عِبَادَة *i.e.* divine worship, which implies that after having repented of his sins, a Muslim becomes resigned to the will of God. The third stage is that of حمد *i.e.* glorifying God, which means that a Muslim is not only resigned to the will of God but he praises and glorifies Him even in adversity.

The fourth stage pertains to the attribute of سَآئِح which means that in this stage a believer forsakes his home for the sake of God and devotes his whole attention to Him. The fifth spiritual stage which a Muslim attains is that of رَاكِع which signifies that he begins to serve God with all his soul and body, every part of his body being dedicated to His service. See also note on 2 : 44. In the sixth stage the believer becomes a سَاجِد (one who falls prostrate before God) which symbolizes the highest stage of nearness to God, when a believer not only severs, as it were, his connection with the world, but also loses his ownself, and throws himself on the earth, mixing with the dust. The Holy Prophet is reported to have said that in the attitude of prostration a believer is in a position of extreme nearness to God.

When a true believer has reached the stage of سَاجِد *i.e.* close nearness to God, his next duty is to bring the straying sheep into the fold of the Master. So now he becomes God's preacher, enjoining what is good and forbidding what is evil. This is the seventh stage to which a true Muslim can and should rise. The next, and in a way the final, stage is that of God's *Khalīfa i.e.* a divine Reformer, which is referred to in the words, "who watch the limits set by God," *i.e.* those who are, as it were, the guardians of the Law of God. The expression الْحَافِظُوْن لِحُدُوْدِ اللّٰه may also mean, those who strictly observe the ordinances of God.

113. It is not for the Prophet and those who believe that they should ask *of God* forgiveness for the idolaters, even though they may be kinsmen, after it has become plain to them that they are the people of Hell.[1262]

مَا كَانَ لِلنَّبِيِّ وَالَّذِيْنَ اٰمَنُوْۤا اَنْ يَّسْتَغْفِرُوْا لِلْمُشْرِكِيْنَ وَلَوْ كَانُوْۤا اُولِيْ قُرْبٰى مِنْۢ بَعْدِ مَا تَبَيَّنَ لَهُمْ اَنَّهُمْ اَصْحٰبُ الْجَحِيْمِ ۝

114. And [a]Abraham's asking forgiveness for his father was only because of a promise he had made to him, but when it became clear to him that he was an enemy to Allah, he dissociated himself from him. [b]Surely, Abraham was most tender-hearted, *and* forbearing.[1263]

وَمَا كَانَ اسْتِغْفَارُ اِبْرٰهِيْمَ لِاَبِيْهِ اِلَّا عَنْ مَّوْعِدَةٍ وَّعَدَهَاۤ اِيَّاهُ ۚ فَلَمَّا تَبَيَّنَ لَهٗۤ اَنَّهٗ عَدُوٌّ لِّلّٰهِ تَبَرَّاَ مِنْهُ ۭ اِنَّ اِبْرٰهِيْمَ لَاَوَّاهٌ حَلِيْمٌ ۝

---

[a]19 : 48 ; 26 : 87 ; 60 : 5.   [b]11 : 76.

1262. Commentary :

When a true believer is he who possesses the qualities mentioned in the preceding verse, he can never hesitate to sever his connection with disbelievers if and when called upon to do so. It is in two ways that it can become "plain" that an idolater or a disbeliever is an inmate of Hell: *firstly*, if and when God informs His Prophet through some revelation that a certain idolater will not believe and will die as a disbeliever ; *secondly*, when an idolater actually dies without repenting of idolatry. In either case it is not permissible to pray for such idolaters. In ordinary circumstances, however, it is not disallowed to pray for disbelievers. The Holy Prophet is reported to have once said, "There lived a Prophet who, even though he was severely wounded by his people, went on praying to God, saying, 'My Lord, forgive my people, for they know not what they are doing.'" It was really to himself that the Holy Prophet referred in this saying. He was referring to the treatment he received at the hands of the people of Ṭā'if, and to the prayer that he, while bleeding and wounded, offered for them,

1263. Important Words :

اَوَّاه (most tender-hearted) is the intensive adjective from اوه. They say, اوه or تَأَوَّهُ *i.e.* he said, Ah ! or Alas ! ; he moaned or uttered a moan ; or he gave prolonged utterance to distress or complaint. اَوَّاه means, one who is often saying, Ah ! or Alas ! from a motive of love or pity or fear ; one often moaning or mourning or sorrowing ; compassionate or tender-hearted ; one often praying ; one who praises God greatly or glorifies Him much ; one who addresses himself with earnest supplication to God, confident that his prayer will be accepted ; one inviting much or often to what is good (Lane).

Commentary :

The preceding verse declares that praying for disbelievers, after it has become clear that they are inmates of Hell, is forbidden. The present verse explains a prayer which Abraham offered for his idolatrous father on the basis that he had made a promise to do so. Abraham, however, was not slow in dissociating himself from his father as soon as it became clear to him that he was an enemy of God. The verse ends with words expressive of high praise for Abraham. See also 6 : 75.

115. And it is not for Allah to cause a people to go astray after He has guided them until He makes clear to them that which they ought to guard against. Surely, Allah knows all things well.

116. Surely, *it is Allah to Whom belongs the kingdom of the heavens and the earth. He gives life and causes death. And you have no friend nor helper beside Allah.

117. Allah has certainly turned with mercy to the Prophet and *to* the Emigrants and the Helpers who followed him in the hour of distress after the hearts of a party of them had well-nigh swerved. He again turned to them with mercy. Surely, He is to them Compassionate, Merciful.[1264]

وَمَا كَانَ اللهُ لِيُضِلَّ قَوْمًا بَعْدَ إِذْ هَدَاهُمْ حَتّٰى يُبَيِّنَ لَهُمْ مَّا يَتَّقُوْنَ إِنَّ اللهَ بِكُلِّ شَيْءٍ عَلِيْمٌ ۝

إِنَّ اللهَ لَهُ مُلْكُ السَّمٰوٰتِ وَ الْأَرْضِ يُحْيِ وَ يُمِيْتُ وَ مَا لَكُمْ مِّنْ دُوْنِ اللهِ مِنْ وَّلِيٍّ وَّ لَا نَصِيْرٍ ۝

لَقَدْ تَّابَ اللهُ عَلَى النَّبِيِّ وَالْمُهٰجِرِيْنَ وَالْأَنْصَارِ الَّذِيْنَ اتَّبَعُوْهُ فِيْ سَاعَةِ الْعُسْرَةِ مِنْ بَعْدِ مَا كَادَ يَزِيْغُ قُلُوْبُ فَرِيْقٍ مِّنْهُمْ ثُمَّ تَابَ عَلَيْهِمْ إِنَّهُ بِهِمْ رَءُوْفٌ رَّحِيْمٌ ۝

*39:45; 57:3.

1264. Commentary:

It is clear from this verse that the word تاب (turned with mercy) does not necessarily mean "turning with mercy by way of accepting repentance". It also means, as in the present verse, "bestowing favour upon a person, or being gracious to him", for it has been used here with regard to the Holy Prophet and those who cheerfully followed him in the hour of distress. Indeed, in the case of the Holy Prophet and his faithful followers it was not an occasion for granting forgiveness but for bestowing reward. As it was an "hour of distress" for the Muslims, the expedition to Tabūk is rightly known as غزوة العسرة (*Ghazwat al-'Usra*) *i.e.* the expedition of distress.

118. And *He has turned with mercy* to the three *a*whose *case* was deferred, until the earth became too strait for them with *all* its vastness, and their souls were *also* straitened for them, and they became convinced that there was no refuge from Allah save unto Himself. Then He turned to them with mercy that they might turn *to Him*. Surely, it is Allah Who is Oft-Returning *with compassion and is* Merciful.[1265]

وَعَلَى الثَّلٰثَةِ الَّذِيْنَ خُلِّفُوْا ۛ حَتّٰى اِذَا ضَاقَتْ عَلَيْهِمُ الْاَرْضُ بِمَا رَحُبَتْ وَضَاقَتْ عَلَيْهِمْ اَنْفُسُهُمْ وَظَنُّوْا اَنْ لَّا مَلْجَاَ مِنَ اللّٰهِ اِلَّاۤ اِلَيْهِ ۭ ثُمَّ تَابَ عَلَيْهِمْ لِيَتُوْبُوْا ۭ اِنَّ اللّٰهَ هُوَ التَّوَّابُ الرَّحِيْمُ ۟ ﴿١١٨﴾

---

*a*9 : 106.

1265. **Commentary :**

The reference here is to Ka'b bin Mālik, Hilāl bin Umayya and Murāra bin Rabī'a already referred to in 9 : 106. These were sincere Muslims but failed to join the expedition to Tabūk, and therefore the Holy Prophet, on his return to Medina, ordered their complete social ostracism. They continued under this interdiction for no less than fifty days, when on their sincere repentance, and after they had come out of this severe ordeal successfully, they were granted pardon, as mentioned in this verse. One of these three men, Ka'b bin Mālik, relates his own story, which may be summed up as follows :—

" Hitherto it had been a custom with the Holy Prophet to conceal the object of an intended expedition to the very last. But the journey now to be undertaken was so distant and the heat of the season so excessive and the enemy against whom he was called upon to march so powerful that he thought it necessary to give his followers a timely warning so that they might be able to make the necessary preparation.

"I went to the market every day to make the needful purchases, but came back without doing anything, thinking that I would do the necessary preparation next day, for I was well able to do so. In this way I went on postponing from day to day until the army started from Medina. Even then I thought I would be able to make the necessary

arrangements next day and join the army on the way. But the next day also I did nothing and put off till the day following. The result of this procrastination was that the army had travelled such a long distance from Medina that I had to give up the idea of making any attempt to join it from behind.

"When I heard that the Holy Prophet was coming back to Medina, grief seized me. On his return to Medina, those who had remained behind came to him and offered false excuses for their absence. He accepted their excuses, pardoned them, and left their cases in the hand of God. I also went to him and saluted him and he smiled with the smile of one who is angry and asked me the reason of my absence. I replied, 'By God, if there had been another person in your place, O Prophet of God, I think I might have escaped his anger by offering an excuse, for I am clever in argument. But, by God, I know that if I tell you a false story, you will be pleased with me, but in that case the All-Knowing God will bring about circumstances which will make you angry with me ; and if I speak to you the truth, you may feel angry, but I hope God will pardon me. By God, I have no pretext to offer for my absence ; I was never stronger and never better off than I was at the time when I stayed behind.' The Holy Prophet said, 'As for this man, he has

R. 15   119.   O ye who believe ! ^afear Allah and be with the truthful.¹²⁶⁶

يَا أَيُّهَا الَّذِينَ آمَنُوا اتَّقُوا اللهَ وَكُونُوا مَعَ الصّٰدِقِينَ ﴿١١٩﴾

^a3 : 103 ; 5 : 36 ; 39 : 11 ; 57 : 29.

spoken the truth.' Then he said to me, 'Go away, until God gives His decision about you.' On enquiry, I learnt that the Holy Prophet had said the same thing to two other persons, Murāra b. Rabī'a and Hilāl b. Umayya. He laid all the three of us under an interdict, forbidding the Faithful to hold any intercourse with us. My two companions, who were old and weak, did not leave their homes. I was strong and healthy and went about from place to place but no one spoke to me. Everybody shunned me or regarded me with an altered mien. I sought the Mosque, sat down near the Prophet, and saluted him, but my salutation was not returned. While I was in this predicament, there came to me a messenger with an epistle from the King of the Banū Ghassān, expressing his sympathy with me in my present plight and inviting me to his court, where he promised to treat me with respect and honour. 'This is another trial', said I to myself, and repairing to a burning oven, I cast the King's letter into the fire, saying to the messenger, 'This is my reply to the letter.'

"On the forty-first day came the further command that we should separate even from our wives, whereupon I sent away my wife to her parents, and was left all alone to undergo in its severest rigour the punishment meted out to us. My heart was dying away and the whole world appeared to grow narrow to me. My other companions also were in a pitiable condition. They kept weeping day and night in their homes. At last, on the fifty-first day, the Prophet of God received a revelation bringing the welcome news that God had turned to us with mercy and had accepted our repentance. A friend on horseback came galloping to me to be the first to convey to me the happy news, but another friend

forestalled him by ascending the nearest hill and crying therefrom at the top of his voice : 'Rejoice, O Ka'b b. Mālik.' I concluded that I was pardoned and hastened to the Holy Prophet and found him in the Mosque. He received me with a radiant countenance and said, 'Rejoice, O Ka'b, for this is the happiest day that has ever dawned upon you since you were born.' My soul was lifted up from the depths of despondency and in the transports of gratitude, I offered my whole wealth in atonement of my error. 'Nay,' said the Holy Prophet, 'Keep a part of your wealth and give away the rest, to be spent in the cause of God.' I also said to the Holy Prophet, 'It is through my speaking the truth that God has done me this favour. So I make a solemn promise that I will never speak but the truth so long as I live.' And by God, I have strictly adhered to this promise to the present day and hope God will help me to observe this promise in the future as well'' (Bukhārī ch. on *Maghāzī*).

The above narration forcefully leads one to the conclusion that :—

(1) The Holy Prophet kept strict discipline among his followers but this discipline was tempered with mercy ;

(2) In spite of this discipline the Holy Prophet was loved and revered by his followers to an extraordinary degree ;

(3) His true followers always strove their best to set an unparalleled example of sacrifice, devotion and piety.

1266. Commentary :

This verse directly following the verses that speak

120. It was not proper for the people of Medina and those around them from among the Arabs of the desert that they should have remained behind the Messenger of Allah or that they should have preferred their own lives to his. That is because there distresses them neither thirst nor fatigue nor hunger in the way of Allah, nor do they tread a track which enrages the disbelievers, nor do they cause an enemy any injury whatsoever, but there is written down for them a good work on account of it. Surely, Allah suffers not the reward of those who do good to be lost.[1267]

121. And they spend not any sum, small or great, nor do they traverse a valley, but it is written down for them, that *Allah may give them the best reward for what they did.[1268]

مَا كَانَ لِأَهْلِ الْمَدِينَةِ وَمَنْ حَوْلَهُمْ مِّنَ الْأَعْرَابِ اَنْ يَّتَخَلَّفُوْا عَنْ رَّسُوْلِ اللهِ وَلَا يَرْغَبُوْا بِأَنْفُسِهِمْ عَنْ نَّفْسِهِ ذٰلِكَ بِأَنَّهُمْ لَا يُصِيْبُهُمْ ظَمَأٌ وَّلَا نَصَبٌ وَّلَا مَخْمَصَةٌ فِيْ سَبِيْلِ اللهِ وَلَا يَطَؤُنَ مَوْطِئًا يَّغِيْظُ الْكُفَّارَ وَلَا يَنَالُوْنَ مِنْ عَدُوٍّ نَّيْلًا اِلَّا كُتِبَ لَهُمْ بِهِ عَمَلٌ صَالِحٌ اِنَّ اللهَ لَا يُضِيْعُ اَجْرَ الْمُحْسِنِيْنَ ۞

وَلَا يُنْفِقُوْنَ نَفَقَةً صَغِيْرَةً وَّلَا كَبِيْرَةً وَّلَا يَقْطَعُوْنَ وَادِيًا اِلَّا كُتِبَ لَهُمْ لِيَجْزِيَهُمُ اللهُ اَحْسَنَ مَا كَانُوْا يَعْمَلُوْنَ ۞

*16 : 97-98 ; 24 : 39 ; 39 : 36.

of hypocrites and those weak in faith, lays down one of the most important rules of conduct that contribute to the building up of a person's moral character and to his spiritual growth and development. This consists (1) in one's own effort to perfect his righteousness by developing the fear of God and (2) in seeking the company of the truthful and sticking to it. As a matter of fact, to keep company with the righteous and the truthful is highly essential. It serves to remove moral and spiritual rust from one's heart, and exercises a very wholesome influence on it. It leads a believer to the fountain of purity and righteousness. It provides a moral and spiritual environment for man. That was one of the advantages enjoyed by those who accompanied the Holy Prophet to Tabūk.

1267. **Important Words :**

موطئا (track) is derived from وطئ. They say وطئ الشيء i.e. he trod upon the thing with his feet or he trampled upon the thing. موطأ therefore, means, a place trod upon ; a footstep or footprint (Lane).

Commentary :

The verse relates some of the great advantages which would have accrued to the laggers-behind, if they had accompanied the Holy Prophet to Tabūk. See also the following verse.

1268. **Commentary :**

See the preceding verse with which the present one is linked up.

122. ^aIt is not possible for the believers to go forth all together. Why, then, does not a party from every section of them go forth that they may become well-versed in religion, and that they may warn their people when they return to them, so that they may guard *against evil?*[1269]

وَمَا كَانَ الْمُؤْمِنُونَ لِيَنْفِرُوا كَآفَّةً ۚ فَلَوْلَا نَفَرَ مِنْ كُلِّ فِرْقَةٍ مِنْهُمْ طَآئِفَةٌ لِيَتَفَقَّهُوا فِي الدِّينِ وَلِيُنْذِرُوا قَوْمَهُمْ إِذَا رَجَعُوٓا إِلَيْهِمْ لَعَلَّهُمْ يَحْذَرُونَ ۝

R. 16 123. O ye who believe! ^bfight such of the disbelievers as are near to you and ^clet them find hardness in you; and know that Allah is with the righteous.[1270]

يَآأَيُّهَا الَّذِينَ اٰمَنُوا قَاتِلُوا الَّذِينَ يَلُونَكُمْ مِنَ الْكُفَّارِ وَلْيَجِدُوا فِيكُمْ غِلْظَةً ۚ وَاعْلَمُوٓا أَنَّ اللّٰهَ مَعَ الْمُتَّقِينَ ۝

124. And whenever a *Sūra* is sent down, there are some of them who say: 'Which of you has this *Sūra* increased in faith?' But ^dthose who believe have their faith increased thereby and they rejoice.[1271]

وَإِذَا مَآ أُنْزِلَتْ سُورَةٌ فَمِنْهُمْ مَّنْ يَّقُولُ أَيُّكُمْ زَادَتْهُ هٰذِهٖ إِيمَانًا ۚ فَأَمَّا الَّذِينَ اٰمَنُوا فَزَادَتْهُمْ إِيمَانًا وَّهُمْ يَسْتَبْشِرُونَ ۝

^a3 : 105. ^b2 : 191. ^c48 : 30. ^d8 : 3.

1269. Commentary :

As weaknesses in faith and works resulted from lack of knowledge and training, the present verse speaks of the way in which such weaknesses could be removed. The Arabs of the desert were quite ignorant of the teachings of Islam (9 : 97). The verse suggests a practical method of instructing them in the tenets and principles of the Faith. A certain number from every tribe or section were required to come to Medina for instruction in the teachings of Islam, and then go back to their respective people and teach them what they had themselves learned. It was indeed the easiest, the most effective and practical method of learning the principles and teachings of the New Faith and imparting them to others.

1270. Commentary :

The words, *such of the disbelievers as are near to*

you, signify those hypocrites who lived among the Muslims and intermixed with them. Muslims were enjoined to fight them as a class and not each and every one of them individually. They were to fight them by exposing their malpractices and hypocritical deeds and by bringing these to the notice of the Holy Prophet.

The words, *and let them find hardness in you*, mean that, like a hard thing which refuses to receive impressions, a Muslim should not allow himself to be influenced by his evil desires and the evil persons who surround him.

1271. Commentary :

The question, *which of you has this Sūra increased in faith*, refers to the contention of the hypocrites that the Quranic *Sūras* increase none in faith. This objection of the hypocrites is answered in the words that follow.

125. But as for *those in whose hearts is a disease, it adds *further* filth to their *present* filth, and they die while they are disbelievers.[1272]

126. Do they not see that they are tried every year once or twice? Yet they do not repent, nor would they be admonished.[1273]

127. And whenever a Sūra is sent down, *they look at one another, *saying,* 'Does any one see you?' Then they turn away. *Allah has turned away their hearts because they are a people who would not understand.[1274]

*2 : 11.　　*24 : 64.　　*61 : 6.

1272. Commentary:

Divine revelation is like rain-water. If the seed is good and the soil favourable, rain is sure to help in producing a good crop; but if the seed and the soil are bad, the crop is bound to be bad in spite of good rain. As the soil of the hearts of the hypocrites was unclean and corrupt, the water of divine revelation only served to add to their filth; for with the coming down of heavenly rain the filth that lay hidden in the hearts of the disbelievers also came out.

1273. Commentary:

The hypocrites are here asked the pertinent question: Is not the fact that events are taking place every now and then by which their faith is tried and true and sincere Muslims are distinguished from those insincere and false, sufficient to open their eyes to the truth that God Himself is the author of Islam, and that in order to protect His religion and make it prosper, He is always separating the faithful from the faithless, so that Muslims may become purified of all

dross and impurities and Islam may come to possess a band of sincere and devoted followers? This fact alone, they are told, is sufficient to increase and strengthen the faith of those who have the seed of truth in their hearts. The verse also helps to explain 9 : 101 above, where it is said that God will punish the hypocrites "twice".

1274. Commentary:

The hypocrites used to sit among Muslims when worldly matters were being discussed; but when the recital of the Quran began, they would quietly slink away. The verse means to say that as these men refuse to listen to the word of God and turn away from it, so, as a punishment for this act of theirs, God has turned away their hearts from truth. This helps to explain expressions like "leading astray" etc., used about God in the Quran. His "leading astray" only means that when evil-minded men go astray and persist in their evil course, God leaves them alone and allows them to wander away from the truth, stamping them as lost.

128. Surely, a Messenger has come unto you from among yourselves; grievous to him is that you should fall into trouble; *he is* ardently desirous of your *welfare; and* [a]to the believers *he is* compassionate *and* merciful.[1275]

لَقَدْ جَآءَكُمْ رَسُوْلٌ مِّنْ اَنْفُسِكُمْ عَزِيْزٌ عَلَيْهِ مَا عَنِتُّمْ حَرِيْصٌ عَلَيْكُمْ بِالْمُؤْمِنِيْنَ رَءُوْفٌ رَّحِيْمٌ ۝

129. But if they turn away, say, [b]'Allah is sufficient for me. There is no God but He. In Him do I put my trust, and [b]He is the Lord of the mighty Throne.'[1276]

فَاِنْ تَوَلَّوْا فَقُلْ حَسْبِيَ اللّٰهُ ۖ لَآ اِلٰهَ اِلَّا هُوَ ۖ عَلَيْهِ تَوَكَّلْتُ وَهُوَ رَبُّ الْعَرْشِ الْعَظِيْمِ ۝

---

[a]9 : 61   [b]39 : 39 ; 21 : 23 ; 23 : 117 ; 27 : 27 ; 40 : 16.

1275. Commentary :

This verse applies to both believers and disbelievers, the opening part of it applying to the latter and the closing part to the former. To disbelievers the verse says : It grieves the Prophet to see you fall into trouble *i.e.* although you subjected the Prophet to all manner of persecutions and privations, yet his heart is so full of the milk of human kindness that no amount of persecution on your part can make him bitter against you or make him wish you ill. He is so kind and sympathetic to you that he cannot bear to see you turn away from the path of righteousness and thus put yourselves in trouble. To believers the verse says : The Prophet is compassionate and merciful *i.e.* he cheerfully shares with you your sorrows and afflictions. Moreover, like an affectionate father he treats you with kindness and mercy.

The attributes "compassionate and merciful" applied here to the Holy Prophet are also applied to God. As a matter of fact, the attributes of God are of two kinds : (1) تنزیهی *i.e.* those that make Him distinct from His creation *e.g.* رحمان (One Whose mercy extends to all) ; these are never applied to any one except God. (2) تشبیهی *i.e.* those in which He resembles other beings *e.g.* رحیم (Merciful) ; for mercy is an attribute which

may be shared, in however meagre a degree, by others also.

1276. Commentary :

The verse, which is the last of the present *Sūra*, purports to say to disbelievers that it is for their own good that the Prophet invites them to truth and that their refusal to listen to him would do him no harm.

The clause, *He is the Lord of the mighty Throne,* implies a beautiful and dignified refutation of the charge that the Prophet was aiming at temporal power. The clause may mean something like this : "I seek the establishment of no temporal kingdom in Arabia or anywhere else. On the contrary, my aim and object is the establishment of the Kingdom of God on earth, in the wake of which material prosperity and temporal power, very much greater than the kingdom of Arabia, are destined to come to me and my followers and no power on earth can stop that".

The words, *In Him do I put my trust, and He is the Lord of the mighty Throne,* with which the *Sūra* comes to an end, also provide the essence of the spirit of Islam, *i.e.,* (1) that the God of Islam is Supreme over all, and (2) that a true Muslim should put his trust in Him alone.